Unemployment Rate in Canada since World War II

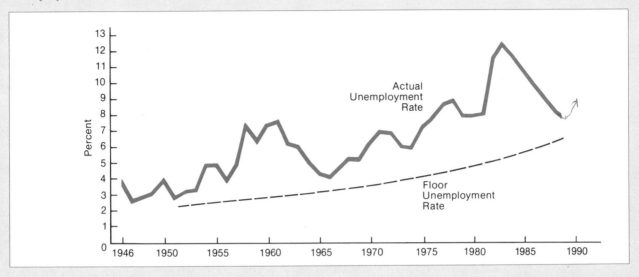

Rates of Change of Wages and Prices in Canada, 1949–1989

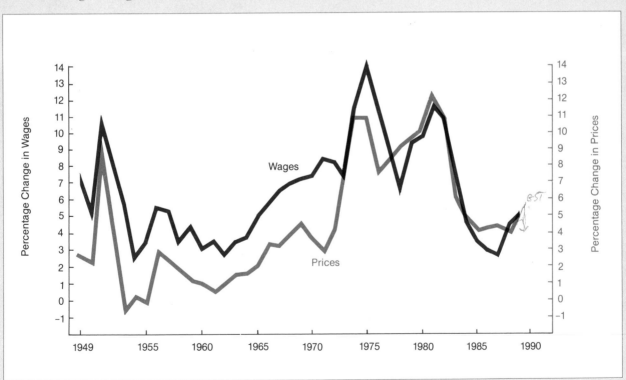

ECONOMICS
Principles and Policy
THIRD CANADIAN EDITION

P.261 — concept of bond prices

4 5+6
7 8

ECONOMICS

Principles and Policy

THIRD CANADIAN EDITION

William J. Baumol
New York University and
Princeton University

Alan S. Blinder
Princeton University

William M. Scarth
McMaster University

Harcourt Brace Jovanovich, Canada
Toronto   Montreal   Orlando   San Diego   London   Sydney   Tokyo

To my four children,
Ellen, Daniel,
and now Sabrina and Jim
W.J.B.

For Scott, who is now Beyond the Final Exam,
and William, who is on his way
A.S.B.

To Brian, David,
and the memory of Michael
W.M.S.

Editorial Director: Scott Duncan
Developmental Editor: Sarah J. Duncan
Editorial Assistant: Lee Donald
Production Co-ordinator: Sue Ann Becker
Editor and Project Co-ordinator: Darlene Zeleney
Cover and Interior Design: Jack Steiner Graphic Design
Technical Art: Nick Owocki
Typesetting: CompuScreen Typesetting Ltd.
Printing and Binding: John Deyell Company

Canadian Cataloguing in Publication Data

Baumol, William J.
   Economics : principles and policy

3rd Canadian ed.
Includes index.
ISBN 0-7747-3163-X

1. Economics.   I. Blinder, Alan S.   II. Scarth, William
M., 1946- .   III. Title.

HB171.5.B38 1991   330   C90-095059-5

95 94 93 92 91 1 2 3 4 5
Printed and bound in Canada

Cover: John Korner, b. 1913. *Favourite Harbour, VI*, 1956–57. Oil on canvas. 91.5 cm × 127.5 cm. The National Gallery of Canada. The publisher would like to thank Mr. Koerner for his permission to reproduce the painting, and Susan Campbell, of the National Gallery of Canada, for her assistance in obtaining permission.

Preface

For decades, the "principles of economics" book has been expected to codify the entire discipline of economics. In recent years, this has become increasingly difficult, but also more imperative. The explosion of economic knowledge has made it impossible to put all of economics between two covers. But at the same time, more and more public policy issues either are basically economic in nature or involve important economic considerations. Intelligent citizens can no longer afford to be innocent of economics.

This dilemma has guided the preparation of this book in two ways. First, we have studiously avoided the encyclopedic approach and abandoned the fiction, so popular among textbook writers, that literally everything is of the utmost importance. Second, we have tried to highlight those important ideas that are likely to be of lasting significance—principles that you will want to remember long after the course is over because they offer insights that are far from obvious, because they are of practical importance, and because they are widely misunderstood by intelligent laypeople. A dozen of the most important of these ideas have been selected as **12 Ideas for Beyond the Final Exam** and are called to the reader's attention whenever they occur through the use of the book's logo ▰ .

This method of highlighting key ideas has proved very popular with users of the previous editions of our book, many of whom have suggested that we go even farther in the direction of weeding out material of lesser importance. In this edition, we have decided to follow these suggestions. There seems to be an unwritten law that, with every new edition, a principles textbook will drift farther away from the focus that was its original raison d'être: New material is added, but old material has a habit of remaining in place, with the result that both readability and focus deteriorate. Because both students and instructors have told us that the comparative advantage of our textbook is precisely in its consistent focus and readability, we resolved firmly, in preparing this third edition, to avoid the common pitfall that has harmed other textbooks.

Armed with this resolve, we approached the revision process boldly, and shortened the book significantly: It now consists of thirty-two chapters as opposed to the last edition's forty. This streamlining was not achieved by simply dropping the later chapters of the textbook for which instructors never seemed to find time in the course of the academic year. After all, those second-edition chapters contained important material on such issues as income distribution, the process of growth, problems encountered by the planned economies, and prevailing criticisms of mainstream economics. Instead, these and other important discussions have been thoroughly updated and integrated into the core material of the textbook. They need no longer be sacrificed to time constraints along with the more peripheral material that formerly occupied the later parts of the book.

Take, for example, our new organization of material in the microeconomics portion of the textbook, which focusses heavily on what the market does well and what it does poorly, as well as on the trade-off between equality and efficiency. These fundamental issues cannot be discussed adequately without some exploration of income distribution and of the actual experiences of the planned economies. Thus, in Chapter 24, which explains how the "invisible hand" does its job in the idealized world of perfect competition, the analytical discussion is supplemented by material on the actual experience of three major economies representing different types and degrees of planning—the Soviet Union, China, and Japan. (The discussion of the Soviet Union has been extensively rewritten, and new material on Eastern Europe added.) The remarkable and extremely rapid changes taking place within Eastern Bloc countries give new immediacy to this whole set of issues—after all, the transition from planning to markets may be the most burning economic issue of our time.

Other examples of our revision strategy include the integration, in Chapter 18, of material on productivity and growth (which formerly occupied two chapters), and the weaving together of our discussions of factor pricing, the tax system, and the poverty problem into two chapters (Chapters 29 and 30) from the second edition's four. The component parts of these two new chapters are designed in such a way that students and instructors can opt either to cover the material in full or to pick and choose the parts on which they wish to concentrate.

In short, with this revision, our book focusses on the central insights of our discipline even more effectively than did the earlier editions. It would have been easy to make the book *appear* more concise and less encyclopedic, without properly integrating material that was scattered throughout the earlier editions. For example, we could have adopted a two-column text design to shorten the book significantly, but decided against this format because it leaves no room in the margins for our definitions of key terms and concepts (a feature that users have found very helpful) or for the reader's own annotations.

Readability without Sacrificing Rigour

All modern economics textbooks abound with "real-world" examples, but we have tried to go beyond this, to elevate the examples to pre-eminence. For in our view, the policy issue or everyday economic problem ought to lead the student naturally to the economic principle, not the other way around. For this reason, many chapters *start* with a real policy issue or a practical problem that may seem puzzling or paradoxical to non-economists, and then proceed to describe the economic analysis required to remove the mystery. In doing this, we have tried to utilize technical jargon and diagrams only where there is a clear need for them, never for their own sake.

Still, economics is a somewhat technical subject and, except for a few rather light chapters, this is a book for the desk, not for the bed. We have, however, made strenuous efforts to simplify the technical level of the discussion as much as we could without sacrificing content. Fortunately, almost every important idea in economics can be explained in plain English, and this is what we have tried to do. Yet, even while reducing the technical difficulty of the book, we have incorporated some elements of economic analysis that have traditionally been left out of introductory books but that are really too important to omit.

Foremost among these is our extensive treatment of prices and inflation in Parts Two through Four. For years, textbooks devoted many chapters to unrealistic, but presumably simpler, economic models, in which prices never rose. The original American edition of this book was the first introductory textbook to put inflation into the story from the very beginning, rather than as an afterthought—a practice we maintain and expand in this third Canadian edition.

Another example is our treatment of monetary and fiscal policy options for a small open economy such as Canada's. Unlike other textbooks, ours does not shy away from a full application of aggregate supply and demand analysis in this area. And instead of separating our explanation of theory from our discussion of historical policy episodes, we thoroughly integrate the two by making full and rigorous use of the analytical tools to explain the policy experiences.

A third example of our commitment to a rigorous study of central analytical issues is our treatment of the market mechanism's ability, under ideal circumstances, to allocate society's resources in the most efficient manner possible. Many introductory-textbook authors, thinking the topic too difficult for beginning students, give little more than some general hints about this important result. We offer a genuine proof and an extensive discussion of precisely what the result does—and does not—imply about the efficiency of real-world market economies.

To summarize, then, our revision has been guided by two objectives—readability and rigour. The majority of students taking a principles course in economics do not plan to specialize in the field. What they want and need is to obtain a basic level of literacy in economic affairs, so that they can think independently when evaluating public issues. A book cannot meet this need if it is too technical, and addresses itself only to those going on to advanced studies in economics. In a word, the book will fail if it is not readable. But an introductory economics textbook will also fail if it tries so hard to be accessible that it glosses over fundamental points. (After all, in economics, a little learning can be a particularly dangerous thing!) Hence, a book that purports to explain economic reasoning cannot sacrifice rigour any more than it can succeed without being readable. By combining an untiring effort to maintain the literary style that readers have appreciated in our earlier editions with a "hard line" on topic selection, we have tried to meet both objectives, and to achieve a consistent focus on central themes and rigorous analysis in the process.

Macroeconomics

Students are invariably interested in learning enough macroeconomics within an introductory course to enable them to make sense of (or at least evaluate) such things as major statements by the Governor of the Bank of Canada. This is simply not possible without an analysis that stresses the cost-increasing effects of a lower Canadian dollar, which requires an integrated analysis of aggregate demand *and* supply. We use this integrated analysis directly in our discussion of policy episodes.

The macroeconomic section of the book starts with a brief history of macroeconomic events in Canada and an initial use of the aggregate demand and supply curves (Chapter 4). In the same chapter, there is a full discussion of the costs associated with unemployment and inflation, and an explanation of how national product (gross domestic product) is measured. In other words, measurement issues relating to all the major macroeconomic variables are now contained within one chapter; furthermore, the different parts of the chapter are self-contained, so that they can be read at any time during the term of study, at the instructor's discretion. In Chapters 5 through 9, we move on to multiplier theory, fiscal policy, and the supply-side effects of tax changes. The effects of personal income-tax changes, sales tax policy, and corporate tax concessions are thoroughly examined.

Chapter 10 introduces financial considerations. Firms finance their investment expenditures in two ways: They sell stocks and bonds (this is the set of options discussed in Chapter 10), and they borrow from the banks. Chapter 11 introduces the student to the operations of the latter by explaining the money supply and the chartered banking system. The study of central banking that follows (Chapter 12) stresses that pegging the exchange rate forces the Bank of Canada to conduct "open-market operations" in the foreign-exchange market, in just the same way that it does in domestic bond markets when initiating monetary policy. The nature of the foreign-exchange market is explained at this stage, and monetary policy and exchange-rate policy are discussed simultaneously. The chapter ends with a full discussion of several public statements issued by the Governor of the Bank of Canada concerning the viability of an independent interest-rate policy for Canada and other aspects of monetary policy.

The next two chapters integrate the analyses of fiscal and monetary/exchange-rate policy. Chapter 13 provides an updated discussion of the monetarist–Keynesian debate from the perspective of a closed economy. This approach allows us to outline the policy options available to the United States, whose economy has such a direct impact on our own. Chapter 14 analyzes the relative effectiveness of monetary and fiscal policies under alternative exchange-rate regimes for a small open economy such as Canada's. Several policy episodes are used to illustrate the direct importance of the economic analysis. The potential use of exchange-rate policy to limit the damage caused by foreign trade restrictions is fully discussed in Chapter 14.

The macroeconomics half of the book ends with four "issues" chapters, which can be read in any order. Each of these remaining four chapters deals with a central issue that is both highly topical and of enduring importance. The questions raised are as follows:

- *Chapter 15*: How was our international monetary system developed and why do we observe such vast swings in currency values?

- *Chapter 16*: Are large government budget deficits bad?

- *Chapter 17*: What is the nature of the trade-off between inflation and unemployment?

- *Chapter 18*: How can productivity growth be increased in both the developed and the less developed economies?

This final chapter of the macroeconomics portion of the book has been extensively revised; it focusses on the rise of the service sector in Western economies and on the consequent concern about the phenomenon often referred to as "deindustrialization."

Many of the macroeconomics chapters will look familiar to users of the previous edition, although few paragraphs have survived untouched. Some of the changes worth noting in this third Canadian edition are as follows:

- The basic algebraic treatment of multiplier derivations is now integrated into the text, rather than tucked away in appendices.

- The multiplier is now quite generally defined in terms of the slope of the "total expenditure schedule," so that whenever complicating factors are added, the unifying principle behind the changes in the multiplier formula is more apparent.

- The appendix on discounting now appears in the chapter on investment spending (Chapter 6).

- The material that explains how the central bank intervenes in the foreign-exchange market (Chapter 12) has been totally revised; it is now briefer and clearer.

- The discussion of the purchasing-power parity theory of exchange-rate determination in Chapter 15 has been expanded.

There are new or extensively revised boxed inserts on many topical issues, such as the following:

- Reforming unemployment insurance (page 89)
- How the CPI is measured (page 92)
- Corporate tax concessions (page 204)
- Changes in Canada's money (page 231)
- Reforming deposit-insurance and reserve-requirement regulations (page 245)
- Designing Europe's new central bank (page 249)

- Bank of Canada policy statements (page 264)
- Why the national debt is a burden (page 344)
- Economists versus religious leaders on macroeconomic policy (page 371)
- Labour's reaction to changes in the workplace (page 383)

Other boxed inserts fall under the rubric "At the Frontier," a feature introduced in the second edition and expanded in the third, which offers straightforward introductory descriptions of work that currently occupies the attention of academic economists. These glimpses into exciting new developments give students some awareness of the fact that economics is a living and evolving discipline, not one that is confined to the insights of the distant past. In the macroeconomics portion of the book, these boxed inserts include the following topics:

- Unemployment and inflation as co-ordination failures (page 145)
- The Lucas critique of estimated models of the economy (page 290)

All of our boxed inserts are intended to stimulate the student's interest and to demonstrate that investing a serious effort in understanding economic reasoning is a worthwhile and relevant endeavour.

Microeconomics

The discussion of microeconomics is organized around the central theme that we believe deals with the most significant lessons to be learned in an introductory economics course: what a market system does well, and what it does poorly.

Part One introduces this central theme and some of the fundamental ideas of economics (such as scarcity, opportunity cost, markets, and prices). A host of topical examples are used to illustrate these concepts and to convey the power of supply and demand analysis. They include "green" products at grocery stores, the proliferation of materials for recycling, species extinction, minimum-wage laws, rent controls, and the drug problem. Both the beginning (Chapters 2 and 3) and the end (Chapter 32) of the microeconomics portion of the book emphasize the fundamentally important issue of the environment. By starting with, and then returning to, this issue, we are able to maintain our focus on the theme of what the market does well and what it does poorly.

Our deeper excursion into microeconomic reasoning begins with Part Five. The chapters in this part of the book acquaint students with the central analytical tools of microeconomics and use those tools to explain how both consumers (Chapters 19 and 20) and producers (Chapters 21 and 22) make decisions that best serve their own interests. The extensive revisions in these chapters often reflect the suggestions of users of the last two editions of our book. For example:

- Three different methods are now presented to explain the consumer's optimal purchase rule: (1) basic intuition, applied to an example involving two goods; (2) marginal utility theory, applied to an example involving one good (which represents a small part of the consumer's budget. This method measures utility in terms of the consumer's willingness to part with income in order to acquire the good in question.); and (3) indifference curve analysis. Instructors can select their preferred combination of methods to explain this important concept.

- The relationship among the total, average, and marginal product curves and among the three corresponding cost curves is much more clearly explained.

- The formula for a monopolist's price-over-cost markup is derived and explained.

- Much greater emphasis is placed on the trade-off between equity and efficiency throughout the microeconomics portion of the book. In several chapters, the issue is explained with the aid of graphs depicting consumer and producer surplus.

Part Six examines how the decisions of consumers and firms interact in the marketplace, and provides an extensive examination of the virtues and vices of free markets. The early chapters of Part Six (Chapters 23 and 24) extol the remarkable accomplishments of an idealized system of markets, while the later chapters (Chapters 25, 26, and 27) discuss some of the market system's principal failings, particularly in the areas of monopoly power and externality effects. Chapter 28 discusses the free-trade debate, and ends with a clear, schematic explanation of how the government's main instruments of economic policy can best be assigned to our major economic goals. In this way, Part Six sets the stage for Part Seven, in which we address several important microeconomic policy issues.

The four chapters in Part Seven are devoted to answering the following four questions of current concern:

- *Chapter 29*: What determines the distribution of income?

- *Chapter 30*: What sorts of reforms in the tax and welfare systems represent the most efficient ways of reducing the problems of poverty and discrimination?

- *Chapter 31*: How have our competition laws and our experience with government regulation of industry contributed to promoting competitive behaviour?

- *Chapter 32*: What guidance does economic analysis offer for solving the problems of pollution and resource depletion?

All four of these chapters maintain our fundamental emphasis on identifying the equity and the efficiency aspects of microeconomic policy issues. Only by exploring the implications of policy on these two fronts can we fully appreciate the differences in the views that are held on these issues. And only by stressing this distinction can we defend our preference for certain policies—that is, for the policies that promote our objectives of equity and equality with the least sacrifice of economic efficiency.

The microeconomics portion of the book is replete with topical discussions. For example, in the text there are discussions of the GST (Chapter 30), the Free Trade Agreement (Chapter 28), and the use of input–output analysis in economic planning (Chapter 24). Furthermore, there are new or revised boxed inserts on the following subjects:

- The rising cost of medical care (page 413)

- How the concept of elasticity is applied in legal battles (page 443)

- The transition to free markets in Eastern Europe (page 538)

- Government bail-outs of corporations (page 620)

- Labour-union problems (page 668)

- Agricultural marketing boards (page 722)

- Recent experience with the new Competition Act (page 745)

- Pollution (page 756)

- An economist's answer to criticisms (such as those often published by David Suzuki) of our discipline's approach to issues of environmental protection

We have also expanded our "At the Frontier" series of boxed inserts in the microeconomics sections of the book, treating subjects such as the following:

- Experimental economics (page 57)

- Game theory (page 580)

- The theory of contestable markets (page 582)

- Principal agents and asymmetric information (page 597)

- Rent-seeking (page 648)

Canada and the Rest of the World

In both the macro and micro sections of the book, the material on the openness of the Canadian economy is given centre stage. Perhaps the most popular feature of the previous editions of this book, as we noted earlier, is the full integration of macroeconomic theory with the discussions of policy episodes in a way that properly emphasizes the fact that monetary policy and exchange-rate policy are one and the same thing. In the microeconomics sections, the material on comparative advantage and tariff policy is not tucked away, but appears in the core set of chapters on the pros and cons of free markets. Also, since the legal approaches to limiting market power (that is, regulation and competition laws) have met with rather limited success, it is frequently stressed that tariff cuts can be used to make Canadian markets contestable. Thus, tariff policy is discussed as one among several instruments for stimulating competition. Of course, the gains from international trade do not depend solely on Canada's small domestic markets and incomplete exploitation of the economies of large-scale production. The principle of comparative advantage in the standard situation of constant costs is fully explained in Chapter 28, which also contains two important new sections: One discusses the advantages and disadvantages of the Free Trade Agreement with the United States and the other explains the proper assignment of policy instruments to goals, as noted earlier.

Note to the Student

Most courses will begin with Part One, where we have touched most of the traditional bases while keeping the introductory materials briefer than they are in most other texts. Courses dealing with macroeconomic theory and policy in the first term will proceed next to Parts Two through Four, while courses commencing with microeconomics will skip to Parts Five through Seven.

Whatever the nature of your course, we would like to offer one suggestion. Unlike some of the other courses you may be taking, principles of economics is cumulative—each week's lesson builds on what you have learned before. You will save yourself a lot of frustration (and also a lot of work) if you keep up on a week-to-week basis. To help you do this, there is a chapter summary, a list of important terms and concepts, and a selection of discussion questions at the end of each chapter. In addition to these aids, many students will find the *Study Guide*, designed specifically to accompany this text, helpful as a self-testing and diagnostic device. When you encounter difficulties in the *Study Guide*, you will know which sections of the text you need to review.

Note to the Instructor

The ordering of chapters in the book is based on courses that treat macroeconomics before microeconomics, but it lends itself equally well to courses that reverse that sequence. The macroeconomic analysis is found in Parts Two through Four. The microeconomics material occupies Chapters 2 and 3 and Parts Five through Seven. Because our *detailed* study of microeconomics does not begin until Chapter 19, it may appear to readers that the book shortchanges microeconomics. In fact, no such problem exists. There are fifteen chapters in the macroeconomics block, fourteen chapters in the microeconomics block, and three chapters in the introductory section (Part 1). Since two of the chapters in Part 1 discuss microeconomic material (scarcity and choice and an initial pass at supply and demand analysis), the book actually contains *more* chapters on microeconomics. The following chart summarizes the book's basic structure:

```
┌─────────────────────────┐
│  I  Getting Acquainted  │
│     with Economics      │
│     (3 chapters)        │
└─────────────────────────┘
```

```
┌─────────────────────────────┐     ┌─────────────────────────────┐
│ II  Macroeconomics:         │     │  V  Essentials of           │
│     Aggregate Supply and    │     │     Microeconomics:         │
│     Demand Analysis         │     │     Consumers and Firms     │
│     (5 chapters)            │     │     (4 chapters)            │
│                             │     │                             │
│ III Fiscal, Monetary, and   │     │ VI  The Market System:      │
│     Exchange-Rate Policy    │     │     Virtues and Vices       │
│     (6 chapters)            │     │     (6 chapters)            │
│                             │     │                             │
│ IV  Macroeconomic Issues    │     │ VII Microeconomic Issues    │
│     (4 chapters)            │     │     (4 chapters)            │
└─────────────────────────────┘     └─────────────────────────────┘
```

Given that a reasonable pace for covering material is roughly one chapter per week on average, the following suggested course outlines should be suitable for many teaching situations.

OUTLINE FOR A ONE-TERM COURSE IN MICROECONOMICS

Chapter Number	Material Covered
1	Methodology
2	Scarcity and choice
3	Basic supply and demand
19 ⎫ 20 ⎬	Consumer theory
21 ⎫ 22 ⎬	Theory of the firm
23	Perfect competition
24	Laissez faire versus planning
25	Monopoly
27	Other sources of market failure
28	Comparative advantage and free trade

Plus any *two* of the following:

29	Income distribution
30	Tax reform
31	Competition policy
32	Environmental issues

OUTLINE FOR A ONE-TERM COURSE IN MACROECONOMICS

Chapter Number	Material Covered
1	Methodology
3	Basic supply and demand
4	Measuring macroeconomic performance
5 6 7 8 9	Multiplier analysis, fiscal policy, aggregate demand and supply, the self-correcting mechanism
11 12	Money and banking
13 14	Integration of fiscal, monetary, and exchange-rate policy

Plus any *two* of the following:

15	International policy co-ordination
16	The deficit
17	Phillips curves
18	Productivity and growth

Chapters 10 and 26 have been omitted from these course outlines. Chapter 10, on firms and the stock market, can (and most probably will) be read by students on their own. It is not demanding analytically, and most students are very interested in the subject. Chapter 26, on monopolistic competition and oligopoly, can be included by instructors who wish to place extra emphasis on theory, but its inclusion would necessitate the exclusion of one of the microeconomic "issues" chapters. However, it should be noted that the latter four chapters are divided into self-contained sections to allow instructors to focus on particular issues without having to cover the complete chapter. For example, the topic of regulation occupies half of Chapter 31, and that of pollution occupies half of Chapter 32; this material can be combined to create the equivalent of one chapter, to the exclusion of the other sections in Chapters 31 and 32.

Two things should be clear from our sample course outlines: (1) the book works very well for instructors who prefer to start their courses with microeconomics; (2) it is structured to accommodate the time constraints that confront most instructors.

Concerning the *Study Guide*, and whether you should recommend it for your students, we offer the following advice. Since such a guide should be especially useful for the student who is having difficulty, the core material in our *Study Guide* is pitched at a fairly basic level. However, in contrast to previous editions, we have added a number of much more challenging questions this time, so that the *Study Guide* will be of greater value to the more advanced students as well. Every chapter now has two practice tests, each of which contains both true/false and multiple-choice questions. The first test is more basic, while the second is more challenging. More-advanced students who are fairly confident that they understand the material may want to skim the Chapter Review, the Basic Exercises, the Definition Quiz, and the first practice test, and concentrate their attention on the more difficult practice test and the

Supplementary Exercises. By structuring the *Study Guide* in this way, we have tried to ensure that students of varying levels of ability will be able to benefit from this learning aid. As instructors, we know that even the best students can benefit from extra practice. Judging by the comments we have received from users, we expect that the introduction of a more challenging practice test and some additional, more difficult, Supplementary Exercises in each chapter will be a welcome addition to the *Study Guide*.

As with previous editions, a computerized *Test Bank* is available for the use of instructors. The third edition of this teaching aid has been significantly expanded. Also available is a fully revised *Instructor's Manual* and a set of *Transparency Masters*.

Once again, our textbook is available in separate, paperback *Microeconomics* and *Macroeconomics* editions. The introductory chapters (Part One) and the chapter on free trade are included in both volumes. Users of these split editions will have no difficulty locating material in the textbook's ancillaries, as the chapter and page numbers in the paperback volumes conform exactly to those used in the combined text.

In trying to improve the book from one edition to the next, we rely heavily on our own experiences as teachers. But our experience using the book is small compared with that of the community of instructors who have been and who will be using it. If you encounter problems, or have suggestions for improving the book, we urge you to let us know by writing to Bill Scarth in care of the publisher. Such letters are invaluable, and we are glad to receive them, even if they are critical.

With Thanks

Finally, and with great pleasure, we turn to the customary acknowledgments of indebtedness. Some of these have been accumulating now through five American editions of the book. The many American instructors whose comments were invaluable in planning this edition have been individually listed in the fifth American edition. Friends and colleagues who have made helpful suggestions directly for the Canadian editions include: John Burbidge, Don Dawson, Martin Dooley, Jim Johnson, Mel Kliman, Wayne Lewchuk, Andy Muller, Gord Myers, Les Robb, Byron Spencer, Mike Veall, and Doug Welland of McMaster University; Doug Burgess of Burgess–Graham Securities; Michael Hare of the University of Toronto; Tom Powrie, Brian Scarfe, and Sten Drugge of the University of Alberta; Hugh Young of the Department of Finance in Ottawa; Tony Myatt and Charles Waddell of the University of New Brunswick; Peter Kennedy of Simon Fraser University; Waclaw Dajnowiec of Ryerson Polytechnical Institute; Irwin Gillespie of Carleton University; Jack Guthrie of Camosun College; Robert Allan of the University of British Columbia; Lionel Ifill of Algonquin College; Ted Horbulyck of the University of Calgary; Chris Debresson of Concordia University; John Sayre of Capilano College; Mary-Ann Dimond and Robert Dimond of Brock University; Maurice Boote of Trent University; John Farrugia of Mohawk College; Arnold Frenzel and Peter Sinclair of Wilfrid Laurier University; Rob Jeacock and Raimo Marttala of Malaspina College; Thierry Neubert of John Abbott College; and Bram Cadsby of the University of Guelph. We wish to thank all of these individuals, as well as the many students who took the time to send their comments and suggestions to the publisher. Many of the suggestions made by instructors and students alike have been incorporated into this third edition. We are particularly indebted to Don Dawson of McMaster University, who provided thorough and invaluable input for the chapter on industrial organization.

The book you hold in your hand was not done by us alone. The fine people at Harcourt Brace Jovanovich, Canada, worked tirelessly and effectively to turn our manuscript into the book you see. Valuable help was contributed by Sarah Duncan, Scott Duncan, Sue Ann Becker, Denise Wake, Riça Night, Jack Steiner, Nick Owocki, and Elizabeth Stone. Most important has been the tireless support of our editor and project co-ordinator, Darlene Zeleney. Darlene has been a central player in this project for seven years now, and as time passes she finds more and more ways to help. She is always cheerful and effective, and her contribution to the book is fundamental.

And finally, there are our wives, Hilda Baumol, Madeline Blinder, and Kathy Scarth. They have helped us in so many ways. Their patience, good judgment, and love have made everything go more smoothly than we had any right to expect. We deeply appreciate their invaluable support.

William J. Baumol   **Alan S. Blinder**   **William M. Scarth**

Publisher's Note to Students and Instructors

This textbook is an important part of your course. If you are a student, it will greatly contribute to your present and future studies. If you are the instructor, you chose this textbook from among many as the best one for you and your students. The authors and publishers appreciate this acknowledgment of the considerable time and money we have invested to ensure the book's high quality.

If you are a student, we hope you will find this textbook an invaluable companion in meeting the objectives of your course. As well, it will become an excellent addition to your personal library.

Please remember that this is a copyrighted work and, as such, any photocopying means that the authors lose royalties that are rightfully theirs. This loss will discourage them from writing another edition of this textbook or other books. If this happens we all eventually lose—authors, publishers, instructors, and students.

We are very interested in your reactions to the book, so be sure to send us the stamped reply card at the end of the text. Your input helps us continue to publish high-quality books for your course.

Brief Contents

Contents

10 Firms and Their Financing: Stocks and Bonds 209

11 Money and the Banking System 227

PART IV
Macroeconomic Issues   309

15 Policy Co-ordination in the World Economy   311

16 Budget Deficits and the National Debt   329

PART V
Essentials of Microeconomics: Consumers and Firms   403

PART VI
The Market System: Virtues and Vices
501

31 Regulation of Industry and Competition Policy   719

Getting Acquainted with Economics

1

The Problems and Tools of the Economist

Why does public discussion of economic policy so often show the abysmal ignorance of the participants? Why do I so often want to cry at what public figures, the press, and television commentators say about economic affairs?

ROBERT M. SOLOW

Economics is a broad-ranging discipline, both in the questions it asks and in the methods it uses to seek answers. Many definitions of economics have been proposed, but we prefer to avoid any attempt to define the discipline in a single sentence or paragraph. Instead, this chapter will introduce you to economics by letting the subject matter speak for itself.

The first part of this chapter is intended to give you some idea of the types of problems that can be approached through economic analysis and the kinds of solutions that economic principles suggest. Many of the world's most pressing problems are economic in nature. So a little knowledge of basic economics is essential to anyone who wants to understand the world in which he or she lives.

The second part briefly introduces the methods of economic inquiry and the tools that economists use, while the appendix zeroes in specifically on the use and misuse of graphs. These are tools you may find useful in your life as a citizen, consumer, and worker long after the course is over.

Ideas for Beyond the Final Exam

As university professors, we realize it is inevitable that you will forget much of what you learn in this course—perhaps with a sense of relief—soon after the final exam. There is not much point bemoaning this fact; elephants may never forget, but people do. Nevertheless, some economic ideas are so important that you will want to remember them well beyond the final exam. If you do not, you will have shortchanged your own education. To help you pick out a few of the most crucial concepts, we have selected twelve ideas from among the many contained in this book. Some offer critical and enduring insights into the workings of the economy. Others bear on important policy issues that often appear in the newspapers. Still others point out common misunderstandings that occur among even the most thoughtful lay observers. As the quotation that opens this chapter suggests, many learned judges, politicians, business leaders, and university administrators who failed to understand or misused these economic principles could have made far wiser decisions than they did.

Each of the 12 **Ideas for Beyond the Final Exam** will be discussed in depth as it occurs in the course of the book; you should not expect to understand these ideas fully after reading this first chapter. Nonetheless, we think it useful to sketch them briefly here both to introduce you to economics and to provide a selective preview of what is to come.

IDEA 1: The Trade-Off between Inflation and Unemployment

At the start of the 1980s, Canadian policy-makers waged all-out war on inflation. The war was won: Inflation was reduced dramatically. But casualties were heavy: The national unemployment rate, which had averaged 6.8 percent during the 1970s, ran a stunning 11.5 percent in 1982 and 1983, and remained above 9 percent until 1987.

Economists maintain that this conjunction of events was no coincidence. Owing to features of our economy that we will study in Parts Two, Three, and Four, there is an agonizing *trade-off between inflation and unemployment in the short run*, meaning that most policies that bring down inflation also cause unemployment to rise. Since this trade-off poses the fundamental dilemma of national economic policy, we will devote all of Chapter 17 to examining it in detail.

IDEA 2: The Illusion of High Interest Rates

Is it more costly to borrow money at 5 percent interest or at 13 percent interest? That would appear to be an easy question to answer, even without a course in economics. But, in fact, it is not. An example will show why.

Around 1960, banks were lending money to home buyers at annual interest rates of about 5 percent. Twenty years later, these rates had risen to 13 percent. Yet economists maintain that it was actually cheaper to borrow in 1980 than in 1960. Why? Because inflation in 1980 was running at about 10 percent per year, while in 1960 it stood at only about 1 percent.

Why is information on inflation relevant to deciding how costly it is to borrow? Consider the position of a person who lends $100 for one year at a rate of 13 percent interest when the inflation rate is at 10 percent. At the end of the year the lender gets back his $100 plus $13 interest. But over that same year, because of inflation, he loses $10 *in terms of what his money can buy*. That is, in terms of *purchasing power*, the lender gains only $3 on his $100 loan, or 3 percent.

Now consider someone who lends $100 at 5 percent interest when prices are rising only 1 percent a year. This lender gets back the original $100 plus $5 in interest and loses only $1 in purchasing power from inflation—for a net gain of $4, or a 4 percent return on his loan.

As we will learn in Chapter 4, the failure to understand this principle has caused troubles for our tax laws, and in Chapter 16 we will see that it has even led to misunderstanding of the size and nature of the government budget deficit.

IDEA 3: The Consequences of Budget Deficits

Large federal budget deficits have been the focus of all of the Canadian government's budgets in recent years. The conflicting claims and counterclaims that have marked the debate over budget deficits are bound to confuse laypeople. Some critics claim that deficits hold dire consequences—including higher interest rates, more inflation, a stagnant economy, and an irksome burden on future generations of Canadians. Others deny these charges.

Who is right? In Chapter 16, we will learn that there is no easy answer—a budget deficit may be sound or unsound policy, depending on its size and on the reasons for its existence. However, whether or not the deficit represents sound policy, if it is generally believed to be unsound, its existence limits the government's ability to undertake new policies.

IDEA 4: The Overwhelming Importance of Productivity

In Geneva a worker in a watch factory now turns out roughly one hundred times as many mechanical watches per year as his ancestor did three centuries earlier. The

productivity of labour (output per worker hour) in cotton production has probably gone up more than a thousandfold in two hundred years. It is estimated that production per hour of labour in manufacturing in North America has gone up about seven times in the past century. This means that we can enjoy about seven times as much clothing, housewares, and luxury goods as were available to a typical citizen one hundred years before.

Economic issues such as inflation, unemployment, and monopoly are important to us all and will receive great attention in this book. But in the long run nothing has as great an effect on our material well-being and the amounts society can afford to spend on hospitals, schools, and social amenities as the rate of growth of productivity. Chapter 18 points out that, because productivity compounds like the interest on savings in a bank, what appears to be a small increase in productivity growth can have a huge effect on a country's standard of living over a long period of time. Since 1800, for example, productivity in North America is estimated to have grown only a bit more than 1.5 percent a year on the average. But that was enough to increase the output of manufactured goods per person about twenty times—a truly incredible amount.

IDEA 5: Mutual Gains from Voluntary Exchange

One of the most fundamental ideas of economics is that in a **voluntary exchange** both parties must gain something, or at least expect to gain something. Otherwise, why would they both agree to the exchange? This principle may seem self-evident, and it probably is. Yet it is amazing how often it is ignored in practice.

For example, it was widely believed for centuries that governments should interfere with international trade because one country's gain from a swap must be the other country's loss (see Chapter 28). Analogously, some people feel instinctively that if Mr. A profits handsomely from a deal with Mr. B, then Mr. B must have been exploited. Laws sometimes prohibit mutually beneficial exchanges between buyers and sellers—as when rental housing units are eliminated because the rent is "too high" (Chapter 3), or when a willing worker cannot be hired because the wage rate is "too low" (Chapters 3 and 29).

In each of these cases and in many more, well-intentioned but misguided reasoning blocks the mutual gains that arise from voluntary exchange—and thereby interferes with one of the most basic functions of an economic system (see Chapter 2).

IDEA 6: The Surprising Principle of Comparative Advantage

The Japanese economy produces many products that Canadians buy in huge quantities—including cars, TV sets, cameras, and electronic equipment. Canadian manufacturers have complained about the competition and demanded protection against the flood of imports that, in their view, threatens Canadian standards of living. Is this view justified?

Economists think not. But what if a combination of higher productivity and lower wages were to permit Japan to produce *everything* more cheaply than we could? Would it not then be true that Canadians would have no work and that our nation would be impoverished?

A remarkable result, called the **law of comparative advantage**, shows that even in this extreme case the two nations should still trade and that each can gain as a result! We will explain this principle fully in Chapter 28 (where we will also note some potentially valid arguments in favour of protecting domestic industry). But for now a simple parable will make the reason clear.

Suppose Sam grows up on a farm and is a whiz at ploughing, but he is also a successful country singer who earns $2000 a performance at hotels and nightclubs.

Should Sam refuse some singing engagements to leave time for ploughing? Of course not. Instead he should hire Alfie, a much less efficient farmer, to plough for him. Sam is the better farmer, but he earns so much more by specializing in singing that it pays him to leave the farming to Alfie. Alfie, though a poorer farmer than Sam, is an even worse singer. Thus Alfie earns a living by specializing in the job at which he at least has a *comparative* advantage (his farming is not quite as bad as his singing), and both Alfie and Sam gain. The same is true of two countries. Even if one of them is more efficient at everything, both countries can gain by producing the things they do best *comparatively.*

IDEA 7: Attempts to Repeal the Laws of Supply and Demand: The Market Strikes Back

When a commodity is in short supply, its price naturally tends to rise. Sometimes disgruntled consumers badger politicians into "solving" the problem by imposing a legal ceiling on the price. Similarly, when supplies are abundant—say, when fine weather produces extraordinarily abundant crops—prices tend to fall. This, naturally, makes suppliers unhappy, and they often succeed in getting legislation enacted that prohibits low prices by imposing price floors. But such attempts to repeal the laws of supply and demand usually backfire and sometimes produce results virtually the opposite of those that were intended.

Where rent controls are adopted to protect tenants, housing grows scarce because the law makes it unprofitable to build and maintain apartments. When minimum-wage legislation is enacted to protect low-wage workers, low-wage jobs disappear. Price floors are placed under agricultural products, and surpluses pile up. History provides spectacular examples of the way in which free markets strike back at attempts to interfere with the way they would otherwise work. For example, when the armies of Spain surrounded Antwerp in 1584, hoping to starve the city into submission, profiteers kept Antwerp going by smuggling food and supplies through enemy lines. However, when the city fathers adopted price controls to end their "unconscionable" prices, supplies suddenly dried up and the city soon surrendered.

As we will see in Chapter 3 and elsewhere in this book, such consequences of interference with the price mechanism are no accident. They follow inevitably from the way free markets work. Despite the many examples from history, many policy-makers still call for interference with the price mechanism. A common example, which surfaced again in 1990, is the suggestion that our government limit the trade in financial assets across our border, so that Canadian interest rates could remain lower than those in the United States.

IDEA 8: Externalities: A Shortcoming of the Market Cured by Market Methods

Markets are very efficient in producing the goods that consumers want in the quantities in which they are desired. Markets do so by offering large financial rewards to those who respond to what consumers want to buy and who make these products available economically. Similarly, the market mechanism minimizes waste and inefficiency by causing inefficient producers to lose money.

This system works well as long as an exchange between a seller and a buyer affects only those two parties. But often an economic transaction affects third parties that were not consulted. Examples abound: The utility that supplies electricity to your home also produces soot and pollutants that despoil the air and affect the health of others; after a farmer sprays his crops with toxic pesticides, the poison may seep into the ground water and affect the health of neighbouring communities.

Such social costs—called **externalities** because they affect parties *external* to the economic transaction that causes them—escape the control of the market mechanism, since there is normally no financial incentive motivating polluters to minimize the damage they do. The electric company and the farmer do not include environmental damage in their cost calculations. As a consequence, it pays firms to make their products as cheaply as possible, disregarding externalities that may damage the quality of life.

Yet, as we will learn in Chapters 27 and 32, there is a way for the government to use the market mechanism to control undesirable externalities. If the public utility and the farmer are charged for the harm they cause to the public, just as they are charged when they use tangible resources such as coal and fertilizer, then they will have an incentive to reduce the amount of pollution they generate. Thus, in this case, economists believe that market methods are often the best way to cure one of the market's most important shortcomings.

IDEA 9: Rational Choice and True Economic Costs

Despite dramatic improvements in our standard of living since the Industrial Revolution, we have not come anywhere near a state of unlimited abundance, and so we must constantly make choices. If you purchase a house, you may not be able to afford to eat at expensive restaurants as often as you used to. If a firm decides to retool its factories, it may have to postpone plans for new executive offices. If a government expands its road networks, it may be forced to reduce its outlays on school buildings.

Economists say that the true costs of such decisions are not the number of dollars spent on the house, the new equipment, or the roads, but rather *the value of what must be given up in order to acquire the item*—the restaurant meals, the new executive offices, or the new schools. These are called **opportunity costs** because they represent the *opportunities* the individual, firm, or government must forgo to make the desired expenditure. Economists maintain that opportunity costs must be considered in the decision-making process if rational choices are to be made (see Chapter 2).

The cost of a university or college education provides a vivid example that is probably close to your heart. How much do you think it *costs* to go to university? Most likely you would answer this question by adding together your expenditures on tuition, room and board, books, and the like and then deducting any scholarship funds or government grants you may receive. Economists would not. They would first want to know how much you could be earning if you were not attending university. This may sound like an irrelevant question, but because you give up these earnings by attending university, they must be added to your tuition bill as a cost of your education. Nor would economists accept the dormitory bill for room and board as a measure of your living costs. They would want to know by how much this exceeds what it would have cost you to live at home, and only this extra cost would be counted as an expense. On balance, a university or college education probably costs more than you think.

IDEA 10: The Importance of Marginal Analysis

Many pages in this book will be spent explaining and extolling the virtues of a type of decision-making process called **marginal analysis** (see especially Chapters 19 and 22), which can best be illustrated by an example.

Suppose that an airline is told by its accountants that the full cost of transporting one passenger from Montreal to Edmonton is $350. Can the airline profit by offering a reduced rate of $250 to students who fly on a standby basis? The surprising answer is: Probably yes. The reason is that the airline is committed to pay most of the $350 cost per passenger whether the plane carries 20 passengers or 120 passengers. Marginal analysis says that full costs—which include costs of maintenance, landing rights, ground crews, and so on—are irrelevant to an airline interested in making as much profit as possible. The only costs that are relevant in deciding whether to carry standby passengers for reduced rates are the extra costs of writing and processing additional tickets, the food and beverages these passengers consume, the additional fuel required, and so on. These costs are called **marginal costs**, and they are probably quite small in this instance. Any passenger who pays the airline more than its marginal cost will add something to the company's profit, so it probably is more profitable to let the students ride for the reduced fare than to fly the plane with some empty seats.

There are many real cases in which decision-makers, not understanding marginal analysis, have rejected advantageous possibilities like the reduced fare in our hypothetical example. These people were misled by calculating in terms of *average* rather than *marginal* cost figures—an error that can be quite costly.

IDEA 11: The Cost Disease of the Service Sector

There is a distressing phenomenon occurring throughout the industrialized world. Many community services have apparently been growing poorer—fewer postal deliveries, larger university classes, less reliable garbage pickups—while the public is paying more and more for them. Indeed, the costs of providing public services have risen consistently faster than has the rate of inflation. A natural response is to attribute the problem to government inefficiency. But this is certainly not the whole story, because private services have also grown more costly.

As we shall see in Chapter 27, one of the major causes of the problem is economic. And it has nothing to do with the inefficiency (or corruption) of public employees; rather, it has to do with the dazzling growth in efficiency of private manufacturing industries! Because technological improvements make workers more productive in manufacturing, wages rise. And they rise not only for the manufacturing workers but also for postal workers, teachers, and other public employees because workers can leave industries with low-paying jobs and compete for jobs in high-paying industries. But for personal services, technology is not easily changed. Since it still takes one person to drive a postal truck and one teacher to teach a class, the cost of these services is forced to rise. The same sort of cost disease affects other services, such as medical care, restaurant cooking, retailing, and automobile repair.

This is important to understand not because it excuses the financial record of our governments, but because an understanding of the problem suggests what we should expect the future to bring and, perhaps, indicates what policies should be advocated to correct it.

IDEA 12: Increasing Output May Require Sacrificing Equality

Many people support tax cuts on the grounds that they spur productivity and efficiency by providing greater incentives for working, saving, and investing. The provision of such incentives was one of the primary reasons the federal government introduced its two-part tax reforms effective in 1987 and 1991.

But there is at least one problem with this approach: to provide stronger incentives for success in the economic game, the gaps between the "winners" and the "losers" must necessarily be widened. For it is these gaps, after all, that provide the incentives to work harder, to save more, and to invest productively.

However, some observers feel that the unequal distribution of income in our society is unjust, that it is inequitable for the super-rich to sail yachts and give expensive parties while poor people live in slums and eat inadequate diets. People who hold this view are disturbed by the fact that tax cuts are quite likely to make the distribution of income even more unequal than it already is.

This example illustrates a genuine and pervasive dilemma. There is often a *trade-off* between the *size* of a nation's output and the degree of *equality* with which that output is distributed. As illustrated by the example of tax cuts, programs that increase production often breed inequality. And, as we shall see in Chapter 30, many policies designed to divide the proverbial economic pie more equally inadvertently cause the size of the pie to shrink. But, as we shall also see, economists make many useful suggestions about how this trade-off can be minimized.

Epilogue

These, then, are a dozen of the more fundamental concepts to be found in this book— ideas that we hope you will retain **Beyond the Final Exam**. Do not try to learn them perfectly right now, for you will hear much more about each of them as the book progresses. Instead, keep them in mind as you read—we will point them out to you as they occur by the use of the book's logo ✊ —and look back over this list at the end of the course. You may be amazed to see how natural, or even obvious, they will seem then.

Inside the Economist's Tool Kit

Now that you have some idea of the kinds of issues economists deal with, you should know something about how they grapple with these problems.

Economics as a Discipline

Economics has something of a split personality. Clearly the most rigorous of the social sciences, it nevertheless looks decidedly more "social" than "scientific" when compared with physics.

An economist is a jack of several trades, borrowing modes of investigation from numerous fields. Mathematical reasoning is used extensively in economics, but so is historical study. And neither looks quite the same as when practised by a mathematician or a historian. Statistical inference, too, plays an important role in economic inquiry, but economists have had to modify standard statistical procedures to fit the kinds of data they deal with—data that are not generated under the controlled conditions of the laboratory.

An introductory course in economics cannot make you an economist, but it should help you approach social problems from a pragmatic and dispassionate point of view. Answers to all society's problems will not be found in this book. But you should learn how to pose questions in ways that will help produce answers that are both useful and illuminating.

The Need for Abstraction

Some students find economics unduly abstract and "unrealistic." The stylized world envisioned by economic theory seems only a distant cousin to the world they see around them. There is an old joke about three people—a chemist, a physicist, and an economist—stranded on an isolated island with an ample supply of canned food but no implements with which to open the cans. In debating what to do, the chemist suggests lighting a fire under the cans, thus expanding their contents and causing the cans to burst. The physicist doubts that this will work. He advocates building a catapult with which they can smash the cans against some nearby boulders. Then, they turn to the economist for his suggestion. He thinks for a moment and announces, "Let's assume we have a can opener."

Economists *do* make unrealistic assumptions, and you will encounter many of them in the pages that follow. But this propensity to abstract from reality results from the incredible complexity of the real world, not from any fondness economists have for sounding absurd.

Compare the chemist's task of explaining the interactions of compounds in a chemical reaction with the economist's task of explaining the interactions of people in an economy. Are molecules ever motivated by greed or altruism, by envy or ambition? Do they ever emulate other molecules? Do forecasts about them influence their behaviour? People, of course, do all these things, and many, many more. It is therefore immeasurably more difficult to predict human behaviour than it is to predict chemical reactions. If economists tried to keep track of every aspect of human behaviour, they could surely never hope to understand the nature of the economy. Thus:

Abstraction from details is necessary to understand the functioning of anything as complex as the economy.

Abstraction means ignoring many details in order to focus on the most important factors in a problem.

To appreciate why the economist **abstracts** from details, put yourself in the following hypothetical situation. You have just arrived, for the first time in your life, in Montreal. You are now at Hôpital Jean-Talon. This is the point marked *A* in Figures 1–1 and 1–2, which are alternative maps of part of Montreal. You want to drive to the Hôpital St. Mary, marked *B* on each map. Which map would you find more useful? You will notice that Map 1 (Figure 1–1) has the full details of the Montreal road system. Consequently, it requires a major effort to read it. In contrast, Map 2 (Figure 1–2) omits many minor roads so that the major arteries stand out more clearly.

Most strangers to the city would prefer Map 2. With its guidance they are likely to find Hôpital St. Mary in a reasonable amount of time, even though a slightly shorter route might have been found by careful calculation and planning using Map 1. Map 2 seems to *abstract* successfully from a lot of confusing details while retaining the essential aspects of the city's geography. Economic theories strive to do the same.

Map 3 (Figure 1–3), which shows little more than the major routes that pass through the greater Montreal area, illustrates a danger of which all theorists must

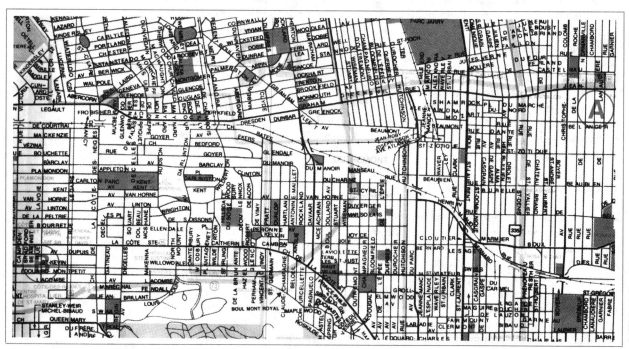

FIGURE 1–1
Map 1

Map 1 gives complete details of the road system of Montreal. If you are like most people, you will find it hard to read and not very useful for figuring out how to get from Hôpital Jean-Talon (point A) to Hôpital St. Mary (point B). For this purpose, the map carries far too much detail, though for some other purposes (for example, locating some small street) it may be the best map available.

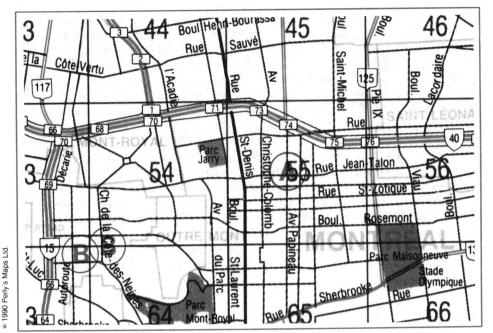

FIGURE 1–2
Map 2

Map 2 shows a very different perspective of Montreal. Minor roads are eliminated—we might say, *assumed away*—in order to present a clearer picture of where the major arteries go. As a result of this simplification, several ways of getting from Hôpital Jean-Talon (point *A*) to Hôpital St. Mary (point *B*) stand out clearly. For example, we can drive west on Hwy. 40 to Hwy. 15 or take Rue Jean-Talon over to Chemin de la Côte-des-Neiges. While we might find a shorter route by poring over the details of Map 1, most of us will feel more comfortable with Map 2.

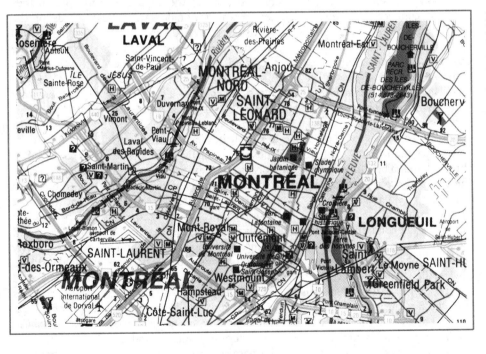

FIGURE 1–3
Map 3

Map 3 strips away still more details of the Montreal road system. In fact, only major roads remain. This map may be useful for passing through the city or getting around it, but it will not help the tourist who wants to see the sights of Montreal. For this purpose, too many details are missing.

beware. Armed only with the information provided on this map, you might never find Hôpital St. Mary. Instead of a useful idealization of the Montreal road network, the map-makers have produced a map that is oversimplified for our purpose. Too much has been assumed away. Of course, this map was never intended to be used as a guide to Hôpital St. Mary, which brings us to a very important point:

There is no such thing as one "right" degree of abstraction for all analytic purposes. The optimal degree of abstraction depends on the objective of the analysis. A model that is a gross oversimplification for one purpose may be needlessly complicated for another.

Economists are constantly treading the thin line between Map 2 and Map 3, between useful generalization about complex issues and gross distortions of the pertinent facts. How can they tell when they have abstracted from reality just enough? There is no objective answer to this question, which is why applied economics is as much art as science. One of the factors distinguishing good economics from bad economics is the degree to which analysts are able to find the factors that constitute the equivalent of Map 2 (rather than Maps 1 or 3) for the problem at hand. It is not always easy to do.

For example, suppose you are interested in learning why different people have different incomes, why some are fabulously rich while others are pathetically poor. People differ in many ways—too many to enumerate, much less to study. The economist must ignore most of these details in order to focus on the important ones. The colour of a person's hair or eyes probably is not important to the problem at hand, but the colour of his or her skin certainly might be. Height and weight may not matter, but education probably does. Proceeding in this way, we pare Map 1 down to the manageable dimensions of Map 2. But there is a danger of going too far. To make it easy to analyze a problem, we can end up stripping away some of the crucial features, and winding up with Map 3.

The Role of Economic Theory

A person "can stare stupidly at phenomena; but in the absence of imagination they will not connect themselves together in any rational way." These words of the renowned American philosopher–scientist C. S. Peirce succinctly express the crucial role of theory in scientific inquiry. What precisely do we mean by theory? To the economist or the natural scientist, the word *theory* does not mean what it does in common parlance. In scientific usage, a theory is *not* an untested assertion of alleged fact. The statement that saccharine causes cancer is not a theory; it is a *hypothesis* that will prove to be either true or false after the right sorts of experiments have been completed.

A **theory** is a deliberate simplification of factual relationships whose purpose is to explain how those relationships work.

Instead, a **theory** is a deliberate simplification (abstraction) of factual relationships that attempts to explain how those relationships work. It is an *explanation* of the mechanism behind observed phenomena. For example, astronomers' data describe the paths of the planets, and gravity forms the basis of theories that are intended to explain these data. Similarly, economists have data suggesting that government policies can affect the degree of a country's prosperity. Economic theory seeks to describe and explain how government policies affect the path of the national economy.

Economic theory has acquired an unsavoury public image in recent years—partly because of inaccurate predictions by some economists, partly because doctrinal disputes have spilled over into the news media, and partly because some politicians have found it expedient to scoff at economists. This bad image is unfortunate because theorizing is not a luxury but a necessity. Economic theory provides a logical structure for organizing and analyzing economic data. Without theory, economists would be able only to observe the world; with theory, they can attempt to understand it.

People who have never studied economics often draw a false distinction between *theory* and *practical policy*. Politicians and business people, in particular, often reject abstract economic theory as something that is best ignored by "practical" policymakers. The irony of these statements is that:

It is precisely the concern for policy that makes economic theory so necessary and important.

If there were no possibility of changing the economy through public policy, economics might be a historical and descriptive discipline, asking, for example, What happened in Canada during the Great Depression of the 1930s? or, How is it that industrial pollution got to be so serious in the twentieth century?

But deep concern about public policy forces economists to go beyond such historical and descriptive questions. To analyze policy options, they are forced to deal with possibilities that have not actually occurred. For example, to learn how to prevent depressions, they must investigate whether the Great Depression could have been avoided by more astute government policies. Or to determine what environmental programs will be most effective, they must understand how and why a market economy produces pollution and what might happen if government placed taxes on industrial waste discharges and automobile emissions. As Peirce pointed out, not even a lifetime of ogling at real-world data will answer such questions.

Indeed, the facts can sometimes be highly misleading. Statistics often indicate that two variables behave very similarly, moving up and down together. But this **correlation** does not prove that either of these variables *causes* the other. For example, in rainy weather, people tend to drive their cars more slowly, and there are also more traffic accidents. But this correlation does not mean that slow driving causes accidents. Rather, both phenomena can be attributed to a common underlying factor (more rain) that leads both to more accidents and to slower driving. Thus, just looking at the degree of correlation (the degree of similarity) in the behaviour of two sets of statistics (like accidents and driving speeds) may not tell us much about cause and effect. We need to use theory as part of the analysis.

Because most economic issues hinge on some question of cause and effect, only a combination of theoretical reasoning and data analysis can hope to provide solutions. Simply observing correlations in data is not enough. We must understand how, if at all, different government policies will lead to a lower unemployment rate or how a tax on emissions will reduce pollution.

Two variables are said to be **correlated** if they tend to go up or down together. But correlation need not imply causation.

What Is an Economic "Model"?

An **economic model** is a representation of a theory or a part of a theory, often for the purpose of illuminating cause-and-effect relationships. The notion of a "model" is familiar enough to children, and economists (in common with other scientists) use the term in much the same way that children do.

A child's model automobile or airplane looks and operates much like the real thing, but it is much smaller and much simpler, and so it is much easier to manipulate and understand. Engineers for General Motors and Boeing also build models of cars and planes. While their models are far bigger and much more elaborate than a child's toys, they use them for much the same purposes: to observe the workings of these vehicles "up close," to experiment with them in order to see how they might behave under different circumstances ("What happens if I do this?"). From these experiments, they make educated guesses as to how the real-life version will perform.

Economists use models for similar purposes. A. W. Phillips, the famous engineer-turned-economist who discovered the "Phillips curve" (discussed in Chapter 17), was talented enough to construct a working model of the determination of national income in a simple economy using coloured water flowing through pipes. For years this contraption, depicted in Figure 1–4, graced the basement of the London School of Economics. However, most economists lack Phillips's manual dexterity, so economic models are generally built with paper and pencil rather than with hammer and nails.

Because many of the models used in this book are depicted in diagrams, we explain the construction and use of various types of graphs in the appendix to this chapter. But sometimes economic models are expressed only in words. The statement "Business people produce the level of output that maximizes their profits" is the basis for a behavioural model whose consequences are explored in some detail in Parts Five through Seven. Don't be put off by seemingly abstract models. Think of them as useful road maps, and remember how hard it would be to find your way around Montreal without one.

An **economic model** is a simplified, small-scale version of some aspect of the economy. Economic models are often expressed in equations, by graphs, or in words.

FIGURE 1-4
The Phillips Machine
The late Professor A. W. Phillips, while teaching at the London School of Economics in the early 1950s, built this machine to illustrate Keynesian theory. This is the same theory that we will explain later in this book, using words and diagrams, but Phillips's background as an engineer enabled him to depict the theory with the help of tubes, valves, and pumps. Economists, on the whole, tend not to be very good plumbers; only Phillips and Irving Fisher before him used water and pipes to build models of this sort. Most economists rely on paper and pencil instead. But the two sorts of models perform the same function: They simplify reality in order to make it understandable.

Reasons for Disagreements: Imperfect Information and Value Judgments

"If all the earth's economists were laid end to end, they could not reach an agreement," or so the saying goes. If economics is a scientific discipline, why do economists seem to quarrel so much? Politicians and reporters are fond of pointing out that economists can generally be found on both sides of every issue of public policy. Physicists, on the other hand, do not debate whether the earth revolves around the sun or vice versa.

The question reflects a misunderstanding of the nature of science. Disputes are normal at the frontier of any science. As a matter of fact, physicists formerly did argue over whether the earth revolves around the sun. Nowadays, they argue about antimatter, the "big bang," and other esoteric phenomena. These arguments often go unnoticed by the public, because most of us do not understand what modern physicists are talking about. But because economics is a *social* science, its disputes are aired in public, and almost everyone is personally concerned with the subject matter. Sometimes it seems as though anyone who has ever bought or sold anything fancies himself an amateur economist.

Furthermore, there is much more agreement among economists than is commonly supposed. For example, virtually all economists, regardless of their politics, agree that taxing polluters is one of the best ways to protect the environment, and that free trade among nations is preferable to the erection of barriers through tariffs and quotas. The list could go on and on. It is probably true that the issues about which economists agree *far* exceed those about which they disagree.

Finally, many of the disputes among economists are not disputes at all. Economists, like everyone else, come in all political persuasions: conservative, middle-of-the-road, radical. Each may have different values and hold a different view of what is best for society, so each may have a different opinion on the "right" solution to any problem of public policy. In addition, not all of the pertinent facts about the issue in question may be known.

Value judgments are propositions that cannot be proven true or false; they simply are or are not consistent with a particular moral code.

While economists can contribute the best theoretical and factual knowledge there is on a particular issue, the final decision on policy questions often rests either on information that is not currently available or on tastes and ethical opinions (the things we call **value judgments**), or on both.

The following example concerning unemployment and inflation might help to illustrate why pure scientific analysis often fails to lead to a specific policy conclusion.

Government policies that succeed in shortening a recession are virtually guaranteed to cause higher inflation for a while. Using tools that we will describe in Parts Two, Three, and Four, many economists believe they can even measure how much more inflation the economy will suffer as the price of fighting a recession. Is it worth it? An economist cannot answer this question: The decision rests on value judgments about the moral trade-off between inflation and unemployment (about who is made better and worse off in each case)—judgments that can be made only by the citizenry through its elected officials.

Earlier in this chapter we said that economics cannot provide all the *answers*, but it can teach you how to ask the right *questions*. Now you know some of the reasons why. By the time you finish studying this book, you should have a good understanding of when the right course of action turns on disputed facts, when on value judgments, and when on some combination of the two.

Summary

1. To help you get the most out of your first course in economics, we have devised a list of *twelve important ideas* that you will want to remember *Beyond the Final Exam*. Here we list them, very briefly, indicating where each idea occurs in the book.

   1) Most government policies that reduce inflation are likely to intensify the unemployment problem, and vice versa. (Chapter 17)

   2) Interest rates that appear very high may actually be very low if they are accompanied by rapid inflation. (Chapter 4)

   3) Budget deficits may or may not be advisable, depending on circumstances. (Chapter 16)

   4) In the long run, productivity is almost the only thing that matters for a nation's material well-being. (Chapter 18)

   5) In a voluntary exchange, both parties must expect to benefit. (Chapters 3 and 29)

   6) Two nations can gain from international trade, even if one is more efficient at making everything. (Chapter 28)

   7) Lawmakers who try to repeal the "law" of supply and demand are liable to open a Pandora's box of troubles they never expected. (Chapter 3)

   8) Externalities cause the market mechanism to misfire, but this defect of the market can be remedied by market-oriented policies. (Chapters 27 and 32)

   9) To make a rational decision, the opportunity cost of an action must be measured, because only this calcu-

   lation will tell the decision-maker what he has given up. (Chapter 2)

   10) Decision-making often requires the use of marginal analysis to isolate the costs and benefits of a particular decision. (Chapters 19 and 22)

   11) The operation of free markets is likely to lead to rising prices for public and private services. (Chapter 27)

   12) Most policies that equalize income will exact a cost by reducing the nation's output. (Chapter 30)

2. Because of the great complexity of human behaviour, economists are forced to abstract from many details, make generalizations that they know are not quite true, and organize what knowledge they have according to some theoretical structure.

3. Economists use simplified models to understand the real world and predict its behaviour, much as a child uses a model railway to learn how trains work.

4. While these models, if skilfully constructed, can illuminate important economic problems, they can rarely answer the questions that confront policy-makers. For this purpose, value judgments are needed, which the economist is no better equipped than anyone else to make.

5. A course in economics seeks to teach the student how to formulate the right questions, questions that point to the value judgments or unknown pieces of data that must be obtained in order to make an intelligent decision. It does not try to provide all the answers.

Concepts for Review

Voluntary exchange
Comparative advantage
Productivity
Externalities

Marginal analysis
Marginal costs
Abstraction and generalization
Theory

Correlation versus causation
Economic model
Value judgments

Questions for Discussion

1. Think about how you would construct a "model" of how your university is governed. Which officers and administrators would you include and exclude from your model if the objective were
   a. to explain how decisions on tuition payments are made?
   b. to explain the quality of the football team?
   Relate this to the map example in the chapter.

2. Relate the process of "abstraction" to the way you take notes in a lecture. Why do you not try to transcribe every word the lecturer utters? Why do you not just write down the title of the lecture and stop there? How do you decide, roughly speaking, on the correct amount of detail?

3. Explain why a government policy-maker cannot afford to ignore economic theory.

Appendix
The Use and Misuse of Graphs

Constructing Graphs

We have noted that economic models are often analyzed and explained with the help of graphs, but that is not the only reason for you to study how they work. You are likely to encounter them often, and in various areas of your life—from reading the daily newspaper to discussing your health with your physician.

In this appendix we show, first, how to read a graph that depicts a relationship between two variables. Second, we define the term *slope* and describe how it is measured and interpreted. Third, we explain how the behaviour of three variables can be shown on a two-dimensional graph. Fourth, we discuss how misinterpretation is avoided by adjusting many economic graphs to accommodate changes in the purchasing power of the dollar, in the population of the nation, and in other pertinent developments. And finally, we examine several other common ways in which graphs can be misleading if not drawn and interpreted with care.

Two-Variable Diagrams

Much of the economic analysis to be found in this and other books requires that we keep track of two **variables** simultaneously. For example, in studying the operation of markets, we will want to keep one eye on the price of a commodity and the other on the quantity that is bought and sold.

For this reason, economists frequently find it useful to display actual or hypothetical figures in a *two-dimensional graph*, which simultaneously represents the behaviour of two economic variables. The numerical value of one variable is measured along the bottom of the graph (called the *horizontal axis*), starting from the **origin** (the point labelled "0"), and the numerical value of the other is measured along the side of the graph (called the *vertical axis*), also starting from the origin. Both variables are equal to zero at the origin.

Figure 1–5 is a typical graph of economic analysis. The same (imaginary) *demand curve* is represented by the dots in Figure 1–5(a) and the heavy coloured line in Figure 1–5(b). The graphs show the price of natural gas on their vertical axes and the quantity of gas people want to buy at each such price on the horizontal axes. Each dot in Figure 1–5(a) represents one of the pairs of observations in Table 1–1. The dots are then just connected in Figure 1–5(b) by means of the continuous green curve labelled *DD*.

Economic diagrams are generally read as one reads latitudes and longitudes on a map. On the demand curve in Figure 1–5, the point marked *a* represents a hypothetical combination of price and quantity demanded in Halifax. By drawing a horizontal line leftward from that point to the vertical axis, we learn that the average price for gas in Halifax is $30 per thousand cubic metres. By dropping a line straight down to the horizontal axis, we find that 80 million cubic metres are wanted by consumers at this price, just as the statistics in Table 1–1 show. The other points on the graph give similar information. For example, point *b* indicates that if natural gas in Halifax cost only $20 per thousand cubic metres, the quantity demanded would be higher—it would reach 120 million cubic metres.

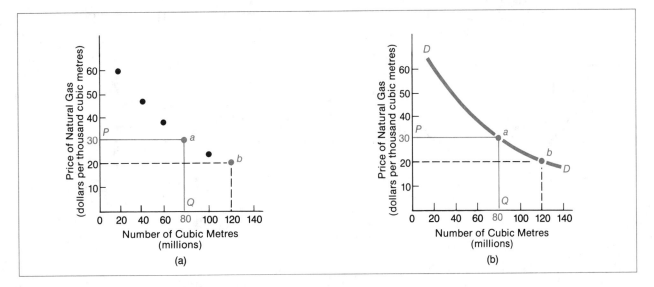

FIGURE 1-5

A Demand Curve for Natural Gas in Halifax

These figures show the relationship between the price of natural gas and the quantity of it that will be demanded. In Figure 1-5(a), each point represents one of the pairs of data given in Table 1-1. For example, the point labelled *a* indicates that at a price of $30 per thousand cubic metres (point *P*), the quantity demanded will be 80 million cubic metres (point *Q*). In Figure 1-5(b), the points have been connected by the coloured line. This curve gives us an easy-to-read image of the relationship between price and quantity demanded.

TABLE 1-1

Quantities of Natural Gas Demanded at Various Prices

Price ($ per thousand cubic metres)	20	30	40	50	60
Quantity demanded (millions of cubic metres)	120	80	60	40	22

Notice that information about price and quantity is *all* we can learn from the diagram. The demand curve will not tell us about the kinds of people who live in Halifax, the size of their homes, or the condition of their furnaces. It tells us the price and the quantity demanded at that price—no more, no less. But on that subject, it does tell us that when price declines, there is an increase in the amount of gas consumers are willing and able to buy.

A diagram abstracts from many details, some of which may be quite interesting, in order to focus on the two variables of primary interest—in this case, the price of natural gas and the amount of gas that is demanded at each price. All the diagrams used in this book share this basic feature. They cannot tell the reader the "whole story" any more than a map's latitude and longitude figures for a particular city can make someone an authority on that city.

The Definition and Measurement of Slope

One of the most important features of the diagrams used by economists is the rapidity with which the line, or curve, being sketched runs uphill or downhill as we move to the right. The demand curve in Figure 1-5 clearly slopes downhill (the price falls) as we follow it to the right (that is, as more gas is demanded because of the lower price). In such instances we say that *the curve has a negative slope, or is negatively sloped, because one variable falls as the other one rises.*

The **slope of a straight line** is the ratio of the vertical change to the corresponding horizontal change as we move to the right along the line, or as it is often said, the ratio of the "rise" over the "run."

The four panels of Figure 1-6 show all the possible slopes for a straight-line relationship between two unnamed variables called *Y* (measured along the vertical axis) and *X* (measured along the horizontal axis). Figure 1-6(a) shows a negative slope, much like our demand curve. Figure 1-6(b) shows a positive slope, because variable *Y* rises (we go uphill) as variable *X* rises (we move to the right). Figure 1-6(c) shows a *zero* slope, where the value of *Y* is the same, irrespective of the value of *X*. Figure 1-6(d) shows an *infinite*

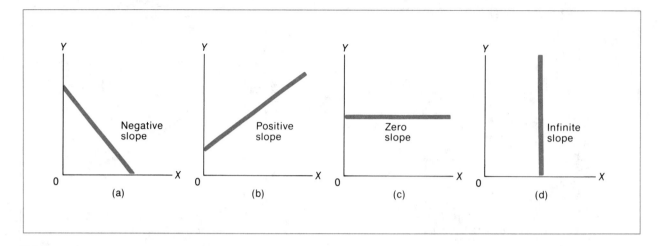

FIGURE 1-6
Different Types of Slope of a Straight-Line Graph
In Figure 1-6(a), the curve goes downward as we read from left to right, so we say it has a negative slope. The slopes in the other figures can be interpreted similarly.

slope, meaning that the value of X is the same, irrespective of the value of Y.

Slope is a numerical concept, not just a qualitative one. The two panels of Figure 1–7 show two positively sloped straight lines with different slopes. The line in Figure 1–7(b) is clearly steeper. But by how much? The labels should help you compute the answer. In Figure 1–7(a) a horizontal movement, AB, of 10 units (13 – 3) corresponds to a vertical movement, BC, of 1 unit (9 – 8). So the slope is $BC/AB = \frac{1}{10}$. In

Figure 1–7(b), the same horizontal movement of 10 units corresponds to a vertical movement of 3 units (11 – 8). So the slope is $\frac{3}{10}$, which is larger.

By definition, the slope of any particular straight line is the same no matter where on that line we choose to measure it. That is why we can pick any horizontal distance, AB, and the corresponding slope triangle, ABC, to measure slope. But this is not true of lines that are curved.

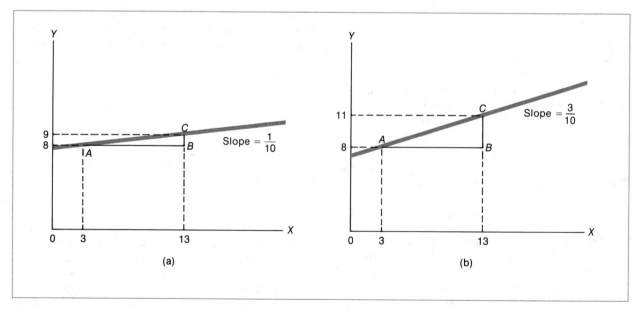

FIGURE 1-7
How to Measure Slope
Slope indicates how much the graph rises per unit move from left to right. Thus, in Figure 1-7(b), as we go from point A to point B, we go 13 - 3 = 10 units to the right. But in that interval, the graph rises from the height of point B to the height of point C; that is, it rises 3 units. Consequently, the slope of the line is $BC/AB = 3/10$.

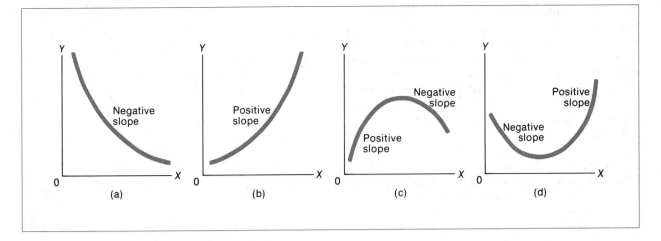

FIGURE 1-8
Behaviour of Slopes in Curved Graphs
As Figures 1-8(c) and 1-8(d) indicate, where a graph is not a straight line it may have a slope that starts off as positive but becomes negative farther to the right, or vice versa.

A curved line also has slope, but the numerical value of the slope is different at every point.

The four panels of Figure 1-8 provide some examples of **slopes of curved lines**. The curve in Figure 1-8(a) has a negative slope everywhere, while the curve in Figure 1-8(b) has a positive slope everywhere. But these are not the only possibilities. In Figure 1-8(c) we encounter a curve that has a positive slope at first but a negative slope later on. Figure 1-8(d) shows the opposite case: a negative slope followed by a positive slope.

It is possible to measure the slope of a smooth curved line numerically *at any particular point*. This is done by drawing a *straight* line that *touches*, but does not *cut*, the curve at the point in question. Such a line is called a **tangent to the curve**.

The slope of a curved line at a particular point is the slope of the straight line that is tangent to the curve at that point.

In Figure 1-9 we have constructed tangents to a curve at two points. Line *tt* is tangent at point *C*, and line *TT* is tangent at point *F*. We can measure the slope of the curve at these two points by applying the definition. The calculation for point *C*, then, is as follows:

$$\text{Slope at point } C = \text{Slope of line } tt = \frac{\text{Distance } BC}{\text{Distance } AB}$$
$$= \frac{6-2}{10-0} = \frac{4}{10} = +0.4.$$

A similar calculation yields the slope of the curve at point *F*, which, as we can see from Figure 1-9, must be smaller:

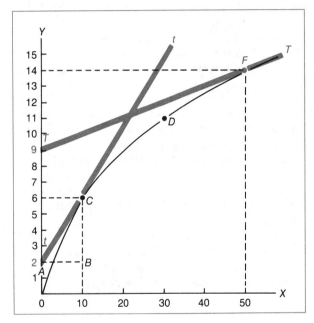

FIGURE 1-9
How to Measure Slope at a Point on a Curved Graph
To find the slope at point *F*, draw the line *TT*, which is tangent to the curve at point *F*; then measure the slope of the straight-line tangent *TT* as in Figure 1-7. The slope of the tangent is the same as the slope of the curve at point *F*.

$$\text{Slope at Point } F = \text{Slope of line } TT$$

$$= \frac{14-9}{50-0} = \frac{5}{50} = +0.1.$$

EXERCISE
Show that the slope of the curve at point *D* is between +0.1 and +0.4.

What would happen if we tried to apply this graphical technique to the high point in Figure 1–8(c) or to the low point in Figure 1–8(d)? Take a ruler and try it. The tangents that you construct should be horizontal, meaning that they should have a slope of exactly zero. It is always true that where the slope of a smooth curve changes from positive to negative, or vice versa, there will be at least a single point with a zero slope.

Curves that have the shape of a hill, such as Figure 1–8(c), have a zero slope at their *highest* point. Curves that have the shape of a valley, such as Figure 1–8(d), have a zero slope at their *lowest* point.

Rays through the Origin and 45° Lines

The point at which a straight line cuts the vertical (*Y*) axis is called the *Y-intercept*. For example, the *Y*-intercept of line *tt* in Figure 1–9 is 2, while the *Y*-intercept of line *TT* is 9. Lines whose *Y*-intercept is zero have so many special uses that they have been given a special name: a **ray through the origin**, or a **ray**.

Figure 1–10 contains three rays through the origin, and the slope of each is indicated in the diagram. The ray in the centre—whose slope is 1—is particularly useful in many economic applications because it marks off points where *X* and *Y* are equal (as long as *X* and *Y* are measured in the same units). For example, at point *A* we have *X* = 3 and *Y* = 3; at point *B*, *X* = 4 and *Y* = 4; and a similar relation holds at any other point on that ray.

How do we know that this is always true for a ray whose slope is 1? If we start from the origin (where both *X* and *Y* are zero) and the slope of the ray is 1, we know from the definition of slope that:

$$\text{Slope} = \frac{\text{Vertical change}}{\text{Horizontal change}} = 1.$$

This implies that the vertical change and the horizontal change are always equal, so the two variables must always remain equal.

Rays through the origin with a slope of 1 are called 45° **lines** because they form an angle of 45° with the horizontal axis. If a point representing some data is above the 45° line, we know that the value of *Y* exceeds the value of *X*. Conversely, whenever we find a point below the 45° line, we know that *X* is larger than *Y*.

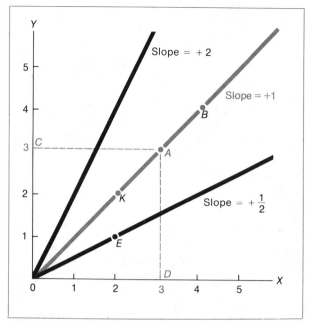

FIGURE 1–10
Rays through the Origin
Rays are straight lines drawn through the zero point on the graph (the *origin*). Three rays with different slopes are shown. The middle ray, the one with slope = +1, has two properties that make it particularly useful in economics: (1) it makes a 45° angle with either axis, and (2) any point on that ray (for example, point *A*) is exactly equal in distance from the horizontal and vertical axes (length *DA* = length *CA*). So if the items measured on the two axes are in equal units, then at any point on that ray, such as *A*, the number on the *X*-axis (the abscissa) will be the same as the number on the *Y*-axis (the ordinate).

Squeezing Three Dimensions into Two: Contour Maps

Sometimes, because a problem involves more than two variables, two dimensions just are not enough, which is unfortunate since paper is only two dimensional. When we study the decision-making process of a business firm, for example, we may want to keep track simultaneously of three variables: how much labour it employs, how much machinery it uses, and how much output it creates.

Luckily, there is a well-known device for collapsing three dimensions into two, namely a *contour map*. Figure 1–11 is a contour map of Mont Tremblant, near Montreal. On several of the irregularly shaped "rings" we find a number indicating the height above sea level at that particular spot on the mountain. Thus, unlike the more usual sort of map, which gives only latitudes and longitudes, this contour map exhibits three pieces of information about each point: latitude, longitude, and altitude.

Figure 1–12 looks more like the contour maps encountered in economics. It shows how some third

FIGURE 1-11
A Geographic Contour Map
All points on any particular contour line represent geographic locations that are at the same height above sea level.

variable, called Z (think of it as a firm's output, for example), varies as we change either variable X (think of it as a firm's employment) or variable Y (think of it as the use of a firm's machines). Just as with the map of Mont Tremblant, any point on the diagram conveys three pieces of data. At point A, we can read off the values of X and Y in the conventional way (X is 30 and Y is 40), and we can also note the value of Z by

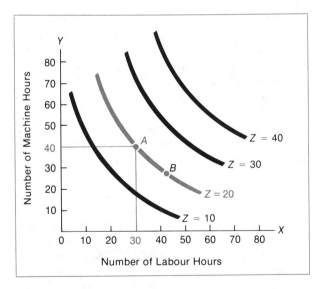

FIGURE 1-12
An Economic Contour Map
In this contour map, all points on a given contour line represent different combinations of labour and capital capable of producing a given output. For example, all points on the curve $Z = 20$ represent input combinations that can produce 20 units of output. Point A on that line means that the 20 units of output can be produced using 30 labour hours and 40 machine hours. Economists call such maps *isoquant maps* or *production indifference maps*.

checking to see on which contour line point A falls. (It is on the $Z = 20$ contour.) So point A is able to tell us that 30 hours of labour and 40 hours of machine time produce 20 units of output.

While most of the analyses presented in this book are based on the simpler two-variable diagrams, contour maps find applications as well, especially in Chapter 19 and the appendix to Chapter 21.

Perils in the Interpretation of Graphs

The preceding materials contain just about all you will need in order to understand the simple graphics used in economic models. We turn now to the second objective of this appendix: to show how statistical data are portrayed on graphs and some of the pitfalls to watch out for.

The Interpretation of Growth Trends

Probably the most common form of graph in empirical economics is a year-by-year (or perhaps a month-by-month) depiction of the behaviour of some economic variable—such as the percentage of the labour force that has been unemployed, as shown in the graph on the inside front cover of this book. **Time-series graphs** are a type of two-variable diagram in which time is always the variable measured along the horizontal axis. Such graphs can be quite illuminating, offering an instant visual grasp of the course of the relevant events. *However, if misused,* they can easily mislead those who are not experienced in dealing with them, and misinterpretations can easily, if unintentionally, be caused by people who draw graphs without sufficient care.

A fine example of such problems can be seen by referring ahead to Figures 16–1 and 16–2 on pages 331 and 332. The first of these figures shows a time-series chart of Canada's national debt that illustrates the possibility of misinterpretation. Consider the increase in the national debt from the mid-1950s to the mid-1960s—it appears to be substantial. But this oversimplified chart fails to alert the reader to two relevant facts: (1) that there was substantial population growth in Canada during that decade, and (2) that Canadians' incomes were rising rapidly at the time, with a consequent increase in the quantity of all sorts of debts, such as home mortgages. The real issue involved in the question of the national debt is whether it rises *more rapidly* than do the population and the average income per person, and Figure 16–1 essentially ignores that central issue. The relevant factors can, however, be accounted for if the national debt is expressed as a *fraction* of national income (that is, national product), and the results of this "correction" are shown in Figure 16–2. There, we see that the national debt, when measured as a fraction of the income Canadians had available to service that debt, actually declined over the decade in question. There is a general lesson to be learned from this example:

The facts, as portrayed in a time-series graph, most assuredly do not "speak for themselves." Because almost everything grows in a growing economy, one must use judgment in interpreting growth trends. Depending on what kind of data are being analyzed, it may be essential to correct for population growth, for rising prices, for rising incomes, or for all three.

Distorting Trends by Choice of the Time Period

In addition to watching for possible misinterpretations of growth trends, users of statistical data must be on guard for distortions of trends caused by unskilfully chosen first and last periods for the graph. A brief reference to the stock-market price indexes that we hear discussed on the nightly news should be sufficient to make this point. Suppose you were presented with a time-series graph of the TSE index (the Toronto Stock Exchange price index) from 1929 to 1932 or from August to December 1987. Most people know that there were major stock-market crashes during these periods. But suppose you didn't know this. If all the information you had was the dramatic downhill pictures for these years, you would conclude that stocks are a terrible investment. On the other hand, if you saw a time-series graph covering the entire period from the 1920s to the 1990s, you would see the true picture: investment in stocks is profitable at some times and unprofitable at others, but over the long term, the general increase in stock prices has been dramatic.

The deliberate or inadvertent distortion resulting from an unfortunate or unscrupulous choice of time period for a graph must constantly be watched for.

There are no rules that can give absolute protection from this difficulty, but several precautions can be helpful:

1. Make sure that the first date shown on the graph is not an exceptionally high or low point. In comparison with 1929—a year of unusually high stock-market prices—the years immediately following are bound to give the impression of a downward trend.

2. For the same reason, make sure that the graph does not end in a year that is extraordinarily high or low (although this may be unavoidable if the graph simply ends with figures that are as up-to-date as possible).

3. Make sure that (in the absence of some special justification) the graph does not depict only a very brief period, which can easily be atypical.

Dangers of Omitting the Origin

Frequently, the value of an economic variable described on a graph does not fall anywhere near zero during the period under consideration. For example, Canada's **bank rate** (the interest rate that the chartered banks must pay to the Bank of Canada when borrowing reserves) rose during early 1990 from 12.15 percent to 12.8 percent. This means that a graph representing the behaviour of the bank rate in early 1990 would have a good deal of wasted space between the horizontal axis of the graph, where the interest rate is zero, and the level of the graph representing a 12 percent interest rate. In that area there are simply no data to plot. It is therefore tempting simply to eliminate this wasted space by beginning the graph just below the 12 percent interest-rate level. This was done at the time by *Maclean's*, as reproduced in our Figure 1–13.

What is wrong with the drawing? The answer is that it vastly exaggerates the size of the increase in the interest rate that is depicted. It makes it look as though the interest rate quadrupled. In fact, however, the bank rate increased by only about one-twentieth of its initial value during this period.

Omitting the origin in a graph is dangerous because it always exaggerates the magnitudes of the changes that have taken place.

Sometimes, it is true, the inclusion of the full graph would waste so much space that it is undesirable to include it. In that case, a good practice is to put a very clear warning on the graph to remind the reader that some space has been omitted. Figure 1–14 shows one way of doing so.

EXERCISE
Using the data shown in Figure 1–13, draw the *full* graph, from the point of zero interest rate, on a sheet of graph paper. Notice the difference in its effect from that of Figure 1–13. Notice also the amount of wasted space.

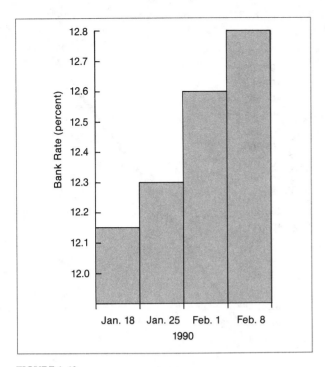

FIGURE 1–13
A Graph Showing Omission of the Origin
A hasty glance at this figure seems to show that the bank rate quadrupled during the first few weeks of 1990.
SOURCE: Adapted from *Maclean's*, February 19, 1990, page 35.

Unreliability of Steepness and Choice of Units

The last problem we will consider has consequences very similar to the one we have just discussed. The problem is that we can never trust the impression we get from the steepness of an economic graph. A graph of stock-market prices that moves uphill sharply (has a large positive slope) appears to suggest that prices are rising rapidly, while another graph in which the rate of climb is much slower seems to imply that prices are going up sluggishly. Yet, depending on how one draws the graph, exactly the same statistics can produce a graph that rises very quickly or one that climbs very slowly.

One reason for this is that 100 points on the stock-market index, for example, can be represented in a graph by a height of either, say, one centimetre or three centimetres. Clearly, if the larger size is chosen to represent a one-unit change in the variable, the movement of that variable up or down will appear much more dramatic than it would if the smaller size were used. Another reason for graphs being rather arbitrary is that, in economics, there are no fixed units of measurement. Coal production can be measured in kilograms, hundredweight (hundreds of pounds), or tons. Prices can be measured in cents, dollars, or mil-

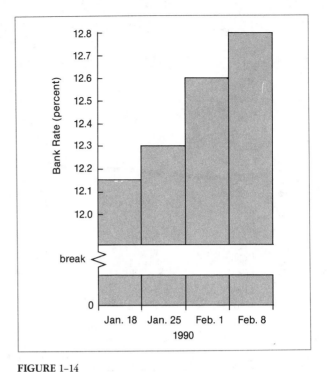

FIGURE 1–14
A Break in a Graph
A good way of warning the reader that the full graph has not been included is to put a break in the graph, as illustrated here.

lions of dollars. Time can be measured in days, months, or years. Any of these choices is perfectly legitimate, but it makes all the difference to the rapidity with which a graph using the resulting figures rises or falls.

An example will bring out the point. Suppose that we have the following (imaginary) figures on daily coal production from a mine, which we measure both in hundredweight and in tons (remembering that 1 ton = 20 hundredweight):

YEAR	PRODUCTION IN TONS	PRODUCTION IN HUNDREDWEIGHT
1975	5000	100,000
1980	5050	101,000
1985	5090	101,800

Look at Figures 1–15(a) and 1–15(b), one graph showing the figures in tons and the other showing them in hundredweight. The line looks quite flat in Figure 1–15(a) but quite steep in Figure 1–15(b).

Unfortunately, we cannot solve the problem by agreeing always to stick to the same measurement units. Litres may be the right unit for measuring demand for milk, but they will not do for measuring demand for cloth or coal. A penny may be the right

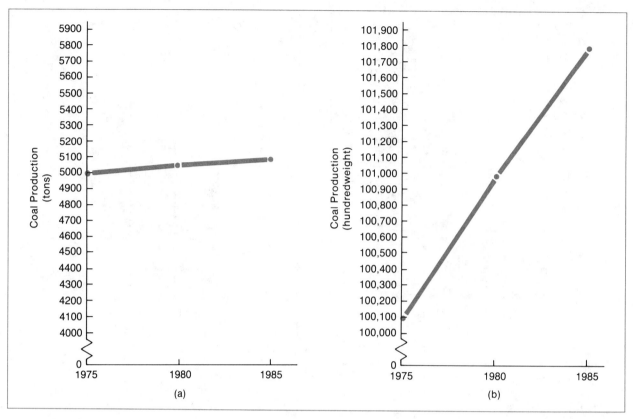

FIGURE 1–15
Slope Depends on Units of Measurement
(a) Coal production is measured in tons, and production seems to be rising very slowly. (b) Production is measured in hundredweight (hundred-pound units), so the same facts now seem to say that production is rising spectacularly.

monetary unit for jelly beans, but it is not a very convenient unit for the cost of airplanes or cars.

A change in units of measurement stretches or compresses the axis on which the information is represented, which automatically changes the slope of a graph. Therefore, we must never place much faith in the apparent implications of the slope of an ordinary graph in economics.

In Chapter 20, on demand analysis, we present an approach that economists have adopted to deal with this problem. Instead of calculating changes in

"absolute" terms—such as tons of coal—they use as their common unit the *percentage* increase. By using percentages rather than absolute figures, the problem can be avoided. The reason is simple. If we look at our hypothetical figures on coal production again, we see that whether we measure the increase in output from 1975 to 1980 in tons (from 5000 to 5050) or in hundredweight (from 100,000 to 101,000), the *percentage* increase is the same. Fifty is 1 percent of 5000, and 1000 is 1 percent of 100,000. Since a change in units affects both the numbers *proportionately*, the result is a washout—it does nothing to the percentage calculation.

Summary

1. Because graphs are used so often to portray economic models, it is important for students to acquire some understanding of their construction and use. Fortunately, the graphics used in economics are usually not very complex.

2. Most economic models are depicted in two-variable diagrams. We read data from these diagrams just as we read the latitude and longitude on a map: each point represents the values of two variables at the same time.

3. In a few instances, three variables must be shown at

once. In these cases, economists use contour maps, which, as the name suggests, show "latitude," "longitude," and "altitude" all at the same time.

4. Often, the most important property of a line or curve drawn on a diagram will be its slope, which is defined as the ratio of the "rise" over the "run," or the vertical change divided by the horizontal change. Curves that go uphill as we move to the right have positive slopes, while curves that go downhill have negative slopes.

5. By definition, a straight line has the same slope wherever we choose to measure it. The slope of a curved line changes, but the slope at any point on the curve can be calculated by measuring the slope of a straight line tangent to the curve at that point.

6. A time-series graph is a particular type of two-variable diagram that is useful in depicting statistical data. Time is measured along the horizontal axis, and some variable of interest is measured along the vertical axis.

7. While time-series graphs are invaluable in helping us condense a great deal of information in a single picture, they can be quite misleading if they are not drawn and interpreted with care. For example, growth trends can be exaggerated by inappropriate choice of units of measurement or by failure to correct for some obvious source of growth (such as rising population). Omitting the origin can make the ups and downs in a time series appear much more extreme than they actually are. Or, by a clever choice of the starting and ending points for the graphs, the same data can be made to tell very different stories. Readers of such graphs—and they include anyone who ever reads a newspaper—must be on guard for problems like these or they may find themselves misled by "the facts."

Concepts for Review

Variable	Tangent to a curve	Ray through the origin, or ray
Two-variable diagram	Y-intercept	45° line
Horizontal and vertical axes	Slope of a straight (or curved) line	Contour map
Origin (of a graph)	Negative, positive, zero, and infinite slope	Time-series graph

Questions for Discussion

1. Look for a graph in your local newspaper, on the financial page or elsewhere. What does the graph try to show? Is someone trying to convince you of something with this graph? Check to see if the graph is distorted in any of the ways mentioned in this appendix.

2. Portray the following hypothetical data on a two-variable diagram:

Enrolment Data: University of Nowhere

ACADEMIC YEAR	TOTAL ENROLMENT	ENROLMENT IN ECONOMICS COURSES
1987–1988	3000	300
1988–1989	3100	325
1989–1990	3200	350
1990–1991	3300	375
1991–1992	3400	400

Using a ruler, draw in a straight line to summarize the trend in the data in your graph. Measure the slope of this line, and explain what this number means.

3. Sam believes the number of dates he gets per week depends on the number of dabs of aftershave lotion he uses. He concludes from experience that the following figures are typical:

Number of dabs	0	1	2	3	4
Number of dates	1	3	4	5	6

Put these numbers into a graph like Figure 1–5(a). Measure and interpret the slopes between adjacent dots.

4. Suppose that between 1987 and 1988 expenditures on dog food rose from $35 million to $70 million and the price of dog food doubled. What do these facts imply about the popularity of dog food?

5. Suppose that between 1980 and 1990 the population of North America went up 10 percent and the number of people attending professional wrestling matches rose from 3,000,000 to 3,100,000. What do these facts imply about the growth in popularity of professional wrestling?

2

Scarcity and Choice

Our necessities are few but our wants are endless.

INSCRIPTION FOUND IN A
FORTUNE COOKIE

This chapter examines a subject that many economists consider to be *the* fundamental issue of economics: the fact that since virtually no resource is available in unlimited supply, people must consequently make decisions consistent with their limited means. A wild-eyed materialist may dream of a world in which everyone owns a yacht and five automobiles, but the earth almost certainly lacks the resources needed to make that dream come true. The scarcity of resources, both natural and synthetic, makes it vital that we stretch our limited resources as far as possible.

This chapter introduces a method of analyzing the choices available to decision-makers, given the resources at their command. The same sort of analysis, based on the concept of *opportunity cost*, will be shown to apply to the decisions of business firms, of governments, and of society as a whole. Many of the most basic ideas of economics —such as *efficiency*, *division of labour*, *exchange*, and the *role of markets*—are introduced here for the first time and are shown to be means for making the unpleasant choices forced upon us by the scarcity of resources constraining all economic decisions. This chapter also introduces a broad question that constitutes the central theme of this text:

What does the market do well and what does it do poorly?

The "Indispensable Necessity" Syndrome

It is natural but not rational for people to try to avoid facing up to the hard choices that scarcity makes necessary. This happened, for example, when governments of countries such as Mexico, Brazil, and Poland were forced by their enormous foreign debts to tighten their belts sharply during the 1980s. Scarcity of foreign currency meant that these governments and their economies had to cut down severely the quantities of consumer goods and productive inputs they bought from abroad.

Budget cuts force politicians and administrators to make some hard decisions about which services to cut. As they struggle with these decisions, they learn to their dismay that their constituents are often unwilling to accept *any* reductions. It seems that any proposal for cuts that would bring us closer to living within our means is met with the cry that each of the items slated for reduction is *absolutely* essential.

Yet, regrettable as it is to have to give up anything, reduced budgets mean that *something* must go. If everyone reacts by declaring *everything* to be indispensable, the decision-maker is in the dark and is likely to end up making cuts that are bad for everyone. When the budget must be reduced, it is critical to determine which cuts are likely to prove *least damaging* to the people affected.

It is nonsense to assign top priority to everything. No one can afford everything. An optimal decision is one that chooses the most desirable alternative *among the possibilities permitted by the quantities of scarce resources available.*

Scarcity, Choice, and Opportunity Cost

Resources are the instruments provided by nature or by people that are used to obtain the goods and services humans want. Natural resources include minerals, the soil (usable for agriculture, building land, and so on), water, and air. Labour is another resource that is scarce, partly because of time limitations (the day having only 24 hours). Factories and machines are resources made by men and women. These three types of resources are often referred to as "land, labour, and capital."

One of the basic themes of economics is that the **resources** of decision-makers, no matter how large they may be, are always limited, and that as a result everyone has some hard decisions to make. The federal government agonizes over difficult budget decisions every year, even though it spends billions of dollars annually. Even Philip II, of Spanish Armada fame and ruler of one of the greatest empires of history, had to cope with rebellions on the part of his troops, whom he was often unable to pay or to supply with even the most basic provisions. His government actually went bankrupt about half a dozen times.

But far more fundamental than the scarcity of funds is the scarcity of physical resources. The supply of fuel, for example, has never been limitless, and an increased scarcity of fuel would force us to make some hard choices. We might have to keep our homes cooler in winter and warmer in summer, live closer to our jobs, or give up such fuel-using conveniences as dishwashers. While energy is the most widely discussed scarcity these days, the general principle of scarcity applies to all the earth's resources —iron, copper, uranium, and so on.

Even goods that can be produced are in limited supply because their production requires fuel, labour, and other scarce resources. Wheat and rice can be grown, but nations have nonetheless suffered famines because the land, labour, fertilizer, and water needed to grow these crops were unavailable. We can increase our output of cars, but the increased use of labour, steel, and fuel in auto production will mean that something else, perhaps the production of refrigerators, will have to be cut back. This all adds up to the following fundamental principle of economics, one we will encounter again and again in this text:

Virtually all resources are scarce, meaning that humanity has less of them than we would like. So choices must be made among a *limited* set of possibilities, in full recognition of the inescapable fact that a decision to have more of one thing means we must give up some of another thing.

In fact, one popular definition of economics is "the study of how best to use limited means in the pursuit of unlimited ends." While this definition, like any short statement, cannot possibly cover the sweep of the entire discipline, it does convey the flavour of the type of problem that is the economist's stock in trade.

The Principle of Opportunity Cost

Economics examines the options left open to households, business firms, governments, and entire societies by the limited resources at their command, and it studies the logic of how **rational decisions** can be made from among the competing alternatives. One overriding principle governs this logic—a principle we have already introduced in Chapter 1 as one of the **12 Ideas for Beyond the Final Exam.** With limited resources, a decision to have more of something is simultaneously a decision to have less of something else. Hence, the relevant *cost* of any decision is its **opportunity cost**—the value of the next best alternative that is given up. Rational decision-making, be it in industry, government, or households, must be based on opportunity-cost calculations.

To illustrate opportunity cost, we can continue the example in which production of additional cars requires the production of fewer refrigerators. While the production of a car may cost $12,000 per vehicle, or some other money amount, its real cost to society is the refrigerators it must forgo to get an additional car. If the labour, steel, and fuel needed to make a car are sufficient to make eight refrigerators, we say that the opportunity cost of a car is eight refrigerators. The principle of opportunity cost is of such general applicability that we devote most of this chapter to elaborating it.

Opportunity Cost and Money Cost

Since we live in a market economy where (almost) everything "has its price," students often wonder about the connection between the opportunity cost of an item and its market price. What we just said seems to divorce the two concepts. We stressed that the true cost of a car is not its market price but the value of the other things (like refrigerators) that could have been made instead. This *opportunity cost* is the true sacrifice that society makes to get a car.

But isn't the opportunity cost of a car related to its money cost? The answer is that the two are often very closely tied because of the way a market economy sets the prices of the steel and electricity that go into the production of cars. Steel is valuable because it can be used to make other goods. If the items that can be made from steel are themselves valuable (that is, if those items are valued highly by consumers), the price of steel will be high. But if the goods that can be made from steel have very little value, the price of steel will be low. Thus, if a car has a high opportunity cost, then a well-functioning price system will assign high prices to the resources that are needed to produce cars, and therefore a car will also command a high price. In sum:

If the market is functioning well, goods that have high opportunity costs will tend to have high money costs, and goods whose opportunity costs are low will tend to have low money costs.

Yet it would be a mistake to treat opportunity costs and explicit monetary costs as identical. For one thing, there are times when the market does *not* function well and hence does not assign prices that accurately reflect opportunity costs. Many such examples will be encountered in this book, especially in Chapters 27 and 32.

Moreover, some valuable items may not bear explicit price tags at all. We have already encountered one example of this in Chapter 1, where we contrasted the opportunity cost of going to college or university with the explicit money cost. We learned that one important item typically omitted from the money-cost calculation is the value of the student's time—that is, the wages he or she could have earned by working instead of attending university. These forgone wages, which are given up by students in order to acquire an education, are part of the opportunity cost of a postsecondary education just as surely as are tuition payments.

Other common examples are goods and services that are given away "free." You incur no explicit monetary cost to acquire such an item. But you may have to pay implicitly by waiting in line. If so, you incur an opportunity cost equal to the value of the next best use of your time.

Production, Scarcity, and Resource Allocation

Consumers do not obtain all the goods and services they would want to acquire if those goods and services were provided free (at a zero price); that is what we mean when we say that outputs are scarce. Scarcity forces consumers to make choices. The scarcity of goods and services is, in turn, attributable to the scarcity of the land, labour, and capital used to produce **outputs**.

These resources are, after all, the means (instruments) of production, the **inputs** whose services co-operate in the production process, on the farm and in the factory, to

A **rational decision** is one that best serves the objective of the decision-maker, whatever that objective may be. The term "rational" connotes neither approval nor disapproval of the objective itself.

The **opportunity cost** of any decision is the forgone value of the next best alternative that is not chosen.

Outputs are the goods and services that consumers want to acquire. **Inputs** or **means of production** are the natural resources, labour, and produced plant and equipment used to make the outputs.

yield the commodities that people consume as well as the produced means of production (machines, locomotives, and so on).

Scarcity of such input resources, then, means that the economy cannot produce all the bread, hats, cars, and computers that consumers would want if they could be made available in limitless amounts at a zero price. Somehow it must be decided whether or not to assign more fuel to the production of refrigerators, which will mean having less fuel to use in the production of airplanes, washing machines, or toys.

The decision on how to **allocate resources** among the production of commodities and among the organizations that produce them is made in different ways in different types of economies. In a centrally planned economy, such as the Soviet Union has been, many such decisions are made by government bureaus. In a market economy, such as Canada, the United States, or Great Britain, no one group or individual makes such resource-allocation decisions explicitly. Rather, they are made automatically, often unobserved, by what are called "the forces of supply and demand." For example, if consumers want more beef than farmers now supply, scarcity will make it profitable for ranchers to hire more labour to increase their herds, thus reallocating labour and other inputs away from other production activities and into increased production of beef.

The allocation of resources refers to the decision on how to divide the economy's scarce input resources among the different outputs produced in the economy and among the different firms or other organizations that produce those outputs.

Scarcity and Choice for a Single Firm

The nature of opportunity cost is perhaps clearest in the case of a single business firm that produces two outputs from a fixed supply of inputs. Given the existing technology and the limited resources at its disposal, the more of one good the firm produces, the less of the other it will be able to produce. And unless management carries out an explicit comparison of the available choices, weighing the desirability of each against the others, it is unlikely that it will make rational production decisions.

Consider the example of a farmer whose available supplies of land, machinery, labour, and fertilizer are capable of producing the various combinations of soybeans and wheat listed in Table 2–1. Obviously, the more land and other resources he devotes to production of soybeans, the less wheat he will be able to produce. Table 2–1 indicates, for example, that if he produces only soybeans, he can harvest 40,000 bushels. But, when soybean production is reduced to only 30,000 bushels, the farmer can also grow 38,000 bushels of wheat. Thus, the opportunity cost of obtaining 38,000 bushels of wheat is 10,000 fewer bushels of soybeans. Or, put the other way around, the opportunity cost of 10,000 bushels of soybeans is 38,000 bushels of wheat. The other numbers in Table 2–1 have similar interpretations.

TABLE 2–1
Production Possibilities Open to a Farmer

BUSHELS OF SOYBEANS	BUSHELS OF WHEAT	LABEL IN FIGURE 2–1
40,000	0	A
30,000	38,000	B
20,000	52,000	C
10,000	60,000	D
0	65,000	E

A production possibilities frontier shows the different combinations of various goods that a producer can turn out, given the available resources and existing technology.

Figure 2–1 is a graphical representation of the same information. Point *A* corresponds to the first line of Table 2–1, point *B* to the second, and so on. Curves like *AE* appear at several points in this book; they are called **production possibilities frontiers**. Any point *on or below* the production possibilities frontier is attainable. Points above the frontier cannot be achieved with the available resources and technology.

The production possibilities frontier always slopes downward to the right. Why?

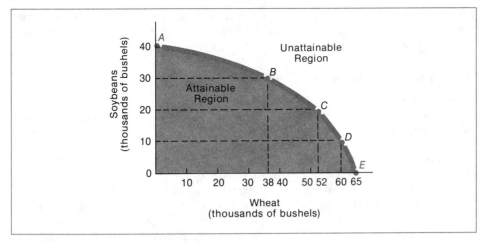

FIGURE 2–1
Production Possibilities Frontier for Production by a Single Firm
With a given set of inputs, the firm can produce only those output combinations given by points in the shaded area. The production possibilities frontier, AE, is not a straight line but one that curves more and more as it nears the axes. That is, when the firm specializes in only one product, those inputs that are especially adapted to the production of the other good lose at least part of their productivity.

Because resources are limited. The farmer can *increase* his wheat production (move to the right in Figure 2–1) only by devoting more of his land and labour to growing wheat, meaning that he must simultaneously *reduce* his soybean production (move downward) since less of his land and labour is available for growing soybeans.

Notice that in addition to having a negative slope, our production possibilities frontier, curve AE, has another characteristic—it is "bowed outward." Let us consider a little more carefully what this curvature means.

Suppose our farmer is initially producing only soybeans, so that he uses for this purpose even land that is much more suitable for wheat cultivation (point A). Now suppose he decides to switch some of his land from soybean production to wheat production. Which part of his land will he switch? Obviously, if he is sensible, he will use the part best suited to wheat growing. If he shifts to point B, soybean production falls from 40,000 bushels to 30,000 bushels as wheat production rises from zero to 38,000. A sacrifice of only 10,000 bushels of soybeans "buys" 38,000 bushels of wheat.

Imagine now that the farmer wants to produce still more wheat. Figure 2–1 tells us that the sacrifice of an additional 10,000 bushels of soybeans (from 30,000 down to 20,000) will yield only 14,000 more bushels of wheat (see Point C). Why? The main reason is that inputs tend to be specialized. As we noted, at point A the farmer was using resources for soybean production that were much more suitable for growing wheat. Consequently, their productivity in soybeans was relatively low, and when they were switched into wheat production the yield was very high. But this cannot continue forever. As more wheat is produced, the farmer must utilize land and machinery that are better suited to producing soybeans and less well-suited to producing wheat. This is why the first 10,000 bushels of soybeans forgone "buys" the farmer 38,000 bushels of wheat while the second 10,000 bushels of soybeans "buys" him only 14,000 bushels of wheat. Figure 2–1 and Table 2–1 show that these returns continue to decline as wheat production expands: the next 10,000-bushel reduction in soybean production yields only 8000 bushels of additional wheat, and so on.

We can now see that the *slope* of the production possibilities frontier represents graphically the concept of *opportunity cost*. Between points C and B, for example, the opportunity cost of acquiring 10,000 additional bushels of soybeans is 14,000 bushels of forgone wheat, and between points B and A, the opportunity cost of 10,000 bushels of soybeans is 38,000 bushels of forgone wheat. In general, as we move upward to the left along the production possibilities frontier (toward more soybeans and less wheat), the opportunity cost of soybeans in terms of wheat increases. Or, putting the same thing differently, as we move downward to the right, the opportunity cost of acquiring wheat by giving up soybeans increases.

The Principle of Increasing Costs

The **principle of increasing costs** states that as the production of one good expands, the opportunity cost of producing another unit of this good generally increases.

We have just described a very general phenomenon, which is applicable well beyond farming. The **principle of increasing costs** states that as the production of one good expands, the opportunity cost of producing another unit of this good generally increases.

This principle is not a universal fact; there can be exceptions to it. But it does seem to be a technological regularity that applies to a wide range of economic activities. As our example of the farmer suggests, the principle of increasing costs is based on the fact that resources tend to be specialized, at least in part, so that some of their productivity is lost when they are transferred from doing what they are relatively good at doing to what they are relatively bad at doing. In terms of diagrams like Figure 2–1, the principle simply asserts that the production possibilities frontier is bowed outward.

Perhaps the best way to understand this idea is to contrast it with a case in which there are no specialized resources. Figure 2–2 depicts a production possibilities frontier for producing black shoes and brown shoes. Because the labour and capital used to produce black shoes are just as good at producing brown shoes, the frontier is a straight line. If the firm cuts back its production of black shoes by 10,000 pairs, it always gets 10,000 additional pairs of brown shoes. No productivity is lost in the switch because resources are not specialized.

Scarcity and Choice for the Entire Society

Like an individual firm, the entire economy is also constrained by its limited resources and technology. If society wants more aircraft and tanks, it will have to give up some boats and automobiles. If it wants to build more factories and stores, it will have to build fewer homes and sports arenas. In general:

FIGURE 2–2
A Production Possibilities Frontier with No Specialized Resources
Resources that produce black shoes are just as good at producing brown shoes. So there is no loss of productivity when black-shoe production is decreased in order to increase brown-shoe production. For example, if the firm moves from point *A* to point *B*, black-shoe output falls by 10,000 pairs and brown-shoe output rises by 10,000 pairs. The same would be true if it moved from point *B* to point *C* or from point *C* to point *D*. The production possibilities frontier is therefore a straight line.

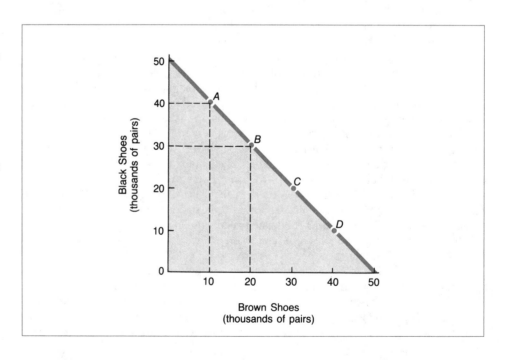

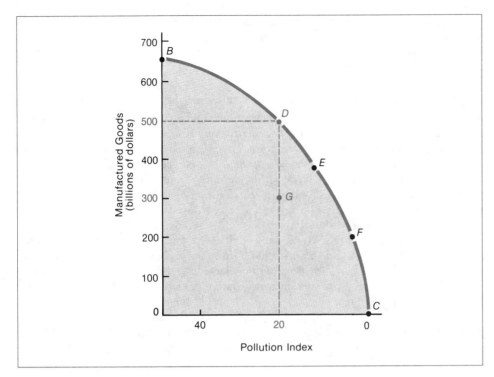

FIGURE 2-3
The Production
Possibilities Frontier for
the Entire Economy
This production possibilities
frontier is curved because
resources are not perfectly
transferable from goods
production to emission
treatment operations. The limits
on available resources place a
ceiling, C, on the availability of
clean air (a reading of zero on
the pollution index), and a
ceiling, B, on the output of
manufactured goods.

The position and shape of the production possibilities frontier that constrains the choices of the economy are determined by the economy's physical resources, its skills and technology, its willingness to work, and its investments in factories, research, and innovation.

Since the debate over environmental issues has been so active in recent years, let us illustrate the nature of society's choices by the example of choosing between clean air and manufactured goods. Just like a single firm, the economy as a whole has a production possibilities frontier for these items determined by its technology and the available resources of land, labour, capital, and raw materials. This production possibilities frontier may look like curve BC in Figure 2-3.

If most workers are employed at factories, coal mines, and refineries, the production of manufactured goods will be large but the availability of clean air will be small. If resources are transferred from the mines and factories to emission treatment operations, the mix of output can be shifted toward cleaner air at some sacrifice of manufactured goods (the move from D to E). However, something is likely to be lost in the transfer process—some of the machines and chemicals that helped produce the manufactured goods will not help in the emission treatment operations. As summarized in the description of the principle of increasing costs, physical resources tend to be specialized, so the production possibilities frontier probably curves downward and toward the axes.

We may even reach a point where the only resources left are items that are not very useful outside factories. In that case, even a very large additional sacrifice of goods yields very little cleaner air. That is the meaning of the steep segment, FC, on the frontier. At point C the air is only slightly cleaner than at F, even though at C goods production has been given up entirely.

The downward slope of society's production possibilities frontier implies that hard choices must be made. Our nation's pollution problems can be solved only by decreasing material consumption, not by rhetoric nor by wishing it so. The curvature of the production possibilities frontier implies that, as emission treatment increases, it becomes progressively more expensive to "buy" cleaner air by sacrificing manufactured goods.

Application: Economic Growth in Canada and Japan

Among the economic choices that any society must make, there is one very important choice that illustrates well the concept of opportunity cost. This choice is embodied in the question "How fast should the economy grow?"[1] At first, the question may seem ridiculous. Since **economic growth** means, roughly, that the average citizen has more and more goods and services, is it not self-evident that faster growth is always better?

> **Economic growth** occurs when an economy is able to produce more goods and services for each consumer.

Again, the fundamental problem of scarcity intervenes. Economies do not grow by magic. Scarce resources must be devoted to the process of growth. Cement and steel that could be used to make swimming pools and stadiums must be diverted to build more machinery and factories. Wood that could be made into furniture and toys must be used for hammers and ladders instead. Grain that could be eaten must be used as seed to plant additional acres. By deciding how large a quantity of resources to devote to future needs rather than to current consumption, society in effect *chooses* (within limits) how fast it will grow.

In diagrammatic terms, economic growth means that the economy's production possibilities frontier shifts outward—that it moves further away from the origin in the graph, as in the move from *FF* to *GG* in Figure 2–4(a). Why? Because such a shift means that the economy can produce more of both the outputs shown in the graph.

[1] Economic growth will be studied in detail in Chapter 18.

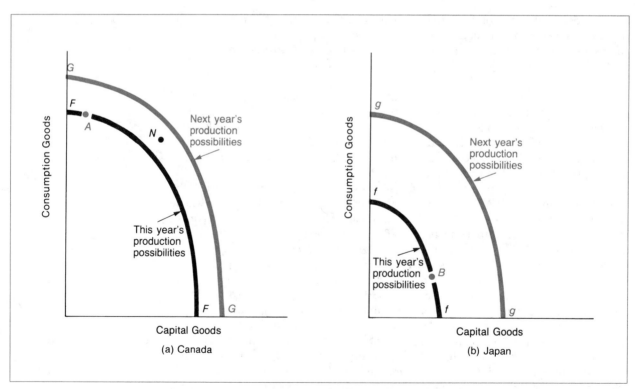

FIGURE 2–4
Growth in Two Economies
Growth shifts the production possibilities frontiers *FF* and *ff* (black) outward to the frontiers *GG* and *gg* (green), meaning that each economy can produce more of both goods than it could before. If the shift in both economies occurs in the same period of time, then the Japanese economy (b) is growing faster than the Canadian economy (a) because the outward shift in (b) is much greater than the one in (a).

Thus, in the figure, after growth has occurred, it is possible to produce the combination of products represented by point *N* (or any other point between the old frontier, *FF*, and the new frontier, *GG*). Before growth occurred, point *N* was beyond the economy's means because it was outside the production possibilities frontier.

How does growth occur? That is, what shifts an economy's production frontier outward? There are many ways in which this can occur. For example, workers may acquire greater skill and learn to produce more output in an hour. Perhaps even more important, the economy may construct more capital goods, temporarily giving up some consumption goods to provide the resources to build the factories and machines. Finally, inventions like the steam engine, AC electricity, and industrial robots can and do increase the economy's productive capacity, thereby shifting the production frontier outward.

Figure 2–4 illustrates the nature of the choice by depicting production possibilities frontiers for **consumption goods**, which are consumed today (like food and electricity), versus **capital goods**, which provide for future consumption (like farm equipment and electricity generating plants), for two different societies.

Figure 2–4(a) depicts a society like Canada's that devotes a relatively small quantity of resources to growth, preferring current consumption instead. It chooses a point like *A* on this year's production possibilities frontier, *FF*. At *A*, consumption is relatively high and production of capital goods is relatively low, so the production possibilities frontier shifts only to *GG* next year. Figure 2–4(b) depicts a society much more enamoured of growth, like Japan's. It selects a point like *B* on its production possibilities frontier, *ff*. At *B*, consumption is lower and investment is higher, so its production possibilities frontier moves all the way to *gg* by next year. Over the years, Japan has grown faster than Canada, but this more rapid growth has had a price—an *opportunity cost*. The Japanese must give up some of the current consumption that Canadians enjoy. Citizens of the Soviet Union have also made large sacrifices in current consumption, as Soviet bureaucrats have tried to maximize growth through massive levels of capital-goods production.

An economy grows by giving up some current consumption and producing capital goods instead for the future. The more capital it produces, the faster will its production possibilities frontier shift outward over time.

It should be noted, however, that the production of capital goods is not the only way to shift the economy's production possibilities frontier outward. New technology —the process of invention and innovation—is probably the primary means by which economies have increased the output they can produce with a given quantity of resources. Increased education and training of the labour force is generally believed to yield a similar result.

The Concept of Efficiency

So far in our discussion of scarcity and choice, we have assumed that either the single firm or the whole economy always operates *on* its production possibilities frontier rather than *below* it. In other words, we have tacitly assumed that, whatever it decides to do, the firm or economy does it *efficiently*. Economists define *efficiency* as the absence of waste. An efficient economy utilizes all of its available resources and produces the maximum amount of output that its technology permits.[2]

To see why any point on the economy's production possibilities frontier in Figure 2-3 represents an efficient decision, suppose for a moment that society has decided to settle for air with a purity level of 20. According to the production possibilities frontier, if this level of clean air is to be attained, then the maximum amount of

A **consumption good** is an item that is available for immediate use by households and that satisfies wants of members of households without contributing directly to future production by the economy.

A **capital good** is an item that is used to produce other goods and services in the future, rather than being consumed today. Factories and machines are examples.

[2]A more formal definition of *efficiency* is offered in Chapter 24.

manufactured goods that can be made is $500 billion (point *D* in Figure 2–3). The economy is, therefore, operating efficiently if it actually produces $500 billion worth of goods rather than some smaller amount, such as $300 billion (as at point *G*). Point *D* is efficient while point *G* is not.

Note that the concept of efficiency does not tell us which point on the production possibilities frontier is *best*; it only tells us that no point that is *not* on the frontier can be best, because any such point represents wasted resources. For example, should society ever find itself at point *G*, the necessity of making hard choices would (temporarily) disappear. It would be possible to increase both the production of goods *and* air purity by moving to a point such as *E*.

Why, then, would an economy ever find itself at a point below its production possibilities frontier? There are a number of ways in which resources are wasted in real life. The most important of them, unemployment, is an issue that will take up a substantial part of this book (Parts Two, Three, and Four). When many workers are unemployed, the economy finds itself at a point like *G*, below the frontier, because by putting the unemployed to work in both manufacturing and emission treatment jobs the economy could produce more goods and have cleaner air. The economy would then move from point *G* to the right (cleaner air) and upward (more goods) toward a point like *E* on the production possibilities frontier. Only when no resources are wasted by unemployment or misuse is the economy *on* the frontier.

Inefficiency can also occur in other ways (even with full employment). A prime example is that of inputs not being assigned to the right task—as when wheat is grown on land best adapted to soybean growing, while soybeans are grown on land best suited to wheat production. Another important type of inefficiency occurs when large firms produce goods or services that are best turned out by small enterprises able to pay closer attention to detail, or when small firms produce outputs best suited to large-scale production. A final example is the outright waste that occurs as a result of favouritism (promotion of an incompetent brother-in-law), discrimination (promotion of a man, when a more-competent woman is available for the job), or wasteful job creation (for example, when union rules require a railway to continue to employ a fireman on a diesel locomotive, where there is no longer a need for one). Each of these inefficiencies results in the community's obtaining less output than it could, given the amounts of input used in the production process.

The Three Co-ordination Tasks of Any Economy

In deciding how to use its scarce resources, society must somehow make three sorts of decisions. First, as we have just emphasized, it must figure out **how to utilize its resources efficiently**; that is, it must find a way to get *on* its production possibilities frontier. Second, it must decide **what combination of goods to produce**—what quantity of manufactured goods versus cleaner air, and so on; that is, it must select one specific point on the production possibilities frontier. Finally, it must decide **how much of each good to distribute to each person**, doing so in a sensible way so that meat does not go to vegetarians and wine to teetotallers.

Certainly, each of these decisions could be made by a central planner who would tell people how to produce, what to produce, and what to consume.[3] But many of the decisions can also be made without central direction, through a system of prices and markets whose directions are dictated by the demands of consumers and the costs of producers. Let us consider each task in turn.

Specialization, Division of Labour, and Exchange

Efficiency in production is one of the economy's three basic tasks. Many features of society contribute to efficiency; others interfere with it. While different societies

[3] Planning is considered in more detail in Chapter 24.

pursue the goal of economic efficiency in different ways, one source of efficiency is so fundamental that we must single it out for special attention: the tremendous gains in productivity that stem from **specialization**, and the consequent **division of labour**.

Adam Smith, the founder of modern economics, first marvelled at this mainspring of efficiency and productivity on a visit to a pin factory. In a famous passage near the beginning of his monumental book *The Wealth of Nations* (1776), he described what he saw:

One man draws out the wire, another straightens it, a third cuts it, a fourth points it, a fifth grinds it at the top for receiving the head; to make the head requires two or three distinct operations; to put it on is a peculiar business, to whiten the pins is another; it is even a trade by itself to put them into the paper.[4]

Smith observed that when the work to be done was divided in this way, each worker became quite skilled in his particular specialty, and the productivity of the group of workers as a whole was enhanced enormously. As Smith related it:

I have seen a small manufactory of this kind where ten men only were employed.... Those ten persons ... could make among them upwards of forty-eight thousand pins in a day.... But if they had all wrought separately and independently, ... they certainly could not each of them have made twenty, perhaps not one pin in a day.[5]

In other words, through the miracle of division of labour and specialization, ten workers accomplished what would otherwise have required thousands. An enormous increase in specialization was the secret of the Industrial Revolution, which helped lift humanity out of the abject poverty that had for so long been its lot.

But specialization created a problem. With division of labour, people no longer produced only what they wanted to consume themselves. The workers in the pin factory had no use for the thousands of pins they produced each day; they wanted to trade them for things like food, clothing, and shelter. Specialization thus made it necessary to have some mechanism by which workers producing pins could **exchange** their wares with workers producing such things as cloth and potatoes.

Without a system of exchange, the productivity miracle achieved by the division of labour would have done society little good. With it, standards of living rose enormously. As we observed in Chapter 1:

> Division of labour means breaking up a task into a number of smaller, more specialized tasks so that each worker can become more adept at his or her particular job.

Mutual Gains from Voluntary Exchange

Unless there is deception or misunderstanding of the facts, a voluntary exchange between two parties must make both parties better off. Even though no additional goods are produced by the act of trading, the welfare of society is increased because each individual acquires goods that are more suited to his or her needs and tastes. This simple but fundamental precept of economics is one of our 12 **Ideas for Beyond the Final Exam**.

While goods can be traded for other goods, a system of exchange works better when everyone agrees to use some common item (such as pieces of paper) for buying and selling goods and services. Enter *money*. Then workers in pin factories, for example, can be paid in money rather than in pins, and they can use this money to purchase cloth and potatoes. Textile workers and farmers can do the same.

[4]Adam Smith, *The Wealth of Nations* (New York: Random House, Modern Library Edition, 1937), page 4.
[5]Ibid., page 5.

Biographical Note: Adam Smith (1723–1790)

Adam Smith, who was to become the leading advocate of freedom of international trade, was born the son of a customs official in 1723 and ended his career in the well-paid post of collector of customs for Scotland. He received an excellent education at Glasgow College, where, for the first time, some lectures were being given in English rather than Latin. A fellowship to Oxford University followed, and for six years he studied there mostly by himself, since, at that time, teaching at Oxford was virtually nonexistent.

After completing his studies, Smith was appointed professor of logic at Glasgow College and, later, professor of moral philosophy, a field which then included economics as one of its branches. Fortunately, he was a popular lecturer, because in those days a professor's pay in Glasgow depended on the number of students who chose to attend his lectures. At Glasgow, Smith was responsible for helping young James Watt find a job as an instrument maker. Watt later invented a key improvement in the steam engine, which made its use possible in factories, trains, and ships. So in this and many other respects, Smith was present virtually at the birth of the Industrial Revolution, whose prophet he was destined to become.

After thirteen years at Glasgow, Smith accepted a highly paid post as a tutor to a young Scottish nobleman with whom he spent several years in France, a customary way of educating nobles in the eighteenth century. Primarily because he was bored during these years in France, Smith began working on *The Wealth of Nations*. In 1776, several years after his return to England, the book was published and rapidly achieved popularity.

The Wealth of Nations contains many brilliantly written passages. It was one of the first systematic treatises in economics, contributing to both theoretical and factual knowledge about the subject. Among the main points made in the book are the importance for a nation's prosperity of freedom of trade and the division of labour permitted by more widespread markets; the dangers of governmental protection of monopolies and imposition of tariffs; and the superiority of self-interest—the instrument of the "invisible hand"—over altruism as a means of improving the economy's service to the general public.

The British government was grateful for the ideas for new tax legislation that Smith proposed, and to show its appreciation, appointed him to the lucrative sinecure of collector of customs, which, together with the lifetime pension awarded him by his former pupil, left him very well off financially, although he eventually gave away most of his money to charitable causes.

In the eighteenth century, the intellectual world was small, and among the many people with whom Smith was acquainted were David Hume, Samuel Johnson, James Boswell, Benjamin Franklin, and Jean Jacques Rousseau. Smith got along well with everyone except Samuel Johnson, who was noted for his dislike of Scots. Smith was absent-minded and apparently timid with women, being visibly embarrassed by the public attention of the eminent ladies of Paris during his visits there. He never married and lived with his mother most of his life. When he died, the Edinburgh newspapers recalled only that when Smith was four years old he was kidnapped by gypsies. But thanks to his writings, he is remembered for a good deal more than that.

These two principles—specialization and exchange (assisted by money)—working in tandem led to a vast improvement in the well-being of humanity. This process of specialization and exchange is extended when one country's citizens trade with those of other countries. Indeed it can be shown that even if the citizens of one country are more efficient at producing *everything* than are the citizens of the other country, *both* countries benefit from specializing and trading. We explain this *principle of comparative advantage* fully in Chapter 28. We show there that a country can obtain points *beyond* its own production possibilities curve by engaging in foreign trade.

Markets, Prices, and the Three Co-ordination Tasks

We have emphasized above that two important principles—specialization and exchange—have led to a vast improvement in material welfare. But what forces induce workers to join together so that the fruits of the division of labour can be enjoyed? And what forces establish a smoothly functioning system of exchange so that each person can acquire what he or she wants to consume? One alternative is to have a central authority telling people what to do. But Adam Smith explained and extolled another way of organizing and co-ordinating economic activity—the use of markets and prices.

Smith noted that people were very good at pursuing their own self-interest, and that a **market system** was a very good way to harness this self-interest. As he put it, with clear religious overtones, in doing what is best for themselves, people are "led by an invisible hand" to promote the economic well-being of society.

Since we live in a market economy, the outlines of the process by which the invisible hand works are familiar to all of us.[6] Firms are encouraged by the profit motive to use inputs efficiently. Valuable resources (such as energy) command high prices, so producers do not use them wastefully. The market system also guides firms' output decisions and, hence, those of society. A rise in the price of wheat, for example, will persuade farmers to produce more wheat and fewer soybeans. And a rise in the price of environmentally friendly products will persuade firms to produce more of these items as well, as the boxed insert on page 40 illustrates. Indeed, this profit incentive seems to be more effective than public exhortations that call for some change in human nature.

Finally, a price system determines who gets what goods through a series of voluntary exchanges. Each consumer uses his income to buy the things he likes best among those he can afford. But the ability to buy goods is not divided equally. Workers with valuable skills and owners of scarce resources are able to sell what they have at attractive prices. With the incomes they earn, they can then purchase the goods and services they want most, within the limits of their budgets. Those with less to sell must live more frugally.

This, in broad terms, is how a market economy solves the three basic problems facing any society: how to produce any given combination of goods efficiently, how to select an appropriate combination of goods, and how to distribute these goods sensibly among the people. As we proceed through the following chapters, you will learn much more about these issues. You will see that they constitute the central theme that permeates not only this text but the work of economists in general. As you progress through the book, keep in mind the following two questions: **What does the market do well and what does it do poorly?** There are plenty of answers to both questions. As you will learn in coming chapters,

1. Society has many important goals. Some of them, such as producing goods and services with maximum efficiency (minimum waste), can in certain circumstances be achieved extraordinarily well by letting markets operate more or less freely.

2. Free markets will not, however, achieve all of society's goals. For example, as we will see in Part Two, they often have trouble keeping unemployment and inflation low. And there are even some goals—such as protection of the environment—for which the unfettered operation of markets may be positively harmful.

3. But even in cases where the market does not perform at all well, there may be ways of harnessing the power of the market mechanism to remedy its own deficiencies, as you will learn in Part Seven of this book.

A **market system** is a form of organization of the economy in which decisions on resource allocation are left to the independent decisions of individual producers and consumers acting in their own best interest without central direction.

[6]This topic is studied in detail in Chapter 24.

Firms Cash In on Consumers' Green Awareness

"Green is such a selling point that it is in businesses' own interest to appear environmentally friendly," said a spokesman for Friends of the Earth, a British environmental group. The organization said it gets 30 to 40 calls a day from companies asking "How can I go green?"

The supermarket is the most visible representative of green awareness.

This summer, the Canadian grocery chain Loblaws introduced a line of environmentally friendly products under the brand name Green that includes re-refined motor oil, toilet paper made from recycled fibre, biodegradable soaps and cleansers, and phosphate-free detergents—all packaged in recycled paper.

In four weeks Loblaws sold $5 million worth of these products, double the company's forecast.

Britain's Body Shop chain promotes natural cosmetic products that are not tested on animals and are packaged in refillable containers.

From an initial investment of $12,500 in 1976, Body Shop has grown to a network of 400 stores in 34 countries that grossed $125 million last year.

In Sweden concern about chlorine emissions has caused

shops to run out of supplies of unbleached paper, and the country's huge forestry export industry has revamped its pulp and paper production technology in line with environmental demands.

SOURCE: *The Mail-Star*, Halifax, December 2, 1989, page C2.

Radicalism, Conservatism, and the Market Mechanism

Since economic debates often have political and ideological overtones, we think it important to close this chapter by stressing that the central theme that we have just outlined is neither a defence of nor an attack upon the capitalist system. Nor is it a "right-wing" position. One does not have to be a conservative to recognize that the market mechanism can be a helpful instrument for the pursuit of economic goals. A number of socialist countries, including Yugoslavia and Hungary, have openly and deliberately organized parts of their economies along market lines, and now the rest of Eastern Europe is moving swiftly in that direction.

The point is not to confuse means and ends in deciding on how much to rely on market forces. Radicals and conservatives surely have different goals, and they may also differ in the means they advocate to pursue these goals. But means should be chosen on the basis of how effective they are in achieving the adopted goals, not on some ideological prejudgment.

For example, many people assign a higher priority to pollution control than some conservatives do. Consequently, these individuals may support very strict controls even if such controls cut into business profits; conservatives may prefer things the other way around. Nevertheless, for reasons explained in Chapter 32, each side may want to use the market mechanism to achieve its goals. Indeed, each side may conclude that, should it lose the political struggle and the other side's position be adopted, less damage will be done to its own goals if market methods are used.

Certainly, there are economic problems with which the market cannot deal. Indeed, we have just noted that the market is the *source* of a number of significant problems. But the evidence leads economists to believe that many economic problems are best handled by market techniques. The analysis in this book is intended to help you identify the strengths and weaknesses of the market mechanism. We urge you to forget the slogans you have heard—whether from the left or from the right—and make up your own mind after you have learned the material covered in this book.

Summary

1. Supplies of all resources are limited. Because resources are scarce, a rational decision is one that chooses the best alternative among the options that are possible with the available resources.

2. It is irrational to assign highest priority to everything. No one can afford everything, and so hard choices must be made.

3. With limited resources, if we decide to obtain more of one item, we must give up some of another item. What we give up is called the *opportunity cost* of what we get; this is the true cost of any decision. The concept of opportunity cost is one of the 12 **Ideas for Beyond the Final Exam**.

4. The allocation of resources refers to the division of the economy's scarce inputs (fuel, minerals, machines, labour, and so on) among the economy's different outputs and the enterprises that produce them.

5. When the market is functioning effectively, firms are led to use resources efficiently and to produce the things that consumers want most. In such cases, opportunity costs and money costs (prices) correspond closely. When the market performs poorly or when important items of cost do not get price tags, opportunity costs and money costs can be quite different.

6. A firm's production possibilities frontier shows the combinations of goods the firm can produce with a given quantity of resources, given the state of technology. The frontier usually is not a straight line but is bowed outward because resources tend to be specialized.

7. The principle of increasing costs states that as the production of one good expands, the opportunity cost of producing another unit of this good generally increases.

8. The economy as a whole has a production possibilities frontier whose position is determined by its technology and by the available resources of land, labour, capital, and raw materials.

9. If a firm or an economy ends up at a point below its production possibilities frontier, it is using its resources inefficiently or wastefully. This is what happens, for example, when there is unemployment.

10. Economic growth means there is an outward shift in the economy's production possibilities frontier. The faster the growth, the faster this shift will occur. But growth requires a sacrifice of current consumption, and this is its opportunity cost.

11. Efficiency is defined by economists as the absence of waste. It is achieved primarily by gains in productivity brought about through specialization, division of labour, and a system of exchange.

12. If an exchange is voluntary, both parties must benefit even though no new goods are produced. This is another of the 12 **Ideas for Beyond the Final Exam**.

13. Every economic system must find a way to answer three basic questions: How can goods be produced most efficiently? How much of each good should be produced? How should goods be distributed?

14. The market system works very well in solving some of society's basic problems, but it fails to remedy others and may, indeed, create some of its own. Where and how it succeeds and fails constitute the theme of this book and characterize the work of economists in general.

Concepts for Review

Scarcity
Choice
Opportunity cost
Inputs (means of production)
Production possibilities frontier
Allocation of resources

Principle of increasing costs
Economic growth
Consumption goods
Capital goods
Efficiency
Specialization

Division of labour
Exchange
Market system
Three co-ordination tasks

Questions for Discussion

1. Discuss the resource limitations that affect:
   a. the poorest person on earth
   b. the richest person on earth
   c. a firm in Switzerland
   d. a government agency in China
   e. the population of the world

2. If you were president of your university, what would you change if your budget were cut by 5 percent? By 20 percent? By 50 percent?

3. If you were to drop out of university, what things would change in your life? What, then, is the opportunity cost of your education?

4. A person rents a house for which he pays the landlord $10,000 a year. Money in the bank earns 9 percent interest a year. The house is offered for sale at $140,000. Is this a good deal for the potential buyer? Where does opportunity cost enter the picture?

5. Construct graphically the production possibilities frontier for the Grand Republic of Glubstania given in the table below. Does the principle of increasing cost hold in the Glubstanian economy?

6. Consider two alternatives for Glubstania in the year 1992. In case (a) its inhabitants eat 60 million pork muffins and build only 12,000 noodle-making machines. In case (b) the population eats only 15 million pork muffins but builds 36,000 noodle machines. Which case will lead to a more generous production possibilities frontier for Glubstania in 1992? (*Note*: In Glubstania, noodle machines are used to produce pork muffins.)

7. Sam's Snack Shop sells two brands of potato chips. Brand X costs Sam 75 cents per bag, and Brand Y costs him $1. Draw Sam's production possibilities frontier if he has $60 budgeted to spend on potato chips. Why is it not "bowed out"?

Glubstania's 1992 Production Possibilities

PORK MUFFINS (millions per year)	NOODLE MACHINES (thousands per year)
75	0
60	12
45	22
30	30
15	36
0	40

3

Supply and Demand: An Initial Look

Reformers have the idea that change can be achieved by brute sanity.

GEORGE BERNARD SHAW

I f the issues of scarcity, choice, and co-ordination constitute the basic *problem* of economics, then the mechanism of supply and demand is its basic investigative tool. Supply and demand analysis is used in this book to study issues as seemingly diverse as inflation and unemployment, the international value of the dollar, government regulation of business, and protection of the environment. So careful study of this chapter will pay rich dividends.

The chapter describes the rudiments of supply and demand analysis in steps. We begin with demand, then add supply, and finally put the two sides together. *Supply and demand curves*—graphs that relate price to quantity supplied and quantity demanded, respectively—are explained and used to show how prices and quantities are determined in a free market. Influences that shift either the demand curve or the supply curve are catalogued briefly. And the analysis is used to explain such things as why airlines often run "sales" and why the prices of personal computers and recycled items have recently fallen so dramatically. Our discussion also involves several examples of government involvement in markets, such as rent controls, minimum-wage laws, subsidization of our court system, and certain aspects of our drug laws.

Indeed, one major theme of this chapter is that governments around the globe and throughout recorded history have attempted to tamper with the price mechanism. We will see that these bouts with Adam Smith's invisible hand have often produced undesired side effects that surprised and dismayed the authorities. And we will show that many of these unfortunate effects were not accidents but inherent consequences of interfering with the operation of free markets. The invisible hand fights back!

Fighting the Invisible Hand

Adam Smith was a great admirer of the price system. He extolled its accomplishments —both as a producer of goods and as a guarantor of individual freedoms. Many people since Smith's time have shared his enthusiasm, but many others have not, and they have tried to do better by legislative decree. There have been countless instances in which the public's sense of justice was outraged by the prices charged on the open market, particularly when the sellers of the expensive items did not enjoy great popularity—landlords, moneylenders, and oil companies are good examples.

Attempts to control interest rates (which may be thought of as the price of borrowing money) go back hundreds of years before the birth of Christ, at least to the code of laws compiled under Hammurabi in Babylonia about 1800 B.C. Our historical legacy also includes a rather long list of price ceilings on foods and other products imposed in the reign of Diocletian, emperor of the declining Roman Empire. More recently, Canadians have been offered the "protection" of a variety of price controls. Ceilings have been placed on prices of some items (such as energy, apartment rents, and insurance premiums) to protect buyers, while floors have been placed under prices of other items (such as farm products) to protect sellers. Many if not most of these measures were adopted in response to popular opinion, and there is a great outcry whenever it is proposed that any one of them be weakened or eliminated.

Yet, somehow, everything such regulation touches seems to end up in even greater disarray than it was before. For example, rent controls lead to a decreased supply of rental accommodation, and surplus agricultural products have had to be destroyed or stored indefinitely. The list could go on. Still, legislators continue to turn to controls whenever the economy does not work to their satisfaction. We still have rent controls in four Canadian provinces, a web of controls over energy prices was dismantled only in the 1980s, and agricultural price-support schemes still abound.

Interferences with the "Law" of Supply and Demand

Public opinion frequently encourages legislative attempts to "repeal the law of supply and demand" by controlling prices. The consequences are usually quite unfortunate, exacting heavy costs from the general public and often aggravating the problem the legislation was intended to cure. This is another of the **12 Ideas for Beyond the Final Exam**, and it will occupy our attention throughout this chapter.

To understand what goes wrong when markets are tampered with, we must first learn how they operate when they are unfettered. This chapter takes a first step in that direction by studying the machinery of supply and demand. Then, at the end of the chapter, we return to the issue of price controls, presenting case studies of rent controls and the minimum wage to illustrate the problems that can arise.

Every market has both buyers and sellers. We begin our analysis on the consumers' side of the market.

Demand and Quantity Demanded

Non-economists are apt to think of consumer demands as fixed amounts. For example, when the production of a new type of machine tool is proposed, management asks "What is its market potential? How many will we be able to sell?" Similarly, government bureaus conduct studies to determine how many engineers will be "required" in succeeding years.

Economists respond that such questions are not well posed—that there is no *single* answer to such a question. Rather, they say, the "market potential" for machine tools or the number of engineers that will be "required" depends on a great number of things, *including the price that will be charged for each.*

The **quantity demanded** of any product normally depends on its price. Quantity demanded also has a number of other determinants, including population size, consumer incomes, tastes, and the prices of other products.

Because of the central role of prices in a market economy, we begin our study of demand by focussing on the relationship between quantity demanded and price. Shortly, we will bring the other determinants of quantity demanded back into the picture.

Consider, as an example, the quantity of milk demanded. Almost everyone purchases at least some milk. However, if the price of milk is very high, its "market potential" may be very small. People will find ways to get along with less milk, perhaps by switching to tea or coffee. If the price declines, people will be encouraged

Price Controls in the Eighteenth Century

The following excerpts illustrate the unfortunate results that have followed from two of the many attempts to override market forces with legislation that have occurred over the years. In these examples, price ceilings made it unprofitable for suppliers to operate, so that scarcities and lost jobs were the unintended by-products.

The French Revolution

During the twenty months between May 1793 and December 1794, the Revolutionary Government of the new French Republic tried almost every experiment in wage and price controls which has been attempted before or since. . . .

. . . [The] first Law of the Maximum, as it was called, provided that the price of grain and flour in each district of France should be the average of local market prices which were in effect from January to May 1793. . . .

. . . By the summer of 1794, demands were coming from all over the country for the immediate repeal of the Law. In some towns in the South the people were so badly fed that they were collapsing in the streets from lack of nourishment. The department of the Nord complained bitterly that their shortages all began just after the passage of the by now hated Law of the Maximum. "Before that time," they wrote to the Convention in Paris, "our markets were supplied, but as soon as we fixed the price of wheat and rye we saw no more of those grains. The other kinds not subject to the maximum were the only ones brought in. The deputies of the Convention ordered us to fix a maximum for all grains. We obeyed and henceforth grain of every sort disappeared from the markets. What is the inference? This, that the establishment of a maximum brings famine in the midst of abundance. What is the remedy? Abolish the maximum."

. . . When Robespierre and his colleagues were being carried through the streets of Paris on their way to their executions, the mob jeered their last insult: "There goes the dirty Maximum."

Early Canada—Louisbourg

During 1750 rules were made as to the price that must be charged for fresh cod fish. It was, by this order, explicitly forbidden for fishermen to refuse to sell their fish at the posted price provided only that the buyer was solvent. To appreciate the serious nature of this law, it is necessary to remember that the bulk of New France's wealth was derived from the cod fishery. Of course, from time to time this regulation led to desperate circumstances for the fishermen and there is some reason to believe that it was responsible for the decline in the fishery in that area of New France.

SOURCE: Robert L. Schuettinger, "The Historical Record: A Survey of Wage and Price Controls over Fifty Centuries," in *Tax-Based Incomes Policies—A Cure for Inflation?* edited by M. Walker (Vancouver: The Fraser Institute, 1982), pages 67, 73–76.

---

to drink more milk. They may give their children larger portions or switch away from juices and sodas. Thus:

There is no *one* demand figure for milk, for machine tools, or for engineers. Rather, there is a different quantity demanded for each possible price.

The Demand Schedule

Table 3–1 displays this information for milk in what we call a **demand schedule**, which shows how much consumers are able and willing to buy (during a specified time period) at different possible prices. The table indicates the quantity of milk that will be demanded in a year at prices ranging from $1 to 40¢ per litre. We see, for example, that at a relatively low price, like 50¢ per litre, customers wish to purchase 70 million litres per year. But if the price rises to, say, 90¢ per litre, quantity demanded falls to 50 million litres.

Common sense tells us why this should be so.[1] First, as prices rise, some customers will reduce their consumption of milk. Second, higher prices will induce

A **demand schedule** is a table showing how the quantity demanded of some product during a specified period of time changes as the price of that product changes, holding all other determinants of quantity demanded constant.

[1] This common-sense answer is examined more fully in Chapter 19.

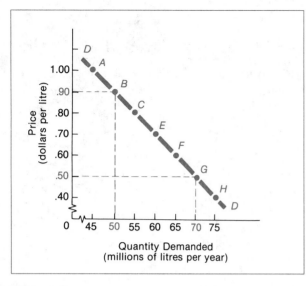

FIGURE 3–1
Demand Curve for Milk
This curve shows the relationship between price and quantity demanded. To sell 70 million litres per year, the price must be only 50¢ (point G). If, instead, price is 90¢, only 50 million litres will be demanded (point B). To sell more milk, the price must be reduced. That is what the negative slope of the demand curve means.

TABLE 3–1
Demand Schedule for Milk

PRICE (dollars per litre)	QUANTITY DEMANDED (millions of litres per year)	LABEL IN FIGURE 3–1
1.00	45	A
0.90	50	B
0.80	55	C
0.70	60	E
0.60	65	F
0.50	70	G
0.40	75	H

some customers to drop out of the market entirely—for example, by switching to soda or juice. On both counts, quantity demanded will decline as the price rises.

As the price of an item rises, the quantity demanded normally falls. As the price falls, the quantity demanded normally rises.

The Demand Curve

The information contained in Table 3–1 can be summarized in a graph, which we call a **demand curve**, displayed in Figure 3–1. Each point in the graph corresponds to a line in the table. For example, point B corresponds to the second line in the table, indicating that at a price of 90¢ per litre, 50 million litres per year will be demanded. Since the quantity demanded declines as the price increases, the demand curve has a negative slope.[2]

Notice the last phrase in the definitions of the demand schedule and the demand curve: "holding all other determinants of quantity demanded constant." These "other determinants" include consumer incomes and preferences, the prices of soda and orange juice, and perhaps even advertising by the dairy association. We will examine the influences of these factors later in the chapter. First, however, let's look at the sellers' side of the market.

A **demand curve** is a graphical depiction of a demand schedule. It shows how the quantity demanded of some product during a specified period of time will change as the price of that product changes, holding all other determinants of quantity demanded constant.

Supply and Quantity Supplied

Like quantity demanded, the quantity of milk that is supplied by dairy farmers is not a fixed number but also depends on many things. Obviously, if there are more dairy farms, or larger ones, we expect more milk to be supplied. Or, if bad weather deprives the cows of their feed, they may give less milk. As before, however, let's turn our attention first to the relationship between **quantity supplied** and one of its major determinants—price.

[2]If you need to review the concept of *slope*, refer back to Chapter 1, especially pages 17–20.

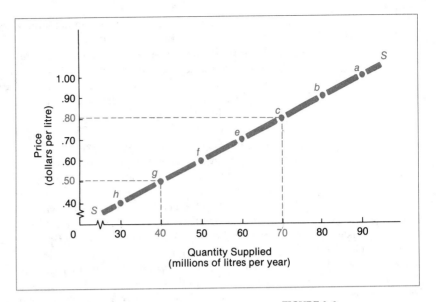

TABLE 3-2
Supply Schedule for Milk

PRICE (dollars per litre)	QUANTITY SUPPLIED (millions of litres per year)	LABEL IN FIGURE 3-2
1.00	90	a
0.90	80	b
0.80	70	c
0.70	60	e
0.60	50	f
0.50	40	g
0.40	30	h

FIGURE 3-2
Supply Curve for Milk
This curve shows the relationship between the price of milk and the quantity supplied. To stimulate a greater quantity supplied, price must be increased. That is the meaning of the positive slope of the supply curve.

Economists generally suppose that a higher price calls forth a greater quantity supplied. Why? Remember our analysis of the principle of increasing cost in Chapter 2 (page 32). According to that principle, as more of any farmer's (or the nation's) resources are devoted to milk production, the opportunity cost of obtaining another litre of milk increases. Farmers will therefore find it profitable to raise milk production only if they can sell the milk at a higher price—high enough to cover the higher costs incurred when milk production expands.

Looked at the other way around, we have just concluded that higher prices normally will be required to persuade farmers to raise milk production. This idea is quite general and applies to the supply of most goods and services.[3] As long as suppliers want to make profits, and the principle of increasing costs holds:

As the price of an item rises, the quantity supplied normally rises. As the price falls, the quantity supplied normally falls.

The Supply Schedule and the Supply Curve

The relationship between the price of milk and its quantity supplied is recorded in Table 3-2, which we call a **supply schedule**. The table shows that a low price like 50¢ per litre will induce suppliers to provide only 40 million litres, while a higher price like 80¢ will induce them to provide much more—70 million litres.

As you might have guessed, when information like this is plotted on a graph, it is called a **supply curve**. Figure 3-2 is the supply curve corresponding to the supply schedule in Table 3-2. It slopes upward because quantity supplied is higher when price is higher.

Notice again the same phrase in the definition: "holding all other determinants of quantity supplied constant." We will return to these "other determinants" a bit later. But first we are ready to put demand and supply together.

Equilibrium of Supply and Demand

To analyze how price is determined in a free market, we must compare the desires of consumers (demand) with the desires of producers (supply) and see whether the two sets of plans are consistent. Table 3-3 and Figure 3-3 are designed to help us do this.

[3]This analysis is carried out in much greater detail in Chapters 21 and 22.

A **supply schedule** is a table showing how the quantity supplied of some product during a specified period of time changes as the price of that product changes, holding all other determinants of quantity supplied constant.

A **supply curve** is a graphical depiction of a supply schedule. It shows how the quantity supplied of some product during a specified period of time will change as the price of that product changes, holding all other determinants of quantity supplied constant.

Table 3–3 brings together the demand schedule from Table 3–1 and the supply schedule from Table 3–2. Similarly, Figure 3–3 puts together the demand curve from Figure 3–1 and the supply curve from Figure 3–2 on a single graph. Such a graphic device is called a **supply–demand diagram**, and we will encounter many of them in this book. Notice that, for reasons already discussed, the demand curve has a negative slope and the supply curve has a positive slope. Most supply–demand diagrams are drawn with slopes like these.

There is only one point in Figure 3–3, point *E*, at which the supply curve and the demand curve intersect. At the price corresponding to point *E*, which is 70¢ per litre, the quantity supplied is equal to the quantity demanded. This means that, at a price of 70¢ per litre, consumers are willing to buy just what producers are willing to sell.

At a lower price, such as 50¢, only 40 million litres of milk will be supplied (point *g*), whereas 70 million litres will be demanded (point *G*). Thus, quantity demanded will exceed quantity supplied. There will be a **shortage** equal to 70 – 40 = 30 million litres. Alternatively, at a higher price, such as $1, quantity supplied will be 90 million litres (point *a*) while quantity demanded will be only 45 million (point *A*). Quantity supplied will exceed quantity demanded, so there will be a **surplus** equal to 90 – 45 = 45 million litres.

Since 70¢ is the price at which quantity supplied and quantity demanded are equal, we say that 70¢ per litre is the **equilibrium price** in this market. Similarly, 60 million litres per year is the **equilibrium quantity** of milk.

TABLE 3–3
Determination of the Equilibrium Price and Quantity of Milk

PRICE (dollars per litre)	QUANTITY DEMANDED	QUANTITY SUPPLIED	SURPLUS OR SHORTAGE?	PRICE WILL:
	(millions of litres per year)			
1.00	45	90	Surplus	Fall
0.90	50	80	Surplus	Fall
0.80	55	70	Surplus	Fall
0.70	60	60	Neither	Remain the same
0.60	65	50	Shortage	Rise
0.50	70	40	Shortage	Rise
0.40	75	30	Shortage	Rise

FIGURE 3–3
Supply–Demand Equilibrium
In a free market, price and quantity are determined by the intersection of the supply curve and the demand curve. In this example, the equilibrium price is 70¢ and the equilibrium quantity is 60 million litres of milk per year. Any other price is inconsistent with equilibrium. For example, at a price of 50¢, quantity demanded is 70 million litres (point *G*), while quantity supplied is only 40 million litres (point *g*), so that price will be driven up by the unsatisfied demand.

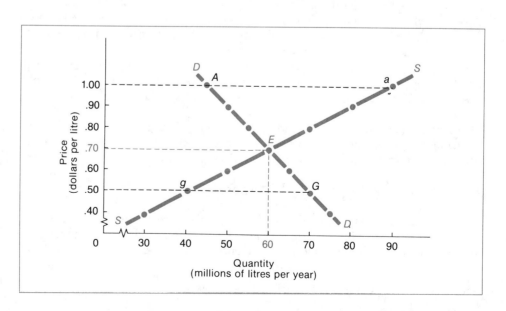

The term "equilibrium" merits a little explanation, since it arises so frequently in economic analysis. An **equilibrium** is a situation in which there are no inherent forces that produce change—that is, a situation that does not contain the seeds of its own destruction. Think, for example, of a pendulum at rest at its centre point. If no outside force (such as a person's hand) comes to push it, the pendulum will remain where it is; it is in *equilibrium*.

But if someone gives the pendulum a shove, its equilibrium will be disturbed and it will start to move upward. When it reaches the top of its arc, the pendulum will, for an instant, be at rest again. But this is not an equilibrium position. A force known as gravity will pull the pendulum downward, and thereafter its motion from side to side will be governed by gravity and friction. Eventually, we know, the pendulum must return to the point at which it started, which is its only equilibrium position. At any other point inherent forces will cause the pendulum to move.

The concept of equilibrium in economics is similar and can be illustrated by our supply and demand example. Why is no price other than 70¢ an equilibrium price in Table 3-3 or Figure 3-3? What forces will change any other price?

Consider first a low price like 50¢, at which quantity demanded (70 million) exceeds quantity supplied (40 million). If the price were this low, there would be many frustrated customers unable to purchase the quantities they desire. They would compete with one another for the available milk. Some would offer more than the prevailing price, and, as customers tried to outbid one another, the market price would be forced up. In other words, a price below the equilibrium price cannot persist in a free market because a shortage sets in motion powerful economic forces that push price upward.

Similar forces operate if the market price is *above* the equilibrium price. If, for example, the price should somehow get to be $1, Table 3-3 tells us that quantity supplied (90 million) would far exceed quantity demanded (45 million). Producers would be unable to sell their desired quantities of milk at the prevailing price, and some would find it in their interest to undercut their competitors by reducing price. This process of competitive price-cutting would continue as long as the surplus persisted, that is, as long as quantity supplied exceeded quantity demanded. Thus, a price above the equilibrium price cannot persist indefinitely.

We are left with only one conclusion. The price 70¢ per litre and the quantity 60 million litres is the only price–quantity combination that does not sow the seeds of its own destruction. It is the only *equilibrium*. Any lower price must rise, and any higher price must fall. It is as if natural economic forces place a magnet at point *E* that attracts the market just as gravity attracts the pendulum.

The analogy to a pendulum is worth pursuing further. Most pendulums are more frequently in motion than at rest. However, unless they are repeatedly buffeted by outside forces (which, of course, is exactly what happens to pendulums used in clocks), pendulums gradually return to their resting points. The same is true of price and quantity in a free market. Markets are not always in equilibrium, but, if they are not interfered with, we have good reason to believe that they normally are *moving toward equilibrium*.

An **equilibrium** is a situation in which there are no inherent forces that produce change. Changes away from an equilibrium position will occur only as a result of "outside events" that disturb the status quo.

The Law of Supply and Demand

In a free market, the forces of supply and demand generally push price toward its equilibrium level—the price at which quantity supplied and quantity demanded are equal.

Like most economic "laws," the law of supply and demand is occasionally disobeyed. Markets sometimes display shortages or surpluses for long periods of time. Prices sometimes fail to move toward equilibrium. But, by and large, the "law" seems a fair generalization. It is right far more often than it is wrong.

The last interesting aspect of the analogy concerns the "outside forces" of which we have spoken. A pendulum that is being blown by the wind or pushed by a hand does not remain in equilibrium. Similarly, many outside forces can disturb a market equilibrium. A frost in Florida will disturb equilibrium in the market for oranges. A strike by miners will disturb equilibrium in the market for coal.

Many of these outside influences actually *change the equilibrium price and quantity* by shifting either the supply curve or the demand curve. If you look again at Figure 3–3, you can see clearly that any event that causes *either* the demand curve *or* the supply curve to shift will also cause the equilibrium price and quantity to change. Such events constitute the "other determinants" that we held constant in our definitions of supply and demand curves. We are now ready to analyze how these outside forces affect the equilibrium of supply and demand, beginning on the demand side.

Shifts of the Demand Curve

Returning to our example of milk, we noted earlier that the quantity of milk demanded is probably influenced by a variety of things other than the price of milk. Changes in population, consumer income, and the prices of alternative beverages, such as soda and orange juice, presumably cause changes in the quantity of milk demanded, even if the price of milk is unchanged.

Since the demand curve for milk depicts only the relationship between the quantity of milk demanded and the price of milk, holding all other factors constant, a change in any of these other factors produces a *shift of the entire demand curve*. That is:

A change in the price of a good produces a **movement along a fixed demand curve**. By contrast, a change in any other variable that influences quantity demanded produces a **shift of the demand curve**. If consumers want to buy *more* at any given price than they wanted previously, the demand curve shifts to the right (or outward). If they desire *less* at any given price, the demand curve shifts to the left (or inward).

To make this general principle more concrete and to show some of its many applications, let us consider some specific examples.

1. *Consumer incomes.*   If average incomes increase, consumers may purchase more of many foods, including milk, even if the price of milk remains the same. That is, *increases in income normally shift demand curves outward to the right*, as depicted in Figure 3–4(a). In this example, the quantity demanded at the old equilibrium price of 70¢ increases from 60 million litres per year (point E on demand curve D_0D_0) to 75 million (point R on demand curve D_1D_1). We know that 70¢ is no longer the equilibrium price, since at this price quantity demanded (75 million) exceeds quantity supplied (60 million). To restore equilibrium, price will have to rise. The diagram shows the new equilibrium at point T, where the price is 80¢ per litre and the quantity (demanded and supplied) is 70 million litres per year. This illustrates a general result.

    Any factor that causes the demand curve to shift outward to the right and does not affect the supply curve will raise both the equilibrium price and the equilibrium quantity.[4]

    Everything works in reverse if consumer incomes fall. Figure 3–4(b) depicts a leftward (inward) shift of the demand curve that results from a decline in

---

[4] This statement, like many others in the text, assumes that the demand curve is downward-sloping and the supply curve is upward-sloping.

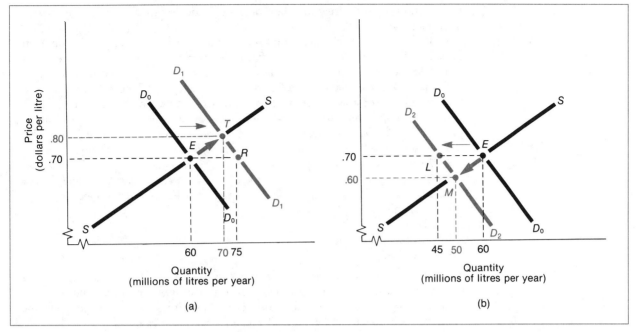

FIGURE 3–4
The Effects of Shifts of the
Demand Curve

A shift of the demand curve will
change the equilibrium price
and quantity in a free market. In
part (a), the demand curve
shifts outward from D_0D_0 to
D_1D_1. As a result, equilibrium
moves from point E to point T;
both price and quantity rise. In
part (b), the demand curve
shifts inward from D_0D_0 to D_2D_2,
and equilibrium moves from
point E to point M; both price
and quantity fall.

consumer incomes. For example, the quantity demanded at the previous equilibrium price (70¢) falls from 60 million litres (point E) to 45 million (point L on demand curve D_2D_2). At the initial price, quantity supplied must begin to fall. The new equilibrium will eventually be established at point M, where the price is 60¢ and both quantity demanded and quantity supplied are 50 million. In general:

Any factor that shifts the demand curve inward to the left and does not affect the supply curve will lower both the equilibrium price and the equilibrium quantity.

2. **Population.** Population growth should affect quantity demanded in more or less the same way as do increases in average incomes. A larger population will presumably wish to consume more milk, even if the price of milk and average incomes are unchanged, thus shifting the entire demand curve to the right as in Figure 3–4(a). The equilibrium price and quantity both rise. Similarly, a decrease in population should shift the demand curve for milk to the left, as in Figure 3–4(b), causing equilibrium price and quantity to fall.

3. **Consumer preferences.** If the dairy industry mounts a successful advertising campaign extolling the benefits of drinking milk, families may decide to raise their quantities demanded. This would shift the entire demand curve for milk to the right, as in Figure 3–4(a). Alternatively, a medical report on the dangers of high cholesterol may persuade consumers to drink less milk, thereby shifting the demand curve inward, as in Figure 3–4(b).

Again, these are quite general phenomena. *If consumer preferences shift in favour of a particular item, that item's demand curve will shift outward to the right, causing both equilibrium price and quantity to rise. Conversely, if consumer preferences shift away from an item, that item's demand curve will shift inward to the left, causing equilibrium price and quantity to fall.*

4. **Prices and availability of related goods.** Because soda, orange juice, and coffee are popular drinks that compete with milk, a change in the price of any of these beverages can be expected to shift the demand curve for milk. If any of these alternative drinks become cheaper, some consumers will switch away from milk. Thus the demand curve for milk will shift to the left, as in Figure 3–4(b). The

introduction of an entirely new beverage—say, coconut milk—can be expected to have a similar effect.

But other price changes shift the demand curve for milk in the opposite direction. For example, suppose that cookies, a commodity that goes well with milk, become less expensive. This may induce some consumers to drink more milk and thus shift the demand curve for milk to the right as in Figure 3-4(a).

Common sense normally will tell us in which direction a price change for a related good will shift the demand curve for a good in question. *Increases in the prices of goods that are substitutes for the good in question (as soda is for milk) move the demand curve to the right, thus raising both the equilibrium price and quantity. Increases in the prices of goods that are normally used together with the good in question (such as cookies and milk) shift the demand curve to the left, thus lowering both the equilibrium price and quantity.* (See Discussion Question 10 at the end of the chapter.)

Applications:
(1) Why Airlines Run Sales

Anyone who travels knows that airline companies reduce fares sharply to attract more customers at certain times of the year when air traffic is light. Yet there is no reason to think that air transportation gets any cheaper at these times. Our supply and demand diagram makes it easy to understand why airlines run such "sales."

Given the number of planes in the airlines' fleets, the supply of seats is relatively fixed, as indicated by the steep supply curve SS in Figure 3-5, and it is more or less the same in all seasons. During times when people want to travel less, the demand curve for seats shifts leftward from its normal position, $D_0 D_0$, to a position such as $D_1 D_1$. Hence, equilibrium in the air traffic market shifts from point E to point A. Thus, both price and quantity decline at certain times of the year, not because of the generosity of the airlines but because of the discipline of the market.

(2) Why Housing Prices Vary

The same analysis can be used to explain variations in housing prices. During the period of high oil prices in the 1970s, average incomes rose in Alberta and so did the size of the province's population. The demand curve for homes, especially in Calgary and Edmonton, shifted to the right, and there was much building and big increases in

FIGURE 3-5
Seasonal Changes in Airline Fares
During seasons of slack demand for air travel, the demand curve shifts leftward from $D_0 D_0$ to $D_1 D_1$. In consequence, the market equilibrium point shifts from E to A, causing both price and quantity to decline.

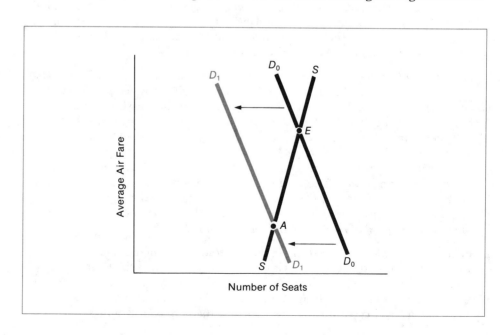

housing prices. Then a period of low oil prices followed in the 1980s; average incomes and the size of the population fell in Alberta. The demand curve for houses shifted back to the left, so housing prices fell.

(3) Why the Weather Affects Prices

December 1989 saw record cold temperatures in Southern Ontario, and the price for heating fuels jumped by 20 percent in January 1990. It is easy to understand why: just think of Figure 3–5, applying it to the example of heating fuel and envisioning it in reverse. The cold weather caused a large rightward shift in the demand curve for heating fuels, and since the supply curve is relatively fixed in the short run, the price rose significantly.

Shifts of the Supply Curve

Like quantity demanded, the quantity supplied on a market typically responds to a great number of influences other than price. The weather, the cost of feed, the number and size of dairy farms, and a variety of other factors all influence how much milk will be brought to market. Since the supply curve depicts only the relationship between the price of milk and the quantity of milk demanded, holding all other factors constant, a change in any of these other factors will cause the entire supply curve to shift. Thus:

A change in the price of the good causes a **movement along a fixed supply curve**. But price is not the only influence on quantity supplied. And, if any of these other influences changes, **the entire supply curve shifts**.

Let us consider what some of these other factors are, and how they shift the supply curve.

1. *Size of the industry.*   We begin with the most obvious factor. If more farmers enter the milk industry, the quantity supplied at any given price probably will increase. For example, if each farm provides 60,000 litres of milk per year when the price is 70¢ per litre, then 1000 farmers provide 60 million litres and 1300 farmers provide 78 million. Thus, the more farms that are attracted to the industry, the greater will be the quantity of milk supplied at any given price and, hence, the farther to the right will be the supply curve.

   Figure 3–6(a) illustrates the effect of an expansion of the industry from 1000 farms to 1300 farms—a rightward shift of the supply curve from S_0S_0 to S_1S_1. Notice that at the initial price of 70¢, the quantity supplied after the shift is 78 million litres (point I on supply curve S_1S_1), which exceeds the quantity demanded of 60 million (point E on supply curve S_0S_0). We can see in the graph that the price of 70¢ is too high to be the equilibrium price; so price must fall. The diagram shows the new equilibrium at point J, where the price is 60¢ per litre and the quantity is 65 million litres. The general point is that:

   Any factor that shifts the supply curve outward to the right and does not affect the demand curve will lower the equilibrium price and raise the equilibrium quantity.

   This must *always* be true if the industry's demand curve has a negative slope because the greater quantity supplied can be sold only if price is decreased to induce customers to buy more.[5]
   Figure 3–6(b) illustrates the opposite case: a contraction of the industry from 1000 farms to 625 farms. The supply curve shifts inward to the left and equilib-

---

[5]Graphically, whenever a positively sloped curve shifts to the right, its intersection point with a negatively sloping curve must always move lower (just try drawing it yourself).

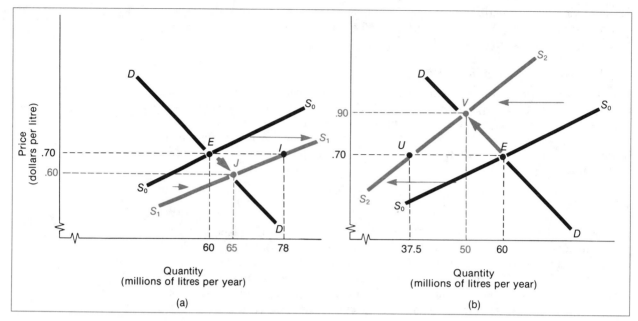

FIGURE 3-6
Effects of Shifts of the Supply Curve
A shift of the supply curve will change the equilibrium price and quantity in a market. In part (a), the supply curve shifts outward to the right, from S_0S_0 to S_1S_1. As a result, equilibrium moves from point E to point J; price falls as quantity increases. Part (b) illustrates the opposite case—an inward shift of the supply curve from S_0S_0 to S_2S_2. Equilibrium moves from point E to point V, which means that price rises as quantity falls.

rium moves from point E to point V, where price is 90¢ and quantity is 50 million litres. In general:

Any factor that shifts the supply curve inward to the left and does not affect the demand curve will raise the equilibrium price and will reduce the equilibrium quantity.

Even if no farmers enter or leave the industry, results like those depicted in Figure 3-6 can be produced by expansion or contraction of the existing farms. If farms get larger by adding more land, expanding the herds, and so on, the supply curve shifts to the right as in Figure 3-6(a). If farms get smaller, the supply curve shifts to the left, as in Figure 3-6(b).

2. **Technological progress.** Another influence that shifts supply curves is technological change. Suppose someone discovers that cows give more milk if Mozart is played during milking. Then, at any given price of milk, farmers will be able to provide a larger quantity of output; that is, the supply curve will shift outward to the right, as in Figure 3-6(a). This, again, illustrates a quite general influence that applies to most industries: *cost-reducing technological progress shifts the supply curve outward to the right.* Thus, as Figure 3-6(a) shows, the usual consequences of technological progress are lower prices and greater output.

3. **Prices of inputs.** Changes in input prices also shift supply curves. Suppose that farm workers become unionized and win a raise. Farmers will have to pay higher wages and consequently will no longer be able to provide 60 million litres of milk profitably at a price of 70¢ per litre [point E in Figure 3-6(b)]. Perhaps they will provide only 37.5 million (point U on supply curve S_2S_2). This example illustrates that *increases in the prices of inputs that suppliers must buy will shift the supply curve inward to the left.*

4. *Prices of related outputs.*   Dairy farms produce more than milk. If cheese prices rise sharply, farmers may decide to use some raw milk to make cheese, thereby reducing the quantity of milk supplied. On a supply–demand diagram, the supply curve would shift inward, as in Figure 3–6(b).

Similar phenomena occur in other industries, and sometimes the effect goes in the opposite direction. For example, suppose the price of beef goes up, which increases the quantity of meat supplied. That, in turn, will cause a rise in the number of cowhides supplied at any given price of leather. Thus, a rise in the price of beef will lead to a rightward shift in the supply curve of leather. In general: *A change in the price of one good produced by a multiproduct industry may be expected to shift the supply curves of all the other goods produced by that industry.*

Applications:
(1) A Computer in Every Home?

A few decades ago, no one owned a home computer. Now there are millions in North America, and enthusiasts look toward the day when computers will be as common-place as television sets. What happened to bring the computer from the laboratory into the home? Did people suddenly develop a craving for computers?

Hardly. What actually happened is that scientists in the early 1970s invented the microchip—a major breakthrough that drastically reduced both the size of computers and, more important, the cost of manufacturing them. Within a few years, microcomputers were in commercial production. And microchip technology continued to improve throughout the 1970s and 1980s, leading to ever smaller, better, and cheaper computers. Today, for less than a thousand dollars, you can buy a desktop machine whose computing powers rival those of the giant computers of the early 1960s.

In terms of our supply and demand diagrams, the rapid technological progress in computer manufacturing shifted the supply curve dramatically to the right. As Figure 3–7 shows, a large outward shift of the supply curve should bring down the equilibrium price and increase the equilibrium quantity—which is just what happened in the computer industry. The figure calls attention to the fact that consumers naturally buy

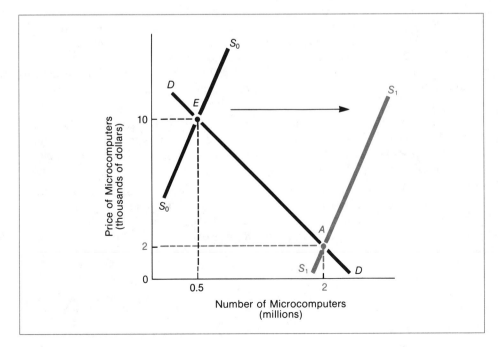

FIGURE 3–7
Technological Change and the Computer Market
The invention of the microchip and subsequent improvements in microchip technology caused the supply curve of micro-computers to shift outward to the right—moving from $S_0 S_0$ to $S_1 S_1$. Consequently, equilibrium shifted from point E to point A. The price of microcomputers fell from $10,000 to $2000, and the quantity increased from 0.5 million to 2 million per year.

more computers as the price of computers falls (*a movement along* demand curve *DD* from *E* to *A*), even if the demand curve does not *shift*.

(2) A Glut of Recycled Items

Concern for the environment has led to the organization of recycling programs for numerous items such as newsprint and glass bottles. Initially these schemes made money, but with the dramatic increase in people's willingness to participate by separating their garbage, the market for such goods became flooded. With the supply curve shifting dramatically to the right (as more "suppliers" entered the market), the price for recycled items has fallen to very low levels, and many municipalities are simply storing them until the price rises again.

The price can be expected to rise when more factories become equipped to process the used products. For example, the machines that paper mills need to produce newsprint from used paper are different from the ones they currently own, which produce newsprint from pulp. Until more of the new machines are built, the recycled paper cannot be used in large quantities. Although this temporary outcome is discouraging for environmentalists, the current low prices for recycled items are indeed inducing firms to build the new equipment that will enable them to take advantage of these low prices. And in the longer run, this is exactly what environmentalists want.[6]

Restraining the Market Mechanism: Price Ceilings

As we have noted already, lawmakers and rulers have often been dissatisfied with the outcomes of the operation of the market system. All through the ages, legislators have done battle with the invisible hand. Sometimes, rather than trying to make adjustments in the workings of the market, governments have sought to raise or to lower the prices of specific commodities by decree. In many of these cases, those in authority felt that the prices set by the market mechanism were, in some sense, immorally low or immorally high. Penalties were therefore imposed on anyone offering the commodities in question at prices lower or higher than those determined by the authorities.

A **price ceiling** is a legal maximum on the price that may be charged for a commodity.

But the market has proven itself a formidable foe that strongly resists attempts to circumvent its workings. In case after case where **price ceilings** are imposed, virtually the same set of consequences ensues:

1. The economy develops a persistent shortage of the items whose prices are controlled. Queuing, direct rationing, or any of a variety of other devices, usually inefficient and unpleasant, have to be substituted for the distribution process provided by the price mechanism. *Example*: In 1990, consumers in the Soviet Union were placing orders for sitting-room furniture that were scheduled for delivery in 2011.

2. An illegal or "black" market often arises to supply the commodity. There are usually some individuals who are willing to take the risks involved in meeting unsatisfied demands illegally, if legal means will not do the job. *Example*: Although it is illegal in most places, ticket "scalping" occurs at most popular sporting events.

3. The prices charged on the black market are almost certainly higher than those that would prevail in a free market. After all, black marketeers expect compensation for the risk of being caught and punished. *Example*: Goods that are illegally smuggled into a country, such as drugs, are normally quite expensive.

---

[6]Another reason that the price for recycled items will not remain depressed for too long is that laws are being passed that effectively push the demand curve to the right. Thirty states south of the border now have some form of compulsory recycling laws. In Canada a similar trend is evident; for example, the city of Toronto passed a law effective January 1991 requiring 50 percent recycled content in the newsprint used by its newspapers.

At the Frontier: Experimental Economics

In theory, supply and demand curves determine price. But does reality work the way theory claims? One way of answering this question is to consider actual historical events. This is what we have done in this chapter, and we have seen that supply and demand analysis explains observed variations in the price of a range of items, from houses to recycled goods, very well. But another way of answering the question is to run controlled experiments the way physicists do.

For a long time it was believed that the option of laboratory experimentation was not available to economists. How can an economist re-create an entire economy, or even a single market, in a laboratory? How can one supply realistic motivation for the people who participate in such an experiment, so that they will act as they would in making an actual decision, with real money at stake?

Because economists have long felt that experimental methods were beyond their grasp, they have relied mostly on statistical inference to test their theories. But the statistical approach is an imperfect solution because it does not allow us to isolate perfectly just *one* influence at a time, as in a scientifically controlled experiment.

This view of experimentation in economics has recently begun to change. Economists still rely mainly on statistical analysis, but they have also begun to experiment. Market experiments are now conducted to test theories about the behaviour of large firms, about economic incentives to help protect the environment, about the responses of consumers to changing tax rules, about government programs that provide financial assistance to poor people, and about a wide variety of other subjects. Dozens of experiments are now under way.

Who are the subjects of these experiments? You guessed it. They are often university students who volunteer to participate. What leads them to volunteer? One reason may be that the experiments are interesting; but there is also money to be earned. In fact, that is what provides the motivation for the participants to act as they would in a real market. Let's look at one such experiment, conducted at two schools in the United States.* The objective was to see whether demand and supply curves do in fact determine price in the way the theory claims.

Students were divided into two groups, sellers and buyers. Each was given some money to start, and the amount of money remaining at the end depended on the purchases and sales he or she made. Sellers acquired "goods" from the experimenter (who acted like a wholesaler) at a price, and then tried to sell them to one of the buyers. Sellers could pocket any difference between the price they paid to the experimenter and the price they received for selling the good. Similarly, buying students could maximize the amount of money they took away from the game by paying the lowest price possible for the goods they purchased. Since the experimenter specified how these gains to the buying students depended on the prices they paid, he was able to derive, at the theoretical level, what the market-clearing price would be.

How did the actual prices turn out in the experiment? Each time a sale was completed by voluntary interaction of buyers and sellers, the agreed-upon price was recorded. The experiment was repeated five times, each repetition involving about 15 to 25 transactions. The actual prices were generally lower than the theoretical equilibrium value, but they were almost always very close. And, in each of the five experiments, the price came closer and closer to the theoretical figure as more transactions were completed and students acquired more experience. In the last two experiments, the average prices were within 2.2 percent of the predicted equilibrium. Apparently, the experiments do work, and so does the theory—as a reasonable approximation of reality.

* See C. R. Plott, "Externalities and Corrective Policies in Experimental Markets," *The Economic Journal*, vol. 93, March 1983, pages 106–27.

---

4. In each case, a substantial portion of the price falls into the hands of the black-market supplier instead of going to those who produce the good or who perform the service. *Example*: A constant complaint in the series of hearings that have marked the history of theatre-ticket price controls in New York City has been that the "ice" (the illegal excess charge) falls into the hands of ticket scalpers rather than going to those who invested in, produced, or acted in the play.

These points and others are best illustrated by considering some concrete examples of price ceilings.

Case Studies:
(1) Rent Controls

New York is the only major city in North America that has had rent controls continuously since World War II. The objective of rent control is, of course, to protect the consumer from high rents. But more than 95 percent of Canadian economists

FIGURE 3-8
Supply–Demand Diagram for Housing

When market forces are permitted to set rents, the quantity of dwellings supplied will equal the quantity demanded. But when a rent ceiling forces rent below the market level, the number of dwellings supplied (point C) will be less than the number demanded (point B). Thus, rent ceilings induce housing shortages.

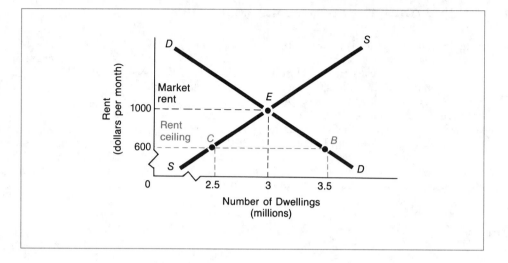

believe that rent control does not help cities or their inhabitants and that, in the long run, it makes almost everyone worse off. Let's use supply–demand analysis to see what actually happens.

Figure 3–8 is a supply–demand diagram for rental units in New York. Curve *DD* is the demand curve and curve *SS* is the supply curve. Without controls, equilibrium would be at point *E*, where rents average $1000 per month and 3 million units are occupied. Effective rent controls must set a ceiling price below the equilibrium price of $1000, because otherwise the rent level would simply settle at the point determined by market forces. But with a low rent ceiling, such as, say, $600, the quantity of housing demanded will be 3.5 million (point *B*) while the quantity supplied will be only 2.5 million (point *C*).

The diagram shows a shortage of 1 million apartments. This theoretical concept of a "shortage" shows up in New York City as an abnormally low vacancy rate— typically about half the U.S. national urban average.

As we expect, rent controls have spawned a lively black market in New York. The black market works to raise the effective price of rent-controlled apartments in many ways, including bribes, "key money" paid to move up on waiting lists, and requirements that prospective tenants purchase worthless furniture at inflated prices.

According to the diagram, rent controls reduce the quantity supplied from 3 million to 2.5 million apartments. What do we see in New York? First, some property owners, discouraged by the low rents, have converted apartment buildings into office space or other uses. Second, some apartments have not been maintained adequately. After all, rent controls create a shortage that makes even dilapidated apartments easy to rent. Third, some landlords have actually abandoned their buildings rather than pay rising tax and fuel bills. These abandoned buildings rapidly become eyesores and eventually pose threats to public health and safety.

With all these problems, why do rent controls persist in New York City? And why did Canada have rent controls in all ten provinces in 1975, and why do we still have controls in four provinces today? Part of the explanation is that many people simply do not understand the problems that rent controls cause. Another part is that landlords are unpopular politically. But a third, and important, part of the explanation is that not everyone is hurt by rent controls, and those who benefit from controls fight hard to preserve them. In New York, for example, many tenants pay rents that are only a fraction of what their apartments would fetch on the open market. This last point illustrates another very general phenomenon:

Virtually every price ceiling or floor creates a class of people with a vested interest in preserving the regulations because they benefit from them. These people naturally use

Rent Control in Ontario

Jack Harvey says he's being held hostage by the provincial government's policy on affordable housing. . . .

The landlord and real estate company president is boarding up his units in an apartment complex on Main Street East rather than rent them out.

The city denied Mr. Harvey permission to renovate the building under the province's Bill 11 because the renovations would probably lead to a rent increase and decrease the supply of affordable housing in the area.

Mr. Harvey wants to upscale the 21-unit building. But when permission was denied by the city, he refused to rent units as they were vacated and currently has 14 vacant apartments.

"The government can't expect landlords to subsidize low income people. . . . We're not allowed to change our own property," said Mr. Harvey.

The government can stop him from raising rents above affordable housing levels, but it can't force him to rent, Mr. Harvey said. . . .

"I'll leave it empty for a year and then I'll go for a demolition permit. Then I'll tear it down and let it go as a commercial property. That way there'll be no headaches and no hassles.". . .

The landlord said he's trying to sell off all his rental properties in Ontario because of the rent-control laws and Bill 11.

He's already sold five properties and reinvested his money in rental properties in New Brunswick, where he said the Landlord and Tenant Act doesn't discourage landlords.

SOURCE: Adapted from Christina Dona, "Housing Laws Unfair Complains Landlord," *The Hamilton Spectator*, September 7, 1988.

---

their political influence to protect their gains, which is one reason why it is so hard to eliminate price ceilings or floors.

The effects of rent control in New York and in several European cities have prompted Swedish economist Assar Lindbeck to quip: "In fact, next to bombing, rent control seems in many cases to be the most efficient technique so far known for destroying cities. . . ."[7]

Canadian cities have not, however, been "destroyed" by rent controls, and one reason is that provincial-government subsidies for apartment construction have been increased. In a study of rent controls in Toronto, it is reported that the proportion of apartment starts that depended on government support increased from 13 percent in 1974 to 91 percent in 1977, after rent control was introduced.[8] The boxed insert on this page features a newspaper article that illustrates some of the effects of rent control in Ontario.

(2) Services Provided Outside the Market

There are numerous other examples of price ceilings throughout the economy. Just think of where there are long waiting periods—in the judicial system, at airports, and even in the area of human-organ transplants. In each of these cases, which we elaborate below, shortages have emerged because the institutional arrangements have not permitted market forces to determine an appropriate price—or, in the economist's jargon, a "market-clearing price." In a number of these cases, the most extreme form of price ceiling prevails—the rule that no price is permitted at all. (In a supply and demand diagram, the effect of this is to push the maximum price line down to the level of the quantity axis.)

Waits of several years for a trial date are not uncommon in our judicial system. Individuals cannot pay a fee to move their case forward in the queue; that is, the maximum allowed price for acquiring an earlier time in the schedule is zero. Despite

---

[7] Assar Lindbeck, *The Political Economy of the New Left: An Outsider's View*, Second Edition (New York: Harper & Row, 1977), page 39.

[8] Basil A. Kalymon, "Apartment Shortages and Rent Control," in *Rent Control: Myths and Realities*, edited by W. Block and E. Olsen (Vancouver: The Fraser Institute, 1981), page 241.

this maximum price within the government-run court system, individuals do have a private-sector alternative that allows them to pay a higher price for a speedy settlement. This option is possible because much of the backlog in our court system is caused by the numerous civil suits that must be heard. These cases do not involve any alleged violation of law; rather, one private citizen brings suit against another over some disagreement. Many of these cases are already being settled out of court (that is, without the involvement of a judge), but the demand on judges' time could be further relieved if private arbitrators were more commonly used. Some are now in operation in Canada, and more than twenty U.S. states have successfully opted for a court-annexed arbitration system to relieve pressure on the judicial system. But it is difficult for private arbitration options to develop more fully when their overhead costs are not subsidized as they are within the publicly funded judicial system. In any event, the fact that the private alternative is gaining popularity *despite* this cost disadvantage proves that the price ceiling of zero that prevails in the public system is the source of the perpetual "shortage" of judicial services.

Airport congestion is an example of what is known as a peak-load problem. Airlines and individual airplane owners must pay fees established by the government for using the various services offered by airport terminals—use of runways, ground services, and so on—and these fees are set at a level that allows the market for the services to clear at most times during the week. But because the government does not allow the charges to be increased temporarily at peak-demand times during the week, there is no incentive for smaller airlines and individual airplane owners to schedule their flights during less busy times. Consequently, severe congestion occurs at most major airports during rush hours.

Our final example is perhaps the most controversial. Present law prohibits the sale of human organs for transplant, and thereby sets a maximum price of zero for such transactions. It is hard to think of an arrangement that could maximize excess demand (that is, create a shortage) more effectively. With the added incentive of financial reward, more people would be likely to become donors; under the current system, far too many would-be recipients must wait for their transplants for long periods of time, or do without. Admittedly, this issue is sensitive and subject to persuasive ethical arguments against changing the present law. Nonetheless, the existing shortages can certainly be attributed to the zero price ceiling.

It is important to note here that economic analysis can be brought to bear only on positive questions (propositions that can be proved or disproved), not on normative issues (propositions that involve value judgments). We are not arguing that human organs *should* be sold at a market-determined price; we are simply noting that a number of the problems in this area follow inexorably from our ethical preference to disallow this practice. It *is* the economist's job to inform individuals of the trade-offs involved—but we cannot make the choices.

All of these examples show that numerous inefficiencies and inequities could be lessened if prices were allowed to be more flexible. Some of the outcomes might not be regarded as fair, but it must be remembered that income can also be redistributed in ways that do not override market forces (as we will see in Chapter 30).

Restraining the Market Mechanism: Price Floors

Interferences with the market mechanism are not always designed to keep prices low. Agricultural price supports and minimum wages are two notable examples in which the law keeps prices *above* free-market levels. **Price floors** are typically accompanied by a standard set of symptoms:

A **price floor** is a legal minimum on the price that may be charged for a commodity.

1. A surplus develops as some sellers cannot find buyers. *Example*: Empty seats on airlines were the norm, not the exception, before the airline industry was deregulated in the 1970s and 1980s.

2. Where goods, rather than services, are involved, the surplus creates a problem of disposal. Something must be done about the excess of quantity supplied over quantity demanded. *Example*: The government has often been forced to purchase, and then store, large amounts of surplus agricultural commodities.

3. To get around the regulations, sellers may offer discounts in disguised—and often unwanted—forms. *Example*: With transatlantic air fares heavily regulated, airlines offer bargains on the land portions of package holidays to the U.K. that are often not fully used.

4. Regulations that keep prices artificially high encourage overinvestment in the industry. Even inefficient businesses whose high operating costs would doom them in an unrestricted market can survive beneath the shelter of a generous price floor. *Example*: This is why the airline and trucking industries both underwent painful "shake-outs" of the weaker companies in the 1980s, following deregulation.

Once again, some specific examples might be useful.

Case Studies:
(1) Farm Price Supports

Perhaps you have seen news items about farmers having to throw away surplus eggs, milk, or other agricultural products. The surpluses are by-products of various government programs designed to raise the incomes of farmers. For many products, a price higher than the equilibrium price is maintained through the provincial marketing boards, which stipulate production limits for each farmer. For other products, a high price is maintained because the government buys up any output that the market does not absorb at the higher price.

One example is the Canadian Dairy Commission, under Agriculture Canada. One of its purposes is to stabilize the price of dairy products at a level high enough to permit reasonable incomes to be earned by all existing dairy farmers. Generally, this involves a support price well above the free-market level, which causes a surplus to develop, as indicated in Figure 3–9. To maintain the price above the free-market level, the government must buy the surplus milk and other dairy products. But this creates a

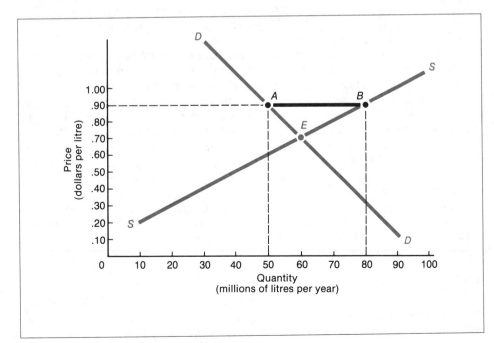

FIGURE 3-9
Price Supports for Milk
In this diagram, which repeats the supply and demand curves from Figure 3-3, the support price for milk (90¢ per litre) is above the equilibrium price (70¢). Quantity supplied is 80 million litres per year (point B), while quantity demanded is only 50 million (point A). To keep the price at 90¢, the government must buy 30 million litres of milk per year and store it as cheese or milk powder, or dispose of it.

problem. Milk is so highly perishable that it must be turned into cheese or butter or dried milk before it can be stored. Buying and storing these products is costly, so the products are often simply disposed of. Even given this practice, the OECD has estimated that Canadian taxpayers spend $100,000 per worker in the farm industries in Canada that are supported by policies of this sort. Similar problems have developed in the United States and in Europe. One solution to the surplus wine that has resulted from price-support programs in Europe has been to convert it to automobile fuel (gasohol), at much expense to the taxpayer (a situation that wine-lovers find discouraging).

This analysis does not imply that individual farm incomes should be lower than they are. It simply shows how the basic forces of supply and demand lead to inefficiencies under the current methods for maintaining farm incomes.

(2) The Minimum Wage

We can use Figure 3–9 once again, to discuss the effects of minimum-wage legislation. Imagine that units of unskilled labour are measurd along the quantity axis, and the wage paid to unskilled labour along the price axis. If the market-clearing wage (given by point E) is deemed "unacceptably low" by legislators, a minimum wage (at the height on the price axis of line AB) can be imposed. Employment (the quantity of labour demanded) falls to the quantity represented by point A, while the supply of labour increases to the quantity represented by point B. Unemployment (that is, excess supply of labour) therefore rises from zero to the amount represented by distance AB. We will analyze minimum-wage laws more thoroughly in Chapter 29; for now, just read the boxed insert in that chapter entitled "Minimum-Wage Law No Help to Unskilled" (page 642). It shows that youth unemployment in Canada is highest in the provinces that have the highest minimum wages, just as our supply and demand analysis predicts.

Fixed Exchange Rates

The **exchange rate** states the price at which one currency can be bought in terms of another currency.

One price that is often set by government policy is the international value of the Canadian dollar, known as the **exchange rate**. Through its agent, the Bank of Canada, the federal government often stands ready to buy or sell quantities of foreign currencies in whatever amounts are required to stabilize the price of the Canadian dollar. For example, for a period during 1984, the government tried to keep the value of the Canadian dollar from falling below a price of 75 cents (U.S.). It tried to maintain this price floor by trading currencies in the foreign-exchange market. Whenever private traders who desired U.S. dollars or other foreign currencies could not find a trader who would buy Canadian dollars at this price (exchange rate), the Canadian authorities would buy up the otherwise unwanted Canadian currency. The authorities did this by selling off part of their foreign-currency reserves. Thus the foreign-exchange rate can be fixed in precisely the same manner as in the milk-price supports discussed above. The only difference is that there are no direct storage costs for holding inventories of foreign currencies. Because of this, and because a fluctuating value of the Canadian dollar is often thought to deter foreign trade, this price is heavily managed and sometimes absolutely fixed.

Unfortunately, we must wait until Chapters 14 and 15 to assess the costs and benefits of this form of market intervention. It turns out that it very much determines which government policies the Minister of Finance can or cannot use to fight unemployment and inflation.

A Can of Worms

Our case studies illustrate some of the major side effects of price floors and ceilings but barely hint at others. And there are yet more difficulties that we have not even mentioned. For the market mechanism is a tough bird that imposes suitable retribution on those who seek to circumvent it by legislative decree. Here is a partial list of other problems that may arise when prices are controlled.

Favouritism and Corruption

When price ceilings create a shortage, someone must decide who gets the limited quantity that is available. This can lead to political favouritism, to corruption in government, or even to discrimination along racial or religious lines.

Unenforceability

Attempts to control prices are almost certain to fail in industries with numerous suppliers, simply because the regulating agency must monitor the behaviour of so many sellers. Some ways will be found to evade or to violate the law, and something akin to the free-market price will generally re-emerge. But there is a difference: since the evasion mechanism, whatever its form, will have some operating costs, those costs must be borne by someone. That someone is normally the consumer.

Auxiliary Restrictions

Fears that a system of price controls will break down invariably lead to regulations designed to shore up the shaky edifice. Consumers may be told when and from whom they are permitted to buy. The powers of the police and the courts may be used to prevent the entry of new suppliers. Occasionally, an intricate system of market subdivision is imposed, giving each class of firms its protected category of operations in which others are not permitted to compete. Laws banning conversion of rent-controlled apartments to condominiums are one example.

Limitation of Volume of Transactions

To the extent that controls succeed in affecting prices, they can be expected to reduce the volume of transactions that occur. Curiously, this is true whether the regulated price is above or below the free market's equilibrium price. If it is set above the equilibrium price, quantity demanded will be below the equilibrium quantity. On the other hand, if the imposed price is set below the free-market level, quantity supplied will be cut down. Since sales volume cannot exceed either the quantity supplied or the quantity demanded, a reduction in the volume of transactions (and, hence, in employment) is likely to result.

Misallocation of Resources

Departures from free-market prices are likely to produce misuse of the economy's resources because the connection between production costs and prices is broken. Also, just as more complex locks lead to more sophisticated burglary tools, more complex regulations lead to the use of yet more resources for their avoidance. New jobs are created for executives, lawyers, and economists. It may well be conjectured that at least some of the expensive services of these professionals could have been used more productively elsewhere.

Economists put it this way. Free markets are capable of dealing with the three basic co-ordination tasks outlined in Chapter 2: deciding *what* to produce, *how* to produce it, and *to whom* the goods should be distributed. Price controls throw a monkey wrench into the market mechanism. Though the market is surely not flawless and government interferences often have praiseworthy goals, good intentions are not enough. Any government that sets out to repair what it sees as a defect in the market mechanism must take care lest it cause serious damage elsewhere. As a prominent economist once quipped, societies that are too willing to interfere with the operation of free markets soon find that the invisible hand is nowhere to be seen.

Economics and Drugs

Current events in the drug trade are reminiscent of the alcohol business in the United States back in the 1920s under Prohibition. The Colombian drug lords compare with Al Capone and the other underworld figures, who were the object of intense police crackdowns. But the liquor continued to flow....

In the end, we all know, Al Capone and the criminals were driven out of the liquor trade. But it is only through legend and television that we came to believe that flying squads of gun-wielding law enforcement agents shut down the underworld business....

The historical reality, of course, is that Al Capone and his associates were driven out of the business by an economic development: deregulation. With the legalization of alcohol, the criminals were quickly replaced by legitimate corporations.

Imagine what would happen if cocaine were deregulated and legalized. The first result would be an end to the violence, both in the producing countries such as Colombia and on the streets of our cities. The guns and the killing are not the consequence of drugs, they are the result of governments trying to use force to stop the production and sale of a product for which there is a demand.

Another effect would be the saving of billions of dollars—the money now spent by law enforcement agencies and police departments across North America to stop the import, distribution, and sale of drugs. Economically, legalization would also remove the vast black-market profits that are the major attraction to those who get into the business.

The social consequences of drug deregulation were suggested recently by Kildare Clarke, associate medical director of the emergency department at Kings County Hospital in New York. In an article in *The New York Times* favouring legalization, Dr. Clarke wrote: "By removing black-market profits, it would substantially reduce the violence that

goes with the illegal trade and the street crime that supports drug habits. It would stop the killing of police officers and innocent bystanders caught in the crossfire. It would allow better controls, reducing the chance of death by overdose or transmission of AIDS by dirty needles."

Dr. Clarke says legalization would probably lead to an initial increase in drug use, but education and training would be part of the deregulation process. He cites alcohol as an example. "Today, we are educating the public about the long-term effects of alcohol, providing treatment for those in need and, over all, dealing with alcohol in a far more rational fashion than we are coping with drugs."

SOURCE: Adapted from Terence Corcoran, "Economic Thinking on Drug Trade Leads to Deregulation Conclusion," *The Globe and Mail*, September 2, 1989, page B2.

A Simple but Powerful Lesson

The lessons you have learned in this chapter may seem elementary, even obvious. And, in many respects, they are. But they are also very important, indeed, indispensable. Although the law of supply and demand is one of the simplest principles in economics, it is also one of the most powerful. Yet, astonishing as it may seem, many people in authority, even highly intelligent people, fail to understand it or to apply it accurately to concrete situations.

For example, as this chapter was being written, *The New York Times* carried a dramatic front-page picture of the president of Kenya setting fire to a large pile of elephant tusks that had been confiscated from poachers. The accompanying story explained that the burning was intended as a symbolic act to persuade the world to halt the ivory trade.[9] As economists, we are in no position to comment on the likely psychological impact of burning elephant tusks, though we doubt that it touched the

[9] *The New York Times*, July 19, 1989, page A–1.

consciences of criminal poachers. The economic effect, however, was clear. By reducing the supply of ivory on the world market, the burning of tusks will force up the price of ivory, which will raise the illicit rewards reaped by those who slaughter elephants. That can only encourage more poaching—precisely the opposite of what the Kenyan government sought to accomplish.

Similar reasoning has been applied to cast doubt on the efficacy of the recent war on drugs. To the extent that drug-interdiction programs succeed in stopping illegal drugs at the border, they reduce the supply and drive up street prices. But that, in turn, raises the rewards for potential smugglers and attracts more criminals to the "industry." Many economists believe that any successful anti-drug program must concentrate on reducing *demand*, which would lower the street price of drugs, not on reducing *supply*, which can only raise it. The newspaper excerpt from *The Globe and Mail* in the accompanying boxed insert shows an appreciation of this reasoning. It is included in our text to help you see the broad applicability of supply and demand analysis. We do not mean to suggest that legalization of drugs is a better way to lower prices than is a program of education. The latter would shift the demand curve for drugs to the left as people became more aware of their harmful effects.

Summary

1. The quantity of a product that is demanded is not a fixed number. Rather, quantity demanded depends on such factors as the price of the product, consumer incomes, and the prices of other products.

2. The relationship between quantity demanded and price, holding all other things constant, can be displayed graphically on a demand curve.

3. For most products, the higher the price, the lower the quantity demanded. So the demand curve usually has a negative slope.

4. The quantity of a product that is supplied also depends on its price and many other influences. A supply curve is a graphical representation of the relationship between quantity supplied and price, holding all other influences constant.

5. For most products, the supply curve has a positive slope, meaning that higher prices call forth greater quantities supplied.

6. A market is said to be in equilibrium when quantity supplied is equal to quantity demanded. The equilibrium price and quantity are shown by the point on a graph where the supply and demand curves intersect. In a free market, price and quantity will tend to gravitate to this point.

7. A change in quantity demanded that is caused by a change in the price of the good is represented by a movement along a fixed demand curve. A change in quantity demanded that is caused by a change in any other determinant of quantity demanded is represented by a shift of the demand curve.

8. This same distinction applies to the supply curve: Changes in price lead to movements along a fixed supply curve; changes in other determinants of quantity supplied lead to shifts of the whole supply curve.

9. Changes in consumer incomes, tastes, technology, prices of competing products, and many other influences cause shifts in either the demand curve or the supply curve and produce changes in price and quantity that can be determined from supply–demand diagrams.

10. An attempt by government regulations to force prices below or above their equilibrium levels is likely to lead to shortages or surpluses, black markets in which goods are sold at illegal prices, and a variety of other problems. This is one of the **12 Ideas for Beyond the Final Exam.**

Concepts for Review

Quantity demanded
Demand schedule
Demand curve
Quantity supplied
Supply schedule
Supply curve

Equilibrium
Shifts in versus movements along
    supply and demand curves
Price ceiling
Price floor
Exchange rate

Supply–demand diagram
Shortage
Surplus
Equilibrium price and quantity

Questions for Discussion

1. How often do you go to the movies? Would you go less often if a ticket cost twice as much? Distinguish between your demand curve for movie tickets and your "quantity demanded" at the current price.

2. What would you expect to be the shape of a demand curve
   a. for a medicine that means life or death for a patient?
   b. for the gasoline sold by Sam's gas station, which is surrounded by many other gas stations?

3. The following are the assumed supply and demand schedules for T-shirts in British Columbia:

DEMAND SCHEDULE		SUPPLY SCHEDULE	
PRICE (dollars)	QUANTITY DEMANDED (per month)	PRICE (dollars)	QUANTITY SUPPLIED (per month)
16	60,000	16	180,000
14	80,000	14	140,000
12	100,000	12	100,000
10	120,000	10	60,000
8	140,000	8	20,000

   a. Plot the supply and demand curves and indicate the equilibrium price and quantity.
   b. What effect will a decrease in the price of cotton (a production input) have on the equilibrium price and quantity of T-shirts, assuming all other things remain constant? Explain your answer with the help of a diagram.
   c. What effect will a decrease in the price of sweat-shirts (a substitute commodity) have on the equilibrium price and quantity of T-shirts, assuming again that all other things are held constant? Use a diagram in your answer.

4. Assume that the supply and demand schedules for soybeans in Glubstania are the following:

PRICE (dollars)	QUANTITY DEMANDED	QUANTITY SUPPLIED
	(millions of bushels per year)	
3.50	10	75
3.00	25	55
2.50	40	40
2.00	55	20
1.50	70	15

   a. What is the equilibrium price and quantity of soybeans?
   b. In order to protect the incomes of farmers, the government sets a minimum price of $3 per bushel. How many bushels will be sold now?
   c. Consumers protest and, as a result, the government abolishes the $3/bushel price floor and imposes instead a $2 maximum price per bushel. How many bushels of soybeans will be sold now?
   d. While this price ceiling is in effect, a drought reduces the soybean crop. What effects will this have on the soybean market?

5. Show how the following demand curves are likely to shift in response to the indicated changes:
   a. The effect on the demand curve for umbrellas when rainfall decreases.
   b. The effect on the demand curve for apple juice when the price of orange juice declines.
   c. The effect on the demand curve for coffee when sugar prices fall.

6. Drinking water is costly to supply. Draw a supply–demand diagram showing how much water would be bought if water were supplied by a private industry controlled by supply and demand. In the same diagram show how much would be consumed if water were supplied by a city government at zero charge. What do you conclude from these results about areas of the country in which water is in short supply?

7. On page 63 it is claimed that either price floors or price ceilings reduce the actual quantity exchanged in a market. Use a diagram, or diagrams, to support this conclusion, and explain the common sense behind it.

8. The same rightward shift of the demand curve may produce a very small or a very large increase in quantity, depending on the slope of the supply curve. Explain with diagrams.

9. The following two diagrams show supply and demand curves for two substitute commodities: tapes and compact discs (CDs).
   a. On the upper diagram, show what happens when technological progress makes it cheaper to produce CDs.
   b. On the lower diagram, show what happens to the market for tapes.

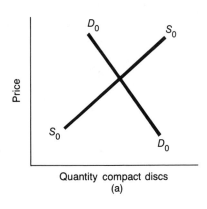

(a)

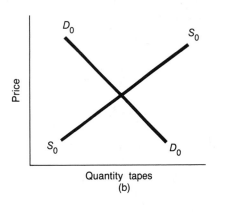

(b)

10. (More difficult.) Consider the market for milk discussed in this chapter (Tables 3–1 through 3–3 and Figures 3–1 through 3–3). Suppose the government decides to fight kidney stones by levying a tax of 30¢ per litre on sales of milk. Follow these steps to analyze the effects of the tax:

 a. Construct the new supply curve (to replace Table 3–2) that relates quantity supplied to the price consumers pay. (*Hint*: Before the tax, when consumers paid 70¢, farmers supplied 60 million litres. With a 30¢ tax, when consumers pay 70¢ farmers will receive only 40¢. Table 3–2 tells us they will provide only 30 million litres at this price. This is one point on the new supply curve. The rest of the curve can be constructed in the same way.)

 b. Graph the new supply curve constructed in part (a) on the supply–demand diagram depicted in Figure 3–3. What are the new equilibrium price and quantity?

 c. Does the tax succeed in its goal of reducing the consumption of milk?

 d. How much does the equilibrium price increase? Is the price rise greater than, equal to, or less than the 30¢ tax?

 e. Who actually pays the tax, consumers or producers? (This may be a good question to discuss in class.)

11. Use a supply–demand diagram to examine the legalization of marijuana. Explain how each curve would shift. On the basis of your analysis, what would you predict concerning the price of marijuana and the quantity of it that is used?

12. Often, when the price of a product rises significantly, some consumers suggest boycotting the product. The idea is to reduce producer profits by forcing the price lower through reduced demand.

 a. Who gains from such a boycott?

 b. Would you join such a boycott?

 c. How would your analysis be different if the commodity were fresh fish as opposed to wine?

Macroeconomics: Aggregate Supply and Demand Analysis

4

National Product, Unemployment, and Inflation

Nothing so weakens governments as inflation.

J.K. GALBRAITH

When men are employed they are best contented.

BENJAMIN FRANKLIN

Economics has traditionally been divided into two fields: microeconomics and macroeconomics. These rather inelegant words are derived from the Greek— "micro" means something small and "macro" means something large. Although they were not specifically described as such, the basic notions and subject matter of **microeconomics** were introduced in Chapters 2 and 3. This chapter does the same for **macroeconomics**.

We begin the chapter by investigating the dividing line between microeconomics and macroeconomics: How do the two parts of the discipline differ and why? Next, we stress that while the *questions* studied by macroeconomists differ from those addressed by microeconomists, the underlying *tools* each group uses are almost the same. Supply and demand provide the basic organizing framework for constructing macroeconomic models, just as they do for microeconomic models. Third, we define some important macroeconomic concepts, such as recession, gross domestic product, unemployment, and inflation. In the process, we look briefly at the broad sweep of Canadian economic history to obtain some evaluation of the prevalence and seriousness of the macroeconomic problems of recession and inflation. We also preview what is to come in subsequent chapters by introducing the notion of government management of the economy.

In Parts Three and Four of this textbook, we will explain how economic planners attempt to strike a balance between high employment and low inflation, why these goals cannot be attained with machinelike precision, and why improvement on one front generally spells deterioration on the other. A great deal of attention will be paid to the *causes* of inflation and unemployment.

But before getting involved in such important issues of theory and policy, we pause in this chapter to take a rather close look at the twin evils themselves: Why is it that a rise in unemployment is generally considered bad news? Why is inflation so loudly deplored? Can we measure the costs of unemployment and inflation? The answers to some of these questions may at first seem obvious, but we will see that there is more to them than meets the eye.

This chapter examines the major macroeconomic variables—how they are measured and why we care about them. Your instructor may wish to cover this material as a single unit at the outset of your course in macroeconomics. Alternatively, he or she may wish to discuss how each variable is measured as each one is encountered in the development of our macroeconomic model. The three sections of the chapter can be read separately if this is the alternative your instructor prefers. Finally, some instructors may simply suggest that students read the material on unemployment and inflation (as well as Appendix A on national income accounting) on their own. Whatever your situation, be sure to read the first section—Gross Domestic Product and Stabilization Policy (pages 72–84)—now; this is the material that will enable you to understand the chapters that follow. Note that data for the three most widely followed macroeconomic variables that we discuss in this chapter—national income, unemployment, and inflation—as well as for two other popular macroeconomic time series—the interest rate and the exchange rate—are graphed on the inside covers of this book for your convenience.

Gross Domestic Product and Stabilization Policy

Aggregation and Macroeconomics

In microeconomics we study *the behaviour of individual decision-making units*. The dairy farmers and consumers of Chapter 3 are individual decision-making units. How do they decide what courses of action are in their own best interests? How are these millions of decisions co-ordinated by the market mechanism, and with what consequences? Questions like these are the substance of microeconomics and are taken up in Parts Five through Seven.

Although Plato and Aristotle might wince at the abuse of their language, microeconomics applies to the decisions of some astonishingly large units. Exxon and the American Telephone and Telegraph Company, for instance, have annual sales that exceed the total production of many nations. Yet an American economist who studies the pricing policies of AT&T is a microeconomist, whereas someone who studies inflation in Trinidad–Tobago is a macroeconomist. So the micro versus macro distinction in economics is certainly not predicated solely on size.

What, then, is the basis for this time-honoured distinction? Whereas microeconomics focusses on the decisions of individual units (no matter how large), macroeconomics concentrates on *the behaviour of entire economies* (no matter how small). Rather than looking at the price and output decisions of a single company, macroeconomists study the overall price level, unemployment rate, and other things that we call *economic aggregates*.

What is an "economic aggregate"? Nothing but an *abstraction* that people find convenient in describing some salient feature of economic life. For example, while we observe the prices of butter, telephone calls, and movie tickets every day, we never observe "the price level." Yet many people (not only economists) find it both meaningful and natural to speak of "the cost of living"—so natural, in fact, that Statistics Canada's monthly attempts at measuring it are widely publicized by the news media.

Among the most important of these abstract notions is the concept of *national product*, which represents the total production of a nation's economy. The process by which real objects like hairpins, baseballs, wheat, and theatre tickets get combined into an abstraction called national product is termed **aggregation**, and it is one of the foundations of macroeconomics. We can illustrate it by a simple example.

Aggregation means combining many individual markets into one overall market.

Imagine a nation called Agraria, whose economy is far simpler than the Canadian economy: Business firms in Agraria produce nothing but foodstuffs to sell to consumers. Rather than deal separately with all the markets for pizzas, candy bars, hamburgers, and so on, macroeconomists group them all into a single abstract "market for output." Thus, when macroeconomists in Agraria announce that output in Agraria rose 10 percent this year, are they referring to more potatoes or hot dogs, more soybeans or green peppers? The answer is: They do not care. In the aggregate measures of macroeconomics, output is output, no matter what form it takes.

Amalgamating many markets into one means that distinctions among different products are ignored. Can we really believe that no one cares whether the national output of Agraria consists of $800,000 worth of pickles and $200,000 worth of ravioli rather than $500,000 each of lettuce and tomatoes? Surely this is too much to swallow. Macroeconomists clearly do not believe that no one cares; instead, they rest the case for aggregation on two foundations.

1. While the *composition* of demand and supply in the various markets may be terribly interesting and important for *some* purposes (such as how income is distributed and what kinds of diets the citizens enjoy or endure), it may be of little consequence for the economy-wide issues of inflation and unemployment—the issues that concern macroeconomists.

2. During economic fluctuations, markets tend to move in unison. When demand in the economy rises, there is more demand for potatoes *and* tomatoes, more demand for artichokes *and* pickles, more demand for ravioli *and* hot dogs.

Though there are exceptions to these two principles, both seem serviceable enough as approximations. In fact, if they were not, there would be no discipline called macroeconomics, and this book would be only half as long as it is. (Lest this cause you a twinge of regret, bear in mind that many people believe unemployment and inflation would be far more difficult to control without macroeconomics, which would be even more regrettable.)

These two principles—that markets normally move together and that the composition of demand and supply may be unimportant for some purposes—enable us to draw a different kind of dividing line between the territories of microeconomics and macroeconomics.

In macroeconomics, we typically assume that most details of resource allocation and income distribution are of secondary importance to the study of the overall rates of inflation and unemployment. In microeconomics, we typically ignore inflation and unemployment and focus instead on how individual markets allocate resources and distribute income.

To use a well-worn metaphor, the macroeconomist analyzes the determination of the size of the economic pie, paying scant attention to what is inside it or to how it gets divided among the dinner guests. A microeconomist, on the other hand, assumes that the pie is of the right size and shape and frets over its ingredients and its division. If you have ever baked or eaten a pie, you will realize that either approach alone is a trifle myopic, but the separation of issues in economics textbooks is necessary solely for the sake of pedagogical clarity. In reality, the crucial interconnection between macroeconomics and microeconomics is always with us.

Supply and Demand in Macroeconomics

Some students reading this book will be taking a course that concentrates on macroeconomics, while others will be studying microeconomics. The discussion of supply and demand in Chapter 3 serves as an invaluable introduction to both fields because the basic apparatus of supply and demand is just as important in macroeconomics as it is in microeconomics.

Figure 4–1 shows two diagrams that should look familiar from Chapter 3. In Figure 4–1(a), there is a downward-sloping demand curve, labelled *DD*, and an upward-sloping supply curve, labelled *SS*. The axes labelled "Price" and "Quantity" do not specify what commodity they refer to because this is a multipurpose diagram. To

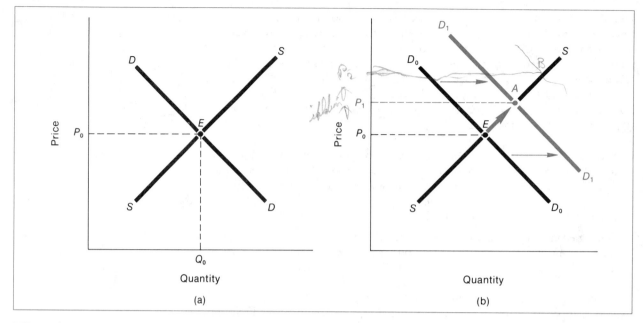

FIGURE 4-1
Two Interpretations of a Shift in the Demand Curve
Part (a) shows an equilibrium at point *E*, where demand curve *DD* intersects supply curve *SS*. Part (b) shows how this equilibrium moves from point *E* to point *A* if the demand curve moves outward. If this graph represents the market for milk as it did in Chapter 3, then it shows an increase in the price of milk. But if the graph represents the aggregate market for "national product," then it shows inflation—a rise in the general price level. → *growth in GDP* — (*But possibly very little if any 'real' growth*)

The **aggregate demand curve** shows the quantity of national product that is demanded at each possible value of the price level.

The **aggregate supply curve** shows the quantity of national product that is supplied at each possible value of the price level.

Inflation refers to a sustained *increase* in the general price level.

start on familiar terrain, first imagine that this is a picture of the market for milk, so the price axis measures the price of milk while the quantity axis measures the quantity of milk demanded and supplied. As we know, if there are no interferences with the operation of a free market, equilibrium will be at point *E* with a price P_0 and a quantity of output Q_0.

Next, suppose something happens to shift the demand curve outward. For example, we learned in Chapter 3 that an increase in consumer incomes might do this. Figure 4–1(b) shows this shift as a rightward movement of the demand curve from D_0D_0 to D_1D_1. Equilibrium has shifted from *E* to *A*, so both the price level and output have risen.

Now let us reinterpret Figure 4–1 as representing an abstract market for "national product." This is one of those abstractions—an economic aggregate—that we described earlier. Consistent with this reinterpretation, think of the price measured on the vertical axis as being another abstraction—the overall price index, or "cost of living."[1] Then curve *DD* in Figure 4–1(a) is called an **aggregate demand curve**, and curve *SS* is called an **aggregate supply curve**. We will explain where these curves come from in Chapters 5 through 8.

With this reinterpretation, Figure 4–1(b) can depict the macroeconomic problem of inflation. We see from the figure that the outward shift of the aggregate demand curve, whatever its cause, pushes the price level up from P_0 to P_1. If aggregate demand keeps shifting out month after month, the economy will suffer from inflation, that is, a sustained increase in the general price level.

The other principal problems of macroeconomics, recession and unemployment, also can be illustrated on a supply–demand diagram, this time by shifting the demand curve in the opposite direction. Figure 4–2 repeats the supply and demand curves of Figure 4–1(a) and in addition depicts a leftward shift of the aggregate demand curve

[1] Both of these aggregates are explained more fully later in this chapter.

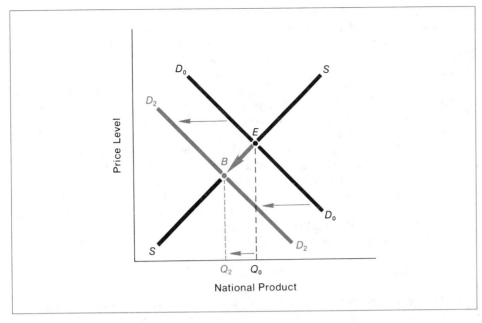

FIGURE 4–2
An Economy Slipping into a Recession

In this aggregate supply-demand diagram, there is an initial equilibrium at point E, where demand curve D_0D_0 intersects supply curve SS. When the demand curve shifts inward from D_0D_0 to D_2D_2, equilibrium moves to point B, and output falls from Q_0 to Q_2.

from D_0D_0 to D_2D_2. Equilibrium now moves from point E to point B so that national product (total output) declines from Q_0 to Q_2. This is what we normally mean by a recession.

A recession is a period of time during which the total output of the economy declines.

Gross Domestic Product

The economy's total output, as we have just seen, is one of the major variables of concern to macroeconomists. While there are several ways to measure it, Statistics Canada focusses on the **gross domestic product**, a term you have probably encountered in the news media. The gross domestic product, or "GDP" for short, is the most comprehensive measure of the output of all the factories, offices, and shops in the Canadian economy. Specifically, it is the sum of the money values of all final goods and services produced in Canada within the year.

Several features of the definition of GDP need to be underscored.[2] First, you will notice that:

We add up the *money values* of things.

The GDP consists of a bewildering variety of goods and services: mousetraps and computers, bologna and caviar, ballet performances and rock concerts, cars and textbooks. How are we to combine all of these into a single number? To an economist, the natural way to do this is first to convert every good and service into *money* terms. If we want to add 10 apples and 20 oranges, we first ask: How much *money* does each cost? If apples cost 20¢ and oranges cost 25¢, then the apples count for $2 and the oranges for $5, so the sum is $7 worth of "output." The market *price* of each good or service is used as an indicator of its *value* to society simply because *someone* is willing to pay that much money for it.

This decision raises the question of what prices to use in valuing the different outputs. The official data offer two choices. First, we can value each good and service at the price at which it was actually sold during the year. If we do this, the resulting measure is called **nominal GDP**, or *money GDP*, or *GDP in current dollars.* This seems like a perfectly sensible choice. But as a measure of output, it has one serious

Gross domestic product (GDP) is the sum of the money values of all final goods and services produced in the economy during a specified period of time, usually one year.

know other mones

Nominal GDP is calculated by valuing all outputs at current prices.

[2] The definition of GDP is explored in greater detail in Appendix A, pages 103–109.

drawback: nominal GDP rises when prices rise, even if there is no increase in actual production. For example, if hamburgers cost $1.50 this year but cost only $1.25 last year, then 100 hamburgers will contribute $150 to this year's nominal GDP but only $125 to last year's. But 100 hamburgers are still 100 hamburgers—output has not grown.

For this reason, government statisticians have devised an alternative measure that corrects for inflation by valuing all goods and services at some fixed set of prices. (Currently, the prices of 1981 are used.) For example, if the hamburgers were valued at $1.25 each in both years, $125 worth of hamburger output would be included in GDP in each year. When we treat every output in this way, we obtain the **real GDP** or *GDP in constant dollars*. (The news media often refer to it as "GDP corrected for inflation.") Throughout most of this book and certainly when we are discussing the nation's output, it is the real GDP that we shall be concerned with. The distinction between nominal and real GDP leads us to a working definition of a *recession* as a period in which *real* GDP declines. For example, between 1981 and 1982, nominal GDP rose from $356 billion to $375 billion, but real GDP *fell* from $356 billion to $344 billion. *ie only prices rose not actual ie real output/production*

The next important aspect of the definition of GDP is that:

Real GDP is calculated by valuing all outputs at the prices that prevailed in some agreed-upon year (currently 1981). Therefore, real GDP is a far better measure of changes in national production.

= GDP in constant dollars

The GDP for a particular year includes only goods and services produced during that year. Sales of items produced in previous years are explicitly excluded.

ie

For example, suppose you buy a perfectly beautiful 1974 Plymouth next week and are overjoyed by your purchase. The national income statistician will not share your glee because she already counted your car in the GDP in 1974 when it was first produced and sold; the car will never be counted again. The same holds true for houses. An old house (unlike an old car) often will sell for more than its original purchasers paid, yet the resale value of the house does not count in the GDP since it was already counted in the year it was built. For the same reason, transactions on the stock market and other exchanges of existing assets are not included in the gross domestic product.

Third, you will note the use of the phrase **final goods and services** in the definition. The adjective "final" is the key word here. For example, when a supermarket buys milk from a farmer, the transaction is not included in the GDP because the supermarket does not want the milk for itself. It buys milk only for resale to consumers. Only when the milk is sold to consumers is it considered a final product. When the supermarket buys it, economists consider it an **intermediate good**.

Final goods and services are those that are purchased by their ultimate users.

An **intermediate good** is a good purchased for resale or for use in producing another good.

The GDP does not include sales of intermediate goods or services.

Fourth, the definition includes the phrase *produced in Canada*. Before 1986, Statistics Canada focussed on an alternative aggregate called the **gross national product (GNP)**, which is the sum of all final goods and services produced within the year by *Canadian-owned* factors of production. Since some firms that operate within Canada are foreign-owned, GDP typically exceeds GNP by about 3 percent. The two series move up and down together through time, so either is a good indicator of the changes in job possibilities. Almost all other countries focus on GDP, although the United States focusses on GNP.

They □ ed to GDP in 3Q 1991.

The GDP measures the quantity of the goods and services produced within an economy, regardless of who owns the factors of production. In contrast, the GNP measures the output of an economy's nationals. For Canada, for example, GDP includes the output of U.S.-owned plants operating within Canada, but it excludes the output of Canadian-owned plants located in the United States; GNP excludes the output of the American subsidiaries but includes that of the foreign operations of Canadian-owned firms.

Finally, although the definition does not state this explicitly:

For the most part, only goods and services that pass through organized markets count in the GDP.

The definition reflects the statisticians' confession that they could not hope to measure the value of many of the economy's most important activities, such as housework, do-it-yourself repairs, and leisure time. While these are certainly economic activities that result in currently produced goods or services, they all lack that important measuring rod—a price.

This omission results in certain oddities. For example, suppose that each of two neighbouring families hires the other to clean house, generously paying $1000 a week for the services. Each family can easily afford such generosity since it collects an identical salary from its neighbour. Nothing real changes, but GDP goes up by about $100,000 a year.

Limitations of the GDP: What GDP Is Not

Having discussed what the GDP *is*, it is worth pausing to expand upon what it *is not*. In particular:

Gross domestic product is not a measure of the nation's economic well-being.

Here are several reasons why:

1. *Only market activity is included in GDP.*   Work done by homemakers and do-it-yourselfers certainly contributes to the nation's well-being, but, as already noted, it is not measured in the GDP because it has no price tag.

One important implication of this exclusion is seen when we try to compare the GDPs of developed and less developed countries. Canadian students are always incredulous when told that the per-capita GDP of the poorest African countries is less than $300 a year. Surely, no one could survive in Canada on less than $5.75 a week. How can Africans do it? One part of the answer, of course, is that these people are incredibly poor. But another part of the answer is that:

International GDP comparisons are vastly misleading when the two countries differ greatly in the fraction of economic activity that each conducts in organized markets.

This fraction is relatively large in Canada and relatively small in the less developed countries, so when we compare their respective measured GDPs we are not comparing the same economic activities at all. Many things that get counted in the Canadian GDP are not counted in the GDPs of less developed nations, where transactions outside organized markets are much more common. Similarly, while neither country's statistics include, for example, output that is consumed by the farmer's own family, this omission is substantial in relation to the GDP of a less developed nation, but relatively insignificant in relation to Canada's GDP today. So it is ludicrous to think that people in less developed countries, poor as they are, survive on what to Canadians would amount to less than $6 a week.

A second implication of the restriction is that GDP statistics take no account of the "underground economy." This includes not just criminal activities but also a great deal of legitimate business activity that is conducted in cash (or by barter) to escape the tax collector. Naturally, we have no good data on the size of the underground economy, but some observers think it may amount to 10 percent or more of Canadian GDP; in some countries, it is surely a much bigger share than this.

2. **GDP places no value on leisure.**   As a country gets richer, one of the things that happens is that its citizens take more and more leisure time. The steady decrease in the length of the typical work week in Canada is clear evidence of this. As a result, the gap is steadily widening between official GDP and some truer measure of national well-being that would include the value of leisure time. For this reason, growth in GDP systematically *understates* the growth in national well-being. But there are also reasons why the GDP *overstates* how well off we are; we consider these next.

3. **"Bads" as well as "goods" get counted in GDP.**   Suppose there is a natural disaster or a major accident—as when the Ocean Ranger oil-drilling rig sank off the coast of Newfoundland in 1982. Surely the well-being of the nation was diminished by this catastrophe. Much expensive equipment was lost, and of course, many people were killed. Yet the disaster may well have caused GDP to rise. Replacing the machinery and the extra government spending for relief, searches, and investigations all added to national product. Yet no one would think that the nation was better off for its higher GDP.

   Wars represent an extreme example of this phenomenon. Mobilization for outright war always causes a country's GDP to rise rapidly. But citizens called into the army could be producing civilian output. Factories needed to produce armaments could instead be making cars, washing machines, and televisions. A country at war is surely worse off than a country at peace, but this fact will not be reflected in its GDP accounts.

4. **Ecological costs are not netted out of the GDP.**   Many of the activities in a modern industrial economy that produce goods and services also have undesirable side

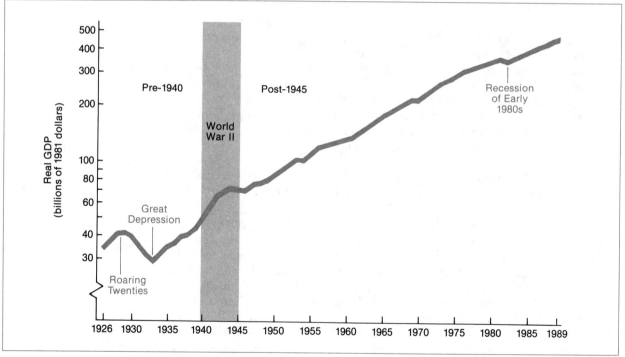

FIGURE 4–3

Real Gross Domestic Product of Canada, 1926–1989

This time-series chart displays the behaviour of real gross domestic production in Canada from 1926 to 1989. (Here real GDP is measured in 1981 prices.) The Great Depression (1929–33) stands out vividly. The years during World War II are shaded. Does the line look smoother to the right of this shaded area? Notice that the vertical axis is calibrated by what is called a "ratio scale," wherein the distance between 1000 and 100 is the same as that between 100 and 10. The effect of this scale is to represent any given percentage change by the same vertical distance, no matter when that change occurs.

SOURCE: Historical Statistics of Canada, and Statistics Canada.

effects on the environment. Automobiles provide enjoyment and a means of transportation, but they also despoil the atmosphere. Factories pollute rivers and lakes while manufacturing valuable commodities. Almost everything seems to produce garbage, which creates the problem of what to do with it. None of these ecological costs is deducted from the GDP in an effort to give us a truer measure of the *net* increase in economic welfare that our economy produces. Is this foolishness? Not if we remember the job that national income statisticians are trying to do: They are measuring the economic activity conducted through organized markets, not national welfare. Our main interest in the GDP stems from its being a measure of the amount of job-creating economic activity that is taking place. Thus, the fact that it is not intended to measure well-being is not a relevant limitation.

The Economy on a Roller Coaster

Having defined several of the basic concepts of macroeconomics, let us breathe some life into them by perusing the economic history of Canada. Figures 4–3 and 4–4 provide a capsule summary of this history since 1926. Figure 4–3 charts the behaviour of real GDP over a period of more than sixty years. The pronounced upward slope of the line indicates that the main feature has been *economic growth*. But the figure also shows that recessions—periods during which the real GDP decreased—have occurred. The ups and downs that are evident in Figure 4–3 are often referred to as *business cycles*.

The history of the price level (Figure 4–4) displays a broadly similar pattern, but one that differs in some important respects. Prices also have been generally rising— that is, inflation has been much more common than deflation—but there have been

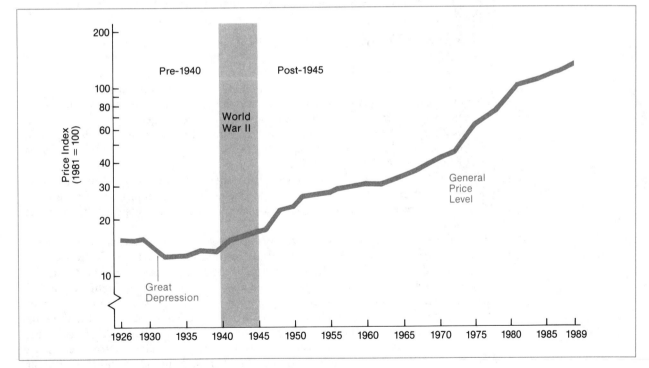

FIGURE 4–4
The Price Level in Canada, 1926–1989
This time-series chart portrays the behaviour of the Canadian price level from 1926 to 1989. (The specific price index used is called the *GDP deflator* and it is defined as the ratio of nominal GDP divided by real GDP.) Once again, the vertical axis has a ratio scale, and the World War II years are shaded. The difference between the 1926–40 period and the 1946–89 period is quite pronounced.
SOURCE: Historical Statistics of Canada, and Statistics Canada.

two exceptions: stable prices during the 1920s and the later 1930s, and falling prices during the early 1930s (the Great Depression).

The following exercise may be enlightening. Cover the portions of Figures 4–3 and 4–4 that deal with the period beginning in 1940, the portions to the right of the shaded area in each figure. The picture that emerges is of an economy on a roller coaster. In Figure 4–3, the up-and-down movement around the underlying growth trend is quite pronounced. In Figure 4–4 we see mainly **deflation**, with hardly any upward trend at all. Indeed, prices at the eve of World War II were lower than they were in the mid-1920s.

Now do the reverse. Cover the data prior to 1946 in both figures and look only at the postwar period. There is, indeed, a difference. The upward trend in real GDP predominates more, and business cycles are much less severe. While perfection has not been achieved, things do look much better. When we turn to the price level, however, things look rather worse. Gone is any period of falling prices such as those that occurred before World War II; even periods of reasonable price stability are rather rare.

This quick inspection of the data suggests that something has happened. The Canadian economy behaved differently in 1946–89 than it did before World War II. Many economists attribute this shift in the economy's behaviour to lessons the government has learned about managing the economy—lessons that we will be learning in Parts Three and Four. When you look at the pre-1940 data, you are looking at an unmanaged economy that went through booms and recessions for "natural" economic reasons. The government did little about either. When you examine the post-1945 data, on the other hand, you are looking at an economy that has been managed by government policy—sometimes successfully and sometimes unsuccessfully. While the recessions are less severe, a cost seems to have been exacted: The economy appears to be more inflation-prone than it was in the more distant past.

> Deflation refers to a sustained *decrease* in the general price level.

The Great Depression of the 1930s

As you look at these graphs, the Great Depression of the 1930s is bound to catch your eye. The decline in economic activity from 1929 to 1933 was the most severe in our nation's history, and the rapid deflation was most unusual. The Depression is far behind us now, but those who lived through it will never forget it.

While statistics usually conceal the true drama of economic events, this is not so in the case of the Great Depression—here, they stand as bitter testimony to its severity. From its 1929 high to its 1933 low, the production of goods and services dropped 30 percent, and the price level fell 18.5 percent. The unemployment rate rose to 20 percent in 1933. From the data alone, one can conjure up pictures of soup lines, beggars on street corners, closed factories, and homeless families (see the boxed insert on the next page).

The Great Depression was a worldwide event; no country was spared its ravages. This traumatic episode literally changed the history of many nations. In Germany, it facilitated the ascendancy of the Nazi party. In the United States, it enabled Franklin Delano Roosevelt's Democratic party to engineer one of the most dramatic political realignments in history and to push through a host of political and economic reforms.

The worldwide depression also caused a much-needed revolution in the thinking of economists. Up until the 1930s, the prevailing economic theory held that a capitalist economy, while it occasionally misbehaved, had a "natural" tendency to cure recessions or inflations by itself. The roller coaster bounced around but did not normally run off the tracks. This optimistic view was not confined to academia. It characterized the views of most politicians (certainly including Prime Minister William Lyon McKenzie King) and business leaders as well.

The stubbornness of the Great Depression shook almost everyone's faith in the ability of the economy to right itself. In Cambridge, England, this questioning attitude

Ten Lost Years

During the worst years of the Great Depression, about 25 percent of Canadian families were forced onto "relief." The loss of work for city dwellers was compounded by the loss of work for farmers due to dust, drought, and grasshoppers. The Canadian government provided rent for cheap, overcrowded accommodation and money for food (about $10 to $15 per month for a family). These desperate times have been described by Canadian author Barry Broadfoot in his *Ten Lost Years*. The quotation below and the photograph are from his moving descriptions.

For the men who had been taught that their main goal was to be a good family provider, the depression was a degrading time. Fathers and older sons became transients, so that those remaining at home would have more food and more room to sleep. They would pick fruit, harvest crops, and hop a train, hoping to find work elsewhere. Thousands of men were riding back and forth across the country on top of trains or in boxcars. The men lived in "hobo jungles" on the edges of large cities, where they built small shacks and tents from old boards, cardboard, and blankets.

The government worried that the unemployed might start a revolution, so they started relief camps far from the cities and ran them in a military fashion. The government felt this was a practical solution to the problem, and the men were clothed and fed. However, many men felt they had been forced to the camps and that they worked under slave conditions.

You've got to realize this, in the relief camps of the Thirties we weren't treated as humans. We weren't treated as animals, either, and I've always thought we were just statistics written into some big ledger in Ottawa. I was 18 and had come out west from Brantford because there was no work for a young fellow in that part of Ontario....

Interior of main sleeping hut, Relief Project No. 27, Ottawa Air Station, Rockliffe, Ontario, 6 March 1933.

(National Archives of Canada)

I headed for Vancouver where at least I wouldn't freeze to death, but we were harassed there and kicked around and so I joined up for a relief camp.

It was one of several up the old Hope-Princeton Trail, made up of board and canvas tents, and buildings they called cabooses where we slept. There was about 150 of us in this one, guys as young as 16 and up to 35 or 45, I should guess, and the thing was, we were all single and no jobs, stony broke and no future and the politicians considered us as dangerous. Their thinking was that if we were isolated then we wouldn't be hanging around vacant lots and jungles listening to Communist troublemakers.

SOURCE: Excerpts from *Ten Lost Years, 1929–1939*, by Barry Broadfoot. Copyright © 1973 by Barry Broadfoot. Reprinted by permission of Doubleday Company, Inc.

---

led John Maynard Keynes, one of the world's most respected economists, to write *The General Theory of Employment, Interest, and Money* (1936). Probably the most important book in economics of the twentieth century, it carried a rather revolutionary message. Keynes discarded the notion that the economy always gravitated toward high levels of employment, replacing it with the assertion that—if a pessimistic outlook led business firms and consumers to curtail their spending plans—the economy might be condemned to stagnation for years.

While this doleful prognosis sounded all too realistic at the time, Keynes closed his book on a hopeful note, for he showed how government actions might prod the economy out of its depressed state. The lessons he taught the world then are the lessons we shall be learning in Parts Three and Four. They show how governments can manage their economies so that recessions will not turn into depressions and depressions will not last as long as the Great Depression. While Keynes was working on *The General Theory*, he wrote his friend George Bernard Shaw, "I believe myself to be writing a book on economic theory which will largely revolutionize . . . the way the world thinks about economic problems." In many ways, he was right, though parts of the Keynesian message remain controversial to this day.

From World War II to the Present

The Great Depression finally ended when the country engaged in war at the end of the 1930s. With total spending at extraordinarily high levels during the war, mostly because of government expenditures, the economy boomed and the unemployment rate fell to less than 2 percent.

Wartime spending of this magnitude usually leads to inflation, but much of the potential inflation during World War II was contained by price controls. With prices held below the levels at which quantity supplied equalled quantity demanded, many goods had to be rationed, and shortages of consumer goods were quite common. All of this ended with a burst of inflation when controls were lifted after the war.

The period from the end of the war until the early 1960s resembled the earlier period of growth with recessions before 1929. The main difference was that the recessions between 1945 and 1965 were noticeably shorter and less severe than their prewar counterparts. Moderate but persistent inflation also became a fact of life. This period of sustained growth, reasonably low unemployment, and non-accelerating inflation was thought by many to be the result of "The New Economics," a term the media created for the policy of economic management prescribed by Keynes in the 1930s. For a while it looked as if we could avoid both unemployment and inflation. But the optimistic verdicts were premature in both cases.

Inflation was the first problem to crop up, beginning in about 1965. Its major cause, as it had been so many times in the past, was high levels of wartime spending—this time for the Vietnam War by the United States. Demand for Canadian goods was very high during this period, partly because of record-level exports to the United States, and partly because we followed a fixed exchange-rate policy. As we explain in Part Three, by not letting the international value of the Canadian dollar rise, our government blocked a major route by which demands for our exports could have been held in check.

Then things began to get much worse for the oil-importing nations of the world. A 1973 war between Israel and the Arab nations led to a quadrupling of the price of oil by the Organization of Petroleum Exporting Countries (OPEC). At the same time, poor harvests in 1973 and 1974 in many parts of the globe kept world food prices rising rapidly. Prices of other raw materials also skyrocketed. Naturally, higher costs of fuel and other materials were soon reflected in the prices of manufactured goods.

For these reasons, the inflation rate in the United States rose to above 12 percent during 1974. Meanwhile, the U.S. economy was slipping into a severe recession and, between late 1973 and early 1975, its unemployment rate almost doubled. Thus, both the twin evils of macroeconomics—inflation and unemployment—were unusually virulent in 1974 and 1975. Indeed, a new term—**stagflation**—was coined to refer to the simultaneous occurrence of economic *stag*nation and rapid in*flation* in the United States.

Canada suffered less unemployment and more inflation than the United States during the mid-1970s for two reasons. First, using policies that stimulated demand, the Canadian government cushioned the recession that would have followed from the large drop in export sales to the United States. Second, the government did not allow the Canadian consumer price of oil to increase to world levels. Nevertheless, the stimulation of the general demand for goods was sufficient to cause inflation to rise dramatically in Canada.

The price of oil began to "misbehave" again in 1979, when the revolution that deposed the Shah of Iran sparked chaos in the world oil market. In a series of price increases, OPEC more than doubled the price of its oil during 1979. The consequences of OPEC's actions were similar to those of 1973–75: stagflation returned. By 1980, the Canadian unemployment rate was 7.5 percent, and the inflation rate was more than 10 percent.

During the early 1980s, Canada followed the United Kingdom's and the United

States' contractionary high interest-rate policies to curb inflation. The policy worked but at a tremendous cost. Inflation fell to 5.8 percent in 1983 (and then to 4 percent by 1986), but unemployment soared to 11.9 percent in 1983 (more than twice what it was in 1973). It was not until 1986 that the unemployment rate fell below 10 percent. By the end of the 1980s, Canada's inflation rate was 5 percent, and the unemployment rate stood at 7.5 percent.

The main purpose of the macroeconomic chapters of this textbook is to explain these ups and downs in unemployment and inflation, and to examine whether policy can do anything to limit such swings.

The Problem of Macroeconomic Stabilization

Our brief discussion of Canadian economic history has involved numerous references to the fact that government policies have indeed contributed to our macroeconomic performance, both good and bad. Let us now commence a more formal discussion of this connection.

We can provide a preliminary analysis of **stabilization policy**, the name given to government programs designed to prevent or shorten recessions and to counteract inflation, by using the basic tools of aggregate-supply and aggregate-demand analysis. To facilitate this, we will refer back to Figures 4–1 and 4–2 on pages 74 and 75.

Figure 4–1(b) gives a simplified view of government policy to fight unemployment. We suppose that, in the absence of government intervention, the economy would reach an equilibrium at point E, where demand curve D_0D_0 crosses supply curve SS. Now, if the output corresponding to point E is so low that many workers are unemployed, *the government can reduce unemployment if it can increase aggregate demand*. In the diagram, this action shifts the demand curve to D_1D_1, causing equilibrium to move to point A. In general:

Recessions and unemployment are often caused by insufficient aggregate demand. When this is so, government policies that augment demand—such as increases in government spending—can be an effective way to increase output and reduce unemployment.

The opposite type of demand management is often called for when inflation is the main macroeconomic problem. Figure 4–2 illustrates this case. Here again, point E, the intersection of demand curve D_0D_0 and supply curve SS, is the equilibrium that would be reached in the absence of government policy. But now we suppose that the price level corresponding to point E is considered "too high," meaning that the *change* in the price level from the previous period to this one would be too rapid if the economy moved to point E. A government program that reduces demand from D_0D_0 to D_2D_2 (for example, a reduction in government spending) can keep prices down and thereby reduce inflation. Thus:

Inflation is frequently caused by aggregate demand racing ahead too fast. When this is the case, government policies that reduce aggregate demand can be effective anti-inflationary devices.

This is a brief summary of the intent of stabilization policy. When demand behaviour is the source of economic instability, the government can limit both recession and inflation by managing aggregate demand, pushing it ahead when it would otherwise lag and restraining it when it would otherwise grow too quickly.

Sound simple? It's not. In reality, managing aggregate demand is a lot more complicated than shifting around lines on graphs with pencil and paper. We will spend much of Parts Three and Four examining the methods of demand management

> Stabilization policy is the name given to government programs designed to prevent or shorten recessions and to counteract inflation (that is, to *stabilize* prices).

and learning why these methods do not always lead to the results that policy-makers hope for.

One problem is that the economy is sometimes plagued by both unemployment and inflation *at the same time*. In this case, the tools of demand management, even if wielded with great precision, are simply not up to the task. In Part Four we will see why demand management is not enough and study some suggestions for dealing with unemployment and inflation at the same time.

Another problem is that sometimes, in an attempt to stabilize the economy, the government slows the rate at which the economy grows over the longer term. This happens, for example, when the government fights inflation in a way that makes it less profitable for firms to invest in new plant and equipment. This reduces aggregate demand now, but it also *reduces potential output in the future*. It is important to keep the distinction between growth policy and stabilization policy clearly in mind, and this can best be done by looking ahead to Figure 4–6 (on page 91). This graph shows both the variations in actual GDP and the smoother trend in what we call potential GDP. Growth policy aims to raise the growth of potential GDP (and in terms of the graph, this means making the slope of the potential GDP line steeper). Stabilization policy aims to limit the gaps between actual and potential GDP. Given constraints of space and time, we have limited our macroeconomic analysis in this book almost exclusively to the stabilization issue. The last chapter on macroeconomics (Chapter 18), however, is devoted exclusively to growth policy.

Before embarking on the important task of examining stabilization policy, we devote the remainder of this chapter to a discussion of the twin macroeconomic evils, unemployment and inflation.

Unemployment

Nowadays, unemployment does not have the dire consequences for most families that it did in the 1930s. Part of the sting has been taken out of temporary unemployment by our system of unemployment insurance (discussed below), and there are other social-welfare programs to support the incomes of the poor (see Chapter 30). Yet most families still do suffer a painful loss of income when their breadwinner becomes unemployed.

Even families that are well protected by unemployment compensation suffer when joblessness strikes. Ours is a work-oriented society. A man's "place" has always been in the office or factory or shop, and this has become increasingly true for women as well. A worker forced into idleness by a recession endures a psychological cost that is no less real for our inability to measure it. Enforced joblessness is a demoralizing mental burden on the unemployed worker. High unemployment leads to a higher incidence of psychological disorders, divorces, suicides, and the like.

Nor are the costs only psychological. Accumulated work experience is a valuable asset. When forced into idleness, workers not only cease accumulating experience, but lengthy periods of unemployment may make them "rusty," and thus less productive when they are re-employed. Short periods of unemployment exact different kinds of costs. A record of steady employment is important in applying for a new job, and a worker who has frequently been laid off will lack this record of reliability.

The **unemployment rate** is the number of unemployed people, expressed as a percentage of the labour force. The *labour force* is the number of people employed or seeking employment.

It is important to realize that these costs, whether large or small in total, are distributed most unevenly across the population. At the bottom of the severe recession of 1981–84, the **unemployment rate** among all workers was 12.5 percent. This is a much higher rate than the 7.5 percent figure with which we started and ended the 1980s. It is also important to note that the 1983 situation was even worse for certain groups. For example, the unemployment rate in Newfoundland was 19 percent, and the unemployment rate among those 15 to 24 years old was 23 percent.

Counting the Unemployed: The Official Statistics

Statistics Canada is responsible for measuring unemployment. How do they do it? How accurate are their measurements?

Statistics Canada's basic method for counting the unemployed is quite direct: it asks people. Specifically, a survey of 48,000 households is conducted each month. The sample is designed to represent all persons 15 years of age and over residing in Canada, with the exception of the following: full-time members of the armed forces, inmates of institutions, residents of the Yukon and Northwest Territories, and those living on Indian reserves. The census-taker asks several questions about the employment status of each member of the household. On the basis of these answers, each person is categorized as being *employed*, *unemployed*, or *not in the labour force*.

The first category is simplest to define. It includes everybody currently working at a job, including part-time workers. Although some part-time workers work less than a full week because they choose to, others do so only because they cannot find a suitable full-time job. Nevertheless, these workers are not considered "unemployed," though many would consider them "underemployed."

The second category is a bit trickier. For those not currently working, Statistics Canada first determines whether they are temporarily laid off from a job to which they expect to return. If so, they are counted as unemployed. The remaining workers are asked whether they actively sought work during the previous week. If they did, they are also counted as unemployed. But if they did not, they are classified as not in the labour force; that is, since they failed to look for a job they are not considered unemployed.

This seems a reasonable way to draw the distinction—after all, we would not want to count all university students who work during the summer months as unemployed between September and May. Yet, there is a problem: Research has shown that many unemployed workers give up looking for jobs after a time. These so-called **discouraged workers** are victims of poor job prospects, just like the officially unemployed. Ironically, when they give up hope, the official unemployment statistics decline! Some critics have therefore argued that an estimate should be made of the number of discouraged workers and that these people should be added to the rolls of the unemployed.

A **discouraged worker** is an unemployed person who gives up looking for work and is therefore no longer counted as part of the labour force.

Statistics Canada now publishes a wide range of low-employment indicators that allow us to assess the reduction in employment opportunities whenever aggregate demand grows slowly. For example, it now indicates not only the number of discouraged workers, but also the number of workers who involuntarily take a cut in the length of their work week. Figures from the large recession of the 1980s give us some sense of the wide variations indicated by these other measures: In addition to a 5 percentage-point increase in the measured unemployment rate, the number of workers in the ranks of the employed who were forced to work shorter hours in 1982 was double the figure that prevailed during the remainder of the decade. Thus, involuntary part-time work, loss of overtime or shortened work hours, and discouraged workers are all examples of "hidden" or "disguised" unemployment. And those who are concerned about these phenomena argue that we should include them in the official unemployment rate because, when we do not, the magnitude of the problem is *underestimated*.

There is, however, an opposing school of thought that argues that the official unemployment rate really *overestimates* the unemployment problem. First, they argue, the unemployment rate of 1991 is not directly comparable to the unemployment rate of, say, 1955 because the composition of the labour force has changed dramatically over these years. Specifically, a larger fraction of all workers are young and female today than was the case thirty years ago. These groups have always had higher rates of unemployment than adult males. Therefore, even if adult men, adult women, and teenagers each had the *same* unemployment rates in 1991 that they had in 1955, the unemployment rate for the entire population would have been higher in

1991 than in 1955.[3] Second, they argue, to count as unemployed, a person need only *say* that he is looking for work, even if he is not really interested in finding a job. No one knows to what extent the unemployment problem is overstated on account of this, but some think that it may be considerable.

Types of Unemployment

Frictional unemployment is unemployment that occurs as a result of the normal workings of the labour market. It includes people who are temporarily between jobs because they are moving or changing occupations, or for similar reasons.

Providing jobs for those who are willing to work is one principal goal of macro-economic policy. How are we to define this goal? One clearly *incorrect* answer would be "a zero measured unemployment rate." Ours is a dynamic and highly mobile economy. Households move from one province to another. Individuals quit jobs to look for better positions or to "retool" for more attractive occupations. These phenomena and many more produce some minimal amount of unemployment—people who literally are *between* jobs. Economists call this the level of **frictional unemployment**.

The critical distinguishing feature of frictional unemployment is that it is short-lived. A frictionally unemployed person has every reason to expect to find a new job soon. People tend to think of frictional unemployment as irreducible, but that is not the case. During World War II, for example, unemployment in this country fell below 2 percent—substantially below the frictional level. Frictional unemployment is irreducible only in the sense that—under normal circumstances—it is socially undesirable to reduce it.

Geographical and occupational mobility play important roles in our market economy—enabling people to search for better jobs. Similarly, waste is avoided by allowing inefficient firms to be replaced by new firms. Inhibition of either of these phenomena must hamper the workings of the market economy. But, if these adjustment mechanisms are allowed to operate, there will always be some temporarily unemployed workers looking for jobs just as there will always be some firms that have unfilled positions and are looking for workers. These gaps are the genesis of frictional unemployment.

Structural unemployment refers to workers who have lost their jobs because they have been displaced by automation, because their skills are no longer in demand, or for similar reasons.

A second type of unemployment is often difficult to distinguish from frictional unemployment, but it has very different implications. **Structural unemployment** arises when jobs are eliminated by changes in the structure of the economy, such as automation or permanent changes in demand. The crucial difference between frictional and structural unemployment is that, unlike frictionally unemployed workers, structurally unemployed workers cannot realistically be considered "between jobs." Instead, they may find their skills and experience unwanted in the changing economy in which they live. They are thus faced with either a prolonged period of unemployment or the necessity of making a major change in their occupation. For older workers, learning a new occupation may be nearly impossible.

Cyclical unemployment is the portion of unemployment that is attributable to a decline in the economy's total production. Cyclical unemployment rises during recessions and falls as prosperity is restored.

The remaining type of unemployment, **cyclical unemployment**, will occupy our attention most in this book. Cyclical unemployment arises when the overall level of economic activity declines. Whenever the unemployment rate rises ominously or falls precipitously, the data are almost certainly reflecting significant changes in cyclical unemployment.

What Is "Full Employment"?

After World War II, the Canadian federal government committed itself to pursue a policy of full employment. In the White Paper of April 1945 it was stated that "the government will be prepared, in periods when unemployment threatens, to incur deficits and increases in the national debt resulting from its employment and income

---

[3] If you do not understand why, consider the following analogy. Suppose your university class contains a mixture of "A" students and "C" students. If, between your first year and your final year, more "C" students enter the class as transfers from other universities, your class's overall average grade will decline even if every student earns the same grades in the final year that he or she did in first year.

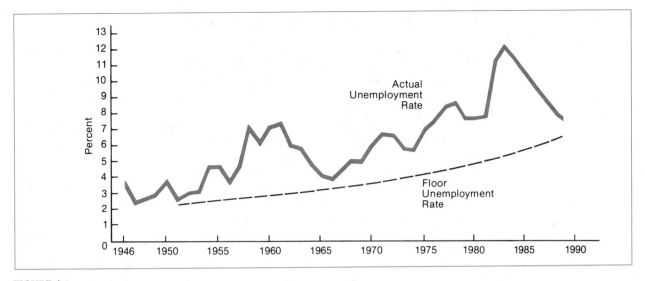

FIGURE 4-5
Unemployment Rate in Canada since World War II
The unemployment rate has risen dramatically since the war, but cyclical unemployment does not account for all of this increase. Cyclical unemployment was high in the recessions of 1958-62, 1970-71, 1977-78, and the early 1980s. The increase in the floor unemployment rate has resulted from structural factors such as demographic changes (the baby boom and the increased labour-force participation of females) and certain institutional changes (the unemployment-insurance provisions instituted in 1971).   SOURCE: Statistics Canada

policy." The government has consistently followed this part of its plan, but follow-through has been less obvious on the other part: "In periods of buoyant employment and income, budget plans will call for surpluses." Part of the reason for this excess of budget deficits over surpluses over the years is that the government seems to be constantly optimistic about what "full employment" is.

During the prosperous years of the late 1940s and early 1950s, unemployment rates were consistently below 4 percent, dropping as low as 2.2 percent in 1947. This led the Economic Council of Canada (formed in the early 1960s) to select 3 percent as a definition of full employment. By this it was meant that 3 percent was the normal level of frictional unemployment in Canada. However, as Figure 4-5 shows, the unemployment rate has never fallen below 3.5 percent since 1956. As a result, economists now feel that the 3 percent target is unrealistic, and most now define full employment as involving an overall unemployment rate of about 7 or 7.5 percent. Actually, detailed studies by both the Economic Council of Canada and the Bank of Canada, published in 1989, are even more discouraging. They estimate the full-employment level of the unemployment rate to be in the 7.5–8 percent range.

There are several reasons for this upward adjustment over time. First, there is the changed composition of the labour force that we discussed above. The largest increase has been among females and youth, while some of the rapid growth in job vacancies since the mid-1970s has been in the processing, fabricating, and extractive fields—occupations that have traditionally employed males aged 25–54. Estimates show that about half the increase in the "floor" unemployment rate shown in Figure 4-5 is due to this mismatching of trends and to other related structural factors. Another reason for the rise in the floor unemployment rate is the increased generosity of the unemployment-insurance legislation that took effect in 1971 and that reduced the incentive for an individual to get off the unemployment rolls. Why work if unemployment benefits and other programs provide an income nearly as large as the salary one could earn on the job? This lack of incentive to work makes low unemployment harder to achieve. Finally, many economists have claimed that substantial increases in the minimum-wage levels during the 1970s have made it harder to employ teenagers and other workers whose productivity is low. If, for example, workers' productivity is exceeded by the legal minimum wage, who will hire them?

Unemployment Insurance: The Invaluable Cushion

A surprising feature of the 1980s is the equanimity with which the electorate tolerated high unemployment rates. One major reason for this is our system of **unemployment insurance**, first established in 1941. Thanks to this system, many—but, as we shall see, not all—Canadian workers need never experience the complete loss of income that so many suffered during the 1930s.

In recent years the benefits paid to an unemployed worker have been set at 60 percent of his or her average weekly insurable earnings (to a given maximum amount). These payments are taxable, but the individual can earn up to 25 percent of his or her benefits through part-time or temporary work, without a reduction in benefits. There has generally been a two-week waiting period following the start of unemployment before benefits are paid. Though a 40 percent drop in earnings poses problems, especially if there are no other earners in the family, families covered by unemployment insurance simply do not go hungry when they lose their jobs, and they are only rarely dispossessed of their homes.

Who is eligible to receive these benefits? Precise qualifications vary from region to region, but some stipulations apply quite generally. First, the period of employment required to establish eligibility has varied between ten and twenty weeks, depending on the unemployment rate in the region. This means that persons just joining the labour force (for instance, new graduates from high school, university, or community college) or re-entering after a protracted absence (such as women resuming paid work after many years of child rearing) are not eligible until they acquire the requisite weeks of employment. Further, while there are certain exceptions, people who quit their last job must wait several extra weeks to collect benefits. And people who are unwilling or unable to work cannot receive unemployment benefits at all; a recipient of benefits must be conducting an active search for employment. The final restriction imposed by the plan concerns the maximum time period for which benefits can be received. This limit depends on the individual's employment history and the prevailing unemployment rates in both the country and the region, and, in 1989, it could not exceed fifty weeks.

Over the years, the government has extended the unemployment-insurance program, although legislation proposed in 1989 was aimed at restricting it (see the boxed insert on the next page). Changes introduced in 1971 included several new groups, such as seasonally unemployed fishermen, pregnant women (with sufficient work experience), people with extended sickness, and those attending retraining programs. Since 1977, some unemployment-insurance funds have been used to keep people working rather than to compensate them for not working. There have been a series of job-sharing plans. For example, if all employees work four days a week instead of five, the company pays the wages for four days and the insurance fund pays wages for the fifth day.

The importance of unemployment insurance to the unemployed is obvious. But there are also significant benefits to citizens who never become unemployed. During recession years many billions of dollars are paid out in unemployment benefits, and since recipients probably spend most of their benefits, unemployment insurance limits the severity of recessions by providing additional purchasing power when and where it is most needed.

The unemployment-insurance system is one of several "cushions" that have been built into our economy since the 1930s to prevent the possibility of another Great Depression. By giving the money to those who become unemployed, the system helps prop up aggregate demand during recessions.

While the Canadian economy is now probably "depression proof," this should not be a cause for too much rejoicing, for the recession of the early 1980s demonstrated that we are far from being "recession proof." Also, many have become concerned

Reforming Unemployment Insurance

Three major studies (by the Macdonald Royal Commission, Newfoundland's Royal Commission on Employment, and the Forget Commission—all released in 1985 and 1986) have examined Canada's unemployment-insurance system, and all of them recommended changes. The basic concern stems from the fact that the system is no longer a self-sustained *insurance* program to supply income to people laid off until they get another job. If the system were a pure insurance scheme, those who quit their jobs without any provocation would not receive benefits. Today, however, such people simply have an extra six-week wait before benefits commence. It is as if, as the National Citizens' Coalition argued in its brief to the Forget Commission, the housing-insurance industry simply deferred a claims payment to a person known to have burned down his own home!

Those who support the existing unemployment-insurance program feel that it is appropriate for the system to go beyond a simple insurance function to be a permanent *income-support* policy. However, the critics argue that unemployment insurance is poorly suited to providing ongoing income support because it does not systematically reach those in poverty. (See Chapter 30 for a discussion of preferred alternatives.)

According to the royal commissions, the existing program has accentuated the economic-dependency problem faced by regions with high unemployment rates. A whole social structure has arisen around unemployment insurance. For instance, in Newfoundland, "getting your stamps" (that is, working ten weeks to qualify for insurance payments for the rest of the year) is accepted as an overriding concern. Government make-work projects are often arranged so that the maximum number of individuals will obtain the ten-weeks-of-work qualification. Some private companies also spread work around in this fashion, despite the negative effect on productivity. The Macdonald Commission concluded that the unemployment-insurance system, having moved well beyond the functions of a pure insurance scheme (by providing fairly generous payments for long intervals

after only short qualification periods), "reinforces the continuation of temporary and unstable jobs in high-unemployment and low-wage regions."

In 1990, the government passed a bill that put tighter limits on the unemployment-insurance system. The revisions lengthened the qualifying period to as long as 20 weeks (from the previous maximum of 14 weeks) and reduced the maximum payment period from 50 to 35 weeks. The range depends on regional unemployment rates.

One motivation behind these changes was that they would reduce the cost of unemployment insurance to the government by about ten percent, even after some of the savings were used to expand retraining programs. The changes did *not* represent an attempt to change the system from a redistributive scheme to a true insurance program (as the royal commission recommended). Access to the system was simply being restricted, so that less redistribution would now occur.

about costly side effects and the large drain on public funds ($13 billion a year as of 1990) caused by the unemployment-insurance system, as the boxed insert on this page explains.

The Economic Costs of High Unemployment

The fact that unemployment insurance and other social-welfare programs replace a significant fraction of lost income has led some skeptics to claim that unemployment is no longer a serious problem. But the fact is that the program *spreads the costs* of the problem among many people instead of letting them all fall on the shoulders of an unfortunate few.

Fire insurance provides a useful analogy. If your home is covered by fire insurance and it burns down, your family will probably suffer only a small financial loss because the insurance company will pay most of the expenses. Where does it get the money? It cannot be created out of thin air. Rather, the company must have collected the funds from the many other families who purchased insurance but did not suffer any fire damages. Thus, one family's loss of perhaps $80,000 is covered by the insurance payments of 400 families each paying $200 a year. In this way, the costs of the catastrophe are spread among hundreds of families and, in the process, made much more bearable.

But despite the insurance, society loses a valuable resource—a house. It will take a great deal of wood, cement, nails, paint, and labour to replace the burnt-out home. *An insurance policy cannot insure society against losses of real resources.*

The case is precisely the same with insurance against unemployment. All workers and employers pay for the insurance policy by making UI contributions. With the funds so collected, the government compensates the victims of unemployment. Thus, instead of letting the costs of unemployment fall entirely on the minority of workers who are out of work, the system of payroll taxes and unemployment benefits *spreads* the costs over the entire population. But it does not eliminate the basic economic cost.

When the economy does not generate enough jobs to employ all those who are willing to work, a valuable resource is lost. Potential goods and services that might have been enjoyed by consumers are lost forever. This is the real economic cost of high unemployment, and no insurance plan can eliminate it.

And these costs are by no means negligible. Table 4–1 summarizes the idleness of workers and machines and the resulting loss of national output for some of the years of lowest economic activity in recent decades. The first column lists the unemployment rate and thus measures unused labour resources. The second lists the percentage of industrial capacity that Canadian manufacturers were actually using and thus indicates the extent of unused plant and equipment. And the third column shows how much more output (real GDP) could have been produced if these labour and capital resources had been fully employed.

While these years are extreme examples, the inability to utilize all of the nation's available resources has been a recurrent problem for our economy. The black line in Figure 4–6 shows the actual real GDP in Canada from 1960 to 1989, while the green line shows the real GDP we *could have* produced if "full employment" had been

Potential gross domestic product is the real GDP the economy would produce if its labour and other resources were fully employed.

maintained. This last statement defines a concept called **potential GDP**. As our previous discussion of full employment pointed out, it *is* possible to push employment beyond its normal full-employment level. This occurs whenever the unemployment rate dips below the "full-employment unemployment rate"—a rate now thought to be about 7 percent. Consequently, it *is* possible for actual GDP to exceed potential GDP. Figure 4–6 shows several instances where this happened. But it also shows that, more typically, actual GDP falls short of potential GDP. The total shortfall of actual GDP below potential GDP since 1960 provides some startling information.

TABLE 4–1
The Economic Costs of High Unemployment

YEAR	UNEMPLOYMENT RATE (percent)	CAPACITY UTILIZATION RATE (percent)	PERCENTAGE OF REAL GDP LOST DUE TO IDLE RESOURCES
1961	7.1	72	6.4
1971	6.4	80	2.7
1977	8.1	80	2.9
1983	11.9	67	8.4

SOURCES: Statistics Canada, and Figure 4–5.

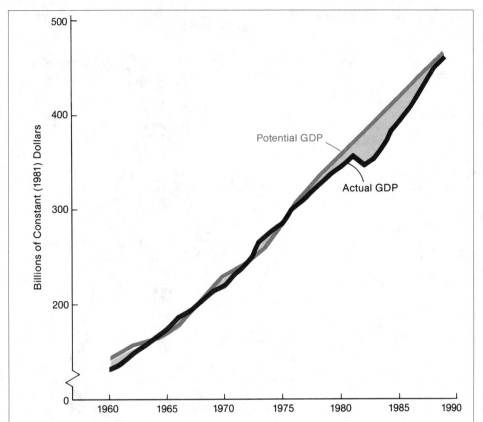

FIGURE 4-6
Actual and Potential GDP in Canada, 1960–1989
This chart compares the growth of actual GDP (black line) with that of potential GDP (green line). There have been three lengthy periods during which real GDP remained below its potential (1960-64, 1969-72, and 1975 to the present), but only two brief periods during which GDP was above potential (1965-66 and 1973-74).
SOURCE: Economic Council of Canada, *Annual Review* (1979), and the Department of Finance, unpublished data, integrated by the authors.

The cumulative gap between actual and potential GDP over the years 1960–89 (all evaluated in 1981 prices), which is shown by the shaded area in Figure 4–6, is an astounding $230 billion. At 1989 levels of output, this loss in output as a result of unemployment would represent approximately six months' worth of production. And there is no way to redeem these losses. The labour wasted in 1989 cannot be utilized in 1990.

Those who argue that unemployment is nothing to worry about today because of unemployment insurance, or because unemployment is concentrated among certain kinds of workers (such as teenagers), or because many unemployed workers become re-employed within a few weeks should ponder Figure 4–6. Is the loss of this much output really no cause for worry? Would these optimists react the same way if the government collected a fraction of the output of every factory in Canada and dumped it into the sea? Waste is waste no matter who ultimately pays the cost.

Inflation

Both the human and the economic costs of inflation are less obvious than the costs of unemployment. But this does not necessarily make them any less real, for if one thing is crystal clear about inflation, it is that people do not like it. (We leave the details of measuring inflation to Appendix B, but the basic idea is conveyed in the boxed insert on page 92.)

Public-opinion polls consistently show that inflation ranks high on people's list of major national problems, sometimes ahead of unemployment. Surveys also find that inflation, like unemployment, causes a deterioration in consumers' sense of well-being —it makes people unhappy. Why?

Price-Checkers Provide Raw Material of CPI

The dour image of John Crow, governor of the Bank of Canada, flickers on dozens of television sets at a downtown Toronto department store while Joan Mayhew busily inspects their price tags.

On the mid-day news, Mr. Crow warns yet again that the inflation genie must be stuffed back into the bottle. Ms Mayhew is oblivious.

But like Mr. Crow, she is a public servant, and both spend their days watching inflation.

One of 86 price-checkers for Statistics Canada, Ms Mayhew is gathering the raw material for the monthly consumer price index, Canada's most widely watched measure of inflation. . . .

Ms Mayhew's equipment includes a tape-measure; a fold-out magnifying glass used to count threads; and a thick, dog-eared manual that describes hundreds of consumer goods in meticulous detail. Larded among its pages are actual samples of leathers, fabrics and stitching that can be held up against a garment to check for authenticity.

The trick is to compare equal items month after month, year after year, so that price is the only thing that changes. "Pure price movement," the statisticians in Ottawa like to call it.

But Ms Mayhew . . . knows first-hand that marketers thrive on change, making it difficult to make direct comparisons.

In the women's swimwear department, for example, the one-piece bathing suits this spring have sprouted an appendage.

"Back draping, with bow over fanny," Ms Mayhew scribbles. "I'll have to think of something more sophisticated when I write it up and send it to Ottawa."

A good 20 minutes is spent inspecting a $12.99 polyester-and-cotton nightie until Ms Mayhew finally judges it the equal of nighties priced in previous months.

Statistics Canada collects more than 100,000 such prices—from milk to magazines, dental fillings to diapers—in 82 urban centres each month. The so-called CPI basket includes more than 300 goods and services. . . .

SOURCE: Excerpted from Dean Beeby, "Price-Checkers Provide Raw Material of CPI," *The Globe and Mail*, April 11, 1990, page B6.

At first, the question may seem ridiculous. During times of inflation, people must keep paying higher prices for the same quantities of goods and services they had before. So more and more income is needed just to maintain the same standard of living. Is it not obvious that this erosion of **purchasing power**—that is, the decline in what money will buy—makes everyone worse off?

This would indeed be the case were it not for one very significant fact. The wages people earn are also prices—prices for labour services. During a period of inflation, wages also rise and, in fact, the average wage typically rises more or less in step with prices. Thus, contrary to popular myth, workers as a group are not usually victimized by inflation.

> The **purchasing power** of a given sum of money is the volume of goods and services it will buy.

The purchasing power of wages—often called the **real wage**—is not systematically eroded by inflation. Sometimes wages rise faster than prices, and sometimes prices rise faster than wages. The fact is that, in the long run, wages tend to outstrip prices as new capital equipment and innovation increase output per worker.

> The **real wage rate** is the wage rate adjusted for inflation. It indicates the volume of goods and services that the money wage will buy.

Figure 4–7 illustrates this simple fact. The green line shows the annual rate of increase of consumer prices in Canada for each year since 1949, while the black line shows the annual rate of wage increases. The difference between the two indicates the growth rate of real wages. For the first 25 years, money wages rose faster than prices,

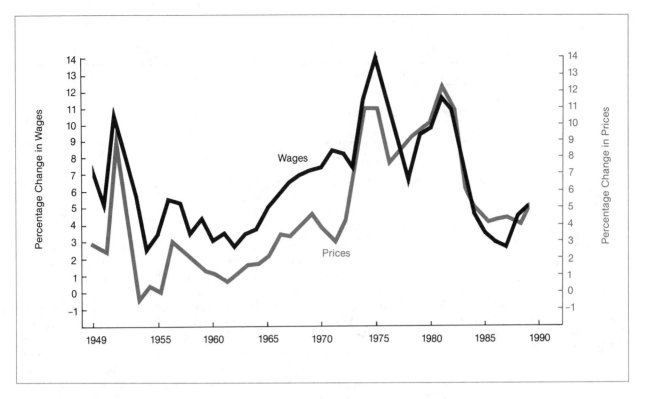

FIGURE 4-7
Rates of Change of Wages and Prices in Canada, 1949–1989
This chart compares the rate of price inflation (green line) with the rate of growth of money (nominal) wages in the postwar period. The patterns are clearly quite similar, with wages and prices normally accelerating or decelerating together. Notice that the traditional gap of wage increases over price increases has not prevailed in recent years.
SOURCE: Statistics Canada. The price index is the Consumer Price Index, and the wage series is average weekly wages and salaries (industrial composite).

reflecting the steady advance of technology and of labour productivity. So the black line was above the green line. The years from 1976 to 1987 stand out as a period in which money wages often did not rise faster than prices. This single fact goes a long way toward explaining why people have been so dissatisfied with economic performance since the mid-1970s.

The feature of Figure 4-7 that virtually jumps off the page is the way the two lines dance together. Money wages normally rise rapidly when prices rise rapidly, and slowly when prices rise slowly. But you should not draw any hasty conclusions from this association. We cannot, for example, learn from this figure whether rising prices cause rising wages or whether rising wages cause rising prices. Remember the warnings given in Chapter 1 about trying to infer causation just by looking at data. But analyzing cause and effect is not our purpose right now. We merely want to explode the myth that inflation inevitably erodes real wages.

Why is this myth so widespread? Imagine a world without inflation in which wages are rising 2 percent a year because of the increasing productivity of labour. Now imagine that, all of a sudden, inflation sets in and prices start rising 4 percent a year, but that nothing else changes. Figure 4-7 suggests that, with perhaps a small delay, money-wage increases will accelerate to 2 percent plus 4 percent, or 6 percent, a year.

Will workers view this change with equanimity? Probably not. To each worker, the 6 percent wage increase will be seen as something he earned by the sweat of his brow. In his view, he *deserves* every penny of his 6 percent raise. And, in a sense, he is right, because "the sweat of his brow" earned him a 2 percent increment in purchasing power that, when the inflation rate is 4 percent, can only be achieved by increasing his wages by a total of 6 percent. An economist would divide the wage increase in the following way:

REASON FOR WAGE INCREASE	AMOUNT
Higher productivity	2%
Compensation for higher prices	4%
Total	6%

"Sure, you're raising my allowance. But am I actually gaining any purchasing power?"

An item's **relative price** is its price in terms of some other item, rather than in terms of dollars.

But the worker will probably keep score differently. Feeling that he earned the entire 6 percent by his own merits, he will view inflation as having "robbed" him of 4 percent of his just deserts. The higher the rate of inflation, the more of his raise the worker will feel robbed of.

Of course, nothing could be farther from the truth. Basically, the economic system is rewarding the worker with *the same 2 percent real-wage increment for higher productivity regardless of the rate of inflation.* The "evils of inflation" are often exaggerated because of a failure to understand this mechanism.

A second reason for misunderstanding the effects of inflation is that people are in the habit of thinking in terms of the number of dollars it takes to buy something rather than in terms of the *purchasing power* of these dollars. For example, if inflation doubles both prices and wages, workers will have to labour exactly the same amount of time as before to earn the price of a loaf of bread. But because they now pay $1 a loaf instead of 50¢, they feel that the price of bread is scandalously high. In fact, nothing has really changed. Nevertheless, people cling to an outmoded idea of what bread *should* cost.

A third misperception results from failure to distinguish between a *rise in the general price level* and a change in **relative prices**, that is, a rise in the price of one commodity relative to that of another. To see the distinction most clearly, imagine first a *pure inflation* in which *every* price rises by 10 percent during the year, so that relative prices do not change. Table 4–2 gives an example in which movie tickets go up from $6 to $6.60, candy bars from $1 to $1.10, and automobiles from $12,000 to $13,200. After the inflation, just as before, it will still take 6 candy bars to buy a movie ticket, 2000 movie tickets to buy a car, and so on. A person who manufactures candy bars in order to purchase movie tickets is neither helped nor harmed by the inflation. Neither is a car dealer with a sweet tooth.

But real inflation is not like this. When there is 10 percent general inflation—meaning that the average price rises by 10 percent[4]—some prices may jump 20 percent or more while others actually fall. Suppose that, instead of the price increases shown in Table 4–2, prices rise as shown in Table 4–3. Movie prices go up by 25

[4]The way statisticians figure out "average" price increases is discussed in Appendix B.

TABLE 4–2
A Rise in the Price Level

	LAST YEAR'S PRICE (dollars)	THIS YEAR'S PRICE (dollars)	PERCENTAGE INCREASE
Candy bar	1.00	1.10	10
Movie ticket	6.00	6.60	10
Automobile	12,000.00	13,200.00	10

TABLE 4–3
A Change in Relative Prices

	LAST YEAR'S PRICE (dollars)	THIS YEAR'S PRICE (dollars)	PERCENTAGE INCREASE
Candy bar	1.00	1.00	0
Movie ticket	6.00	7.50	25
Automobile	12,000.00	12,600.00	5

percent, but candy prices do not change. Surely, candy manufacturers who love movies will be disgruntled because it now costs 7.5 candy bars instead of 6 to get into the theatre. They will blame inflation for raising the price of movie tickets, even though their real problem stems from the *increase in the price of movies relative to candy*. (They would have been hurt just as much if movie tickets had remained at $6 while the price of candy fell to 80¢.)

Since car prices have risen by only 5 percent, theatre owners in need of new cars will be delighted by the fact that an auto now costs only 1680 movie admissions (just as they would have cheered if car prices had fallen to $10,080 while movie tickets remained at $6). However, they are unlikely to attribute their good fortune to inflation —as indeed they should not. What has actually happened is that *cars became cheaper relative to movies*.

Because real-world inflation proceeds at *uneven* rates, relative prices are constantly changing. There are gainers and losers, just as some would gain and others lose if relative prices changed without any general inflation. Inflation, however, gets a bad name because losers often blame inflation for their misfortune while gainers rarely credit inflation for their good luck. Alas, nobody loves inflation.

These three kinds of misconceptions may go a long way toward explaining why respondents to public-opinion polls consistently list inflation as a major national issue, and why higher inflation rates depress consumers.

Inflation does not systematically erode the purchasing power of wages. Nor does it lead to "unfair" prices. Nor is it usually to blame when some goods become more expensive relative to others.

But not all the costs of inflation are mythical. Let us now turn to some of the real costs.

Inflation as a Redistributor of Income and Wealth

We have just seen that the *average* person is neither helped nor harmed by inflation. But almost no one is exactly average! Some people gain from inflation and others lose. It is hard to say anything more systematic than this about the effects of inflation on particular prices and wages.

But inflation does have systematic effects on the distribution of income and wealth. Senior citizens trying to scrape by on pensions or other fixed incomes suffer badly from inflation. Since they earn no wages, it is little solace to them that wages are keeping pace with prices. Their private pension incomes tend not to.[5]

This example actually illustrates a much more general problem. We can think of pensioners as people who "lend" money to an organization (the pension fund) when they are young in order to be "paid back" with interest when they are old. Because of the rise in the price level during the intervening years, the unfortunate pensioners get paid back in less valuable dollars than those they originally loaned. In general:

Those who lend money are usually victimized by rising inflation.

While lenders lose heavily, borrowers do quite well. For example, home-owners who borrowed money from banks in the form of mortgages back in the 1950s, when interest rates were 3 or 4 percent, gained enormously from the surprisingly virulent inflation of the late 1960s and 1970s. They paid back dollars of much lower value than those that they borrowed. And the same is true of other borrowers.

---

[5] This is *not* true, however, for Canada's Old Age Security plan. These benefits are financed out of tax revenues rather than directly through accumulated savings, and benefit levels are generally increased to compensate recipients for changes in the price level.

Borrowers usually gain from rising inflation.

Since the redistribution caused by inflation generally benefits borrowers at the expense of lenders, and since both lenders and borrowers can be found at every income level, we must conclude that:

Inflation does not always steal from the rich to aid the poor, nor does it always do the reverse.

Why, then, is the redistribution caused by inflation so widely condemned? Because its victims are selected capriciously. Nobody legislates this redistribution. Nobody enters into it voluntarily. The gainers do not earn their spoils, and the losers do not deserve their fate. Moreover, there have been particular classes of people whom inflation has systematically robbed of purchasing power year after year—old-age pensioners, people who have saved money and "loaned" it to banks, and workers on long-term contracts or those whose wages and salaries do not adjust easily for some other reason. Even if people "on the average" suffer no damage from inflation, that offers little consolation to those who are hurt by it persistently and systematically. This is the fundamental indictment of inflation.

Inflation redistributes income in an arbitrary way that distorts society's distribution of income. The actual income distribution should reflect the interplay of the operation of free markets and the deliberate efforts of government to alter the distribution. Inflation interferes with and distorts this process.

Real versus Nominal Interest Rates

But wait. Must inflation always rob lenders to bestow gifts upon borrowers? If both parties see inflation coming, won't lenders demand that borrowers pay a higher interest rate as compensation for the coming inflation? Indeed they will. For this reason, economists draw a conceptual distinction between inflation that is *expected* and inflation that comes as a *surprise*.

What happens when inflation is fully expected by both parties? Suppose Diamond Jim wants to borrow $1000 from Scrooge, and both agree that, in the absence of inflation, which erodes the value of money, a fair rate of interest would be 4 percent on a one-year loan. This means that Diamond Jim would pay back $1040 at the end of the year for the privilege of having $1000 now.

If both expect prices to increase by 6 percent, Scrooge may reason as follows: "If Diamond Jim pays me back $1040 a year from today, that money will buy less than what $1000 buys today. Thus I'll really be *paying him* to borrow from me! I'm no philanthropist. Why don't I charge him 10 percent instead? Then he'll pay back $1100 at the end of the year. With prices 6 percent higher, this will buy roughly what $1040 is worth today. So I'll get the same 4 percent increase in purchasing power that we would have agreed on in the absence of inflation, and won't be any worse off. That's the least I'll accept."

Diamond Jim may follow a similar chain of logic. "With no inflation, I was willing to pay $1040 a year from now for the privilege of having $1000 today, and Scrooge was willing to lend it. He'd be crazy to do the same with a 6 percent inflation. He'll want to charge me more. How much should I pay? If I offer to him $1100 a year from now, that will have roughly the same purchasing power as $1040 today, so I won't be any worse off. That's the most I'll pay."

This kind of thinking will lead Scrooge and Diamond Jim to write a contract with a 10 percent interest rate—4 percent as the normal lending charge (Scrooge being compensated for temporarily parting with his money), and 6 percent as compensation for the expected inflation. Then, if the expected 6 percent inflation actually materializes, neither party will have been made better or worse off than was expected at the time the contract was signed.[6]

This example illustrates a very general principle. The 4 percent increase in purchasing power that Diamond Jim agrees to hand over to Scrooge is called the **real rate of interest**. And the 10 percent contractual interest charge that Diamond Jim and Scrooge write into the loan agreement is called the **nominal rate of interest**. The nominal rate of interest is arrived at by adding the **expected rate of inflation** to the real rate of interest. Expected inflation is added to compensate the lender for the loss in purchasing power that he is expected to suffer as a result of inflation. Thus:

Inflation that is accurately predicted need not redistribute income between borrowers and lenders. If the *expected* rate of inflation that is embodied in the nominal interest rate closely approximates the *actual* rate of inflation, no one gains and no one loses. However, to the extent that expectations prove incorrect, inflation will still redistribute income.

It need hardly be pointed out that errors in predicting the rate of inflation are the norm, not the exception. Published forecasts bear witness to the fact that economists have great difficulty in predicting the rate of inflation. The task is no easier for businesses, consumers, and banks. This is one reason inflation is so widely condemned as unfair and undesirable. It sets up a guessing game that no one likes.

The **real rate of interest** is the percentage increase in purchasing power that the borrower pays to the lender for the privilege of borrowing. It indicates the increased ability to purchase goods and services that the lender earns.

The **nominal rate of interest** is the percentage by which the money the borrower pays back exceeds the money that he borrowed, making no adjustment for any fall in the purchasing power of money that results from inflation.

Inflation and the Tax System

So inflation imposes costs on society because it is hard to predict. But other costs, perhaps even more serious ones, arise from high inflation even when it is predicted accurately. These costs stem from the fact that our taxation system was designed for an inflation-free economy and may malfunction when inflation is high.

Our tax law does not recognize the distinction between nominal and real interest rates. The law simply taxes nominal interest regardless of how much real interest it represents. As a result, strange things happen when there is high inflation. Our example of Scrooge's loan to Diamond Jim will illustrate the problem.

The top line of Table 4–4 shows how taxation affects the loan agreement where there is no inflation and the nominal and real interest rates are the same, at 4 percent. Scrooge earns $40 in nominal interest income (column 3). Since there is no inflation, this also represents $40 in real interest income (column 5). If Scrooge pays 50 percent of his income in taxes, his tax bill rises by $20 (column 6), leaving him with $20 after

[6]EXERCISE: Who gains and who loses if the inflation turns out to be only 4 percent instead of the 6 percent that Scrooge and Diamond Jim expected? What if the inflation rate is 8 percent?

TABLE 4–4
Inflation and the Taxation of Interest Income

(1)	(2)	(3)	(4)	(5)	(6)	(7)	(8)	(9)
	NOMINAL		LOSS OF PURCHASING	REAL				EFFECTIVE RATE OF
INFLATION RATE (percent)	INTEREST RATE (percent)	INTEREST INCOME (dollars)	POWER DUE TO INFLATION (dollars)	INTEREST INCOME (dollars)	TAXES PAID (dollars)	REAL INCOME AFTER TAX	(as a percentage of $1000 loan)	TAXATION (percent)
						(dollars)		
0	4	40	0	40	20	20	2	50
6	10	100	60	40	50	–10	–1	125

tax (column 7). This $20 amounts to 2 percent of the $1000 originally loaned (column 8). Because his $20 tax payment is half of his $40 in real interest income, Scrooge's effective tax rate is 50 percent (column 9), just as Parliament intended.

Now let's consider the same transaction when the inflation rate is 6 percent and Scrooge and Diamond Jim settle on a 10 percent nominal interest rate. Scrooge collects $100 in interest (column 3). But, with 6 percent inflation, the purchasing power of the $1000 he lends declines by $60 (column 4). Thus his real interest income is again $40 (column 5). However, the tax collector taxes the $100 nominal interest income, not the $40 real interest income, so Scrooge must pay $50 (50 percent of $100) in taxes (column 6). As we can see in column 7, his after-tax real income on the loan is –$10. Or, putting the same point a different way, the effective real after-tax interest rate he earns is –1 percent! As column 9 shows, the effective tax rate on Scrooge's real interest income is 125 percent, far larger than the 50 percent rate intended by Parliament.

So a tax system that works well at zero inflation misfires at 6 percent inflation because it taxes nominal, rather than real, interest. This little example illustrates a general, and very serious, problem:

Because it fails to recognize the distinction between nominal and real interest rate, our tax system levies high and presumably unintended tax rates on interest income when there is high inflation. And similar problems arise in the taxation of dividends, corporate profits, and other items.[7] Many economists feel that these high tax rates discourage saving, lending, and investing, and that high inflation therefore retards economic growth. Thus, inflation has major costs that are not purely redistributive.

These problems have eased up slightly in recent years, partly because inflation has receded somewhat, and partly because personal income-tax rates were lowered in 1987. But the fundamental reform that would eliminate these problems is *comprehensive* indexation of the tax system (indexation is explained on the next page in reference to the personal income-tax system), and such a reform is not being considered.

Why do inappropriate tax laws stay on the books so long? One reason is a general lack of understanding of the difference between real and nominal interest rates. People seem not to understand that it is normally the *real* rate of interest that matters in an economic transaction because only that rate reveals how much borrowers pay (and lenders receive) *in terms of the goods and services which that money can buy.* They focus on the high nominal rates caused by inflation, even if these rates correspond to very low real interest rates.

Here is an example from a different area—that of monetary policy—that may help you appreciate how widespread and important this interest-rate illusion is. Throughout the first half of the 1970s, Western governments increased their countries' money supplies at record rates because they thought credit had to be made more available to lower the apparent high borrowing costs. But it was only nominal, not real, interest rates that were high. Real interest rates had never been lower. The extra money simply worsened the inflation and widened the gap between the real and nominal interest rates.

---

[7] A particularly serious problem arises in the taxation of capital gains. Capital gains are the difference between the price at which one sells an asset and the price at which one bought it. In Canada, some capital gains are tax-exempt but others are taxed without any adjustment for changes in their purchasing power resulting from inflation. An example will bring out the point. Between 1971 and 1980 the price level doubled, approximately. Consider a piece of land that was purchased for $50,000 in 1971 and sold for $75,000 in 1980. The owner lost purchasing power in the transaction because $75,000 in 1980 dollars purchased far less than $50,000 in 1971 dollars. (Indeed, the selling price was only $37,500 in 1971 dollars.) Yet, since the tax authorities do not correct for inflation, the owner was forced to pay some tax on the nominal capital gain of $25,000, as though there had been a profit rather than a loss.

Some reforms of the tax system have occurred. Since 1975, the authorities have properly separated the real and nominal interest rates in all discussions of their monetary policies. Also, in 1973, the federal government indexed the major provisions in the personal income-tax system.

Without indexing, inflation generates increasingly larger amounts of government revenue without any change in tax rates. One reason for the increase in revenue is that the deductions and credits allowed on the tax form decline as a proportion of income in an inflationary situation, so that a larger proportion of income is subject to tax. The other reason for the unintended increase in revenues is that individuals are pushed into successively higher income-tax brackets as nominal incomes rise because of inflation. Thus, even if wages rise as rapidly as prices, people's real *after-tax* incomes fall.

The case for indexing rests generally on two arguments. One argument is that, in the absence of indexing, a greater share of national income flows automatically to the government with inflation, and it is felt by many that decisions about the division of resources between the public and private sectors should be made explicitly by legislation rather than by the amount of inflation in the economy. The second argument is that indexing improves the equity or fairness of the personal income tax. Without indexing, inflation erodes the value of the allowed income-tax credits.

The Canadian indexing system works as follows: The limits on each income bracket and the value of the tax credits are multiplied annually by a factor that takes account of the amount of inflation during the previous year. An illustration may make this more clear. The basic income exemption for a taxpayer was $1600 and the tax rate was 19 percent for taxable income between $1000 and $2000 in Canada in 1973. If prices had risen 10 percent in 1973, the value of the exemption would have increased to $1760, and taxable income between $1100 and $2200 would have been taxed at a rate of 19 percent in 1974. (The actual inflation adjustment factor for 1974 was 6.6 percent.) There have been changes in the indexation formula in recent years. The government limited the inflation-adjustment factor in the tax system to 6 and 5 percent respectively in 1983 and 1984. Since 1986, the indexation factor has been limited to the excess of the previous year's inflation over 3 percent. One reason the government has cut back the extent of indexation is because it is trying to limit its very large budget deficit.

Other Costs of Inflation

Another cost of inflation is that rapidly changing prices make it risky to enter into long-term contracts. In an extremely severe inflation, the "long term" may be only a few days. But even moderate inflation can have remarkable effects on long-term loans. Suppose a corporation wants to borrow $1 million to finance the purchase of some new equipment and needs the loan for twenty years. If the inflation rate averages 4 percent over this period, the $1 million it repays at the end of twenty years will be worth only $456,387 in today's purchasing power. If inflation averages 8 percent instead, it will be worth $214,548. Lending or borrowing for this long a period is obviously a big gamble. With the stakes this high, neither lenders nor borrowers may want to get involved in long-term contracts. But without long-term loans, business investment becomes impossible. The economy stagnates.

The preceding litany of costs of inflation alerts us to one very important fact: *predictable inflation is far less burdensome than is unpredictable inflation.* When will inflation be most predictable? When it proceeds year after year at more or less the same rate. Thus the *variability of the inflation rate* is a crucial factor. Inflation of 4 percent a year for three consecutive years will exact far lower social costs than inflation that is 2 percent in the first year, zero in the second, and 10 percent in the third. In general:

Steady inflation is much more predictable than variable inflation and therefore has much smaller social and economic costs.

But the *average level of the inflation rate* is also important. Partly because of the incomplete indexing provisions in taxes and the interest-rate illusions mentioned above, a steady inflation of 6 percent a year is more damaging than a steady inflation of 4 percent a year.

Economists distinguish between **creeping inflation** and **galloping inflation** partly on their average level and partly on their variability. Under creeping inflation, prices rise for a long time at a moderate and fairly steady rate. Postwar Sweden provides a good example. During the thirteen-year period from 1954 to 1967, prices climbed a total of 64 percent (compared with only 33 percent in Canada), for an average annual inflation rate of 3.9 percent. And the pace of inflation was remarkably steady, rarely dropping below 2.5 percent or rising above 5 percent.

Galloping inflation refers to inflation that proceeds at an exceptionally high rate, perhaps for only a relatively brief period. Galloping inflation is generally characterized by accelerating rates of inflation so that the rate of inflation is higher this month than it was last month.

Germany after World War I suffered through one of the more severe inflations in history. Wholesale prices increased over 140 percent in 1921 and a colossal 4100 percent during 1922. At this point, what had been very serious galloping inflation simply got out of control. Between December 1922 and November 1923, when a hard-nosed reform finally broke the inflationary spiral, wholesale prices in Germany increased by almost 100 million percent! But even this experience was dwarfed by the great Hungarian inflation of 1945–46, the greatest inflation of them all. For a period of one year, the rate of inflation averaged about 20,000 percent *per month.* And in the final month, the price level skyrocketed 42 quadrillion percent!

While the distinction between creeping and galloping inflation is a quantitative one, we refrained from putting any specific numbers into the definitions. This is because different societies at different points in time have very different conceptions about what rate constitutes creeping inflation and what rate constitutes galloping inflation. For example, in Canada today, annual rates of inflation in the 3 to 4 percent range are generally considered to be "creeping," while rates in the 25 to 30 percent range would surely be construed as "galloping." In most Latin American countries, however, inflation consistently in the 25 to 30 percent range is viewed as "creeping." And in the Canada of the 1950s, a 7 percent annual inflation might have been branded "galloping."

The Costs of Creeping versus Galloping Inflation

If you review the costs of inflation that have been discussed in this chapter, you will see why the distinction between creeping and galloping inflation is so fundamental. Many economists feel we can live reasonably well, indeed can prosper, in an environment of creeping inflation. No one feels we can survive very well under galloping inflation.

Creeping inflation refers to inflation that proceeds for a long time at a moderate and fairly steady pace.

Galloping inflation refers to inflation that proceeds at an exceptionally high rate, perhaps for only a relatively brief period.

These children in Germany during the hyperinflation of the 1920s are building a pyramid with cash, worth no more than the sand or sticks used by children elsewhere.

Under creeping inflation, the rate at which prices rise is relatively easy to predict and to take into account in setting interest rates. Under galloping inflation, where prices are rising at ever-increasing rates, this is very difficult, and perhaps impossible, to accomplish. The potential redistributions become monumental, and as a result, lending and borrowing may cease entirely.

Any inflation makes it difficult to write long-term contracts. With creeping inflation, the "long term" may be twenty years, or ten years, or five years. But with galloping inflation, the "long term" may be measured in weeks or even hours. Railway fares may go up while you are in the middle of your journey. When it is impossible to enter into contracts of any duration longer than a few minutes, economic activity becomes paralyzed. We conclude:

The horrors of galloping inflation either are absent in creeping inflation or are present in such muted forms that they can scarcely be considered horrors. And there is no evidence to support the proposition that creeping inflation must turn into galloping inflation.

Summary

1. Microeconomics studies the decisions of individuals and firms, how these decisions interact, and how they influence the allocation of society's resources and the distribution of income. Macroeconomics looks at the behaviour of entire economies and studies the pressing social problems of inflation and unemployment.

2. While their respective subject matters differ greatly, the basic tools of microeconomics and macroeconomics are virtually identical. Both rely on the supply and demand analysis introduced in Chapter 3.

3. Gross domestic product (GDP) is obtained by adding up the money values of all final goods and services produced within the country in a given year. It is meant to be a measure of the *production* of the economy, not of the increase in its *well-being*. For example, the GDP places no value on housework or other do-it-yourself activities or on leisure time. On the other hand, even commodities that might be considered as "bads" rather than "goods" are counted in the GDP (for example, activities that harm the environment).

4. One major cause of inflation is that aggregate demand may grow more quickly than aggregate supply. In such a case, a government policy that reduces aggregate demand may be able to check the inflation. Similarly, recessions often occur because aggregate demand grows too slowly. In this case, a government policy that stimulates demand may be an effective way to fight the recession.

5. Unemployment exacts heavy financial and psychological costs from those who are its victims, costs that are borne quite unevenly by different groups in the population. Unemployment is measured by a government survey. Some critics claim that the survey methods understate the unemployment problem, while others contend that the methods overstate the problem.

6. Frictional unemployment arises when people are between jobs for normal reasons. Structural unemployment arises from shifts in the pattern of demand or from technological change that results in certain skills becoming obsolete. Cyclical unemployment is the portion of unemployment that rises in recessions and falls when the economy booms.

7. Unemployment insurance replaces about 60 percent of the lost income of unemployed workers who are insured. But not all the unemployed are covered by insurance, and no insurance program can bring back the lost output that could have been produced had these people been working.

8. People have many misconceptions about inflation. For example, many people believe that inflation systematically erodes real wages, are appalled by rising prices even when wages are rising just as fast, and blame inflation for any unfavourable changes in relative prices. All of these are myths.

9. Other costs of inflation are real, however. For example, inflation often redistributes income from lenders to borrowers. This redistribution can be eliminated by adding the expected rate of inflation to the interest rate, but expectations often prove to be quite inaccurate.

10. The real rate of interest is the nominal rate of interest minus the expected rate of inflation. Since the real rate of interest indicates the command over real resources that the borrower surrenders to the lender, it is of primary economic importance.

11. Yet public attention is often riveted on nominal rates of interest, and this confusion can lead to costly policy mistakes when high inflation converts high nominal interest rates into very low real interest rates. This is one of the 12 **Ideas for Beyond the Final Exam**.

12. Despite indexing of the basic personal income-tax system in 1973, our tax system levies very heavy taxes on interest income when inflation is high, since nominal, not real, interest income is taxed.

13. Creeping inflation, which proceeds at moderate and

fairly predictable rates year after year, carries far lower social costs than galloping inflation, which proceeds at high and variable rates. The notion that creeping infla-tion inevitably leads to galloping inflation is a myth with no foundation in economic theory and no basis in historical fact.

Concepts for Review

Aggregation
Aggregate demand and
    aggregate supply curves
Inflation
Deflation
Recession
Gross domestic product (GDP)
Nominal versus real GDP
Final goods and services
Intermediate goods

Stagflation
Stabilization policy
Unemployment rate
Labour force
Discouraged workers
Frictional unemployment
Structural unemployment
Cyclical unemployment
Full employment
Unemployment insurance

Potential GDP
Purchasing power
Real wages
Relative prices
Real rate of interest
Nominal rate of interest
Expected rate of inflation
Indexed taxes

Questions for Discussion

1. Try asking a friend who has not studied economics in which year he or she thinks prices were higher: 1928 or 1940? (You can find the correct answer by referring to Figure 4–4.) Most people your age think that prices have always risen. Why do you think they have this opinion?

2. Which of the following transactions are included in the gross domestic product, and by how much does each raise GDP?
   a. Smith pays a carpenter $6000 to build a garage.
   b. Smith purchases $1000 worth of lumber and materials and builds himself a garage, which is worth $6000.
   c. Smith goes to the woods, cuts down a tree, and uses the wood to build himself a garage that is worth $6000.
   d. The Jones family sells its old house to the Reynolds family for $100,000. The Joneses then buy a newly constructed house from a builder for $150,000.
   e. Your school purchases a used computer from another institution, paying $400,000.
   f. Your school purchases a new computer from IBM, paying $2 million.
   g. You lose $200 in a Las Vegas casino.
   h. You lose $200 in the stock market.
   i. You sell a used economics textbook to your bookstore for $15.
   j. You buy a used economics textbook from your bookstore for $20.

3. Give some reasons why the gross domestic product is not a suitable measure of the well-being of a nation. (Have you noticed newspaper accounts that seem to use GDP for this purpose?)

4. "Since unemployed workers receive unemployment benefits and other benefits that make up for most of their lost wages, unemployment is no longer a social problem." Comment.

5. Do you think that Statistics Canada overestimates or underestimates the number of people that are unemployed? Why?

6. Why is it so difficult to define "full employment"? What unemployment rate should the government be shooting for today?

7. Show why each of the following complaints is based on a misunderstanding about inflation:
   a. "Inflation must be stopped because it robs workers of their purchasing power."
   b. "Inflation is a terrible social disease. It leads to unconscionably high prices for basic necessities."
   c. "Inflation makes it impossible for working people to afford many of the things they were hoping to buy."
   d. "Inflation must be stopped today, for if we do not stop it, it will surely accelerate to ruinously high rates and lead to disaster."

8. What is the after-tax *real interest rate* on a bond paying 13 percent nominal interest per year, if the tax rate is 20 percent and the rate of inflation is:
   a. zero
   b. 2 percent
   c. 5 percent
   d. 12 percent

9. Suppose you agree to lend money to your friend, on the day you both enter university, at what you both expect to be a zero *real* rate of interest. Payment is to be made at graduation, with interest at a fixed *nominal* rate. If inflation proves to be *lower* during your four years in university than what you both had expected, who will gain and who will lose?

10. Add a third line to Table 4–4 showing what would happen if the inflation rate went to 12 percent and the real interest rate remained 4 percent.

Appendix A
National Income Accounting

Defining GDP: Exceptions to the Rules

Earlier in this chapter we noted that

Gross domestic product (GDP) is the sum of the money values of all final goods and services produced within an economy during a specified period of time, usually one year.

However, this definition of GDP has certain exceptions that we have not yet explained.

First, the treatment of government output involves a minor departure from the principle of using market prices. Outputs of private industries are sold on markets, so their prices are observed. But "outputs" of government offices are not sold; indeed, it is sometimes even difficult to define what those outputs are. Lacking prices for outputs, national income accountants fall back on the only prices they have: prices for the inputs from which the outputs are produced. Thus:

Government outputs are valued at the cost of the inputs needed to produce them.

This means, for example, that if a clerk at the Ministry of Transportation earns $8 an hour and spends half an hour torturing you with explanations of why you cannot get a driver's licence, that particular government "service" is considered as being worth $4 and will increase GDP by that amount.

Second, some goods that are not actually sold on markets during the year are nonetheless counted in that year's GDP. These are the goods that are produced during the year but not sold; that is, goods that firms stockpile as *inventories*. Goods that are added to inventories count in the GDP even though they do not pass through markets.

National income statisticians treat inventories as if they were "bought" by the firms that produced them, even though this "purchase" never takes place.

Finally, the treatment of investment goods runs slightly counter to the rule that only final goods are to be counted. In a broad sense, factories, generators, machine tools, and the like might be considered as intermediate goods. After all, their owners want them only for use in producing other goods, not for any innate value that they possess. But this would present

a real problem, for factories and machines normally are never sold to consumers. So when would we count them in GDP? National income statisticians avoid this problem by defining investment goods as final products demanded by the firms that buy them.

Now that we have a more complete definition of just what the GDP is, let us turn to the problem of actually measuring it. National income accountants have devised three ways to perform this task, and we consider each of them in turn.

GDP as the Sum of Final Goods and Services

The first way to measure GDP seems to be the most natural; we simply add up the final demands of all consumers, business firms, the government, and foreigners. Using the symbols C (consumer spending by households), I (investment spending by firms), G (government spending on new goods and services), X (exports—spending by foreigners on goods that we produce), and IM (imports—spending by Canadians on goods produced elsewhere),[8] we have:

$$GDP = C + I + G + X - IM.$$

The I that appears in the actual Canadian national accounts is called **gross private domestic investment**. The word "gross" will be explained presently. "Private" indicates that government investment is considered part of G, and "domestic" just means that machinery sold by Canadian firms to foreign companies is included in exports, rather than in I. Gross private domestic investment in Canada has three components: business investment in plant and equipment, residential construction (home building),[9] and inventory investment. We repeat again that *only* these three things are **investment** in national income accounting terminology.

As defined in the national income accounts, **investment** includes only newly produced capital goods, such as machinery, factories, and new homes. It does not include exchanges of existing assets.

---

[8] These components are explained in greater detail in Chapter 5.
[9] Thus purchases of new homes are considered part of I rather than part of C.

In common parlance, all sorts of activities that are not part of the GDP are often called "investment." People are said to "invest" in the stock market when they purchase shares. Or wealthy individuals "invest" in works of art. But since transactions like these merely exchange one type of asset (money) for another (stock or art works), they are not included in the GDP.

The symbol *G*, for government purchases, represents the *volume of current goods and services purchased by all levels of government*. Thus, anything the government pays to its employees is counted in *G*, as are its purchases of paper, pencils, airplanes, statues, word processors, and so forth.

Few citizens realize that *most of what the federal government spends its money on is not for purchases of goods and services*. Instead, it is on **transfer payments**—literally, money given away—either to individuals or to other levels of government.

The importance of the conceptual distinction lies in the fact that *G* represents the part of the national product that government uses up for its own purposes —to pay for armies, bureaucrats, paper, and ink— whereas transfer payments merely represent shuffling of purchasing power from one group of citizens to another group. Except for the administrators needed to run the programs, real economic resources are not used up in this process.

In adding up the nation's total output as the sum of $C + I + G + X - IM$, we are summing the shares of GDP that are used up by consumers, investors, governments, and foreigners, respectively. Since transfer payments merely give someone the capability to spend on *C*, it is logical to exclude them from our definition of *G*, including in *C* only the portion of these transfer payments that is spent. If we included them in *G*, the same spending would get counted twice: once in *G* and then again in *C*.

Table 4–5 shows the GDP for 1989 computed as the sum of $C + I + G + X - IM$.

GDP as the Sum of All Factor Payments

There is another way to count up the national product—that is, *by adding up all the incomes earned in the economy*. Let's see how this method handles some typical transactions. Suppose Canadian General Electric builds a generator and sells it to Ontario Hydro for $1 million. The first method of calculating GDP simply counts the $1 million as part of *I*. The second method asks: What incomes resulted from the production of this generator? The answer might be something like this:

Wages of C.G.E. employees	$400,000
Interest to bondholders	$50,000
Rentals of buildings	$50,000
Profits of C.G.E. shareholders	$100,000

The total is $600,000. The remaining $400,000 is accounted for by inputs that C.G.E. purchased from other companies: steel, circuitry, tubing, and so on.

But if we traced this $400,000 back farther, we would find that it is accounted for by the wages, interest, and rentals paid by these other companies, *plus* their profits, *plus* their purchases from other firms. In fact, for *every* firm in the economy, there is an accounting identity that says:

$$\text{Revenues from sales} = \begin{cases} \text{Wages paid} + \\ \text{Interest paid} + \\ \text{Rentals paid} + \\ \text{Profits earned} + \\ \text{Purchases from} \\ \quad \text{other firms.} \end{cases}$$

Why must this always be true? Because profits are the balancing item; they are what is *left over* after the firm has made all its other payments. In fact, this accounting identity is really just the definition of profits: sales revenue less all costs of production.

Now apply this accounting identity to *all the firms in the economy*. Total purchases from other firms are precisely what we call *intermediate goods*. What, then, do we get if we subtract these intermediate transactions from both sides of the equation?

TABLE 4–5
Gross Domestic Product in 1989 as the Sum of Final Demands

		AMOUNT (billions of dollars)
Personal consumption expenditures (*C*)		381.1
Gross private domestic investment (*I*)		128.1
Government purchase of goods and services (*G*)		141.7
Net exports (*X* – *IM*)		-2.4
exports (*X*)	159.4	
imports (*IM*)	161.8	
Gross domestic product (*Y*)		648.5

SOURCE: Statistics Canada

$$\left.\begin{array}{c}\text{Revenues from sales}\\\text{minus}\\\text{Purchases from}\\\text{other firms}\end{array}\right\} = \left\{\begin{array}{l}\text{Wages paid +}\\\text{Interest paid +}\\\text{Rentals paid +}\\\text{Profits earned.}\end{array}\right.$$

On the right-hand side, we have the sum of all factor incomes: payments to labour, land, and capital. On the left-hand side, we have total sales minus sales of intermediate goods. This means that we have only sales of *final* goods, which is precisely our definition of GDP. Thus, the accounting identity for the entire economy can be rewritten as:

$$\text{GDP} = \text{Wages} + \text{Interest} + \text{Rents} + \text{Profits},$$

and this gives national income accountants another way to measure the GDP.

Table 4–6 shows 1989's GDP measured by the sum of all incomes. A few details have been omitted in our discussion. The sum of wages, interest, rents, and profits actually adds up to only $506.1 billion (whereas GDP was $648.5 billion). We call this sum the **net domestic income at factor cost** because it is the sum of all factor payments. But the actual selling prices of goods include another category of income that we have

ignored so far: sales taxes, excise taxes, and the like. National income statisticians call these *indirect business taxes*, and when we add these into national income we obtain the **net domestic product**.

The only difference between this and the GDP is **depreciation** of the nation's capital stock.

Depreciation is the value of the portion of the nation's capital equipment that is used up within the year. It tells us how much output is needed just to keep the economy's capital stock intact.

The difference between "gross" and "net" simply refers to whether depreciation is included or excluded. We add depreciation to get GDP. Thus, GDP is a measure of all final output taking no account of the capital used up in the process (and therefore in need of replacement).

In Table 4–6 you can hardly help noticing the preponderant share of employee compensation in total national income—70 percent. Labour is by far the most important factor of production. Corporate profits before tax account for 12 percent of national income (9 percent of GDP), perhaps less than the public thinks. If, by some magic stroke, we could eliminate all corporate profits without upsetting the performance of the economy, the average worker would get a raise of about 17 percent!

GDP as the Sum of Values Added

It may strike you as strange that national income accountants include only *final* goods and services in GDP. Aren't *intermediate* goods part of the nation's product? They are, of course. The problem is that, if all intermediate goods were included in GDP, we would wind up double- and triple-counting things and therefore getting an exaggerated impression of the amount of economic activity that is actually going on.

To explain why, and to show how national income accountants cope with this difficulty, we must introduce a new concept called **value-added**.

The **value added** by a firm is its revenue from selling a product minus the amounts paid for goods and services purchased from other firms.

The intuitive sense of the concept is clear: If a firm buys some inputs from other firms, does something to them, and sells the resulting product for a price higher than it paid for the inputs, we say that the firm has "added value" to the product. If we sum up the values added in this way by all the firms in the economy, we must get the total value of all final products. Thus:

TABLE 4–6
Gross Domestic Product in 1989 as the Sum of Incomes

	AMOUNT (billions of dollars)
Wages, salaries, and supplementary labour income	356.2
plus	
Corporation profits before profits taxes	60.5
plus	
Interest and miscellaneous investment income	52.1
plus	
Rents and net income of farmers and unincorporated business	37.3
equals	
Net domestic income at factor cost	506.1
plus	
Indirect business taxes (less subsidies) and miscellaneous items	72.3
equals	
Net domestic product	578.4
plus	
Depreciation	70.1
equals	
Gross domestic product	648.5

SOURCE: Statistics Canada

GDP can be measured as the sum of the values added by all firms.

To verify that this is so, look back at the accounting identity at the top of page 105. The left-hand side of this equation, sales revenue minus purchases from other firms, is precisely the firm's value-added. Thus:

Value-added = Wages + Interest + Rents + Profits.

Since the second method we gave for measuring GDP is to add up wages, interest, rents, and profits, we see that the value-added approach must also yield the same answer.

The value-added concept is particularly useful in avoiding double-counting. Often it is hard to distinguish intermediate goods from final goods. Paint bought by a painter, for example, is an intermediate good. But paint bought by a do-it-yourselfer is a final good. What happens, then, if the professional painter has some paint left over and uses it to refurbish his own garage? The intermediate good becomes a final good. You can see that the line between intermediate goods and final goods is a fuzzy one in practice.

If we measure GDP by the sum of values added, however, it is not necessary to make such subtle distinctions. In this method, *every* purchase of a new good or service counts, but we do not count the entire selling price, only the part that represents value added.

To illustrate this idea, consider the data in Table 4–7 and how they would affect GDP as the sum of final products. Our example begins when a farmer who grows soybeans sells them to a mill for $3 a bushel. This transaction does *not* count in the GDP, because the miller does not purchase the soybeans for his own use. The miller then grinds up the soybeans and sells the resulting bag of soy meal to a factory that produces soy sauce. The miller receives $4, but GDP still has not increased because the ground beans are also an intermediate product. Next, the factory turns the beans into soy sauce, which it sells to your favourite Chinese restaurant for $8. Still no effect on GDP. But then the big moment arrives: The restaurant sells the sauce to you and other customers as a part of your meals, and you eat it. At this point, the $10 worth of soy sauce becomes a final product and is included in the GDP. Notice that if we had also counted the three intermediate transactions (farmer to miller, miller to factory, factory to restaurant), we would have come up with $25—two and one-half times too much.

Why is it too much? The reason is straightforward. Neither the miller nor the factory owner nor the restaurateur values the product we have been considering *for its own sake*. Only the customers who eat the final product (the soy sauce) have had an increase in their material well-being. So only this last transaction counts in the GDP. However, as we shall now see, value-added calculations enable us to come up with the right answer ($10) by counting only *part* of each transaction. The basic idea is to count at each step only the contribution to the value of the ultimate final product that is made at that step, excluding the values of items produced at earlier steps.

Ignoring the minor items (such as fertilizer) that the farmer purchases from others, the entire $3 selling price of the bushel of soybeans is new output produced by the farmer; that is, the whole $3 is value-added. The miller then grinds the beans and sells them for $4. He has added $4 – $3 = $1 to the value of the beans. When the factory turns this soy meal into soy sauce and sells it for $8, it has added $8 – $4 = $4 more in value. And finally, when the restaurant sells it to hungry customers for $10, a further $2 of value is added.

The right-hand column of Table 4–7 shows this chain of creation of value-added. We see that the value-added by all four firms totals $10, which is exactly the same as the restaurant's selling price. This is as it must be, for only the restaurant sells the soybeans as a final product.

TABLE 4–7
An Illustration of Final and Intermediate Products and Value-Added

ITEM	SELLER	BUYER	PRICE (dollars)	VALUE-ADDED (dollars)
Bushel of soybeans	Farmer	Miller	3	3
Bag of soy meal	Miller	Factory	4	1
Bottle of soy sauce	Factory	Restaurant	8	4
Bottle of soy sauce used as seasoning	Restaurant	Consumers	10	2
		Totals:	25	10

Addendum: Contribution to GDP
Final products......................$10
Sum of values added...............$10

Alternative Measures of the Income of the Nation

Economists use the term *national income* in two different ways. The most common usage is as a general term indicating the size of the income of the nation as a whole, without being specific about exactly how this income is to be measured. This is the sense in which the term "national income" is used in this book. The second use of the term refers to particular concepts in national income accounting, which we now consider.

The first and most obvious candidate for a particular measure of national income is GNP. GNP measures the total income created by the employment of all Canadian-owned factors of production, while GDP measures the total amount of employment-creating production activity in the nation. To calculate GNP, we must add to GDP the investment income of Canadians that is derived from their ownership of factors that are employed in other countries. Also, we must subtract the investment income earned by foreigners from the employment of their capital equipment in Canada. The amount of foreign-owned capital equipment employed in Canada is greater than the amount of Canadian-owned capital employed else-

where. Thus, Canada's national income is less than its national production. (In 1989, GNP was $626.2 billion, while GDP was $648.5 billion.)

As a measure of national income, GNP has several drawbacks. First, it includes some output that represents income to no one—output that simply replaces worn-out machinery and buildings (depreciation). When we deduct this depreciation, we obtain net national product (NNP), as shown in Figure 4–8.

Second, because of sales taxes and related items (indirect business taxes), part of the price paid for each good and service does not represent the income of any individual. When we deduct these indirect business taxes from NNP, we arrive at net national income at factor cost (refer again to Figure 4–8).

There are two other measures of income. *Personal income* is meant to be a better measure of the income that actually accrues to individuals. It is obtained from national income by *subtracting* corporate profits taxes, retained earnings, and payroll taxes (because these items are never received by individuals) and then *adding in* transfer payments to individuals (because these sources of income are not part of the wages, interest, rents, or profits that constitute the national income). As Figure 4–8 suggests, this adding

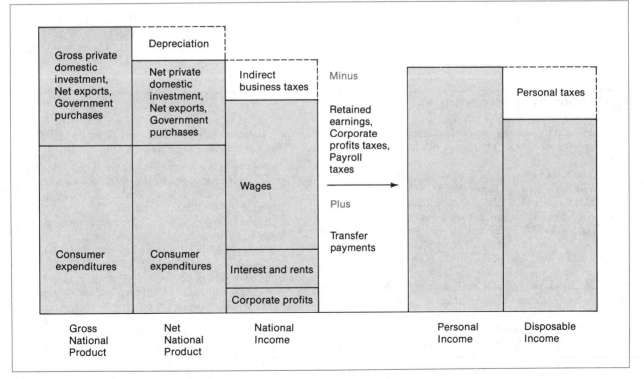

FIGURE 4–8

Alternative Measures of the Income of the Nation

This bar chart indicates the relationships among five alternative measures of the total income of the nation, starting with the largest and most comprehensive measure (GNP) and ranging down to the measure that most closely approximates the spendable income of consumers (disposable income). The data used were for 1989.

and subtracting normally results in a number that is rather close to national income. Finally, if we subtract personal income taxes from personal income, we obtain *disposable income*.

Among all the concepts of the nation's income depicted in Figure 4–8, only two are used frequently in the construction of models of the economy: gross national product (GNP) and disposable income (*DI*).

Since the models presented in this book ignore depreciation and indirect business taxes, GNP is basically identical to national income (see Figure 4–8). Similarly, since we ignore retained earnings, GNP and *DI* differ only by the amounts of taxes and transfers (again, see Figure 4–8). Finally, since we ignore foreign investment income, GNP and GDP coincide.

Summary

1. Gross domestic product (GDP) is the sum of the money values of all final goods and services produced during a year and sold on organized markets. There are, however, certain exceptions to this definition.
2. One way to measure the GDP is to add up the final demands of consumers, investors, governments, and foreigners: GDP = $C + I + G + X - IM$.
3. A second way to measure the GDP is to start with all the

factor payments—wages, interest, rents, and profits—that constitute the national income, and then add indirect business taxes and depreciation.
4. A third way to measure the GDP is to sum up the values added by every firm in the economy (and then once again add indirect business taxes and depreciation).
5. Except for possible bookkeeping and statistical errors, all three methods must give the same answer.

Concepts for Review

National income accounting
Gross domestic product (GDP)
Gross national product (GNP)
Inventories

Gross private domestic investment
Government purchases
Transfer payments
Net exports

Depreciation
Value-added
Disposable income *(DI)*

Questions for Discussion

1. Which of the following transactions are included in the gross domestic product, and by how much does each raise GDP?
   a. You buy a new car, paying $13,000.
   b. You buy a used car, paying $5000.
   c. IBM builds a $100 million factory to make computers.
   d. An unemployed worker receives a government cheque for $250 in unemployment-insurance benefits.
   e. General Motors builds 2000 Cadillacs at a cost of $18,000 each. Unable to sell them, it holds them as inventories.
   f. Mr. Black and Mr. Blue, each out for a Sunday drive, have a collision in which their cars are destroyed. Black and Blue each hire a lawyer to sue the other, paying the lawyers $1500 each for services rendered. The judge throws the case out of court.
   g. You sell a $100 painting to your roommate.

2. Explain the difference between final goods and intermediate goods. Why is it sometimes difficult to apply this distinction in practice? In this regard, why is the concept of value-added useful?

3. Explain the difference between government spending

and government purchases of goods and services (*G*). Which is larger?

4. The following is a complete description of all economic activity in Trivialand for the year 1991. Draw up versions of Tables 4–5 and 4–6 for Trivialand, showing GDP computed in two different ways.
   a. Trivialand has thousands of farmers but only two big business firms: Specific Motors (an auto company) and Super Duper (a chain of food markets). There is no government and no depreciation.
   b. Specific Motors produced 1000 small cars, which it sold at $6000 each, and 100 trucks, which it sold at $8000 each. Consumers bought 800 of the cars, and the remaining 200 cars were exported to the United States. Super Duper bought all the trucks.
   c. Sales at Super Duper markets amounted to $14 million, all of it sold to consumers.
   d. All the farmers in Trivialand are self-employed and sell all their wares to Super Duper.
   e. The costs incurred by all the businesses were as follows:

	SPECIFIC MOTORS (dollars)	SUPER DUPER (dollars)	FARMERS (dollars)
Wages	3,800,000	4,500,000	0
Interest	100,000	200,000	700,000
Rent	200,000	1,000,000	2,000,000
Purchases of food	0	7,000,000	0

5. (More difficult.) Now complicate Trivialand in the following ways and answer the same questions. In addition, calculate national income, personal income, and disposable income.

a. The government bought 50 cars, leaving only 150 cars for export. In addition, the government spent $800,000 on wages for accountants and clerks and made $1,200,000 in transfer payments.
b. Depreciation for the year amounted to $600,000 for Specific Motors and $200,000 for Super Duper. (The farmers had no depreciation.)
c. The government levied sales taxes amounting to $500,000 on Specific Motors and $200,000 on Super Duper (none on farmers). In addition, the government levied a 10 percent income tax on all wages, interest, and rental income.
d. In addition to the food and cars mentioned in Question 4, consumers in Trivialand imported 500 computers from Canada at $2000 each.

Appendix B
How Statisticians Measure Inflation

Index Numbers for Inflation

Inflation is generally measured by the change in some index of the general price level. For example, between 1973 and 1989, the Consumer Price Index (CPI), which stood at 100 in 1981, rose from 47.6 to 151.1, an increase of 217 percent. The meaning of the *change* is clear enough. But what is the meaning of the 47.6 figure for 1973 and the 151.1 figure for 1989?

These numbers are **index numbers**; each expresses the cost of a market basket of goods *relative to its cost in some base period*. Since the CPI uses 1981 as its base period, the CPI of 151.1 for 1989 means that it cost $151.10 in 1989 to purchase the same basket of goods and services that cost $100 in 1981.

Now, the particular basket of consumer goods and services under scrutiny did not really cost $100 in 1981. When constructing index numbers, it is conventional to set the index at 100 in the base year. How is this conventional figure used in obtaining index numbers for other years? Very simply. Suppose the budget needed to buy the roughly 350 items included in the CPI was $500 per month in 1981 and $755 per month in 1989. Then the index is defined by the following rule:

$$\frac{\text{CPI in 1989}}{\text{CPI in 1981}} = \frac{\text{Cost of market basket in 1989}}{\text{Cost of market basket in 1981}}.$$

Since the CPI in 1981 is set at 100:

$$\frac{\text{CPI in 1989}}{100} = \frac{\$755}{\$500} = 1.51$$

or

$$\text{CPI in 1989} = 151.$$

Exactly the same sort of equation enables us to calculate the CPI in any other year. We have the rule:

$$\text{CPI in given year} = \frac{\text{Cost of market basket in given year}}{\text{Cost of market basket in base year}} \times 100.$$

Of course, not every combination of consumer goods that cost $500 in 1981 rose to $755 by 1989. For example, a colour TV set that cost $500 in 1981 might have sold for $450 in 1989, but a $500 insurance bill in 1981 might have ballooned to $900. Since no two families buy precisely the same bundle of goods and services, no two families suffer precisely the same increase in their cost of living unless all prices rise at the same rate. Economists refer to this phenomenon as the **index number problem**.

When relative prices are changing, there is no such thing as a perfect price index that is correct for every consumer. Any statistical index will understate the increase in the cost of living for some families and overstate it for others. At best, the index can represent the situation of an "average" family.

The Consumer Price Index

The most closely watched price index is surely the **Consumer Price Index**, which is calculated and announced each month by Statistics Canada. When you read in the newspaper or see on television that the "cost of living" rose by 0.5 percent last month, chances are the reporter is referring to the CPI.

The CPI is measured by pricing the items on a list representative of a typical urban household budget. To know what items to include and in what amounts, Statistics Canada conducts an extensive survey of spending habits roughly twice every decade. This means that the *same* bundle of goods and services is used as a standard for several years, whether or not spending habits change.[10]

For example, Statistics Canada's 1986 family expenditure survey examined the spending patterns of Canadians living in the country's urban communities of 30,000 people or more. (The results of that survey are still in use today to calculate the current CPI.) In addition to the overall CPI, a separate one is published for each of the sixteen major cities within this group.

A simple example will help us understand how the CPI is constructed. Imagine that students purchase only three items—hamburgers, jeans, and movie tickets (at bargain prices, as you can see)—and that we want to devise a cost-of-living index (call it SPI, for "student price index") for them. First we would conduct a survey of spending habits in the base year (suppose it is 1986). Table 4–8 represents the hypothetical results. You will note that the frugal students of that day spent only $100 per month: $56 on hamburgers, $24 on jeans, and $20 on movies.

TABLE 4–8
Results of Student Expenditure Survey, 1986

	AVERAGE PRICE (dollars)	AVERAGE QUANTITY PURCHASED PER MONTH	AVERAGE EXPENDITURE PER MONTH (dollars)
Hamburger	0.80	70	56
Jeans	24.00	1	24
Movie ticket	5.00	4	20
			Total $100

[10] Economists call this a *base-period weight index* because the relative importance it attaches to each price depends on how much money consumers actually chose to spend on it during the base period.

TABLE 4–9
Prices in 1991

ITEM	PRICE (dollars)	PERCENTAGE INCREASE OVER 1986
Hamburger	1.00	25
Jeans	24.00	0
Movie ticket	5.50	10

Table 4–9 presents hypothetical prices for these same three items in 1991. Each price has risen by a different amount, ranging from zero percent for jeans to 25 percent for hamburgers. By how much has the SPI risen? Pricing the 1986 student budget at 1991 prices, we find that what once cost $100 now costs $116, as the following calculation shows:

Cost of 1986 Student Budget in 1991 Prices

70 hamburgers at $1	$70
1 pair of jeans at $24	24
4 movie tickets at $5.50	22
	Total $116

Thus the SPI, based on 1986 = 100, is

$$\text{SPI} = \frac{\text{Cost of budget in 1991}}{\text{Cost of budget in 1986}} = \frac{\$116}{\$100} \times 100 = 116.$$

So the SPI in 1991 stands at 116, meaning that a student's cost of living has increased 16 percent over the five years.

How to Use a Price Index to "Deflate" Monetary Figures

One of the most common uses of price indexes is in the comparison of monetary figures relating to two different points in time. The problem is that, if there has been inflation, the dollar is not a good measuring rod because it is worth less now than it was worth in the past.

Here is a simple example. Suppose that the average student spent $100 per month in 1986 and that this monthly spending figure had grown to $110 per month in 1991. If there was an outcry that students had become spendthrifts, how would you answer the charge?

The obvious answer is that a dollar in 1991 does not buy what it did in 1986. Specifically, our SPI shows us that it takes $1.16 in 1991 to purchase what $1 would purchase in 1986. To compare the spending habits of students in the two years, we must divide the

1991 spending figure by 1.16. Specifically, *real* spending per student in 1991 (where "real" is defined by 1986 dollars) is:

$$\text{Real spending in 1991} = \frac{\text{Nominal spending in 1991}}{\text{Price index of 1991}}.$$

Thus,

$$\text{Real spending in 1991} = \frac{\$110}{1.16} = \$94.83.$$

In sum, this calculation shows that, despite appearances to the contrary, the change in nominal spending from $100 to $110 actually represented a *decrease* in real spending.

This calculation procedure is called **deflating by a price index**, and it serves to translate non-comparable monetary figures into more directly comparable real figures.

Deflating is the process of finding the real value of some monetary magnitude by dividing by some appropriate price index.

Calculation of real wages, discussed earlier in this chapter, is an example of deflating nominal figures. The real wage is a worker's nominal (money) wage divided by the CPI. Real wages increase only if the numerator (the money wage) increases more rapidly through time than the denominator (the CPI). Thus, when considering the *percentage rates of change* of monetary figures, we subtract. Consider the following examples. In 1986 money wages increased by 2.8 percent in Canada, while the CPI rose by 4.1 percent.

Thus real wages actually fell by 4.1 – 2.8 or 1.3 percent. In contrast, in 1989, money wages and the CPI both rose by 5 percent, so real wages were constant.

The GDP Deflator

In macroeconomics, one of the most important of the monetary magnitudes that we have to deflate is the nominal gross domestic product (GDP). The price index used to do this is called the **GDP deflator**. Our general principle for deflating a nominal magnitude tells us how to go from nominal GDP to real GDP:

$$\text{Real GDP} = \frac{\text{Nominal GDP}}{\text{GDP deflator}} \times 100.$$

As with the CPI, the 100 simply serves to establish the base of the index as 100, rather than 1.00.

Economists sometimes consider the GDP deflator to be a better measure of overall inflation in the economy than the Consumer Price Index. The main reason for this is that the two price indexes are based on different market baskets. As already mentioned, the CPI is based on the budget of a typical urban family. By contrast, the GDP deflator is constructed from a market basket that includes *every* item in the GDP—that is, every final good and service produced in the economy. Thus, in addition to prices of consumer goods, the GDP deflator includes the prices of airplanes, lathes, and other goods purchased by business. It also includes government services. For this reason, the measures of inflation that these two indexes give are rarely the same. Usually their disagreements are minor, but sometimes they can be quite substantial.

Summary

1. Inflation is measured by the percentage increase in an index number of prices, which shows how the cost of some basket of goods has changed over a period of time.
2. Since relative prices are changing all the time and since different families purchase different items, no price index can represent precisely the change in the cost of living for every family.
3. The Consumer Price Index (CPI) tries to measure the cost of living for an "average" urban household by pricing a "typical" market basket every month.
4. Price indexes like the CPI can be used to *deflate* monetary figures to make them more comparable. This amounts to dividing the monetary magnitude by the appropriate price index.
5. The GDP deflator is a better measure of economy-wide inflation than is the CPI because it includes the price of every good and service in the economy.

Concepts for Review

Index number
Index number problem
Consumer Price Index

Deflating by a price index
GDP deflator

Questions for Discussion

1. Fill in the blanks in the following table of GDP statistics. Compute the percentage change in each of the three variables over this three-year period. What is the relationship among these percentage changes?

	1987	1988	1989
Nominal GDP	550.3		648.5
Real GDP	426.4	447.8	
GDP deflator		134.3	140.8

2. Use the following data to compute the Student Price Index for 1991, using the base 1972 = 100.

	PRICE IN 1972 (dollars)	QUANTITY PER MONTH IN 1972	PRICE IN 1991 (dollars)
Button-down shirts	10	1	25
Loafers	25	1	55
Sneakers	10	3	35
Textbooks	12	12	30
Jeans	12	3	25
Restaurant meals	5	11	14

3. (More difficult.) The example in the appendix showed that the Student Price Index rose by 16 percent from 1986 to 1991. You can understand the meaning of this better if you:
   a. Use Table 4–8 to compute the fraction of total spending accounted for by each of the three items in 1986. Call these the "expenditure weights."
   b. Compute the weighted average of the percentage increases of the three prices shown in Table 4–9, using the expenditure weights you have just computed.
   c. You should get 16 percent as your answer. This shows that "inflation," as measured by the SPI, is a weighted average of the percentage price increases of all the items that are included in the index.

5

Income and Spending: The Powerful Consumer

Men are disposed, as a rule and on the average, to increase their consumption as their income increases, but not by as much as the increase in their income.

JOHN MAYNARD KEYNES

I n Chapter 4 we saw how the strength of aggregate demand influences the performance of the economy. When aggregate demand is growing briskly, the economy is likely to be booming, though it may also be having trouble with inflation. When aggregate demand stagnates, a recession is likely to follow.

This chapter begins our detailed study of the theory of national income determination. The theory is based on the concepts of aggregate demand and aggregate supply. In this and the next two chapters, we construct a simplified model of aggregate demand and learn why the *aggregate demand curve* of Chapter 4 has a negative slope. Then Chapter 8 completes the model by adding the **aggregate supply curve**. This first model of the macroeconomy can teach us much about the causes of unemployment and inflation. But it is too simple to deal with policy issues because the government, foreign, and financial sectors are ignored. These omissions are remedied in later chapters, where government spending, taxation, interest rates, and exchange rates are given appropriately prominent roles.

Since consumer spending accounts for almost two-thirds of total demand, it is natural to begin the analysis there. First we need some definitions of alternative concepts of economic activity—distinguishing carefully among total *spending* (aggregate demand), total *output*, and total *income*. Next, we turn to the interactions among these three concepts, using a convenient pictorial device that shows how they are all interrelated. Then we note that government attempts to influence consumer spending have sometimes succeeded and sometimes failed, and we pose the question: Why?

The bulk of this chapter is devoted to this question. To answer it, we first describe the important relationship between consumer income and consumer spending, and we use this relationship to show how government policies have worked when they have been successful. Then we discuss some complications that arise from the fact that consumer income, though crucial, is not the only factor governing consumer spending. One of these complications gives us the first of several reasons why the aggregate demand curve slopes downward. Another holds the clue to why the government's income-tax policies have sometimes failed to influence consumer spending as expected. Also, the analysis explains why the Canadian federal government has tried to arrange sales-tax changes to avoid the problems associated with income-tax policy.

Aggregate Demand, National Product, and National Income

We have already introduced the concept of **gross domestic product** as the standard measure of the total output of the economy.

Aggregate demand is the total amount that all consumers, business firms, government agencies, and foreigners are willing to spend on final goods and services.

Consumer expenditure, symbolized by the letter *C*, is the total amount spent by consumers on newly produced goods and services (excluding purchases of new homes, which are considered investment goods).

Investment spending, symbolized by the letter *I*, is the sum of the expenditures of business firms on new plant, equipment, and inventories, plus the expenditures of households on new homes. Financial "investments" are not included, nor are resales of existing physical assets.

Government purchases, symbolized by the letter *G*, refers to all the goods (such as airplanes and paper clips) and services (such as school teaching and police protection) purchased by all levels of government. It does not include government **transfer payments** to individuals (such as welfare benefits) nor transfer payments from one level of government to another.

Net exports, symbolized by *X – IM*, is the excess of foreign expenditures on our products over our purchases of their goods (Canadian exports minus Canadian imports).

National income is the sum of the incomes of all the individuals in the economy earned in the forms of wages, interest, rents, and profits. It is calculated *before* any income taxes have been deducted.

For the most part, goods are produced in a market economy only if they can be sold. **Aggregate demand** is the total amount that all consumers, business firms, government agencies, and foreigners wish to spend on all final goods and services. The downward-sloping aggregate demand curve of Chapter 4 suggested that aggregate demand is a *schedule*, not a fixed number. And several reasons why aggregate demand depends on the price level will emerge in coming chapters. But the level of aggregate demand also depends on a variety of other factors, such as consumer incomes, various government policies, and events in foreign countries. We can understand the nature of aggregate demand best if we break it up into its major components, which were briefly discussed in Chapter 4, Appendix A.

Consumer expenditure ("consumption" for short) is simply the total demand for all consumer goods and services. This is the focus of the current chapter, and we shall represent it by the letter *C*.

Investment spending, which we represent by the letter *I*, is the amount that firms spend on factories, machinery, and the like, plus the amount that families spend on new homes. Notice that this is a very different usage of the word "investment" from that found in common parlance. Most people speak of "investing" in the stock market or in a bank account, but this kind of "investment" merely swaps one form of financial asset (such as money) for another form (such as a share of stock). When economists speak of "investment," they mean instead the purchase of some *new physical asset*, like a drill press or an oil rig or a home. It is only this kind of investment that leads directly to additional demand for newly produced goods in the economy.

Another major component of aggregate demand is **government purchases** of goods and services; that is, things like paper, typewriters, airplanes, ships, and labour that are bought by all levels of government—federal, provincial, and municipal. We use the letter *G* to denote this variable.

Finally, the last major component of aggregate demand is **net exports**. This consists of exports, which we represent by the letter *X*, and imports, which we denote by *IM*. Exports are the sum of all expenditures by foreigners on Canadian-produced final goods (such as wheat, fish, and snowmobiles) and services (such as transportation, hotel, and restaurant services purchased by foreigners while vacationing in Canada). Canadian expenditures on imports from other countries must be subtracted when calculating total demand for domestic production, since the spending by households, firms, and governments includes their expenditures on the products from other countries.

Given all these abbreviations, we have the following shorthand definition of aggregate demand.

Aggregate demand is the sum $C + I + G + X - IM$.

The last concept we need is a measure of the total *income* of all the individuals in the economy. There are two versions of this: one for before-tax incomes, called **national income**, and one for after-tax incomes, called **disposable income.**[1] The term "disposable income" is meant to be descriptive: It tells us how many dollars consumers actually have available to spend or to save. Because it plays such a prominent role in this chapter, we shall need an abbreviation for it as well; we call it *DI*.

The Circular Flow of Spending, Production, and Income

Enough definitions. How do these three concepts—national product, aggregate demand, and national income—interact in a market economy? We can answer this best with a rather elaborate diagram (Figure 5–1). For obvious reasons, Figure 5–1 is called

[1]More detailed information on these and other concepts was provided in Appendix A of Chapter 4.

a **circular flow diagram**. It depicts a large circular tube in which a fluid is circulating in a clockwise direction. There are several breaks in the tube where either some of the fluid leaks out or additional fluid is injected.

Let us examine this system beginning on the far left. Here, at point 1 on the circle, we find consumers. Disposable income (*DI*) is flowing into them, and two things are flowing out: consumption (*C*), which stays in the circular flow, and saving (*S*), which "leaks out." This just says that consumers normally spend less than they earn and save the balance. The "leakage" to savings does not disappear, of course, but it flows into the financial system. We postpone a consideration of what happens there until Chapters 10 and 11.

The upper loop of the circular flow represents expenditures, and as we move clockwise to point 2, we encounter the first "injection" into the flow: investment spending (*I*). The diagram shows this as coming from "investors"—a group that includes both business firms and consumers who buy new homes. As the circular flow moves beyond point 2, it is bigger than it was before. Total spending has increased from *C* to *C* + *I*.

At point 3 there is yet another injection. The government adds its demand for goods and services (*G*) to those of consumers and investors (*C* + *I*). At point 4 there is another leakage, which allows some of the demands for goods and services to flow out to foreign producers. Demand for Canadian products is less than the total expenditures of households, firms, and governments by the amount of these imports. At point 5 there is the final injection—exports. Thus, by the time we have passed point 5 and have added in the foreign purchases, we have accumulated the full amount of aggregate demand, *C* + *I* + *G* + *X* – *IM*.

Disposable income is the sum of the incomes of all the individuals in the economy after all taxes have been deducted.

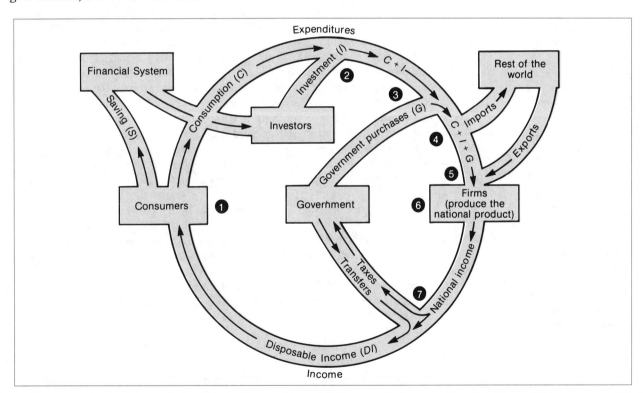

FIGURE 5–1

The Circular Flow of Expenditure and Income

The upper half of this circular flow diagram depicts the flow of expenditures on goods and services that comes from consumers (point 1), investors (point 2), government (point 3), and foreigners (point 5) and goes to the firms that produce the output (point 6). Some of the expenditures are spent on imports (point 4) and so never reach firms operating domestically. The lower half of the diagram indicates how the income paid out by firms (point 6) flows to consumers (point 1), after some is siphoned off by the government in the form of taxes and part of this is replaced by transfer payments (point 7).

The circular flow diagram shows this aggregate demand for goods and services arriving at the business firms, located at point 6 on the extreme right of the diagram. Responding to this demand, firms produce the national product. As the circular flow emerges from the firms, however, we have renamed it *national income*. Why? Because, except for a few details that do not significantly affect the point (and that were explained in Appendix A of Chapter 4):

National income and national product must be equal.

Why is this the case? When a firm produces and sells $100 worth of output, it pays most of the proceeds to its workers, to people who have lent it money, and to the landlord who owns the property on which it is located. All of these payments are *income* to some individuals. But what about the rest? Suppose, for example, that the wages, interest, and rent that the firm pays add up to $90, while its output is $100. What happens to the remaining $10? The answer is that the owners of the firm receive it as *profits*. But these owners are also citizens of the country, so their incomes count in national income, too. Thus, when we add up all the wages, interest, rents, *and profits* in the economy to obtain the national income, we must arrive at the value of the national output.

A slight complication occurs when some of the firms are foreign-owned, as is the case in Canada. In this case, some of the profits earned in Canada add to another country's national income, not ours. This is partly compensated for by the fact that some Canadians earn profits by being part owners of firms that operate outside Canada. To allow for these activities, we could complicate our circular flow diagram with an additional leakage and injection between points 6 and 7. The leakage is incomes paid to foreigners operating within Canada, and the injection is incomes received by Canadians operating in other countries. These flows do not exactly cancel off, so national product and national income are not exactly equal. As we stated in Chapter 4, national product is called *gross domestic product* (GDP); it measures the total amount of employment-creating economic activity that takes place within Canada. National income is called *gross national product* (GNP); it measures the total income of Canadian factors of production wherever they are employed. We have followed the convention of ignoring the difference between these two aggregates for two reasons. First, we wish to keep the circular flow diagram simplified; second, the cyclical swings in GNP and GDP are virtually identical. Employment variations depend on these cyclical swings, not on the absolute level of either GNP or GDP.

The lower loop of the circular flow diagram traces the flow of income by showing national income leaving the firms and heading for consumers. But there is a detour along the way. At point 7, the government does two things. First, it siphons off a portion of the national income in the form of taxes. Second, it adds back government **transfer payments** to individuals, such as disability compensation and government pension benefits, which are sums of money that certain individuals receive as *grants* from the government rather than as payments for services rendered to employers.

Transfer payments are sums of money that certain individuals receive as *grants* from the government rather than as payments for services rendered to employers.

When taxes are subtracted from GDP, and transfer payments are added, we obtain disposable income:[2]

$$DI = \text{GDP} - \text{Taxes} + \text{Transfer payments}.$$

Disposable income flows unimpeded to consumers at point 1, and the cycle repeats itself.

[2] As above, this definition omits a few minor details, which are explained in Appendix A of Chapter 4.

Figure 5–1 raises several complicated questions. Although we pose them here, we will not try to answer them at this early stage. The answers will be made clear in subsequent chapters.

1. Is the output that the firms produce at point 6 (the GDP) equal to aggregate demand? If so, what makes these two quantities equal? If not, what happens?

2. Is the flow of spending and income growing larger or smaller as we move clockwise around the circle, and why?

Chapter 6 provides the answers to questions 1 and 2.

3. Are the government's accounts in balance, so that what flows in at point 7 (taxes minus transfers) is equal to what flows out at point 3 (government purchases)? What happens if they are not?

This important question is first addressed in Chapter 9 and then recurs many times, especially in Chapter 16, which discusses budget deficits.

4. Is our international trade balanced, so that exports equal imports? More generally, what factors determine net exports, and what are the consequences of trade deficits or surpluses?

These questions are answered in Chapter 9.

But we cannot discuss these issues profitably until we first understand what goes on at point 1 (where consumers make decisions) and point 2 (where investors make decisions). We turn next, therefore, to the determinants of consumer spending.

Demand Management and the Powerful Consumer

As we suggested in Chapter 4, the government sometimes wants to shift the aggregate demand curve. There are a number of ways in which it can try to do so. One direct approach is to alter its own spending (G), becoming extravagant when private demand is weak and miserly when private demand is strong. But the government can also take a more indirect route by using taxes and other policy tools to influence *private* spending decisions.

A government desiring to change private spending can concentrate its energies on consumer spending (C), on investment spending (I), or on net exports ($X - IM$). At various times in our history, the Canadian government has elected to pursue one of these courses of action. Its favourite target has been firms' investment spending, which it tries to manipulate with variations in the corporate tax system. We discuss these in Chapter 9. For the present, we discuss attempts to alter household consumption and consider some illuminating policy experiments that were tried in the United States. Also, we describe the Canadian government's attempt to benefit from this U.S. experience.

While there are many things it can do to alter consumer spending, the government's principal weapon is the personal income tax. Any reduction in personal taxes leaves consumers with more disposable income to spend. Any increase in taxes leaves them with less. The linkage from taxes to disposable income to consumer spending seems direct and unmistakable, and, in a way, it is. But a look at the history of some major U.S. tax changes aimed at altering C is sobering. The varying degrees of success both of the measures themselves and of the predictions of their effects explain why economic research into the relationship between taxes and consumption continues.

The U.S. Experience with Income-Tax Changes

The year 1964 was a good one for economists. For years they had been proclaiming that a cut in personal taxes would be an excellent way to stimulate a stagnating economy. But the plea fell on deaf ears until President John F. Kennedy was persuaded of the basic logic of the argument. Under his successor, Lyndon B. Johnson, the U.S. Congress reduced personal taxes by about 18 percent. The legislation was designed to spur consumer spending, and it succeeded admirably. Consumers reacted just about as the textbooks of the day predicted, the economic situation improved rapidly and markedly, and economists smiled knowingly. By 1968, the macroeconomic problem confronting the United States was precisely the opposite of that in 1964: there was too much demand (due to spending associated with the Vietnam War) rather than too little. It appeared logical, then, to prescribe the opposite medicine, and economists were quick to suggest an increase in personal income taxes to force consumers to spend less.

The U.S. government enacted a temporary 10 percent rise in personal tax payments (calling it a "surcharge"). This attempt to cut aggregate demand by reducing C enjoyed only modest success.

The next major change in U.S. tax laws for stabilization purposes also met with partial success at best. In the spring of 1975, the American economy neared the bottom of what was then its worst postwar recession. The government decided to return to each taxpayer part of the taxes paid in 1974, and income-tax rates were reduced for the balance of 1975. However, consumers confounded the government's wishes by *saving* a good deal of their rebates rather than spending them.

Finally, a series of reductions in personal income-tax rates was engineered by President Ronald Reagan. Tax rates in the United States fell by about 23 percent between 1981 and 1984, and consumer spending increased by more or less the amounts that economists predicted.

What went wrong in the United States in 1968 and 1975 that did not go wrong in 1964 and in the 1980s? This chapter will attempt to provide some answers. We begin by exploring the important relationship between consumer income and consumer spending, more or less retracing the chain of logic that led American economists to the right conclusion in 1964. Once this is accomplished, we turn to some of the complications that made things go awry in 1968 and 1975.

Canada's Attempt at Sales-Tax Reduction

In the 1978 Budget, the Canadian federal government tried to avoid the problems encountered by the Americans by relying on *sales-tax* changes rather than *personal income-tax* policies. Toward the end of the chapter, we examine the effects of this approach, and explain why it was not tried again.

Consumer Spending and Income: The Important Relationship

An economist interested in predicting how consumer spending will respond to a change in personal income-tax payments must first ask how C is related to disposable income, for an increase in taxes is a decrease in after-tax income and a reduction in taxes is an increase in after-tax income. This section, therefore, will examine what we know about the response of consumer spending to a change in disposable income.

Figure 5–2 depicts the historical paths of C and DI for Canada since 1961. The association is obviously rather close and certainly suggests that consumption will rise whenever disposable income does and fall whenever income falls. The difference between the two lines is personal saving. The only puzzling feature of Figure 5–2 is the apparent bulge in savings that has occurred since about 1970. The main reason for this is the inflation in this period. When there is no sustained inflation, real and

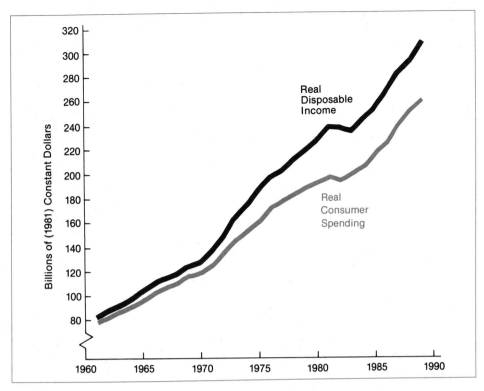

FIGURE 5–2
Consumer Spending and Disposable Income in Canada since 1961
This time-series chart shows the behaviour of consumer spending and disposable income in Canada since 1961. The correspondence between the two variables is very close. The distance between the two lines represents measured consumer saving. The bulge in savings since 1970 results largely from a measurement problem that is based on the large inflation premium that has become incorporated within nominal interest rates.
SOURCE: Statistics Canada.

nominal interest rates coincide, so that households do not need to save any of their interest earnings to keep the real value of their bonds and shares constant. With a sustained inflation, however, much of the received nominal interest rate is the inflation premium, and *all* of this part of interest must be saved just to keep real asset holdings constant. (Real asset holdings can be constant only if nominal holdings of bonds and stocks increase as rapidly as the inflation rate.) To be comparable with the earlier (non-inflationary) period, then, the consumer spending series for the last twenty years should be adjusted for the gap that has emerged between the real and nominal interest rates.

There is a mirror image of this overstatement of household savings in inflationary times. The *dis*saving by the other sectors (firms and governments) is overstated in the standard data by the same amount and for the same reason. We return to this point when discussing the size of the government budget deficit in Chapter 16. This discussion represents another application of the important **12 Ideas for Beyond the Final Exam**: the difference between nominal and real interest.

Of course, knowing that consumer expenditures, *C*, will move in the same direction as disposable income, *DI*, is not enough for policy planners. They need to know *how much* one will go up when the other rises a given amount. Figure 5–3 presents the same data that we saw in Figure 5–2 but in a way designed to help answer the "how much" question.

Economists call such pictures **scatter diagrams**, and they are very useful in predicting how one economic variable (in this case, consumer spending) will change in response to a change in another economic variable (in this case, disposable income). Each dot in the diagram represents the data on *C* and *DI* corresponding to a particular year. For example, the point labelled "1980" shows that real consumer expenditures in 1980 were $192 billion (which we read off the vertical axis), while real disposable incomes amounted to $227 billion (which we read off the horizontal axis). Similarly, each year from 1961 to 1989 is represented by its own dot in Figure 5–3.

How can such a diagram assist the fiscal policy planner? Imagine that you are an American economist in 1963 and you must decide whether to recommend to the

A scatter diagram is a graph showing the relationship between two variables (such as consumption and disposable income). Each year is represented by a point in the diagram. The co-ordinates of each year's point show the values of the two variables in that year.

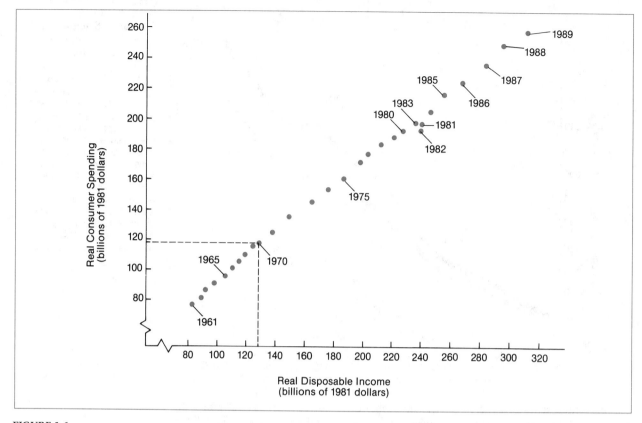

FIGURE 5-3

Scatter Diagram of Consumer Spending and Disposable Income in Canada, 1961–1989

This diagram shows the same data as depicted in Figure 5-2 but in a different manner. Each point on the diagram represents the data for both consumer spending and disposable income during a particular year. For example, the point labelled "1980" indicates that in that year consumer spending was $192 billion while disposable income was $227 billion. Diagrams like this one are called "scatter diagrams."

government a tax cut of $5 billion, $10 billion, or $15 billion. You have forecasts of what consumer expenditures are expected to be if taxes are not reduced. This, plus other forecasts of investment, government spending, and net exports, has led you to conclude that aggregate demand in 1964 will be insufficient if taxes are not reduced. To assist you, the pre-1964 scatter diagram for the United States is given in Figure 5-4. With no more training in economics than you have right now, what would you do?

One rough-and-ready approach is to get a ruler, set it down on Figure 5-4, and sketch a straight line that comes as close as possible to hitting all the points. Try that now. You will not be able to hit each point exactly, but you will find that you can come remarkably close. The line you have just drawn summarizes, in a very rough way, the consumption–income relationship that is the focus of this chapter. You can see at once that it confirms something you might have guessed—that a rise in income is associated with a rise in consumer spending. The slope of the line is certainly positive.

The slope of your line is very important. That line has been drawn into Figure 5-5, and we note that its slope is:

$$\text{Slope} = \frac{\text{Vertical change}}{\text{Horizontal change}} = \frac{\$90 \text{ billion}}{\$100 \text{ billion}} = 0.90.$$

Since the horizontal change involved in the move from *A* to *B* represents a rise in disposable income of $100 billion (from $900 billion to $1000 billion), and the corresponding vertical change represents the associated $90 billion rise in consumer

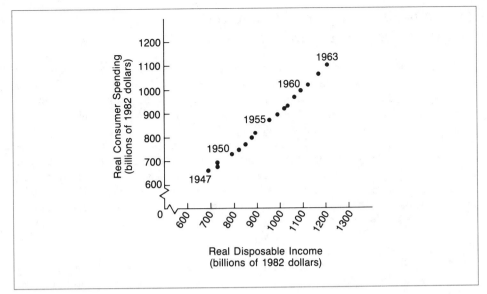

FIGURE 5–4
**Scatter Diagram of
Consumer Spending and
Disposable Income in the
United States, 1947–1963**
This scatter diagram indicates
the information that policy
planners might have used in
deciding upon the size of the
1964 income-tax cut in the
United States.

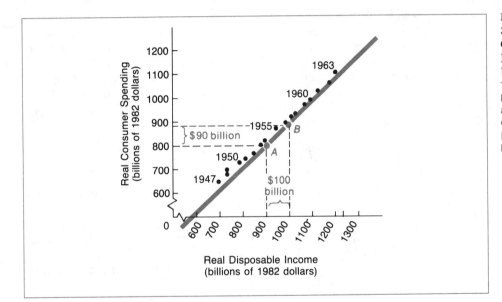

FIGURE 5–5
**Scatter Diagram of
Consumer Spending and
Disposable Income in the
United States, 1947–1963**
This diagram is the same as
Figure 5–4 except for the
addition of a straight line that
comes about as close as
possible to fitting all the data
points.

spending (from $800 billion to $890 billion), the slope of the line indicates how spending responds to changes in disposable income. In this case, we see that each additional $1 of income leads to 90¢ of additional spending.

In terms of the policy issue of 1964, this line can therefore help provide an answer to the question: How much more consumer spending will be induced by tax cuts of $5 billion, $10 billion, or $15 billion if the effects are similar to those observed in the past? First, we need to keep in mind that each dollar of tax cut increases disposable income by $1. Then we apply Figure 5–5's finding that each additional dollar of disposable income increases consumer spending by 90¢, and conclude that tax cuts of $5 billion, $10 billion, and $15 billion would be expected to increase consumer spending by $4.5 billion, $9 billion, and $13.5 billion, respectively. Similar questions addressed by U.S. economists in 1964 led to a decision to cut taxes by about $9 billion.

Later in this and other chapters, we will encounter several reasons why this procedure, while basically valid, must be used with great caution.

The Consumption Function and the
Marginal Propensity to Consume

The **consumption function** is the relationship between total consumer expenditure and total disposable income in the economy, holding all other determinants of consumer spending constant.

The **marginal propensity to consume** (MPC) is the ratio of the change in consumption to the change in disposable income that produces the change in consumption. On a graph, it appears as the slope of the consumption function.

$$MPC = \frac{\Delta C}{\Delta DI}$$

It has been said that economics is just systematized common sense. Let us, then, try to organize and generalize what has been a completely intuitive discussion thus far. One thing we have learned is that there is a close and apparently reliable relationship between consumer spending, *C*, and disposable income, *DI*. Economists call this relationship the **consumption function**.

A second fact we have picked up from these figures is that the slope of the consumption function is fairly constant. We infer this from the fact that the straight line in Figure 5–5 comes close to touching every point. If the slope of the consumption function had changed a lot, it would not be possible to do so well with a single straight line. Because of its importance in such applications as the tax-cut example, economists have given a special name to this slope—the **marginal propensity to consume**, or MPC for short. The MPC tells us how many more dollars consumers will spend if disposable income rises by $1 billion.

The MPC is best illustrated by an example, and for this purpose we turn away from both Canadian and U.S. data for a moment and look at the consumption and income data of a hypothetical country called Macroland (see Table 5–1). The data for Macroland resemble those for Canada and the United States, except that in Macroland, *C* and *DI* figures happen to be nice round numbers, which facilitates computation.

Columns 1 and 2 of Table 5–1 show annual consumer expenditure and disposable income from 1986 to 1991. These two columns constitute Macroland's consumption function and are plotted in Figure 5–6. Column 3 in the table shows the marginal propensity to consume (MPC), which is the slope of the line in Figure 5–6; it is derived from the first two columns. We can see that between 1988 and 1989, *DI* rose by $50 billion (from $300 billion to $350 billion) while *C* rose by $40 billion (from $250 billion to $290 billion). Thus the MPC was:

$$\frac{\text{Change in consumption}}{\text{Change in disposable income}} = \frac{\$40 \text{ billion}}{\$50 \text{ billion}} = 0.80.$$

As you can easily verify, the MPC between any other pair of years in Macroland was also 0.80.

This explains why the slope of the line in Figure 5–5 was so crucial in estimating the effect of a tax cut. Since the slope is the MPC, it tells us how much *additional* spending will be induced by each dollar *change* in disposable income. For each $1 of tax cut, economists expect consumption to rise by $1 times the marginal propensity to consume. Thus:

To estimate the *initial* effect of a tax cut on consumer spending, economists must first estimate the MPC and then multiply the amount of the tax cut by the estimated MPC.

TABLE 5–1
Consumption and Income in Macroland

	(1) CONSUMPTION, *C* (billions of dollars)	(2) DISPOSABLE INCOME, *DI* (billions of dollars)	(3) MARGINAL PROPENSITY TO CONSUME, MPC
1986	170	200	
1987	210	250	0.8
1988	250	300	0.8
1989	290	350	0.8
1990	330	400	0.8
1991	370	450	0.8

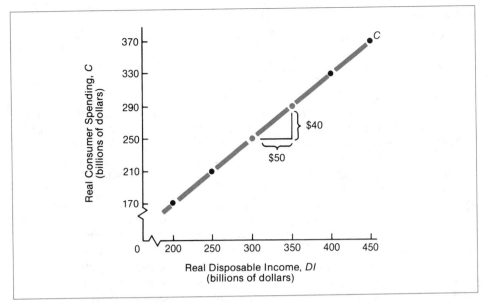

FIGURE 5-6
The Consumption
Function of Macroland
This diagram is similar to Figure
5-5, except that it applies to a
hypothetical (and blissfully
simple!) economy called
Macroland. As can be seen, a
straight-line consumption
function passes through every
point exactly. The slope of this
line is 0.8, which is the marginal
propensity to consume in
Macroland.

But since they never know the true MPC with certainty, this prediction is always subject to some margin of error.[3]

Some students are confused by the fact that the MPC has roughly the same value whether disposable income is at a high or a low level. They are aware of both poor individuals who consume all their income and very rich individuals who consume very little of their income. These simple facts seem to be inconsistent with the notion of a propensity to consume that is independent of income level. But there is actually no inconsistency here, and this can be clarified by distinguishing the **average propensity to consume (APC)** from the MPC. The APC is defined as the ratio of *overall* consumption to disposable income, that is, C/DI, and this ratio *does* fall as we consider individuals with higher income. But, as noted above, the MPC is $\Delta C/\Delta DI$, and this reaction to *changes* in income is essentially independent of income level. Thus, while it is true that the APC is not constant across income levels, the MPC is. As we will see, our economic policy analysis depends only on the MPC, not the APC, so the fact that the MPC is roughly independent of income is very useful for simplifying that analysis.

While we are defining terms, we might usefully introduce two others that often arise: the **marginal propensity to save (MPS)** and the **average propensity to save (APS)**. These terms are defined in an analogous fashion to the MPC and the APC:

$$MPS = \frac{\Delta S}{\Delta DI} \qquad APS = \frac{S}{DI}.$$

Since savings (S) is defined as disposable income not consumed, the following three relationships hold:

$$C + S = DI$$
$$MPC + MPS = 1$$
$$APC + APS = 1.$$

These relationships mean that our policy analysis can be conducted as long as we have data on *either* the MPC or the MPS, since one can be deduced from the other.

---

[3] The word "initial" in the first sentence is an important one. Later chapters explain why the effects discussed in this chapter are only the beginning of the story.

Movements along versus Shifts of the Consumption Function

Among the most important reasons that the sort of calculation we described earlier does not always yield precise results is that the consumption function does not always stand still; sometimes it shifts.

You will recall from Chapter 3 the important distinction between a *movement along* a demand curve and a *shift of* the curve. A demand curve depicts the relationship between quantity demanded and only *one* of its many determinants—price. Thus, a change in price causes a movement *along* the demand curve, but a change in any other factor that influences quantity demanded causes a *shift of the entire demand curve.*

Because consumer spending is influenced by factors other than disposable income, a similar distinction is vital to understanding real-world consumption functions. Look back at the definition of the consumption function in the margin of page 122. A change in disposable income leads to a **movement along the consumption function** because the consumption function depicts the relationship between *C* and *DI*. This movement is what we have been considering so far. But consumption also has other determinants, and a change in any of these "other determinants" of consumer spending will **shift the entire consumption function**, as indicated in Figure 5–7. These unexpected shifts account for many of the errors in forecasting consumption. To summarize:

Any change in disposable income moves us *along* a given consumption function. But a change in any of the other variables that influence consumption results in a *shift* of the entire consumption schedule (see Figure 5–7).

Let us now list some of the "other variables" that can shift the consumption function.

Other Determinants of Consumer Spending

Wealth

One factor affecting consumption is consumers' *wealth*, which is a source of demand in addition to income. Wealth and income are different things. A wealthy person may currently have very little *income*. Similarly, a high-income individual who spends all he earns will not accumulate wealth. To appreciate the importance of the distinction,

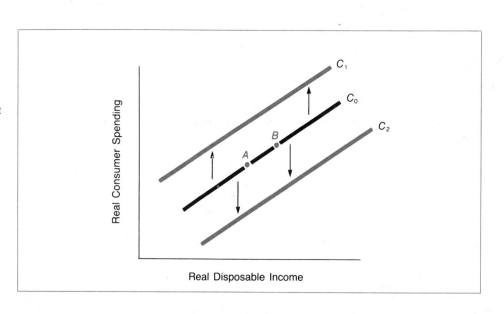

FIGURE 5–7
Shifts of the Consumption Function
An increase in disposable income causes a movement along a fixed consumption function, such as the movement from point A to point B on consumption function C_0. But a change in any other determinant of consumer spending will cause the whole consumption function to shift upward (consumption function C_1) or downward (consumption function C_2).

consider two consumers, both earning $35,000 this year. One of them has $100,000 in the bank, while the other has no assets at all. Who do you think will spend more this year? Presumably the one with the big bank account.

The general point is that current income is not the only source of funds that households have; they can also finance spending by withdrawals from their bank accounts or by cashing in other forms of wealth. Even a perception that their wealth has increased can cause households to spend more and save less. For example, a stock-market boom can raise the consumption function (see the shift from C_0 to C_1 in Figure 5-7); conversely, a collapse of stock prices can lower it (see the shift from C_0 to C_2).

Interest Rates

The interest rate can also cause shifts in the consumption function. For one thing, the value of certain forms of wealth (stocks and bonds) varies with the level of interest rates, as we explain in Chapter 10. For another, people are more apt to save when the return that can be earned on those savings is high. Since higher savings means less consumption, then, for any given level of disposable income, an increase in the interest rate shifts the consumption function down while a fall in the interest rate shifts the consumption function up.

The Price Level

A good deal of consumer wealth is held in forms whose values are fixed in money terms. Money itself is the most obvious example of this, but government bonds, savings accounts, and corporate bonds are all assets with fixed face values in money terms. The purchasing power of any **money fixed asset** obviously declines whenever the price level rises, which means that the asset can buy less. For example, if the price level rises by 10 percent, a $1000 government bond (if sold) will buy about 10 percent less than it could when prices were lower. Consequently:

A money fixed asset is an asset with a face value fixed in terms of dollars, such as money itself, government bonds, and corporate bonds.

Higher overall prices, by eroding the purchasing power of consumer wealth, decrease the demand for goods and services. Lower overall prices, by enhancing the purchasing power of consumer wealth, increase the demand for goods and services. For these reasons a change in the price level will shift the entire consumption function. Specifically:

A higher price level leads to lower real wealth and therefore to less spending *at any given level of real income*. Thus, a higher price level leads to a lower consumption function (such as C_2 in Figure 5-7). Conversely, a lower price level leads to a higher consumption function (such as C_1 in Figure 5-7).

Students are often confused on this point, so it is worth repeating that the depressing effect of the price level on consumer spending works through real *wealth*, not through real *income*. The consumption function is a relationship between *real* consumer income and *real* consumer spending. Thus any decline in real income, regardless of its cause, moves the economy *leftward along a fixed consumption function*; it does not shift the consumption function. By contrast, any decline in *real wealth* will *shift the whole consumption function downward*, meaning that there is less spending at any given level of real income.

The Inflation Rate

Prices may be high and rising slowly, or they may be low but rising rapidly. Therefore, the depressing effect of a high *price level* on real consumer spending must be distinguished from any effect on spending of the *rate of inflation* (that is, the rate at which prices are rising).

The effect of the inflation rate on consumer spending appears to be small. In the past, economists believed that high rates of inflation caused consumers to spend more to "beat" the inflation. That is, people were thought to purchase goods ahead of their needs in order to avoid the higher prices that loomed on the horizon. But behaviour during the inflationary period since 1974 shows that consumer spending was actually unusually low. We explained this on pages 118–19 in terms of the inflation premium that gets embedded in nominal interest rates during inflationary times. Because these effects counteract one another and because we wish to keep our model economy simplified, we ignore these complications and assume that the position of the consumption function is influenced by the *price level*, but not by the *inflation rate*.

Expectations of Future Incomes

It will hardly be considered earth shattering to suggest that consumers' expectations about future income may affect how they spend today. This final determinant of consumer spending turns out to hold the key to answering the question we posed earlier. Why did the U.S. tax policy that succeeded so well in 1964 and the early 1980s fail to alter consumer spending as much in 1968 and 1975?

To understand how expectations of future incomes affect current consumer expenditures, consider the abbreviated life histories of three consumers given in Table 5-2. The reason for giving our three imaginary individuals such odd names will be apparent shortly.

The consumer named "No Change" earned $100 in each of the four years considered in the table. The consumer named "Temporary Rise" earned $100 in three of the four years but had a good year in 1975. The consumer named "Permanent Rise" enjoyed a permanent rise in income in 1975 and was clearly the richest.

TABLE 5-2
Incomes of Three Consumers, 1974–1977

CONSUMER	INCOME IN EACH YEAR				TOTAL INCOME
	1974	1975	1976	1977	
No Change	100	100	100	100	400
Temporary Rise	100	120	100	100	420
Permanent Rise	100	120	120	120	460

Now let us use our common sense to figure out how much each of these consumers might have spent in 1975. Temporary Rise and Permanent Rise had the same income that year. Do you think they spent the same amount? Not if they had some ability to foresee their future incomes, because Permanent Rise was richer in the long run. Now compare No Change and Temporary Rise. Temporary Rise had 20 percent higher income in 1975 ($120 versus $100) but only 5 percent more over the four-year period ($420 versus $400). Do you think her spending was closer to 20 percent above No Change's or closer to 5 percent above it? Most people guess the latter.

The point of this example is that it is reasonable for consumers to decide on their *current* consumption spending by looking at their *long-run* income prospects. This should not be a shocking idea to most students. How many of you are spending only what you earn this year? Probably not very many. And this is not because you are all foolish spendthrifts. On the contrary, you are rational planners. Knowing that your education gives you a reasonable expectation of future income prospects much greater than those you now have, you are no doubt spending with that in mind.

Now what does all this have to do with the failure of the 1975 income-tax rebate in the United States? Imagine that the three rows in Table 5-2 now represent the entire economy under three different government policies. Recall that 1975 was the year of the rebate. The first row (No Change) shows the unchanged path of disposable income if no tax cut was enacted. The second (Temporary Rise) shows an increase in disposable income attributable to a tax cut *for one year only*. The bottom row

(Permanent Rise) shows a policy that increases *DI* in *every future year* by cutting taxes permanently in 1975. Which of the two lower rows do you imagine would have generated more consumer spending in 1975? The bottom row (Permanent Rise), of course. What we have concluded, then, is this:

Permanent cuts in income taxes cause greater increases in consumer spending than do temporary cuts of equal magnitude.

The application of this analysis to the case of the 1975 tax cut is immediate. The rebates were clearly one-time increases in income like that experienced by Temporary Rise in Table 5–2. Hence, no future income was affected. It is not surprising that statistical studies show the 1975 tax cut had little effect on consumer spending.

Much the same situation prevailed in 1968, when the U.S. Congress enacted a temporary 10 percent increase in income taxes to help finance the Vietnam War. Consumers considered the resulting decrease in their disposable income as only a *temporary* loss and did not curtail their spending as much as government officials had hoped. The general lesson is:

A permanent increase in income taxes provides a greater deterrent to consumer spending than does a temporary increase of equal magnitude.

We have, then, what appears to be a general principle, backed up both by historical evidence and common sense. Permanent changes in income taxes have a more significant impact on consumer spending than do temporary changes.

Sales-Tax Changes

A sales-tax change does not affect consumption by changing household incomes. Instead, alterations in sales taxes change the relative prices of buying a good now versus buying it in the future. Indeed, the more *temporary* a sales-tax change is, the more *effective* it is.

For example, if a sales tax is cut for a six-month period and households know the cut is temporary, they will probably accelerate some purchases to fit within the six-month period. But if they expect the lower price will apply indefinitely, they may respond more sluggishly, so less spending is transferred to the recession period. This suggests that temporary sales-tax changes should be far more effective measures for managing aggregate demand than are temporary income-tax changes.

Unfortunately, in Canada, the conventional division of powers between the federal and provincial governments has given rise to a significant problem for implementing sales taxes as a demand-management tool. Retail sales taxes have traditionally fallen under the jurisdiction of provincial governments, while aggregate demand management is a federal government responsibility. The federal government has controlled the manufacturers' sales tax, which is levied at the wholesale level, but this tax has raised relatively little revenue.

The federal government's Budget of 1978 represented an attempt to overcome this implementation problem (and it therefore illustrates the government's appreciation of the lessons we have learned from the U.S. experience with temporary income-tax changes). The federal government transferred some of its personal income-tax revenue to the provinces in return for a specified temporary sales-tax cut by the provinces. A full agreement was reached with all provinces except Alberta and Quebec. Alberta was excluded because there was no sales tax there. The Quebec government decided that political points could be scored by refusing to agree to the deal and by publicly decrying the meddling in provincial matters by the federal government. After two months of intense political wrangling, the federal government simply paid all Quebec taxpayers directly an income-tax rebate of either $85 or the person's federal tax payable (whichever was less). For a long time this episode reduced interest in federal–provincial co-operation on sales-tax adjustment for macroeconomic objectives—which is unfortunate, in the light of the lessons of this chapter.

As this book goes to press, however, we are fast approaching the implementation date for the federal government's controversial GST—the goods and services tax. Public discussion has focussed on some of the most controversial aspects of the new tax, and we will discuss these major advantages and disadvantages in some detail in Chapter 30. Here, we simply note that the GST finally gives the federal government a more predictable and powerful lever to use in its attempts to adjust consumer expenditure for stabilization purposes. Whether the government will choose to use this lever for short-run policy adjustment remains to be seen. The lessons of the 1960s and 1970s may have dimmed in the memory of Canada's policy-makers, because the government made no mention, when it was promoting the new tax, of this particular implication for stabilization policy.

The Predictability of Consumer Behaviour

We have now learned enough to see why the economist's problem in predicting how consumers will react to an increase or decrease in taxes is not nearly as simple as suggested earlier in this chapter.

The principal problem seems to be anticipating how taxpayers will view any changes in the income-tax law. If the government *says* that an income-tax cut is permanent, will consumers *believe* it and increase their spending accordingly? Perhaps not, if the government has a history of raising taxes after promising to keep them low. Similarly, when the government explicitly announces that an income-tax increase is temporary, will consumers always believe this? Or might they greet such an announcement with a hefty dose of skepticism? This is quite possible if there is a long history of "temporary" tax increases that stayed on the books indefinitely.

Thus the effectiveness of any *future* tax-policy move may well depend on the government's *past* track record. A government that repeatedly uses a succession of so-called "permanent" income-tax cuts and income-tax increases for short-run stabilization purposes may find consumers beginning to ignore the tax changes entirely. (The story of the boy who cried wolf is not yet required reading for fiscal policy planners, but it probably should be recommended.) As we noted above, however, consumers tend not to ignore temporary changes in sales taxes, and with the new GST, the government has acquired the means to exploit that principle.

There is much more that can be said about the determinants of consumption, but it is best to leave the rest to more advanced courses. For we are now ready to apply our knowledge of the consumption function to the construction of the first model of the whole economy. While it is true that income determines consumption, the consumption function in turn helps to determine the level of income. If that sounds like circular reasoning, read the next chapter!

Summary

1. Aggregate demand is the total amount of goods and services that consumers, businesses, government units, and foreigners are willing to purchase. It can be expressed as the sum $C + I + G + X - IM$ where C is consumer spending, I is investment spending, G is government purchases, and $X - IM$ is exports minus imports.

2. Economists reserve the term "investment" to refer to purchases of newly produced factories, machinery, and homes.

3. National product is the total output of final goods and services of the economy. It is most commonly measured by the gross domestic product (GDP).

4. National income is the sum of the *before-tax* wages, interest, rents, and profits earned by all individuals in the economy. If we ignore incomes earned by Canadian-owned factors of production operating in other countries and by foreign-owned factors of production operating here, national income must by necessity be equal to national product.

5. Disposable income is the sum of the incomes of all individuals in the economy, *after taxes and transfers*, and is the chief determinant of consumer expenditure.

6. All of these concepts and others can be depicted in a circular flow diagram that shows expenditures from all four sources flowing into business firms and national income flowing out.

7. The government has often tried to manipulate aggregate demand by influencing private expenditure decisions.

8. The close relationship between consumer spending (C) and disposable income (DI) is called the consumption function. Its slope, which is used to predict the change in consumption that will be caused by a change in income taxes, is called the marginal propensity to consume (MPC).

9. Changes in disposable income move us along a given consumption function. Changes in any of the other variables that affect C will shift the entire consumption function. Among the most important of these other variables are total consumer wealth, the price level, and expected future incomes.

10. Because consumers hold assets whose value is fixed in money terms, they lose out when prices rise. The resulting decline in consumer demand when prices rise helps explain why the aggregate demand curve slopes downward.

11. Future income prospects help explain why U.S. tax policy did not affect consumption as much as was hoped in 1968 and 1975. This is because the 1968 tax increase and the 1975 tax cut were both temporary and therefore left future incomes unaffected. By contrast, the U.S. tax cuts of 1964 and 1981–84 were "permanent," and affected future as well as current incomes. It is no surprise, then, that the 1964 and 1981 actions had stronger effects on spending than did the 1968 or 1975 actions.

12. Temporary sales-tax changes affect consumption by changing the ratio of current to future prices, and therefore their impact does not depend on any change in people's permanent income position. However, while aggregate demand management is a federal responsibility, control over retail sales taxes has until recently been held by the provincial governments. A federal sales tax eliminates this disjunction by placing control of sales taxes in the hands of the government responsible for macroeconomic policy.

Concepts for Review

Aggregate demand
Consumer expenditure (C)
Investment spending (I)
Government purchases (G)
Exports (X)
Imports (IM)
$C + I + G + X - IM$

National income (GNP)
Gross domestic product (GDP)
Disposable income (DI)
Circular flow diagram
Transfer payments
Scatter diagram
Consumption function

Marginal propensity to consume (MPC)
Movements along versus shifts of the consumption function
Money fixed assets
Temporary versus permanent tax changes

Questions for Discussion

1. What is the difference between "investment" as the term is used by most people and "investment" as defined by an economist? Which of the following acts constitute "investment" according to the economist's definition?
   a. General Motors constructs a new assembly line.
   b. You buy 100 shares of General Motors stock.
   c. A small steel company goes bankrupt, and Stelco purchases its factory and equipment.
   d. Your family buys a newly constructed home from a developer.
   e. Your family buys an older home from another family. (*Hint:* Are any *new* products demanded by this action?)

2. What would the circular flow diagram (Figure 5–1) look like in an economy with no government and no foreign trade? Draw one for yourself.

3. On a piece of graph paper, construct the scatter diagram for Simpleland from the data given below. Use a ruler to draw in a line of best fit (the consumption function), and determine the MPC. If taxes were permanently increased by 500 in Simpleland, what would be the likely change in consumer spending?

	CONSUMER SPENDING	DISPOSABLE INCOME
1986	1750	2000
1987	2050	2500
1988	2450	3000
1989	2900	3500
1990	3350	4000

4. "The more repeatedly a government uses temporary income-tax and sales-tax cuts during recessions, and temporary income-tax and sales-tax surcharges during inflationary periods, the more irrelevant such an ongoing stabilization policy becomes." Discuss this statement.

5. Aggregate household saving is the difference between disposable income and consumer expenditure ($S = DI - C$). Use the data in Table 5–1 to derive the savings function in Macroland. Economists define the marginal propensity to save (MPS) as the slope of the savings function. It shows how much savings increases per unit increase in DI. What is the MPS in Macroland? What is the relationship between the MPC and the MPS?

6. If taxes are cut *temporarily* and consumer spending does not increase much, what must happen to consumer saving?

6

Demand-Side Equilibrium: Unemployment or Inflation?

Investment . . . is a flighty bird, which needs to be controlled.

J. R. HICKS

As we learned in Chapter 4, the interaction of aggregate demand and aggregate supply determines whether the economy will stagnate or prosper and whether our resources of labour and capital will be fully employed or unemployed. This is the second of a series of chapters devoted to studying this important process.

A simplified model of aggregate demand is constructed in this and the next chapter, and the supply side is added in Chapter 8. This first model of the economy teaches us much about the causes of unemployment and inflation, but it is too simple to deal with policy issues because the government and the financial system are largely ignored. Chapters 10 to 14 remedy these omissions, thereby making it possible to study how government policies affect unemployment and inflation. Thus, by Chapter 14 we will have provided a model that is capable of dealing with a wide variety of policy issues.

In Chapter 5 we examined the largest component of aggregate demand, which is consumer expenditure (C); here, we turn our attention first to the most volatile component, investment (I), and discuss its determinants and the reasons why investment spending is so variable and so difficult to predict.[1] Then, rather than waiting for a full discussion of the other components of aggregate demand, government purchases (G), and net exports $(X - IM)$, we construct an abbreviated model of the determination of national income based only on the C and I components. We use this model to provide a preliminary description of how the state of aggregate demand influences the level of the gross domestic product and to consider a question of great importance to policy-makers: Can the economy be expected to achieve full employment of its resources if the government does not intervene?

The Extreme Variability of Investment

The first thing to be said about investment spending is that it is extraordinarily variable.

Unlike consumer spending, which follows movements in disposable income with great (though not perfect) reliability, investment spending swings from high to low levels with annoying rapidity. During recessions, for example, the decline in investment generally constitutes the greatest part of the total drop in real GDP, despite the fact

---

[1] We repeat the warning given in the previous chapter about the meaning of the word *investment*. It *includes* spending by businesses and individuals on *newly produced* factories, machinery, and houses. But it *excludes* sales of *used* industrial plants, equipment, and homes, and it *also excludes* purely financial transactions, such as the purchase of stocks and bonds.

that investment is a much smaller portion of GDP than is consumption. What accounts for these movements of investment demand?

Business Confidence and Expectations about the Future

While many factors influence business people's desires to invest, John Maynard Keynes (the economist who first used models of the sort we build in this chapter) laid great stress on the *state of business confidence*. Today's business confidence depends on *expectations about the future*.

While it is tricky to measure, it does seem obvious that businesses will build more factories and purchase more new machines when their expectations are optimistic. Conversely, their investment plans will be very cautious if the economic outlook appears bleak. Keynes pointed out that psychological perceptions like these are subject to abrupt shifts (as we have seen in the behaviour of stock prices), so that fluctuations in investment can be a major cause of instability in aggregate demand—hence, Hicks's analogy to a "flighty bird."

Unfortunately, neither economists nor, for that matter, psychologists have any very good ideas about how to *measure*—much less how to *control*—business confidence. Therefore, economists usually focus on several more objective determinants of investment—determinants that are easy to quantify and more easily influenced by government policy.

The Level and Growth of Demand

There will be a strong incentive to invest when firms find that demand is pressing against their capacity. Under these circumstances, firms are very likely to feel that new factories and machinery can be employed profitably. By contrast, if there is a great deal of spare capacity (unused machinery, empty factories, and so on), business managers will not find investment attractive.

Since it takes a substantial amount of time to order machinery or to build a factory, investment plans are made with an eye on the future. Even when pressures on current capacity are not particularly severe, a firm experiencing rapid growth in sales is likely to start investing *now* so that it will have adequate capacity when it is needed in the future. Conversely, slow growth of output will discourage investment. Government stabilization policy thus has another handle on investment spending, for by stimulating aggregate demand it can induce business firms to invest more, though the precise amount may be hard to predict.

The Rate of Interest

The interest rate is the determinant of investment that is studied most extensively by economists, and it will play a pivotal role in later chapters. A good deal of business investment is financed by borrowing, and the interest rate indicates how much firms must pay for that privilege.

The amount that businesses will want to invest depends on the real interest rate they have to pay on their borrowings. The lower the real rate of interest, the more investment spending there will be.

The reason for this relationship is explained more fully in the appendix to this chapter.

In Chapter 12 we will study in some detail how the government can influence the rate of interest. Since interest rates affect investment, policy-makers have a handle on aggregate demand—a handle they do not hesitate to use. The point is that, unlike business confidence, interest rates are visible and manipulable, at least for short periods. Therefore, even if investment responds much more dramatically to changes in confidence than to changes in interest rates, interest rates attract more attention as a potential instrument of government policy.

Biographical Note:
John Maynard Keynes (1883–1946)

John Maynard Keynes, the son of a prominent upper-class British economist, was something of a child prodigy. After an outstanding scholastic career at Eton and Cambridge, Keynes took the civil service examination. His second-place score was not good enough to land him the position he wanted and should have had (in the Treasury), so in 1907 he found himself in the India Office. Some years later, reflecting on the fact that his lowest score on the exam was in the economics section, he suggested with characteristic immodesty, "The examiners presumably knew less than I did."* He was probably right.

While Keynes disliked his work at the India Office, his time there was not wasted. It was during that period that he wrote his *Treatise on Probability* (1909), which drew the admiration of Bertrand Russell and won Keynes's election as a lifetime Fellow of Cambridge's King's College.

During World War I, Keynes was called to the Treasury to assist in planning various financial aspects of the war. There his "unique combination of the guts of a burglar and the intellect of a first-class economist"‡ established him as a dominant figure. At the war's end, he represented the British Treasury at the peace conference in Versailles. The conference was a turning point in Keynes's life, though it was one of his few failures. He sought unsuccessfully to persuade the Allies to take a less punitive attitude toward the vanquished Germans and then left the conference in protest to work on his *Economic Consequences of the Peace*, which created a furor when it was published in 1919. In it Keynes argued that the Germans could never meet the harsh economic terms of the treaty and that its viciousness posed the threat of continued instability and perhaps another war in Europe.

No longer welcome in government, Keynes returned to Cambridge and to his circle of literary and artistic friends in London's Bloomsbury district—a group that included Virginia Woolf, Lytton Strachey, and E. M. Forster. In 1925 he married the ballerina Lydia Lopokova.

Between the wars, Keynes devoted himself to making money, to economic theory, and to political economy. He made both himself and King's College rich by speculating in international currencies and commodities—allegedly by studying the morning's newspapers while still in bed each day. As a scholar, he wrote the *Tract on Monetary Reform* (1923), a stunning denunciation of the gold standard, which was published two years before Churchill once again tied the pound to gold. In 1936, he published his masterpiece, *The General Theory of Employment, Interest, and Money*, upon which modern macroeconomics is based. Finally, as a political activist, he used newspaper and magazine articles and visits to Whitehall and Washington to urge governments to lift their economies out of the Depression (which began for Britain in the 1920s) through policies that we would now call "Keynesian."

A heart attack in 1937 reduced Keynes's activities somewhat, but he returned to the Treasury during World War II and conducted several delicate financial negotiations with the Americans. Then, as the capstone to a truly remarkable career, he represented the United Kingdom—and by all accounts dominated the proceedings—at the conference in Bretton Woods, New Hampshire, in 1944, that established an international financial system that would serve the Western world for twenty-seven years. (See Chapter 15.)

He died of a heart attack at his home on Easter Sunday of 1946 as Lord Keynes, Baron of Tilton, a man who had achieved almost everything that he sought and who had only one regret: He wished he had drunk more champagne.

*Quoted in E. A. G. Robinson, "John Maynard Keynes," in R. Lekachman, ed., *Keynes' General Theory: Reports of Three Decades* (New York: St. Martin's Press, Inc., 1964), page 25.
‡Robert Lekachman, *The Age of Keynes* (New York: Random House, 1966), page 27. This book contains a marvellous biography of Keynes, as does Robert Heilbroner's *The Worldly Philosophers*, 4th edition (New York: Simon and Schuster, 1972).

Tax Provisions

The government has still another way to influence investment spending—by altering various provisions of the tax law. For example, the tax law sets maximum **depreciation allowances**, which govern how firms may deduct the costs of investment from their taxable income. In many of its budgets in the last 40 years, the federal government has made these allowances more generous in a variety of ways. The idea was simple. More generous depreciation allowances lead to bigger tax deductions, and hence smaller tax bills, for firms that invest. This enhances the profitability of investment and so should encourage more investment.

Depreciation allowances are tax deductions that businesses may claim when they spend money on investment goods.

A Simplified Circular Flow

Let us now put consumption and investment together and see how they interact, using as our organizing framework the circular flow diagram introduced in the last chapter. For this purpose, we simplify the circular flow somewhat by leaving out the government and the foreign sector.

There are two reasons for doing this. The first is pedagogical: The workings of the model are much clearer if we strip away some of its complications. But there is an equally important reason. One of the crucial questions surrounding government attempts to stabilize the economy is whether the economy would *automatically* gravitate toward full employment if the government simply left it alone. John Maynard Keynes, contradicting the teachings of generations of economists before him, claimed it would not. But Keynes's views remain controversial. We can study this issue best by imagining an economy that has no government, so that all the aggregate demand comes from the private sector. This is just what we do in this chapter.

Look now at Figure 6–1, which is the same as Figure 5–1 of the last chapter, except that the government and foreign sectors have been omitted. The first thing you may notice is that, with the government and foreign trade out of the picture, there is no longer any leakage out of the national income for imports and taxes (nor are there transfer payments), so there is no important difference between national income and disposable income. Second, there is no government or foreign component of total spending; instead, spending is represented by the sum $C + I$.

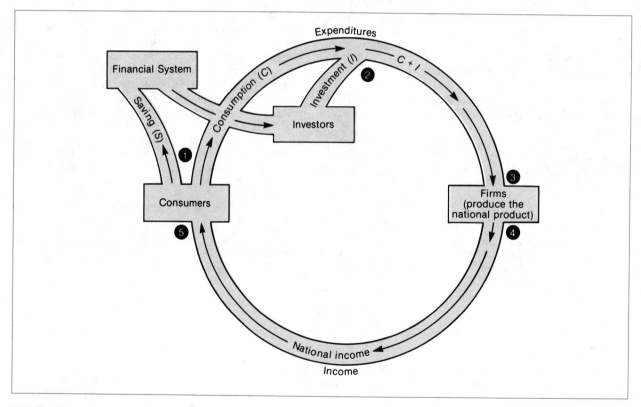

FIGURE 6–1
A Simplified Circular Flow
Here we show a simplified version of the circular flow of income and expenditures that we introduced in Chapter 5. The simplification amounts to shutting off the pipes leading into and out of the government and the rest of the world. Thus, this circular flow represents an economy with no government or foreign trade. Notice that aggregate demand now has only two components (consumer spending and investment spending) and that the entire national income flows to consumers without taxation.

The Meaning of Equilibrium GDP

We can use Figure 6–1 to begin the construction of a simple model of the determination of national income. A first step is to understand the term "equilibrium income."

As was explained in the last chapter, national *product* and national *income* must, of necessity, be equal. But the same cannot automatically be said of total *spending*. Look again at Figure 6–1 and imagine that, for some reason, the total expenditures $(C + I)$ that are being made at point 3 are greater than the output that is being produced by the business firms at point 4.

Two things may happen in such a situation. Since consumers and firms together are buying (in the forms of C and I) more than firms are producing, business firms are being forced to take goods out of their warehouses to meet customer demands. Thus, inventory stocks must be falling. These inventory reductions are a signal to retailers of a need to increase their orders, and to manufacturers of a need to step up their production. Consequently, production is likely to rise. At some later date, if there is evidence that the high level of aggregate demand is not just a temporary aberration, either manufacturers or retailers (or both) may also respond to the buoyant sales performances by raising their prices. Economists therefore say that neither output nor the price level is in **equilibrium** when aggregate demand exceeds the current rate of production.

It is clear from the definition of equilibrium that the economy cannot be in equilibrium when aggregate demand exceeds production, for the falling inventories demonstrate to firms that their production and pricing decisions were not quite appropriate.[2] Thus, since we normally use GDP to measure output:

> Equilibrium refers to a situation in which consumers and firms have no incentive to change their behaviour. They are content to continue with things as they are.

The equilibrium level of GDP cannot be one at which total spending exceeds output because firms will notice that inventory stocks are being depleted. They may first decide to increase production sufficiently to meet the higher demand. Later they may decide to raise prices as well.

Now imagine the other case, in which the flow of total spending reaching firms falls short of current production. Some output cannot be sold and winds up as additions to inventories. The inventory pile-up acts as a signal to firms that at least one of their decisions was wrong. Once again, they will probably react first by cutting back on production, causing the GDP to fall. If the imbalance persists, they may also lower prices in order to stimulate sales. But they certainly will not be happy with things as they are. Thus:

The equilibrium level of GDP cannot be one at which total spending is less than output because firms will not allow inventories to continue to pile up. They may decide to decrease production, or they may decide to cut prices in order to stimulate a demand. Normally, firms are reluctant to cut prices until they are quite certain that the low level of demand is not a temporary phenomenon. So they rely more heavily on reductions in output.

Equilibrium on the Demand Side of the Economy

You may have noticed that we have now determined, through a process of elimination, the level of national income and product that is consistent with people's desires to spend. We have reasoned that whenever GDP is below total spending $(C + I)$, the GDP will rise, and that whenever GDP is above $C + I$, the GDP will fall. Equilibrium can occur, then, only when there is just enough spending to absorb the current level of

---

[2] All the models in this book assume, strictly for simplicity, that firms never want to change their inventories. Deliberate changes in inventories are treated in more advanced courses.

production. Under such circumstances, producers conclude that their price and output decisions are correct, and they have no incentive to change them. We conclude that:

The **equilibrium level of GDP on the demand side** is the one at which total spending equals production. In such a situation, firms find their inventories remaining at desired levels, so there is no incentive to change output or prices.

The simple circular flow diagram, then, has helped us to understand the concept of equilibrium level of GDP on the demand side. It has also shown us how the economy is driven toward that equilibrium. It leaves unanswered, however, three important questions.

1. How large is the equilibrium level of GDP?
2. Will the economy suffer from unemployment, inflation, or both?
3. Is the equilibrium level of GDP on the demand side consistent with firms' desires to produce? That is, is it also an equilibrium on the *supply* side?

The first two questions will occupy our attention in this chapter; the third question is reserved for Chapter 8.

Constructing the Total Expenditure Schedule

Our first objective is to determine precisely the equilibrium level of GDP and to see what factors it depends upon. To make the analysis more concrete, we turn to a numerical example. Specifically, we examine the relationship between aggregate demand and GDP in Macroland, the hypothetical economy that was introduced in the last chapter.

Columns 1 and 2 of Table 6–1 repeat the consumption function of Macroland that we first encountered in Table 5–1. They show how consumer spending, C, depends on national income, which we now begin to symbolize by the letter Y. However, one thing has changed here. The consumption function in Chapter 5 related C to *disposable* income (DI), whereas the consumption function in Table 6–1 relates C to *national* income (Y). This change is legitimate because, in this chapter, we have eliminated the government and the foreign sector from the picture. With no taxes and no transfer payments, there is no difference between DI and Y. Because (as we showed in Chapter 5) national income must equal national product, Y can be used to represent either income or output.

TABLE 6–1
Total Expenditure in Macroland (billions of dollars)

(1) INCOME (Y)	(2) CONSUMPTION (C)	(3) INVESTMENT (I)	(4) TOTAL EXPENDITURE ($C + I$)
200	170	70	240
250	210	70	280
300	250	70	320
350	290	70	360
400	330	70	400
450	370	70	440
500	410	70	480
550	450	70	520
600	490	70	560

This table illustrates the derivation of the total expenditure schedule, which is shaded in green. It is derived from the consumption schedule, columns 1 and 2, and from the investment schedule, columns 1 and 3, by simple addition. This is because total spending is the sum $C + I$.

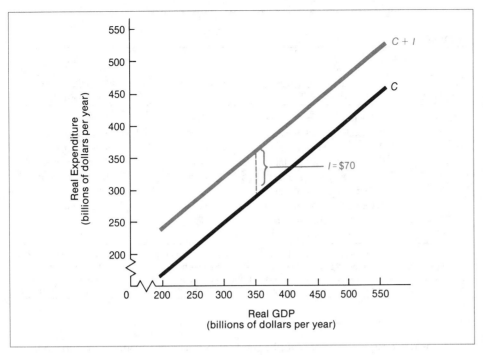

FIGURE 6-2
Construction of the Total Expenditure Schedule
This figure shows in a diagram what Table 6-1 showed numerically—the construction of a total expenditure schedule from its components. Line *C* is the consumption function that we first encountered in Figure 5-6, except that GDP, not disposable income, is measured along the horizontal axis. Line *C* + *I* is the total expenditure schedule and is obtained by adding investment (assumed always to be $70 billion in this example) to the consumption function.

Column 3 provides the other component of aggregate demand, *I*, through the simplifying assumption that investment spending is $70 billion in Macroland, regardless of the level of GDP. By adding together the second and third columns, we calculate *C* + *I*, or total expenditure, which is displayed in column 4. Columns 1 and 4, shaded in green, show how total expenditure depends on income in Macroland. We call this the **total expenditure schedule**.

Figure 6-2 shows the construction of the expenditure schedule graphically. The line labelled *C* is the consumption function of Macroland and simply duplicates Figure 5-6 of the last chapter, except that *Y*, not *DI*, appears on the horizontal axis. It plots on a graph the numbers given in columns 1 and 2 of Table 6-1. The line labelled *C* + *I* depicts the total expenditure schedule that we have just derived by plotting the data in columns 1 and 4 of the table. That is, at each level of GDP measured along the horizontal axis, the height of the *C* + *I* line indicates the sum of consumption plus investment.

The difference between the two lines, therefore, is investment. In the diagram, the lines are parallel—that is, the distance between them is always the same. This distance is $70 billion—the volume of investment assumed in the example. If investment were not always $70 billion, either the two lines would move closer together (at income levels at which investment was below $70 billion) or grow farther apart (at income levels at which investment was above $70 billion). For example, our list of determinants of investment spending suggested that *I* might be larger at higher levels of GDP. Because of this added investment—which is called **induced investment**—the resulting *C* + *I* schedule would have a steeper slope than the *C* schedule.

A **total expenditure schedule** shows how total spending varies with the level of national income (GDP).

Induced investment is that part of investment spending that rises when GDP rises and falls when GDP falls.

The Mechanics of Income Determination

We are now ready to determine the equilibrium level of GDP in Macroland. Look first at Table 6-2, which presents the logic of our circular flow argument in tabular form. The first two columns of this table reproduce the expenditure schedule that was constructed in Table 6-1. The other columns explain the process by which equilibrium is approached. Let us see why a GDP of $400 billion must be the equilibrium level.

TABLE 6–2
The Determination of Equilibrium Output

(1) OUTPUT (Y) (billions of dollars)	(2) TOTAL SPENDING (C + I) (billions of dollars)	(3) BALANCE OF SPENDING AND OUTPUT	(4) INVENTORIES ARE:	(5) PRODUCERS WILL RESPOND BY:
200	240	Spending exceeds output	Falling	Producing more
250	280	Spending exceeds output	Falling	Producing more
300	320	Spending exceeds output	Falling	Producing more
350	360	Spending exceeds output	Falling	Producing more
400	400	Spending equals output	Constant	Not changing production
450	440	Output exceeds spending	Rising	Producing less
500	480	Output exceeds spending	Rising	Producing less
550	520	Output exceeds spending	Rising	Producing less
600	560	Output exceeds spending	Rising	Producing less

Columns 1 and 2 are the total expenditure schedule derived in the previous table. The remaining columns explain how the equilibrium level of national income can be derived from these data. For example, reading across the first row we see that when GDP is $200 billion, total spending is $240 billion. Thus spending exceeds production (by $40 billion), so that inventories must be falling. Producers are likely to respond to this drop in inventory stocks by raising their rate of production. The other rows are read similarly, and together they show that only $400 billion can be the equilibrium level of GDP. This is the only output level that firms will not want to change.

Consider first any output level below $400 billion. For example, when GDP is $350 billion, C is $290 billion and I is $70 billion for a total of $360 billion (column 2), which is $10 billion more than production. With spending greater than output (column 3), inventories will be falling (column 4). As the table suggests, this will be a signal to producers to raise their output (column 5). Clearly, then, no output level below Y = $400 billion can be an equilibrium. Output is too low.

A similar line of reasoning can eliminate any output level above $400 billion. Consider, for example, Y = $450 billion. The table shows that total spending is $440 billion if national income is $450 billion. So $10 billion of the GDP is unsold. This raises producers' inventory stocks and signals them that their rate of production is too high.

Just as we concluded from our circular flow diagram, then, equilibrium will be achieved only when total spending (C + I) is equal to GDP (Y). In symbols, our condition for equilibrium GDP is:

$$C + I = Y.$$

The table shows that this occurs only at a GDP of $400 billion. This, then, must be the equilibrium level of GDP.

Figure 6–3 shows this same conclusion graphically, by adding a 45° line to Figure 6–2. Why a 45° line? Recall that a 45° line marks all points on a graph at which the value of the variable measured on the horizontal axis is equal to the value of the variable measured on the vertical axis. In this convenient graph of the expenditure schedule, gross domestic product (Y) is measured on the horizontal axis and total expenditure (C + I) is measured on the vertical axis. So the 45° line shows all the points at which output and spending are equal: that is, where Y = C + I. The 45° line therefore displays all the points at which the economy *can possibly* be at equilibrium, for if C + I is not equal to Y, firms will not be content with their current output levels.

Now we must compare these potential equilibrium points with the actual combinations of spending and output that the economy can attain, given the behaviour of consumers and investors. That behaviour, as we have seen, is described by the C + I line in Figure 6–3, which shows how total expenditure varies as income changes. The economy will *always* be on the C + I line because only points on the C + I line are consistent with the spending plans of consumers and investors. Similarly, *if* the

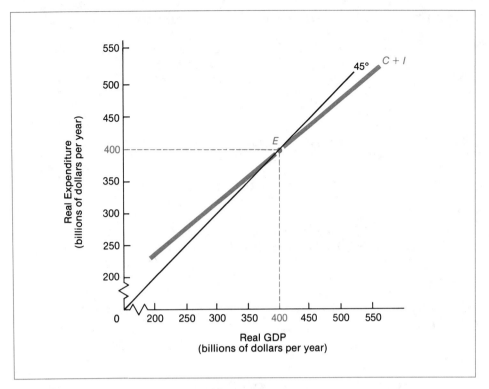

FIGURE 6-3

Income–Expenditure Diagram

This figure adds a 45° line—which marks off points where expenditure and output are equal—to
Figure 6-2. Since the condition for equilibrium GDP is that expenditure and output must be equal, this line
can be used to determine the equilibrium level of GDP. In this example, equilibrium is at point *E*, where GDP
is $400 billion—precisely as we found in Table 6-2.

economy is in equilibrium, it *must* be on the 45° line. As Figure 6–3 shows, these two
requirements together imply that the only viable equilibrium is at point *E*, where the
C + *I* line intersects the 45° line. Only this point is consistent both with equilibrium
and with the actual desires to consume and invest.

Notice that to the left of the equilibrium point, *E*, the *C* + *I* line lies above the
45° line. This means that total spending exceeds total output, as we have already noted
in words and with numbers. Hence inventories will be falling and firms will conclude
that they should increase production. The opposite is true to the right of equilibrium
point *E*; here, spending falls short of output, inventories are rising, and firms will cut
back production.

Diagrams like this one will recur so frequently in this and the next several
chapters that it will be convenient to have a name for them. Let us, therefore, call
them **income–expenditure diagrams** since they show how expenditures vary with
income. Sometimes we shall also refer to them simply as **45° line diagrams**. In later
chapters, when we add in other components of spending (by the government and by
foreigners), we will no longer refer to the total expenditure line in these diagrams as
just the *C* + *I* line. We will draw many more total expenditure lines, but they will have
become *C* + *I* + *G* + *X* – *IM* lines. The theoretical reasoning that we are learning now
will apply in just the same way—only the detailed label for the total expenditure line
will be more cumbersome. To ensure that you do not become confused about the
equilibrium condition as we add in new components, remember this general rule:

An income–expenditure
diagram, also called a 45°
line diagram, plots total
real expenditure (on the
vertical axis) against real
income (on the horizontal
axis). The 45° line marks
off points where income
and expenditure are equal.

Equilibrium output on the demand side occurs at the level where the total expenditure
schedule intersects the 45° line.

The Simple Algebra of Income Determination

We have just presented our model of demand-side equilibrium both graphically and in tabular form. It can also be explained with some simple algebra.

Written as an equation, the consumption function of Macroland is:

$$C = 10 + 0.8Y.$$

This is simply the equation of a straight line with intercept 10 and slope 0.8. Investment in Macroland is assumed to be 70, regardless of the level of income. So the sum $C + I$ is:

$$C + I = 10 + 0.8Y + 70 = 80 + 0.8Y.$$

This is the equation of the $C + I$ curve found in Figure 6–3.

Since the equilibrium quantity of GDP demanded is defined by:

$$Y = C + I,$$

we can solve for the equilibrium value of Y algebraically by substituting $80 + 0.8Y$ for $C + I$. Thus, we have:

$$Y = C + I = 80 + 0.8Y.$$

To solve this equation for Y, first subtract $0.8Y$ from both sides to get:

$$0.2Y = 80.$$

Then divide both sides by 0.2 to obtain the answer:

$$Y = 400.$$

This, of course, is precisely the solution we found by graphical and tabular methods.

The method of solution is easily generalized to deal with any set of numbers in our equations. Suppose the consumption function is:

$$C = a + bY.$$

(In our example, $a = 10$ and $b = 0.8$.) Then the equilibrium condition that $Y = C + I$ implies:

$$Y = a + bY + I.$$

Subtracting bY from both sides leads to:

$$(1 - b)Y = a + I,$$

and dividing through by $1 - b$ gives:

$$Y = \frac{a + I}{1 - b}.$$

This formula, which is certainly not to be memorized, is valid for any numerical values of a, b, and I (so long as b is between zero and one).

The Aggregate Demand Curve

Chapter 4 sketched a framework for macroeconomic analysis by introducing aggregate demand and aggregate supply curves that relate aggregate quantities demanded and supplied to the price level. Yet the price level has not even been mentioned so far in our discussion of equilibrium. It is now time to remedy this omission, for only by explicit analysis of the determination of the price level will we be able to deal with important issues relating to inflation.

Fortunately, no further mechanical apparatus is required. The price level can be brought into our income–expenditure analysis by recalling something we learned in the last chapter: At any given level of real income, higher prices lead to lower real consumer spending. One reason, you will recall, is that consumers own assets whose values are fixed in money terms, and which therefore lose purchasing power when prices rise. With real wealth lower, consumers spend less and therefore total spending in the economy falls. In reality, however, another, much more powerful, reason for this dependency of the position of the total expenditure schedule on the price level comes from foreign trade: The higher our price level, the more households shift their purchases toward imported items, leaving a reduced level of spending for domestically produced goods. For both these reasons, then, a rise in the price level will lower the consumption function depicted in Figure 6–2 and, hence, the total expenditure schedule as well. Conversely, a fall in the price level will raise both the C and $C + I$ schedules in the diagram.

What, then, do changes in the price level do to the equilibrium level of real GDP on the demand side? Common sense says that, with lower spending, equilibrium GDP should fall. And Figure 6–4, on page 142, shows that this conclusion is correct. The top panel in the figure shows that the total expenditure line shifts down when the price level rises from 100 to 200. In this example, the equilibrium value for national income on the demand side falls from \$400 billion to \$300 billion, since consumers have reduced their spending. Indeed, for every conceivable level of prices, there is a different position for the $C + I$ line and therefore a different level of equilibrium output on the demand side. We can summarize all these possibilities with a series of if–then propositions. For example, if price equals 100, then equilibrium quantity demanded is 400. This combination of values for price and output is recorded in the lower, summary panel as point E_1. Similarly, if price equals 200, then equilibrium quantity demanded is 300, and this combination is recorded in the summary panel as point E_2. The line connecting all such summary points for all possible combinations of price and output is the aggregate demand curve. To review, then:

A rise in the price level leads to a lower equilibrium level of real aggregate quantity demanded. This relationship between the price level and the equilibrium quantity of real GDP demanded is depicted in the lower panel of Figure 6–4 and is precisely what we called the **aggregate demand curve** in earlier chapters. It comes directly from the 45° line diagram. Thus, points E_1, and E_2 in the lower panel of Figure 6–4 correspond to the points bearing the same labels in the upper panel.

We have also seen that:

An income–expenditure diagram like the one in Figure 6–3 can be drawn up only for a *specific* price level. At different price levels, the $C + I$ schedule will be different and, hence, the equilibrium quantity of GDP demanded will be different.

As we shall now see, this finding is critical to understanding the genesis of unemployment and inflation.

FIGURE 6–4

Derivation of the Aggregate Demand Curve

Higher prices lower the position of the total expenditure line ($C + I$), leading to a lower aggregate quantity demanded. The equilibrium quantity demanded for each possible price level is summarized in the lower panel. This summary line is the aggregate demand curve.

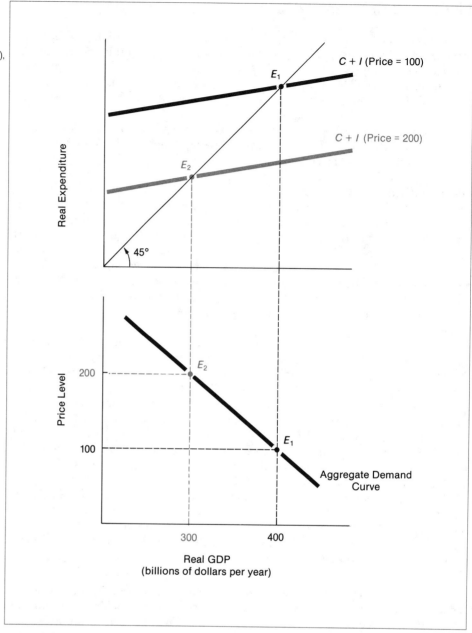

Demand-Side Equilibrium and Full Employment

We now turn to the second major question of this chapter: Will the economy achieve an equilibrium at full employment without inflation, or will there be unemployment, inflation, or both?

In the income–expenditure diagrams used so far, the equilibrium level of GDP demanded has been shown as the intersection of the total expenditure schedule and the 45° line, regardless of whatever level of GDP might correspond to full employment of the nation's available resources. However, as we will see now, when equilibrium GDP exceeds the full-employment level of output, the result is inflation. And when equilibrium falls below full employment, there will be unemployment and recession.

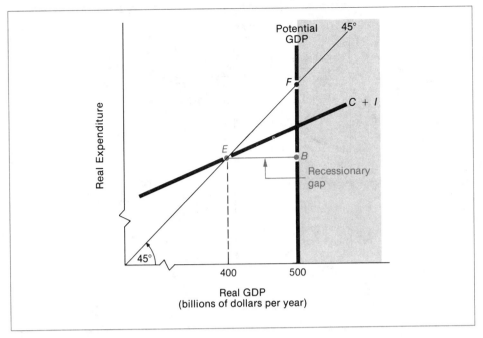

FIGURE 6–5
A Recessionary Gap
Sometimes equilibrium GDP
may fall below potential GDP, so
that some workers are
unemployed. This diagram
illustrates such a case. The
horizontal distance *EB* between
equilibrium GDP and potential
GDP is called the recessionary
gap.

This fact was one of the principal messages of Keynes's *The General Theory of Employment, Interest, and Money*. Since he was writing during the Great Depression, it was natural for him to stress the case in which equilibrium falls short of full employment so that there are unemployed resources. Figure 6–5 illustrates this possibility. A vertical line has been erected at the full-employment level of GDP (called "potential GDP"), which is assumed to be $500 billion in the example. We see that the *C + I* curve cuts the 45° line at point *E*, which corresponds to a GDP (*Y* = $400 billion) below potential GDP. In this case, the *C + I* curve is too low to lead to full employment. Such a situation might arise because either consumers or investors are unwilling to spend at normal rates or because the price level is "too high," thereby depressing the *C + I* curve. Unemployment must occur because not enough output will be demanded to keep the entire labour force busy.

The distance between the equilibrium level of output demanded and the full-employment level of output (that is, potential GDP) is called the **recessionary gap**—and is shown by the horizontal distance from *E* to *B*.

It is clear from Figure 6–5 that full employment can be reached only by raising the total spending schedule to eliminate the recessionary gap. Specifically, the *C + I* schedule must move upward until it cuts the 45° line at point *F*. Can this happen without government intervention? We know that a sufficiently large drop in the price level could do the job. But is that a realistic prospect? We will study this question after we have brought the supply side into the picture. But first let us consider the other case, in which equilibrium GDP exceeds full employment.

Figure 6–6 illustrates this possibility. The expenditure schedule intersects the 45° line at point *E*, where GDP is $600 billion. But this exceeds the full-employment level, *Y* = $500 billion. A case like this can arise when consumer or investment spending is unusually buoyant or when a "low" price level pushes the *C + I* curve upward.

To reach an equilibrium at full employment in Figure 6–6, the price level would have to rise enough to drive the *C + I* schedule *down* until it passed through point *F*. The horizontal distance *BE*—which indicates the amount by which the quantity of GDP demanded exceeds potential GDP—is called the **inflationary gap**. If there is an inflationary gap, a higher price level or some other means of reducing total expenditure is necessary to reach an equilibrium at full employment.

The **recessionary gap** is the amount by which the equilibrium level of real GDP falls short of potential GDP.

The **inflationary gap** is the amount by which equilibrium real GDP exceeds the full-employment level of GDP.

FIGURE 6-6
An Inflationary Gap

Sometimes equilibrium GDP may lie above potential GDP, meaning that there are more jobs than required for full employment. This diagram illustrates such a case. The horizontal distance *BE* between potential GDP and equilibrium GDP is called the inflationary gap. It is gradually eliminated by rising prices, which pull the *C + I* schedule down until it passes through point *F*.

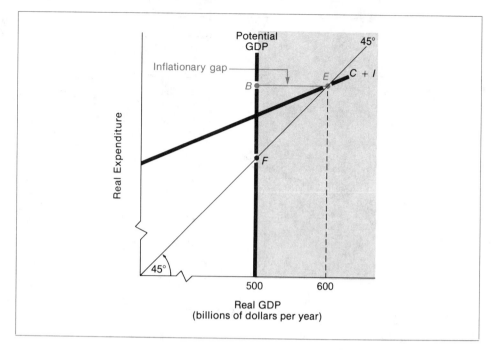

In sum, only if the price level and the spending plans of consumers and investors are "just right" will the total expenditure line (the *C + I* line in this first simplified model) intersect the 45° line precisely at full employment, so that neither a recessionary gap nor an inflationary gap occurs. Are there reasons to expect this outcome? Does the economy have a self-correcting mechanism that automatically eliminates recessionary or inflationary gaps and propels it toward full employment? And how is it that inflation and unemployment sometimes occur together? These are questions we are not quite ready to address because we have yet to bring *aggregate supply* into the picture, and, as we learned in Chapter 4, the price level is determined by the interaction of *both* aggregate demand *and* aggregate supply. However, it is not too early to get an idea about why things can go wrong, why the economy can find itself far away from full employment.

The Co-ordination of Saving and Investment

To understand what goes wrong with the economy in a recession, it is useful to pose the following question: How can the full-employment level of GDP fail to be an equilibrium?

To find an answer, look back at the simplified circular flow diagram (Figure 6-1 on page 134). Suppose that firms produce the full-employment level of GDP, and this becomes the national income that emerges at point 4 in the diagram. This full-employment level of income then flows to consumers at point 5, who save some of it and spend the rest. The saving, you will note, "leaks out" of the circular flow at point 1. So, once we pass this point, consumption is less than full-employment GDP. But then, at point 2, an additional source of spending enters: investment. Recalling that the condition for equilibrium is that the sum *C + I* equals the GDP, we have the following conclusion:

The economy will reach an equilibrium at full employment only if the amount that consumers wish to save out of full-employment incomes is precisely equal to the amount that investors want to invest. If these two magnitudes happen to be unequal, then full employment will not be an equilibrium for the economy.

At the Frontier: Unemployment and Inflation as Co-ordination Failures

The idea that recessions are times when the market system fails to perform properly is a very old one, predating Keynes. As we have seen in this chapter, Keynes attributed this failure to a *lack of co-ordination* between the decisions of savers and those of investors. If savers want to save more out of full-employment income than investors want to invest, full employment cannot be an equilibrium for the economy. GDP must be lower and unemployment must be higher.

In recent years, economic theorists have begun to formalize Keynes's common-sense notion that co-ordination failures may be the root cause of recessions and unemployment. Although normally couched in mathematical terms, the basic idea is elementary and is well illustrated by the parable of the football game.

Picture a crowd watching a football game. Something exciting happens and the fans rise from their seats. The people in the front rows stand up first, and those seated behind them are forced either to stand or to give up watching the game. Soon all the people in the stadium are on their feet. But with everyone standing, no one can see any better than when everyone was sitting, and the fans are enduring the further discomfort of standing. (Never mind that sitting in stadium seats can hardly be called comfortable!) So all of the fans in the stadium would be better off if they agreed to sit down. But co-ordinating the decisions of tens of thousands of fans is virtually impossible. So everyone stands.

In the terminology of economics, the football stadium has *two equilibria*—a superior one, with everyone sitting, and an inferior one, with everyone standing. In practice, we all know what happens. The crowd rises to its feet on every exciting play, sits during lulls in the action, and then rises again at the slightest hint of excitement. Thus it vacillates between the good equilibrium and the bad equilibrium.

Now, what does all this have to do with unemployment? Recall Keynes's idea that unemployment arises because the decisions of savers and investors are not co-ordinated. Left to their own devices, individuals acting in their own best interests often choose actions that lead to the inferior equilibrium with high unemployment (analogous to standing at the football game), even though there is a superior equilibrium with low unemployment (like sitting at the game). Although people prefer the equilibrium with low unemployment, they may be unable to co-ordinate their decisions in order to produce it.

If high unemployment does in fact arise from *co-ordination failures*, the government might be able to do something to cure it. Keynes certainly thought so. But the football analogy reminds us that a central authority may not find it easy to solve the co-ordination problem.

The co-ordination–failure idea may also help to explain why it is so hard to stop inflation. Nobody wants prices to rise. Everyone would prefer that they be stable. But stopping inflation is also a bit like watching a football game. Think of yourself as the seller of a product. If all the other sellers in the economy would hold their prices steady, you would be happy to hold yours steady, too. Hence zero inflation appears to be an equilibrium for the economy, just as sitting at the football game is an equilibrium for the football stadium. But if you believe that others will continue to raise their prices at, say, 5 percent per year, you will probably want to increase yours as well. Hence 5 percent inflation may also be an equilibrium, like standing at a football game. Everyone in society may agree that the equilibrium with 5 percent inflation is inferior, but since a commitment cannot be obtained in advance that no one will raise prices, society can easily get stuck with that 5 percent inflation, just as football fans must frequently stand at ball games.

Specifically, we can see from the circular flow diagram that if saving exceeds investment at full employment, then the total demand arriving at the firms (point 3) will fall short of total output because the added investment spending is not enough to replace the leakage to saving. With demand inadequate to support production at full employment, we know that the GDP must fall below potential. There will be a recessionary gap. Conversely, if investment exceeds saving when the economy is at full employment, then total demand ($C + I$) will exceed potential GDP and production will rise above the full-employment level. There will be an inflationary gap.

Now this discussion does nothing but restate what we already know in different words. In symbols, our previous equilibrium condition was $C + I = Y$. If we note that Y is also the sum of consumption plus saving, $Y = C + S$, it follows that $C + I = C + S$, or $I = S$, is a restatement of the equilibrium condition. But this restatement holds the key to understanding why the economy can find itself stuck below full employment (or above it, for that matter), for *the people who do the investing are not the same people as those who do the saving.* In a modern capitalist economy, investing is done by one group of individuals (corporate executives and home buyers) while saving is done by another group.[3] It is easy to imagine that their plans may not be well co-ordinated. If they are not, we have just seen how either unemployment or inflation can arise.

Notice that these problems would never arise if the acts of saving and investing were not separated. Imagine a primitive economy of farmers, each of whom invests only in his own farm. There is no borrowing or lending and no financial system. In this world, any farmer wanting to buy a new plough or tractor (that is, wanting to *invest*) would have to refrain from consuming part of his income (that is, would have to *save*). Therefore, the amount that all farmers together planned to save out of full-employment income would of necessity be equal to the amount of planned investment. Total spending and production would always have to be equal at full employment.

Almost the same holds true in a centrally planned economy like that of China or the Soviet Union. But there, the state decides how much will be invested and has a great deal of leverage over how much saving people do. If the planners do their calculations correctly, they can force saving to be equal to investment at full employment. Consequently, business fluctuations have not been a major problem in planned economies. However, many of these economies have recently opted to embrace market principles; ever since, they have found that they, too, must deal with unemployment and inflation.

Keynes observed that modern market economies differ from either primitive societies or centrally planned societies in this fundamental way and that this separation of decisions within the market system is what leaves them vulnerable to recessions. However, one should not conclude that in order to avoid unemployment and recession the Canadian economy should revert either to a primitive form of capitalism or to rigid central planning. These "remedies" are far worse than the disease. Fortunately, there are policies the government can follow in an advanced capitalist economy to ease the pain of unemployment and recession—policies that we shall be studying in the following chapters.

[3]In a modern economy, it is not only households that save. Businesses also save, in the form of retained earnings. Nonetheless, households are the ultimate source of the saving needed to finance investment.

Summary

1. Investment is the most volatile component of aggregate demand, largely because it is tied so closely to the state of business confidence and to expectations about the future performance of the economy.

2. Government policy cannot influence business confidence in any reliable way, so policies designed to alter investment spending are aimed at more objective, though possibly less important, determinants of investment. Among these are interest rates, the overall state of aggregate demand, and corporate tax incentives.

3. The equilibrium level of national income on the demand side is the level at which total spending just equals production (GDP). In this chapter we ignore government and foreign demand, so total spending is the sum of consumption plus investment. Thus, in symbols, the condition for equilibrium is $Y = C + I$.

4. Income levels below equilibrium are bound to rise because, when spending exceeds output, firms will see their inventory stocks being depleted and will react by stepping up production.

5. Income levels above equilibrium are bound to fall because, when total spending is insufficient to absorb total output, inventories will pile up and firms will react by curtailing production.
6. The determination of the equilibrium level of GDP on the demand side can be portrayed on a convenient "income–expenditure diagram" as the point at which the total expenditure schedule—defined in this most simplified model as the sum of the consumption and investment schedules—crosses the 45° line. The 45° line is significant because it marks off points at which spending and output are equal (that is, at which $C + I = Y$), and this is the basic condition for equilibrium.
7. An income–expenditure diagram can be drawn up only for a specific price level, however. Thus the equilibrium GDP so determined depends on the price level.
8. Because higher prices reduce our export sales and because they lower the purchasing power of consumers' wealth and hence reduce their spending, equilibrium real GDP demanded is lower when prices are higher. This downward-sloping relationship is known as the aggregate demand curve.
9. Equilibrium GDP can be above or below potential GDP, which is defined as the GDP that would be produced if the labour force were fully employed.
10. If equilibrium GDP exceeds potential GDP, the difference is called an inflationary gap. If equilibrium GDP falls short of potential GDP, the resulting difference is called a recessionary gap.
11. Such gaps can occur in a decentralized economy because the saving that consumers want to do at full-employment income levels may differ from the investing that investors want to do. This problem is not likely to arise in a planned economy or in a primitive economy.

Concepts for Review

Depreciation allowances	$C + I = Y$	Recessionary gap
Equilibrium level of GDP	Income–expenditure (or 45° line) diagram	Inflationary gap
Total expenditure schedule	Aggregate demand curve	Co-ordination of saving
Induced investment	Full-employment level of GDP (or potential GDP)	and investment

---

Questions for Discussion

1. Why would someone interested in stabilization policy want to study a model of an economy in which there is no government?

2. Analysts of the economy often argue that the rate of business investment in Canada is too low. Does this chapter give you any ideas about what is meant by the phrase "too low"? What factors do you think accounted for the low level of investment spending in the early 1980s? (You may want to discuss this last issue with your instructor.)

3. Why is no arbitrary level of GDP an equilibrium for the economy? (Explain the economic mechanism involved.)

4. From the following data, construct an expenditure schedule on a piece of graph paper. Then use the income–expenditure (45° line) diagram to determine the equilibrium level of GDP.

INCOME	CONSUMPTION	INVESTMENT
1100	990	120
1150	1035	120
1200	1080	120
1250	1125	120
1300	1170	120

5. From the following data, construct an expenditure schedule on a piece of graph paper. Then use the income–expenditure (45° line) diagram to determine the equilibrium level of GDP.

INCOME	CONSUMPTION	INVESTMENT
1100	1020	90
1150	1050	105
1200	1080	120
1250	1110	135
1300	1140	150

Compare your answer with your answer to Question 4.

6. Suppose investment spending were always $250, and consumer spending depended on the price level in the following way:

PRICE LEVEL	CONSUMER SPENDING
80	740
90	720
100	700
110	680
120	660

On a piece of graph paper, use these data to construct an aggregate demand curve. Why do you think this example supposes that consumption declines as the price level rises?

7. Does the economy this year seem to have an inflationary gap or a recessionary gap? (If you do not know the answer from reading the newspaper, ask your instructor.)

8. From the data in Question 4, construct the saving schedule and the investment schedule on a piece of graph paper. (In doing so, remember that any income that is not consumed must have been saved.) Use these constructions to find the equilibrium level of GDP. (*Hint*: You may find *negative* saving at some income levels. There is nothing wrong with this. You do negative saving any time you draw down your bank account balance.)

9. Do the same thing with the data in Question 5.

10. Find the equilibrium level of GDP demanded in an economy in which investment is fixed at $250 and the consumption function is:

$$C = 250 + 0.5Y.$$

Show that saving equals planned investment in equilibrium.

11. Imagine an economy in which consumer expenditure is represented by the following equation:

$$C = 50 + 0.75Y.$$

Imagine also that investors want to spend $500 at every level of income: $I = 500$.
   a. What is the equilibrium level of income?
   b. If the full-employment level of income is $2000, is there a recessionary or an inflationary gap? If so, how much?
   c. What will happen to the equilibrium level of income if investors become pessimistic about the country's future and reduce their investment to $400?
   d. Is there a recessionary or an inflationary gap now? How much?

12. Ivyland has the following consumption function:

$$C = 100 + 0.75Y.$$

Firms in Ivyland always invest $200.
   a. Find the equilibrium level of GDP.
   b. How much is saved?
   c. Suppose consumers are given an inducement to save, so that the consumption function falls to $C = 50 + 0.75Y$, but at the same time firms boost investment spending to $240. Answer questions (a) and (b) under these new circumstances.

Appendix
Discounting and Present Value

Frequently, in business and economic problems, it is necessary to compare sums of money received (or paid) at different dates. Consider, for example, the purchase of a machine that costs $11,000 and will yield a revenue of $14,520 two years from today. If the machine can be financed by a two-year loan bearing 10 percent interest, it will cost the firm $2200 in interest

Costs and Benefits of Investing in a Machine

	End of Year 1	End of Year 2
Benefits		
Revenue derived from the machine	0	$14,520
Costs		
Interest	$1,100	1,100
Repayment of principal on loan	0	11,000
Total	$1,100	$12,100

payments and $11,000 in principal repayment by the end of the second year (see the table below). Is the machine a good investment?

The total costs of owning the machine over the two-year period ($1100 + $12,100 = $13,200) are less than the total benefits ($14,520). But this is clearly an invalid comparison, because the $14,520 in future benefits is not worth $14,520 in terms of today's money. Adding up dollars received (or paid) at different dates is a bit like adding apples and oranges. The process that has been invented for making these magnitudes comparable is called **discounting**, or **computing the present value** of a future sum of money.

To illustrate the concept of present value, let us ask how much $1 received a year from today is worth *in terms of today's money*. If the rate of interest is 10 percent, the answer is about 91 cents. Why? Because if we invest 91 cents today at 10 percent interest, it will grow to 91 cents plus 9.1 cents in interest = 100.1 cents in a year. Similar considerations apply to any rate of interest. In general:

If the rate of interest is i, the present value of \$1 to be received in a year is: $\dfrac{\$1}{(1+i)}$.

This is so, because in a year $\dfrac{\$1}{(1+i)}$ will grow to

$$\dfrac{\$1}{(1+i)}(1+i) = \$1.$$

What about money to be received two years from today? Using the same reasoning, \$1 invested today will grow to $\$1 \times (1.1) = \$1.10$ after one year and to $\$1 \times (1.1) \times (1.1) = \$1 \times (1.1)^2 = \$1.21$ after two years. Consequently, the present value of \$1 to be received two years from today is:

$$\dfrac{\$1}{(1.1)^2} = \dfrac{\$1}{1.21} = 82.64 \text{ cents.}$$

A similar analysis applies to money received three years from today, four years from today, and so on.

The general formula for the present value of \$1 to be received N years from today when the rate of interest is i is:

$$\dfrac{\$1}{(1+i)^N}.$$

The present value formula highlights the two variables that determine the present value of any future flow of money: the rate of interest (i) and how long you have to wait before you get it (N). Clearly, the higher the interest rate, the smaller is the present value of any future sum. When firms invest in a machine, it is often the case that most of the costs are incurred immediately, while most of the revenues arrive well into the future. Thus, the higher the interest

rate, the more likely it is that the present value of the revenue will not exceed the cost of the machine, and so overall investment spending by firms will be less. This inverse dependence of investment spending on the level of interest rates was emphasized in the text.

Let us apply this analysis to the specific example that we used to start this appendix. The present value of the revenue is easy to calculate since it all comes two years from today. Since the rate of interest is assumed to be 10 percent ($i = 0.1$) we have:

$$\text{Present value of revenues} = \dfrac{\$14{,}520}{(1.1)^2}$$

$$= \dfrac{\$14{,}520}{1.21}$$

$$= \$12{,}000.$$

The present value of the costs is a bit trickier in this example since they occur at two different dates. The present value of the first interest payment is $\$1100/(1 + i) = \$1100/1.1 = \$1000$. And the present value of the final payment of interest plus principal is:

$$\dfrac{\$12{,}100}{(1+i)^2} = \dfrac{\$12{,}100}{(1.1)^2} = \dfrac{\$12{,}100}{1.21} = \$10{,}000.$$

Now that we have expressed each sum in terms of its present value, it is permissible to add them up. So the present value of all costs is:

$$\text{Present value of costs} = \$1000 + \$10{,}000$$
$$= \$11{,}000.$$

Comparing this to the \$12,000 present value of the revenues clearly shows that the machine is really a good investment. This same calculation procedure is applicable to all investment decisions.

Summary

To determine whether a loss or a gain will result from a decision whose costs and returns will come at several different periods of time, the figures represented by these gains and losses must all be discounted to obtain their present value. For this, one uses the present value formula for X dollars receivable N years from now:

$$\text{Present value} = \dfrac{X}{(1+i)^N}.$$

One then adds together the present values of all the returns and all the costs. If the sum of the present values of the returns is greater than the sum of the present values of the costs, then the decision to invest will promise a net gain.

Concepts for Review

Discounting
Present value

Questions for Discussion

1. Compute the present value of $1000 to be received in four years if the rate of interest is 15 percent.

2. A government bond pays $100 in interest each year for three years and also returns the principal of $1000 in the third year. How much is it worth in terms of today's money if the rate of interest is 10 percent? If the rate of interest is 15 percent?

7

Changes on the Demand Side: Multiplier Analysis

A definite ratio, to be called the *Multiplier*, can be established between income and investment.

JOHN MAYNARD KEYNES

I n the last chapter we derived the economy's *aggregate demand curve*, which shows how the equilibrium quantity of real GDP demanded depends on the price level—holding all other factors constant. But often these "other factors" do not remain constant and, as a consequence, the entire aggregate demand curve shifts. This chapter is the first of several that are devoted to enumerating these "other factors" and explaining how and why they make the aggregate demand curve shift.

The central concept of this short chapter is the *multiplier*—the idea that an increase in spending will bring about an *even larger* increase in overall demand. We approach this idea from three different perspectives, each of which provides the reader with different and significant insights into the multiplier process. First, the multiplier is illustrated graphically using the income–expenditure diagram from Chapter 6. Next, we reach the same conclusion through the use of a numerical example, and finally, we offer an algebraic statement.

At the end of the chapter, we use multiplier analysis to explain why a drive to increase national saving might not succeed.

The Magic of the Multiplier

Because investment spending is subject to such abrupt swings, it is often the cause of business fluctuations in Canada and elsewhere. Let us, therefore, ask what would happen to equilibrium income in our fictitious country, Macroland, if firms there suddenly decided to spend more on investment goods. As we shall see, such a decision would have a *multiplied* effect on GDP in Macroland. This is indeed the case in the Canadian economy.

For simplicity, we begin by assuming that the price level is fixed—an assumption we maintain *only* for this short chapter. Refer first to Table 7–1, which looks very much like Table 6–1 (page 134). The only difference is that we assume here that, for some reason, firms in Macroland now want to invest $20 billion more than they previously did—for a total of $90 billion. The multiplier principle says that Macroland's GDP will rise by more than the $20 billion increase in investment. Specifically, the multiplier is defined as the ratio of the change in equilibrium GDP (Y) divided by the original change in spending that causes the change in GDP. In shorthand, when we deal with the multiplier for investment (I), the formula is:

$$\text{Multiplier} = \frac{\text{Change in } Y}{\text{Change in } I}.$$

The multiplier is the ratio of the change in equilibrium GDP (Y) divided by the original change in spending that causes the change in GDP.

TABLE 7-1

Total Expenditure in Macroland after the Rise in Investment Spending (billions of dollars)

(1) INCOME (Y)	(2) CONSUMPTION (C)	(3) INVESTMENT (I)	(4) TOTAL EXPENDITURE (C + I)
200	170	90	260
250	210	90	300
300	250	90	340
350	290	90	380
400	330	90	420
450	370	90	460
500	410	90	500
550	450	90	540
600	490	90	580

This table shows the construction of a total expenditure schedule for Macroland after investment has risen to $90 billion. As indicated by the shaded numbers, only income level Y = $500 billion is equilibrium on the demand side of the economy because only at this level is total spending (C + I) equal to production (Y).

Let us verify that the multiplier is indeed greater than 1. Table 7–1 shows how to derive a new expenditure schedule by adding up C and I at each level of Y, just as we did in Chapter 6. If you compare the last column of Table 7–1 to that of Table 6–1, you will see that the new expenditure schedule lies uniformly above the old one by $20 billion. Figure 7–1 illustrates this diagrammatically. The schedule marked $C + I_0$ is derived from the last column of Table 6–1, while the higher schedule marked $C + I_1$ is derived from the last column of Table 7–1. The two $C + I$ lines are parallel and $20 billion apart.

So far no act of magic has occurred—things look just as you might expect. But one more step will bring the multiplier rabbit out of the hat. Let us see what the upward shift of the $C + I$ line does to equilibrium income. In Figure 7–1 equilibrium moves outward from point E_0 to point E_1, that is, from $400 billion to $500 billion. The difference is an increase in national income of $100 billion. All this from a $20 billion stimulus to investment? That is the magic of the multiplier.

FIGURE 7-1
Illustration of the Multiplier
This figure depicts the multiplier effect of a rise in investment spending of $20 billion. The expenditure schedule shifts upward from $C + I_0$ to $C + I_1$, thus moving equilibrium from point E_0 to point E_1. The rise in income is $100 billion, so the multiplier is $100/$20 = 5.

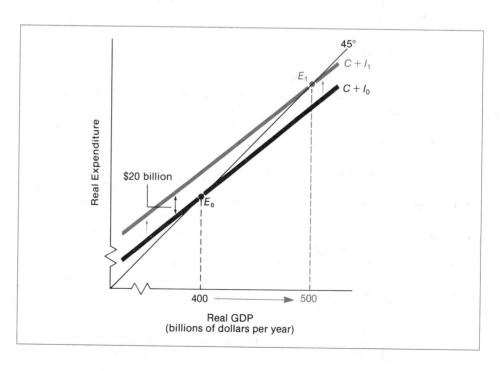

Because the change in I is $20 billion and the change in equilibrium Y is $100 billion, by applying our definition, the multiplier is:

$$\text{Multiplier} = \frac{\text{Change in } Y}{\text{Change in } I} = \frac{\$100 \text{ billion}}{\$20 \text{ billion}} = 5.$$

This tells us that, in our example, every additional dollar of investment demand will add $5 to the equilibrium GDP!

This does indeed seem mysterious. Can something be created from nothing? Let us, therefore, check to be sure that the graph has not deceived us. The first and last columns of Table 7–1 show in numbers what Figure 7–1 shows in a picture. Notice that, at any income level less than $500 billion, spending $(C + I)$ exceeds output (Y). As we know, this cannot be an equilibrium situation because inventories would be disappearing. On the other hand, at any income level greater than $500 billion, inventories would be piling up, since $C + I$ is less than Y.

Only at $Y = \$500$ billion are spending and production in balance, as Table 7–1 shows. This is $100 billion higher than the $400 billion equilibrium GDP obtained in the discussion of Table 6–1, where investment was only $70 billion. Thus a $20 billion rise in investment leads to a $100 billion rise in equilibrium GDP. The multiplier really is 5.

Demystifying the Multiplier: How It Works

The multiplier result seems peculiar at first, but it loses its mystery once we remember the circular flow of income and expenditure and the simple fact that one person's spending is another person's income. To illustrate the logic of the multiplier and see why it is exactly 5 in our model economy, let us look more closely at what actually happens if businesses decide to spend an additional $1 million on investment goods. If GDP is to rise by $5 million and $Y = C + I$, consumer spending must rise by $4 million. Let's see how.

Suppose that Generous Motors—a major corporation in Macroland—decides to spend $1 million to retool a factory to manufacture pollution-free electronically powered automobiles. Its $1 million expenditure goes to construction workers and owners of construction companies as wages and profits. That is, it becomes their *income*.

But the owners and workers of the construction firms will not simply keep their $1 million in the bank. They will spend some of it. If they are "typical" consumers, their spending will be $1 million times the marginal propensity to consume (MPC).[1] In our example, the MPC is 0.8. So let us assume that they spend $800,000 and save the rest. *This $800,000 expenditure is a net addition to the nation's demand for goods and services exactly as GM's original $1 million expenditure was*. So, at this stage, the $1 million investment has already pushed GDP up some $1.8 million.

But the process by no means stops here. Shopkeepers receive the $800,000 spent by construction workers, and these shopkeepers in turn also spend 80 percent of their new income. This accounts for $640,000 (80 percent of $800,000) in additional consumer spending in the "third round." Next follows a fourth round in which the recipients of the $640,000, in their turn, spend 80 percent of this amount, or $512,000, and so on. At each stage in the spending chain, people spend 80 percent of the additional income they receive, and the process continues.

Where does it all end? Does it all end? The answer is that it does, indeed, eventually end—with GDP a total of $5 million higher than it was before Generous Motors spent the original $1 million. The multiplier, as stated, is 5.

---

[1] You may want to review the definition of MPC in Chapter 5 (page 122).

TABLE 7-2
The Multiplier Spending Chain

(1) ROUND	(2) SPENDING IN THIS ROUND (dollars)	(3) CUMULATIVE TOTAL (dollars)
1	1,000,000	$1,000,000
2	800,000	1,800,000
3	640,000	2,440,000
4	512,000	2,952,000
5	409,600	3,361,600
6	327,680	3,689,280
7	262,144	3,951,424
8	209,715	4,161,139
9	167,772	4,328,911
10	134,218	4,463,129
. . .	. . .	. . .
20	14,412	4,942,354
. . .	. . .	. . .
50	18	4,999,929
. . .	. . .	. . .
"Infinity"	0	5,000,000

This table shows how the multiplier unfolds through time. Round 1 is GM's initial spending, which leads to $1 million in additional income to construction workers. Round 2 shows the construction workers spending 80 percent of this amount, since the marginal propensity to consume is 0.8. The other rounds proceed accordingly, with spending in each successive round equal to 80 percent of that in the previous round. Technically, the full multiplier of 5 is reached only after an "infinite" number of rounds. But, as can be seen, we are quite close to the full amount after 20 rounds.

Table 7-2 displays the basis for this conclusion. In the table, "round 1" represents GM's initial investment, which creates $1 million in income for construction workers; "round 2" represents the construction workers' spending, which creates $800,000 in income for shopkeepers. The rest of the table proceeds accordingly. Each entry in column 2 is 80 percent of the previous entry, and column 3 tabulates the running sum of column 2.

We see that after 10 rounds of spending the initial $1 million investment has mushroomed to nearly $4.5 million, and the sum is still growing. After 20 rounds, the total increase in GDP is more than $4.9 million—near its eventual value of $5 million. While it takes quite a few rounds of spending before the multiplier chain is near 5, we see from the table that it approaches 4 within seven periods.

Figure 7-2 provides a graphical presentation of the numbers in the last column of Table 7-2. Notice how the multiplier builds up rapidly at first, and then tapers off to approach its ultimate value (5 in this example) gradually.

Algebraic Statement of the Multiplier

Figure 7-2 and Table 7-2 probably make a persuasive case for the fact that the multiplier eventually reaches 5. But for the remaining skeptics we offer a simple algebraic proof.[2] Most of you learned about an "infinite geometric progression" in high school. This is simply an infinite series of numbers, each one of which is a fixed fraction of the previous one. This fraction is called the "common ratio." A geometric progression beginning with 1 and having a common ratio equal to 0.8 looks like this:

$$1 + 0.8 + (0.8)^2 + (0.8)^3 + \ldots .$$

[2]Students who blanch at the sight of algebra should not be put off. Anyone who can balance a chequebook (even many who cannot!) will be able to follow the argument.

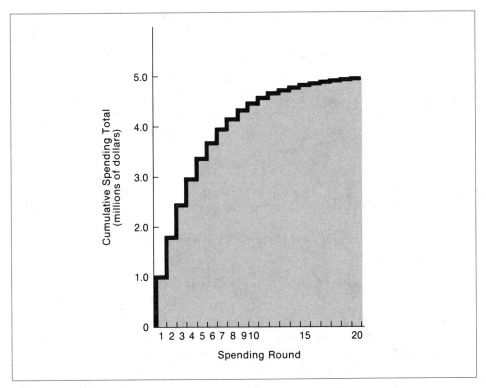

FIGURE 7–2
How the Multiplier Builds
This diagram portrays the numbers from Table 7-2 and shows how the multiplier builds through time. Notice how the effect grows quickly at first and how the full effect is almost reached after 15 rounds.

More generally, a geometric progression beginning with 1 and having a common ratio R is:

$$1 + R + R^2 + R^3 \dots.$$

A simple formula enables us to sum such a progression as long as R is less than 1.[3]

The formula is:[4]

$$\begin{matrix} \text{Sum of infinite} \\ \text{geometric progression} \end{matrix} = \frac{1}{1 - R}.$$

Now we can recognize that the multiplier chain in Table 7–2 is just an infinite geometric progression with 0.8 as its common ratio. That is, each \$1 spent by GM leads to a $0.8 \times \$1$ expenditure by construction workers, which in turn leads to a $(0.8) \times (0.8 \times \$1) = (0.8)^2 \times \$1$ expenditure by the shopkeepers, and so on. Thus, for each initial dollar of investment spending, the progression is:

$$1 + 0.8 + (0.8)^2 + (0.8)^3 + (0.8)^4 + \dots.$$

---

[3] If R exceeds 1, nobody can possibly sum it—not even with the aid of a modern computer!
[4] The proof is simple. Let the symbol S stand for the (unknown) sum of the series:

$$S = 1 + R + R^2 + R^3 + \dots.$$

Then, multiplying by R,

$$RS = R + R^2 + R^3 + \dots.$$

By subtracting RS from S, we obtain:

$$S - RS = 1$$

or

$$S = \frac{1}{1 - R}.$$

Applying the formula for the sum of such a series, we find that:

$$\text{Multiplier} = \frac{1}{1 - 0.8} = \frac{1}{0.2} = 5.$$

Notice how this result can be generalized. If we did not have a specific numerical value for the marginal propensity to consume but simply called it "MPC," the geometric progression would have been:

$$1 + \text{MPC} + (\text{MPC})^2 + (\text{MPC})^3 + \ldots,$$

which has the MPC as its common ratio. Applying the same formula for summing a geometric progression to this more general case gives us the following general result:

Oversimplified Formula for the Multiplier

$$\text{Multiplier} = \frac{1}{1 - \text{MPC}}.$$

We call this formula "oversimplified" because it ignores many factors that are important in the real world. One of them is *inflation*, a complication to which we will turn in the next chapter. A second is *income taxation*, and a third is *imports*; both of these points will be elaborated in Chapter 9. These complications enter the picture as additional components of the total expenditure line: instead of remaining simply the $C + I$ line, the total expenditure schedule becomes the $C + I + G + X - IM$ line. In this more general context, it is useful to remember the multiplier formula as:

$$\text{Multiplier} = \frac{1}{1 - \text{slope of total expenditure line}}.$$

In the simpler model of this chapter, the only reason the total expenditure line has any slope is because of the MPC. This is why the more general formula reduces to the "oversimplified" version, $1/(1 - \text{MPC})$, in this case. Two further factors, interest rates and exchange rates, arise from the financial system. We explain these complications in Chapters 13 and 14, after money and banking have been explained. As it turns out, *all* of these factors *reduce* the size of the multiplier.

The *simplified multiplier formula* ignores the effects of inflation, taxation, imports, interest rates, and exchange rates. Later chapters show how all these factors lower the multiplier.

We can begin to appreciate just how unrealistic the "oversimplified" formula is by considering some real numbers for the Canadian economy. The marginal propensity to consume (MPC) has been estimated many times; it is about 0.9. From our oversimplified formula, then, it would seem that the multiplier should be:

$$\text{Multiplier} = \frac{1}{1 - 0.9} = \frac{1}{0.1} = 10.$$

In fact, the actual multiplier for the Canadian economy is believed to be less than 2. This is quite a discrepancy! But it does not mean that anything we have said about the multiplier so far is incorrect. Our story is simply incomplete. As we progress through the following chapters, you will learn why the multiplier is less than 2 even though the MPC is close to 0.9. For now we simply point out that:

While the multiplier is larger than 1 in the real world, it cannot be calculated with any degree of accuracy from the oversimplified formula. The actual multiplier is *lower* than the formula suggests.

The Multiplier Effect of Consumer Spending

Business firms that invest are not the only initiators of the magic of the multiplier; consumers, the government, and foreigners can start it too. But since we do not introduce the government and foreigners until Chapter 9, let us now see how the multiplier works when the process is initiated by an upsurge in consumer spending.

First, we need to distinguish between two types of change in consumer spending. When C rises because income rises—that is, when consumers move outward *along a fixed consumption function*—we call the increase in C an **induced increase in consumption**. However, if instead C rises because the entire consumption function *shifts* up, we call the rise an **autonomous increase in consumption**. The name indicates that consumption changes independently of income, and Chapter 5's discussion pointed out that a number of events, such as a change in the price level or in the value of the stock market, can initiate such a shift.

Let us suppose that, for some reason, consumer spending rises autonomously by $20 billion. In this case, our table of aggregate demand must be revised to look like Table 7–3. Comparing this to Table 7–1 on page 152, we note that each entry in column 2 is $20 billion *higher* than the corresponding entry in Table 7–1 (because consumption is higher) and each entry in column 3 is $20 billion *lower* (because investment is lower).

The equilibrium level of income is clearly Y = $500 billion once again. Indeed, the entire expenditure schedule is the same as it was in Table 7–1. The initial rise of $20 billion in spending leads to an ultimate rise of $100 billion in GDP, just as occurred in the case of higher investment spending. In fact, Figure 7–1 applies to this case without any changes. The multiplier for autonomous changes in consumer spending, then, is also 5 ($100/$20).

The reason is straightforward. It does not matter who—business investors or consumers—injects an additional dollar of spending into the economy. Wherever it comes from, 80 percent of it will be respent if the MPC is 0.8, and the recipients of this second round will in turn spend 80 percent of their additional income, and so on and on. And that is what constitutes the multiplier process. In the next chapter we will learn, not surprisingly, that this same multiplier applies equally well to the third component of aggregate demand—government purchases of goods and services.

An **induced increase in consumption** is an increase in consumer spending that stems from an increase in consumer incomes. It appears on a graph as a movement along a fixed consumption function.

An **autonomous increase in consumption** is an increase in consumer spending without any increase in incomes. It appears on a graph as a shift of the entire consumption function.

TABLE 7–3
Total Expenditure after Consumers Decide to Spend $20 Billion More (billions of dollars)

(1) INCOME (Y)	(2) CONSUMPTION (C)	(3) INVESTMENT (I)	(4) TOTAL EXPENDITURE (C + I)
200	190	70	260
250	230	70	300
300	270	70	340
350	310	70	380
400	350	70	420
450	390	70	460
500	430	70	500
550	470	70	540
600	510	70	580

This table shows the construction of the total expenditure schedule for Macroland following an autonomous increase of $20 billion in consumption rather than in investment. Notice that columns 2 and 3 differ from the corresponding columns in Table 7-1, but column 4 is the same in both tables. Thus the expenditure schedule in the 45° line diagram is the same as in the earlier example.

The Multiplier in Reverse

A good way to check your understanding of the multiplier process is to run it in reverse: What happens if, for example, consumers autonomously decide to spend less? For example, suppose a wave of thriftiness comes over the people of Macroland so that, no matter what their total income, they now want to spend $20 billion *less* than they did previously.

A decision to spend $20 billion less out of any given level of income is, by definition, a *downward* shift of the total expenditure schedule by $20 billion. This is shown in Figure 7–3, where the $C + I$ schedule falls from $C_0 + I$ to $C_1 + I$. The vertical distance between these two parallel lines is the $20 billion drop in spending.

There are two ways of calculating the multiplier. First, our oversimplified multiplier formula tells us that the multiplier is:

$$\frac{1}{1 - \text{MPC}} = \frac{1}{1 - 0.8} = \frac{1}{0.2} = 5.$$

So a $20 billion drop in spending will lead to a multiplier effect of $100 billion. Alternatively, we can read this conclusion from Figure 7–3. Here the economy's equilibrium point moves down the 45° line from point E_0 to E_1; income drops from $400 billion to $300 billion—a decline of $100 billion.

Now compare the analysis of a decline in spending that is summarized in Figure 7–3 with our previous analysis of an increase in spending, as shown in Figure 7–1 on page 152. You will see that everything is simply turned in the opposite direction. The multiplier works in both directions.

The Paradox of Thrift

The last example of multiplier analysis teaches an important lesson: It shows that an increase in the desire to save will lead to a cumulative fall in GDP. And, *because saving depends on income*, the resulting decline in national income will pull saving down.

FIGURE 7–3
The Multiplier in Reverse
This diagram shows the multiplier effect of an autonomous decline in consumer spending of $20 billion. The decline appears as a downward shift of $20 billion in the expenditure schedule, which falls from $C_0 + I$ to $C_1 + I$. Equilibrium, which is always at the intersection of the expenditure schedule and the 45° line, moves from point E_0 to point E_1, and income falls from $400 billion to $300 billion.

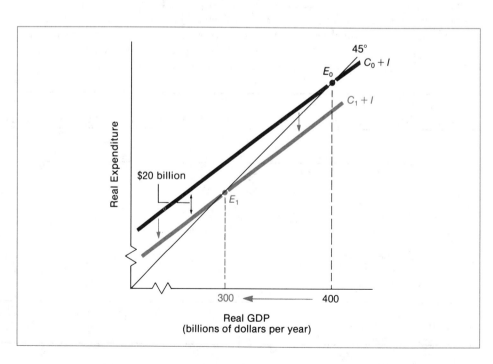

Let us be a bit more specific about this. Before the upsurge in saving, consumers were spending $330 billion out of a total national income of $400 billion, as we can see in Table 6–1 on page 136. Hence $70 billion was being saved. In Figure 7–3, income falls to $300 billion. Since investment is still $70 billion and $C + I$ must add up to Y, we know that consumption at point E_1 must be $230 billion. So total saving is still $70 (= $300 – $230) billion. The effort to save more has been totally frustrated by the decline in GDP.

This remarkable result is called the **paradox of thrift**, because it shows that, while saving may pave the road to riches for an individual, if the nation as a whole decides to save more, the result may be a recession and lower incomes for all. The paradox of thrift is important because it is contrary to most people's thinking, and it means that greater saving may be a mixed blessing if it is not accompanied by equally greater investment. The paradox of thrift reminds us that it is not always accurate to think of the nation's economic problems as simply a big version of an individual family's economic problems.

The **paradox of thrift** is the fact that an effort by a nation to save more may simply reduce national income and fail to raise total saving.

The Simple Algebra of the Multiplier

In Chapter 6, we worked out a general expression for the equilibrium level of GDP when the price level is fixed, investment is some fixed number, I, and the consumption function is:

$$C = a + bY.$$

The answer obtained there (which can be found on page 140) was:

$$Y = \frac{a + I}{1 - b}.$$

From this formula it is easy to derive the oversimplified multiplier formula algebraically and to show that it applies equally well to a change in investment or to a change in autonomous consumer spending. To do this, suppose that *either I or a* increased by one unit. In either case, the sum $C + I$ would rise from:

$$C + I = a + bY + I,$$

to:

$$C + I = a + bY + I + 1.$$

Using the equilibrium condition that Y must be equal to $C + I$, we can solve for Y just as we did in Chapter 6:

$$Y = C + I,$$

so that:

$$Y = a + bY + I + 1,$$

and therefore:

$$(1 - b)Y = a + I + 1,$$

or:

$$Y = \frac{a + I + 1}{1 - b}.$$

By comparing this with our previous expression for Y, we see that a one-unit change in *either* a or I changes equilibrium GDP by:

$$\text{change in } Y = \frac{a + I + 1}{1 - b} - \frac{a + I}{1 - b}$$

$$\text{change in } Y = \frac{a + I + 1 - (a + I)}{1 - b}$$

or:

$$\text{change in } Y = \frac{1}{1 - b} \cdot$$

Recalling that b is the marginal propensity to consume, we see that this is precisely the oversimplified multiplier formula.

The Multiplier and the Aggregate Demand Curve

At this point we must recall something that was mentioned at the start of this chapter: Income–expenditure diagrams such as those in Figures 7–1 and 7–3 can be drawn up only for a given price level. A different price level leads to a different total expenditure curve. This means that our oversimplified multiplier formula measures *the increase in real GDP demanded, that is, the increase in the level of GDP that would occur if the price level were fixed*. In other words, it measures the *horizontal shift* of the economy's aggregate demand curve.

Figure 7–4 illustrates this conclusion by supposing that the price level that underlies Figure 7–1 is $P = 100$. The top panel simply repeats Figure 7–1 and shows how an increase in investment spending from $70 billion to $90 billion leads to an increase in GDP from $400 billion to $500 billion.

The bottom panel shows two downward-sloping aggregate demand curves. The first, labelled $D_0 D_0$, depicts the situation when investment is $70 billion. Point E_0 on this curve indicates that, at the given price level ($P = 100$), the equilibrium quantity of GDP demanded is $400 billion. It corresponds exactly to point E_0 in the top panel. The second aggregate demand curve, $D_1 D_1$, depicts the situation after investment has risen to $90 billion. Point E_1 on this curve indicates that the equilibrium quantity of GDP demanded when $P = 100$ has risen to $500 billion, which corresponds exactly to point E_1 in the top panel.

As Figure 7–4 shows, the horizontal distance between the two aggregate demand curves is exactly equal to the increase in real GDP shown in the income–expenditure diagram—in this case, $100 billion. Thus:

An autonomous increase in spending leads to a horizontal shift of the aggregate demand curve by an amount given by the oversimplified multiplier formula.

Thus everything we have said about the multiplier applies to shifts of the economy's aggregate demand curve. If businesses decide to increase their investment spending or if the consumption function shifts up, the aggregate demand curve moves horizontally to the right—as indicated in Figure 7–4. If investment decreases or if the consumption function shifts down, the aggregate demand curve moves horizontally to the left. In subsequent chapters we will learn, not surprisingly, that the same shifts occur with changes in either of the other two components of total spending: government purchases and net exports.

Thus the aggregate demand curve cannot be expected to stand still. Autonomous changes in spending by consumers, investors, government units, or foreigners all cause the aggregate demand curve to move around. But to understand the consequences of shifts of aggregate demand, we must bring the aggregate supply curve into the picture. That is the task of the next chapter.

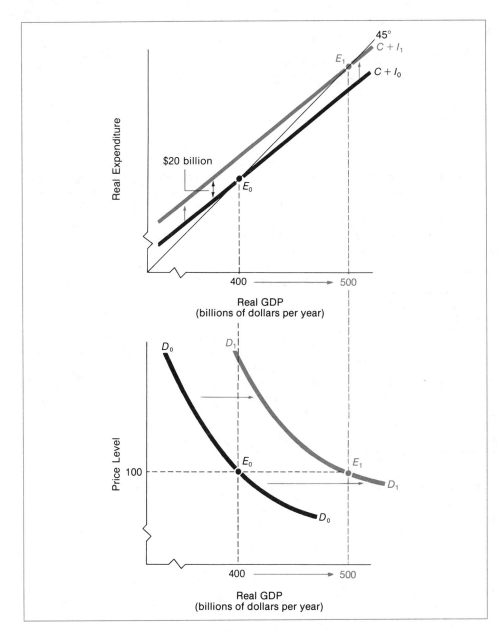

FIGURE 7–4
Two Views
of the Multiplier
The top panel repeats Figure 7–1. The bottom panel shows two aggregate demand curves. Curve D_0D_0, which applies when investment is $70 billion, shows that equilibrium GDP on the demand side comes at $Y = \$400$ billion when $P = 100$ (point E_0). Curve D_1D_1, which applies when investment is $90 billion, shows that equilibrium GDP on the demand side comes at $Y = \$500$ billion when $P = 100$ (point E_1). The horizontal distance between points E_0 and E_1 in the bottom panel indicates the oversimplified multiplier effect.

Summary

1. Any autonomous increase in expenditure has a multiplier effect on GDP; that is, it increases GDP by more than the original increase in spending.

2. The reason for this multiplier effect is that one person's additional expenditure constitutes a new source of income for another person, and this additional income leads to still more spending, and so on.

3. The multiplier also works in reverse: an autonomous decrease in any component of aggregate demand leads to a multiplied decrease in national income.

4. A simple formula for the multiplier says that its numerical value is $1/(1-\text{MPC})$. This formula, which is too simple to give accurate results, measures the horizontal shift

of the aggregate demand curve. (A more general version of the formula is $1/[1$ minus slope of total expenditure line].)

5. The *simplified* multiplier formula ignores the effects of inflation, taxation, imports, interest rates, and exchange rates. Later chapters show how all these factors lower the multiplier.

6. If the nation as a whole decides to save more, that is, to consume less, the resulting decline in national income may serve to make everyone poorer. This possibility that thriftiness, while helpful for the individual, may be disastrous for an entire nation is called the paradox of thrift.

Concepts for Review

The multiplier

Autonomous increase in consumption

Induced increase in consumption

Paradox of thrift

Questions for Discussion

1. Try to remember where you last spent a dollar. Explain how this dollar will lead to a multiplier chain of increased income and spending. (Who received the dollar? What will he or she do with it?)

2. Use both numerical and graphical methods to find the multiplier effect of the following shift in the consumption function in an economy in which investment is always $110.

INCOME	CONSUMPTION BEFORE SHIFT	CONSUMPTION AFTER SHIFT
$510	$430	$470
540	450	490
570	470	510
600	490	530
630	510	550
660	530	570
690	550	590
720	570	610

(*Hint*: What is the marginal propensity to consume?)

3. Turn back to Discussion Question 4 in Chapter 6 (page 147). Suppose investment spending rises to $130 and the price level is fixed. By how much will the equilibrium GDP increase? Derive the answer both numerically and graphically.

4. Explain the paradox of thrift. Why do you think it is called a paradox?

5. Consider an economy with the following savings function:

$$S = -100 + 0.4Y.$$

Suppose investment spending increases from 400 to 500. By how much do output and consumption change? Relate your answers to the multiplier formula.

6. Consider an economy with the following savings and investment functions:

$$S = -200 + 0.2Y$$
$$I = 0.1Y$$

What is equilibrium GDP? What is the value of the autonomous consumer-spending multiplier on GDP?

8

Supply-Side Equilibrium: Unemployment *and* Inflation?

I n Chapter 6 we learned that the level of prices, in conjunction with the economy's consumption and investment schedules, governs whether the economy will experience a recessionary or an inflationary gap. If the $C + I$ schedule is "too low," a *recessionary gap* will arise, while a $C + I$ schedule that is "too high" leads to an *inflationary gap*. Which sort of gap actually occurs is of some importance because, as we shall see in this chapter, a recessionary gap normally spells unemployment while an inflationary gap means inflation.

The tools provided in Chapter 6, however, are not sufficient to determine which sort of gap will arise, because the position of the $C + I$ schedule depends on the price level—and the price level is determined by *both* aggregate demand *and* aggregate supply. Thus, the task of the present chapter is to bring the supply side of the economy into the picture.

We begin by explaining how the *aggregate supply curve* is derived from business costs. Next we consider the interaction of aggregate supply and aggregate demand and the joint determination of output and the price level. With this apparatus in hand, we return to the phenomena of recessionary and inflationary gaps and study how the economy adjusts to each type. Doing this puts us in a position to deal with the crucial question raised in earlier chapters: Does the economy have an efficient self-correcting mechanism? As we shall learn, the economy is better at curing inflationary gaps than recessionary gaps. We also use aggregate supply–aggregate demand analysis to explain the vexing problem of *stagflation*—the simultaneous occurrence of high unemployment *and* high inflation—which has plagued the economy since the mid-1970s. The chapter ends by explaining how inflation affects the multiplier.

The Mystery of Stagflation

The analysis of demand-side equilibrium presented in Chapter 6 seems to suggest that while we can have *either* unemployment (from a recessionary gap) *or* inflation (from an inflationary gap), we should not have both at the same time. And, for many decades, this seemed to be the way things worked out. The Great Depression witnessed severe unemployment and falling prices; World War II led to an inflationary boom; there was very little inflation during the 1958–62 recession.

But things started to change in the 1970s. The inflation rate fell only slightly during the 1971 recession, and it rose dramatically during the 1971–76 period, when unemployment also rose. Inflation also increased during the 1980 recession. These events have made clear that inflation and unemployment can co-exist. In this chapter, we will see that economic theory can explain why stagflation occurs.

The Aggregate Supply Curve

In earlier chapters we noted that *aggregate demand* is a schedule, not a fixed number. The quantity of real GDP that will be demanded depends on the price level, as summarized in the economy's *aggregate demand curve*.

Analogously, the concept of *aggregate supply* does not refer to a fixed number but, rather, to a schedule (to a supply *curve*). The volume of goods and services that will be provided by profit-seeking enterprises depends on the prices they obtain for their outputs, wages and other production costs, the state of technology, and other things. The relationship between the price level and the quantity of real GDP supplied, *holding all other determinants of quantity supplied constant*, is called the economy's **aggregate supply curve**.

> The **aggregate supply curve** shows, for each possible price level, the quantity of goods and services that all the nation's businesses are willing to produce, holding all other determinants of aggregate quantity supplied constant.

A typical aggregate supply curve is drawn in Figure 8–1. It slopes upward, meaning that as prices rise more output is produced, *other things held constant*. It is not difficult to understand why this curve slopes upward. Producers in the Canadian economy are motivated mainly by profit. Since the profit made by producing a unit of output is simply the difference between the price at which it is sold and the unit cost of production,

$$\text{Profit per unit} = \text{Price} - \text{Cost per unit},$$

it is clear that the response of production to a rising price level (henceforth, *P*) depends on the response of costs.[1]

One critical fact affecting this response is that labour and other inputs used by firms normally are available at *relatively fixed prices* for some period of time—though certainly not forever. There are many reasons for this. Some workers and firms enter into long-term labour contracts that set money wages up to three years in advance. Even where there are no explicit contracts, employees typically have their wages increased only about once per year. During the interim period, money wages are fixed. Much the same is true of other factors of production. Many firms get deliveries of raw materials under long-term contracts according to which suppliers have agreed to provide the materials at prearranged prices. None of these contracts lasts forever, of course, but many of them last long enough to be of importance.

[1] For a full discussion of business output decisions and how they respond to costs, see Chapter 22. For those who have already studied that chapter, it should be helpful to note that, roughy speaking, we can think of the aggregate supply curve as the whole-economy analogue of the firm's marginal cost curve (see Chapter 22).

FIGURE 8–1
An Aggregate Supply Curve
This graph shows a typical aggregate supply curve. It has a positive slope (that is, it rises as we move to the right), meaning that the quantity of output supplied rises as the price level rises.

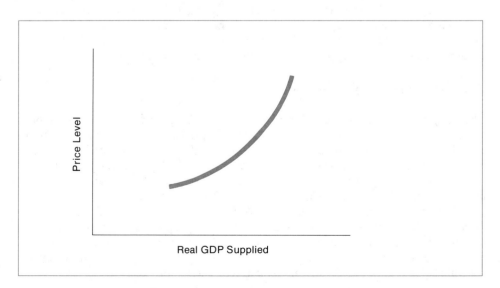

Why is it significant that firms often purchase inputs like labour and raw materials at prices that stay fixed for considerable periods? Because firms decide how much to produce by comparing selling prices with costs of production, and production costs obviously depend on input prices. If the selling prices of the firm's products rise while wages and other factor costs are relatively fixed, production becomes more profitable, and so firms are persuaded to increase output.

A simple example will illustrate the idea. Suppose a firm uses one hour of labour time to manufacture a gadget that sells for $9. If workers earn $8 per hour and the firm has no other production costs, its profit per unit is:

$$\text{Profit per unit} = \text{Price} - \text{Cost per unit}$$
$$= \$9 - \$8$$
$$= \$1.$$

Let us assume that this level of profit is just enough to compensate firms for the risks involved and so make the current production level worthwhile. Now what happens if the price of a gadget rises to $10, but wage rates remain constant? The firm's profit per unit becomes:

$$\text{Profit per unit} = \text{Price} - \text{Cost per unit}$$
$$= \$10 - \$8$$
$$= \$2.$$

With production more profitable, it is likely that the firm will supply more gadgets.

The same process operates in reverse. Suppose selling prices fall while input costs are relatively fixed. Since this squeezes their profit margins, firms may react by cutting back on production. For example, if the price of a gadget fell from $9 to $8.50, profit per unit would fall from $1 to 50¢, and the firm would probably produce less.

The behaviour we have just described is summarized by the upward slope of the aggregate supply curve: Production rises when the price level (P) rises, and falls when P falls. In other words:

The aggregate supply curve slopes upward because firms normally can purchase labour and other inputs at fixed costs for some period of time. Thus, higher selling prices make production more attractive.

The phrase "for some period of time" alerts us to the possibility that the aggregate supply curve may not stand still for long. If wages or prices of other inputs change, as they surely will during inflationary times, the aggregate supply curve will shift.

Shifts of the Aggregate Supply Curve

We have concluded so far that, for any given level of wages and other input prices, there will be an upward-sloping aggregate supply curve relating aggregate quantity supplied to the price level. But what factors determine the *position* of this curve? What things can make it shift?

The Money Wage Rate

Our previous discussion suggests that the most obvious determinant of the position of the aggregate supply curve is the money wage rate. Wages are the major element of cost for most firms, typically accounting for something like 70 percent of all expenses. Higher wages spell higher costs, thereby lowering profits at any given price.

Let us return to our example and consider what would happen to a gadget producer if the money wage rose to $8.75 per hour while the price of a gadget remained $9. Profit per unit would decline from $9 - $8 = $1 to $9 - $8.75 = $0.25.

With profits squeezed, the firm would probably cut back on production, since the lower level of profit would be less than that which had previously just made it worthwhile for the firm to bear the associated risks.

This is the typical reaction of firms in our economy to a rise in wages. Therefore, a wage increase leads to a decrease in aggregate quantity supplied at current prices. Graphically, the aggregate supply curve shifts to the left (or inward), as shown in Figure 8–2. In this diagram, when wages are low, firms are willing to supply $400 billion in goods and services at a price level of 100 (point *A*). After wages increase, however, these same firms are willing to supply only $350 billion at this price level (point *B*). By similar reasoning, the aggregate supply curve will shift to the right (or outward) if wages fall. Thus:

A rise in the money wage rate causes the aggregate supply curve to shift inward, meaning that the quantity supplied at any price level declines. A fall in the money wage rate causes the aggregate supply curve to shift outward, meaning that the quantity supplied at any price level increases.

Prices of Other Inputs and Taxes

In this regard, there is nothing special about wages. An increase in the price of *any* input that firms buy, or in the level of any sales or payroll tax that firms must pay, will shift the aggregate supply curve in the same way. That is:

The aggregate supply curve is shifted inward by an increase in the price of any input to the production process, or by a tax levied on that input, and is shifted outward by a decrease in the price.

While there are many inputs other than labour, one that has attracted much attention in recent years is energy. Increases in the price of energy push the aggregate supply curve inward more or less as shown in Figure 8–2. Sales taxes do the same thing, since the price received by firms for their products must be high enough to cover any

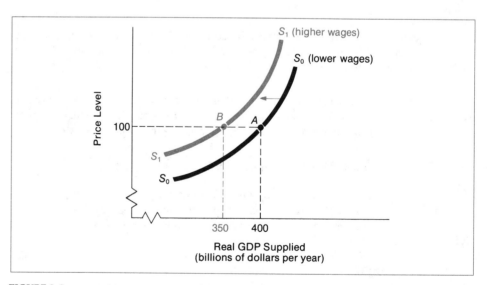

FIGURE 8–2

A Shift of the Aggregate Supply Curve

This diagram shows what happens to the economy's aggregate supply curve when money wages rise. Higher wages shift the supply curve inward from S_0S_0 to S_1S_1, leading, for example, to an output level of $350 billion (point *B*), rather than $400 billion (point *A*), when the price level is 100. The aggregate supply curve will shift inward in the same manner if the price of any other input (such as energy) increases. Since some inputs are imported, a fall in the foreign value of the Canadian dollar also shifts the supply curve inward.

existing sales tax. This is why taxes like our GST create stagflation during the period in which they are introduced.

The Exchange Rate

Since some production inputs are imported intermediate goods, a fall in the foreign value of the Canadian dollar raises business costs. Thus, the **exchange rate** is an important shift variable for the aggregate supply curve as well.

The **exchange rate** is the price at which one currency can be bought, stated in terms of another currency.

The aggregate supply curve is shifted inward by a depreciation in the foreign value of the Canadian dollar, and outward by an appreciation in its foreign value.

Technology and Productivity

Another factor that determines the position of the aggregate supply curve is the state of technology. Suppose, for example, that a technological breakthrough increases the **productivity** of labour. If money wages do not change, such an improvement in productivity will *decrease* business costs and thus improve profitability and encourage more production.

Productivity is the amount of output produced by a unit of input.

Once again, our gadget company will help us understand how this works. Suppose the price of a gadget stays at $9 and the hourly wage rate stays at $8, but gadget workers become much more productive. Specifically, suppose the labour input required to manufacture a gadget falls from one hour (which costs $8) to three-quarters of an hour (which costs $6). Then profit per unit rises from $9 – $8 = $1 to $9 – $6 = $3. The lure of higher profits should induce gadget manufacturers to increase production. In brief, we have concluded that:

Improvements in productivity shift the aggregate supply curve outward.

Figure 8–2 can be viewed as applying to a *decline* in productivity. As you will learn in Chapter 18, the slow growth of productivity has been a problem for Canada in the 1970s, and it remains a source of concern. Many people feel that this productivity slowdown contributed to the stagflation of the 1970s.

Available Supplies of Labour and Capital

The last determinant of the position of the aggregate supply curve is obvious, but we list it anyway for the sake of completeness. The bigger the economy—as measured by its available supplies of labour and capital—the more it is capable of producing. So:

As the labour force grows and as the capital stock is increased by investment, the aggregate supply curve will shift outward (to the right), meaning that more output will be produced at any given price level.

These, then, are the major "other things" that we hold constant when drawing up an aggregate supply curve: wage rates, prices of other inputs (such as energy), sales taxes and payroll taxes, the exchange rate, technology, the labour force, and the capital stock. While a change in the price level moves the economy *along a given supply curve*, a change in any of these other determinants of aggregate quantity supplied *shifts the entire supply schedule*.

The Shape of the Aggregate Supply Curve

One other feature of the aggregate supply curve depicted in Figure 8–1 merits comment. We have drawn our supply curve with a characteristic curvature: It is relatively flat at low levels of output and gets steeper at high levels of output (as we move to the right). There is a reason for this.

When economic activity is weak, product demand slack, and capacity utilization low, firms are likely to respond to an upsurge in demand by bringing their unused capital and labour resources back into production. Therefore, their unit costs of production do not rise much as output expands. As a result, they will find it neither necessary nor advisable to raise prices much. Rapidly rising output with relatively unchanged prices means an aggregate supply curve that is relatively flat.

By contrast, if the economy is booming, demand is buoyant, and production is straining capacity, firms will be able to increase output only by hiring more workers, acquiring more capital, or putting workers on overtime. Whatever they do, unit costs of production rise. Price increases will thus become necessary and, incidentally, they will not be resisted forcefully on the demand side. In this case, the aggregate supply curve is steep. Thus:

The slope of the aggregate supply curve, which tells us the price increase that is associated with a unit increase in quantity supplied, generally rises as the degree of resource utilization rises.

Equilibrium of Aggregate Demand and Supply

In Chapter 6 we learned that the level of prices is a crucial determinant of whether equilibrium GDP is below full employment (a recessionary gap), precisely at full employment, or above full employment (an inflationary gap). We are now in a position to analyze which type of gap, if any, will actually occur in any particular case by combining the analysis of aggregate supply just completed with the analysis of aggregate demand from the last two chapters to determine *simultaneously* the equilibrium level of real GDP (Y) and the equilibrium price level (P).

Figure 8–3 shows the mechanics graphically. The aggregate demand curve DD and the aggregate supply curve SS intersect at point E, where real GDP is $400 billion and the price level is 100. As can be seen in the graph, at any higher price level, such as 120, aggregate quantity supplied would exceed aggregate quantity demanded. There would be a glut on the market as firms found themselves unable to sell all their output. As inventories piled up, firms would compete more vigorously for the available customers, thereby forcing prices down. The price level would fall, as would production.

At any price level lower than 100, such as 80, quantity demanded would exceed quantity supplied. There would be a shortage of goods on the market. With invento-

FIGURE 8–3
Equilibrium of Real GDP and the Price Level
This diagram shows how the equilibrium levels of real GDP and the price level are simultaneously determined by the intersection of the aggregate demand curve (*DD*) and the aggregate supply curve (*SS*). In this example, equilibrium occurs at point *E*, with a real GDP of $400 billion and a price level of 100.

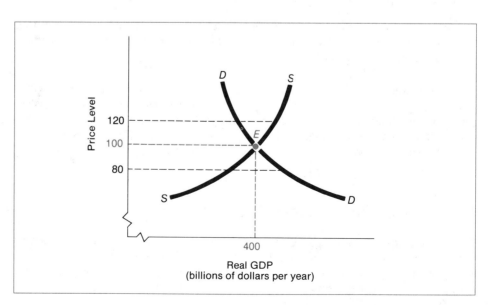

TABLE 8-1
The Determination of the Equilibrium Price Level

(1) PRICE LEVEL (P)	(2) AGGREGATE QUANTITY DEMANDED (billions of dollars)	(3) AGGREGATE QUANTITY SUPPLIED (billions of dollars)	(4) BALANCE OF SUPPLY AND DEMAND	(5) PRICES WILL:
75	440	360	Quantity demanded exceeds quantity supplied	Rise
80	430	370	Quantity demanded exceeds quantity supplied	Rise
100	400	400	Quantity demanded equals quantity supplied	Remain the same
120	380	420	Quantity supplied exceeds quantity demanded	Fall
150	360	440	Quantity supplied exceeds quantity demanded	Fall

ries disappearing and customers knocking on their doors, firms would be encouraged to raise prices. The price level would rise and so would production.

Only when the price level is 100 are the quantities of real GDP demanded and supplied equal. Hence, only the combination $P = 100$, $Y = \$400$ billion is an equilibrium.

Table 8-1 illustrates this same conclusion in another way, using a tabular analysis similar to that of Chapter 6 (refer back to Table 6-2 on page 138). Columns 1 and 2 constitute an aggregate demand schedule corresponding to the aggregate demand curve DD in Figure 8-3. Columns 1 and 3 constitute an aggregate supply schedule with the general shape discussed in this chapter. It corresponds exactly to aggregate supply curve SS in the figure.

It is clear from the table that equilibrium occurs only at $P = 100$ and $Y = \$400$ billion. At any other price level, aggregate quantities supplied and demanded would be unequal, with consequent upward or downward pressure on prices. For example, at a price level of 80, customers demand $430 billion worth of goods and services, but firms wish to provide only $370 billion. The price level is too low and will be forced upward. Conversely, at a price level of, say, 120, quantity supplied ($420 billion) exceeds quantity demanded ($380 billion), implying that the price level must fall.

Recessionary and Inflationary Gaps Revisited

Let us now reconsider a question we posed, but could not answer, in Chapter 6: Will equilibrium occur at, below, or above full employment?

We could not give a complete answer to this question in Chapter 6 because we had no way to determine the equilibrium price level, and therefore no way to tell which type of gap, if any, would arise. The aggregate supply and demand analysis summarized in Figure 8-3 gives us the information we need to determine the price level. But we find that our answer is nonetheless the same as it was in Chapter 6: Anything can happen.

The reason is that nothing in Figure 8-3 tells us where full employment is; it could be above the $400 billion equilibrium level or below it. Depending on the locations of the aggregate demand and aggregate supply curves, then, we can reach equilibrium above full employment (an inflationary gap), at full employment, or below full employment (a recessionary gap).

All three possibilities are illustrated in Figure 8-4. The three upper panels are familiar from Chapter 6. As we move from left to right, the $C + I$ schedule rises from $C + I_0$ to $C + I_1$ to $C + I_2$, leading respectively to a recessionary gap, an equilibrium at full employment, and an inflationary gap. In fact, the upper left-hand diagram is a repeat of Figure 6–5 (page 143), and the upper right-hand diagram repeats Figure 6–6 (page 144). We stressed in Chapter 6 that any one of the three cases is possible, depending on the price level and on the consumption and investment schedules.

In the three lower panels, the equilibrium price level is determined at point E by the intersection of the aggregate supply curve (SS) and the aggregate demand curve (DD). But the same three possibilities emerge nonetheless.

In the lower left-hand panel, aggregate demand is too small to provide jobs for

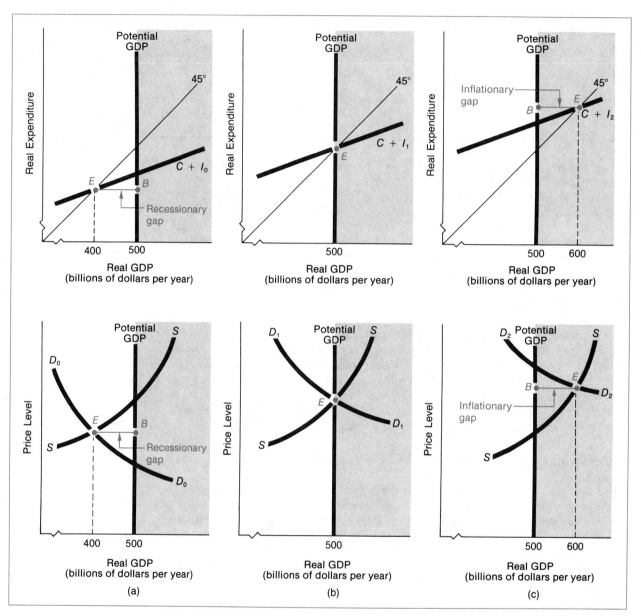

FIGURE 8–4

Recessionary and Inflationary Gaps Revisited

This figure shows three possible types of equilibrium on two different diagrams. In the top row, income–expenditure diagrams from Chapter 6 are used to depict a recessionary gap, an equilibrium at full employment, and an inflationary gap. In the bottom row, these same three situations are shown on aggregate supply and demand diagrams. In each case, the aggregate supply curve is the same (SS), equilibrium occurs at point E, and full employment GDP is $500 billion.

In part (a), the aggregate demand curve D_0D_0 is relatively low, so that equilibrium falls below full employment. There is a recessionary gap measured by the distance EB, or $100 billion. In part (b), the aggregate demand curve D_1D_1 is higher, and equilibrium occurs precisely at full employment. There is no gap of either kind. In part (c), the aggregate demand curve D_2D_2 is so high that equilibrium occurs beyond full employment. There is an inflationary gap measured by the distance BE, or $100 billion.

the entire labour force, so there is a recessionary gap equal to distance *EB*, or $100 billion. This corresponds precisely to the situation depicted on the income-expenditure diagram immediately above it.

In the lower right-hand panel, aggregate demand is so high that the economy reaches an equilibrium well beyond full employment. There is an inflationary gap equal to *BE*, or $100 billion, just as in the diagram immediately above it.

In the lower middle panel, the aggregate demand curve D_1D_1 is at just the right level to produce an equilibrium at full employment. There is neither an inflationary nor a recessionary gap, as in the diagram just above it.

Thus, it may seem that we have done nothing but restate our previous conclusions. But, in fact, we have done much more. Because now that we have studied the determination of the equilibrium price level, we are in a position to examine how the economy adjusts to either a recessionary gap or an inflationary gap.

Adjusting to an Inflationary Gap: Inflation

We have already suggested that an inflationary gap sets the stage for inflation. As we shall see now, this happens because the economy, if left to its own devices, produces an inflation that eventually eliminates an inflationary gap. In other words, the gap self-destructs, although the process may be slow and painful. Let us see how this works.

Suppose equilibrium GDP is above potential, as in the lower right-hand panel of Figure 8–4. Jobs are plentiful and labour is in great demand. Although some workers are unemployed, this minimal unemployment is less than the frictional (and structural) level—that is, less than the number we expect to be jobless because they are moving, changing occupations, and so on, or because the existing job vacancies do not match the skills and aspirations of the unemployed (labour-force composition problems). Because of the low level of unemployment, many firms have trouble finding workers. They may even be having trouble hanging on to their current employees, as other firms try to lure them away with higher wages.

Such a situation is bound to lead to rising money wages, and rising wages add to business costs, thus shifting the aggregate supply curve inward. (Remember, the aggregate supply curve is drawn for a *given* money wage.) But as the aggregate supply curve shifts inward—eventually moving from S_0S_0 to S_1S_1 in Figure 8–5, for example—the size of the inflationary gap steadily declines. Thus, inflation erodes the inflationary gap, eventually leading the economy to an equilibrium at full employment (point *F* in Figure 8–5).

There is a straightforward way of looking at how this self-correcting process works. The trouble arises in the first place because consumers and investors are demanding more output than the economy is capable of producing at normal operating rates. To paraphrase an old cliché, there is too much demand chasing too little supply. Naturally, prices will be rising in such an environment. And the rising prices will eat away at the purchasing power of consumers' wealth, forcing them to cut back on consumption, as explained in Chapter 5. Also emphasized in Chapter 5 was the reaction of foreigners. With higher domestic prices, the competitiveness of our products in the world market is reduced, and our export sales suffer. Eventually, both foreign and domestic demand for our goods will be scaled down to the economy's capacity to provide those goods; at this point, the self-correcting process stops. That, in essence, is the unhappy process by which the economy cures itself of the problem of excessive aggregate demand.

One caveat should be entered. The conclusion that an inflationary gap sows the seeds of its own destruction holds *only in the absence of further forces propelling the aggregate demand curve outward*. But in Chapter 7 we encountered several forces that might shift the aggregate demand curve outward. As you can see by manipulating the aggregate demand–aggregate supply diagram, if aggregate demand is shifting out at the same time that aggregate supply is shifting in, there will certainly be inflation, but

FIGURE 8-5

The Elimination of an Inflationary Gap

When the aggregate supply curve is S_0S_0 and the aggregate demand curve is DD, the economy will initially reach equilibrium (point E) with an inflationary gap. The resulting inflation of wages will push the supply curve inward until it has shifted to the position indicated by curve S_1S_1. Here, with equilibrium at point F, the economy is at normal full employment. But, during the adjustment period from E to F, there will have been inflation.

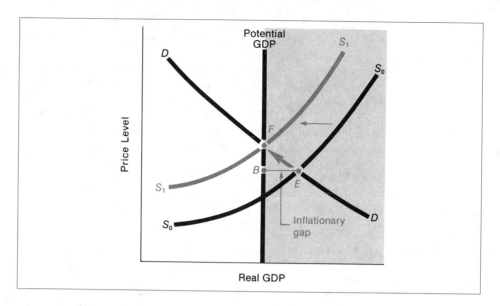

the inflationary gap may not shrink. (Try this as an exercise, to make sure you understand how to use the apparatus.) As a historical proposition, then, not all inflationary episodes have come to a smooth and gradual end. At times, the self-correcting mechanism is overridden by rapid expansion of aggregate demand—which is sometimes even caused by government policy!

Demand Inflation and Stagflation

Simple as it is, this adjustment model teaches us a number of important lessons about inflation in the real world. First of all, Figure 8–5 reminds us that the real culprit in this particular inflation is the excessive level of aggregate demand. The aggregate demand curve is initially so high that it intersects the aggregate supply curve at an output level higher than full employment. The resulting intense demand for workers pushes wages higher; and higher wages spell higher prices. While excessive demand is not the only possible cause of inflation in the real world, it certainly is the cause in our example.

However, business managers and journalists are very likely to blame inflation on rising wages. In a superficial sense, of course, they are right, because higher wages do indeed lead firms to raise their prices. But in a deeper sense they are wrong. Both rising wages and rising prices are only symptoms of an underlying malady: too much aggregate demand. Blaming labour for inflation in such a case is a bit like blaming high medical costs for making us ill.

Second, we see that output falls while prices rise as the economy adjusts from point E to point F in Figure 8–5. This process thus provides our first (but not our last!)

Stagflation is inflation that occurs while an economy is having a recession (or growing very slowly).

explanation of the phenomenon of **stagflation**. We see that:

A period of stagflation is part of the normal aftermath of a period of excessive aggregate demand.

It is easy enough to understand why stagflation occurs in this case. When aggregate demand is excessive, the economy will (temporarily) produce beyond its normal capacity. Labour markets tighten and wages rise. Machinery and raw materials may also become scarce and so start rising in price. Faced by higher costs, the natural reaction of business firms is both to produce less and to charge a higher price. This is stagflation.

Let us review what we have learned about inflationary gaps thus far.

If aggregate demand is exceptionally high, the economy may reach an equilibrium above full employment (an inflationary gap). When this occurs, the tight situation in the labour market soon forces wages to rise. Since wages are business costs, prices rise and there is inflation. With cuts in consumer purchasing power, the inflationary gap begins to close. As the inflationary gap is closing, output falls while prices continue to rise, so the economy experiences stagflation until the inflationary gap is eliminated. At this point, a long-run equilibrium is established with a higher price level and with GDP equal to potential GDP.

Examples from Canadian History

The stagflation that follows a period of excessive aggregate demand is, you will note, a rather benign form of the dreaded disease. After all, although output is falling, it nonetheless remains above potential GDP, and unemployment is low. The Canadian experience of the late 1960s and early 1970s provides "textbook" examples of inflationary gaps that extinguished themselves in this way. During the 1966–69 period, the Canadian economy was booming, unemployment got down to 4 percent, and jobs were plentiful. According to official estimates of potential GDP, there was an inflationary gap.

Our analysis suggests that wages should have been accelerating, and indeed they were. The bright green bars in Figure 8–6 illustrate this acceleration. The dark green bars show that the rate of price inflation followed the rate of increase of wages—rising from 2.4 percent a year to over 4.6 percent. This is, again, in line with what our model predicts.

The upsurge in inflation naturally ate away at the inflationary gap, which was gone by 1969. Price inflation subsequently fell back to 2.9 percent by 1971. Despite outcries about "excessive" wage demands having "caused" inflation, it is clear that the ultimate cause of the acceleration in both wages and prices was the excessive aggregate

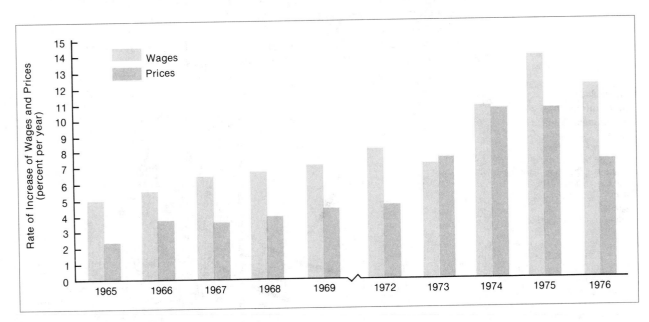

FIGURE 8–6

Growth Rates of Wages and Prices in Canada, 1965–1969 and 1972–1976

These data illustrate what happened when an inflationary gap arose in the late 1960s. Notice the acceleration of both wages and prices. By 1969, the gap was eliminated and wage increases levelled off. Price increases subsequently fell back to 2.9 percent in 1971. Another inflationary gap appeared in 1973–74. Again wage increases first accelerated and then levelled off after the inflationary gap was eliminated.
SOURCE: Statistics Canada.

demand caused by large increases in government expenditure and exports (due to the boom in the United States that resulted from the Vietnam War).

The second example of an inflationary gap occurred in 1973–75, as the Canadian government overstimulated aggregate demand in an attempt to avoid a recession following the OPEC oil price increases in 1973. Again, Figure 8–6 shows the acceleration in wages and prices that occurred. As the inflation eliminated the inflationary gap (as the higher wages shifted the aggregate supply curve to the left), the unemployment rate rose (from 5.4 percent in 1974 to 7.1 percent in 1976). Once again, the economy behaved just as our simple model suggests. We should note that at the start of the 1990s some observers were voicing their concern that, because the unemployment rate in Canada was once again dropping below the full-employment level, the economy could be on the verge of another stagflationary episode of this sort.

Adjusting to a Recessionary Gap: Deflation or Unemployment?

Let us now consider what can happen when the economy finds itself in equilibrium *below* full employment—that is, when there is a *recessionary* gap. This might be caused, for example, by inadequate consumer spending or by anemic investment spending. Figure 8–7 illustrates such a case with an impression of the economic situation of the early 1980s, when we were involved in the worst recession of the post–World War II period.

You might expect that we could just run our previous analysis in reverse: High unemployment leads to falling wages; falling wages reduce business costs and shift the aggregate supply curve outward, so firms cut prices; falling wages and prices eliminate the recessionary gap by propping up consumer spending; and full employment is restored. The economy moves smoothly from point E to point F in Figure 8–7. Very simple, but rather misleading in our modern economy.

Why is it misleading? While the economy may have operated like this long ago, it certainly does not work this way now. The history of Canada and other similar Western economies shows *many examples* of falling wages and prices before World War II but *none* since then. Not even the severe recession of 1981–84, during which unemployment climbed above 12 percent, was able to force average prices and wages down (although it certainly slowed their rate of increase).

FIGURE 8–7
The Elimination of a Recessionary Gap?
At point E, there is a recessionary gap because the aggregate demand curve DD crosses the aggregate supply curve S_0S_0 below the level of potential GDP. If wages fall, the aggregate supply curve gradually shifts outward until it reaches the position indicated by supply curve S_1S_1. Here the economy has attained a full-employment equilibrium at point F. But if wages refuse to fall, the economy gets stuck with a recessionary gap and a long period of unemployment.

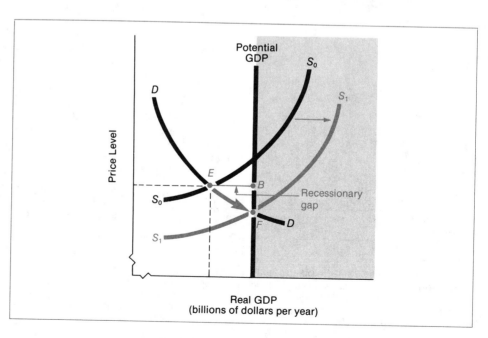

Exactly *why* wages and prices are relatively rigid in the downward direction in our modern economy has been a subject of intense controversy among economists for years. And the controversy continues.

Some economists emphasize institutional features such as minimum-wage laws, union contracts, and a variety of government regulations that place legal floors under particular wages and prices. Because most of these institutions are of relatively recent vintage, this theory successfully explains why wages and prices are more rigid now than they were before World War II. However, most of the Canadian economy is not subject to legal restraints on cutting wages and prices. So it seems doubtful that legal restrictions can provide a complete explanation.

Other observers subscribe to the theory that workers have a profound psychological resistance to accepting a wage reduction. This theory certainly has the ring of truth. Think how you would react if your boss announced that she was cutting your hourly wage rate. You might quit, or you might devote less care and attention to your job. Genuine wage "concessions" are rare enough to make news headlines. For example, Chrysler workers accepted pay cuts in the early 1980s, but only when it appeared that the company was in grave danger of going bankrupt.

While no one doubts that wage cuts are bad for morale, the psychological theory has one major drawback. It fails to explain why the psychological resistance to wage cuts apparently started only after World War II. Until a satisfactory answer to this question is provided, many economists will remain skeptical.

Yet another theory is based on the old adage "you get what you pay for." The idea is that workers differ in productivity, but that the productivity of individual employees is hard for the employer to identify. Firms therefore worry that a general wage reduction will result in the loss of their best workers, since these are the ones who have the best opportunities elsewhere in the economy. Rather than take this chance, firms prefer to maintain high wages even in recessions.

A fourth explanation is based on a fact we emphasized in Chapter 4—that until the 1980s, business cycles were far less severe in the postwar period than they had been in the prewar period. Because of postwar governments' commitment to full employment, firms and workers came to believe that recessions would not turn into depressions. Thus, workers and firms may have decided to wait out the bad times rather than accept wage or price reductions that they would later regret. It is this explanation that was favoured by the Reagan and Thatcher administrations in the United States and the United Kingdom. They rejected the previous approaches, which involved an "inflationary bias." They observed that previous governments had always stimulated aggregate demand sufficiently to keep unemployment from rising too much, causing labour leaders to take employment for granted, and to push for large wage increases. Either some wage-and-price-control scheme seemed to be necessary to combat labour's quite natural reaction to the inflationary gap, or labour had to be stopped from taking employment for granted. By essentially dropping any commitment to full employment and by bluntly announcing that they would not permit an inflationary gap, these governments attempted to reduce the downward inflexibility of wages.

There are other theories as well, none of which commands anything like universal acceptance. But, regardless of the cause, we might as well accept the fact that, in the modern Canadian economy, prices and wages will rise when demand is strong but generally will not fall as dramatically when demand is weak. During recessions, wages do fall to some extent, but not enough to prevent protracted downswings.

The implications of the relative downward rigidity of wages are quite serious, for a recessionary gap cannot cure itself without deflation. And if wages and prices will not fall significantly, *the economy gets stuck at a point such as E in Figure 8–7—that is, at a point below full employment.* Keynes was the first economist to point out that wage rigidity would lead to a long-lasting equilibrium below full employment and to distinguish that condition from the full-employment equilibrium that we have just been considering.

When aggregate demand is low, the economy may get stuck in an *unemployment equilibrium*. There is a recessionary gap, but wages and prices refuse to fall; so the gap persists. The economy endures a prolonged period in which production is below potential GDP.

Does the Economy Have a Self-Correcting Mechanism?

Now a situation like this would, presumably, not last forever. As the recession lengthened and perhaps deepened, more and more workers would be unable to obtain jobs at the prevailing high wages. Eventually their resistance to wage cuts, whatever its cause, would be worn down by their need to be employed. Firms, too, would become increasingly willing to cut prices as the period of weak demand lasted longer and longer, and managers became convinced that the slump was not merely a temporary aberration. Prices and wages did, in fact, fall during the Great Depression of the 1930s. And they might fall again if a sufficiently drastic depression were allowed to occur. (Their rates of increase certainly slowed in the weak markets of the early 1980s.)

Nowadays, however, the political leaders of all three major parties in Canada believe it is folly to wait for falling wages and prices to eliminate a recessionary gap. But while they agree that *some* government action is both necessary and appropriate under recessionary conditions, there is still vocal—and highly partisan!—debate over how much and what kind of intervention is warranted.

One reason for this disagreement is that the **self-correcting mechanism** does operate—if only weakly—to cure recessionary gaps. Recent history provides a vivid illustration.

The Economy in the 1980s: A Case Study

As the 1980s opened, the Canadian economy was operating not too far below full employment, but the inflation rate was very high. A policy-induced recession (to fight inflation) drove the unemployment rate up from only 7.5 percent in 1980 to 12.0 percent in 1983. Throughout this period, the recessionary gap was growing larger, not smaller. Does this mean that the self-correcting mechanism failed to work? Not quite. It just worked weakly, and with some delay.

Between 1980 and 1981, as the recessionary gap increased, wage and price inflation accelerated slightly, as Figure 8–8 shows. According to our model of the self-correcting mechanism, this is not supposed to happen. But then, with unemployment and the recessionary gap setting postwar records, things began to change. While wages and prices did not actually decline, their rates of increase did slow down markedly in 1982–83. By 1983, as you can see in Figure 8–8, the rate of inflation had fallen to just over half its 1980 level. The rates of wage and price increases stayed lower for the next three years. Inflation was significantly lowered, but at substantial cost. More than a million unemployed workers and hundreds of bankrupted businesses were the casualties of the war against inflation. As late as the end of 1986, the annual unemployment rate had not fallen below 9 percent, and it did not reach the 1980 starting value of 7.5 percent until 1989. Thus, it took almost a decade for the self-correcting mechanism to bring us back to full employment. The self-correcting mechanism is a rocky road to full employment.

Our overall conclusion about the economy's ability to right itself, then, runs something like this:

The economy does indeed have a self-correcting mechanism that tends to eliminate either unemployment or inflation. However, this mechanism is much more efficient at curing inflationary gaps through inflation than at curing recessionary gaps through deflation. Also, its ability to curb inflation is sometimes overridden by increases in aggregate demand. Thus, the self-correcting mechanism cannot always be relied on.

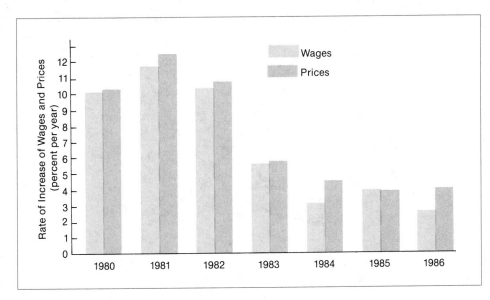

FIGURE 8-8
Growth Rates of Wages and Prices in Canada, 1980-1986
These data illustrate what happened when the Canadian economy developed a large recessionary gap in 1980-83. Notice that wage and price inflation did not slow down in 1980-81 but then did drop markedly in 1982 and 1983 and stayed lower for several years.
SOURCE: Statistics Canada.

Stagflation from Supply Shifts

We have so far encountered one type of stagflation in this chapter—the stagflation that often follows in the aftermath of an inflationary boom. However, the same model does not fit the facts of the more serious stagflationary episodes of 1973–75 and 1978–80 in the United States. What happened during these "mysteries"?

What was going on during those years that caused so much more unemployment *and* inflation than expected? What were the causes of this more virulent type of stagflation? Several things, but the principal villain was the rising price of energy.

In 1973, the Organization of Petroleum Exporting Countries (OPEC) reached a collusive agreement to limit production; it succeeded in quadrupling the price of crude oil in only a few months. American consumers found the prices of gasoline and home-heating fuels increasing sharply. American businesses found that one of the most important inputs to the production process—energy—rose drastically in price, thus increasing the cost of doing business. In 1979, the world oil market went into a panic again following the ousting of the Shah of Iran. Oil prices escalated as buyers scrambled to secure supplies and to build inventories. Seizing the opportunity, OPEC this time doubled the price of oil.

Higher energy prices, we observed earlier, shift the economy's aggregate supply curve inward in the manner illustrated in Figure 8–2 (page 166). If the aggregate supply curve shifts inward, as it surely did for the United States in 1973–75 and again in 1978–80, production will be reduced. And in order to reduce demand to the available supply, prices will have to rise. The result is the worst of both worlds: falling production and rising prices.

This conclusion is shown in Figure 8–9, which superimposes an aggregate demand curve, *DD*, on the two aggregate supply curves of Figure 8–2. The economy's equilibrium shifts upward to the left, from point *E* to point *A*. Thus, output falls while prices rise.

Stagflation is the typical result of adverse supply shifts.

The numbers used in Figure 8–9 are roughly indicative of what happened in the United States between 1973 (represented by supply curve $S_0 S_0$ and point *E*) and 1975 (represented by supply curve $S_1 S_1$ and point *A*). Real production fell by about $50 billion, while the price level rose almost 20 percent.

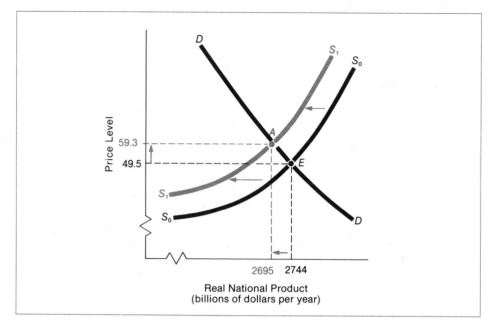

FIGURE 8–9

Stagflation from a Shift in Aggregate Supply

This diagram illustrates how stagflation arises if the aggregate supply curve shifts inward to the left (from S_0S_0 to S_1S_1). If the aggregate demand curve does not change, equilibrium moves from point E to point A. Output falls as prices rise, which is what we mean by stagflation. The diagram indicates roughly what happened in the United States during 1973–75, when higher energy prices caused stagflation.

Why didn't Canada suffer the adverse supply shocks to the same extent as the United States during the 1970s? The answer is that our government followed a rather different policy. Much to the chagrin of the oil-producing provinces, the federal government prevented domestic oil prices from rising as much as world prices did. For oil consumers in the eastern provinces who relied on imported oil, the government paid the difference between the high world price and the much lower domestic price. To a large extent, therefore, the Canadian policy precluded any big leftward shift of the aggregate supply schedule.

Another aspect of Canadian policy was also important. The authorities correctly predicted the recession that followed the OPEC crisis in the United States and elsewhere, and they knew that this would decrease the demand for Canadian-produced goods. In an attempt to override this expected leftward shift of our aggregate demand curve, the government stimulated aggregate demand rather dramatically. (The specific policies involved are discussed in the next few chapters.) As a result, Canada had an inflationary gap in 1973–74, not a recessionary gap as did the United States.

Was Canada's reaction to the world oil-price shocks a good policy? By comparing our experience with that of the United States, we see that Canadians suffered less unemployment. However, Canada's inflation performance was somewhat worse. Also, citizens of the oil-producing provinces remain bitter about the big loss in their income caused by the ceiling imposed on domestic oil prices. Finally, to some extent, the Canadian policy only delayed, and did not eliminate, the adverse supply shifts. The Canadian oil price was gradually increased each year for a decade after 1974. Also, to cover part of the mushrooming budget deficit (partly caused by the government's oil-price subsidy to eastern consumers during the 1970s), the federal government raised the manufacturers' sales tax during the 1980s. This increased business costs and shifted the aggregate supply curve inward, thereby worsening the recession of the 1980s instead of the one in the 1970s.

Inflation and the Multiplier

When we introduced the concept of the multiplier in Chapter 7, we said that there were several reasons why its actual value is smaller than that suggested by the oversimplified multiplier formula. We are now in a position to understand one of these reasons:

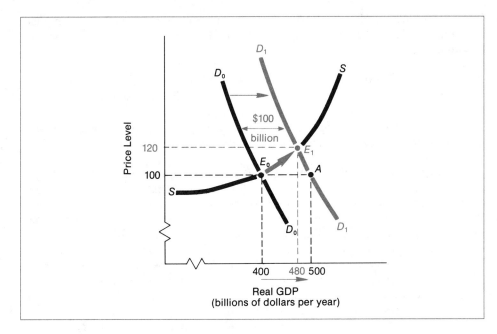

FIGURE 8-10
Inflation and the Multiplier
This figure illustrates the complete analysis of the multiplier, including the effect of inflation. The simple multiplier of Chapter 7, which ignored changes in the price level, appears here as a *horizontal* shift of $100 billion in the aggregate demand curve, meaning that the multiplier would be $100/$20 = 5 if prices did not rise. However, when aggregate demand shifts from D_0D_0 to D_1D_1, prices rise. In the diagram, the price level increases from 100 to 120 or by 20 percent. Consequently, equilibrium real income increases from $400 billion to only $480 billion—for a rise of $80 billion, or a multiplier of $80/$20 = 4.

Inflation reduces the size of the multiplier.

The basic idea is quite simple. In Chapter 7, we described a multiplier process in which one person's spending became another person's income, which led to further spending by the second person, and so on. But this story is confined to the demand side of the economy. Let us therefore consider what is likely to happen on the supply side as the multiplier process unfolds. Will the additional demand be taken care of by firms without raising prices?

If the aggregate supply curve is upward sloping, the answer is no; more goods will be provided only at higher prices. Thus, as the multiplier chain progresses, pulling income and employment up, prices will also rise. And this, as we know from Chapter 5, will dampen consumer spending because rising prices reduce the purchasing power of consumers' wealth, and also divert demand away from domestically produced goods. So the multiplier chain will not proceed as far as it would have in the absence of inflation. How much inflation results from the rise in demand? How much of the multiplier chain is cut off by inflation? The answers depend on the slope of the economy's aggregate supply curve.

For a concrete example of the analysis, let us return to the $20 billion increase in investment spending used in Chapter 7. As we learned there (see especially pages 160–61) $20 billion in additional investment spending eventually leads—through the multiplier process—to *a horizontal shift of $100 billion in the aggregate demand curve*. But to know the actual price level and the actual quantity that will ultimately be produced, we must bring the aggregate supply curve into the picture.

Figure 8-10 does this. Here we show the $100 billion horizontal shift of the aggregate demand curve, from D_0D_0 to D_1D_1, that is derived from the oversimplified multiplier formula (which ignores rising prices). The aggregate supply curve, *SS*, then tells us how this expansion of demand is apportioned between higher output and higher prices. We see that as the economy's equilibrium moves from point E_0 to point E_1, real GDP does not rise by $100 billion. Instead, prices rise, which, as we know, tends to cancel out part of the rise in quantity demanded. So output increases from $400 billion to $480 billion—an increase of only $80 billion. Thus, in our example, inflation reduces the multiplier from $100/$20 = 5 to $80/$20 = 4. In general:

As long as the aggregate supply curve is upward sloping, any increase in aggregate demand will push up the price level. This will, in turn, drain off some of the higher real demand. Thus, inflation reduces the multiplier below that suggested by the oversimplified formula.

Notice also that the price level in this example has been pushed up (from 100 to 120, or 20 percent) by the rise in investment demand. This, too, is a general result:

As long as the aggregate supply curve is upward sloping, any outward shift of the aggregate demand curve will cause some rise in prices in the economy.

The economic behaviour behind these results certainly cannot be considered surprising. Firms faced with large increases in quantity demanded at their original prices respond to the changed circumstances in two natural ways: They raise production (so GDP rises), and they raise prices (so the price level rises). But this rise in the price level reduces the purchasing power of the bank accounts and bonds held by consumers, and they, too, react in the natural way: They cut down on their spending. Also, to avoid the higher domestic prices, they switch some of their spending over to imports. These reactions amount to a movement *along* aggregate demand curve D_1D_1 in Figure 8–10 from point A to point E_1.

Higher prices thus play their usual dual role in a market economy: They encourage suppliers to produce more and, at the same time, encourage demanders to consume fewer domestically produced goods. In this way, equilibrium is re-established at higher levels of output and higher prices through the process of inflation.

Figure 8–10 also shows us exactly where the oversimplified multiplier formula goes wrong. By ignoring the effects of the higher price level, the oversimplified formula supposes the economy moves horizontally from point E_0 to point A. As the diagram clearly shows, output does not actually rise this much. Output *would* rise this much *only* if the aggregate supply curve were horizontal. (Verify this for yourself by pencilling in an imaginary horizontal aggregate supply curve through points E_0 and A in Figure 8–10.) That is, the oversimplified multiplier formula tacitly assumes that the aggregate supply curve is horizontal. Normally, this is an unrealistic assumption, and that is one reason why the oversimplified formula exaggerates the size of the multiplier.

As a summary, it may be useful to put together what we have learned about multiplier analysis in Chapters 7 and 8.

STEPS IN CALCULATING OVERALL EFFECTS ON REAL OUTPUT

1. Shift the total expenditure schedule in the 45° line diagram vertically by the amount of the autonomous shift in spending (as, for example, in Figure 7–1 on page 152).

2. Use the 45° line diagram, or the oversimplified multiplier formula, to calculate the multiplier effect on the GDP that *would* occur *if* the price level, wage rates, interest rate, exchange rate, and level of imports stayed constant (see again Figure 7–1).

3. Now move from the 45° line diagram to an aggregate supply and demand diagram like Figure 8–10 to see how the price level will react. Enter the multiplier effect calculated in Step 2 as a horizontal shift of the aggregate demand curve in the supply–demand diagram.

4. The supply–demand diagram shows what *would* happen to real output and the price level *if* wages, the interest and exchange rates, and imports were constant.[2]

---

[2] The change in the price level in turn has an effect on the position of the total expenditure line in the 45° line diagram. See Discussion Question 10 at the end of the chapter.

We consider this remaining proviso in following chapters. It turns out that the exchange rate and interest rates will remain roughly constant in the face of a shift in autonomous expenditure *if* the central bank follows a fixed exchange-rate policy (as explained in Chapter 14). However, the assumption that imports and wages remain unchanged in the face of an expenditure increase is not plausible. The analysis in Chapter 13 indicates that when more-plausible assumptions about the response of wages are made, our model predicts a larger effect of aggregate demand increases on the price level and a smaller effect on real output.

A Role for Stabilization Policy

Chapter 6 emphasized the volatility of investment spending, and Chapter 7 noted that changes in investment have multiplier effects on aggregate demand. This chapter has taken the next step by showing how shifts in the aggregate demand curve cause fluctuations in both real GDP growth and inflation—fluctuations that are widely decried as undesirable. It also suggested that the economy's self-correcting mechanism works rather slowly, thereby leaving room for government stabilization policy to improve the workings of the free market. Can the government really do this? If so, how? These are the questions for Parts Three and Four of this book.

Summary

1. The economy's aggregate supply curve relates the quantity of goods and services that will be supplied to the price level. It normally slopes upward to the right because the costs of labour and other inputs are relatively fixed in the short run, meaning that higher selling prices make input costs relatively "cheaper" and therefore encourage greater production.

2. The position of the aggregate supply curve can be shifted by changes in wage rates, prices of other inputs, the exchange rate, technology, or the quantities of labour and capital available for employment.

3. The aggregate supply curve normally gets steeper as output increases. This means that, as output and capacity utilization rise, any given increase in aggregate demand leads to more inflation and less growth of real output.

4. The equilibrium price level and the equilibrium level of real GDP are jointly determined by the intersection of the economy's aggregate supply and aggregate demand schedules. This intersection may come at full employment, below full employment (a recessionary gap), or above full employment (an inflationary gap).

5. If there is an inflationary gap, the economy has a self-correcting mechanism that erodes the gap through a process of inflation. Specifically, unusually strong job prospects push wages up, shifting the aggregate supply curve to the left and reducing the inflationary gap.

6. One consequence of this self-correcting mechanism is that if a surge in aggregate demand opens up an inflationary gap, part of the economy's natural adjustment to this event will be a period of stagflation; that is, a period in which prices are rising while output is falling.

7. The economy also has a self-correcting mechanism that erodes a recessionary gap. However, this mechanism works much more slowly and less reliably than the inflationary-gap mechanism because it relies on falling wages to shift the aggregate supply curve outward, and wages do not fall easily.

8. An inward shift of the aggregate supply curve will cause output to fall while prices rise; that is, it will cause stagflation. Among the events that have caused such a shift are the abrupt increases in the price of foreign oil in the 1970s and the falling foreign-currency value of the Canadian dollar in the 1980s.

9. Among the reasons that the oversimplified multiplier formula is wrong is the fact that it ignores any inflation that may be caused by an increase in aggregate demand. Such inflation decreases the multiplier by reducing consumer spending, because consumers as a group suffer a loss of purchasing power when prices rise.

Concepts for Review

Aggregate supply curve
Productivity
Equilibrium of real GDP and the price level

Inflationary gap
Self-correcting mechanism
Stagflation

Recessionary gap
Inflation and the multiplier

Questions for Discussion

1. In an economy with the following aggregate demand and aggregate supply schedules, find the equilibrium levels of real output and the price level. Graph your solution. If full employment comes at $2800 billion, is there an inflationary or a recessionary gap?

AGGREGATE QUANTITY DEMANDED (in billions)	PRICE LEVEL	AGGREGATE QUANTITY SUPPLIED (in billions)
3000	75	2400
2950	80	2450
2800	90	2600
2700	110	2700
2600	140	2800

2. Suppose a worker receives a wage of $12 per hour. Compute the *real* wage (money wage deflated by the price index) corresponding to each of the following possible price levels: 85, 95, 100, 110, 120. What do you notice about the relationship between the real wage and the price level? Relate this to the slope of the aggregate supply curve.

3. In 1989, capacity utilization averaged 89 percent in Canada. In 1982 it averaged 70 percent. In which year do you think the economy found itself on a steeper portion of its aggregate supply curve? Explain why.

4. Explain why a tax such as the GST shifts the aggregate supply curve inward to the left. What are the consequences of such a shift?

5. Comment on the following statement: "Inflationary and recessionary gaps are nothing to worry about because the economy has a built-in mechanism that cures either type of gap automatically."

6. Give *two* different explanations of how stagflation comes about in an economy.

7. Why do you think wages tend to be rigid in the downward direction?

8. Add the following aggregate supply and aggregate demand schedules to the data in Question 3 of Chapter 7 (page 162) to see how inflation affects the multiplier.

(1) PRICE LEVEL	(2) AGGREGATE DEMAND (when investment is $120)	(3) AGGREGATE DEMAND (when investment is $130)	(4) AGGREGATE SUPPLY
90	$1210	$1310	$1110
95	1205	1305	1155
100	1200	1300	1200
105	1195	1295	1245
110	1190	1290	1290
115	1185	1285	1335

Draw these schedules on a piece of graph paper. Then:
a. Notice that the difference between columns 2 and 3 (the aggregate demand schedule at two different levels of investment) is always $100. Discuss how this relates to your answer in the previous chapter.
b. Find the equilibrium GDP and the equilibrium price level both before and after the increase in investment. What is the value of the multiplier?

9. Use an aggregate supply and demand diagram to show that multiplier effects are smaller when the aggregate supply curve is steeper. Which case gives rise to more inflation—the steep aggregate supply curve or the flat one? What happens to the multiplier if the aggregate supply curve is vertical?

10. (More difficult.) Assume that investment spending rises. Draw a set of graphs illustrating the Steps in Calculating Overall Effects on Real Output listed on page 180. Your aggregate supply–demand diagram from steps 3 and 4 will show a change in the price level. How would this change in the price level affect the 45° line diagram you used in step 1? In view of this, use the 45° line diagram to show that inflation reduces the multiplier.

11. Suppose a politician promises that, if elected, he will stimulate the economy so that jobs are created *and* the real incomes of those already employed are higher. Use aggregate supply and demand analysis to see how (or whether) this can be accomplished.

Fiscal, Monetary, and Exchange-Rate Policy

9

Fiscal Policy

Facts do not cease to exist because they are ignored.

ALDOUS HUXLEY

I n Part Two, we constructed and analyzed a model of an economy with no government and no foreign sector. We concluded that such an economy has only weak tendencies to move toward high employment with low inflation. Furthermore, we hinted that well-designed government policies might improve the economy's performance. It is now time to pick up on that hint—and to get acquainted with some of the difficulties the government must overcome if it is to conduct a successful stabilization policy. Furthermore, we can no longer continue with our simplification of ignoring the foreign sector. Canada's exports and imports comprise a full quarter of its national product, and net exports are almost as volatile a component of aggregate demand as is investment. Thus, to make our model fit the Canadian economy, our task in this chapter is to put the government and the foreign sector back into the picture.

Traditionally, the government has used its taxing and spending powers to influence the demand side of the economy. So this chapter begins there, in the traditional domain of *fiscal policy*. We expand the basic model to allow for government purchases of goods and services and for net exports as components of aggregate demand. We also introduce an income tax that makes disposable income less than national income. As we shall see, none of these complications requires any fundamental change in the way we analyze the determination of GDP and the price level, although taxes and imports do reduce the multiplier.

We close the chapter by explaining how taxes affect aggregate supply as well as aggregate demand.

Government Purchases and Equilibrium Income

The federal Minister of Finance normally presents a budget to Parliament each year. This economic report outlines the government's proposed **fiscal policy**. In these statements, the finance minister outlines taxing and spending proposals, explains the effects that government economists expect these proposals to have on aggregate demand and supply, and offers an explanation indicating why this is the right policy at that time.

This chapter is concerned with how these important budget decisions are, or should be, made. If you were a member of Parliament, how would you evaluate the budget? How much spending is the right amount? How much taxation is appropriate? Perhaps more to the point, how can you as a voter decide whether your elected representatives have made sound decisions?

Before attempting to answer questions like these, we must integrate the government into our model of the determination of national income and the price level. We

The government's **fiscal policy** is its plan for spending and taxation. It is designed to steer aggregate demand in some desired direction.

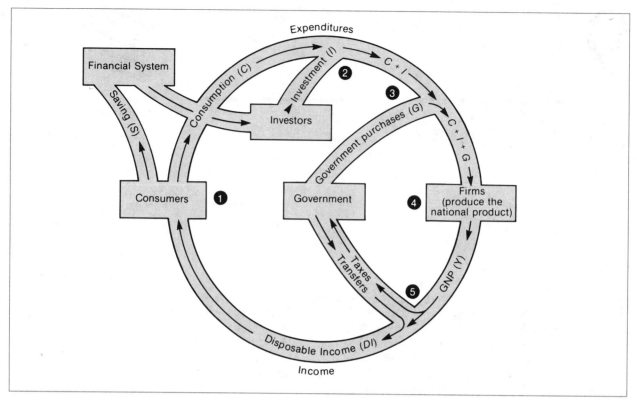

FIGURE 9–1
The Circular Flow of Expenditure and Income with No Foreign Trade

do this in stages, starting first with **government purchases of goods and services** (*G*), then adding taxes, and finally the foreign sector. Thus, in considering once again the circular flow of income and expenditure (see Figure 9–1), we ignore for the moment the flows of tax revenues and transfer payments at point 5 (and we continue to simplify by ignoring exports and imports until later in this chapter). The discussion that now follows relies on graphs and algebra. If you prefer to work through the tables of data from which the graphs are drawn, read through the Basic Exercise for Chapter 9 in the accompanying *Study Guide*.

How would the equilibrium level of GDP be determined in an economy in which the government bought goods but did not levy taxes or make transfers? The circular flow diagram shows us the answer, just as it did in an economy with no government (Chapter 6). If the size of the circular flow of income and expenditure is to be maintained, then the total amount of new goods and services that firms produce at point 4 (*Y*) must be equal to the sum of the demands of consumers at point 1 (*C*), investors at point 2 (*I*), and government at point 3 (*G*). We thus obtain the following restatement of the condition for equilibrium on the demand side of the economy:

For any given price level, equilibrium GDP on the demand side of the economy occurs when the sum of consumption demand, investment demand, and government demand for goods and services just equals output. In symbols:

$$Y = C + I + G.$$

The reasoning behind this equilibrium condition is precisely the same as it was in Chapter 6. At income levels below equilibrium, the sum $C + I + G$ would exceed Y;

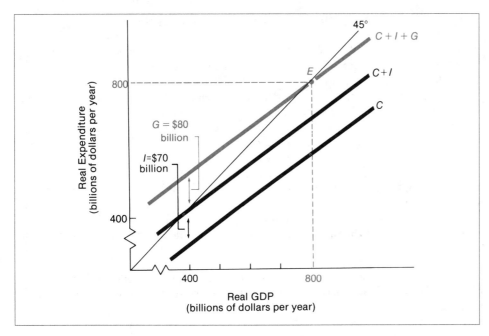

FIGURE 9-2
Income Determination with Government Spending
This diagram adds government purchases of goods and services (G) to the income-expenditure diagrams that we have been using. The C + I + G curve is the total expenditure schedule, and the point where it crosses the 45° line (point E) marks the equilibrium level of GDP. The C + I + G line is parallel to the C + I line because of the assumption that whatever the level of GDP, government spending remains at $80 billion.

and so inventories would be disappearing, signalling firms that they should raise their production. Conversely, at income levels above equilibrium, $C + I + G$ would be less than Y, so that unwanted inventories would be accumulating and firms would have incentives to cut back production.

Figure 9-2 depicts these principles graphically. The line labelled C is the same consumption function we used in previous chapters. The line labelled $C + I$ adds a fixed $70 billion in investment to this; again, this amount is taken from previous chapters (see, for example, page 137). Finally, the line labelled $C + I + G$ adds an additional $80 billion in government spending (which is assumed to be fixed at this amount, whatever the level of GDP) to the $C + I$ line. This gives us our new total expenditure schedule. Just as in previous chapters, the equilibrium of the economy is at point E, where the total expenditure schedule crosses the 45° line. This is because the 45° line includes all the points at which $C + I + G$ add up to Y.

In Chapter 7 we stated that when government spending was introduced, the multiplier for G would be the same as the multiplier for autonomous changes in C and I. We can now demonstrate this conclusion.

If you flip back to page 138, you will see that the equilibrium reached there was at a level of output $Y = \$400$ billion. Now, in an economy that is identical with the one in Chapter 6 except for the $80 billion in government spending, we see that the equilibrium is at $Y = \$800$ billion. Thus an $80 billion increment in G (from zero to $80 billion) has pushed GDP up by $400 billion. In this example, then, the multiplier for government spending is $\$400/\$80 = 5$, which, you will recall, was also the value of the multiplier for autonomous increases in investment or consumption.

The two multipliers are identical because the logic behind them is identical. In Chapter 7 we studied an example of a multiplier spending chain set in motion when Generous Motors spent $1 million to build a factory. This process could equally well have been kicked off by the federal government's buying $1 million worth of new cars from GM. Thereafter, each recipient of additional income would spend 80 percent of it (the assumed marginal propensity to consume) until $5 million in new income had eventually been created.

The qualification that we placed on the oversimplified multiplier formula in Chapter 8 also applies here. Government spending normally leads to some inflation, which pulls down consumer spending and thus reduces the value of the multiplier below our illustrative figure of 5.

Income Taxes and the Consumption Schedule

You can see, then, that it takes little effort to bring government purchases into our model of income determination. Let us turn our attention next to taxes and in particular to the personal income tax.

For present purposes, the most important aspect of taxes is that they create a discrepancy between gross domestic product (GDP) and disposable income (*DI*), as can be seen in the circular flow diagram (Figure 9–1). Tax revenues flow out of the circular flow and into the hands of the government. (The effects of the transfer payments, which enter the circular flow at point 5, will be considered presently.)

We learned in Chapter 5 that there is a close and reliable relationship between consumer spending and *disposable* income. Therefore, if we want to construct a relationship between consumer spending and GDP, we first have to allow for the fact that taxes are deducted from GDP before *DI* is arrived at. The importance of this piece of accounting is that when taxes are increased, disposable income falls—and hence so does consumption—*even if GDP is unchanged*. As a result:

An increase in personal income taxes shifts the consumption schedule in our 45° line diagram downward. Similarly, a reduction in taxes shifts the consumption schedule upward.

The specific manner in which the consumption schedule shifts depends on the nature of the tax change. One way to reduce taxes is to introduce a flat, per-person tax credit. The increase in disposable income from this legislation is the *same* regardless of the level of GDP; hence the increase in consumer spending is the same. In a word, the *C* schedule shifts upward in a parallel manner, as shown in Figure 9–3(a).

But often tax policy is designed to make the change in disposable income depend

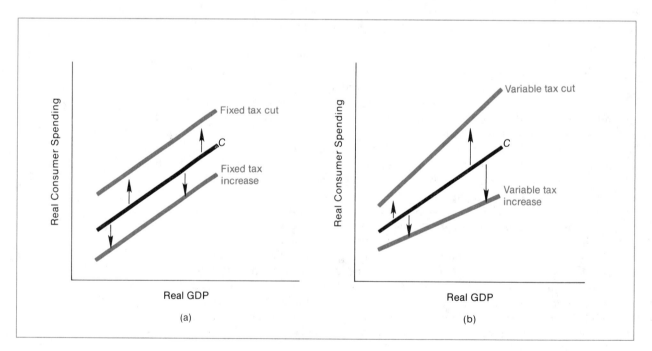

FIGURE 9–3

How Tax Policy Shifts the Consumption Schedule

Because consumption depends on disposable income, not GDP, any change in taxes will shift the consumption schedule relating consumption to GDP. Part (a) shows how the curve shifts for changes in taxes of fixed amounts. Part (b) shows how the *C* curve shifts if the tax cut (or tax increase) is larger at high incomes than at low incomes.

on the level of income; normally the changes are larger at high income levels than at low ones. This is true, for example, when the government changes tax *rates*. Since this sort of tax policy changes disposable income more when GDP is higher, the upward or downward shift in the *C* schedule is sharper at high income levels than at low ones. Figure 9–3(b) illustrates how this type of tax policy shifts the consumption schedule.

Tax Policy and Equilibrium Income

We are now in a position to put taxes into our model of income determination. To do this, we must first adjust the consumption schedule we have been using to allow for an income tax.

Table 9–1 does this on the assumption that taxes are 25 percent of GDP. Column 1 shows alternative values of GDP ranging from $250 billion to $550 billion, and column 2 indicates that taxes are always one-quarter of this amount. Column 3 subtracts column 2 from column 1 to arrive at disposable income (*DI*). Column 4 then shows the amount of consumer spending corresponding to each level of *DI*. Note that columns 3 and 4 are derived from the same consumption function that we have studied in earlier chapters (*C* = 10 + 0.8*DI*). But the consumption schedule that we need for our 45° line diagram relates *C* to *Y*, not to *DI*—that is, it relates spending to total consumer income, not to income net of taxes—and the schedule is therefore found in columns 1 and 4.

To derive the new expenditure schedule for an economy with taxes, we need only replace the old consumption schedule with this new one. This is done diagrammatically in Figure 9–4. The inclusion of taxes has lowered the total expenditure schedule. Since the 45° line is given in the diagram, we can immediately locate the equilibrium level of GDP at point *E*. Here, gross domestic product is $400 billion, consumption is $250 billion, investment is $70 billion, and government purchases are $80 billion.

Once we adjust the expenditure schedule to include the effects of taxes, the determination of national income proceeds exactly as before. The effects of government spending and taxation, therefore, are fairly straightforward; they can be summarized as follows:

Government purchases of goods and services add to total spending directly through the *G* component of *C* + *I* + *G*. Taxes indirectly *reduce* total spending by lowering disposable income, and thus reduce the *C* component of *C* + *I* + *G*. On balance, then, the government's actions may raise or lower the equilibrium level of GDP, depending on how much spending and taxing it does.

TABLE 9-1
Derivation of a Consumption Schedule with Income Taxation

(1) GROSS DOMESTIC PRODUCT (billions of dollars)	(2) TAXES (billions of dollars)	(3) DISPOSABLE INCOME (GDP minus taxes) (billions of dollars)	(4) CONSUMPTION (billions of dollars)
250	62.5	187.5	160
300	75.0	225.0	190
350	87.5	262.5	220
400	100.0	300.0	250
450	112.5	337.5	280
500	125.0	375.0	310
550	137.5	412.5	340

Because taxes (column 2) must be subtracted from gross domestic product (column 1) to get disposable income (column 3), this table shows how an income tax lowers the consumption schedule (column 4) in a concrete example.

FIGURE 9–4
Income Determination with Government Spending and Taxation

This diagram adds a 25 percent income tax to the model economy portrayed in Figure 9-2. Because of this, the C schedule is shifted down (and hence the C + I and C + I + G schedules are also shifted down). Equilibrium is at point E, where the C + I + G schedule crosses the 45° line. Thus equilibrium GDP is $400 billion, the same as it was in the economy with no government. This, however, is certainly not a general result; government actions can either raise or lower GDP.

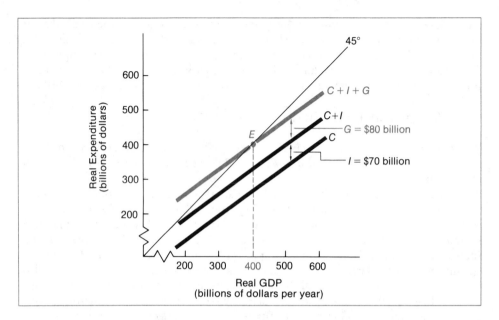

Notice one interesting feature of our example. With purchases of $80 billion and taxes equal to 25 percent of GDP, the economy's equilibrium is at $Y = \$400$ billion (see Figure 9–4), the same as it was with $G = 0$ and no taxes. But tax receipts are $100 billion when GDP is $400 billion. This means that $100 billion in taxes must have decreased GDP by the same amount as $80 billion in spending increased it. Apparently:

The multiplier for changes in taxes is smaller than the multiplier for changes in government purchases.

Let us see why.

Multipliers for Tax Policy

Because the multipliers for tax changes work indirectly via consumption, they must be worked out in two steps.

Step 1. Before turning to the 45° line diagram, we must figure out what any proposed change in the tax law is likely to do to the consumption schedule.

Step 2. We can then enter this effect as a shift of the $C + I + G$ schedule in the 45° line diagram, and work out the multiplier.

A reduction in income taxes provides a convenient example of this two-step analysis, because we have already done Step 1 in an earlier chapter. Specifically, in Chapter 5 we studied how consumer spending would respond to a cut in income taxes. We concluded that if the tax reduction were viewed as permanent, consumers would increase their spending by an amount equal to the tax cut times the marginal propensity to consume. (If you need review, turn back to pages 122 and 126–27.)

This is the shift that must be entered in the 45° line diagram to complete Step 2, and Figure 9–5 displays such a shift. The tax cut raises the expenditure schedule from $C_0 + I + G$ to $C_1 + I + G$ by raising its C component. The diagram then shows the multiplier effect on GDP, which rises from Y_0 to Y_1.

In our numerical example, income-tax receipts rise from zero to $100 billion. So step 1 instructs us to multiply the $100 billion in added income taxes by the marginal

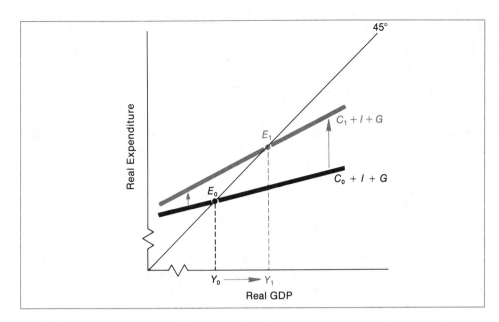

FIGURE 9-5
The Multiplier for a Reduction in Income Taxes
In this example, the $C + I + G$ schedule is shifted upward, from $C_0 + I + G$ to $C_1 + I + G$, by a tax cut. Equilibrium GDP therefore increases from Y_0 to Y_1.

propensity to consume (MPC), which is 0.8, to get $80 billion as the estimated vertical shift of the consumption schedule at $Y = \$400$ billion. Notice that this is precisely equal to the $80 billion increase in government purchases. So, in this example, the *downward* shift of the C schedule exactly offsets the *upward* shift of the G schedule when $Y = \$400$, leading to no net change in the height of the $C + I + G$ schedule. That is why the equilibrium level of GDP did not change when we introduced the government.

Thus we see that the multiplier for income taxes is lower than the multiplier for government purchases because, while G is a direct component of $C + I + G$, taxes are not. Taxes work indirectly, first by changing disposable income and then by changing C. That is why we had to multiply the $100 billion change in taxes by 0.8 to get the $80 billion shift of the C schedule. Economically, some of the change in disposable income affects *saving* rather than *spending*, so a one-dollar tax cut does not pack as much punch as a dollar of G. The fact that the multipliers for G and taxes differ in this way has an interesting implication:

If government purchases and taxes rise by equal amounts, the equilibrium level of GDP on the demand side will rise. If G and taxes fall by equal amounts, the equilibrium level of GDP on the demand side will fall.

Thus fiscal policies that keep the deficit the same do not keep aggregate demand the same—a lesson that politicians frequently forget.

Government Transfer Payments

Finally, we should mention the last major tool of fiscal policy: **government transfer payments**. How are transfers treated in our models of income determination—like purchases of goods and services (G) or like taxes?

The answer follows readily from the circular flow diagram (Figure 9-1). The important thing to understand about transfer payments is that they intervene between gross domestic product (Y) and disposable income (DI) in precisely the *opposite* way from income taxes. Specifically, starting with the wages, interest, rents, and profits that constitute the national income, we *subtract* income taxes to calculate disposable income. We do so because these taxes represent the portion of incomes that are *earned* but never *received* by consumers. But then we must *add* transfer payments because they represent sources of income that are *received* though they were not *earned* in the process of production. Thus, transfer payments are basically *negative taxes*, and giving a consumer $1 in the form of a transfer payment is equivalent to reducing his or her taxes by $1.

So to answer our question, in terms of the 45° line diagram, *increases in transfer payments can be treated simply as decreases in taxes*. And we see that Figure 9–5, which we devised to illustrate a tax cut, can also be used to illustrate a rise in unemployment benefits, in social insurance benefits, or in any other such transfer payment. Similarly, the analysis of a decrease in transfer payments would proceed exactly like the analysis of an increase in taxes.

The Multiplier Revisited

We now have acquired most of the tools we need to understand how fiscal policy decisions are made. But, before members of Parliament vote on the budget, they should have an idea of the magnitude of the multiplier. Our figure of 5 is too high, and we can now understand how the income tax works to lower its value. But before getting involved in the mechanics, let us understand the basic reason.

As we learned in Chapter 7, the multiplier works through a chain of spending and respending, as one person's expenditure becomes another's income. But through taxation some of the additional income leaks out of the circular flow at each stage. Specifically, if the income-tax rate is 25 percent, when Generous Motors spends $1 million on salaries, workers actually receive only $750,000 in *after-tax* (or disposable) income. If workers spend 80 percent of this amount (based on a marginal propensity to consume of 0.8), spending in the next round will be only $600,000. Notice that this is only *60 percent* of the original expenditure, not *80 percent* as in our earlier example. Thus the multiplier chain for each original dollar of spending shrinks from:

$$1 + 0.8 + (0.8)^2 + (0.8)^3 + \ldots = \frac{1}{1 - 0.8} = \frac{1}{0.2} = 5$$

to:

$$1 + 0.6 + (0.6)^2 + (0.6)^3 + \ldots = \frac{1}{1 - 0.6} = \frac{1}{0.4} = 2.5 \, .$$

This is clearly a very large reduction in the multiplier. We thus have a second reason why our oversimplified multiplier formula of Chapter 7 gives an exaggerated impression of the size of the multiplier:

REASONS THE OVERSIMPLIFIED MULTIPLIER FORMULA IS WRONG

1. It ignores price-level changes, which serve to reduce the size of the multiplier.
2. It ignores income taxes, which serve to reduce the size of the multiplier.

Later in this chapter, and in later chapters, we shall encounter still more reasons.

This conclusion about the multiplier can be made quite explicit by working through a simple algebraic version of the model economy. In so doing, we deal only with a simplified model in which prices do not change. While it is possible to work out the corresponding algebra for the more realistic aggregate-demand–aggregate-supply analysis with variable prices, the analysis is rather complicated and is best left to more advanced courses.

To start, we return to our numerical example: The government spends $80 billion on goods and services ($G = 80$), and levies an income tax equal to 25 percent of GDP. So, if the symbol T denotes tax receipts,

$$T = 0.25Y.$$

Since the consumption function we have been working with is

$$C = 10 + 0.8DI,$$

where DI is disposable income, and since disposable income and GDP are related by the accounting identity

$$DI = Y - T,$$

it follows that the C schedule used in the 45° line diagram is described by the algebraic equation:

$$
\begin{aligned}
C &= 10 + 0.8(Y - T) \\
&= 10 + 0.8(Y - 0.25Y) \\
&= 10 + 0.8(0.75Y) \\
&= 10 + 0.6Y.
\end{aligned}
$$

We can now apply the equilibrium condition for an economy with a government, which is

$$Y = C + I + G.$$

Since investment in this example is $I = 70$, substituting for C, I, and G into this equation gives:

$$
\begin{aligned}
Y &= 10 + 0.6Y + 70 + 80 \\
0.4Y &= 160 \\
Y &= 400.
\end{aligned}
$$

This is all there is to finding equilibrium GDP in an economy with a government, but no foreign sector.

To find the multiplier for government spending, increase G by 1 and resolve the problem:

$$
\begin{aligned}
Y &= C + I + G \\
Y &= 10 + 0.6Y + 70 + 81 \\
0.4Y &= 161 \\
Y &= 402.5.
\end{aligned}
$$

So the multiplier is $402.5 - 400 = 2.5$, as stated in the text.

To find the multiplier for an increase in fixed taxes, change the tax schedule to:

$$T = 0.25Y + 1.$$

Disposable income is then

$$DI = Y - T = Y - (0.25Y + 1) = 0.75Y - 1,$$

so the consumption function is

$$
\begin{aligned}
C &= 10 + 0.8DI \\
&= 10 + 0.8(0.75Y - 1) \\
&= 9.2 + 0.6Y.
\end{aligned}
$$

Solving for equilibrium GDP as usual gives

$$Y = C + I + G$$
$$Y = 9.2 + 0.6Y + 70 + 80$$
$$0.4Y = 159.2$$
$$Y = 398.$$

So a $1 increase in fixed taxes lowers Y by $2. The tax multiplier is –2.

Now let us proceed to a more general solution, using symbols rather than specific numbers. The equations of the model that involves no foreign sector are as follows:

$$(1) \qquad Y = C + I + G$$

is the equilibrium condition, as usual;

$$(2) \qquad C = a + b\,DI$$

is the same consumption function we have used in Chapters 6 and 7;

$$(3) \qquad DI = Y - T$$

is the accounting identity relating disposable income to GDP; and

$$(4) \qquad T = T_0 + tY$$

is the tax function, where T_0 represents fixed taxes (which were zero in our numerical example) and t represents the tax rate (which was 0.25 in the example). Finally, I and G are just fixed numbers.

We begin the solution by substituting equations (3) and (4) into equation (2) to derive the consumption schedule relating C to Y:

$$C = a + b\,DI$$
$$C = a + b(Y - T)$$
$$C = a + b(Y - T_0 - tY)$$
$$(5) \qquad C = a - bT_0 + b(1 - t)Y.$$

You will notice that a change in fixed taxes (T_0) shifts the intercept of the C schedule while a change in the tax rate (t) changes its slope, as explained on pages 188–89.

Next, substitute equation (5) into equation (1) to find equilibrium GDP:

$$Y = C + I + G$$
$$Y = a - bT_0 + b(1 - t)Y + I + G$$
$$[1 - b(1 - t)]Y = a - bT_0 + I + G$$

or

$$(6) \qquad Y = \frac{a - bT_0 + I + G}{1 - b(1 - t)}.$$

Equation (6) shows us that G has the same multiplier as I or a, and that this multiplier is:

$$\text{Multiplier} = \frac{1}{1 - b(1 - t)}.$$

To see that this is in fact the multiplier,[1] raise G or I or a by 1 unit. In each case, equation (6) would be changed to read:

$$Y = \frac{a - bT_0 + I + G + 1}{1 - b(1 - t)}.$$

Subtracting equation (6) from this expression gives the change in Y stemming from a one-unit change in G or I or a:

$$\text{Change in } Y = \frac{1}{1 - b(1 - t)}.$$

We noted in Chapter 7 (page 156) that if there were no income tax ($t = 0$), a realistic value for b (the marginal propensity to consume) would yield a multiplier of 10, which is much bigger than the true multiplier. Now that we have added taxes to the model, our multiplier formula produces more realistic numbers, but only for an economy with a relatively less significant foreign sector, such as the United States. Reasonable values for the parameters for the U.S. economy are $b = 0.9$ and $t = 0.33$. The multiplier formula then gives:

$$\text{Multiplier} = \frac{1}{1 - \dfrac{9}{10}\left(1 - \dfrac{1}{3}\right)} = \frac{1}{1 - \dfrac{9}{10} \times \dfrac{2}{3}}$$

$$= \frac{1}{1 - \dfrac{6}{10}} = \frac{1}{\dfrac{4}{10}} = 2.5,$$

which is not far from its actual estimated value of nearly 2.

Finally, we can see from equation (6) that the multiplier for a change in fixed taxes (T_0) is:

$$\text{Tax multiplier} = \frac{-b}{1 - b(1 - t)}.$$

For the example considered earlier, $b = 0.8$ and $t = 0.25$, so the formula gives:

$$\frac{-0.8}{1 - 0.8(1 - 0.25)} = \frac{-0.8}{1 - 0.8(0.75)}$$

$$= \frac{-0.8}{1 - 0.6} = \frac{-0.8}{0.4} = -2.$$

According to these figures, each \$1 *increase* in T_0 *reduces* Y by \$2.

Equilibrium Income with Exports and Imports

The complete circular flow diagram that we studied in Chapter 5 (Figure 5–1, page 115) involved one additional injection and leakage of funds, which we have so far

[1] To see that this is the multiplier formula, either follow the argument in the text or differentiate Y (as defined in equation [6]) with respect to G. This gives $dY/dG = 1/[1 - b(1 - t)]$.

ignored. The additional sector is the rest of the world. *Exports* (*X*) represent foreign purchases of our goods and thus constitute the final injection. *Imports* (*IM*) represent purchases by Canadians that do *not* involve sales by firms producing in Canada, and so they represent an important leakage of funds. Using the same reasoning as before, we now obtain the final restatement of the condition for equilibrium on the demand side of the economy:

For any given price level, equilibrium GDP on the demand side occurs when the sum of consumption, investment, government, and net exports just equals GDP. In symbols:

$$Y = C + I + G + X - IM.$$

While both exports and imports depend on many factors, the predominant one is national income. Some of the additional consumption and investment goods that Canadian consumers and firms buy as income rises are foreign goods. So to construct a simple model of an economy with international trade:

We assume that our imports rise as our GDP rises and fall as our GDP falls.

Similarly, our exports are the imports of other countries, so it is natural to assume that our exports depend on *their* GDPs, not on *ours*. Thus:

We assume that our exports are insensitive to our own GDP.

These two assumptions enable us to bring international trade into our income determination model. Graphically, we simply have to shift the $C + I + G$ schedule up by the magnitude of exports, and then shift the $C + I + G + X$ line down by the quantity of imports. Because the level of exports is independent of our GDP, this shift up in the total expenditure line is a parallel one. But because the level of imports rises as our GDP rises, the shift down in the total expenditure line is not parallel. It shifts down more at the high-GDP end, so that the slope of the total expenditure line is made less steep by imports. Like taxes, then, imports make the multiplier smaller. We have two conclusions:

When net exports are positive, world trade raises equilibrium GDP. When net exports are negative, world trade lowers equilibrium GDP.

International trade lowers the value of the multiplier.

Thus international trade gives us yet another reason why the oversimplified multiplier formula given in Chapter 7 (page 156) overstates the true value of the multiplier.

As before, this conclusion about the multiplier can be made very clear by extending our algebraic treatment of the model economy. (Note that the following equations are numbered in relation to those in the preceding section.)

For an economy *with* foreign trade, the equilibrium condition is:

$$(1a) \quad Y = C + I + G + X - IM,$$

and we add an import function:

$$(7) \quad IM = i_0 + iY,$$

where i is the marginal propensity to import. Substitution of equation (5) (from page 194) and equation (7) into equation (1a) yields the revised expression for equilibrium output:

$$(6a) \quad Y = \frac{a - bT_0 + I + G + X - i_0}{1 - b(1 - t) + i}.$$

The expenditure multiplier for this open economy is therefore:

$$\frac{1}{1 - b(1 - t) + i}$$

The presence of a positive propensity to import (i greater than zero) reduces the multiplier. For the plausible parameter values ($b = 0.9$, $t = 0.33$, and $i = 0.2$) the multiplier formula gives a most realistic answer for Canada, 1.67.

The Canadian and World Economies

In Canada we export about one-quarter of our national product, and as a result we are extremely vulnerable to business conditions in the rest of the world. Since the lion's share of our exports is to the United States, whenever it has a recession, our spending schedule shifts down by a significant amount (exports decrease), and we have a recession too.

But our heavy reliance on foreign trade is not all bad. Our high tendency to import means that Canada's total expenditure line is quite flat so that our multiplier is quite small. Thus, the openness of our economy is a mixed blessing. It exposes us to additional shocks to aggregate demand, especially from the United States, but it also means that domestically generated shocks have a smaller multiplier effect than they would in an economy less involved in foreign trade.

One final point concerning exports and imports should be stressed. Both are affected by the exchange rate, tariffs, and the level of prices both here and abroad. As a result, these variables become important influences on aggregate demand. If foreigners put a tax on their imports (that is, a **tariff**), effectively raising the price of our goods in their country, our exports fall. This shifts our $C + I + G + X - IM$ line down, moving our aggregate demand curve to the left. Similarly, if we put a tariff on our imports, raising the price of foreign goods here, less domestic spending leaks out of the circular flow, so aggregate demand is increased.

A tariff is a tax on imports.

When recessions occur, countries are often tempted to raise tariffs to "export" their unemployment problem. However, all countries cannot do this simultaneously, and an attempt to do this can involve a series of retaliations—a situation that very much restricts world trade. As a result, most Western countries have stated for many years that they are against using tariffs to stimulate domestic demand. Nonetheless, countries seem to be continually tempted by what they see as the short-run advantages of becoming more protectionist.

The exchange rate is also an important influence on exports and imports. The lower the foreign value of the Canadian dollar, the less it costs foreigners to buy our exports and the more it costs Canadians to buy foreign imports. Thus:

A depreciation of the Canadian dollar raises net exports ($X - IM$), shifts the $C + I + G + X - IM$ line up, and so moves the aggregate demand curve to the right. For the same reason, an appreciation of the Canadian dollar lowers net exports and shifts the aggregate demand curve to the left.

Our general summary is:

Government expenditures, tax rates, transfer payments, exports, tariffs, and the exchange rate are all important variables that shift the aggregate demand curve.

Changes in the domestic price level do not shift the aggregate demand curve because the influence of price is already captured in the slope of the curve. The dependence of exports and imports on prices is one of the reasons the aggregate demand curve slopes down.

Planning Expansive Fiscal Policy

Now, at last, you are ready to pretend that you are a member of Parliament deciding how to respond to the finance minister's proposed budget. Suppose that the economy would have a GDP of $400 billion if last year's budget were simply repeated. Suppose further that your goal is to achieve a fully employed labour force and that staff economists tell you that your goal can be achieved with a GDP of approximately $500 billion. Further, just to keep the calculations manageable, suppose that the price level is fixed. (We will drop this unrealistic assumption in just a few pages.) What budget should you support?

First we must consider what options are available if we want to raise GDP by $100 billion. We are not yet in a position to discuss exchange-rate policy, and we have argued that tariffs should be avoided, but there are other options that this chapter has taught us: the government can raise government purchases, reduce taxes, or increase transfer payments by enough to close the recessionary gap between actual and potential GDP.

Figure 9–6 illustrates the problem, and its cure through higher government spending, on our 45° line diagram. Figure 9–6(a) shows the equilibrium of the economy if no changes are made in the budget. With an assumed expenditure multiplier of 2, you can figure out that an additional $50 billion of government spending will be needed to push the GDP up $100 billion and eliminate the recessionary gap ($100 billion/2 = $50 billion).

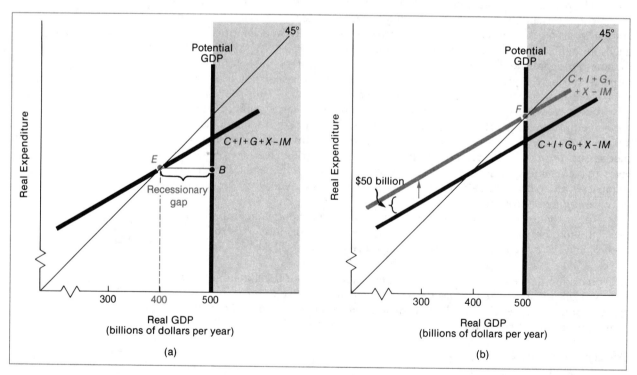

FIGURE 9–6

Fiscal Policy to Eliminate a Recessionary Gap

This diagram shows, with more precision than can actually be achieved in practice, how fiscal policy can eliminate a recessionary gap. Part (a) shows the gap: Equilibrium GDP ($400 billion) falls short of potential GDP ($500 billion). Part (b) shows how fiscal policy—by moving the C + I + G + X − IM line up just enough—can wipe out this gap and restore full employment. With a multiplier of 2, a rise in G of $50 billion or a cut in taxes large enough to shift C up by $50 billion would do the trick.

So you might vote to raise G by \$50 billion, hoping to move the $C + I + G + X - IM$ line in Figure 9–6(a) out to the position indicated in Figure 9–6(b), thereby achieving full employment. Of course you might prefer to achieve the required fiscal stimulus by lowering income taxes, rather than by increasing expenditures. (We have learned that this would require a tax cut of more than \$50 billion.) Or you might prefer to rely on more generous transfer payments. The point is that there are a variety of budgets capable of pushing the economy up to full employment by increasing GDP by \$100 billion. Figure 9–6 applies equally well to any of them.

Planning Restrictive Fiscal Policy

The preceding example assumed that the basic problem of fiscal policy is to overcome a deficiency of aggregate demand, as is often the case. But at other times the problem is that demand is excessive relative to the economy's capacity to produce. In this case, fiscal policy should assume a restrictive stance in order to reduce inflation.

It does not take much imagination to run our previous analysis in reverse. If, under a continuation of current budget policies, there would be an inflationary gap, contractionary fiscal policy could eliminate it. By cutting spending programs out of the budget, by raising taxes, or by some combination of these policies, the government could pull the $C + I + G + X - IM$ schedule down to a non-inflationary position and achieve an equilibrium at full employment.

Notice the difference between this way of eliminating an inflationary gap and the natural self-correcting mechanism of the economy that we discussed in Chapter 8. There we observed that if the economy were left to its own devices, a cumulative but self-limiting process of inflation eventually would eliminate the inflationary gap and return the economy to full employment. Here we see that it is not necessary to put the economy through the inflationary wringer. Instead, a restrictive fiscal policy can limit aggregate demand to the level that the economy can produce at full employment.

The Choice between Spending Policy and Tax Policy

In principle, fiscal policy can nudge the economy in the desired direction equally well by changing government spending or by changing taxes. For example, if the government wants to expand the economy, it can raise G or lower taxes. Either policy shifts the total expenditure schedule upward, as depicted in Figure 9–6, thereby raising the equilibrium GDP on the demand side.

In terms of our aggregate demand and supply diagram, either policy shifts the aggregate demand curve outward from D_0D_0 to D_1D_1 in Figure 9–7. As a result, the economy's equilibrium moves from point E to point A. Both real GDP and the price level rise. As this diagram points out, any combination of higher spending and lower taxes that produces the same aggregate demand curve leads to the same increases in real GDP and prices.

How, then, do we decide whether it is better to raise spending or to cut taxes? The answer depends mainly on how large a public sector we want, and this is a contentious issue.

One point of view, expressed most eloquently in the writings of Canadian-born economist John Kenneth Galbraith, is that there is something amiss when a country as wealthy as the United States has such an impoverished public sector. In Galbraith's view, America's most pressing needs are not for more designer jeans, sports cars, and VCRs, but rather for better schools, more efficient public-transportation systems, and cleaner city streets and lakes. Those who agree with him believe that we should *increase* G when the economy needs stimulus and pay for these improved public services by *increasing taxes* when the economy needs to be reined in.

An opposing opinion, advocated by conservative politicians in all the Western countries, is that the government sector is already too large; that we are foolish to rely

FIGURE 9-7
**Expansionary
Fiscal Policy**

Any of a variety of expansionary
fiscal policies will push the
aggregate demand curve
outward to the right, as depicted
by the shift from D_0D_0 to D_1D_1 in
this aggregate supply and
demand diagram. The
economy's equilibrium moves
upward to the right along
aggregate supply curve SS,
from point E to point A.
Comparing A with E, we note
that output is higher but prices
are also higher. The
expansionary policy has caused
some inflation.

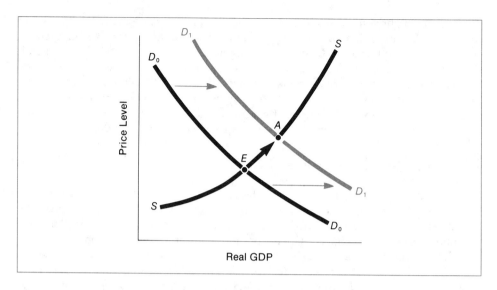

on government to do things that private individuals and businesses could do better on
their own; and that the growth of government interferes too much in our everyday
lives and in so doing circumscribes our freedom. Those who hold this view argue for
tax cuts when macroeconomic considerations call for expansionary fiscal policy, and
for *reductions in public spending* when restrictive policy is required.

This is an important point, and one on which so many people are confused. Too often
the use of fiscal policy for economic stabilization is erroneously associated with a large
and growing public sector—that is, with "big government." This need not be the case.
Individuals favouring a smaller public sector can advocate an active fiscal policy just as
well as those who favour a larger public sector. Advocates of big government budgets
should seek to expand demand (when appropriate) through higher government
spending and contract demand (when appropriate) through tax increases. By contrast,
advocates of small public budgets should seek to expand demand by cutting taxes and
reduce demand by cutting government expenditures.

There are potentially legitimate arguments against an active stabilization policy,
as we noted in Chapter 8. For example, the downward rigidity of wages may be
strengthened if workers can count on the government's active commitment to full
employment. But this issue is entirely separate from questions concerning the relative
worth of big or small government.

Some Harsh Realities

The mechanics outlined so far in this chapter make the fiscal policy planner's job look
rather simple. The elementary diagrams suggest, rather misleadingly, that the authorities can drive GDP to any level they please simply by manipulating their spending and
tax programs. It seems as though they should be able to hit the full-employment bull's-
eye every time.

But, in fact, a better analogy is that of using a gun of uncertain accuracy to shoot
through dense fog at an erratically moving target. The target is moving because, in the
real world, the investment schedule and the export schedule (and, to a lesser extent,
the consumption schedule) are constantly shifting on account of changes in expectations, new technological breakthroughs, changes in trade agreements and consumers'
tastes, and the like. This means that the policies decided upon today, which are to take
effect at some future date, may no longer be appropriate by the time that future date
rolls around. Policy must be based, to some extent, on *forecasting*, and no one has yet

discovered a foolproof method of economic forecasting. Since our forecasting ability is so modest and since fiscal policy decisions sometimes take a long time to be carried out, the government may occasionally find itself fighting the last inflation just when the new recession gets under way.

A second misleading feature of our diagrams is that multipliers are not known with as much precision as our examples may suggest. It is therefore impossible to "fine tune" every wobble out of the economy's growth path through fiscal policy; economics is simply not that precise a science. The point is even more cogent with respect to income-tax policy, for here we get involved in trying to guess whether consumers will view tax changes as permanent or temporary.

A third complication is that our target—full-employment GDP—may be only dimly visible, as if through a fog. Especially when the economy's last experience with full employment is very far in the past, economists may have difficulty estimating the GDP level that represents full employment. In fact, as was mentioned in Chapter 4, controversy exists over how much unemployment constitutes "full employment" right now.

Finally, in trying to decide whether to push the economy out of a position of unemployment, legislators would like to know what the inflationary costs will be. As Figure 9-7 reminds us, any expansionary fiscal policy that closes a recessionary gap by increasing aggregate demand also pushes prices higher, that is, causes more inflation. This undesired side effect may make the government hesitant to use fiscal policy to end a recession.

Taxes and the Aggregate Supply Schedule

But must this undesired effect always occur? Can we stimulate the economy through fiscal policy *without* worsening inflation? In principle, we can, if the government's instruments can be used to shift the aggregate supply schedule to the right, without having any noticeable impact on the position of the aggregate demand curve. Such a policy would deliver what would often be regarded as the best of both worlds—higher real output and lower prices (as shown in Figure 9-8). But *does* the government actually have any instruments that can have this supply-side effect? The following policies, most of which are tax cuts aimed at stimulating firms' investment in cost-saving techniques, are the ones that are usually suggested.

1. *Accelerated Depreciation.* As mentioned in Chapter 6, a company investing in a machine or factory is not permitted to take the entire cost of that asset as a tax

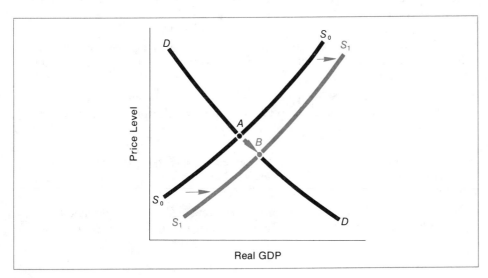

FIGURE 9-8
Tax Cuts and Aggregate Supply
The basic idea of tax cuts is that they can cause the economy's aggregate supply curve to shift outward to the right. If the effect of the tax cut on aggregate demand can be neutralized by another policy, so that the position of the curve does not change, the tax cut will lead to the equilibrium point *B* instead of the equilibrium point *A*. Comparing *B* with *A*, we see that the program leads to lower prices and higher output.

write-off in the year it is purchased. Instead, it must spread the cost over the lifetime of the asset in a series of **depreciation allowances**, which Revenue Canada calls **capital cost allowances**. These are annual tax deductions that in total add up to the value of the asset. Naturally, firms prefer to take their depreciation allowances sooner rather than later, because higher depreciation allowances in the early years of an investment mean lower immediate tax burdens.

For a long time, Canadian policy-makers felt that an effective way to provide greater incentives for investment was to speed up ("accelerate") depreciation allowances. For example, if the government reduces the "lifetime" of a machine for tax purposes from, say, seven years to five, then obviously firms will get the tax savings from depreciation faster. This is precisely the course of action that has been taken in Canada. For much of the 1970s and 1980s, the official lifetime (for tax purposes) of a machine in the manufacturing and processing sector was two years.

2. *Reducing the Corporation Income Tax.*   By letting companies retain more of their pre-tax income, it is argued, government will provide both greater investment incentives (by raising the profitability of investments) and more investable funds (by letting companies keep more of their earnings).[2] More investment should lead to increased efficiency (lower unit costs), which we show graphically as a shift down of the aggregate supply curve.

3. *Reducing Taxes on Capital Gains.*   Many investments, particularly financial investments such as stocks and bonds, often lead to **capital gains and losses.** For example, if Mr. Cabot purchases Canadian Pacific shares in 1960 for $10,000 and sells them in 1990 for $100,000, the law says he has reaped a $90,000 *capital gain*, and must pay tax. Lower taxes on capital gains provide greater incentives for individuals and firms to invest more. Partly for these reasons, the Canadian government has given favourable tax treatment for capital gains.

A **capital gain** is an increase in the market value of a piece of property, such as a common share of stock or a parcel of land, that occurs during the period between when it is bought and when it is sold. A **capital loss** is a decrease in that property's value.

Not all tax cuts are aimed directly at spurring investment. If there is to be more investment, someone must be providing the saving to finance it. Thus, our tax system has long involved:

4. *Lower Taxes on Income from Savings.*   The extreme form of this strategy is to simply exempt from taxation all income from interest and dividends. Since income must be either consumed or saved, this would, in effect, change our present personal income tax into a tax on consumer spending. While this has not been adopted explicitly in Canada, the general shift away from income taxation and toward an increased reliance on consumption taxes (the new GST) is accomplishing this increased incentive for saving. Retirement Savings Plans (RSPs) serve the same purpose.

Of course, capital is not the only factor of production. Aggregate supply can be expanded by increasing the supply of labour services as well. It is for this reason that our government has legislated:

5. *Lower Personal Income-Tax Rates.* Such cuts encourage people to work harder and for longer hours and induce them to spend more time at productive activities and less time worrying about how to avoid taxes.

Aggregate supply depends on the state of technology and the availability of raw materials. So the tax system has encouraged technological progress and resource exploration by offering:

6. *Tax Credits for Research and Exploration.* Canadian corporate tax law has consistently allowed companies that spend money on research and development

---

[2] This will be explained in greater detail in Chapter 13.

(R & D) and resource exploration to have dramatic reductions in their tax bills. The hope is obvious: Tax incentives should increase spending on R & D, and more R & D should lead to improvements in technology. Similarly, tax incentives should increase spending on drilling for oil (etc.), and more energy resources and other raw materials should lead to lower business costs.

Finally, business costs can be decreased by:

7. *Reducing Sales and Payroll Taxes.* If firms are allowed to pay less to the government in the form of sales taxes or Canada pension and unemployment insurance contributions, they can afford to lower their selling prices (so the aggregate supply curve should shift down). Given the government's goals of higher output and lower prices, the implementation of the GST in 1991 can be viewed as counterproductive: Because this type of sales tax shifts the aggregate supply curve to the left, it results in stagflation.

How have these policies worked out in practice? Critics have had no quarrel with the analytical basis of the approach; if the aggregate supply curve *can* be shifted to the right as a result of fiscal policy, then that is desirable. But critics have also argued that advocates of tax cuts exaggerate the *magnitude* of their beneficial effects and ignore some of their undesirable side effects. Here is a list of the main criticisms.

1. *The Small Magnitude of Supply-Side Effects.* It is easy to design tax cuts that, for example, make working more *attractive* financially; that is, they raise take-home pay. All you have to do is cut tax rates. Doing this, however, does not guarantee that people will actually work more. Instead, they may find themselves able to afford the goods and services they want with fewer hours of labour and react by working *less*. Similarly, if tax cuts raise the return on savings, people may find their savings goals easier to achieve and may react by saving less. Most of the statistical evidence suggests that it is unrealistic to expect tax reductions to lead to very substantial increases in labour supply, household savings, or firms' investment spending. Foreign ownership is the major reason why firms' investment spending does not respond much, as explained in the boxed insert on the next page.

2. *Demand-Side Effects.* If you cut personal taxes, individuals *may possibly* work more, but they *will certainly* spend more. If you reduce business taxes and successfully encourage expansion of industrial capacity, business firms will necessarily demand more investment goods.

    The response to this criticism is to link the tax cuts to reductions in government spending that would cancel out the demand-side effects. Whatever the demand stimulus caused by the tax cuts, some expenditure reduction big enough to neutralize it can be implemented. By combining these two programs into a fiscal package, it may be possible to obtain the situation depicted in Figure 9–8: a rise in aggregate supply with no accompanying rise in aggregate demand.

    The problem with this strategy is that if *large* tax cuts are made, then *large* spending cuts must accompany them. But it is simply not plausible to expect governments to make sufficiently large expenditure cuts. For example, when the Conservatives came into power in 1984, their "Agenda for Economic Renewal" stated that their goal was to "reduce the deficit through expenditure reductions and not through major tax increases." But despite this resolve and a large electoral majority, the Conservatives legislated significant tax increases during the 1980s. The budget deficit was no smaller at the end of the decade, and this was because the government simply would not cut its expenditures sufficiently.

3. *Problems in Timing.* The most popular types of supply-side tax cuts in Canada seek to encourage greater business investment. But investment does not create new

Corporate Tax Concessions in Canada

At the policy level, the Canadian federal government has been using corporate tax concessions as its favourite instrument of fiscal policy for more than thirty years. Its intention has been to stimulate investment spending. While this policy is an attempt to raise aggregate demand and therefore create jobs while the new equipment is constructed and installed, the government has consistently stressed the supply-side motivation of its policies. The idea is to get new and better equipment in place so that Canadian labour is more productive and the level of potential GDP is increased.

Perhaps the most dramatic use of corporate tax concessions came in the 1972 Budget, when the corporate profits tax rate was cut from 50 percent to 40 percent, and firms in the manufacturing and processing sector were allowed to claim for tax purposes that machines and equipment were fully worn out within two years of purchase. An election occurred before the budget was passed, and the Liberals just managed to stay in office with a minority government. Most analysts credit the NDP's criticism of the tax concessions as an important reason for the decline in the government's support (although others criticized, too, as the cartoon from the *Toronto Star* indicates). The political problem facing the Conservatives was that they wanted to support the tax concessions, but they had to express concern about their unpopularity. They decided to support the government, provided that it conducted a study of the effectiveness of the tax cuts.

In the study, the Department of Finance surveyed companies and simply asked them whether the tax cuts had *any* effect on their investment spending. Only 47 percent of the firms said yes. This low proportion is due to the fact that

Tit for tat

Reprinted by permission of the *Toronto Star*.

many firms in Canada are foreign-owned. When foreign-owned firms file for corporation profits taxes in their home country (say, the United States) they are allowed a tax credit equal to the amount of taxes already paid in other countries (like Canada). Thus, if the Canadian government collects less revenue as a result of our tax concessions, the foreign-owned firm qualifies for precisely that much less of a tax credit when filing in the United States. The end result is that the Canadian government has given revenue to the American government, and the firm (and its investment spending) is unaffected.

industrial capacity overnight. It takes time to plan new investment projects, arrange the financing, get delivery on machinery, build factories, and then actually put these things into operation. The crucial point is that the *expenditures* on investment goods come before the *expansion of capacity*. Thus, even if supply-side policies are successful, aggregate *demand* expands first and aggregate *supply* follows later.

4. *Effect on the Distribution of Income.* The preceding objections all pertained to the likely effects of tax cuts on aggregate supply and demand. But there is a very different problem that bears mention: Most supply-side initiatives would increase income inequality. Why? Because, while raising the incomes of the wealthiest members of our society may not be their primary aim, most of these incentives cannot help but concentrate benefits on the rich simply because it is the rich who earn most of the capital gains, interest, and dividends and who own most of the corporations.

Indeed, this tilt toward the rich is almost an inescapable corollary of supply-side logic. Its basic aim is to increase the incentive for working and investing; that is, to increase the gap between the rewards of those who succeed in the economic game (by working hard, investing well, and so on) and of those who fail. It can hardly be surprising therefore, that supply-side policies tend to increase economic inequality.

5. *Increase in the Deficit.* You can hardly help noticing that most of the policies suggested for shifting the aggregate supply curve to the right involve reductions in one tax or another. Thus, unless some other tax is raised or spending is cut, such strategies are bound to raise the government budget deficit.

The response to this criticism is that lower tax rates need not lead to lower tax revenues if the tax base grows quickly enough. For example, suppose the GDP starts at $400 billion when the tax rate is 25 percent; the government collects $100 billion in tax revenues. Then, if the tax rate is cut to 20 percent, but GDP grows to $500 billion as a result, tax receipts will remain at $100 billion.

But is this numerical illustration plausible? We have learned enough in this chapter to see that the answer is no. If the GDP starts at $400 billion, a cut in the tax rate from 25 percent to 20 percent lowers tax revenues initially by $20 billion (from $100 billion to $80 billion). For this to cause a $100 billion increase in the GDP (from $400 billion to $500 billion), the tax multiplier would have to be $100/$20 = 5. This is about three times as large as the actual multiplier.

On balance, most economists have reached the conclusion that while numerous tax changes have effects on the position of the aggregate supply curve, the effects of those same policies on the aggregate demand curve are at least as important. Thus, it is very difficult to use fiscal policy to attack either unemployment or inflation without there being an undesired effect on the other target. Furthermore, international tax agreements and the large degree of foreign ownership in Canada make corporate tax incentives an inefficient fiscal tool (in the sense that much revenue is lost per unit of investment spending stimulated).

The one tax rate in which increases or cuts are generally considered to have an immediate and significant shift effect on the aggregate supply curve is the sales-tax rate. Thus, as we noted earlier, the short-run effect of imposing a new goods and services tax is similar to that of an oil-price increase—it leads to stagflation. Government authorities do not like to admit to causing such things. Instead, they direct our attention to the longer-term benefits of the GST—namely, that because it encourages higher savings (and therefore higher investment) by discouraging consumption, it can be expected to raise Canadian incomes in the future.

Summary

1. The government's fiscal policy is its plan for managing aggregate demand and supply through its spending and taxing programs. It is announced and described in the federal budget.

2. Government purchases of goods and services (G) and net exports ($X - IM$) are direct components of the total spending. Therefore, they have the same multiplier as do autonomous changes in consumption or investment.

3. When income taxes are introduced, there is a difference between GDP and disposable income. Since consumer spending (C) depends on disposable income, any change in taxes will shift the consumption schedule on a 45° line diagram.

4. Shifts in the consumption function caused by tax policy are subject to the same multiplier as autonomous shifts in the consumption schedule. The income tax reduces the size of this common multiplier, however, just as it reduces the size of the multiplier for G, I, or X. High tendencies to import also reduce the size of the multiplier.

5. Government transfer payments are treated like negative taxes, not like government purchases of goods and services, because they influence total spending only indirectly through their effect on consumption.

6. The net effect of the government on aggregate demand —and hence on equilibrium output and prices— depends on whether the expansionary effects of its spending are greater or smaller than the contractionary effects of its taxes.

7. The multiplier for changes in taxes is smaller than the multiplier for changes in government purchases.

8. If the multipliers were known precisely, it would be possible to plan fiscal policies to eliminate either a recessionary or an inflationary gap. Recessionary gaps

can be cured by raising *G*, cutting taxes, or increasing transfers. Inflationary gaps can be cured by cutting *G*, raising taxes, or reducing transfers.

9. Active stabilization policy can be carried out either by means that tend to expand the size of government (by raising either *G* or taxes when appropriate) or by means that hold back the size of government (by reducing either *G* or taxes when appropriate).

10. Expansionary fiscal policy can lessen recessions, but it normally exacts a cost in terms of higher inflation. This

dilemma has led to interest in tax cuts designed to stimulate aggregate supply. If successful, they can expand the economy and reduce inflation at the same time —a desirable outcome.

11. But critics point out five problems of supply-side tax cuts: They also stimulate aggregate demand; the beneficial effects on aggregate supply may be small; the demand-side effects occur before the supply-side effects; they make the income distribution more unequal; and large tax cuts lead to large budget deficits.

Concepts for Review

Fiscal policy
Government purchases of goods and services (*G*)
Net exports (*X* – *IM*)

Tariffs
Government transfer payments
Effect of income taxes and imports on the multiplier

Supply-side tax cuts
Depreciation allowances
Capital gains and losses

Questions for Discussion

1. Consider an economy involved in no foreign trade, in which tax collections are always $200 and in which the three components of aggregate demand are as follows:

GDP	TAXES	DI	C	I	G
$480	$200	$280	$210	$100	$215
540	200	340	255	100	215
600	200	400	300	100	215
660	200	460	345	100	215
720	200	520	390	100	215

Find the equilibrium of this economy graphically. What is the marginal propensity to consume? What is the multiplier? What would happen to equilibrium GDP if government purchases were reduced by $30 and the price level were unchanged?

2. Now consider a related economy in which investment is also $100, government purchases are also $215, and the price level is also fixed. But taxes now vary with income, and as a result the consumption schedule looks like the following:

GDP	TAXES	DI	C
$480	$160	$320	$255
540	180	360	285
600	200	400	315
660	220	440	345
720	240	480	375

Find the equilibrium graphically. What is the marginal propensity to consume? What is the tax rate? Use your diagram to show the effect of a decrease of $30 in government purchases. What is the multiplier? Compare this answer with your answer to Question 1 above. What do you conclude?

3. Explain why *G* has the same multiplier as autonomous shifts in *C* or *I*, while taxes have a different multiplier.

4. Return to the hypothetical economy in Question 1 and suppose that *both* taxes and government purchases are increased by $60. Find the new equilibrium under the assumption that consumer spending continues to be exactly three-quarters of disposable income (as it is in Question 1).

5. Discuss the difference between a government purchase of a good or service and a government transfer payment.

6. Suppose that you are in charge of the fiscal policy of the economy in Question 1. There is an inflationary gap with income at $660, and you want to reduce income to $600. What specific actions can you take to achieve this goal?

7. Now put yourself in charge of the economy in Question 2, and suppose that full employment comes at a GDP of $720. How can you push income up to that level?

8. (More difficult.) Return to Question 1 and once again assume that you want to lower GDP to $600 but are now required to do so while maintaining a balanced budget. By how much do you have to raise government purchases and taxes?

9. (More difficult.) Consider an economy with a horizontal aggregate supply curve. Investment is fixed at $900,

government purchases are $1300, the consumption function is:

$$C = 300 + 0.75DI,$$

and taxes are 20 percent of GDP—making disposable income (DI) equal to 80 percent of GDP. Find the equilibrium level of GDP. How would this equilibrium change if taxes were abolished? Compare your answer with the examples in this chapter.

10. Consider the following fictitious economy.

GDP	SAVINGS	IMPORTS
$500	$50	$10
600	70	20
700	90	30
800	110	40
900	130	50
1000	150	60
1100	170	70
1200	190	80

Investment and exports are $100 and $110, respectively. What is the equilibrium value of GDP? What is the multiplier? What is equilibrium GDP if exports drop to $80?

11. Find the equilibrium level of GDP in an economy described by the following set of equations:

$$C = 10 + 0.9DI$$
$$I = 200$$
$$G = 360$$
$$T = 100 + 0.33Y.$$

Next, find the multipliers for government purchases and for fixed taxes. If it is desired to lower GDP by $100, what are some policies that would do the trick?

12. This is a variant of the previous problem that approaches things the way a fiscal policy planner might. In an economy whose consumption function and tax function are as given in Question 11 and with investment fixed at $200, find the value of G that would make GDP equal to $1400.

13. You are given the following information about an economy.

$$C = 20 + 0.8(Y - T)$$
$$I = 100$$
$$G = 520$$
$$T = 0.25Y$$

a. Find equilibrium GDP and the budget deficit.
b. Suppose the government, unhappy with the budget deficit, decides to cut government spending by precisely the amount of the deficit in (a). What actually happens to the budget deficit and why?

14. (More difficult.) In the economy considered in Question 13, suppose the government, seeing that it has not wiped out the deficit, keeps cutting G until it succeeds in balancing the budget. What level of GDP will then prevail?

15. You are given the following information about an economy.

$$C = 50 + 0.8(Y - T)$$
$$I = 100$$
$$G = 100$$
$$X = 70$$
$$T = 0.2Y$$
$$IM = 0.21Y$$

Find the equilibrium values for GDP, budget surplus, and trade surplus.

10

Firms and Their Financing: Stocks and Bonds

The action of the stock market must necessarily be puzzling at times since otherwise everyone who studies it only a little bit would be able to make money in it.

B. GRAHAM, D. L. DODD, AND S. COTTLE

For several chapters now, we have been developing our model economy by allowing for numerous injections and withdrawals of funds in the circular flow of income and expenditure. To refresh your memory of the details of that circular flow chart, see Figure 5–1 on page 115.) The three injections of funds are investment spending by firms, government spending, and exports; the three withdrawals of funds are household savings, taxes, and imports. But our discussion of these flows of funds has been incomplete, since we have not explained what goes on within the two blocks of the chart labelled "financial system" and "rest of the world." Once we extend our discussion to rectify these simplifications, we will be able to explain how interest rates and the exchange rate are determined and how these financial variables affect unemployment and inflation. We commence this detailed excursion into the financial parts of our economy in this chapter.

How are household savings collected and channelled over to firms to finance business investment expenditures on new plant and equipment? Basically, there are three methods. In the first, the existing owners of firms simply extend ownership rights to a wider group of individuals by selling new stocks or shares in their companies. In the second, firms effectively go into debt by selling "IOU" slips called "bonds." The third method also involves firms' going into debt—in this case, by taking out bank loans. It is the banks that collect up household savings (in deposit accounts) and make these funds available to firms. As it turns out, in order to understand how the financial part of the economy works, we need not consider all three options. We can simplify our model economy by restricting firms to only one financing option: taking out bank loans. Hence, in the next two chapters, we will formally extend our model by focussing on banking. But in the meantime, since many students are interested in the stock and bond markets, we include a brief discussion of these financing options here. And since, from the point of view of our formal model-building, this chapter on stocks and bonds is really an extended "aside," your instructor may choose to leave it for you to read on your own.

The stock market is really something of an enigma. No other economic activity is reported in such detail in so many newspapers and followed with such concern by so many people; yet no activity seems to have been so successful in eluding those who devote themselves to predicting its future. There is no shortage of well-paid "experts" who are prepared to forecast the future of the market. But there are real questions about what these experts deliver. For example, a widely noted study of leading analysts' predictions of company earnings (on which they based their stock-price forecasts) reported:

We wrote to nineteen major Wall Street firms ... among the most respected names in the investment business.

We requested—and received—past earnings predictions on how these firms felt earnings for specific companies would behave over both a one-year and a five-year period. These estimates ... were ... compared with actual results to see how well the analysts forecast short-run and long-run earnings changes.

Bluntly stated, the careful estimates of security analysts (based on industry studies, plant visits, etc.) do little, if any, better than those that would be obtained by simple extrapolation of past trends.

For example ... the analysts' estimates were compared [with] the assumption that every company in the economy would enjoy a growth in earnings of about 4 percent over the next year (approximately the long-run rate of growth of the national income). It turned out that ... this naïve forecasting model ... would make smaller errors in forecasting long-run earnings growth than ... [did] the forecasts of the analysts.

When confronted with the poor record of their five-year growth estimates, the security analysts honestly, if sheepishly, admitted that five years ahead is really too far in advance to make reliable projections. They protested that while long-term projections are admittedly important, they really ought to be judged on their ability to project earnings changes one year ahead.

Believe it or not, it turned out that their one-year forecasts were even worse than their five-year projections.[1]

Later in this chapter we will be in a position to give the explanation many economists offer for this poor performance record.

Firms in Canada

It is customary to divide firms into three groups: *corporations, partnerships*, and *sole proprietorships* (businesses having a single owner). Over three-quarters of the firms in the manufacturing sector are corporations, and these firms account for an even higher proportion of sales. But while economic power resides in the corporations, this form of business organization actually constitutes a *minority* of Canadian business firms, measured in terms of the total number of enterprises.

Just what are the three basic forms of organization of business firms, and what induces organizers of a firm to choose one form rather than another?

Sole Proprietorships

A **sole proprietorship** is a business firm owned by a single person.

The **sole proprietorship** is the form of business organization involving the fewest legal complications. Most small retail firms, most farms, and many small factories are run as sole proprietorships. To start a sole proprietorship, an individual simply decides to go into business and opens up a new firm or takes over an existing firm. Aside from special regulations, such as health requirements for a restaurant or zoning restrictions that limit business activity to particular geographical areas, the individual does not need anyone's permission to go into business. This is one of the main advantages of the sole-proprietorship form of organization. But probably its main attraction is that the owner can be his or her own boss and the firm's sole decision-maker. No partners or shareholders have to be consulted when the proprietor wants to expand or change the company's product line or modify the firm's advertising policy.

Unlimited liability is a legal obligation of a firm's owner(s) to pay back company debts with whatever resources he or she owns.

On the other hand, a sole proprietorship has two basic disadvantages, difficulties that make it almost impossible to organize large-scale enterprises as proprietorships. First, the owner has **unlimited liability** for the debts of the firm. If the firm goes out

[1] Burton G. Malkiel, *A Random Walk Down Wall Street* (New York: W. W. Norton & Company, Inc., 1973), pages 140–41.

of business leaving unpaid bills, the former owner can be forced to pay them out of personal savings. The owner can be made to sell the family home or any other personal assets, no matter how unrelated to the business, so that the proceeds can be used to pay off the company's obligations. Often sole proprietors guard themselves against this danger by signing away all their property to other members of their families or to others whom they feel they can trust. But, there are many tales of tragedy that begin with the signing away of all of one's possessions—King Lear's betrayal by his daughters might well serve as the classic warning to those proprietors who are apt to be too trusting.

A second and equally basic shortcoming of the sole proprietorship is that it inhibits expansion of the firm by making it difficult to raise money. People outside the company are reluctant to put money into a firm over which they exercise no control. This means that the proprietorship's capital is usually no greater than the amount its owner is willing and able to put into it, plus the amount that banks or other commercial lenders are willing to provide.

SUMMARY

The two main advantages of the sole proprietorship are:

1. It leaves full control in the hands of the owner.
2. It involves little legal complication.

Its two main disadvantages are:

1. The unlimited liability of the owner for the obligations of the company.
2. The difficulty of increasing the amount of funds that can be raised for the firm.

Partnerships

Measured in terms of the amount of their capital, **partnerships** tend to be larger than proprietorships but smaller than corporations. However, the largest partnerships greatly exceed the smallest corporations in terms of both their financing and their influence. For example, the most prestigious law firms are partnerships. When you call a law firm and are greeted by "Smith, Jones, LaRoche, and Cohen, good morning," you are almost certainly being treated to a partial listing of the company's current or past senior partners (the partners who own the largest share of the firm or who founded the firm).

The advantage of the partnership over the proprietorship is that it brings together the funds and expertise of a number of people and permits them to be combined to form a company larger than any one of the owners could have financed or managed alone. If one cannot hope to run a particular type of firm with an inventory of less than $2 million, a person who is not rich may be unable to get into the business without the aid of a partner. A partnership may also bring together a variety of specialists, as often happens in a medical practice.

But the partnership has disadvantages, some of them substantial. Decision-making in a partnership may be harder than in any other type of firm. The sole proprietor need consult no one before acting; the corporation appoints officers who are authorized to decide things for the company. But in a partnership it may be necessary for every partner to agree before any steps are taken by the firm, and this is the primary bane of this form of enterprise. A partnership has been compared to two people in a horse costume, each supplying two of the legs, each prepared to go in a different direction, and each unable to move without the other.

Furthermore, in a partnership, as in a proprietorship, the individual partners have unlimited liability, meaning that they can conceivably be in danger of losing their personal possessions to pay off company debts. Finally, the partnership suffers from unique legal complications. A partnership agreement is like a marriage contract

A **partnership** is a firm whose ownership is shared by a fixed number of proprietors.

entered into solely for the financial advantage of the participants, and so there is likely to be considerable haggling about the terms. And under the law, if a partner dies, or decides to leave the firm, or the others decide to buy that person's share in the enterprise, the partnership may have to be dissolved and haggling about the contract may start all over again.

SUMMARY

The benefits of the partnership to the owners of the firm are:

1. Access to larger quantities of financial capital.
2. Opportunity to combine expertise.

Its disadvantages are:

1. The need to obtain the agreement of many if not all partners to all major decisions.
2. Unlimited liability of the partners for the obligations of the company.
3. The legal complications, including possible dissolution of the partnership, when there is *any* change in ownership.

Corporations

A **corporation** is a firm that has the legal status of a fictional person. This fictional person is owned by a number of persons, called its shareholders, and is run by a set of elected officers (usually headed by a president) and a board of directors, whose chairman is often also in a powerful position to influence the affairs of the firm.

Limited liability is a legal obligation of a firm's owners to pay back company debts only with the money they have already invested in the firm.

Most big firms are **corporations**, a form of business that has quite a different legal status from that of a proprietorship or a partnership. Because a corporation is a person in the eyes of the law, its earnings, like those of other persons, are taxed. If a corporation pays some of its earnings to its shareholders as dividends, those dividends are also taxable.

But this disadvantage is counterbalanced by an important advantage: Any debt of the corporation is regarded as an obligation of that fictitious person, not as a liability of any shareholder. This means that the shareholders benefit from the protection of **limited liability**—they can lose no more than the money they have put into the firm. Creditors cannot force them to sell their personal possessions to help repay any outstanding debts incurred by the firm.

Limited liability is the main secret of the success of the corporate form of organization. Thanks to that provision, individuals from every part of the world are willing to put money into firms whose operations they do not understand and whose managements they do not know. A giant firm may produce computers, locomotives, and electrical generators; it may have, as subsidiaries, publishing houses and shoe factories. Few of its shareholders will know or care about all the firm's activities. Yet each investor knows that by providing money to the firm in return for a share of its ownership, no more is risked than the amount of money provided. This has permitted corporations to obtain financing from literally millions of shareholders, each of whom receives in return a claim on the firm's profits and, at least in principle, a portion of the company's ownership.

As indicated, the profits of a corporation are subject to taxation. Smaller and privately held corporations get taxed at special low rates, but the larger firms with high profits pay tax at a rate of about 40 percent of income (varying somewhat depending on the nature of the company's business and the province where it is located). The Canadian personal income-tax system involves some tax relief on dividend income. Without such relief, if an individual were to invest in shares of a corporation paying tax at a 40 percent rate, any earnings of the corporation passed on to the individual in dividends would first have been cut almost in half by corporate taxes and then be subject to taxation as income to the individual.

Corporations are directed by a hired group of managers: a chairman of the board of directors, a president, various vice presidents, and so on. These executives are legally employees of the owners of the firm, who, as we will see, are the shareholders of the corporation. This arrangement has great advantages. It prevents the quarrels and indecision that are often problems for partnerships. On the other hand, since the management is made up of hired personnel, it cannot always be trusted to do what is best for the owners. Managers are often accused of looking after their own interests first and, if necessary, sacrificing those of the shareholders (the owners).

Corporations escape another problem that troubles partnerships. As we saw, if a partner wants to leave the firm, the entire enterprise may have to be reorganized. But in a corporation, any owner who wants to quit just sells her shares on the stock market, while the corporation goes on exactly as before. In this way, at least in theory, a corporation can continue forever.

SUMMARY

The benefits of the corporate form of enterprise to its owners are:

1. Limited liability.
2. Access to large quantities of capital.
3. Ease of operation with the help of a hired management.
4. Permanence: The firm is not dissolved or reorganized each time an owner leaves.

Its disadvantages are:

1. "Double" taxation of dividend payments to the owners if dividend income is not taxed at lower rates at the personal income-tax level.
2. The possibility that hired managers will act in their own interests rather than in the interests of the owners.

Financing Corporate Activity

Our discussion of the earnings of an investor in corporate securities introduces a subject of interest to millions of Canadians—*stocks* and *bonds*. When a corporation needs money to add to its plant or equipment or to finance other types of real investment, taking out a bank loan is not its only option: It can get the funds it needs by printing new shares of stock or new bonds and selling them to people who are interested in investing their money. What enables the firm to get money in exchange for printed paper? Doesn't the process seem a bit like counterfeiting? If done improperly, there are grounds for this suspicion. But carried out appropriately, it is a perfectly rational economic process.

As long as the funds derived from a new issue of shares or bonds are used effectively to increase the firm's capacity to produce and earn a profit, then these funds will automatically yield the means for any required repayment and for the payment of appropriate amounts of dividends or interest to the purchasers. There have been times when this did not happen. It is alleged that one of the favourite practices of the more notorious nineteenth-century manipulators of the market was "watering" of company stock—issuing shares with little or nothing to back them up. The term is derived from the practice of some cattle dealers, who would force their animals to drink large quantities of water just before bringing them to be weighed for sale.

Another major source of funds is **ploughback** or **retained earnings**. For example, if a company earns $30 million after taxes and decides to pay out only $10 million in dividends and invest the remaining $20 million back into the firm, that $20 million is called ploughback.

When business is profitable enough that management has the funds to reinvest in the company, it will often prefer ploughback to other sources of funding. One reason for this preference is that it is less risky to management. This source of funds does not require prior approval by the appropriate provincial securities commission, as do other sources. Moreover, ploughback does not depend on the availability of eager customers for the new securities. (An issue of such new securities turns into a disappointment if there is little demand for them when they are offered to the public.)

Ploughback or **retained earnings** is the portion of a corporation's profits that management decides to keep and invest back into the firm's operations rather than to pay out directly to shareholders in the form of dividends.

Above all, a ploughback decision generally does not lead anyone to re-examine the efficiency of management's operation in the way that a new stock issue invariably does. In these instances, the provincial securities commission, potential buyers of the shares, and their professional advisers all scrutinize the company carefully.

A second reason for the attractiveness of ploughback is that issuing new shares or bonds is usually an expensive and lengthy process. The company is required by the provincial securities commission to gather data in its prospectus—a document describing the financial condition of the company—before the new issue is approved. Not only is this costly, but the many months of delay that are involved require the firm to wait for the funds when it needs them quickly. This delay also subjects the firm to the risk of a change in stock-market conditions (during the period of delay a brisk demand for new shares and bonds may conceivably dwindle or even evaporate).

Stocks and Bonds

A **common stock** of a corporation is a piece of paper that gives the holder a share of the ownership of the company.

A **bond** is simply an IOU by a corporation that promises to pay the holder of the piece of paper a fixed sum of money at the specified *maturity* date, and some other fixed amount of money (the *coupon* or the *interest payment*) every year up to the date of maturity.

We turn now to the major sources of corporate financing besides ploughback and direct borrowing from banks—the corporate securities, like **common stocks** and **bonds**. A share of stock represents ownership of part of the corporation. For example, if a company issues 100,000 shares, then a person who owns 1000 shares actually owns 1 percent of the company and is entitled to 1 percent of the company's *dividends*, which are the corporation's annual payments to shareholders. The shareholder's vote counts for 1 percent of the total votes in an election of corporate officers or in a referendum on corporate policy.

Bonds differ from stocks in several ways. First, whereas the purchaser of a corporation's stock *buys* a share of its ownership and receives some control over its affairs, the purchaser of a bond simply *lends* money to the firm. Second, whereas shareholders have no idea how much they will receive for their shares when they sell them or how much they will receive in dividends each year while they own them, bondholders know with a high degree of certainty how much money they will be paid if they hold their bonds to maturity. For instance, a bond with a face value of $1000 and an $80 coupon that matures in 1996 will provide to its owner $80 per year every year until 1996, and in addition it will repay the $1000 to the bondholder in 1996. Unless the company goes bankrupt, there is no doubt about this repayment schedule. Third, bondholders have a *legally prior claim* on company earnings, which means that nothing can be paid by the company to its shareholders until interest payments to the company's bondholders have been met. For all these reasons, bonds are considered less risky for their buyers than stocks. An important exception is "junk bonds"—a very risky type of bond that became popular in the 1980s. Junk bonds were used heavily by groups of people attempting to purchase enough stocks of some corporation to acquire control of that firm. More will be said later about such takeover activities and the use of junk bonds to finance them (see the boxed insert on pages 220–21).

In reality, some of the differences between stocks and bonds are not as clear-cut as we have just described. Two misconceptions are particularly worth noting. First, the ownership of the company represented by the holding of a few shares of its stock may be more apparent than real. A holder of 0.002 percent of the shares of General Motors —which is a *very large* investment—exercises no real control over GM's operations. In fact, some economists believe that the ownership of large corporations is so diffuse that no shareholder or shareholder group has *any* effective control over management. In this view, the management of a corporation is a largely independent decision-making body; as long as it keeps enough cash flowing to shareholders to prevent discontent and rebellion, management can do anything it wants within the law. Looked at in another way, this last conclusion really says that shareholders are merely another class of people who provide loans to the company. The only real difference between shareholders and bondholders, according to this interpretation, is that shareholders' loans are riskier and therefore entitled to higher payments.

Second, bonds *can* be quite risky to the bondholder. People who try to sell their bonds before maturity may find that the market price for bonds happens to be low, so that if they need to raise cash in a hurry, they may have to sell at a substantial loss. Also, bondholders may be exposed to losses from inflation. Whether the $1000 promised the bondholder at the 1996 maturity date represents substantial purchasing power depends on what happens to the general price level in the meantime. And no one can predict the price level this far in advance with any accuracy. Finally, a firm can issue bonds for which there is little backing; that is, the firm may own little valuable property that it can use as a guarantee of repayment to the lender (the bondholder). This was often true of the junk bonds of the 1980s and helps to explain their extreme riskiness.

Bond Prices and Interest Rates

Why is investment in bonds risky? That is, what makes their price go up and down? The main element in the answer is that changes in interest rates cause bond prices to change. There is a straightforward relationship between bond prices and interest rates. Whenever one goes up, the other must go down. For example, suppose that the Hudson's Bay Company had issued some fifteen-year bonds when interest rates were comparatively low, so that the company had to offer to pay only 6 percent to find buyers for these bonds. People who invested $1000 in new Hudson's Bay bonds received in return a contract that promised them $60 per year for fifteen years plus the return of their $1000 at the end of that period. Suppose further that two years later interest rates in the economy rise so that new fifteen-year bonds of companies of similar quality pay 12 percent. Now for $1000 one can buy a contract that offers $120 per year. Obviously, under these circumstances no one will pay as much as $1000 for a bond that promises only $60 per year. Consequently, the market price of the two-year-old Hudson's Bay bonds must fall. There are bonds in existence now that were issued years ago at interest rates of 6 percent. In today's markets, with much higher interest rates, such bonds sell for a price well below their original value. Alternatively, bonds from the early 1980s, when interest rates were higher than they are today, command a price greater than their face value.

When interest rates in the economy rise, there must be a fall in the prices of previously issued bonds with their lower interest earnings. For the same reason, when interest rates in the economy fall, the prices of previously issued bonds must rise.

It follows that as interest rates in the economy change because of changes in monetary policy or for other reasons, bond prices will also fluctuate. That is one reason why investment in bonds can be risky.

Corporate Choice between Stocks and Bonds

We have seen why a corporation may prefer to finance its real investment, such as construction of factories and equipment, through ploughback or retained earnings rather than the issue of new stocks or bonds. But suppose it has decided to do the latter. How does it determine whether bonds or stocks suit its purposes better?

Two considerations are of prime importance. Although issuing bonds generally causes more risk to the firm than issuing new shares of stock, the corporation usually expects to pay more money to shareholders over the long run than to bondholders. In other words, to the firm that issues them, bonds are cheaper but riskier. The decision about which is better for the firm therefore involves a trade-off between the two considerations.

Why are bonds risky to the corporation? When it issues $20 million in new bonds at 10 percent, the company commits itself to pay out $2 million every year for the life of the bond. It is obligated to pay that amount each year, whether that year happens to be one in which business is booming or one in which the firm is losing money. That is a big risk. If the firm is unable to meet its obligation to bondholders in some year, it faces bankruptcy.

The issue of new shares does not burden the company with any such risk since the company does not promise to pay the shareholders *any* fixed amount. Shareholders simply receive whatever is left of the company's net earnings after payments to bondholders. If nothing is left to pay the new shareholders in some years, legally speaking, that is just their bad luck.

Why, then, do shareholders normally obtain higher average expected payments from the company than do bondholders? To arrive at the answer, we must look at the risk–return trade-off from the investor's point of view. In the case of bonds, the company assumes as much risk as possible by guaranteeing a specified payment to the bondholder. In the case of stocks, however, the company assumes little or no risk, leaving it all to the shareholder.

The situation is reversed for the individual who provides the money: Bonds are safer than stocks. Since this is true, no investor will want to buy stocks rather than bonds unless she can expect a sufficiently higher return on the stocks to make up for their added risk. So if a company offers both stocks and bonds, their prices and prospective returns must offer a higher (but riskier) average rate of return to shareholders than to bondholders.

To the firm that issues them, bonds are riskier than stocks because they commit the firm to make a fixed annual payment even in years when it is losing money. For the same reason, stocks are riskier than bonds to the buyers of securities. That is why shareholders expect to be paid more money than bondholders.

Are there any rules for a firm to follow when it decides on the trade-off between risk and cost in choosing whether to issue stocks or bonds? There is no general rule, but some principles do hold. For example, new, relatively risky firms find it hard to raise money by issuing stocks because investors want protection from the perils of investing in an unproven company. For similar reasons, very safe companies prefer stock- to bond-financing because the safety of the firm means that shareholders will not have to be paid much more than bondholders.

Buying Stocks and Bonds

Although stocks and bonds can be purchased through any brokerage firm, not all brokers charge the same fees. For many years, the charges to small investors were fixed by collusive agreement and did not vary from broker to broker. The Toronto Stock Exchange was deregulated in 1983, and as a result, some bargain brokerage facilities are available.

Rational planning by an individual of what stocks, bonds, and other financial investments to hold requires more than just careful examination of the merits and demerits of individual securities. It is important to select a combination of securities that meet one's needs effectively. Such a combination of holdings is called the individual's **portfolio** of investments. For example, an individual who is saving to send children to university in ten years does not need securities that pay money out regularly in the meantime, while a retired person who depends on periodic payments from her holdings will want securities that provide such a stream of payouts conveniently.

A far more important consideration in deciding what to include in a portfolio is the fact that the risks of the portfolio are affected by the combination of securities it includes, and the portfolio may well be far less risky than any of the individual securities it contains. The secret is **diversification**, meaning not putting all one's eggs

Diversification refers to an increase in the number and variety of stocks, bonds, and other such items held by the owner of a portfolio. If the individual owns airline shares, diversification requires the purchase of stocks or bonds in a very different industry, such as a hydro-electric power company.

in one basket. If Joe Jones holds only shares of company A and the company goes bankrupt, then all may be lost. However, if Joe Jones divides up his holdings among companies A, B, and C, the portfolio may perform satisfactorily even if company A goes broke. Moreover, suppose company A specializes in producing luxury items, which do well in prosperous periods but very badly during recessions, while company B sells cheap clothing, whose cyclical demand pattern differs greatly from that of company A. If Jones holds shares in both companies, the overall risk is smaller than if he owns shares in only one of the companies.

All other things being equal, a portfolio containing many different types of securities tends to be less risky than a portfolio with fewer types of securities.

Increasingly, institutional investors have adopted portfolios composed of a broad range of stocks typifying those offered by the entire stock market. By owning a representative basket of stocks, money managers can reduce the risks of owning individual stocks and ensure that their portfolio is not significantly outperformed by the overall market.

Institutional money managers have been making increasing use of computers to decide on their portfolios and to buy or sell huge portfolios of stocks simultaneously and rapidly. And since 1982 some traders have allowed their computers to decide when to jump in and make massive sales or purchases. This is called *program trading*, and it is a controversial practice. Some observers have argued that it has exacerbated price fluctuations, especially during the stock-market crash of October 1987.

Following a Portfolio's Performance

Newspapers carry daily information on stock and bond prices. Figure 10–1 is an excerpt from a stock-market report in *The Globe and Mail*. In the first two columns, before the company name, the report gives the stock's highest and lowest price in the current year. In the highlighted example, the price of InterHome Energy, an oil and gas pipeline company, is reported to have ranged between $50.50 and $42.75. Next, after the name of the stock, there appears the annual dividend per share ($2.00). The next four figures indicate that day's highest price, lowest price, and the price at which the last transaction of the day took place (all $48.87 in this case), and the change in

52-week High	52-week Low	Stock	Div	High /bid	Low /ask	Close /last	Change	Vol
225	115	ISG Technologies		187	175	180	+3	17827
25	24¼	ITT Cda 2 p B	1.80	$24¼	24¾	24¼		nt
25¾	24½	Imasco Financial p A	2.25	$24¾	25	24¾		nt
40½	33⅜	Imasco	1.28	$37⅛	36⅞	36⅞	-⅛	6387
350	285	Imasco 6% p A	.292	315	315	315	+15	400
25	23	Imasco 7.375% p C	1.844	$23⅝	24	23½		nt
23⅞	21	Imperial Life III p C	1.844	$22⅞	23⅛	23¼		nt
180	100	Imperial Metals		133	130	133	+3	2500
65¼	53¼	Imperial Oil A	1.80	$59¼	58⅝	59⅛	+⅛	88376
44¼	26	Inco	1.156	$36¼	35⅛	36	+¾	278635
23½	20⅛	Inco 7.85% p B	1.962	$21½	22	21¾		nt
11⅛	460	Innopac Inc	.24	$5⅞	5⅞	5⅞	+¼	1000
9¾	5⅛	Inspiration Res	a.12	$5⅞	6⅛	5½		nt
85	45	Intensity Res o		65	70	70		nt
34	10	Inter Cable o		11	17	11		nt
170	75	Inter Cable p A	r1.00	50	75	75		nt
9⅞	6¾	Inter-City Prodcts		$7	6⅞	6⅞		10366
26	25¼	Inter-City Prodcts p C		$25½	25½	25½	+¼	100
380	350	Inter-Prov Divr Hld		350	380	350		nt
50½	42¾	InterHome Ener Inc	2.00	$48⅞	48⅞	48⅞	-⅛	1732
24	11¾	Intera A		$20¾	21¼	20¾		nt
76	20	Interaction Res o		28	26	28	+2	10500
8⅜	5	Intermetco	.28	$5	5	5		4900
47	11	Interquest		40	40	40		10000
142½	108½	IBM	a4.84	$133¼	132	135		z77
365	335	Intl Colin Energy		340	330	340		z103

FIGURE 10–1
Excerpt from a Stock-Market Page
This table from *The Globe and Mail* gives the highest and lowest price in the current year; the current dividend rate; the highest, lowest, and final price of the stock on that day; the change in price from the day before; and the number of shares traded on that day.
SOURCE: From "Toronto Quotations for July 26, 1990, prepared by the Toronto Stock Exchange," *The Globe and Mail*, Toronto, July 26, 1990, page B10.

FIGURE 10–2

Excerpt from a Bond Price Table

This table from *The Globe and Mail* shows the issuing company (or branch of government); the annual interest payment); the date on which the bond will be redeemed at face value; its approximate current price; the effective yield (that is, the average amount earned per year on the bond if held to its redemption date, expressed as a percentage of the current price); and the change in the price from the previous day. SOURCE: From "Canadian Bonds," *The Globe and Mail*, Toronto, July 26, 1990, page B8.

Issuer	Coupon	Maturity	Price	Yield	$ Chg
GOVERNMENT OF CANADA					
Canada	9.00	1 Sep 91	96.450	12.540	NC
Canada	11.50	6 Mar 92	99.600	11.760	NC
Canada	10.25	1 Jun 92	97.650	11.682	+0.100
Canada	12.25	6 Jun 92	101.050	11.585	NC
Canada	10.75	1 May 93	98.950	11.186	+0.150
Canada	9.50	1 Sep 93	95.175	11.392	+0.100
Canada	11.75	15 Oct 93	101.250	11.260	+0.150
Canada	10.25	1 Feb 94	97.325	11.195	+0.100
Canada	9.25	15 Dec 94	93.625	11.124	+0.150
Canada	11.75	1 Mar 95	102.225	11.111	+0.150
. . .					
PROVINCIAL					
Alberta	10.00	15 Jun 94	95.325	11.522	+0.100
Alberta Tel	9.50	8 Jul 97	91.000	11.410	+0.200
BC	9.25	27 Nov 91	96.250	12.388	NC
BC	11.63	22 Mar 94	100.125	11.571	+0.150
BC	11.25	16 Aug 00	100.275	11.202	+0.200
Hydro Quebec	10.00	26 Sep 11	89.325	11.337	NC
Hydro Quebec	11.00	15 Aug 20	97.125	11.337	NC
Manitoba	11.00	15 Aug 00	100.375	10.936	+0.200
New Brunswick	9.75	15 Aug 99	90.800	11.406	+0.200
. . .					
CORPORATE					
Avco Fin	12.38	11 Jul 95	100.125	12.335	+0.250
Bell Canada	10.50	15 May 98	94.875	11.507	+0.125
Bell Canada	10.35	15 Dec 09	92.875	11.258	+0.125
Bell Canada	11.45	15 Apr 10	100.625	11.365	-0.125
BC Telephone	10.50	12 Jun 00	94.375	11.462	+0.250
BC Telephone	12.00	31 May 10	104.000	11.480	+0.125
Bank of NS	10.35	19 Jul 01	92.375	11.595	+0.125
Cdn Imp Bank	12.45	1 Dec 00	104.750	11.641	+0.125
Cdn Util	10.20	30 Nov 09	91.375	11.303	+0.125
Imperial Oil	9.88	15 Dec 99	90.875	11.486	NC
Maclean Hunt	12.20	19 Jul 95	100.625	12.026	NC
Nova Corp	12.63	15 Apr 10	101.500	12.413	+0.125

that price from the previous day (down ⅛). The final column shows the number of shares traded that day (1732).

Figure 10–2, also from *The Globe and Mail*, gives similar information about bonds. The first thing to notice here is that a company may have several bonds differing in maturity dates and coupon values (the annual interest payments). For example, Bell Canada has three different bonds shown. The one that is highlighted is labelled Bell Canada 10.50 15May98, meaning that these are bonds that yield an annual interest payment of 10.5 percent of their face value (this is called the "coupon"), and that their maturity (redemption) date is May 15, 1998. Since other bonds are available that earn yields in excess of 10.5 percent, it is not surprising that people are not prepared to pay the full face value of $100 to acquire one of these bonds. The price quoted for this bond is $94.87, which is about what investors did pay for the bond on the day shown in the table. Anyone paying $94.87 for this bond, holding it until May 15, 1998, collecting $10.50 interest each year, then redeeming the bond for $100, will have made an investment that yielded an average 11.5 percent per year, which is shown as "yield" in the table. The last column shows the change in price from the previous trading day (up 12.5 cents).

Stock Exchanges and Their Functions

Stock exchanges have existed in Europe since the thirteenth century. In North America the first trading of company shares took place in the early eighteenth century when merchants met at the foot of Wall Street in New York City. This early trading market was not restricted to shares. Wheat, tobacco, and slaves were also involved. The Montreal Stock Exchange is Canada's oldest, with records of trading dating back to 1832, followed by Toronto (1852), Vancouver (1907), and Alberta (1913). There is also a commodities exchange in Winnipeg.

The Toronto Stock Exchange, located near Bay Street in Toronto, is the largest in Canada, and it ranks fifth in the world by size (after the New York and American

Stock Exchanges in New York City, and those in Tokyo and London). This is where the expression "power of Bay Street" comes from. The leading brokerage firms hold "seats" on the stock exchange, which enable them to trade directly on the floor of the exchange.

Someone who wants to buy shares on the Toronto Stock Exchange must use a broker, who will deal with a firm that has a seat on the Exchange. Suppose you live in New Brunswick and want to buy 200 shares of the Royal Bank. The broker you approach may be employed by a firm that holds a seat on the Exchange, or she may work through another firm that holds one. The broker who is to fill your order sends a trader to the area on the floor of the Exchange where Royal Bank stock is traded. The trader's responsibility is to buy the shares for you at the lowest possible price. Other traders will be trying to sell Royal Bank shares at the highest possible price for their clients. The traders shout their willingness to buy (bids) or their willingness to sell (offers or "asks") specified amounts of stock at specified prices until two traders agree on a price at which to do business with each other, at which time the sale is completed. This process is sometimes called the "auction-market" process.

Nowadays, a growing percentage of shares are traded through brokers on a basis known as "over the counter." This method of trade does not involve a public market at all. It is not a place where many buyers and sellers meet to make exchanges simultaneously. Rather, it is run by a number of firms, each operating more or less independently of the others. When a buyer brings an order to such a firm, the broker simply shops around by telephone, seeking to find someone to match the purchase demand with a corresponding supply offer, or the broker may buy or sell for his own account the shares supplied or demanded by the order. Thus, each broker does the job that is done by a trader on one of the exchanges. Obviously, over-the-counter trading is a much less structured and less organized affair than is trading on the exchanges.

With the advent of computers and improved electronic means of communication, it is now possible to automate the over-the-counter market via an electronic network through which every buy or sell order is announced to brokers simultaneously across the country, as are the price and quantity of every completed transaction. In the United States, thousands of stocks, including stocks of many Canadian companies, are traded on such a network. In Canada, a similar system, called CATS (Computer Assisted Trading System), is used through the stock exchanges for the trading of some of the less active stocks. On the Tokyo Stock Exchange, the majority of listed stocks are traded using an automated system that is patterned on the TSE's CATS. Many analysts expect that we are not too many years away from an integrated global system in which the major stock exchanges will be fully linked electronically, with twenty-four-hour trading days.

Stock Exchanges and Corporate Capital Needs

While corporations often raise the funds they need by selling stocks, they do not normally do so through any of the stock exchanges. When new shares are offered by a company in Canada, the new issue is usually handled through a trust company. In contrast, the stock markets trade almost exclusively in "second-hand securities"— stocks in the hands of those who had bought them earlier and who now wish to sell them.

The stock market does not provide funds to corporations that need the financing to expand their productive activities. The markets provide money only to persons who already hold shares of stock previously issued by the corporations.

Yet stock exchanges have two functions that are of critical importance for the financing of corporations. First, by providing a second-hand market for shares, they make it much less risky for an individual to invest in a company. Investors know that

Corporate Takeovers

The Recent Surge in Takeovers

In recent years the stock market and the managements of a number of corporations have been shaken by attempts by "outsiders" to take over firms that they do not currently control. A company is said to have undergone a **takeover** when a group of financiers not currently in control of the firm buys a sufficient amount of company stock to gain control. Often, the new controlling group fires the current management and substitutes a new chairman, president, and other top officers.

A company becomes a tempting target for a takeover attempt if its earnings seem very low compared to their potential level—possibly because the firm's current management is not very competent—or if the price of its shares is very low in comparison with the value of its plant, equipment, and other assets. Sometimes the group seeking the takeover really wants one particular asset of the company: its tax credits. Both federal and provincial governments give firms credit against their corporate tax for a variety of reasons. But for those credits to be useful, the firm must have enough profits from which to subtract the credits. If the firm is not in this position, it is advantageous for some more profitable company to acquire it with its tax credits (to subtract from the overall profits of the merged enterprise) even if the new management cannot run that particular business any more effectively than did the old management.

An attempt to acquire the company by a group unfriendly to current management is called a "hostile takeover." Naturally, current management will try to fight off such an attempt since the officers of the corporation do not want to lose their high-paying jobs. They can fight back in many ways. For example, they can try to arrange instead for a "friendly takeover" by a group of investors whom they like better. (Such a group is sometimes called a "white knight.") Alternatively, management may attempt to sabotage the company deliberately (an action called a "poison pill"), often by selling some of its most valuable parts in order to make what is left of the firm unattractive to the group attempting the takeover. Or management may seek to bribe the takeover group by offering them a very high price for the shares they have already managed to acquire. (Indeed, takeovers are often attempted in the hope that management will be forced to offer such a bribe—known as "greenmail"—to those who threaten to take the company over.)

Since the mid-1980s, when a large number of takeover battles broke out, the issue has received a good deal of publicity and set off a heated debate. People who argue for few or no legal restrictions on takeover activity point out that this is perhaps the most effective means of ridding companies of incompetent managements, thereby helping to keep the economy at peak efficiency. They also point out that a takeover attempt helps to drive up the price of an undervalued company's shares, bringing them into line with the firm's true economic value.

Those who advocate strict regulation or inhibition of takeovers argue that shareholders who are innocent bystanders can be badly hurt in the process—for example, when management pays a large bribe to the takeover group or sells off a valuable part of the company. Moreover, a group seeking to buy, say, 7 percent of the company's shares will try to do so as secretly as possible, hoping to obtain the stock cheaply; in effect, they cheat those who sell them the shares. Opponents of takeovers also point out that planning and carrying out strategies and counterstrategies uses up and, arguably, wastes a valuable resource: the time of bright,

their money is not locked in—if they need the money, they can always sell their shares to other investors at the price the market currently offers. This reduction in risk makes it far easier for corporations to issue new shares. Second, the stock market determines the current price of the company's shares. That, in turn, determines whether it will be hard or easy for a corporation to raise money by selling new stock. For example, suppose a company initially has one million shares and wants to raise $10 million. If the price is $40 per share, an issue of 250,000 shares can bring in the required funds, leaving the original shareholders with four-fifths of the company's ownership. But if the price of the stock is only $20 per share, then 500,000 new shares will have to be issued, cutting the original shareholders back to two-thirds of the ownership of the company. This is a less attractive proposition.

Some believe that the price of a company's stock is closely tied to the efficiency with which its productive activities are conducted, the effectiveness with which it matches its product to consumer demands, and the diligence with which it goes after profitable innovation. In this view, those firms that can make effective use of funds because of their efficiency are precisely the corporations whose stock prices will usually be comparatively high. In this way the stock market tends to channel the economy's investment funds to those firms that can make best use of the money. In sum:

talented people. That is, these critics say quite rightly, take-over activity absorbs some of the nation's most capable individuals in financial manipulation rather than in productive and innovative activity.

Finally, the critics can point to the fact that takeovers have often been financed by junk bonds. The "raiders" of a firm issue such bonds to raise the money they need to buy up the stocks that will give them control of the target corporation. These bonds are frequently backed only by the profits that the raiders expect their new acquisition to generate. Such profits may arise because the new owners bring in a more efficient management or because they sell off at a high price a valuable portion of the corporation's activities (one of it successful products, for example), which they purchased cheaply because the corporation's stock price was low before the takeover.

These junk bonds are considered risky because of the danger that the promised profits may never materialize. A takeover financed in this way is called a "leveraged buyout," because the raiders risk little of their own money in the process. Instead, their limited resources are levered upward with the aid of other people's money—the money supplied by the purchasers of the junk bonds. Critics of this process also note that it leaves the firm saddled with a heavy debt—its new obligation to the junk bonds' purchasers.

Foreign Takeovers of Canadian Firms

An issue that always surfaces when takeovers occur in Canada is the decades-old argument over foreign ownership. When the Conservative government took power in 1984, it welcomed foreign investment, dismantling the Foreign In-vestment Review Agency (FIRA) and the National Energy Program (NEP), which the former Liberal government had used to discourage foreign ownership of Canadian firms. Recent trends have reflected these changes in policy. Back in 1970, about 30 percent of all non-financial firms in Canada were foreign-owned. This proportion fell to about 20 percent by 1985, but rose back to the 30 percent level by 1990. (The comparable figures for the United States and the European Community are 8 percent and 6 percent, respectively.) Many observers expect foreign takeovers to increase further as the recent Free Trade Agreement with the United States makes Canadian companies even more attractive to European and Japanese firms.

Economic nationalists are critical of foreign investment because they feel that foreign-owned firms are not obliged to obey Canadian government policies as fully as do Canadian-owned firms. For example, Mel Hurtig, a founder of the Council of Concerned Canadians, considers the levels of foreign ownership in Canada a "recipe for disaster."* However, research does not support the hypothesis that foreign-owned firms are less responsible corporate citizens.

Thus, to gain a clearer perspective on the issue of foreign ownership, we must examine the benefits that Canadians get from the activity of these firms, and determine whether they exceed the losses in dividend and profit payments that go out of the country to foreign owners. We must also weigh in the costs of the tax concessions that are often given to domestic firms to stave off foreign ownership, and the costs of the decreased competitiveness that follows from obstructing the entry of foreign firms.

*The Globe and Mail, November 28, 1989, page A7.

If a firm has a promising future, its shares will tend to command a high price on the stock exchanges. The high price of its shares will make it easier for the firm to raise capital by permitting it to amass a large amount of money through the sale of a comparatively small number of new shares of stock. Thus, *the stock market helps to allocate the economy's resources to those firms that can make the best use of those resources.*

However, some observers are skeptical about the claim that the price of a company's shares is closely tied to the company's efficiency. They believe that the demand for a company's stock is disproportionately influenced by short-term developments in the company's profitability and that little attention is paid to management decisions promoting the company's long-term growth in earnings. These critics sometimes liken the stock market to a gambling casino, where hunch, rumour, and superstition have a critical influence on prices (more will be said about this later in the chapter).

The Issue of Speculation

Individuals who engage in **speculation** deliberately invest in risky assets, hoping to obtain a profit from the expected changes in the prices of these assets.

Dealings in securities are often viewed with hostility and suspicion because they are thought to be an instrument of **speculation**. When something goes wrong in the market, say, when there is a sudden fall in prices, *speculators* are often blamed. The word "speculators" is used by editorial writers as a term of strong disapproval, implying that those who engage in the activity are parasites who produce no benefits for society and often do it considerable harm.

Economists disagree vehemently with this judgment. They say that speculators perform two vital economic functions:

1. They sell *protection from risk* to other people, much as a fire insurance policy affords protection from risk to a homeowner.

2. They help to smooth out price fluctuations by purchasing items when they are abundant (and cheap) and holding them and reselling them when they are scarce (and expensive). In that way, they play a vital economic role in helping to alleviate and even prevent shortages.

Some examples from outside the securities markets will make the role of speculators clear. A ticket broker attends a preview of a new musical comedy and suspects that it will be a hit. She decides to speculate by buying a large block of tickets for future performances. In this way, she takes over some of the producer's risk, for the producer now has some hard cash and a reduced inventory of risky tickets. If the show turns out to be a flop, the broker will be stuck with the tickets. If it is a hit, she can, where the law allows it, sell them at a premium (and be denounced as a speculator or a "scalper"). Similarly, speculators enable farmers or producers of metals and other commodities whose future price is uncertain to get rid of their risk. A farmer who has planted a large crop but who fears its price may fall before harvest time can protect himself by signing a *contract for future delivery* at an agreed-upon price at which the speculator will purchase the crop when it comes in. In that case, if the price happens to fall, it is the speculator and not the farmer who will suffer the loss. Of course, if the price happens to rise, the speculator will reap the gain—that is the nature of risk bearing. The speculator who has agreed to buy the crop at the preset price, regardless of market conditions at the time the sale takes place, has, in effect, sold an insurance policy to the farmer. Surely this is a useful function.

The second role of speculators is perhaps even more important; in effect, they accumulate and store goods in periods of abundance, making them available in periods of scarcity. Suppose the speculator has reason to suspect that next year's crop of a storable commodity will not be nearly as abundant as this year's. He will buy some now, when it is cheap, for resale when it becomes scarce and expensive. In the process, he will smooth out the swing in prices by adding his purchases to the total market demand in the period of low prices (which tends to bring the price up), and bringing in his supplies during the period of high prices (which tends to push the price down).[2]

Thus, the successful speculator will help to relieve matters during periods of extreme shortage. There are cases in which he literally helps to relieve famine by releasing the supplies he has deliberately hoarded for such an occasion. Of course, he is cursed for the high prices he charges on such occasions. But those who curse him do not understand that prices might have been even higher if the speculator's foresight and avid pursuit of profit had not provided for the emergency. On the securities market, famine and severe shortages are not an issue, but the fact remains that successful speculators tend to reduce price fluctuations by increasing demand when prices are low and contributing to supply when prices are high.

[2]For a diagrammatic analysis of this function, see Discussion Question 6 at the end of this chapter.

Far from aggravating instability and fluctuations, speculators work as hard as they can to iron out fluctuations, for that is how they make their profits.

Even among government officials, journalists, and other thoughtful individuals, it is widely believed that speculators perform no real service for the economy, that their activity generally aggravates high prices and increases scarcity in times of shortages, and that they add to the instability of the economy in other ways. These impressions are virtually the reverse of the truth. Whether or not speculators are personally virtuous is not the point. The fact is that in earning their profits they make several vital contributions to the workings of the economy: (1) They take over risks from individuals seeking protection from risk; (2) They tend to add to supplies in periods of shortages; and (3) They work to depress prices when prices are unusually high and to raise prices when prices are unusually low—*for that is how speculators earn profits— by buying things when they are cheap in anticipation of their resale when they become expensive.*

Stock Prices as Random Walks

The beginning of this chapter cited evidence that the best professional securities analysts have a forecasting record so miserable that investors may do as well by predicting earnings by hunch, superstition, or any purely random process as they would by following the advice of a professional. Similarly, it has been said that an investor is well advised to pick stocks by throwing darts at the stock-market page— since it is far cheaper to buy a set of darts than to obtain the apparently useless advice of a professional analyst. Indeed, there have been at least two experiments, one by a U.S. senator and one by *Forbes* magazine, in which stocks picked by dart throwing actually outperformed the mutual funds, whose stocks are selected by the experts. Does this mean that analysts are incompetent people who do not know what they are doing? Not at all. Rather, there is strong evidence that they have undertaken a task that is basically impossible.

How can this be so? The answer is that to make a good forecast of any variable— GDP, population, or fuel use—there must be something in the past whose behaviour is closely related to the future behaviour of the variable whose path we wish to predict. If a 10 percent rise in this year's consumption always produces a 5 percent rise in next year's GDP, this fact can help us predict future GDP on the basis of current observations. But if we want to forecast the future of a variable whose behaviour is completely unrelated to the behaviour of *any* current variable, there is no objective evidence that can help us make that forecast. Throwing darts or gazing into a crystal ball is no less effective than analysts' calculations.

There is a mass of statistical evidence that the behaviour of stock prices is largely unpredictable. In other words, the behaviour of stock prices is essentially random; the paths they follow are what statisticians call **random walks**. A random walk is like the path followed by a drunk. All we know about his position after his next step is that it will be given by his current position plus whatever random direction his next haphazard step will take. The relevant feature of randomness, for our purposes, is that it is by nature unpredictable, which is just what the word *random* means.

If the evidence that stock prices approximate a random walk stands up to research in the future as it has so far, it is easy enough to understand why the stock-market predictions are as poor as they are. The analysts are trying to forecast behaviour that is basically random; in effect, they are trying to predict the unpredictable.

Two questions remain. First, does the evidence that stock prices follow a random walk mean that investment in stocks is a pure gamble and never worthwhile? And, second, how does one explain the random behaviour of stock prices? To answer the

The time path of a variable, such as the price of a stock, is said to constitute a **random walk** if its magnitude in one period (say, May 2, 1988) is equal to its value in the preceding period (May 1, 1988) plus a completely random number. That is:

Price on May 2, 1988
= Price on May 1, 1988
+ Random number,

where the random number (positive or negative) might be obtained by a roll of dice or some such procedure.

first question, it is false to conclude that investment in stocks is generally not worthwhile. The statistical evidence is that, over the long run, stock prices *as a whole* have had a fairly marked upward trend, perhaps reflecting the long-term growth of the economy. Evidence *does* indicate that stock prices are likely to rise if one waits long enough for them to do so. Thus, the random walk does not proceed in just any direction—rather, it represents a set of erratic movements *around the basic trend in stock prices*.

Moreover, it is not in the *overall* level of stock prices that the most pertinent random walk occurs, but in the performance of one company's shares compared with another's. For this reason professional advice may be able to predict that investment in the stock market is likely to be a good thing over the long haul. But, if the random-walk evidence is valid, there is no way professionals can tell us *which* of the available stocks is most likely to go up—that is, which combination of shares is best for the investor to buy.

The only appropriate answer to the second question is that no one is sure of the explanation. There are two widely offered hypotheses—each virtually the opposite of the other. The first asserts that stock prices are random because clever professional speculators are able to foresee almost perfectly every influence that is *not* random. For example, suppose a change occurs that makes the probable earnings of some company higher than had previously been expected. Then, according to this view, the professionals will instantly become aware of this change and immediately buy enough to raise the price of the stock accordingly. Then, by the time investment "advice" is widely distributed, the only thing for the stock price to do between this year and next is wander randomly, because the professionals cannot predict random movements and hence cannot force current stock prices to anticipate them.

The other explanation of random behaviour of stock prices is at the opposite

JUST A NORMAL DAY AT THE NATION'S MOST IMPORTANT FINANCIAL INSTITUTION...

pole from the view that all non-random movements are wiped out by supersmart professionals. This view holds that people who buy and sell stocks have learned that they cannot predict future stock prices. As a result they react to any signal, however irrational and irrelevant it appears. If the president catches cold, stock prices fall. If an astronaut's venture is successful, prices go up. For, according to this view, investors are, in the last analysis, trying to predict, not the prospects of the economy or of the company whose shares they buy, but the supply and demand behaviour of other investors, which will ultimately determine the course of stock prices. Since all investors are equally in the dark, their groping can only result in the randomness that we observe. The classic statement of this view of stock-market behaviour was provided by John Maynard Keynes, a successful professional speculator himself:

Professional investment may be likened to those newspaper competitions in which the competitors have to pick out the six prettiest faces from a hundred photographs, the prize being awarded to the competitor whose choice most nearly corresponds to the average preferences of the competitors as a whole; so that each competitor has to pick not those faces which he himself finds prettiest, but those which he thinks likeliest to catch the fancy of the other competitors, all of whom are looking at the problem from the same point of view. It is not a case of choosing those which, to the best of one's judgment, are really the prettiest, nor even those which average opinion genuinely thinks the prettiest. We have reached the third degree where we devote our intelligences to anticipating what average opinion expects the average opinion to be. And there are some, I believe, who practise the fourth, fifth, and higher degrees.[3]

This view may help to explain the dramatic rise in the stock market from 1982 to 1987—and then its headline-catching crash in October 1987—when all the while no major change in the underlying profitability of most companies had occurred.

[3] John Maynard Keynes, *The General Theory of Employment, Interest, and Money* (New York: Harcourt Brace Jovanovich, 1936), page 156.

Summary

1. The three basic types of firms are corporations, partnerships, and sole proprietorships. Most Canadian firms are sole proprietorships, but most Canadian manufactured goods are produced by corporations.

2. Corporate investors have greater protection from risk than do individual proprietorships or partnerships because they have *limited liability*—they cannot be asked to pay more than they have invested in the firm.

3. Corporations finance their activities by ploughback (that is, by retaining and channelling part of their earnings back into the company), by the sale of stocks and bonds, and by direct borrowing.

4. A stock is a share in the ownership of the company. A bond is an IOU by a company for money lent to it by the bondholder. Many observers argue that the purchase of a stock also really amounts to a loan to the company—a loan that is riskier than the purchase of a bond.

5. If interest rates rise, bond prices will fall. In other words, if some bond amounts to a contract to pay 8 percent and the market interest rate goes up to 10 percent, people will no longer be willing to pay the old price for that bond.

6. If stock prices correctly reflect the future prospects of different companies, promising firms are helped to raise money because they are able to sell each stock they issue at a favourable price.

7. Bonds are relatively risky for the firms that issue them, but they are fairly safe for their buyers, because they are a commitment by the firm to pay a fixed annual amount to the bondholder whether or not the company made money that year. But stocks, which do not promise any fixed payment, are relatively safe for the company and risky for their owner.

8. A portfolio is a collection of stocks, bonds, and other assets with a single owner. The greater the number and variety of securities and other assets it contains, the less risky it is.

9. Speculation affects stock-market prices, but (contrary to what is widely assumed) there is reason to believe that speculation actually *reduces* the frequency and size of price fluctuations. Speculators are also useful to the economy because they undertake risks that others wish to avoid, thereby, in effect, providing others with insurance against risk.

10. Statistical evidence indicates that *individual* stock prices behave randomly.

Concepts for Review

Sole proprietorship
Unlimited liability
Partnership
Corporation
Limited liability

Ploughback or retained earnings
Common stock
Bond
Portfolio diversification
Stock exchanges

Takeover
Speculation
Random walk

Questions for Discussion

1. Why would it be difficult to run General Motors as a partnership or an individual proprietorship?

2. Do you think it is fair to tax a corporation more than a partnership doing the same amount of business? Why or why not?

3. If you hold shares in a corporation and management decides to plough back the company's earnings some year instead of paying dividends, what are the advantages and disadvantages to you?

4. Suppose interest rates in the economy are 12 percent and a safe bond promises to pay $10 a year in interest forever. What do think the price of the bond will be? Why?

5. Suppose in the economy in the previous example, interest rates suddenly fall to 10 percent. What will happen to the price of the bond that pays $10 per year?

6. Show in diagrams that if a speculator were to buy when price is high and sell when price is low he would increase price fluctuations. Why would it be in his best interest *not* to do so? (*Hint:* Draw two supply–demand diagrams, one for the high-price period and one for the low-price period. How would the speculator's activities affect these diagrams?)

7. If stock prices really are a random walk, can you nevertheless think of good reasons for getting professional advice before investing?

8. Hostile takeovers often end up in court when current managements attempt to block them and raiders accuse those managements of selfishly sacrificing the interests of shareholders. The courts often look askance at "coercive" offers by raiders—an offer to buy, say, 20 percent of the company's shares by a certain date, from the first shareholders who offer to sell. By contrast, they take a more favourable attitude toward "non-coercive" offers to buy any and all shares supplied to the raider at an announced price. Do you think the courts are right to reject coercive offers but prevent management from blocking non-coercive offers? Why?

9. In "program trading," computers decide when to buy or sell shares on behalf of large institutional investors, and carry out those transactions at electronic speeds. Critics claim that this is a major reason for the sharp fluctuations in stock prices that occurred in the 1980s. Is this criticism plausible? What other influences may have been important?

11

Money and the Banking System

[Money] is a machine for doing quickly and commodiously what would be done, though less quickly and commodiously, without it.

JOHN STUART MILL

The circular flow diagrams that were used in earlier chapters to explain equilibrium GDP (see, for example, Figure 5–1 on page 115) had a "financial system" in their upper left-hand corners. Savings flowed into this system and investment flowed out. Something obviously goes on inside the financial system to channel the saving into investment, and it is time we learned what this something is.

There is another, equally important reason for studying the financial system. *Fiscal policy* is not the only lever the government has on the economy's aggregate demand curve. It also exercises significant control over aggregate demand by manipulating *monetary and exchange-rate policy*. If we are to understand monetary and exchange-rate policy (the subjects of Chapters 12 to 14), we must first acquire some understanding of the financial system.

The present chapter has three major objectives. It first seeks to explain the nature of money—what it is, what purposes it serves, and how it is measured. Once this is done, we turn our attention to the banking system, explaining its historical origins, the nature of banking as a business, and why this industry is so heavily regulated. Finally, we learn how banks create money—a subject that is of great importance because it is simply impossible to understand monetary policy without knowing how money is created.

At the end of the chapter, we will see why government authorities must exercise control over the supply of money in a modern economy, and this leads naturally into the discussion in Chapter 12 of *central banking*, that is, the techniques used to implement monetary and exchange-rate policy. In Chapters 13 and 14, we integrate what we will by then have learned about money and monetary policy into our model of income determination, as the culmination of our study of macroeconomic theory.

Policy Issue: Competition among Banks

Until the mid-1980s there were only thirteen regular chartered banks in Canada, and the "big five" still account for over 90 percent of all bank deposits across the country. Each of these five companies has more than 1000 branches. Recent changes in financial regulations permit the operation of foreign banks in Canada (hence they have considerably increased in number), but the new rules have not yet changed the dominant position of the five major banks.

This heavy concentration of a few firms is in stark contrast to the U.S. banking system, where branching across state (and, in some cases, county) lines was traditionally forbidden. As a result, there are 14,000 separate banks in the United States. In 1980 significant legal changes were made in the United States to deregulate the operations of their many banks. One of the purposes of this deregulation was to provide benefits to households through increased industry competition.

With Canada's highly concentrated banking industry, it would seem that increased competition would be desirable here too. This was the thrust of the changes in the last two revisions to Canada's Bank Act. But to form a judgment on deregulation, we must first address an even more basic question: Why were banks so heavily regulated in the first place?

One reason is that governments often feel compelled to regulate any monopolized industry. The intention is that government regulation can ensure that "the public interest" gets some weight in the decision-making process of these private firms. The Canadian banking industry did certainly become more concentrated through time. The country had fifty-one banks in 1874; by 1914, that number was down to twenty-two. During that period, there were seventeen new banks established; however, there were also twenty-five failures and twenty-one mergers. But industry concentration cannot be the only reason for regulation, since the U.S. banks have historically been subject to even more regulation than banks in Canada.

A major reason for regulation is simply that the major "output" of the banking industry—the nation's supply of money—is of vital importance to the health of the economy. Bank managers presumably do what is best for their shareholders. That, at any rate, is their job. But, as we shall see, what is best for bank shareholders may not be best for the whole economy. Therefore, the government does not allow bankers to determine the level of the nation's money supply by profit considerations alone.

Another reason for the extensive regulation of banks is concern for the safety of depositors. In a free-enterprise system, new businesses are born and die every day, and no one save those people immediately involved takes much notice of these goings-on. When a firm goes bankrupt, shareholders lose money and employees may lose their jobs. (The latter may not even happen if new management takes over the assets of the bankrupt firm.) But, except for the case of very large firms, that is about it.

A **run on a bank** occurs when many depositors withdraw cash from their accounts simultaneously.

But banking is different. If banks were treated like other firms, depositors would lose money whenever one went bankrupt. That is bad enough by itself, but the real danger comes in the case of a **run on a bank**. When depositors get jittery about the security of their money, they may all rush in at once to cash in their accounts. For reasons we will learn in this chapter, most banks could not survive a "run" like this and would be forced into insolvency. Worse yet, this disease is highly contagious. If Mrs. Smith hears that her neighbour has just lost her life savings because the Victoria Street National Bank went broke, she is quite likely to rush to her own bank to make a hefty withdrawal.

Without modern forms of bank regulation, therefore, one bank failure might lead to another, and indeed, as noted above, bank failures certainly did occur in the past. They were much more common in the United States. For instance, failures were not an important feature of the Great Depression in Canada, while 2200 banks failed in 1932 alone in the United States. Failures of banks in the United States are relatively rare nowadays, although there were forty-two in the recession year of 1982 and more in recent years. Failures have been infrequent in Canada, because "head office" can always bail out any local branch that may get into difficulties. But including "near banks" (such as trust companies), twenty-two institutions failed in Canada during the 1980–85 period. Not surprisingly, the governments in both Canada and the United States have taken steps to ensure that the infectious disease of bank failure, if it occurs, will not spread. This is done in several ways as discussed later in this chapter.

Barter versus Monetary Exchange

Barter is a system of exchange in which people directly trade one good for another, without using money as an intermediate step.

Money is so much a part of our day-to-day existence that we are likely to take it for granted, failing to appreciate all that it accomplishes. But it is important to realize that money is very much a social contrivance. Like the wheel, it had to be invented. The most obvious way to trade commodities is not by the use of money, but by **barter**—a system in which people exchange one good directly for another. And the best way to appreciate what monetary exchange accomplishes is to imagine a world without it.

Under a system of direct barter, if Farmer Jones grows corn and has a craving for spinach, he has to find a spinach farmer with a taste for corn. If he finds such a person (this was called the *double coincidence of wants* by the classical economists), they make the trade. If this sounds easy, try to imagine how busy Farmer Jones would be if he had to repeat the sequence for every commodity he consumed in a week. For the most part, the desired double coincidences of wants are more likely to turn out to be double wants of coincidence, where Jones gets no spinach and the spinach farmer gets no corn. Worse yet, with so much time spent looking for trading partners, Jones would have far less time to grow corn.

Money greases the wheels of exchange and thus makes the whole economy more productive.

Under a monetary system, the corn farmer gives up his corn for money. He does so not because he wants the money per se, but because of what that money can buy. Money makes Farmer Jones's shopping tasks much easier, for it allows him simply to locate a spinach farmer who wants money. And what spinach farmer does not?

For these reasons, monetary exchange replaced barter at a very early stage of human civilization, and only extreme circumstances, such as massive wars and runaway inflations, have been able to bring barter (temporarily) back.

The Conceptual Definition of Money

Monetary exchange is the alternative to barter. In a system of monetary exchange, people trade **money** for goods when they purchase something and trade goods for money when they sell something, but they do not trade goods directly for other goods. This defines money's principal role as the **medium of exchange**. But once it has become accepted as the medium of exchange, whatever object is serving as money is bound to take on other functions as well. For one, it will inevitably become the **unit of account**, that is, the standard unit for quoting prices. Thus, if inhabitants of an idyllic tropical island use coconuts as money, they would be foolish to quote prices in terms of sea shells.

Money may also come to be used as a **store of value**. If Farmer Jones temporarily produces and sells corn of more value than he wants to consume right away, he may find it convenient to store the difference in the form of money until he wants to use it. This is because he knows that money can be "sold" easily for goods and services at a later date, whereas land, gold, and other stores of value might not be. Of course, if money pays no interest and inflation is substantial, he may decide to forgo the convenience of money and store his wealth in some other form, rather than see its purchasing power rapidly eroded. So this role of money is far from inevitable.

Since money may not always serve as a store of value and since there are many stores of value other than money, it is best not to include the store-of-value function as part of our conceptual definition of money. Instead, we simply label as "money" whatever serves as the medium of exchange.

Money is the standard object used in exchanging goods and services. In short, money is the **medium of exchange**.

The **unit of account** is the standard unit for quoting prices.

A **store of value** is an item used to store wealth from one point in time to another.

What Serves as Money?

Anthropologists and historians will testify that a bewildering variety of things have served as money in different times and places. Cattle, stones, candy bars, cigarettes, woodpecker scalps, porpoise teeth, and giraffe tails are a few of the more colourful examples. In the early settlements in Quebec, playing cards were used as money; this and some other memorable events in the development of the Canadian money system are described in the boxed insert on page 231.

In primitive or less organized societies, the commodities that serve as money generally have value in themselves. If not used as money, cattle can be slaughtered for food, cigarettes can be smoked, and so on. But such **commodity money** generally runs into several severe difficulties. To be useful as a medium of exchange the commodity must be divisible. This makes cattle a very poor choice. It must also be of uniform, or at least readily identifiable, quality so that inferior substitutes are easy to recognize. This may be why woodpecker scalps never achieved great popularity. The medium of exchange must also be storable and durable, which presents a serious problem for candy-bar or banana money. Finally, because commodity moneys need to be carried and stored, it is helpful if the item is compact, that is, has high value per unit of volume and weight. (See the boxed insert on page 232.)

All of these traits make it sensible that gold and silver have circulated as money since the first coins were struck about 2500 years ago. Since the metals have high value in non-monetary uses, a lot of purchasing power can be carried without too much weight. Pieces of gold are also storable, divisible (with a little trouble), and of identifiable quality (with a little more trouble).

Some of the same characteristics suggest that paper makes an ideal money. Since we can print any number on it that we want, we can make paper money as divisible as we please and also make it possible to carry a large value in a lightweight and compact form. Paper is easy to store and, with a little cleverness, we can make counterfeiting very hard. (Again, see the boxed insert on the next page). The Chinese originated paper money in the eleventh century.

Paper cannot, however, serve as a commodity money because its value per square inch in alternative uses is so small. A paper currency that is repudiated by its issuer can, perhaps, be used as wallpaper or to wrap fish, but these uses will surely represent only a small fraction of the paper's value as money. Contrary to the popular expression, such a currency literally *is* worth the paper it is printed on, which is to say that it is not worth very much. Thus paper money is always **fiat money**.

Modern Canadian money is fiat money. Look at a $5 bill. To the left of Laurier's picture, it states: "This note is legal tender." Nowhere on the certificate is there a promise, stated or implied, that the Canadian government will exchange the paper for anything else. A $5 bill is convertible into five loon coins, or twenty quarters, or fifty dimes, or a hundred nickels, or any other similar combination, but not into gold, chocolate, or any other commodity.

Why do people hold these pieces of paper? Only because they know that others are willing to accept them for things of intrinsic value—food, rent, shoes, and so on. If this confidence ever evaporated, these dollar bills would cease serving as a medium of exchange and, given that they make ugly wallpaper, would become virtually worthless.

A **commodity money** is an object in use as a medium of exchange that also has a substantial value in alternative (non-monetary) uses.

Fiat money is money that is decreed as such by the government. It is of little value as a commodity, but it maintains its value as a medium of exchange because people have faith that the issuer will stand behind the pieces of printed paper and limit their production.

Changes in Canada's Money

From a very early date, some North American Indian tribes used wampum as money. It consisted of small cylinders or tubes, about two centimetres long, made from sea shells. Two colours, white and blue, indicated different amounts. The use of wampum continued well after the coming of the Europeans, and because the colonists lacked a supply of coins sufficient for their needs, it was declared legal currency for a time. Although wampum ceased to be legally recognized in 1670, it continued to circulate among colonists until 1704 and among the Indians until 1825.

Early European Canadians also used a random assortment of English, French, Portuguese, Spanish, and Mexican coins. The scarcity and confusion of this currency led to a number of expedients over the years. One such measure was the famous playing-card money, first issued in New France in 1685. It consisted of playing cards cut into quarters and marked with the seal of the treasurer in wax and the autograph of the governor. Although this currency had been intended as a one-season stopgap (when ships carrying coins failed to arrive in Quebec), it proved popular and—because the amount issued was strictly limited—reliable and non-inflationary. Thus, it continued to be issued and used until the fall of Quebec in 1759.

Another interesting solution to a currency shortage occurred in Prince Edward Island. During the later eighteenth century, a large, silver Spanish coin was in wide circulation throughout Eastern Canada. Its value varied from centre to centre but was highest in Halifax. Thus, whenever merchants in P.E.I. received those coins, they sent them to Halifax to take advantage of the higher purchasing power there. The result by the end of the century was a grave shortage of coins in P.E.I., which prompted that colony's governor to obtain a supply and have their centres punched out. These "P.E.I. dollars" were accepted on the island, but not off it, so the currency shortage was solved.

Private banks and eventually government issued paper currency in the 1800s, but there were serious problems at first. All an individual had to do to create currency was to "found" a fictitious bank with a prestigious-sounding name, have some notes printed on quality paper (usually in New York), and issue them. Of course, some paper currency was sound, but some wasn't, and many people were suspicious of it. Confusion was rife, and it took many years and many regulations to end it. The final step came in 1934 with the creation of the Bank of Canada, which now issues the country's only legal tender. The first Bank of Canada notes (dollar bills) were issued in separate French and English versions in 1935.

Changes in our currency system are still occurring today. For example, the new dollar coin, with a loon on one face, was issued in 1987. Charles Lynch, a popular newspaper columnist, wrote of this development:

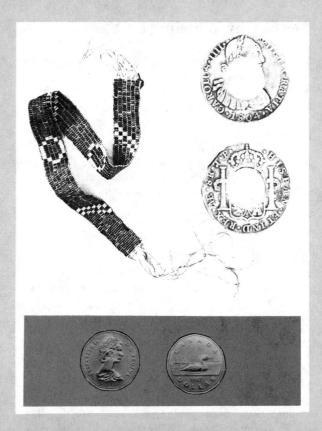

The new design ensures that from now on, we'll talk no more of dollars—it will be loons.... One cautionary note comes from Australia, where they put a kangaroo on their dollar coin and it became known, forevermore, as a roo. If the Australians measure their wealth in roos, there is danger that we might shorten ours to loos. And people who say they're going to spend a loo would be assumed to be answering the call of nature. [*]

A more recent development is the new $50 bill, issued in 1989. It has a modern optical-scanning device—a one-centimetre patch of thin film—on the upper left-hand corner. The patch looks gold from one angle and green from another; it is similar to the hologram image that appears on certain credit cards. This change was made necessary by major advances in the technology of forgery, such as high-quality colour photocopiers. The layer of film roughly doubles the cost of producing a $50 bill, bringing it to 5.5¢ per note. Each bill lasts about three and a half years.

[*]Charles Lynch, *The Hamilton Spectator*, April 15, 1987, page A7.

Dealing by Wheeling on Yap

Primitive forms of money still exist in some remote places, as this extract from a newspaper article suggests.

YAP, Micronesia—On this tiny South Pacific Island ... the currency is as solid as a rock. In fact, it is rock. Limestone to be precise.

For nearly 2000 years the Yapese have used large stone wheels to pay for major purchases, such as land, canoes, and permission to marry. Yap is a U.S. trust territory, and the dollar is used in grocery stores and gas stations. But reliance on stone money ... continues.

Buying property with stones is "much easier than buying it with U.S. dollars," says John Chodad, who recently purchased a building lot with a 30-inch stone wheel. "We don't know the value of the U.S. dollar."

Stone wheels don't make good pocket money, so for small transactions, Yapese use other forms of currency, such as beer. . . .

Besides stone wheels and beer, the Yapese sometimes spend *gaw*, consisting of necklaces of stone beads strung together around a whale's tooth. They also can buy things with *yar*, a currency made from large sea shells. But these are small change.

The people of Yap have been using stone money ever since a Yapese warrior named Anagumang first brought the huge stones over from limestone caverns on neighboring Palau, some 1500 to 2000 years ago. Inspired by the

moon, he fashioned the stone into large circles. The rest is history. . . .

By custom, the stones are worthless when broken. You never hear people on Yap musing about wanting a piece of the rock. . . .

SOURCE: Adapted from Art Pine, "Hard Assets, or Why a Loan in Yap Is Hard to Roll Over," *The Wall Street Journal*, March 29, 1984, page 1.

But don't panic. This is not likely to occur. Our current monetary system has evolved over hundreds of years during which *commodity money* was first replaced by *"full-bodied" paper money*—paper certificates that were backed by gold or silver of equal value held in the issuer's vaults. Then the full-bodied paper money was replaced by certificates that were only partially backed by gold and silver. Finally, we arrived at our present system, in which paper money has no "backing" whatsoever. Like a hesitant swimmer who first dips her toes, then her legs, then her whole body into a cold swimming pool, we have "tested the water" at each step of the way—and found it to our liking. It is unlikely that we will ever take a step back in the other direction.

How the Quantity of Money Is Measured

As we will learn in coming chapters, the amount of money circulating in the economy is of profound importance for the determination of national income and the price level. Thus it becomes important for the government to know how large the money supply is at any given time.

Our conceptual definition of money describes it as the medium of exchange. But this raises questions about just what items should be included and what items excluded when we count up the money supply. Some items are easy. All of our coins, the small change of our economic system, clearly should count as money. So should paper money, which accounts for a far greater volume of transactions. But we cannot stop here if we want to include the main vehicle for making payments in our society,

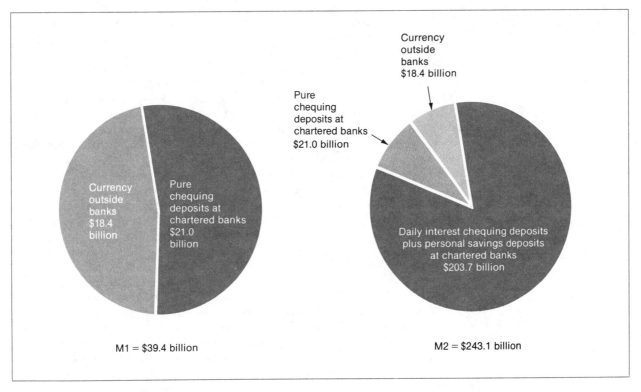

FIGURE 11-1
Definitions of the Money Supply (January 1990)
SOURCE: Bank of Canada *Review.*

because the lion's share of our nation's payments are made neither in metal nor in paper money but by cheque.

Chequing deposits are bookkeeping entries in bank ledgers. Many people think of cheques simply as a convenient way to give coins or dollar bills to someone else. But, in fact, cheques serve directly as money, and Canada has more money in the form of chequing deposits than it has in the form of currency. For example, if you pay the grocer $50 by cheque, no dollar bills or coins normally will change hands. Instead, that cheque will travel back to your bank, where $50 will be deducted from the bookkeeping entry that records your account and added to the bookkeeping entry for your grocer's account. (If you and the grocer hold accounts at different banks, more books get involved, but still no coins or bills are likely to be moved.) Since so many transactions are made by cheque, it seems imperative that chequing deposits be included in any specific definition of the money supply.

One popular definition of the money supply stops here; it includes only currency held outside chartered bank vaults, plus chequing deposits at chartered banks. In the official statistics, this narrowly defined concept of money is called **M1**. The left-hand side of Figure 11-1 shows the composition of M1 as of January 1990.

But there are other types of accounts that allow withdrawals by cheque and that therefore are candidates for inclusion in the money supply. Strictly speaking, withdrawals from the savings account at your bank can require up to seven days' prior notice. However, in practice this procedure is not followed, and people regard their savings-account holdings as equivalent to money. Furthermore, since many banks offer convenient electronic transfers of funds from one account to another, either by telephone or by pushing a button on an automated teller, savings balances can serve the same purposes as chequing balances. For this reason, savings accounts are included in the other, broader statistical definition of the money supply known as **M2**.

The narrowly defined money supply, usually abbreviated **M1**, is the sum of all coins and paper money in circulation, plus pure chequing deposits at chartered banks.

The broadly defined money supply, usually abbreviated **M2**, is the sum of currency in public hands, plus chequing and all savings deposits at chartered banks.

The composition of M2 as of January 1990 is shown on the right-hand side of Figure 11–1. You can see that the savings accounts predominate, dwarfing everything that is included in M1.

Some economists do not want to stop counting at M2; they prefer still broader definitions of money that include other closely related assets. For example, many people do their "banking" at trust companies or credit unions; this is especially true in Quebec, with its caisses populaires. The problem with extending the definition of the money supply by including the deposits at these institutions is that there is no clear-cut place to stop. Furthermore, there is no obvious line of demarcation between these assets, which *are* money, and assets that are merely *close substitutes* for money—so-called **near moneys**.

If we define an asset's **liquidity** as the ease with which it can be converted into cash, then there is a range of assets of varying degrees of liquidity. Everything in M1 is completely "liquid"; savings accounts included in M2 are a bit less so; and so on, until we encounter such things as short-term government bonds, which, while still quite liquid, would not normally be included in the money supply. Any number of different "M's" can be defined—and have been—by drawing the line in different places.

There are still more complexities. For example, credit cards clearly serve as a medium of exchange. So should they be included in the money supply? Yes, you say. But how would we do this? How much money does your credit card represent? If you think about questions like this for a while, you will realize that there are no good answers—which is one reason why research on the definition of money continues. But, in a first course in economics, we do not want to get bogged down in complex definitional issues. So we will simply adhere to the convention that *"money" consists only of coins, paper money, and deposits at chartered banks that require essentially no notice for withdrawal.*

Now that we have defined money and seen how it can be measured, we turn our attention to the principal creators of money—the banks.

How Banking Began

When Adam and Eve left the Garden of Eden, they did not encounter a bank. Banking had to be invented, and some time passed before it came to be practised as it is today. With a little imagination, we can see how the first banks must have begun.

When money was made of gold, consumers and merchants found it inconvenient to have to carry it around and to weigh and assay it for purity every time a transaction was made. So it is not surprising that the practice developed of leaving one's gold in the care of a goldsmith, who had safe storage facilities, and carrying in its place a receipt from the goldsmith stating that John Doe did indeed own five ounces of gold of a certain purity. When people began trading goods and services for the goldsmiths' receipts, rather than for the gold itself, the receipts became an early form of paper money.

At this stage, paper money was fully backed by gold. But gradually the goldsmiths began to notice that the amount of gold they were actually required to pay out in a day was but a small fraction of the total gold they had stored in their warehouses. Then one day some enterprising goldsmith hit upon a momentous idea that must have made him fabulously wealthy.

His thinking probably ran something like this. "I have 2000 ounces of gold stored away in my vault, for which I collect storage fees from my customers. If I get much more, I'll need an expensive new vault. But in the last year, I was never called upon to pay out more than 100 ounces on a single day. What harm could it do if I lent out, say, half the gold I now have? I'll still have more than enough to pay off any depositors who come in for a withdrawal, so no one will ever know the difference. And I could earn 30 additional ounces of gold each year in interest on the loans I make (at 3 percent interest on 1000 ounces). With this profit, I could lower my service charges to depositors and so attract still more deposits. I think I'll do it."

Near moneys are liquid assets that are close substitutes for money.

An asset's **liquidity** refers to the ease with which it can be converted into cash.

With this resolution, the modern system of **fractional reserve banking** was born. This system has three important features—features that are crucially important to this chapter.

Fractional reserve banking is a system under which bankers keep in their vaults as reserves only a fraction of the funds they hold on deposit.

1. *Bank profitability.*   By getting deposits at zero interest and lending some of them out at positive interest rates, goldsmiths made a profit. The history of banking as a profit-making industry was begun and has continued to this date. *Banks, like other enterprises, are in business to earn profits.*

2. *Bank discretion over the money supply.*   When goldsmiths decided that they could get along by keeping only a fraction of their total deposits on reserve in their vaults and lending out the balance, they acquired the ability to *create money.* Previously, when they were keeping 100 percent reserves, each gold certificate represented exactly one ounce of gold. So whether people decided to carry their gold or leave it with their goldsmiths, money supply was not affected—it was set by the actual volume of gold.

   With the advent of fractional reserve banking, however, new paper certificates were added whenever goldsmiths lent out some of the gold they held on deposit. The loans, in effect, created new money—in other words, they put more paper certificates into circulation. In this way, the total amount of money came to depend on the amount of gold that each goldsmith felt it necessary to maintain as reserves in his vault. For any given volume of gold on deposit, the lower the reserves the goldsmiths kept, the more loans they could make, and therefore the more money there would be. While we no longer use gold to back our money, this principle remains true today. *Bankers' business decisions influence the supply of money.*

3. *Exposure to runs.*   A goldsmith who kept 100 percent reserves never had to worry about a run on his vault. Even if all his depositors showed up at the door at once, he always had enough gold to return their deposits. But as soon as the first goldsmith decided to get by with only fractional reserves, the possibility of a run on the vault became a real concern. If that first goldsmith who lent out half his gold had found 51 percent of his customers at his door one unlucky day, he would have had a lot of explaining to do. Similar problems have worried bankers for centuries. *The danger of a run on the bank has induced bankers to keep prudent reserves and to lend out money carefully.*

Principles of Bank Management: Profits versus Safety

Bankers have a reputation, probably deserved, for conservatism in politics, dress, and business affairs. From what has been said so far, the economic rationale for this conservatism should be clear. Today's chequing deposits are pure fiat money. For years now these deposits have been "backed" by nothing more than the bank's promise to convert them into currency on demand. Thus, banks depend entirely on people's trust and so have had to acquire a reputation for prudence. This they did (and continue to do) in two principal ways. First, they had to maintain a sufficiently generous level of reserves to minimize their vulnerability to runs. Second, they had to be somewhat cautious in making loans and investments, since any large losses on their loans could undermine the confidence of depositors.

   It is important to realize that banking under a system of fractional reserves is an inherently risky business that is rendered relatively safe only by cautious and prudent management. The history of bank failures in the United States before World War II bears sober testimony to the fact that many bankers were neither cautious nor prudent. Why? Because this is not a recipe for high profits. Bank profits are maximized by keeping reserves as low as possible, by making at least some risky investments, and by giving loans to borrowers of questionable credit standing (because these borrowers will pay the highest interest rates). The art of bank management is to strike the appropriate balance between the lure of profits and the need for safety. When a banker errs by being too stodgy, his bank will earn inadequate profits. When he errs by taking unwarranted risks, his bank may not survive at all.

Bank Regulation

The public authorities apparently have decided that the balance struck by profit-minded bankers often would not be at the place where society would like it struck. So government has thrown up a web of regulations designed to insure the safety of depositors and to control the supply of money.

The principal innovation guaranteeing the safety of bank deposits is **deposit insurance**. Today most bank deposits are insured against loss by the federal government, up to an amount of $60,000 per account regardless of what happens to the bank. Thus, while bank failures may spell disaster for the bank's shareholders, they do not give many depositors cause for concern. Deposit insurance eliminates the motive for customers to rush to their bank just because they hear some bad news about the bank's finances. Many observers give this innovation much of the credit for the pronounced decline in bank failures in the United States since 1933 (the year in which deposit insurance was started there). It had 2200 bank failures in 1932, and 60 in 1934. In Canada, our deposit-insurance system was created in 1967. The Canada Deposit Insurance Corporation, which administers this insurance, does not apply it to stocks, bonds, foreign-currency deposits, or people's deposits in the country's numerous investment companies. But for every failure of an institution whose deposits *are* insured, the government has extended protection to *all* deposits, no matter how large, even though coverage is not required to exceed $60,000 per account. There has recently been much debate about whether our current form of deposit insurance is such a good idea. See the boxed insert on page 245, which clarifies the issues involved.

In addition to insuring depositors against loss, the government takes steps to see that banks do not get into financial trouble. For one thing, various regulatory authorities conduct periodic *bank examinations and audits* in order to keep tabs on the financial condition and business practices of the banks under their purview. For another, laws and regulations *limit the kinds and quantities of assets in which banks may invest*. For example, banks have been limited in the amount of common stock they may purchase, and it wasn't until 1954 that banks were allowed to make household mortgages. Both these forms of regulation were clearly aimed at maintaining bank safety.

A final type of regulation also has some bearing on safety, but it is motivated primarily by the government's desire to control the money supply. We have seen that the amount of money any bank will issue depends on the amount of reserves it elects to keep. For this reason, most banks are subject by law to minimum **required reserves**. While banks may (and sometimes do) keep reserves in excess of these legal minimums, they may not keep less. It is this regulation that places an upper limit on the money supply. The rest of this chapter is concerned with the details of this mechanism.

How Bankers Keep Books

Before we can fully understand the mechanics of modern banking and the process by which money is "created," we must acquire at least a nodding acquaintance with the way in which bankers keep their books. The first thing to know is how to distinguish assets from liabilities.

An **asset** of a bank is something of value that the bank *owns*. This "thing" may be a physical object, such as the bank building, a computer, or a vault, or it may be just a piece of paper, such as the IOU of a customer to whom the bank has made a loan. A **liability** of a bank is something of value that the bank *owes*. Most bank liabilities take

Deposit insurance is a system that guarantees that depositors will not lose money even if their bank goes bankrupt.

Required reserves are the minimum amount of reserves (in cash or the equivalent), mandated by law, that banks must maintain. Normally, required reserves are proportional to the volume of deposits.

An **asset** of an individual or a business firm is an item of value that the individual or firm owns.

TABLE 11–1
Balance Sheet of Bank-a-mythica, December 31, 1990

ASSETS		LIABILITIES AND NET WORTH	
Assets		**Liabilities**	
Reserves	$1,000,000	Chequing deposits	$5,000,000
Loans outstanding	4,500,000		
Total	$5,500,000		
Addendum: Bank Reserves		**Net Worth**	
Actual reserves	$1,000,000	Shareholders' equity	500,000
Required reserves	1,000,000		
Excess reserves	0	Total	$5,500,000

the form of bookkeeping entries. For example, if you have a chequing account in the Victoria Street Bank, your bank balance there is a liability of the bank. (It is, of course, an asset for you.)

There is an easy test to see whether some piece of paper or bookkeeping entry is a bank's asset or a liability. Ask yourself whether, if this paper were converted into cash, the bank would receive the cash (if so, it is an asset) or pay it out (if so, it is a liability). This test makes it clear that loans to customers are bank assets (when the loans are repaid, the bank collects), while customers' deposits are bank liabilities (when deposits are cashed in, the bank must pay up). Of course, to the customers, things are just the opposite; the loans are liabilities and the deposits are assets.

When accountants draw up a complete list of all the bank's assets and liabilities, the resulting document is called the bank's **balance sheet**. Typically, the value of all the bank's assets exceeds the value of all its liabilities. (On the rare occasions when this is not the case, the bank is in serious trouble.) In what sense, then, do balance sheets "balance"?

They balance because accountants have invented the concept of **net worth**. Specifically, they have defined the net worth of a bank to be the difference between the value of all its assets and the value of all its liabilities. Thus, by definition, when accountants add net worth to liabilities, the sum they get must be the same as the value of the bank's assets. In short:

$$\text{Assets} = \text{Liabilities} + \text{Net worth.}$$

Table 11–1 illustrates this with the balance sheet of a fictitious bank, Bank-a-mythica, whose finances are extremely simple. On December 31, 1990, it had only two kinds of assets (listed on the left-hand side of the balance sheet)—$1 million in cash, which it held as reserves, and $4.5 million in outstanding loans to its customers, that is, in customers' IOUs. And it had only one type of liability (listed on the right-hand side)—$5 million in chequing deposits. The difference between total assets ($5.5 million) and total liabilities ($5 million) was the bank's net worth ($500,000), shown on the right-hand side of the balance sheet.

The Limits to Money Creation by a Single Bank

Let us now turn to the process of deposit creation. Many bankers will deny that they have any ability to "create" money. (The very phrase has a suspiciously hocus-pocus sound to it.) But they are not quite right. For although any individual bank's ability to create money is severely limited in a system with many banks, the banking system as a whole can achieve much more than the sum of its parts. Through the modern alchemy

A **liability** of an individual or a business firm is an item of value that the individual or firm owes. Many liabilities are known as "debts."

A **balance sheet** is an accounting statement listing the values of all the assets on the left-hand side and the values of all the liabilities and **net worth** on the right-hand side.

Net worth is the value of all assets minus the value of all liabilities.

of **deposit creation**, it can turn one dollar into many dollars. But to understand this important process, we had better proceed in steps, beginning with the case of a single bank, our hypothetical Bank-a-mythica.

According to the balance sheet in Table 11–1, Bank-a-mythica is holding cash reserves in its vault that are equal to 20 percent of its deposits ($1 million in cash is equal to 20 percent of the $5 million in deposits). Let us assume that this is the minimum reserve ratio prescribed by law and that the bank strives to keep its reserves down to the legal minimum; that is, it strives to keep its **excess reserves** at zero.

Now let us suppose that on January 2, 1991, an eccentric miser comes into Bank-a-mythica and deposits $100,000 in cash in his chequing account. The bank now has acquired $100,000 more in cash reserves and $100,000 more in chequing deposits. But since deposits are up by $100,000, *required* reserves are up by only 20 percent of this amount, or $20,000, leaving $80,000 in *excess* reserves. Table 11–2 illustrates the effects of this transaction on Bank-a-mythica's balance sheet. (Tables like this one, which show *changes* in balance sheets rather than the balance sheets themselves, will help us follow the money-creation process.)

If Bank-a-mythica does not want to hold excess reserves, it will be unhappy with the situation illustrated in Table 11–2, for it is holding $80,000 in excess reserves on which it earns no interest. So as soon as possible it will lend out the extra $80,000—let us say to Hard-Pressed Construction Company. This loan leads to the balance sheet changes shown in Table 11–3: Bank-a-mythica's loans rise by $80,000, while its holdings of cash reserves fall by $80,000.

By combining Tables 11–2 and 11–3, we arrive at Table 11–4, which summarizes all the bank's transactions for the week. Cash reserves are up $20,000, loans are up $80,000, and now that the bank has had a chance to adjust to the inflow of deposits, it no longer holds excess reserves.

TABLE 11–2
Changes in Bank-a-mythica's Balance Sheet, January 2, 1991

ASSETS		LIABILITIES	
Reserves	+ $100,000	Chequing deposits	+ $100,000
Addendum: Changes in Reserves			
Actual reserves	+ $100,000		
Required reserves	+ 20,000		
Excess reserves	+ $ 80,000		

Bank-a-mythica receives a $100,000 cash deposit. It now holds excess reserves of $80,000, since required reserves rise by $20,000 (20 percent of $100,000).

TABLE 11–3
Changes in Bank-a-mythica's Balance Sheet, January 3–6, 1991

ASSETS		LIABILITIES	
Loans outstanding	+ $80,000	No change	
Reserves	− $80,000		
Addendum: Changes in Reserves			
Actual reserves	− $80,000		
Required reserves	No change		
Excess reserves	− $80,000		

Bank-a-mythica gets rid of its excess reserves by making a loan of $80,000 to Hard-Pressed Construction Company.

TABLE 11–4
Changes in Bank-a-mythica's Balance Sheet, January 2–6, 1991

ASSETS		LIABILITIES	
Reserves	+ $20,000	Chequing deposits	+ $100,000
Loans outstanding	+ 80,000		
Addendum: Changes in Reserves			
Actual reserves	+ $20,000		
Required reserves	+ 20,000		
Excess reserves	No change		

When it receives $100,000 in cash deposits, Bank-a-mythica keeps only the required $20,000 in reserves and lends out the remaining $80,000 to Hard-Pressed Construction Company. Its excess reserves return to zero.

Looking at Table 11–4 and keeping in mind our specific definition of money, it appears at first that the chairman of Bank-a-mythica is right when he claims not to have engaged in the nefarious practice of "money creation." All that happened was that, in exchange for the $100,000 in cash it received, the bank issued the miser a chequing balance of $100,000. This does not change M1; it merely converts one form of money into another.

But wait. What happened to the $100,000 in cash that the eccentric man brought to the bank? The table shows that $20,000 was retained by Bank-a-mythica in its vault. Since this currency is no longer in circulation, it no longer counts in the official money supply. (Notice that Figure 11–1 included only "currency outside banks.") But the other $80,000, which the bank lent out, is still in circulation. It is held by Hard-Pressed Construction, which probably will redeposit it in some other bank. But even before this happens, the original $100,000 in cash has supported a rise in the money supply: There is now $100,000 in the chequing deposit of the miser and $80,000 of cash in circulation, making a total of $180,000. The money-creation process has begun.

Multiple Money Creation by a Series of Banks

Let us now trace the $80,000 in cash and see how the process of money creation gathers momentum. Suppose that Hard-Pressed Construction Company, which banks across town at the National Bank, deposits the $80,000 into its bank account. National's reserves increase by $80,000. But because deposits are up by $80,000, *required* reserves rise by only 20 percent of this amount, or $16,000. If the management of the National Bank behaves like that of Bank-a-mythica, the $64,000 of excess reserves will be lent out.

Table 11–5 shows the effects of these events on the National Bank's balance sheet. (The preliminary steps corresponding to Tables 11–2 and 11–3 are not shown separately.) At this stage in the chain, the original $100,000 in cash has led to $180,000 in deposits—$100,000 at Bank-a-mythica and $80,000 at the National Bank—and $64,000 in cash, which is still in circulation (in the hands of the recipient of National's loan—Al's Auto Shop). Thus, from the original $100,000, a total of $244,000 has been added to the money supply ($180,000 in chequing deposits plus $64,000 in cash).

But, to coin a phrase, the bucks do not stop here. Al's Auto Shop will presumably deposit the proceeds from its loan into its own account at its bank, the Provincial Bank, leading eventually to the balance sheet adjustments shown in Table 11–6 when the Provincial makes an additional loan rather than hold on to excess reserves. You can see how the money-creation process continues.

Table 11–7 is a convenient tabular summary of the balance sheet changes of the first five banks in the chain on the assumptions that each bank holds exactly the 20 percent required reserves (no excess reserves), and that each loan recipient redeposits the proceeds in the next bank. But the chain does not end there, for the Main Street Movie Theatre, which received the $32,768 loan from the Fifth Bank, then deposits these funds into the Sixth Bank. It has to keep only 20 percent of this deposit, or $6,553.60, on reserve and will lend out the balance. And so the chain continues.

TABLE 11–5
Changes in National Bank's Balance Sheet

ASSETS		LIABILITIES	
Reserves	+ $16,000	Chequing deposits	+ $80,000
Loans outstanding	+ 64,000		
Addendum: Changes in Reserves			
Actual reserves	+ $16,000		
Required reserves	+ 16,000		
Excess reserves	No change		

Hard-Pressed Construction deposits its $80,000 in the National Bank, which sets aside the required $16,000 in reserves (20 percent of $80,000) and lends $64,000 to Al's Auto Shop.

TABLE 11–6
Changes in Provincial Bank's Balance Sheet

ASSETS		LIABILITIES	
Reserves	+ $12,800	Chequing deposits	+ $64,000
Loans outstanding	+ 51,200		
Addendum: Changes in Reserves			
Actual reserves	+ $12,800		
Required reserves	+ 12,800		
Excess reserves	No change		

When Al deposits his $64,000 in the Provincial, it retains $12,800 as required reserves (20 percent of $64,000) and lends out the remaining $51,200.

TABLE 11–7
The Process of Multiple Money Creation

BANK	(1) DEPOSIT RECEIVED	(2) REQUIRED RESERVES	(3) EXCESS RESERVES	(4) NEW LOANS	(5) ADDITION TO THE MONEY SUPPLY
Bank-a-mythica	+$100,000	+$ 20,000	+$80,000	+$ 80,000	0
National Bank	+ 80,000	+ 16,000	+ 64,000	+ 64,000	+$ 80,000
Provincial Bank	+ 64,000	+ 12,800	+ 51,200	+ 51,200	+ 64,000
Fourth Bank	+ 51,200	+ 10,240	+ 40,960	+ 40,960	+ 51,200
Fifth Bank	+ 40,960	+ 8,192	+ 32,768	+ 32,768	+ 40,960
.	.	.	.	.	.
.	.	.	.	.	.
.	.	.	.	.	.
.	.	.	.	.	.
All other banks	+ 163,840	+ 32,768	—	+ 131,072	+ 163,840
Totals	+$500,000	+$100,000	0	+$400,000	+$400,000

Where does it all end? The last two lines of Table 11-7 show what eventually happens to all other banks and to the entire banking system. The initial deposit of $100,000 in cash ultimately leads to a total of $500,000 in new deposits (column 1) and a total of $400,000 in new loans (column 4). The money supply (column 5) rises by $400,000. The initial transaction at Bank-a-mythica merely exchanges one form of money (currency in circulation) for another (chequing deposits) and hence has no net effect on the money supply. But all the other transactions in the chain increase the money supply by the amount of new deposits.

So there really is some hocus-pocus. Somehow, an initial deposit of $100,000 leads to $500,000 in new bank deposits—an expansion of $5 for every original dollar —and a net increase of $400,000 in the money supply. We had better understand why this is so. But first let us verify that the calculations in Table 11-7 are correct.

If you look carefully at the table, you will see that each column of numbers forms a *geometric progression;* specifically, each entry is equal to exactly 80 percent of the entry that preceded it. Recall that in the discussion of the multiplier in Chapter 7 we learned how to sum an infinite geometric progression, which is just what each of these chains eventually will be. In particular, if the common ratio is R, the sum of an infinite geometric progression is

$$1 + R + R^2 + R^3 + \ldots = \frac{1}{1 - R}.$$

By applying this formula to the chain of chequing deposits in column 1 of Table 11-7, we get:

$$
\begin{aligned}
&\$100,000 + \$80,000 + \$64,000 + \$51,200 + \ldots \\
=\ &\$100,000 \times (1 + 0.8 + 0.64 + 0.512 + \ldots) \\
=\ &\$100,000 \times (1 + 0.8 + 0.8^2 + 0.8^3 + \ldots) \\
=\ &\$100,000 \times \frac{1}{1 - 0.8} = \frac{\$100,000}{0.2} = \$500,000.
\end{aligned}
$$

Proceeding similarly, we can verify that both columns 4 and 5 sum to $400,000 and that column 2 sums to $100,000. (Check these as exercises.)

So the numbers in Table 11-7 seem to be correct. Let us, therefore, think through the logic behind them. The chain of deposit creation can end only when there are no more excess reserves to be loaned out; that is, when the entire $100,000 in cash is tied up in required reserves. That explains the last entry in column 2. But with a reserve ratio of 20 percent, excess reserves disappear only when chequing deposits expand by $500,000—which is the last entry in column 1. Finally, since balance sheets must balance, the sum of all newly created assets (reserves plus loans) must equal the sum of all newly created liabilities ($500,000 in deposits). That leaves $400,000 for new loans —which is the last entry in column 4.

More generally, if the reserve ratio is some number R (rather than the $\frac{1}{5}$ in our example), each dollar of deposits requires only a fraction R of a dollar in reserves. Hence, deposits must expand by $1/R$ for each dollar of new reserves that is injected into the system. This suggests the general formula for multiple money creation:

OVERSIMPLIFIED MONEY-MULTIPLIER FORMULA
If the reserve ratio maintained by banks is some fraction, R, an injection of $1 of new reserves into the banking system can lead to the creation of $1/R$ in new deposits. That is, the so-called "money multiplier" is given by either of the following:

Change in deposits $= (1/R) \times$ Change in reserves;

Change in money supply $= (1/R) \times$ Change in excess reserves.

Notice that these equations correctly describe what happens in our example. The initial deposit of $100,000 in cash at Bank-a-mythica creates $80,000 in excess reserves (the top entry in column 3 of Table 11–7). Applying a multiplier of $1/R = 1/0.2 = 5$ to this $80,000, we conclude that the money supply will rise by $400,000—which is just what happens.

One implication of these money-multiplier relationships is that a change in the form in which the public holds its money (say from cash to deposits, as in our example of the eccentric miser) affects the overall money supply less than does a government issue of new currency. In our example, the money supply increases by $400,000: Although there is now $500,000 in new deposits, there is $100,000 less in public-held currency. In the case of newly issued currency, a $100,000 issue of new notes leads to $500,000 more in bank deposits, without *any* reduction in public-held currency.

The Process in Reverse: Multiple Contractions of the Money Supply

Let us now briefly consider how this deposit-creation mechanism operates in reverse—as a system of deposit *destruction*. In particular, suppose that our eccentric miser comes back to Bank-a-mythica to withdraw $100,000 from his chequing account and return it to his mattress, where it rightfully belongs. Bank-a-mythica's *required* reserves will fall by $20,000 as a result of this transaction (20 percent of $100,000), but its *actual* reserves will fall by $100,000. The bank will be $80,000 short, as indicated in Table 11–8(a).

How does it react to this discrepancy? As some of its outstanding loans are routinely paid off, the bank will cease granting new ones until it has accumulated the necessary $80,000 in required reserves. The data for Bank-a-mythica's contraction are shown in Table 11–8(b), assuming that borrowers pay off their loans in cash.[1]

But where did the borrowers get this money? Probably by making withdrawals from other banks. In this case, let us assume it all came from the National Bank, which loses an $80,000 deposit and $80,000 in reserves. It finds itself short some $64,000 in reserves [see Table 11–9(a)] and therefore must reduce its loan commitments by $64,000 [see Table 11–9(b)]. This, of course, causes some other bank to suffer a loss of reserves and deposits of $64,000, and the whole process repeats just as it did in the case of deposit expansion.

After the entire banking system has become involved, the picture will be just as

---

[1] In reality, they would probably pay with cheques drawn on other banks. Bank-a-mythica would then cash these cheques to acquire the reserves.

TABLE 11–8
Changes in the Balance Sheet of Bank-a-mythica

(a) ASSETS		(a) LIABILITIES		(b) ASSETS		(b) LIABILITIES
Reserves	−$100,000	Chequing deposits	− $100,000	Reserves	+ $80,000	
				Loans outstanding	− 80,000	
Addendum: Changes in Reserves				**Addendum: Changes in Reserves**		
Actual reserves	− $100,000			Actual reserves	+ $80,000	
Required reserves	− 20,000			Required reserves	No change	
Excess reserves	− $ 80,000			Excess reserves	+ $80,000	

When Bank-a-mythica loses a $100,000 deposit, it must reduce its loans by $80,000 to replenish its reserves.

TABLE 11-9
Changes in the Balance Sheet of National Bank

(a)				(b)		
ASSETS		LIABILITIES		ASSETS		LIABILITIES
Reserves	− $80,000	Chequing deposits	− $80,000	Reserves	+ $64,000	
				Loans outstanding	− 64,000	
Addendum: Changes in Reserves				**Addendum: Changes in Reserves**		
Actual reserves	− $80,000			Actual reserves	+ $64,000	
Required reserves	− 16,000			Required reserves	No change	
Excess reserves	− $64,000			Excess reserves	+ $64,000	

National Bank's loss of an $80,000 deposit forces it to cut back its loans by $64,000.

shown in Table 11–7, except that all the *plus* signs will be *minus* signs. Deposits shrink by $500,000, loans fall by $400,000, bank reserves are reduced by $100,000, and the money supply falls by $400,000. As suggested by our money-multiplier formula with $R = 0.2$, the decline in deposits is $1/0.2 = 5$ times as large as the decline in excess reserves.

During the height of the radical student movements of the late 1960s, a circular appeared in Cambridge, Massachusetts, urging citizens to withdraw all funds from their chequing accounts on a prescribed date, hold them in cash for one week, and then redeposit them. This act, the circular argued, would surely wreak havoc upon the capitalist system. Obviously, some of these radicals were well-schooled in modern money mechanics, for the argument was basically correct. The tremendous multiple contraction of the banking system and consequent multiple expansion that a successful campaign of this sort could have caused might have disrupted the local financial system quite seriously. But history records that the appeal met with little action.

Why the Money-Creation Formula Is Oversimplified

So far, our discussion of the process of money creation has made it all seem rather mechanical. If all proceeds according to formula, each $1 in new reserves will lead to a $1/R$ increase in deposits. But in reality things are not this simple. Just as we did in the case of the expenditure multiplier, we must stress that the oversimplified formula for money creation is accurate only under very particular circumstances. These circumstances require that:

1. Every recipient of a bank loan must redeposit the proceeds of that loan into another bank rather than hold it in cash.

2. Every bank must hold reserves no larger than the legal minimum.

Let us see what happens to the chain of deposit creation when either of these assumptions is violated.

Suppose first that the business firms and individuals who receive bank loans decide not to redeposit all of the proceeds into their bank accounts. For example, Hard-Pressed Construction Company and all the other borrowers might decide to hold half of their loan proceeds in cash and deposit only the remaining half. The National Bank would receive only a $40,000 deposit and could, therefore, make only a $32,000 loan. The Provincial Bank would then receive only $16,000 (half of $32,000), and so on. The whole chain of deposit creation would be reduced drastically. Thus:

If individuals and business firms decide to hold more cash, the multiple expansion of the money supply will be curtailed because fewer dollars of cash will be available to be used as reserves to support new chequing deposits. Consequently, the money supply will be smaller.

The basic idea here is simple. Each $1 of cash held by a bank can support several dollars (specifically, $1/R$) of money. But each $1 held by an individual is exactly one dollar of money; it supports no bank deposits. Hence, any time cash leaves the banking system, the money supply will decline. And any time cash enters the banking system, the money supply will rise.

Next, suppose that Bank-a-mythica's management becomes conservative, perhaps because the outlook for loan repayments worsens because of a recession. The bank might then decide to keep more reserves than the legal requirement (say, 30 percent) and lend out less than the $80,000 assumed in Table 11–4 (say, $70,000). If this happens, then the National Bank will receive a smaller injection of cash reserves than that shown in Table 11–5. And if the National's management is as jittery as Bank-a-mythica's, it too will hold more in reserves and lend out less. Thus:

If banks wish to keep excess reserves, the multiple expansion of the money supply will be restricted. A given amount of cash will support a smaller supply of money than would be the case if banks held no excess reserves. The appropriate adjustment to our formula is automatically involved if R is measured by the actual reserve ratio rather than the (smaller) required reserve ratio.

The Need for Monetary Control

If we pursue this point a bit further, we will see why government regulation of the money supply is so important for economic stability. We have just suggested that banks will wish to keep excess reserves when they do not foresee profitable and secure opportunities to make loans. This is likely to happen during the downswing and around the bottom of a business contraction. If it occurs, the propensity of banks to hold excess reserves will turn the money-creation process into one of money destruction. Thus:

During a recession, profit-oriented banks would be prone to reduce the money supply by increasing their excess reserves—if the monetary authorities did not intervene. As we will learn in subsequent chapters, the money supply is an important influence on aggregate demand, so such a contraction of the money supply would exacerbate the severity of the recession.

On the other hand, banks will want to squeeze the maximum possible money supply out of any given amount of cash reserves by keeping their reserves at the bare minimum when the demand for bank loans is buoyant, profits are high, and many investments suddenly start to look profitable. This reduced incentive to hold excess reserves in prosperous times means that:

During an economic boom, the behaviour of profit-oriented banks is likely to make the money supply expand, adding undesirable momentum to the booming economy and paving the way for a burst of inflation. The authorities must intervene to prevent this.

Regulation of the money supply, then, is necessary because bankers, in the pursuit of profit, might otherwise provide the economy with a widely fluctuating money supply that dances to the tune of the business cycle. Precisely how the authorities can keep the money supply under control is the subject of the next chapter.

Reform of Deposit Insurance and Reserve Requirements

Despite its usefulness for both reducing the frequency of runs on banks and maintaining confidence in the financial system, deposit insurance involves some undesirable incentive effects. While it lowers the costs to depositors of the failure of insured institutions, it also raises the probability of those very failures.

The reason for this is that insurance eliminates the need for depositors to assess and monitor the riskiness of the financial institutions they deal with, and thereby also eliminates the need for them to demand higher yields in compensation for riskier ventures. This in turn removes the discipline on managers of financial institutions that would otherwise force them to pay higher costs when undertaking greater risks. Since managers face no trade-off between the risks they take in their lending and the interest costs they must pay for deposited funds, deposit insurance in effect makes regulation of financial institutions all the more necessary to maintain the solvency of the various institutions.

One proposal to deal with these problems has been advanced by two Nobel Prize–winning economists—James Tobin (a liberal adviser to Democratic presidents in the United States) and Milton Friedman (a conservative adviser to Republican presidents). They have advocated that banks be required to hold 100 percent reserves against that subset of deposits that is federally insured. This would certainly solve the confidence problem, and it would give depositors a choice. They could have a higher rate of return on other (uninsured) forms of deposits, but they would have to assess whether the increased risk was worth it. Financial institutions would not be penalized by this scheme, since another facet of the proposal is that the central bank pay interest on all bank reserves.

As this book goes to press, the Canadian government's long-awaited bill on changes in financial regulations has not appeared. The plan, however, is to adopt a scheme very different from that favoured by the Nobel laureates. The

new arrangement follows from the widespread interest in deregulation that prevailed during the 1980s. The new scheme *eliminates* required reserves altogether. Clearly, crises of confidence can still occur, and the unfortunate disincentive effects of deposit insurance remain. Nevertheless, under the new arrangement, chartered banks will be free to compete on an equal footing with other financial institutions (which have never been subject to required reserve regulations).

Even in the absence of reserve requirements, the Bank of Canada will still be able to control the amount of bank reserves, because the chartered banks will continue to hold deposit accounts at the central bank for cheque-clearing purposes. The Bank will still be able to use its standard tools to change the size of the reserves.

Summary

1. It is more efficient to exchange goods and services by using money as a medium of exchange than by bartering them directly.

2. In addition to being the medium of exchange, whatever serves as money is likely to become the standard unit of account and a popular store of value.

3. Throughout history, all sorts of things have served as money. Commodity moneys gave way to full-bodied paper money (certificates backed 100 percent by some commodity, such as gold), which in turn gave way to partially backed paper money. Nowadays our paper money has no commodity backing whatsoever; that is, it is pure fiat money.

4. The most widely used definition of the Canadian money supply is M1, which includes coins and paper money held outside banks, plus pure chequing deposits. However, many economists prefer the M2 definition, which adds to M1 savings deposits and most notice deposits held at chartered banks.

5. Under our modern system of fractional reserve banking, banks keep cash reserves equal to only a fraction of their total deposit liabilities. This is the key to banks' profitability, since their remaining funds can be loaned out at interest. But it also leaves them potentially vulnerable to runs.

6. Because of this vulnerability, bank managers are generally conservative in their investment strategy, and they also keep a prudent level of reserves. Even so, the government keeps a watchful eye over banking practices.

7. Before bank mergers and deposit insurance, bank failures were fairly common. Some still occur, particularly in the United States.

8. As a whole, the banking system can create several dollars of deposits for each dollar of cash reserves it receives. Under certain assumptions, the ratio of new money to new excess reserves will be $1/R$, where R is the required reserve ratio.

9. The same process works in reverse, as a system of money destruction, when cash is withdrawn from the banking system.

10. Because banks and individuals may want to hold more cash when the economy is shaky, the money supply would probably contract under such circumstances if the monetary authorities did not intervene. Similarly, the money supply would probably expand rapidly in boom times if it were unregulated.

Concepts for Review

Run on a bank
Barter
Unit of account
Money
Medium of exchange
Store of value
Commodity money

Fiat money
M1 versus M2
Near moneys
Liquidity
Fractional reserve banking
Deposit insurance
Required reserves

Asset
Liability
Balance sheet
Net worth
Deposit creation
Excess reserves

Questions for Discussion

1. Suppose that no banks keep excess reserves and no individuals or firms hold on to cash. If someone suddenly discovers $4 million in buried treasure, explain what will happen to the money supply if the required reserve ratio is one-sixth (16.67 percent).

2. How would your answer to Question 1 differ if the reserve ratio were 25 percent? If the reserve ratio were 100 percent?

3. Each year during the Christmas shopping season, consumers and stores wish to increase their holdings of cash. Explain how this could lead to a multiple contraction of the money supply. (As a matter of fact, the authorities prevent this contraction from occurring by methods explained in the next chapter.)

4. Excess reserves make a bank less vulnerable to runs. Why, then, don't bankers like to hold excess reserves? What circumstances might persuade them that it would be advisable to hold excess reserves?

5. Use tables such as Tables 11–2 and 11–3 to illustrate what happens to bank balance sheets when each of the following transactions occurs:

a. You withdraw $100 from your chequing account to purchase textbooks at the book store.

b. Paul steals $150 in cash from Patty and deposits it into his chequing account.

c. Mary Q. Contrary withdraws $600 in cash from her account at Bank-a-mythica, carries it to the West coast, and deposits it into her account at the National Bank.

6. For each of the transactions listed in Question 5, what will be the ultimate effect on the money supply if the required reserve ratio is 10 percent? (Assume that the oversimplified money-multiplier formula applies.)

7. Suppose the required reserve ratio and the public's currency/deposit ratio were 10 percent and 15 percent, respectively. Assume that banks hold no excess reserves. By how much would bank deposits increase if there were a new injection of $1 million cash into the system? Try to develop the appropriate revision in the money-multiplier formula that is relevant in this case.

12

Central Banking and Monetary Policy

Victorians heard with grave attention that the Bank Rate had been raised. They did not know what it meant. But they knew that it was an act of extreme wisdom.

J. K. GALBRAITH

F rom what we learned in Chapter 11 about the normal practices of profit-oriented banks, we might expect the money supply to expand rapidly during prosperous times and to grow sluggishly, or even to shrink, during recessions. Fortunately, the historical record for *postwar* Canada does not exhibit this pattern. Why not? One reason is that Canada's *central bank*, the Bank of Canada, has prevented it from happening.

The Bank of Canada is a very special kind of bank. Its customers are banks rather than individuals, and it performs some of the same services for them that your bank performs for you. Though it turns out to be quite an effective profit-maker, its actions are not guided by the profit motive. Instead, the Bank of Canada acts in what it perceives to be the national interest. Just how the Bank of Canada regulates the money supply and the international value of the Canadian dollar and why its performance has fallen short of perfection are the main subjects of this chapter.

The Bank of Canada

The Bank of Canada was officially created by the Bank of Canada Act of 1934. It was originally a privately owned bank with approximately 12,000 individual shareholders. In 1938, complete nationalization took place when the federal government bought all the shares. The Bank of Canada is now a Crown corporation, and all its profits accrue to the government.

Before the creation of the Bank of Canada, much of our currency was dollar bills, or notes, issued by the various chartered banks. In 1934, 53 percent of the currency was Dominion of Canada notes, while 47 percent was private bank liabilities. In 1950, all chartered bank notes were withdrawn from circulation.

One of the reasons for the creation of the Bank of Canada was to provide more stability for the economy. During the first four years of the Great Depression, the Canadian money supply fell by 12.5 percent. While no chartered banks failed, this contraction in the money supply accentuated the fall in aggregate demand that took place. Now the Bank of Canada tries to control Canada's money supply in an attempt to have the "appropriate" level of aggregate demand.

The Independence of the Bank of Canada

Canadians have had five governors of their central bank. According to the original act, the governor was appointed for seven years, and once appointed, he could not be removed by the government. This institutional independence of the governor was looked upon as a source of pride by some and as an anti-democratic embarrassment by others. (The issue of the degree of independence a central bank should have has also been an active topic of debate in the European countries, as described in the accompanying boxed insert.) The proponents of central bank independence argue that it enables monetary-policy decisions to be made on objective, technical criteria and keeps monetary control out of the "political thicket." Without this independence, it is argued, there would be a tendency for politicians to force the Bank of Canada to expand the money supply too rapidly, thereby contributing to chronic inflation and undermining faith in the financial system.

Opponents of this view counter that there is something profoundly undemocratic about having an unelected banker and his advisers make decisions that affect the well-being of all Canadians. Monetary policy, they argue, ought to be formulated by the elected representatives of the people, just like fiscal policy. Those who argue for government control over the Bank can point to historical instances in which monetary and fiscal policy have been at loggerheads—with the Bank of Canada undoing or even overwhelming the effects of fiscal-policy decisions.

This conflict did not occur under our first governor, Graham Towers, who headed the central bank from 1935 to 1954. However, the second governor, James Coyne (1955 to 1961), was the centre of a dramatic conflict with the Conservative government headed by John Diefenbaker. During the severe recession of the late 1950s, Diefenbaker's government used expansionary fiscal policy in an attempt to create jobs. Coyne was more concerned with avoiding inflation and a possible depreciation of the Canadian dollar. Thus, he put a tight limit on the growth of the money supply and operated a contractionary monetary policy. This counteracted the government's fiscal policy. After much wrangling, the government's constitutional advisers suggested that an act be passed declaring the governor's seat to be vacant. The government could not fire Mr. Coyne, but they could define his position out of existence. Although the Senate refused to pass this bill, Mr. Coyne felt that he had had his chance to have his reasoning officially recorded during the Senate hearings, and he resigned.

When our third governor, Louis Rasminsky (1961 to 1973), took office, he formally acknowledged that the government had the final power "to direct the Bank as to the policy which the Bank is to carry out." This principle was officially included in the 1967 revision of the Bank of Canada Act. As a result, our fourth governor, Gerald Bouey (1974 to 1987), and the fifth and current governor, John Crow (who was appointed in 1987), have had to take their basic instructions from the government. However, should Mr. Crow consider the government's dictates to be irresponsible monetary policy, he can resign and explain his reasons. Since this would be extremely embarrassing for the government, from a political point of view, the governor still has a significant degree of power. For example, throughout the 1980s, the governor consistently warned the government that the Bank of Canada would not print up new money to buy up large numbers of the government bonds being issued to cover the record budget deficits. Several recent annual reports of the Bank stress that the government must get better control of its deficit. Hence, the governor of the Bank is not a pawn of the government.

Controlling the Money Supply: Reserve Requirements

Chapter 11 taught us one important way in which the monetary authorities can control the money supply: by varying the minimum required reserve ratio. The lower the reserve ratio, the more the chartered banks can loan out, and therefore the more deposit money they can create. However, since the 1967 revision of the Bank Act, the main reserve ratio has been fixed by law, and so the reserve requirement is no longer an instrument of monetary control.[1]

[1] The Bank of Canada can still manipulate the level of *secondary* reserve requirements, which are what the chartered banks must hold in short-term bonds, excess cash, and day-to-day loans (as a proportion of their total deposits). But the Bank does not use secondary reserve requirements as an instrument of monetary policy.

Europe's Politicians Debate the Framework of a New Central Bank

The twelve governments within the European Community are moving toward economic and monetary union. If they have a single currency, they will need a new central Bank of Europe. But different member countries have voiced strong opinions on the way the Bank should be structured.

West Germany has been emphatic that the new Bank must be as politician-proof as its own Bundesbank. Britain, on the other hand, wants the Bank to be less independent, and to be accountable to the European Parliament. But since this Parliament will not have serious power until individual countries embrace much more complete *political* union (not just economic union), Britain's position really amounts to stalling on economic union. While it is tempting to favour the democratic approach, and not let the central banker be too independent, it is a fact that the countries with the most independent central banks have had the most envied inflation records.

Some analysts are predicting that the compromise option for Europe may rest in modelling the new Bank after that of the Netherlands. Normally the Dutch central bank conducts its policy independently, but the government can override its decisions. If the Bank objects to this intervention, the government can have its way only if it publishes the Bank's explanation of its policy along with the government's own reasons for ignoring this advice. It is presumed that this would lead to a vote of no confidence in the government and, as a result, such a deadlock has never materialized. While the Dutch system appears to grant a little more power to the central bank than does the Canadian system, the major

difference may simply be that the Dutch procedure has been spelled out more formally.

The reserve requirements that rule today are those that were set in the 1980 revision of the Bank Act. Chartered banks must hold at least the following amounts in their vaults or in their deposits at the Bank of Canada: 10 percent of their chequing deposit obligations; 2 percent of the first $500 million of savings and notice deposit obligations; 3 percent of the remaining savings and notice deposits; 3 percent of their foreign-currency deposit obligations.

The fact that there are several different reserve requirements means that the actual money-creation formula is more complicated than the one we derived in Chapter 11. The fact that the reserve requirement is less stringent on deposit accounts that formally require prior notice of withdrawals is an anachronism. The reserves are not required for public confidence, given the existing deposit insurance. Unfortunately, this anachronism has a cost, since it makes monetary control more difficult. Chartered banks can vary deposit interest rates and service charges for cheques to induce the public to change the proportion of the deposits it holds in chequing accounts. By doing so, the chartered banks (not the central bank) can control the overall reserve requirement ratio.

Controlling the Money Supply: Open-Market Operations

The Bank of Canada buys and sells in the nation's bond markets, and this is its main method of affecting chartered bank reserves. Since these operations involve the Bank

Open-market operations refer to the Bank of Canada's purchase or sale of government securities through transactions in the open bond market.

of Canada as simply one (sometimes large) participant in the bond markets that are open to anyone, they are called **open-market operations**. To appreciate the mechanics of this policy, we must consider the balance sheet of the central bank; this is presented in Table 12–1.

We see from Table 12–1 that the majority of the Bank of Canada's purchases are limited to one class of assets: Government of Canada bonds. The Bank purchases either newly printed bonds issued by the government to cover some of its current budget deficit, or existing government bonds previously held by members of the private sector. The latter operation, which is called an open-market purchase, allows the Bank to increase the money supply even if there is no current budget deficit, as we shall presently see. Unlike the chartered banks, the Bank of Canada returns all bond-interest earnings to the government.

The other major asset purchased by the Bank is foreign exchange. Some of these holdings are gold (since gold was the original international medium of exchange), and the rest are stocks of various major foreign currencies. Our discussion of the reasons for and the implications of the Bank's purchasing or selling foreign exchange is postponed until later in this chapter. What we emphasize now is simply the fact that exchange-rate policy is carried out by the Bank of Canada.[2]

Table 12–1 also shows that the bulk of the Bank of Canada's "liabilities" is the stock of currency that is used by chartered banks and the general public. We also see that the Bank of Canada serves as a bank for the chartered banks. A large part of the reserves held by the chartered banks to satisfy the reserve requirement laws are held in the form of chequing deposits at the Bank of Canada. The cheque-clearing process between any two chartered banks is accomplished by the banks' writing cheques (to each other) drawn against their own accounts at the Bank of Canada. The federal government also holds an account with the Bank of Canada, and, of course, it has deposit accounts at the various chartered banks as well. The government uses all of these accounts to store tax revenue as it comes in and to write cheques to make payments.

An open-market purchase of federal government bonds (previously held by the general public) by the Bank of Canada on January 2, 1991, is illustrated in Table 12–2.

The +$100,000 entry on the asset side of the Bank of Canada's balance sheet indicates its purchase of bonds from some members of the general public on the open market. The Bank of Canada pays for the bonds by cheque, and the bond dealer gives the cheques to the members of the public for whom he sold the bonds. The members of the public then deposit the cheques totalling $100,000 in their chartered banks, and this is recorded as the +$100,000 entry on the liability side of the chartered banks'

[2]The third asset, advances, is explained on page 252.

TABLE 12–1
The Consolidated Balance Sheet of the Bank of Canada and the Exchange Fund Account, January 1990

ASSETS (billions of dollars)		LIABILITIES (billions of dollars)	
Government of Canada bonds	21.25	Notes in circulation (currency)	19.62
		Deposits:	
Gold and foreign-currency reserves	15.65	of chartered banks	2.35
		of federal government	0.01
Advances	0.55	Miscellaneous accounts and net worth	15.47

SOURCE: Bank of Canada *Review*.

TABLE 12–2
Changes in the Balance Sheets of the Bank of Canada and the Chartered Banks Following an Open-Market Purchase of Bonds

CHANGES IN BALANCE SHEET OF BANK OF CANADA, JANUARY 2, 1991

ASSETS		LIABILITIES	
Government bonds	+$100,000	Currency outstanding	
Foreign exchange		Deposits:	
		of federal government	
Advances to chartered banks		of chartered banks	+$100,000

CHANGES IN BALANCE SHEET OF CHARTERED BANKS, JANUARY 2, 1991

ASSETS		LIABILITIES	
Reserves:		Deposits:	
vault cash		of general public	+$100,000
deposits at the Bank of Canada	+$100,000	of federal government	
Loans		Advances from Bank of Canada	
Addendum: Changes in Reserves			
Actual reserves	+$100,000		
Required reserves	+ $20,000		
Excess reserves	+ $80,000		

A multiple expansion of loans and deposits begins as the chartered banks get rid of their excess reserves by making new loans totalling $80,000.

balance sheet. The other entries on the balance sheets indicate the cheque-clearing process. The chartered banks send the cheques back to the Bank of Canada, and the central bank pays the chartered banks by simply granting them an increase of $100,000 in their deposits at the Bank of Canada. This cheque-clearing operation requires two entries on the balance sheet, since the chartered banks' deposits are both their own asset *and* the Bank of Canada's liability.

The net result of this transaction is that the chartered banks' reserves increase by the same amount as do their deposits. Given the low reserve requirements, most of this increase is excess reserves; so the chartered banking system is now in a position to commence the process of multiple expansion in loans and deposits that we described in Chapter 11. For example, if we continue to assume a reserve requirement ratio of 0.2 for our illustration, the open-market purchase of bonds by the Bank of Canada eventually results in an increase of the public's deposits in chartered banks equal to $500,000. We need not repeat the details of that multiple expansion process. Our purpose here is only to explain how the Bank of Canada actually creates the initial increase in reserves that starts the expansion of the money supply. By a similar process, an open-market sale of government bonds by the Bank of Canada would involve minus signs on the four entries in Table 12–2 and so lead to a multiple contraction of chartered bank loans and deposits.

Open-market operations constitute the major tool of monetary policy by which the Bank of Canada varies the rate of growth of the money supply.

The Bank of Canada buys bonds whenever it wants to increase the money supply, and sells bonds whenever it wants to decrease the money supply.

To anticipate our discussion of exchange-rate policy in later sections of this chapter, we emphasize one important point now: *It does not matter what type of asset the Bank of*

Canada buys or sells; the effect on the money supply is the same. Thus, as we shall see, Bank of Canada purchases of foreign exchange constitute an expansionary monetary policy, and Bank of Canada sales of foreign-exchange reserves constitute a contractionary monetary policy.

Controlling the Money Supply: Changes in the Bank Rate

The **bank rate** is the rate of interest charged by the Bank of Canada when reserves are loaned to the chartered banks (advances from the central bank). It is used as a signal of the direction of monetary policy.

If the chartered banks ever become over-extended in loan operations and do not have the reserves required by the Bank Act, they can borrow the reserves from the Bank of Canada. The rate of interest charged by the Bank of Canada for these advances is called the **bank rate**. Since the chartered banks rarely require an advance from the central bank, the bank rate is usually employed only as a summary signal, so that the private sector is aware of the behind-the-scenes operations of the Bank. For example, if the Bank has been selling government bonds and intends to continue this action, it raises the bank rate. This represents an easily understood signal that the Bank is trying to reduce the money supply and tighten credit. Thus, changes in the bank rate merely reflect the stance of monetary policy as defined by the more basic tool of open-market operations.

Many people misunderstand the role of bank-rate announcements, since these changes are often *followed by* adjustments in the prime lending rates charged by chartered banks. Given this observed sequence of events, it appears that the bank rate is the fundamental causal influence. In fact, the Bank of Canada's contraction of reserves (due to open-market bond sales) is the real cause of loans becoming scarce and chartered bank loan rates increasing. However, the chartered banks can achieve a gain in public relations by waiting for the central bank to raise the bank rate before increasing their loan rates. Then they can talk about having to "pass on cost increases" to their customers.

Before 1979, the bank rate was changed by the Bank of Canada on a relatively infrequent basis. In the autumn of 1979, however, the true role of the bank rate became more transparent as the Bank of Canada adopted a policy of adjusting it on a weekly basis. Every week the federal government auctions its new issue of treasury bills, a type of bond that it uses to obtain operating funds. The yield on the treasury bills is determined in a free market by supply and demand. The bank rate is now set every week at one-quarter of one percentage point above that week's treasury bill yield. This arrangement made explicit what had been true for years: The bank rate is set to be *consistent with* going market interest rates; it *does not determine* market interest rates. Monetary policy has its fundamental effects on market interest rates by affecting the quantity of bonds and reserves that are available to the private sector through open-market operations.

Controlling the Money Supply: Other Instruments

The Bank of Canada has two other means by which it can influence the money supply; these are referred to as deposit-switching and moral suasion.

Deposit-switching means moving government funds from the central bank to a chartered bank (or vice versa). It works on the money supply in much the same way as do open-market operations. To see this, we consider what happens when the federal government switches some of its deposit holdings from the Bank of Canada to one of its deposit accounts in a chartered bank. The government starts the process by writing a cheque to itself (actually, this manipulation is done for the government by the Bank of Canada) and gives the cheque to the chartered bank. When the bank credits the government's deposit account there, it sends the cheque back to the Bank of Canada (in the cheque-clearing process) so that the chartered bank can be reimbursed for honouring the cheque. The chartered bank receives credit in the form of increased deposits at the Bank of Canada. But just as in the case of an open-market purchase of bonds by the central bank, the chartered bank now has excess reserves, and a multiple expansion of loans and deposits can commence. The Bank of Canada uses deposit-switching to regulate the money supply over short-term time intervals.[3]

Moral suasion refers to informal pressure that the governor of the Bank of Canada can bring to bear on the chartered banks. Since the governor can easily contact the key people at the major banks, he can directly explain to them what actions he will take if the chartered banks do not follow some specified recommendation (such as slowing the rate of growth in loans to the public).

Now that we have completed our discussion of the technical means the Bank can use to regulate the money supply, we must explain why Canada has to have a flexible exchange rate if these tools are to have the desired effect on the money supply.

Flexible Exchange Rates: A Prerequisite for Independent Control of the Money Supply

The Bank of Canada often intervenes in the foreign-exchange market on a daily basis, in order to control the value of the Canadian dollar. Since this intervention involves either buying or selling foreign exchange, the quantity of central bank liabilities outstanding becomes residually determined. This means that the more the Bank tries to fix a particular price for the Canadian dollar (the exchange rate), the more it loses the ability to fix the nation's money supply at any particular value. Thus, exchange-rate policy and monetary policy are one and the same. Because of this connection, we will now provide a more thorough explanation of exchange rates and how they can be fixed by the central bank. We will explain the distinction between a policy of fixed exchange rates and one of floating exchange rates, then discuss how the choice of policy affects the ability of the Bank of Canada to control the nation's money supply.

If international trade is to take place, there must be a way to transform one currency (say, yen) into another (in our case, dollars). The rates at which such transformations are made are called **exchange rates**. There is an exchange rate between every pair of currencies. For example, $1 Canadian is currently (May 1990) the equivalent of about 5 French francs. The exchange rate between the franc and the dollar, then, may be expressed as "5 francs to the dollar" (meaning that it costs 5 francs to buy a dollar) or about "20 cents to the franc" (meaning that it costs 20 cents to buy a franc).

Under our present system, currency rates change frequently. When another currency gets more expensive in terms of dollars, we say that it has **appreciated** relative to the dollar. Alternatively, we can look at this same event in terms of the dollar buying less foreign currency, meaning that the dollar has **depreciated** relative to another currency.

What is a depreciation to one country must be an appreciation to the other.[4]

In Chapter 15, we will examine some of the more dramatic appreciations and depreciations in the world's major currencies, and explain the principal factors behind such realignments.

The **exchange rate** states the price, in terms of one currency, at which another currency can be bought.

A nation's currency is said to **appreciate** when exchange rates change so that a unit of its own currency can buy more units of foreign currency. The currency is said to **depreciate** when exchange rates change so that a unit of its currency can buy fewer units of foreign currency.

[3]EXERCISE: Construct a table like Table 12–2 summarizing the effects of deposit-switching.

[4]While depreciation and appreciation are the terms used to describe movements of exchange rates in free markets, another set of terms is used to describe decreases and increases in currency values when these values are set by government decree. When an officially set exchange rate is altered so that a unit of a nation's currency can buy *fewer* units of foreign currency, we say there has been a *devaluation* of that currency. When the exchange rate is altered so that the currency can buy *more* units of foreign currency, we say there has been a *revaluation*.

Exchange-Rate Determination in a Free Market

Floating exchange rates, also known as **flexible exchange rates**, are rates determined in free markets by the law of supply and demand.

Floating exchange rates (also called **flexible exchange rates**) are exchange rates determined entirely by the forces of supply and demand (with no government interference), just like the prices of apples, or typewriters, or haircuts.

To analyze the process of exchange-rate determination in a simplified context, imagine that Canada and the United States are the only two countries on earth, so there is only one exchange rate to be determined. Figure 12–1 depicts the determination of this exchange rate at the point (denoted E in the figure) where demand curve DD crosses supply curve SS. At this price ($1.18 Canadian per U.S. dollar), we know that the number of U.S. dollars demanded is equal to the number of U.S. dollars supplied.

In a free market, exchange rates are determined by the law of supply and demand. If the rate were below the equilibrium level, the quantity of foreign exchange demanded would exceed the quantity of foreign exchange supplied, and the price of foreign exchange would be bid up. If the rate were above the equilibrium level, quantity supplied would exceed quantity demanded, and the price of foreign exchange would fall. Only at the equilibrium exchange rate is there no tendency for the exchange rate to change.

As usual, supply and demand determine price. What we must ask in this case is: Where do the supply and demand come from? Why does anyone demand a U.S. dollar?

From the Canadian point of view, the demanders of U.S. dollars are Canadian importers of goods and Canadian buyers of foreign financial assets. Suppliers of U.S. dollars to the foreign-exchange trading market are Canadian exporters and foreign purchasers of Canadian financial assets. As you read the following explanation, pretend that you are an exporter or an importer: this will help you make the discussion more concrete, and allow you to see why the slopes of the curves drawn in Figure 12–1 are appropriate.

If the U.S. dollar rises in value, the sales revenue earned by Canadian exporters is worth more in terms of Canadian dollars. Exporters' costs, on the other hand, are denominated in Canadian dollars and so are not increased. The resulting increase in profitability stimulates more export activity, and the final outcome is that more foreign exchange is earned. Exporters must supply this foreign exchange to the trading market in order to turn it into Canadian dollars (to pay their domestic costs). Since more foreign exchange is brought to the market when the foreign currency has

FIGURE 12–1
Determination of Exchange Rates in a Free Market
In a free market, an exchange rate, like any price, will be determined by the intersection of the demand and supply curves. Point E depicts this point for the exchange rate between the Canadian dollar and the U.S. dollar, which settles at $1.18 Canadian per U.S. dollar. Newspapers often quote the inverse of this number as the exchange rate; that is, they say that it takes 85 cents (U.S.) to buy one Canadian dollar.

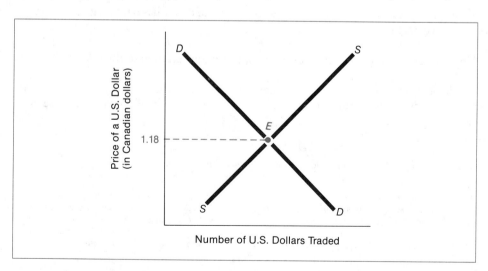

increased in value, we show the supply curve of U.S. dollars with a positive slope. Conversely, from the point of view of importers, it becomes necessary to economize on purchases from the United States when the U.S. dollar becomes more expensive; in other words, demand for foreign exchange falls. This is why the demand-for-foreign-exchange curve has a negative slope.

An important point to note is that the position of both the demand and the supply curves for foreign exchange depends on the trade in financial assets across borders, not just on the trade in goods and services. For example, if something happens to make Canadian bonds more appealing to foreigners (like an increase in Canadian interest rates or an expected appreciation in the value of the Canadian dollar), both demand and supply curves for foreign exchange shift positions. To acquire our bonds, foreigners must offer to exchange their currency for ours (to obtain what they need for payment in our bond market). Similarly, Canadians' demand for foreign exchange decreases when Canadian-issued securities become more appealing. These reactions mean that the demand for U.S. dollars shifts to the left, and the supply of U.S. dollars shifts to the right, resulting in a falling value for the U.S. dollar (and therefore a rising value for the Canadian dollar). We discuss the importance of these sorts of shifts in the next section, and in several later chapters.

Fixed Exchange Rates

Some exchange rates today are truly floating, determined by the forces of supply and demand without government interference, in the manner we have just described. But many are not. For this reason, we turn our attention next to the opposite of floating exchange rates, a system of **fixed exchange rates**, or rates that are set by governments. Under such a system the exchange rate, being fixed, is not closely watched. Instead, international financial specialists focus on a country's *balance of payments*—a term we can now define.

To understand what the balance of payments is, look at Figure 12–2 on page 256, which depicts the Canadian situation in 1989. More foreign exchange was entering Canada than was demanded by private participants in this trading market. Since the Bank of Canada wanted to limit any appreciation of the Canadian dollar, it bought up the otherwise unwanted incoming supply of foreign exchange (equal to distance *AB* in Figure 12–2). This increase in the official holdings of foreign-exchange reserves is called the **balance of payments surplus**. All that is physically needed to accumulate these foreign-exchange reserves is a quantity of Canadian dollars with which to trade. Since the Bank of Canada prints these, there is technically no limit to the size of the balance of payments surplus that we can maintain. Nevertheless, if we print up domestic currency very rapidly, the growth in the nation's money supply will outstrip our ability to produce goods, and inflation will result. Ultimately, then, the limit imposed on running a balance of payments surplus indefinitely comes from our reluctance to incur the resulting inflation.

The opposite kind of payment imbalance is a **balance of payments deficit**, which is illustrated in Figure 12–3. At the artificially low price for foreign exchange being maintained in this example, domestic residents are demanding more U.S. dollars (to pay for imports) than they are earning through export sales to the United States. This excess demand for foreign exchange is the balance of payments deficit, represented by distance *AB* in Figure 12–3. When a country runs a deficit, it is depleting its official holdings of foreign-exchange reserves by the amount of the private excess demand each period (for example, each year). The country must pay for "living beyond its means" in this way by drawing down its accumulated reserves. The Bank of Canada can maintain the particular exchange rate as long as it has enough reserves to keep selling off amount *AB* each period—the amount that is not voluntarily forthcoming from private traders. When the Bank of Canada's supply is included, the overall supply and demand are equal at the going exchange rate.

Fixed exchange rates are rates that are set by government decisions and maintained by central bank actions.

The **balance of payments surplus** is the amount by which the quantity supplied of foreign exchange (per year) exceeds the quantity demanded. Balance of payments surpluses arise whenever the value of foreign exchange is pegged at an artificially high level —that is to say, when the value of the *domestic* currency is pegged at an artificially low level.

The **balance of payments deficit** is the amount by which the quantity supplied of foreign exchange (per year) falls short of the quantity demanded. Balance of payments deficits arise whenever the value of foreign exchange is pegged at an artificially low level— that is to say, when the value of the *domestic* currency is pegged at an artificially high level.

FIGURE 12-2

A Balance of Payments Surplus

When more foreign exchange comes into a country than is used, the central bank must buy up the excess (distance *AB*) to keep the value of foreign exchange from being bid down.

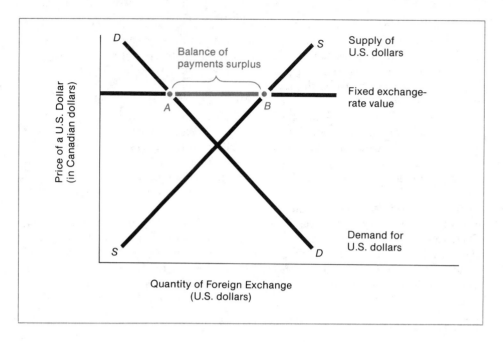

FIGURE 12-3

A Balance of Payments Deficit

When less foreign exchange is earned than the amount a country's citizens are spending, the central bank must supply the extra foreign currency (distance *AB*) to make the excess foreign-currency purchases possible and to keep the value of the *domestic* currency from being bid down.

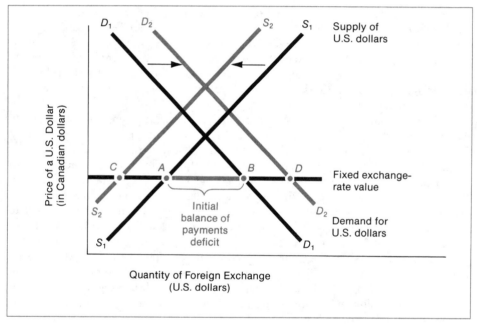

Generally speaking, then, the Bank of Canada can fix the exchange rate by maintaining large amounts of both Canadian dollars and foreign exchange. The Bank simply has to stand ready to be a major buyer or seller of foreign exchange.

The Bank of Canada buys U.S. dollars whenever the U.S. dollar starts to slip in value just a bit, and it sells U.S. dollars whenever that currency starts to rise a bit in value. If the Bank makes purchases or sales that are big enough, it can essentially prevent the price of foreign exchange from changing at all.

But things are never perfectly symmetrical: We could run a balance of payments surplus forever, since there is no physical limit on the amount of *domestic* currency that the Bank of Canada can print (in order to buy up the otherwise unwanted incoming foreign exchange). But we simply cannot run a balance of payments deficit indefinitely, since we will run out of *foreign-exchange* reserves. When this happens, the Bank has nothing more to trade with, and must back out of the market. Private currency speculators can predict this development because data on the size of the reserve holdings and on the balance of payments deficit (which shows the speed with which the reserves are running out) are published regularly. Once speculators become convinced that the domestic currency will fall in value (which has to occur when the central bank stops supporting it), they will want to take advantage of the almost certain change in the exchange rate. Intent on avoiding capital losses, they will sell off all their assets that are denominated in the currency that is about to devalue. So foreigners dramatically decrease their supply of U.S. dollars to the Canadian foreign-exchange market pictured in Figure 12–3, and Canadians increase their demand for U.S. dollars in a big way, since they too want to avoid the expected capital losses. Thus, the demand and supply curves move to the positions marked in green in Figure 12–3, and the balance of payments deficit shoots up from *AB* to amount *CD*. The very fear of the devaluation essentially guarantees that it will occur, since with the much larger payments deficit, the foreign-exchange reserves that are needed to peg the exchange rate will be depleted that much sooner.

Sometimes different countries' central banks make loans of reserves to one another through the International Monetary Fund (IMF), so that an individual central bank can outlast the speculators. But if the IMF thinks that the borrowing country is trying to peg an inordinately high value for its currency (which must be the case if there was a noticeable payments deficit in the first place), it will normally refuse to make the loan.

This discussion has made clear a weakness of the system of fixed exchange rates. In principle, imbalances in exchange rates could be cured either by a devaluation by the country with a balance of payments deficit or by an upward revaluation by the country with a balance of payments surplus. In practice, though, it is almost always the deficit countries that are forced to act.

Why do the surplus countries refuse to revalue? One reason is a stubborn refusal to recognize some basic economic realities. They view the disequilibrium as the problem of the deficit countries and believe that the deficit countries, therefore, should take the corrective steps. This, of course, is nonsense. Some currencies are overvalued *because* some other currencies are undervalued. In fact, the two statements mean exactly the same thing.

The other reason exporters in Germany, Japan, and other surplus countries resist upward revaluations of their currencies is that such action would make their products more expensive to foreigners and thus cut into their export sales. And these exporters have the political clout to make their views stick. Meanwhile, because the values of the mark and the yen on world markets are artificially held down, German and Japanese consumers are put in the unenviable position of having to pay more for imported goods. Rather than buy these excessively expensive foreign goods, they watch domestically produced goods go overseas in return for pieces of paper (dollars, francs, pounds, and so on).

A more thorough investigation of the reasons that countries try to fix their exchange rates takes place in Chapter 15. Here we simply stress that fixing the exchange rate necessarily involves the country's central bank in either buying up or selling off foreign exchange. Thus, pegging the exchange rate involves the Bank of Canada's performing an open-market operation in the foreign-exchange market rather than in the domestic bond market. The implications for the money supply are the same. This can be appreciated by simply moving the +$100,000 entry on the asset side of the Bank of Canada balance sheet in Table 12–2: The effect on chartered bank reserves is the same whether this entry is on the government-bond line or on the foreign-exchange line. But there is one important difference. In the case of an open-market operation in the domestic bond market, it is the central bank that determines the amount by which chartered bank reserves are changed. In the case of pegging the exchange rate, however, it is the private participants in the foreign-exchange market who determine this amount, *not* the central bank. In this case, the growth in bank reserves is determined by the gap between the private demand and supply curves for foreign exchange. This trade-off can be summarized as follows:

The Bank of Canada can control *either* our exchange rate *or* our money supply but *not* both.

The Money-Supply Mechanism: A Summary

This completes our discussion of the Bank of Canada's methods of controlling the money supply. We can now begin to integrate what we have just learned about the financial system into the macroeconomic model presented in Chapters 6 through 9, and to study how money affects the national economy. For this purpose, the analyses of the last chapter and the present one can be summed up in the following statement:

As interest rates rise, banks normally find it more profitable to expand their volume of loans and deposits, thus increasing the supply of money. However, the Bank of Canada can shift the relationship between the money supply and interest rates by employing its principal weapon of monetary control: open-market operations.

These ideas are depicted graphically in Figure 12–4. Part (a) shows a typical money-supply schedule labelled *MS*, illustrating that bank behaviour makes the money stock rise as interest rates rise.[5] Notice that the sensitivity of the money supply to interest rates is rather weak in the diagram—a large rise in the rate of interest (from 7 percent to 9 percent) induces only a small increase in the supply of money (from $54 billion to $55 billion). The drawing is deliberately constructed that way because that is what the statistical evidence shows.

[5] There are many interest rates in the economy. However, they all tend to move up and down together. Hence, for present purposes, we can speak of "the" rate of interest.

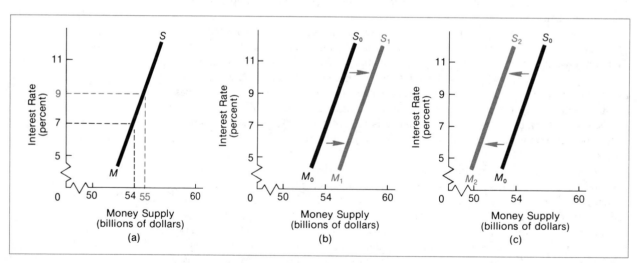

FIGURE 12–4
The Supply Schedule for Money
Part (a) shows a typical supply schedule for money. It is rising as we move toward the right, meaning that banks will supply more money when interest rates are higher. Part (b) illustrates what happens to the money-supply schedule when the Bank of Canada purchases securities in the open market. With this expansionary policy, the supply schedule shifts outward. Part (c) depicts the effect of a sale of bonds by the Bank of Canada. With this contractionary policy, the supply schedule shifts inward.

The curve in Figure 12–4(a) shows the money-supply schedule corresponding to some specific monetary policy. Figure 12–4(b) portrays how the money-supply schedule responds to an *expansionary change in monetary policy*, such as an open-market purchase of government bonds. The money-supply schedule shifts outward from M_0S_0 to M_1S_1, as indicated by the arrows. After banks have adjusted to the change, there is more money at any given interest rate. Figure 12–4(c) shows what happens in the reverse case—*contractionary monetary policy*, such as an open-market sale of securities. The money-supply schedule shifts inward from M_0S_0 to M_2S_2.

The diagrams make things look rather more precise than they actually are. Since the Bank of Canada's control over the money-supply schedule is imperfect in the short run, the actual *MS* schedule is obscured by a bit of fog. In what follows, we portray all the graphs as clean straight lines only for pedagogical simplicity. The Bank of Canada wishes things were so simple in the real world!

The Demand for Money

Just as we must know something about both the supply of and the demand for wheat before we can predict how much will be sold and at what price, it is necessary to know something about the **demand for money** if we are to understand the amount of money actually in existence and the prevailing interest rate.

The definition of money given in Chapter 11 suggests the most important reason that people hold money balances: The medium of exchange is needed to carry out purchases and sales of goods and services. Since the *nominal* gross domestic product (GDP) is considered to be the best measure of the total *money* value of all goods and services traded in the economy, it seems safe to assume that the higher the nominal GDP, the higher will be the demand for money. And, indeed, an impressive amount of statistical evidence supports this supposition. Notice that nominal GDP and hence the demand for money rise if *either* real output or the price level rises—a fact that will assume some importance in the next chapter.

But the nominal value of output is not the only factor affecting the demand for money; interest rates matter, too. At first, that may seem surprising because some forms of money, such as currency and some chequing deposits, pay no interest. Why, then, are interest rates relevant? They are relevant because money is only one of a variety of forms in which individuals can hold their wealth. Holders of money *give up* the opportunity to hold one of these other assets, such as government bonds, in order to gain the convenience of money. In so doing, they *give up* the interest that they could have earned on one of these alternative assets.

This is another example of the concept of *opportunity cost*.[6] On the surface, it seems virtually costless to hold money. But, *compared with the best alternative*, this action is not costless at all. For example, if the best alternative to holding $100 in cash is to put those funds into a government bond that pays 9 percent interest, then the opportunity cost of holding that money is $9 per year (9 percent of $100).

How, then, should the rate of interest influence the quantity of money that people demand? It is natural to assume that when interest rates are high people will make strenuous efforts to economize on their holdings of money balances, efforts that would not be worthwhile at lower interest rates. In a word, rational behaviour of consumers and business firms should make the demand to hold money *decline* as the interest rate *rises*. And once again, careful analysis of the data shows this to be true. To summarize:

People and business firms hold money primarily to finance their transactions. Therefore, the quantity of money demanded increases as real output rises or as prices rise. However, the quantity of money demanded decreases as the rate of interest rises because the rate of interest is the opportunity cost of holding money balances.

[6]If you need to review this concept, see Chapter 2.

FIGURE 12-5
The Demand Schedule for Money

The downward-sloping curve *MD* is a typical demand schedule for money. It slopes down because money is a less-attractive asset when interest rates on alternative assets are higher. The entire curve is shifted if either the number of transactions (which is often measured by real GDP) or the average price of a transaction (which is measured by the price level) changes. Thus, the curve shifts to the right if nominal GDP rises and to the left if nominal GDP falls.

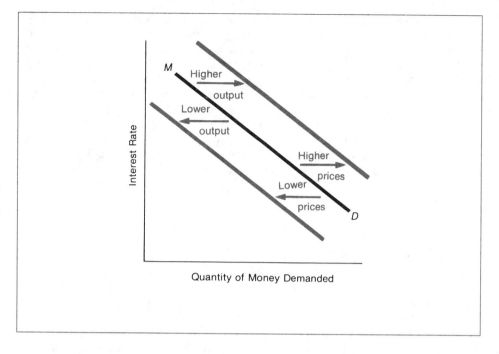

It is possible to portray the demand for money by a graphical device, as shown in Figure 12-5. There we show a downward-sloping demand schedule for money (the curve labelled *MD*)—the quantity of money demanded decreases as the rate of interest rises. But since the quantity of money demanded also depends on real output and the price level, we must hold both real output and the price level constant in drawing up such a curve. Changes in either of these variables will shift the *MD* curve in the manner indicated in the diagram because at higher levels of nominal GDP, demand for money is higher; and at lower levels of nominal GDP, it is lower (no matter what the level of interest rates).

Equilibrium in the Money Market When Foreign and Domestic Financial Markets Are Independent

As is usual in supply and demand analysis, it is useful to put both sides of the market together on a single graph. Figure 12-6 combines the money-supply schedule of Figure 12-4(a) (the curve labelled *MS*) with the money-demand schedule of Figure 12-5 (the curve labelled *MD*).

There is no curve representing foreigners' actions in this market, since, for the moment, we are assuming that funds cannot flow across international borders, so that interest rates in Canada are entirely independent of, and able to diverge from, the level of U.S. interest rates. Point *E* is the equilibrium of the money market. The diagram thus shows that *given* real output and the price level (which locates the *MD* curve) and *given* the monetary policy (which locates the *MS* curve), the money market is in equilibrium at an interest rate of 9 percent and a money stock of $55 billion.

We can see why 9 percent is the equilibrium interest rate by considering other values. At any interest rate above 9 percent, the quantity of money supplied would exceed the quantity demanded, and the interest rate (the price for renting money) would therefore decline. At any interest rate below 9 percent, more money would be demanded than supplied, so the interest rate would rise to eliminate the scarcity.

Since the interest rate to which we have been referring is the yield on non-monetary assets such as bonds, it might be instructive to consider the market equilibration process through a direct focus on the bond market as well. As we learned in

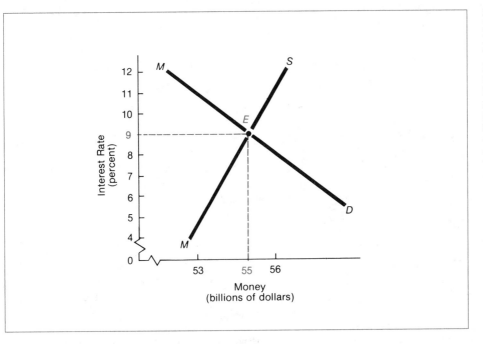

FIGURE 12–6
Equilibrium in the Money Market with Foreign Transactions Omitted
Equilibrium in the market for money is determined by the intersection of demand curve *MD* and supply curve *MS*. At point *E*, the interest rate is 9 percent, and the money supply is $55 billion. At no other interest rate would the demand for and the supply of money be in balance.

Chapter 10, a bond is a contract in which the seller promises to pay the buyer a fixed sum of money each year for a specified number of years, and then to pay back the principal value. For example, if the stated yield (the "coupon rate," which is printed on the bond along with the fixed maturity value) is 9 percent, and the bond is purchased at "par" value (the same value it will have at maturity) of $100, then the actual yield and the coupon rate coincide at 9 percent. But if new bonds paying 10 percent become available, no one will want to own the bonds that were already in existence. As people attempt to sell the old bonds in order to buy the new ones, the price of the old bonds will fall by an amount that allows the new purchaser to get a 10 percent yield—the 9 percent coupon payment, plus a capital gain. The new purchaser gets a capital gain because he buys the bond at less than $100, but sells it at maturity at full price. This illustrates one of the principles we learned in Chapter 10—that competition forces the prices of existing bonds to vary inversely with the prevailing level of bond yields in the market.

Now we can apply this reasoning to Figure 12–6. As noted earlier, at any rate of interest *above* 9 percent, there is an excess supply of money. This is just a formal way of saying that, when interest rates are high, people find that they are holding more of their wealth in the form of money than they would like or, conversely, that they hold too little of it in higher-interest-earning forms (for the sake of our discussion, in bonds). "Too much money" in one's financial portfolio is just another way of saying "not enough bonds" (or other non-monetary forms of holding wealth). To fix this imbalance, people will use their money to buy bonds from one another. In the process, the price of bonds is bid up, and their effective yield is thereby reduced. In other words, returning to Figure 12–6, the interest rate begins to fall toward the equilibrium point.

Monetary Policy

Since the central bank can shift the position of the money-supply curve, it can alter the equilibrium point in domestic money markets through its **monetary policy**. Expansionary monetary-policy actions involve purchasing government securities in the open market. This action provides additional excess reserves to the banking system, thus encouraging banks to increase their loans and deposits. As money becomes more plentiful, interest rates drop.

Monetary policy refers to actions that the Bank of Canada takes in order to change the equilibrium of the money market—that is, to alter either the money supply or the exchange rate.

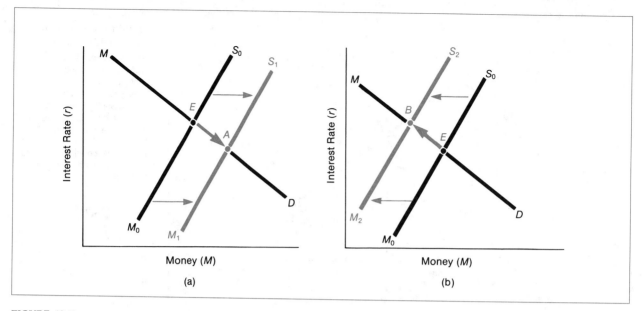

FIGURE 12-7

The Effects of Monetary Policy on the Money Market

The two parts of this figure show the effects of monetary policy on the money supply (M) and the rate of interest (r). In part (a), expansionary monetary policies shift the supply schedule from M_0S_0 to M_1S_1 and push the equilibrium from point E to point A; M rises as r falls. In part (b), contractionary policies pull the supply schedule from M_0S_0 to M_2S_2, causing equilibrium to move from point E to point B; M falls as r rises.

Our supply–demand analysis of the money market shows this in Figure 12–7(a). By shifting the money-supply schedule outward from M_0S_0 to M_1S_1, the central bank moves the market equilibrium from point E to point A—thus forcing the interest rate down. Contractionary monetary-policy actions, such as selling securities in the open market, have the opposite effect. They push interest rates up, as Figure 12–7(b) shows. In summary, we can say:

Monetary policies that expand the money supply normally lower interest rates. Monetary policies that reduce the money supply normally raise interest rates.

During the early 1980s the U.S. central bank rigidly restricted the growth of the U.S. money supply to fight inflation. The theory was that the resulting high interest rates would discourage investment spending and so decrease aggregate demand. Those high interest rates caused much concern in Canada and other Western countries.

Equilibrium in the Money Market When Foreign and Domestic Financial Markets Are Integrated

In the previous section, we discussed the determination of the level of interest rates without any reference to the level of foreign interest rates. While this analysis is useful for a country like the United States, it is unrealistic for Canada. Since it is so easy for Americans to buy Canadian bonds and vice versa and since Canadian bonds constitute a small proportion of the North American financial market, the North American interest rate is essentially determined by U.S. monetary policy in the manner we have just described. Competition among sellers of bonds precludes a different rate of interest from being "made in Canada."

Figure 12-8, which reproduces the demand and supply curves from Figure 12-6, shows how this works. Assume that the value of the U.S. interest rate has just risen from 9 to 11 percent. Equilibrium in the Canadian market cannot remain at point E,

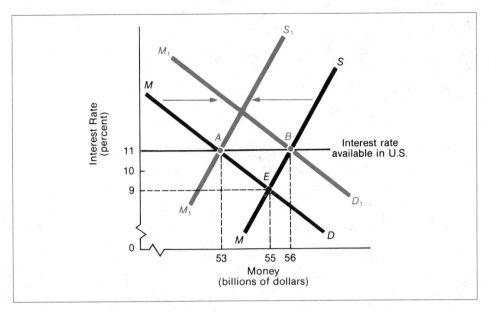

FIGURE 12–8
Equilibrium in the Money Market When the Availability of Foreign Bonds
Pegs the Rate of Interest
Under fixed exchange rates, the Bank of Canada must accept the otherwise unwanted Canadian currency (given by distance AB). This decreases the amount of money in circulation so MS shifts left and equilibrium obtains at point A. Under flexible exchange rates, the Canadian dollar depreciates (because of the excess supply, AB). This raises import costs and stimulates exports. The resulting increase in nominal GDP shifts MD to the right and equilibrium obtains at point B.

since that outcome involves Canadians earning only 9 percent on their bonds, while 11 percent is available through buying U.S. bonds. Thus, households and firms will choose to be at point A on their demand-for-money curve. Given this choice by demanders, and given the interest rate of 11 percent, there is an excess supply of domestic money equal to the distance AB in Figure 12–8 ($3 billion in our example).

How is this disequilibrium resolved? There are two possible methods of resolution, depending on whether the country has adopted a fixed or a flexible exchange-rate policy.

Fixed Exchange Rates

Under a fixed exchange-rate regime, the Bank of Canada must intervene in the money market to support the exchange rate. In our example, there is excess supply of Canadian dollars, equal to $3 billion and shown by distance AB in Figure 12–8. The mirror image of this excess supply of Canadian dollars is the equivalent excess demand for U.S. dollars, which savers need to buy the desired U.S. bonds. Since the U.S. dollar is in demand while the Canadian dollar is not, a fall in the value of the Canadian dollar will occur unless the Bank intervenes. To avoid the fall in the value of the Canadian dollar, the Bank of Canada must buy up the otherwise unwanted 3 billion Canadian dollars by selling the corresponding amount of U.S. dollars from the country's foreign-exchange reserves. As a result of this foreign-exchange operation, there will be less Canadian money circulating than before (by amount AB). So the money-supply curve will be shifted to the left by this distance (to position $M_1 S_1$), and the supply and demand curves will intersect the interest-rate line at point A. Thus, a complete equilibrium can be obtained under fixed exchange rates, but only with an adjustment that amounts to a contractionary monetary policy—an open-market sale of foreign exchange.

Bank of Canada Policy

The following excerpts illustrate how directly the Bank of Canada relies on the economic analysis that we have covered in this chapter. The first two date from Gerald Bouey's time as governor of the Bank. The third and fourth are from John Crow, the current governor.

1984

OTTAWA—Bank of Canada Governor Gerald Bouey says he cannot ease up on high interest rates at the expense of the Canadian dollar because this would risk further inflation. . . .

In the Bank of Canada's annual report . . . Mr. Bouey said that he will do everything within reason to fight rising prices—including resisting "sharp downward movements" in the value of the Canadian dollar.

The Bank of Canada allowed interest rates to rise on Thursday, in order to attract liquid capital into Canada and thus keep the value of the dollar up. . . .

. . . At a press conference in which he released the annual report, Mr. Bouey told reporters that the central bank had little choice except to let interest rates go up. . . .

In his report, the central bank chief warned that it would be folly for the Government to deliberately try to devalue the currency in order to lower interest rates and create jobs. Such a move could only weaken private sector confidence in the Government's determination to bring down inflation.

If that were to happen, he said, interest rates might dip for a short period but then they would rise again. . . .

Mr. Bouey said interest rates in Canada can come down significantly only if the United States lowers its federal deficit. This, by alleviating fears of inflation among Wall Street financiers, would let U.S. interest rates, and thus Canadian rates, come down.

He said that while he supports the idea of reducing the Canadian deficit, such a reduction would lower interest rates only minimally. Canadian interest rates, he said, are in large measure set in the U.S.

SOURCE: *The Globe and Mail*, Toronto, March 17, 1984, page 1.

1986

The Canadian dollar rebounded strongly to 70.42 U.S. cents on currency exchanges yesterday as the Bank of Canada fired every monetary weapon in its arsenal, sending speculators scrambling for cover.

In what was the most vigorous defence of the dollar in some time, the central bank moved aggressively into financial markets to buy Canadian dollars. . . .

The federal Government also said it had concluded an

A policy of fixed exchange rates involves giving up the ability to conduct an independent monetary policy. Under fixed exchange rates, the private agents involved in the foreign-exchange market dictate what open-market operation the Bank of Canada must conduct to peg the exchange rate. Both the magnitude and the direction of this open-market operation are determined for the central bank.

Flexible Exchange Rates

How is full equilibrium achieved under a flexible-rate policy? Without intervention by the Bank of Canada, the attempt by private agents to trade away Canadian for U.S. dollars means that the Canadian dollar will depreciate in value. This makes our imports more expensive and so raises our price level. It also makes our exports cheaper for foreigners to buy and so raises aggregate demand. Both of these influences raise nominal GDP in Canada and so shift the money-demand curve to the right. The depreciation of the Canadian dollar continues until the excess supply of Canadian dollars is eliminated by the demand-for-money curve shifting out to position M_1D_1 in Figure 12–8. Thus, a complete equilibrium is obtained under flexible exchange rates at point B; the adjustment involves inflation and an increase in aggregate demand.

When foreign interest rates increase, competition forces Canadian interest rates to increase. Our only policy choice is whether we want aggregate demand to expand or contract along with this rise in interest rates. Contraction follows if the Bank of

unprecedented borrowing of $2-billion (U.S.) to bolster its international monetary reserves. The record borrowing in a single day sent a clear message that Ottawa is prepared to protect the currency from further erosion on North American exchanges.

SOURCE: Alexander Bruce, *The Globe and Mail*, Toronto, February 6, 1986, page A1.

1987

I am often asked why the Bank pays so much attention to the exchange value of the Canadian currency. The answer is simple. Domestic price stability is the primary contribution that monetary policy can make to good economic perform-

ance. And the most important single price in the Canadian economy is the price of the Canadian dollar.

A decline in the dollar relative to other currencies directly raises the price of our imports and the domestic price of all those Canadian made goods which compete against imports or may be exported. These price increases can lead to concerns about inflation and can feed back into wages and other prices. . . .

It is inherently dangerous to rely on currency depreciation to improve international competitiveness. If depreciation sets off a spiral of price and wage increases, we wind up less rather than more competitive. . . . The only sure way to bring about a sustainable improvement in competitiveness is by keeping our domestic costs and prices down. That should be the principal focus of monetary policy.

SOURCE: John Crow, Speech, Calgary, 19 May 1987.

1990

. . . It might seem . . . that a good approach to monetary policy is to make sure that it is always sufficiently expansionary to lessen or even entirely avoid any tendency for the currency to appreciate . . . and to help the currency to depreciate in order to offset any potential loss of export competitiveness when there is any strong inflation of domestic costs. . . . However, a monetary policy that is directed in this way has surrendered control over monetary expansion.

SOURCE: The 1989 *Annual Report of the Bank of Canada, 1989*, tabled in February 1990, page 9.

Canada fixes the exchange rate, since the Bank must absorb the excess supply of Canadian dollars that results from bond-holders' switching to foreign bonds. The Bank can refuse to supply foreign currency in exchange for the Canadian dollars that bond-holders want to sell, but then the Canadian dollar depreciates. This raises the price of imports and stimulates aggregate demand and so leads to inflation.

The applicability of this analysis can be demonstrated in two ways. First, we can illustrate the direct connection between Canadian and U.S. interest rates that exists in the data; second, we can consider the reports of the Bank of Canada. Figure 12–9 (on page 266) certainly verifies that Canada's pattern of interest rates has followed that of the United States. The graph demonstrates that a significant interest-rate differential has emerged only when a significant change in the exchange rate was expected by market participants. Some have argued that Canada might be able to increase its interest-rate differential with the United States by enacting laws that regulate financial institutions in such a way as to control the international flow of funds. The Economic Council of Canada has recently considered this question by studying the experience that Japan, West Germany, France, and the United Kingdom have had with such policies. The Council concluded that the controls did not work and noted that these countries are abandoning them.

The only policy decision that exists for the Bank of Canada is whether we follow a fixed or a flexible exchange-rate policy. As the accompanying boxed insert explains,

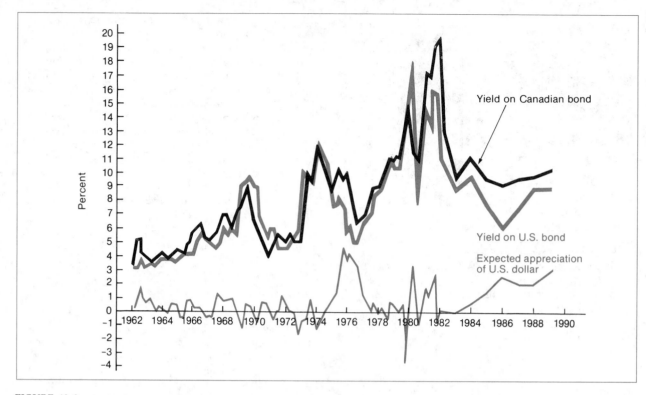

FIGURE 12–9

Canadian and U.S. Interest Rates and the Expected Appreciation of the U.S. Dollar, 1962–1989

This graph shows that a significant interest-rate differential has emerged only when a significant change in the exchange rate was expected by market participants.

SOURCE: Bank of Canada *Review*.

the Bank of Canada relies on this analysis and has chosen to fight inflation rather than unemployment and therefore to resist depreciation of the Canadian dollar. It is possible to criticize the Bank for caring too much about inflation, but it cannot be blamed for high interest rates.

Conclusion and Preview

We now understand how the Bank of Canada is organized, what tools it has available for regulating the money supply, how monetary policy is connected with exchange-rate policy, and how interest rates and exchange rates are determined. We can now investigate how these monetary-policy decisions affect unemployment, inflation, and the overall state of the economy, a task to which we turn in the next chapter.

Summary

1. The Bank of Canada is the country's central bank, which serves as a bank for the chartered banks. It is the institution that conducts Canada's monetary and exchange-rate policy.
2. The Bank of Canada relies primarily on open-market operations to change the reserves available to the chartered banks.

3. Open-market purchases of government bonds or foreign exchange by the Bank of Canada increase the money supply. Open-market sales of government bonds or foreign exchange by the Bank decrease Canada's money supply.
4. The bank rate is the rate the chartered banks must pay the Bank of Canada if they need to borrow reserves.

Since very little borrowing of reserves occurs, the weekly adjustment in the bank rate serves only as a signal of the direction of monetary policy. A decrease in the bank rate indicates that the Bank of Canada has been conducting policies that increase the money supply.

5. The Bank of Canada does not have perfect control over the money supply in the short run, because it cannot predict perfectly how far the process of deposit creation or destruction will go.

6. An exchange rate states the value of one currency in terms of another. Thus, exchange rates influence the patterns of world trade in important ways.

7. If governments do not interfere, exchange rates will be determined in free markets by the usual laws of supply and demand. This is called a system of floating or flexible exchange rates.

8. The supply of foreign exchange in a country is derived from foreigners' desires to purchase that country's goods and services or to invest in its assets. Any change that increases that supply of foreign exchange will cause the value of foreign exchange to depreciate, and will therefore cause the value of the country's *domestic* currency to appreciate.

9. The demand for foreign exchange within a country is derived from the desire of that country's citizens to purchase foreign goods and services or to invest in foreign assets. Any change that increases that demand for foreign exchange will cause the value of foreign exchange to appreciate, and will therefore cause the value of the country's *domestic* currency to depreciate.

10. Exchange rates can be fixed at non-equilibrium levels by governments that are willing and able to mop up any excess of foreign exchange supplied over quantity demanded or provide any excess of foreign exchange demanded over quantity supplied. In the first case, the country suffers from a balance of payments surplus; in the second, it has a balance of payments deficit.

11. When the Bank of Canada fixes the exchange rate, it performs an open-market operation in the foreign-exchange market instead of the domestic bond market. As a result, the central bank cannot set both the money supply and the exchange rate.

12. The money-supply schedule shows that more money is supplied at higher interest rates because, as interest rates rise, banks find it more profitable to expand their loans and deposits. This schedule can be shifted by Bank of Canada policy.

13. The money-demand schedule shows that less money is demanded at higher interest rates because interest is the opportunity cost of holding money. This schedule shifts when output or the price level changes.

14. The equilibrium money stock (M) and the equilibrium rate of interest (r) are determined by the intersection of the money-supply and money-demand schedules, as long as foreign and domestic financial markets are independent.

15. Central bank policy can shift this equilibrium. Expansionary policies cause M to rise and r to fall. Contractionary policies reduce M and increase r.

16. Canadian interest rates are determined in the United States. Increased foreign interest rates are accompanied by inflation if we let the Canadian dollar depreciate, and by a contraction in the money supply and aggregate demand if the Bank of Canada pegs the exchange rate.

Concepts for Review

Bank of Canada
Reserve requirements
Exchange rate
Appreciation
Depreciation
Supply of and demand for foreign exchange
Floating, or flexible, exchange rates
Open-market operations
Contraction and expansion of the money supply

Bank rate
Fixed exchange rates
Balance of payments deficit and surplus
Interest-rate differential
Supply of money
Demand for money
Equilibrium in the money market
Controlling M versus controlling exchange rate

Questions for Discussion

1. Why does a modern industrial economy need a central bank?

2. Do you think it is a good idea to have an independent central bank? Explain your reasons.

3. Suppose there is $60 billion of cash in existence, and all of it is held in bank vaults as *required* reserves (that is, banks hold no *excess* reserves). How large will the money supply be if the required reserve ratio is 16⅔ percent? 20 percent? 25 percent?

4. Show the balance sheet changes that would take place if the Bank of Canada purchased an office building from the Bank of Commerce for a price of $100 million. Compare this to the effect of an open-market purchase of securities such as that shown in Table 12–2. What do you conclude?

5. Suppose that the Bank of Canada purchases $8 million

worth of government bonds from Joe Tycoon, who banks at the Bank of Montreal. Show the effects on the balance sheets of the central bank, the Bank of Montreal, and Joe Tycoon. (*Hint*: What will Joe Tycoon do with the $8 million cheque he receives from the Bank of Canada?) Does it make any difference if the Bank of Canada buys bonds from a bank or from an individual?

6. Why would the Bank of Canada's control over the money supply be tighter if all chartered bank deposits were subject to the same reserve requirements?

7. Explain why former Bank of Canada Governor Bouey stated that he would resign rather than carry out written instructions from the government to try to lower interest rates by allowing the Canadian dollar to depreciate.

8. The following is a quotation from *The Globe and Mail* (January 27, 1990, page B1):

When Mr. Crow tried to reduce interest rates this month by a mere quarter of a percentage point, the inflows of money that had been pushing up the dollar abruptly reversed. In just two weeks, the Canadian dollar lost everything it had gained in the previous seven months.

Use economic reasoning to explain the developments reported in this passage.

13

Stabilization Policy for a Closed Economy

The love of money is the root of all evil.

THE NEW TESTAMENT

Lack of money is the root of all evil.

GEORGE BERNARD SHAW

I n this chapter and the next, we bring together our analysis of income determination and the price level from Chapters 5 through 9 and our analysis of money and monetary policy from Chapters 11 and 12. In doing so, we complete the construction of our model of the entire macroeconomy. We will then use this model to see how and to what extent the Bank of Canada's ability to manage the money supply also enables it to manage the level of aggregate demand—and hence to influence unemployment and inflation.

We begin the chapter by integrating the financial system into the Keynesian $C + I + G + X - IM$ model described in Chapters 5 through 9. The mechanisms by which monetary policy affects aggregate demand are spelled out and analyzed, and we learn an additional reason why the aggregate demand curve slopes downward.

Then we turn to a very old and very simple macroeconomic model—the *quantity theory of money*, and its modern reincarnation, *monetarism*—for an alternative view of the effects of money on the economy. Although the monetarist and Keynesian theories seem to be two contradictory views of how monetary and fiscal policy work, we will see that the conflict is more apparent than real. In fact, the disagreement is akin to hearing an Anglophone say, "Yes," and a Francophone say, "Oui." The uninitiated hear two different languages, but knowledgeable listeners understand that they mean the same thing.

Although one major objective of this chapter is to show that differences between the two theories are greatly exaggerated, there *are* significant differences between the two schools of thought—not outright contradictions but differences in emphasis. These differences occupy the rest of this chapter.

The model economy on which we base this chapter's analysis rests on the unrealistic but simplifying assumption that a country's financial markets operate independently of foreign financial markets. That is, to apply this chapter's analysis to Canada would be to assume that Canadian interest rates can diverge from the level of U.S. interest rates indefinitely.

This picture of the Canadian economy is *not* realistic. Nevertheless, this chapter is valuable for two reasons. One is pedagogical; it permits the clearer exposition of the Keynesian–monetarist controversy and the foreign-exchange market complications in two separate steps. The second advantage comes from Canadian students' need to know and understand their neighbour to the south. An analysis in which domestic policies affect interest rates in a lasting way *is* appropriate for the United States. Thus, the material in this chapter can facilitate an informed opinion about options for U.S. policies—which, of course, have a direct bearing on Canada. In Chapter 14, we will consider the case that is more realistic for Canada—that of integrated financial markets.

A Study Hint

Because this chapter integrates so many aspects of the macroeconomic theory we have already constructed, it requires you to keep many things in mind at the same time. In this respect, it needs careful study. Fortunately, however, it does not introduce any new technical apparatus. Literally everything we need can be borrowed from earlier chapters. The following is a list of the things we will be referring to in the pages to come, indicating where you should look if you need to review any of them:

- How aggregate supply and aggregate demand interact to determine the price level (Chapters 4 and 8).
- How the circular flow of income and expenditure determines equilibrium output (Chapter 6).
- The analysis of the multiplier (Chapters 7 and 9).
- The workings of fiscal policy (Chapter 9).
- How the supply of and the demand for money interact to determine the quantity of money and the interest rate, and how the central bank can influence this equilibrium (Chapter 12).

Before proceeding with this integration of material, we clarify some important vocabulary. The words "money" and "income" are used almost interchangeably in common parlance. This is a pitfall we must learn to avoid.

Money is a snapshot concept. It is the answer to questions like: "How much money do you have right now?" or "How much money did you have at 3:32 P.M. on Friday, November 5?" To answer questions like these, you would add up the cash you are or were carrying and whatever bank balances you have or had and answer something like: "I have $126.33," or "On Friday, November 5, at 3:32 P.M., I had $31.43."

Income, by contrast, is more like a motion picture; it comes to you only over a period of time. If you are asked "What is your income?" you must respond by saying "$500 *per week*," or "$2000 *per month*," or "$30,000 *per year*," or something like that. Notice that there is a unit of time attached to each of these responses. If you just say "My income is $452.19," without indicating whether it is per week or per month or per year, no one will understand what you mean.

That the two concepts are very different is easy to see. Nominal GDP in 1989 was about $649 billion, while the money stock (M1) was only about $41.2 billion. While money and income are very different, they are certainly related. This chapter is precisely about that relationship. Specifically, we will look at how the stock of *money* in existence at any moment in time influences the rate at which people will be earning *income*—that is, how money affects the GDP.

Interest Rates and Total Expenditure

To begin, we go back to the analysis of Chapters 5 to 9, where we learned that aggregate demand is the sum of consumption spending (C), investment spending (I), government purchases of goods and services (G), and net exports ($X - IM$). We know that *fiscal policy* controls G directly and influences both C and I through the tax laws. We now want to find out how *monetary policy* influences $C + I + G + X - IM$.

Most economists agree that, of the four components of aggregate demand, investment (I) is the most sensitive to monetary policy. *Business investment* in new factories and machinery is sensitive to interest rates for reasons that have been explained in earlier chapters.[1] Since the rate of interest that must be paid on borrowings is one element of the cost of making an investment, business executives will find investment prospects less attractive as interest rates rise. Therefore, they will

---

[1]See, for example, Chapter 6, page 132.

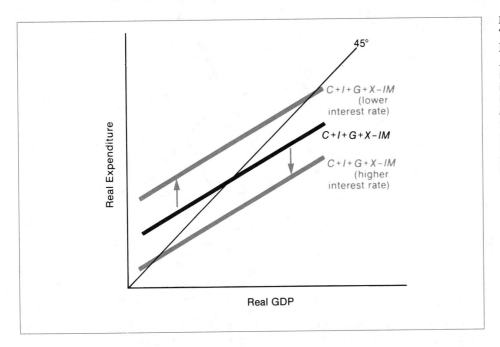

FIGURE 13-1
The Effect of Interest Rates on Aggregate Demand
Because interest rates are an important determinant of investment spending, *I*, the *C + I + G + X - IM* schedule shifts whenever the rate of interest changes. Specifically, as shown here, lower interest rates shift the curve upward and higher interest rates shift it downward.

spend less. For similar reasons, *investment in housing* by individuals may also be deterred by high interest rates. Since the interest cost of a home mortgage is a major component of the total cost of owning a home, fewer families will want to buy a new home when interest rates are high than when interest rates are low. We conclude:

Higher interest rates lead to lower investment spending. But investment (*I*) is a component of total spending (*C + I + G + X – IM*). Therefore, when interest rates rise, total spending falls. In terms of the 45° line diagram of previous chapters, a higher interest rate leads to a lower *C + I + G + X – IM* schedule. Conversely, a lower interest rate leads to a higher *C + I + G + X – IM* schedule. (See Figure 13–1.)

Monetary Policy in the Keynesian Model

The effect of interest rates on spending provides the mechanism by which monetary policy affects aggregate demand in the Keynesian model. We know from our analysis of the money market in Chapter 12 that monetary policy affects the rate of interest. Let us, therefore, outline the effects of monetary policy in the Keynesian model, starting first on the demand side of the economy.

Suppose the central bank,[2] seeing the economy stuck with unemployment and a recessionary gap, raises the money supply. We learned in Chapter 12 that it would normally do this by purchasing government securities in the open market. With the demand schedule for money (temporarily) fixed, such an increase in the supply of money has the effect that an increase in supply always has in a free market—it lowers the price. (See Figure 13–2.) In this case, the price of renting money is the rate of interest (*r*), so *r* falls.

Next, for reasons we have just outlined, investment spending (*I*) rises in response to the lower interest rates. But, as we learned in Chapter 7, such a rise in investment kicks off a multiplier chain of increases in output and employment. Thus, finally, we have completed the links from the money supply to the level of aggregate demand. In brief, monetary policy works as follows:

---

[2]For the sake of convenience, we refer to the central bank as the Bank of Canada throughout this chapter. Bear in mind, however, that the analysis of the next chapter is the one more applicable to the Canadian economy.

FIGURE 13-2
**The Effect of
Expansionary Monetary
Policy on the Money
Supply and Rate of Interest**
An expansionary monetary
policy pushes the money-supply
schedule outward from M_0S_0 to
M_1S_1, causing equilibrium in the
money market to shift from point
E_0 to point E_1. The money
supply rises from \$55 billion to
\$59 billion, while the interest
rate falls from 9 percent to 7
percent.

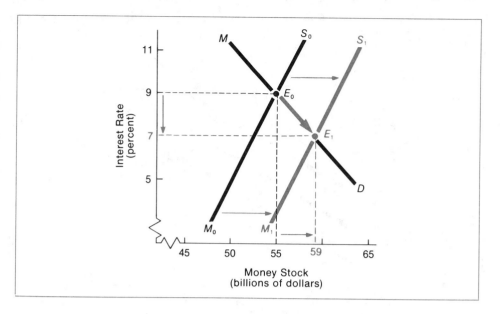

A higher money supply leads to lower interest rates, and these lower interest rates encourage investment, which has multiplier effects on aggregate demand.

The process operates equally well in reverse. By contracting the money supply, the Bank of Canada can force interest rates up, causing investment spending to fall and pulling down aggregate demand via the multiplier mechanism.

This, in outline form, is how monetary policy operates in the Keynesian model. Since the chain of causation is fairly long, the following schematic diagram may help clarify it.

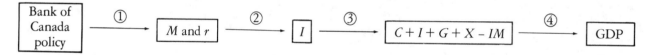

In this causal chain, link 1 indicates that the actions of the Bank of Canada affect money and interest rates. Link 2 stands for the effect of interest rates on investment. Link 3 simply notes that investment is one component of total spending. And link 4 is the multiplier, relating an autonomous change in investment to the ultimate change in aggregate demand.

Let us next review what we have learned about each of these links in previous chapters. In the process, we will see what Keynesians must study if they are to estimate the effect of monetary policy.

Link 1 was the subject of the last chapter, and Figure 13-2 reviews the analysis. Given the initial level of real GDP and prices, the demand schedule for money is shown by curve MD. The Bank of Canada's expansionary action shifts the supply schedule out from M_0S_0 to M_1S_1, resulting in an increase in the money stock from \$55 billion to \$59 billion in this example and a decline in the interest rate from 9 percent to 7 percent. Thus the first thing a Keynesian economist must know is how sensitive interest rates are to changes in the supply of money.

Link 2 translates the drop in the interest rate into an increase in investment spending (I), which we take to be \$10 billion in this example. To estimate this effect in practice, a Keynesian economist must study the sensitivity of investment to interest rates.

Link 3 instructs us to enter this \$10 billion rise in I as an autonomous shift in the $C + I + G + X - IM$ schedule of a 45° line diagram. Figure 13-3 carries out this step.

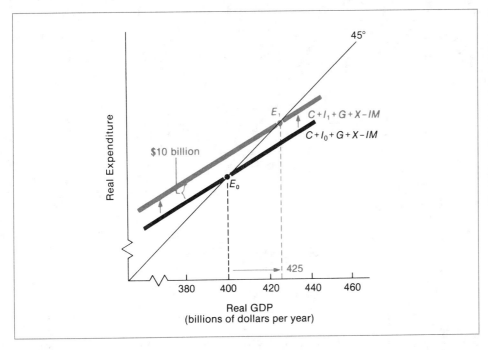

FIGURE 13-3
The Effect of Expansionary Monetary Policy on Aggregate Demand
Expansionary monetary policies, which lower the rate of interest, will cause the $C + I + G + X - IM$ schedule to shift upward from $C + I_0 + G + X - IM$ to $C + I_1 + G + X - IM$, as shown here. In this example, since the multiplier is 2.5, a $10 billion rise in investment leads, via the multiplier process, to a $25 billion rise in GDP.

The expenditure schedule rises from $C + I_0 + G + X - IM$ to $C + I_1 + G + X - IM$.

Finally, link 4 applies multiplier analysis to this vertical shift in the expenditure schedule in order to predict the eventual increase in real GDP demanded. In this example, we assume a multiplier of 2.5, so multiplying $10 billion by 2.5 gives the final effect on aggregate demand—a rise of $25 billion. This is shown in Figure 13-3 as a shift in equilibrium from E_0 (where GDP is $400 billion) to E_1 (where GDP is $425 billion). Of course, the size of this multiplier itself must also be estimated. To summarize:

The effect of monetary policy on aggregate demand depends on the sensitivity of interest rates to the money supply, on the responsiveness of investment spending to the rate of interest, and on the size of the multiplier.

Money and the Price Level in the Keynesian Model

One need only recall the inflation of past decades to realize that we have forgotten something. What happens to the price level? To answer this, we must simply remember once again that prices and output are determined jointly by aggregate demand *and* aggregate supply. The analysis of monetary policy that we have completed so far has shown us how an increase in the money supply shifts the aggregate demand curve; that is, it increases the *aggregate quantity demanded at any given price level*. But to learn what happens to the price level and to real output, we must bring *aggregate supply* into the picture as well.

Specifically, in considering shifts in aggregate demand caused by *fiscal* policy in Chapter 9, we noted that an upsurge in total spending normally induces firms to increase output somewhat *and* to raise prices somewhat. This is just what an aggregate supply curve shows. Whether prices or real output exhibit the greater response depends mainly on the degree of capacity utilization. An economy operating near full employment has only a limited ability to increase production; it therefore responds to greater demand mainly by raising prices. On the other hand, an economy with a substantial amount of unemployed labour and unused capital is able to increase output a great deal without significantly raising prices.

Now this analysis of output and price responses applies equally well to monetary

FIGURE 13–4
The Inflationary Effects of Expansionary Monetary Policy
Raising the money supply normally causes inflation. When expansionary monetary policy causes the aggregate demand curve to shift outward from D_0D_0 to D_1D_1, the economy's equilibrium shifts from point E to point B. Real output expands (in this case by $20 billion), but prices also rise (in this case by 3 percent).

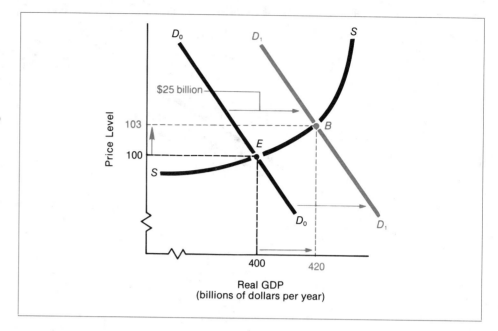

policy or, for that matter, to anything else that raises aggregate demand. We conclude, then, that:

Expansionary monetary policy causes some inflation under normal circumstances. But how much inflation it causes depends on the state of the economy. If the money supply is expanded when unemployment is high and there is much unused industrial capacity, then the result may be little inflation. If, however, increases in the money supply occur when the economy is fully employed, then the main result is inflation.

The effect of a rise in the money supply on the price level is depicted graphically on an aggregate supply-and-demand diagram in Figure 13–4. The curved shape of aggregate supply curve SS reflects the assumptions that output rises with little inflation when the economy is depressed, while prices rise with little gain in output when the economy is near full employment.

In the example we have been using, the Bank of Canada's actions raise the money supply by $4 billion, and this increases aggregate demand (through the multiplier) by $25 billion. We enter this in Figure 13–4 as a horizontal shift of $25 billion in the aggregate demand curve, from D_0D_0 to D_1D_1. The diagram shows that this expansionary monetary policy raises the economy's equilibrium from point E to point B—the price level therefore rises from 100 to 103, or 3 percent. The diagram also shows that real GDP rises by only $20 billion, which is less than the $25 billion stimulus to aggregate demand. The reason, as we know from earlier chapters, is that rising prices stifle demand.

By taking account of the effect of an increase in the money supply on the price level, we have completed our story about the role of monetary policy in the Keynesian model. We can thus expand our schematic diagram of monetary policy as follows:

$$\boxed{\begin{array}{c}\text{Bank of}\\\text{Canada}\\\text{policy}\end{array}} \xrightarrow{\text{\textcircled{1}}} \boxed{M \text{ and } r} \xrightarrow{\text{\textcircled{2}}} \boxed{I} \xrightarrow{\text{\textcircled{3}}} \boxed{C + I + G + X - IM} \xrightarrow{\text{\textcircled{4}}} \boxed{Y \text{ and } P}$$

The last link now recognizes that *both* output *and* prices normally are affected by changes in the money supply.

Why the Aggregate Demand Curve Slopes Downward

This analysis of the effect of money on the price level puts us in a better position to understand why higher prices reduce aggregate quantity demanded; that is, why the aggregate demand curve slopes downward. In earlier chapters, we explained this phenomenon in part by observing that rising prices reduce the purchasing power of certain assets held by consumers, especially money and government bonds, and that this in turn retards consumption spending. There is nothing wrong with this analysis. But, quantitatively, higher prices have much more important effects on aggregate demand through other channels, which we are now in a position to understand.

Money is demanded primarily to conduct transactions, and we saw in Chapter 12 that a rise in the *average money cost* of each transaction—as a result of a rise in the price level—will increase the quantity of money demanded. It simply takes more cash to buy a given amount of goods at higher prices. This means that when expansionary policy of any kind pushes the price level up, more money will be demanded at any given interest rate.

But if the supply of money is *not* increased, an increase in the quantity of money demanded at any given interest rate must force the cost of borrowing money—the rate of interest—to rise. As we know, increases in interest rates reduce investment and, hence, reduce aggregate demand. This, then, is a major reason why the economy's aggregate demand curve has a negative slope, meaning that aggregate quantity demanded is lower when prices are higher.

At higher price levels, the quantity of money demanded is greater. Given a fixed supply schedule, a higher price level must lead to a higher interest rate. Since high interest rates discourage investment, the aggregate quantity demanded is lower when the price level is higher; that is, the aggregate demand curve slopes downward to the right.

We have also noted at several points earlier that there is another reason for the downward slope of the aggregate demand curve. The higher the domestic price level, the more expensive are a country's goods relative to foreign products. As a result, both domestic residents and foreigners buy fewer of that country's domestically produced goods. This means that net exports $(X - IM)$ fall, leading to an overall drop in aggregate demand when the domestic price level rises. In Canada's economy, this mechanism has a quantitatively significant effect.

Velocity and the Quantity Theory of Money

We have now seen how money influences real output and the price level in the Keynesian model. But there is another way to look at these matters using a model that, while much older than the Keynesian model, is at the heart of modern critiques of Keynesian economics. This model is known as the **quantity theory of money**, and it is easy to understand once we have introduced one new concept—*velocity*.

We learned in Chapter 11 that because barter is so cumbersome, virtually all economic transactions in advanced economies are conducted by the use of money. This means that if there are, say, $500 billion worth of transactions in the economy during a particular year and there is an average money stock of $50 billion during that year, then each dollar of money must get used an average of ten times during the year.

The number 10 in this example is called the **velocity of circulation**, or just **velocity** for short, because it indicates the speed at which money circulates. For example, a particular dollar bill might be used to pay for a haircut in January; the barber might use it to buy a sweater in March; the storekeeper might then use it to buy gasoline in May; the gas station owner could pay it out to a painter who paints his house in October; and the painter might spend it on a Christmas present in December. This would mean that the dollar was used five times during the year, so that velocity would be 5. If a dollar were used only four times during the year, its velocity would be only 4, and so on. Similarly, a $20 bill circulating with a velocity of 8 would be the

Velocity indicates the number of times per year that an "average dollar" is spent on goods and services. It is the ratio of nominal GDP to the number of dollars in the money stock. That is:

$$\text{Velocity} = \frac{\text{Nominal GDP}}{\text{Money stock}}.$$

monetary instrument used to finance $160 worth of transactions in that year.

No one has data on all the transactions in the economy. To make velocity an operational concept, we must settle on a precise definition of transactions that we can actually measure. The most popular choice is gross domestic product in current dollars (nominal GDP), even though it ignores many transactions that use money—such as sales of existing assets. If we accept nominal GDP as a measure of the money value of transactions, we are led to a concrete definition of velocity as the ratio of nominal GDP to the number of dollars in the money stock. Since nominal GDP is the product of real GDP times the price level, we can write this definition as:

$$V = \frac{\text{Value of transactions}}{\text{Money stock}} = \frac{\text{Nominal GDP}}{M} = \frac{P \times Y}{M}.$$

By multiplying both sides of the equation by M, we arrive at an identity called the **equation of exchange** that relates the money supply and nominal GDP:

The equation of exchange states that the money value of GDP transactions must be equal to the product of the average stock of money times velocity. That is: $M \times V = P \times Y$.

$$\text{Money supply} \times \text{Velocity} = \text{Nominal GDP}.$$

Alternatively, stated in symbols, we have:

$$M \times V = P \times Y.$$

Here we have quite an obvious link between the stock of money, M, and the nominal value of the nation's output. But it is only a matter of arithmetic, not of economics. For example, it does not imply that the Bank of Canada can raise nominal GDP by increasing M. Why not? Because V might simultaneously fall by enough to prevent $M \times V$ from rising. That is, if there were more dollar bills in circulation than before but each bill changed hands more slowly, total spending would not necessarily rise.

The *quantity theory of money* transforms the equation of exchange from an accounting identity into an economic model *by assuming* that changes in velocity are so minor that, for practical purposes, velocity can be taken to be a constant.

You can see that if V never changed, the equation of exchange would be a marvellously simple model of the determination of nominal GDP—one that is far simpler than the Keynesian model. To see this, we need only to turn the equation of exchange around to read,

$$P \times Y = V \times M.$$

This equation says, for example, that if the Bank of Canada wants to increase nominal GDP by 12.7 percent, it need only raise the money supply by 12.7 percent. In such a simple world, economists could use the equation of exchange to *predict* nominal GDP simply by predicting the quantity of money. And policy-makers could *control* nominal GDP simply by controlling the money supply.

In the real world things are not so simple, because velocity is not a fixed number. But this does not necessarily destroy the usefulness of the quantity theory. We explained in Chapter 1 why all economic models make assumptions that are at least mildly unrealistic—without such assumptions they would not be models at all, just tedious descriptions of reality. The question is whether the assumption of constant velocity is a useful abstraction from annoying detail or a gross distortion of facts.

Figure 13-5 sheds some light on this question by showing the behaviour of velocity since 1953. You will undoubtedly notice an upward trend throughout this period. Quite clearly, *velocity is not constant over long periods of time*. Also we see some rather substantial fluctuations of velocity about its trend. Such fluctuations have led most economists to the conclusion that *velocity is not constant in the short run either*. It seems, then, that the strict quantity theory of money is not an adequate model of aggregate demand.

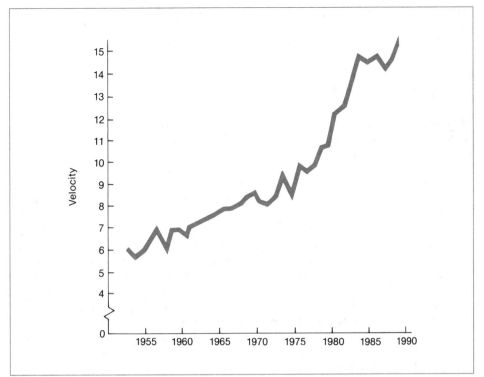

FIGURE 13-5
Velocity of Circulation, 1953-1989
Velocity displays both a trend and short-run fluctuations. (The money supply here is measured as M1.)
SOURCE: Historical Statistics of Canada (series J22), and Bank of Canada *Review*, selected issues.

The Determinants of Velocity

Since it is abundantly clear that velocity is a variable, not a constant, we can use the equation of exchange as a model of GDP determination only by examining the determinants of velocity. What factors decide whether V is 6 or 8 or 10; that is, whether a dollar is used to buy goods and services six or eight or ten times a year?

Perhaps the principal factor is the *frequency with which paycheques are received.* This can best be explained through a numerical example. Consider a worker who earns $24,000 a year, paid to her in twelve monthly paycheques of $2000 each. Suppose that she spends the whole $2000 over the course of each month and maintains a minimum balance in her chequing account of $500. Each payday her bank balance will shoot up to $2500 and then be gradually whittled down as she makes withdrawals to purchase goods and services. Finally, on the day before her next paycheque arrives, her chequing balance will be just $500. Over the course of a typical month, then, her average chequing account balance will be $1500 (halfway between $2500 and $500).

Now suppose her employer switches to a twice-a-month payroll. Her paycheques come twice as often but are reduced to $1000 each. There is no reason for her rate of spending to change, but her *cash balances* will change. For now her chequing balance will rise only to $1500 on payday (the $500 minimum balance plus the $1000 paycheque), and it will still be drawn down gradually to $500. Her average cash balance will therefore decline to $1000 (halfway between $1500 and $500). Why is this so? Because, with the next paycheque coming sooner than before, it is not necessary to keep as much cash in the bank in order to carry out a given quantity of transactions.

But what does this have to do with velocity? Notice that when she was on a monthly payroll, this worker's personal velocity was:

$$V = \frac{\text{Annual income}}{\text{Average cash balance}} = \frac{\$24,000}{\$1500} = 16.$$

When she switched to a semimonthly payroll, velocity rose to:

$$V = \frac{\text{Annual income}}{\text{Average cash balance}} = \frac{\$24,000}{\$1000} = 24.$$

The general lesson to be learned is that:

More frequent wage payments mean that people can conduct their transactions with lower average cash balances. Since they will want to hold less cash, money will circulate faster. In other words, velocity will rise.

A second factor influencing velocity is the *efficiency of the payments mechanism,* including how quickly cheques clear through banks, the use of credit cards, and other methods of transferring funds. It is easy to see how this works.

The example in the previous paragraph assumed that our worker holds her entire paycheque in the form of money until she uses it to make a purchase. But, given that many forms of money pay little or no interest, this method may not be the most rational behaviour. If it is possible to convert interest-bearing assets into money on short notice and at low cost, a rational individual might use her paycheque to purchase such assets and then use credit cards for most purchases, making periodic transfers to her chequing account as necessary. For the same amount of total transactions, then, she would require lower money balances. This means that money would circulate faster: Velocity would rise.

The incentive to limit cash holdings depends on the ease and speed with which it is possible to exchange money for other assets. This is what we mean by the "efficiency of the payments mechanism." As computerization has speeded up the bookkeeping procedures of banks, as financial innovations have made it possible to transfer funds rapidly between chequing accounts and other assets, and as credit cards have come to be used instead of cash, the need to hold money balances has declined. By definition, then, velocity has risen.

Fortunately such basic changes in the payments mechanism usually take place only gradually and are therefore often easy to predict. But this is not always so. For example, a host of financial innovations introduced in the 1980s—some of which were mentioned in Chapter 11's discussion of the definitions of money—have given analysts fits in predicting velocity.

A third determinant of velocity is the *rate of interest.* The basic motive for economizing on money holdings is that money (at least M1) pays little or no interest, while many alternative stores of value pay higher rates. The higher these alternative rates of interest, the greater the incentive to economize on holding money. Therefore, as interest rates rise, people want to hold less money. So the existing stock of money circulates faster, and velocity rises.

It is this factor that most directly undercuts the usefulness of the quantity theory of money as a guide for monetary policy. For in the last chapter we learned that expansionary monetary policy, which increases *M*, normally also decreases the interest rate. But if interest rates fall, other things equal, velocity (*V*) will also fall. Thus, *when the central bank raises the money supply (M), the product M × V may go up by a smaller percentage than does M itself.*

One component of the interest rate is worth singling out for special attention: *the expected rate of inflation.* We explained in Chapter 4 why an "inflation premium" equal to the expected inflation rate often gets built in to market interest rates.[3] Thus, in many instances, high inflation is the principal cause of high nominal interest rates.

---

[3] If you need review, turn back to pages 96–97.

High rates of inflation, which erode the purchasing power of money, therefore lead both individuals and businesses to hold as little money as they can get by on—actions that increase velocity.

To summarize this discussion of the determinants of velocity:

Velocity is not a strict constant but depends on such things as the frequency of payments, the efficiency of the financial system, the rate of interest, and the rate of inflation. Only by studying these determinants of velocity can we hope to predict the level of nominal GDP from knowledge of the money supply.

Monetarism: The Quantity Theory Modernized

The foregoing does not mean, however, that the equation of exchange cannot be a useful framework within which to organize macroeconomic analysis. It can be. And during the past forty years, a group of economists called *monetarists* have convincingly demonstrated that this is so.

Monetarists recognize that velocity is not a constant. But they stress that it is fairly *predictable*—certainly in the long run and probably also in the short run. This leads them to the conclusion that the best way to study economic activity is to start with the *equation of exchange:* $M \times V = P \times Y$. From here, careful study of the determinants of M (which we provided in the previous two chapters) and of V (which we just completed) can be used to *predict* the behaviour of nominal GDP. Similarly, given an understanding of movements in V, control over the money supply gives the central bank *control* over nominal GDP.

These are the central tenets of **monetarism**. When something happens in the economy, monetarists ask two questions:

1. What does this event do to the stock of money?

2. What does this event do to velocity?

From the answers, they assert that they can predict the path of nominal GDP.

By comparing the monetarist approach with the Keynesian approach that we described earlier in this chapter, we can put both doctrines into perspective and understand the limitations of each. As we mentioned earlier, they differ more in style than in substance. Keynesians divide aggregate demand into four compartments— marked "C," "I," "G," and "$X - IM$"—and unite them all with the equilibrium condition that $C + I + G + X - IM = Y$. In Keynesian analysis, money affects the economy by first affecting interest rates.

Monetarists, on the other hand, organize their knowledge into two alternative boxes—labelled "M" and "V"—and then use a simple identity, $M \times V = P \times Y$, to bring this knowledge to bear in predicting aggregate demand. In the monetarist model, the role of money in the national economy is not necessarily limited to working through interest rates.

The bit of arithmetic that multiplies M by V to get P multiplied by Y is neither more nor less profound than the one that adds C, I, G, and $X - IM$ to get Y. And certainly both identities are correct. The only substantive difference is that the monetarist equation leads to a prediction of *nominal* GDP, that is, the demand for goods and services measured in money terms, whereas the Keynesian equation leads to a prediction of *real* GDP, that is, the demand for goods and services measured in dollars of constant purchasing power.

Why, then, do we not simply mesh the two theories—using the monetarist approach to study nominal GDP and the Keynesian approach to study real GDP? It seems that by doing so we could use the separate analyses of real and nominal GDP to obtain a prediction of the future behaviour of the price level, which, of course, is the source of any difference in behaviour between real and nominal GDP.

Monetarism is a mode of analysis that uses the equation of exchange to organize macroeconomic predictions.

The reason that this appealing procedure will not work helps point out the major limitation of each theory. *Taken by itself, either theory is incomplete.* Each gives us a picture of the *demand* side of the economy without saying anything about the *supply* side. To try to predict both the price level and real output solely from these demand-oriented models would be like trying to predict the price of spinach by studying only the behaviour of consumers and ignoring that of farmers. It just will not work. In terms of our earlier aggregate supply and demand analysis:

Both the monetarist and Keynesian analyses are ways of studying the *aggregate demand curve*. In neither case is it possible to learn anything about both output and the price level without also studying the *aggregate supply curve*.

Economists thus are forced to choose between two alternative ways of predicting aggregate demand. If the monetarist route is chosen, the economist will use velocity and the money supply to study the demand for *nominal* GDP and then turn to the supply side to estimate how any predicted change in nominal income gets apportioned between changes in production and changes in prices. The schematic diagram on page 272, with its emphasis on interest rates, plays little role in the monetarist analysis of the transmission mechanism for monetary policy. On the other hand, an economist working with the Keynesian $C + I + G + X - IM$ approach will start by using that schematic diagram to predict how monetary policy affects the demand for *real* GDP. Then he will turn to the aggregate supply curve to estimate the inflationary consequences of this real demand.

Which approach works better? There is no generally correct answer for all economies in all periods of time. Therefore, it is not surprising that some economists prefer one approach while others favour the alternative.

Reconciling the Keynesian and Monetarist Views

We have already come quite a long way toward reconciling the Keynesian and monetarist views of how the economy operates. Keynesian analysis lends itself naturally to the study of fiscal policy, since G is a part of $C + I + G + X - IM$. But we have learned in this chapter that Keynesian economics also provides a powerful and important role for monetary policy: An increase in the money supply reduces interest rates, which, in turn, stimulates the demand for investment.

Monetarist analysis provides an obvious and direct route by which monetary policy influences both output and prices. But can the monetarist approach also handle fiscal policy? It can, because fiscal policy has an important effect on the rate of interest. And it is not hard to understand how this effect operates.

Let's see what happens to real output and the price level following, say, a rise in government purchases of goods and services. We learned in Chapter 9 that both real GDP (Y) and the price level (P) rise. But Chapter 12's analysis of the demand for money taught us that rising Y and P push the demand curve for money outward to the right. With no change in the supply curve for money, the rate of interest must rise. So expansionary fiscal policy raises interest rates.

If the government uses its spending and taxing weapons in the opposite direction, the same process works in reverse. Falling output and (possibly) falling prices shift the demand curve for money inward to the left. With a fixed supply curve for money, equilibrium in the money market leads to a lower interest rate. Thus:

Monetary policy is not the only type of policy that affects interest rates. Fiscal policy also affects interest rates. Specifically, increases in government spending or tax cuts normally push interest rates higher, whereas restrictive fiscal policies normally pull interest rates down.

The fact that fiscal policy affects interest rates gives it a role in the monetarist model despite the fact that the equation of exchange, $M \times V = P \times Y$, does not include either government spending or taxation among its variables. Any of the government policies that a Keynesian would call expansionary—higher spending, lower taxes, and so on—pushes up the rate of interest. And rising interest rates push up velocity because people want to hold less money when the interest they can earn on alternative assets increases. So it is through the V term in $M \times V$ that fiscal policy does its work in the monetarist framework. The equation of exchange, $M \times V = P \times Y$, then implies that nominal GDP must rise when government spending increases, even if M is fixed. The given supply of money can finance more transactions when velocity is higher. Conversely, restrictive fiscal policies, like tax increases and expenditure cuts, reduce the quantity of money demanded and lower interest rates. The consequent drop in velocity lowers income through the equation of exchange, because the money supply circulates more slowly.

The translation, then, seems to be complete. The Keynesian story about how fiscal policy works can be phrased in the monetarist dialect. And the monetarist tale about monetary policy can be told with a Keynesian accent. Furthermore, both modes of analysis help only to explain the mysteries of aggregate *demand* and must be supplemented by an analysis of aggregate *supply* to be complete. We must conclude then, that:

The differences between Keynesians and monetarists have been grossly exaggerated by the news media. Indeed, when it comes to matters of basic economic theory, there are hardly any differences at all.

But this does not mean that Keynesians and monetarists must agree on everything any more than the fact that English prose can be translated into French implies that English and French Canadians always see eye to eye. There are important differences of emphasis and policy that we will take up in the remainder of this chapter.

The Multiplier Formula Once Again

But first, the fact that expansionary fiscal policy pushes up interest rates has another important consequence that we should mention. Recall that higher interest rates deter private investment spending. This means that when the government raises the G component of $C + I + G + X - IM$, one of the side effects of its action will be to reduce the I component (by raising interest rates). Consequently, the sum $C + I + G + X - IM$ will not rise as much as simple multiplier analysis might suggest. In a word, the surge in government demand (G) discourages some private demand (I). This phenomenon provides another reason why the oversimplified multiplier formula, $1/(1 - \text{MPC})$, exaggerates the size of the multiplier:

Because any rise in G (or, for that matter, any autonomous rise in C or I or $X - IM$) pushes interest rates higher, and hence deters some investment spending, the increase in the sum $C + I + G + X - IM$ is smaller than what the oversimplified multiplier formula predicts.

Combining this observation with our previous analysis of the multiplier, we now have a more complete list of:

REASONS WHY THE OVERSIMPLIFIED
MULTIPLIER FORMULA IS WRONG

1. It ignores price-level changes, which reduce the size of the multiplier.

2. It ignores the income tax, which reduces the size of the multiplier.

3. It ignores imports, which reduce the size of the multiplier.

4. It ignores the rising interest rates that accompany any autonomous increase in spending, which also reduce the size of the multiplier.

Should Stabilization Policy Rely on Fiscal or Monetary Policy?

Although the Keynesian and monetarist approaches can be thought of as two languages, it is well known that language can influence attitudes in many subtle ways. And it must be admitted that Keynesians and monetarists have not lacked things to argue about.

For years they conducted a spirited and well-publicized debate over whether the government should rely mainly on fiscal policy or monetary policy to manage aggregate demand. While one would guess from reading the newspapers that this is the most important issue in the Keynesian–monetarist debate today, it is in fact the *least* important. It is unimportant because, as we have seen, each approach allows a role for each type of policy.

Nonetheless, the Keynesian language biases things subtly toward thinking that fiscal policy is central simply because fiscal actions influence aggregate demand so directly. G is, after all, a part of $C + I + G + X - IM$. Monetarists, on the other hand, see a more indirect channel that works through interest rates and velocity, and they wonder if something might not go wrong along the way.

The roles are reversed in the analysis of monetary policy. To monetarists, the effect of the money supply on aggregate demand is simple—it follows directly from the equation of exchange: $M \times V = P \times Y$. While monetary policy also affects aggregate demand in the Keynesian model, the mechanisms are rather complex, and there is obviously room for a slip-up. Monetary expansion might not affect the interest rate very much, or a fall in the interest rate might not induce much additional investment. Thus some Keynesians have their doubts when monetarists attribute great stabilizing powers to monetary policy.

During the 1960s and early 1970s the choice between fiscal and monetary policy dominated the debate between the more partisan Keynesians and monetarists. Extreme monetarists claimed that fiscal policy was futile, while extreme Keynesians argued that monetary policy was useless. We shall see in the next chapter that each of these conclusions, under certain circumstances, can be perfectly correct *if* the country's financial markets are integrated with those of the rest of the world (as Canada's are). Specifically, it turns out that monetary policy cannot have a significant effect on aggregate demand if a country follows a fixed exchange-rate policy, while fiscal policy has no significant effect on aggregate demand if a flexible exchange-rate policy is followed. However, a country such as the United States is much more capable of setting its own level of interest rates, and for it, the analysis of this chapter is directly relevant. U.S. evidence has rejected the extreme claims of both Keynesians and monetarists, so now both groups agree that both fiscal and monetary policy have significant effects on aggregate demand. Although Keynesians still tend to look more toward fiscal policy and monetarists tend to rely more on monetary policy, this is not a major difference between the two groups.

More important than the issue of which type of policy is more *powerful* is the related question, Which type of medicine—fiscal or monetary—cures the patient more *quickly*? In our discussions of fiscal and monetary policy so far, we have ignored such subtle questions of timing and proceeded as if the authorities instantly noticed the need for stabilization policy, decided upon a course of action, and administered the appropriate medicine. In reality, each of these steps takes time.

First, delays in data collection and processing mean that the latest macroeconomic data pertain to the economy as it was a few months ago. Second, one of the prices of democracy is that the government often takes a good deal of time to decide what should be done, to muster the necessary political support, and to put its decisions into effect. Finally, our economy is a bit like a sleeping elephant—it reacts rather sluggishly to moderate fiscal and monetary prods. As it turns out, these **lags in stabilization policy**, as they are called, play a pivotal role in the choice between fiscal and monetary policy. It is not hard to see why.

One of the main policy tools for manipulating consumer spending (*C*) is the personal income tax, and Chapter 5 documented why the fiscal-policy planner can feel fairly secure that each $1 of tax reduction will lead to about 90¢ of additional spending *eventually*. But not all of this will happen at once.

First, consumers must learn about the tax change. Then, more time may elapse before many consumers are convinced that the change is permanent. Finally, there is simple force of habit: Households need time to adjust their spending habits when circumstances change. For all these reasons, consumers may increase their spending by only 30¢ to 50¢ for each $1 of additional income within the first few months after a tax cut. Only gradually, over a period of perhaps several years, will they raise their spending until they are finally consuming 90¢ of each additional dollar of income.

Lags are much longer for investment (*I*), which, while it also can be influenced by fiscal policy (tax incentives), provides the main vehicle by which monetary policy affects aggregate demand. Planning for capacity expansion in a large corporation is a long, drawn-out process. Ideas must be submitted and approved. Plans must be drawn up, funding acquired, orders for machinery or contracts for new construction placed. And most of this occurs *before* any appreciable amount of money is spent. Economists have found that much of the response of investment to changes in interest rates or tax provisions is delayed for several years.

The fact that *C* responds more quickly than *I* has important implications for the choice among alternative stabilization policies. The reason is that the most common varieties of fiscal policy affect aggregate demand either directly (*G* is a component of $C + I + G + X - IM$) or work through consumption with a relatively short lag, while monetary policy has its major effects on investment. Therefore:

Conventional types of fiscal-policy actions, such as changes in *G* or in personal taxes, probably affect aggregate demand much more promptly than do monetary-policy actions.

Notice that the statement says nothing about which instrument is more *powerful*. It simply asserts that the fiscal weapon, whether it is stronger or weaker, acts more *quickly*. This important fact has been used to build a case that fiscal policy should bear the major burden of economic stabilization. But before you jump to such a conclusion, you should realize that the sorts of lags we have been discussing are not the only ones affecting the timing of stabilization policy.

Apart from these lags in expenditure, which are beyond the control of policy-makers, there are further lags that result from the behaviour of the policy-makers themselves! We are referring here to the delays that occur while the policy-makers are studying the state of the economy, contemplating what steps they should take, and putting their decisions into effect. And here most observers believe that monetary policy has an important edge; that is:

Policy lags are normally much shorter for monetary policy than for fiscal policy.

The reasons are apparent. The Governor of the Bank of Canada meets frequently with his advisers, so monetary-policy decisions are made almost every month. And once the Bank of Canada decides on a course of action, it normally can be executed almost instantly by buying or selling bonds on the open market.

Contrast this with fiscal policy. Federal budgeting procedures operate on an annual budget cycle. Except in rare circumstances, *major* fiscal-policy initiatives that affect spending can occur only at the time of the budget. Tax laws can be changed at any time, but the wheels of Parliament grind slowly, and it may take many months before Parliament acts on a bill to change taxes. In sum, one has to be very optimistic to suppose that important fiscal-policy actions can be taken on short notice.

Where does the combined effect of expenditure lags and policy lags leave us? With nothing conclusive, unfortunately. As the late Arthur Okun put it, the debate over whether the nation should rely only on monetary policy or only on fiscal policy is a bit like arguing whether a safe car is one with good headlights or one with good brakes. It is unwise to drive at night unless you have both.

Controversy Surrounding the Aggregate Supply Curve

One of the main disputes in the Keynesian–monetarist debate today is over the shape of the economy's aggregate supply curve. As we have noted, both the Keynesian and the monetarist models must be supplemented by an aggregate supply curve if they are to tell us anything about output and prices. Most Keynesians tend to think of the aggregate supply curve as fairly flat in the short run (like the supply curves in Figure 13–6), so that large increases in output can be achieved with rather little inflation. Monetarists, by contrast, picture the supply curve as quite steep (like the ones in Figure 13–7), so that prices are very responsive to changes in output. The differences for public policy are substantial.

In the Keynesian view, expansionary fiscal or monetary policy that raises the aggregate demand schedule can buy large gains in real GDP at little cost in terms of inflation. This is shown in Figure 13–6(a). Here, stimulation of demand raises the aggregate demand curve from D_0D_0 to D_1D_1 and moves the economy's equilibrium

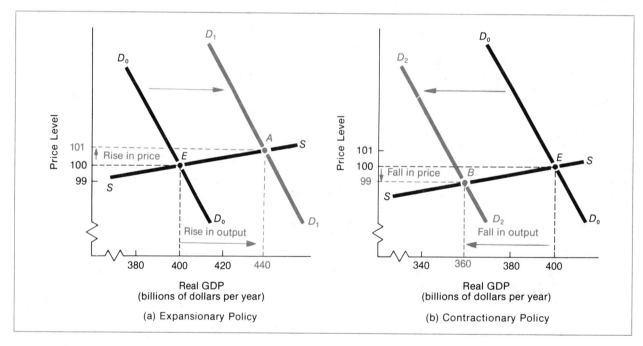

FIGURE 13–6
Stabilization Policy with a Flat Aggregate Supply Curve: The Keynesian Case
These two diagrams show that stabilization policy is much more effective as an anti-recession policy than as an anti-inflation policy when the aggregate supply curve is very flat. In part (a), monetary or fiscal policies push the aggregate demand curve outward from D_0D_0 to D_1D_1, causing equilibrium to shift from point E to point A. It can be seen that output rises substantially (from \$400 billion to \$440 billion), while prices rise only slightly (from 100 to 101, or 1 percent). So the policy is quite successful. In part (b), contractionary policies are used to combat inflation by pushing the aggregate demand curve inward from D_0D_0 to D_2D_2. Prices do fall slightly (from 100 to 99) as equilibrium shifts from point E to point B, but real output falls much more dramatically (from \$400 billion to \$360 billion). So the policy has had little success. Keynesians tend to believe in this case.

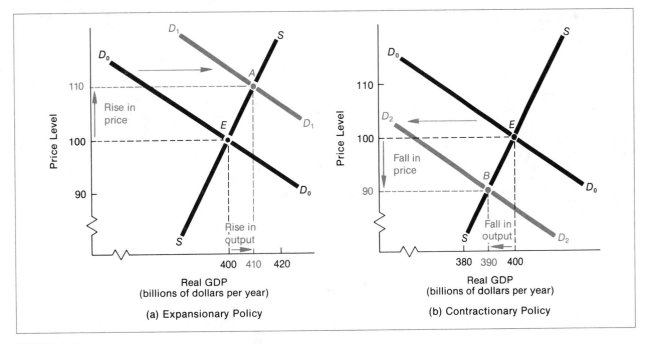

FIGURE 13-7
Stabilization Policy with a Steep Aggregate Supply Curve: The Monetarist Case
These two diagrams show that stabilization policy is much more effective at fighting inflation than at fighting recession when the aggregate supply curve is steep. In part (a), expansionary policies that push aggregate demand outward from D_0D_0 to D_1D_1 raise output by only $10 billion but push up prices by 10 percent, as equilibrium moves from point E to point A. So demand management is not a good way to end a recession. In part (b), contractionary policies that pull aggregate demand inward to D_2D_2 are successful in that they lower prices markedly (from 100 to 90, or 10 percent) but reduce output only slightly (from $400 billion to $390 billion). Monetarists tend to believe in this case.

from point E to point A. There is a substantial rise in output ($40 billion) with only a pinch of inflation (1 percent).

Conversely, when the supply curve is so flat, a restrictive stabilization policy is not a very effective way to cure inflation; instead, it serves mainly to reduce real output, as Figure 13-6(b) shows. Here, a leftward shift of the aggregate demand curve moves equilibrium from point E to point B, lowering real GDP by $40 billion but cutting the price level by merely 1 percent.

The monetarists see things differently. To them, the aggregate supply curve is so steep that expansionary fiscal or monetary policies are likely to cause a good deal of inflation without adding much to real GDP. [See Figure 13-7(a), where expansionary policies shift equilibrium from E to A.] Similarly, contractionary policies are effective ways of bringing down the price level without much sacrifice of real output, as shown by the shift from E to B in Figure 13-7(b).

The resolution of this debate is of fundamental importance for the proper conduct of stabilization policy. If the Keynesian view is right, stabilization policy is much more effective at combating recession than inflation. If the monetarist view is correct, the reverse is true.

Why does the argument persist? Why can't economists determine whether the aggregate supply curve is flat or steep and stop arguing? The answer is that supply conditions in the real world are far more complicated than our simple diagrams suggest. Some industries may have flat supply curves while other have steep ones. For reasons explained in Chapter 8, supply curves shift over time. And, unlike many laboratory scientists, economists cannot perform the controlled experiments that would reveal the shape of the aggregate supply curve directly. Instead, they must use statistical inference to make educated guesses.

Although empirical research on aggregate supply is proceeding, our understanding of aggregate supply remains much less settled than our understanding of aggregate

FIGURE 13-8

An Aggregate Supply Curve with Both Steep and Flat Regions

As this diagram suggests, either the Keynesians or the monetarists may be right under the appropriate circumstances. The Keynesian view of a flat supply curve is likely to be most accurate when there is much unemployment and unused capacity. The monetarist view of a steep supply curve is likely to be more accurate when there is full employment and high capacity utilization.

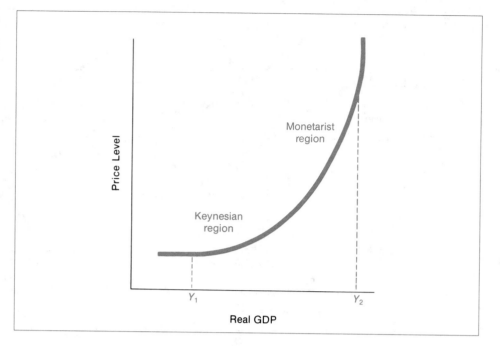

demand. Nevertheless, many economists believe that the outline of a consensus view has emerged. This view stresses that the steepness of the aggregate supply schedule depends on the degree of slack in the economy.

If industry has a great deal of spare capacity, then increases in demand will not call forth large price increases. Similarly, when many workers are unemployed, employment can rise without causing much acceleration in the rate at which wages are growing. In a word, the aggregate supply curve is quite flat. On the other hand, when businesses are producing near capacity and unemployment is near the frictional level, greater demand for goods will induce firms to raise their prices, and the resulting greater demand for labour will push wages up faster. In brief, the aggregate supply schedule will be steep.

Figure 13-8 shows a version of the aggregate supply curve that embodies these ideas. It has the same general shape as most of the supply curves that we have used in this book. At low levels of GDP, like Y_1, it is nearly horizontal; then its slope starts to rise gradually until at very high levels of GDP, like Y_2, it becomes almost vertical. The implication is that any change in aggregate demand will have most of its effect on *output* when economic activity is slack (the Keynesian case) but on *prices* when the economy is operating near full employment (the monetarist case). In summary:

1. Keynesians believe that the aggregate supply curve is rather flat in many circumstances, especially when the economy is operating at low levels of resource utilization. They therefore stress the effects of demand management on output and belittle the effects on prices.

2. Monetarists believe that the aggregate supply curve is rather steep in many circumstances, especially when the economy has little slack. They therefore emphasize the effects of demand management on prices and belittle the effects on real output.

3. A middle-of-the-road view holds that the Keynesian case is quite strong when there is a great deal of unemployment, while the monetarist case is stronger when the economy is near full employment. Not all economists accept this middle-of-the-road view, but many do.

Should We Have a Stabilization Policy At All?

We have yet to consider what may be the most fundamental and controversial issue of all: Is it likely that the government can conduct a successful stabilization policy? Or are its well-intentioned efforts likely to be harmful, so that it would be better to adhere to fixed rules?

This controversy has raged for several decades now, with no end in sight. That Keynesians favour discretionary stabilization policy while monetarists favour non-interventionist rules is not surprising, given their political differences. As it happens, monetarists tend to be politically conservative while many Keynesians are liberal. So it is natural that Keynesians should be more intervention-minded and monetarists more inclined to keep the government's hands off the economy. But much more than political ideology propels the debate. We want to understand the economic issues.

Monetarists point to the lags and uncertainties that surround the operation of both fiscal and monetary policies—lags and uncertainties that we have stressed in this chapter. Will the Bank of Canada's actions have the desired effects on the money supply? How long will these actions have significant effects on interest rates? How will they affect spending, and how long will it take before the effects appear? Can fiscal-policy actions be taken promptly? Will consumers view tax changes as temporary or permanent? How large is the expenditure multiplier? The list could go on.

Monetarists look at this formidable catalogue of difficulties, add a dash of skepticism about our ability to forecast the economy's future, and conclude that stabilization policy is likely to do more harm than good. They advise both the fiscal and monetary authorities to pursue a passive policy rather than an active one—adhering to fixed rules that, while they will not iron out all the bumps in the economy's growth path, will at least keep it roughly on track in the long run.

Keynesians, though they admit that perfection is unattainable, are much *more optimistic* than the monetarists about the possibility of achieving a successful stabilization policy. And they are much *less optimistic* than the monetarists about how smoothly the economy would function in the absence of demand management. They therefore advocate discretionary increases in government spending (or decreases in taxes) and more rapid growth of the money supply when the economy has a recessionary gap. By this policy mix, they believe, government can keep the economy closer to its full-employment growth path.

Naturally, each side can point to evidence that buttresses its own view. Keynesians like to remind us of successful tax cuts that helped create jobs. Monetarists remind us of numerous instances when the government refused to limit excess aggregate demand, thereby causing inflation.

The historical record of fiscal and monetary policy is far from glorious. It shows that while there were many instances in which appropriate stabilization policy *could have been* helpful, the authorities instead either took inappropriate steps or did nothing at all. (We examine some of these mistakes in Chapter 14.) It seems, therefore, that the question of whether the government should adopt passive rules or attempt an activist stabilization policy merits a closer look. As we shall see, the lags in the effects of policy play a pivotal role in the debate.

Lags and the Rules-versus-Discretion Debate

The reason that lags lead to a fundamental difficulty for stabilization policy—a difficulty so formidable that it has led many economists to conclude that attempts to stabilize economic activity are likely to do more harm than good—can be explained best by reference to Figure 13-9. Here we chart the behaviour of both actual and potential GDP over the course of a business cycle in a hypothetical economy in which no stabilization policy is attempted. At point *A*, the economy begins to slip into a recession and does not recover to full employment until point *D*. Then, between

FIGURE 13–9

A Typical Business Cycle

This is a stylized representation of the relationship between actual and potential GDP during a typical business cycle. The imaginary economy slips into a recession at point *A*, bottoms out around point *B*, and is in a recovery period until point *D*. After point *D*, it enters an inflationary boom that lasts until point *E*.

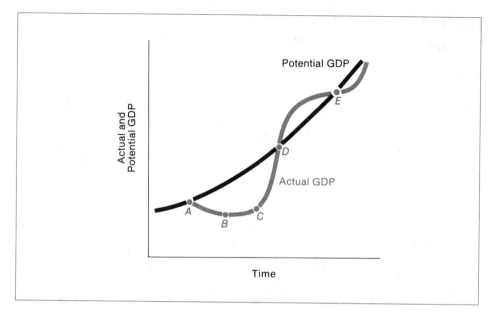

points *D* and *E*, the economy overshoots and is in an inflationary boom.

The case for stabilization policy runs like this. The recession is recognized to be a serious problem at point *B*, and appropriate actions are taken. These have their major effects around point *C* and thus curb both the depth and length of the recession.

But suppose the lags are really much longer than this. Suppose, for example, that delays in taking action postpone policy initiatives until point *C* and that stimulative policies do not have their major effects until after point *D*. Then policy will be of little help during the recession, and will actually do harm by overstimulating the economy during the ensuing boom. Thus:

In the presence of long lags, attempts at stabilizing the economy can actually destabilize it.

Because of this, some economists, like Milton Friedman, have argued that we are better off letting the economy alone and relying on its natural self-corrective forces to cure recessions and inflations. Instead of embarking on periodic programs of monetary and fiscal stimulus or restraint, they advise policy-makers to stick to *fixed rules*; that is, to rigid formulas that ignore current economic events.

Automatic Stabilizers

The rule most emphasized by monetarists is that the central bank simply keep the money supply growing at a constant rate. For fiscal policy, monetarists usually recommend that the government resist temptations to manage aggregate demand and rely instead on **automatic stabilizers**—features of the economy that reduce its sensitivity to shocks. Examples of automatic stabilizers are not hard to find in the federal budget. The personal income tax is the most obvious example.

The ability of the income tax to act as a shock absorber derives from the fact that it makes disposable income—and thus consumer spending—less sensitive to fluctuations in GDP. When GDP rises, disposable income (*DI*) rises also, but by less than the rise in GDP because part of the income is siphoned off by the government. This helps limit the upward fluctuation in consumption spending. And when GDP falls, *DI* falls less sharply because part of the loss is absorbed by the government rather than by consumers. So consumption does not drop as much as it otherwise might. Thus, as we noted in Chapter 9, income taxes lower the value of the multiplier. In truth, the

An automatic stabilizer is any arrangement that automatically serves to support aggregate demand when it would otherwise sag and to hold down aggregate demand when it would otherwise surge ahead. In this way, an automatic stabilizer reduces the sensitivity of the economy to shifts in demand.

unloved personal income tax is a modern institution that helps insure us against a repeat performance of the Great Depression.

There are many other automatic stabilizers in our economy. For example, in Chapter 4 we studied the Canadian system of unemployment insurance. This serves as an automatic stabilizer in a similar way. When GDP begins to fall and people lose their jobs, unemployment benefits prevent the disposable incomes of the jobless from falling as much as their earnings. As a result, unemployed workers can maintain their spending, and consumption need not fluctuate as dramatically as employment.

And the list could continue. The basic principle is the same: Each of these automatic stabilizers, in one way or another, serves as a shock absorber, thereby lowering the multiplier. And each does so without the need for any decision-maker to take action. In a word, they work *automatically*.

Believers in fixed rules assert that we should forget about discretionary policy and rely solely on automatic stabilizers and the economy's natural self-correcting mechanisms. Are they right? As usual, the answer depends on many factors.

How Fast Does the Economy's Self-Correcting Mechanism Work?

We stressed in Chapter 8 that the economy does have a self-correcting mechanism. If the economy can cure recessions and inflations very quickly by itself, then the case for intervention is weak. For if such problems typically last only a short time, then lags in discretionary stabilization policy mean that the medicine will often have its major effects only after the disease is over. (In terms of Figure 13–9, point D comes very close to point A.)

While the more extreme advocates of rules argue that this is what indeed happens, most economists agree that the economy's self-correcting mechanism is slow and not terribly reliable, even when supplemented by the automatic stabilizers. On this count, then, a point is scored for the Keynesians and discretionary policy.

How Long Are the Lags in Stabilization Policy?

As we explained, long lags before stabilization measures are adopted or take effect make it unlikely that policy can do much good, while short lags point in the other direction. Thus, advocates of fixed rules emphasize the length of lags, while proponents of discretion discount them.

Who is really right depends on the circumstances. In the most optimistic scenario, fiscal-policy actions are taken promptly, and the economy feels much of the stimulus from expansionary policy less than a year after slipping into a recession. While far from an instant cure, such timely actions would certainly be felt soon enough to do some good. But, as we have seen, more pessimistic scenarios raise the possibility that policy may actually be destabilizing. History offers examples of both types of scenarios. No general conclusion can be drawn.

How Accurate Are Economic Forecasts?

One way to cut down the policy-making lag is to have good economic forecasts. If we could see a recession coming a full year ahead of time (which we certainly *cannot* do), even a rather slow-acting policy response would still be timely. (In terms of Figure 13–9, the coming recession would be predicted well before point A arrived.) Unfortunately, however, to forecast Canadian economic performance, we must be able to predict U.S. interest rates, foreign-government policies that affect our export performance, and such intangibles as people's expectations about inflation in times to come. The evidence is that forecasting is certainly not good enough to support so-called "fine tuning," that is, attempts to keep the economy always within a hair's breadth of full employment. But it probably is good enough if our interest in using discretionary stabilization policy is simply to avoid sizable gaps between actual and potential GDP. The boxed insert on the next page briefly discusses the techniques used by economists to forecast economic performance.

At the Frontier: Are Econometric Models Useful for Policy Analysis?

To make conditional—or "what if?"—predictions about the effects of government policy, a statistical version of the kind of model we have been constructing since Chapter 5 is required. At several points in the text (for example, on pages 192–95) we illustrated how our model of the economy could be represented algebraically. Economists use actual data and statistical methods to estimate all the a's and b's in equations such as $C = a + bDI$. The applied models, called econometric models, sometimes involve hundreds of equations, and both the estimation and simulations are done by computer. Econometric models are routinely used to produce numerical estimates of the effects that government policies might have. But some economists are highly critical of such procedures.

One major shortcoming of standard econometric models was first pointed out by Prof. Robert E. Lucas, Jr., of the University of Chicago. He argued that changes in economic policy often alter people's behaviour, thereby making the future different from the past.* Econometric models are essentially a complicated way of summarizing the statistical patterns found in historical data, and when we use such a model to assess the likely effects of policy, we tacitly assume that the future will be like the past. If this proves to be untrue, the conclusions we reach may be quite wrong.

But why should a change in policy upset historical behaviour patterns? A non-economic example may help explain why.† If you watch Canadian football, you know that teams almost always punt on third down when they have three or more yards to go. Now suppose the rules were changed to allow a team four downs (as in the American game) rather than three. Someone who knew nothing about football, but simply extrapolated past behaviour, would continue to expect teams to punt on third down. But, in fact, the rule change would probably make punting on third down a rare event (as we know from watching American football).

Professor Lucas argued that many government policy changes are like rule changes in football: they may induce people, acting in their own best interests, to alter their behaviour. We encountered one example of this in Chapter 5, when we discussed why consumers will react less strongly to a *temporary* drop in income than to a *permanent* one (see pages 126–27). Suppose economists have estimated the marginal propensity to consume, and hence the multiplier. Now

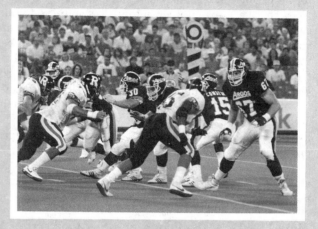

suppose stabilization policy improves, making recessions shorter and shallower. Consumers who understand this will assume that any income loss from a recession is now more transitory than it used to be. In consequence, they will cut their spending by less. So the marginal propensity to consume should decline, making our previous econometric estimate (based on past behaviour) a bad one.

Virtually all economists concede that Lucas is correct *in principle*. However, they continue to debate how important his criticism is *in practice*. Some ignore the problem and continue to use econometric models for policy analysis. Others are working on complex new methods that use economic theory and statistical analysis to deduce people's *objectives* from their observed *behaviour*. The idea is that, even if observed behaviour (punting on third down) changes when the rules change, underlying objectives (winning football games) do not. Although the new methods, which are far too complicated to explain here, are quite difficult to apply, progress is being made in this area.

---

* Robert E. Lucas, Jr., "Econometric Policy Evaluation: A Critique," in K. Brunner and A. H. Meltzer, eds., *The Phillips Curve and Labor Markets*, Carnegie-Rochester Conference Series, No. 1 (Amsterdam: North Holland, 1976).
† This example is from Thomas J. Sargent, *Rational Expectations and Inflation* (New York: Harper and Row, 1986), pages 1–2.

Other Dimensions of the Rules-versus-Discretion Debate

While lags and forecasting play major roles in the debate between advocates of rules and advocates of discretionary policy, these are not the only issues on which they diverge.

The Size of Government

One argument that is bogus but nonetheless often heard is that an activist fiscal policy must inevitably lead to a growing public sector. Since proponents of fixed rules tend also to be opponents of big government, they view this as undesirable. Of course, others think that a large public sector is just what society needs. This argument is, however, completely beside the point because, as we explained in Chapter 9 (pages 199–200), one's opinion about the proper size of government should have nothing to do with one's view on stabilization policy. When recessions occur, advocates of big government can call for greater spending while advocates of small government can insist on tax cuts. Similarly, if there is a need to contract aggregate demand to fight inflation, the public sector can be made smaller by cutting expenditures or bigger by raising taxes. While such choices may be quite momentous from other points of view, they simply do not bear on the question of whether we should fight the recession or the inflation.

Uncertainties Caused by Government Policy

Advocates of rules are on stronger ground when they argue that frequent changes in tax laws, government spending programs, or monetary conditions will make it difficult for firms and consumers to formulate and carry out rational plans. They argue that by adhering to fixed rules, which are known to businesses and consumers, the authorities can provide a more stable environment for the private sector. Variations in the GDP gap, they say, would be smaller in an environment free from large and unpredictable changes in monetary and fiscal conditions. One of the points stressed by advocates of rules is that the downward flexibility of wages and prices has been undermined by the government's commitment to activist stabilization policy during the postwar years. Why lower your wage or price during a recession if you expect that the government is about to stimulate demand?

A Political Business Cycle

Advocates of rules use a final argument that is political rather than economic. Fiscal policy, they note, is decided by elected politicians. At least when elections are on the horizon, these men and women are likely to be at least as concerned with keeping their offices as with doing what is right for the economy. This leaves fiscal policy subject to all sorts of political manipulations, meaning that inappropriate actions may be taken to attain short-run political goals. In a system of purely automatic stabilization, its proponents argue, a rule of law would replace the rule of men, and this peril would be eliminated.

There is certainly a *possibility* that politicians could deliberately *cause* economic instability to help their own re-election. Some observers of these "political business cycles" claim that several leaders have taken full advantage of the opportunity, stimulating the economy before an election, and contracting it afterwards. Furthermore, even if there is no insidious intent, politicians may take the wrong actions for perfectly honourable reasons; it certainly is easy to find examples of large errors in the history of Canadian stabilization policy (as noted in the next chapter).

So, taken as a whole, the political argument against discretionary policy seems to have a great deal of merit. But what are we to do about it? It is foolhardy to believe that fiscal and monetary decisions could or should be made by a group of objective and non-partisan technicians. Steering the economy is not like steering a rocket to the moon. Because policy actions that help on the employment front normally do harm on the inflation front and vice versa, the "correct" policy action is almost always an inherently political matter. In a democracy, if we take such decisions out of the hands of elected officials, in whose hands shall we put them?

This harsh fact may seem worrisome in view of the possibilities for political chicanery, but it should not bother us any more (or any less!) than similar manoeuvring in other areas of policy-making. After all, the same thing applies to international relations, formulation of the law, and so on. Politicians make all these decisions for us, subject only to sporadic accountability at election times. Is there really any reason why economic decisions should be different?

Conclusion: What Should Be Done?

Where do all these considerations leave us? On balance, is it better to conduct discretionary policy as best we can, knowing full well that we will never do it perfectly? Or is it wiser to rely on fixed rules and automatic stabilizers? In weighing the pros and cons that we have discussed in this chapter, one's basic view of the economy is central. Some economists believe that the economy, if left unmanaged, would generate a series of ups and downs that are hard to predict, but that it would correct each of them by itself in a relatively short period of time. They conclude that, because of long lags and poor forecasts, our ability to anticipate whether the economy will be heading up or down by the time policy actions have their effects is quite limited. And so they are led to advocate fixed rules.

Other economists liken the economy to a giant glacier with a great deal of inertia. This means that if we observe an inflationary or recessionary gap today, it is likely still to be there a year or two from now because the self-correcting mechanism works so slowly. In such a world, accurate forecasting is not imperative, even if policy lags are long. If we base policy on a forecast of a \$10 billion gap between actual and potential GDP a year from now and the gap turns out to be only \$5 billion, then we still will have done the right thing despite the horrible forecast. Holders of this view of the economy, then, are likely to advocate the use of discretionary policy.

While there is no consensus on this issue either among economists or among politicians, a prudent view might be that:

The case for active discretionary policy is strong when the economy has a serious deficiency or excess of aggregate demand. However, advocates of fixed rules are right that it is unwise to try to iron out every little wiggle in the growth path of GDP.

But the decision cannot be made solely on economic grounds. Political judgments enter as well. In the end:

The question of whether the government should take an active hand in managing the economy, which is one of the main bones of contention between Keynesians and monetarists today, is as much a matter of ideology as of economics. Liberals have always looked to government activism to solve social problems, while conservatives have consistently pointed out that many efforts of government fail despite the best of intentions.

Since no one can decide whether liberal or conservative political attitudes are the "correct" ones on purely objective criteria, the rules-versus-discretion debate is likely to go on for quite some time.

Summary

1. Monetarist and Keynesian analyses are two different ways of studying the determination of aggregate demand. Neither is a complete theory of the behaviour of the economy until aggregate supply is brought into the picture.

2. Investment spending (I), including business investment and investment in new homes, is sensitive to interest rates (r). Specifically, I is lower when r is higher.

3. This fact explains how monetary policy works in the Keynesian model. Raising the money supply (M) leads to a lower r; the lower interest rates stimulate more investment spending, and this investment stimulus, via the multiplier, then raises aggregate demand.

4. However, prices are likely to rise as output rises. The amount of inflation caused by increasing the money supply depends on the levels of unemployment and of capacity utilization. There will be much inflation when the economy is near full employment but little inflation when there is a great deal of slack.

5. An important reason why the aggregate demand curve slopes downward is that higher prices increase the demand to hold money in order to finance transactions. Given the money supply, this pushes interest rates up, which, in turn, discourages investment.

6. A second reason why the aggregate demand curve slopes downward is that higher domestic prices make our exports less competitive internationally so net export demand falls.

7. Velocity (V) is the ratio of nominal GDP to the stock of money. It indicates how quickly money circulates, that is, how many times money changes hands in a year.

8. Among the determinants of velocity is the rate of interest (r). At higher interest rates, people find it less attractive to hold money because most money pays no interest. Thus, when r rises, money circulates faster, and V rises.

9. Monetarism is a type of analysis that focusses attention on velocity and the money supply (M). Though monetarists realize that V is not constant, they believe that it is predictable enough to make it a useful tool for policy analysis and forecasting.

10. Because expansionary fiscal policy raises output and prices, and hence increases the demand for money, it pushes interest rates higher. This is how a monetarist explains the effect of fiscal policy. Because higher r leads to higher velocity, it leads to a higher product $M \times V$ even if M is unchanged.

11. While Keynesian and monetarist theories both lead us to expect that fiscal *and* monetary policies can each affect aggregate demand, Keynesians tend to believe more in the effectiveness of fiscal policy while monetarists tend to believe more in the effectiveness of monetary policy.

12. Because fiscal-policy actions affect aggregate demand either directly through G or indirectly through C, the expenditure lags between fiscal actions and their effects on aggregate demand are probably fairly short. By contrast, monetary policy operates mainly on investment, I, which responds very slowly to changes in interest rates.

13. However, the policy-making lag normally is much longer for fiscal policy than for monetary policy. Hence, when the two lags are combined, it is not clear which type of policy acts more quickly.

14. Keynesians believe that the aggregate supply curve is rather flat in the short run. This means that increases in aggregate demand will add much to the nation's real output and add little to the price level. Stabilization policy thus has much to recommend it as an anti-recession device, but it has little power to combat inflation.

15. Monetarists believe that the aggregate supply curve is very steep. This means that increases in aggregate demand increase real output rather little and succeed mostly in pushing up prices. Consequently, while stabilization policy can do much to fight inflation, it is not a very effective way to cure unemployment.

16. The Keynesian view probably is most applicable to an economy with much unemployment, while the monetarist view applies best to an economy producing near capacity levels.

17. The Canadian economy has a number of automatic stabilizers that make it less vulnerable to shocks than it would otherwise be. Among these are the personal income tax and unemployment benefits.

18. When there are long lags in the operation of fiscal and monetary policy, attempts to stabilize economic activity may actually destabilize it.

19. Many monetarists believe that our imperfect knowledge of the channels through which stabilization policy works and the long lags involved make it unlikely that discretionary stabilization policy can succeed.

20. Keynesians recognize these difficulties but do not believe they are as serious as monetarists think. On the other hand, Keynesians place much less faith in the economy's ability to cure recessions and inflations on its own. They therefore think that discretionary policy is advisable.

Concepts for Review

Why the aggregate demand curve slopes downward
Quantity theory of money
Velocity
Equation of exchange

Effect of interest rate on velocity
Monetarism
Effect of monetary policy on inflation
Effect of fiscal policy on interest rates
Lags in stabilization policy

Shape of the aggregate supply curve
Rules versus discretionary policy
Automatic stabilizers

Questions for Discussion

1. How much money (including cash and chequing account balances) do you typically have at any particular moment? Divide this into your total income over the past 12 months to obtain your own personal velocity. Are you typical of the nation as a whole?

2. Use the concept of opportunity cost to explain why velocity is higher at higher interest rates.

3. How does monetarism differ from the quantity theory of money? How does it differ from Keynesian analysis?

4. Explain why both business investments and purchases of new homes are expected to decline when interest rates rise.

5. Explain what a $40 billion increase in the money supply will do to real GDP under the following assumptions:

a. Each $20 billion increase in the money supply reduces the rate of interest by 1 percentage point.
b. Each 1 percentage point decline in interest rates stimulates $30 billion of new investment spending.
c. The expenditure multiplier is 2.5.
d. There is so much unemployment that prices do not rise noticeably when demand increases.

6. Explain how your answer to Question 5 would differ if each of the assumptions were changed. Specifically, what sorts of changes in the assumptions would make monetary policy very weak?

7. Using graphs, explain why the aggregate demand curve has a negative slope.

8. Distinguish between the expenditure lag and the policy lag in stabilization policy. Does monetary policy or fiscal policy have the shorter expenditure lag? What about the policy lag?

9. Explain why their contrasting views on the shape of the aggregate supply curve lead Keynesians to argue much more strongly for stabilization policies to fight unemployment while monetarists argue much more strongly for stabilization policies to fight inflation.

10. Consider an economy in which government purchases are 50; taxes and net exports are zero; the consumption function is:

$$C = 100 + 0.8Y;$$

and investment spending (I) depends on the rate of interest (r) in the following way:

$$I = 500 - 800r.$$

Find the equilibrium GDP if the central bank makes the rate of interest (a) 5 percent ($r = 0.05$); (b) 10 percent.

11. What is the value of the government expenditure multiplier on GDP in the economy of Question 10?

12. Name some automatic stabilizers and explain how and what they "stabilize."

13. Which of the following events would strengthen the argument for the use of discretionary policy, and which would strengthen the argument for rules?
    a. Structural changes make the economy's self-correcting mechanism faster and more reliable than before.
    b. New statistical methods are found that improve the accuracy of economic forecasts.

14. Suppose you are given the following econometric model:

$$C = 18 + 0.9DI$$
$$DI = Y - T$$
$$T = 10 + \tfrac{1}{3}Y$$
$$Y = C + I + G + X - IM.$$

The model generates predictions for Y, DI, T, and C when independent forecasts for I, G, and $X - IM$ are made. If expectations are that $I = 200$, $G = 880$, and $X - IM = 0$, what forecast does the model make for overall output? If this forecast proves to be inaccurate, does this mean the econometric model is flawed?

14

Stabilization Policy for a
Small Open Economy

The truth is never pure and
rarely simple.

OSCAR WILDE

I n Chapter 13 we explained how fiscal and monetary policy affect GDP, the price
level, and the level of interest rates. We now must admit, however, that we cut the
story short by assuming that Canadian interest rates can move independently of
foreign interest rates. On the contrary, as we stressed in Chapter 12, interest-rate
differentials cause large flows of funds across the border as asset holders strive to
acquire bonds giving a higher yield. These flows of funds represent shifts in the
demand and supply curves for foreign exchange. Such shifts must result in one of two
things: a movement of the exchange rate (if we are on a flexible-rate policy) so that
net exports will change; or a change in the domestic money supply (if we are on a
fixed exchange-rate policy). In either case, there are further effects on aggregate
demand. We now complete the analysis by examining four separate cases:

1. Fiscal policy under fixed exchange rates.

2. Fiscal policy under flexible exchange rates.

3. Monetary policy under fixed exchange rates.

4. Monetary policy under flexible exchange rates.

Our conclusion is that the usefulness of monetary and fiscal policies as demand-
management tools depends critically on the government's exchange-rate policy. In
addition to analyzing options for domestic stabilization policy, we consider the effects
on Canada of two key macroeconomic disturbances from abroad: increases in interest
rates in the United States and increases in world trade restrictions. Thus, although this
is one of the shorter chapters in the book, it is *indispensable* to a proper understanding
of macroeconomic policy.

Fiscal Policy under a Fixed Exchange-Rate Regime

Consider an increase in government spending. Our earlier analysis suggested that this
policy leads to an increase in real GDP and the price level, and that the higher nominal
value of transactions induces households and firms to try to acquire more money. As a
result, the money-demand curve shifts to the right, and there is an increase in the
Canadian interest rate. This review of our earlier analysis is summarized by the shift
from point A to point B in each panel of Figure 14–1. Both real GDP and the price
level increase, from $400 billion to $420 billion and from 100 to 105, respectively
[Figure 14–1(a)], and there is what we now recognize as a *temporary* increase in the

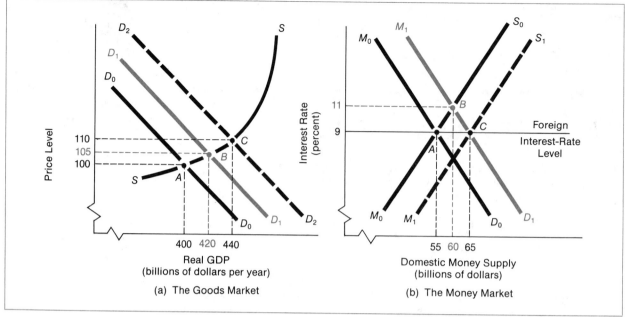

FIGURE 14-1

Fiscal Policy with International Capital Flows

An increase in government spending shifts the aggregate demand curve from D_0D_0 to D_1D_1 [panel (a)]. The resulting higher nominal GDP shifts the money-demand curve from M_0D_0 to M_1D_1 [panel (b)]. The higher rate of interest attracts foreign funds into Canada so that either the Canadian dollar appreciates (and net exports fall, returning the demand curves to D_0D_0 and M_0D_0) under flexible exchange rates, or the Bank of Canada buys the incoming foreign funds (so that the domestic money supply increases to M_1S_1, and aggregate demand is further stimulated to D_2D_2) under fixed exchange rates.

Canadian interest rate to 11 percent [Figure 14-1(b)]. In this example, Canadian interest rates now exceed foreign interest rates by two percentage points.

Now let us trace the international effects of the higher Canadian interest rate depicted in Figure 14-1(b). It causes foreign investors to send more funds into Canada as they shift their portfolios of assets to acquire more of the now-appealing high-yield Canadian bonds. To acquire our bonds, they need our currency; therefore, they sell foreign exchange to obtain our currency. Similarly, Canadians reduce their demand for foreign exchange as they have increased incentive to hold their own bonds.

The net effect on the foreign-exchange market is that the Canadian dollar is more in demand so Canada's balance of payments must move in the direction of a surplus. Under a fixed exchange-rate regime, the Bank of Canada avoids any appreciation of the Canadian dollar by buying up the otherwise unwanted quantity of foreign exchange, for which purpose it issues more Canadian money.

The higher quantity of domestic money is shown by a shift to the right of the money-supply line in Figure 14-1(b) from M_0S_0 to M_1S_1. This easing of domestic credit conditions, which necessarily follows from the Bank of Canada's intervention in the foreign-exchange market, eliminates the interest-rate differential. The final outcome in the domestic money market is given by point C in Figure 14-1(b). The return of the Canadian interest rate to its original level reverses any cut-back of investment spending that originally occurred, so aggregate demand is stimulated further, as shown by the aggregate demand curve shifting further to position D_2D_2 in Figure 14-1(a).

We conclude that the initial direct expansionary effect of the fiscal policy (the movement from point A to point B) is *reinforced* by the subsequent effects of the policy that are induced by the Bank of Canada's intervention to keep the exchange rate fixed (the movement from point B to point C). In our example, then, the expansionary fiscal policy raises real GDP from $400 billion to $440 billion and raises the price level from 100 to 110. The reason for these large effects is that the Bank of Canada was forced, by its commitment to fix the exchange rate, to perform a complementary monetary policy. The open-market purchase of foreign exchange increases the Canadian money supply (to $65 billion in our example). The interest rate rises from 9 percent to 11 percent only *temporarily*; in the end, the Canadian interest rate has returned to the level of foreign interest rates.

Fiscal Policy under a Flexible Exchange-Rate Regime

Now consider the same increase in government spending when exchange rates are floating freely. The initial effects are the same as in Figure 14–1 (to which we continue to refer): higher GDP (shown by the move from A to B), Canadian interest rates rising above foreign rates, and an increased demand for Canadian dollars on the foreign-exchange market. Under flexible exchange rates, the Bank of Canada makes no attempt to buy up the otherwise unwanted quantity of foreign exchange, so the Canadian dollar appreciates in value. With no transactions by the Bank of Canada, the money supply is constant so the money-supply schedule remains at position M_0S_0 in Figure 14–1(b). But the appreciating Canadian dollar makes our imports cheaper, and foreigners find our exports more expensive. As a result, *net exports fall*; the aggregate demand curve shifts back to the left from D_1D_1 toward D_0D_0 in Figure 14–1(a).

How far will this process go? The induced appreciation of the Canadian dollar must continue as long as the Canadian interest rate remains above foreign rates. Hence, the process can come to an end only when the aggregate demand curve has shifted leftward enough to re-establish the original equilibrium point A. With prices and real output back at their original levels, the demand-for-money curve will be back at its original position, so Canadian interest rates will be back down to the level of foreign interest rates. At this point, savers' shift of funds across the border stops. In the end, then, the initial direct expansionary effect of fiscal policy is eventually completely eliminated by the induced exchange-rate effects.

The effort to raise real GDP by government spending fails under flexible exchange rates; aggregate demand is affected only temporarily, since all that the higher government spending does is *replace* pre-existing export demand for Canadian products.

This scenario is a perfect description of the Canadian situation during the late 1950s and early 1960s. We were in a recession, with high unemployment and very little inflation. James Coyne, the governor of the Bank of Canada, felt that unemployment was not a concern of the central bank. Technically he was right; the Bank of Canada Act states that the Bank's job is to preserve the value of our currency, and that means keeping the purchasing power of our dollar from being eroded by inflation. Coyne tried to ensure that this would not occur by restricting the quantity of money in the system. This policy put upward pressure on interest rates, and the resulting increase in the foreign demand for our bonds pushed up the value of the Canadian dollar. The problem was that both the temporarily higher interest rates (which lowered investment spending) and the more expensive Canadian dollar (which lowered net exports) made the unemployment problem worse. The Department of Finance ran large deficits in an attempt to lessen unemployment, but as we have just learned, fiscal policy has no lasting effect on aggregate demand under flexible exchange rates. It is no wonder that the Diefenbaker government wanted Coyne to resign; it was left with fiscal policy as the only tool for "curing" the recession, and that is essentially a useless tool in a flexible exchange-rate setting. It is not surprising that major Canadian economists ran a full-page item in leading newspapers at the time, urging the Bank of Canada to relieve the constraint it had placed on stabilization policy.

Monetary Policy under a Fixed Exchange-Rate Regime

We now consider monetary policy in each of the polar-case exchange-rate regimes. Suppose the Bank of Canada wants to fight inflation and so decreases the domestic money supply. The analysis in Chapter 13 suggested that this policy leads to a decrease in GDP and the price level, and a higher interest rate due to tighter credit conditions. This is illustrated in Figure 14–2. The decrease in the domestic money supply is shown by the leftward shift of the money-supply line (from M_0S_0 to M_1S_1) in Figure 14–2(b). The resulting tighter credit conditions are indicated by the fact that Canadian interest rates have risen from 9 percent to 11 percent, at point B in panel (b). The higher borrowing costs mean lower investment spending by firms, so the aggregate demand curve shifts left from D_0D_0 to D_1D_1 in panel (a). Thus, the economy moves from point A to point B in both panels of Figure 14–2. The initial effects of the contractionary monetary policy in this example are to reduce real GDP from $400 billion to $380 billion, to reduce the price index from 100 to 95, and to raise borrowing costs from 9 percent to 11 percent. As we have seen before, however, the resulting gap between foreign and domestic interest rates cannot last.

The interest-rate differential causes portfolio shifts on the part of bond-holders toward Canadian bonds. Foreigners will supply more foreign exchange to the trading market, to get the Canadian dollars that are required to pay for the high-yield Canadian bonds. Canadians will demand less foreign exchange, since they now have a decreased demand for foreign financial assets. These reactions to the temporary interest-rate differential mean upward pressure on the value of the Canadian dollar. Under a fixed exchange-rate regime, the Bank of Canada precludes this appreciation of the dollar by buying the otherwise unwanted quantity of foreign exchange. That is, Canada sustains an increase in the balance-of-payments surplus, and the Bank of Canada issues more domestic currency to pay for this accumulation of foreign-exchange reserves. Since the money supply increases automatically as a result of this

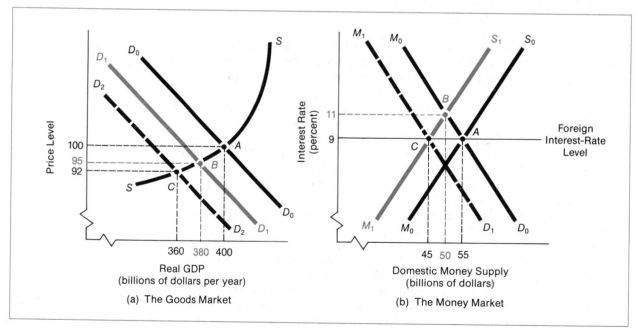

FIGURE 14–2

Monetary Policy with International Capital Flows

A decrease in the money supply shifts the money-supply curve from M_0S_0 to M_1S_1 [panel (b)]. The resulting higher borrowing costs reduce aggregate demand from D_0D_0 to D_1D_1 [panel (a)]. The higher rate of interest also attracts foreign funds into Canada so that either the Canadian dollar appreciates (and net exports fall, pushing aggregate demand down to D_2D_2) under flexible exchange rates, or the Bank of Canada buys the incoming foreign funds (so that the domestic money supply increases back to supply curve position M_0S_0) under fixed exchange rates.

open-market purchase of foreign exchange, the money-supply curve in Figure 14–2(b) shifts back to the right. This easing of credit conditions causes Canadian interest rates to start falling back down from 11 percent, and as a result, the aggregate demand curve starts to shift back to the right, from position D_1D_1 in Figure 14–2(a). Thus, the original decreases in real GDP and the price level are reversed.

How far will this process go? The increase in the money supply that is induced by the flow of foreign funds into Canada must continue as long as the Canadian interest rate is significantly above foreign rates. Hence, the process comes to an end when the money-supply line shifts far enough to the right that it returns to position M_0S_0, and the interest rate is 9 percent, at point A in Figure 14–2(b). But if borrowing costs return to their original level, investment spending by firms will be restored to its initial level. Thus, the aggregate demand curve will return to its starting position, D_0D_0, in Figure 14–2(a). In the end, then, we return to point A in both panels of Figure 14–2 and there is no lasting effect of monetary policy.

By committing themselves to issue or withdraw money according to the outcome in the foreign-exchange market, the authorities have relinquished the ability to set the domestic money supply at any independently specified value.

In spite of the fact that the flexible exchange-rate version of this model ex-plained the Coyne Affair so well, the Bank of Canada ignored it again by trying a rather dramatic contractionary monetary policy to fight inflation in 1969. We were then in a fixed exchange-rate regime. The money supply was cut in mid-1969, and Canadian interest rates rose. The effect on the balance of payments was dramatic. We had a surplus of $65 million in 1969; then, with foreign currency attracted by high Canadian interest rates, the balance-of-payments surplus rose to $1663 million in 1970 (a twenty-five-fold increase!) although the Bank maintained the fixed exchange-rate policy only until May of that year. The Bank tried to insulate the domestic money supply from the balance-of-payments surplus by using open market operations in the bond market. That is, as rapidly as it was issuing new Canadian money to buy the incoming foreign exchange, it tried to balance this by selling government bonds to decrease chartered bank reserves. However, the Bank soon realized that selling bonds to the general public (to get the new money back out of the system) produced a vicious circle. Big bond issues are purchased only if the interest rate involved is favourable. Thus, the big bond sales further raised interest rates, caused a larger inflow of foreign exchange (resulting in an even larger balance-of-payments surplus), and forced the government to sell even more bonds, etc., etc., if the money supply was to remain contracted.

The government finally realized it was trapped in this vicious circle, and it broke the chain in May 1970 by removing the promise to fix the exchange rate. As the model predicts, the value of the Canadian dollar increased noticeably immediately following this decision. It is ironic that after moving to a floating-rate policy (which we have just shown to be a necessary condition for conducting a successful monetary policy), the Bank gave up its fight against inflation and embarked on an expansionary monetary policy. This was "effective" (given the new floating exchange-rate environment), and the acceleration of inflation was the result.

Monetary Policy under a Flexible Exchange-Rate Regime

To discuss monetary policy under flexible exchange rates we consider the same decrease in money supply and continue to refer to Figure 14–2. The initial effects are the same: lower real GDP, lower price level, the Canadian interest rate climbing higher than foreign rates, and the interest-rate differential causing foreign funds to flow into Canada. The difference is that without the Bank of Canada's involvement in the foreign-exchange market there is no further movement in the position of the money-supply curve from $M_1 S_1$. Instead, the Canadian dollar appreciates as the foreign funds enter the country, and this makes our imports cheaper to buy and our exports more expensive for foreigners to buy. As our net exports fall, the aggregate demand curve shifts leftward in the direction of $D_2 D_2$, so the price level and real GDP are further reduced.

How far will this process go? The appreciation of the Canadian dollar must continue as long as the Canadian interest rate is significantly above foreign interest rates. The process ends when the aggregate demand curve has shifted down sufficiently to lower nominal GDP enough to shift the demand-for-money curve to position $M_1 D_1$ in panel (b). At this stage, the economy is at point C in both panels of Figure 14–2. In our example, the price index has fallen from 100 to 92, and real GDP has fallen to $360 billion. The money supply has fallen to the $45 billion level, and the interest rate has returned to its original value of 9 percent, which is the level of foreign interest rates. Since the interest rate differential is eliminated, we see that:

In a small open economy, monetary policy works through the sensitivity of net exports to the exchange rate, not through the sensitivity of investment spending to the interest rate.

We have analyzed a *contractionary* monetary policy in the flexible exchange-rate case to allow you to compare its effects directly with those described in our preceding discussion of actual policy taken in 1969–70 under fixed exchange rates. As we noted earlier, however, after moving to a flexible exchange-rate regime on May 1970, the government adopted an *expansionary* monetary policy, which characterized the 1971–74 period. The same reasoning can be used in reverse to explain how expansionary monetary policy does have a lasting expansionary effect on aggregate demand, but only under floating rates. The rate of growth of Canada's money supply rose from 4.7 percent in 1969 to 19.9 percent in 1974. Given that the average annual growth in Canada's real output since 1953 has been less than 4.7 percent, this policy clearly involved an excessive stimulation of spending. The Bank of Canada finally accepted this interpretation and, in September 1975, reversed its policy position. During the 1975–82 period, the Bank emphasized repeatedly that it was attempting to ensure that Canada's money supply did not increase at more than a specified rate (to be lowered systematically so that inflation could be gradually reduced). The news media referred to this period as "Canada's experiment with monetarism." One interesting question is why the Bank permitted the overstimulation of aggregate demand in the 1971–74 period. The answer to this question will make clear the underlying cause of inflation.

The key to the answer is found in the 1971 *Annual Report* of the Bank of Canada. The report notes that the expansion in Canada's money supply was needed to "avoid contributing to undue appreciation of our currency," which would have "exacerbated the difficulties of important export and import competing industries and impeded the expansion of economic activity." Essentially, the Bank was concerned about unemployment, not inflation, and felt that rising interest rates and the resulting increase in the foreign value of the Canadian dollar would aggravate unemployment.

It is true that *if* foreign countries were not experiencing inflation, the higher value of the Canadian dollar would have hurt our exports, since a given amount of foreign currency earned as sales receipts would translate into fewer Canadian dollars to be used for financing domestic production costs. This is what the Bank of Canada was trying to avoid, and it probably regarded this possibility with particular concern since this is exactly what had happened in the 1958–61 period of tight monetary policy that came to be known as the Coyne Affair. However, there was an important difference in the 1970s: foreign countries *were* experiencing inflation. And as long as the Canadian dollar did not appreciate at a rate *higher* than that of foreign inflation, Canadian exporters would *not* be subject to a cost squeeze *at all*. Given the foreign environment, then, the Bank's inappropriate resistance to currency appreciation led to the overly expansive aggregate-demand policy of the 1971–74 period.

Looking back on the matter, the Bank of Canada does not dispute this judgment of its policy error. Also, since 1975 the Bank has reverted to maintaining a fundamental concern about inflation, not unemployment, as is made clear in the quotes from Bank governors Gerald Bouey and John Crow (see the boxed insert back in Chapter 12, pages 264–65).

Review of Aggregate Demand Policy Options

1. Fiscal policy has a lasting effect on aggregate demand under fixed exchange rates. The temporary rise in interest rates following the expansion attracts foreign funds, which the Bank of Canada must absorb to peg the exchange rate. The increase in the domestic money supply that the Bank must allow, in order to buy the incoming foreign exchange, reinforces the initial fiscal expansion.

2. Fiscal policy has no lasting effect on aggregate demand under a floating exchange rate. Any initial expansion of demand just causes temporarily higher interest rates, which attract foreign funds. The Canadian dollar appreciates, forcing a contraction in net export demands.

3. Monetary policy has no lasting effect on aggregate demand under fixed exchange rates. Any initial expansion of demand involves temporarily lower domestic interest rates, which cause foreign funds to leave the country. The Bank of Canada must accept the domestic currency that is relinquished as foreign exchange is purchased to buy foreign bonds. The resulting decrease in domestic money circulating counteracts the original policy.

4. Monetary policy has a lasting effect on aggregate demand under a floating exchange rate. An expansion of demand by the central bank initially involves lower domestic interest rates. As foreign funds leave the country, the Canadian dollar depreciates. The resulting stimulation of net exports reinforces the initial expansionary monetary policy.

These strong conclusions depend on the assumption that Canada is a "small" open economy—that is, that it has absolutely no ability to maintain interest rates at values that differ significantly from those in the United States. This assumption is not completely true, but as we noted in Chapter 12 (pages 265–66) it is very close to being so. Although the aggregate demand effects summarized above are *far* more relevant than those discussed in Chapter 13, we should probably temper them a little bit. Capital flows across the U.S.–Canadian border are not instantaneous. The following summary table gives the conclusions in this slightly weaker form.

Effects on Aggregate Demand of:

	FISCAL POLICY	MONETARY POLICY
Under a fixed exchange-rate regime	Strong	Weak
Under a flexible exchange-rate regime	Weak	Strong

To utilize this summary table, we must know what Canada's exchange-rate policy is. However, there is no simple answer to this question. We had a flexible exchange-rate regime in the 1950s, a fixed exchange-rate regime in the 1960s, and a mixture of the two since 1970.[1]

[1] The historical development of the international monetary system is discussed in the next chapter.

Officially, Canada is currently following a policy of floating exchange rates, but the Bank of Canada often heavily manages the rate (in many instances, to avoid a depreciation that is deemed inflationary). The Bank's intervention is, at times, dramatic. (Again, recall the boxed insert on pages 264–65.)

Exchange Rates and Aggregate Supply

We emphasized in Chapter 9 that the exchange rate is a shift variable for the aggregate supply curve. Since some imports are intermediate products, an appreciating Canadian dollar lowers one component of domestic costs and shifts the aggregate supply curve down. Similarly, a depreciating Canadian dollar raises this component of domestic costs and shifts the aggregate supply curve up. With this reminder, we are in a position to extend our discussion beyond aggregate demand and to derive the complete real GDP and price-level effects of monetary and fiscal policies under each exchange-rate regime.

An increase in government spending under fixed exchange rates is shown in Figure 14–3(a). We have already shown that there is a lasting effect on aggregate demand in this case, which is indicated by the rightward shift of the aggregate demand curve from $D_0 D_0$ to $D_1 D_1$. Since the exchange rate is fixed, the aggregate supply curve does not move. We conclude that expansionary fiscal policy under fixed exchange rates raises both prices and real output.

The same increase in government spending under flexible exchange rates is shown in Figure 14–3(b). We discovered earlier that there is no lasting effect on

FIGURE 14-3
Fiscal and Monetary Effects on Aggregate Demand and Supply
Both monetary and fiscal policies have direct aggregate-supply effects under a floating exchange-rate regime, since the exchange rate affects the costs of imported intermediate products.

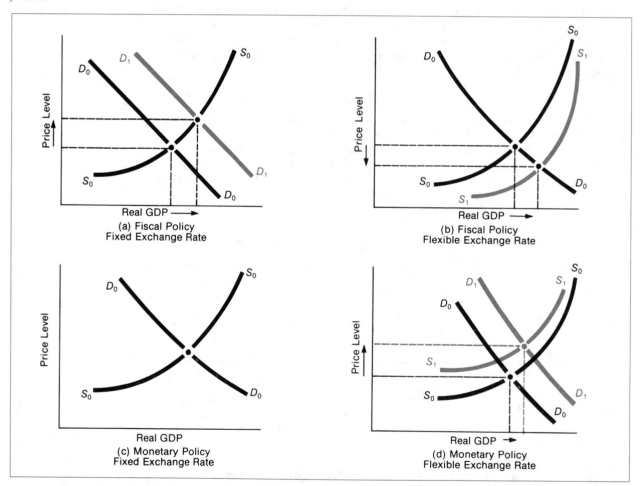

(a) Fiscal Policy
Fixed Exchange Rate

(b) Fiscal Policy
Flexible Exchange Rate

(c) Monetary Policy
Fixed Exchange Rate

(d) Monetary Policy
Flexible Exchange Rate

aggregate demand in this case, so there is no rightward shift of the aggregate demand curve. The reason is that the appreciation of the Canadian dollar reduces net exports and lowers aggregate demand by as much as the higher government spending raises it. There is nothing to counteract the above-noted cost-saving effect of the currency appreciation, however, so the aggregate supply curve shifts down from S_0S_0 to S_1S_1. We conclude that expansionary fiscal policy under flexible exchange rates raises real GDP and lowers the price level because its only effects are from the aggregate supply side.

An increase in the domestic money supply is considered in the remaining two panels of Figure 14–3. Since there is no lasting effect on aggregate demand under fixed exchange rates nor any shift in the supply curve without an exchange-rate change, neither curve is shifted in Figure 14–3(c). We conclude that monetary policy has no effect on real GDP or the price level under fixed exchange rates. A more accurate description of this outcome is that an independent monetary policy cannot be set if the central bank has already committed the money supply to be whatever is required to peg the exchange rate.

An increase in the money supply is possible if the central bank does not intervene in the foreign-exchange market. This policy is considered in Figure 14–3(d). Since there is a lasting effect of the monetary expansion on aggregate demand, the demand curve shifts to the right from D_0D_0 to D_1D_1. However, the reason for this is that the depreciation in the Canadian dollar raises net exports. This depreciation also raises business costs, so the aggregate supply curve shifts up from S_0S_0 to S_1S_1. We conclude that expansionary monetary policy under flexible exchange rates results in higher prices, and (at best) in only a small increase in real GDP.

Review

Before we can have an informed opinion concerning the effects of government policy on unemployment and inflation, we must know what the government's exchange-rate policy is. Although a noticeable variation in the value of the Canadian dollar took place during the 1980s (it ranged between 70 cents U.S. and 86 cents U.S.), the government's policy was (and remains) one of significant management of the exchange rate. Thus we can take the fixed exchange-rate predictions of our analysis as roughly appropriate for *short-run* policy predictions. As a result, we cannot expect Canada to have a monetary policy that is much different from that in the United States. Fiscal policy can be used as an independent instrument, but as we have just seen in Figure 14–3(a), it involves the standard short-run trade-off between the real GDP and price-level goals. A further constraint on the use of fiscal policy is that it is difficult to conduct it in a flexible manner when the budget deficit is as large as it has been in recent years—a subject we discuss in greater detail in Chapter 16.

Foreign Interest-Rate Increases and Aggregate Supply

We considered the aggregate-demand effects of an increase in foreign interest rates in Chapter 12 (pages 262–66). Here we bring in the aggregate-supply effects that are involved if the exchange rate is allowed to float.

Until Canadian interest rates are pulled up to the level of foreign interest rates through competition, investors will sell Canadian bonds to buy the higher-yield foreign bonds. To accomplish this shift, investors must buy foreign currency by selling Canadian dollars. If the exchange rate is flexible, this shift causes a fall in the value of the Canadian dollar. The depreciation of the Canadian dollar stimulates foreign demand for our exports, so that the aggregate demand curve shifts out from D_0D_0 to D_1D_1 in Figure 14–4(a). The depreciated Canadian dollar also increases business costs, so the aggregate supply curve moves from S_0S_0 to S_1S_1. The net result is significant upward pressure on the price level, and perhaps even a decrease in production.

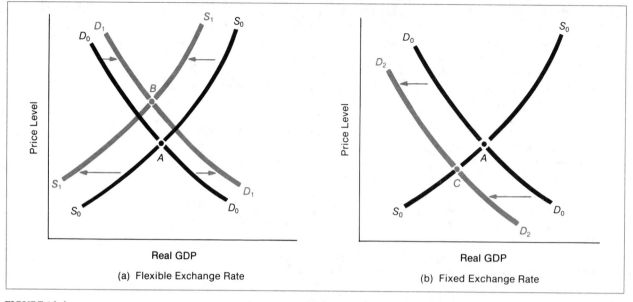

FIGURE 14-4

Aggregate-Demand and Aggregate-Supply Effects of Foreign Interest-Rate Increases

Foreign interest-rate increases lead investors to trade Canadian bonds for foreign bonds, and this requires exchanging Canadian dollars for foreign currencies. If there is a floating exchange rate [panel (a)], the depreciation of the Canadian dollar stimulates export demand (so demand shifts from $D_0 D_0$ to $D_1 D_1$) and increases business costs (so supply shifts from $S_0 S_0$ to $S_1 S_1$). We move from point A to point B in panel (a). If the exchange rate is fixed [panel (b)], the Bank of Canada buys the previously circulating Canadian currency to avoid depreciation, so the domestic money supply shrinks and aggregate demand shifts from $D_0 D_0$ to $D_2 D_2$. Without a change in the exchange rate, there is no direct effect on business costs, so no shift of the aggregate supply curve occurs. We move from point A to point C in panel (b). Output can fall under either exchange-rate regime, but more inflation occurs under a floating rate.

A lower level of production is particularly likely in the short run, since the increase in business costs occurs without a lag. In contrast, there is often a significant lag following an exchange-rate change, before foreign buyers decide that a change is permanent enough to warrant switching orders from one country to another.

To maintain a fixed exchange rate after an increase in foreign interest rates, the Bank of Canada must sell foreign exchange. Investors who desire high-yield bonds will be trading in Canadian dollars to get the necessary foreign exchange. As the previously circulating Canadian dollars are absorbed by the Bank of Canada (in payment for its sales of foreign exchange), the domestic money supply shrinks. As a result, the aggregate demand curve shifts in from $D_0 D_0$ to $D_2 D_2$ in Figure 14-4(b). With no change in the exchange rate under a fixed exchange-rate policy, there is no direct effect on business costs, so there is no shift in the aggregate supply curve.

To summarize, an increase in foreign interest rates leaves Canada with the following alternatives:

1. Peg the exchange rate, so the higher interest rate is accompanied by lower output and downward pressure on prices [a move from point A to point C in Figure 14-4(b)]; or

2. Float the exchange rate, so the higher interest rate is accompanied by higher prices, and probably a mild slump in output [a move from point A to point B in Figure 14-4(a)].

One's choice between these alternatives depends (among other things) on one's beliefs about the costs of unemployment versus the costs of inflation.

As we learned in Chapter 12, the Bank of Canada permitted some depreciation of the Canadian dollar in the face of U.S. interest-rate increases in the early 1980s, but the exchange rate was heavily managed. The Bank followed this policy because, ever since 1975, it has regarded the costs of inflation to be very high.

Foreign Trade Restrictions

If the dramatic increase in U.S. interest rates was, for Canada, the major foreign macroeconomic shock of the first half of the 1980s, trade restrictions threatened by the United States and other countries were considered the biggest foreign disturbance of the second half of the decade. In fact, the main purpose of signing the Free Trade Agreement with the United States in 1989 was to try to avoid these restrictions. But what policy should Canada adopt when our trading partners *do* impose restrictions? Should we peg or float the exchange rate?

Trade restrictions imposed by our trading partners force a reduction in our export sales. The initial effect, then, is a decrease in total spending, $C + I + G + X - IM$, in Canada. From the viewpoint of macroeconomic analysis, the effect of the foreign country's policy is just the same as the effect of a decrease in domestic government expenditure; as far as the curve shifts are concerned, it makes no difference whether it is the G component or the X component of aggregate demand that is affected initially. Thus, to understand the macroeconomic effects of foreign tariffs or quotas, all we have to do is recall the effects of a contractionary domestic fiscal policy. The top two panels of Figure 14–3 showed what happens with an expansionary fiscal policy; now we simply read these two shifts in reverse.

We saw that fiscal policy has lasting aggregate-demand effects under fixed exchange rates. Foreign tariffs, then, cause a lasting leftward shift in Canada's aggregate demand curve. With a fixed exchange rate, there is no change in the Canadian-dollar price of imported intermediate goods, so there is no direct effect on business costs, and thus no shift in the position of the aggregate supply curve. As should be clear from our reverse reading of Figure 14–3(a), then, foreign countries' trade restrictions cause recession (lower real GDP) and pressure for lower prices in Canada, if the exchange rate is pegged.

Could a true float of the exchange rate avoid this recession? We have already learned that a change in G leads to no lasting aggregate-demand effects for a small open economy on a flexible exchange rate. [This is why we showed no shift in the position of the aggregate demand curve in Figure 14–3(b).] The same reasoning applies for changes in the X component of aggregate demand. But that reasoning also reveals that a foreign tariff will have an adverse aggregate-supply-side effect. Recall that the temporary effect of a drop in Canadian aggregate demand is a lower domestic interest rate. Funds leave the country, and the Canadian dollar depreciates. The cheaper Canadian dollar stimulates our export sales, which tends to counteract the effects of the foreign tariff (this is why there is no lasting effect on aggregate demand). But, as we have already learned, the cheaper Canadian dollar makes intermediate imports more expensive. This increase in business costs shifts the aggregate supply curve upward, and the result in Canada is stagflation (higher prices and lower real output).

Unfortunately, then, exchange-rate policy cannot be used to insulate the domestic economy from the effects of foreign trade restrictions; a recession occurs under either exchange-rate regime. Nevertheless, since many economists think that the empirical magnitude of the aggregate-demand effect under fixed exchange rates is bigger than the aggregate-supply effect under flexible exchange rates, they believe a floating exchange rate can be a partial buffer against foreign trade restrictions.

A Concluding Comment

We have now completed our development of the tools of aggregate supply and demand. This chapter has shown that our analytical model has direct application for understanding past errors in Canadian macroeconomic policy and for clarifying the country's stabilization-policy options in the face of future macroeconomic disturbances.

But to fully understand macroeconomic issues as they are usually discussed in the media, the reader should complete four more tasks, and we have provided four more chapters in this macroeconomic section of the book to facilitate this accomplishment. First, you must be aware of certain historical and institutional arrangements that are involved in the international monetary system. Second, you must understand how trade deficits and government budget deficits are related, and whether a large government debt is or is not a great burden to a country's citizens. Third, you must understand how aggregate demand-and-supply analysis can be recast so as to permit direct analysis of the potential trade-off between unemployment and the inflation *rate* (rather than restrict attention to discussions of real GDP and the price *level*). Fourth, you should have some understanding of what affects labour productivity and the rate of growth of potential GDP. Each of the remaining four chapters in this part of the text is devoted to one of these important applications of our macroeconomic analysis.

Summary

1. The usefulness of monetary and fiscal policies as tools of demand management depends critically on the government's exchange-rate policy.
2. Fiscal policy has no lasting effect on aggregate demand under a floating exchange rate. Any initial expansion of demand just causes temporarily higher interest rates, which attract foreign funds. The Canadian dollar appreciates, forcing a contraction in net export demands. The truth of this proposition was dramatically illustrated by the conflict between the Bank of Canada and John Diefenbaker's Conservative government, known as the Coyne Affair.
3. Fiscal policy has a lasting effect on aggregate demand under fixed exchange rates. The temporary rise in interest rates following the expansion attracts foreign funds, which the Bank of Canada must absorb to peg the exchange rate. The increase in the domestic money supply, which the Bank must allow to buy the incoming foreign exchange, reinforces the initial fiscal expansion.
4. Monetary policy cannot be used as an independent instrument in a fixed exchange-rate regime. Any initial expansion of demand involves temporarily lower domestic interest rates, which cause foreign funds to leave the country. The Bank of Canada must accept the domestic currency that is relinquished as foreign exchange is purchased to buy foreign bonds. The resulting decrease in domestic money circulating counteracts the original pol-

icy. The truth of this proposition was dramatically illustrated in the 1969–70 period, when Canada tried a contractionary monetary policy with a pegged exchange rate, while the U.S. policy was expansionary due to the Vietnam war.

5. Monetary policy has a lasting effect on aggregate demand under a floating exchange rate. An expansion of demand by the Bank of Canada initially involves lower domestic interest rates. As foreign funds leave the country, the Canadian dollar depreciates. The resulting stimulation of net exports reinforces the initial expansionary monetary policy.

6. Both monetary and fiscal policies can have direct aggregate-supply effects under a floating exchange-rate regime. Since the exchange rate affects the costs of imported intermediate products, it affects business costs and shifts the position of the aggregate supply curve.

7. Although we have had a floating exchange rate, the Bank of Canada has for many years followed a policy of heavily managing its short-run value. As a result, our monetary policy has largely been determined by events in the United States. Under these circumstances, fiscal policy remains an independent instrument that can be used for demand management, but it involves the standard short-run trade-off: Higher levels of real GDP can be had only with increases in the price level.

Concepts for Review

Interest-rate differential
Foreign exchange market intervention

Fixed exchange rates
Floating, or flexible, exchange rates

Questions for Discussion

1. Why did the Bank of Canada resist appreciation of the Canadian dollar in the early 1970s?

2. Why did the Bank of Canada resist depreciation of the Canadian dollar in the 1980s?

3. In the text we examined an expansionary fiscal policy and a contractionary monetary policy, under both exchange-rate regimes. Show that the conclusions in the table on page 301 would be equally valid for a contractionary fiscal policy and an expansionary monetary policy.

4. Does exchange-rate policy make a difference for the effects of a foreign tariff on the Canadian economy?

5. Examine the effects of a tariff levied in Canada against our imports. What happens to prices and the level of employment?

6. Which of the following policies puts lasting upward pressure on the price level?
   a. An increase in the reserve requirement ratio under flexible exchange rates.
   b. An increase in corporate depreciation allowances that stimulates investment spending, under flexible exchange rates.

PART IV

Macroeconomic Issues

15

Policy Co-ordination in the World Economy

All decent people live beyond their incomes nowadays and those who aren't respectable live beyond other people's. A few gifted individuals manage to do both.

SAKI

T his chapter takes a look at the system that has been set up to handle the international movement of money—the **international monetary system**. We have already discussed the two polar forms of international monetary arrangements—the fixed exchange-rate regime and the flexible exchange-rate regime, at least from one small country's point of view. But now we wish to consider how the system as a whole works. In the first part of this chapter, we examine why some countries' currencies appreciate while others' depreciate. In the second part, we discuss how the *balance of payments* is measured. In the third part, we trace the historical development of the international monetary system, starting with the old *gold standard*, then the so-called *gold-exchange system* that prevailed from 1944 until 1971, and finally the current *mixed* system—which is a curious admixture of fixed and floating exchange rates. By comparing how the different systems have worked over the years, we can gain an understanding of the ongoing controversy over whether the major trading nations should seek greater exchange-rate stability than exists now.

In the final part of the chapter, we focus on the gaping trade deficit of the United States, which emerged in the 1980s—the largest trade deficit ever run by any nation in the history of the world. How much of the policy reaction to this deficit should come from the United States, and how much should come from countries running large trade surpluses, such as Japan? Because Canada is so exposed to the effects of foreign trade, the manner in which the major trading countries respond to their trade imbalances is of great importance to us.

What Determines Exchange Rates?

When exchange rates are flexible, they are determined by the forces of supply and demand. But what factors move the supply and demand curves? Economists believe that the principal determinants of exchange-rate movements are rather different in the long, medium, and short runs. So we turn in the next three sections to the analysis of exchange-rate movements over these three "runs." We begin with the long run.

The Purchasing-Power Parity Theory: The Long Run

As long as there is free trade across national borders, exchange rates should eventually adjust so that the same product costs the same number of dollars (or the same amount of any other currency) in every country, except for differences attributable to transportation costs and the like. This simple statement forms the basis of the major theory of exchange-rate determination in the long run.

The **purchasing-power parity theory of exchange-rate determination** holds that the exchange rate between any two national currencies adjusts to reflect differences in the price levels in the two countries.

An example will bring out the basic truth in this theory and also suggest some of its limitations. Suppose that Swedish and Canadian steel are identical and that these two nations are the only producers of steel for the world market. Suppose further that steel is the only tradeable good that either country produces.

Question: If Canadian steel costs $200 per tonne and Swedish steel costs 1000 kronor per tonne, what must be the exchange rate between the dollar and the krona?

Answer: Since 1000 kronor or $200 each buy a tonne of steel, they must be of equal value. Hence, each krona must be worth 20 cents. Why? A higher dollar price for a krona, such as 25 cents, would mean that steel cost $250 per tonne (1000 kronor at 25 cents each) in Sweden but only $200 per tonne in Canada. Then all foreign customers would shop for their steel in Canada. Similarly, any exchange rate below 20 cents to the krona would send all the steel business to Sweden.

The purchasing-power parity theory is used to make long-run predictions about the effects of inflation on exchange rates. To continue our example, suppose that over a five-year period, prices in Canada rise by 25 percent while prices in Sweden rise by 50 percent. The purchasing-power parity theory predicts that the krona will depreciate relative to the dollar. It also predicts the amount of the currency depreciation. Say that after the inflation, Canadian steel costs $250 per tonne (one-quarter more than $200), while Swedish steel costs 1500 kronor per tonne (50 percent more than 1000 kronor). For these two prices to be equivalent, 1500 kronor must be worth $250, or one krona must be worth 16.7 cents. The value of the krona, therefore, must have fallen from 20 cents to 16.7 cents.

According to the purchasing-power parity theory, differences in domestic inflation rates are a major cause of adjustments in exchange rates. For instance, if one country has a faster rate of inflation than another, then its exchange rate must be depreciating.

Using algebra, the purchasing-power parity theory can be stated quite simply:

$$P_C = EP_S,$$

where P_C and P_S stand for the levels of prices in Canada and Sweden, and E stands for the exchange rate, measured as the number of Canadian dollars it takes to buy one krona. Thus, the theory is simply the "law of one price" that competition should maintain in the long run, when all contracts can be readjusted and goods can be transported across borders. (The equation would be more complicated if we allowed for transportation costs and tariffs, but we are abstracting from these details to make a basic point.)

This equation can be used to emphasize a point that we made in Chapter 12— that a floating exchange rate is a prerequisite for an independent monetary policy, which is, in turn, a requirement for an independent inflation policy. Rewriting the purchasing-power parity relationship in terms of changes in each variable, we have:

$$\Delta P_C = E\Delta P_S + P_S\Delta E.$$

Then, dividing through by $P_C = EP_S$, we obtain:

$$\frac{\Delta P_C}{P_C} = \frac{E\Delta P_S}{EP_S} + \frac{P_S\Delta E}{EP_S},$$

Purchasing-Power Parity and the Big Mac

In September 1986, *The Economist* used a well-known international commodity to assess the purchasing-power parity theory. As this article shows, the theory did not work very well, probably because it is not practical for arbitrageurs to buy hamburgers in one country and sell them in another.

Depressing though it may be to gourmets, the Big Mac hamburger ... is sold in 41 countries, with only the most trivial changes of recipe. That ought to say something about comparative prices. Think of the hamburger as a medium-rare guide to whether currencies are trading at the right exchange rates.

... The theory of purchasing-power parity (PPP) for currencies ... argues that an exchange rate between two currencies is in equilibrium (at PPP) when it equates the prices of a basket of goods and services in both countries—or, in this case, that rate of exchange which leaves hamburgers costing the same in each country. Comparing actual exchange rates with PPPs is one indication of whether a currency is under- or over-valued.

In Washington, a Big Mac costs $1.60 (U.S.); in Tokyo, our Makudonarudo correspondent had to fork out 370 yen ($2.40).

Dividing the yen price by the U.S. dollar price yields a Mac-PPP of $1 equals 231 yen; but on September 1 the dollar's actual exchange rate stood at 154 yen. The same method gives a Mac-PPP against the West German mark of 2.66 marks, compared with a current rate of 2.02 marks. Conclusion: on Mac-PPP grounds, the dollar looks undervalued against the yen and the mark....

The hamburger standard provides the United States with strong evidence for its contention that Asian ... newly industrializing countries ought to increase the value of their currencies.... A hamburger costs 64 per cent more in Washington than in Hong Kong—on Mac-PPP grounds,

the dollar is 64 per cent overvalued against the Hong Kong dollar. It is also 23 per cent too high against the Singapore dollar.

The hamburger standard has its limitations.... PPP simply indicates where exchange rates should be in the long run if price levels were the only difference between countries. In fact, there are many other differences.

So even though PPPs are handy for converting living standards into a common currency, they are not necessarily the best way to judge the exchange rate needed to bring the current account of the balance of payments into "equilibrium."

Confused? Some economics can be hard to digest.

SOURCE: *The Globe and Mail*, September 18, 1986, page B1; reprinted from *The Economist*.

---

and therefore:

$$\frac{\Delta P_c}{P_c} = \frac{\Delta P_s}{P_s} + \frac{\Delta E}{E} \ .$$

This relationship states that, over the long haul, the Canadian dollar will appreciate each year by an amount equal to the excess of the Swedish inflation rate ($\Delta P_s/P_s$) over the Canadian inflation rate ($\Delta P_c/P_c$). Another way of putting this is to say that Canada can have a lower inflation rate (say, 5 percent) than Sweden (say, 10 percent) only if we let the Canadian dollar appreciate by 5 percent each year. Other things being equal, we expect an appreciation of our currency to hurt our exports. However, although the appreciation in our example is making us less competitive by 5 percent each year, we are at the same time getting more competitive by virtue of the fact that we are inflating less rapidly than Sweden. This 5 percent advantage just makes up for the appreciation in our currency, so competitive positions stay constant. Clearly, of we pegged the exchange rate (set $\Delta E/E$ to zero), the two countries would have the same inflation rates over the longer term.

The purchasing-power parity theory has proved to work quite well in explaining longer-term trends. But to understand shorter-run changes in exchange rates, we must consider several complications that the theory ignores.

First, changes in any of the interferences with free trade, such as tariffs and quotas, can upset simple calculations based on purchasing-power parity. For example, if Swedish prices rise faster than Canadian prices but, at the same time, foreign countries erect tariff barriers to keep out Canadian (but not Swedish) steel, then the krona might not have to depreciate.

Second, some goods and services cannot be traded across national frontiers. Land and buildings are only the most obvious examples; most services can be traded only to a limited extent (as when tourists from one country have their hair cut in another). Inflation rates for goods and services that are *not tradeable* have little bearing on exchange rates.

Third, few of the world's tradeable goods are as uniform as the Swedish and Canadian steel in our example. A Volvo and a Buick, for example, are not identical products. So the price of a Volvo *in Canadian dollars* can rise faster than the price of a Buick without driving Volvos out of the market entirely. On balance:

Most economists believe that other factors are much more important than relative price levels for exchange-rate determination in the short run. But in the long run, purchasing-power parity plays an important role.

Economic Activity and Exchange Rates: The Medium Run

Consumer spending increases quite regularly when income expands, and decreases when income contracts; the same is true for imported goods. Thus, as we stressed in Chapter 9:

A country's imports will rise quickly when its economy is booming and slowly when its economy is stagnating. Holding other things equal, a country that grows faster than the rest of the world normally finds its currency depreciating because its imports grow faster than its exports, so that its demand curve for foreign currency shifts outward more rapidly than its supply curve.

The recent policy controversy involving the United States, West Germany, and Japan is a case in point. As the U.S. dollar fell during the second half of the 1980s, the U.S. government tried to persuade the Germans and Japanese to give their economies a boost—as a way to spur U.S. exports and prop up the dollar.

Interest Rates and Exchange Rates: The Short Run

While economic activity is important for exchange-rate determination in the medium run, "other things" are often not equal in the short run. Specifically, as we stressed in the last chapter, one factor that often seems to call the tune in determining exchange-rate movements in the short run is *interest-rate differentials*. There is an enormous fund of so-called "hot money"—owned by banks, multinational corporations, and wealthy individuals of all nations—amounting to more than $1 trillion (U.S.), which travels around the globe in search of the highest interest rates.

Holding other things equal, countries with high interest rates are able to attract more funds than are countries with low interest rates. Thus a rise in a country's interest rates will often lead to an appreciation of its currency, and a drop in its interest rates will lead to a depreciation.

As the boxed insert in Chapter 12 (pages 264–65) made clear, the Bank of Canada routinely relies on temporary interest-rate differentials to keep the Canadian dollar from depreciating. Most experts in international finance agree that international money is so volatile that interest-rate movements are the chief determinant of exchange-rate fluctuations in the short run.

Market Determination of Exchange Rates: Summary

We can summarize this discussion of exchange-rate determination in free markets in the following three points:

1. Currency values will generally be *appreciating* in countries whose inflation rates are lower than those in the rest of the world, because buyers in foreign countries will demand their goods and thus drive up their currencies.

2. Currency values can also be expected to rise in countries whose levels of economic activity are lower than average, because these countries will be importing rather little.

3. We expect to find appreciating currencies in countries whose interest rates are high because these countries will attract capital from all over the world.

Reversing each of these points, currencies will be *depreciating* in countries with relatively high inflation rates, or high levels of economic activity, or low interest rates.

Fixed Exchange Rates and the Definition of the Balance of Payments

From our discussion of fixed exchange rates in Chapter 12 (pages 255–58) it may seem that measuring a nation's balance-of-payments position is a simple task: We simply count up the private supply of foreign exchange coming into the country and subtract the quantity of foreign exchange being used up to make payments to foreigners. The difference is the balance-of-payments surplus. Conceptually, this is all there is to it. But, in practice, the difficulties are great because we never have statistics on the exact amount of foreign exchange demanded and supplied. There is no way to observe this directly.

If we look at actual market transactions, we will see that the quantity of foreign exchange actually *purchased* and the quantity actually *sold* on the foreign-exchange market are identical. Unless someone has made a bookkeeping error, this must always be so. How, then, can we recognize a balance-of-payments surplus or deficit? Easy, you say. Just look at the transactions of the central bank, whose purchases or sales must make up the difference between private supply and private demand. If the Bank of Canada is selling off foreign-exchange reserves, its sales measure our balance-of-payments deficit. If the Bank is buying up incoming foreign exchange, its purchases represent our balance-of-payments surplus. Thus, we measure the balance of payments by *excluding official transactions among governments*.

The Canadian Balance-of-Payments Accounts

Using 1989 as an example, Table 15–1 shows the official Canadian balance-of-payments accounts. The top section of the table summarizes Canada's trade in currently produced goods and services—the so-called *current account*. The positive or negative sign attached to each entry indicates whether the transaction represented a *gain* (+) or a *loss* (−) of foreign currency.

Looking first at the top of the table, we see that in merchandise transactions Canadians exported $4.6 billion more than they imported, leading to a surplus in merchandise trade (lines 1–3). The trade of services netted an amount more than six times larger, but in this case it was a deficit: Lines 4 and 5 indicate that Canadians spent more on foreign travel and on making interest payments to foreigners to service

TABLE 15–1

Canadian Balance-of-Payments Accounts, 1989 (billions of dollars)

Current Account			
1) Merchandise exports	+138.9		
2) Merchandise imports	−134.3		
3) Balance of merchandise trade		+ 4.6	
4) Service exports			
(Foreign travel in Canada, Canadian interest and dividend receipts from abroad)		+28.2	
5) Service imports			
(Canadian travel abroad, foreign interest and dividend receipts from Canada)		−57.5	
6) Net transfer payments		+ 5.1	
7) Balance on current account			−19.6
Capital Account			
8) Net direct foreign investment in Canada		− 1.1	
9) Net short- and long-term portfolio investment in Canada		+26.6	
10) Balance on capital account (excluding the government's transactions)			+25.5
Summary			
11) Errors and omissions			−2.8
12) Balance of payments			+3.1

SOURCE: Bank of Canada *Review*.

our international debt than we received from foreign tourists and from our investments abroad. The transfer payments in line 6 include items such as gifts and foreign aid. Line 7 gives the net result of all trading in goods and services—the balance on current account. This entry means that during 1989 Canada spent $19.6 billion more than it received.

Lines 8 to 10 record trades of financial assets; this section is called the *capital account* of the balance of payments. Line 8 indicates that in 1989 Canadians purchased more shares in foreign companies than foreigners purchased in Canadian companies. Line 9 indicates that Canadians sold $26.6 billion of long- and short-term bonds to foreigners, more than foreigners sold to Canadians. The balance on the capital account is given in line 10. It indicates that $25.5 billion entered Canada during 1989, as a result of all the recorded trades of stocks and bonds across the border that year.

There is one other line in the table—line 11, errors and omissions. This entry shows that during 1989, $2.8 billion flowed out of Canada in unidentified forms. While part of this discrepancy simply comes from errors in data collection and computation, the lion's share reflects the Canadian government's inability to monitor all the flows of money, goods, and services across its borders. As a result, the overall balance of payments shows a surplus of $3.1 billion.

The surplus in the balance of payments indicates that Canada's official holdings of foreign exchange rose by $3.1 billion during 1989 to reflect the fact that Canadians spent less than they earned in private transactions with the rest of the world (25.5 − 19.6 − 2.8 = 3.1).[1]

A Bit of History: The Gold Standard

About the only time exchange rates were truly fixed was under the old **gold standard**, at least when it was practised in its ideal form.[2]

Under the gold standard, fixed exchange rates were maintained by an automatic equilibrating mechanism that went something like this: All currencies were defined in

---

[1] If you need to review what a balance-of-payments surplus or deficit means for a country's money supply, turn back to pages 255–58.

[2] As a matter of fact, although the gold standard lasted (on and off) for hundreds of years, it was rarely practised in its ideal form. Except for a brief period of fixed exchange rates in the late nineteenth and early twentieth centuries, there were periodic adjustments of exchange rates even under the gold standard.

terms of gold; indeed, some were actually made of gold. When a nation had a deficit in its balance of payments, this meant, essentially, that more gold was flowing *out* than was flowing *in*. Since the domestic money supply was based on gold, losing gold to foreigners meant that the quantity of money automatically fell. Thus, "monetary policy" *automatically* turned restrictive, and interest rates rose, attracting foreign capital. At the same time, the restrictive monetary policy pulled down national output and prices, thus discouraging imports and encouraging exports. The balance-of-payments problem quickly rectified itself. This meant, however, that:

Under the gold standard, no nation had control of its domestic monetary policy, and therefore no country could control its domestic economy very well.

At least in principle, the effects on surplus countries were perfectly symmetrical under the gold standard. A balance-of-payments surplus led, via gold inflows, to an increase in the domestic money supply whether the surplus country liked the idea or not. This raised prices (which decreased exports) and raised real GDP (which increased imports). Because of these automatic adjustments, nations rarely reached the point at which devaluations or revaluations were necessary. Exchange rates were fixed as long as countries abided by the rules of the gold-standard game.

In addition to the complete loss of control over domestic monetary conditions, the gold standard posed one other serious difficulty.

A fundamental problem with the gold standard was that the world's commerce was at the mercy of gold discoveries.

Discoveries of gold meant higher prices in the long run and higher real economic activity in the short run, through the standard monetary-policy mechanisms that we studied in Chapters 11 to 13. And when the supply of gold from discoveries did not keep pace with the growth of the world economy, prices had to fall in the long run and employment had to fall in the short run.

An examination of the periods containing the world's great gold discoveries during the last several centuries provides a direct test of our understanding of these arrangements. These periods are precisely the times when there were major world inflations, just as our analysis suggests.

The Bretton Woods System and the International Monetary Fund

The gold standard collapsed amid the financial chaos of the Great Depression of the 1930s and World War II. Without it, the world struggled through an almost complete breakdown in international trade.

Then, as World War II drew to a close, with much of Europe in ruins and with the United States holding the lion's share of the free world's reserves, officials of the industrial nations met at Bretton Woods, New Hampshire, in 1944 to try to establish a stable monetary environment that would facilitate world trade. Since the U.S. dollar was the only "strong" currency at that time, it was natural for them to turn to the dollar as the basis of the new international economic order.

That is just what they did. The Bretton Woods agreements re-established a system of fixed exchange rates based not on the old gold standard but on the free convertibility of the U.S. dollar into gold. The United States agreed to buy or sell gold to maintain the $35 per ounce price that had been established by President Franklin Roosevelt in 1933. The other signatory nations, which had almost no gold in any case, agreed to buy and sell U.S. dollars to maintain their exchange rates at agreed-on levels. Thus all currencies were indirectly on a modified "gold standard." A holder of French francs, for example, could exchange these for U.S. dollars at (roughly) 5 francs per dollar and then exchange these into gold at $35 per ounce. In this way, the value of the franc was fixed at 175 francs per ounce of gold (5 francs per dollar times 35 dollars per ounce). The new system was dubbed the **gold-exchange system**, and often referred to as the **Bretton Woods system**.

The **International Monetary Fund (IMF)** was set up to police and manage this new system. Using funds that had been contributed by member countries, the IMF was empowered to make loans to countries that were running low on reserves. Only in the case of a "fundamental disequilibrium" in a nation's balance of payments was a change in exchange rates to be permitted, for it was believed that only relatively fixed exchange rates could provide the stable climate needed to restore world trade.

Of course, the Bretton Woods conferees did not define clearly what a "fundamental disequilibrium" was, nor could they have. As the system evolved, it came to mean a chronic deficit in the balance of payments of sizable proportions. Such nations would then devalue their currencies relative to the U.S. dollar. So the system was not really one of fixed exchange rates but rather one where rates were "fixed until further notice."

Several flaws in the Bretton Woods system were consistent with those evident in our discussion of the pure system of fixed exchange rates in Chapter 12 (pages 255–58). First, since devaluations were permitted only after a long run of balance-of-payments deficits, these devaluations (a) could be clearly foreseen, and (b) normally had to be quite large. Speculators then saw opportunities for profit and would "attack" weak currencies with a wave of selling.

This problem led many economists to question whether the system of fixed exchange rates was really providing the stable climate for world trade that had been intended. Was a system in which rates were constant for long periods and then altered by very large amounts really more conducive to international trade than one in which overvalued currencies would gradually depreciate, as they would under a system of floating rates?

The second problem arose from the custom that deficit nations were expected to devalue when forced to, while surplus nations (mainly Germany and Japan) could resist upward revaluations. But the United States was in a special position. The only exchange rate it set was between the U.S. dollar and gold, but that exchange rate was not relevant for any trading relationships. The United States was therefore the one nation in the world that had no way to devalue its currency relative to other currencies, no matter how "fundamental" the disequilibrium in its balance of payments became. The only way exchange rates between the U.S. dollar and foreign currencies could change was if the surplus nations revalued their currencies upward relative to the U.S. dollar. They did not do this frequently enough, so the United States, with its chronically overvalued currency, ran persistent balance-of-payments deficits.

While this represented an adjustment problem for the system as a whole, it was a benefit for the United States. Whenever other countries had large balance-of-payments deficits, they had to do something about it before they ran out of foreign-exchange reserves. But the United States could not run out of "foreign exchange," since it could simply print more. This certainly was convenient for the United States. It could import more than it exported and could buy up ownership in companies operating in other countries, and all it had to give in return were U.S. dollars, which it could print at essentially no cost.

Adjustment Mechanisms under the Bretton Woods System

Under the Bretton Woods system, devaluation was viewed as a last resort, to be used only after other methods of adjusting to payments imbalances had failed. What were these other methods?

We have already encountered most of them in our discussion of exchange-rate determination in free markets (see pages 311–15). Any factor that increases the demand for, say, British pounds or that reduces the supply will push the value of the pound upward if it is free to adjust. If, however, the exchange rate is pegged, it is the balance-of-payments deficit rather than the exchange rate that will adjust when supply of or demand for a nation's money changes. Specifically, the British balance-of-payments deficit will shrink if either the demand for pounds increases or the supply decreases.

Referring back to our earlier discussions of the factors that underlie the demand and supply curves, then, we see that one way a deficit nation can improve its balance of payments is to *reduce its aggregate demand*, thus discouraging imports and cutting down its demand for foreign currency. Another is to *slow its rate of inflation*, thus encouraging exports and discouraging imports. Finally, it can *raise its interest rates* in order to attract more foreign capital.

In a word, under the Bretton Woods system, deficit nations were expected to follow restrictive monetary and fiscal policies *voluntarily* just as they would *automatically* have done under the old gold standard. However, just as under the gold standard, this medicine was often unpalatable, so deficit nations frequently resorted to a bewildering variety of **exchange controls**—laws and regulations that made it very difficult for its nationals to sell their own currency to get foreign exchange. Many countries still have such controls.

Exchange controls are laws restricting the exchange of one nation's currency for another's.

Surplus nations could, of course, have taken the opposite measures: pursuing expansive monetary and fiscal policies to increase economic growth and lower interest rates. But they often did not relish the inflation that would come with such actions and, once again, left the burden of adjustment to the deficit nations. The general point about fixed exchange rates is that:

Under a system of fixed exchange rates, the government of a country loses some control over its domestic economy. There may be times when balance-of-payments considerations force it to contract its money supply and therefore its economy, even though domestic needs are calling for expansion. Conversely, there may be times when the domestic economy needs to be reined in, but balance-of-payments considerations force an expansionary monetary policy.

The Bretton Woods system worked fairly well for a number of years, but it finally broke down because of its inability to "devalue" the U.S. dollar with respect to the other world currencies. During the mid-1960s, the size of the U.S. balance-of-payments deficit grew tremendously, primarily because of that country's large expenditures on the Vietnam war and on domestic social programs, and because the stock of U.S. dollars in foreign hands had reached a level that was many times larger than the U.S. government's holdings of gold. The demand for U.S. dollars fell, and the demand for gold rose, as many speculators anticipated that the United States would effectively increase its reserves of gold by raising the official price well above $35 per ounce. But the larger U.S. balance-of-payments deficits meant that the *world money supply was growing very rapidly*. So the late 1960s was just like one of the earlier periods of large gold discoveries, and as in those periods, a world inflation ensued. Since the other nations had no way of stopping the overly expansive U.S. monetary policy, the only way they could control their own inflation rates was to cut the link with the U.S. dollar. Many countries floated their exchange rate, as Canada did in 1970. The Bretton Woods system ended when the monetary policy of the base-currency country, the United States, became irresponsible in the eyes of the other countries.

In August 1971, President Nixon formally abolished the Bretton Woods system by announcing that the United States would no longer peg the value of the dollar by buying and selling gold. Actually, the system had already ended.

Most observers today agree that the gold-exchange system could not have survived the incredible events of the 1970s in any case. The worldwide inflationary boom of 1972, the poor food harvests in 1972–74, the huge increases in the price of oil in 1973–74 and again in 1979–80, and the great worldwide recessions of 1974–76 and the early 1980s all helped create a world in which the major countries were experiencing dramatically different inflation rates.

For example, between 1975 and 1985 inflation averaged 4 percent per year in West Germany, 7 percent in the United States, 11 percent in Great Britain, and 15 percent in Italy. As the purchasing-power parity theory reminds us, large differences in inflation rates call for *major* changes in currency values. The Bretton Woods system was ill-suited to handle such major changes.

Why Try to Fix Exchange Rates?

In view of these and other severe problems with the Bretton Woods system, why did the international financial community work so hard to maintain fixed rates for so many years? The answer is that floating exchange rates, determined in free markets by supply and demand, also pose problems.

Chief among these is the possibility that freely floating rates may prove to be highly variable rates, which add an unwanted element of riskiness to foreign trade. For example, if the exchange rate is 20 cents to the French franc, then a 2000-franc Parisian dress will cost $400. But should the franc appreciate to 25 cents, this same dress would cost $500. A Canadian department store thinking of buying this dress may need to place its order far in advance and will want to know the cost *in dollars*. It may be worried about the possibility that the value of the franc will rise, so that the dress will cost more than $400. And such worries can inhibit trade.

There are two answers to this concern. First, we can hope that freely floating rates will prove not to be very volatile. Prices of many domestic consumer goods, for example, are determined by supply and demand in free markets and yet do not fluctuate unduly. Second, speculators can relieve business firms of exchange-rate risks— for a fee, of course. Consider the department store example. If French francs cost 20 cents today, the department store manager can assure herself of paying exactly $400 for the dress several months from now by arranging for a speculator to deliver francs to her at 20 cents on the day she needs them. If the franc appreciates in the interim, it is the speculator, not the department store, that will take the financial beating. (And, of course, if the franc depreciates, the speculator will pocket the profits.)

This role of speculation was described more fully in our discussion of the stock market in Chapter 10 (see pages 222–23). The fears that speculative activity in free markets will lead to wild gyrations in prices, while occasionally valid, are more often unfounded. The reason is quite simple. International currency speculators, if they are to make profits, must buy a currency when its value is low (thus helping to support the currency by pushing up its demand curve) and sell it when its value is high (thus holding down the price by adding to the supply curve).

This means that, if they are successful, speculators will be coming into the market as *buyers* just when demand is weak (or when supply is strong), and as *sellers* just when demand is strong (or supply is scant). In doing so, they will help limit price fluctuations. Looked at the other way around, speculators can destabilize prices only if they are systematically willing to lose money.[3]

Notice the stark contrast to the system of fixed exchange rates in which speculation often led to wild "runs" on currencies that were on the verge of devaluation.

Speculative activity, which may very well be destabilizing under fixed rates, is likely to be stabilizing under floating rates.

We do not mean to imply here that there are no difficulties at all under floating exchange rates. At the very least, speculators will demand a fee for their services—a

"Then it's agreed. Until the dollar firms up, we let the clamshell float."
Drawing by Ed Fisher
© 1971,
The New Yorker Magazine, Inc.

[3] See Discussion Question 10 at the end of the chapter.

fee that adds to the costs of trading across national borders. In addition, it may be impossible to eliminate all exchange-rate risks through speculation. Currently, for example, contracts offered in speculative markets cover at most a few months. Thus no business can protect itself from exchange-rate changes over a period that is measured in years.

The experience under floating rates since 1973 has delivered clear verdicts on two issues. First, exchange rates have proven to be quite volatile—more volatile than many of the advocates of floating rates anticipated. Second, international trade has flourished despite this volatility. Apparently exchange-rate risk is not as burdensome as some people feared.

The Current Mixed System

Our current international financial system—where some currencies are still pegged to some other key currency, others are floating freely, and many more are floating subject to government interferences—has evolved gradually since 1971. Though it continues to change and adapt, at least three features are evident.

The first is the decline in the notion that exchange rates should be fixed for relatively long periods of time. The demand by many countries in the early 1970s that the world quickly return to fixed exchange rates had largely subsided by the mid-1970s. Even where rates are still pegged to the U.S. dollar, devaluations and revaluations are now much more frequent—and smaller—than they were in the 1944–71 period. Most free-world currency rates change slightly on a day-to-day basis, and market forces generally determine the basic trends, up or down. Even advocates of greater fixity in exchange rates generally propose that governments keep rates within certain *ranges*, rather than literally fix them.

Second, some central banks do not hesitate to intervene to moderate exchange movements whenever they feel that such actions are appropriate. Typically, these interventions are aimed at ironing out transitory fluctuations. But there have been instances in which central banks have, for a time, opposed basic trends in exchange rates. Deficit nations have bought their own currencies to prevent them from depreciating. Surplus nations have sold their own currencies to prevent them from appreciating. While we certainly no longer have many fixed exchange rates, many of the major currencies are floating less than freely. The terms "dirty float" or "managed float" have been coined to describe this mongrel system.

The quotations from the governors of the Bank of Canada in the boxed insert on pages 264–65 (as well as the statement quoted in Discussion Question 8 of Chapter 12, page 268) verify that this is the policy followed in Canada. These tendencies are also illustrated in Figure 15–1, on page 322, where the balance-of-payments data show that the Bank of Canada has limited fluctuations in the exchange rate. The surpluses in the early 1970s and the late 1980s prove that the Bank of Canada was accumulating foreign-exchange reserves (that is, selling Canadian dollars) to limit the rise in the value of the Canadian dollar that did take place in those periods. Similarly, the deficits during 1976–78 and the mid-1980s prove that the Bank of Canada was selling off foreign-exchange reserves (that is, buying Canadian dollars) to limit the fall in the value of the Canadian dollar.

Incidentally, most analysts attribute the rise in the Canadian dollar in the 1969–70 period to the temporarily higher interest rates and the lower inflation rate in Canada (compared to the United States). Similarly, the fall in the Canadian dollar in the later 1970s and the early 1980s was due to the higher inflation rate in Canada and our attempt to maintain interest rates lower than those of the United States.

The third unmistakable feature of the present international monetary system is the virtual elimination of any role for gold. The trend away from gold actually began before President Nixon's dramatic announcement in 1971, and by now it is only a minor exaggeration to say that gold plays no role in the world's financial system.

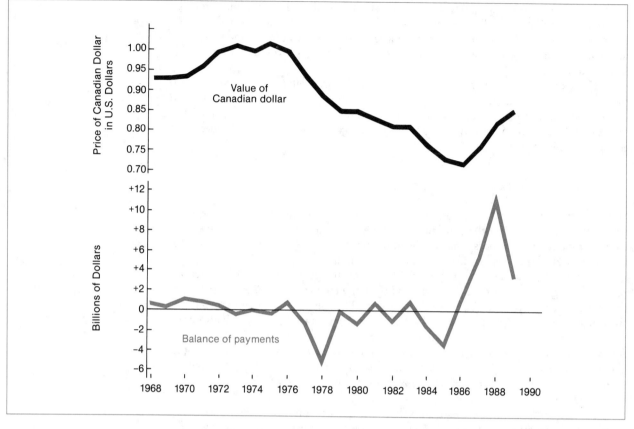

FIGURE 15–1

Canada's Balance of Payments and the Value of the Canadian Dollar

This graph shows that the Bank of Canada has resisted movements in the exchange rate. The balance-of-payments surpluses in the early 1970s indicate that the Bank was accumulating foreign-exchange reserves (that is, selling Canadian dollars) to limit the rise in the Canadian dollar that took place. Also, balance-of-payments deficits occurred in 1976–78 and most of the 1980s, since the Bank was buying up Canadian dollars to limit the fall in our currency's value that was taking place. The large surpluses in the late 1980s reflect the large flows of funds into Canada as foreign investors purchased our high-yield bonds. The Canadian dollar rose in the late 1980s but the Bank's actions limited that rise.

SOURCE: Bank of Canada, *Review*.

Nowadays there is a *free market* in gold, which enables those who wish to invest in it —dentists, jewellers, industrial users, speculators, and ordinary citizens who think of gold as a good store of value—to buy or sell as they wish. Indeed, it may be the case today that gold is considered a good investment solely because everyone believes that everyone *else* thinks it is! The price of gold, determined each day by the law of supply and demand, has proved to be quite volatile. Fortunes have been made and lost by investors in gold.

Recent Developments in International Financial Markets

The European Monetary System

The countries of the European Community (EC), which seek to become a unified free-trade area by 1992, have a long-range goal of establishing a single currency for the Common Market. Floating rates would make this goal impossible. So in 1973 some of the member countries entered into an agreement whereby exchange rates among their currencies could remain relatively *fixed* while Common Market currencies as a group would rise or fall *relative to the rest of the world*. In 1979 the arrangement was strengthened and formalized in the **European Monetary System (EMS)**. The EMS makes periodic adjustments to exchange rates that get out of line with the others, and it is widely regarded as the first step, albeit a small one, toward a unified European currency. In practice, the German mark is the dominant currency in the EMS, playing a role within Europe analogous to that played by the U.S. dollar under the Bretton Woods system. However, some countries, most notably the United Kingdom, are reluctant to surrender control of monetary policy to the EMS. And, as of this writing, no one has figured out how, if at all, to integrate Eastern Europe into the system.

The LDC Debt Problem[4]

The enormous debts of many less developed countries (LDCs) and the difficulties they are having in meeting their burdensome interest payments have frequently grabbed the headlines in recent years. Many experts feel that the still-unresolved LDC debt problem poses a serious threat to the stability of the international monetary system.

The seeds of the problem were sown in the 1970s. When real interest rates were low, many of these countries, particularly those in Latin America, borrowed heavily to finance their development. Then, in the 1980s, well-managed and poorly managed countries alike were hit by four shocks. First, the worldwide recession of the 1980s made it harder for them to earn foreign currency by exporting goods to the industrialized countries; their markets simply contracted. Second, real interest rates rose dramatically, making the burden of paying interest on the debt much harder to bear. Third, many of their currencies depreciated, while their debts were denominated in U.S. dollars. This imparted an immediate increase in their debt burden. Fourth, the prices of primary commodities (which the LDCs export to earn most of their foreign exchange) plummeted in the 1980s to levels not experienced since the 1930s.

Beginning with Mexico's problems in 1982, the 1980s were marked by a series of near-crises in the international financial system as countries such as Argentina, Brazil, Peru, the Philippines, and others postponed or scaled back payments and renegotiated their debt obligations. Citizens of many of these countries suffered severe declines in their standards of living, and some banks absorbed sizable losses. But, so far, a series of special arrangements negotiated by governments and banks has managed to keep the system afloat and avoid a panic.

Yet no one is declaring the problem solved. In fact, the heavy indebtedness of some European countries is now deepening the problem. Many business people, politicians, and economists doubt that the LDCs will ever be able to repay their debts in full and advocate some sort of partial forgiveness of interest or principal, perhaps on a selective basis. Such an approach on the part of the developed countries was being adopted by 1990.

The Link between the Budget Deficit and the Trade Deficit

During the 1980s, there was a dramatic change in the U.S. policy mix toward a contractionary monetary policy and an expansionary fiscal policy (through tax cuts). This led to massive federal budget deficits that had to be financed by selling government bonds. Our macroeconomic analysis (in Chapters 13 and 14) has shown that *both* fiscal expansion and monetary contraction lead to higher domestic interest rates. This is what happened in the United States. The high American interest rates attracted foreign funds, which appreciated the U.S. dollar dramatically during the first half of the 1980s. Consequently, American imports soared, while U.S. exporters suffered a profit squeeze. The resulting fiscal deficit essentially caused the world's largest-ever current-account trade deficit. It is useful to elaborate on this link by using a little bit of algebra.

We begin by recalling two definitions: that GDP equals disposable income (DI) plus taxes (T), or

[4]For more on this problem, see Chapter 18, especially page 395.

$$Y = DI + T,$$

and that disposable income can be either consumed or saved:

$$DI = C + S.$$

These two definitions jointly imply that

$$Y = C + S + T,$$

which simply says that national income can be spent, saved, or taxed away.

Now remember the equilibrium condition for GDP in an open economy:

$$Y = C + I + G + X - IM.$$

Equating these two expressions for Y gives

$$C + I + G + X - IM = C + S + T.$$

Subtracting C from both sides and grouping terms in a natural way leads to this conclusion:

$$G - T = (S - I) - (X - IM).$$

In words, the government budget deficit must be equal to the surplus of savings over investment plus the trade deficit. This fundamental equation suggests that there is a potentially tight connection between the budget deficit and the trade deficit. Let us examine how this link worked out in the case of the United States in the 1980s. Since the Reagan tax cuts led to a large budget deficit, the United States could have avoided a large trade deficit only by saving much more or investing much less. The latter is not an appetizing option, and, in any case, generous business tax cuts in 1981 shielded investment spending from the effects of high interest rates. (Investment actually rose as a share of U.S. national product.) That leaves saving, which did not increase significantly. With S not rising and I not falling, our equation leaves only one possibility: a rise in $G - T$ must be reflected in a fall in $X - IM$. The government budget deficit thus led to a massive trade deficit.

This story may seem overly mechanical. It may also appear to differ from the one we told earlier; after all, the last paragraph never mentioned interest rates or exchange rates. One last piece of arithmetic, however, will both show that the two stories are equivalent and bring out the intuition behind our fundamental equation.

As we noted earlier in this chapter, the current account and capital account surpluses must sum to zero under a regime of floating exchange rates (see the discussion on page 315, and remember that official transactions do not exist under flexible exchange rates). Thus (as long as we simplify by ignoring payments to service foreign debts),

$$(X - IM) + \text{Capital inflows} = 0.$$

Using this to replace $X - IM$ in the previous equation gives:

$$G - T = (S - I) + \text{Capital inflows}.$$

This last equation is simply common sense: If U.S. savers will not save enough to meet the borrowing requirements of both the U.S. government and American firms engaged in investment activity, the balance must be borrowed from foreigners.

It is no mystery what happens next. To attract foreign capital, the United States,

International Policy Co-ordination—"All Together Now: You First"

Starting in the mid-1970s, the Group of Seven ("G-7" for short)—the major Western industrial democracies, including the United States, Japan, West Germany, France, Great Britain, Canada, and Italy—started meeting once a year to discuss international financial issues. As the headline from *The Globe and Mail*—"All Together Now: You First"—suggests, however, the sessions are long on rhetoric and short on real commitments. Some excerpts from the article follow.

From the dollar to the debt strategy, the world's financial players have all got religion. There's only one hitch: no one is prepared to dig deep for the collection plate....

The seven major industrial countries, including Canada, agree that the U.S. currency is too high.... But brave talk of economic policy co-ordination soon evaporates when a long-term cure for the dollar's ills means swallowing bitter pills at home. As a result, the G-7 is reduced to tactical interventions in foreign exchange markets, ... in hopes the dollar has peaked....

The current test of policy co-ordination among the G-7 partners is the overheated U.S. dollar. Last week, in an effort to put some muscle into the [most recent] G-7 communiqué, key central banks intervened on foreign exchange markets to push down the dollar....

In the absence of substantial economic policy changes in the United States, West Germany, and Japan, a co-ordinated attack on the currency will not end the large current-account imbalances that contribute to the dollar's strength. And there are strong domestic forces at play in all three countries that conflict with any [of them] taking drastic measures.

In the United States, the Federal Reserve Board is trapped between its desire to keep alive the seven-year cycle of moderate growth and its fear about a resurgence in inflation. A sharp drop in U.S. interest rates—coupled with higher rates abroad—could check the dollar's rise but fuel inflation at home.

Similarly, West Germany and Japan put domestic considerations first.

But there are dark clouds on the horizon. IMF officials

see no threat of a world recession next year but IMF research director Jacob Frenkel warns that large imbalances between the major economies "are a significant cause of concern" because they are expected to widen in the next year.

"Unless there are further policy measures, I don't see them shrinking to more sustainable levels," he told reporters, noting that persistent trade deficits in the United States sow the seeds of protectionism.

But if policy co-ordination is a "Weight-Watchers" club, as Mr. Frenkel put it, no one wants to go on a diet alone. As a result, the G-7 partners are "drifting until the next crisis," said John Williamson, an international finance expert at the Institute for International Economics.

SOURCE: Adapted from Jennifer Lewington, "Much Agreeing, Limited Resolve on Issues. It Seems to Be: 'All Together Now: You First,'" *The Globe and Mail*, October 3, 1989, pages C1–C2.

like any country, must offer interest rates higher than those available elsewhere. As a result capital flows into the United States, the value of the U.S. dollar is driven up, and the expensive dollar leads to a trade deficit. Thus the adjustments of interest rates and exchange rates that we discussed earlier are precisely the way the economy matches the budget deficit with a trade deficit.

Concluding Comment

That the major economies of the world are linked suggests the need for greater policy co-ordination among nations. But since the national interests of particular nations often differ, countries are understandably reluctant to surrender any of their sovereignty. Hence international policy co-ordination remains an elusive goal (see the boxed inserts on this page and on page 326). Economically speaking, we all live in one world. Politically, however, we live in a world of separate nation-states.

The Arithmetic of U.S.–Japanese Economic Relations

The huge U.S. trade deficit with Japan is a significant source of friction between the two countries and has led to frequent calls for protectionist measures in the United States. Our fundamental equation,

$$G - T = (S - I) - (X - IM),$$

teaches us that part of the problem traces to different saving habits in the two countries.

The Japanese people are among the biggest savers in the world. So $S - I$ is a large positive number in Japan. Like the U.S. government, the Japanese government has a budget deficit. However, Japan's $G - T$ is far smaller than its $S - I$. It follows that, in order to balance the international books, Japan must generate a trade surplus.

The contrast between the United States and Japan in this regard is marked. While the American people and government together are big net borrowers, the Japanese people and government together are big net savers. In an integrated world financial system, it is, therefore, natural that the Japanese should be lending to the Americans. In short, Japan should have capital *outflows* and the United States should have capital *inflows*—which is just what has been happening in recent years.

Remember too that:

Current account surplus + Capital account surplus = 0;

the implication is that Japan should have a current account *surplus*, and that the United States should have a current account *deficit*. Once again this is only natural.

Being an island nation almost devoid of natural resources, Japan must run huge trade deficits in primary products. Much of this trade is with developing countries. To offset this trade deficit in primary products, Japan needs a surplus in trade in manufactured goods. And who is likely to be the leading customer for these goods? The biggest consumers on earth—the Americans.

So it is natural for the United States to run a bilateral deficit in trading goods with Japan. That does not, however, justify a huge deficit, nor does it suggest that the Japanese are blameless in the matter. For one thing, Japan has long been among the most protectionist of all the advanced industrial nations. Much of this protectionism has been subtle, coming not through high tariffs but through bureaucratic regulations that make importing difficult. But Japan also has its share of high tariffs and quotas. So one possible solution to the U.S.–Japan trade problem is to persuade Japan to open its markets more. However, no one really thinks that the Americans could sell nearly as much in Japan as the Japanese sell in the United States, even in a completely free market.

Macroeconomic policy might be a more effective tool. Look once again at the fundamental equation. If Japan stimulated its economy by means of a more expansionary fiscal policy, its $G - T$ would rise and its $X - IM$ would fall. If, at the same time, the United States reduced its budget deficit, its $G - T$ would fall and its $X - IM$ would rise. In all likelihood, the trade imbalance between the two countries would narrow. And, to add a note from the Canadian perspective, if Japan alone took action, our exports would expand; if, on the other hand, only the United States took action, our exports would contract.

Summary

1. Several factors are important in the determination of exchange rates. In the long run, purchasing-power parity plays a major role in exchange-rate movements. The purchasing-power parity theory states that relative price levels in any two countries determine the exchange rate between their currencies. Therefore, countries with relatively low inflation rates normally will have appreciating currencies.

2. Over shorter periods, the pace of economic activity and the level of interest rates exert a greater influence on the exchange rate.

3. The balance of payments is difficult to measure, since many transactions across borders are difficult to monitor. However, the estimated accounts show that Canada typically has a surplus on merchandise trade, a deficit on the services account (which is due mostly to the interest payments on our foreign debt), and a surplus on the capital account (which is due to the fact that our foreign debt is increasing).

4. In the early part of this century, the world was on a particular system of fixed exchange rates called the gold standard, in which the value of every nation's currency was fixed in terms of gold. But this created problems because nations could not control their own money supplies and because the world could not control its total supply of gold.

5. After World War II, the gold standard was replaced by the gold-exchange (or Bretton Woods) system, where rates were again fixed or, rather, fixed until further notice. In this system, the U.S. dollar was the basis of international currency values.

6. The gold-exchange system served the world well and helped restore world trade, but it got into trouble when U.S. monetary policy became overly expansionary, imposing inflation on everyone. The system provided no way to remedy this situation.

7. After 1971, the world gradually moved to a system of relatively free exchange rates, though there are plenty

of exceptions. We now have a thoroughly mixed system of "dirty" or "managed" floating, which continues to evolve and adapt.

8. Canada's managed currency value fell between 1976 and 1986, mostly because of our relatively inferior inflation performance; in the latter part of the 1980s, our currency value rose because upward pressure was maintained on Canadian interest rates.

9. Floating rates are not without their problems. For example, importers and exporters justifiably worry about fluctuations in exchange rates. Though these problems seem manageable, some people think that a return to fixed exchange rates is desirable.

10. Under floating exchange rates, investors who speculate on international currency values provide a valuable service by assuming the risks of those who do not wish to speculate. Normally, speculators stabilize rather than destabilize exchange rates, because that is how they make profits.

11. Budget deficits and trade deficits are linked by the fundamental equation $G - T = (S - I) - (X - IM)$. This also implies that $G - T = S - I +$ capital inflows. It follows from this equation that the U.S. trade deficit must be cured by some combination of lower budget deficits, higher savings, and lower investment. A change in the U.S. policy mix toward easier monetary policy and smaller budget deficits is one way to reduce that country's trade deficit without contracting the U.S. economy (and therefore the Canadian economy) and without imposing the costs of protectionist policies on all the trading partners involved (including the Americans themselves).

12. International co-ordination of economic policies is important, but it is elusive in a world of sovereign nations.

Concepts for Review

Purchasing-power parity	Gold-exchange system (Bretton Woods system)	The LDC debt problem
Current account	International Monetary Fund (IMF)	Budget deficits and trade deficits
Capital account	Exchange controls	$G - T = (S - I) - (X - IM)$
Balance of payments	"Dirty" or "managed" floating	
Gold standard	The European Monetary System (EMS)	

Questions for Discussion

1. If the Canadian dollar depreciates relative to the Japanese yen, will the Sony stereo you have longed for become more or less expensive? What effect do you think this will have on Canadian demands for Sonys? Does the demand curve for yen, therefore, slope upward or downward? Explain.

2. During the 1980s, inflation in West Germany has generally been below that in Canada. What, then, does the purchasing-power parity theory predict should have happened to the exchange rate between the mark and the dollar? Your instructor will be able to tell you whether this is what actually happened.

3. Use supply and demand diagrams to analyze the effect on the exchange rate between the Canadian dollar and the British pound if:
   a. Britain's flow of North Sea oil decreases.
   b. British dockworkers refuse to unload ships that arrive with cargo from Canada but continue to load ships that sail from Britain.
   c. Both Britain and Canada slip into recession, but the Canadian recession is far more severe.
   d. Polls suggest that Thatcher's Conservative government will be replaced by radicals who vow to nationalize all foreign-owned assets.

4. How are the problems of a country faced with a balance-of-payments deficit similar to those posed by a government regulation that holds the price of milk above the equilibrium level? (*Hint*: Think of each in terms of a supply–demand diagram.)

5. Look at the Canadian balance-of-payments accounts table in the text (Table 15–1 on page 316). Figure out where each of the following actions you could have taken in 1989 would have been recorded in these accounts:
   a. You spent the summer travelling in Europe.
   b. Your uncle in France sent you $50 as a birthday present.
   c. You bought a new Toyota.
   d. You sold stock on the Tokyo stock market.
   e. You drove over the American border carrying Canadian records in your truck and sold them to a friend in the United States. (*Hint*: Would your sale have been recorded anywhere?)

6. For each of the transactions listed in Question 5, indicate how it would affect:
   a. The Canadian balance of payments, if exchange rates were fixed.
   b. The international value of the Canadian dollar, if exchange rates were floating.

7. Under the old gold standard, what do you think happened to world prices when there was a huge gold strike in California in 1849? What do you think hap-

pened when the world went without any important new gold strikes for twenty years or so?

8. Explain why the members of the Bretton Woods conference in 1944 wanted to establish a system of fixed exchange rates. What was the flaw that led to the ultimate breakdown of the system in 1971?

9. Suppose you want to reserve a hotel room in Paris for the coming summer but are worried that the value of the franc may rise between now and then, making the room too expensive for your budget. Explain how a speculator could relieve you of this worry. (Don't actually try it. Speculators deal only in very large sums!)

10. On page 320, it is pointed out that successful speculators buy a currency when demand is weak and sell it when demand is strong. Use supply and demand diagrams for two different periods (one with weak demand, the other with strong demand) to show why this will limit price fluctuations.

11. Use the following statistics to produce a balance-of-payments table for Canada, identifying separately the current and capital accounts. (Assume no statistical discrepancy.)

	BILLIONS OF DOLLARS
Canadian income on foreign investment in Canada	10
Canadian government grants to foreigners	30
Merchandise exports	550
Canadian tourist expenditures abroad	30
Canadian private direct investment abroad	120
Merchandise imports	650

a. Does the balance of payments show a surplus or a deficit?

b. What would happen to the exchange rate under a regime of flexible exchange rates?

12. Explain the economic theory behind the following paragraph from *The Globe and Mail* (December 4, 1989, page B1):

Later in the week, given another boost by the Bank of Canada's high interest rate policy, the dollar broke through the 86-cent mark briefly—its first time at that level since 1980. Some economists see 87 cents as a possibility. That thought sends shudders through Canada's manufacturing and resource sectors.

16

Budget Deficits and the National Debt

Blessed are the young, for they shall inherit the national debt.

HERBERT HOOVER

There is a widespread belief that there is something inherently wrong with government budget deficits. Opinion polls consistently show that the public wants smaller deficits, and politicians of all parties constantly rail against deficits. Yet our federal budgets have shown a deficit in twenty-four of the last thirty-two years.

Why is the federal budget so frequently in the red? What kinds of problems do large deficits pose for the economy, both now and in the future? Should we strive to balance the budget? And, if so, by what means? These are the questions to be addressed in this chapter.

We begin by explaining why the principles of stabilization policy that we learned in Part Three do not lead to the conclusion that the budget should always be balanced. (Neither, however, do they lead to the conclusion that it should always be in deficit!) Then we try to get the facts straight. We discuss the size of the national debt, and how it grew so large. Then we turn to the federal budget deficit and why some economists claim that it is badly mismeasured.

With the facts established, we examine the alleged ill effects of deficits. We shall see that many popular arguments against deficits are based on faulty reasoning. But not all are. In particular, we devote special attention to three potentially severe costs of deficit spending: It can be inflationary, it can "crowd out" private investment spending or export sales, and it can increase foreign indebtedness.

Should the Budget Be Balanced?

The basic principles of fiscal policy that we discussed in Chapter 9 certainly do not lead to the conclusion that the government should always balance its budget. Instead, they point to the desirability of budget *deficits* when private demand $(C + I + G + X - IM)$ is too weak and budget *surpluses* when private demand is too strong. The budget should be balanced, according to these principles, only when $C + I + G + X - IM$ approximately equals the full employment level of output. This may sometimes occur, but it will not necessarily be the norm.

In brief, according to this approach, the focus of fiscal policy should be on *balancing aggregate supply and aggregate demand*, not on balancing the budget. The reason why a balanced budget may not achieve a balanced economy is clear from our earlier discussion of stabilization policy.

Consider the fiscal policy that would be followed by a government that believed in balanced budgets. If private spending sagged for some reason, the multiplier would pull GDP down. Since personal and corporate tax revenues fall sharply when GDP declines, the budget would start to swing into the red. To a true budget-balancer, this would be a signal either to reduce spending or to raise taxes—exactly the opposite of the appropriate policy response.

Thus, attempts to balance the budget—which occurred during the early part of the Great Depression—prolong and deepen recessions.

Budget balancing can also lead to inappropriate fiscal policy when an economic boom begins. If rising tax revenues induce a budget-balancing government to spend more or cut taxes, fiscal policy will accentuate the boom—with inflationary consequences.

This analysis explains why a balanced budget should not be expected to be the norm. Further, it suggests that the budget should be balanced over the time interval of one complete business cycle, not over the arbitrary time period of one year. But if the government had been balancing the budget over the cycle, we could not have had fifteen budget deficits in the last fifteen years, since the recession phase of every business cycle lasts for a much shorter period than fifteen years. What explains this outcome? Before attempting an answer, we should get the facts straight.

Deficits and Debt: Some Terminology

First some critical terminology. The title of this chapter contains two terms that seem similar but mean different things: *budget deficits* and the *national debt*. We must learn to distinguish between the two.

The **budget deficit** is the amount by which the government's expenditures exceed its receipts during some specified period of time, usually one year. For example, during fiscal year 1989–90, the federal government spent $30.5 billion more than it collected in tax revenue, so the deficit was $30.5 billion.[1]

The **national debt**, also called the public debt, is the total value of the government's indebtedness at a moment in time. Thus, for example, the national debt at the end of fiscal year 1989–90 was roughly $350 billion.

The two concepts—debt and deficit—are closely related because the government accumulates *debt* by running *deficits* or reduces its debt by running surpluses. The relationship between the debt and the deficit can be explained by a simple analogy. As you run water into a bathtub ("run a deficit"), the accumulated volume of water in the tub ("the debt") rises. Alternatively, if you let water out ("run a surplus"), the total amount of water in the tub ("the debt") falls. Analogously, budget deficits raise the national debt while budget surpluses lower it.

Having made this distinction, let us look first at the size and nature of the accumulated public debt and then at the annual budget deficit.

The **budget deficit** is the amount by which the government's expenditures exceed its receipts during a specified period of time, usually one year.

The **national debt** is the federal government's total indebtedness at a moment in time. It is the result of previous deficits.

Some Facts about the National Debt

How large a public debt do we have? How did we get it? Who owns it? Is it really growing rapidly?

To begin with the simplest question, the public debt is enormous. At the end of fiscal 1989–90 it amounted to more than $350 billion, or more than $13,400 for every man, woman, and child in Canada. When we compare the debt with the gross domestic product—the volume of goods and services our economy produces in a year—it does not seem so large after all. With nominal GDP averaging about $670 billion during the years 1989–90 the debt was about 52 percent of the nation's yearly output. By contrast, many families who own homes owe *several years'* worth of income to the

[1] The fiscal year of the Canadian government ends on March 31. Thus, fiscal year 1989–90 ran from April 1, 1989, to March 31, 1990.

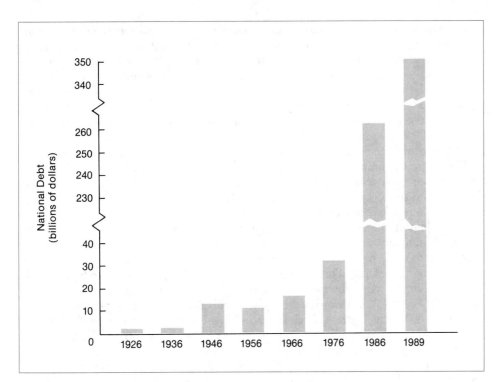

FIGURE 16–1
**The Canadian National
Debt, 1926–1989**
This graph charts the behaviour
of the public debt in Canada.
Except for the last eighteen
years, most of the increase can
be accounted for by World War
II and the severe recession during the Diefenbaker–James
Coyne period (late 1950s and
early 1960s). But since the early
1970s, the debt has grown very
rapidly.
SOURCE: Department of Finance.

bank that granted them a mortgage. Many corporations also owe their bondholders much more than 50 percent of a year's sales.

But before these analogies make you feel too comfortable, we should point out that simple analogies between public and private debt are almost always misleading. A family with a large mortgage debt also owns a home with a value that presumably exceeds the mortgage. A solvent business firm has assets (factories, machinery, inventories, and so forth) that far exceed its outstanding bonds in value.

Is the same thing true of the Canadian government? Nobody knows for sure. How much are the parliament buildings worth? Or the national parks? Because these government assets are *not* sold on markets, no one can tell whether the federal government's assets exceed its debt or not.

Figure 16–1 charts the increase in the national debt from 1926 to 1989. You will notice that most of the debt was acquired during World War II, during the deep recession of 1958–62, or since the mid-1970s. The 1980s included a very severe recession, and the growth of the debt was enormous. Indeed, if the breaks in the graph had not been used here, the 1989 bar would have been more than three times as high as the one shown! Thus, the full extent of the growth in the debt is not evident from just a casual glance at Figure 16–1.

Because of the federal government's heavy reliance on income taxes, its overall tax revenues fall when economic activity falls, as it did in the early 1980s. The fact that we have had a series of recessions is one of the main reasons the national debt has increased. But there are other causes and, as we shall see later, the *cause* of the debt is quite germane to the question of whether or not the debt is a burden. So it is important to remember that:

Before 1973, the major portion of the Canadian national debt could be attributed to the costs of financing the war and to the losses of tax revenues that accompany recessions. And while recessions have continued to fuel the growth of the debt, other significant factors came into play after 1973.

One important cause of the increase in the debt after 1973 was the indexation of the personal income-tax system, which was introduced that year by the Liberal government. This scheme dramatically reduced the government's revenue during inflationary times.[2] The government did not reduce its expenditures by a similar amount. During the 1980s, however, a much more significant influence came into play: the government's rapidly growing interest-payment obligations on the national debt began to deplete its revenues dramatically. This component of government spending alone had reached $40 billion per year in 1990.

The growth of the debt looks enormous in Figure 16–1. Indeed, as already noted, two breaks in the graph were necessary to avoid its covering the entire height of the page. But we must remember that everything grows in a growing economy. Private debt and business debt have also grown rapidly since 1926, so it would be surprising indeed if the public debt had not grown as well.

In addition, the debt is measured in dollars and, in an inflationary environment, the purchasing power of each dollar declines every year. A good way to put the numbers into some perspective is to express each year's national debt as a fraction of that year's nominal GDP. This is done in Figure 16–2. Here, in contrast to Figure 16–1, we see an unmistakable downward trend from the dizzying heights of World War II until 1975. In 1947, the national debt was the equivalent of thirteen months' national income. By 1975, this figure had been whittled down to less than two months' income. If we use this as a crude indicator of the nation's ability to "pay off" its debt, then the burden of the debt was certainly far smaller in 1975 than it was in 1947.

However, in the last few years, the national debt has been growing very fast. In just fifteen years since 1975, the debt has risen to the equivalent of more than six months' GDP. This is one of the reasons many economists are alarmed by our persistently large budget deficits.

[2]Indexing the tax system is explained on page 99.

FIGURE 16–2
Ratio of Public Debt to National Product
This graph takes the data used to construct Figure 16–1 and divides each year's debt by the nation's total production of that year. We can see that the debt grew relative to national product during the Great Depression, World War II, the recessions of 1958–62 and the 1980s, and in the period following the indexation of the personal income-tax system.
SOURCE: Department of Finance.

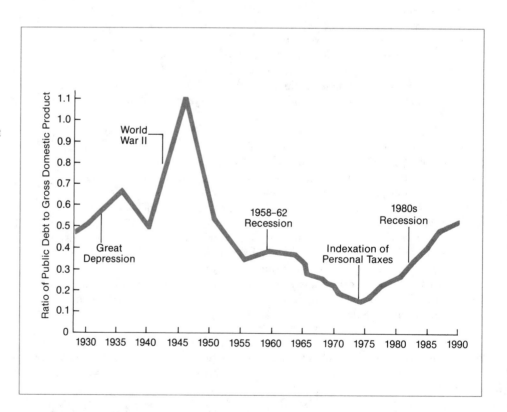

Interpreting the Budget Deficit

We have seen that the national debt grew unusually rapidly in the 1980s. The reason, of course, is that the federal government's annual budget deficits were much larger than they had been previously.

Figure 16–3 shows the budget deficit year by year for the entire decade. You will note that these deficit figures are smaller than those reported earlier in the chapter. The earlier data are taken from the *Public Accounts of Canada*, which records the actual receipts and payments of government on a fiscal-year basis, as reported to Parliament. The deficits depicted in Figure 16–3 (and noted in the remaining tables in this chapter) are defined on a national-accounts basis, because the government calculates its inflation and cyclical adjustments (to be discussed below) using deficits measured on a national-accounts basis. The main differences between the public-accounts and the national-accounts methods of measurement are that the latter involves the calendar year and records revenue items on the basis of when revenues were earned (not when they were actually paid). To interpret these deficit figures, we must first consider what many economists view as a serious measurement problem—the way interest payments are treated in the government's budget.

Inflation Accounting for Interest Payments*

At first blush, government accountants seem to treat interest payments in the sensible way: Every dollar of interest that the government pays on the national debt is counted as a dollar of spending—just like purchases of supplies, old age security payments, and the salaries of civil servants. This seems the natural thing to do. But it ignores the fundamental distinction between real and nominal interest rates that we emphasized in Chapter 4. To review the analysis:

*This section contains difficult material that may be skipped in shorter courses.

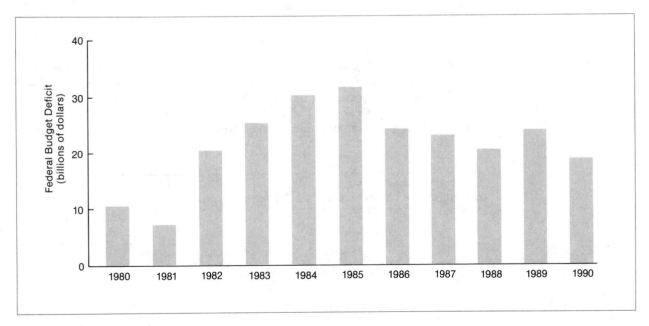

FIGURE 16–3
Federal Budget Deficits, 1980–1990*
The federal deficit tripled during this period, but it has been coming back down slowly in recent years.
*Measured on a national-accounts basis.
SOURCE: Department of Finance, February 1990 budget projections.

The **real interest rate** tells us the amount of purchasing power the borrower turns over to the lender for the privilege of borrowing. To this we must add an **inflation premium**, equal to the expected rate of inflation, to get the **nominal interest rate**. The inflation premium compensates the lender for the expected erosion of the purchasing power of his money and is best thought of as repayment of principal.[3]

The last sentence has important implications for the government budget—implications that few people understand.

From an economic point of view, the portion of the government's interest payments that merely compensates lenders for inflation should be counted as *repayment of principal*, not as *interest expense*, because it simply returns to lenders the purchasing power of their original loans. Only the *real* interest that the government pays should be treated as an expenditure item in the budget. Breaking up interest payments in this way is called **inflation accounting**. Since even quite sophisticated people have trouble understanding inflation accounting, it is worth taking the time to illustrate the idea with an analogy and a simple example.

> Inflation accounting means adjusting standard accounting procedures for the fact that inflation lowers the purchasing power of money.

Imagine that you lend a roommate, who is enrolled in a chemistry course, a bar of radium that you happen to own. Your roommate uses the radioactive bar in experiments for a year and then returns it to you. Has your loan been repaid in full? Certainly not. Because of the natural process of radioactive decay, the bar you get back is smaller than the bar you originally loaned. To pay you back in full, your roommate must give you enough additional radium to replace the portion that has been eroded during the year.

The analogy to interest rates on loans is straightforward: Inflation erodes the purchasing power of money just as radioactive decay erodes radium. So, in figuring out how many dollars constitute repayment of principal, we must take inflation into account. Let's illustrate this with a concrete example, comparing a loan made at zero inflation (no decay) with a loan made at 10 percent inflation (rapid decay).

First, suppose the government borrows $1000 for a year when the inflation rate is zero, paying 2 percent interest. At the end of the year it must pay back $1000 in principal and $20 in interest, for a total of $1020. Of this, only $20—the interest payment—is an expenditure item in the budget. The repayment of principal does not appear in the budget since it is not spending. The loan transaction is summarized quite simply in column 1 of Table 16–1.

Now, let us see how inflation (erosion of the purchasing power of money) complicates the accountant's job. Suppose the same transaction takes place when the rate of inflation is 10 percent. If the real rate of interest is still 2 percent, the nominal rate of interest must be about 12 percent.

Specifically, to compensate the lender for 10 percent inflation—and nothing

[3]If you need further review, see pages 95–96.

TABLE 16–1
Accounting for a $1000 Loan at a 2 Percent Real Interest Rate

	(1)	(2)	(3)
		AT 10 PERCENT INFLATION	
	AT ZERO INFLATION	CONVENTIONAL ACCOUNTING	INFLATION ACCOUNTING
Interest (included in budget)	$ 20	$ 122	$ 22
plus			
Principal (excluded from budget)	1000	1000	1100
equals			
Total payment	$1020	$1122	$1122

more—the government must return $1.10 for each dollar originally borrowed. A real interest rate of 2 percent means that the government must return 2 percent more than this, or $1.02 \times \$1.10 = \$1.122$ per dollar borrowed. Thus, each dollar of lending earns 12.2 cents in interest, making the nominal interest rate 12.2 percent.

If the nominal interest rate is 12.2 percent, a government that borrows $1000 at the start of the year will have to repay $1,122 at year's end. Conventional accounting procedures will treat $1000 of this as repayment of principal (and hence not as an expenditure) and $122 as interest (which is an expenditure). This conventional accounting treatment is indicated in column 2 of Table 16–1.

But these numbers are misleading: $1000 at the end of the year is not adequate repayment of principal, because inflation has eroded the real value of money. The correct inflation-accounting treatment recognizes that it takes $1100 at the end of the year to buy what $1000 bought at the beginning of the year. So $1100 is treated as repayment of principal, leaving only $22 ($1122 – $1100) to be treated as interest. The correct inflation accounting is shown in column 3 of Table 16–1.

To recapitulate, the proper economic treatment of a loan in an inflationary environment must recognize that more dollars (in our example, $1100) must be returned to the lender in order to give back the purchasing power of the original loan ($1000). Only the excess of the nominal interest payment ($122) over the compensation for inflation ($100) should be counted as interest.

This example holds the following lesson for interpreting budget-deficit figures:

Inflation distorts the government budget under conventional accounting procedures by exaggerating interest expenses.

The example also suggests how this error can be corrected:

To correct the deficit for inflation, we must subtract the inflation premium from the interest paid on the national debt, thereby counting only *real* interest payments.

This treatment, by the way, corresponds exactly to the way inflation accounting is done by major corporations.

As Table 16–2 shows, making the inflation adjustment to interest payments would have reduced reported deficits by an average of almost $6 billion in recent years.

TABLE 16–2
Inflation Accounting and the Deficit

	ACTUAL DEFICIT* (billions of dollars)	INFLATION ADJUSTMENT (billions of dollars)	INFLATION-ADJUSTED DEFICIT (billions of dollars)
1980	−10.7	+ 4.2	− 6.5
1981	− 7.3	+ 5.9	− 1.4
1982	−20.3	+ 4.8	−15.5
1983	−25.0	+ 3.6	−21.4
1984	−30.0	+ 3.6	−26.4
1985	−31.4	+ 4.4	−27.0
1986	−24.0	+ 6.2	−17.8
1987	−22.9	+ 5.5	−17.4
1988	−20.5	+ 7.7	−12.8
1989	−23.9	+ 8.7	−15.2
1990	−18.9	+11.1	− 7.8

*Measured on a national-accounts basis. The 1990 figure is a projection made before it became clear that GDP growth in 1990 would be depressed and that interest rates would remain high. Thus, more-accurate entries for the last row in this table would be much larger, but these figures were not available from the government when this book went to press.

SOURCE: Department of Finance, February 1990 budget projections.

Starting in 1982, however, the federal government began running large deficits even after correction for inflation accounting.

The Cyclically Adjusted Budget

The second major issue in making sense of the budget deficit is not a problem of measurement, but one of interpretation. As we learned in Chapter 9, the government's taxing and spending decisions affect the level of economic activity. For example, higher spending or lower taxes lead—via the multiplier process—to higher aggregate demand and therefore to a higher GDP. This makes it natural to think that big deficits signify expansionary fiscal policy.

But that view may be incorrect because the state of the economy also affects the budget. In particular, *recessions tend to enlarge the budget deficit*. The reason is simple. Remember that the deficit is the difference between government expenditures and tax receipts; that is:

$$\text{Deficit} = G + \text{Transfers} - \text{Taxes}.$$

The government's most important sources of tax revenue—income taxes, corporate profit taxes, sales taxes, and payroll taxes—all shrink when GDP falls because firms and people pay less tax when they earn less. Similarly, some forms of government spending, notably transfer payments such as unemployment benefits, rise when GDP falls because more people are out of work. Since spending goes up and tax receipts go down as GDP falls:

The deficit rises in a recession (and falls in a boom), even when there is no change in fiscal policy.

Because the deficit changes even when policy does not, the deficit is a poor measure of the government's fiscal policy. For this reason, many economists feel that we should pay less attention to the actual deficit or surplus and more attention to the deficit or surplus in what is called the **cyclically adjusted budget**. This is a hypothetical construct that replaces both the spending and the tax receipts in the *actual* budget with estimates of how much the government *would be* spending and receiving, *given* current tax rates and expenditure rules, *if* the economy were operating at its average level of unemployment.

Since it is based on the spending and taxing the government would be doing at normal levels of unemployment, rather than on actual expenditures and receipts, the cyclically adjusted budget is not sensitive to the state of the economy. It will change only when policy changes. For this reason, most economists believe it is a better measure of the thrust of fiscal policy than is the actual deficit. Using this new concept, we can provide a useful restatement of our previous conclusion about the effect of a recession on the budget deficit:

When unemployment rises, the actual budget deficit grows larger while the cyclically adjusted budget remains unchanged.

This simple observation helps us understand the genesis of the large budget deficits of the early 1980s: They were partly attributable to the consistently high unemployment rates that marked this period. Table 16–3 shows just how important the distinction between the actual deficit and the cyclically adjusted deficit has been in recent years. For 1982, for example, one-third of the actual deficit was due to the recession. Nevertheless, even the cyclically adjusted budget has been deeply in the red in recent years.

The cyclically adjusted budget is the hypothetical budget we *would have* if the economy were operating with an average level of unemployment.

TABLE 16-3
Unemployment and the Federal Deficit

	ACTUAL DEFICIT* (billions of dollars)	CYCLICAL ADJUSTMENT† (billions of dollars)	CYCLICALLY ADJUSTED DEFICIT (billions of dollars)
1980	−10.7	+0.4	−10.3
1981	− 7.3	−0.1	− 7.4
1982	−20.3	+7.1	−13.2
1983	−25.0	+7.2	−17.8
1984	−30.0	+4.2	−25.8
1985	−31.4	+1.9	−29.5
1986	−24.0	+1.0	−23.0
1987	−22.9	−0.7	−23.6
1988	−20.5	−3.7	−24.2
1989	−23.9	−3.6	−27.5
1990	−18.9	+0.2	−18.7

* See note to Table 16-2.
† For 1990, based on a cyclically adjusted unemployment rate of 8 percent and growth of cyclically adjusted output of 3.2 percent. Due to the uncertainties in estimating cyclically adjusted unemployment and output, or average rates of unemployment and output growth that can be sustained over economic cycles, the year-to-year change in the cyclically adjusted deficit may be a more reliable indicator of discretionary fiscal policy than the levels.

SOURCE: Department of Finance, February 1990 budget projections.

Conclusion: What's New about the Recent Deficits?

Table 16-4 puts our two major adjustments—for inflation and for unemployment—together and compares recent actual deficits (column 1) with their corresponding cyclically adjusted, inflation-corrected deficits (column 4). The difference between the two columns is startling. There has been a major swing in the federal budget position, but only since 1982 has the cyclically adjusted, inflation-corrected budget been consistently in substantial deficit. Much of the actual deficit is understandable, given the high levels of inflation and recession prevailing in the early 1980s. But these considerations account for only about one-third of the total of the last three years' deficits as shown in Table 16-4. It is because the *corrected* deficit never approached such levels in peacetime until the 1980s that there has been such concern.

TABLE 16-4
Actual and Adjusted Budget Deficits

	(1) ACTUAL DEFICIT* (billions of dollars)	(2) INFLATION ADJUSTMENT (billions of dollars)	(3) CYCLICAL ADJUSTMENT (billions of dollars)	(4) ADJUSTED DEFICIT (billions of dollars)
1980	−10.7	+ 4.2	+0.4	− 6.1
1981	− 7.3	+ 5.9	−0.1	− 1.5
1982	−20.3	+ 4.8	+7.1	− 8.4
1983	−25.0	+ 3.6	+7.2	−14.2
1984	−30.0	+ 3.6	+4.2	−22.2
1985	−31.4	+ 4.4	+1.9	−25.1
1986	−24.0	+ 6.2	+1.0	−16.8
1987	−22.9	+ 5.5	−0.7	−18.1
1988	−20.5	+ 7.7	−3.7	−16.5
1989	−23.9	+ 8.7	−3.6	−18.8
1990	−18.9	+11.1	+0.2	− 7.6

*See note to Table 16-2.

SOURCE: Tables 16-2 and 16-3.

Bogus Arguments about the Burden of the Debt

Having gained some perspective on the facts, let us now turn to some of the arguments advanced by those who claim that by running budget deficits we are placing an intolerable burden on future generations.

Argument 1: Our children and grandchildren will be burdened by heavy interest payments. To meet these payments, there will have to be higher taxes.

Answer: It is certainly true that a higher debt will necessitate higher interest payments and, other things being equal, this will lead to higher taxes paid by our children and grandchildren. But think who will receive the higher interest payments as income: our children and grandchildren! Thus one group of future Canadians will, essentially, be making interest payments to another group of future Canadians. While some people will gain and others will lose, the future generation as a whole will come out even. We conclude that:

As long as the national debt is owned by domestic citizens, the future interest payments merely shuffle money from one group of Canadians to another. These transfers may or may not be desirable, but they hardly constitute a burden to the nation as a whole.

However, this argument *is* valid for that portion of our debt that is held by foreigners. Paying the interest on this portion of the debt *will* be a burden on future generations of Canadians. (We should also note that it is not just the government debt owned by foreigners that is at issue here. If the bonds issued by our governments are bought by domestic residents and if this then forces our private companies to issue bonds to foreigners, the burden on future Canadians is just as severe in terms of interest obligations to foreigners.) Hence:

Higher foreign-owned debt does represent a burden to future Canadians as a group.

Argument 2: It will ruin the nation when we have to repay the enormous debt.

Answer: A first answer to this merely rephrases the answer to the previous argument: Only the part owned by foreigners involves any burden; the rest is paid by one group of Canadians to another. But there is a much more fundamental point. *Unlike a private family, the nation need never pay off its debt.* Instead, each time the principal is due, the government can simply "roll it over" by floating more debt. Indeed, this is precisely what the government does.

Is this a bit of chicanery? How can the government get away with borrowing money that it never intends to pay back? The answer is found by recognizing the fallacy of comparing the government to a family or individual. People cannot be extended credit in perpetuity because they will not live that long. Sensible lenders will not extend long-term credit to very old people because their heirs cannot be forced to pay up. But the Canadian government will never "die"; at least, we hope not! So this problem does not arise. In this respect, the government is in much the same position as a large corporation. General Motors never worries about paying off its debt. It too rolls it over by floating new debt all the time.

Argument 3: It will bankrupt the nation. Like any family or any business firm, a nation has a limited capacity to borrow. If it exceeds this limit, it is in danger of being unable to pay its creditors. It may go bankrupt, with calamitous consequences for everyone.

Answer: This is another example of a false analogy. What is claimed about private debtors is certainly true. But the Canadian government need never fear defaulting on its debt. Why? First, because it has enormous power to raise revenues by taxation. If you had such power, you would never have to fear bankruptcy either.

Furthermore, a good part of the Canadian national debt is an obligation to pay *Canadian* dollars: Each debt certificate obligates the government to pay the holder so many Canadian dollars on a prescribed date. But the Canadian government is the source of these dollars; it prints them! *No nation need ever fear defaulting on debts that call for repayment in its own currency.* At the very worst, it can always print whatever money it needs to pay off its creditors.

It does not follow, however, that acquiring debt through budget deficits is therefore always a good idea. Sometimes it is clearly a bad idea. Printing money to pay the debt will expand aggregate demand and cause inflation, and this will often be undesirable. The point is not that budget deficits are either good or bad—we already know that they can be either under the appropriate circumstances. Rather, the point is that worrying about a possible default on the national debt is quite unnecessary, unless a very significant portion of that debt, or the debts of the nation's households and firms, are obligations to pay *foreign* currencies. A large foreign debt cannot be paid simply by printing more domestic currency. This is a problem for a number of less developed countries, but Canada's foreign debt is not at such levels.

Having cleared the air of these fallacious arguments, we are now in a position to explore some real problems that may arise when the government spends more than it takes in through taxation.

Budget Deficits and Inflation

One indictment of deficit spending that certainly *does* have validity under most circumstances is the charge that it is inflationary. Why? Because when government policy pushes up aggregate demand, firms may find themselves unwilling or unable to produce the higher quantities that are being demanded at the going prices. Prices will therefore have to rise.

Figure 16–4 is an aggregate supply and demand diagram that shows this analysis graphically. Initially, equilibrium is at point E_0—where demand curve D_0D_0 and supply curve SS intersect. Output is $400 billion, and the price index is at 100. The diagram

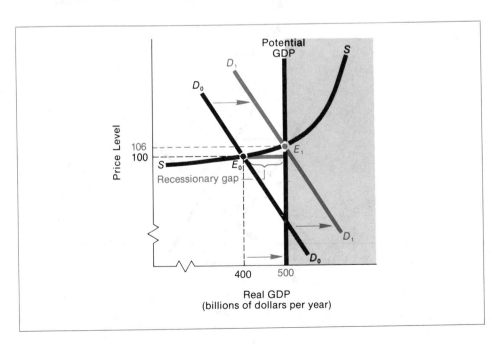

FIGURE 16–4

The Inflationary Effects of Deficit Spending

In this diagram, expansionary fiscal policy pushes the aggregate demand curve out from D_0D_0 to D_1D_1, causing equilibrium to move from E_0 (where there is unemployment) to E_1 (where there is full employment). But because aggregate supply curve SS slopes upward, the price level is pushed up from 100 to 106; that is, there is a 6 percent inflation.

indicates that the economy is operating below full employment; there is a recessionary gap. If the government does nothing to reduce the resulting unemployment, we know from Chapter 8 that this recessionary gap will linger for a long time. The economy will suffer through a prolonged period of unemployment.

Rather than permit such a long recession, we know that the government can raise its spending or cut its taxes enough to shift the aggregate demand schedule upward from D_0D_0 to D_1D_1. Such a policy can wipe out the recessionary gap and the associated unemployment—but not without an inflationary cost. The diagram shows that the new equilibrium price level is at 106, or 6 percent higher than before the government acted.

Thus the cries that budget deficits are "inflationary" have the ring of truth. How much truth, of course, depends on the slope of the aggregate supply curve. Deficit spending will not cause much inflation if the economy has lots of slack and the aggregate supply curve consequently is flat. But deficit spending will be highly inflationary in a fully employed economy with a steep aggregate supply curve.

The Monetization Issue

Some people worry about the inflationary consequences of deficits for a rather different reason. They fear that the Bank of Canada may have to "monetize" part of the deficit, by which they mean that the Bank may feel compelled to purchase some of the newly issued government debt. Let us explain, first, why the Bank might make such purchases, and second, why these purchases are called **monetizing the deficit**.

The central bank is said to **monetize the deficit** when it purchases the bonds that the government issues.

Deficit spending, we have just noted, normally drives up both real GDP and the price level. As we have emphasized before, such an economic expansion shifts the demand curve for money outward to the right—as depicted in Figure 16-5. The figure shows that, if the Bank of Canada takes no actions to shift the money-supply curve, interest rates will rise (from point A to point B).

Suppose now that the Bank does not want interest rates to rise. What can it do? To prevent the incipient rise in interest rates, it must engage in expansionary monetary policies that shift the supply curve for money outward to the right—from M_0S_0 to M_1S_1 in Figure 16-5. And, as noted in Chapter 12, expansionary monetary policies normally take the form of open-market purchases of government bonds. For this reason, deficit spending sometimes induces the Bank of Canada to increase its purchases of government bonds, that is, to buy up some of the newly issued debt.

FIGURE 16-5

Monetization and Interest Rates

If expansionary fiscal policy pushes real GDP and the price level higher, the demand curve for money will shift outward from M_0D_0 to M_1D_1. Equilibrium in the money market shifts from point A to point B, so interest rates rise. If the Bank of Canada does not want a fiscal expansion to raise interest rates, it must increase the money supply. To keep the rate of interest constant, the Bank of Canada will have to shift the money-supply curve outward from M_0S_0 to M_1S_1. Points A and C correspond to the same rate of interest.

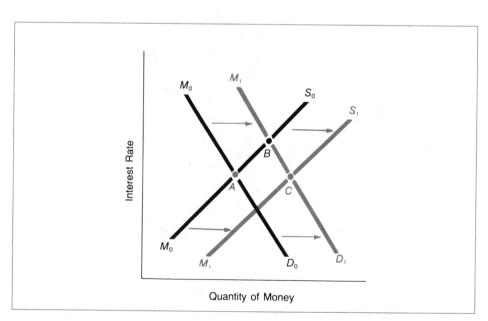

Even if the Bank of Canada makes no explicit response to the pressure for higher interest rates, the reaction of foreign bond-holders forces the same result. As foreigners move to acquire the relatively high-yield Canadian bonds, they must enter the foreign-exchange market to get the required amount of Canadian dollars to buy the bonds. This puts upward pressure on the value of the Canadian dollar. The Bank of Canada frequently resists any significant appreciation of the Canadian dollar, to avoid a potential squeeze on the profits of Canadian exporters. This requires intervention in the foreign-exchange market, to make available the additional Canadian dollars demanded by the foreign investors. Thus, the pursuit of maximum interest yields by foreign bond-holders keeps Canadian interest rates from rising significantly, and a managed exchange-rate policy by the Bank of Canada means that the domestic money supply must increase following newly issued government debt.

Why is this process called *monetizing* the deficit? The reason is simple. As we learned in Chapter 12, open-market purchases of bonds or foreign exchange by the central bank give the chartered banks more reserves, which leads, eventually, to an increase in the money supply. By this indirect route, then, larger budget deficits may lead to an expansion of the money supply. To summarize:

If the Bank of Canada takes no countervailing actions, an expansionary fiscal policy that raises the budget deficit will raise real GDP and prices, thereby shifting the demand curve for money outward and putting upward pressure on interest rates. If the Bank does not want either interest rates or the exchange rate to rise, it can engage in expansionary open-market operations, that is, purchase more government debt or foreign exchange. If the Bank of Canada does this, the money supply will increase. In this case, we say that part of the deficit is *monetized*.

Monetized deficits are more inflationary than non-monetized deficits for the simple reason that expansionary monetary and fiscal policies together are more inflationary than expansionary fiscal policy alone. When both policies expand simultaneously, the aggregate demand curve shifts farther to the right—referring back to Figure 16–4, it moves outward from position D_1D_1. This creates even more inflationary pressure.

Many economists and business leaders were concerned about monetization in the 1980s. The reason is simple arithmetic. When budget deficits are extremely large, even a small percentage of monetization can lead to a substantial increase in bank reserves and the money supply.

Deficits, Interest Rates, and Crowding Out

So far we have been looking for possible burdens of the national debt on the *demand* side of the economy. But a serious burden also comes on the *supply* side because large budget deficits discourage investment and therefore retard the growth of our nation's capital stock. The mechanism is easy to understand.

We have just seen that budget deficits create pressure for higher interest rates unless the Bank of Canada engages in substantial monetization. But the rate of interest (r) is a major determinant of investment spending (I). In particular, higher r leads to lower I. And if we do less spending on I today, we will have a smaller capital stock tomorrow. This, according to most economists, is the true sense in which a large national debt may put a burden on future generations:

Because of the large national debt, we may bequeath less physical capital to future generations. If they inherit less plant and equipment, these generations will be burdened by a lower productive capacity—a lower potential GDP—and this means lower income per person.

Crowding out occurs when deficit spending by the government forces private investment spending or exports to contract.

There is another way of looking at this problem—a way that explains why it is often called the **crowding-out effect**. Consider what happens in financial markets when the government engages in deficit spending. When it spends more than it takes in through tax revenues, the government must borrow the balance from private citizens. It does this by issuing bonds, and these bonds compete with corporate bonds and other financial instruments for the available supply of funds. When some private savers are persuaded to buy government bonds, there must be a decline in the funds remaining to invest in private bonds. Thus some private firms that wish to borrow to finance new capital equipment will get "crowded out" of the financial markets as the government claims an increasing share of the economy's total pool of saving.

Some critics of deficits who have taken this lesson to its illogical extreme argue that each $1 of deficit spending by government crowds out exactly $1 of private spending, so that expansionary fiscal policy has no net effect on total demand. In their view, when G rises, I falls by the same amount, so that $C + I + G + X - IM$ is unchanged. Other analysts feel that as long as a severe recession exists, firms will not be borrowing to expand anyway. According to this view, crowding out becomes a real issue only if the deficit remains large after the economy improves.

Some analysts challenge the relevance of the crowding-out problem even when the economy is recovering. They argue that the notion of "room in the bond market" for both government and private borrowing makes limited sense for Canada. We always have the option of foreign borrowing, so the relevant bond market is very big relative to all Canadian participants. With the option of foreign borrowing, there should be little increase in interest rates following deficit finance, so there should be little crowding out of investment.

We must remember, however, that foreign borrowing involves foreign exchange entering the country. This foreign exchange must be converted to domestic currency to finance the increased domestic expenditures. If the exchange rate is flexible, it is the international value of the Canadian dollar that gets bid up, not the domestic rate of interest. But an appreciating Canadian dollar makes our exports more expensive to foreigners, so there is still a crowding-out effect—exports are crowded out by the increase in government spending. Investment spending by these exporting firms also diminishes, without an increase in interest rates.

Exchange-rate crowding out can be avoided if the Bank of Canada fixes the exchange rate. Thus, we can summarize as follows:

Both interest-rate and exchange-rate reasons for crowding out can be avoided, but only by monetizing the deficit and/or by allowing the foreign-owned portion of the national debt to rise. Either option yields a burden: either inflation or large interest-payment obligations to foreigners in the future.

The True Burden of the National Debt

With this analysis of crowding out, we are in a position to understand why budget deficits might or might not impose a burden on future generations: When government budget deficits take place in a high-employment economy, the crowding-out effect becomes important, so the deficits will exact a burden, either by leaving a smaller capital stock to future generations or by leaving them a bigger interest-payment obligation to foreigners. However, deficits in a slack economy may well lead to more investment rather than less since economic activity is stimulated. In this case, the debt may be a blessing rather than a burden.

Which case applies to the Canadian national debt? To answer this, let us go back to the historical facts and recall how we have accumulated such a large debt. The first cause was the financing of World War II. This debt was contracted in a fully employed economy and thus undoubtedly constituted a burden in the formal sense. It left future generations with less capital because some of our nation's resources were diverted from private investment into government production. The bombs, ships, and planes that it financed were used up in the war, not bequeathed as capital to future generations.

Yet what were the alternatives? We could have tried to finance the entire war by taxation, and thus placed the burden on consumption rather than on investment. But that would truly have been extremely hard on that generation and maybe even impossible, given the colossal wartime expenditures. Or we could have printed money, but that would have unleashed an inflation that nobody wanted. Or we could have just done much less government spending and would therefore have contributed less toward winning the war. So, in retrospect, the generations alive today and in the future may not feel unduly burdened by the decisions of the people in power in the 1940s.

The second major contributor to the national debt has been a series of recessions. But these are precisely the circumstances under which increasing the debt might prove to be a blessing rather than a burden. So, if we look for the classic type of deficits to which the valid burden-of-the-debt argument applies—deficits acquired in a fully employed peacetime economy—we do not find many in the Canadian record *until after 1973*.

It is in this context that current budget deficits are a sharp departure from the past. Our examination of inflation adjustments and cyclical adjustments showed that large deficits would exist today even if the Canadian economy had normal levels of unemployment and no inflation. This is not something that has happened before, at least not on an ongoing basis. It poses a real threat of crowding out and/or increased interest obligations to foreigners, and thus it represents a serious potential burden on future generations.

The Burden of the National Debt

Let us now summarize our evaluation of the burden of the national debt and thereby clarify one of the 12 **Ideas for Beyond the Final Exam** introduced in Chapter 1. First, the arguments that a large national debt may lead the nation into bankruptcy or unduly burden future generations who have to make onerous payments of interest and principal are mostly bogus. They are important arguments only if the country is significantly in debt to foreigners. Second, before 1973, the actual public debt of the Canadian federal government was mostly contracted as a result of the war and recessions—precisely the circumstances under which the valid burden-of-the-debt argument does not apply. Third, the national debt *will* be a burden if it is contracted in a fully employed peacetime economy, because in that case it will reduce the nation's capital stock and increase its foreign indebtedness. The large deficits of recent years are quite worrisome from this point of view.

Conclusion: What Should Be Done about the Deficit?

It is a matter of simple arithmetic that you close a budget deficit by raising taxes and/or reducing spending. Either of these routes is a contractionary fiscal policy that will retard the growth of real GDP. Given this fact of life, should we try to close the deficit? The correct answer would be no, if the cyclically adjusted, inflation-corrected deficit were zero. But even after these adjustments, the federal government deficit is very large, so some closing of the deficit is called for.

If contractionary fiscal policy is so obviously needed, why haven't we seen more action from the government? The reason seems to be that the political process is not very good at apportioning pain. Whenever a tax is raised or a spending program cut, someone will be hurt. Many of these "someones" vote, and politicians know that. Despite this, the government raised taxes significantly during the latter half of the 1980s. But expenditures have not been cut much, and of course the interest-payment obligations are feeding on themselves and getting bigger every year.

Deficit Clouds Future: Ageing Population, the Poor Will Be the Victims of Debt Squeeze

In its final annual report for the 1980s, the Economic Council of Canada warned that the deficit problem was becoming severe. The report was summarized in *The Globe and Mail*'s lead story for November 2, 1989, and the title of our box is adapted from that headline. Excerpts from the article are given here.

Canada faces a bleak future unless steps are taken to cut the federal deficit and deal with the problems of an ageing population and the gap between rich and poor, the Economic Council of Canada predicted yesterday.

In its annual review of the economy, the government-appointed economic research agency said the burgeoning cost of servicing the federal debt is leaving future generations with a huge burden and is strangling the government's ability to initiate programs to deal with the changing needs of Canadians....

To tackle the deficit problem, the council suggests a two-year freeze on five areas of government spending, including capital assistance and subsidies to business, transfer payments to the provinces, indexing of family allowances and hiring of federal public servants....

The council says that this persistent deficit problem occurs at a time when the population is ageing rapidly, with the proportion of Canadians over 65 expected to increase to 21 percent of the population in 30 years' time and 30 percent by the year 2040. That, in turn, will mean new and different demands on the federal treasury.

"The pressure of debt service is already forcing painful cuts in current commitments, with the result that there is no room to introduce new expenditure programs," the council said, adding: "Delaying deficit reduction could seriously erode the legacy that we will leave to future generations."

The council also noted increasing polarization in the distribution of wealth. After rapid wage growth in the 1960s and 1970s, the real earnings of an average worker have virtually stood still, with real family income depending in-

creasingly on higher participation by married women in the work force.

"Generally speaking, our parents were much better off than their parents when they retired," the report says. "Today, however, unless Canada's economic performance greatly improves, our children can expect only modest improvement over our situation when they retire, even though as husband and wife they may have worked full time for much of their lives."

SOURCE: Adapted from Alan Freeman, "Deficit Clouds Future, Economists Warn: Aging Population, the Poor Victims of Debt Squeeze," *The Globe and Mail*, November 2, 1989, pages A1–A2.

By 1990, the polls suggested that Canadians did not want further tax increases. They would accept cuts in government spending in three areas—defence, arts and culture, and foreign aid. But these three areas did not represent enough spending to make a significant dent in the deficit. The government simply had to start making some reductions in the big spending areas—in subsidies for regional development and agriculture, in transfers to provinces for health and education, and in numerous social programs. Despite the fact that the polls advised against these reductions, the government made some initial cuts in some of these areas in its 1990 budget.

In addition to the fact that people do not want these particular programs cut back, *any* expenditure reductions will lead to some job losses in the short run. Thus, one of the very real costs of the deficit is that it constrains the government's ability to stimulate job creation.

Is there any way around the problem that steps taken to close the deficit are contractionary? One possible answer to this problem is that fiscal and monetary policies could be better co-ordinated. If fiscal policy must turn contractionary to reduce the deficit, monetary policy can turn expansionary to counteract the effects on aggregate demand. In this way, we can hope to shrink the deficit without shrinking the economy in the process. Such a change in the policy "mix" would put downward pressure on interest rates, since both tighter budgets and easier money tend to push interest rates down in the short run.

The problem with this policy mix is that it would lead to a depreciation in the foreign value of the Canadian dollar. Pressure for lower interest rates in Canada leads to foreign investors' selling off Canadian bonds in favour of higher yields elsewhere. A depreciated Canadian dollar *stimulates* aggregate *demand* (through higher net export sales), but it *contracts* aggregate *supply* (by raising business costs). Despite this unfavourable supply-side effect, quite a few economists, including those at the Economic Council of Canada, have advocated a shift in the policy mix toward tighter budgets and easier monetary policy. However, the history of the 1980s has given us precisely the opposite combination: loose fiscal policy and tight money. If this continues, deficits will persist and will become increasingly burdensome (see the accompanying boxed insert).

Summary

1. Rigid adherence to budget balancing would make the economy less stable by reducing aggregate demand (via tax increases and reductions in G) when private spending is low and raising aggregate demand when private spending is high.

2. The national debt has grown dramatically since the early 1970s. Before then it grew only because of recessions and World War II.

3. Inflation makes the deficit look bigger than it really is because all nominal interest payments are counted as expenditures. Under inflation accounting, only real interest payments count as expenditures, and the corrected deficit is seen to be much smaller than it appears.

4. Part of the reason for large budget deficits in the 1980s was the fact that the economy was operating well below full employment. The cyclically adjusted deficit, which uses estimates of what the government's receipts and outlays would be at average unemployment rates, was smaller than the official deficit for much of the period.

5. If we correct the official deficit for inflation and cyclical variations, we find that large deficits in the cyclically adjusted, inflation-corrected budget began only in 1982, and continued through the rest of the decade.

6. Arguments that the public debt will burden future generations, who will have to make huge payments of interest and principal, are based on false analogies. In fact, many of these payments are simply transfers from some Canadians to other Canadians. However, some debt is foreign-owned, and the associated interest obligations *do* represent a burden in the future.

7. Under normal circumstances, budget deficits are somewhat inflationary. They are even more inflationary if they are "monetized"; that is, if the Bank of Canada buys some of the newly issued government debt in the open market to keep interest rates from rising or to fix the exchange rate.

8. Unless the deficit is substantially monetized, deficit spending forces interest rates higher and discourages private investment spending. This is called the crowding-out effect. If there is a great deal of crowding out, then deficits really do impose a burden on future generations by leaving them a smaller capital stock to work with.

9. Even if foreigners purchase most of the newly issued Canadian debt, so that interest rates do not rise, the increased foreign demand for Canadian dollars results in an appreciation of the Canadian dollar so that export demand is crowded out. Also, interest obligations to foreigners are increased.

10. Crowding out may not be very important when unemployment is high. Indeed, higher output levels may induce firms to raise investment spending. But when the economy is near full employment, the proponents of the crowding-out hypothesis are probably right: High government spending just displaces private investment and exports.

11. Whether or not deficits are a burden depends on how and why the government ran these deficits in the first place. If deficits are contracted to fight recessions, it is possible that more investment is actually stimulated. Deficits contracted to carry on wars certainly impair the future capital stock, though they may not be considered a burden for non-economic reasons. Since these two cases account for most of Canada's national debt that was incurred before 1973, this debt cannot reasonably be considered a serious burden. However, a noticeable part of the debt incurred since 1973 does represent an overly expansionary fiscal policy and a rapidly growing burden.

12. Since the size of the deficit depends on the state of the economy and since the state of the economy is affected by the deficit, simple correlations between the deficit and other economic variables cannot be used to deduce causation.

Concepts for Review

Budget deficit
National debt
Real versus nominal interest rates
Inflation accounting

Cyclically adjusted budget
Foreign indebtedness
Monetization of deficits
Interest-rate crowding out

Exchange-rate crowding out
Burden of the national debt

Questions for Discussion

1. Explain the difference between the budget deficit and the national debt. If we reduce the deficit, will the debt stop growing?

2. Explain the following statement made by the Economic Council in its 1989 Annual Report (as quoted in *The Globe and Mail*, December 18, 1989, page B2):

   The primary budgetary balance—which excludes net interest payments—must generate a surplus sufficient to offset the growth in interest costs, in order to avoid an increase in the debt/GDP ratio. In other words, increases in revenue and/or reductions in government expenditure are needed simply to overcome the escalating momentum of public debt.

3. Comment on the following: "Deficit spending paves the road to ruination. If we keep it up, the whole nation will go bankrupt. Even if things do not go this far, what right have we to burden our children and grandchildren with these debts while we live high on the hog?"

4. Calculate the budget deficit and the inflation-corrected deficit for an economy with the following data:
   Government expenditures other than interest = $80
   Tax receipts = $85
   Interest payments = $60
   Interest rate = 12 percent
   Inflation rate = 10 percent
   National debt at start of year = $500.
   (*Note*: 12 percent interest on an $800 debt is $60.)

5. Explain why the cyclically adjusted budget might show a surplus while the actual budget is in deficit.

6. If the Bank of Canada begins to increase the money supply more rapidly than before, what will happen to the government budget deficit? (*Hint*: What will happen to tax receipts and interest expenses?) If the government wants to offset the effects of the Bank's actions on aggregate demand, what might it do? How will this affect the deficit?

7. Given the current state of the economy, do you think the Bank of Canada should monetize a sizable proportion of the deficit? (*Note*: There is no one correct answer to this question. It is a good question to discuss in class.)

8. Explain both interest-rate and exchange-rate mechanisms for crowding out. Given the current state of the economy, do you think crowding out is an issue?

9. Evaluate each of the following statements. (*Note*: The facts in each case are correct; concentrate on the conclusion that is reached.)
   a. "In 1978, we had a small deficit and strong GDP growth. In 1982, we had a huge deficit and a recession. Therefore, deficit spending does not stimulate the economy."
   b. "If we compare 1981 with 1983, we find a much larger deficit but much lower inflation in 1983. Therefore, it is clear that deficit spending is not inflationary."

17

The Trade-Off between Inflation and Unemployment

All progress is precarious, and the solution of one problem brings us face to face with another problem.

MARTIN LUTHER KING

T he worldwide trend toward higher inflation was arrested during the 1980s. As inflation declined throughout the Western world, the rate of inflation in Canada fell from 11 percent to 5 percent. In the United States, it fell from 10 percent to 4 percent; in Great Britain, from 20 percent to 6 percent; in West Germany, from 6 percent to about zero. As this was happening, the Western economies all suffered severe recessions. In Canada, for example, the unemployment rate topped 10 percent for the first time since the Great Depression; indeed, it reached 11.9 percent in 1983.

Most economists believe that this conjunction of events was no coincidence. Rather, they insist, the period of high unemployment was the price we paid to reduce the rate of inflation. Although some optimists claim that it is possible to reduce inflation without suffering from unemployment, the world clearly paid a heavy price for the disinflation of the 1980s. Was this price inevitable, or could we have avoided it? That is the question for this chapter.

You may recall from Chapter 1 that the existence of an agonizing trade-off between inflation and unemployment is one of the 12 **Ideas for Beyond the Final Exam**. The importance of this trade-off can hardly be overestimated. It is probably the one area of macroeconomics where confusion is most widespread. And because this confusion can have disastrous consequences for the conduct of stabilization policy, the trade-off merits the comprehensive examination that we give it in this chapter. Without a thorough understanding of the dimensions of this trade-off, it is impossible for a citizen to make an informed judgment about macroeconomic policy.

Demand-Side Inflation versus Supply-Side Inflation: A Review

Let us begin our investigation of the trade-off by reviewing some of what we have learned about inflation in earlier chapters.

One major cause of inflation, though not the only one, is *excessive growth of aggregate demand*. What happens if, for some reason, consumers, investors, the government, or foreigners decide to increase spending? We know, first of all, that such an autonomous increase in spending will have a multiplier effect on aggregate demand; that is, each additional $1 of *C*, *I*, *G*, or *X* – *IM* will lead to perhaps $2 of additional demand, assuming we are on a fixed exchange rate. Second, we know that such a stimulus to aggregate demand will normally pull up *both* real output *and* prices.

The reason, to review our earlier findings, is that firms normally will find it profitable to supply the additional output only at higher prices.

Figure 17–1, which is familiar from earlier chapters, displays this conclusion. Initially, the economy is at point A, where aggregate demand curve D_0D_0 intersects aggregate supply curve SS. Then something happens to increase demand, and the aggregate demand curve shifts horizontally to D_1D_1. The new equilibrium is at point B, where both prices and output are higher than they were at A.

The slope of the aggregate supply curve measures the amount of inflation that accompanies any specified rise in output and therefore embodies the most important aspects of the trade-off between unemployment and inflation. We concluded in Chapter 13 that this trade-off will be favourable when the economy is operating at low levels of capacity utilization and high levels of unemployment. Under such circumstances, firms can expand their operations substantially without running into higher costs. On the other hand, if demand stimulus occurs in a fully employed economy,

FIGURE 17–1
Inflation from the Demand Side

An increase in aggregate demand, whether it comes from consumers, investors, the government, or foreigners, shifts the aggregate demand curve outward from D_0D_0 to D_1D_1. The economy's equilibrium moves from point A to point B. Since point B corresponds to a higher price level than does point A, there is *inflation* (that is, a rising price level) as the economy moves from A to B.

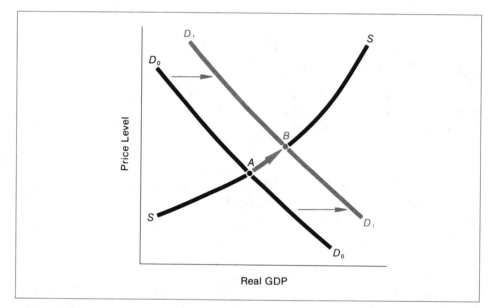

FIGURE 17–2
Inflation from the Supply Side

A decrease in aggregate supply—which can be caused by such factors as an autonomous increase in wages or an increase in the price of foreign oil—can cause inflation. When the aggregate supply curve shifts to the left, from S_0S_0 to S_1S_1, the equilibrium point moves from A to B. Comparing B with A, we see that the price level is higher, which means there must have been *inflation* (rising prices) in the interim. Notice also that adverse supply shifts make real output decline while prices are rising; that is, they produce *stagflation*.

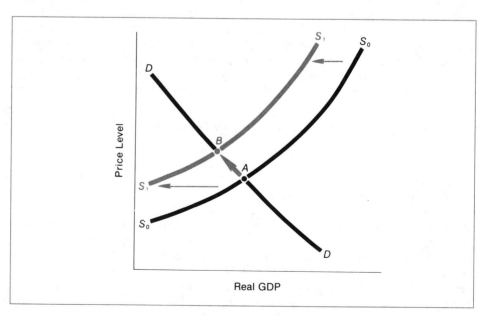

firms will find it quite difficult to raise output and so will respond mostly by raising prices. Thus, the trade-off is very unfavourable when unemployment is low.

But we have learned in this book (especially in Chapter 8) that inflation need not always emanate from the demand side. Restrictions in the growth of aggregate supply —caused, for example, by an increase in the price of foreign oil—can shift the economy's aggregate supply curve inward (or upward). This is illustrated in Figure 17–2, where the aggregate supply curve shifts from S_0S_0 to S_1S_1, and the economy's equilibrium consequently moves from point A to point B. Prices rise as output falls; we have *stagflation*. Thus, while inflation can be initiated from either the demand side or the supply side of the economy, there is a crucial difference. Demand-side inflation is normally accompanied by rising real GDP (see Figure 17–1), while supply-side inflation may well be accompanied by falling GDP (see Figure 17–2). This is an important distinction, as we shall see in this chapter.

Applying the Model to a Growing Economy

You may have noticed that our simple model of aggregate supply and aggregate demand determines an equilibrium price level and an equilibrium level of real GDP. But in the real economy, we do not see an unchanged price level and an unchanged level of real GDP for long periods of time. Instead, the price level and the level of real GDP change every year.

This is illustrated in Figure 17–3, which is a scatter diagram of the Canadian

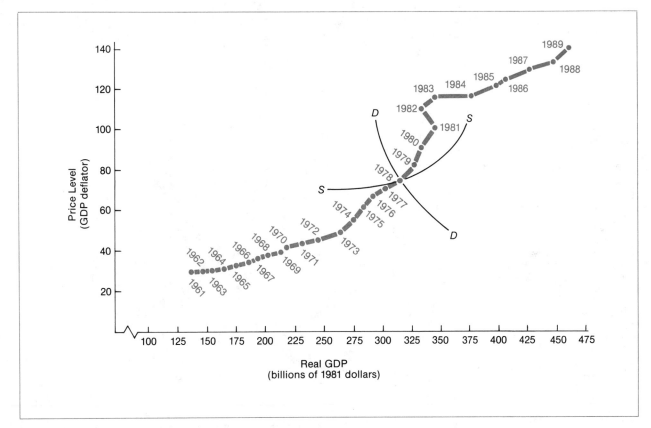

FIGURE 17–3

The Price Level and Real Output in Canada, 1961–1989
This scatter diagram shows, for each year from 1961 to 1989, the price level (GDP deflator) and real GDP for Canada. Clearly the normal state of affairs is for both variables to rise from one year to the next.
SOURCE: Statistics Canada

price level and the level of real GDP for every year from 1961 to 1989. The points are labelled for your convenience, and it is quite clear that the general march of the economy through time is upward and to the right—toward higher prices and higher levels of output.

It is certainly no mystery why this occurs. The economy's aggregate supply and aggregate demand curves change each year. Aggregate supply normally grows because there are more workers, more machinery, and more factories each year and because technology is improving. Aggregate demand normally grows because, with a growing population, there is more demand for both consumer and investment goods by both domestic and foreign residents and because the government increases its spending and the Bank of Canada increases the money supply. We can think of each point in Figure 17–3 as the intersection of an aggregate supply curve and an aggregate demand curve for that particular year. To help you visualize this, the curves for 1978 are sketched in the diagram.

One thing is clear from this diagram: If we want to apply our theoretical model to the real world, we must recognize that the normal state of affairs is for *both* the aggregate demand curve *and* the aggregate supply curve to shift to the right each year. As a consequence, we expect to find both the price level and real GDP rising from year to year.

Figure 17–4 illustrates this idea. The numbers are chosen so that curves D_0D_0 and S_0S_0 approximately represent the end of 1988, and the curves D_1D_1 and S_1S_1 approximately represent the end of 1989. Thus the equilibrium late in 1988 was at point A, with real GDP of $448 billion and a price level of 134, while the equilibrium one year later was at point B, with real GDP at $460 billion and the price level at 141. The green arrow in the diagram shows how equilibrium moved during 1989. It points upward and to the right, meaning that both prices and output increased.

FIGURE 17–4
Aggregate Supply and Demand Analysis of a Growing Economy
This diagram illustrates how the aggregate supply and demand analysis of earlier chapters can be applied to a real-world economy, in which both the supply curve and the demand curve normally shift outward from one year to the next. In this example, demand curve D_0D_0 and supply curve S_0S_0 represent the Canadian economy in late 1988. Equilibrium was at point A, with a price level of 134 and real GDP of $448 billion. Demand curve D_1D_1 and supply curve S_1S_1 represent the end of 1989. During the year, the price index rose by 7 points (about 5.2 percent) and output increased by $12 billion (about 2.7 percent).

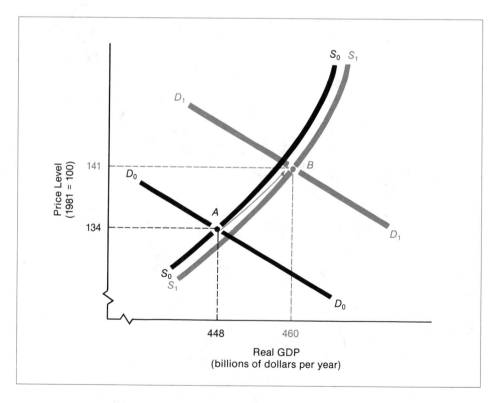

Demand-Side Inflation and the Phillips Curve

Let us now use our theoretical model to rerun history. Suppose that during 1989 the aggregate demand curve had grown faster than it actually did. What difference would this have made for the performance of the national economy? Figure 17–5 provides the answers. Here the demand curve D_0D_0 and both supply curves are exactly as they were in the previous diagram, but the demand curve D_2D_2 is farther to the right than the demand curve D_1D_1 in Figure 17–4. Equilibrium is at point A late in 1988 and point C late in 1989. Comparing point C in Figure 17–5 with point B in Figure 17–4, we see that output would have increased more during 1989 ($22 billion versus $12 billion) and prices would also have increased more (to 145 instead of 141); that is, there would have been more inflation. This is generally what happens when the growth rate of aggregate demand speeds up.

For any given rate of growth of the aggregate supply curve, a faster rate of growth of the aggregate demand curve will lead to more inflation and faster growth of real output.

It is left for the reader to draw another figure (as an exercise) showing the aggregate demand curve shifting to the right *less than* the distance shown in Figure 17–4. This is the opposite case from the one just considered. It shows that a smaller demand shift would have entailed *less inflation* and *slower growth of real output* than actually took place. This again is generally the case.

For any given rate of growth of the aggregate supply curve, a slower rate of growth of the aggregate demand curve will lead to less inflation and slower growth of real output.

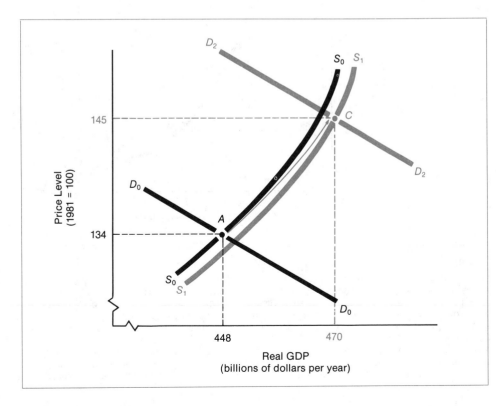

FIGURE 17–5
The Effects of Faster Growth of Aggregate Demand
In this hypothetical example, we imagine that, because either private citizens spent more or the government pursued more expansionary policies, aggregate demand grew faster between late 1988 and late 1989 than it did in Figure 17–4. The consequence is that in this diagram the price level rises 11 points (about 8.2 percent) during 1989, compared with the 7 points (5.2 percent) in Figure 17–4. Growth of real output is also greater: $22 billion here and only $12 billion in the previous figure.

If we put these two findings together, we have a very clear prediction from our theory:

If fluctuations in the economy's real growth rate from year to year are caused primarily by variations in the rate at which the aggregate demand curve shifts outward, then the data should show that the most rapid inflation occurs during years when output expands most rapidly, and the slowest inflation occurs when output expands more slowly.

Does the theory fit the facts? We will put it to the test in a moment, but first let us translate it into a prediction about the relationship between inflation and unemployment. Faster growth of real output naturally means faster growth in the number of jobs and, hence, *lower unemployment*. Conversely, slower growth of real output means slower growth in the number of jobs and, hence, *higher unemployment*. Thus, the unemployment rate and the growth rate of output should be inversely related—the faster the economy grows the lower the unemployment rate, and the slower the economy grows the higher the unemployment rate.

Figure 17-6 illustrates this idea. The actual unemployment rate in Canada in late 1989 was about 7.5 percent, and the inflation rate was about 5.2 percent. This is point *b* in Figure 17-6, which corresponds to equilibrium point *B* in Figure 17-4. The faster growth rate of demand depicted by point *C* in Figure 17-5 would have led to higher inflation and lower unemployment. For the sake of a concrete example, we suppose that unemployment would have been 7 percent and inflation would have been 8.2 percent; this is point *c* in Figure 17-6. This figure shows quite graphically the principal empirical implication of our theoretical model:

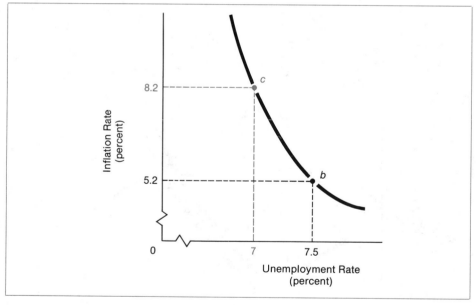

FIGURE 17-6
Origins of the Phillips Curve
The two previous diagrams indicated two different rates of growth of real GDP between late 1988 and late 1989 and two different inflation rates. Since each different real growth rate corresponds to a different rate of unemployment, we can put the information contained in the two preceding diagrams together in a scatter diagram to show the relationship between inflation and unemployment. Points *b* and *c* in this figure correspond to points *B* and *C* in Figures 17-4 and 17-5, respectively. The inflation numbers are read directly from the previous two graphs. The unemployment numbers are fabricated to represent the fact that faster growth is associated with lower unemployment (point *c*) while slower growth is associated with higher unemployment (point *b*). Scatter diagrams like this one are called "Phillips curves," after their inventor, A. W. Phillips.

If fluctuations in economic activity are primarily caused by variations in the rate at which the aggregate demand curve shifts outward from year to year, then the data should show that low unemployment rates are associated with high inflation rates and high unemployment rates are associated with low inflation rates.

Now we are ready to look at real data. Do we actually observe such an inverse relationship between inflation and unemployment? Almost 35 years ago, economist A. W. Phillips plotted data on unemployment and the rate of change of *wages* (not prices) for several extended periods of British history on a series of scatter diagrams, one of which is reproduced as Figure 17–7. He then sketched in a curve that seemed to "fit" the data. This type of curve, which is now called a **Phillips curve**, shows that wage inflation normally is high when unemployment is low and is low when unemployment is high. So far, so good.

Phillips curves have also been constructed for *price* inflation, and one of these for Canada in the 1950s and 1960s is shown in Figure 17–8. The curve appears to fit the data fairly well, although there are two exceptions, 1953 and 1955. According to our theory, these facts suggest that economic fluctuations in England between 1861 and 1913 and in Canada between 1952 and 1969 probably were accounted for primarily by changes in the growth of aggregate demand; that is, by changes in the spending habits

A **Phillips curve** is a graph depicting the rate of unemployment on the horizontal axis and either the rate of inflation or the rate of change of money wages on the vertical axis. Phillips curves are normally downward sloping, indicating that higher inflation rates are associated with lower unemployment rates.

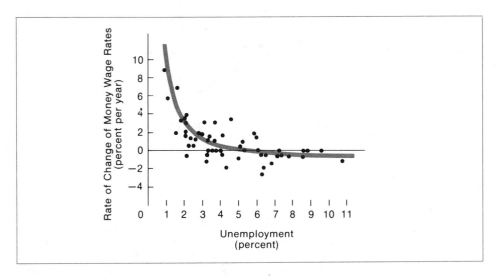

FIGURE 17–7
The Original Phillips Curve
This scatter diagram, reproduced from the original article by A. W. Phillips, shows the rate of change of money wages and the rate of unemployment in the United Kingdom between 1861 and 1913. Each year is represented by a point in the diagram.
SOURCE: A. W. Phillips, "The Relationship Between Unemployment and the Rate of Change of Money Wages in the United Kingdom, 1861–1957," *Economica*, New Series, vol. 25, November 1958.

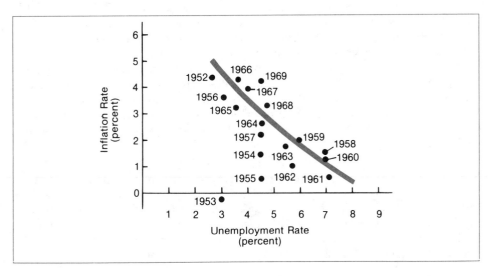

FIGURE 17–8
A Phillips Curve for Canada
This Phillips curve relates price inflation (using the national-output price deflator rather than wage inflation) to the unemployment rate in Canada for the years 1952–69. Though it misses badly in two instances (1953 and 1955), it generally "fits" the data fairly well.

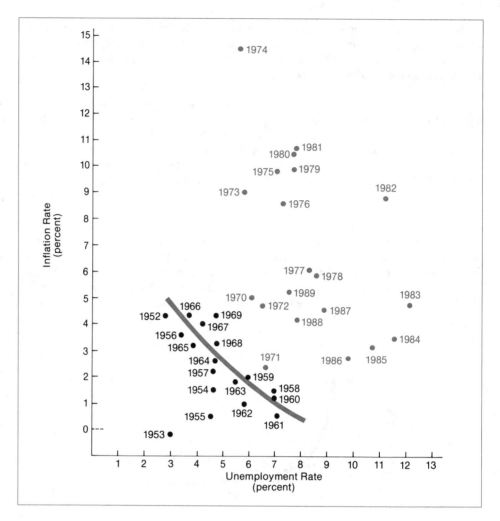

of consumers, investors, foreigners, and the government. The simple model of demand-side inflation does seem to describe what happened.

During the 1960s and early 1970s, economists often thought of the Phillips curve as a "menu" of the choices available to policy-makers. In this view, policy-makers could opt for low unemployment and high inflation—as was done in 1967. Or they might prefer higher unemployment coupled with lower inflation—as, for example, in 1961. The Phillips curve, it was thought, described the *quantitative* trade-off between inflation and unemployment. And, for a number of years, it worked rather well.

Then something happened. The economy in the 1970s behaved far worse than expected in terms of the Phillips curve shown in Figure 17–8. In particular, given the unemployment rates in each of those years, inflation was astonishingly high by historical standards. This is shown in Figure 17–9, which simply adds to Figure 17–8 the points for 1970–89. Clearly something had gone wrong with the old view of the Phillips curve as a menu for policy choices. But what?

Supply-Side Inflation and the Collapse of the Phillips Curve

There are two major answers to this question, and the truth no doubt contains elements of each. We begin with the simpler explanation, which claims that much of the inflation of the 1970s did not emanate from the demand side. Instead, the 1970s were full of adverse "supply shocks"—events such as crop failures and oil-price increases—that pushed the economy's aggregate supply curve inward, to the left. What kind of Phillips curve will be generated when economic fluctuations come from the supply side?

Figure 17-2 has already given us the answer: The price level increases, and real output falls. Falling output means fewer jobs available, so unemployment increases. Thus:

If fluctuations in economic activity emanate mainly from the supply side, higher rates of inflation will be associated with higher rates of unemployment, and lower rates of inflation will be associated with lower rates of unemployment.

There were numerous supply shocks during the 1970s. Food prices boomed between 1972 and 1974 and again in 1978. World energy prices soared in 1973–74 and again in 1979–80. The Canadian government shielded our economy from some of these shocks (as we discussed in Chapter 8), but we were not completely insulated. As noted in Chapter 4, a model involving both demand-side *and* supply-side inflation shocks can easily explain our unemployment and inflation experience since 1970.

What the Phillips Curve Is Not

There is, however, another view of what went wrong in the 1970s. This one holds that policy-makers misinterpreted the Phillips curve and tried to pick unsustainable combinations of inflation and unemployment that were not in fact on the menu. Specifically, the Phillips curve is a *statistical relationship* between inflation and unemployment that we expect to emerge *if changes in the growth of aggregate demand are the predominant factor accounting for economic fluctuations*. But the curve was widely misinterpreted as depicting a number of *alternative equilibrium points* that the economy could achieve and from which policy-makers could choose.

We can understand the flaw in this reasoning by quickly reviewing an earlier lesson. We know from Chapter 8 that the economy has a **self-correcting mechanism** that will cure both inflations and recessions *eventually* even if the government does nothing. Why is this relevant here? Because it tells us that many combinations of output and prices cannot be maintained indefinitely. Some will "self-destruct." Specifically, if the economy finds itself far away from the normal "full-employment" level of unemployment, forces will be set in motion that tend to erode the inflationary or recessionary gap.

For example, consider the case of a recessionary gap where aggregate supply curve S_0S_0 intersects aggregate demand curve DD as in Figure 17–10. With equilibrium output well below potential GDP at point A, there is unused industrial capacity and unsold output. So firms will not raise prices very much. At the same time, the availability of unemployed workers eager for jobs limits the rate at which labour can push up wage rates. But wages are the main component of business costs, so when wages decline (relative to what they would have been without a recession) so do costs. And lower costs stimulate greater production. This idea is depicted in Figure 17–10 as an outward shift of the aggregate supply curve—from S_0S_0 to S_1S_1.

As can be seen in the figure, the outward shift of the aggregate supply curve brought on by the recession causes equilibrium output to rise as the economy moves from point A to point B. Thus the recessionary gap begins to shrink. This process continues until the aggregate supply curve reaches the position indicated by S_2S_2 in Figure 17–10. Here wages have fallen enough to eliminate the recessionary gap, and the economy has reached a full-employment equilibrium at point C.[1]

---

[1] This simple analysis assumes the aggregate demand curve does not move during the adjustment period. If it is shifting to the right, the recessionary gap will disappear even faster, but inflation will not slow down as much. EXERCISE: Construct the diagram for the case involving changing demand by adding a shift in the aggregate demand curve to Figure 17–10.

FIGURE 17-10
The Elimination of a Recessionary Gap

When the aggregate supply curve is S_0S_0 and the aggregate demand curve is DD, the economy will reach an equilibrium with a recessionary gap (point A). The resulting deflation of wages will cause the aggregate supply curve to shift outward (downward) from S_0S_0 to S_1S_1 and eventually to S_2S_2. Here, with equilibrium at point C, the recessionary gap is gone and the economy is back at "full employment."

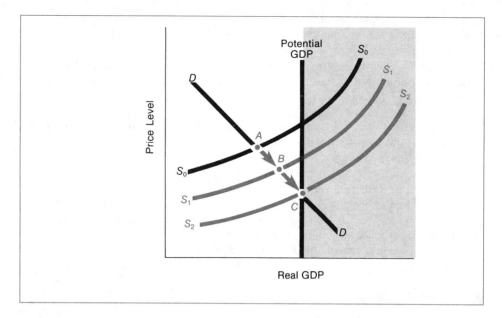

FIGURE 17-11

The Vertical Long-Run Phillips Curve

In the long run, points like a, where unemployment is above the normal "full-employment" unemployment rate, are unsustainable. The economy's natural self-correcting mechanism (which was described in Figure 17-10) will erode the recessionary gap by reducing both inflation and unemployment. In the diagram, this will force the economy toward a point such as c. The long-run choices, therefore, are among points such as c and f, which constitute what is called the *vertical (long-run) Phillips curve*, not among points such as d and a on the downward-sloping (short-run) Phillips curve.

We can relate this idea to our discussion of the origins of the Phillips curve with the help of Figure 17-11, which is a hypothetical Phillips curve. Point a in Figure 17-11 corresponds to point A in Figure 17-10: It shows the initial recessionary gap with unemployment (at 9.5 percent) above full employment, which we assume to occur at 7.5 percent. But we have seen that point A in Figure 17-10—and therefore also point a in Figure 17-11—is not sustainable. The economy tends to rid itself of the recessionary gap through the process of disinflation that we have just described. The adjustment path from A to C that we analyzed in Figure 17–10 would appear on our Phillips curve diagram as a movement toward less inflation and less unemployment—something like the green arrow from point a to point c in Figure 17–11.

Similarly, points representing inflationary gaps—such as point d in Figure 17–11—are not sustainable. They are also gradually eliminated by the self-correcting mechanism that we studied in Chapter 8. To review briefly, wages are forced up by the abnormally low unemployment, and this in turn pushes prices higher. Higher prices deter export spending by foreigners, and they reduce investment spending by forcing up interest rates. And they also deter consumer spending by lowering the purchasing power of consumer wealth. The inflationary process continues until the amount people want to spend is brought into balance with the amount firms want to supply at normal full employment. During such an adjustment period, unemployment and inflation are both rising—as indicated by the green path from point d to point f in Figure 17–11.

Putting these two conclusions together, we see that:

On a Phillips curve diagram, neither points corresponding to an inflationary gap (such as d in Figure 17–11) nor points corresponding to a recessionary gap (such as a in Figure 17–11) can be maintained indefinitely. Inflationary gaps lead to rising unemployment and rising inflation. Recessionary gaps lead to falling inflation and falling unemployment. All the points that are sustainable in the long run (such as c, e, and f in Figure 17–11) correspond to the same rate of unemployment, which is therefore called the **natural rate of unemployment**. The natural rate corresponds to what we have so far been calling the "full-employment" unemployment rate—the one that exists when actual and potential GDP coincide.

Now we can see why the Phillips curve connecting points d, e, and a does not represent a menu of policy choices. While we can move from a point such as e to a point such as d by stimulating aggregate demand sufficiently, there is no way that we can *stay* at point d. Unemployment cannot be kept this low indefinitely. Instead, policy-makers must choose from among points such as e, f, and c, all of which are vertically above one another at the natural rate of unemployment. For rather obvious reasons, the line connecting these points has been dubbed the **vertical (long-run) Phillips curve**. It is this vertical Phillips curve (connecting points such as e, f, and c) that represents the true long-run "menu" of policy choices.

Our conclusions about the Phillips curve can be summarized in three statements:

> The economy's self-correcting mechanism always tends to push the unemployment rate back toward a specific rate of unemployment that we call the **natural rate of unemployment**.
>
> The **vertical (long-run) Phillips curve** shows the menu of inflation/unemployment choices available to society in the long run. It is a vertical straight line at the natural rate of unemployment.

SUMMARY

1. To the extent that economic fluctuations emanate from the demand side, we expect to find an inverse relationship between unemployment and inflation—a downward-sloping Phillips curve.

2. In the short run, it is possible to "ride up the Phillips curve" toward lower levels of unemployment by stimulating aggregate demand. Conversely, by restricting the growth of demand, it is possible to "ride down the Phillips curve" toward lower rates of inflation (see, for example, point a in Figure 17–11). There is, thus, a *trade-off between unemployment and inflation*. Stimulating demand will improve the unemployment picture but worsen inflation; restricting demand will lower inflation but aggravate the unemployment problem.

3. However, there is no such trade-off in the long run. The economy's self-correcting mechanism ensures that unemployment eventually will return to the "natural rate," no matter what happens to aggregate demand. In the long run, faster growth of demand leads only to higher inflation, not to lower unemployment, and slower growth of demand leads only to lower inflation, not to higher unemployment.

Fighting Inflation with Fiscal and Monetary Policy

Let us now apply this analysis to a concrete policy problem, one that has vexed our ministers of finance for years. How should the government's ability to manage aggregate demand through fiscal and monetary policy be used to fight inflation?

To create a somewhat realistic example, let us imagine that a new government takes office when the inflation rate is 10 percent and the unemployment rate is 7.5 percent—point *e* in Figure 17–11. Suppose the new government adopts a policy of restricting the growth of aggregate demand by contractionary fiscal and/or monetary policy, thereby opening up a recessionary gap. In a word—though no politician would ever use such blunt language—the government decides to fight inflation by causing a recession.

At first, the economy "rides down" the short-run Phillips curve from point *e* to point *a* in Figure 17–11. The recession pushes unemployment up from 7.5 percent to 9.5 percent but reduces inflation from 10 percent to 7 percent. Lower inflation has been "bought" by causing higher unemployment. This scenario roughly describes what happened in Canada in the early 1980s, except that the recession was much more severe in reality than in the example.

But the anti-inflation dividends of recession do not end there. The economy's self-correcting mechanism begins to work and gradually erodes the recessionary gap. Inflation continues to decline as the economy recovers and unemployment falls. In the example, inflation falls from 7 percent to 5 percent as the economy recovers along the path from *a* to *c* in Figure 17–11. In the actual Canadian case, inflation continued to decline as recovery progressed, but the economy did not return to full employment until 1989.

When all the dust has settled, the economy in our hypothetical example has moved from point *e* to point *c* in Figure 17–11. Comparing these two points shows that, in the end, there is less inflation and no more unemployment. In what sense, then, do policy-makers have to face up to a trade-off between inflation and unemployment? The answer is that:

The cost of reducing inflation by restrictive fiscal and monetary policies is a *temporary* rise in unemployment.

Figures 17–12 and 17–13 are intended to give the flavour of what the real menu of choices looks like to a policy-maker who is considering embarking on such a program. Figure 17–12 contrasts the behaviour of the inflation rate over time under a "status quo policy" (which leaves the unemployment rate unchanged at 7.5 percent) with the behaviour under a restrictive anti-inflationary policy (which deliberately slows the growth rate of aggregate demand and makes unemployment rise).

Inflation will continue at 10 percent per year if the government does not restrain the growth of demand and unemployment remains at 7.5 percent. This is the status quo policy path shown in black in Figure 17–12. It corresponds to the case where the economy remains indefinitely at point *e* in Figure 17–11.

On the other hand, if a restrictive policy is followed and the growth of aggregate demand is restrained, inflation will begin to fall, slowly at first but then with increasing speed. In the example, we suppose that the inflation rate falls little in the first year, more in the second year, and is essentially down to 5 percent after three years. This is the restrictive-policy path shown in green in Figure 17–12. It corresponds to the path from *e* to *a* to *c* in Figure 17–11.

The shaded area in the figure summarizes the difference between these two paths and therefore depicts the payoff to anti-inflation policy. But there are also costs. Figure 17–13 gives a rough impression of how the unemployment rate might behave under the two alternative policies. The status quo policy keeps the unemployment rate at 7.5 percent, which is the natural rate. The restrictive policy results in a recession: Unemployment rises gradually from 7.5 percent to 9.5 percent and then gradually falls

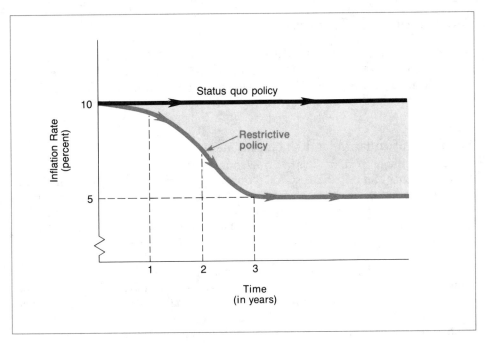

FIGURE 17–12
The Payoff to Anti-Inflation Policy
If a recession is caused by restrictive fiscal and monetary policy, the inflation rate will not respond very much at first. Gradually, however, inflation will yield to the slack caused by the restrictive policy. In this example the inflation rate begins at 10 percent, falls only to 9 percent after one year, but is down to 7.5 percent after two years, and 5 percent after three years. The shaded area indicates the gains that the policy has reaped on the inflation front.

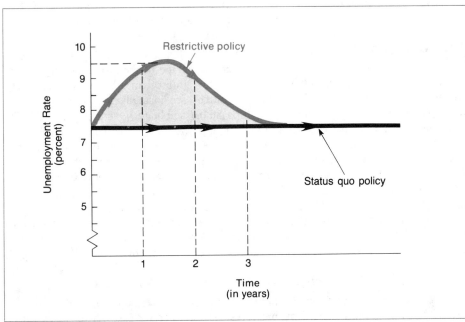

FIGURE 17–13
The Cost of Anti-Inflation Policy
The inflation gains depicted in the preceding figure do not come to us without cost. The restrictive policy increases unemployment for a period; that is, it induces a recession. In this example, the unemployment rate takes about a year to rise from 7.5 percent to 9.5 percent (the recession period), and then takes more than two years to return to 7.5 percent (the recovery period). The shaded area indicates the extra unemployment that must be endured in order to get the inflation rate down from 10 percent to 5 percent.

back to the natural rate of 7.5 percent. The shaded area in Figure 17–13 shows what it costs to get the inflation rate down: For over three years unemployment is above the natural rate.

Notice the differences in timing between Figure 17–12 and Figure 17–13. In the early stages of the disinflation program (say, the first year), progress against inflation is meagre even though the losses on the unemployment front are substantial. This reflects an underlying reality that we have mentioned before: Inflation gives way only grudgingly to economic slack. Because of this, policy-makers who embark on a disinflationary course must be patient. The costs in terms of unemployment, although temporary, come sooner. The gains on the inflation front, though more durable, appear later.

What Should Be Done?

Should the government pay the recessionary cost of fighting inflation? When the benefits depicted in Figure 17–12 are balanced against the costs shown in Figure 17–13, have we made a good bargain? While each of you will have to answer this question for yourself, our analysis has highlighted three critical issues on which your answer should rest.

The Costs of Inflation and Unemployment

We spent a major part of Chapter 4 examining the social costs of inflation and unemployment. Most of the costs of the extra unemployment depicted in Figure 17–13, we concluded, are easy to translate into dollars and cents. Basically, we only need to estimate the real GDP that is lost each year. However, the costs of inflation are harder to put a price tag on, and hence the benefits from reducing inflation are harder to measure. Thus, there is considerable controversy over the costs and benefits of using recession to fight inflation.

Some economists and public figures, including Bank of Canada Governor John Crow, believe that inflation is extremely costly, and so they look with favour on the trade-off that is embodied in Figures 17–12 and 17–13. Indeed, Mr. Crow wants to drive the inflation rate down to zero. Others have a lower estimate of the costs of inflation and find recession a terribly high price to pay. Some observers believe that we paid an excessively high price to reduce inflation from 11 percent to 4 percent in 1980–86, while others applaud the policy and maintain that the price was worth paying.

The Position of the Economy

We have stated several times in this book that the shape of the economy's aggregate supply curve, and hence the shape of the short-run Phillips curve, depends very much on the degree of resource utilization. If resources are virtually fully employed, the aggregate supply curve (and thus the Phillips curve) will be rather steep, which means that the inflation gains will be substantial and the unemployment costs will be minimal. On the other hand, if there is a great deal of unemployed labour and unutilized industrial capacity, the aggregate supply curve (and hence the short-run Phillips curve) may be nearly horizontal. In that case, a great deal of unemployment will be needed to achieve even a slight reduction in inflation. The short-run Phillips curves we have drawn in this chapter have this characteristic shape.

Because the short-run Phillips curve is shaped this way, the trade-off depicted in our last two diagrams will look more favourable when the economy is in a boom and less favourable when there is already a good deal of unemployment.

The Efficiency of the Economy's Self-Correcting Mechanism

We have stressed that once government policy causes a recession, it is the economy's natural self-correcting mechanism that cures the recessionary gap. The obvious question here is: How long do we have to wait? If the self-correcting mechanism—which works through reductions in the rate of wage inflation—is slow and halting, the costs of fighting inflation will be enormous. On the other hand, if wage inflation responds promptly, the recession necessary to bring down inflation may not be very severe.

This is another issue that is surrounded by controversy. Most economists believe that the weight of the evidence points to very sluggish wage behaviour. The rate of wage inflation appears to respond only slowly to economic slack. In terms of our Figure 17–11 (page 356), this means that the economy will traverse the path from *a* to *c* at an agonizingly slow pace, so that a very long recession will be necessary if there is to be any appreciable effect on inflation.

But a significant minority opinion finds this assessment far too pessimistic. Economists in this group argue that the costs of reducing inflation are not nearly so severe and that the key to a successful anti-inflation policy is its effect on people's *expectations*. But, to understand this argument, we must first examine why expectations are relevant to the Phillips curve trade-off.

Inflationary Expectations and the Phillips Curve

The explanation starts with some more review. Recall from Chapter 8 that the main reason the economy's aggregate supply curve slopes upward—that is, why output increases as the price level rises—is that businesses typically purchase labour and other inputs under long-term contracts that stipulate the cost of the input in *money* terms (for example, the nominal wage rate). If such contracts are in force when prices go up, then *real* wages fall as prices rise. From businesses' point of view, labour becomes cheaper in real terms, and firms are induced to expand employment and output. Buying cheaply and selling dearly is, after all, the route to higher profits. Long-term contracts that set the nominal wage rate, then, explain why higher prices lead to more output; that is, why the aggregate supply curve slopes upward.

Table 17–1 illustrates how this works in a concrete example. We suppose that workers and firms agree today that the money wage to be paid a year from now will be $10 per hour. The table then shows the real wage that corresponds to each alternative rate of inflation.[2] Clearly, the higher the inflation rate, the higher the price level at the end of the year and the lower the real wage.

TABLE 17–1
Money and Real Wages under Inflation

INFLATION RATE (percent)	PRICE LEVEL ONE YEAR FROM NOW	MONEY WAGE ONE YEAR FROM NOW (dollars per hour)	REAL WAGE ONE YEAR FROM NOW (dollars per hour)
0	100	10.00	10.00
4	104	10.00	9.62
8	108	10.00	9.26
12	112	10.00	8.93

Lower real wages provide an incentive for the firm to increase output, as we have just noted. But lower real wages also impose losses of purchasing power on workers. Thus, there is a sense in which workers are being "cheated" by inflation if they sign a contract specifying a fixed money wage in an inflationary environment.

Why would workers sign such a contract if they can see inflation coming? Would it not be more reasonable to insist on being compensated for inflation in advance? After all, firms should be willing to provide compensation for expected inflation by paying higher money wages because they realize that doing so does not raise real wages.

Table 17–2 illustrates how the money wage specified in a contract can be adjusted for expected inflation. For example, if 4 percent inflation is expected, the contract could stipulate that the wage rate be increased to $10.40 (which is 4 percent more than $10) at the end of the year. That would keep the real wage at $10, the same as it would be under zero inflation. The remaining money wage figures in Table 17–2 are derived similarly.

If workers and firms actually adjust money wages in the way suggested in Table 17–2, then the expected real wage will not decline as the expected price level rises. (In the example, the expected future real wage is always $10 per hour.) Then, if expectations prove correct, prices and wages will go up together, leaving the real wage unchanged. Workers will not lose from inflation and firms will not gain. But, of course,

---

[2]Each real-wage figure is obtained by dividing the $10 nominal wage by the corresponding price level a year later and multiplying by 100. Thus, for example, when the inflation rate is 4 percent, the real wage at the end of the year is ($10/104) × 100 = $9.62.

TABLE 17–2
Money and Real Wages under Expected Inflation

EXPECTED INFLATION RATE (percent)	EXPECTED PRICE LEVEL ONE YEAR FROM NOW	MONEY WAGE ONE YEAR FROM NOW (dollars per hour)	EXPECTED REAL WAGE ONE YEAR FROM NOW (dollars per hour)
0	100	10.00	10.00
4	104	10.40	10.00
8	108	10.80	10.00
12	112	11.20	10.00

that means that there will be no special incentive for firms to produce more as prices rise. In a word, the aggregate supply curve will become *vertical*. In general:

If workers can see inflation coming and if they receive compensation for it in advance so that inflation does not erode *real* wages, then the economy's aggregate supply curve will not slope upward. It will be a vertical line at the level of output corresponding to potential GDP.

Such a curve is shown in part (a) of Figure 17–14. Since we derived the Phillips curve from the aggregate supply curve earlier in the chapter, it follows that even the *short-run* Phillips curve will become vertical under these circumstances [see part (b) of Figure 17–14].[3]

If this analysis is correct, it has profound implications for the trade-off and for the costs and benefits of inflation-fighting. This can be seen by referring back to Figure 17–11, where we depicted the strategy of fighting inflation by causing a recession. We concluded there that in order to move from point *e* (representing 10 percent inflation) to point *c* (representing 5 percent inflation), the economy would have to take a detour through point *a*; that is, it would have to endure a recession. If, however, even the *short-run* Phillips curve were *vertical* rather than downward sloping, this detour would not be necessary. It would be possible for inflation to fall without unemployment rising. The economy could jump directly from point *e* to point *c*.

[3] See Discussion Question 10 at the end of the chapter.

FIGURE 17–14
A Vertical Aggregate Supply Curve and the Corresponding Vertical Phillips Curve

If workers foresee inflation and if they also receive full compensation for it in advance, then inflation will no longer erode real wages. In that case, firms will have no incentive to raise production as prices rise, and the aggregate supply curve will be vertical as in part (a). Since we derived the short-run Phillips curve from the aggregate supply curve, the short-run Phillips curve will also become vertical [part (b)].

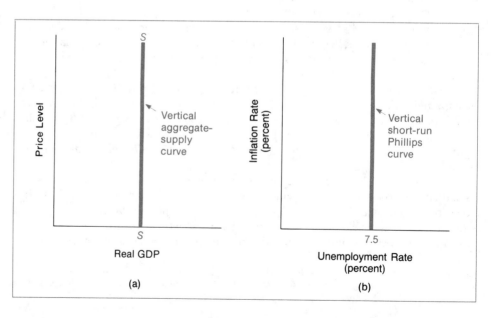

Is this analysis correct? Can we really slay the inflationary dragon so painlessly? As a piece of pure logic, the argument is impeccable. Yet things do not seem to have worked out this way. In practice, inflation-fighting has been very costly. We must, therefore, ask ourselves whether the premises on which the analysis rests are realistic. There are several reasons why many economists think the expectations argument should not be applied uncritically to the modern economy.

1. The argument is predicated on the notion that inflation can be accurately foreseen. But many contracts for labour and other raw materials cover such long periods of time that the expectations that were held when the contracts were written may be very different from the current reality. If a restrictive policy reduces inflation below the rate firms and workers were expecting when they made their wage agreement, real wages will wind up higher than was intended, and hence firms will want to reduce employment and produce less.

2. Many people believe that inflationary expectations are quite sluggish, that they do not adapt quickly to changes in the economic environment. If, for example, the government embarks on an anti-inflation policy, workers will continue to expect high inflation for quite a while. Thus they will continue to insist on high rates of increase in money wages. Then, if inflation actually slows down, real wages will wind up rising faster than anyone expected. Firms will therefore find labour "too expensive" relative to current selling prices, and unemployment will result. With lags in the reaction of expectations, then, the short-run Phillips curve retains its downward slope and inflation-fighting is costly.

The Theory of Rational Expectations

These two points, and others we have not mentioned, have persuaded most economists that the expectations argument, while valid in part, should not be taken to extremes. Most economists nowadays accept the notion that the Phillips curve is downward sloping in the short run, and hence that a short-run trade-off does exist. But a vocal minority of economists, believers in the doctrine of **rational expectations**, disagrees. To explain this point of view, we must first explain what rational expectations are. Then we will be in a position to understand why the hypothesis of rational expectations has such radical implications for the Phillips curve.

What Are "Rational" Expectations?

In many economic problems, people must formulate expectations about what the future will bring. For example, those who invest in the stock market need to forecast the future prices of the shares they buy and sell. And we have just discussed why workers and businesses may want to forecast the future price level before they agree on a money wage. *Rational expectations* is a hypothesis about how such forecasts are made.

As used by economists, a forecast (an "expectation") of a future variable is considered rational if the forecaster makes *optimal* use of all information that is both *available* and *relevant*. Let us elaborate on the italicized words in this definition, using as an example a hypothetical stock-market investor who has rational expectations.

First, believers in the doctrine of rational expectations recognize that *information is limited*. An investor who is interested in buying Canadian Pacific shares would like to know how much profit the company will make in the coming years. Armed with such information, she could predict the future price of CP stock more accurately. But that information is not available; no one knows it. Her forecast of the future price of CP stock is not "irrational" just because she does not know CP's future profits. On the other hand, if CP shares normally go down on Fridays and up on Mondays, she should be aware of this fact.

Rational expectations are forecasts that, while not necessarily correct, are the best that can be made given the available data. Rational expectations, therefore, cannot err *systematically*. If expectations are rational, forecasting errors are pure random numbers.

Second, *not all information is important*. Some publicly available facts may be irrelevant to predicting the variables of interest. If so, a rational forecaster can afford to be ignorant of them. For example, anyone who cares to can find out how many babies were born last year in Fredericton. But this fact may not tell you much about the future performance of Canadian Pacific. So our investor need not have this information to be rational. However, if there is a clear Friday/Monday pattern in CP share prices, she had better know what day of the week it is!

Finally, we have the word *optimal*. As used by economists, this means using proper statistical inference to process all the relevant information that is available before making a forecast. Thus, to have rational expectations, your forecasts do not have to be correct, but they cannot have systematic errors that could have been avoided by applying better statistical methods. This requirement, while exacting, is not quite as outlandish as it may seem. A good billiards player makes expert use of the laws of physics, even though he may have no understanding of the theory. Similarly, an experienced stock-market investor may make good use of information even without formal training in statistics.

Rational Expectations and the Trade-Off

Let us now see how the doctrine of rational expectations has been applied to deny that any trade-off between inflation and unemployment exists—even in the short run.

Even though rational expectationists recognize that inflation cannot always be predicted accurately, they claim that workers will not make *systematic* errors in forecasting inflation. Note that Point 2 above suggests that inflationary expectations are typically *too low* when inflation is rising and *too high* when inflation is falling. Rational expectationists deny that this is possible. Workers, they argue, will always make the best possible forecast of inflation, using all the latest data and the best available economic models. Such forecasts will not err systematically in one direction or the other regardless of whether inflation is rising or falling. Consequently:

If expectations are rational, the difference between the *actual* rate of inflation and the *expected* rate of inflation (the forecasting error) will be a pure random number.

Now recall that the basic expectationist argument summarized in the previous section claims that employment is affected by inflation only to the extent that inflation differs from what was expected. It follows, therefore, that:

If expectations are rational and there are no long-term contracts, the inflation rate can be reduced without the need for a period of high unemployment. The short-run Phillips curve is vertical.

Except for some random—and totally unpredictable—gyrations due to forecasting errors, unemployment will always remain at the natural rate.

The implications of rational expectations for the conduct of economic policy are really quite revolutionary, *at least when long-term contracts are not important*. According to this view, the government's ability to manipulate aggregate demand does not give it any control over real output and unemployment because the aggregate supply curve is vertical—even in the short run. Any *predictable* change in aggregate demand will lead to a change in the expected rate of inflation and hence will leave real wages unaffected.

The government can influence output only by making *unexpected* changes in aggregate demand. But this is not easy to do when expectations are rational because people are well informed about what policy-makers are up to. According to the rational expectationists, if the monetary and fiscal authorities typically react to high inflation by reducing aggregate demand, people will soon come to anticipate this reaction. And, as just mentioned, anticipated reductions in aggregate demand will not affect unemployment because they will not cause *unexpected* changes in inflation.

An Evaluation

The hypothesis of rational expectations is now embraced by many economists, but the proposition that inflation can be reduced without significant output losses is not. There are many reasons for this.

For one, Point 1 above remains valid even if expectations are rational. When long-term contracts are made, people get locked into provisions that, while rational when they were made, may seem irrational from today's point of view. For example, consider a labour contract drawn up in 1980 that specified a money wage rate to be paid in 1983. Given what people knew in 1980, it may have been rational to expect the 1983 price level to be 30 percent higher than the 1980 price level. So the money wage may have been set to rise 33 percent over the three years. Then inflation slowed dramatically. If the money wage specified in the contract was actually paid, the real wage was higher than had been intended. But no one had behaved irrationally. Thus, the hypothesis of rational expectations is *necessary* to defend the proposition that inflation can be reduced without a temporary recession, but it is not *sufficient* without the following qualification: There must be no long-term contracts.

Since long-term contracts do exist, it is perhaps not surprising that the facts have not been kind to the costless disinflation proposition. The theory suggests that unemployment should hover around the natural rate most of the time. Yet this does not seem to be the case. The theory also denies that predictable monetary- and fiscal-policy actions will have effects on real output. Yet most observers think they can identify episodes in the past, such as the policy-induced recession of the early 1980s, where such actions had significant effects on real GDP and unemployment.

At this writing, there is a great deal of controversy over how best to apply the idea of rational expectations to macroeconomic issues. The issues are far from resolved. But the evidence to date has led most economists to reject the extreme costless disinflation proposition and to affirm the existence of a short-run trade-off between inflation and unemployment. In the longer run, however, the rational-expectations view should be more or less correct, for two reasons. First, the longer the time horizon, the fewer fixed nominal contracts there are; second, people will not hold systematically wrong expectations indefinitely. As Abraham Lincoln said, you cannot fool all of the people all of the time.

Why Economists (and Politicians) Disagree

This chapter has now taught us some of the reasons why economists often disagree about the proper conduct of national economic policy. And it also helps us understand some of the related political debates.

Should the government take stern actions to reduce inflation? You will say *yes* if you believe that (1) inflation is more costly than unemployment; (2) the short-run Phillips curve is steep; (3) expectations react quickly; and (4) the economy's self-correcting mechanism works smoothly and rapidly. These views on the economy tend to be held by monetarists and rational expectationists and by the (generally conservative) politicians who listen to them.

But you will say *no* if you believe that (1) unemployment is more costly than inflation; (2) the short-run Phillips curve is flat; (3) expectations react sluggishly; and (4) the self-correcting mechanism is slow and unreliable. These views are held by many Keynesian economists, so it is not surprising that the (generally liberal) politicians who follow their advice often oppose the use of recession to fight inflation.

The tables turn, however, when the question is whether to use demand management to bring a recession to a rapid end. The Keynesian view of the world—that unemployment is costly, that the short-run Phillips curve is flat, that expectations adjust slowly, and that the self-correcting mechanism is unreliable—leads to the conclusion that the benefits of fighting unemployment are high while the costs are low. And so Keynesians are eager to fight recessions. The monetarist and rational-expectationist positions on these four issues are precisely the reverse, and so are the policy conclusions. The (generally conservative) politicians who take advice from monetarists therefore typically oppose strong measures to fight recession.

The Dilemma of Demand Management

So we have seen that the makers of monetary and fiscal policy face an agonizing trade-off. If they stimulate aggregate demand to reduce unemployment, they will aggravate inflation. If they restrict aggregate demand to fight inflation, they will cause higher unemployment.

But wait. Early in the chapter we learned that when inflation comes from the supply side, inflation and unemployment will be *positively* associated: We will suffer from more of both or enjoy less of each. Does this mean that monetary and fiscal policy-makers can escape the trade-off between inflation and unemployment? Certainly not.

Adverse shifts in the aggregate supply curve can cause both inflation and unemployment to rise together and thus can destroy the Phillips curve relationship. Nevertheless, anything that monetary and fiscal policy can do will make unemployment and inflation move in opposite directions. The reason is that monetary and fiscal policy give the government a significant amount of control over only the *aggregate demand* curve, not the *aggregate supply* curve.

Thus, no matter what the source of inflation and no matter what happens to the Phillips curve, the makers of monetary and fiscal policy must still face up to the disagreeable trade-off between inflation and unemployment. This is a principle that many policy-makers have failed to recognize and one of the 12 Ideas that we hope you will remember well **Beyond the Final Exam.**

Naturally, the unpleasant nature of this trade-off has led to a vigorous search for a way out of the dilemma. Both economists and public officials have sought a policy that might offer improvements on both fronts simultaneously, or that might ease the pain of either unemployment or inflation. The rest of this chapter will consider some of these ideas.

Attempts to Reduce the Trade-Off Directly

One class of such policies attempts to reduce the natural rate of unemployment. For example, vocational training and retraining programs, if successful, help unemployed workers with obsolete skills acquire abilities that are currently in demand. In doing so, these programs help alleviate upward pressures on wage rates in jobs where qualified workers are in short supply. For example, if an unemployed textile worker is taught to assemble computers, then progress is made against both inflation and unemployment, since one former textile worker leaves the ranks of the unemployed while one new worker helps alleviate the shortage of skilled labour in the computer industry.

Although the idea sounds appealing and has attracted many adherents, successes achieved through training programs have, in practice, been rather limited. Too often, people are trained for jobs that do not exist by the time they finish their training—if indeed they ever existed. Even when successful, these programs are quite expensive, which restricts the number of workers that can be accommodated. Despite these difficulties, revised versions of these retraining schemes continue to be developed.

The Canada Employment Centres also try to improve the match of workers to jobs, seeking to improve the funnelling of information from prospective employers to prospective employees. Firms are encouraged to list their job vacancies with the centres and to inspect the centres' lists of people looking for work. Unemployed workers and people wanting to change jobs are encouraged to register with the Canada Employment Centres and to study its lists of openings. In this way, it is hoped, the simultaneous occurrence of unemployed workers and unfilled jobs will be reduced. Increasingly, computerization is being used to improve the dissemination of information from centre to centre and region to region.

The centres also co-ordinate direct job-creation schemes, which are intended to provide jobs for persons whose unemployment insurance has run out. The federal government has also tried schemes such as the Industry and Labour Adjustment Program, which paid two-thirds of workers' former wages (after their unemployment insurance had expired—until retirement if necessary) if the workers were over 45 years of age and had been released by declining, low-productivity industries. This experimental program involved an attempt to raise aggregate productivity, since it was a substitute for continually propping up industries in which Canada is not competitive.

Another federal government program aimed at reducing frictional unemployment is one involving relocation grants. If the unemployed live in one province and job vacancies occur in others, the government moving allowance permits the family to move and therefore the worker to take the job. (Some analysts argue, however, that other grants to high-unemployment regions tend to cancel out the effectiveness of the moving allowances.)

While these government programs are intended to improve the Phillips curve, many other schemes—such as government regulations ranging from agricultural price supports, to control of airline-passenger fares, to requirements that trucks return empty after delivering their loads—have been criticized on the grounds that they make prices higher at any given level of unemployment. Over recent years many of these government interferences with free-market processes have come under vigorous verbal assault, with the result that some deregulation has now occurred in the airline, trucking, and telecommunications industries.[4]

Incomes Policy

Yet another way to improve the trade-off, an approach that has been tried intermittently in Canada, is **incomes policy**. As practised in this country, incomes policy has run the gamut from verbal admonitions all the way to outright prohibition of wage and price increases beyond a certain guideline (in the 1975–78 period). In some foreign countries that rely upon incomes policy more heavily than we do, a still more bewildering variety of alternative measures has emerged. Indeed, there may be only one common thread linking these disparate policies: No hard evidence exists that any of them has succeeded *permanently* in improving the trade-off between unemployment and inflation. Note that the emphasis here is on the word "permanently," for many attempts at incomes policy—including some in this country—have had temporary success.

The Canadian 1975–78 episode stands out as perhaps the most successful use of incomes policy in a Western economy since World War II. All studies show that our controls program lessened the magnitude of the temporary increases in unemployment that accompanied the contractionary aggregate demand policy at the time. The reason for the relative success of the Canadian experience is given later in this chapter.

To laypeople, controls seem a relatively painless way to try to improve the trade-off between inflation and unemployment. Large corporations, it is argued, have the market power to raise prices even when price rises are not justified by cost increases. Controls might stop this behaviour. Opponents of controls respond that market power, which undoubtedly exists, can explain *high* prices. But why, they ask, would a

Incomes policy is a generic term used to describe a wide variety of measures aimed at curbing inflation *without* reducing aggregate demand.

[4]For a full discussion of regulation and deregulation, see Chapter 31.

firm with market power wait until this month to raise prices when it could have done so last month or the month before? They answer that large corporations raise prices only when changes in demand or cost considerations make it profitable to do so, not because they have a residue of unused market power. Most economists would agree, and therefore believe that the fundamental way to limit inflation is to limit excess demand.

A second justification for controls is that inflation gathers substantial momentum once workers, consumers, and business managers begin to expect that it will continue. **Inflationary expectations** encourage workers to demand higher wage increases. Firms, in turn, are willing to grant the workers' demands because they believe they will be able to pass the cost increases on to consumers in a general inflationary environment. Consumers contribute their part to the shell game by purchasing durable goods ahead of their needs in anticipation of higher prices in the future, an action that increases demand and helps fuel the inflation engine. Thus, to a great extent, *inflation occurs because people expect it to occur.*

In terms of our aggregate supply and demand analysis, inflationary expectations shift the aggregate supply curve upward because workers insist on—and get—higher money wages to compensate them for the coming inflation. Phrased in terms of the Phillips curve, this means that *inflationary expectations shift the Phillips curve upward*, so that any given rate of unemployment corresponds to a higher rate of inflation.

This analysis provides the best intellectual case for controls. A tough and thorough program of wage and price controls, it is argued, can break the vicious cycle of inflationary expectations. By announcing a controls program, the government serves notice on workers that they do not need anticipatory wage increases to preserve their purchasing power. Firms are warned that they may not be able to pass on higher costs to consumers. And consumers may conclude that buying now to beat future price increases is a poor strategy. By breaking inflationary expectations, supporters argue, a controls program can shift the Phillips curve down and so reduce the costs (in terms of temporary unemployment) of lowering inflation.

Under the right conditions, this argument may be correct. However, many economists question whether this line of reasoning is generally valid. For example, it may be that astute workers, business executives, and consumers realize that no controls program can remain in force forever—at least not in a free-market economy like ours. They may then view the temporary dip in the inflation rate caused by controls as an aberration soon to be corrected and therefore not as a major event that warrants changing their long-term expectations.

Another problem with implementing a controls program is that workers and firms may anticipate it. Reports that a controls program *may* begin can cause wage and price increases "just in case."

Why cannot wage–price controls be a permanent feature of the Canadian economy? We learned the answer to this back in Chapter 3 (pages 56–60). When price ceilings are effective, they force the price below the equilibrium price, so that quantity demanded exceeds quantity supplied.

With price no longer serving as the rationing device, some other method of rationing is necessary. One possibility is simply long lines of eager buyers waiting their turn. Scenes like this are quite typical in the Soviet Union. Another is government ration coupons, giving the owner the right to buy stated quantities of certain items—a device used successfully for many goods during World War II and, more recently, by Lithuania in 1990 when the Soviet Union cut off supplies to that country. Neither of these measures is likely to be popular with the electorate in peacetime. And both are likely to spawn a black market, which erodes respect for law and order at the same time that it abrogates the effects of controls. Controls give law-abiding citizens an incentive to break the law in an effort to circumvent the controls.

And the problems spawned by price controls go deeper than this. To appreciate the point, let us consider the specific example of fixing the price of hamburgers. Among the principal factors determining the equilibrium price of hamburgers are the prices of various raw agricultural commodities such as beef. But prices of raw agricultural commodities cannot be controlled by the government because they are so dependent on the weather and other acts of nature. If price controls fix the price of hamburgers while the price of beef skyrockets, it may become unprofitable to sell burgers. If so, firms will start leaving the hamburger industry.

With hamburgers unavailable, consumers will increase their purchases of other goods, thereby putting upward pressure on the prices of goods such as fish and soybeans. Thus, price controls on hamburgers will cause the hamburger industry to contract and necessitate additional price controls on fish and soybeans. And so it goes. Each extension of price controls to a new commodity requires additional controls to support it, in a never-ending chain. Thus, for price controls to be effective, they must be nearly universal—which is, of course, next to impossible except in times of acute national crisis.

This analysis also explains why wage and price controls have almost always failed to work. Most governments that have used controls (for example, the British during the 1960s and 1970s) saw them as "solving" the inflation problem and thereby freeing monetary and fiscal policy to be used without restraint for achieving employment objectives. As a result, aggregate demand policy and incomes policy were often inconsistent. Monetary and fiscal policy pushed demand curves to the right, while the incomes policy made it unlawful for the prices to adjust to equilibrium. Most analysts have likened these policy episodes to putting a pot of water on the stove, wiring on the lid, and turning the burner on high. Little steam emerges for a while, but eventually it all blasts out. This is exactly what happened with the many European experiments with controls, and with controls in the United States during the 1970s. Lower inflation rates prevailed while the controls were in effect, but these were counterbalanced by higher inflation rates during the year or so after controls were lifted. Instead of improving the trade-off, the controls managed only to increase the *variability* of inflation. In Chapter 4 we pointed out that the *variability* of inflation often exacts more serious social costs than does its *average level*. In this sense, these controls programs were counterproductive, and this is why most economists say that they "failed."

The Canadian experiment in the 1970s avoided this problem to some degree, since it was imposed as a *complement* to, not a *substitute for*, contractionary aggregate demand policy. During this period, the government used monetary and fiscal policy to limit the rightward shifts of demand curves, and the controls were intended only to shorten the lags in the downward revision of inflationary expectations.

The famous Canadian economist Harry Johnson likened incomes policies to a farmer's attempts to make his donkey behave. The policy always begins as gentle ear-stroking but seems eventually to turn into ear-twisting and then attempts to grope for more sensitive parts of the animal.

A more constructive incomes policy is one that does not try to force the donkey to ignore its private interest but instead tries to change the signals facing the donkey so that its private interest and the public interest coincide. This is the idea behind **tax-based incomes policy (TIP)**. Just as a donkey can be coaxed into behaving with the offer of a carrot, firms and workers can be led to restrict wage and price increases to a certain limit with the promise of a tax break that is conditional on this behaviour. Australia has implemented such a policy, and the Economic Council of Canada has suggested that tax-based incomes policies warrant further study.

Tax-based incomes policy uses the tax system to provide incentives favouring non-inflationary behaviour.

Profit-Sharing

Several countries seem to have had success in eliminating some of the downward inflexibility in wage rates. This makes the economy's self-correcting mechanism work faster, so that anti-inflation policy involves a smaller and less prolonged recession. One way of achieving some of this improvement in the trade-off may be through the adoption of an alternative compensation scheme for workers known as **profit-sharing**. In this system, workers are paid a base wage plus a share of the firm's profits. Since part of workers' pay comes from profits rather than from straight wages, labour costs automatically fall whenever business turns sour.

Profit-sharing is a system of compensating labour in which workers receive both a fixed base wage and a share of the firm's profits.

Japan has had extensive profit-sharing for years and has achieved lower rates of *both* inflation and unemployment than we have had in North America. However, profit-sharing is not the only institutional difference between Japan and North America, and we do not know what practical problems might arise with more extensive use of it here. Organized labour has certainly been cool to the idea of letting earnings fluctuate with company profits. Nevertheless, the potential benefits are large enough to justify the intensive scrutiny that profit-sharing is now receiving.

Indexing

Indexing refers to provisions in a law or a contract whereby monetary payments are automatically adjusted whenever a specified price index changes. Wage rates, pensions, interest payments on bonds, income taxes, and many other things can be indexed in this way, and have been. Sometimes such contractual provisions are called *escalator clauses*.

Indexing, which refers to provisions in a law or contract whereby monetary payments are automatically adjusted whenever a specific price index changes, presents a very different approach to the inflation–unemployment dilemma. Whereas the other proposals discussed in the last few pages are all designed to improve the trade-off, the primary purpose of indexing is *to reduce the social costs of inflation.*

The mechanics of indexing can be explained best through an example. In Canada one of the most common forms of indexed contract is an *escalator clause* in a wage agreement. An escalator clause provides for an automatic increase in money wages—without the need for new contract negotiations—any time the price level rises by more than a specified amount. Nowadays, about half of all workers employed by large unionized firms in Canada are covered by some sort of escalator or cost-of-living clause.

Interest payments on bonds or savings accounts can also be indexed, although this is not currently done in Canada.[5] The mechanics here are quite simple. If you had an indexed savings account, your bank might guarantee you a 1 percent *real interest rate* on your savings by automatically increasing your balance by the amount of inflation. For example, suppose you deposited $1000 on January 1 and withdrew it on December 31. An ordinary savings account, paying 6 percent interest, would pay you $1060 at the end of the year—your original $1000 plus 6 percent interest—regardless of the prevailing rate of inflation. But if this were an indexed bank account paying 1 percent, and prices rose by 10 percent during the year, your balance at year-end would be $1110—your original $1000 plus 1 percent real interest ($10) plus 10 percent ($100) to compensate you for your loss of purchasing power. The *nominal interest rate* would thus be 11 percent.[6] In general, the nominal rate would be 1 percent *plus* the rate of inflation. Thus, if inflation turned out to be less than 5 percent that year, you would receive less than $1060.

Indexing is not designed to keep either wages or interest rates *high*, but to make real wages and interest payments independent of inflation—to cut down the chances that purchasing power will be eroded by inflation.

The most extensive government use of indexing to be found in Canada today is in certain transfer payments. Canada Pension Plan benefits are fully indexed so that retirees are not victimized by inflation. A variety of government income-maintenance and social-insurance programs also pay benefits that are tied directly to prices. Some economists believe that Canada should adopt a much more widespread system of indexing. Why? Because, they argue, it would take most of the sting out of inflation. To

[5] Some other countries, with much higher inflation than ours, do extensive indexing of interest rates. Brazil and Israel are notable examples.

[6] The distinction between real and nominal interest rates, one of our **12 Ideas for Beyond the Final Exam**, was discussed in detail in Chapter 4.

Ethical Reflections on the Economic Crisis

Many Canadians were shocked by the depth of the recession of the 1980s. The Canadian Conference of Catholic Bishops made public its *Ethical Reflections on the Economic Crisis* in January 1983, and much public discussion followed. The following two statements capture the general thrust of the bishops' views:

1. Unemployment rather than inflation should be recognized as the primary problem, and expansion in aggregate demand is needed to lower unemployment.
2. A wage-and-price-control policy is a more balanced and equitable instrument for controlling inflation than is a contractionary demand policy.

Both comments stem from the bishops' deep concern for the poor. But each statement involves both a positive element (one that can be proved true or false) and a normative element (an opinion); more specifically, each involves an economic issue and a moral issue. The bishops, in their capacity as spiritual advisers, can comment on the latter. Economists, in their role as technical advisers, must limit their evaluation of these policy suggestions to the positive, or factual, aspects. We consider each statement in turn.

1. Statement One involves the proposition that unemployment can be traded off with inflation (a factual issue) and the view that the costs of unemployment are more important than the costs of inflation (a moral issue). We have learned that it is very unlikely that unemployment and inflation can be traded off in the long run, so that *in the long run* (but not the short run!), moral disagreements concerning the relative burdens of unemployment and inflation are not critical for the conduct of policy.
2. Statement Two involves the assumption that wage and price controls work, even when aggregate demand policy is expansionary (a factual question) and the view that unemployment is more important than the misallocation of resources that follows from controls (a moral question). Unfortunately, history has given a very

clear answer regarding the factual question: While controls can work for a year or two, they have *never* provided any *lasting* help in fighting inflation when used as a substitute for (rather than a complement to) contractionary demand policy. If controls do not work, moral debates concerning their costs are beside the point.

The point of this discussion is to emphasize that while economists *cannot* referee moral disputes, they can contribute toward minimizing them by drawing attention to, and commenting on, the positive aspects of policy disagreements. As we have seen in these examples, the factual issue *can* be logically prior to the moral question. Nevertheless, the current state of economic analysis permits this strong conclusion *only* if one is prepared to stress the *longer run*. In the short run, there *is* an unemployment–inflation trade-off, and controls *can* reduce the magnitude of the temporary recession that must accompany a disinflation policy. Regarding short-run policy options, then, heated debate will continue even if all participants are careful to separate positive and normative issues.

---

see how indexing would accomplish this, let us review some of the social costs of inflation that we enumerated in Chapter 4.

One important cost is the capricious redistribution of income caused by unexpected inflation or deflation. We saw that borrowers and lenders normally incorporate an *inflation premium* equal to the *expected rate of inflation* into the nominal interest rate. Then, if inflation turns out to be higher than expected, the borrower has to pay to the lender only the agreed-upon nominal interest rate, including the premium for expected inflation; he does not have to compensate the lender for the (higher) actual inflation. Thus the borrower enjoys a windfall gain and the lender loses out. The opposite happens if inflation turns out to be lower than was expected. Again the borrower pays the lender the agreed-upon nominal interest rate, but now his rate includes an inflation premium that overcompensates the lender for the actual inflation. But if interest rates on loans were indexed, none of this would occur. Borrowers and lenders would agree on a fixed *real* rate of interest, and then the borrower would compensate the lender for whatever *actual inflation* occurred. No one would have to guess what the inflation rate would be.

A second social cost we mentioned in Chapter 4 stems from the fact that our tax system levies taxes on nominal interest and nominal capital gains. As we learned, this flaw in the tax system leads to extremely high effective tax rates in an inflationary environment. But indexing could fix this problem easily. We need only rewrite the tax code so that only real interest payments and real capital gains are taxed.

A final problem noted in Chapter 4 is that uncertainty over future price levels makes it difficult to enter into long-term contracts—rental agreements, construction agreements, and so on. One way out of this problem is to write indexed contracts, which specify all future payments in real terms.

In the face of all these benefits and others we have not mentioned here, why do many economists oppose a move toward more complete indexing? One reason is the fear that indexing will lead to an acceleration of inflation. With the costs of inflation reduced so markedly, they argue, what will persuade governments to pay the price of fighting inflation? What will stop them from inflating more and more? They fear that the answer to these questions is, Nothing. Voters who stand to lose nothing from inflation are unlikely to pressure their legislators to stop it. Opponents of indexing worry that a mild inflationary disease could turn into a ravaging epidemic in a highly indexed economy. Hyperinflation often involves dramatic political changes.

Controversies over Stabilization Policy

This has been a long chapter, but it has allowed us to apply our macroeconomic theory thoroughly to the pressing policy issues of unemployment and inflation. You have made a significant investment of time in mastering the economic reasoning involved; we hope that you now regard that investment as worthwhile, given the long-standing and deep concern about these twin macroeconomic maladies. Economists and politicians are not the only ones who have entered the debate over what Canada's stabilization policies should be, as the boxed insert on page 371 makes clear. We hope that you now feel more comfortable in arriving at your own position in this debate.

Summary

1. Inflation can be caused either by rapid growth of aggregate demand or by sluggish growth of aggregate supply.

2. When fluctuations in economic activity emanate from the demand side, prices will rise rapidly when real output grows rapidly. Since rapid growth means more jobs, unemployment and inflation will be inversely related.

3. This inverse relationship between unemployment and inflation is called the Phillips curve. It explains Canadian data for the 1950s and 1960s rather well but fails miserably to account for the 1970s.

4. One reason for this failure is that the Phillips curve was misinterpreted as a menu of *long-run* policy choices for the economy. This view is incorrect because the economy's self-correcting mechanism guarantees that neither an inflationary gap nor a recessionary gap can last indefinitely.

5. Because of the self-correcting mechanism, the economy's true long-run choices lie along a *vertical* Phillips curve, which shows that the so-called *natural rate of*

unemployment is the only unemployment rate that can persist indefinitely.

6. In the short run, the economy can move up or down its short-run Phillips curve. *Temporary* reductions in unemployment can be achieved at the cost of higher inflation. Similarly, *temporary* increases in unemployment can be used to fight inflation.

7. Whether it is advisable to use unemployment to fight inflation depends on four principal factors: the relative social costs of inflation versus unemployment, the efficiency of the economy's self-correcting mechanism, the current position of the economy, and how quickly inflationary expectations adjust.

8. If workers expect inflation to occur and if they demand (and receive) compensation for inflation, output will be independent of the price level. Both the aggregate supply curve and the short-run Phillips curve are vertical in this case.

9. However, errors in predicting inflation will still change

real wages and hence will still change the quantity of output that firms wish to supply. Thus, *unpredicted* movements in the price level will lead to the normal sort of upward-sloping aggregate supply curve.

10. According to the hypothesis of rational expectations, errors in predicting inflation will be purely random. This means that, except for some random (and uncontrollable) gyrations, the aggregate supply curve is vertical even in the short run.

11. Many economists reject the "no trade-off in the short run" view of the world. Some deny that expectations are "rational" and believe instead that people tend, for example, to underpredict inflation when it is rising. They point out that contracts signed years ago cannot possibly embody expectations that are "rational" in terms of what we know today.

12. When fluctuations in economic activity are caused by shifts of the aggregate supply curve, output will grow slowly (causing unemployment to rise) when inflation speeds up. Hence, the rates of unemployment and inflation will be positively related.

13. Many observers feel that the adverse supply shifts during the 1970s help explain why the Phillips curve collapsed.

14. Even if inflation is initiated by supply-side problems, so that inflation and unemployment occur together, the monetary and fiscal authorities still face this trade-off: Anything they do to improve unemployment is likely to worsen inflation, and anything they do to reduce inflation is likely to aggravate unemployment. The reason is that monetary and fiscal policy mainly influence the aggregate demand curve, not the aggregate supply curve. This is one of our 12 Ideas for Beyond the Final Exam.

15. Policies that improve the functioning of the labour market—including retraining programs and various types of employment services—can improve the trade-off between inflation and unemployment by lowering the natural rate of unemployment. To date, however, Western governments have had only modest success with these measures.

16. Many varieties of incomes policies have been used in this and other countries in an effort to improve the trade-off between inflation and unemployment. While some have led to notable temporary improvements, a surge of inflation often follows the controls period.

17. Controls interfere with the workings of our market economy, but one argument in favour of short-term wage–price controls is that they can reduce inflationary expectations. This robs inflation of some of its momentum and reduces the magnitude of the temporary recession that must accompany contractionary aggregate demand policy.

18. New policy suggestions involve using tax incentives and profit-sharing to encourage more desirable wage and price increases.

19. Indexing is another way to approach the trade-off problem. Instead of trying to improve the trade-off, it concentrates on reducing the social costs of inflation. Opponents of indexing worry, however, that the economy's resistance to inflation may be lowered by indexing.

Concepts for Review

Demand-side inflation	Trade-offs between unemployment and inflation in the short run and in the long run	Incomes policy
Supply-side inflation		Tax-based incomes policy
Phillips curve		Profit-sharing
Self-correcting mechanism	Inflationary expectations	Indexing
Natural rate of unemployment	Rational expectations	
Vertical (long-run) Phillips curve	Stagflation caused by supply shocks	

Questions for Discussion

1. Some observers during the 1970s claimed that policy-makers no longer faced a trade-off between inflation and unemployment. Why did they think this? Were they correct?

2. "There is no sense in trying to shorten recessions through fiscal and monetary policies because the effects of these policies on the unemployment rate are sure to be temporary." Comment on the truth of this statement and on its relevance for policy formulation.

3. Why is the economy's self-correcting mechanism more efficient at eliminating inflationary gaps than it is at eliminating recessionary gaps?

4. Why is it said that decisions on fiscal and monetary policy are, at least in part, political decisions that cannot be made on the basis of "objective" economic criteria?

5. Does the economy have a recessionary gap or an inflationary gap today? What should be done about this? What facts would you want to know in preparing an answer to this question?

6. What is a "Phillips curve"? Why did it seem to work so much better in the 1950s and 1960s than it did in the 1970s?

7. Explain the dilemma that policy-makers face when there is an episode of supply inflation. What would you

recommend if there were a severe bout of supply inflation today?

8. Why do expectations about inflation affect the wages resulting from labour–management bargaining?

9. What is meant by "rational" expectations? Why does the doctrine of rational expectations have such stunning implications for economic policy? Would believers in rational expectations want to shorten a recession by expanding aggregate demand? Would they want to fight inflation by reducing aggregate demand?

10. Show that, if the economy's aggregate supply curve is vertical, fluctuations in the growth of aggregate demand produce only fluctuations in inflation with no effect on output. Relate this to your answer to the previous question.

11. Suppose that a program of wage–price controls is under consideration by the government. What are the possible benefits to the nation from such a program? What are the possible costs? How would you go about balancing the benefits against the costs?

12. At the time of writing (mid-1990), ordinary savings accounts paid approximately 10 percent *nominal* interest. Would you prefer to trade yours in for an indexed bank account that paid a zero *real* rate of interest? What if the real interest rate offered was 4 percent? What do your answers to these questions reveal about your personal attitudes toward inflation?

13. The 1990s opened with Canada's unemployment rate at 7.5 percent, the inflation rate (of the CPI) at 5 percent, and a large government budget deficit. Discuss the arguments for and against expansionary policy at that time.

18

Productivity, Growth, and Development

The three great causes most favourable to [growth in] production are accumulation of capital, fertility of soil, and inventions to save labour.

T. R. MALTHUS

In our discussions of stabilization policy, we were concerned with minimizing the gap between the actual and potential levels of national production. But because, over the longer run, the fluctuations in this gap cancel one another out, our primary concern shifts to ensuring that growth in the *potential* level of output can occur. This shift in focus is natural, since real GDP per capita is the basic limit on our material welfare. We turn to the longer-run horizon in this chapter, to consider our prospects for a rising standard of living.

The chapter is divided into three major sections. The first considers the factors affecting productivity, or growth in the potential level of output; the second explores the costs and benefits of growth; and, in the third, we turn to the special problems of the less developed countries (LDCs) and look at the measures that have been proposed to increase their rate of growth.

Productivity

As far as the last two centuries are concerned, the current state of affairs is unprecedented: In the industrialized countries the quantity and quality of food, clothing, and comforts have reached levels that were never dreamed possible by earlier generations. The change has been so revolutionary that it is difficult to grasp its magnitude. A person in North America today can produce in an hour perhaps twenty times as much as it was possible to produce in 1800. In 1800, about 90 percent of the North American labour force had to work on farms; all that farm labour barely managed to produce enough food to provide adequate nutrition for the populace. Today, only about 3 percent of workers earn their living on farms, yet those few farm workers provide an outpouring of surpluses that the government constantly struggles to contain.

Vast Changes in Living Standards

North America has always been a privileged land with relatively high levels of nutrition. In the eighteenth century, an average male (white, native-born) who reached the age of 10 could expect to live to somewhere between 50 and 55 years of age. By contrast, an English *nobleman* at that time could expect to live only to between 39 and 46 years of age.

In the mid-nineteenth century, low incomes, local weather conditions, crop cycles, an almost complete lack of refrigeration, and limited transport of goods bound a large part of even the North American population to a minimal and nutritionally inferior variety of foods. Such uninspiring staples as potatoes, lard, cornmeal, and salt pork were the mainstays of diets, particularly outside the population centres. Most travellers' accounts of meals in nineteenth-century America mentioned the ubiquity of some kind of one-pot stew that constituted the main meal of the day for the family.

Nevertheless, most North Americans were right to feel that they lived in a land of unprecedented abundance, for that one-pot stew was quite sure to be there every day. For many centuries most Europeans had devoted nearly half their food budgets to breadstuffs, and for most of them, the "bread" was of very inferior quality. Often it took the form of gruel—what we would think of today as a hot breakfast cereal—served in a single bowl with a single spoon, both of which were passed around the table to feed the entire family. In bad years, even gruel was unavailable. Famine continued to threaten Europe until the beginning of the nineteenth century, and earlier it had constituted a normal fact of existence.

Food shortages were not the only manifestation of very poor living conditions. Even the housing of relatively well-off nineteenth-century North Americans (a very small proportion of the population) was primitive by modern standards. Baths, for example, were rare, even in the cities. No homes had electricity and few had gas. Fewer still had hot running water, and not even 2 percent had indoor toilets and cold running water. Boston, one of the more advanced North American cities, with a population of nearly 200,000 in 1860, had only 31,000 sinks, 4,000 baths and 10,000 water closets (about half of which were extremely primitive affairs). Outdoor privies were the norm, and baths, for the great majority, a luxury (with the latter still feared by many to be unhealthy). There were also large slum areas. The worst evils of these overcrowded slums were insufficient light and air; narrow airshafts conveyed foul air and disease and served as inflammatory flues when fire broke out. There were no private water closets or washing facilities in these buildings, and cellars and courtyards were foul.

In brief, by today's standards, life in North America just a hundred years ago was hard and primitive, even though living conditions were vastly improved from earlier centuries. Today, of course, things are entirely different. Only about 15 percent of Canadian housing units lack complete plumbing (defined as hot and cold piped water, a flush toilet, and a bathtub or shower, for the exclusive use of that housing unit), only 1 percent lack a flush toilet, and only 0.5 percent lack running water. More than three-quarters of households have electric washing machines; two-thirds have a clothes dryer; and virtually all have an electric refrigerator. Eighty percent of households have one or more cars, and almost 90 percent have a colour television.

This revolution in manner of living was made possible by an unprecedented rate of growth in human efficiency in producing output. Before reporting the facts, it is necessary to describe the two basic concepts, *labour productivity* and *output per capita*, usually employed to measure, respectively, the productive efficiency of the working population and the resulting average level of economic well-being.

Labour productivity refers to the amount of output turned out with the use of a *given* amount of labour. Obviously, an increase in productivity means that a human being has become a more effective instrument of production. This can be the result of harder work, better training, more or better equipment, innovative technology, or a variety of other causes.

The **standard of living**, on the other hand, is more naturally measured by real **GDP per capita**—that is, by total output divided by the number of people among whom it will be distributed. The more output there is for each person, the better off, in economic terms, the average person must be.

The fantastic magnitude of the increases in both labour productivity and output per capita since, say, 1800 is best appreciated by contrasting them with the dismal average record of many previous centuries. In Europe, after a long decline, living standards had been increasing intermittently since the eleventh century—the century in which William the Conqueror acquired England. Yet, it is estimated that even by the time of the American Civil War (1860) neither labour productivity nor GDP per

Labour productivity refers to the amount of output a worker turns out in an hour (or a week or a year) of labour. It can be measured as total national output (GDP) in a given year divided by the total number of hours of work performed for pay in the country during that year. That is, labour productivity is defined as GDP per labour hour.

Gross domestic product (GDP) per capita is the economy's total output divided by the number of people among whom it will be distributed—that is, the economy's population.

capita had returned to the levels that had been achieved in Rome about sixteen centuries earlier. Thus, on the average, productivity and GDP per capita did not grow at all for some sixteen hundred years. The number of innovations in consumer goods during those sixteen centuries was remarkably small, even for those wealthy enough to buy them. Indeed, some significant amenities, notably elaborate bathing facilities and efficient home-heating devices, had disappeared since the fall of Rome.

In contrast, the period since, say, the 1830s has been characterized by an endless explosion of innovations. The railway and the steamship revolutionized transportation. Steel-making technology changed drastically. The chemical and electronics industries were born and produced hundreds of new products that we now take for granted. Today, the process has reached the point where our one unchanging expectation for the future is that it will be characterized by constant change.

Impressive growth of labour productivity has also characterized the past century. Japanese productivity has risen about 2500 percent; French and West German productivity levels each went up about 1500 percent; productivity in the United States and Canada increased about 1100 percent; and even British productivity jumped by an astonishing 600 percent. To see the implications of this dramatic rise in productivity for living standards (as measured by output per capita) we must first note what has happened to labour time spent by the typical worker.

In the industrialized free-market countries, the number of hours worked per year has fallen significantly—by about 40 percent on the average. This is partly the result of a fall in work hours per day—typically, from about 12 hours per day in 1870 to some 7.5 hours in 1979. Also, the usual work week has declined from six days to five days. But most surprising is the almost total absence of any vacations for most of the population in 1870. The two- or four-week vacation is largely a twentieth-century invention, another luxury made possible by the rise in productivity. Largely because of this sharp fall in labour expended, output per person did not rise nearly as quickly as productivity. Yet the increases in per-capita output have also been spectacular. Output per person went up almost 2100 percent in Japan, 1900 percent in West Germany, 800 percent in the United States and Canada, and 400 percent in Great Britain.

To take the Canadian case as an example, the average income of a Canadian in 1870 (in dollars whose purchasing power has been corrected for inflation) was only about one-eighth as large as it is today. To imagine living on an income so small, one must look at Egypt, Bolivia, or the Philippines, whose per-capita income today has been calculated to be on a par with that of an average Canadian in 1870.

After some 1600 years of zero average growth in labour productivity and living standards, both of these measures exploded in the nineteenth and twentieth centuries in the world's industrialized countries, reaching levels previously unimaginable.

Significance of the Growth of Productivity

As we pointed out in our list of **12 Ideas for Beyond the Final Exam:**

Productivity Is Everything in the Long Run
It is hardly an exaggeration to say that, in the long run, almost nothing counts for the determination of a nation's standard of living but its *rate of productivity growth.*

Over long periods of time, small differences in rates of productivity growth compound, like interest in a bank account, and can make an enormous difference to a society's prosperity. Nothing contributes more to reduction of poverty, to increases in leisure, and to the country's ability to finance education, public health, environmental protection, and the arts.

To take a rather exaggerated example, let us compare living standards today with those that prevailed in the year 1800. Suppose productivity had increased at a rate of 1 percent per year between then and now. At this rate of growth, the average Canadian today would command about six times as many goods and services as his or her forebears did in 1800. If productivity growth had been 3 percent, the average living standard would be an incredible *275* times as high as it was in 1800. (In fact, Canadian productivity growth has averaged slightly less than 2 percent.)

Productivity growth can make an enormous difference for a nation's standing in the hierarchy of the world's economies. It has been remarked that the United States' success in keeping its annual productivity growth about one percentage point ahead of Great Britain's for about a century transformed America from a minor, developing country into a superpower and transformed Great Britain from the world's pre-eminent power into a second-rate economy. It is Japan's 3 percent average annual productivity-growth rate since 1870 which transformed that country from one of the world's poorest into a nation with one of the highest GDPs in the world.

Convergence in Productivity Performance

Not only have all the industrial countries grown in productivity and income per capita; they have also become more and more similar to one another in terms of both these measures. In other words, those industrial countries that were farthest behind in 1870 have been catching up with those that were ahead. Most people are aware of this convergence process in general terms; they know, for example, that the productivity gap between the United States and Japan has narrowed dramatically. It is less well known, however, that the rate of such convergence is slowing down, and that in terms of *overall levels*, the United States and Canada are still ahead of many other major industrialized countries. (For example, in 1989, West Germany and Japan were in fourth and sixth place, respectively.)

Why are countries growing more alike in productivity and average standards of living? No one has the entire answer, but a good part of the story is probably the speed-up of the international spread of new technology. Today's better communications permit innovative techniques to move from one country to another far more quickly than in the past. Better and more widespread education permits countries to learn technical details from one another and to train their labour forces rapidly to make use of them. At the beginning of the eighteenth century, when the Newcomen steam engine (the predecessor of Watt's steam engine) was invented in England, it took half a century for the engine to spread to Western European countries and the American colonies. In contrast, the innovations in transistor and semiconductor technology since World War II have, on average, taken about two and a half years to spread among countries.

All industrial countries benefit from the process of shared information; each learns from the innovations that occur in all the others. The British, the French, and the Germans benefit from American computer technology while the United States and others benefit from Japanese advances in robotics.

There is one crucial asymmetry. Countries that are behind can learn a great deal from countries that are ahead, but the latter have less to learn from the former. This is generally believed to be a prime explanation of the convergence phenomenon. Lagging countries can and do grow more quickly than leaders because the lagging ones have more to learn from the others and more to gain by imitation. Meanwhile, the growing speed and efficiency of communications speeds up the entire process.

Lagging countries have more to learn from leading countries than leading countries can learn from lagging ones. This fact and the growing speed with which innovations are spread help to explain why the world's industrialized economies are growing more equal. However, a number of the poorest countries are falling farther behind.

Later in this chapter, we will discuss in detail the handicaps that specialist observers blame for the poor performance of many less developed countries (LDCs). Here we will only note briefly why the forces of equalization just described for the more developed countries do not work for a number of the LDCs.

Two influences are pertinent. First, the poor educational levels in the LDCs and the resulting scarcity of qualified engineers and technicians are a serious impediment to imitation and effective use of the complex technological advances of the industrialized countries. So the LDCs do not benefit by learning from other countries nearly to the extent that the wealthier nations do. Second, the absence of products to which sophisticated production techniques can readily be applied makes it hard to participate in growth gains from learning and imitation. A country that depends on products such as bananas and peanuts for most of its income has little use for new robot designs or automated manufacturing processes, though it can and often does benefit from agricultural innovations. Thus, while the LDCs can and do learn to some degree from the technology of the industrialized economies, they suffer serious handicaps in this process, handicaps to which the industrialized countries are largely immune.

Determinants of Productivity Growth

By international standards, Canada's productivity-growth performance has been quite good. But between the mid-1960s and the mid-1980s there was a marked slowdown in our productivity growth, which caused much concern about our future living standards. Today, this concern is expressed primarily in the notion that Canada's manufacturing sector is being competed away and that we are becoming nothing more than a service economy. We shall first discuss several of the reasons why observers feel that Canada's productivity-growth rate is lower than it could be, and then evaluate the prevalent concern about "deindustrialization."

Probably the most widely cited cause of productivity-growth slowdowns is what many regard as *insufficient investment in plant and equipment*. The more a society invests, the more plant and equipment an average member of the labour force has available to work with. More and better equipment enables him or her to turn out more output per hour, so productivity grows. Thus investment and the savings that make investment possible are crucial for productivity growth.

Another prime suspect in the slowing of productivity growth is *expenditure on applied research*. Innovation is one of the main sources of productivity growth. New and more efficient productive procedures—from the steam engine to robotics—have multiplied the output a worker is capable of producing. However, innovation requires more than a new idea. It usually needs careful research to get out the "bugs" and to make the new procedures operational. This work is called **research and development (R & D)**. Because R & D is a critical step between the original invention and its final adoption by business enterprise, a big drop in R & D expenditures can do substantial damage to productivity growth.

About half of Canada's R & D expenditures are made by businesses, and the other half by government and non-profit institutions. Published data indicate that, of the eight major countries of the Organization for Economic Cooperation and Development (OECD), Canada has the lowest ratio of R & D outlays in relation to national income.

Government regulation is also sometimes blamed for slowdowns in productivity growth. In the 1960s and 1970s, regulations for protection of the health and safety of workers and for protection of the environment were strengthened. These absorbed some of the investment outlays of business and increased the costs of production.

Probably part of the slowdown in productivity growth resulted from the sharply *rising price of energy* that occurred in the late 1970s and that led to many economic changes. The building-insulation business grew; demand for large, gas-guzzling cars plunged. Much plant and equipment had to be changed to adapt to new patterns of

> Research and development (R & D) refers to systematic efforts undertaken to invent new or improved products or productive techniques and to make them ready to market or for use in production processes.

consumer and business demand induced by rising energy prices and to substitute fuel-efficient equipment for items that had been installed when energy was cheap.

Some portion of the slowdown is probably also attributable to the fact that the years between 1974 and 1984 were not generally characterized by healthy business conditions. Several recessions, and inflation of unprecedented severity and duration, occurred in the major Western economies, and these are not conditions that encourage business investment and innovation.

Finally, productivity-growth problems in Canada have been linked to the fact that, historically, the Canadian tariff has protected some domestic industries from competitive pressures. Since some producers are insulated from these pressures, there is nothing to force them to adjust the scale of plant in order to push the average cost of production down to its minimum possible point. This is essentially the problem of *short production runs*. Fixed costs are relatively important for firms operating for a small market such as Canada's. Furthermore, most technological improvements reduce variable costs more than fixed costs. Thus, technological improvements reduce average costs more for firms that are not in existence solely to service a small domestic market.

We must bear in mind that some worsening of our relative performance in productivity growth is to be expected, given the international convergence process that we discussed in the preceding section. However, despite these problems, Canada's performance did improve noticeably during the latter half of the 1980s.

Productivity and the Deindustrialization Thesis

A **service** is an industry that does not turn out any physical products. Telecommunications, medical care, teaching, police protection, and the work of lawyers are examples of service industries. Some, like telecommunications, use highly sophisticated equipment, and their productivity has grown rapidly. In many other services, such growth has been very slow.

Let us now turn to the popular notion that lagging productivity growth is turning Canada into a service economy—the "deindustrialization" thesis. The trends are said to portend a future in which Canada suffers chronic and apparently incurable problems in its trade with other countries because its manufactured products are not competitive with those of foreign countries. As a result, it is argued, Canada will be forced either to bear heavy unemployment or to see its labour force driven into low-paying jobs in the **service industries**, thus transforming the nation into an economy in which people earn their living by flipping hamburgers and washing dishes. The deindustrialization story, oversimplified, asserts that slow productivity growth in manufacturing allows other countries to steal our industrial markets away.

At first glance, the data seem to confirm this hypothesis. Between 1965 and 1988 the share of the Canadian labour force engaged in the service sector *rose* 24 percent, just as predicted by the deindustrialization thesis. But, as shown in Table 18-1, the story breaks down when we seek to identify the countries that have supposedly stolen our industrial markets. The data for ten leading industrial countries show that *every* country listed (other than the United States) increased the share of its labour force in the services *by a greater percentage than we did*. If Canada's 24 percent rise in the share of employment in services represents a move toward a service economy, what are we to make of the 33 percent rise in West Germany, the 44 percent increase in France, and the 31 percent increase in Japan? Which country was "industrialized" by the "deindustrialization" of North America? Or are all industrial nations becoming service economies and, if so, why?

It turns out that there is a straightforward answer in which productivity plays a key role; but it is very different from the deindustrialization parable. The simple explanation is that, throughout the industrial world, productivity has grown considerably faster in manufacturing than it has in most services. For example, productivity has grown far faster in automobile manufacturing than it has in selling real estate. This means that, though manufacturing outputs have grown, less and less of each nation's labour force has been needed to produce them. So a declining share of each nation's jobs has been provided in the manufacturing sector.

Moreover, after correction for inflation, the ratio of the *outputs* of the manufacturing and service sectors of the industrial economies has remained roughly unchanged

TABLE 18-1
Share of Labour Force in the Service Industries, 1965–1988

COUNTRY	1988 (percent)	1965–1988 (percent *increase*)
Australia	69.4	27
Canada	70.9	24
France	63.1*	44
Great Britain	69.7	36
Italy	57.8	58
Japan	58.5	31
Netherlands	69.3†	32
Sweden	67.3	45
United States	71.3	20
West Germany	55.7	33

*Data for France are for 1987.
†Data for the Netherlands are for 1986.
SOURCE: U.S. Department of Labor, Bureau of Labor Statistics, *Handbook of Labor Statistics* (Washington, D.C.. U.S. Government Printing Office, 1989), pages 559–60.

over the years, while national unemployment rates have shown no long-term tendency to rise. With manufacturing taking a declining share of the labour force and unemployment not rising, the share of employment in services naturally had to grow.

A hypothetical example makes the point clear. If, over a certain period of time, productivity in automobile manufacturing doubled but automobile output rose only 50 percent, there must have been a 25 percent *reduction* in the number of workers employed in that industry. And if, over the same period of time, productivity in the real estate industry stayed still while sales volume rose 50 percent, this industry must have employed 50 percent *more* workers than before. Thus, with both industries expanding their outputs in exactly the same proportion, some labour must have shifted out of the auto industry, with its high productivity growth, into the real estate industry, with its stagnant rate of productivity. This is the true sense in which *all* the industrial nations are becoming service economies. The share of their outputs constituted by manufactures has generally not fallen, but the share of employment in the service sector has risen universally.

Unemployment and Productivity Growth

Popular discussions of productivity growth often warn that rapid increases in labour productivity are not as beneficial as they are cracked up to be. We are told that each productivity increase reduces the demand for labour because it means that fewer work hours are needed to produce a given output. As a result, according to this view, productivity growth must create unemployment. Second, it is argued (perhaps somewhat inconsistently) that if an economy's productivity growth lags behind that of other countries, it will lose jobs to foreign workers, its industry will suffer, and its exports will fall. However, the data do not support either of these conclusions, at least for the long run.

If the long-run unemployment spectre were a reality, we would expect that the 1100 percent increase in output per labour hour in Canada and the United States, the 600 percent increase in Great Britain, and the 1500 percent rise in Germany since 1870 would have had devastating effects on the demand for labour in these countries. After all, with productivity rising almost elevenfold during the last century, output per capita in North America could have been kept about constant if the employed labour force had been cut to one-eleventh its initial size as a share of the population. Even with a 50 percent fall in the number of hours an average person works per year, we might expect perhaps nine-elevenths of the labour force to be unemployed. In fact, nothing of the sort has happened. There is no evidence suggesting any *long-term* rise in unemployment.

How have leading industrialized countries maintained employment in the face of rising productivity? The answer, of course, is that output per capita has hardly remained constant. The demand for consumer goods and services, schools, hospitals, and factories has expanded explosively as productivity growth has increased the purchasing power in the hands of the public. That growth in demand has sufficed to prevent any long-term increase in unemployment.

The absence of any long-term unemployment trend also undermines the (nearly) opposite apprehension of deindustrialization. Great Britain, for example, which has been lagging behind the most in productivity growth among industrialized countries, did not suffer from perpetually rising unemployment or from unemployment problems markedly more serious than those of other countries.

Neither rapid absolute productivity growth nor a slow relative productivity-growth rate need subject a country to long-run increases in unemployment rates.

Before offering an explanation for this fact, we turn to the widely held view that a persistent lag in a nation's productivity growth will place it at an increasing competitive disadvantage in international trade and that it will thereby be excluded increasingly from its export markets, with devastating effects upon its industries.

Here again we use Great Britain, with its exceedingly poor productivity record, to examine these claims. It is true that the British *share* of exports declined from over 40 percent of the world's total in 1870 to less than 10 percent a century later. But that is only because other countries' foreign sales went up even more rapidly than did Britain's. The fact is that the country's total exports have risen spectacularly: In the course of a century, the volume of British exports of goods and services increased about 900 percent.

The Real Cost of Lagging Productivity: Lagging Wages and Living Standards

From what has just been said, it may seem that lagging in productivity growth is not so bad. After all, with no trend toward rising unemployment, with exports increasing, with the share of employment in manufacturing more or less keeping up with other countries', what is so terrible about Great Britain's fate? Indeed, these observations may make one wonder how Great Britain was able to score these apparent successes despite its comparatively poor productivity performance.

The secret, which also shows the true price the British had to pay, is to be found in that country's lagging real wages. In the nineteenth century, British workers were the best-paid in Europe. According to one estimate (which admittedly is not very reliable), in about 1860 an English worker's wages permitted the purchase of about two and a half times the quantity of goods and services that a German worker's did. Yet by 1988, the purchasing power of a German worker's wages was almost twice as great as that of a British worker's. In other words, in a little more than a century the relative position of workers in the two countries had almost been reversed.

How are lagging British wages related to the country's productivity lag? The answer is straightforward. If Britain cannot compete on world markets by virtue of growing efficiency (productivity), it still can sell its products by providing cheap British labour. Of course, Britain does not volunteer to adopt low real wages; rather, market forces make this happen automatically, since inefficiently produced goods cannot be sold in the international marketplace unless those goods are produced by relatively cheap inputs. Hence, the invisible hand forces British wages to lag behind. Labour simply cannot extract higher wages from an economy that has little to give.

Increased Flexibility in the Workplace

In the fall of 1990, the Canadian Auto Workers union and the Ford Motor Company signed a landmark contract that gives the company the right to make fundamental changes in the way production takes place, without having to consult in detail with the union. In return, the company promises fair treatment of existing workers; for example, Ford is to provide retraining allowances and at least a full year's notice if any jobs are to be lost in the future. This arrangement allows management to experiment with new methods of organizing production, some of which have been very successful in Japan. The union's acceptance of management's right to be this flexible is a marked change from its attitude of only one year earlier, as the following excerpt from *The Globe and Mail* indicates. It is encouraging that management has acknowledged workers' right to significant compensation in the face of potentially dramatic changes and that workers will accept that compensation in order to allow management to experiment in ways that may bring productivity growth and therefore higher wages. This new attitude on both sides is much more constructive than the unco-operative stance that is reflected in the article below.

... Union locals have been under pressure from some employers to accept the team concept, under which workers operate as basically self-supervising teams led by team leaders who are also members of the bargaining unit.

The CAW sees efforts by management to redesign the structure of work as part of a sophisticated plan to extend its power and weaken that of workers and their unions....

The CAW position is that the union is not opposed to "positive" changes in the workplace, but that management's goal is to transfer workers' loyalty from the union to the company so that employees totally identify with the company's goal.

The union, however, is not rejecting all roles other than policing the collective agreement. It says it wants to play a part in industrial health and safety, [in] worker training, and in the introduction of technology.

Management's goals are to achieve greater flexibility and improve competitiveness, offering in return what the CAW regards as the carrot of increased job satisfaction and greater worker control. But the union maintains that the partnership offered and the promises of greater security are false.

CAW president Robert White says the union supports and understands the need for quality and improved produc-

tivity, but it rejects any efforts, under whatever name, that jeopardize workers' rights, undermine workplace conditions, and erode the independence of the union....

Mr. White said the "ideology of competitiveness" is at the heart of management's program. But accepting competitiveness as a rationale for reorganizing work would lead to continuing concessions by workers to compete with low-wage countries, he said....

SOURCE: Wilfred List, "CAW Rejects Concept of Work Teams as Not in Workers' Interests," *The Globe and Mail*, October 23, 1989, page B3.

A country with lagging productivity is likely to be condemned to become an exporter of cheap labour. That is the only way it can keep its industry viable, maintain its exports, and preserve domestic jobs. This is the real danger that Canada faces if its productivity performance is unsatisfactory for any substantial period of time.

Further problems are related to lagging productivity. Besides holding down living standards, a decline in productivity growth makes it difficult politically and psychologically to finance a variety of social programs that many Canadians consider important. Improvements in health care, education, and the arts, environmental protection, attempts to reduce poverty, and many other such activities generally require higher expenditures and therefore higher taxes. If productivity is growing rapidly, these taxes are not too painful because there is enough left over for workers' take-home pay to rise. But if productivity growth is slow, any substantial increase in expenditure for social purposes is likely to cut into workers' real incomes. So it is no accident that the slowdown in productivity has created pressures to reduce spending on social programs.

A lag in productivity growth can also be expected to cause continuous shifts in the products that a country can turn out most profitably. For example, we have observed a decline in the marketability of Canadian clothing, footwear, steel, and automobiles relative to the products of other countries. Meanwhile, the demand for Canadian agricultural products, telecommunications equipment, energy, and other items has risen. In the long run, the decline of one industry, if accompanied by the rise of another, is not a bad thing at all. But in the shorter run it may be very costly and painful to the community. A young steelworker can be retrained if he loses his job, but the process may still involve months of unemployment. An older worker may find himself in far more serious trouble. Factories in dying industries must be abandoned and replaced by new plants to house the growing industries. Families must be uprooted, leaving friends and relatives, to follow the geographic movement of job opportunities. Flourishing communities are sometimes transformed into ghost towns. Thus, even if the long run holds a new job for every one that was lost, and even if the shift does not involve the impoverishment of Canadian workers (which it does), transition is a costly and painful process.

It is for such reasons that it makes sense for us to embrace any changes in the workplace that will enhance productivity. As the boxed insert on page 383 suggests, this view has been resisted by workers in the past, but seems increasingly to be gaining acceptance.

In Chapter 28, we shall discuss the law of comparative advantage, which tells us that as Canada loses its competitiveness in some industries there must necessarily be other industries in which its *comparative* advantage increases—that is, in which it becomes comparatively less *in*efficient. It is industries in the latter category that will then produce Canada's exports. Nonetheless, our standard of living will definitely suffer if productivity growth continues to lag.

Growth and Its Costs and Benefits

Population Growth: Is Less Really More?

Adam Smith, like many of his successors, took it for granted that expansion of productive capacity is inherently desirable. But he also took it for granted, apparently without examining the matter very closely, that growth in the size of population is to be wished for. His reason was that a larger population provides a larger work force, and a larger work force makes a larger national output possible. Few economists since Smith's time have argued in this way. Nowadays we usually measure a nation's prosperity not in terms of its total output but in terms of its output *per person*. India has a national product about twice as large as Sweden's. But with a population more than 100 times as large as Sweden's, India remains a poor country while Sweden is highly prosperous. The point is that:

If the objective of growth is the material welfare *of the individuals* who make up a country, then the proper measure of the success of a program of economic development is how much it adds to output per person. The relevant index is not total output. It is total output *divided by total population*—that is, *output per capita*.

From this point of view, the appropriate objective of growth is not, as the old cliché puts it, "the greatest good for the *greatest number*"—it is the greatest good *per person* in the economy. Per-capita figures tell this story well. To make the appropriate comparison of well-being in Sweden and India, we note that per-capita national income in Sweden is about $15,690 (U.S.) a year, whereas in India, even after a generous adjustment to correct for lower prices in that country, the figure is $300 a year. If the goal of society is the elimination of poverty, illiteracy, and inadequate medical care, sheer increase in population is a questionable pursuit.

In 1798, the Reverend Thomas R. Malthus (who was to become England's first professor of political economy) published *An Essay on the Principle of Population.* This book was to have a profound effect on people's attitudes toward population growth. Malthus argued that sexual drives and other influences induce people to reproduce themselves as rapidly as their means permit. Unfortunately, he said, when the number of humans increases, the production of food and other consumption goods generally cannot keep up.

As the earth becomes more crowded, people must work each piece of farmland more intensively than before, and they must look for new land to farm. But neither of these ways to increase production will help enough to meet the increased need. There are limits to what a given piece of land can produce. Moreover, as people put soil under cultivation, they will naturally tend to pick the best lots first. Thus, as they extend the area that is cultivated, people will be forced to make use of increasingly inferior farmland.

Together, these two phenomena lead to the noted *law of diminishing returns* to additional labour used with a fixed supply of land, a relationship we will discuss in detail in Chapter 21. This hypothesis states that if we use more and more labour to cultivate a fixed stock of land, we will eventually reach a point at which each additional labourer will contribute less additional output than the previous labourer. Ultimately, as the labour force increases, output per worker will decline.

Malthus and his followers concluded that the tendency of humankind to reproduce itself must constantly exert pressure on the economy to keep living standards from rising. Wages will gravitate toward some minimal subsistence level—the lowest income on which people are willing to marry and raise a family. If wages are above subsistence, the population can and will grow. But, as we have seen, rising population without any rise in available land must reduce output per worker because of the law of diminishing returns. Thus, a wage that is above subsistence will set forces into motion that will drive wages down toward subsistence.

Sometimes, according to Malthus, the population will grow beyond the capability of the economy to support it. Then the number of people will be brought back into line by means that are far more unpleasant than a decrease in wages—by starvation and disease or by wars that produce the required number of casualties.

Later in the nineteenth century and during the first half of the twentieth century, the gloomy Malthusian vision seemed to lose credibility. New technology and improved agricultural practices generally enabled the output of food and other agricultural products to increase faster than the population (at least in the wealthier industrialized nations). In addition, it turned out that as living standards rose, people became less anxious to reproduce, and so the expansion of population slowed substantially. All in all, it began to look as though population growth constituted no significant threat—it was something with which human technological skills and ingenuity could cope.

More recently, however, there has been renewed concern over population. With improvements in medicine—notably improved hygiene in hospitals, the use of such public-health measures as swamp drainage, and the discovery of antibiotics—death rates have plunged in the developing countries, especially for infants. At the same time, birth-control programs in most of these countries have, at least until quite recently, not been very successful. As a result, the populations of developing countries have continued to expand dramatically, eating up a good proportion of any output increases obtained through their governments' economic-development programs.

It has been widely concluded that significant improvement in living standards in the developing areas is impossible without a substantial reduction in their population growth. But the neo-Malthusians, as one dedicated group is sometimes called, go further than this, arguing that a rapid approach to birth rates so low that populations cease expanding—that is, to *zero population growth*—is virtually a matter of life and death even for the most prosperous nations. It is illuminating to consider the logic of their argument.

The Crowded Planet: Exponential Population Growth

In advocating his position, Malthus adopted a line of argument that has caught many imaginations ever since:

Population, when unchecked, increases in a geometrical ratio. Subsistence increases only in an arithmetical ratio. A slight acquaintance with numbers will shew the immensity of the first power in comparison of the second.[1]

Exponential growth is growth at a constant percentage rate.

In modern discussions, such a "geometric" growth pattern is referred to as **exponential growth**, or "compounded growth" or "snowballing." Exponential growth is growth at a constant *percentage* rate. For example, at a 10 percent growth rate, a population of 100 persons will increase by 10 persons a year, but a population of a million persons will increase by 100,000 persons a year. Thus, although the *rate* of growth is the same for large and small populations, the *numbers* are dramatically different. The bigger the population, the more it will add annually. And each year's growth implies still larger growth in the following year. It is like a snowball rolling downhill, accumulating more snow the bigger it gets and so expanding faster and faster all the time.

If the population doubles (grows 100 percent) in 35 years, it will quadruple (grow another 100 percent) in 70 years, increase 8-fold in 105 years, 16-fold in 140 years, and so on indefinitely. The doubling sequence (2, 4, 8, 16, 32, 64, and so on) is the basic pattern of exponential growth. By projecting the world's population into the future on the assumption that population will grow exponentially at about its current rate, it can be easily calculated that by the year 2165 the population will have grown to about 92 billion—almost 20 times as many inhabitants on the earth as there are today.

It turns out that in his assumptions about exponential growth, Malthus was being conservative. He did not begin to spell out the wonders and the horrors that his premise implied. Consider some calculations by one leading authority on population (who has derived his conclusions simply by carrying through the arithmetic of exponential growth rates):

- *If population were to grow at today's rates for another 600 to 700 years, every square foot of the surface of the earth would contain a human being;*

- *If it were to expand at the same rate for 1200 years, the combined weight of the human population would exceed that of the earth itself;*

- *If that growth rate were to go on for 6000 years (a very short period of time in terms of biological history), the globe would constitute a sphere whose diameter was growing with the speed of light.*[2]

---

[1] Thomas R. Malthus, *An Essay on the Principle of Population* (London, 1798), page 20.

[2] Ansley J. Coale, "Man and His Environment," *Science*, vol. 179 (October 9, 1970), pages 132–36. Copyright 1970 by the American Association for the Advancement of Science.

And none of this is conjecture. It is *sure* to come about *if* the present (exponential) rate of growth of the earth's population continues unabated.

Of course, none of this can really happen. Our finite earth just does not have room for that sort of expansion. The fate of humanity is not determined by the rules of arithmetic—it depends on the course of nature and on the behaviour of the human race. It is true that if the number of humans continues to swell until it presses upon the earth's capacity, the process will ultimately be brought to a halt in a Malthusian apocalypse. Disease, famine, and war must finally put a stop to the expansion process.

But there is a better alternative. People can choose to stop raising large families. There is no inevitability about the family of six or ten children. As we have just noted, there has in fact been a decline in the rate of expansion in the wealthier societies—so much so that in North America in the last few years the rate of reproduction has reached what can ultimately give us zero population growth. Even in the developing nations, as we will see later in this chapter, the birth rate has recently been declining.

A more balanced view of the matter recognizes the serious difficulties that rapid population growth can lead to and suggests that its encouragement will not serve the interests of society. Yet, it does *not* imply that a great catastrophe is necessarily at hand or that the appropriate reaction is panic.

Requirements for Increased Growth

What can be done to increase the growth rate of an economy? Unfortunately, no one has a handy list of sure-fire recipes.

Growth can be attributed to a number of factors that no one knows how to explain: (1) *inventiveness*, which produces the new technology and other innovations that have contributed so much to economic expansion; (2) *entrepreneurship*, the leadership that recognizes no obstacles and undertakes the daring industrial ventures needed to move the economy ahead; and (3) *the work ethic* that leads a work force to high levels of productivity. No one really knows what features of economic organization and social psychology actually lead a community to adopt these goals, as Great Britain is said to have done at the beginning of the nineteenth century, as the United States is reputed to have done in the first half of the twentieth century, and as Japan is apparently doing today. We do know, however, that:

Growth requires two things that people can influence directly:

1. A large expenditure on *capital equipment*: factories, machinery, transportation, and telecommunications equipment.
2. The devotion of considerable effort to research and development from which innovations are derived.

Both these types of expenditures help to increase the economy's ability to *supply* goods. In the last several chapters, we have stressed that the level (and, consequently, the growth) of national income is determined by the interaction of aggregate supply and aggregate demand. It is the need for capital equipment in any growth process that provides a vital link between aggregate demand and aggregate supply, for an economy acquires a larger capital stock by investing. Recall that aggregate demand is the sum of consumption, investment, government spending, and net exports, $Y = C + I + G + X - IM$. But I is the key part of Y that creates more capital for the future.

The *composition* of aggregate demand is a major determinant of the rate of economic growth. If a larger fraction of total spending goes toward investment rather than toward consumption, government purchases, or exports, the capital stock will grow faster and the aggregate supply schedule will shift more quickly to the right.

Over the years, many governments have used the tax system in an attempt to encourage savings, investment, research, and innovation. More recently a very different approach to productivity stimulation, called **industrial strategy**, has been advocated by researchers and embraced by many politicians. The idea is to follow the example of the Japanese and the French by setting up a government planning agency to encourage the particular industries that, in the judgment of the agency, can make the largest contribution to the nation's productivity growth. If it judged that industry A had poor growth prospects while industry B promised the possibility of extraordinary growth, the agency could use such means as tax breaks, loans, and informal pressure to induce a flow of capital and labour out of industry A and into industry B. This, together with some industry-by-industry advice and other attempts to influence business decisions, would, it is hoped, make a major contribution to productivity growth in Canada.

Many economists object that no government agency can do as well as the forces of the market in picking probable future winners and losers. The profit motive already spurs investors to identify the winners and back them with their resources, while withdrawing funds from the likely losers. Private investors do make mistakes. But, in the view of many observers, the mistakes of government agencies are likely to be far more frequent, more serious, and more difficult to reverse, since the individual decision-makers involved do not stand to gain or lose to the same extent as do private entrepreneurs. For this and other reasons, critics of industrial strategy worry that an avowed policy of "picking winners" might degenerate into a habit of "backing losers." This seems to have happened in countries such as Britain and Sweden.

Perhaps more in line with the way economists think is a proposal that might be described as market-mechanism industrial policy. This policy would provide reductions in business taxes, but not uniformly for all firms. Rather, firms would be given a rebate based on the rate of increase in their productivity. The faster a firm increased its productivity, all other things being equal, the lower the tax bill it would have to pay at year's end. Such a plan would increase the profitability of investment in industries in which it is easy to raise productivity and reduce the profitability of investment in industries in which it is hard to raise productivity. In this way, the program could induce business people to make the type of decisions that a government agency under an industrial strategy would strive for. But by avoiding government intervention on an industry-by-industry basis—with its mixture of subsidies, tax breaks, and special stimuli—a market-based approach might achieve the same end at lower economic cost and with less government interference in individual decisions.

Accumulating Capital by Sacrificing Consumption: The Case of the Soviet Union

The importance of the *composition* of demand stands out sharply if we turn away from Canada and consider a *centrally planned* economy, such as the Soviet Union was, at least until very recently.

After the Russian Revolution in 1917, when the Soviet Union undertook to expand its industrial output very rapidly, it was clear from the earliest stage of planning that a tremendous amount of capital equipment would be required to carry out the expansion. Not only did the Soviets have to build modern factories and acquire sophisticated machinery, they also needed a **social infrastructure**—a transportation network to bring raw materials to the factories and take finished products to the markets, an efficient telecommunications system, and schools in which to train the population sufficiently to be an effective labour force. All this and much more was needed, and all of it required labour, raw material, and fuel for its construction.

Obviously, such a use of resources has its *opportunity cost*. Fuel and steel that are employed to build a train become unavailable for the production of refrigerators and washing machines. The real price of accumulating plant, equipment, and infrastructure is paid in the form of consumer goods that must be given up in order to build that capital equipment. In other words:

Through saving, the public gives up some consumption, which is the price it must pay for the accumulation of plant, equipment, and infrastructure. Without this sacrifice, growth generally cannot occur.

This is the hard lesson that the inhabitants of the Soviet Union have been living with for over half a century. The Soviet leadership had been determined to promote rapid economic growth and had imposed on the general public whatever sacrifices of current consumption were deemed necessary for the purpose. Only in the most recent decades has an increase in the supply of consumer goods been assigned any priority. As a result, Soviet living standards have been rising very slowly, particularly because the demands of the military forces have joined those of the growth planners in competing for the resources that might otherwise go into consumption. This is undoubtedly one of the main reasons for the recent upheavals in the U.S.S.R. and the Eastern European countries.

The reason for this harsh trade-off is clear enough. If the economy is producing at its full potential—and the Soviet economy generally has been—then real output, Y, cannot be increased further. Since $Y = C + I + G + X - IM$ and since exports are needed to finance imports, a decision to devote more resources to the production of heavy machinery (which is in I) or armaments (which are in G) is simultaneously a decision to forgo some consumption. Where resources are already fully employed, it is simply not possible to have both more guns and more butter.

The Payoff to Growth: Higher Consumption in the Future

We may seem to be painting a rather grim picture of growth, and indeed, the process has often been harsh in the U.S.S.R. and in other nations that have enforced a high rate of economic growth. But it is also true that if the growth process is successful, the sacrifice of consumption that it requires is only a temporary loss. Consumers give up goods and services now in order to make possible the construction of a productive capacity that will permit them to consume even more goods and services at a later date. After all, from the consumers' point of view, that is what growth is all about. It is not an end in itself, but a means to an end—a standard of living higher than they could have attained without the process of economic expansion.

At least in a consumer-oriented economy, the decision to save in order to promote economic growth is simply an *exchange between present and future consumption*. Consumers sacrifice consumption now in order to be able to increase consumption in the future by more than they gave up in the past. Economies would remain stagnant if people were unwilling to make this trade.

Growth Without Sacrificing Consumption: Something for Nothing?

Of course, some growth can be achieved without much sacrifice of present consumption. At least one of the main engines of growth can be powered with relatively small increases in the nation's stock of factories, equipment, and infrastructure. Research and development can teach society new and more efficient ways of using the nation's productive resources. Thus, *innovation*—the process of putting inventions into operation—can permit an economy to get more output from the same inputs without requiring significant *expansion* of capital stock.

Everyone knows that this has in fact occurred. From the invention of the steam engine to that of the modern computer, our economy has benefited from a stream of inventions—some sensational, some more routine—that together have increased enormously the productivity of the nation's resources. Another way of describing this process is to say that while a substantial proportion of growth is *embodied* in increased quantities of plant, equipment, and infrastructure, a very large proportion of the economy's growth is *disembodied*. That is, it is attributable to better ideas—to improved methods of finding and using the same quantities of resources.

Embodied growth has two serious costs that disembodied growth avoids. First, embodied growth necessarily speeds up the use of society's depletable resources: its iron ore, its petroleum supplies, and its stocks of other minerals and fuels. Second, the resources that are used up in a process of embodied growth must ultimately end up on society's garbage heap. The physical laws of conservation of matter and energy tell us that no raw material can ever disappear. It can be transformed into smoke or solid waste, but unless it is recycled *entirely* (something that is both beyond the capability of our technology and impractical for other reasons), the greater the quantity of resources used in the productive process, the greater the quantity of wastes that must result.

Economist Kenneth Boulding has likened our planet to a spaceship hurtling through the solar system but constrained by terrestrial littering laws to keep its garbage on board. In spaceship Earth, we can transform waste materials into other forms—as by melting old bottles for reuse or converting them into energy, or by burning combustible garbage for heat—but we cannot simply toss them overboard.

Both of these environmental concerns—resource depletion and waste disposal—lead us to favour disembodied over embodied growth. To the extent that we can succeed in increasing the productivity of our resources, we can reduce both the rate at which they are depleted and the severity of the community's waste-disposal problems.

One final remark on disembodied growth is in order. Economists are fond of pointing out that there is no such thing as a free lunch. Except in rare instances, improvements in technology are not "manna from heaven." They result, instead, from the work of scientists and technicians in government and industrial laboratories, from the labour of inventors in their basements or garages, and from the effort of management specialists studying the organization of factories and assembly lines. This means that labour (along with other resources) is diverted from other activities into the production of knowledge. *In a fully employed economy, the opportunity costs of investing in the discovery of new knowledge are the consumption of and physical investment in goods that would otherwise have been produced.* So even here, we cannot get something for nothing.

Is More Growth Really Better?

A number of writers have raised questions about the desirability of faster economic growth as an end in itself, at least in the wealthier industrialized countries. Yet faster growth does mean more wealth, and to most people the desirability of wealth is beyond question. "I've been rich and I've been poor—and I can tell you, rich is better," a noted stage personality is said to have told an interviewer, and most people seem to have the same attitude about the economy as a whole. To those who hold this belief, a healthy economy is one that is capable of turning out vast quantities of shoes, food, cars, and TV sets. An economy whose capacity to provide all these things is not expanding is said to have succumbed to the disease of *stagnation*.

Economists from Adam Smith to Karl Marx saw great virtue in economic growth. Marx argued that capitalism, at least in its earlier historical stages, was a vital form of economic organization by which society got out of the rut in which the medieval stage of history had trapped it. Marx believed that "the development of the productive powers of society... alone can form the real basis of a higher form of society." Marx went on to tell us that only where such great productive powers have

The Poverty of Affluence

Does affluence make us better off? American psychologist Paul Wachtel argues that it may not, as this excerpt from his book on the subject suggests.

... The growth economy ... creates more needs than it satisfies and leaves us feeling more deprived than when we had "less." ... It is ironic that the very kind of thinking which produces all our riches also renders them unable to satisfy us. Our restless desire for more and more has been a major dynamic for economic growth, but it has made the achievement of that growth largely a hollow victory. Our sense of contentment and satisfaction ... depends upon our frame of reference, on how what we attain compares to what we expected. If we get farther than we expected we tend to feel good. If we expected to go farther than we have then even a rather high level of success can be experienced as disappointing. In America, we keep upping the ante. Our expectations keep accommodating to what we have attained. "Enough" is always just over the horizon, and like the horizon it recedes as we approach it. ... The sense of economic distress and disappointment currently sweeping America has [little] to do with real deprivation and much [to do] with assumptions and expectations.

SOURCE: Paul L. Wachtel, *The Poverty of Affluence: A Psychological Portrait of the American Way of Life* (New York: The Free Press, A Division of Macmillan Inc., 1983), pages 16–17.

---

been unleashed can one have "a society in which the full and free development of every individual forms the ruling principle."[3] In other words, only a wealthy economy can afford to give all individuals the opportunity for full personal satisfaction through the use of their special abilities in their jobs and through increased leisure activities.

Yet the desirability of further economic growth for a society that is already wealthy has been questioned on grounds that undoubtedly have a good deal of validity. It is pointed out that the sheer increase in quantity of products has imposed an enormous cost on society in the form of pollution, crowding, proliferation of wastes that need disposal, and debilitating psychological and social effects. It is said that industry has transformed the satisfying and creative tasks of the artisan into the mechanical and dehumanizing routine of the assembly line. It has dotted our roadsides with junkyards, filled our air with smoke, and poisoned our food with dangerous chemicals. The question is whether the outpouring of frozen foods, talking dolls, CB radios, and headache remedies is worth its high cost to society. As one well-known economist put it:

The continued pursuit of economic growth by Western Societies is more likely on balance to reduce rather than increase social welfare.... Technological innovations may offer to add to men's material opportunities. But by increasing the risks of their obsolescence it adds also to their anxiety. Swifter means of communications have the paradoxical effect of isolating people; increased mobility has led to more hours commuting; increased automobilization to increased separation; more television to less communication. In consequence, people know less of their neighbors than ever before in history.[4]

Virtually every economist agrees that these concerns are valid, though many question whether economic growth is their major cause. Nevertheless, they all emphasize that pollution of air and water, noise and congestion, and the mechanization of the work process are very real and very serious problems. There is every reason for society to undertake programs that grapple with these problems. Chapter 32, which deals with problems of the environment and natural resources, examines these issues more closely and describes some policies to deal with them.

[3] Karl Marx, *Capital*, vol. I (Chicago: Charles H. Kerr Publishing Co., 1906), page 649.

[4] E. J. Mishan, *The Costs of Economic Growth* (New York: Frederick A. Praeger Publishers, 1967), pages 171, 175.

Despite the costs of growth in terms of human and environmental damage, there is strong evidence that if the economy's total output were kept at its present level, the community would pay a high price over and above the loss of additional goods and services.

First, it would not be easy to carry out a decision to prevent further economic growth. Mandatory controls are abhorrent to most Canadians. We could not *order* people to stop inventing means to expand productivity. Nor would it make any sense to order every firm and industry to freeze its output level, since changing tastes and needs require some industries to expand their outputs at the same time that others are contracting. But who would decide which should grow and which should contract, and how should such decisions be made? *The achievement of zero economic growth might very well require government intervention on a scale that would become expensive and even repressive.*

Second, without continued growth, it would be no easy matter to finance effective programs of environmental protection. To improve the purity of our air and water and to clean up urban neighbourhoods, billions of dollars must be made available every year. Continued growth would enable the required resources to be provided without any reduction in the availability of consumer goods. But without such growth, we might actually be forced to cut back on our programs to protect the environment. Society could thus end up with less goods and a worse environment.

Finally, zero economic growth might seriously hamper efforts to eliminate poverty both within our economy and throughout the world. Much of the earth's population today lives in a state of extreme want. And though wealthier nations have been reluctant to provide more than token amounts of help to the **less developed countries (LDCs)**, less wealth would mean there would be even less to share. So perhaps the only hope for improved living standards in the impoverished countries of Africa, Asia, and Latin America lies in continued increases in output.

Problems of the Less Developed Countries

Living in the LDCs

More than three-quarters of the world's population lives in areas whose average per-capita income is $2000 (U.S.) or less per year, evaluated (as well as it is possible to do) in terms of today's prices. Table 18–2 shows that there are countries in which annual per-capita income is $300 (U.S.) or less. Even after adjustment for differences in measurement of national product in the United States and the poorer countries, this probably comes to an annual income figure of less than $1000.

To Canadians, such a figure is not only likely to seem incredible, it is all but incomprehensible. Few of us can *really* imagine what life would be like if our family income were reduced to, say, $2000 per year. It is even hard to envision survival on such amounts. It must be emphasized that these figures do *not* represent the living standards of a small group of outcasts from their own societies. Rather, they are *typical* of perhaps a majority of those who live in Asia, Africa, and Latin America.

What can life be like in such circumstances? No brief description can really bridge the gulf between our range of experience and theirs. Yet it can offer us a glimpse into a way of life that few of us will want to share.

Inhabitants of many of the less developed countries live with their large families in one-room shanties or apartments, their water supplies are scanty, polluted, and often miles from home, their only source of energy is that of man and beast, and their sparse harvests are wrung from miserable soil in goods years, with starvation

TABLE 18–2
National Income in Various Countries, 1989

	PER-CAPITA INCOME (U.S. dollars)
Developed Countries	
United States	18,430
Sweden	15,690
Canada	15,100
West Germany	14,460
Less Developed Countries	
Egypt	710
Bolivia	570
Haiti	360
China	300
India	300
Ethiopia	120

SOURCE: Population Reference Bureau Inc., *1989 World Population Data Sheet.*

threatened perhaps every five years when the rains do not come and the crops fail.[5] With no surplus in production, no good can be put into reserves, and the old, the infirm, and the very young are likely to perish.

The life of a male in an LDC is hard enough, with its low nutritional level, its lack of equipment to help in work, and its frequency of debilitating diseases. But his life is luxurious compared with that of his wife. She is usually married by the age of 14 and bears eight or ten children. If (as is true of some 80 percent of the population) she lives in a rural area, she may have to trudge miles every day to fetch water for the family. She sews all the family's clothes by hand and cooks its meals. There is not enough money for pre-ground flour, so part of the woman's daily work is to pound the grain by hand for food for the family—perhaps an additional two hours of hard labour. She also tends the gardens that produce food for the family, although, except in Moslem countries where women are sequestered, she is also expected to put in a full day in the fields during the six months of the agricultural season.

Another duty of the woman in an LDC is to bring produce, wood, or whatever she has to trade to market a couple of times a week, and she must often walk as many as ten miles each way with bundles as heavy as she can carry on her back or on her head. She has no respite in the raising of her children, since they are likely not to have a school to attend when they are well or a hospital to go to when they are sick.

In the LDCs, infant mortality rates are 15 times higher than ours, and life expectancy is more than 20 years shorter. There is little question about the quality of life in less developed lands.

Most of the inhabitants of many LDCs are shockingly poor. Malnutrition and disease are widespread. The sheer process of living and surviving taxes the people to the utmost and makes them old before their time.

[5] For example, in Africa the unpredictability of rainfall (and therefore of food production), along with political instability and chronic inability to buy food, has resulted in continuing undernourishment for an estimated one-quarter of the population—more than 100 million people who do not eat enough to carry on an active working life (World Bank Annual Report, 1989).

Recent Trends

Despite population increases, some LDCs (particularly in the Far East) have succeeded in breaking out of the stagnation trap. In those more successful economies, if growth continues as it has recently, an average family in some underdeveloped areas can look forward to a doubling of its living standards in less than 30 years. Or, put another way, standards of living will be increasing faster than they did in Canada in the nineteenth century!

Although such good news applied to a number of LDCs in several parts of the world during the 1970s, the 1980s were not as favourable, particularly because of severe debt problems, which we shall discuss a bit later. Also, it must be remembered that even when the *percentage* increases in per-capita incomes in the LDCs are similar to those in the industrialized countries, *absolute* incomes continue to rise more quickly in the richer lands. For example, where per-capita income is $100 a year, a 2.5 percent growth rate translates into a $2.50 annual improvement; where per-capita income is $5000 a year, the same 2.5 percent rate of growth adds $125 a year to the income of the average person.

A few numbers will indicate how discouraging the relative performance of the LDCs as a group has been. A study of some 70 countries by a group of noted economists[6] calculated a standard index of degree of inequality (called the "Gini index") for three subsets of these countries: the industrialized countries, the middle-income countries, and the LDCs. The study covered the 30-year period from 1950 to 1980, which includes the 1970s, usually considered a decade of extraordinary progress for the LDCs. For the industrialized countries, the index of inequality fell by almost 60 percent over the 30-year period, meaning that the poorer of the industrial countries had done a very effective job of catching up with the richer ones. The countries of the middle-income group also came closer to one another, but only to a modest degree, with their inequality index falling 4 percent in three decades. But for the LDCs the index actually rose 9 percent, meaning that these poorest of countries were increasingly diverging among themselves into relatively richer and relatively poorer groups.

Even more important, the disparity between the LDCs and the other two groups has been increasing. The average annual growth rates of real GDP were 3.1 percent (compounded) for the industrial countries, 3 percent for the middle-income countries, and only 1.5 percent for the LDCs.

With average growth rates half as big as those of the more-affluent economies, the LDCs as a group have fallen farther behind the rest of the world for much of the period since World War II.

A continuing problem within the LDCs is the high population-growth rate. While in North America and Western Europe net population growth has generally fallen to (or almost to) zero, the population explosion continues in some of the LDCs, particularly in Africa. In many LDCs, the annual growth rate of population continues to be about 12 times as high as it is in industrialized countries. Clearly, the more closely population growth approximates growth in national income, the more slowly standards of living will rise, since there will be that many more people among whom the additional product must be divided.

Impediments to Development in the LDCs

No one has produced a definitive list of causes of the poverty of the LDCs, just as no one can pretend to have produced a foolproof prescription for its cure. Yet there is general agreement on the main conditions contributing to the economic problems of

---

[6] Robert Summers, Irving B. Kravis, and Alan Heston, "Changes in World Income Distribution," *Journal of Policy Modelling*, vol. 6 (May 1986), pages 237–69.

The Debt Crisis of the Developing Countries

Although there had been previous isolated cracks in the international debt terrain, it was not until 1982 that the problem erupted in dramatic proportions. In August of that year, Mexico announced that it was unable to meet its debt obligations to foreign creditors, although it was taking steps to rectify the situation. In response, the U.S. government mounted a rescue operation, involving the creditor banks, the International Monetary Fund (IMF), and other creditor governments. The package included a strict program of adjustment for the Mexican economy and a rescheduling of much of the debt. Nervous banks began to cut back lending to other countries that appeared to be heavily indebted, with Brazil the most obvious target. As long as the banks had been willing to continue lending, the debtor countries had had the foreign exchange necessary to continue servicing their accumulated debt, i.e., making scheduled payments of interest and amortization of principal. As the banks cut back, the debtors found debt-service obligations increasingly difficult to meet. One by one, Brazil, Argentina, and many other debtor countries found it necessary to seek debt relief from their creditors, while implementing programs of economic adjustment monitored by the IMF.

SOURCE: United States, *Economic Report of the President*, February 1984, page 71.

The debt problem threatens to undermine growth in many LDCs. It was caused by overborrowing and overspending during the 1970s when prosperity and growth seemed easy to sustain; by the high oil prices of the 1970s, which hurt the oil-importing LDCs; by the fall in oil prices in the early 1980s, which hurt the oil-exporting LDCs; and by high interest rates, which hurt them all.

The debt crisis is forcing widespread adoption of austerity policies—reducing already low consumption levels so that less has to be imported and more goods are left over for export. It prevents any ambitious investment programs for the same reason, thus impeding future growth. It is indeed a major problem for the LDCs and, incidentally, for the shareholders of large banks in the industrialized countries to whom the money is owed and who fear the loss of their loans.

For further discussion of the debt crisis, review the material in Chapter 15, page 323.

LDCs. These include lack of physical capital, rapid growth of populations, lack of education, unemployment, and social and political impediments to business activity. Let us examine each of these in turn.

Scarcity of Physical Capital

The LDCs are obviously handicapped by their lack of modern factories and machinery. In addition, they lack infrastructure—good roads, railways, port facilities, and so on. But capital is not easy to acquire. If it is to be provided by the populations of the LDCs themselves, they must save the required resources—that is, as we saw earlier in this chapter, they must give up consumption in order to free the resources needed to build plants, equipment, and roads. That is comparatively easy in a rich community, where substantial saving still leaves the public well off in terms of current consumption. But in an LDC, where malnutrition is a constant threat, the bulk of the inhabitants cannot save except at enormous sacrifice to their families. Moreover, in many of the LDCs, tradition imputes little virtue to investment in business, so that even the wealthy are not terribly eager to put their savings into productive equipment. Thus:

Because of poverty, which makes saving difficult, if not impossible, and because of traditions that do not encourage investment, the LDCs' growth rates of domestically financed capital are lower than those in the developed countries.

One way to help matters is to obtain the funds for investment from abroad. There is a long tradition of foreign investment in developing countries. For example, throughout much of Canadian history, we drew capital from abroad, to finance such projects as the national railway. In recent decades a considerable share of the resources going to the LDCs from abroad has come from foreign governments as part of their aid programs. While some of the resources provided in this way have been used wastefully, informed observers generally agree that the waste incurred under these programs has not been intolerably large, and they conclude that these capital transfers from the rich countries to the poor have at least worked in the right direction.

Capital can also be transferred to an LDC when a private firm chooses to invest money in such a country to build a factory or to explore for oil in order to increase its own profits. This too seems to have been helpful to the LDCs. In earlier days, it sometimes gave an unacceptable degree of political influence to the foreign firms, particularly when the LDC was a colony of an industrial country. In recent years this difficulty may have become rarer. Nowadays, it is more often the outside firm that is afraid of the government of the LDC rather than vice versa, with foreign proprietors frequently fearful of rigid control by the government of the LDC in which it invests. Sometimes it even fears outright expropriation—that the government will simply take over its property in the LDC with, or even without, compensation, because of the hostile attitudes that residents of many LDCs hold toward large foreign companies.

It is difficult for a resident of an industrialized country like Canada to realize how much hatred and resentment is felt in less developed countries toward the "northern imperialist powers." This resentment is focussed in particular on **multinational corporations**—companies such as IBM, Royal Dutch Shell, Volkswagen, and Unilever—which have their headquarters in an industrialized country and their operations in a variety of less developed countries. Multinationals may first process their own raw materials in one country, ship them to another to make them into parts, and assemble them in still a third. Some of these corporations, among them the oil companies, specialize in the extraction and/or marketing of raw materials, while others, such as IBM and Volkswagen, specialize in manufacturing. Many LDCs regard these and other giant foreign corporations as instruments of imperialist exploitation, not as firms that happen to carry on their activities wherever the dictates of efficiency require, contributing benefits to each of the countries in which they operate.

It is true that foreign firms hope to make more money out of an LDC than they put into it, but that is only natural, since otherwise their investment would not have been expected to be profitable, and the funds would therefore not have been invested in the first place. But there are usually *mutual gains* from trade. Investment will be useful to the LDCs if in the process of earning these profits foreign firms build factories and infrastructure, and provide jobs that leave the community wealthier than it would otherwise have been. The evidence is that this is in fact what foreign private investment has typically accomplished in recent decades.

A problem with foreign business investment that is more serious is the danger that foreign firms will fail to train native personnel in the skills necessary to run the factories built by those companies. Often the foreign firm brings in its own managers, engineers, and technicians, and the work force from the LDCs is kept in menial jobs in which on-the-job training is minimal. In recent years the LDCs have begun to deal with this problem by restricting immigration of foreign personnel, giving them work permits only for limited periods and requiring at least some minimum employment of native personnel in key positions.

Another danger posed by foreign investment is that it may prevent future financial independence. Profits are a major source of the funds used for investment. If foreign investment takes over the LDCs' most profitable industries, then newly formed capital—new plant and equipment—will also be owned predominantly by foreigners.

Population Growth

Population growth is often described as the primary villain in the LDCs. We have already noted that their populations grow far more rapidly than those of the wealthier countries. And though the growth rate has recently been declining in many of the less developed countries, the population of the LDCs overall is expanding at a rate that will double in less than thirty years, requiring a doubling of housing, schools, hospitals, and so on simply to maintain standards of living at their existing, low, levels. This represents a heavy real cost for an LDC.

The growth in population has been stimulated by improvements in medical care, which have reduced death rates dramatically. Today, in some areas, death rates (ratio of deaths to population) are only one-quarter or one-fifth as high as birth rates. While formerly it was not unusual for half a nation's children to die before the age of 20, today in many countries this is true of only some 4 percent of those populations. This dramatic decline can be attributed primarily to inexpensive public-health measures—reduction in stomach diseases through purer water supplies, reduction in the incidence of malaria by the draining of swamps, insecticide spraying of the breeding grounds of infectious mosquitoes, eradication of smallpox by vaccination, and so forth. The more expensive treatment of illness, using modern medical techniques and miracle drugs, seems to have contributed far less.

But not all LDCs suffer from serious population problems. India, Indonesia, and Egypt are frequently cited examples of population pressures. On the other hand, many African countries and parts of Latin America still have populations so small that they are denied economies of large-scale communication and transportation. The economy of a sparsely settled country whose electric power and telecommunication lines must traverse great unpopulated areas is under a costly handicap.

Governments in a number of LDCs have been struggling to find workable ways to cut population growth. Programs set up to distribute contraceptives and propaganda against large families have achieved modest success, but in some countries with particularly severe population problems the governments have been dissatisfied with the results of these voluntary efforts. In India, a program making use of compulsory sterilization aroused the anger of the public and finally led to the downfall of the government.

Ironically enough, it was Communist China that, along with Singapore, decided to employ strong financial incentives for population control. In China, government support is provided for a first child. For a second, the support is withdrawn and some financial penalties imposed; for a third child, the penalties are really prohibitive for most people. But there is much more to the program than such relatively benign financial incentives. For example, in urban areas (where most of the citizens work in state-operated enterprises and are monitored more closely than rural residents), the success of the one-child policy has been assured by extreme authoritarian coercion. The state-operated factories all conduct a program of birth-control monitoring. Women workers are required to keep a record of their menstrual cycles, which they must submit to an assigned monitor; a woman who misses a menstrual period is forced to have an abortion. Such coercive measures have, indeed, been successful in reducing birth rates to averages of approximately one child per couple in the cities and two children per couple in rural areas (where five or six children used to be the norm). Population experts have warned, however, that the one-child program may prove disastrous for China's economy, not only because family enterprises have always played an important role in that country, but also because, twenty years hence, the support of a tremendous ageing population will have to be borne by a significantly depleted labour force.

Education and Technical Training

Everyone knows that educational levels in the LDCs are much lower than they are in the wealthier countries. There are fewer graduates of elementary schools, far fewer graduates of high schools, and enormously fewer graduates of postsecondary institutions. The percentage of the population that is literate is much lower than in industrialized nations. The issue is how much of a handicap this constitutes for economic growth.

If, by "education," we refer to general learning rather than technical (trade) schooling, the evidence is that it makes considerably less difference for economic growth than is often believed. For example, the number of jobs that clearly require secondary education rarely seems to exceed 10 percent of the labour force. Various studies that have investigated whether there is a statistical relationship between the economic growth of an economy and its typical educational level have found only weak correlations between the two. Other suggestive evidence can easily be cited. For example, in 1840, when Great Britain ruled the markets of the world, only 59 percent of the British adult population was literate, while in the United States, Scandinavia, and Germany, then all relatively undeveloped, the figure was about 80 percent.

All of this is not meant to imply that education is worthless. On the contrary, it obviously offers many benefits in and of itself, which need not be discussed here. But it does suggest that if a government invests in education *purely as a means to stimulate economic growth*, only a very limited outlay is justifiable on these grounds.

Matters are quite different when we turn to technical training. There is apparently a high payoff to the training of electricians, machinists, draftsmen, construction workers, and the like. While the number of persons involved need not be very high in proportion to the population, the role played by such specialists is crucial. However, the LDCs would find it a very heavy drain upon their scarce foreign currency to send young people abroad to learn these skills in the numbers called for by the needs of the economy. One of the main inhibitions to adequate training in these areas is that in many countries such skills are held in low esteem and considered inferior to training in the liberal arts. Consequently, technical education is often handicapped by low budgets, low teacher salaries—which discourage good people from entering the field—and the prejudice of potential students against such fields.

Training in improved farming methods also has a great deal to contribute. In many of the LDCs, agricultural methods produce yields far lower than the best of the known techniques can offer. As one leading observer, Nobel Prize–winner Sir W. Arthur Lewis, has remarked:

If this gap could be closed, the economies of these countries would be unrecognizable. Indeed ... no impact can be made on mass living standards without revolutionizing agricultural performance.[7]

There seem to be no easy ways to provide the necessary education to the farmers who cannot spare the time to attend schools, and training their children also involves a number of critical obstacles. Religious beliefs often lead parents to object to schooling of their children, particularly of girls; in areas where literacy is low (where the problem is generally most serious), truly literate and knowledgeable teachers are almost impossible to find in any substantial numbers; and children who do complete schooling tend to leave the farms and move to the cities.

Programs to provide help to the peasants on their own farms have had only limited success. Indeed, lack of training is only part of the problem. Many other things are needed to make modern farming methods possible—for example, the use of modern machinery is generally appropriate only for farms larger than the two hectares (or five acres) that are the norm in many countries. Roads and storage facilities must be built. Credit must be made available to farmers. Financial arrangements must be changed so the farmer need no longer give up half his crop to landlords and tax collectors whom he can surely regard as little more than parasites and who undermine his incentives for improved productivity.

[7]W.A. Lewis, *Development Economics: An Outline* (Morristown, N.J.: General Learning Press, 1974), page 25.

Unemployment

One of the most noteworthy features of the growth of the LDCs has been an increase in unemployment as population shifted out of agriculture into the cities. Increased schooling has stimulated the migration out of rural areas, as has unionization, which has often produced a huge gap between urban and rural wages. Government investment policies have also favoured construction of schools, hospitals, and other facilities in the cities, and as a result, large numbers of migrants have entered the cities to swell the ranks of the unemployed. The unemployment rate among young urban workers has been particularly high; indeed, rates as high as 50 percent are not unheard of.

These figures are compounded by the phenomenon of **disguised unemployment**. For example, ten persons may do a job for which only six are needed. The statistics show no unemployment among the ten workers, even though four of them really contribute nothing to output. Some observers believe that this is such a widespread problem in rural areas that even a substantial reverse migration of the urban unemployed back to the farms would add very little to production, at least in some of the LDCs.

An important consequence of all this is that in many LDCs unemployment may not be accompanied by any substantial reduction in output, in contrast to the situation in industrialized economies. But this does not mean that unemployment in the LDCs is not a serious problem. What it does mean is that it may sometimes be desirable for those economies to avoid the use of labour-saving equipment, partly because it will result in better use of an abundant resource and partly because it will contribute to the solution of a serious social problem. Thus, increased output is desirable perhaps primarily because it helps to sop up unemployed labour. This is in contrast to the usual situation in the developed countries in which increased employment is desirable perhaps primarily because it increases income and output.

Social Impediments to Entrepreneurship

As we saw earlier in this chapter, one of the magic ingredients of economic growth is **entrepreneurship**. It is clear that the LDCs need entrepreneurs if their economies are to grow rapidly. But in many of these economies, there are serious inhibitions to entrepreneurship. Traditional social values often accord relatively low status to business activity. Indeed, those traditional values may even prevent businesses from seeking ways to attract and please their customers and their work force. In addition, high positions in business in many LDCs are often determined by family connections and inheritance, not by ability.

In the LDCs, growth will be inhibited until customs can be modified to increase the social status of economic activity, to make it respectable for private business people and managers of public enterprises to do their best to attract business and increase productivity, and to assign responsibility on the basis of ability rather than family connections.

Government Inhibition of Business Activity

In addition to social impediments to business, the political situation in the LDCs often is detrimental to business success. Business is not helped by unstable governments or by the uncertainty that accompanies such an environment, especially if there is a high likelihood of revolution. Foreign investment will be discouraged where there is fear of expropriation or of unstable currencies that may fall in value and wipe out profits.

In addition, in the normal course of events, governments in the LDCs are often inclined to interfere with business activity in a variety of ways that seem relatively innocuous—but whose effects can be deadly. For example, as a matter of prestige, currency exchange rates are often set so high that exports from the LDC cannot compete on the world market.

Help from Industrialized Economies

We have just seen that two of the primary needs of the LDCs are technical skills and capital resources. Happily, these are precisely the things that the more prosperous nations are in a position to offer. We have the trained teachers, classrooms, laboratories, and equipment necessary to provide an education of the highest quality to students from the LDCs.

However, there is a danger here that has received a great deal of attention—the so-called **brain drain**. This refers to the temptation for students from LDCs to try to stay in the countries where they have studied and enjoy the higher living standard, rather than to return home where their abilities are needed so badly.

There are several ways to deal with this. For example, one can require students to return to their homelands for at least some given number of years after completion of the educational program, or one can offer higher wages for trained people in the LDCs to make returning more attractive. Yet the problem is there, and the large number of doctors, teachers, and other skilled personnel from LDCs who are seeking jobs in the developed countries suggests that it is not negligible.

A second major contribution to the LDCs that the wealthier countries can make is to offer trained technicians and technical advice. Such counselling and personnel can be very helpful as a temporary measure, but in the long run they can prove detrimental if provision for the training of local personnel for the ultimate replacement of the foreign technicians and advisers is not built into the program.

Third, the world can help the LDCs through research. One of the hardest problems for the developing world is what to do in the rural areas that suffer from inadequate rainfall, where several hundred million people live in both Asia and Africa. These people are badly in need of new dry-farming techniques. Until some are discovered, their poverty will increase as their numbers grow. An international research organization devoted to food production in problem areas in the LDCs would have much to contribute.

Fourth, and perhaps most important, the developed countries can help by promoting freedom of trade and investment. This will help those LDCs whose exports could readily be expanded but are now being held back by barriers to trade. Exports of most primary and agricultural products are inhibited by tariffs and other restrictions in the developed world. Many feel that the most useful single action we can take to aid the LDCs is to remove these impediments to their export earnings, since with those earnings they could develop more-diversified economies.

Finally, assistance from the developed to the less developed countries can take the form of money or physical resources provided either as loans made on favourable terms or as outright grants (gifts). Unfortunately, many countries (including Canada) find it politically expedient to cut foreign-aid expenditures when trying to reduce overall budget deficits. For example, in 1990, foreign aid was already less than one-half of 1 percent of GDP, and the expenditure cuts on foreign aid introduced in that year represented almost *one-quarter of the total cuts* in federal government expenditures.

The "North–South" Controversy and Commodity Price Stabilization

The conflict of interests between the LDCs and the industrialized countries has come to be called, somewhat inaccurately, the "North–South confrontation," with the "North" referring to the wealthy nations and the "South" denoting the poor countries. The international trade arrangements, which the North considers to constitute a free market for the unhampered exchange of goods for the mutual benefit of all participants, are widely viewed in the South as a thinly disguised instrument of old-fashioned imperialism to be used to exploit the poorer economies.

A major cause of this discontent is the prices of the commodities, such as cocoa and sugar, which the South considers to be unfairly low and distressingly unstable. There has been considerable pressure for international agreements that will take steps to reduce the upswings and downswings of these prices. It has been proposed that a stabilization fund be organized and used to buy such commodities when their prices are falling and to sell them when their prices are rising. That is, by shifting demand outward when prices are relatively low, the fund would raise these prices; by shifting demand downward when prices are comparatively high, it would force these prices downward.

But negotiations have stalled over at least two issues. First, the industrialized countries want much of the money for the stabilization fund to be supplied by the less developed countries themselves, while the latter want most of the fund to be financed by the industrialized countries who buy these products. But the second issue is perhaps more serious. The North intends the stabilization fund to do only what its name implies: to iron out fluctuations in commodity prices, not to raise or lower those prices on the average. But to many southern countries "stabilization" actually is a diplomatic way of referring to their desire to *raise* commodity prices, something the North is reluctant to do.

Summary

1. Productivity growth over the past century has made a tremendous contribution to standards of living. Real per-capita income is nearly eight times as large as it was in 1870. Never in previous history have economic conditions improved so much.

2. For the first time in history famine is no longer a constant threat in the world's industrialized countries. That is because productivity in agriculture has increased greatly. In 1800 about 90 percent of the North American labour force was needed to feed its population—and did so poorly. Today, only about 3 percent of the North American labour force works on farms, and yet it produces great abundance.

3. Over long periods, a small increase in the rate of productivity growth can compound to make an enormous difference in the economic well-being of a nation. This is one of the 12 **Ideas for Beyond the Final Exam**.

4. There is evidence suggesting that at least a small set of the world's leading economies are converging towards similar living standards and similar productivity levels.

5. Lagging productivity holds back a nation's real wages and per-capita incomes. In the long run, however, it will generally not cause unemployment or inability to export enough to pay for the nation's imports.

6. The share of the Canadian labour force employed in the services has increased substantially. But so has that of every industrial free-market economy. A major cause is probably the rapid rise of manufacturing productivity, which makes fewer workers necessary in that economic sector.

7. A rapidly rising population poses a threat to growth of per-capita incomes. On our finite planet, exponential growth (growth at a constant percentage rate) is, in general, impossible except for relatively brief periods.

8. Increases in growth depend heavily on entrepreneurship, accumulation of capital equipment, and research and development.

9. Saving is necessary for the accumulation of resources with which to produce factories, machinery, and other capital equipment. Thus, saving is a critical requisite for growth, particularly in less developed countries.

10. Many observers argue that even if continued growth does not lead to catastrophically rapid depletion of resources (as some have predicted), its desirability is nevertheless questionable because it produces pollution, overcrowding, and many other undesirable consequences.

11. Those who favour growth argue that without it there is no chance of ridding the world of poverty.

12. Standards of living in many LDCs are extremely low; per-capita incomes that are equivalent to $2000 (U.S.) a year are common. Life expectancy is low and daily living is very difficult, particularly for women.

13. Growth in the LDCs is impeded by shortages of capital caused by poverty, traditions that do not encourage investment, rapid population growth, poor education, unemployment, lack of entrepreneurship, and government impediments to business.

14. Industrialized countries can help the LDCs by providing capital through loans and grants, by offering training and education to people from those lands, and by encouraging freedom of trade with the LDCs.

15. Many LDCs have borrowed so heavily that simply keeping up with the interest payments is a great burden on their economies. Some have defaulted on the loans; others have imposed austerity programs that are hard on their people and make growth even more difficult.

Concepts for Review

Productivity	Research and development (R & D)	Embodied growth
Standard of living	Service industries	Disembodied growth
GDP per labour hour	Deindustrialization	Less developed countries (LDCs)
GDP per capita	Exponential population growth	
Real wages	Exchange between present and future consumption	

Questions for Discussion

1. Try to describe what family budgets were like 120 years ago when North American income per person (GDP per capita) was about one-eighth as high as it is today.

2. List some of the inventions that have increased agricultural output in the past century.

3. List some of the inventions that have increased manufacturing output in the last century.

4. List some of the new consumer products of the past century. Which of them became generally available only after World War II?

5. List some inventions widely used in North America that originated elsewhere.

6. List some North American inventions widely used abroad.

7. If growing productivity has vastly reduced the amount of labour needed to produce a given output, why has it not caused massive and growing unemployment?

8. If output per capita in a country doubles every twenty-five years, how much will it grow in a century?

9. Suppose population grows at a constant exponential rate and doubles every 12 years. How many times will it have grown in 36 years? How many years does it require to expand to 32 times its initial level?

10. Which do you think are more similar: production methods in a North American and a West German factory today; or production methods in the same North American factory today and the methods used there twenty-five years ago?

11. After the political upheavals in the Communist-bloc countries in Eastern Europe in 1989, it became clear that one of those countries' most urgent needs is productivity growth. What are they doing about it?

12. Can you think of any innovations that permit growth without proportionate increases in use of inputs?

13. Name as many undesirable consequences of growth as you can think of. Are the undesirable consequences of growth more likely to be considered serious in a less developed country or in an industrialized country? Why?

14. Discuss the advantages and disadvantages to an LDC of a Canadian manufacturing company's investing in that country.

15. If you were economic adviser to the president of an LDC, what might you suggest that he or she do to encourage increases in saving and investment?

16. Discuss what you have read in the newspapers and heard from other sources about the Japanese "growth miracle." What does it portend for the future of the Japanese economy? For that of Canada? (The Japanese economy is described in some detail in Chapter 24, pages 544–46.)

17. It has been noted that crime overlords who organize drug empires, and the managements of law firms that specialize in stimulation of litigation, are often, in fact, successful entrepreneurs. Discuss whether these persons contribute to the growth of their economies.

ALSO AVAILABLE!

Student Study Guide

To Accompany

ECONOMICS
PRINCIPLES & POLICY
THIRD CANADIAN EDITION
William J. Baumol, Alan S. Blinder & William M. Scarth

Designed to help you in your study of Introductory Economics, the **Student Study Guide** contains numerous tools tied directly to the text. An ideal aid to help you better understand the principles of economics, the Study Guide contains the following features:

Chapter Reviews: Provides a Summary Discussion of the major points of each chapter.

Learning Objectives: Highlights economic concepts which you should be able to grasp by the end of each chapter.

Self-Tests and Definition Quizzes: Allow you to self-test your knowledge of chapter content in preparation for the actual quiz.

Important Terms and Concepts: List the important items from the chapter which you should be able to define.

Supplemental Exercises: More advanced exercises which require greater knowledge of Economic principles of mathematical complexity.

Appendix: Additional exercises designed to further illustrate topics discussed in the appendices.

Economics: Principles & Policy
Third Canadian Edition
Study Guide, William M. Scarth & Craig Swan
- ISBN: 0-7747-3164-8 **HBJ Canada**, 1991

Essentials of Microeconomics: Consumers and Firms

19

Consumer Choice and the Individual's Demand Curve

Everything is worth what its purchaser will pay for it.

PUBLILIUS SYRUS (1st century B.C.)

I t is clear from our initial look at supply and demand in Chapter 3 that if we are to understand how markets function and how they react to changes in the economic environment, we will have to delve more deeply into the nature of both demand and supply. What influences determine the shapes and positions of the demand and supply curves? How do the curves shift in response to various events? The purpose of Part Five is to answer questions like these and thereby to provide the analytical tools we will need to pursue the central theme of this book: the virtues and shortcomings of the market mechanism.

We begin on the demand side of the market. In this chapter we emphasize that the market-demand curves of Chapter 3 depend on choices made by individual consumers, and we explore the logic underlying these choices. Thus, in contrast with Chapter 3, where we dealt with curves describing the combined demand of all consumers in the market, here we will consider the demand curve of an individual consumer. Since such a demand curve tells us how much of a good a consumer wants to purchase at each possible price, its origins must in some sense rest in consumer psychology. But since economists claim no qualifications for making deep pronouncements about consumer psychology, our exploration will not go very far below the surface. It will, however, describe some powerful tools used in the analysis of consumer choice and cast some light on a number of important issues, including the negative slope of the individual consumer's demand curve.

In Chapter 20 we take up some further aspects of demand curves that are essential for understanding the workings of the market mechanism and expand our analysis from demand curves for single consumers to demand curves for a total market. Then, in Chapters 21 and 22, we turn our attention to the supply side of the market.

A Puzzle:
Should Water Be Worth More than Diamonds?

When Adam Smith was lecturing at the University of Glasgow in the 1760s, he introduced the study of demand by posing a puzzle. Common sense, he said, suggests that the price of a commodity must somehow depend on what that good is worth to consumers—on the amount of *utility* that commodity offers. Yet, Smith pointed out, there are cases in which a good's utility apparently has little influence on its price.

Two examples he gave were diamonds and water. He noted that water, which is essential to life and therefore undoubtedly of enormous value to most consumers, generally sells at a very low price, while diamonds, on the other hand, cost thousands of dollars even though they hardly constitute anything resembling a necessity. A century later, this puzzle, called the **diamond–water paradox**, helped stimulate the invention of what is perhaps the most powerful set of tools in the economist's toolkit —*marginal analysis*. Fortunately, we need wait only a few pages, not a century, to learn how marginal analysis—a general method for making optimal decisions—helps to resolve the paradox.

Marginal Analysis

The intuition behind marginal analysis is very straightforward. Suppose you have $100 of spending money available for the coming month and that you are trying to decide how to divide this entire budget between two items: beer and pizza. (We are not suggesting that you *should* limit your purchases to these two items! We have just chosen two commonly consumed items to provide a simple exposition of the basic idea behind marginal analysis.) Both beer and pizza yield satisfaction (or utility) but it seems that for virtually everyone, the additional satisfaction obtained from the tenth piece of pizza is less than that obtained from the first piece. Assuming, then, that the addition to satisfaction falls as you consume either more pizza or more beer, it is not likely to be rational for you to exhaust your budget on just one item or the other.

But how do you decide the optimal combination of beer and pizza? You will maximize the total satisfaction that can be obtained from your $100 if you arrange your purchases so that the additional satisfaction you get from spending the very last dollar is the same whether you spend it on beer *or* pizza. If this is not the case, you will have made a mistake. For example, if you are getting, say, 10 units of satisfaction per dollar spent on pizza and only 5 units of satisfaction per dollar spent on beer, it means two things. First, you should spend your next dollar on pizza; and second, you could have had more satisfaction if you had spent your last dollar on pizza instead of beer as well. But as you transfer more of your expenditure over to pizza, you will move closer to satiation, and the amount of satisfaction you derive per unit of pizza will begin to fall. Your transfer of funds toward pizza should therefore stop when the additional amount of satisfaction per dollar spent on pizza falls to the point that it is no longer greater than that for beer. Thus, if you made no mistakes (that is, if your judgment was not clouded by the consumption of the beer itself), you could have maximized satisfaction only by arranging your purchases so that in the end, the *additional satisfaction per dollar spent* on both (or all) commodities was the *same*. In the economist's language, this means that sensible buyers will equalize the "marginal utility per dollar spent" on all commodities, in accordance with the *optimal purchase rule*.

There are two ways we can make this discussion of the household's optimal purchase rule more precise, and each method has advantages and disadvantages. The advantages of the first formal analysis, which assumes that any one good is a very small part of an individual's whole budget (income), are that it affords a simple derivation of the optimal purchase rule and that it can be used to explain *consumer surplus*. This concept will arise frequently in later chapters to explain why various distortions such as monopoly, tariffs, price regulations, and various taxes are "bad" on efficiency grounds. The disadvantages of this "one-good-at-a-time" analysis are that it gives insufficient emphasis to the fact that a consumer's budget is limited, and it may give the mistaken impression that economists have to treat utility as a cardinal concept (and that consumers need to be able to measure units of satisfaction). The second formalization of the optimal purchase rule, to which we refer as "indifference curve analysis" and which we discuss in the final sections of this chapter, avoids these problems. The disadvantage of this second approach is that it is more advanced. However, this book is written in such a way that these sections can be omitted without threatening your understanding of later chapters.

Total and Marginal Utility

As noted above, economists have constructed a simple theory of consumer choice based on the hypothesis that each consumer spends his or her income in the way that yields the greatest amount of satisfaction, or *utility*. This seems a reasonable starting point, since it says little more than that people do what they prefer. But, to make the theory operational, we need a way to measure utility.

A century ago, economists thought that utility could be measured directly in some kind of psychological units (sometimes called "utils"), after somehow reading the consumer's mind. But gradually it came to be realized that this task was unnecessary and perhaps impossible. How many utils did you get from the last movie you saw? You probably cannot answer that question because you have no idea what a util is.

But you may be able to answer a different question, such as: How many hamburgers would you give up to get that movie ticket? If you answer "three," we still do not know how many utils you get from a movie. But we do know that you get more than you get from a hamburger. Hamburgers, rather than utils, become the unit of measurement, and we can say that the utility of a movie (to you) is three hamburgers.

Early in the twentieth century, economists concluded that this more indirect way of measuring utility was all they needed to build a theory of consumer choice. We can measure the utility of a movie ticket by asking how much of some other commodity (like hamburgers) you are willing to give up for it. Any commodity will do for this purpose. But the simplest choice, and the one we will use in this book, is money.[1]

Thus, we are led to define the **total utility** of some bundle of goods to some consumer as *the largest sum of money she will voluntarily give up in exchange for it*. For example, suppose Jennifer is considering purchasing six kilograms of bananas. She has determined that she will not buy them if they cost more than $4.44, but she will buy them if they cost $4.44 or less. Then the *total utility* of six kilograms of bananas to her is $4.44—the maximum amount she is willing to spend to have them.

Total utility measures the benefit Jennifer derives from her purchases. It is total utility that really matters. But to understand which decisions most effectively promote *total* utility we must consider the related concept of **marginal utility**. This term refers to the *additional utility that an individual derives by consuming one more unit of any good*.

Table 19–1 helps clarify the distinction between marginal utility and total utility and shows how the two are related. The first two columns show how much *total* utility

The **total utility** of a quantity of goods to a consumer (measured in money terms) is the maximum amount of money he or she is willing to give in exchange for it.

The **marginal utility** of a commodity to a consumer (measured in money terms) is the maximum amount of money he or she is willing to pay *for one more unit* of it.

[1] *NOTE TO INSTRUCTORS*: You will recognize that while not using the terms, we are distinguishing between neoclassical *cardinal utility* and *ordinal utility*. Moreover, throughout the book "marginal utility in money terms," or "money marginal utility," is simply a synonym for the marginal rate of substitution between money and the commodity in question.

TABLE 19–1
Total and Marginal Utility of Bananas (Measured in Money Terms)

NUMBER OF KILOGRAMS	TOTAL UTILITY (in dollars)	MARGINAL UTILITY (in dollars)	POINT IN FIGURE 19–1
0	0		
1	1.20	1.20	A
2	2.32	1.12	B
3	3.20	0.88	C
4	3.92	0.72	D
5	4.28	0.36	E
6	4.44	0.16	F
7	4.52	0.08	G
8	4.52	0	H

(measured in money terms) Jennifer derives from various quantities of bananas ranging from zero to eight kilograms. For example, a single kilogram is worth (no more than) $1.20 to her, two kilograms are worth $2.32, and so on. The *marginal* utility is the *difference* between any two successive total-utility figures. For example, if the consumer already has three kilograms (worth $3.20 to her), an *additional* kilogram brings her total utility up to $3.92. Her marginal utility is thus the difference between the two, or 72¢.

Remember: Whenever we use the terms *total utility* and *marginal utility*, we are defining these in terms of the consumer's willingness to part with money for the commodity—not in some unobservable (and imaginary) psychological units.

The "Law" of Diminishing Marginal Utility

With these definitions we can now state in precise terms the simple hypothesis about consumer tastes that we mentioned above: The more of a good a consumer has, the less will be the *marginal* utility of an additional unit.

In general, this is a plausible proposition. The idea is based on the assertion that every person has a hierarchy of uses to which he or she will put a particular commodity. All of these uses are valuable, but some are more valuable than others. Let's consider bananas again. Jennifer may use them to give to her family to eat, to feed a pet monkey, to make banana cream pie (which is a bit rich for her tastes), or to give to a brother-in-law for whom she has no deep affection. If she has only one kilogram, it will be used solely for the family to eat. The second, third, and fourth kilograms may be used to feed the monkey; and the fifth may go into the banana cream pie. But the only use she has for the sixth kilogram, alas, is to give it to her brother-in-law.

The point is obvious. Each kilogram of bananas contributes something to the satisfaction of Jennifer's needs for the product. But each additional kilogram contributes less (relative to money) than did its predecessor because the use to which it can be put has a lower priority. This, in essence, is the logic behind the **"law" of diminishing marginal utility**.

The third column of Table 19–1 illustrates this concept. The marginal utility (abbreviated MU) of the first kilogram of bananas is $1.20; that is, Jennifer is willing to pay up to $1.20 for the first kilogram. The second kilogram is worth no more than $1.12, the third kilogram only 88¢, and so on until, after the fifth kilogram, the consumer is willing to pay only 16¢ for an additional kilogram (the MU of the sixth kilogram is 16¢).

The numbers in the first and third columns in the table are shown in Figure 19–1 by points *A*, *B*, *C*, and so on. Note that as we move to the right in the graph, the height of the points falls (for example, point *B* is lower than point *A*). This again illustrates

The **"law" of diminishing marginal utility** asserts that additional units of a commodity are worth less and less to a consumer in money terms. As the individual's consumption increases, the marginal utility of each additional unit declines.

FIGURE 19–1
A Typical Marginal Utility or Demand Curve
This demand curve is derived from the consumer's table of marginal utilities by following the optimal purchase rule. The points in the graph correspond to the numbers in Table 19–1.

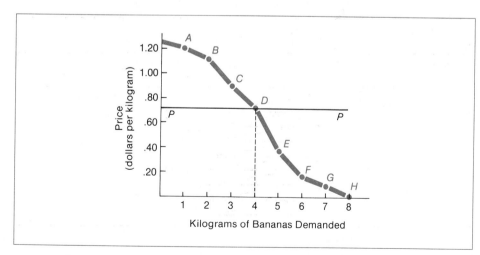

the "law": marginal utility diminishes as the quantity of product obtained by the consumer rises.

The assumption upon which this "law" is based is plausible for most consumers and for most commodities. But, like most laws, there are exceptions. For some people, the more they have of some good that is particularly significant to them, the more they want. Consider the needs of addicts and collectors, for example. The stamp collector who has a few stamps may consider the acquisition of one more to be mildly amusing. The person who has a large and valuable collection may be prepared to go to the ends of the earth for another stamp. Similarly, the alcoholic who finds a dry martini quite pleasant when he first starts drinking may find one more to be absolutely irresistible once he has already consumed four or five. Economists, however, generally treat such cases of *increasing marginal utility* as anomalies. For most goods and most people, marginal utility probably declines as consumption increases.

The Optimal Purchase Rule

Now let us put the concept of marginal utility to work in analyzing consumer choice. Every consumer has a limited amount of money to spend. Which items will he or she buy, and in what quantities? The theory of consumer choice is based on the hypothesis that consumers will spend their money in the way that *maximizes their total utility*. This hypothesis leads to the following **optimal purchase rule**:

It always pays the consumer to buy more of any commodity whose marginal utility (measured in money) exceeds its price, and less of any commodity whose marginal utility is less than its price. When possible, the consumer should buy the quantity of each good at which price (P) and marginal utility (MU) are exactly equal; that is, at which

$$P = \text{MU},$$

because only these quantities will maximize the *total utility* he or she gains from the purchases given the fact that the money available must be divided up among all the goods bought.[2]

Notice that while our concern is with *total* utility, the rule is framed in terms of *marginal* utility. Marginal utility is not important for its own sake, but rather as an instrument used to calculate the level of purchases that maximizes total utility.

To see why this rule works, refer to the table and graph of marginal utilities of bananas (Table 19–1 and Figure 19–1). Suppose the supermarket is selling bananas for 72¢ a kilogram (line *PP* in the graph) and Jennifer considers buying only two kilograms. We see that this is not a wise decision, because the marginal utility of the third kilogram of bananas (88¢) is greater than its 72¢ price. If Jennifer were to increase her purchase to three kilograms, the additional kilogram would cost 72¢ but yield 88¢ in marginal utility (point *C*); thus the additional purchase would bring her a clear net gain of 16¢. Obviously, at the 72¢ price she is better off with three kilograms of bananas than with two.

Similarly, at this price, five kilograms (point *E*) is *not* an optimal purchase because the marginal utility of the fifth kilogram is less than its 72¢ price. Jennifer would be better off with only four kilograms, since that would save her 72¢ with only a 36¢ loss in utility—a net gain of 36¢ from the decision to buy one kilogram less. In

[2] We can equate a dollar price with marginal utility only because we measure marginal utility in money terms (or, as the matter is usually put by economists, because we deal with the marginal rate of substitution of money for the commodity in question). If marginal utility were measured in some psychological units not directly translatable into money terms, a comparison of *P* and MU would have no meaning. However, MU could also be measured in terms of any commodity other than money. (*Example*: How much root beer is Jennifer willing to trade for an additional banana?)

sum, our rule for optimal purchases tells us that Jennifer should not end up buying a quantity at which MU is far higher than price (points *A*, *B*, and *C*) because from any such point she is better off buying more. Similarly, she should not end up at points *E*, *F*, *G*, or *H*, where MU is below price, because from any such point she is better off buying less. Rather, Jennifer should buy four kilograms (point *D*), where $P = $ MU, since any purchase above this amount yields a marginal utility that is less than price, and any purchase below this amount leaves MU greater than *P*.

It should be noted that price is an objective, observable figure determined by the market, while marginal utility is subjective and reflects the tastes of the consumer. Since consumers lack the power to influence the price, they must adjust their purchases to make the marginal utility of each good equal to the price given by the market.

From Marginal Utility to the Demand Curve

We can use the optimal purchase rule to show that the "law" of diminishing marginal utility implies that demand curves typically slope downward to the right; that is, they have negative slopes. For example, it is possible to use the list of marginal utilities in Table 19–1 to determine precisely how many bananas Jennifer would buy at any particular price. Table 19–2 gives several alternative prices and the optimal purchase quantity corresponding to each. (To make sure you understand the logic behind the optimal purchase rule, verify that the entries in the right-hand column of Table 19–2 are in fact correct. Note that for simplicity of explanation the illustrative prices have been chosen to equal the marginal utilities in Table 19–1. In-between prices would make the optimal choices involve fractions of a kilogram.) This *demand schedule*, which relates quantity demanded to price, may be translated into Jennifer's *demand curve* shown in Figure 19–1. This demand curve is simply the line connecting the marginal utility points, *A*, *B*, *C*, and so on. You can see that it has the characteristic negative slope commonly associated with demand curves.

Let us examine the logic underlying the negatively sloped demand curve a bit more carefully. If Jennifer is purchasing the optimal number of bananas and then the price falls, she will find that her marginal utility of bananas is now above the suddenly reduced price. For example, Table 19–1 tells us that at a price of 88¢ per kilogram it is optimal to buy three kilograms, because the marginal utility (MU) of the fourth kilogram is 72¢. But if price is reduced to anything less than 72¢, it then pays to purchase the fourth kilogram because its MU exceeds its price. This additional kilogram of bananas will lower the marginal utility of the next (fifth) kilogram of bananas to 36¢ in the example, so if the price exceeds 36¢ it will not pay the consumer to buy the fifth kilogram, just as is prescribed in the optimal purchase rule.

Note the critical role of the "law" of diminishing marginal utility. If *P* falls, a consumer who wishes to maximize total utility will see to it that MU falls. According

TABLE 19–2
List of Optimal Quantity to Purchase at Alternative Prices

PRICE (in dollars)	QUANTITY TO PURCHASE
0.08	7
0.16	6
0.36	5
0.72	4
0.88	3
1.12	2
1.20	1

to the "law" of diminishing marginal utility, the only way to do this is to increase the quantity purchased.

While this explanation is a bit abstract and mechanical, it can easily be rephrased in practical terms. We have seen that the various uses to which an individual puts a commodity have different priorities. For Jennifer, giving bananas to her family has a higher priority than using them to make pie, which in turn is of higher priority than giving them to her brother-in-law. If the price of bananas is high, Jennifer will buy only enough for the high-priority uses—those that offer a high marginal utility. When price declines, however, it pays to purchase more of the good—enough for some lower-priority uses. This is the essence of the analysis. It tells us that the same assumption about consumer psychology underlies both the "law" of diminishing marginal utility and the negative slope of the demand curve. They are really two different ways of describing the assumed attitudes of consumers.

The Diamond–Water Paradox: The Puzzle Resolved

We can use marginal utility analysis to solve Adam Smith's diamond–water paradox—his observation that the price of diamonds is much higher than the price of water even though water seems to offer far more utility. The resolution of the diamond–water paradox is based on the distinction between marginal and total utility.

The *total* utility of water—its life-giving benefit—is indeed much higher than that of diamonds, just as Smith observed. But price, as we have seen, is not related directly to total utility. Rather, the optimal purchase rule tells us that price will tend to be equal to *marginal* utility. And there is every reason to expect the marginal utility of water to be very low while the marginal utility of diamonds is very high. Water is extremely plentiful in many parts of the world, and so its price is generally quite low. Consumers use correspondingly large quantities of water. By the principle of diminishing marginal utility, therefore, the marginal utility of water to a typical household will be pushed down to a very low level.

On the other hand, diamonds are very scarce. As a result, the quantity of diamonds consumed is not large enough to drive the MU of diamonds down very far and so buyers are willing to pay high prices for them. The scarcer the commodity, the higher its *marginal utility* and its market price, regardless of the size of its *total* utility.

Thus, like many paradoxes, the diamond–water puzzle has a straightforward explanation. In this case, all one has to remember is that:

Scarcity raises price and *marginal* utility but not necessarily *total* utility.

Consumer Surplus

Economists often want to calculate how much consumers are hurt by having to pay high prices for the commodities that they purchase. For example, because we levy taxes on imported goods and because these tariff costs are included in the price that individuals pay for the goods, consumers are not receiving the benefits of the lower prices that would exist without trade restrictions. How can we estimate the magnitude of these consumer losses?

We can use marginal utility analysis to explain how economists answer this question. Let's return briefly to the numerical example given in Table 19–1. At the price of 72¢ per kilogram, Jennifer decides to buy four kilograms of bananas for a total payment of $4 \times 72¢ = \$2.88$. But how much is Jennifer actually willing to pay for these four kilograms? The answer is equal to the total utility she derives from the four kilograms of bananas, which is \$3.92. Her total willingness to pay exceeds what she has to pay since the value to her of the first few kilograms exceeds the addition to her utility provided by the last (or marginal) unit she purchases. This surplus exists because of the "law" of diminishing marginal utility. Economists note that all con-

FIGURE 19–2
Consumer Surplus

Given this demand curve, which is the same as that shown in Figure 19-1, the total utility from buying 4 kilograms of bananas is equivalent to the whole shaded area. But the total expenditure is only the portion of the shaded area below the price line, *PP*. The upper, triangular portion is the surplus utility gained by the consumer.

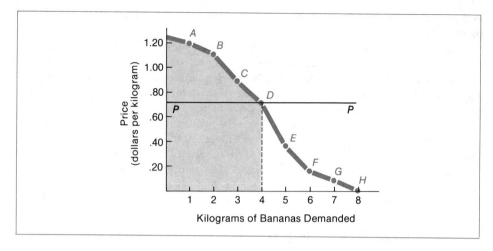

Consumer surplus is the amount by which an individual's total willingness to pay for an item exceeds what he or she has to pay to buy it.

sumers receive a surplus of utility when the market allows them to buy more than one unit of any commodity at a constant price that equals their marginal utility. Economists call this **consumer surplus**. In our example, Jennifer's consumer surplus is the difference between the total utility she receives from the four kilograms of bananas ($3.92) and the total amount she must pay for the four kilograms ($2.88), or $1.04. These amounts are readily recognizable in Figure 19–2. The total utility received from consuming four kilograms of bananas is approximated by the area under the marginal utility curve up to quantity level 4. This is because the sum of the marginal utilities for all four kilograms gives the total utility received. This area is shaded in Figure 19–2. But Jennifer has to pay only four times the going market price (4 × 72¢ = $2.88). This total expenditure is equal to that part of the shaded region in Figure 19–2 that is below line *PP*, the line that defines the going market price. Consumer surplus is the leftover part of the shaded region—that is, the triangle that is below the marginal utility curve but above the market price line *PP*.

We can now see how economists use the concept of consumer surplus. Suppose new trade restrictions raise the price of bananas from 72¢ per kilogram to $1.50 per kilogram. How much is Jennifer, our representative consumer, hurt by this development? The price has risen so much that Jennifer decides not to purchase any bananas. The total utility she could have derived from banana consumption falls by $3.92. But that amount overstates her loss because she now has the $2.88 (which she previously spent on bananas) available to spend on other commodities. Thus, her net losses are equal to the consumer surplus that she previously enjoyed ($1.04). In later chapters, we will use this insight to discuss the burden imposed by several specific taxes and tariffs, as well as by monopoly. As long as economists can obtain a statistical estimate of the demand curve for any commodity, the consumer surplus can be measured easily.

Economists are not the only ones who recognize and use the concept of consumer surplus. Many firms use pricing policies that offer lower prices only to customers who buy relatively large quantities in each market period. (One method is to sell large and small boxes of the item, with the per-kilogram price lower for the large boxes than for the small boxes. Another method is the quantity discount: one pair of socks for $6, six pairs for $25.) The point of this policy is to charge a high price per kilogram to those buyers who buy only a small quantity (and who therefore have a high marginal utility) and to offer the lower price only to those who buy a large quantity. This strategy allows the firm to acquire some of what would otherwise be consumer surplus (if all individuals were permitted to buy the item at the lower price).

The Dutch auction is the classic example of a pricing policy designed to extract consumer surplus from buyers. At the beginning of such an auction, an item is offered for sale at a very high price. The auctioneer keeps lowering the price until someone bids, and the good is then sold at that price to that one bidder. To guard against the

Consumer Surplus Applied: The Issue of Free Medical Care

The diagram in this box illustrates the marginal utility that is derived from medical care. Because *some* medical care is essential to life, the left-hand end of the marginal utility curve never actually touches the vertical axis. This means that the area "under" the marginal utility curve for medical care is infinite. And because medical care is of such great importance to an individual, many take the view that it should be provided free (that is, at a zero user charge at the individual level). Of course, many individuals pay medical-insurance premiums, but the amount they pay each year is independent of the number of visits they have with their doctors. Hence, the additional cost per visit (the user charge) is zero.

But the notion that medical care should be free because it is so important to people confuses *total utility* with *marginal utility*. Beyond a certain amount—say, distance *OA*—further medical care is of very little use to an individual. As with all goods and services, if enough medical care is "consumed," the *marginal* utility of the last units consumed is very low. But if the *price* of an item or a service is zero, individuals will expand their use of it until its marginal utility is essentially zero. Hence, if a very small user charge were imposed for medical care—say, equal to distance *OP*—we could save a tremendous quantity of resources without reducing individuals' utility very much at all.

With the user charge, individuals will choose quantity *OA*, so their loss of utility is equal to area *ABC*. This is a trivial proportion of the overall area under the marginal utility curve (which approaches infinity). Thus, the charge brings a dramatic saving in resources (distance *OA* is much shorter than *OB*) for a very little proportionate loss in total

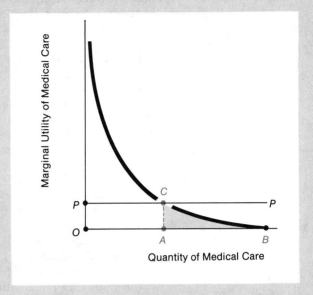

utility. Given that governments are desperately looking for ways of saving resources in areas that involve goods or services provided through the public sector, they should find even rather small user charges tempting. However, some people cannot afford even a small user fee, and many policy-makers do not find it appealing to have one rule for the poor (a zero user fee) and another for everyone else. Hence, user fees are often rejected on equity grounds, even though this decision involves a large cost on efficiency grounds, as our analysis has shown.

---

chance that some other individual may get the item, each individual is tempted to make a bid equal to his full willingness to pay. This is not so true with the kind of auctions common in Canada, which start with a low price and allow an indefinite number of bids, a system that gives each individual many opportunities to have another chance.

The concept of consumer surplus allows us to be quite explicit about one of our **12 Ideas for Beyond the Final Exam**. It used to be thought that neither party to a fair exchange can make a net gain, because each must pay the other just what the good is worth. But this view of the matter makes no sense. If neither party makes any net gain from a trade, why would either take the time and trouble to carry out the transaction? Economists recognized several centuries ago that where an exchange is entirely voluntary and there is no cheating or misrepresentation, there must be a net gain for *both* parties—*there must be mutual gains from trade.*

The same must be true when a consumer makes a purchase from a supermarket or an appliance store: she must expect a net gain from the transaction, or else she will simply not bother to buy. Even if the seller "overcharges" (by whatever standard that is judged), the size of the consumer's net gain may be reduced, but it will not be eliminated altogether. If the seller is so greedy as to charge a price that does wipe the net gain out altogether, the punishment will fit the crime: The consumer will refuse to buy, and the greedy seller's would-be gain will never materialize.

As we have already noted, the net gain that the consumer obtains from a purchase is called consumer surplus. There are numerous current policy issues that can be better understood by appreciating this concept, as the boxed insert on the preceding page illustrates.

Prices, Income, and Quantity Demanded*

Our study of marginal analysis has enabled us to examine the relationship between the price of a commodity and the quantity that will be purchased. But the quantity of the good demanded by a consumer also depends on the consumer's income. Let us first consider briefly how a change in income affects quantity purchased. Then we will use this information to learn more about the effects of a price change.

The Demand Consequences of a Change in Income

The consumer's purchase of commodity X depends on both his income and the price of X. Let us consider what happens to the amount of X a consumer will buy when his real income rises. It may seem almost certain that he will buy more X than before, but that is not necessarily so. A rise in real income can either increase or decrease the quantity of X purchased.

Why might it do the latter? There are some goods and services that people buy only because they cannot afford any better. They eat bologna three days a week and filet mignon twice a year, but they would rather have it the other way around. They use margarine instead of butter or purchase most of their clothing secondhand. If their real income rises, they may then buy more filet mignon and less bologna, more butter and less margarine, more new shirts and fewer secondhand shirts. Thus, a rise in real income will reduce the quantities of bologna, margarine, and secondhand shirts demanded. Economists have given the rather descriptive name **inferior goods** to the class of commodities for which quantity demanded falls when income rises.

The upshot of this discussion is that we cannot draw definite conclusions about the effects of a rise in consumer incomes on quantity demanded. For most commodities, if incomes rise and prices do not change, there will be an increase in quantity demanded. (Such items are often called *normal goods*.) But for the inferior goods there will be a decrease in quantity demanded.

The Two Effects of a Change in Price

A fall in the price of some good—say, heating oil—has two consequences. First, it makes fuel oil cheaper relative to electricity, gas, or coal. We say, then, that the *relative price* of fuel oil has fallen. Second, this price decrease leaves homeowners with more money to spend on movie admissions, soft drinks, or clothing. In other words, the decrease in the price of fuel oil *increases the consumer's real income*—her power to purchase other goods.

While a fall in the price of a commodity always produces these two effects simultaneously, our analysis will be easier if we separate the effects from one another and study them one at a time.

1. *The income effect of a change in price.* As we have just noted, a fall in the price of a commodity leads to a rise in the consumer's *real* income—the amount that her wages will purchase. The consequent effect on quantity demanded is called the **income effect** of the price fall.

    The income effect caused by a fall in a commodity's price is much the same as if the consumer's wages had risen: She will buy more of any commodity that is not an inferior good. The process producing the income effect has three stages: (1) the price of the good falls; causing (2) an increase in the consumer's real income; which

An **inferior good** is a commodity whose quantity demanded falls when the purchaser's real income rises, all other things remaining equal.

The **income effect** is a *portion* of the change in quantity of a good demanded when its price changes. A rise in price cuts the consumer's purchasing power (real income), which leads to a change in the quantity demanded of that commodity. That change is the income effect.

---

*The remainder of this chapter, starting with this section, contains rather more difficult material, which, in shorter courses, may be omitted without loss of continuity.

leads to (3) a change in quantity demanded. Of course, if the price of a good rises, it will produce the same effect in reverse. The consumer's real income will decline, leading to the opposite change in quantity demanded.

2. *The substitution effect of a change in price.*   A change in the price of a commodity produces another effect on quantity demanded that is rather different from the income effect. This is the **substitution effect**, which is the effect on quantity demanded attributable to the fact that the new price is now higher or lower than before *relative to the prices of other goods*. The substitution effect of a price change is the portion of the change in quantity demanded that can be attributed *exclusively* to the resulting change in relative prices rather than to the associated change in real income.

There is nothing mysterious or surprising about the effect of a change in relative prices when the consumer's real income remains unchanged. Whenever it is possible for the consumer to switch between two commodities, she can be expected to buy more of the good whose relative price has fallen and less of the good whose relative price has risen. For example, some years ago the telephone company instituted sharp reductions in the prices of evening long-distance telephone calls relative to daytime calls. The big decrease in the relative price of evening calls brought about a large increase in calling during the evening hours and a decrease in daytime calling, just as the telephone company had hoped. Similarly, a fall in the relative price of fuel oil will induce more of the people who are building new homes to install oil heat instead of electric heat.

When the price of any commodity X rises relative to the price of some other commodity Y, a consumer whose real income has remained unchanged can be expected to buy less X and more Y than before. Thus, *if we consider the substitution effect alone*, a decline in price always increases quantity demanded and a rise in price always reduces quantity demanded.

These two concepts, the income effect and the substitution effect, which many beginning economics students think were invented to torture them, are really quite useful. Let us consider an example of how economists use them. Suppose the price of hamburgers declines while the price of cheese remains unchanged. The *substitution effect* clearly induces the consumer to buy more hamburgers in place of grilled cheese sandwiches, because hamburgers are now comparatively cheaper. What of the *income effect*? Unless hamburger is an inferior good, the income effect leads to the same decision. The fall in price makes consumers richer, which induces them to increase their purchases of all but inferior goods. This example alerts us to two general points:

If a good is not inferior, it must have a downward-sloping demand curve, since income and substitution effects reinforce each other. However, an inferior good may violate this pattern of demand behaviour because the income effect of a decline in price leads consumers to buy less.

Do *all* inferior goods, then, have upward-sloping demand curves? Certainly not, for we have the substitution effect to reckon with, and the substitution effect always favours a downward-sloping demand curve. Thus, we have a kind of tug-of-war in the case of an inferior good. If the *income effect* predominates, the demand curve slopes upward; if the *substitution effect* prevails, the demand curve slopes downward.

Economists have concluded that the substitution effect generally wins out; so while there are many examples of inferior goods, there are few examples of upward-sloping demand curves. When might the income effect prevail over the substitution effect? Certainly not when the good in question (say, margarine) is a very small fraction of the consumer's budget, for then a fall in price makes the consumer only slightly "richer" and therefore creates a very small income effect. But the demand

The **substitution effect** is the change in quantity demanded of a good resulting from a change in its relative price, exclusive of whatever change in quantity demanded may be attributable to the associated change in real income.

The Theory of Consumer Choice and White Rats

A few years ago, a team of economists and psychologists studied whether the theory of consumer choice that we have just outlined—including the different income and substitution effects of a price change—applies to animal species other than *homo sapiens*. According to their research, it does.*

In one experiment, standard laboratory rats were placed in experimental chambers equipped with two levers; pressing one lever rewarded them with a prescribed amount of commodity A (say, water) while pressing the other rewarded them with a prescribed amount of commodity B (say, food). The rats were given a limited "budget," in that they could press the levers only a fixed number of times per day. Once they had exhausted their "income" by pressing the levers, say, 250 times, the lights above the levers would go out, signalling the rats that their presses would no longer result in rewards. Apparently, the little creatures learned the meaning of the lights quite quickly.

In this controlled environment, *income effects* could be observed by varying the permitted number of lever presses per day. The results showed clearly that when more lever presses were allowed, rats chose to consume more of both goods. Apparently, none of the goods, such as food, water, root beer, and Tom Collins mix, was an inferior good from the rats' point of view.

Measuring *substitution effects* was a bit trickier since, as we have stressed, a price change sets in motion *both* an income effect *and* a substitution effect. In the experiment, the "price" of each commodity was controlled by varying the

amount of food or liquid produced by each lever press. Substitution effects were measured, for example, by raising the "price" of food (that is, reducing the amount of food yielded by each press), while at the same time allowing the rat enough additional lever presses to compensate him for his loss of purchasing power. As the analysis of this chapter has suggested, the rats responded to this change in their environment by "buying" less food.

Putting the two effects together, then, a higher price of food led to less consumption of food via the income effect and also to less consumption of food via the substitution effect. The demand curves of these rats were indeed negatively sloped.

---

*John H. Kagel, Raymond C. Battalio, Howard Rachlin, and Leonard Green, "Demand Curves for Animal Consumers," *Quarterly Journal of Economics*, vol. 96, February 1981, pages 1–16.

---

curve could slope upward if an inferior good constitutes a substantial portion of the consumer's budget.

We conclude this discussion of income and substitution effects with a warning against an error that is frequently made. Many students mistakenly close their books thinking that price changes cause substitution effects while income changes cause income effects. This is incorrect. As the foregoing example of hamburgers made clear:

Any change in price sets in motion both a substitution effect and an income effect, both of which affect quantity demanded.

Indifference Curve Analysis

Our analysis of consumer demand, while correct as far as it goes, has one shortcoming: By treating the consumer's decision about the purchase of each commodity as an isolated event, it conceals the necessity of choice imposed on the consumer by his limited budget. It does not indicate explicitly the hard choice behind every purchase decision—the sacrifice of some goods to obtain others. The idea, of course, is implicit because the purchase of a commodity involves a trade-off between that good and money. If you spend more money on rent, you have less to spend on entertainment. If you buy more clothing, you have less money for food. But to represent the consumer's choice problem explicitly, economists have invented two geometric devices, the *budget line* and the *indifference curve*, which we now describe.

Geometry of the Available Choices: The Budget Line

Suppose, for simplicity, that there were only two commodities produced in the world, cheese and records. The decision problem of any household then would be to determine the allocation of its income between these two goods. Clearly, the more it spends on one the less it can have of the other. But just what is the trade-off? A numerical example will answer this question and also introduce the graphical device that economists use to portray the trade-off.

Suppose that cheese costs $2 per kilogram, records sell at $3 each, and our consumer has $12 at his disposal. He obviously has a variety of choices—as displayed in Table 19–3. For example, if he buys no records, he can go home with six kilograms of cheese, and so on. Each of the combinations of cheese and records that the consumer can afford can be shown in a diagram in which the axes measure the quantities of each commodity that are purchased. In Figure 19–3, kilograms of cheese are measured along the vertical axis, number of records is measured along the horizontal axis, and each of the combinations enumerated in Table 19–3 is represented by a labelled point. For example, point A corresponds to spending everything on cheese, point E corresponds to spending everything on records, and point C corresponds to buying two records and three kilograms of cheese.

If we connect points A through E by a straight line, the green line in the diagram, we can trace all the possible ways to divide the $12 between the two goods. For example, point D tells us that if the consumer buys three records, there will be only enough money left to purchase one and a half kilograms of cheese. This is readily seen to be correct from Table 19–3. Line AE is therefore called the **budget line**.

The **budget line** for a household represents graphically all the possible combinations of two commodities that it can purchase, given the prices of the commodities and some fixed amount of money at its disposal.

TABLE 19-3
Alternative Purchase Combinations for a $12 Budget

NUMBER OF RECORDS (at $3 each)	EXPENDITURE ON RECORDS (in dollars)	REMAINING FUNDS (in dollars)	KILOGRAMS OF CHEESE (at $2 per kg)	LABEL IN FIGURE 19-3
0	0	12	6.0	A
1	3	9	4.5	B
2	6	6	3.0	C
3	9	3	1.5	D
4	12	0	0.0	E

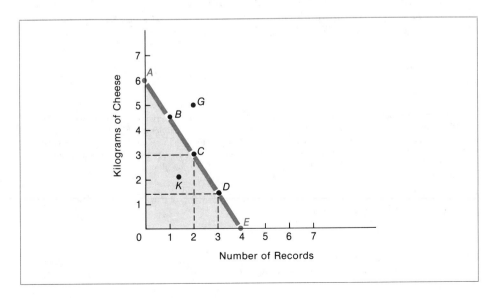

FIGURE 19-3
A Budget Line
This budget line shows the different combinations of cheese and records the consumer can buy with $12 if cheese costs $2 per kilogram and records cost $3 each. At point A the consumer buys six kilograms of cheese and has nothing left over for records. At point E he spends the entire budget on records. At intermediate points (such as C) on the budget line, the consumer buys some of both goods (two records and three kilograms of cheese).

Properties of the Budget Line

Let us now use r to represent the number of records purchased by our consumer and c to indicate the amount of cheese he acquires. Thus, at $2 per kilogram, he spends on cheese a total of $2 \times$ (number of kilograms of cheese bought) $= 2c$ dollars. Similarly, he spends $3r$ dollars on records, making a total of $2c + 3r = \$12$, if the entire $12 is spent on the two commodities. This is the equation of the budget line. It is also the equation of the straight line drawn in the diagram.[3]

We note also that the budget line represents the *maximal* amounts of the commodities that the consumer can afford. Thus, for any given purchase of records, it tells us the greatest amount of cheese his money can buy. If our consumer wants to be thrifty, he can choose to end up at a point below the budget line, such as K. Clearly, then, the choices he has available include not only those points on the budget line AE but also any point in the shaded triangle formed by the budget line AE and the two axes. By contrast, points above the budget line, such as G, are not available to the consumer given his limited budget. A bundle consisting of five kilograms of cheese and two records would cost $16, which is more than he has to spend.

The position of the budget line is determined by two types of data: the prices of the commodities purchased and the income at the buyer's disposal. We can complete our discussion of the graphics of the budget line by examining briefly how a change in either of these magnitudes affects its location.

Obviously, any increase in the income of the household increases the range of options available to it. Specifically, *increases in income produce parallel shifts in the budget line*, as shown in Figure 19–4(a). The reason is simply that a, say, 50 percent increase in available income, if entirely spent on the two goods in question, would permit the family to purchase exactly 50 percent more of *either* commodity. Point A in Figure 19–3 would shift upward by 50 percent of its distance from the origin, while point E would move to the right by 50 percent.[4] Figure 19–4(a) shows three such budget lines corresponding to incomes of $9, $12, and $18, respectively.

Finally, we can ask what happens to the budget line when there is a change in the price of some commodity. In Figure 19–4(b), we see that when the price of records *decreases*, the budget line moves outward, but the move is no longer parallel because the point on the cheese axis remains fixed. Once again, the reason is fairly straightforward. A 50 percent reduction in the price of records permits the family's $12 to buy twice as many records as before: Point E is moved rightward to point H, at which eight records are shown as obtainable. However, since the price of cheese has not changed, point A, the amount of cheese that can be bought for $12, is unaffected. Thus we have the general result that *a reduction in the price of one of the two commodities swings the budget line outward along the axis representing the quantity of that item while leaving the location of the other end of the line unchanged.*

---

[3] The reader may have noticed one problem that arises in this formulation. If every point on the budget line AE is a possible way for the consumer to spend his money, there must be some manner in which he can buy fractional records. Perhaps the purchase of one and a half records can be interpreted to include a down payment of $1.50 on a record on his next shopping trip! Throughout this book it is convenient to assume that commodities are available in fractional quantities when drawing diagrams. This makes the graphs clearer and does not really affect the analysis.

[4] An algebraic proof is simple. Let M (which is initially $12) be the amount of money available to our household. The equation of the budget line can be solved for c, obtaining

$$c + -(3/2)r = M/2.$$

This is the equation of a straight line with a slope of $-3/2$ and with a vertical intercept of $M/2$. A change in M, the quantity of money available, will not change the *slope* of the budget line; it will lead only to parallel shifts in that line.

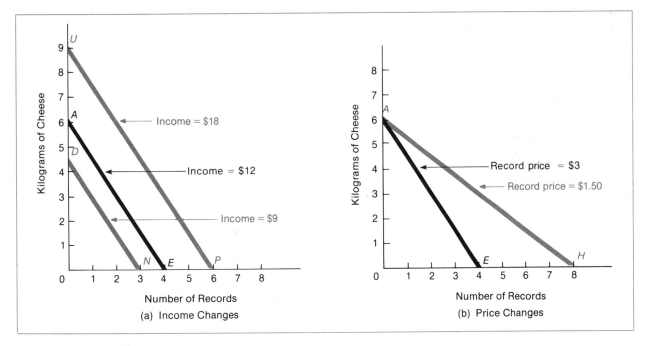

FIGURE 19-4

The Effect of Income and Price Changes on the Budget Line

A change in the amount of money in the consumer's budget causes a parallel shift in the budget line [panel (a)]. A rise in the budget from $12 to $18 raises the budget line from *AE* to *UP*. A fall from $12 to $9 lowers the budget line from *AE* to *DN*. On the other hand, a fall in the price of records causes the end of the budget line on the records axis to swing away from the origin [panel (b)]. A fall in record price from $3 to $1.50 swings the price line from *AE* to coloured line *AH*. This happens because at the higher price, $12 buys only four records, but at the lower price, it buys eight records.

What the Consumer Prefers: The Indifference Curve

The budget line tells us what choices are *available* to the consumer, given the size of his income and the commodity prices fixed by the market. We next must examine the consumer's *preferences* in order to determine which of these possibilities he will want to choose.

After much investigation, economists have determined what they believe to be the minimum amount of information they need about a purchaser in order to analyze his or her choices. This information consists of the consumer's *ranking* of the alternative bundles of commodities that are available. Suppose, for instance, the consumer is offered a choice between two bundles of goods—bundle *W*, which contains three records and one kilogram of cheese, and bundle *T*, which contains two records and three kilograms of cheese. The economist wants to know only whether the consumer prefers *W* to *T*, *T* to *W*, or whether he is *indifferent* about which one he gets. Note that the analysis requires no information about *degree* of preference— whether the consumer is wildly more enthusiastic about one of the bundles or just prefers it slightly.

Graphically, the preference information is provided by a group of curves called **indifference curves** (Figure 19-5)—lines connecting all combinations of the commodities in question that are equally desirable to the consumer. But before we examine these curves, let us see how such a curve is interpreted. A single point on an indifference curve tells us nothing about preferences. For example, point *R* on curve *I*a simply represents the bundle of goods composed of four records and one-half kilogram of cheese. It does *not* suggest that the consumer is indifferent between one-half kilogram of cheese and four records. For the curve to tell us anything, we must consider at least two of its points, for example, points *S* and *W*. Since they represent

An **indifference curve** is a line connecting all combinations of the commodities in question that are equally desirable to the consumer.

FIGURE 19-5

Three Indifference Curves for Cheese and Records

Any point in the diagram represents a combination of cheese and records (for example, *T* represents two records and three kilograms of cheese). Any two points on the same indifference curve (for example, *S* and *W*) represent two combinations of the goods that the consumer likes equally well. If two points, such as *T* and *W*, lie on different indifference curves, the one on the higher indifference curve is preferred by the consumer.

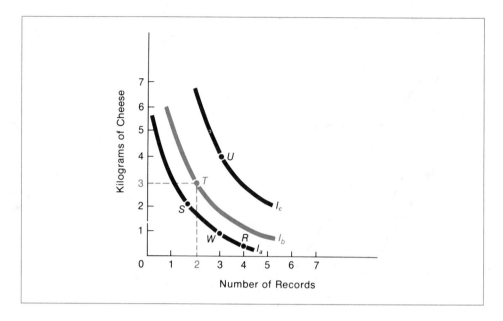

two different combinations that are on the same indifference curve, they are equally desirable to our consumer.

Properties of Indifference Curves

We do not know yet which bundle, among all the bundles he can afford, our consumer prefers; we know only that a choice between certain bundles will lead to indifference. So before we can use an indifference curve to analyze the consumer's choice, we must examine a few of its properties. Most important for us is the fact that:

As long as the consumer desires *more* of each of the goods in question, *every* point on a higher indifference curve (that is, a curve farther from the origin in the graph) will be preferred to *any* point on a lower indifference curve.

In other words, among indifference curves, higher is better. The reason is obvious. Given two indifference curves—say, I_b and I_c in Figure 19-5—the higher curve will contain points lying above and to the right of some points on the lower curve. Thus, point *U* on curve I_c lies above and to the right of point *T* on curve I_b. This means that at *U* the consumer gets more records *and* more cheese than at *T*. Assuming that he desires both commodities, our consumer must prefer *U* to *T*. Since every point on curve I_c is, by definition, equal in preference to point *U*, and the same relation holds for point *T* and all other points along curve I_b, *every* point on curve I_c will be preferred to *any* point on curve I_b.

This at once implies a second property of indifference curves: They never intersect. This is so because if an indifference curve, I_b, is anywhere above another, I_a, then I_b must be above I_a everywhere, since every point on I_b will be preferred to every point on I_a.

Another property that characterizes the indifference curve is its *negative slope*. Again, this holds only if the consumer wants more of both commodities. Consider two points, such as *S* and *R*, on the same indifference curve. If the consumer is indifferent between them, one cannot contain more of *both* commodities than the other. Since point *S* contains more cheese than does point *R*, *R* must offer more records than *S* does, or the consumer would not be indifferent about which he gets. This means that if, say, we move toward the one with the larger number of records, the quantity of cheese must decrease. The curve will always slope downhill toward the right, a negative slope.

A final property of indifference curves is the nature of their curvature—the way they round toward the axes. As drawn, they are "bowed in"—they flatten out (their slopes decrease in absolute value) as they extend from left to right. To understand why this is so we must first examine the economic interpretation of the slope of an indifference curve.

The Slopes of an Indifference Curve and a Budget Line

In Figure 19-6 the average slope of the indifference curve between points M and N is represented by RM/RN. RM is the quantity of cheese the consumer gives up in moving from M to N. Similarly, RN is the increased number of records acquired in this move. Since the consumer is indifferent between bundles M and N, the gain of RN records must just suffice to compensate him for the loss of RM kilograms of cheese. Thus, the ratio RM/RN represents the terms on which the consumer is just willing—*according to his own preferences*—to trade one good for the other. If RM/RN equals two, the consumer is willing to give up (no more than) two kilograms of cheese for one additional record. The *slope of an indifference curve*, then, referred to as the **marginal rate of substitution** between the commodities involved, represents the maximum amount of one commodity the consumer is willing to give up in exchange for one more unit of another commodity.

The slope of the budget line BB in Figure 19-6 is also a rate of exchange between cheese and records. But it no longer reflects the consumer's subjective willingness to trade. Rather, the slope represents the rate of exchange the *market* offers to the consumer when he gives up cheese in exchange for records. Recall that the budget line represents all commodity combinations a consumer can get by spending a fixed amount of money. The budget line is thus a curve of constant expenditure. At current prices, if the consumer reduces his purchase of cheese by amount DE in Figure 19-6, he will save just enough money to buy an additional amount, EF, of records, since at points D and F he is spending the same total number of dollars. The *slope of a budget line*, then, is the amount of one commodity the market requires an individual to give up in order to obtain one additional unit of another commodity without any change in the amount of money spent.

As you can see, the slopes of the two types of curves are perfectly analogous in

The marginal rate of substitution between two commodities is the maximum amount of one commodity the consumer is willing to give up in exchange for one more unit of the other commodity. Geometrically, it is represented by the *slope of an indifference curve.*

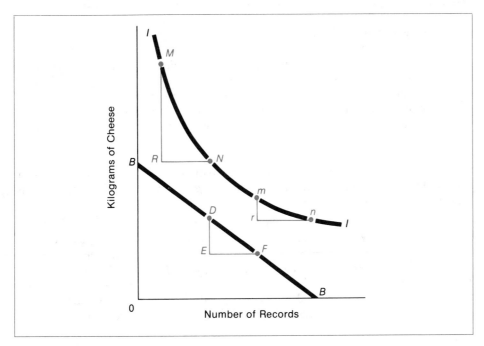

FIGURE 19-6
Slopes of a Budget Line and an Indifference Curve
The slope of the budget line shows how many kilograms of cheese, ED, can be exchanged for EF records. The slope of the indifference curve shows how many kilograms of cheese, RM, the consumer is just willing to exchange for RN records. When the consumer has more records and less cheese (point m as compared with M), the slope of the indifference curve decreases, meaning that the consumer is only willing to give up rm kilograms of cheese for rn records.

their meaning. The slope of the indifference curve tells us the terms on which the *consumer* is willing to trade one commodity for another, while the slope of the budget line reports the *market* terms on which the consumer can trade one good for another.

It is useful to carry our interpretation of the slope of the budget line one step further. Common sense tells us that the market's rate of exchange between cheese and records would be related to their prices, p_c and p_r, and it is easy to show that this is so. Specifically, the slope of the budget line is equal to the ratio of the prices of the two commodities. The reason is straightforward. If the consumer gives up one record, he has p_r more dollars to spend on cheese. But the lower the price of cheese, the greater the quantity of cheese this money will enable him to buy. Purchasing power will be inversely related to its price. Since the price of cheese is p_c per kilogram, these additional funds, p_r dollars, permit him to buy p_r/p_c more kilograms of cheese. Thus the slope of the budget line is p_r/p_c.

Before returning to our main subject, the study of consumer choice, we pause briefly and use our interpretation of the slope of the indifference curve to discuss the third of the properties of the indifference curve—its characteristic curvature—which we left unexplained earlier. With indifference curves being the shape shown, the slope decreases as we move from left to right. We can see in Figure 19–6 that at point m, toward the right of the diagram, the consumer is willing to give up far less cheese for one more record (quantity rm) than he is willing to trade at point M, toward the left. This is because at M he initially has a large quantity of cheese and few records, while at m his initial stock of cheese is low and he has many records. In general terms, the curvature premise on which indifference curves are usually drawn asserts that consumers are relatively eager to trade away a commodity of which they have a large amount but are more reluctant to trade goods of which they hold small quantities. This psychological premise is what is implied in the curvature of the indifference curve.

The Consumer's Choice

We can now use our indifference curve apparatus to analyze how the consumer chooses among the combinations he can afford to buy; that is, the combinations of records and cheese shown by the budget line. Figure 19–7 brings together in the same diagram the budget line from Figure 19–3 and the indifference curves from Figure 19–5.

Since according to the first of the properties of indifference curves the consumer prefers higher to lower curves, he will go to the point on the budget line that lies on the highest indifference curve attainable. This will be point T on indifference curve I_b. He can afford no other point that he likes as well. For example, neither point K below the budget line nor point Z on the budget line gets him on as high an indifference curve, and any point on an indifference curve above I_b, such as point U, is out of the question because it lies beyond his financial means. We end up with a simple rule of consumer choice:

Consumers will select the most desired combination of goods obtainable for their money. The choice will be that point on the budget line at which the budget line is tangent to an indifference curve.

We can see why no point except the point of tangency, T (two records and three kilograms of cheese), will give the consumer the largest utility that his money can buy. Suppose the consumer were instead to consider buying four records and no cheese. This would put him at point Z on the budget line and on indifference curve I_a. But then, by buying fewer records and more cheese (a move to the left on the budget line), he could get to an indifference curve that was higher and hence more desirable without

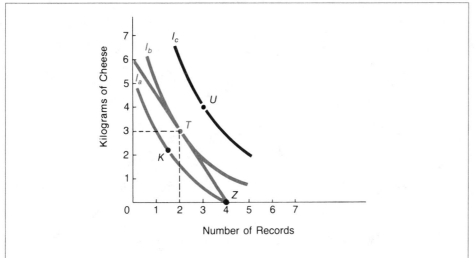

spending any more money. It clearly does not pay to end up at *Z*. Only at the point of tangency, *T*, is there no room for improvement.

At a point of tangency where the consumer's benefits from purchasing cheese and records are maximized, the slope of the budget line equals the slope of the indifference curve. This is true by the definition of a point of tangency. We have just seen that the slope of the budget line is the ratio of the prices of records and cheese. We can therefore restate the requirement for the optimal division of the consumer's money between the two commodities in slightly more technical language:

Consumers will get the most benefit from their money by choosing a combination of commodities whose marginal rate of substitution is equal to the ratio of their prices.

It is worth reviewing the logic behind this conclusion. Why is it not advisable for the consumer to stop at a point like *Z*, where the marginal rate of substitution (slope of the indifference curve) is less than the price ratio (slope of the budget line)? Because by moving upward and to the left along his budget line, he can take advantage of market opportunities to obtain a commodity bundle that he likes better. And this will always be the case if the rate at which the consumer is *personally* willing to exchange cheese for records (his marginal rate of substitution) differs from the rate of exchange offered *on the market* (the slope of the budget line).

Consequences of Income Changes: Inferior Goods

Next, consider what happens to the consumer's purchases when there is a rise in income. We know that a rise in income produces a parallel outward shift in the budget line, such as the shift from *BB* to *CC* in Figure 19–8(a). This moves the consumer's equilibrium from tangency point *P* to tangency point *F* on a higher indifference curve.

A rise in income may or may not increase the demand for a commodity. In the case shown in Figure 19–8(a), the rise in income does lead the consumer to buy more cheese *and* more records. But his indifference curves need not always be positioned in a way that yields this sort of result. In Figure 19–8(b) we see that as the consumer's budget line rises from *BB* to *CC*, the tangency point moves leftward from *H* to *G*, so that when his income rises he actually buys *fewer* records. In this case we infer that records are an *inferior* good.

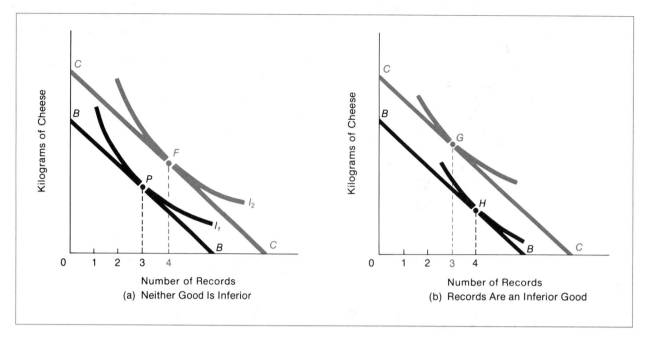

FIGURE 19-8
Effects of a Rise in Income: Inferior Goods
When neither good is inferior [panel (a)], the rise in income causes a parallel shift in the budget line from *BB* to *CC*. The quantity of records demanded rises from three to four, and the quantity demanded of cheese also increases. When records are an inferior good [panel (b)], the upward shift in the budget line from *BB* to *CC* causes the quantity of records demanded to fall from four (point *H*) to three (point *G*).

Consequences of Price Changes: Deriving the Demand Curve

Finally, we come to the main question underlying demand curves: How does our consumer's choice change if the price of one good changes? We learned earlier that a reduction in the price of a record causes the budget line to swing outward along the horizontal axis while leaving its vertical intercept unchanged. In Figure 19–9, we depict the effect of a decline in the price of records on the quantity of records demanded. As the price of records falls, the budget line swings from *BC* to *BD*. The tangency points, *T* and *E*, also move in a corresponding direction, causing the quantity demanded to rise from two to three. The price of records has fallen, and the quantity demanded has risen: The demand curve for records is negatively sloped.

The demand curve for records can be constructed directly from Figure 19–9. Point *T* tells us that two records will be bought when the price of a record is $3. Point *E* tells us that when the price of a record falls to $1.50, quantity demanded rises to three records.[5] These two pieces of information are shown in Figure 19–10 as points *t* and *e* on the demand curve for records. By examining the effects of other possible prices for records (other budget lines emanating from point *B* in Figure 19–9), we can find all the other points on the demand curve in exactly the same way.

The indifference curve diagram also brings out an important point that the demand curve diagram does not show. A change in the *price of records* also has consequences for the *quantity of cheese demanded* because it affects the amount of money left for cheese purchases. In the example illustrated in Figure 19–9, the decrease in the price of records increases the demand for cheese from three to three and three-quarters kilograms.

[5] How do we know that the price of records corresponding to budget line *BD* is $1.50? Since the $12 total budget will purchase at most eight records (point *D*), the price per record must be $12 ÷ 8 = $1.50.

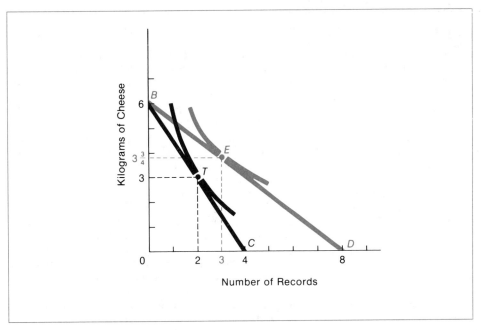

FIGURE 19-9
Consequences of Price Changes

A fall in record price swings the budget line outward from line BC to BD. The consumer's equilibrium point (the point of tangency between the budget line and an indifference curve) moves from T to E. The desired purchase of records increases from two to three, and the desired purchase of cheese increases from three kilograms to three and three-quarters kilograms.

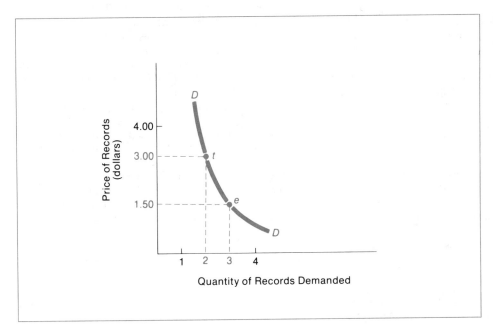

FIGURE 19-10
Deriving the Demand Curve for Records

The demand curve is derived from the indifference curve diagram by varying the price of the commodity in question. Specifically, when the price is $3 per record, we know from Figure 19-9 that the optimal purchase is two records (point T). This information is recorded here as point t. Similarly, the optimal purchase is three records when the price of records is $1.50 (point E in Figure 19-9). This is shown here as point e.

Conclusion

This completes our discussion of the logic behind consumer choice. In the next chapter we will use this analysis as a base upon which to build a theory of demand, thereby taking our first major step toward understanding how the market system operates. Meanwhile, in the current chapter we have laid the foundations for an evaluation of the virtues and shortcomings of the market mechanism as an instrument to serve the consumer's wishes effectively. For tools such as the marginal utility of a purchase and the consumer surplus that this purchase gives to the buyer are instruments used by economists to analyze and evaluate the performance of the market mechanism.

Summary

1. Economists distinguish between total utility and marginal utility. Total utility, or the benefit a consumer derives from a purchase, is measured by the maximum amount of money he or she would give up in order to have the good in question. Rational consumers seek to maximize total utility.

2. Marginal utility is the maximum amount of money a consumer is willing to pay for an additional unit of a commodity. Marginal utility is useful in calculating what set of purchases maximizes total utility.

3. The "law" of diminishing marginal utility is a psychological hypothesis stating that as a consumer acquires more and more of a commodity, the marginal utility of additional units of the commodity will decrease.

4. To maximize the total utility obtained by spending money on some commodity X, given the fact that the other goods can be purchased only with the money that remains after buying X, the consumer must purchase a quantity of X such that the price is equal to the commodity's marginal utility (in money terms).

5. If the consumer acts to maximize utility and if his marginal utility of some good declines when larger quantities are purchased, then his demand curve for the good will have a negative slope. A reduction in price will induce the purchase of more units, leading to a lower marginal utility.

6. Abundant goods tend to have a low price and low marginal utility regardless of whether their total utility is high or low. That is why water can have a low price despite its high total utility.

7. As long as consumers have only to pay a price that equals the marginal utility of the last unit consumed for all units of the item they purchase, they receive a bonus. Economists use the term consumer surplus for this excess of willingness to pay over what is actually paid.

8. An inferior good, such as secondhand clothing, is a commodity consumers buy less of when they get richer, all other things held equal.

9. A rise in the price of a commodity has two effects on quantity demanded: (a) a substitution effect, which makes the good less attractive because it has become more expensive than it was previously, and (b) an income effect, which decreases the consumer's total utility because higher prices cut his purchasing power.

10. Any increase in the price of a good always has a *negative* substitution effect; that is, considering only the substitution effect, a rise in price must reduce the quantity demanded.

11. The income effect of a rise in price may, however, push quantity demanded up or down. For normal goods, the income effect of a higher price (which makes consumers poorer) reduces quantity demanded; for inferior goods, the income effect of higher prices actually increases quantity demanded.

12. Indifference curve analysis permits us to study the interrelationships of the demands for two (or more) commodities. The basic tools of indifference curve analysis are the consumer's budget line and indifference curves.

13. A budget line shows all combinations of two commodities that the consumer can afford, given the prices of the commodities and the amount of money the consumer has available to spend. The budget line is a straight line whose slope equals the ratio of the prices of the commodities. A change in price changes the slope of the budget line. A change in the consumer's income causes a parallel shift in the budget line.

14. Two points on an indifference curve represent two combinations of commodities such that the consumer does not prefer one of the combinations over the other. Indifference curves normally have negative slopes and are "bowed in" toward the origin. The slope of an indifference curve indicates how much of one commodity the consumer is willing to give up in order to get an additional unit of the other commodity.

15. The consumer will choose the point on his budget line that gets him to the highest attainable indifference curve. Normally this will occur at the point of tangency between the two curves. This choice indicates the combination of commodities that gives him the greatest benefits for the amount of money he has available to spend. The consumer's demand curve can be derived from his indifference curve.

Concepts for Review

Diamond–water paradox
Marginal analysis
Total utility
Marginal utility
The "law" of diminishing marginal utility

Optimal purchase rule ($P = \text{MU}$)
Scarcity and marginal utility
Consumer surplus
Inferior goods
Income effect

Substitution effect
Budget line
Indifference curves
Marginal rate of substitution

Questions for Discussion

1. Describe some of the different things you do with water. Which would you give up if the price of water rose a little? If it rose by a fairly large amount? If it rose by a very large amount?

2. Which is greater: your *total* utility from 12 litres of water per day or your total utility from 18 litres per day? Why?

3. Which is greater: your *marginal* utility at 12 litres per day or your marginal utility at 18 litres per day? Why?

4. Some people who do not understand the optimal purchase rule argue that if a consumer buys so much of a good that its price equals its marginal utility, he could not possibly be behaving optimally. Rather, they say, he would be better off quitting when ahead, that is, buying a quantity such that marginal utility is much greater than price. What is wrong with this argument? (*Hint*: What opportunity does the consumer then miss? Is it maximization of marginal or total utility that serves the consumer's interests?)

5. According to Table 19–1, what is Jennifer's loss in consumer surplus if price rises from 72¢ to 88¢ per kilogram of bananas?

6. What inferior goods do you purchase? Why do you buy them? Do you think you will continue to buy them when your income is higher?

7. Which of the following items are likely to be normal goods to a typical consumer? Which are likely to be inferior goods?
   a. Expensive perfume
   b. Paper napkins
   c. Secondhand clothing
   d. Overseas trips

8. Suppose that gasoline and safety pins each rise in price by 20 percent. Which will have the larger income effect on the purchases of a typical consumer? Why?

9. Around 1850, Sir Robert Giffen observed that Irish peasants actually consumed more potatoes as the price of potatoes increased. Use the concepts of income and substitution effects to explain this phenomenon.

10. John Q. Public spends all his income on cheap wine and hot dogs. Draw his budget line when:
    a. His income is $80 and the cost of one bottle of wine and one hot dog is $1.60 each.
    b. His income is $120 and the two prices are as in (a).
    c. His income is $80 and hot dogs cost $1.60 each and wine costs $1.20 per bottle.

11. Draw some hypothetical indifference curves for John Q. Public on a diagram identical to the one you constructed for part (a) of Question 10.
    a. Approximately how much wine and how many hot dogs will Public buy?
    b. How will these choices change if his income increases to $120, as in part (b) of Question 10? Is either good an inferior good?
    c. How will these choices change if wine prices fall to $1.20 per bottle, as in part (c) of Question 10?

12. Explain what information the *slope* of an indifference curve conveys about a consumer's preferences. Use this to explain the typical U-shaped curvature of indifference curves.

20

Market Demand and Elasticity

There was a time when a fool and his money were soon parted, but now it happens to everybody.

ADLAI STEVENSON

Economists who work for business firms are frequently assigned the task of studying consumer demand for the products their companies produce. Business managers count the results of such studies among the most important information they get. Government agencies also gather information about demand, which they use to study a wide variety of issues such as general business conditions and receipts from sales taxes.

The quantity demanded in any market depends on many things: the incomes of consumers, the price of the good, the prices of other goods, the volume and effectiveness of advertising, and so on. Demand analysis deals with all these influences, but it has traditionally focussed on the price of the good in question. The reason is that the market price of a commodity plays a crucial role in influencing both quantity supplied and quantity demanded, and, in equilibrium, price is set at the level that makes these two quantities equal. This role of price was studied in Chapter 3, and we will return to it time and again throughout the book.

We begin this chapter by showing how the market-demand curve for a product is derived from the individual-demand curves of the individual consumers. Next we turn to the "law" of demand, which tells us that quantity demanded decreases as price increases. Third, we pose a question: Who pays for the sales taxes levied on a product—consumers or producers? The important concept of elasticity is introduced as a way to measure the responsiveness of quantity demanded to price, and it is then used to answer this question. Fourth, we turn to variables other than price that influence quantity demanded. And, finally, we explain the importance of the time period to which a demand curve applies and, in an appendix, describe how this can create problems in obtaining demand information from statistical data. Near the end of the chapter we also provide some examples of how knowledge of elasticity can illuminate important policy issues, such as the farm-income problem.

From Individual-Demand Curves to Market-Demand Curves

In the last chapter we studied how *individual-demand curves* are derived from the logic of consumer choice. Each consumer seeks to attain the highest total utility permitted by his limited budget and, in the process, will typically react to a higher price by reducing his quantity demanded. But to understand how the market system works we must derive the relationship between price and quantity demanded in *the market as a whole*—the **market-demand curve**.

If each individual pays no attention to other people's purchase decisions when making his own, it is straightforward to derive the market-demand curve from the customers' individual-demand curves. We simply *add* the negatively sloping

A **market-demand curve** shows how the total quantity demanded of some product during a specified period of time changes as the price of that product changes, holding other things constant.

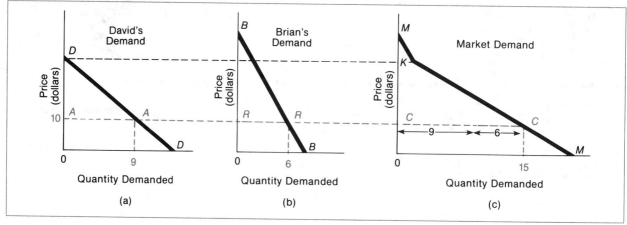

FIGURE 20–1

The Relationship between Total Market Demand and the Demands of Individual Consumers within That Market

If David and Brian are the customers for a product, and at a price of $10 David demands 9 units [line *AA* in part (a)] and Brian demands 6 units [line *RR* in part (b)], then total quantity demanded by the market at that price is 9 + 6 = 15 [line *CC* in part (c)]. In other words, we obtain the market-demand curve by adding horizontally all points on each consumer's demand curve at each given price. Thus, at a $10 price we have length *CC* on the market-demand curve, which is equal to *AA* + *RR* on the individual-demand curves. (The sharp angle at point *K* on the market curve occurs because it corresponds to the price at which David, whose demand pattern is different from Brian's, first enters the market. At any higher price, only Brian is willing to buy anything.)

individual-demand curves *horizontally* as shown in Figure 20–1. There we see three schedules: individual-demand curves *DD* and *BB* for two people, David and Brian, and the total (market-) demand curve *MM*.

Specifically, this market-demand curve is constructed as follows. *Step 1*: Pick any relevant price, say $10. *Step 2*: At that price, determine David's quantity demanded (9 units) from David's demand curve in part (a) of Figure 20–1 and Brian's quantity demanded (6 units) from Brian's demand curve in part (b). Note that these quantities are indicated by line segment *AA* for David and line segment *RR* for Brian. *Step 3*: Add Brian's and David's quantities demanded at the $10 price (segment *AA* + segment *RR* = 9 + 6 = 15) to yield the total quantity demanded by the market at that price [line segment *CC*, with total quantity demanded equal to 15 units, in part (c)]. Now repeat the process for all alternative prices to obtain other points on the market-demand curve until the shape of the entire curve *MM* is indicated. That is all there is to the adding-up process.

The "Law" of Demand

A formal definition of the demand curve for an entire market was given in Chapter 3 and again in the margin of the previous page. We shall pay much attention in this chapter to the "other things" referred to in this definition. But for now, let us focus on price, and note that the total quantity demanded by the market normally moves in the opposite direction from price. Economists call this relationship the **"law" of demand**.

The **"law" of demand** states that a lower price generally increases the amount of a commodity that people in a market are willing to buy. So, for most goods, demand curves have a negative slope.

Notice that we have put the word *law* in quotation marks. By now you will have observed that economic laws are not always obeyed, and we shall see in a moment that the "law" of demand is not without its exceptions. But first let us see why the "law" usually holds.

In Chapter 19 we learned that individual-demand curves are usually downward sloping because of the "law" of diminishing marginal utility. If individual-demand curves slope downward, then we see from the preceding discussion of the adding-up process that the market-demand curve must also slope downward. This is just common sense: If every consumer in the market buys fewer bananas when the price of bananas rises, then the total quantity demanded in the market must surely fall.

But market-demand curves may slope downward even when individual-demand curves do not, because not all consumers are alike. For example, if a bookstore reduces the price of a popular novel, it may draw many new customers, but few customers will be induced to buy two copies. Similarly, people differ in their fondness for bananas. True devotees may maintain their purchases of bananas even at exorbitant prices, while others will not eat a banana even if it is offered free of charge. As the price of bananas rises, the less enthusiastic banana-eaters drop out of the market entirely, leaving the expensive fruit to the more devoted consumers. Thus, the quantity demanded declines as price rises simply because higher prices induce more people to kick the banana habit. Indeed, for many commodities, it is the appearance of new customers in the *market* when prices are lower, rather than the negative slope of *individual* demand curves, that accounts for the law of demand.

This point is also illustrated in Figure 20–1, where we see that at a price higher than 0D only Brian will buy the product. However, at a price below 0D David is also induced to make some purchases. Hence, below point K the market-demand curve lies further to the right than it would have if David had not been induced to enter the market. To put the point another way, a rise in price from a level below D to a level above D will cut quantity demanded for two reasons: first, because Brian's demand curve has a negative slope; and second, because it drives David out of the market.

We conclude, therefore, that the law of demand stands on fairly solid ground. If individual-demand curves are downward sloping, then the market-demand curve surely will be, too. And the market-demand curve may slope downward even when individual-demand curves do not.

Nevertheless, exceptions to the law of demand have been noted. One common exception occurs when quality is judged on the basis of price—the more expensive a product, the better it is believed to be. For example, many people buy brand-name aspirin, even if right next to it on the drugstore shelf there is a "generic" aspirin, with an identical chemical formula, sold at half the price. The consumers who buy branded aspirin may well use comparative price to judge the relative qualities of different brands. They may prefer Brand X to Brand Y because X is slightly more expensive. If Brand X were to reduce its price below that of Y, consumers might assume that it was no longer superior and actually reduce their purchases of it.

Another possible cause of an upward-sloping demand curve is snob appeal. If part of the reason for purchasing a Rolls Royce is to advertise one's wealth, a decrease in the car's price may actually reduce sales, even if the quality of the car is unchanged. Other types of exceptions have also been noted by economists, but, for most commodities, it seems quite reasonable to assume that demand curves have a negative slope, an assumption that is supported by the data.

Application: Who Pays an Excise Tax?

The law of demand has many applications. Suppose, for example, that 18 million pocket books are sold per year, and the government considers placing a $4 tax on each book sold (called an **excise tax**), hoping to collect $72 million in revenue per year ($4 per book times 18 million books). The law of demand tells us that the government will collect less than $72 million. Why? Because the excise tax will push up the price and that will reduce quantity demanded below 18 million.

An **excise tax** is a tax levied as a fixed amount of money per unit of product sold or as a fixed percentage of the purchase price.

Knowing that revenues will rise by less than $72 million is useful, but it is not enough. If quantity demanded is highly responsive to price, a rise in price will cause consumers to cut back more sharply on book purchases—and the government will get less money from its tax—than if consumers are less sensitive to price in their demand for this item. So, to determine its tax receipts, the government needs to estimate *how*

TABLE 20–1
Demand and Supply Schedules for Pocket Books

PRICE (dollars)	QUANTITY SUPPLIED	QUANTITY DEMANDED
	(millions of books per year)	
10	30	0
9	27	1
8	24	3
7	21	9
6	18	18
5	15	27
4	12	36
3	9	45

much the price will rise and *how much* quantity demanded will fall. For this purpose, the government needs a *quantitative measure* of the responsiveness of quantity demanded to price. Such a measure is the main subject of this chapter. But, to see how tax revenues can be estimated, we must detour briefly. In the process, we will also learn who really pays the excise tax.

Table 20–1 presents hypothetical supply and demand schedules for books in a format that is familiar from Chapter 3. You can see that the equilibrium price is $6 per book and the equilibrium quantity is 18 million books per year [point *A* in Figure 20–2(a)]. Now, what happens if the government imposes a $4 per book excise tax? To find the answer we must first determine what a $4 excise tax does to the supply curve.

The Effect of the Tax on the Supply Curve

We do this by answering a series of hypothetical questions about how sellers would react to the tax at different levels of market price.

First, if books sell for $12, including the tax, how many will be supplied? The key point here is that suppliers will receive only $8 per book—$12 minus the $4 tax. Therefore, the tax-free supply schedule in Table 20–1 (third line) tells us that quantity

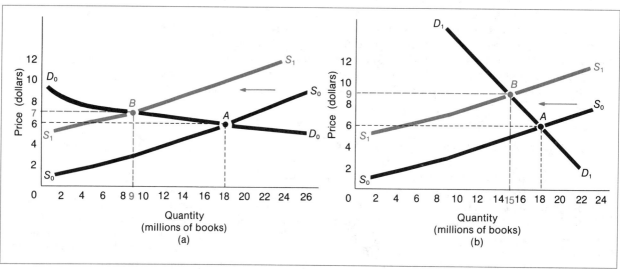

FIGURE 20–2
Who Pays an Excise Tax?

A $4 excise tax shifts the supply curve vertically upward by $4—from S_0S_0 to S_1S_1. The market equilibrium therefore shifts from point *A* to point *B*. In part (a), the demand curve D_0D_0 is rather flat, so the price rises only $1 (from $6 to $7) while the quantity falls dramatically (from 18 million to 9 million). Producers pay most of the tax. In part (b), the demand curve D_1D_1 is much steeper, so the price rises by $3 and quantity falls by much less (only 3 million books). Consumers pay most of the tax.

TABLE 20–2
Effect on the Book Market of a $4 Excise Tax

PRICE INCLUDING TAX (dollars)	PRICE RECEIVED BY SUPPLIERS (dollars)	QUANTITY SUPPLIED	QUANTITY DEMANDED
		(millions of books per year)	
12	8	24	0
11	7	21	0
10	6	18	0
9	5	15	1
8	4	12	3
7	3	9	9
6	2	6	18
5	1	3	27

supplied will be 24 million books per year. Thus, at a price to customers of $12 each, quantity supplied is 24 million books. This information is recorded in the top row of Table 20–2.

The rest of the supply schedule in Table 20–2 is constructed similarly. For example, a $10 price nets the seller $6, which, according to Table 20–1, leads to a quantity supplied of 18 million books. And so on.

A pattern is apparent in Table 20–2. At any given price, suppliers will provide the same quantity after the tax as they previously provided at a price $4 lower. Thus, we conclude that:

An excise tax shifts the supply curve upward by the amount of the tax.

This conclusion is just common sense. After all, suppliers care about the price they receive, not about the price buyers pay. Graphically, our conclusion is depicted in part (a) of Figure 20–2, which shows the demand curve D_0D_0 and the two supply curves—S_0S_0 before tax and S_1S_1 after tax. The two supply curves are parallel and $4 apart.

The Role of the Shape of the Demand Curve

Now we can answer the questions of interest: How much will the market price rise as a result of the tax? How much will the quantity fall? And how much revenue will the government collect?

The answers depend on the responsiveness of quantity demanded to price changes—that is, on the shape of the demand curve. We start with a case in which demand is relatively responsive [part (a) of Figure 20–2]; that is, a small (vertical) change in price leads to a large (horizontal) change in quantity, making the demand curve rather flat.

Figure 20–2(a) shows that in this case the $4 excise tax raises the equilibrium price from $6 per book (point A) to $7 (point B). Because this lowers the quantity sold from 18 million to 9 million books per year, the government will collect only $36 million ($4 times 9 million) rather than $72 million.

In this example, the price rises by only one-fourth as much as the tax (from $6 to $7), so consumers wind up paying only one-fourth of the tax. The other $3 of tax is paid by businesses, which now collect only $3 per book ($7 less $4 tax) instead of $6. But consumers do not always pay such a small fraction of an excise tax. The way the tax burden is shared depends on how responsive quantity demanded is to price. In this example, quantity demanded responds very strongly.[1]

---

[1] The distribution of the tax burden also depends on the responsiveness of quantity *supplied* to price. But we are concentrating on demand here.

Part (b) of Figure 20–2 shows that things work out quite differently if quantity demanded is much less responsive to price. Demand curve D_1D_1 is much steeper than demand curve D_0D_0, meaning that a given change in price elicits a much smaller quantity response.[2] As a result, the equilibrium price rises by much more ($3 instead of $1), and the quantity demanded falls by much less (only 3 million instead of 9 million).

With the unresponsive demand curve D_1D_1, consumers pay three-quarters of the tax and firms pay only one-quarter. And, since the decline in quantity is much smaller in part (b) than in part (a), the government collects more revenue—$60 million per year ($4 times 15 million) in part (b) rather than the $36 million in part (a). The quantity of tax collected and the shape of the demand curve are related for a simple reason. The more responsive the demand curve is, the more the tax will cause quantity demanded to fall, and so the less tax revenues will rise. Thus we conclude that *responsiveness* is the key influence here.

The less responsive consumer demand is to a change in price, the larger is the share of any excise tax that is paid by consumers and the more total tax revenue the government collects, other things being equal.

Consumer demand tends to be relatively unresponsive to changes in the price of goods that are considered necessities (as we explain in greater detail later in the chapter). Is it any wonder, then, that the highest sales taxes in Canada are on gasoline (generally considered a necessity) and on alcohol and tobacco (considered a necessity by a devoted group of consumers)? For example, two-thirds of the price of a bottle of liquor is tax, and the tax rate on gasoline is slightly higher than 50 percent.

Clearly, we need a good way to measure demand responsiveness to price changes —a subject to which we turn next. (Note: The concept of consumer surplus is also relevant here. Question 14 at the end of this chapter shows how it can be used to determine which commodities should be taxed. We also discuss this matter more fully in Chapter 30.)

Elasticity: The Measure of Responsiveness

It is not only governments that need a way to measure the responsiveness of quantity demanded to price. So do other users of demand information, such as business firms, which need it for decisions on pricing of products, on whether to develop new models of their products, and so on. Economists measure this responsiveness by means of a concept they call **elasticity**. A demand curve indicating that consumers respond sharply to a change in price is said to be "elastic" (or "highly elastic"). A demand curve involving a relatively small or insignificant response by consumers to a given price change is called "inelastic."

> The (price) elasticity of demand is the ratio of the *percentage* change in quantity demanded to the *percentage* change in price that brings about the change in quantity demanded.

The precise measure used for this purpose is called the **price elasticity of demand**, or sometimes simply the **elasticity of demand**, and it is defined as the ratio of the *percentage* change in quantity demanded to the associated *percentage* change in price. Specifically:

$$\text{Elasticity of demand} = \frac{\%\text{ change in quantity demanded}}{\%\text{ change in price}}.$$

Thus, demand is called **elastic** if, say, a 10 percent rise in price leads to a reduction in quantity demanded greater than 10 percent. The demand is called **inelastic** if such a price rise reduces quantity demanded by any amount less than 10 percent.

[2] The reader should verify that a fall in price from $7 to $6 per book raises quantity demanded by 9 million books in part (a) but only by about 1 million books in part (b).

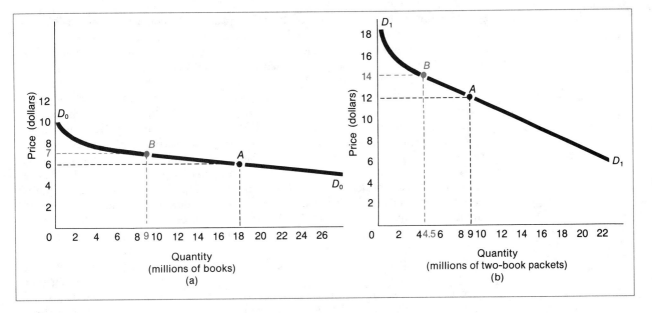

FIGURE 20-3

The Sensitivity of Slope to Units of Measurement

The slope of a curve changes whenever we change units of measurement. Part (a) repeats Figure 20-2(a); the demand curve looks very flat. In part (b), we measure quantity in two-book packets, so all the quantities are cut in half and all the prices are doubled. As a result, the demand curve looks rather steep. But the two demand curves present exactly the same information.

Let us now consider how these definitions can be used to analyze a demand curve. At first, it may seem that the *slope* of the demand curve conveys the information we need: Since curve D_1D_1 is much steeper than curve D_0D_0 in Figure 20-3, any given change in price corresponds to a much larger change in quantity demanded in panel (a) than in panel (b), and thus it is tempting to call the curve in panel (a) "more elastic." But slope will not do the job because the slope of any curve depends on the units of measurement, as we saw in the appendix to Chapter 1, and in economics there are no standardized units of measurement. Cloth output may be measured in metres or yards, milk in litres or quarts, and coal in kilograms or tonnes.[3]

It is because of this problem that economists use the elasticity measure, which is based on *percentage* changes in price and quantity rather than on *absolute* changes. The elasticity formula solves the units problem because percentages are unaffected by units of measurement. If nominal GDP doubles, it goes up by 100 percent, whether

---

[3] An example will illustrate the problem. Figure 20-3(a) repeats the demand curve D_0D_0 from Figure 20-2(a). It looks flat. Specifically, its slope between points A and B is:

$$\text{Slope} = \frac{\text{change in price}}{\text{change in quantity demanded}} = \frac{\$1.00}{9} = 0.11.$$

But suppose we measure quantity in millions of two-book packets, instead of in millions of single books. This is done in Figure 20-3(b), and here the demand curve looks very steep. Between points A and B, price changes by $2 per package (that is, $1 per book) and quantity demanded changes by 4.5 million packages (9 million books). So the slope is now:

$$\text{Slope} = \frac{\text{change in price}}{\text{change in quantity demanded}} = \frac{\$2.00}{4.5} = 0.44.$$

This is quite a change in slope. But nothing has really changed. Points A and B represent exactly the same quantities and prices in both figures. Only the units of measurement have changed.

measured in millions or billions of dollars. If your height doubles between age 5 and age 15, it goes up 100 percent, whether measured in inches or in centimetres.[4]

In the formula that is actually used to measure price elasticity of demand, then, both the change in quantity demanded and the change in price are expressed as *percentages*. In addition to using percentages, the elasticity formula usually used in practice has a second important attribute: The change in quantity is not calculated either as a percentage of the "initial" quantity or as a percentage of the "subsequent" quantity, but *as a percentage of the average of the two quantities*. Similarly, the change in price is expressed as a percentage of the average of the two prices in question. To see why the issue arises, consider, as an example, the demand information presented in Table 20-1 (page 432). At a price of $6, quantity demanded is 18 million books; at a price of $7, quantity demanded is 9 million books. Suppose that a book company is deciding whether to price its product at $6 or $7. The difference in sales volume is 18 million − 9 million = 9 million. This 9-million-unit difference in sales is 50 percent of 18 million but 100 percent of 9 million. Which is the correct figure to use as the percentage change in quantity?

This problem is always with us because any given change in quantity must involve some larger quantity Q_L (18 million in our example) and some smaller quantity Q_S (9 million), so that a given change in quantity must be a relatively small percentage of Q_L and a relatively large percentage of Q_S. Obviously, neither of these can claim to be *the* right percentage change in quantity. We therefore use what appears to be a compromise—the *average* of the two quantities. In terms of our example, we use the average of 18 million and 9 million—that is, 13.5 million—in our calculation of the percentage change in quantity. Thus:

$$\text{Percentage change in quantity} = 9 \text{ million as a percentage of } 13.5 \text{ million}$$
$$= 66\tfrac{2}{3} \text{ percent}$$

Similarly, in calculating the percentage change in price, we take the $1 change in price as a percentage of the average of $7 and $6, giving us $1/$6.50, or 15.4 percent, approximately.[5]

SUMMARY

The elasticity formula has two basic attributes:

1. It deals only in percentages.

2. It calculates percentage change in terms of the average value of the quantities or prices at issue.

In addition, the formula usually drops all minus signs (see footnote 5).

---

[4]Applying the elasticity formula given above to our example illustrates that it really does solve the units problem. In moving from point *A* to point *B* in either version of Figure 20–3, quantity demanded declines by 50 percent—from 18 million to 9 million in panel (a), or from 9 million to 4.5 million in panel (b). Similarly, the percentage rise in price from $6 to $7 in panel (a) or from $12 to $14 in panel (b) is 16.67 percent whether we use dollars, dimes, or pennies.

Mathematically, the reason is straightforward. If H_a and H_b represent height at age 5 and age 15, respectively, the formula for the percentage rise in height is $(H_b - H_a)/H_a$. Since an inch is about 2.5 centimetres, if we switch from inches to centimetres, in this formula both the numerator and the denominator are multiplied by 2.5. These 2.5s then cancel out, leaving the percentage figure unaffected by the switch from inches to centimetres.

[5]Recall that, by the law of demand, when price increases, quantity demanded will normally decrease, and vice versa. That is, when the percentage change in price is positive, the percentage change in quantity demanded will be negative, and vice versa. So our elasticity formula would normally produce a *negative* number. In calculating elasticity it is customary to disregard the minus sign to make the elasticity a *positive* number. That way, a *larger* elasticity number means that demand is *more* responsive to price.

We can now state the formula for price elasticity of demand. Keeping in mind all these features of the formula, we have:

Price elasticity of demand =

$$\frac{\text{Change in quantity as \% of average of the two quantities}}{\text{Change in price as \% of average of the two prices}},$$

so that in our example,

$$\text{Elasticity} = \frac{9 \text{ million as \% of } (18 \text{ million} + 9 \text{ million})/2}{\$1 \text{ as \% of } (\$7 + \$6)/2} = \frac{66.67\%}{15.38\%} = 4.33.$$

For easy reference, the elasticity calculation for an additional example (for a demand curve that we have not drawn) is given in compact form in Table 20–3. For this demand curve, when P is 12, Q is 17, and when P is 8, Q is 23. The change in P is $12 - 8 = 4$, and average P is $(12 + 8)/2 = 10$, so the change in P is 4 as a percentage of 10, or 40 percent. Similarly, the change in Q is $23 - 17 = 6$, and average Q is $(23 + 17)/2 = 20$, so the change in Q is 6 as a percentage of 20, or 30 percent. Hence:

$$\text{Elasticity} = 30/40 = 0.75.$$

TABLE 20–3
Calculation of Price Elasticity of Demand

	PRICE	QUANTITY
Situation 1	$P_1 = 12$	$Q_1 = 17$
Situation 2	$P_2 = 8$	$Q_2 = 23$
Change	$P_1 - P_2 = 12 - 8 = 4$	$Q_2 - Q_1 = 23 - 17 = 6$
Average	$(P_1 + P_2)/2 = 20/2 = 10$	$(Q_2 + Q_1)/2 = 40/2 = 20$
% change	4 as % of 10 = 40%	6 as % of 20 = 30%
	Elasticity = % change in quantity/% change in price = 30/40 = 0.75	

Elasticity and the Shape of Demand Curves

Figure 20–4 shows how elasticity of demand is related to the shape of the demand curve. We begin with two extreme but important cases. Part (a) depicts a demand curve that is simply a vertical line. This curve is called *perfectly inelastic* throughout because its elasticity is zero. This means that consumer purchases do not respond at all to any change in price. That is, quantity demanded remains at 90 units no matter what the price; thus, the percentage change in quantity is always zero and hence the elasticity is zero. Such a demand curve is quite unusual. It may perhaps be expected when the price range being considered already involves very low prices from the point of view of the consumer. It does occur when the item (for example, insulin) is considered absolutely essential by the consumer.

Part (b) of Figure 20–4 shows the opposite extreme: a horizontal demand curve. It is said to be *perfectly elastic* (or "infinitely elastic"). If there is the slightest rise in price, quantity demanded will drop to zero; that is, the percentage change in quantity demanded would be infinitely large. This may be expected to occur where a rival product that is just as good in the consumer's view is available at the going price ($5 in our diagram). In cases where no one will pay more than the going price, the seller will lose all his customers if he raises his price even one penny.

Part (c) depicts a case between these two extremes: a *straight-line* demand curve,

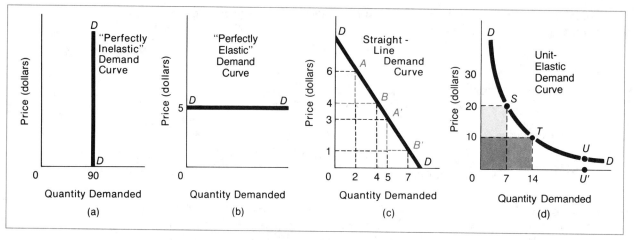

FIGURE 20–4

Demand Curves with Different Elasticities

The vertical demand curve in part (a) is *perfectly inelastic* (elasticity = 0)—quantity demanded remains the same regardless of price. The horizontal demand curve in part (b) is *perfectly elastic*—at any price above $5, quantity demanded falls to zero. Part (c) shows a *straight-line demand curve*. Its *slope* is constant, but its *elasticity* is not. Part (d) depicts a *unit-elastic* demand curve whose constant elasticity is 1.0 throughout. A change in price pushes quantity demanded in the opposite direction but does not affect total expenditure. When price equals $20, total expenditure is price times quantity, or $20 × 7 = $140; and when price equals $10, expenditure equals $10 × 14 = $140.

which is neither vertical nor horizontal. Though the *slope* of a straight-line demand curve is constant throughout its length, its *elasticity* is not.

As we move down a straight-line demand curve, a given numerical change in quantity constitutes an ever smaller percentage change in quantity, while a given numerical change in price constitutes an ever larger percentage change in price. Since elasticity is defined as the percentage change in quantity divided by the percentage change in price, the numerator of the elasticity fraction gets smaller and the denominator gets larger as we move down a straight-line demand curve. Consequently:

Along a straight-line demand curve, the price elasticity of demand grows steadily smaller as we move from left to right. That is so because the quantity keeps getting larger, so that a given numerical change in quantity becomes an ever smaller percentage change, while the price keeps going lower so that a given numerical change in price becomes an ever larger percentage change.

Example: The elasticity of demand between points *A* and *B* in Figure 20–4(c) is:

$$\frac{\text{Change in } Q \text{ as } \% \text{ of average } Q}{\text{Change in } P \text{ as } \% \text{ of average } P} = \frac{2 \text{ as } \% \text{ of } (2+4)/2}{2 \text{ as } \% \text{ of } (4+6)/2}$$

$$= \frac{2/3}{2/5} = \frac{66\frac{2}{3}\%}{40\%} = 1.67 \text{ (approx.)}.$$

But the elasticity of demand between points *A'* and *B'* is:

$$\frac{2 \text{ as } \% \text{ of } (5+7)/2}{2 \text{ as } \% \text{ of } (3+1)/2} = \frac{2/6}{2/2} = \frac{33\frac{1}{3}\%}{100\%} = 0.33 \text{ (approx.)}.$$

If the elasticity of a straight-line demand curve varies from one part of the curve to another, what is the appearance of a demand curve with the same elasticity throughout its length? For reasons given in the next section, it looks like the curve in Figure 20–4(d), which is a curve with elasticity equal to one throughout (a *unit-elastic* demand curve). That is, a unit-elastic demand curve bends in the middle toward the origin of the graph and at either end moves closer and closer to the axes but never touches or crosses the axes.

As we have seen, it is conventional to speak of a curve whose elasticity is greater than one (the percentage change in quantity is greater than the percentage change in price) as an *elastic* demand curve and of one whose elasticity is less than one (the percentage change in quantity is less than the percentage change in price) as an *inelastic* curve. When elasticity is exactly one, we say the curve is unit-elastic. This terminology is convenient for discussing the last important property of the elasticity measure (to which we turn in the next section).

Elasticity and Total Expenditure

The elasticity of demand conveys useful information about the effect of a price change on the buyer's *total expenditure*. In particular, it can be shown that:

If demand is elastic, a fall in price will increase total expenditure. If demand is unit-elastic, a change in price will leave total expenditure unaffected. If demand is inelastic, a fall in price will reduce total expenditure. The opposite outcomes will occur when price rises.

These relationships hold because total expenditure equals price times quantity demanded, $P \times Q$, and a fall in price has two opposing effects on $P \times Q$. It decreases P and, if the demand curve is negatively sloped, it increases Q.

That is, a price decrease has two effects on expenditure: (1) *the price effect*, which decreases expenditure by cutting the amount of money a consumer spends on each unit of the good; and (2) *the quantity effect*, which increases the consumer's total expenditure on the good by raising the number of units of the good that he buys. The net consequence for expenditure depends on the elasticity. If price goes down 10 percent and quantity demanded increases 10 percent (a case of *unit elasticity*), the two effects will cancel out: $P \times Q$ will remain constant. On the other hand, if price goes down 10 percent and quantity demanded rises 15 percent (a case of *elastic* demand), $P \times Q$ will increase. Finally, if a 10 percent price fall leads to a 5 percent rise in quantity demanded (an *inelastic* case), $P \times Q$ will fall.

The connection between elasticity and total expenditure is easily seen in a graph. First we note that:

The total expenditure represented by any point on a demand curve (any price–quantity combination), such as point S in Figure 20–5, is equal to the area of the rectangle under that point (the area of rectangle $ORST$ in the figure). This is so because the area of a rectangle equals height times width $= OR$ times $OT =$ price times quantity, and, by definition, price times quantity equals total expenditure.

To illustrate the connection between elasticity and consumer expenditure, Figure 20–5 shows an elastic portion of a demand curve, DD. At a price of $6 per unit, the quantity sold is four units, so total expenditure is $4 \times \$6 = \$24$. This is represented by the shaded grey rectangle, because the formula for the area of a rectangle is height $\times$ width, which in this case is $4 \times \$6 = \$24$. When price falls to $5 per unit, 12 units are bought. Consequently, the new expenditure ($60 = \$5 \times 12$), now measured by the coloured rectangle, will be larger than the old. In contrast, Figure 20–4(d), the unit-elastic demand curve, shows a case in which expenditure remains constant even though selling price changes. Total spending is $140 whether the price is $20 and 7 units are sold (point S) or the price is $10 and 14 units are sold (point T).

This discussion also indicates why a unit-elastic demand curve must have the shape depicted in Figure 20–4(d), hugging the axes more and more closely but never

FIGURE 20–5

An Elastic Demand Curve
When price falls, quantity demanded rises by a greater percentage, increasing the total expenditure. Thus, when price falls from $6 to $5, quantity demanded rises from 4 to 12, and total expenditure rises from $6 × 4 = $24 to $5 × 12 = $60.

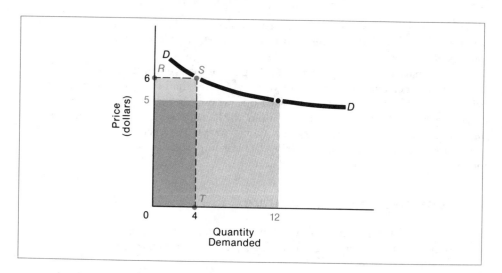

touching or crossing them. We have seen that when demand is unit-elastic, total expenditure must be the same at every point on the curve. It must be the same ($140) at points S and T and U. Suppose that at point U' (or some other point) the demand curve were to touch the horizontal axis. We will see now that this is impossible if expenditure at this point is to remain $140, because if U' lies on the axis, the price at that point must be zero. Therefore, at that point we must have total expenditure = $P \times Q = 0 \times Q =$ zero. We conclude that if the demand curve is unit-elastic throughout, it can never cross the horizontal axis (where $P = 0$) or the vertical axis (where $Q = 0$). Since the slope of the demand curve is negative, the curve simply must get closer and closer to the axes as one moves away from its middle points. That is why a unit-elastic demand curve must always have the shape illustrated in Figure 20–4(d).

All of this indicates why elasticity of demand is so important for business decisions. A firm should not jump to the most obvious conclusion—that an increase in price will add to its profits—for it may find that consumers take their revenge by cutting back on their purchases. In fact, if the demand curve is elastic, the firm will end up selling so many fewer units that its total revenue must actually fall, even though it makes more money than before on each unit it sells. In sum, whether a price rise or a price cut will be the better strategic move for a business firm depends very much on the elasticity of demand for its product.

What Determines Elasticity of Demand?

What kinds of goods have elastic demand curves, meaning that quantity demanded responds strongly to price? And what kinds of goods have inelastic demand curves? Several considerations are relevant.

Nature of the Goods

Necessities, such as basic foodstuffs, have very inelastic demand curves. The quantity of bread or potatoes demanded does not decline very much when the price of bread or potatoes rises. In contrast, many *luxury goods*, such as restaurant meals, have rather elastic demand curves. Statistical estimates of various elasticities confirm this principle. For example, consider the following elasticities, which have been estimated from postwar data: aluminum, 0.4; newspapers, 0.5; purchased meals, 1.1; pleasure boats, 2.4; china and tableware, 8.8.

Availability of Close Substitutes

If consumers can easily get a very good substitute, Y, for a product, X, they will switch readily to Y if the price of X rises sharply. Thus the closer the substitutes for X that are available, the more elastic its demand will be. This factor is a critical determinant of elasticity. The demand for gasoline is inelastic because it is not easy to run a car without it. But the demand for *any particular brand* of gasoline is quite elastic, because another company's product will work just as well. This example suggests a general principle: The demand for narrowly defined commodities (like iceberg lettuce) is more elastic than the demand for more broadly defined commodities (like vegetables).

Fraction of Income Absorbed

The fraction of income absorbed by a particular item is also important. Who will buy less salt if its price rises? But many families will resist buying a second or third car if auto prices go up.

Passage of Time

This factor is relevant because the demand for many products is more elastic in the long run than in the short run. For example, when the price of home heating oil rose in the 1970s, some homeowners switched from oil heat to gas heat. But, at first, very few homeowners switched, so the demand for oil was quite inelastic. It gradually became more elastic as time passed and more homeowners switched, having had the opportunity to purchase and install new equipment and having made up their minds to do so because it became clear that the price change would last more than a very brief period.

Elasticity Is a General Concept

We have spent much time studying the price elasticity of demand. But since elasticity is a very general measure of the responsiveness of one economic variable to another, we now consider other common and similar elasticity measures.

It is clear from what we have said that a firm will be very interested in the price elasticity of the demand curve for its product. But this is not where its interest in demand ends, for, as we have noted, quantity demanded depends on other things besides price, such as the consumer's income. The firm's management will want to know how much a change in consumers' income will affect the demand for its product. Fortunately, the elasticity measure can be helpful here too.

An increase in consumer incomes clearly raises the quantity demanded of most goods. To measure the response we use the *income elasticity of demand*, defined as the ratio of the percentage change in quantity demanded to the percentage change in income.

Economists also use elasticity to measure other analogous responses. For example, to measure the response of quantity *supplied* to a change in the price of a product, economists use the *price elasticity of supply*, defined as the ratio of the percentage change in quantity supplied to the percentage change in price. The logic and analysis of all such elasticity concepts are, of course, perfectly analogous to those for price elasticity of demand.

Cross Elasticity of Demand: Substitutes and Complements

There are many products whose quantities demanded depend on the quantities and prices of other products. Certain goods make one another *more* desirable. For example, cream and sugar can increase the desirability of coffee, and vice versa. The same is true of mustard or ketchup and hamburgers. In some extreme cases, neither of two products ordinarily has any use without the other—an automobile and tires, a pair of shoes and shoelaces, and so on. Such goods, each of which makes the other more valuable, are called **complements**.

The demand curves of complements are interrelated, meaning that a rise in the price of coffee is likely to affect the quantity of sugar demanded. Why? When coffee

Two goods are called **complements** if an increase in the price of one reduces the quantity demanded of the other, all other things remaining constant.

prices rise, less coffee will be drunk and therefore less sugar will be demanded. The opposite will be true of a fall in coffee prices. A similar relationship holds for other complementary goods.

At the other extreme, there are goods that make one another *less* valuable. These are called **substitutes**. Ownership of a motorcycle, for example, may decrease the desire for a bicycle. If your pantry is stocked with cans of tuna, you are less likely to rush out and buy cans of salmon. As you might expect, demand curves for substitutes are also interrelated, but in the opposite direction. When the price of motorcycles falls, people may demand fewer bicycles, so the quantity demanded falls. When the price of coffee goes up, people drink less coffee and instead consume more tea or juice.

There is another elasticity measure that can be used in determining whether two products are substitutes or complements: their **cross elasticity of demand**. This measure is defined much like the ordinary price elasticity of demand, only instead of measuring the responsiveness of the quantity demanded of, say, coffee to a change in the price of coffee, cross elasticity of demand measures the responsiveness of the quantity demanded of coffee to a change in the price of, say, sugar. For example, if a 20 percent rise in the price of sugar reduces the quantity of coffee demanded by 5 percent (a change of *minus* 5 percent in quantity demanded), then the cross elasticity of demand will be

$$\frac{\% \text{ change in quantity of coffee demanded}}{\% \text{ change in sugar price}} = \frac{-5\%}{20\%} = -0.25.$$

Obviously, the producers of breakfast cereal X care a great deal about the cross elasticity of demand for product X with respect to the price of rival cereal Y.

Using the cross elasticity of demand measure, we come to the following rule about complements and substitutes:

If two goods are substitutes, a rise in the price of one of them raises the quantity demanded of the other; so their cross elasticities of demand will normally be positive. If two goods are complements, a rise in the price of one of them tends to decrease the quantity demanded of the other, so their cross elasticities will normally be negative.[6]

This result is really a matter of common sense. If the price of a good goes up and there is a substitute available, people will tend to switch to the substitute. If the price of Japanese cameras goes up and the price of North American cameras does not, at least some people will switch to North American cameras. Thus, a *rise* in the price of Japanese cameras causes a *rise* in the quantity of North American cameras demanded. Both percentage changes are positive numbers and so their ratio, the cross elasticity of demand, is also positive.

On the other hand, if two goods are complements, a rise in the price of one will discourage not only its own use but also the use of the complementary good. Automobiles and car radios are obviously complements. A large increase in the price of cars will depress the sale of cars, and this will in turn reduce the sale of car radios. Thus, a positive percentage change in the price of cars leads to a negative percentage change in the quantity of car radios demanded. The ratio of these numbers, the cross elasticity of demand for cars and radios, is therefore negative.

It should be clear from our discussion of substitute goods that if a rise in the price of firm X causes consumers of its product to switch in droves to competitive product Y, then the cross elasticity of demand for product Y with respect to the price of X is high. That, in turn, means that competition is really powerful enough to prevent firm X from raising its price arbitrarily. This is why the concept of cross elasticity is so

Two goods are called **substitutes** if an increase in the price of one raises the quantity demanded of the other, all other things remaining constant.

The **cross elasticity of demand** for product X to a change in the price of another product, Y, is the ratio of the percentage change in quantity demanded of product X to the percentage change in the price of product Y that brings about the change in quantity demanded.

[6]Because cross elasticities can be positive or negative, it is *not* customary to drop minus signs as we do when calculating ordinary price elasticity of demand.

Elasticity in Practice: Legal Cases

Cross elasticity of demand has many important applications. For example, if a cross elasticity is high and positive, it indicates that the products in question are substitutes for one another. Establishing whether substitutes exist is important in a court of law if the government wishes to show that an industry is monopolized. When the United States Supreme Court ruled as to whether Dupont had monopolized trade in cellophane, it accepted the measured cross elasticity of demand as an important piece of evidence. Even though Dupont sold about 75 percent of the cellophane used in the United States, no monopoly was deemed to exist. The Supreme Court concluded that significant competition existed since a slight decrease in the price of cellophane was observed to cause a large switch in sales from other flexible wrappings to cellophane.

The case of Polaroid v. Kodak provides another example. Kodak had been found guilty of patent infringement when it began to sell instant cameras and film in 1976, and in 1989 a lengthy trial was under way to determine just how much Kodak owed Polaroid in damages. The key issue was to estimate how much profit Polaroid had lost as a result of Kodak's entry into the market. The concepts of price elasticity of demand and cross elasticity of demand both played crucial roles in the presentations of the two sides.

Price elasticity of demand was important in determining whether the explosive growth in instant-camera sales from 1976 to 1979 was in large part attributable to the fall in price resulting from competition by Kodak, or to the increased interest in the product among consumers that was brought about by Kodak's reputation and its access to additional retail outlets. In the latter case, Polaroid might actually have benefited residually from Kodak's entry into the market, rather than losing profit as a result of it.

After 1980, sales of instant cameras and film began to drop sharply. Cross elasticity was crucial in the explanation

of this development, because, at the same time, the prices of 35 millimetre cameras, film, developing, and printing had all begun to fall significantly. If it could be proved that this was the cause of the decline in Polaroid's overall sales, Kodak's instant-photography activity could not be held responsible, and the amount that Kodak would be required to pay to Polaroid would be significantly smaller. If, on the other hand, the cross elasticity of demand between conventional-photography prices and the demand for instant cameras and film proved to be low, then the cause of the decline in Polaroid's sales might have been Kodak's patent-infringing activity, adding to the damage payments to which Polaroid would be entitled. Since the figures involved are in the hundreds of millions (and perhaps even billions) of dollars, it should be obvious why both parties to the case worked so hard to get statistical estimates of the two elasticities.

Just as this book went to press, the case was settled, and Kodak was ordered to pay about $900 million in damages.

---

often cited in litigation before courts or government regulatory agencies when the degree of competition in an industry is an important aspect of the case.

Practical examples illustrating the importance of various elasticity concepts are provided in the two boxed inserts that appear on this and the next page.

Shifts in Demand Curves

Demand is obviously a complex phenomenon. We have studied in detail the dependence of quantity demanded on price, and we have just seen that quantity demanded depends on other variables such as incomes, the prices of substitutes and complements, and factors such as advertising. Because of these "other variables," demand curves often do not retain the same shape and position as time passes. Instead, they shift about. And, as we learned in Chapter 3, shifts in demand curves have predictable consequences for both quantity and price. But in public or business discussions, one often hears vague references to a "change in demand." By itself, this expression does not really mean anything. Remember from our discussion in Chapter 3 that it is vital

The Farm-Income Problem*

In recent years, the real price of wheat has fallen dramatically. The resulting squeeze on farm profits has forced many farmers into bankruptcy, and prairie grain bins have been overflowing. A particularly tragic outcome has been that the world's hungry do not have access to much of this surplus. Why do things seem to get so out of balance in this and a number of other markets for basic commodities?

The proximate answer to this question is that many of the world's farmers receive massive subsidies, which stimulate very large levels of production. The existence of the subsidies is, however, symptomatic. We must appreciate why they were introduced in the first place if we are to come to a deeper understanding of current farm problems.

The key facts are:

1. Technological improvements (new seeds, fertilizers, farming methods, and so on) have increased productivity in agriculture dramatically.

2. People's incomes have grown, but the income elasticity of food demand is low.

3. The price elasticity of food demand is low.

Fact 1 means that the supply curve for most agricultural products has shifted to the right very significantly, but, because of Fact 2, the demand curve has not shifted nearly as much. The general implications for farm revenues can be appreciated by considering what happens when the supply curve shifts to the right while the demand curve is stationary. Fact 3 means that the total-revenue rectangle must be getting smaller, so farm incomes are squeezed. To relieve this problem for farmers, governments have both offered subsidies and embarked on government purchase schemes.

These shifts and policies are illustrated in the accompanying diagram. Before the shift in technology, the equilibrium point is G, and farm revenues are given by rectangle $OCGD$. After the supply-curve shift, the new free-market equilibrium is point H, and farm revenues equal $OBHE$. Since the demand curve is price-inelastic, area $OBHE$ is smaller than $OCGD$; farmers' incomes are endangered. Thus, the government introduces some version of an income-support policy.

One scheme involves the government's buying and stock-piling grain; for example, if the government purchases quantity DF (equals GI) of wheat, the price will return to level OC, and farm revenues will total $OCIF$ (of which $DGIF$ is paid by the government). Only quantity OD of the wheat is actually consumed.

In an alternative scheme, the government lets the price fall but pays farmers the difference between the new market price and the pre-existing price, OC. If the government guarantees a total price of OC to the farmers, they will produce amount OF. This entire quantity will be consumed, and consumers will pay a price of OA (equals FJ). The government must pay the difference between the old and

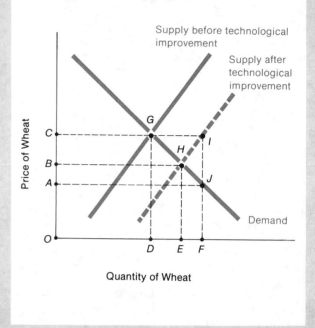

new consumer prices—that is, the amount AC (equals JI) per unit. The total cost to the government of this second policy is amount $ACIJ$. Since the demand curve is price-inelastic, this amount must exceed $DGIF$, the cost of the first policy.

Our knowledge of elasticity suggests that it is not surprising that governments often resort to purchase-and-storage schemes in an attempt to maintain farm incomes. But our analysis shows that this preference for the purchase-and-storage policy over the subsidy scheme is based on a *narrow* view of costs. It is true that the direct cost to government revenues is less with the purchase policy, but a more general view would acknowledge that people do not really care *how* they pay farmers—whether directly when buying the product, or indirectly through their taxes to fund either program. In either case, $OCIF$ is paid to farmers. The only real difference is that, under the subsidy scheme, *all* the product is enjoyed. Since the demand curve represents the aggregate marginal utility curve, and since the area under the marginal utility schedule represents total utility, the value of the output that is *not* wasted under the subsidy policy is $DGJF$. By choosing the purchase-and-storage policy over the subsidy scheme, as we often do, we are throwing away $DGJF$ *every* period—a wasteful choice. This is not just a transfer from one group to another—it is an annual amount of satisfaction that is lost to *everyone*.

*For another boxed insert on farm-income problems (specifically, on agricultural marketing boards), see Chapter 31, pages 722–23.

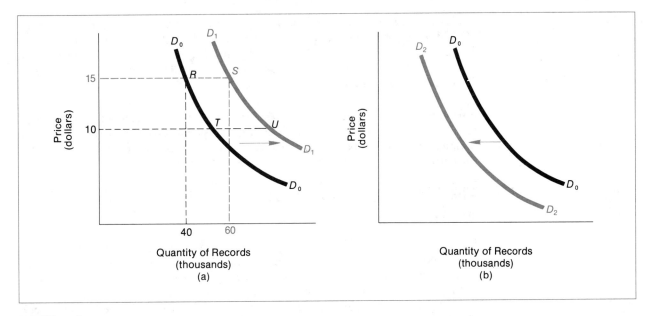

FIGURE 20-6
Shifts in a Demand Curve
A rise in consumer income or an increase in advertising or a rise in the price of a substitute product can all produce a rightward (outward) shift of the demand curve for a product, as depicted by the shift from the black curve D_0D_0 to the green curve D_1D_1 in part (a). This means that at any fixed price (say, $15), the quantity of the product demanded will rise. (In the figure, it rises from 40,000 units to 60,000 units.) Similarly, a fall in any of the variables, such as consumer income, will produce a leftward (inward) shift in the demand curve, as in part (b).

to distinguish between a response to a price change (*which is a movement along the demand curve*) and a change in the relationship between price and quantity demanded (*which is a shift in the demand curve*).

When price falls, quantity demanded generally responds by rising. This is a movement *along* the demand curve. On the other hand, an effective advertising campaign may mean that more goods will be bought at *any given price*. This would be a rightward *shift* in the demand curve. In fact, such a shift can be caused by a change in the value of any of the variables affecting quantity demanded other than price. While the distinction between a shift in a demand curve and a movement along it may at first seem trivial, it is a significant difference in practice and can cause confusion if it is ignored. So let us pause for a moment to consider how changes in some of these other variables shift the demand curve.

As an example, consider the effect of a change in consumer income on the demand curve for records. In Figure 20-6(a), the black curve D_0D_0 is the original demand curve for records. Now suppose that parents start sending more money to their needy sons and daughters in university. If the price of records were to stay the same, we would expect students to use some of their increased income to buy more records. For example, if the price were to remain at $15, quantity demanded might rise from 40,000 (point R) to 60,000 (point S). Similarly, if price had instead been $10 and had remained at that level, there might be a corresponding change from T to U. In other words, the rise in income would be expected to *shift* the entire demand curve to the right from D_0D_0 to D_1D_1. In exactly the same way, a fall in consumer income can be expected to lead to a leftward shift in the demand curve for records, as shown in Figure 20-6(b).

Other variables that affect quantity demanded can be analyzed in the same way. For example, a rise in TV advertising for records might lead to a rightward (outward) shift in the demand curve for records, as depicted in Figure 20-6(a). The same thing might occur if there were an increase in the price of a substitute product, such as CDs or cassette tapes, because that would put records at a competitive advantage. That is, if two goods are substitutes, a rise in the price of one of them will tend to cause the demand curve for the other one to shift outward (to the right). Conversely, if a product that is complementary to records (for example, a record player) becomes more expensive, we would expect the demand curve for records to shift to the left, as in Figure 20–6(b). In summary:

A demand curve is expected to shift to the right (outward) if consumer incomes rise, if tastes change in favour of the product, if substitute goods become more expensive, or if complementary goods become cheaper. A demand curve is expected to shift to the left (inward) if any of these factors goes in the opposite direction.

The Time Dimension of the Demand Curve and Decision-Making

There is one more feature of a demand curve that does not show up on a graph but that is very important nevertheless. A demand curve indicates, at each possible price, the quantity of the good that is demanded *during a particular period of time*. That is, all the alternative prices considered in a demand curve must refer to the *same* time period. We do not compare a price of $10 for January with a price of $8 for September. This feature imparts a peculiar character to the demand curve and makes statistical estimates more difficult than might be supposed, because the available statistics usually give different prices and quantities only for different dates. Why, then, do economists adopt this apparently peculiar approach? The answer is that the time dimension of the demand curve is dictated inescapably by the logic of decision-making.

When a business undertakes to find the best price for one of its products for, say, the next six months, it must consider the range of alternative prices available to it for that six-month period and the consequences of each possible choice. For example, if management is reasonably certain that the best price lies somewhere between $3.50 and $5.00, it should perhaps consider each of four possibilities, $3.50, $4.00, $4.50, and $5.00, and estimate how much it can expect to sell at each of these potential prices during the six-month period in question. The result of these estimates may appear in a format similar to that shown in the table below.

Potential price	$3.50	$4.00	$4.50	$5.00
Expected quantity demanded	75,000	73,000	70,000	60,000

This table, which supplies management with what it needs to know to make a pricing decision, also contains precisely the information an economist uses to draw a demand curve.

The demand curve describes a set of hypothetical responses to a set of potential prices, only one of which can actually be charged. All of the points on the demand curve refer to alternative possibilities for the *same* period of time—the period for which the decision is to be made.

Thus, the demand curve as just described is no abstract notion that is useful primarily in academic discussion. Rather, it offers precisely the information that businesses need for rational decision-making. However, as already noted, the fact that all points on the demand curve are hypothetical possibilities, all for the same period of time, causes problems for statistical evaluation of demand curves. These problems are discussed in the appendix to this chapter.

Summary

1. A market-demand curve for a product can be obtained by summing horizontally the demand curves of each individual in the market; that is, by adding up at each price the quantities demanded by each consumer.

2. The "law" of demand says that demand curves normally have a negative slope, meaning that a rise in price reduces quantity demanded.

3. To measure the responsiveness of quantity demanded to price we use the elasticity of demand, which is defined as the percentage change in quantity demanded divided by the percentage change in price.

4. If demand is elastic (elasticity greater than one), a rise in price will reduce total expenditure. If demand is unit-elastic (elasticity equal to one), a rise in price will not change total expenditure. If demand is inelastic (elasticity less than one), a rise in price will increase total expenditure.

5. The more inelastic is the demand for a commodity, other things being equal, the higher is the share of any excise tax that is paid by consumers, and the higher is the tax revenue collected by the government.

6. Demand is not a fixed number. Rather, it is a relationship showing how quantity demanded is affected by price and other pertinent influences. If one or more of these other variables change, the demand curve will shift.

7. Goods that make each other more desirable (hot dogs and mustard, wristwatches and watch straps) are called *complements*. Goods such that if we have more of one we usually want less of another (steaks and hamburgers, Coke and Pepsi) are called *substitutes*.

8. Cross elasticity of demand is defined as the percentage change in the quantity demanded of one good divided by the percentage change in the price of the other good. Two substitute products normally have a positive cross elasticity of demand. Two complementary products normally have a negative cross elasticity of demand.

9. A rise in the price of one of two substitute commodities can be expected to shift the other's demand curve to the right. A rise in the price of one of two complementary goods is apt to shift the other's demand curve to the left.

10. All points on a demand curve refer to the *same* time period—the time during which the price will be in effect.

Concepts for Review

Market-demand curve	(Price) elasticity of demand	Substitutes
"Law" of demand	Elastic, inelastic, and unit-elastic demand curves	Cross elasticity of demand
Excise tax	Complements	Shift in a demand curve

Questions for Discussion

1. What variables besides price and advertising are likely to affect the quantity of a product that is demanded?

2. Describe the probable shifts in the demand curves for:
   a. airplane trips when there is an improvement in the airlines' on-time performance.
   b. automobiles when air fares rise.
   c. automobiles when gasoline prices rise.
   d. electricity when average temperature in Canada rises during a particular year. (Note: The demand curve for electricity in Ontario and the demand curve for electricity in the Yukon should respond in different ways. Why?)

3. Which of the following goods may conceivably have positively sloping demand curves? Why?
   a. Diamonds.
   b. Copper.
   c. Milk.
   d. Shoelaces.

4. Explain why elasticity of demand is measured in *percentages*.

5. Give examples of commodities whose demand you expect to be elastic and some whose demand you expect to be inelastic.

6. Explain why the elasticity of a straight-line demand curve varies from one part of the curve to another.

7. Calculate the price elasticity of demand when price falls from $6 to $5 in Table 20-1.

8. If the price elasticity of demand for gasoline is 0.20 and the current price is 50 cents per litre, what rise in the price of gasoline will reduce its consumption by 10 percent?

9. A rise in the price of a product whose demand is elastic will reduce the total revenue of the firm. Explain.

10. Which of the following product pairs would you expect to be substitutes and which would you expect to be complements?
    a. Shoes and shoelaces.
    b. Gasoline and big cars.
    c. Bread and crackers.
    d. Butter and margarine.

11. For each of the previous product pairs, what would you guess about their cross elasticity of demand?
    a. Do you expect it to be positive or negative?
    b. Do you expect it to be a large or small number? Why?

12. Explain why the following statement is true: "A firm with a demand curve that is inelastic at its current output level can always increase its profits by raising its price and selling less." (*Hint*: Refer back to the discussion of elasticity and total expenditure on pages 439–40.)

13. Analysts have concluded that public-transit use is in decline. To change this we could either lower the price of public transit or raise the cost of driving a private car. (Car users are currently not charged directly for driving on expressways or for the pollution and congestion costs that they impose.) Analysts have estimated that the cross elasticity of demand is higher than the price elasticity of demand for public transit. What is your advice as an economic adviser?

14. Assume there are two goods, X and Y, with prices P_X and P_Y. The demand functions for each commodity are:

$$X = 5 - 0.5P_X$$
$$Y = 8 - P_Y.$$

Assume that both goods can be purchased from the rest of the world at a constant price: $P_X = 3$ and $P_Y = 2$. What quantity of each good is consumed and what is the price elasticity of demand in that range of the demand curve for each good? Suppose the government needs to raise tax revenue equal to 4, and to do so, imposes an excise tax (which could be called a tariff in this case) on one good or the other. What is the loss of consumer surplus in each case? Which commodity should be taxed if the goal is to minimize the loss of consumer surplus for buyers, while still raising the necessary revenue? What have you learned about how the elasticity of demand determines which good should be taxed?

Appendix
Statistical Analysis of Demand Relationships

The peculiar time dimension of the demand curve, in conjunction with the fact that many variables other than price can influence quantity demanded, makes it surprisingly hard to discover the shape of the demand curve from statistical data. It can be done, but the task is full of booby traps and can usually be carried out successfully only by using advanced statistical methods. Let us see why these two characteristics of demand curves cause problems.

The most obvious way to go about estimating a demand curve statistically is to collect a set of figures on prices and quantities sold in different periods, like those given in Table 20–4. These points can then be plotted on a diagram with price and quantity on the axes, as shown in Figure 20–7. One can then proceed to draw in a line (the dotted line *TT*) that connects these points reasonably well and that appears to be the demand curve. Unfortunately, line *TT*, which summar-

izes the historical data, may bear no relationship to the demand curve we are after.

You may notice at once that the prices and quantities represented by the historical points in Figure 20–7 refer to different periods of time, and that they

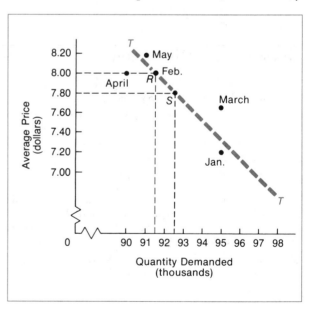

FIGURE 20–7
Plot of Historical Data on Price and Quantity
The dots labelled Jan., Feb., and so on represent actual prices and quantities sold in the months indicated. The green line *TT* is drawn to approximate the dots as closely as possible.

TABLE 20–4
Historical Data on Price and Quantity

	PRICE (dollars)	QUANTITY SOLD
January	7.20	95,000
February	8.00	91,500
March	7.70	95,000
April	8.00	90,000
May	8.20	91,000

all have been *actual*, not *hypothetical*, prices and quantities at some time. This distinction is significant. Over the period covered by the historical data the true demand curve, which is what we really want, may well have shifted because some of the other variables affecting quantity demanded changed.

What actually happened may be as shown in Figure 20-8. Here we see that in January the demand curve was given by *JJ*, but by February the curve had shifted to *FF*, by March to *MM*, and so on. That is, there was a separate and distinct demand curve for each of the relevant months, and none of them need resemble the plot of historical data, *TT*.

In fact, the slope of the historical plot curve, *TT*, can be very different from the slopes of the true underlying demand curves, as is the case in Figure 20-8. This means that the decision-maker can be seriously misled if he selects his price on the basis of the historical data. He may, for example, think that demand is quite insensitive to changes in price (as line *TT* in the diagram seems to indicate), and so he may reject the possibility of a price reduction when in fact the true demand curves show that a price reduction will increase quantity demanded substantially. For example, if in February he charged a price of $7.80 rather than $8, the historical plot would suggest to him a rise in quantity demanded of only 1000 units. (Compare point *R*, with sales of 91,500 units, and point *S*, with sales of 92,500 units, in Figure 20-7.) However, as can

be seen in Figure 20-8, the true demand curve for February (line *FF* in Figure 20-8) promises him an increment in sales of 2500 units (from point *R*, with sales of 91,500, to point *W*, with sales of 94,000) if he reduces February's price from $8 to $7.80. A manager who based his decision on the historical plot, rather than on the true demand curve, might be led into serious error.

In the light of this discussion, it is astonishing how often in practice one encounters demand studies that use apparently sophisticated techniques to arrive at no more than a graph of historical data. One must not allow oneself to be misled by the apparent complexity of the procedures employed to fit a curve to historical data. If these merely plot historical quantities against historical prices, the true underlying demand curve is not likely to be found.

An Illustration: Did the Advertising Program Work?

A few years ago one of the world's largest producers of packaged foods conducted a statistical study to determine the effectiveness of its advertising expenditures, which amounted to nearly $100 million a year. A company statistician collected year-by-year figures on company sales and advertising outlays and discovered, to his delight, that they showed a remarkably close relationship to one another: Quantity demanded rose as advertising rose. The trouble was that the relationship seemed just too perfect. In economics, data about demand and any one of the elements that influence it almost never make such a neat pattern. Human tastes and other pertinent influences are just too variable to permit such regularity.

Suspicious company executives asked one of the authors of this book to examine the analysis. A little thought showed that the suspiciously close statistical relationship between sales and advertising expenditure resulted from a disregard for the principles just presented. The investigator had in fact constructed a graph of *historical* data on sales and advertising expenditure, analogous to *TT* in Figures 20-7 and 20-8 and therefore not necessarily similar to the truly relevant relationship.

The stability of the relationship actually arose from the fact that, in the past, the company had based its advertising outlays on its sales, automatically allocating a fixed percentage of its sales revenues to advertising. The *historical* advertising–demand relationship therefore described only the company's budgeting practices, not the effectiveness of its advertising program. If management had used this curve in planning its advertising campaigns, it might have made some regrettable decisions. *Moral*: Avoid the use of historical curves like *TT* in making economic decisions.

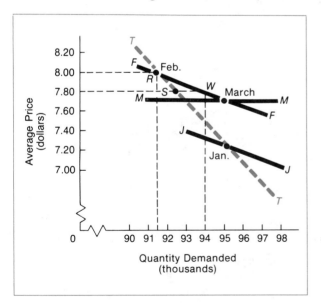

FIGURE 20-8

Plot of Historical Data and True Demand Curves

An analytical demand curve shows how quantity demanded in a particular month is affected by the different prices considered during that month. In the case shown, the true demand curves are much flatter (more elastic) than is the line plotting historical data. This means that a cut in price will induce a far greater increase in quantity demanded than the historical data suggest.

21

Input Decisions and Production Costs

J ust as the consumer must decide what combination of products to buy and how much of each to purchase, the producer must decide how much to produce (the size of the firm's *output*) and what combination of *inputs* (labour, raw materials, machinery, and so on) to buy. And just as there is a key concept—the consumer's utility or preferences—that is crucial for the analysis of the buyer's behaviour, there is a fundamental phenomenon—production cost—that underlies the analysis of the seller's decisions.

Because the firm's decision on how much output to produce depends on costs, to understand the choice of output level, one must first analyze how costs are determined. This chapter will therefore consider the logic of a firm's input decisions, while the next chapter will analyze its output choices.

For pedagogical purposes, this chapter is divided into two parts. In the first part we begin with the simple case in which the firm varies the quantity of only a single input. This will vastly simplify the analysis and enable us to see more easily how to analyze the three key issues of this chapter: how the quantity of input used affects production, how the firm selects the optimal quantity of an input, and how the production relation between inputs and outputs gives the producer the cost information needed to determine output and price.

The second part of the chapter goes over the same territory—production, optimal input use, and the determination of the firm's cost curves—but deals with the more realistic case in which several input quantities can be changed.* Many new insights emerge from the multi-input analysis. Throughout the chapter we assume that the price of each input is fixed by the market and is beyond the control of the firm that buys it.

A Practical Application: Testing Whether a Larger Firm Is More Efficient

Economies of large-scale production are thought to be a pervasive feature of modern industrial society. Automation, assembly lines, and sophisticated machinery are widely believed to reduce production costs dramatically. But if this equipment has enormous capacity and requires a very large investment, small companies will not be able to benefit much from these products of modern technology. In this case, only large-scale production can offer the associated savings in costs. Where such *economies of scale*, as economists call them, exist, production costs per unit will decline as output expands.

---

*Some instructors may prefer to postpone this part until later in the course.

FIGURE 21–1

Historical Costs for Long-Distance Telephone Transmission

By 1991, the dollar cost per circuit mile in the United States had fallen below 8 percent of what it was in 1942. Because prices had more than tripled in that period, the decline in *real* cost was even more sensational. Yet this diagram of historical costs is not legitimate evidence *one way or the other* about economies of scale in telecommunications.
SOURCE: AT&T, recent data estimated.

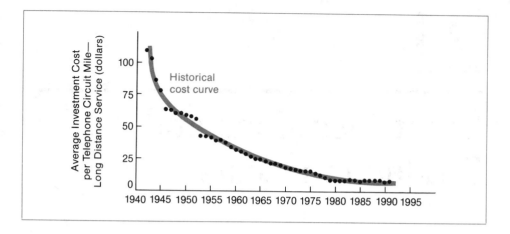

But this favourable relationship between low costs and large size does not characterize every industry. When a court is called upon to decide whether a giant firm is operating against consumers' interests, officials need to know whether the industry has significant economies of scale. Those who want to break up large firms argue that industrial giants concentrate economic power, which is something these individuals wish to avoid. Those who oppose such breakups point out that if significant economies of scale are present, large firms will be much more efficient producers than will a number of small firms. It is crucial, therefore, to be able to decide whether economies of scale are present. What kind of evidence will speak to this issue?

Court cases of this sort have occurred and data like those shown in Figure 21–1 are sometimes offered to the courts. These figures, provided by AT&T in the United States, indicate that since 1942, as the volume of messages rose, the capital cost of long-distance communication by telephone dropped enormously. Yet economists maintain that while this graph may be valid evidence of efficiency, innovation, and perhaps other virtues of the telecommunications industry, it does *not* constitute legitimate evidence, one way or another, about the presence of economies of scale. Specifically, though this information shows that costs fell as the telephone company's volume of business grew, it does *not* show that a large firm is more efficient than a small one. At the end of this chapter we will see precisely what is wrong with such evidence and what sort of evidence really is required to determine whether production by a very large firm is indeed more efficient.

Production, Input Choice, and Cost with One Variable Input

We begin our discussion with the unrealistic single-variable input case. That is, while any business firm uses many different inputs, we will assume for simplicity that it can change the quantity of only one of them. In other words, we are trying to replicate in our theoretical analysis what a physicist or a biologist does in the laboratory when conducting a *controlled* experiment in which only one variable is permitted to change at a time, to study the influence of that variable alone.

Production: An Input's Total, Average, and Marginal Physical Products

Consider, as an example of a firm, farmer Phil Pfister, who grows corn by himself on a 40-hectare plot of land. Ultimately, he can vary all his input quantities: He can hire

TABLE 21-1
Farmer Pfister's Total Physical Product Schedule*

CORRESPONDING LABEL IN FIGURE 21-2	FERTILIZER INPUT (tonnes)	CORN OUTPUT (bushels)
A	0	0
B	1	250
C	2	550
D	3	900
E	4	1200
F	5	1450
G	6	1600
H	7	1650
I	8	1650
J	9	1600

*Data of the sort provided in this table do not represent the farmer's subjective opinion. They are *objective* information of the sort a soil scientist could supply from experimental evidence.

An **input** is any item that the firm uses in its production process. Labour, fuel, raw materials, machinery, and factories are all examples of inputs. The firm's **output** is the good or service it produces. Sometimes the word "output" is used to mean the *quantity* of the good or service that the firm produces.

many or few farmhands, buy more land, or sell some of the land he owns. But suppose for the moment that his only choice is how much fertilizer to apply to his land.

Farmer Pfister has studied the relationship between his **input** of fertilizer and his **output** of corn, and he has concluded that, at least up to a point, more fertilizer leads to more output. The relevant data are displayed in Table 21-1. We can see that the land has been worked so much that nothing will grow on the 40 hectares if no fertilizer is applied. But the application of more and more fertilizer yields additional output; for instance, with four tonnes of fertilizer, output is 1200 bushels. Eventually, however, a saturation point is reached beyond which additional fertilizer actually reduces the corn crop (any amount beyond eight tonnes). These data are portrayed graphically in what we call a **total physical product (TPP) curve** in Figure 21-2. This curve shows how much corn farmer Pfister can produce on 40 hectares of land when different quantities of fertilizer are used.

Two other physical product concepts are added in Table 21-2. **Average physical product (APP)** is simply the total physical product divided by the quantity of variable input utilized. It is the measure of output per unit of input. In our example, it is total corn output divided by number of tonnes of fertilizer used. APP is shown in the last column of Table 21-2, in which the TPP schedule is reproduced. For example, since 4

The firm's **total physical product (TPP)** curve shows what happens to the quantity of the firm's output as one changes the quantity of one of the firm's inputs while holding the quantities of all other inputs unchanged.

The **average physical product (APP)** is the total physical product (TPP) divided by the quantity of input utilized. Thus, APP = TPP/Q_i, where Q_i is the quantity of input.

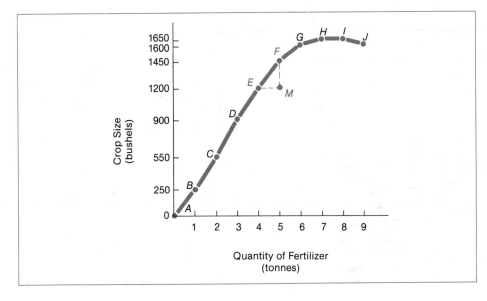

FIGURE 21-2
Total Physical Product with Different Quantities of Fertilizer
This graph shows how Farmer Pfister's corn crop varies as he uses more and more fertilizer on his fixed plot of land. (Other inputs, such as labour, are also held constant in this graph.)

The Canadian Productivity Problem and Average Physical Product

In recent years there has been increasing concern in North America that the productivity of Japanese and other Asian workers is outstripping the productivity of Canadian and American workers. (See Chapter 18 on productivity for further discussion of these issues.) For example, statistics for two auto plants suggest that a Japanese auto worker, on the average, turns out nine engines per day, while his North American counterpart turns out only two. Thus, the productivity of labour in the auto industry is widely measured as the number of units of output produced per hour of labour.

But you will now recognize that the number of engines produced divided by the number of labour hours expended is exactly the same as the average physical product of an hour of labour in auto engine production. In other words, when you read in the newspapers about trends in the productivity of Canadian labour or comparisons between that productivity and productivity in other countries, you will know that the report refers to the average physical product, which we discuss in this chapter.

---

tonnes of fertilizer yield 1200 bushels of corn, the APP of 4 tonnes of fertilizer is $1200/4 = 300$ bushels per tonne. (For a real example, see the boxed insert above.)

If Farmer Pfister is to decide how much fertilizer to use, he must know how much *additional* corn output he can expect from each *additional* tonne of fertilizer. This concept is known as **marginal physical product (MPP)**. Thus, the marginal physical product of, for example, the fourth tonne of fertilizer is the total output of corn when four tonnes of fertilizer are used *minus* the total output when three tonnes are used.

The **marginal physical product (MPP)** of an input is the increase in total output that results from a one-unit increase in the input, holding the amounts of all other inputs constant. Geometrically, it is the slope of the TPP curve. In symbols, $MPP = \Delta TPP / \Delta Q_i.$

The marginal physical product schedule of fertilizer on Farmer Pfister's land is given in the third column of Table 21-2. For example, since 3 tonnes of fertilizer yield 900 bushels of corn and 4 tonnes yield 1200 bushels, the MPP of the fourth tonne is $1200 - 900 = 300$ bushels. The other MPP entries in Table 21-2 are calculated from the total product data in the same way. Figure 21-3(a) displays these numbers graphically in a **marginal physical product curve**.

All three curves—TPP, APP, and MPP—are shown together in Figure 21-3(b). The same information about the production process is contained in any one of the three curves. The TPP curve is the most convenient for making clear the idea of diminishing returns at the intuitive level. The APP curve is important since it reflects the way that productivity data are discussed in news reports. The MPP curve is useful for the firm in deciding the optimal level of an input to be used (as we will see presently).

TABLE 21-2
Farmer Pfister's Schedules for Total, Average, and Marginal Physical Product and Marginal Revenue Product

FERTILIZER INPUT (tonnes)	TOTAL PHYSICAL PRODUCT (corn output in bushels)	MARGINAL PHYSICAL PRODUCT (bushels per tonne)	AVERAGE PHYSICAL PRODUCT (bushels per tonne)	MARGINAL REVENUE PRODUCT (dollars)
0	0		—	—
1	250	250	250	500
2	550	300	275	600
3	900	350	300	700
4	1200	300	300	600
5	1450	250	290	500
6	1600	150	266.7	300
7	1650	50	235.7	100
8	1650	0	206.3	0
9	1600	-50	177.8	-100

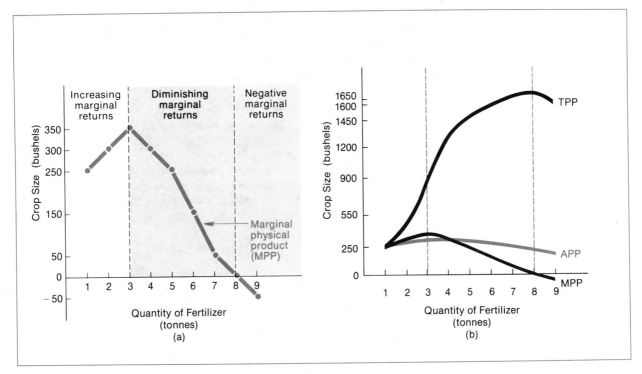

FIGURE 21-3
Farmer Pfister's MPP, TPP, and APP
In panel (a), the graph of marginal physical product (MPP) shows how much *additional* corn Farmer Pfister gets from each application of an additional tonne of fertilizer. The relation between the MPP curve and the total product curve in Figure 21-2 is simple and direct: The MPP curve at each level of input shows the *slope* of the corresponding total product curve. To see why, suppose we want to know what happens when Farmer Pfister increases fertilizer usage from four tonnes to five tonnes; that is, we want to determine the MPP of the fifth tonne. In Figure 21-2 this takes us from point *E* to point *F* on the total product curve, so that output increases from 1200 bushels to 1450 bushels. The difference, 250 bushels, is the marginal physical product of the fifth tonne of fertilizer. It is measured by the slope of the total product curve between points *E* and *F* because it corresponds to the rise in the curve (distance *MF*) resulting from a move to the right by one unit (distance *EM*)—which is precisely the definition of slope. All three curves are shown in panel (b). The APP curve at each level of input shows (as a height) the slope of a ray joining the origin of the graph to each point on the TPP curve. This is because APP = TPP/Q_i. The APP and MPP curves intersect at the level of input use where the tangent to the TPP curve and the ray to the origin are the same line. Note: This makes MPP cut APP at its maximum point.

The "Law" of Diminishing Marginal Returns

The marginal physical product curve in Figure 21-3 shows a pattern that will prove significant for our analysis. Up until three tonnes of fertilizer are used, the marginal physical product of fertilizer is *increasing*; between three tonnes and eight tonnes it is *decreasing*, but still *positive*; and beyond eight tonnes the MPP of fertilizer actually becomes *negative*. The graph has been divided into three zones to illustrate these three cases. The left zone is called the region of **increasing marginal returns**; the middle zone, the region of **diminishing marginal returns**; and the right zone, the region of **negative marginal returns**. In this graph, the marginal returns to fertilizer increase at first and then diminish. This is a typical pattern.

In the increasing marginal returns zone, each additional tonne of fertilizer adds more to TPP than the previous tonne added. In Figure 21-2, this corresponds to output levels 1-3, where the curve is rising with increasing rapidity. In the diminishing returns area, each additional tonne of fertilizer adds less to TPP than the previous tonne added. In Figure 21-2, this corresponds to output levels 4-7, where the TPP curve is still rising but at a diminishing rate. Finally, in the zone of negative marginal returns (outputs greater than 7), additional fertilizer actually reduces production (by damaging the plants).

The "law" of diminishing marginal returns, which has played a key role in economics for two centuries,[1] asserts that when we increase the amount of any one input, *holding the amounts of all others constant*, the marginal returns to the expanding input ultimately begin to diminish. The so-called law is no more than an empirical regularity based on some observation of the facts; it is not a theorem deduced analytically.

The reason why returns to a single input are usually diminishing is straightforward. As we increase the quantity of one input while holding all others constant, the input whose quantity we are increasing gradually becomes more and more abundant compared with the others. As the farmer uses more and more fertilizer with his fixed plot of land, the soil gradually becomes so well fertilized that adding yet more fertilizer does little good. Eventually the plants are absorbing so much fertilizer that any further increase in fertilizer will actually harm them. At this point the marginal physical product of fertilizer becomes *negative*.

The Optimal Quantity of an Input

We now have all the tools we need to see how the firm can decide on the quantity of input that is consistent with maximization of its profits. For this purpose, let us refer back to the first and third columns of Table 21–2, which show Farmer Pfister's marginal physical product schedule. Suppose fertilizer costs $350 per tonne, the farmer's product is worth $2 per bushel, and he is using three tonnes of fertilizer. Is this optimal for him? The answer is no, because the marginal physical product of the fourth tonne is 300 bushels (fourth entry in the marginal physical product column of Table 21–2). This means that although a fourth tonne of fertilizer would cost $350, it would yield an additional 300 bushels, which at the price of $2 would add $600 to his revenue. Thus he would come out $600 – $350 = $250 ahead if he added a fourth tonne.

It is convenient to have a specific name for the additional revenue that accrues to a firm when it increases the quantity of some input by one unit; we call it **marginal revenue product**. So if Farmer Pfister's crop sells at a fixed price (say, $2 per bushel), the marginal revenue product (MRP) of the input equals its marginal physical product (MPP) multiplied by the price of the product:

The **marginal revenue product (MRP)** of an input is the additional revenue the producer is able to earn as a result of increased sales when he uses an additional unit of the input. MRP = MPP × price of product.

$$MRP = MPP \times \text{Price of output.}$$

For example, we have just seen that the marginal revenue product of the fourth tonne of fertilizer to Farmer Pfister is $600, which we obtained by multiplying the MPP of 300 bushels by the price of $2 per bushel. The other entries in the last column of Table 21–2 are obtained in precisely the same way. The concept of MRP enables us to formulate a simple **rule for the optimal use of any input**. Specifically:

When the marginal revenue product of an input exceeds its price, it pays the producer to expand his use of that input. Similarly, when the marginal revenue product of the input is less than its price, it pays the producer to use less of that input.

Let us test this rule in the case of Farmer Pfister. We have observed that three tonnes of fertilizer cannot be enough because the MRP of the fourth tonne ($600) exceeds its price ($350). What about the fifth tonne? Table 21–2 tells us that the MRP of the fifth tonne ($500) also exceeds its price; thus, stopping at four tonnes cannot be optimal. The same cannot be said of the sixth tonne, however. A sixth tonne is not a good idea, since its MRP is only $300, which is less than its $350 cost.

---

[1] The "law" is generally credited to Anne Robert Jacques Turgot (1727–81), one of the great Comptrollers-General of France before the Revolution, whose liberal policies, it is said, represented the old regime's last chance to save itself. But, with characteristic foresight, the king fired him.

Notice the crucial role of diminishing returns in this analysis. Because the "law" of diminishing marginal returns holds true for Pfister's farm, the marginal *physical* product of fertilizer eventually begins to decline. Therefore, the marginal *revenue* product also begins to decline. At the point where MRP falls below the price of fertilizer, it is appropriate for Pfister to stop increasing his purchases. In sum, it always pays the producer to expand his input use until diminishing returns set in and reduce the MRP to the price of the input.

A common expression suggests that it does not pay to continue doing something "beyond the point of diminishing returns." As we see from this analysis, the reality is quite to the contrary: It normally pays to do so! Only when the marginal revenue product of an input has been reduced (by diminishing returns) to the level of the input's price has the proper amount of the input been employed. Thus, the optimal quantity of an input is that at which the MRP is equal to its price (P). In symbols:

$$MRP = P \text{ of input.}$$

This analysis of the firm's input decisions now enables us to proceed to the derivation of the firm's cost curves, which play so crucial a role in its output decisions — the topic of our next chapter.

The Firm's Three Cost Curves

Costs are determined by the production relations that have just been studied and by the prices of the inputs. We can now use our two basic assumptions—that the price of fertilizer is beyond the control of the firm and that the quantities of all inputs other than fertilizer are somehow given—to deduce the firm's costs from the physical product schedules in Table 21–1 and Figure 21–2. We need simply record, for each quantity of output, the amount of fertilizer required to produce it, multiply that quantity of fertilizer by its price, and add this to the cost of the other inputs whose quantities we are holding constant. It is critical to recognize that these must include the opportunity costs of any inputs the farmer contributes himself—his labour or his capital, which he could instead have used elsewhere to earn wages or interest.

Suppose that fertilizer costs $350 per tonne and that the cost of the fixed inputs (capital, labour, and land) is $1000. Then, from Table 21–1, we have the table of total costs shown in Table 21–3. For example, to produce 900 bushels of corn (fourth row), we know from Table 21–1 that it requires 3 tonnes of fertilizer at $350 per tonne, which when added to the $1000 cost of other inputs gives us the total cost, $2050.

TABLE 21–3
A Portion of Farmer Pfister's Total-Cost Schedule

OUTPUT OF CORN (bushels)	TOTAL COST (dollars)
0	$1000
250	$1000 + $350 = $1350
550	$1000 + 2 x $350 = $1700
900	$1000 + 3 x $350 = $2050
1200	$1000 + 4 x $350 = $2400
1450	$1000 + 5 x $350 = $2750
1600	$1000 + 6 x $350 = $3100
1650	$1000 + 7 x $350 = $3450

SOURCE: Obtained from the production data in Table 21-1, assuming fertilizer is the only variable input.

The point of this exercise is that:

The total-product curve tells us the input quantities needed to produce any given output. And from those input quantities and the price of the inputs, we can determine the *total cost* of producing any level of output. This is the amount the firm spends on the inputs needed to produce the output, plus any opportunity costs that arise in that production activity. Thus, the relation of total cost to output is determined by the technological production relations between inputs and outputs and by input prices.

The behaviour of the firm's costs as output changes is obviously critical for output decisions. There are three interrelated cost curves that contain the pertinent information: the **total-cost curve**, the **average-cost curve**, and the **marginal-cost curve**, where marginal cost is a concept analogous to marginal physical product. As we shall see shortly, average and marginal costs are obtained directly from total costs (which we have just determined).

A firm's **total-cost (TC) curve** shows, for each possible quantity of output, the total amount that the firm must spend for its inputs to produce that amount of output plus any opportunity cost incurred in the process.

A firm's **average-cost (AC) curve** shows, for each output, the cost per unit; that is, total cost divided by output.

A firm's **marginal-cost (MC) curve** shows, for each output, the increase in the firm's total cost required if it increases its output by an additional unit. Geometrically, MC is the slope of the TC curve. In symbols, $MC = \Delta TC/\Delta Q$.

Total cost (TC) was just explained. But it is worth stressing that TC is not quite the same as the total expenditure of the firm. Expenditure and cost are not equal because, to an economist, "cost" must include the *opportunity costs* of inputs provided by owners of the firm—even though the owners do not explicitly "charge" for those inputs. Thus, if to produce 1600 bushels of corn, Farmer Pfister must purchase $2100 of fertilizer, and $200 of other inputs, and in addition he himself provides labour time, capital, and land whose opportunity cost is $800 (that is, those inputs could have earned $800 elsewhere), then the total cost of the 1600 bushels equals $2300 in input expenditures plus $800 in opportunity cost, or $3100.

Average cost (AC), also called *unit cost*, is simply total cost divided by output; that is:

$$\text{Average cost} = \frac{\text{Total cost}}{\text{Quantity of output}},$$

or in symbols:

$$AC = \frac{TC}{Q}.$$

To determine the *marginal cost* (MC), we must know what would happen to TC if output were to increase by one unit. For example, the marginal cost of a fifth unit of output, MC_5, is the amount that production of this unit increases total cost. That is, it is equal to the excess of the total cost of the fifth unit, TC_5, over the total cost of the fourth unit, TC_4. Thus $MC_5 = TC_5 - TC_4$. More generally,

$$MC = \frac{\Delta TC}{\Delta Q}.$$

Table 21–4 presents the calculation for marginal cost systematically. For variety, we deal this time with the number of houses built per month by a construction firm that turns out standardized homes. We assume that the firm's total costs have already been determined from the relation between its inputs and its outputs, just as we did in the case of Farmer Pfister. For example, the coloured entries show that the total cost of four houses is $360,000, and of five houses, $425,000.

From the TC data we can next obtain the AC figure for each output. For example, we see that the AC of four houses is $360,000/4 = $90,000. We can also obtain the MC figures from the TC numbers. For example, by subtracting the TC of five houses from the TC of four houses, we see that the MC of producing the fifth house is $425,000 − $360,000 = $65,000. In general:

TABLE 21-4
Hypothetical Total, Average, and Marginal Costs of a Home-Construction Firm

HOUSES BUILT PER PERIOD	TOTAL COST (thousands of dollars)	MARGINAL COST (thousands of dollars)	AVERAGE COST (thousands of dollars)
0	0		—
1	210	210	210
2	270	60	135
3	306	36	102
4	360	54	90
5	425	65	85
6	516	91	86
7	700	184	100

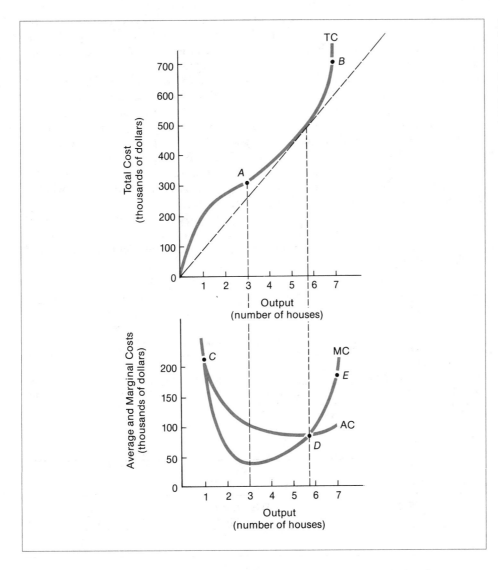

FIGURE 21-4
Total, Average, and Marginal Costs
These cost curves of a hypothetical home-construction firm are based on figures presented in Table 21-4. These curves show how the firm's total, average, and marginal costs behave when the firm changes its decision on how many houses to produce. For any quantity of output, the AC curve in the lower panel shows, as a height, the slope of the ray joining the point on the TC curve for that quantity to the origin (upper panel), and the MC curve shows, as a height, the slope of the tangent to the TC curve at the same quantity. At the quantity level indicated by point *D*, this ray and this tangent are one and the same line; that is why the MC and the AC curves intersect here.

Once we know a firm's total costs for its various outputs, we can calculate its average costs and its marginal costs from the same information.[2]

---

[2]The process also works the other way. If we know AC, we can work backwards to find TC from the formula $TC = AC \times Q$. Similarly, if we know all the firm's marginal costs, we can work backwards to find its total costs.

Figure 21–4 plots the numbers in this table and thus shows the total-, average-, and marginal-cost curves for the construction firm. The shapes of the curves depicted here are considered typical. The TC curve is generally assumed to rise fairly steadily as the firm's output increases. After all, one cannot expect to produce three houses at a lower total cost than two houses. The AC curve and the MC curve are both shown to be shaped roughly like the letter U—first going downhill then gradually turning uphill again.

To explain these characteristic shapes, we must first distinguish between two important types of costs.

Fixed Costs and Variable Costs

Fixed costs are unavoidable overhead costs that do not vary when the firm's output level changes. Any other cost of the firm is called a variable cost.

Total, average, and marginal costs are often divided into two components: **fixed costs** and **variable costs**. A *fixed cost* is the cost of the indivisible inputs that the firm needs to produce any output at all. The total cost of such inputs does not change when the firm changes its outputs by an amount that does not exceed the inputs' production capacity. Any other cost of the firm's operation is called *variable* because the total amount of that cost will increase when the firm's output rises.

The difference between fixed costs and variable costs can be illustrated by comparing the cost of a railway's fuel with that of its track construction. To operate between Winnipeg and Regina a railway must lay a set of tracks. It cannot lay half a set of tracks or a quarter of a set of tracks. We therefore call such an input "indivisible." The construction cost of the railway's tracks will be the same whether one train per month or five trains per day travel the route.[3] Thus, up to a point, track-construction cost is not affected by output size, that is, by volume of traffic. On the other hand, the more trains that pass over those tracks, the higher the railway's total fuel bill will be. We therefore say that fuel costs are variable.

Although variable costs are only part of overall costs (fixed plus variable costs), the variable costs of a firm exhibit patterns of behaviour like those already shown in Table 21–4 and Figure 21–4. However, curves of *total fixed costs* (TFC) and *average fixed costs* (AFC) have very special patterns, which are illustrated in Table 21–5 and Figure 21–5. We see that TFC remains the same, whether the firm produces a lot or a little.[4] As a result, any TFC curve, like the one in Figure 21–5(a), is horizontal—it has the same height at every output.

[3]Note, however, that an increase in traffic will increase annual maintenance and replacement costs, so that replacement and maintenance are variable costs. Note also that opportunity costs can be fixed, variable, or a combination of the two.

[4]Here we assume that the fixed costs are also what economists call *sunk costs*, meaning that the firm has already spent the money in question or signed a contract to do so. Consequently, if it decides to go out of business (produce zero output), it must still spend the money. (Sunk costs are further discussed later in this chapter.)

TABLE 21–5
Hypothetical Fixed Costs of a Home-Construction Firm

HOUSES BUILT PER PERIOD	TOTAL FIXED COST (thousands of dollars)	AVERAGE FIXED COST (thousands of dollars)
0	120	—
1	120	120
2	120	60
3	120	40
4	120	30
5	120	24
6	120	20

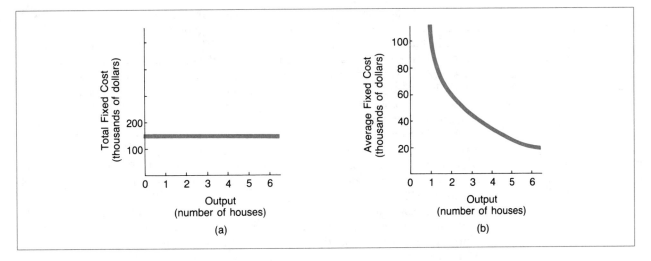

FIGURE 21-5
Fixed-Cost Curves: Total and Average
The total-fixed-cost curve [part (a)] is horizontal because, by definition, TFC does not change when output changes. AFC in part (b) decreases steadily as the TFC is spread among more and more units of output, but because AFC never reaches zero, the AFC curve never crosses the horizontal axis.

Average fixed cost, however, gets smaller and smaller as output increases because with TFC constant, AFC = TFC/Q gets smaller and smaller as output (the denominator) increases. Put another way, any increase in output permits the fixed cost to be spread among more units, leaving less and less of it to be carried by any one unit. For example, when only one house is built, the entire $120,000 of the firm's fixed cost must be borne by that one house. But if the firm constructs two homes, each of them need cover only half the total—$60,000.

However, AFC can never reach zero because even if the firm were to produce, say, a million houses, each would have to bear, on the average, one millionth of the TFC, which is still a positive number, even if it is a very small one. It follows that the AFC curve goes lower and lower as output increases, moving closer and closer to the horizontal axis but never crossing it. This is the pattern shown in Figure 21-5(b).

Since we have simply divided costs into two parts, fixed costs (FC) and variable costs (VC), we also have the rules:

$$TC = TFC + TVC \qquad\qquad AC = AFC + AVC$$

The total-fixed-cost curve is always horizontal because, by definition, total fixed cost does not change when output changes. The average-fixed-cost curve declines when output increases, getting closer and closer to the horizontal axis but never crossing it.

Shapes of the Average-Cost and Total-Cost Curves

The preceding discussion of fixed and variable costs enables us to complete our investigation of the shapes of the total-, average-, and marginal-cost curves. Since the cost curves depend on the physical product curves, these technological relationships should serve to explain the shapes of the cost curves. We will next discuss what they imply about the shapes of the AC and TC curves.

We have drawn the AC curve to be U-shaped in the lower panel of Figure 21-4: The leftward portion of the curve is downward sloping, and the rightward portion is upward sloping. Why should we expect AC to decline when output increases in the leftward portion of the AC curve? Part of the answer is that production technology often exhibits increasing returns in that "start-up" range of output levels, and increasing returns mean decreasing costs. But fixed costs are a major element in the answer too. As we have seen in Figure 21–5(b), the average-*fixed*-cost curve always falls as output increases, and it falls very sharply at the leftward end of the AFC curve. But AC = AFC + AVC, so that the AC curve of virtually any product contains a fixed-cost portion, AFC, which falls when output increases. That is the main reason we can expect the AC curve for any product to have a downward-sloping portion such as *CD* in the lower panel of Figure 21–4—a portion that is said to be characterized by decreasing average cost.

By decreasing average cost, we mean that when quantity goes up by, say, 10 percent, total cost goes up by less than 10 percent, so that average cost, which is the ratio TC/Q, will fall. For example, if when $Q = 100$, TC = $1000, then AC = $1000/$100 = $10. Now, suppose Q rises by 20 percent to 120 units; if TC rises by only 8 percent to $1080, then AC must fall to $1080/120 = $9. All of this is related to the concept of economies of scale, which is discussed later in the chapter. However, we must postpone discussion of that concept because so far in our analysis we have allowed only one input quantity to vary, while the economies-of-scale concept refers to the consequence of changing all input quantities simultaneously.

Similarly, in the range between D and E in the same figure, AC is rising. This, then, is the zone of increasing average costs—a given percentage rise in output requires a greater percentage rise in TC, so that AC = TC/Q must rise. But why does the portion of the AC curve with decreasing average cost come to an end? There are two reasons: (1) the law of diminishing returns, and (2) the administrative (bureaucratic) problems of large organizations.

The first of these phenomena is crucial for our present discussion, in which we are expanding one input (quantity of fertilizer) while holding all other input quantities constant. In that case we can be sure that the law of diminishing returns will work to increase marginal (and average) costs, for reasons we have already considered. Moreover, in reality, where firms can and do vary more than one input quantity, the law of diminishing returns also works to raise MC and AC because a firm may not be able to expand all of its inputs in proportion as its output increases. For example, it may not be able to expand the time the very top management of the company devotes to its operation because there are limits to the number of hours the president can put in. Even if all other inputs double, the president may not be able to double the amount of time she puts in. With some inputs not expanding while others are, diminishing returns to the expanding inputs can be expected because the expanding inputs will grow less and less efficient and that will tend to raise average costs.

The second source of increasing average cost in practice stems from sheer size. Large firms tend to be relatively bureaucratic, impersonal, and costly to manage. As the personal touch of top management is lost and the firm becomes very large, costs will ultimately rise disproportionately, and average cost will ultimately be driven upward.

The point at which average cost begins to rise varies from industry to industry. It occurs at a much larger volume of output in automobile production than in farming—which is why no farms are as big as even the smallest of automobile producers. A large part of the reason is that the fixed costs of automobile production are far greater than those in farming, so the resulting spreading of fixed costs over the increasing number of units of output keeps AC falling in auto production for a far larger range of output than it does in farming. Thus, although firms in both industries may have U-shaped AC curves, the bottom of the U occurs at a far larger output in auto production than in farming.

The typical AC curve of a firm is U-shaped. Its downward-sloping segment is largely attributable to the fact that the firm's fixed costs are spread over larger and larger outputs. The upward-sloping segment is attributable to diminishing returns and the disproportionate rise in administrative cost that occurs as the firm grows larger. The output at which decreasing average cost ends or at which increasing average cost begins varies across industries. The greater the relative size of fixed costs, the higher will tend to be the output at which the switchover occurs.

This, then, indicates the basis for economists' conclusion that AC curves tend to be U-shaped.[5] Since the shape of the TC curve does not play a major role in introductory discussions in microeconomics, only a few words will be said on this subject.

Going back to Figure 21–4 (upper panel), we see that between points 0 and A the TC curve is rising, but at a declining rate (its slope keeps falling). Roughly speaking, this means that in this region TC goes up less rapidly than Q. Farther to the right, however, TC rises at an increasing rate, so that TC goes up more rapidly than Q. Since marginal cost is the increase in total costs divided by the increase in output, MC $= \Delta TC/\Delta Q$, marginal cost at any level of output is just the slope of the total-cost curve at that point. Thus, portion $0A$ of the TC curve in the upper panel of Figure 21–4 corresponds to the falling portion of the MC curve in the lower panel. On the other hand, region AB of the TC curve is the portion of the TC curve corresponding to the rising portion of the MC curve. Thus, the shape of the $0A$ region of the TC curve corresponds to that of the negatively sloped region of the MC curve—both reflect the spreading of fixed costs over an increasing output. And, similarly, diminishing returns and disproportionate increases in administrative costs can account for segment AB of the TC curve, just as they help explain the rising portion of the MC curve.

Long-Run versus Short-Run Costs

The cost to the firm of a change in its output depends very much on the period of time under consideration. The reason is that, at any point in time, many input choices are *precommitted* by past decisions. If, for example, the firm purchased machinery a year ago, it is committed to that decision for the remainder of the machine's economic life, unless the company is willing to take the loss involved in getting rid of it sooner. A precommitted cost is said to be **sunk**.

An input to which the firm is committed for a short period of time, however, is not a fixed commitment when a longer planning horizon is considered. For example, a two-year-old machine with a nine-year economic life is a fixed commitment for the next seven years, but it is not a fixed commitment in plans that extend beyond the seven years. Economists summarize this notion by speaking of two different "runs" for decision-making—the **short run** and the **long run**.

These terms will recur time and again in this book. They interest us now because of their relationship to the shape of the cost curve. In the short run, there is relatively little opportunity for the firm to adapt its production processes to the size of its current output because the size of its plant has largely been predetermined by its past decisions. Over the long run, however, all inputs, including the size of the plant, become adjustable.

Consider the example of Farmer Pfister. Once the crop is planted, he has little discretion over how much of the various inputs to use. Over a somewhat longer planning horizon, he can decide how much labour to employ and how much seed to use. Over a still longer period, he can acquire new equipment and increase or decrease the size of his farm. Much the same is true of big industrial firms. In the short run, management has little control over the production technique. But with some advance planning, different types of machines using different amounts of labour and energy can be acquired, factories can be redesigned, and other choices can be made. Indeed,

A **sunk cost** is a cost to which a firm is precommitted for some limited period, either because the firm has signed a contract to make the payments or because it has already paid for some durable item (such as a machine or a factory) and cannot get its money back.

The **short run** is a period of time briefer than the long run, so that some, but not all, of the firm's sunk commitments will have ended.

The **long run** is a period of time long enough for all the firm's sunk commitments to come to an end.

[5] Empirical evidence confirms this view, though it suggests that the bottom of the U is often long and flat. That is to say, there is often a considerable range of outputs between the regions of scale economies and scale diseconomies. In this intermediate region the AC curve is approximately horizontal, meaning that there AC does not change when output increases.

over the longest run, no inputs remain committed; all of them can be varied in both quantity and design.

It should be noted that the short and long runs do not refer to the same period of time for all firms; rather, they vary in length depending on the nature of the firm's sunk commitments. If, for example, the firm can change its work force every week, its machines every two years, and its factory every twenty years, then twenty years will be the long run, and any period shorter than twenty years will constitute the short run.

The Average-Cost Curve in the Short and Long Runs

As we just observed, which inputs can be varied and which are precommitted depends on the time horizon under consideration. It follows that:

The average- (and total-) cost curve depends on the firm's planning horizon. The average- (and total-) cost curve pertinent to the long run differs from that for the short run because more inputs become variable.

We can, in fact, be much more specific about the relationships between short-run and long-run average-cost (AC) curves. Consider, as an example, the publisher of a small newspaper. In the short run, the firm can choose only the number of typesetters and printers and the quantity of paper and ink it uses, but in the long run, it can also choose between two different sizes of printing press. If the firm purchases the smaller press, the AC curve looks like curve *SL* in Figure 21–6. That means that if the paper is pleasantly surprised and its circulation grows to 50,000 copies per day, its cost will be 12 cents per copy (point *V*). It may then wish it had purchased the bigger press (whose AC curve is shown as *BG*), which would have enabled the firm to cut unit cost to 9 cents per copy (point *W*). However, in the short run nothing can be done about this decision; the AC curve remains *SL*. Similarly, had it bought the larger press, its short-run AC curve would have been *BG* and it would have been committed to this cost curve even if business were to decline sharply.

In the long run, however, the machine must be replaced, and management has its choice once again. If it expects a circulation of 50,000 copies, it will purchase the larger press and its cost will be 9 cents per copy. Similarly, if it expects sales of only 20,000 copies, it will arrange for the smaller press and for average costs of 12 cents per copy (point *U*). In sum, in the long run, the firm will select the press size (that is, the short-run AC curve) that is most economical for the output level it expects to produce. The long-run average-cost curve, then, consists of all the *lower* segments of the short-run AC curves. In Figure 21–6, this composite curve is the coloured curve *STG*. If many different press sizes are possible, the long-run AC curve is a smooth locus that is tangent to all the short-run AC curves.

FIGURE 21–6
Short- and Long-Run Average-Cost Curves for a Newspaper
The publisher has a choice of two printing presses, a small one with AC curve *SL*, and a big one with AC curve *BG*. These are the short-run curves that apply as long as the newspaper is stuck with its chosen press. But in the long run, when it has its choice of press size, it can pick any point on the coloured lower boundary of these curves. This lower boundary, *STG*, is the long-run average-cost curve.

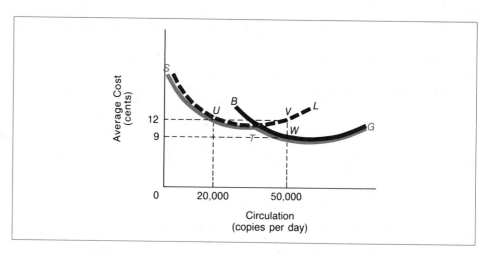

Multiple Input Decisions:
The Choice of Input Combinations*

Casual observation of industrial processes deludes many people into thinking that management really has very little discretion in choosing its inputs. Technological considerations alone, it would appear, dictate such choices. A particular type of furniture-cutting machine may require two operators working for an hour on a certain amount of wood to make five desks, no more and no less. But this is an overly narrow view of the matter; whoever first declared that there are many ways to skin a cat saw things more clearly.

The furniture manufacturer may have several alternative production processes for making desks. For example, there may be simpler and cheaper machines that can change the same pile of wood into five desks using more than two hours of labour. Or still more workers could eventually do the job with simple hand tools, using no machinery at all. The firm will seek the *least costly* method of production. In advanced industrial societies, where labour is expensive and machinery is cheap, it may pay to use the most automated process; in more primitive societies, where machinery is scarce and labour abundant, making desks by hand may be the most economical solution. In other words, one input can generally be *substituted* for another.

A method of analysis that a business firm can use to select the least costly production process is described next. But you should know at the outset that the analysis is applicable well beyond the confines of business enterprises. Non-profit organizations, like your own university, are interested in finding the least costly ways to accomplish a variety of tasks (for example, maintaining the grounds and buildings); government agencies are concerned with meeting their objectives at minimum costs. Even in the household, there are many "cats" that can be "skinned" in different ways. Thus our present analysis of **cost minimization** is widely applicable.

The Marginal Rule for Optimal Input Proportions: An Introduction

The second main topic of this chapter is the optimal choice of input quantities. Common sense guides the principles that can be used to determine what input proportions will minimize the cost of producing a given output. To bring out the logic of those principles, suppose Farmer Pfister is considering whether to use more fertilizer and less pesticide, or vice versa, in producing his contractually required 1600-bushel output of corn. Suppose also that fertilizer costs $350 per tonne, as in our earlier example, while an additional spraying of his land with pesticide costs exactly four times as much—$1400. If the marginal physical product of a tonne of fertilizer is 250 bushels, but the marginal physical product of an additional pesticide spraying is 750 bushels, what should Pfister do?

A little thought indicates the answer: Farmer Pfister should cut down on spraying and increase his use of fertilizer. Why? Because the pesticide costs four times as much as the fertilizer, but yields only three times as much corn; that is, *the ratio of the marginal product of pesticide to the marginal product of fertilizer is less than the ratio of the price of pesticide to the price of fertilizer.*

Let us examine the reasoning a bit more closely. Given the ratios in our example, it must pay the farmer to spend less on pesticide and more on fertilizer, because in doing so he will end up producing the same 1600 bushels of corn, but at a lower input cost. Suppose, for example, that Pfister decides to spend $1400 less on pesticide, thus

---

*Instructors may want to teach this part of the chapter (up to page 472) now or they may prefer to wait until they come to Chapter 29 on the determination of wages, interest rates, profit, and rent.

cutting back one spraying of his land. This reduces his output by 750 bushels (the marginal product of pesticide). How much more fertilizer does he need to undo this output reduction? The answer is that with the MPP of fertilizer equal to 250 bushels, it will take about 3 additional tonnes of fertilizer to make up the shortfall. But, at a price of $350 per tonne, the three tonnes of fertilizer will cost the farmer just $1050. Thus, by trading one pesticide spraying for three tonnes of fertilizer, the farmer ends up saving $1400 – $1050 = $350, and producing the same output.

Such a move will *always* work out in this way. By switching away from the input with the *lower* marginal product per dollar and buying enough more of the input with the *higher* marginal product per dollar, the firm can reduce the money it spends on inputs without any reduction in output. This gives us the first basic rule for attaining the most economical input proportion for the production of a given output quantity:

A firm can reduce the cost of producing a given output quantity by using less of some input, *A*, and making up for it by using more of another input, *B*, whenever the ratio of the price of input *A* to the price of input *B* exceeds the ratio of the marginal physical product of *A* to the marginal physical product of *B*. That is, whenever

$$P_a/P_b > \mathrm{MPP}_a/\mathrm{MPP}_b,$$

costs can be reduced by reducing the proportion of input *A* to input *B* used.

Obviously, the opposite will be true if the relative price of *A* is lower than its relative marginal product. In other words, input proportions *cannot* be optimal if the ratio of the prices of two inputs is not equal to the ratio of their marginal products. That is,

The proportions of any two inputs, *A* and *B*, used by the firm can be optimal only if

$$P_a/P_b = \mathrm{MPP}_a/\mathrm{MPP}_b.$$

This rule also makes common sense. If a unit of input *A* has a marginal product that is, for example, three times as big as that of input *B*, the firm should be willing to pay exactly three times as much money for an additional unit of *A* as it does for an additional unit of *B*, no more and no less.

But what if the market happens to set input prices so that this doesn't work? Suppose the market price of *A* happens to be four times as large as that of *B*, as in our corn-growing example. What can the farmer do about it? We have seen that in this case the farmer will buy less of *A* (pesticide) and more of *B* (fertilizer). That will not change the market *prices* of fertilizer and pesticide. But it will change the *marginal physical products* of the two inputs because of the effects of *the law of diminishing returns*. As Farmer Pfister buys more fertilizer relative to pesticide, the marginal product of fertilizer will ultimately go down, as indicated in Table 21–2 and Figure 21–3(a). For exactly the same reason, as pesticide use falls and it becomes relatively scarce, its marginal product will rise. When the farmer has gone far enough in switching money from pesticide to fertilizer, the ratio of their marginal products will rise from 3:1 up to 4:1. It will then equal the ratio of the prices of the two inputs, so the rule for cost minimization will be satisfied.

Changes in Input Prices and Optimal Input Proportions

The common-sense reasoning behind the rule for optimal input proportions leads to an important conclusion. Suppose the price of fertilizer rises while the price of pesticide remains the same. The rule

$$P \text{ of fertilizer}/P \text{ of pesticide} = \mathrm{MPP} \text{ of fertilizer}/\mathrm{MPP} \text{ of pesticide}$$

Input Substitution on the Range

When at the end of the 1970s the second fuel crisis hit North America, the newspapers carried a story about ranchers in the Southwest United States reportedly hiring additional cowhands to drive cattle on foot instead of carrying them on trucks. In other words, the rising price of oil had led ranchers to substitute the work of cowhands for the gasoline formerly used in driving cattle-carrying trucks. This is no scenario from a Wild West movie but an illustration of the way in which life follows the analytical principles described in the text, substituting inputs whose relative price has not risen for inputs whose relative price has risen.

There are many other illustrations of this phenomenon. It helps to explain the disappearance, in half a century, of personal servants, who were once commonplace in the homes of middle-class families (in the 1920s "every" such home had at least a full-time maid) and the substitution of washing machines, clothes dryers, and dishwashers as real wages rose. It also helps to account for the disappearance of

wooden houses in England as forests disappeared and wood became increasingly expensive compared with other building materials. You can undoubtedly come up with other examples without difficulty.

---

tells us that the optimal use of fertilizer now requires that the MPP of fertilizer must be higher than before. By the "law" of diminishing returns, the MPP of fertilizer is *higher* only when *less* fertilizer is used. Thus a rise in the price of fertilizer leads the farmer to use *less* fertilizer and, if he still wants to produce 1600 bushels of output, to use *more* pesticide. In general:

As any one input becomes more costly relative to other competing inputs, the firm is likely to substitute one input for another; that is, to reduce its use of the input that has become more expensive and to increase its use of competing inputs.

This general principle of input substitution applies in industry just as it does on Farmer Pfister's farm. For some applications of the analysis, see the box above.

The Production Function

To help select the combination of inputs that can produce the desired output most cheaply, economists have invented a concept they call the **production function**. The production function summarizes the technical and engineering information about the relationship between inputs and output in a given firm, taking *all* the firm's inputs into account. It indicates, for example, just how much output Farmer Pfister can produce if he has given amounts of land, labour, fertilizer, and so on.

When there are only two inputs—which are enough to indicate the basic principles involved—a production function can be represented graphically (which we do in the appendix to this chapter) or by a simple table. Table 21–6 indicates Farmer Pfister's production function for the use of two inputs, labour and fertilizer, to produce corn on his farm. To make the table easier to read, most of the numbers that normally would be entered (but that are irrelevant for our purposes) have been replaced by dashes.

The table is read like a city-to-city distance chart. So, to see how much can be produced with two tonnes of fertilizer and three months of labour, we locate the 2 in the column of numbers on the left, which indicates the quantity of fertilizer, and the 3

The **production function** indicates the *maximum* amount of product that can be obtained from any specified *combination* of inputs, given the current state of knowledge. That is, it shows the *largest* quantity of goods that any particular collection of inputs is capable of producing.

TABLE 21–6
A Production Function

			QUANTITY OF LABOUR (months)			
	0	1	2	3	4	5
QUANTITY OF FERTILIZER (tonnes)	1	250	900	1400	1600	—
	2	550	1250	1600	1800	—
	3	900	1450	1750	—	—
	4	1200	1600	—	2400	—
	5	1450	2000	—	—	—
	6	1600	—	—	3900	—
	7	1650	—	—	—	—
	8	1650	2700	3600	4400	5000
	9	1600	—	—	—	—

in the row of numbers across the top, which represents the quantity (in months) of labour. Then, in the spot horizontally to the right of the 2 and vertically below the 3, we find the number 1600, meaning that this input combination can produce 1600 bushels of output per month. Similarly, you should be able to verify that with eight tonnes of fertilizer and three months of labour, 3600 bushels per month can be produced.

The first column of Table 21–6, which corresponds to alternative amounts of fertilizer used in combination with *one* month of labour, is familiar to us already—it is just the total physical product schedule that we have been using for Farmer Pfister working alone with various amounts of fertilizer. The other columns represent alternative production arrangements in which Pfister hires one or more farmhands to help him.

How much labour and fertilizer should Farmer Pfister use if he wants to grow 1600 bushels of corn? The production-function table shows us that there are a variety of alternatives available to him. He can, for example, work alone and use six tonnes of fertilizer. Or he can hire a second worker and use only four tonnes. The coloured entries in Table 21–6 indicate all the different ways in which Farmer Pfister can conceivably meet his 1600-bushel production target.

Which will he choose? Naturally, the one that costs him the least. Table 21–7 shows Farmer Pfister's cost calculations. It is assumed here that fertilizer costs $350 per tonne, that farm labour costs $500 per month, and that Pfister's sunk costs on such items as land and machinery amount to $800 per month. Thus, for example, the first line tells us that Pfister can produce 1600 bushels using only his own labour (which costs $500), six tonnes of fertilizer (which cost $2100), and land and machinery that cost $800 per month, for a total cost of $500 + $2100 + $800 = $3400. The other lines in Table 21–7 can be read the same way. We see that the cheapest way to produce 1600

TABLE 21–7
Production Costs under Alternative Input Combinations Capable of Producing 1600 Bushels

QUANTITY OF LABOUR (months)	COST OF LABOUR (at $500 per month)	QUANTITY OF FERTILIZER (tonnes)	COST OF FERTILIZER (at $350 per tonne)	FIXED COSTS (for land, machinery, etc.)	TOTAL COST
1	$ 500	6	$2100	$ 800	$3400
2	1000	4	1400	800	3200
3	1500	2	700	800	3000
4	2000	1	350	800	3150

bushels of corn is by using three workers and two tonnes of fertilizer, for a total cost of $3000, which is less than any other alternative.

Notice that two types of information are relevant to Farmer Pfister's decision. The *technological information* embodied in the production function tells Pfister all the possible ways that 1600 bushels can be produced; that is, it tells him about the possibilities for factor substitution. Then *financial information*—the prices of the two inputs—is needed to tell him which alternative is the least costly. As we saw from our analysis in the preceding section, if either set of data changes, Farmer Pfister's decision on input combinations is likely to change as well. For example, if fertilizer gets much more expensive, he might switch to an alternative that uses more labour and less fertilizer.[6]

The Firm's Cost Curves

Earlier we calculated the firm's cost curves in the special case where the quantity of only one input—fertilizer—was selected by the firm. Now we can see how the cost curves can be determined in the more realistic case of choices about the quantities of several inputs.

In deciding on the quantity of output that serves its objectives best, the firm must consider alternative production levels and compare their costs. In the present example, an output of 1600 bushels is not likely to be the only possible production level that Farmer Pfister is considering. He might wonder, for example, about the least costly way to produce 1100 bushels or 2100 bushels.

By the same procedures as those outlined in Table 21–7, Farmer Pfister can compute the minimum cost of producing *any* quantity of output, using the logic of the requirement that in such a cost-minimizing decision the relative marginal physical products of any two inputs must equal their relative prices.

Let us suppose that Farmer Pfister has calculated the minimum total costs for alternative production levels displayed in Table 21–8. Here we have the numbers Pfister needs to plot five different points on his *total-cost curve*, which is the curve shown in Figure 21–7. Point A shows the $2700 total cost of 1200 bushels of output,

[6]EXERCISE: Suppose that fertilizer rises in price to $600 per tonne. Construct a new version of Table 21–7 and use it to show that it will be optimal to reduce fertilizer use from two tonnes to zero and to increase the use of labour from three months to five months.

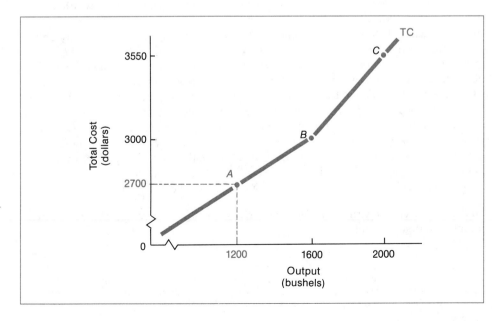

TABLE 21–8
Data for Pfister's Total-Cost Curve

OUTPUT LEVEL (bushels)	TOTAL COST (TC) (dollars)
1200	2700
1600	3000
2000	3550

FIGURE 21–7
Total-Cost Curve
Point A shows that to produce 1200 bushels per month, a total of $2700 in cost must be incurred, just as Table 21–8 indicates.

point B shows the $3000 total cost of 1600 bushels, and point C shows the $3550 total cost of 2000 bushels. As before, by dividing the total cost for each output by the quantity of the output, we obtain the corresponding *average cost*; that is, the cost per unit of output. For example, when output is 1600 bushels, total cost is $3000; so average cost is $3000/1600, or $1.88. Similarly, we can deduce the marginal-cost curve from the total-cost figures, just as we did before.

Economies of Scale

We are now beginning to put together the apparatus we need to address the question posed at the start of this chapter: How can we tell if a firm has substantial **economies of scale**? We are now in a position to give a definition of this concept.

Production is said to involve **economies of scale**, also referred to as **increasing returns to scale**, if, when all input quantities are doubled, the quantity of output is more than doubled.

The scale of operation of a business enterprise is defined by the quantities of the various inputs it uses. To see what happens when the firm doubles its scale of operations, we inquire about the effect on output of a doubling of each and every one of the firm's input quantities. As an example of economies of scale, turn back to the production function for Farmer Pfister in Table 21–6 on page 468 and assume that labour and fertilizer are the only two inputs.[7] Notice that with two months of labour and four tonnes of fertilizer, output is 1600 bushels. What happens if we double both inputs—to four months of labour and eight tonnes of fertilizer? The table shows us that output rises to 4400—that is, it more than doubles. So Farmer Pfister's production function, at least in this range, is said to display **increasing returns to scale** (economies of scale).

Economies of scale seem to be present in many modern industries. Where they are present they foster large firm size because then large firms have a cost advantage over small ones. Automobile production and telecommunications are examples commonly cited.

The reasons for scale economies are technological—that is, the technical nature of an economic activity determines whether or not it is characterized by scale economies. Consider warehouse space as an example of one such type of technical relationship. Imagine that there are two warehouses, each shaped like a perfect cube, but that warehouse A has length, width, and height equal to 100 feet, while in warehouse B those dimensions are each equal to 200 feet. Because the area of a square floor or a square wall is equal to the square of its length, the amount of land and building material (bricks, and so on) of warehouse B will be four times as great as that of warehouse A. However, since the area of a cube equals length times width times height—that is, its area equals the cube of its length—warehouse B will have $2^3 = 8$ times as much storage space as warehouse A. Thus, multiplying each input (roughly) by 4 yields 8 times the storage space. This example is, of course, oversimplified, and omits such complications as the need for stronger supports in taller buildings, the increased difficulty of moving goods in and out of higher storeys, and the like. Still, the basic idea is correct, and shows why, up to a point, the very nature of warehousing creates technological relationships that lead to economies of scale.

We can relate our definition of economies of scale to the shape of the *long-run* average-cost curve instead of the production function. Notice that the definition requires a doubling of *every* input to bring about more than a doubling of output. If all input quantities are doubled, then total cost must double. But if output *more* than doubles as a result, then cost per unit (average cost) must decline. In other words:

Production functions with economies of scale lead to long-run average-cost curves that decline as output expands.

---

[7] This assumption is necessary because the table deals with only two inputs and the definition requires that *all* inputs be doubled simultaneously. So, to be true to the definition, because labour, fertilizer, land, and machinery were all used by the farmer, their quantities would all have to be doubled.

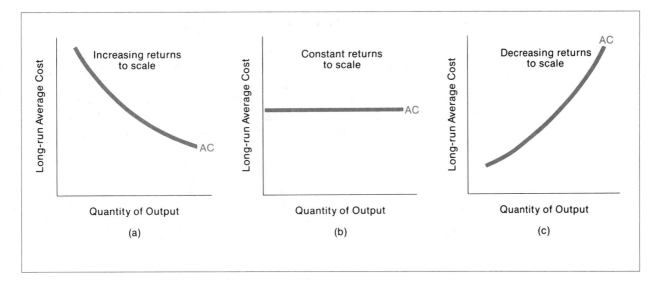

FIGURE 21-8
Three Possible Shapes for the Long-Run Average-Cost Curve
In part (a), long-run average costs are decreasing as output expands because the firm has significant economies of scale (increasing returns to scale). In part (b), constant returns to scale lead to a long-run AC curve that is flat; costs per unit are the same for any level of output. In part (c), which pertains to a firm with decreasing returns to scale, long-run average costs rise as output expands.

An example will clarify the arithmetic behind this rule. We saw earlier (Table 21-7) that it costs $3200 to produce 1600 bushels of corn with two months of labour and four tonnes of fertilizer. The average cost is thus $2 per bushel. If, as the production function states, doubling all inputs (and thus doubling costs to $6400) leads to production of 4400 bushels, then cost per unit will become $6400/4400, or approximately $1.45. Economies of scale in the production function thus lead to *decreasing* average cost as output expands; in this case, average cost decreases by 55 cents—from $2 to $1.45.

A decreasing average-cost curve is depicted in Figure 21-8(a). But this is only one of three possible shapes the long-run average-cost curve can take. A second possibility is shown in part (b) of the figure. In this case we have an example of **constant returns to scale**, where both total cost (TC) and quantity of output (Q) double, so average cost (AC = TC/Q) remains constant. Finally, it is possible that output less than doubles when all inputs double. This would be a case of **decreasing returns to scale**, which leads to a rising long-run average-cost curve like the one depicted in Figure 21-8(c). Thus there is an association between the slope of the AC curve and the nature of the firm's return to scale; the correspondence is precise if the firm does find it efficient to carry out any changes in its output by means of proportionate changes in all of its inputs.

It should be pointed out that the same production function can display increasing returns to scale in some ranges, constant returns to scale in others, and decreasing returns to scale in yet others. Farmer Pfister's production function in Table 21-6 provides an illustration of this. We have already seen that it displays increasing returns to scale when inputs are doubled from two months of labour and four tonnes of fertilizer to four months of labour and eight tonnes of fertilizer. But, looking back at Table 21-6 (page 468), we can see that there are constant returns to scale when inputs double from two months of labour and one tonne of fertilizer (900 bushels of output) to four months of labour and two tonnes of fertilizer (1800 bushels). We can also find a region of decreasing returns to scale. Notice that with two months of labour and two tonnes of fertilizer the yield is 1250 bushels, while with double those inputs—four months of labour and four tonnes of fertilizer—the yield is only 2400 bushels.

Diminishing Returns and Returns to Scale

Earlier in this chapter we discussed the "law" of diminishing marginal returns. Is there any relationship between economies of scale and the phenomenon of diminishing returns? It may seem at first that the two are contradictory. After all, if a producer gets diminishing returns from his inputs as he uses more of each of them, doesn't it follow that by using more of *every* input, he cannot obtain economies of scale? The answer is that there is no contradiction, for the two principles deal with fundamentally different issues.

1. ***Returns to a single input.*** Here we must ask the question: How much can output expand if we increase the quantity of just *one* input, *holding all other input quantities unchanged*?

2. ***Returns to scale.*** Here the question is: How much can output expand if *all* inputs are increased *simultaneously* by the same percentage?

The "law" of diminishing returns provides an answer to the first question while economies of scale pertain to the second.

Table 21-6 shows us that Farmer Pfister's production function satisfies the "law" of diminishing returns to a single input. To see this, we must hold the quantity of one input constant while letting the other vary. The row corresponding to eight tonnes of fertilizer will serve as an example, since an entry is provided for every quantity of labour. Reading across the row, we see from the second entry that the use of one month of labour and eight tonnes of fertilizer yields 1650 bushels of corn. The next entry shows that the same eight tonnes of fertilizer plus one additional month of labour produces a marginal product of 1050 bushels (that is, the total of 2700 bushels produced by the two months of labour minus the 1650 bushels obtained from the first month's labour). In the third column we find that another month of labour (still holding fertilizer use at eight tonnes) brings in a smaller marginal product of 900 (3600 total bushels minus the 2700 bushels produced by the first two months' labour). The "law" of diminishing returns is clearly satisfied.

Returns to scale, on the other hand, describe the production response to a proportionate increase in *all* inputs. We have already seen that this production function displays increasing returns to scale in some ranges, constant returns to scale in others, and decreasing returns to scale in yet others. Thus, the "law" of diminishing returns (to a single input) is compatible with *any* sort of returns to scale. In summary:

Returns to scale and returns to a single input (holding all other input quantities constant) refer to two distinct aspects of a firm's technology. A production function that displays diminishing returns to *a single input* may show diminishing, constant, or increasing returns when *all input quantities are increased proportionately.*

Historical Costs versus Analytical Cost Curves

In the appendix to the previous chapter, we made much of the fact that all points on a demand curve pertain to the *same* period of time, and that a plot of historical data on prices and quantities is normally *not* the demand curve that the decision-maker needs. A similar point relating to cost curves will resolve the problem posed at the beginning of the chapter as to whether declining historical costs are evidence of economies of scale.

All points on any of the cost curves used in economic analysis refer to the same period of time.

One point on the cost curve of an auto manufacturer tells us, for example, how much it costs it to produce 2.5 million cars during 1991. Another point on the curve tells us what happens to the firm's costs if, *instead*, it produces, say, 3 million cars in 1991. Such a curve is called an **analytical cost curve** or, when there is no possibility of confusion, simply a cost curve. This curve must be distinguished from a diagram of **historical costs**, which shows how costs have changed from year to year.

The different points on an analytical cost curve represent *alternative possibilities*, all for the same time period. In 1991, the car manufacturer will produce either 2.5 or 3 million cars (or some other amount), but certainly not both. Thus, at most, only one point on this cost curve will ever be observed. The company may, indeed, produce 2.5 million in 1991 and 3 million in 1992, but the latter is not relevant to the 1991 cost curve. By the time 1992 comes around, the cost curve may well have shifted, so the 1991 cost figure will not apply to the 1992 cost curve. We can, of course, draw a different sort of graph that indicates, year by year, how costs and outputs have varied. Such a graph, which gathers together the statistics for a number of different periods, is not, however, a *cost curve* as that term is used by economists. An example of such a diagram of historical costs was given at the beginning of the chapter in Figure 21–1.

But why do economists rarely use historical cost diagrams and instead deal primarily with analytical cost curves, which are much more difficult to explain and to obtain statistically? The answer is that analysis of real policy problems—such as the desirability of having a single supplier of telephone services—leaves no choice in the matter. Rational decisions require analytical cost curves. Let us see why.

Resolving the Economies-of-Scale Puzzle

Since the 1940s there has been great technical progress in the telephone industry. From ordinary open wire, the industry has gone to microwave systems, telecommunications satellites, and coaxial cables of enormous capacity, and new techniques using laser beams are on the way. Innovations in switching techniques and in the use of computers to send messages along uncrowded routes are equally impressive. All of this means that the *entire* analytical cost curve of telecommunications must have shifted downward quite dramatically from year to year. Innovation must have reduced not only the cost of large-scale operations *but also the cost of smaller-scale operations*.

Now, if we are to determine whether in 1991 a single supplier can provide telephone service more cheaply than can a number of smaller firms, we must compare the costs of *both* large- and small-scale production in 1991. It does no good to compare the cost of a large supplier in 1991 with its own costs as a smaller firm back in 1942, because that cannot possibly give us the information we need. The cost situation in 1942 is irrelevant for today's decision between large and small suppliers because no small firm today would use the obsolete techniques of 1942. Until we compare the costs of the large and small supplier *today* we cannot make a rational choice between single-firm and multi-firm production. It is the analytical cost curve, all of whose points refer to the same period, that, by definition, supplies this information.

Figures 21–9 and 21–10 show two extreme hypothetical cases, one in which economies of scale are present and one in which they are not. Yet both of them are based on the same historical cost data (in black) with their very sharply declining costs. (This curve is reproduced from Figure 21–1.) They also show (in colour) two possible average-cost curves, one for 1942 and one for 1991. In Figure 21–9 the analytical AC curve (in green) has shifted downward very sharply from 1942 to 1991, as technological change reduced all costs. Moreover, both of the AC curves slope downward to the right, meaning that, in either year, the larger the firm the lower its average costs. Thus, the situation shown in Figure 21–9 really does represent a case in which there are economies of large-scale production so that one firm can produce at lower cost than many.

But now look at Figure 21–10, which shows exactly the same historical costs as Figure 21–9. Here, both analytical AC curves are U-shaped. In particular, we note that

FIGURE 21–9

Declining Historical Cost Curve with the Analytical Average-Cost Curve Also Declining in Each Year

The two analytical cost curves shown indicate how the corresponding points (*A* and *B*) on the historical cost diagram are generated by that year's analytical curve. The analytical cost curves are declining, so we know that there are economies of scale in the production activity whose costs are shown.

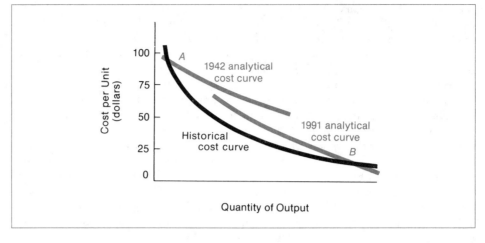

FIGURE 21–10

Declining Historical Cost Curve with U-Shaped Analytical Cost Curves in Each Year

Here the shape of the analytical average-cost curves does not show economies of scale.

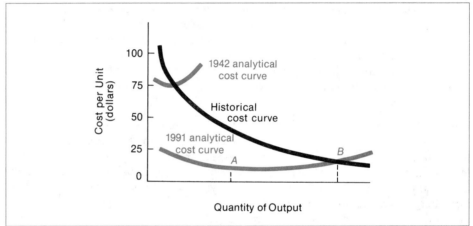

the 1991 AC curve has its minimum point at an output level, *A*, that is less than one-half the current output, *B*, of the large supplier. This means that in the situation shown in Figure 21–10, despite the sharp downward trend of historical costs, a smaller company can produce more cheaply than a large one can. In this case, one cannot justify domination of the market by a single large firm on the grounds that its costs are lower. In sum, the behaviour of historical costs tells us nothing about the cost advantages or disadvantages of a single large firm. More generally:

Because a diagram of historical costs does not compare the costs of large and small firms at the same point in time, it cannot be used to determine whether there are economies of large-scale production. Only the analytical cost curve can supply this information.

Cost Minimization in Theory and Practice

Lest you be tempted to run out and open a business, confident that you now understand how to minimize costs, we should point out that decision-making in business is a good deal harder than we have indicated here. Rare is the business executive who knows for sure what his production function looks like, or the exact shapes of his marginal revenue product schedules, or the precise nature of his cost curves. No one can provide a cookbook for instant success in business. What we have presented here is a set of principles that constitutes a guide to good decision-making.

Business management has been described as the art of making critical decisions on the basis of inadequate information, and in our complex and ever-changing world there is often no alternative to an educated guess. Actual business decisions will at best approximate the cost-minimizing ideal outlined in this chapter. Certainly, there will be mistakes. But when management does its job well and the market system functions smoothly, the approximation may prove amazingly good. While no system is perfect, inducing firms to produce at the lowest possible cost is undoubtedly one of the jobs the market system does best.

Summary

1. A firm's total-cost curve shows the lowest possible cost for producing any given level of output. It is derived from the input combination used to produce any given output and the prices of the inputs.
2. A firm's average-cost (AC) curve shows the lowest possible cost per unit at which it is possible to produce any given level of output. It is derived from the total-cost (TC) curve by simple arithmetic: $AC = TC/Q$.
3. A firm's marginal-cost (MC) curve shows for each output level the increase in total cost resulting from a one-unit increase in output.
4. The long run is a period sufficiently long for the firm's plant to require replacement and for all its current contractual commitments to expire. The short run is any period briefer than that.
5. Fixed costs are costs whose total amounts do not vary when output increases. All other costs are called *variable*. In the short run, fixed costs are *sunk*.
6. At all outputs, the total-fixed-cost (TFC) curve is horizontal, and the average-fixed-cost (AFC) curve declines toward the horizontal axis but never crosses it.
7. $TC = TFC + TVC$;
   $AC = AFC + AVC$;
   $MC = \Delta TC/\Delta Q = \Delta TVC/\Delta Q$.
8. It is normally possible to produce the same quantity of output in a variety of ways by substituting more of one input for less of another. Firms normally seek the least costly way to produce any given output.
9. The marginal physical product of an input is the increase in total output resulting from a one-unit increase in the use of that input, holding the quantities of all other inputs constant.

10. The "law" of diminishing marginal returns states that if we increase the amount of one input (holding all other input quantities constant), the marginal physical product of the expanding input will eventually begin to decline.
11. Profit maximization requires the firm to purchase that quantity of any input at which the input's marginal revenue product is equal to its price.
12. A firm that wants to minimize costs will use those quantities of any two inputs at which the ratio of their marginal physical products is equal to the ratio of the prices of those two inputs.
13. The production function shows the relationship between inputs and output. It indicates the maximum quantity of output obtainable from any given combination of inputs.
14. If a doubling of all the firm's inputs *just* permits it to double its output, the firm is said to have constant returns to scale. If with doubled inputs it can *more than* double its output, it has increasing returns to scale (or economies of scale). If a doubling of inputs produces *less than* double the output, the firm has decreasing returns to scale.
15. With increasing returns to scale, the firm's long-run average costs are decreasing; constant returns to scale are associated with constant long-run average costs.
16. We cannot tell if there are economies of scale (increasing returns to scale) simply by inspecting a diagram of historical cost data. Only the underlying analytical cost curve can supply this information.

Concepts for Review

Total physical product
Average physical product (APP)
Marginal physical product (MPP)
"Law" of diminishing marginal returns
Total-cost curve
Average-cost curve
Marginal-cost curve
Fixed cost

Variable cost
Sunk cost
Short and long runs
Substitutability of inputs
Cost minimization
Marginal revenue product (MRP)
Rule for optimal input use
Production function

Economies of scale (increasing returns to scale)
Constant returns to scale
Decreasing returns to scale
Historical versus analytical cost relationships

Questions for Discussion

1. A firm's total fixed cost is $44,000. Construct a table of total, average, and marginal fixed costs for this firm for output levels varying from 0 to 6 units. Draw the corresponding TFC and AFC curves.

2. With the data in the accompanying table, calculate the firm's AVC and MVC and draw the graphs for TVC, AVC, and MVC.

QUANTITY	TOTAL VARIABLE COSTS (thousands of dollars)
1	40
2	80
3	120
4	176
5	240
6	360

3. From the figures in Questions 1 and 2, calculate TC, AC, and MC for each of the output levels from 1 to 6, and draw the three graphs.

4. If a firm's commitments in 1991 include machinery that will need replacement in five years, a factory building rented for ten years, and a two-year union contract specifying how many workers it must employ, when, from its point of view in 1991, does the firm's long run begin?

5. If the marginal revenue product of a kilowatt hour of electric power is 8 cents and the cost of a kilowatt hour is 12 cents, what can a firm do to increase its profits?

6. A firm hires two workers and rents 15 hectares of land for a season. It produces 150,000 bushels of crop. If it had doubled its land and labour, production would have been 280,000 bushels. Does it have constant, diminishing, or increasing returns to scale?

7. Suppose wages are $25,000 per season and land rent per hectare is $4000. Calculate the average cost of 150,000 bushels and the average cost of 280,000 bushels, using the figures in Question 6 above. (Note that average costs diminish when output increases.) What connection do these figures have with the firm's returns to scale?

8. Farmer Pfister has bought a great deal of fertilizer. Suppose he now buys more *land*, but not more fertilizer, and spreads the fertilizer evenly over all his land. What may happen to the marginal physical product of fertilizer? What is the role of input proportions in the determination of marginal physical product?

9. Labour costs $10 per hour. Nine workers produce 180 bushels of product per hour. Ten workers produce 196 bushels. Land rents for $1000 per hectare per year. With ten hectares worked by nine workers, the marginal physical product of a hectare of land is 1400 bushels per year. Does the farmer minimize costs by hiring nine workers and renting ten hectares of land? If not, which input should he use in larger relative quantity?

10. A firm finds there is a sudden increase in the demand for its product. In the short run, it must operate longer hours and pay higher overtime wage rates. In the long run, however, it will pay the firm to install more machines and not operate them for longer hours. Which do you think will be lower, the short-run or the long-run average cost of the increased output? How is your answer affected by the fact that the long-run average cost includes the new machines the firm buys, while the short-run average cost includes no machine purchases?

Appendix: A Graphic Analysis of Input Decisions

To describe a production function—that is, the relationship between input combinations and size of total output—we can use a graphic device called an **isoquant** instead of the sort of numerical information described in Table 21–6 in the chapter.

An *isoquant* is a curve in a graph showing quantities of *inputs* on its axes. Each isoquant indicates *all* combinations of input quantities capable of producing a *given* quantity of output efficiently; thus, there must be a separate isoquant for each quantity of output.

If you have read the final sections of Chapter 19 on indifference curves and consumer choice, you will recognize a close analogy in logic (and in geometric shape) between consumers' indifference curves and producers' isoquants. Figure 21–11 represents different quantities of labour and land capable of producing given amounts of wheat. The isoquant labelled 220,000 bushels indicates that an output of 220,000 bushels of wheat can be obtained with the aid of *any one* of the combinations of inputs represented by points on the curve. For example, it can be produced by 10 years of labour and 200 hectares of land (point *A*) or, instead, it can be produced by the labour–land combination shown by point *B* on the same curve. Because it lies considerably below and to the right of point *B*, point *A* represents a productive process that uses more labour and less land than shown at point *B*.

The isoquants in a diagram such as Figure 21–11

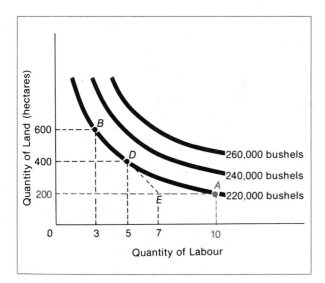

FIGURE 21-11
An Isoquant Map
The figure shows three isoquants, one for the production of 220,000 bushels of wheat, one for 240,000 bushels, and one for 260,000 bushels. For example, the lowest curve shows all combinations of land and labour capable of producing 220,000 bushels of wheat. Point A on that curve shows that 10 years of labour and 200 hectares of land are enough to do the job.

constitute a complete description of the production function. For each combination of inputs, they show how much output can be produced. Since it is drawn in two dimensions, the diagram can deal with only two inputs at a time. In more realistic situations, there may be more than two inputs, and an algebraic analysis must be used. But all the principles we need to analyze such a situation can be derived from the two-variable case.

Characteristics of Isoquants

Before discussing input pricing and quantity decisions, we first examine what is known about the shapes of isoquants. The main characteristics are straightforward and entirely analogous to the properties of consumer-indifference curves discussed in Chapter 19.

Characteristic 1: Higher curves correspond to larger outputs. Points on a higher isoquant represent larger quantities of *both* inputs than the corresponding points on a lower curve. Thus, the higher the curve, the larger the output it represents.

Characteristic 2: The isoquant will generally have a negative slope. It goes downhill as we move toward the right. This means that if we reduce the quantity of one input used and we do not want to cut production, we must use more of another input. For example, if we

want to use less land to produce 220,000 bushels of wheat, we will have to hire more labour to make up for the reduced land input.

Characteristic 3: The curves are typically assumed to curve inward toward the origin near their "middle." This is a reflection of the "law" of diminishing returns to a single input. For example, in Figure 21-11, points B, D, and A represent three different input combinations capable of producing the same quantity of output. At point B a large amount of land and relatively little labour is used, while the opposite is true at point A. Point D is intermediate between the two. Indeed, point D is chosen so that its use of land is exactly halfway between the amounts of land used at A and at B.

Now consider the choice among these input combinations. As the farmer considers first the input combination at B and then the one at D and finally the one at A, he is considering the use of less and less land, making up for it by the use of more and more labour so that he can continue to produce the same output. But the trade-off does not proceed at a constant rate because of diminishing returns in the substitution of labour for land.

When the farmer considers moving from point B to point D, he gives up 200 hectares of land and instead hires two additional years of labour. Similarly, the move from D to A involves giving up another 200 hectares of land. But this time, hiring an additional two years of labour does not make up for the reduced use of land. Diminishing returns to labour as he hires more and more workers to replace more and more land mean that now a much larger quantity of additional labour, five years rather than two, is needed to make up for the reduction in the use of land. If there had been no such diminishing returns, the isoquant would have been a straight line, *DE*. The curvature of the isoquant through points D and A reflects diminishing returns to substitution of inputs.

The Choice of Input Combinations

An isoquant describes only what input combinations *can* produce a given output; it indicates the technological possibilities. A business cannot decide which of the available options suits its purposes best without the corresponding cost information; that is, the relative prices of the inputs.

Just as we did for the consumer in Chapter 19, we can construct a **budget line**—a representation of equally costly input combinations—for the firm. For example, if farmhands are paid $9000 a year and land rents for $1000 per hectare a year, then a farmer who spends $360,000 can hire 40 farmhands but rent no

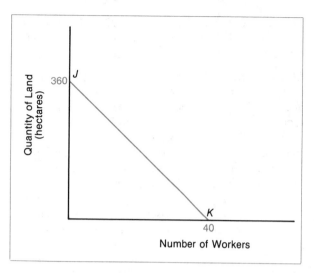

FIGURE 21–12
A Budget Line
The firm's budget line, *JK*, shows all the combinations of inputs it can purchase with a fixed amount of money—in this case $360,000.

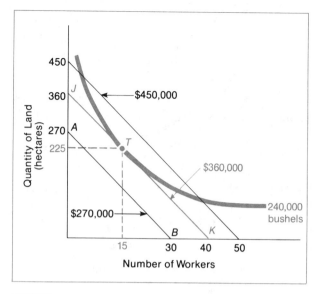

FIGURE 21–13
Cost Minimization
The least costly way to produce 240,000 bushels of wheat is shown by point *T*, where the isoquant is tangent to budget line *JK*. Here the farmer is employing 15 workers and using 225 hectares of land. It is not possible to produce 240,000 bushels on a smaller budget, and any larger budget would be wasteful.

land (point *K* in Figure 21–12), or he can rent 360 hectares but have no money left for farmhands (point *J*). But it is undoubtedly more sensible for him to pick some intermediate point on his budget line, *JK*, at which he divides the $360,000 between the two inputs.

There is an important difference, however, in how this budget line is used. The consumer had a fixed budget and sought the highest indifference curve attainable with these limited funds. The firm's problem in minimizing costs is just the reverse. Its budget is not fixed. Instead, it wants to produce a given quantity of output (say, 240,000 bushels) with the *smallest possible budget*.

A way to find the minimum budget capable of producing 240,000 bushels of wheat is illustrated in Figure 21–13, which combines the isoquant for 240,000 bushels from Figure 21–11 with a variety of budget lines similar to *JK* in Figure 21–12. The firm's problem is to find the lowest budget line that will allow it to reach the 240,000-bushel isoquant. Clearly, an expenditure of $270,000 is too little; there is no point on budget line *AB* that permits production of 240,000 bushels. Similarly, an expenditure of $450,000 is too much, because the firm can produce its target level of output more cheaply. The solution is at point *T*, meaning that 15 workers and 225 hectares of land are used to produce the 240,000 bushels of wheat. In general:

The least costly way to produce any given level of output is indicated by the point of tangency between a budget line and the isoquant corresponding to that level of output.

Cost Minimization, Expansion Path, and Cost Curves

Figure 21–13 shows how to determine the input combination that minimizes the cost of producing 240,000 bushels of output. We can repeat this procedure exactly for any other output quantity, such as 200,000 bushels or 300,000 bushels. In each case, we draw the corresponding isoquant and find the lowest budget line that permits it to be produced. For example, in Figure 21–14 budget line *BB* is tangent to the isoquant for 200,000 units of output and budget line *B'B'* is tangent to the isoquant for 300,000 units of output. In this way, we obtain three tangency points: *S*, which gives us the input combination that produces a 200,000-bushel output at lowest cost; *T*, which gives the same information for a 240,000-bushel output; and *S'*, which indicates the cost-minimizing input combination for the production of 300,000 bushels.

This process can be repeated for as many other levels of output as we like. For each such output we draw the corresponding isoquant and find its point of tangency with a budget line. That tangency point will show the input combination that produces the output in question at lowest cost.

Curve *EE* in Figure 21–14 connects all these cost-minimizing points; that is, it is the locus of *S*, *T*, and *S'*, and all the other points of tangency between an

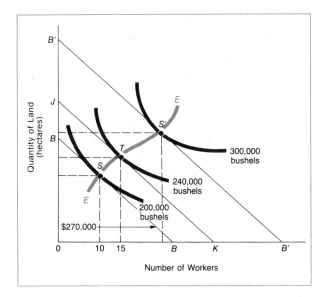

FIGURE 21–14
The Firm's Expansion Path
Each point of tangency, such as *S*, between an isoquant and a budget line shows the combination of inputs that can produce the output corresponding to that isoquant at lowest cost. The locus of all such tangency points is *EE*, the firm's expansion path.

isoquant and a budget line. Curve *EE* is called the firm's **expansion path**, which is defined as the locus of the firm's cost-minimizing input combinations for all relevant output levels.

In Figure 21–13 we were able to determine for tangency point *T* the quantity of output (from the

isoquant through that point) and the total cost (from the tangent budget line). Similarly, we can determine the output and total cost for every other point on the expansion path, *EE*, in Figure 21–14. For example, at point *S* we see that output is 200,000 units and total cost is $270,000.

This is precisely the sort of information we need to find the firm's total-cost curve; that is, it is just the sort of information contained in Table 21–4, from which we first calculated the total-cost curve and then the average-and marginal-cost curves in Figure 21–4. Thus we see that:

The points of tangency between a firm's isoquants and its budget lines yield its expansion path. The expansion path shows the firm's cost-minimizing input combination for each pertinent output level. This information also yields the output and total cost for each point on the expansion path, which is just what we need to draw the firm's cost curves.

Effects of Changes in Input Prices

Suppose now that the cost of renting land increases and the wage rate of labour decreases. This means that the budget lines will differ from those depicted in Figure 21–13. Specifically, with land now more expensive, any given sum of money will rent fewer hectares, so the intercept of each budget line on the vertical (land) axis will shift *downward*. Conversely, with labour cheaper, any given sum of money will buy more

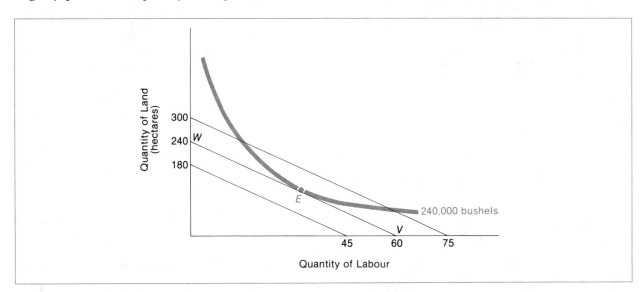

FIGURE 21–15
Optimal Input Choice at a Different Set of Input Prices
If input prices change, the combination of inputs that minimizes costs will normally change, too. In this diagram, land rents for $1500 per hectare (more than in Figure 21–13) while labour costs $6000 per year (less than in Figure 21–13). As a result, the least costly way to produce 240,000 bushels of wheat shifts from point *T* in Figure 21–13 to point *E* here.

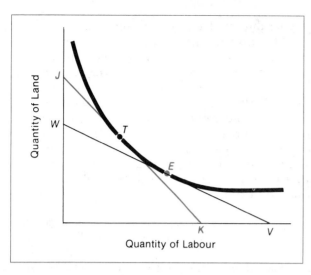

FIGURE 21-16

How Changes in Input Prices Affect Input Proportions

When land becomes more expensive and labour becomes cheaper, the budget lines (such as JK) become less steep than they were previously (see WV). As a result, the least costly way to produce 240,000 bushels shifts from point T to point E. The firm uses more labour and less land.

labour, so the intercept of the budget line on the horizontal (labour) axis will shift to the *right*. A series of budget lines corresponding to a $1500 per hectare rental rate for land and a $6000 annual wage for labour is depicted in Figure 21-15. We see that these budget lines are less steep than those shown in Figure 21-13 and that the least costly way to produce 240,000 bushels of wheat is now given by point E.

To assist you in seeing how things change, Figure 21-16 combines in a single graph budget line *JK* and tangency point *T* from Figure 21-13 and budget line *WV* and tangency point *E* from Figure 21-15. Notice that point *E* lies below and to the right of *T*, meaning that as wages decrease and rents increase the firm will hire more labour and rent less land. As common sense suggests, when the price of one input rises in comparison with that of others, it will pay the firm to hire less of this input and more of other inputs to make up for its reduced use of the more expensive input.

In addition to this substitution of one input for another, a change in the price of an input may induce the firm to alter the level of output that it decides to produce. But this is the subject of the next chapter.

Summary

1. A production function can be fully described by a family of isoquants, each of which shows all the input combinations capable of producing a specified amount of output.

2. As long as each input has a positive marginal physical product, isoquants will have a negative slope and the higher curves will represent larger amounts of output than the lower curves. Because of diminishing returns, these curves characteristically bend toward the origin near their middle.

3. The optimal input combination for any given level of output is indicated by the point of tangency between a budget line and the appropriate isoquant.

4. The firm's expansion path shows, for each of the firm's possible output levels, the combination of input quantities that minimizes the cost of producing that output.

5. From the isoquants and the budget lines tangent to them along the expansion path, one can find the total cost for each output level. From these figures one can determine the firm's total-cost, average-cost, and marginal-cost curves.

6. When input prices change, firms will normally use more of the input that becomes relatively less expensive and less of the input that becomes relatively more expensive.

Concepts for Review

Isoquant
Budget line

Point of tangency between the budget line and the corresponding isoquant
Expansion path

Questions for Discussion

1. Typical Manufacturing Corporation (TMC) produces gadgets with the aid of two inputs: labour and glue. If labour costs $5 per hour and glue costs $5 per litre, draw TMC's budget line for a total expenditure of $100,000. In this same diagram, sketch an isoquant indicating that TMC can produce no more than 1000 gadgets with this expenditure.

2. With respect to Question 1, suppose that wages rise to $10 per hour and glue prices rise to $6 per litre. How are TMC's optimal input proportions likely to change? (Use a diagram to explain your answer.)

3. What happens to the expansion path of the firm in Question 2?

22

Output–Price Decisions and Marginal Analysis

Annual income twenty pounds, annual expenditure nineteen nineteen six, result happiness. Annual income twenty pounds, annual expenditure twenty pounds ought and six, result misery.

CHARLES DICKENS

When computer companies such as NEC introduce ever more powerful laptop computers, they have to decide on the price at which each model should be offered and the number of each to produce. These are clearly among the most crucial decisions the firm makes. These decisions have a vital influence on NEC's labour requirements, on the reception given the product by consumers, and, indeed, on the very survival of the company.

This chapter describes the tools that firms like NEC can use to make decisions on outputs and prices—tools that are equally useful to government agencies and non-profit organizations in making analogous decisions. We begin the chapter by examining the relationship between the firm's price decisions and the quantity of product it sells. We then discuss the assumption of profit maximization before turning to the techniques firms can use to achieve the largest possible profit. We will explore—in words, with numerical examples, and with graphs—several methods of finding the level of output that maximizes profits. Each of these methods teaches us something about the nature of the firm's decision-making process and provides some general lessons about the use of marginal analysis. The analysis will also yield two conclusions that may be somewhat surprising and show that unaided common sense can sometimes be misleading in business decisions. Specifically, it will be shown that a change in fixed costs does not change the levels of price and output that maximize a firm's profits, and that it may be possible for a firm to make a profit by increasing the amount it sells at a price that is, apparently, below cost.

Two Illustrative Cases*

Price and output decisions can perplex even the most experienced business people, as the following real-life illustrations show. At the end of the chapter, we will see how the tools described in it helped in solving the problems.

CASE 1: PRICING A SIX-PACK

The managers of one of America's largest manufacturers of soft drinks became concerned when a rival company introduced a cheaper substitute for one of their leading products. As a result, some of the firm's managers advocated a reduction in the price of a six-pack from $1.50 to $1.35. This stimulated a heated debate. It was agreed that the price should be cut if doing so was not likely to reduce the company's profits. Although some of the managers maintained that the cut made sense because of the demand it would stimulate, others held that the price cut would hurt the company by

*The figures in these examples are doctored to help preserve the confidentiality of the information and to simplify the calculations. The cases, however, are real.

cutting profit per unit of output. The company had reliable information about costs but knew rather little about its consumers' responsiveness to price changes. At this point, consultants were called in to offer their suggestions. We will see how economic analysis enabled them to solve the problem even though the vital demand elasticity figures were unavailable.

CASE 2: MAKING PROFITS BY SELLING BELOW COSTS

In a recent legal battle between two manufacturers of pocket calculators, which we will call Company A and Company B, the latter accused the former of selling 10 million sophisticated calculators at a price of $12, "which [A] knew was too low to cover its costs." B claimed that A was doing this "only to drive [B] out of the business." Company A's records, which were revealed to the court, appeared at first glance to confirm B's accusation. The cost of materials, labour, fuel, direct advertising of the calculator during the dispute, and other such direct costs came to $10.30 per calculator. Company A's accountants also assigned to this product its share of the company's annual expenditure on administration, research, advertising, and the like (which were referred to as "overhead")—a total of $4.25 per calculator. The $12 price clearly did not cover the $14.55 cost attributed to each calculator sold. Yet, economists representing Company A were able to convince the court that manufacture of the calculator was a profitable activity for Company A, so that there was no basis on which to conclude that its only purpose was to destroy B. At the end of the chapter we will explain just how this was possible.

Price and Quantity: One Decision, Not Two

This chapter is about how firms, like those in the preceding cases, select a *price* and a *quantity* of output that best serve their financial interests. While it would seem that firms must choose two numbers, in fact they can pick only one. Once they have selected the *price*, the *quantity* they will sell is up to consumers. Alternatively, firms may decide *how much* they want to sell, but then they must leave it to the market to determine the *price* at which this quantity can be sold.

Management gets its two numbers by making only one decision because the firm's demand curve tells it, for any quantity it may decide to market, the highest possible price its product can fetch. For purposes of illustration, consider a hypothetical firm, Computron, Inc., which produces giant computers. Computron's demand curve, *DD* in Figure 22–1, shows that if the company decides to charge the relatively

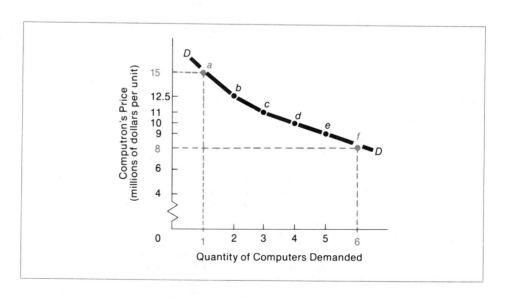

high price of $15 million per computer (point *a* on the curve), then it can sell only one unit per year. On the other hand, if it wants to sell as many as six computers per year, it can do so only by offering its product at the low price of $8 million (point *f*). In summary:

Each point on the demand curve represents a price–quantity pair. The firm can pick any such pair. But it can never pick the price corresponding to one point on the demand curve and the quantity corresponding to another point, since such an output would never be sold at the selected price.

Throughout this chapter, then, we will not discuss price and output decisions separately, for they are merely two different aspects of the same decision. To analyze this decision, we will make a strong assumption about the behaviour of business firms, which, while not literally correct, seems to be a useful simplification of a much more complex reality—the assumption that firms strive for the largest possible total profit.

Do Firms Really Maximize Profits?

Naturally, many people have questioned whether firms really try to maximize profits, to the exclusion of all other goals. Business people are like other human beings: Their motives are varied and complex. Given the choice, many executives might prefer to control the largest firm rather than the most profitable one. Some may be influenced by envy, others by a desire to "do good." Different managers within the same firm may not always agree with one another. So any attempt to summarize the firm's objectives in terms of a single number (profit) is bound to be an oversimplification.

In addition, the exacting requirements for maximizing profits are tough to satisfy. In practice, the required calculations are rarely carried out fully. In deciding on how much to invest, on what price to set for a product, or on how much to allocate to the advertising budget, the firm's managers face an enormous range of available alternatives. And information about each alternative is often expensive and difficult to acquire. As a result, when a firm's management decides on an $18 million construction budget it rarely compares the consequences of that decision in any detail with the consequences of all the possible alternatives—such as budgets of $17 million or $19 million. But unless all the available possibilities are compared, there is no way management can be sure it has chosen the one that brings in the highest possible profits.

Often management studies with care only the likely effects of the proposed decision itself: What sort of plant will it obtain for the money? How costly will it be to operate the plant? How much revenue is it likely to obtain from the sale of the plant's output? Management's concern is *whether the decision will produce results that satisfy the firm's standards of acceptability*—whether its risks will not be unacceptably great, whether its profits will not be unacceptably low, and so on. Such analysis does not necessarily lead to the maximum possible profit, because, though the decision may be good, some of the alternatives that have *not* been investigated may be better.

Decision-making that seeks only acceptable solutions has been called **satisficing** to contrast with optimizing. Some analysts, such as Carnegie-Mellon University's Nobel Prize winner Herbert Simon, have concluded that decision-making in industry and government is often of the satisficing variety.

But even if this is true, it does not necessarily make profit maximization a bad assumption. Recall our discussion of abstraction and model-building in Chapter 1. A map of Montreal that omits thousands of roads is no doubt "wrong" if interpreted as a literal description of the city. Nonetheless, by capturing the most important elements of reality, it may help us understand the city better than a map that is cluttered with too much detail. Similarly, we can learn much about the behaviour of business firms by assuming that they try to maximize profits, even though we know that *all* of them do not act this way *all* of the time.

We will therefore assume throughout this and the next few chapters that the firm has only one objective: It wants to make its total profit as large as possible. Our analytic strategy will be to determine what output level (or price) achieves this goal.

Total Profit: Keep Your Eye on the Goal

Total profit, then, is assumed to be *the* goal of profit-maximizing firms. It is, by definition, the difference between what a firm earns in the form of sales revenue and what it pays out in the form of costs:

$$\text{Total profit} = \text{Total revenue} - \text{Total costs.}$$

Total profit defined in this way is called **economic profit**, to distinguish it from the accountant's definition of profit. The two concepts of profit differ because total cost, in the economist's definition, includes the opportunity cost of any capital, labour, or other inputs supplied by the owner of the firm. Thus, if a small business earns just enough to pay the owner the normal fee for her labour and the use of her capital—say, $35,000 a year—and not a penny more, an economist will say she is earning zero *economic* profit (she is just covering all her costs) while most accountants will say her profit is $35,000.

To analyze how total profit depends on output, we must study the behaviour of total profit's two components: total revenue (TR) and total cost (TC). We know from preceding chapters that both **total revenue** and **total cost** depend on the output–price combination the firm selects.

Total revenue can be calculated directly from the demand curve, since by definition it is the product of price times the quantity that will be bought at that price:

$$\text{TR} = P \times Q.$$

Table 22–1 shows how the total-revenue schedule is derived from the demand schedule for our illustrative firm, Computron. The first two columns simply express the demand curve of Figure 22–1 in tabular form. The third column gives, for each quantity, the product of price times quantity. For example, if Computron markets three computers per year at a price of $11 million per computer, its annual sales revenue will be 3 × $11 million = $33 million.

Figure 22–2 displays Computron's total-revenue schedule in graphical form as

---

TABLE 22–1
Demand Schedule and Total- and Marginal-Revenue Schedules for Computron, Inc.

NUMBER OF COMPUTERS (per year)	PRICE = AVERAGE REVENUE (millions of dollars per computer)	TOTAL REVENUE (millions of dollars per year)	MARGINAL REVENUE (millions of dollars per computer)
0	—	0	—
1	15	15	15
2	12.5	25	10
3	11	33	8
4	10	40	7
5	9	45	5
6	8	48	3

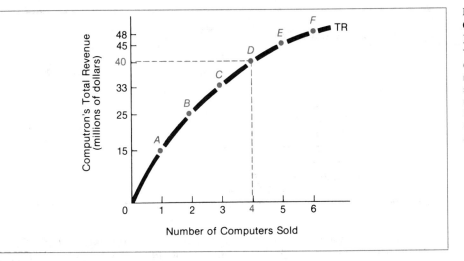

FIGURE 22-2
Computron's Total-Revenue Curve
The total-revenue curve for Computron, Inc., is derived directly from the demand curve, since total revenue is the product of price times quantity. Points A, B, C, D, E, and F in this diagram correspond to points a, b, c, d, e, and f, respectively, in Figure 22-1.

the black TR curve. This graph shows precisely the same information as the demand curve in Figure 22–1, but in a somewhat different form. For example, point *d* on the demand curve in Figure 22–1, which shows a price–quantity combination of *P* = $10 million and *Q* = 4 computers, appears as point *D* in Figure 22–2 as a total revenue of $40 million ($10 million price per unit times 4 units) corresponding to a quantity of four computers. Similarly, each point on the TR curve in Figure 22–2 corresponds to the similarly labelled point in Figure 22–1.

The relationship between the demand curve and the TR curve can be rephrased in a slightly different way. Since the price of the product is the revenue *per unit* that the firm receives, we can view the demand curve as the curve of **average revenue**. Average revenue (AR) and total revenue (TR) are related to one another in the same way as average cost and total cost.[1] Specifically, since

Average revenue (AR) is total revenue (TR) divided by quantity.

$$AR = \frac{TR}{Q} = \frac{P \times Q}{Q} = P,$$

average revenue and price are two names for the same thing.

Finally, the last column of Table 22–1 shows the **marginal revenue** for each level of output, that is, the *addition* to total revenue resulting from the addition of one unit to total output. Its definition and calculation are precisely analogous to those of marginal cost, which were described at length in Chapter 21 (pages 458–60). Thus, in Table 22–1 we see that when output rises from two to three units, total revenue goes up from $25 million to $33 million, so that marginal revenue is $33 million – $25 million = $8 million.

The revenue side is, of course, only half of the profit picture. We must turn to the cost side for the other half. The last chapter explained how the total-cost (TC), average-cost (AC), and marginal-cost (MC) schedules are determined by the firm's production techniques and the prices of the inputs it buys. Rather than repeat this analysis, we simply list the total-, average-, and marginal-cost schedules for Computron in Table 22–2. Figure 22–3 depicts the total-cost curve as the green TC curve.

Notice that total costs at zero output are not zero, because Computron incurs **fixed costs** of $2 million per year even if it produces nothing.[2] For example, Computron will have to pay the rent for its factory and the salary of its president whether it produces one computer, five computers, or ten.

Marginal revenue, often abbreviated MR, is the *addition* to total revenue resulting from the addition of one more unit to total output. Geometrically, marginal revenue is the *slope* of the total-revenue curve. The formula is $MR = \Delta TR / \Delta Q$.

[1] See the appendix to this chapter for a general discussion of the relationship between totals and averages.

[2] For a review of the concept of fixed costs, see Chapter 21, pages 460–61.

TABLE 22-2
Total, Average, and Marginal Costs for Computron, Inc.

NUMBER OF COMPUTERS (per year)	TOTAL COST (millions of dollars)	MARGINAL COST (millions of dollars per computer)	AVERAGE COST (millions of dollars per computer)
0	2		—
1	9	7	9
2	14	5	7
3	21	7	7
4	32	11	8
5	45	13	9
6	60	15	10

To study how total profit depends on output, we bring together in Table 22–3 the total-revenue and total-cost schedules. The last column in Table 22–3, total profit, is just the difference between total revenue and total cost for each level of output. Remembering that Computron's assumed objective is to maximize its profits, it is a simple matter to determine the level of production it will choose. By producing and selling three computers per year, Computron achieves the highest level of profits it is capable of achieving—some $12 million per year. Any higher or lower rate of production would lead to lower profits. For example, profits would drop to $8 million if output were expanded to four units.

Profit Maximization: A Graphical Interpretation

Precisely the same analysis can be presented graphically. In Figure 22–4 we bring together into a single diagram the total-revenue curve from Figure 22–2 and total-cost curve from Figure 22–3. Total profit, which is the difference between total revenue and total cost, appears in the diagram as the *vertical* distance between the TR and TC curves. For example, when output is four units, total revenue is $40 million (point *A*), total cost is $32 million (point *B*), and total profit is the distance between points *A* and *B*, or $8 million.

In this graphical view of the problem, Computron wants to maximize total

FIGURE 22–3
Computron's Total-Cost Curve
The graph shows, for each possible level of output, Computron's total costs. Because Computron has some fixed costs, the level of total cost at zero output is $2 million, not zero.

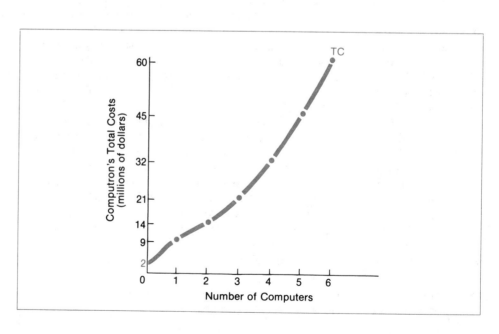

TABLE 22–3
Total Revenues, Costs, and Profit for Computron, Inc.

NUMBER OF COMPUTERS (per year)	TOTAL REVENUE	TOTAL COST	TOTAL PROFIT
		(millions of dollars per year)	
0	0	2	−2
1	15	9	6
2	25	14	11
3	33	21	12
4	40	32	8
5	45	45	0
6	48	60	−12

profit, which is the vertical distance between the TR and TC curves. The curve of total profit is drawn in the lower portion of Figure 22–4. We see that it reaches its maximum value, $12 million, at an output level of approximately three units per year. This is, naturally, the same conclusion we reached with the aid of Table 22–3.

The total-profit curve in Figure 22–4 is shaped like a hill. Though such a shape is not inevitable, we expect a hill shape to be typical for the following reason. If a firm produces nothing, it certainly earns no profit, and it will probably incur a loss if it has

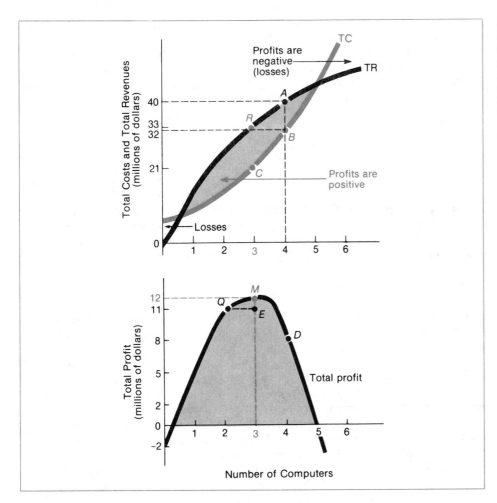

FIGURE 22–4
Profit Maximization: A Graphical Interpretation
Computron's profits are maximized when the vertical distance between its total-revenue curve, TR, and its total-cost curve, TC, is at its maximum. In the diagram, this occurs at an output of three units per year; total profits are CR, or $12 million. The total-profit curve is shown in the lower portion of the figure. Naturally, it reaches its maximum value ($12 million) at three units (point M).

an idle factory on its hands and must spend money to guard it and keep it from deteriorating. At the other extreme, a firm can produce so much output that it swamps the market, forcing price down so low that it again loses money. Only at intermediate levels of output—something between zero and the amount that floods the market—will the company earn a positive profit. Consequently, the total-profit curve will rise from zero (or negative) levels at a very small output, to positive levels in between, and it will fall to negative levels when output gets too large. Thus, the total-profit curve will normally be a hill like the one shown in Figure 22–4.

Marginal Analysis and Maximization of *Total* Profit

We see that there may be many levels of output that yield a positive profit. But the firm is not aiming for just any level of profit. It wants the largest profit that is obtainable. The profit graph shows that the hill reaches its summit ($12 million) when output quantity is approximately $Q = 3$. If the firm produces only 2 units, it earns only $11 million in profit. If $Q = 4$, profit falls to $8 million. So the firm's goal is to get to the top of the hill, where profit is maximized.

If management really knew the exact shape of its profit hill, choosing the optimal level of output would be a simple task indeed. It would only have to locate the point corresponding to M in Figure 22–4, the top of its profit hill. However, management rarely if ever has its information in such a simple form, so a different technique for finding the optimum is required. That technique is **marginal analysis**—the same set of tools that we used in our analysis of consumers maximizing utility in Chapter 19 and the firm minimizing costs in Chapter 21.

Marginal profit is the *addition* to total profit resulting from one more unit of output.

To see how marginal analysis helps solve Computron's problem, we introduce an expository concept: **marginal profit**. Referring back to Table 22–3, for example, we see that an increase in Computron's annual output from two to three computers would raise total profit from $11 million to $12 million. That is, it would generate $1 million in *additional* profits, which we call the *marginal profit* resulting from the addition of the third unit. Similarly, marginal profit from the fourth unit would be:

$$\text{Total profit from 4 units} - \text{Total profit from 3 units} = \$8 \text{ million} - \$12 \text{ million} = -\$4 \text{ million}.$$

The marginal rule for finding the optimal level of output is easy to understand:

If the marginal profit from increasing output by one unit is positive, then output should be increased. If the marginal profit from increasing output by one unit is negative, then output should be decreased. Thus, an output level can maximize total profit only if at that output marginal profit equals zero.

In the Computron example, the marginal profit from the third unit is +$1 million (going from the second to the third unit *adds* $1 million to profit), so it pays to produce the third unit. But marginal profit from the fourth unit is –$4 million (going from the third unit to the fourth *reduces* total profit by $4 million), so the firm should not produce the fourth unit. Since Computron is dealing in whole numbers—for example, it cannot produce 3.12 computers—it cannot achieve a marginal profit of exactly zero. But by producing three units per year it comes quite close.

The profit hill in Figure 22–4 gives us a graphical interpretation of the "marginal profit equals zero" condition. Marginal profit is defined as the additional profit that accrues to the firm when output rises by one unit. So, when output is increased, say, from two units to three units (the distance QE in Figure 22–4), total profit rises by $1 million (the distance EM) and marginal profit is therefore EM/QE. This is precisely the definition of the *slope* of the total-profit curve between points Q and M. In general:

With this geometric interpretation in hand, we can easily understand the logic of the marginal-profit rule. At a point such as Q, where the total-profit curve is rising, marginal profit (= slope) is positive. Profits cannot be maximal at such a point, because we can increase profits by moving farther to the right. A firm that decided to stick to point Q would be wasting the opportunity to increase profits by increasing output. Similarly, the firm cannot be maximizing profits at a point like D, where the slope of the curve is negative, because there marginal profit (= slope) is negative. If it finds itself at a point like D, the firm can raise its profit by decreasing its output.

Only at a point such as M, where the total-profit curve is neither rising nor falling, can the firm possibly be at the top of the profit hill rather than on one of the sides of the hill. And point M is precisely where the slope of the curve—and hence the marginal profit—is zero. *An output decision cannot be optimal unless the corresponding marginal profit is zero.*

The firm is not interested in marginal profit for its own sake, but rather for what it implies about *total* profit. Marginal profit is like the needle on the pressure gauge of a boiler: The needle itself is of no concern to anyone, but if one fails to watch it, the consequences may be quite dramatic.

One common misunderstanding that arises in discussions of the marginal criterion of optimality is the idea that it seems foolish to go to a point where marginal profit is zero. "Isn't it better to earn a positive marginal profit?" This notion springs from a confusion between the quantity one is seeking to maximize (*total* profit) and the gauge that indicates whether such a maximum has in fact been attained (*marginal* profit). Of course it is better to have a positive *total* profit than zero total profit. But a zero value on the *marginal*-profit gauge merely indicates that all is apparently well, that *total* profit may be at its maximum.

Marginal Revenue and Marginal Cost: Guides to an Optimum

A more conventional version of the marginal analysis of profit maximization proceeds directly in terms of the cost and revenue components of profit. For this purpose refer back to Figure 22–4, where the profit hill was constructed from the total-revenue (TR) and total-cost (TC) curves. Observe that there is another way of finding the profit-maximizing solution. We want to maximize the vertical distance between the TR and TC curves. This distance, we see, is not maximal at an output level such as two units, because there the two curves are growing farther apart. If we move farther to the right, the vertical distance between them (which is total profit) will increase. Conversely, we have not maximized the vertical distance between TR and TC at an output level such as four units, because there the two curves are coming closer together. We can add to profits by moving farther to the left (reducing output).

The conclusion from the graph, then, is that total profit (the vertical distance between TR and TC) is maximized only when the two curves are neither growing farther apart nor coming closer together; that is, when their *slopes* are equal. While this conclusion is rather mechanical, we can breathe some life into it by interpreting the slopes of the two curves as **marginal revenue** and **marginal cost**. These concepts, which have already been defined and illustrated, permit us to restate the geometric conclusion we have just reached in an economically significant way:

Profit can be maximized only at an output level at which marginal revenue is (approximately) equal to marginal cost. In symbols:

$$MR = MC.$$

TABLE 22-4
Marginal Revenue and Marginal Cost for Computron, Inc.

NUMBER OF COMPUTERS (per year)	MARGINAL REVENUE	MARGINAL COST
		(millions of dollars per year)
0	—	—
1	15	7
2	10	5
3	8	7
4	7	11
5	5	13
6	3	15

The logic of the MR = MC rule for profit maximization is straightforward.[3] When MR is *not* equal to MC, profits cannot possibly be maximized because the firm can increase its profits either by raising its output or by reducing it. For example, if MR = $16 million and MC = $12 million, the firm can increase its net profit by $4 million by producing and selling one more unit. If MC exceeds MR—say, MR = $7 million and MC = $10 million—the firm loses $3 million on its marginal unit, so it can add $3 million to its profit by reducing output by one unit. Only when MR = MC is it impossible for the firm to add to its profit by changing its output level.

Table 22-4 reproduces marginal-revenue and marginal-cost data for Computron, Inc., from Tables 22-1 and 22-2. The table shows, as must be true, that the MR = MC rule leads us to the same conclusion as Figure 22-4 and Table 22-3. Computron should produce and sell three computers per year.

The marginal revenue of the third computer is $8 million ($33 million from selling three computers less $25 million from selling two) while the marginal cost is only $7 million ($21 million minus $14 million). So the firm should produce the third unit. But the fourth computer brings in only $7 million in marginal revenue while its marginal cost is $11 million—clearly a losing proposition.

Because the graphs of marginal analysis will prove so useful in the following chapters, Figure 22-5(a) shows the MR = MC condition for profit maximization graphically. The black curve labelled MR in the figure is the marginal-revenue schedule from Table 22-4. The curve labelled MC is the marginal-cost schedule. They intersect at point E, which is therefore the point where marginal revenue and marginal cost are equal. The optimal output for Computron is three units.[4] Figures 22-5(b) and 22-5(c), respectively, are reproductions of the TR and TC curves from the upper part of Figure 22-4 and the total-profit curve from the lower portion of that figure. Note how MC and MR intersect at the same output at which the distance of TR above TC is greatest, which is the output at which the profit hill reaches its summit.

Applications:
(1) Fixed Cost and the Profit-Maximizing Price

Our analytic apparatus can now be used to offer a surprising insight. Suppose there is a rise in the firm's fixed cost; say, the rental cost of an indispensable air-filtering

---

[3] You may have surmised by now that just as total profit = total revenue – total cost, it must be true that marginal profit = marginal revenue – marginal cost. This is in fact correct. It also shows that when marginal profit = 0, we must have MR = MC.

[4] One qualification must be entered. Sometimes marginal-revenue and marginal-cost curves do not have the nice shapes depicted in Figure 22-5(a), and they may intersect more than once. In such cases, while it remains true that MC = MR at the output level that maximizes profits, there may be other output levels at which MC is also equal to MR but at which profits are not maximized.

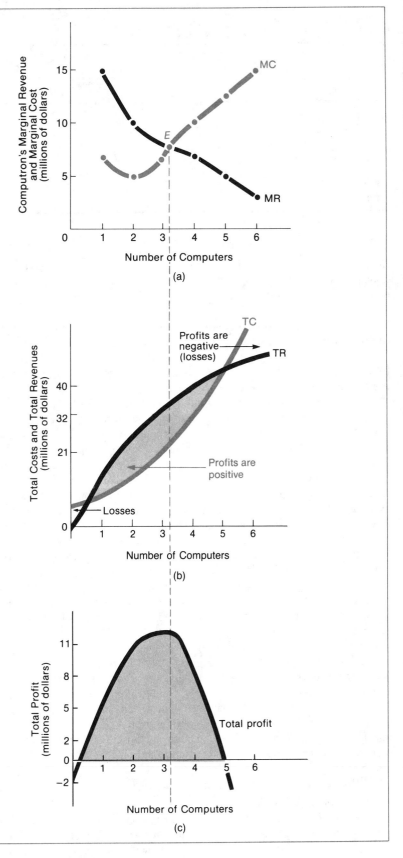

FIGURE 22–5

Profit Maximization: Another Graphical Interpretation

Profits are maximized where marginal revenue (MR) is (approximately) equal to marginal cost (MC), for only at such a point will *marginal profit* be zero. Part (a) shows the MR = MC condition for profit maximization graphically as point *E*, where output is close to three computers. Since Computron does not produce fractions of computers, the best it can do is to produce three of them. The diagram also reproduces from Figure 22-4 the TR and TC curves [part (b)] and the total-profit curve [part (c)], showing how all three agree that the profit-maximizing output is a bit larger than three units.

TABLE 22-5

Total Profit before and after a Rise in Fixed Cost

NUMBER OF COMPUTERS (per year)	TOTAL PROFITS BEFORE FIXED-COST INCREASE	INCREASE IN FIXED-COST PAYMENT (millions of dollars per year)	TOTAL PROFIT AFTER FIXED-COST INCREASE
0	−2	2	−4
1	6	2	4
2	11	2	9
3	12	2	10
4	8	2	6
5	0	2	−2
6	−12	2	−14

machine doubles. What will happen to the profit-maximizing price and output? Should price go up to cover the increased cost? Should the firm push for a larger output (even if that requires a fall in price)? The answer is: neither.

When a firm's fixed cost increases, its profit-maximizing price and output remain completely unchanged, so long as it pays the firm to stay in business.

In other words, there is nothing the firm's management can do to offset the effect of the rise in fixed cost. It must just lie back and take it.

Why is this so? Remember that, by definition, a fixed cost is a cost that does not change when output changes. Computron's air-filtering cost increase is the same whether business is slow or booming, whether production is two or six computers. This is illustrated in Table 22–5, which also reproduces Computron's total profits from Table 22–3. The third column of the table shows that total fixed cost has risen by $2 million per year, no matter what the firm's output. As a result, for each possible output of the firm, total profit is $2 million less than what it would have been otherwise. For example, when output is four units, we see that total profit must fall from $8 million (second column) to $6 million (last column).

Now, because profit is reduced by the same amount at each and every output level, the output level that was most profitable to the firm before the rent increase must still be the output that yields the highest profit. In Table 22–5 we see that $10 million is the largest entry in the last column, which shows profits after the rise in fixed cost. The highest profit is attained, as it was before, when output equals three units. Given the firm's demand curve (Figure 22–1) this, of course, means that the profit-maximizing price will remain $11 million—the price at which it sells three units (point c on the demand curve).

All of this is also shown in Figure 22–6, which shows the firm's total profit hill before and after the rise in fixed cost (reproducing Computron's initial profit hill from Figure 22–4). We see that the cost increase simply moves the profit hill straight downward by $2 million, so that the highest point on the hill is just lowered from point M to point N. But the top of the hill is shifted neither toward the left nor toward the right. It remains at the three-unit output level. Just as we saw before, the profit-maximizing output level remains unchanged when fixed costs rise.

(2) Taxes and the Profit-Maximizing Price

The result we have just described, which applies only to fixed costs and not to variable costs, is important for government policy regarding the taxing of firms. If the government levies a sales tax (a certain amount per unit of the good that the firm produces and sells), the firm's marginal costs will be increased (the MC curve will shift

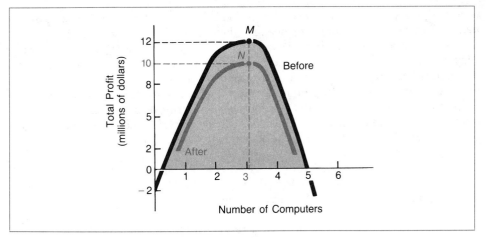

FIGURE 22–6
Fixed Cost Does Not Affect Profit-Maximizing Output
The graph reproduces Computron's initial profit hill from Figure 22–4 (the black curve labelled "before"). A $2 million increase in fixed cost shifts the profit hill downward, to the green curve marked "after." But the original point of maximum profit (point M) and the new one (point N) are at the same output level. This is so because the cost increase pushes the profit hill straight downward.

up). This rise will reduce the profit-maximizing level of output, so one can predict that the firm will pass on some of the sales tax by raising the selling price and lowering the level of inputs (say, by laying off workers). But if the government levies a *licence fee*, that is, an amount a firm must pay to be in business at all, only fixed costs are increased. Consequently, as we have just seen, such a levy will not be passed on in higher prices or cause the firm to lay off any inputs.

The choice between the two types of taxes will depend on the goals of the government. If the tax is meant to reduce profits and to redistribute the resulting income to others, the licence fee is appealing as it involves no unfortunate side effects in terms of higher prices or layoffs. If, on the other hand, the tax is meant to increase the product's price so that, for example, the price more properly reflects the costs of pollution that are involved in its production, the sales tax will be the more appealing option. In this case, because the government is seeking to reduce consumption of the item, higher prices and less production are desirable outcomes.

Marginal Analysis in Real Decision Problems

We can now put the marginal analysis of profit determination to work to unravel the puzzles with which we began this chapter. It should be noted that neither example involves a mechanical application of the MC = MR rule. Both examples are drawn from reality, and reality never works as neatly as a textbook illustration. However, as these cases show, the reasoning taught in the text *does* help to deal with real problems.

CASE 1: THE SODA-PRICING PROBLEM
Our first problem dealt with a firm's choice between keeping the price of a brand of soda at $1.50 per six-pack or reducing it to $1.35 when a competitor entered the market. The trouble was that to know what to do, the firm needed to know its demand curve (and hence its marginal-revenue curve). However, the firm did not have enough data to determine the shape of its demand curve. How, then, could a rational decision be made?

As we indicated, the debate among the firm's managers finally reached agreement on one point: The price should be cut if, as a result, profits were not likely to decline; that is, if *marginal profit* were not negative. Fortunately, the data needed to determine whether marginal profit was positive were obtainable. Initial annual sales were 10 million units, and the firm's engineers maintained emphatically that marginal costs were very close to constant at $1.20 per six-pack over the output range in question. Instead of trying to determine the *actual* increase in sales that would result from the price cut, the team of consultants decided to try to determine the *minimum necessary* increase in quantity demanded required to avoid a decrease in profits.

It was clear that the firm needed additional revenue at least as great as the additional cost of supplying the added volume, if profits were not to decline. The consultants knew that sales at the initial price of $1.50 per six-pack were $15 million ($1.50 per unit times 10 million units). Letting Q represent the (unknown) quantity of six-packs that would be sold at the proposed new price of $1.35, the economists compared the added revenue with the added cost of providing the Q new units. Since MC was constant at $1.20 per unit, the added cost amounted to:

$$\text{Added cost} = \$1.20 \times (Q - 10 \text{ million}).$$

This was to be compared with the added revenue:

$$\text{Added revenue} = \text{New revenue} - \text{Old revenue}$$
$$= \$1.35Q - \$15 \text{ million}.$$

No loss would result from the price change if the added revenue was greater than or equal to the added cost. The minimum Q necessary to avoid a loss therefore was that at which added revenue equalled added cost, or

$$1.35Q - 15 \text{ million} = 1.2Q - 12 \text{ million},$$

or

$$0.15Q = 3 \text{ million}.$$

This would be true if, and only if, Q, the quantity sold at the lower price, would be

$$Q = 20 \text{ million units}.$$

In other words, this calculation showed that the firm could break even from the 15-cent price reduction only if the quantity of its product demanded rose at least 100 percent (from 10 to 20 million units). Since past experience indicated that such a rise in quantity demanded was hardly possible, the price reduction proposal was quickly abandoned. Thus the logic of the MC = MR rule, plus a little ingenuity, enabled the consultants to deal with a problem that at first seemed baffling—even though they had no estimate of marginal revenue.

CASE 2: THE "UNPROFITABLE" CALCULATOR

Our second case study concerned a firm that was apparently losing money on its calculator sales because its $12 price was less than the $14.55 average cost that the company's accountants assigned to the product. This $14.55 included $10.30 of costs arising directly from the manufacture and marketing of the calculators, plus a $4.25 per-calculator share of the company's overall general expenses ("overhead"). Accused of deliberately selling below cost in order to drive a competitor out of business, the company was able to use marginal analysis to show that this was not true and that the price at which the calculators were sold was in fact profitable.

To demonstrate this, the company's witness explained that, if the sales were really unprofitable, the company would have been able to raise its net earnings by ceasing production and sale of the calculators. A moment's consideration shows, however, that the opposite would have happened—that profits would have decreased if the company gave up its annual sale of 10 million calculators. The company's revenues would have been reduced by the (marginal) figure of $12 on each of its 10 million units sold—a revenue reduction of $120 million. But how much cost would it have saved? The answer is that the cost saving would equal only the cost outlay actually *caused* by the production of the calculator—the $10.30 per unit in direct cost.

None of the company's overhead would have been saved by ending calculator production—the company president would not have been fired if the product were discontinued, and the company would probably even have had to increase general expenditures on new product research. Rather, the (marginal) saving would have been the direct cost of $10.30 per calculator times the 10-million-calculator output—a total saving of $103 million. Thus, elimination of the product would have *reduced* total company profit by $17 million per year—the $103 million cost saving minus the $120 million in revenue forgone. In other words, continued production of the calculators was not causing losses; on the contrary, it was contributing $17 million in profits every year. The court concluded that this reasoning was correct, and used this conclusion in its decision.

This case illustrates a point that is encountered frequently. The calculator producer was selling its product at a price that *appeared* not to cover costs, but really did. The same sort of issue frequently faces firms considering the introduction of a new product or the opening of a new branch office. In many such cases the new operation may not cover *average* costs as measured by standard accounting methods. Yet to follow the apparent implications of those cost figures would amount to throwing away a valuable opportunity to add to the net earnings of the firm and, perhaps, to contribute to the welfare of the economy. Only *marginal* analysis can reveal whether the contemplated action is really worthwhile.

Conclusion: The Fundamental Role of Marginal Analysis

In Chapter 19, we saw how marginal analysis helps us to understand the consumer's purchase decisions. In Chapter 21, it helped us understand the firm's input choices, and in this chapter, it enabled us to examine output decisions. The logic of marginal analysis applies not only to economic decisions by consumers and firms but also to those of governments, universities, hospitals, and other organizations. In short, the analysis can be used by any individual or group making economic choices for the use of scarce resources. Thus, one of the most important conclusions that can be drawn from the last four chapters, a conclusion brought out vividly by the two examples we have just discussed, concerns:

The Importance of Marginal Analysis
In any decision about whether to expand an activity, it is always the *marginal* cost and *marginal* revenue that are the relevant factors. A calculation based on *average* figures is likely to lead the decision-maker to miss all sorts of opportunities, some of them critical.

More generally, if one wants to make *optimal* decisions, *marginal analysis* should be used in the planning calculations. This is true whether the decision applies to a business firm seeking to maximize profit or minimize cost, to a consumer trying to maximize utility, or to a less-developed country striving to maximize per capita output. It applies as much to decisions on input proportions and advertising as to decisions about output levels and prices. Indeed, this is such a general principle of economics that it is one of the 12 **Ideas for Beyond the Final Exam.**

A real-life example far removed from profit maximization will illustrate the way in which marginal criteria are useful in decision-making. For some years before women were admitted to Princeton University (and to several other universities), the cost of the proposed change was frequently cited as a major obstacle. It had been decided in advance that any woman coming to the university would constitute a net addition to the student body because, for a variety of reasons involving relations with alumni and other groups, a reduction in the number of male students was not feasible. Presumably on the basis of a calculation of average cost, some critics spoke of figures as high as $80 million.

To economists it was clear, however, that the relevant figure was the *marginal cost*, the addition to total cost that would result from the introduction of the additional students. The women students would, of course, bring to Princeton additional tuition fees (marginal revenues). If these fees were just sufficient to cover the amount they would add to costs, the admission of the women would leave the university's financial picture unaffected.

A careful calculation showed that the admission of women would add far less to the university's financial problems than the *average-cost* figures indicated. One reason was that (at that time) women's course preferences were characteristically different from men's and hence women frequently elected courses that were undersubscribed in exclusively male institutions. Therefore, the admission of one thousand women to a formerly all-male institution required fewer additional courses than if one thousand more men had been admitted.[5] More important, it was found that a number of classroom buildings were underutilized. The cost of operating these buildings was nearly fixed—their total utilization cost would be changed only slightly by the influx of women. The corresponding marginal cost was therefore almost zero and certainly well below the average cost (cost per student).

For all these reasons, it turned out that the relevant marginal-cost figure was much smaller than the figures that had been bandied about earlier. Indeed, this cost was something like a third of the earlier estimates. There is little doubt that this careful marginal calculation played a critical role in the admission of women to Princeton and to some other institutions that made use of the calculations in the Princeton analysis. Subsequent data, incidentally, confirmed that the marginal calculations were amply justified.

A Look Back and a Look Forward

We have now completed four chapters describing how consumers and business managers can make optimal decisions. Will you find executives in head offices calculating marginal cost and marginal revenue in order to decide how much to produce? Hardly. Not any more than you will find consumers in stores computing their marginal utilities in order to decide what to buy. Like consumers, successful business people often rely heavily on intuition and "hunches" that cannot be described by any set of rules.

However, we have not sought a literal *description* of consumer and business behaviour but rather a *model* to help us analyze and predict this behaviour. Just as astronomers construct models of the behaviour of objects that do not think at all, economists construct models of consumers and business people who do think, but whose thought processes may be rather different from those of economists. In the chapters that follow we will use these models to serve the purposes for which they were designed: to analyze the functioning of a market economy and to see what things it does well and what things it does poorly.

[5] See Gardner Patterson, "The Education of Women at Princeton," *Princeton Alumni Weekly*, vol. 69, September 24, 1968.

Summary

1. A firm can choose the quantity of its product it wants to sell or the price it wants to charge. But it cannot choose both because price affects the quantity demanded.
2. In economic theory, it is usually assumed that firms seek to maximize profits. This should not be taken literally, but interpreted as a useful simplification of reality.
3. Marginal revenue is the additional revenue earned by increasing sales by one unit. Marginal cost is the additional cost incurred by increasing production by one unit.
4. Maximum profit requires the firm to choose the level of output at which marginal revenue is equal to marginal cost.

5. Geometrically, the profit-maximizing output level occurs at the highest point of the total-profit curve. There the slope of the total-profit curve is zero, meaning that marginal profit is zero.
6. A change in fixed cost will not change the profit-maximizing level of output.

7. It may pay a firm to expand its output if it is selling at a price greater than marginal cost, even if that price happens to be below average cost.
8. Optimal decisions must be made on the basis of marginal-cost and marginal-revenue figures, not average-cost and average-revenue figures. This is one of the 12 **Ideas for Beyond the Final Exam**.

Concepts for Review

Profit maximization
Satisficing
Total profit
Economic profit

Total revenue and cost
Average revenue and cost
Marginal revenue and cost

Fixed cost
Marginal analysis
Marginal profit

Questions for Discussion

1. "It may be rational for a firm not to try to maximize profits." Discuss the circumstances under which this statement may be true.

2. Suppose the firm's demand curve indicates that at a price of $9 per unit, customers will demand two million units of its product. Suppose management decides to pick *both* price and output, produces three million units of its product, and prices it at $14. What will happen?

3. Suppose a firm's management would be pleased to increase its share of the market, but if it expands its production, the price of its product will fall and so its profits will decline somewhat. What choices are available to this firm? What would you do if you were president of this company?

4. Why does it make sense for a firm to seek to maximize *total* profit, rather than to maximize *marginal* profit?

5. A firm's marginal revenue is $41 and its marginal cost is $19. What amount of profit does the firm fail to pick up by refusing to increase output by one unit?

6. Calculate average revenue (AR) and average cost (AC) in Table 22–3. How much profit does the firm earn at the output at which AC = AR? Why?

7. A firm's total cost is $200 if it produces one unit, $350 if it produces two units, and $450 if it produces three units of output. Draw up a table of total, average, and marginal costs for this firm.

8. Draw average- and marginal-cost curves for the firm in Question 7. Describe the relationship between the two curves.

9. A firm with no fixed costs has the demand and total-cost schedules given in the table below. If it wants to maximize profits, how much output should it produce?

QUANTITY	PRICE (dollars)	TOTAL COST (dollars)
1	6	1
2	5	2.5
3	4	4
4	3	7
5	2	11

10. Review the concept of fixed cost in Chapter 21. Suppose Computron's total costs are increased by $10 million per year. Show in Table 22–2 how this affects Computron's total, average, and marginal costs.

11. Why does it make sense for a change in a firm's fixed cost not to change the output level that maximizes its profit?

12. Consider a firm whose demand curve is $Q = 6 - 0.5P$, where P and Q stand for price and quantity. The firm must pay a rent of 6 per period for its premises, and a constant cost of 2 per unit in production costs. What price will this firm charge? What will be the firm's response if the government imposes a price ceiling of 4 per unit? Explain your answers fully.

Appendix
The Relationships among Total, Average, and Marginal Data

By now you will have noticed that there is a close connection between the average-revenue and average-cost curves and the corresponding marginal-revenue and marginal-cost curves. After all, we deduced our total-revenue figures from the average revenue and then calculated our marginal-revenue figures from the total revenues; a similar chain of deduction applied to costs. In fact:

Marginal, average, and total figures are inextricably bound together. From any one of the three, the other two can be calculated. Total, average, and marginal figures bear relationships to one another that hold for any variable—such as revenue, cost, or profit—that is affected by the number of units in question.

To illustrate and emphasize the wide applicability of marginal analysis, we switch our example from profits, revenues, and costs to a non-economic variable, cooking weights. We do so because calculation of weights is more familiar to most people than calculation of profits, revenues, or costs, and we can use this example to illustrate several fundamental relationships between average and marginal figures. A not-so-expert hamburger-maker is shaping patties and piling them on a platter balanced on a kitchen scale. The data on what he produces are in Table 22-6.[6]

He begins with an empty scale (the total weight of the patties is equal to zero). The first patty he makes weighs exactly 100 grams; marginal and average weight are both 100 grams. If the next patty weighs 140 grams (the marginal weight equals 140 grams), the average weight rises to 120 grams (240 ÷ 2), and so on.

The way to calculate average weight from total weight is quite clear. When, for example, the scale holds four patties with a total weight of 500 grams, the average weight must be 500 ÷ 4 = 125 grams, as shown in the corresponding entry of the third column. In general, the rule for converting totals to averages, and vice versa, is:

Rule 1a. Average weight equals total weight divided by number of items.

Rule 1b. Total weight equals average weight times number of items.

TABLE 22-6
Weights of Hamburger Patties

NUMBER OF PATTIES ON SCALE	TOTAL WEIGHT (grams)	AVERAGE WEIGHT (grams)	MARGINAL WEIGHT (grams)
0	0	—	—
1	100	100	100
2	240	120	140
3	375	125	135
4	500	125	125
5	600	120	100
6	660	110	60

And this rule naturally applies equally well to cost, revenue, profit, or any other variable of interest.

Calculation of *marginal* weight from *total* weight follows the *subtraction* process we have already encountered in the calculation of marginal utility, marginal cost, and marginal revenue. Specifically:

Rule 2a. The marginal weight of, say, the third item equals the total weight of three items minus the total weight of two items.

For example, when the fourth patty is placed on the scale, *total* weight rises from 375 grams to 500 grams, and hence the corresponding marginal weight is 500 – 375 = 125 grams, as is shown in the last column of Table 22-6. We can also go in the opposite direction —from marginal to total—by the reverse, *addition*, process.

Rule 2b. The total weight of, say, three items equals the marginal weight of the first item plus the marginal weight of the second item plus the marginal weight of the third item.

Rule 2b can be checked by referring to Table 22-6. There it can be seen that the total weight of three items, 375 grams, is indeed equal to 100 + 140 + 135 grams, the sum of the preceding marginal weights. A similar relation holds for any other total weight figure in the table, as the reader should verify.[7]

---

[6] Note that in this illustration, "number of patties" is analogous to units of output, "total weight" to total revenue or cost, and so on.

[7] There is an exception in the case of costs. Summing up marginal-cost figures as in Rule 2b leads to total *variable* cost. If there are *fixed* costs, these must be added in to arrive at total (variable plus fixed) costs.

In addition to these familiar arithmetic relationships, there are two other useful relationships. The first of these may be stated as:

Rule 3. In the absence of fixed weight (costs), the marginal, average, and total figures for the first item must all be equal.

This rule holds because when the scale holds only one item, whose weight is X grams, the average weight will obviously be X, the total weight must be X, and the marginal weight must also be X (since the total must have risen from 0 to X grams). Put another way, when the marginal item is alone, it is obviously also the average item, and also represents the totality of all relevant items.

Now for the final and very important relationship:

Rule 4. If marginal weight is lower than average weight, then average weight must fall when the number of items increases. If marginal weight exceeds average weight, average weight must rise when the number of items increases. And if marginal and average weight are equal, the average weight must remain constant when the number of items increases.

These three possibilities are all illustrated in Table 22–6. Notice, for example, that when the third patty is placed on the scale, the average weight rises from 120 to 125 grams. That is because this patty's (marginal) weight is 135 grams, which is above the average, as Rule 4 requires. Similarly, when someone asks for a small hamburger and a 60-gram patty is added to the pile, the average falls from 120 to 110 grams because marginal weight, 60 grams, is below average weight.

The reason Rule 4 works is easily explained with the aid of our example. When the third patty is added, we see that the average rises. At once we know that this patty must be above average weight, for otherwise its addition would not have pulled up the average. Similarly, the average will be pulled down by the addition of a patty whose weight is below the average (marginal weight is less than average weight). And the addition of a patty of average weight (marginal equals average weight) will leave the old average figure unchanged. That is all there is to the matter.

It is essential to avoid a common misunderstanding of this rule: It does *not* state, for example, that if the average figure is rising, the marginal figure must be rising. When the average rises, the marginal figure may rise, fall, or remain unchanged. The addition of two patties both well above average will push the average up in two successive steps even if the second new one is lighter than the first. We see such a case in

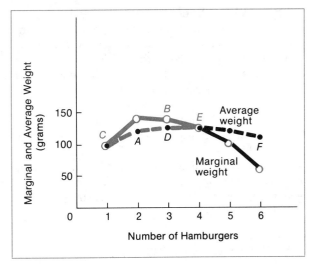

FIGURE 22–7

The Relationship between Marginal and Average Curves
If the marginal curve is above the average curve, the average curve will be pulled upward. Thus, wherever the marginal curve is above the average curve, the average curve must be going upward (green segment of curves). The opposite is true where the marginal curve is below the average curve.

Table 22–6, where the arithmetic shows that while average weight rises successively from 100 to 120 to 125 grams, the marginal weight falls from 140 to 135 to 125 grams.

Graphic Representation of Marginal and Average Curves

We have shown how, from a curve of total profit (or total cost or total anything else), one can determine the corresponding marginal figure. We noted several times in the chapter that the marginal value at any particular point is equal to the *slope* of the corresponding total curve at that point. But for some purposes it is convenient to use a graph that records marginal and average values directly rather than deriving them from the curve of totals.

We can obtain such a graph by plotting the data in a table of average and marginal figures, such as Table 22–6. The result looks like the graph shown in Figure 22–7. Here we have indicated the number of hamburger patties in the pile on the horizontal axis and the corresponding average and marginal weight figures on the vertical axis. The solid dots represent average weights; the small circles represent marginal weights. Thus, for example, point A shows that when two patties are on the scale, their average weight is 120 grams, as was reported on the third line of Table 22–6. Similarly, point B on the graph represents information provided in the next column of the table: that is, that the marginal weight of the third patty is 135 grams. For visual convenience these points have been connected into a marginal curve and an average curve, represented respectively by the solid and the broken curves in the diagram. This is the representation of marginal and average values that economists most frequently use.

Figure 22–7 illustrates two of our rules. Rule 3 says that, for the first unit, the marginal and average values will be the same. And that is precisely why the two curves start out together at point *C*. When there is only one patty on the scale, marginal and average weight *must* be the same. The graph also obeys Rule 4:

Between points *C* and *E*, where the average curve is *rising*, the marginal curve lies *above* the average. (Notice, however, that over part of this range the marginal curve *falls* even though the average curve is rising—Rule 4 says nothing about the rise or fall of the marginal curve.) We see also that over range *EF*, where the average curve is falling, the marginal curve is below the average curve, again in accord with Rule 4. Finally, at point *E*, where the average curve is neither rising nor falling, the marginal curve meets the average curve: Average and marginal weights are equal at that point.

Questions for Discussion

1. Suppose the following is your record of exam grades in Principles of Economics:

EXAM DATE	GRADE	COMMENT
September 30	65	A slow start.
October 28	75	A big improvement.
December 13	90	Congratulations!
January 30	85	Slipped a little.
March 1	95	Well done!

Use these data to make up a table of total, average, and marginal grades for the five exams.

2. From the data in your table, illustrate each of the rules mentioned in this appendix. Be sure to point out an instance where marginal grade falls but average grade rises.

The Market System: Virtues and Vices

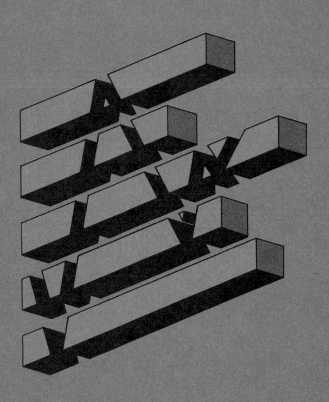

23

The Firm and the Industry under Perfect Competition

Competition . . . brings about the only . . . arrangement of social production which is possible. . . . [Otherwise] what guarantee [do] we have that the necessary quantity and not more of each product will be produced, that we shall not go hungry in regard to corn and meat while we are choked in beet sugar and drowned in potato spirit, that we shall not lack trousers to cover our nakedness while buttons flood us in millions.

FRIEDRICH ENGELS

Besides the consumer demands and the business costs that we studied in the last four chapters, the decisions of firms also depend on the number, size, and behaviour of the other firms in the industry. The strength of the competition faced by a company can profoundly affect its pricing, its output decisions, and its input purchases. Strong competitive pressures, sometimes taking subtle forms, can severely limit the freedom of choice of management in setting prices and can, in the process, protect the interests of consumers. Giant corporations may also find themselves under this sort of pressure, even where there are few rival domestic firms. In recent years, for example, many Canadian companies have found themselves facing stiffening competition from foreign firms.

This chapter and the four chapters that follow it analyze some of the forms that competition—or its absence—can take, and examine some of the implications for general welfare.

Industries differ dramatically in the number of firms that populate them and in the typical size of those firms. Some industries, like the fishing industry, have a great many very small firms; others, like the automobile industry, are composed of a few industrial giants. This chapter deals with a very particular type of market structure—called *perfect competition*—in which firms are numerous and small. We begin by comparing alternative market forms and defining perfect competition precisely. We then use the tools we acquired in Chapter 22 to analyze the behaviour of the perfectly competitive firm and derive its supply curve. Next, we consider the supply curve of *all* the firms in an industry—the *industry supply curve*—and investigate how developments in the industry affect the individual firms.

Application: Can Good Weather Be Bad for Farmers?

If you do your own gardening, you no doubt hope for the best possible weather—a nice mixture of sunshine and rain to help the plants grow. Drought and frost are your mortal enemies. For farmers who produce commodities that are not sold abroad, however, ideal weather sometimes spells disaster. After a bumper crop comes in, farmers often pressure Ottawa, complaining about the low prices that result. Legislators are urged to "protect" the farmer from these low prices, which is to say, to protect them from the consequences of good weather. On the other hand, adverse weather often leaves farmers *as a whole* rather well off. Even though bad weather ruins some farmers (to whom help *is* sometimes given), broad-based political action does not typically appear after droughts, floods, and premature frosts. What accounts for this strange behaviour? The tools we are about to describe—the analysis of competitive supply—will permit us to answer this question at the end of the chapter.

Varieties of Market Structure: A Sneak Preview

A **market** refers to the set of all sale and purchase transactions that affect the price of some commodity.

It will be helpful to open our discussion by explaining clearly what is meant by the word **market**. Economists do not reserve the term to denote only an organized exchange operating in a well-defined physical location. In its more general and abstract usage, *market* refers to a set of sellers and buyers whose activities affect the price at which a *particular commodity* is sold. For example, two separate sales of Canadian Pacific shares in different parts of the country may be considered as taking place in the same market, while the sale of bread and carrots in neighbouring stalls of a market square may, in our sense, occur in totally different markets.

So far, this book has not distinguished among firms in terms of the sort of market in which they operate. We have talked only about firms in general. But in this chapter and the next few we will see that market form makes a great deal of difference to the way in which firms can and do behave. Under some market forms, for example, the firm has no control over price. In others, the firm has the power to adjust price in a way that adds to its profits and that, in the opinion of some people, constitutes exploitation of consumers. Economists distinguish among different kinds of markets according to (1) how many firms they include, (2) whether the products of the different firms are identical or somewhat different, and (3) how easy it is for new firms to enter the market. Table 23–1 summarizes the main features of the four market structures we will study in this and subsequent chapters. It is provided here as a kind of road map of where we are going. *Perfect competition* is obviously at one extreme (many small firms selling an identical product) while *pure monopoly* (a single firm) is at the other. In between are hybrid forms—called *monopolistic competition* (many small firms each selling products slightly different from the others') and *oligopoly* (a few large rival firms)—that share some of the characteristics of perfect competition and some of the characteristics of monopoly.

Perfect competition is not the typical market form in the Canadian economy. Indeed, it is quite rare. Some farming and fishing industries approximate perfect competition, as do some financial markets. Pure monopoly—literally *one* firm—is also infrequent. Most of the products you buy are no doubt supplied by oligopolies or monopolistic competitors—terms we will be defining precisely in Chapter 26.

TABLE 23–1
Varieties of Market Structure

TYPE OF MARKET STRUCTURE	DEFINITION			WHERE TO FIND IT	
	NUMBER OF SELLERS	NATURE OF THE PRODUCT	BARRIERS TO ENTRY	IN THE CANADIAN ECONOMY	IN THIS TEXTBOOK
Perfect competition	Many	All firms produce identical products (example: wheat)	None	Some agricultural markets and parts of retailing come close	Chapter 23
Monopolistic competition	Many	Different firms produce somewhat different products (example: restaurant meals)	Minor	Most of the retailing sector, textiles, and restaurants	Chapter 26
Oligopoly	Few	Firms may produce identical or differentiated products (example: brands of toothpaste)	May be considerable	Much of the manufacturing sector, especially autos, steel, and cigarettes	Chapter 26
Pure monopoly	One	Unique product	May be considerable	Public utilities	Chapter 25

Perfect Competition Defined

You can appreciate just how special perfect competition is once we provide a comprehensive definition. A market is said to operate under **perfect competition** when the following four conditions are satisfied:

1. *Numerous participants.* Each seller and purchaser constitutes so small a portion of the market that the firm's decisions have no effect on the price. This requirement rules out trade associations or other collusive arrangements strong enough to affect price.

2. *Homogeneity of product.* The product offered by any seller is identical to that supplied by any other seller. (Example: Wheat of a given grade is a homogeneous product; different brands of toothpaste are not.) Because the product is homogeneous, consumers do not care from which firm they buy.

3. *Freedom of entry and exit.* New firms desiring to enter the market face no special impediments that the existing firms can avoid. Similarly, if production and sale of the good proves unprofitable, there are no barriers preventing firms from leaving the market.

4. *Perfect information.* Each firm and each customer is well informed about the available products and their prices. They know whether one supplier is selling at a price lower than another is.

These are obviously exacting requirements that are met infrequently in practice. One example might be a market for common shares: There are literally thousands of buyers and sellers of Bell Canada stock; all of the shares are exactly alike; anyone who wishes can enter the market easily; and most of the relevant information is readily available in the daily newspaper. But other examples are hard to find. Our interest in perfect competition is surely not for its descriptive realism.

Why, then, do we spend time studying perfect competition? The answer takes us back to the central theme of this book. It is under perfect competition that the market mechanism performs best in allocating society's resources. So, if we want to learn what markets do well, we can put the market's best foot forward by beginning with perfect competition.

As Adam Smith suggested some two centuries ago, perfectly competitive firms use society's scarce resources with maximum efficiency. And as Friedrich Engels suggested in the opening quotation of this chapter, perfectly competitive firms serve consumers' tastes effectively. So by studying perfect competition, we can learn just how much an *ideally functioning* market system might accomplish. This is the topic of the present chapter and the next one. Then, in Chapters 25 and 26, we will consider other market forms and see how they deviate from the perfectly competitive ideal. Still later chapters (especially Chapter 27 and those in Part Seven) will examine many important tasks that the market does not perform at all well, even under perfect competition. These chapters combined should provide a balanced assessment of the virtues and vices of the market mechanism.

The Competitive Firm and Its Demand Curve

To discover what happens in a market in which perfect competition prevails, we must deal separately with the behaviour of *individual firms* and the behaviour of the *industry* that is constituted by those firms. One basic difference between the firm and the industry under competition relates to *pricing*. We say that:

Under perfect competition, the firm is a *price taker*. It has no choice but to accept the price that has been determined in the market.

The fact that a firm in a perfectly competitive market has no control over the price it charges follows from the definition of perfect competition. The presence of a vast number of competitors, each offering identical products, forces each firm to meet but not exceed the price charged by the others. Like a shareholder with 100 shares of Bell Canada, the firm simply finds out the prevailing price on the market and either accepts that price or refuses to sell. But while the individual firm has no influence over price under perfect competition, the industry does. This influence is not conscious or planned—it happens spontaneously through the impersonal forces of supply and demand, as we observed in Chapter 3.

With two important exceptions, the analysis of the behaviour of the firm under perfect competition is exactly the same as that pertaining to any other firm, so the tools developed in Chapters 21 and 22 can be applied directly. The two exceptions are the special shape of the competitive firm's demand curve and the effects on the firm's profits of freedom of entry and exit. We will consider them in turn, beginning with the demand curve.

In Chapter 22, we assumed that the firm's demand curve always slopes downward; if a firm wished to sell more (without increasing its advertising or changing its product specifications), it had to reduce the price of its product. The competitive firm is an exception to this general principle.

A perfectly competitive firm has a **horizontal demand curve**. This means it can double or triple its sales without any reduction in the price of its product.

How is this possible? The answer is that the competitive firm is so insignificant relative to the market as a whole that it has absolutely no influence over price. The farmer who sells his barley through the exchange in Winnipeg must accept the current quotation his broker reports to him. Because there are thousands of farmers, the Winnipeg price per tonne will not budge because Farmer Jones decides he doesn't like the price and holds back a truckload for storage. Thus, the demand curve for Farmer Jones's barley is as shown in Figure 23–1; the price he is paid in Winnipeg will be $80 per tonne whether he sells one truckload (point *A*) or two (point *B*) or three (point *C*). This is so because price is determined by the *industry's* supply and demand curves, shown in the right-hand portion of the graph.

Short-Run Equilibrium of the Perfectly Competitive Firm

We have pointed out that economists consider the short run to be a period so brief that some relevant arrangements cannot be changed. For example, if the firm has signed a

FIGURE 23–1
Demand Curve for a Firm under Perfect Competition
Under perfect competition, the size of the output of a firm is so small a portion of the total industry output that it cannot affect the market price of the product. Even if the firm's output increases many times, market price remains $80, where it is set by industry supply and demand.

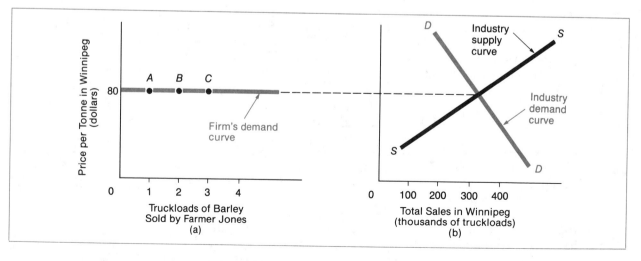

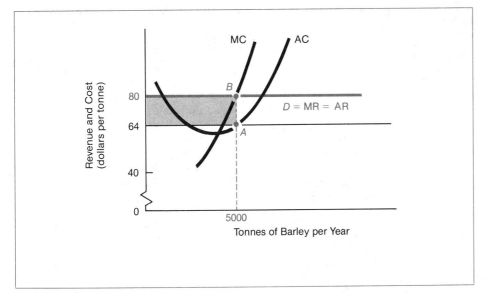

FIGURE 23–2
Short-Run Equilibrium of the Competitive Firm
The profit-maximizing firm will select the output (5000 tonnes per year) at which marginal cost equals marginal revenue (point *B*). The demand curve, *D*, is horizontal because the firm's output is too small to affect market price; thus it is also the marginal-revenue curve. In the short run, demand may be either high or low in relation to cost. Therefore each unit it sells may return a profit (*AB*) or a loss.

five-year rental lease, that firm's long run must be a period greater than five years. Another critical element that does not change in the short run is the number of firms in the industry. Even if an industry is making profits sufficiently high to induce newcomers to open up for business, entrance usually takes time. For the short run, then, we can ignore the possibility of entry or exit and study the decisions of the firms already in the industry. We already have sufficient background to analyze how the competitive firm decides how much to produce. To begin, recall from Chapter 22 that profit maximization requires the firm to pick an output level that makes its *marginal cost equal to its marginal revenue*: $MC = MR$. The only feature that distinguishes the profit-maximizing equilibrium of the competitive firm from that of any other type of firm is its horizontal demand curve.

Because the demand curve is horizontal, the competitive firm's marginal-revenue curve is a horizontal straight line that coincides with its demand curve; hence, $MR = price (P)$. It is easy to see why this is so. If the price does not depend on how much the firm sells (which is what a horizontal demand curve means), then each *additional* unit sold brings in an amount of revenue (the *marginal* revenue) exactly equal to the market price. So marginal revenue always equals price under perfect competition; the demand curve and the MR curve coincide because the firm is a price taker.

Once we know the shape and position of a firm's marginal-revenue curve, we can use this information and the marginal-cost curve to determine its optimal output and profit, as shown in Figure 23–2. As usual, the profit-maximizing output is that at which $MC = MR$ (point *B*). This competitive firm produces 5000 tonnes per year—the output level at which MC and MR are both equal to the market price, $80. Thus:

Because a firm in a perfectly competitive market is a price taker, its marginal-revenue schedule coincides with the going market-price line. Thus the *equilibrium* of a profit-maximizing firm in a perfectly competitive market must occur at an output level at which marginal cost is equal to price, or in symbols:

$$MC = P.$$

The same information is shown in Table 23–2, which gives the firm's total revenue, total cost, and profit for different output quantities. We see from the last column that total profit is maximized at an output of either 4000 or 5000 tonnes, where total profit is $80,000. Table 23–2 also gives marginal costs and marginal revenues. We see that an increase in output from 4000 tonnes to 5000 tonnes incurs a

TABLE 23-2
Revenues, Costs, and Profits of a Competitive Firm

QUANTITY (thousands of tonnes)	TOTAL REVENUE	MARGINAL REVENUE	TOTAL COST	MARGINAL COST	TOTAL PROFIT
	(thousands of dollars)				
0	0				
1	80	80	80		0
2	160	80	140	60	20
3	240	80	180	40	60
4	320	80	240	60	80
5	400	80	320	80	80
6	480	80	440	120	40
7	560	80	640	200	−80

marginal cost ($80,000) that is equal to the corresponding marginal revenue ($80,000), confirming that 5000 tonnes is the profit-maximizing level of output.[1]

Short-Run Profit: Graphic Representation

The analysis so far tells us how the firm can pick the output that maximizes profit. But even if it succeeds in doing so, the firm may conceivably find itself in trouble. If the demand for its product is weak or its costs are high, even the most profitable option may lead to a loss. To determine whether the firm is making a profit or incurring a loss, we must compare total revenue (TR = $P \times Q$) with total cost (TC = AC $\times Q$). Since Q is common to both of these, we need only compare P and AC.

The firm's profit is shown in Figure 23-2. By definition, profit per unit of output is revenue per unit minus cost per unit. To enable us to represent profit per unit graphically we have included in Figure 23-2 the firm's *average-cost* (AC) curve, which was explained in Chapter 21. We see in the figure that average cost at 5000 tonnes per year is only $64 per tonne (point *A*). Since the price, or average revenue (AR), is $80 per tonne (point *B*), the firm is making a profit of AR − AC = $16 per tonne. This profit margin appears in the graph as the vertical distance between points *A* and *B*.

Notice that in addition to showing the *profit per unit*, the graph can be used to show the firm's *total profit*. Total profit is the profit per unit ($16 in this example) times the number of units (5000 per year). Therefore, total profit is represented as the *area* of the shaded rectangle whose height is the profit per unit ($16) and whose width is the number of units (5000).[2] That is, total profit at any output is the area of the rectangle whose base equals the level of output and whose height equals AR − AC. Thus, in this case, profits are $80,000 per year.

The MC = P condition gives us the output that maximizes the perfectly competitive firm's profit. It does not tell us whether the firm is making a profit or a loss. To determine this, we must compare price with average cost.

[1] The MC = MR rule yields the conclusion that the firm should produce exactly 5000 tonnes, while the profits column in Table 23-2 suggests that the firm should be indifferent between operating at 4000 and 5000 tonnes. The source of this slight inconsistency is essentially a measurement error. To calculate marginal costs and marginal revenues accurately, we should increase output one tonne at a time, instead of proceeding in leaps of 1000 tonnes. But that would require too much space!

[2] Recall that the formula for the area of a rectangle is area = height $\times$ width.

The Case of Short-Term Losses

The market is obviously treating the farmer in the graph rather nicely. But what if the market is not so generous in its rewards? What if, for example, the market price is only $40 per tonne instead of $80? Figure 23–3 shows the equilibrium of the firm under these circumstances. The firm still maximizes profits by producing the level of output at which marginal cost is equal to price—point *B* in the diagram. But this time "maximizing" profits really means keeping the loss as small as possible.

At the optimal level of output (3000 tonnes per year), average cost is $60 per tonne (point *A*), which exceeds the $40 per tonne price (point *B*). The firm is therefore running a loss of $20 per tonne times 3000 tonnes, or $60,000 per year. This loss, which is represented by the area of the shaded rectangle in Figure 23–3, is the best the firm can do. If it selected any other output level, its loss would be even greater.

The price-taking firm will always equate MC and P, but in the short run it may wind up with either a profit or a loss.

Shut-Down and Break-Even Analysis

There is, however, a limit to the amount of loss the firm can be forced to accept. If losses get too big, the firm can simply shut down. To understand the logic of the decision between shutting down and remaining in operation, we must return to the distinction between costs that are sunk (the fixed costs) and costs that are variable in the short run. It will be recalled from the discussion of Chapter 21 that costs are sunk if the firm cannot escape them in the short run, either because of a contract (say, with a landlord or a union) or because it has already bought an item (say, a machine) and can get its money back only by operating that item as long as it lasts.

If the firm stops producing, its revenue will fall to zero. Its *escapable* or *variable* costs will also fall to zero. But its sunk or *fixed* costs—such as rent—will remain to plague it. If the firm is losing money, sometimes it will be better off continuing to operate until its obligations to pay sunk costs expire, but sometimes it will do better by shutting down. Two rules govern the decision:

Rule 1.   The firm will not lose money if total revenue (TR) exceeds total cost (TC). In that case, it should not plan to shut down in either the short run or the long run.

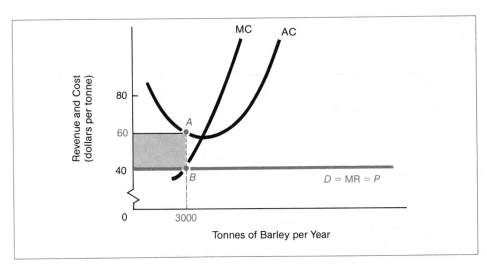

FIGURE 23–3
Short-Run Equilibrium of the Competitive Firm with a Lower Price
In this diagram, the cost curves are the same as in Figure 23-2, but the demand curve (*D*) has shifted down to a market price of $40 per tonne. The firm still does the best it can by setting MC = *P* (point *B*). But since its average cost at 3000 tonnes per year is $60 per tonne, it runs a loss (shown by the shaded rectangle).

Rule 2. The firm should not shut down in the short run if TR exceeds total escapable or variable cost (TVC). It should, nevertheless, plan to close in the long run if TR is less than TC.

The first rule is obvious. If the firm's revenues cover its total costs, then it does not lose money.

The second rule is a bit more subtle. Suppose TR is less than TC. If our unfortunate firm continues in operation, how much will it lose? Clearly it will lose the difference between total cost and total revenue; that is:

Loss if the firm stays in business = TC – TR.

However, if the firm shuts down, both its revenues and its escapable or variable costs become zero, leaving only its sunk costs—the total *fixed* costs (TFC)—to be paid:

Loss if the firm shuts down = TFC.

Rule 2 is illustrated by the two cases in Table 23–3.[3] Case A deals with a firm that loses money but is better off staying in business in the short run. If it closes down, it will lose its $60,000 fixed cost. But if it continues in operation, it will lose only $40,000 because TR ($100,000) exceeds TVC ($80,000) by $20,000, so that its operation contributes $20,000 toward meeting its sunk costs. In case B, on the other hand, continued operation only adds to its losses. If the firm operates, it will lose $90,000 (last entry in Table 23–3), whereas if it shuts down, it will lose only the $60,000 in sunk costs that it must pay in any case, whether it operates or not.

The shut-down decision can also be analyzed graphically. In Figure 23–4, the firm will run a loss whether the price is P_1, P_2, or P_3, because none of these prices is high enough to reach the minimum level of average cost (AC). The *lowest* price that keeps the firm from shutting down can be shown in the graph by introducing one more curve: the **average variable cost (AVC)** curve mentioned in Chapter 21. Why is this curve relevant? Because, as we have just seen, it pays the firm to remain in operation if its total revenue (TR) exceeds its total variable cost (TVC). If we divide both TR and TVC by quantity (Q), we get $TR/Q = P$ and $TVC/Q = AVC$, so this condition may be stated equivalently as the requirement that price exceed AVC. The conclusion is:

The firm will produce nothing unless price lies above the minimum point on the AVC curve.

[3]More generally, we see that the firm will find it advisable to shut down if it is better to lose TFC than to lose TC – TR (that is, if TC – TR > TFC or TC – TFC > TR). Finally, since TC = TFC + TVC, we can express this condition as TVC > TR, which is Rule 2.

TABLE 23–3
The Shut-Down Decision

	CASE A	CASE B
	(thousands of dollars)	
TR	100	100
TVC	80	130
TFC	60	60
TC	140	190
Loss if firm shuts down (TFC)	60	60
Loss if firm does not shut down (TC – TR)	40	90

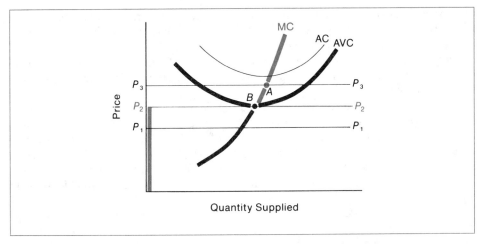

FIGURE 23-4
Shut-Down Analysis
At a price as low as P_1, the firm
cannot even cover its average
variable costs; it is better off
shutting down entirely. At a
price as high as P_3, the firm
selects point A but operates at a
loss (because P_3 is below AC).
However, it is more than
covering its average variable
costs (since P_3 exceeds AVC),
so it pays to keep producing.
Price P_2 is the borderline case.
With this price, the firm selects
point B and is indifferent
between shutting down and
staying open.

Figure 23–4 illustrates this principle by showing an MC curve, an AVC curve, and several alternative demand curves corresponding to different possible prices. Price P_1 is below the minimum average variable cost. With this price, the firm cannot even cover its variable costs and is better off shutting down (producing zero output). Price P_3 is higher. While the firm still runs a loss if it sets MC = P at point A (because AC exceeds P_3), it is at least covering its *escapable* or *variable* costs, and so it pays to keep operating in the short run. Price P_2 is the borderline case. If the price is P_2, the firm is indifferent between shutting down and staying in business and producing at a level where MC = P (point B). P_2 is thus the *lowest* price at which the firm will produce anything. As we see from the graph, P_2 corresponds to the minimum point on the AVC curve.

The Short-Run Supply Curve of the Competitive Firm

Without realizing it, we have now derived the **supply curve of the competitive firm** in the short run. Why? Recall that a supply curve summarizes the answers to such questions as, If the price is so and so, how much will the firm produce? We have now discovered that there are two possibilities, as indicated by the thick coloured line in Figure 23–4.

1. If the price exceeds the minimum AVC, in the short run it pays a competitive firm to produce the level of output that equates MC and P. Thus, for any price above point B, we can read the corresponding quantity supplied from the firm's MC curve.

2. If the price falls below the minimum AVC, then it pays the firm to produce nothing. Quantity supplied falls to zero.

Putting these two observations together, we conclude that:

The short-run supply curve of the perfectly competitive firm is its marginal-cost curve above the point where it intersects the average variable-cost curve; that is, above the minimum level of AVC. If price falls below this level, the firm's quantity supplied drops to zero.

The Short-Run Supply Curve of the Competitive Industry

Having completed the analysis of the competitive firm's supply decision, we turn our attention next to the competitive *industry*. Again we need to distinguish between the short run and long run, but the distinction is different here. The short run for the *industry* is defined as a period of time too brief for new firms to enter the industry or for old firms to leave, so the number of firms is fixed. By contrast, the long run for the industry is a period of time long enough for any firm that so desires to enter (or leave). In addition, the long run must be a period protracted sufficiently to permit each firm in the industry to adjust its output to its own long-run costs.[4] We begin our analysis of industry equilibrium in the short run.

With the number of firms fixed, it is a simple matter to derive the **supply curve of the competitive industry** from those of the individual firms. At any given price, we simply *add up* the quantities supplied by each of the firms to arrive at the industry-wide quantity supplied. For example, if each of 1000 identical firms in the barley industry supplies 4000 tonnes when the price is $60 per tonne, then the quantity supplied by the industry at a $60 price will be 4000 tonnes per firm × 1000 firms = 4 million tonnes.

This process of deriving the *market* supply curve from the *individual* supply curves of firms is perfectly analogous to the way we derived the *market* demand curve from the *individual* demand curves of consumers in Chapter 20. Graphically, what we are doing is *summing the individual supply curves horizontally*, as illustrated in Figure 23–5. At a price of $60, each of the 1000 firms in the industry supplies 4000 tonnes [point *c* in part (a)], so the industry supplies 4 million tonnes [point *C* in part (b)]. At a price of $80 each firm supplies 5000 tonnes [point *e* in part (a)], and so the industry supplies 5 million tonnes [point *E* in part (b)]. Similar calculations can be done for any other price. This indicates, incidentally, that the supply curve of the industry will shift to the right whenever a new firm enters the industry.

The supply curve of the competitive industry in the short run is derived by *summing* the supply curves of all the firms in the industry *horizontally*.

Notice that if the short-run supply curves of individual firms are upward sloping, the short-run supply curve of the competitive industry will be upward sloping, too. We

[4] The short-run and long-run average-cost curves were discussed in Chapter 21, pages 463–64.

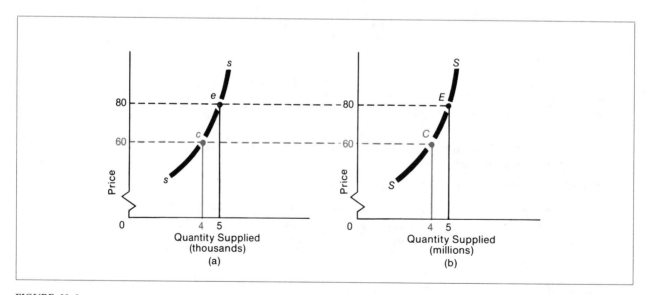

FIGURE 23–5

Derivation of the Industry Supply Curve from the Supply Curves of the Individual Firms

In this hypothetical industry of 1000 identical firms, each individual firm has the supply curve *ss* in part (a). For example, quantity supplied is 4000 tonnes when the price is $60 per unit (point *c*). By *adding up* the quantities supplied by each firm at each possible price, we arrive at the industry supply curve *SS* in part (b). For example, at a unit price of $60, total quantity supplied by the industry is 4 million units (point *C*).

have seen that the firm's supply curve is its marginal-cost curve (above the level of minimum average variable cost), so it follows that rising marginal costs lead to an upward-sloping *industry* supply curve.

Industry Equilibrium in the Short Run

Now that we have derived the industry supply curve, we need only add a market demand curve to determine the price and quantity that will emerge. This is done for our illustrative barley industry in Figure 23–6, where the industry supply curve [carried over from Figure 23–5 (b)] is *SS* and the demand curve is *DD*. Note that for the competitive industry, unlike the competitive firm, the demand curve is normally downward sloping. Why? Each firm by itself is so small that if it alone were to double its output the effect would hardly be noticeable. But if *every* firm in the industry were to expand its output, that would make a substantial difference. Customers can be induced to buy the additional quantities arriving at the market only if the price of the good falls.

Point *E* is the equilibrium point for the competitive industry, because only at the combination of price, $80, and quantity, 5 million tonnes, are neither purchasers nor sellers motivated to upset matters. At a price of $80, sellers are willing to offer exactly the amount consumers want to purchase.

Should we expect price actually to reach, or at least to approximate, this equilibrium level? The answer is yes. To see why, we must consider what happens when price is not at its equilibrium level. Suppose it takes a lower value, such as $60. The low price will stimulate customers to buy more, and it will also lead firms to produce less than at a price of $80. Our diagram confirms that at a price of $60, quantity supplied (4 million tonnes) is lower than quantity demanded (9.4 million tonnes). Thus, unsatisfied buyers will probably offer to pay higher prices, which will force price *upward* in the direction of its equilibrium value, $80.

Similarly, if we begin with a price higher than the equilibrium price, we may readily verify that quantity supplied will exceed quantity demanded. Under these circumstances, frustrated sellers are likely to reduce their prices, so price will be forced downward. In the circumstances depicted in Figure 23–6, then, there is in effect a magnet at the equilibrium price of $80 that will pull the actual price in its direction if for some reason the actual price starts out at some other level.

In practice, there are few cases in which competitive markets, over a long period of time, seem not to have moved toward equilibrium prices. Matters eventually seem

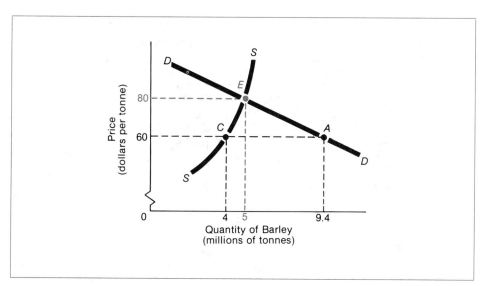

FIGURE 23–6
Supply–Demand Equilibrium of a Competitive Industry
The only equilibrium combination of price and quantity is a price of $80 and a quantity of 5 million tonnes at which the supply curve *SS* and the demand curve *DD* intersect (point *E*). At a lower price, such as $60, quantity demanded (9.4 million tonnes, as shown by point *A* on the demand curve) will be higher than the 4-million-tonne quantity supplied (point *C*). Thus the price will be driven back up toward the $80 equilibrium. The opposite will happen at a price such as $100, which is above equilibrium.

to work out as depicted in Figure 23–6. Of course, numerous transitory influences—a strike that cuts production, a sudden change in consumer tastes, and so on—can jolt any real-world market away from its equilibrium point. And there also have been periods, sometimes of distressingly long duration, when the "bottom has dropped out" of some nearly competitive markets, such as stock exchanges. During such market "crashes," it certainly did not seem that prices were moving toward equilibrium.

Yet, as we have just seen, there are powerful forces that do push prices back toward equilibrium—toward the level at which the supply and demand curves intersect. These forces are of fundamental importance for economic analysis, for if there were no such forces, prices in the real world would bear little resemblance to equilibrium prices, and there would be little reason to study supply–demand analysis. Fortunately, the required equilibrating forces do exist.

Industry and Firm Equilibrium in the Long Run

The equilibrium of a competitive industry in the long run may differ from the short-run equilibrium that we have just studied. There are two reasons. First, in the long run, the number of firms in the industry is not fixed. Second, as we saw in Chapter 21 (pages 463–64), in the long run the firm can vary its plant size and make other changes that were prevented by temporary commitments. Hence, the firm's (and the industry's) long-run cost curves are not the same as its short-run cost curves.

What will lure new firms into the industry or repel old ones? Profits. Remember that when a firm selects its optimal level of output by setting MC = P, it may wind up with either a profit or a loss. Such profits or losses must be *temporary* for a competitive firm, because the freedom of new firms to enter the industry or of old firms to leave it will, in the long run, eliminate them.

Suppose very high profits accrue to firms in the industry. Then new companies will find it attractive to enter the business, and expanded production will force the market price to fall from its initial level. Why? Recall that the industry supply curve is the horizontal sum of the supply curves of individual firms. Under perfect competition, new firms can enter the industry on *the same terms as existing firms*. This means that new entrants will have the *same* individual supply curves as old firms. If the market price did not fall, entry of new firms would lead to an increased number of firms with no change in output *per firm*. Consequently, the total quantity supplied on the market would be higher and would exceed quantity demanded. But, of course, this means that in a free market, entry of new firms *must* push the price down.

FIGURE 23–7
A Shift in the Industry Supply Curve Caused by the Entry of New Firms
This diagram shows what happens to the industry equilibrium when new firms enter the industry. Quantity supplied at any given price increases; that is, the supply curve shifts to the right, from S_0S_0 to S_1S_1 in the figure. As a result, the market price falls (from $80 to $70) and the quantity increases (from 5 million tonnes to 7.2 million tonnes).

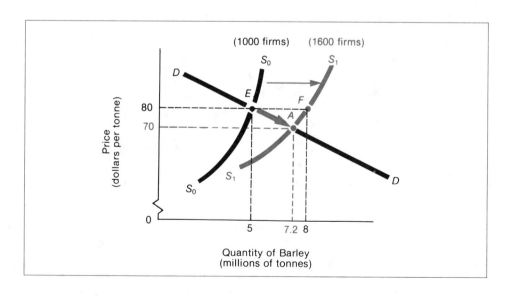

Figure 23-7 shows how the entry process works. In this diagram, the demand curve DD and the original (short-run) supply curve S_0S_0 are carried over from Figure 23-6. The entry of new firms seeking high profits *shifts the short-run supply curve outward to the right*, to S_1S_1. The new market equilibrium is at point A (rather than at point E), where price is $70 per tonne and 7.2 million tonnes are produced and consumed. Entry of new firms reduces price and raises total output. (Had the price not fallen, quantity supplied after entry would have been 8 million tonnes—point F.) Why must the price fall? Because the demand curve for the industry is downward sloping— an increase in output will be purchased by consumers only if the price is reduced.

To see where the entry process stops, we must consider how the entry of new firms affects the behaviour of old firms. At first, this may seem to contradict the notion of perfect competition; perfectly competitive firms are not supposed to care what their competitors are doing. Indeed, these barley farmers do not care. But they do care very much about the market price of barley, and, as we have just seen, the entry of new firms into the barley-farming industry lowers the price of barley.

In Figure 23-8 we have juxtaposed the diagram of the equilibrium of the competitive firm (Figure 23-2 on page 507) and the diagram of the equilibrium of the competitive industry (Figure 23-7). Before entry, the market price was $80 [point E in Figure 23-8(b)] and each of the 1000 firms was producing 5000 tonnes— the point where marginal cost and price were equal [point e in Figure 23-8(a)]. The demand curve facing each firm was the horizontal line D_0 in Figure 23-8(a). There were profits because average costs (AC) at 5000 tonnes per firm were less than price.

Now suppose 600 new firms are attracted by these high profits and enter the industry. Each has the cost structure indicated by the AC and MC curves in Figure 23-8(a). As we have noted, the industry supply curve in Figure 23-8(b) shifts to the right, and price falls to $70 per tonne. Firms in the industry cannot fail to notice this lower price. As we see in Figure 23-8(a), each firm reduces its output to 4500 tonnes in reaction to the lower price (point a). But now there are 1600 firms, so total industry output is $4500 \times 1600 = 7.2$ million tonnes [point A in Figure 23-8(b)].

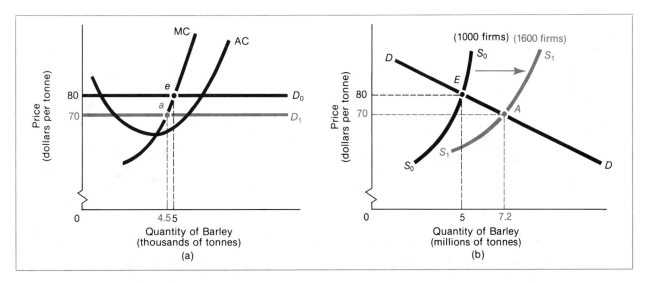

FIGURE 23-8

The Competitive Firm and the Competitive Industry
Here we show the interaction between developments at the industry level [in part (b)] and developments at the firm level [in part (a)]. An outward shift in the industry supply curve from S_0S_0 to S_1S_1 in part (b) lowers the market price from $80 to $70. In part (a), we see that a profit-maximizing competitive firm reacts to this decline in price by curtailing output. When the demand curve of the firm is D_0 ($80), it produces 5000 tonnes (point e). When the firm's demand curve falls to D_1 ($70), its output declines to 4500 tonnes (point a). However, there are now 1600 firms rather than 1000, so total industry output has expanded from 5 million tonnes to 7.2 million tonnes [part (b)]. Entry has reduced profits. But since P still exceeds AC at an output of 4500 tonnes per firm in part (a), some profits remain.

At point *a* in Figure 23–8(a), there are still profits to be made because the $70 price exceeds average cost. Thus the entry process is not yet complete. When will it end? Only when all profits have been competed away. Only when entry shifts the industry supply curve so far to the right [S_2S_2 in Figure 23–9(b)] that the demand curve facing individual firms falls to the level of minimum average cost [point *m* in Figure 23–9(a)] will all profits be eradicated and entry cease.

The two panels of Figure 23–9 show the competitive firm and the competitive industry in long-run equilibrium.[5] Notice that at the equilibrium point [*m* in part (a)], each firm picks its own output level so as to maximize its profit. This means that for every firm $P = MC$. But free entry forces P to be equal to AC in the long run [point *M* in part (b)], for if P were not equal to AC, firms would either earn profits or suffer losses. Thus:

When a perfectly competitive industry is in long-run equilibrium, firms maximize profits so that $P = MC$ and entry forces the price down until it is tangent to the average-cost curve ($P = AC$). As a result, in long-run competitive equilibrium it is true that:

$$P = MC = AC.$$

Thus, even though every firm earns zero economic profit, profits are at the maximum that is attainable.

In the numerical example just presented to explain this long-run efficiency point, we have implicitly assumed that the long-run *industry* supply curve is horizontal. We made this assumption just to simplify the exposition. Let us now clarify where it crept in. When new firms entered the industry, we did not adjust the position of the cost

[5]If the original short-run equilibrium had involved losses instead of profits, firms would have exited from the industry, shifting the industry supply curve inward, until all losses were eradicated and we would end up in a position exactly like Figure 23–9. EXERCISE: To test your understanding, draw the version of Figure 23–8 that corresponds to this case.

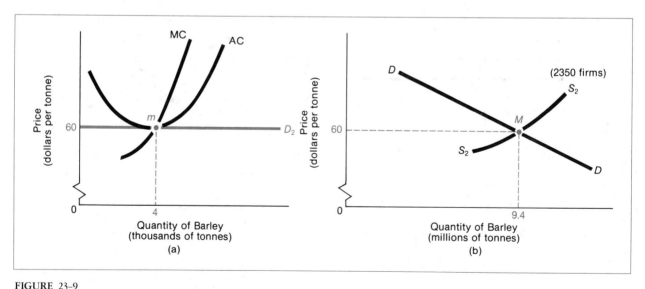

FIGURE 23–9
Long-Run Equilibrium of the Competitive Firm and Industry
By the time 2350 firms have entered the industry, the industry supply curve is S_2S_2 and the market price is $60 per tonne. At this price, the horizontal demand curve facing each firm is D_2 in part (a), so the profit-maximizing level of output is 4000 tonnes (point *m*). Here, since average cost and price are equal, there is no economic profit.

curves for the representative firm. Thus, even though we were discussing a long-run time horizon, we assumed that the new firms built plants just like the old ones and that the old firms chose not to install different sizes or kinds of plants. If, instead, we had assumed, for example, the use of more efficient (lower average cost) techniques, both the MC and the AC curves would have been lower, resulting in an industry supply curve that was negatively sloped. Thus, if increasing returns to scale are possible for each firm, the long-run industry supply curve will be downward sloping.

This possibility is not the only one. Suppose each individual firm has constant returns to scale, but as the industry expands, the demand by the entire industry forces up the price of one of the inputs. This would raise the position of each firm's MC and AC curves, and the long-run industry supply curve would be positively sloped. It is this long-run industry supply curve, whatever its slope, that is relevant to the determination of long-run equilibrium price and quantity in the standard supply–demand diagram.

Zero Economic Profit: The Opportunity Cost of Capital

In our discussion of the long run, something may be troubling you. Why would there be any firms in the industry *at all* if there were no profits to be made? What sense does it make to call a position of zero profit a "long-run equilibrium"? The answer is that the zero-profit concept used in economics does not mean the same thing that it does in ordinary usage.

As has been noted repeatedly, when economists measure average cost, they include the cost of *all* the firm's inputs, *including the opportunity cost of the capital* or any other input, *such as labour*, provided by the firm's owners. Since the firm may not make explicit payments to those who provide it with capital, this element of cost may not be picked up by the firm's accountants. So what economists call *zero economic profit* may correspond to some positive amount of profit as measured by conventional accounting techniques.

For example, if investors can earn 15 percent by lending their funds elsewhere, then the firm must earn a 15 percent rate of return to cover its opportunity cost of capital. Because economists consider this 15 percent opportunity cost to be the *cost of the firm's capital*, they include it in the AC curve. If the firm cannot earn at least 15 percent on its capital, funds will not be made available to it because investors can earn greater returns elsewhere. So, in the economist's language, in order to break even— earn zero **economic profit**—a firm must earn enough to cover not only the cost of labour, fuel, and raw materials but also the cost of its funds, including the opportunity cost of any funds supplied by the owners of the firm.

Economic profit equals net earnings, in the accountant's sense, minus the firm's opportunity cost of capital.

To illustrate the difference between economic profits and accounting profits, suppose Canadian government bonds pay 15 percent and the owner of a small shop earns 10 percent on her business investment. The shopkeeper might say she is making a 10 percent profit, but an economist would say she is *losing* 5 percent on every dollar she has invested in her business. The reason is that by keeping her money tied up in the firm, she gives up the chance to buy government bonds and receive a 15 percent return. With this explanation of economic profit we can now understand the logic behind the zero-profit condition for the long-run industry equilibrium.

Zero profit in the economic sense simply means that firms are earning the normal economy-wide rate of profit in the accounting sense. This condition is guaranteed by freedom of entry and exit.

Freedom of entry guarantees that those who invest in a competitive industry will receive a rate of return on their capital *no greater than* the return that capital could earn elsewhere in the economy. If economic profits are being earned in some industry, capital will be attracted into it. The new capital will shift the industry supply curve to the right, which will drive down prices and profits. This process will continue until the return on capital in this industry is reduced to the return that capital could earn elsewhere—its opportunity cost.

Similarly, freedom of exit of capital guarantees that in the long run, once capital has had a chance to move, no industry will provide a rate of return *lower than* the opportunity cost of capital. For if returns in one industry are particularly low, resources will flow out of it. Plant and equipment will not be replaced as they wear out. As a result, the industry supply curve will shift to the left, and prices and profits will rise toward their opportunity cost level.

Perfect Competition and Economic Efficiency

We have now completed our discussion of the long-run equilibrium of the industry. What about the firm? We have already implicitly answered that in Figure 23–9(a). We see there that in equilibrium the firm's horizontal demand curve D_2D_2 must be just tangent to its long-run AC curve. Why? If the AC curve lay below D_2D_2, the firm could make a profit by producing an output at which P is greater than AC [as in Figure 23–8(a)]. If AC were everywhere above D_2D_2, the firm would suffer a loss because P would be smaller than AC—no matter what output the firm produces. We know neither situation is compatible with competitive equilibrium because positive profits induce entry and losses cause exit. We conclude:

Long-run competitive equilibrium of the firm will occur at the lowest point on the firm's long-run AC curve where that curve is tangent to the firm's horizontal demand curve. Thus, the outputs of competitive industries are produced at the lowest possible cost to society.

Why is it always most efficient if each firm in a competitive industry produces at the point where AC is as small as possible? Our example will bring out the point. Suppose the industry is in long-run equilibrium with 9.4 million tonnes of barley being produced by the 2350 farms (each producing 4000 tonnes). This total amount can also be produced by 4700 farms each producing 2000 or by 1880 farms each producing 5000 tonnes. This is so since $2000 \times 4700 = 4000 \times 2350 = 5000 \times 1880 = 9.4$ million. (Of course the job can be done by other numbers of farms, but for simplicity let us consider only these three possibilities.) The AC figures for the farms are as shown in Table 23–4. An output of 4000 tonnes corresponds to the lowest point on the AC curve, with an AC of $60 per tonne. Which is the cheapest way for the industry to produce its 9.4 million tonne output? That is, what is the cost-minimizing number of firms for the job? Looking at the last column of Table 23–4, we see that the 9.4 million tonne output is produced at the least total cost if it is done by 2350 firms each producing the cost-minimizing output of 4000 tonnes.

Why is this so? The answer is not difficult to see. For a given industry output, it is obvious that total industry cost will be as small as possible if and only if AC for each firm is as small as possible: that is, if the number of firms doing the job is such that each is producing the output at which AC is as low as possible.

TABLE 23–4
Average Cost for the Firm and Total Cost for the Industry

FIRM'S OUTPUT (thousands of tonnes)	FIRM'S AVERAGE COST (thousands of dollars)	NUMBER OF FIRMS	INDUSTRY OUTPUT (millions of tonnes)	TOTAL INDUSTRY COST (millions of dollars)
2	70	4700	9.4	658.0
4	60	2350	9.4	564.0
5	64	1880	9.4	601.6

That this kind of cost efficiency characterizes perfect competition in the long run can be seen in Figures 23–8 and 23–9. Before full long-run equilibrium is reached (Figure 23–8), firms may not be producing in the least costly way. For example, the 5 million tonnes being produced by 1000 firms at points e and E in Figures 23–8(a) and (b) could be produced more cheaply by more firms, each producing a smaller volume, because the point of minimum average cost lies to the left of point e in Figure 23–8(a). This problem is rectified, however, in the long run by entry of new firms seeking profit. We see in Figure 23–9 that after the entry process is complete, every firm is producing at its most efficient (lowest AC) level—4000 tonnes. As Adam Smith might have put it, even though each farmer cares only about his own profits, the barley-farming industry as a whole is guided *by an invisible hand* to produce the amount of barley that society wants at the lowest possible cost.

Why Good Weather Can Be Bad for Farmers

The interactions between the competitive firm and the competitive industry that we have just studied permit us to resolve the puzzle with which we began the chapter: Why is it that farm incomes often decline when the harvest is good and increase when the harvest is bad?

First, we should clarify the point. The statement is not that *every* farmer benefits from a drought or a flood. Obviously, these calamities can ruin the particular farmers who are Mother Nature's victims. The claim is that farmers who are not severely affected by bad weather come out ahead, and the reason is not hard to understand.

Once crops are planted, the supply curve of the farming industry is very nearly vertical. The harvest will be almost the same whether the price is high or low. (Of course, if the commodity is one that is traded abroad, the supply curve for goods available *within* Canada need not be vertical. We will discuss this case later, once we have derived the principles behind international trade.) For a closed market, then, a bumper crop means that the supply curve is far to the right, like S_1S_1 in Figure 23–10, instead of in its "normal" position (which is indicated by S_0S_0 in the figure). Consequently, a bumper crop leads to low prices—equilibrium will be at price P_1 instead of price P_0. As the graph indicates, the drop in price is often quite severe because the demand curves for most farm products are rather *inelastic* (food being a necessity).

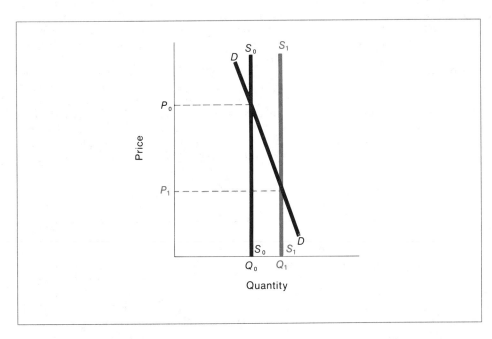

FIGURE 23–10
The Problem with Farm Incomes
The demand curve for most farm products is quite inelastic. Thus if good weather conditions lead to a bumper crop (the supply curve shifts outward from S_0S_0 to S_1S_1), the market price typically falls so much that farm income (the product of price times quantity sold) actually declines. Conversely, farm income often rises when the weather is bad and farm prices are high.

Each farmer's quantity produced may be increased by the good weather. But because the market price falls *by an even greater percentage*, the farmer's total income declines.[6] As noted at the outset of this chapter, this often sends farmers scurrying off to Ottawa crying "Foul!"

On the other hand, suppose bad weather damages the crop but Farmer Jones escapes relatively unscathed. Because of the inelastic market-demand curve, the market price shoots up. (To see this, just use Figure 23–10 in reverse: Suppose S_1S_1 is the supply curve under normal weather conditions and S_0S_0 is the supply curve when the weather is bad.) Farmer Jones's harvest falls slightly, but the price he gets for each unit rises smartly, and Jones comes out ahead of the game.

[6]This is a consequence of the inelasticity of the demand curve. Recall that in Chapter 20 (pages 439–40) we showed that a reduction in price *lowers* total revenue if the demand curve is inelastic. This is the result we are using here.

Summary

1. Markets are classified into several types depending on the number of firms in the industry, the degree of similarity of their products, and the possibility of impediments to entry.

2. The four main market structures are monopoly (single-firm production), oligopoly (production by a few firms), monopolistic competition (production by many firms with somewhat different products), and perfect competition (production by many firms with identical products and free entry and exit).

3. Few industries satisfy the conditions of perfect competition exactly, although some come close. Perfect competition is studied because it is easy to analyze and because it is useful as a yardstick for measuring the performance of other market forms.

4. The demand curve of the perfectly competitive firm is horizontal because its output is so small a share of the industry's production that it cannot affect price. With a horizontal demand curve, price, average revenue, and marginal revenue are all equal.

5. The short-run equilibrium of the perfectly competitive firm is at the level of output that maximizes profits; that is, where MC equals MR equals price. This equilibrium may involve either a profit or a loss.

6. The short-run supply curve of the perfectly competitive firm is the portion of its marginal-cost curve that lies above its average variable-cost curve.

7. The industry's short-run supply curve under perfect competition is the horizontal sum of the supply curves of all its firms.

8. In the long run, freedom of entry forces the perfectly competitive firm to earn zero economic profit; that is, no more than the firm's capital could earn elsewhere (the opportunity cost of the capital).

9. Industry equilibrium under perfect competition is at the point of intersection of the industry's supply and demand curves.

10. In long-run equilibrium under perfect competition, the firm's output is chosen so that average cost, marginal cost, and price are all equal. Output is at the point of minimum average cost, and the firm's demand curve is tangent to its average-cost curve at its minimum point.

11. The competitive industry's long-run supply curve coincides with its long-run average-cost curve.

Concepts for Review

Market
Perfect competition
Pure monopoly
Monopolistic competition
Oligopoly

Price taker
Horizontal demand curve
Short-run equilibrium
Average variable cost
Total variable cost

Supply curve of the firm
Supply curve of the industry
Long-run equilibrium
Opportunity cost
Economic profit

Questions for Discussion

1. Explain why a perfectly competitive firm does not expand its sales without limit if its horizontal demand curve means that it can sell as much as it wants to at the current market price.

2. Explain why a demand curve is also a curve of average revenue. Recalling that when an average-revenue curve is neither rising nor falling, marginal revenue must equal average revenue, explain why it is always true that $P = MR = AR$ for the perfectly competitive firm.

3. Explain why in the short-run equilibrium of the perfectly competitive firm $P = MC$, while in long-run equilibrium $P = MC = AC$.

4. Which of the four attributes of perfect competition (many small firms, freedom of entry, standardized product, perfect information) are primarily responsible for the fact that the demand curve of a perfectly competitive firm is horizontal?

5. Which of the four attributes of perfect competition is primarily responsible for the firm's zero economic profits in long-run equilibrium?

6. It is indicated in the text (pages 510–11) that the MC curve cuts the AVC curve at the *minimum* point of the latter. Explain why this must be so. (*Hint*: Since marginal costs are, by definition, all variable costs, the MC curve can be considered the curve of *marginal variable*

costs. Apply the general relationships between marginals and averages explained in Chapter 22.)

7. Explain why it is not sensible to close a business firm if it earns zero economic profits.

8. If the firm's lowest average cost is $12 and the corresponding average variable cost is $6, what does it pay a perfectly competitive firm to do if:
   a. The market price is $11?
   b. The price is $7?
   c. The price is $4?

9. If the market price in a competitive industry is above its equilibrium level, what do you expect to happen?

10. A few years ago when oil prices were very high, it was proposed to mix alcohol distilled from grain with gasoline to make "gasohol." This obviously would have caused an upward shift in the demand for grain. Use Figure 23–9 to analyze the effects on barley-growing profit and output
    a. in the short run.
    b. in the long run.

11. In this chapter, we asserted that the firm's MC curve goes through the lowest point of its AC curve as well as through the lowest point of its AVC curve. Since the AVC curve lies below the AC curve, how can both these statements be true?

24

The Price System: Laissez Faire versus Economic Planning

Early in the book, we posed a question that provides an organizing framework for our study of microeconomics: What does the market do well, and what does it do poorly? Given what we have learned about demand in Chapters 19 and 20 and about supply in Chapters 21–23, we can now offer a fairly comprehensive answer to the first part of this question: What does the market do well?

We begin by returning to two important themes raised in Chapters 2 and 3: first, that because all resources are scarce, it is critical to utilize them *efficiently*; second, that an economy must have some way to *co-ordinate* the actions of many individual consumers and producers. Specifically, we emphasize that society must somehow choose *how much* of each good to produce, *what input quantities* to use in the production process, and *how to distribute* the resulting outputs among consumers.

As the opening quotations suggest, these tasks are exceedingly difficult for central planners to accomplish effectively. But they are rather simple for a market system, which is why observers with philosophies as diverse as those of Adam Smith and Leon Trotsky have been admirers of the market. But the chapter should not be misinterpreted as a piece of salesmanship, for that is not its purpose.

We have organized this textbook in a way that allows us to give a full account of both the strengths and the weaknesses of the market. Now that we have completed our discussion of perfect competition, it makes sense to explain the market's advantages fully in this chapter and, hence, to make clear why economists view perfect competition as the standard by which to compare other market structures. In the following two chapters, we discuss various forms of monopoly, then devote an entire chapter to cataloguing the market's major shortcomings.

We have divided this chapter into two parts. The first part, like the last several chapters, is analytical; it explains how economic efficiency can be obtained through the operation of *de*centralized markets *under conditions of perfect competition*. The second part is institutional and historical; it explains the experiences of several countries that have relied on varying degrees of central planning instead of (or in addition to) the market. The two parts of the chapter can be read independently of each other. Your instructor may choose to help you through the first part, but leave you to read the second part (on the U.S.S.R., China, and Japan) on your own. The chapter closes with an appendix, which extends the analytical material of the first part of the chapter, and which is optional in shorter courses.

Efficiency and Free Markets

The version of the price system we shall study here is an idealized one in which every good is produced under the exacting conditions of perfect competition. While, as we have seen, a few industries are reasonable approximations of perfect competition, other industries in our economy are as different from this idealized world as the physical world is from a frictionless vacuum tube. But just as the physicist uses the vacuum tube to illustrate the laws of gravity with a clarity that is otherwise unattainable, the economist uses the theoretical concept of a perfectly competitive economy to illustrate the virtues of the market. There will be plenty of time in later chapters to study its vices. Indeed, the next three chapters, as we noted above, discuss the weaknesses of the market, and the whole of Part Seven investigates areas in which many regard the market to operate imperfectly—areas such as income distribution, monopoly, and pollution.

Efficient Resource Allocation: The Concept

The fundamental fact of scarcity limits the volume of goods and services that any economic system can produce. In Chapter 2 we illustrated the concept of scarcity with a graphical device called a *production possibilities frontier*, which we repeat here for convenience as Figure 24–1. The frontier, curve *BC*, depicts all combinations of manufactured goods and clean air that this society can produce given the limited resources at its disposal. For example, if it decides to use pollution-control devices to maintain an air quality level of 20 on the pollution index, it will have enough resources left over to produce *no more than* $500 billion of manufactured goods (point *D*). Of course, it is always possible to produce fewer than $500 billion of manufactured goods—at a point, such as *G*, below the production possibilities frontier. But if society does this, it is wasting some of its productive potential; that is, it is not operating *efficiently*.

FIGURE 24–1
The Production Possibilities Frontier and Efficiency
Every point on the production possibilities frontier, *BC*, represents an efficient allocation of resources, because it is impossible to get more of one item without giving up some of the other. Any point below the frontier, such as *G*, is inefficient, since it wastes the opportunity to obtain more of both goods.

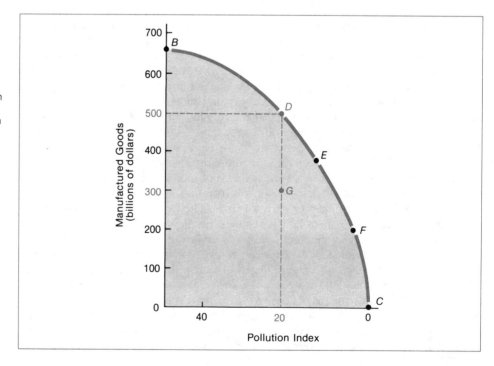

In Chapter 2 we defined efficiency rather loosely as the absence of waste. Since the main subject of this chapter is how a competitive market economy allocates resources efficiently, we now need a more precise definition. It is easiest to define an **efficient allocation of resources** by saying what it is *not*. Suppose it were possible to rearrange things so that some people would have more of the things they want and no one would have to give up anything. Then failure to change the allocation of resources to take advantage of this opportunity would surely be wasteful—that is, *inefficient*. When there are no such possibilities for reallocating resources to make some people better off without making anyone else worse off, we say that the allocation of resources is *efficient*.

Figure 24-1 illustrates the idea. Points below the frontier, such as *G*, are inefficient because, if we start at *G*, we can make *both* clean-air lovers *and* material-consumption lovers better off by moving to a point *on* the frontier, like *E*. Thus *no point below the frontier* can represent an efficient allocation of resources. By contrast, *every point on the frontier* is efficient because, no matter where on the frontier we start, it is impossible to get more of one good without giving up some of the other.

This example brings out two important features of the concept of efficiency. First, it is strictly a technical concept; there are no value judgments stated or implied, and tastes are not questioned. An economy is judged efficient if it is good at producing *whatever* people want. Thus the economy in the example is just as efficient when it produces only manufactured goods at point *B* as when it produces only pollution-control devices at point *C*.

Second, there are normally *many* efficient allocations of resources; in the example, *every* point on frontier *BC* is efficient. As a rule, the concept of efficiency does not permit us to tell which allocation is "best" for society. In fact, the most amazing thing about the concept of efficiency is that it gets us anywhere at all. At first blush, the criterion seems vacuous. It seems to assert, in effect, that anything agreed to unanimously is desirable. If some people are made better off *in their own estimation* and none are harmed, then society is certainly better off by anyone's definition. Yet, as we shall see in this chapter, the concept of efficiency can be used to formulate surprisingly detailed rules to steer us away from situations in which resources are being wasted.

An efficient allocation of resources is one that takes advantage of every opportunity to make some individuals better off in their own estimation while not worsening the lot of anyone else.

Efficiency and the Public Interest

Let us now consider the meaning of efficiency and its connection with pricing. We can start off by indicating that prices can sometimes be *too low* to serve the public interest. That statement raises a point that people untrained in economics always find difficult to accept: *low prices may not always be in the public interest.* The reason is clear enough. If a price is set "too low" (for example, the price of using a crowded airport or the price of oil), then consumers will receive the "wrong" signals. They will be encouraged to crowd the airport even more or to consume more oil, thereby squandering society's precious resources. A historical illustration is perhaps the most striking way to bring out the point. In 1834, some ten years before the great potato famine caused unspeakable misery and death by starvation and brought so many people from Ireland to North America, a professor of economics named Mountifort Longfield lectured at the University of Dublin about the price system. He offered the following remarkable illustration of his point:

Suppose the crop of potatoes in Ireland was to fall short in some year one-sixth of the usual consumption. If [there were no] increase of price, the whole ... supply of the year would be exhausted in ten months, and for the remaining two months a scene of misery and famine beyond description would ensue.... But when prices [increase] the sufferers [often believe] that it is not caused by scarcity.... They suppose that there are provisions enough, but that the distress is caused by the insatiable rapacity of the possessors ... [and] they have generally succeeded in obtaining laws against [the price increases] ... which alone can prevent the provisions from being entirely consumed long before a new supply can be obtained.[1]

Longfield's reasoning can usefully be rephrased. If the crop fails, potatoes become scarcer. If society is to use its very scarce resources efficiently, it must cut back on the consumption of potatoes—which is just what rising prices would do *automatically* if the market mechanism were left to its own devices. However, if the price is held artificially low, then consumers will be using society's resources inefficiently. In this case, the inefficiency shows up in the form of famine and suffering when the year's crop is consumed months before the next crop arrives.

It is not easy to accept the notion that higher prices can serve the public interest better than lower ones. Politicians who voice this view are put in the position of the proverbial father who, before spanking his child, announces, "This is going to hurt me much more than it hurts you!" Since advocacy of higher prices courts political disaster, the political system often rejects the market solution when resources suddenly become more scarce.

The pricing of oil in Canada in the 1970s provided an excellent example. For years after the oil cartel (OPEC) drastically raised prices, legislation in Canada held domestic oil prices below free-market levels. The consequence, as economists were quick to point out, was that Canadian consumers faced a market price for oil that was below the true marginal cost of oil to society. Consumers were therefore encouraged to use too much oil, and our dependence on imported oil increased. Suggestions to end the price controls were rebuffed by policy-makers, who feared the political consequences.

Interferences with the "Law" of Supply and Demand
Recall from Chapter 3 that one of the 12 **Ideas for Beyond the Final Exam** states that interfering with free markets by preventing price increases can sometimes serve the public very badly. In extreme cases it can even create havoc—undermining production and causing extreme shortages of vitally needed products. The reason is that prohibiting price increases in situations of true scarcity prevents the market mechanism from reallocating resources to help cut down the shortage efficiently. The invisible hand is not permitted to do its work.

Of course there are cases in which it is appropriate to resist price increases—where unrestrained monopoly would otherwise succeed in gouging the public and where rising prices fall so heavily on the poor that rationing becomes the more acceptable option. But it is important to recognize that artificial restrictions on prices can produce serious and even tragic consequences—consequences that should be taken into account before a decision is made to tamper with the market mechanism.

Scarcity and the Need to Co-ordinate Economic Decisions

Efficiency becomes a particularly critical issue for the general welfare when we concern ourselves with the workings of the economy as a whole rather than with a narrower topic such as the setting of one price (for potatoes or even oil). An economy may be thought of as a complex machine with literally millions of component parts. If this machine is to function efficiently, some way must be found to make the parts work in harmony.

A consumer in Calgary may decide to purchase two dozen eggs, and on the same day similar decisions are made by thousands of shoppers throughout the country. None of these purchasers knows or cares about the decisions of the others. Yet scarcity

[1] Mountifort Longfield, *Lectures on Political Economy* (Dublin, 1834), pages 53–56.

Pricing to Promote Efficiency: An Example

To consider the connection between pricing and efficiency, let us use a real-life example—the prices that are charged to use Canada's airports.

Congested airports have caused some of the most bitter squabbles about resource use. For example, Montreal's Dorval airport has long been congested *at peak times* (such as 5:00 P.M. on Fridays) but not at other times (such as the middle of Thursday afternoons). Because of the crowding that sometimes occurred, the federal government built the extremely underutilized Mirabel airport. No one denies the dramatic wastage of resources that was involved.

Most of this waste has followed from the presumption that airport congestion must be approached from a purely technical point of view. Officials simply do not question the assumption that more runways, more parking and terminal facilities, and more efficient methods of refuelling and loading are the answers.

The problem is that *all* of these aspects of the issue involve resources that are not currently priced on any market. Transport Canada issues a complete book to airport administrations entitled "Air Service Fee Regulations." In it, the charges for landings, take-offs, plane parking, bridges (the structures used for passengers to enter the planes), and various aspects of terminal use are listed. These charges depend on all kinds of things, such as whether the flight is domestic, trans-border, or trans-ocean; the type of engine on the airplane; and the gross take-off weight of the aircraft. However, *none* of the fees depends at all on the economic value of the use of the airport. Consequently, a very few passengers in a small private aircraft can pay a trivial landing fee and significantly add to congestion at peak times.

To an economist, the problem of peak-load congestion at airports is an obvious outcome of improper pricing. Airport charges for services should differ among airports and among times of the week and year. There should be low prices during those hours when space is abundant, and higher prices during rush hours, when space is scarce. Such a variable price structure would provide the incentive for those who can conveniently change times or location (for example, use the airport at Hamilton instead of Toronto) to do so. As a result, use of the airport could be switched away from the congested periods with the least total sacrifice. This flexibility is precluded by the current rigid price structure. The result is much wastage, including airport lands that could have been (or were) used for farms, homes, parks, productive industries, or simply open space near the cities.

---

requires that these demands must somehow be co-ordinated with the production process so that the total quantity of eggs demanded does not exceed the total quantity supplied. The supermarkets, wholesalers, shippers, and chicken farmers must somehow arrive at consistent decisions, for otherwise the economic process will deteriorate into chaos. And there are many other such decisions that must be co-ordinated. One cannot run machines that are completed except for a few parts that have not been delivered. Planes and cars cannot be used unless there is an adequate supply of fuel.

In an economy that is planned and centrally directed, it is easy to imagine how such co-ordination takes place—though the implementation turns out to be far more difficult than the idea. Central planners set production targets for firms and may even tell firms how to meet these targets. In extreme cases, consumers may even be told, rather than asked, what they want to consume.

In a market system, prices are used to co-ordinate economic activity instead. High prices discourage consumption of the resources that are most scarce, while low prices encourage consumption of the resources that are comparatively abundant. For example, if supplies of oil begin to run out while enormous reserves of coal remain, the price of oil can be expected to rise in comparison with the price of coal. As the price of oil rises, only those for whom oil offers the greatest benefits will continue to buy it. Firms or individuals that can get along almost equally well with coal or gas will switch to these more economical fuels. Some business firms will transform their equipment, and new homes will be built with heating systems that use gas. Only those who find alternative fuels a poor or unacceptable substitute for oil will continue to use

---

oil despite its higher price. In this way, prices are the instrument used by Adam Smith's invisible hand to organize the economy's production.

The invisible hand has an astonishing capacity to handle a co-ordination problem of truly enormous proportions—one that will remain beyond the capabilities of computers at least for the foreseeable future. It is true that, like any mechanism, this one has its imperfections, some of them rather serious. But without understanding the nature of the overall task performed by the market system, it is all too easy to lose sight of the tremendously demanding task that it constantly accomplishes—unnoticed, undirected, and at least in some respects, amazingly well. Let us, then, examine in more detail just what this co-ordination problem is like.

Three Co-ordination Tasks in the Economy

We noted in Chapter 2 that any economic system, whether planned or unplanned, must find answers to three basic questions of resource allocation:

1. *Output selection*: How much of each commodity should be produced?
2. *Production planning*: What quantities of each of the available inputs should be used to produce each good?
3. *Distribution*: How should the resulting goods be divided among the consumers?

These co-ordination tasks may at first appear tailor-made for a regime of governmental central planning. Yet most economists (even, nowadays, those in the centrally planned economies) believe that it is in these tasks that central planning performs most poorly and, paradoxically, that the free market, with its utter lack of conscious planning and central direction, is at its best. To understand how the unguided market manages the miracle of producing co-ordination out of what might otherwise have been chaos, let us look at how each of these questions is answered by a system of free and unfettered markets, the method of economic organization that the eighteenth-century French economists named **laissez faire**. Under laissez faire, the government would prevent crime, enforce contracts, and build roads and other types of public works, but it would not set prices and would interfere as little as possible with the operation of free markets. How does such an unmanaged economy solve the three co-ordination problems?

Laissez faire refers to a program of minimal interference with the workings of the market system. The term means that people should be left alone in carrying out their economic affairs.

Output Selection

In a free-market system, the price mechanism decides what to produce via what we have called the "law" of supply and demand. Where there is a *shortage*—that is, where quantity demanded exceeds quantity supplied—the market mechanism pushes the price up, thereby encouraging more production and less consumption of the commodity in short supply. Where there is a *surplus*—that is, where quantity supplied exceeds quantity demanded—the same mechanism works in reverse: the price falls, which discourages production and stimulates consumption.

We can make these abstract ideas more concrete by looking at a particular example. Suppose millions of people wake up one morning with a craving for omelettes. For the moment, the quantity of eggs demanded exceeds the quantity supplied. But within days the market mechanism swings into action to meet this sudden change in demand. The price of eggs rises, which stimulates the production of eggs. In the first instance, farmers simply bring more eggs to market by taking them out of storage. Over a somewhat longer period of time, chickens that otherwise would have been sold for meat are kept in the chicken coops laying eggs. Finally, if the high price of eggs persists, farmers begin to increase their flocks, build more cages, and so on. Thus, a shift in consumer demand leads to a shift in society's resources; more eggs are wanted, and so the market mechanism sees to it that more of society's resources are devoted to the production of eggs. Some characterize this process as being driven by **consumer sovereignty**.

Similar reactions follow if a technological breakthrough reduces the input quantities needed to produce some item. Electronic calculators are a perfect example. Just twenty years ago, calculators were so expensive that they could be found only in business firms and scientific laboratories. Then advances in science and engineering reduced their cost dramatically, and the market went to work. With costs sharply reduced, prices plummeted and the quantity demanded skyrocketed. Electronics firms flocked into the industry to meet this demand, which is to say that more of society's resources were devoted to producing the calculators that were suddenly in such great demand. These examples lead us to conclude that:

Under laissez faire, the allocation of society's resources among different products depends on two basic influences: consumer preferences and the relative difficulty of producing the goods, that is, their production costs. Prices vary so as to bring the quantity of each commodity produced into line with the quantity demanded.

Notice that no bureaucrat or central planner arranges the allocation of resources. Instead, allocation is guided by an unseen force—the lure of profits, which is the invisible hand that guides chicken farmers to increase their flocks when eggs are in greater demand and guides electronics firms to build new factories when the cost of electronic products falls.

Production Planning

Once the composition of output has been decided, the next co-ordination task is to determine just how those goods are going to be produced. The production-planning problem includes, among other things, the assignment of inputs to enterprises—that is, which farm or factory will get how much of which materials. These decisions can be crucial. If a factory runs short of an essential input, the entire production process may grind to a halt.

As a matter of fact, inputs and outputs cannot be selected separately. The inputs assigned to the growing of coffee rather than of bananas determine the quantities of coffee and bananas that can be obtained. However, it is simpler to think of these decisions as if they occurred one at a time.

Once again, under laissez faire it is the price system that apportions fuels and other raw materials among the different industries in accord with those industries' requirements. The firm that needs a piece of equipment most urgently will be the last to drop out of the market for that product when prices rise. If more grain is demanded by millers than is currently available, the price will rise and bring quantity demanded back into line with quantity supplied, always giving priority to those users who are willing to pay the most for grain. Thus:

In a free market, inputs are assigned to the firms that can make the most productive (most profitable) use of them. Firms that cannot make a sufficiently productive use of some input will be priced out of the market for that item.

This task, which sounds so simple, is actually almost unimaginably complex. It is also one on which many centrally planned systems have floundered. We will return to it shortly, as an illustration of how difficult it is to replace the market by a central-planning bureau. But first let us consider the third of our co-ordination problems.

Distribution of Products among Consumers

The third task of any economy is to decide which consumer gets each of the goods that have been produced. The objective is to distribute the available supplies so as to match

Consumer sovereignty means that consumer preferences determine what goods shall be produced, and in what amounts.

the differing preferences of consumers as well as possible. Coffee lovers must not be flooded with tea while tea drinkers are showered with coffee.

The price mechanism solves this problem by assigning the highest prices to the goods in greatest demand and then letting individual consumers pursue their own self-interests. Consider our example of the rising price of eggs. As the price of eggs rises, those whose craving for omelettes is not terribly strong will begin to buy fewer eggs. In effect, the price acts as a rationing device, apportioning the available eggs among the consumers who are willing to pay the most for them.

But the price mechanism has one important advantage over other rationing devices: It is able to pay attention to consumer preferences. If eggs are rationed by the most obvious and usual means (say, two to a person), everyone ends up with the same quantity—whether he thinks of eggs as the most unpleasant component of his breakfast or as the ingredients of the soufflé for which he has pined all day long. The price system, on the other hand, permits each consumer to set his own priorities. If you just barely tolerate eggs, a rise in their price quickly induces you to get your protein from some other source. But the egg lover is not induced to switch so readily. Thus:

The price system carries out the distribution process by rationing goods on the basis of preferences *and relative incomes*.

Notice the last three words. This rationing process *does* favour the rich, and this is a problem that market economies must confront. However, we may still want to think twice before declaring ourselves opposed to the price system. If equality is our goal, might not a more reasonable solution be to use the tax system to equalize incomes, and *then* let the market mechanism distribute goods in accord with preferences?

We have just seen, in broad outline, how a laissez-faire economy addresses the three basic issues of resource allocation: what to produce, how to produce it, and how to distribute the resulting products. Since it performs these tasks quietly, without central direction and with no apparent concern for the public interest, many radical critics have predicted that such an unplanned system must degenerate into chaos. Yet that does not seem to be the way things work out. Unplanned the market may be, but its results are far from chaotic. In fact, quite ironically, it is the centrally planned economies that often find themselves in economic chaos. Perhaps the best way to appreciate the accomplishments of the market is to consider how a centrally planned system copes with the three co-ordination problems we have just outlined. For this purpose, we will concentrate on just one of them: production planning.

Input–Output Analysis: The Near Impossibility of Perfect Central Planning

Of the three co-ordination tasks of any economy, the assignment of inputs to specific industries and firms has claimed the most attention of central planners. The reason is this: Because the production processes of the various industries are *interdependent*, the whole economy can grind to a halt if the production-planning problem is not solved satisfactorily.

Let's take a simple example. Gasoline is used both by consumers to run cars and by the trucking industry. Unless the planners allocate enough gasoline to trucking, products will not get to market, and unless they allocate enough trucks to haul the gasoline to gas stations, consumers will not be able to get to the market to buy the products. Thus, trucking activity depends on gasoline production but the latter also depends on the former. We seem to be caught in a circle. Although it turns out not to be a vicious circle, both problems must be dealt with together, not separately.

Because the output required from any one industry depends on the output desired from every other industry, planners can be sure that the production of the various outputs is sufficient to meet both consumer and industrial demands only by taking explicit account of the interdependencies among industries. If they change the output target for one industry, every other industry's output target must also be adjusted.

For example, if planners decide to provide consumers with more electricity, then more steel must be produced for more electric generators. But an increase in steel output requires more coal to be mined. More mining in turn means that still more electricity is needed to light the mines, to run the elevators, and perhaps even to run some of the trains that carry the coal, and so on and so on. Any single change in production sets off a chain of adjustments throughout the economy that require still further adjustments.

To decide how much of each output an economy must produce, the planner must use statistics to form a set of equations, one equation for each product, and then solve those equations *simultaneously*. (The simultaneous solution process prevents the circularity of the analysis—electricity output depends on steel production but steel output depends on electricity production—from becoming a vicious circle.) The technique used to solve these complicated equations—**input–output analysis**—was invented by economist Wassily Leontief, and it won him the Nobel Prize in 1973.

The equations of input–output analysis, which are illustrated in the boxed insert on page 532, take account of the interdependence among industries by describing precisely how each industry's target output depends on every other industry's target. Only by solving these equations *simultaneously* for the required outputs of electricity, steel, coal, and so on, can one be sure of a consistent solution that produces the required amounts of each product—including the amount of each product needed to produce every other product.

The example of input–output analysis that appears in the box is not provided so that you can learn how to apply the technique yourself. Its real purpose is to illustrate the *very complicated* nature of the problem that faces a central planner. For the problem faced by a real planner, while analogous to the one in the box, is enormously more complex. In any real economy, the number of commodities is far greater than the three outputs in the example. In Canada, some large manufacturing companies individually deal in hundreds of items and keep thousands of different items in inventory. In planning, it is ultimately necessary to make calculations for each such item. It is not enough to plan the right number of bolts *in total*; we must make sure that the required number *of each size* is produced. (Try to put five million large bolts into five million small nuts.) So, to be sure our plans will really work, we need a separate equation for every size of bolt and one for every size and type of nut. But then, to replicate the analysis described in the boxed insert, we will have to solve simultaneously several *million* equations!

This problem of computation has two dimensions. The first is the sheer size of the matrices that must be inverted to solve such a vast number of simultaneous equations. The second concerns the functional form of the millions of equations involved. For such a large system to be solved, the equations must be linear, but real-world technological relationships are not linear: Because of diminishing returns, production functions are curved relationships. Thus, even with the aid of a powerful computer, the standard input–output analysis explained in the boxed insert could supply, at best, only an approximation of the actual solution. (It might be interesting to note here that by 1989, computer technology had progressed to the point that it could just begin to handle computations of this magnitude—suggesting that, at least from the mathematical perspective, central planning might one day become feasible. Ironically, 1989 also marked the year that countries all over the world were moving away from planning and toward a decentralized, market approach.)

Worse still is the data problem. Each of the three equations in our boxed insert requires *three* pieces of statistical information, making 3×3, or 9, numbers in total. This is because the equation for electricity must indicate on the basis of statistical information how much electricity is needed in steel production, how much is needed in

Input–Output Equations: An Example

Imagine an economy with only three outputs: electricity, steel, and coal; and let E, S, and C represent the dollar value of their respective outputs. Suppose that for every dollar's worth of steel, \$0.20 worth of electricity is used up, so that the total electricity demand of steel manufacturers is $0.2S$. Similarly, assume the coal manufacturers use up \$0.30 of electricity in producing \$1 worth of coal, or a total of $0.3C$ units of electricity. Since E dollars of electricity are produced in total, the amount left over for consumers, after subtraction of industrial demands for fuel, will be

$$E \quad - \quad 0.2S \quad - \quad 0.3C$$
$$\text{(available} \quad \text{(use in steel} \quad \text{(use in coal}$$
$$\text{electricity)} \quad \text{production)} \quad \text{production)}$$

Suppose further that the central planners have decided to supply \$15 million worth of electricity to consumers. We end up with the electricity output equation

$$E - 0.2S - 0.3C = 15.$$

The planner will also need such an equation for each of the two other industries, specifying for each of them the net amounts intended to be left for consumers after the industrial uses of these products. The full set of equations might then be:

$$E - 0.20S - 0.30C = 15$$
$$S - 0.10E - 0.06C = 7$$
$$C - 0.15E - 0.40S = 10 \ .$$

These are typical equations in an input–output analysis. Only, in practice, a typical analysis has hundreds and sometimes thousands of equations with similar numbers of unknowns. This, then, is the logic of input–output analysis.

---

coal production, and how much is demanded by consumers. In a five-industry analysis, 5×5, or 25, pieces of data are needed; a 100-industry analysis requires 100^2, or 10,000, numbers; and a million-item input–output study would need one *trillion* pieces of information. The data-gathering problems are therefore no easy task, to put it mildly. There are still other complications, but we have seen enough to conclude that:

A full, rigorous central-planning solution to the production problem is a tremendous task, requiring an overwhelming quantity of information and some incredibly difficult calculations. Yet this very difficult job is carried out automatically and unobtrusively by the price mechanism in a free-market economy.

How Perfect Competition Achieves Efficiency: What to Produce

Earlier in the chapter we indicated how the market mechanism solves the three basic co-ordination problems of any economy—what to produce, how to produce, and how to distribute the goods to consumers. And we suggested that these same tasks pose almost insurmountable difficulties for central planners. One critical question remains. Is the allocation of resources that the market mechanism selects *efficient*, according to the precise definition of efficiency presented earlier in this chapter? The answer is that, under the idealized circumstances of perfect competition, it is. Since a detailed proof of this assertion for all three co-ordination tasks would be long and time-consuming, we will present the proof only for the first of the three tasks—output selection. The corresponding analyses for the production-planning and distribution problems are quite similar and are reserved for the appendix.

Our question is this: Given the output combination selected by the market mechanism, is it possible to improve matters by producing more of one good and less of another? Might it be "better," for example, if society produced more beef and less lamb? We shall answer this question in the negative, thus showing that, at least in theory, perfect competition does guarantee efficiency in production.

We will do this in two steps. First, we will derive a criterion for efficient output selection, that is, a test which tells us whether or not production is being carried out efficiently. Second, we will examine why that test is *automatically* passed by the prices that emerge from the market mechanism under perfect competition.

Step 1: Rule for Efficient Output Selection

We begin by stating the rule for efficient output selection:

Efficiency in the choice of output quantities requires that, for each of the economy's outputs, the marginal cost (MC) of the last unit produced be equal to the marginal utility (MU) of the last unit consumed.[2] In symbols:

$$MC = MU.$$

Let us use an example to see why this rule *must* be satisfied for the allocation of resources to be efficient. Suppose the marginal utility of an additional kilogram of beef to consumers is $8, while its marginal cost is only $5. Then the value of the resources that would have to be used up to produce one more kilogram of beef (its MC) would be $3 less than the consumers' willingness to pay for that additional kilogram (its MU). In a sense, society could get more (the MU) out of the economic production process than it was putting in (the MC) by increasing the output of beef by one kilogram. It follows that the output at which $MU > MC$ cannot be optimal, since society would be made better off by an increase in that output level.

The opposite is true if the MC of beef exceeds the MU of beef. In that case, the last kilogram of beef must have used up more value (MC) than it produced (MU). It would therefore be better to have less beef and more of something else.

We have therefore shown that, if there is *any* product for which MU is not equal to MC, the economy must be wasting an opportunity to produce a net improvement in consumers' welfare. This is exactly what we mean by using resources *inefficiently*. Just as was true at point G in Figure 24-1, if $MC \neq MU$ for any commodity, it is possible to rearrange things so as to make some people better off while harming no one. It follows that efficiency in the choice of outputs is achieved only when $MC = MU$ for *every* good.[3]

Step 2: The Critical Role of the Price System

The next step in the argument is to show that under perfect competition the price system *automatically* leads buyers and sellers to behave in a way that makes MU and MC equal. To see this, recall from the last chapter that under perfect competition it is most profitable for each beef-producing firm to produce the quantity of beef at which the marginal cost of the beef is equal to the price of beef:

$$MC = P.$$

This must be so because, if the marginal cost of beef were less than the price, the farmer could add to his profits by increasing the size of his herd (or the amount of

---

[2] It will be recalled from Chapter 19 that we measure marginal utility in money terms, that is, as the amount of money that a consumer is willing to give up for an additional unit of the commodity. Economists usually call this the marginal rate of substitution between the commodity and money.

[3] Warning: We will find in Chapter 27 that one reason markets sometimes perform imperfectly is the fact that the marginal cost to the individual decision-maker (this is called "marginal private cost") is not the same as the marginal cost to society ("marginal social cost"). This situation occurs when the individual whose actions cause the cost is able to escape paying it and instead lets someone else bear the burden. For example, Firm X's production causes pollution emissions that increase the laundry bills of households in the neighbourhood. In such a case, the efficiency rule requires that MU = marginal social cost. That rule will obviously be violated—and inefficiency will result—if the behaviour of the market makes MU = marginal private cost.

grain that he feeds his animals), and the reverse would be true if the marginal cost of beef were greater than its price. Thus, under perfect competition, the lure of profits leads each producer of beef (and of every other product) to supply the quantity that makes $MC = P$.

We also learned, in Chapter 19, that it is in the interest of each consumer to purchase the quantity of beef at which the marginal utility of beef in terms of money is equal to the price of beef:

$$MU = P.$$

If he did not do this, we saw, either an increase or a decrease in his purchase of beef would leave him better off.

Putting these last two equations together, we see that the invisible hand enforces the following string of equalities:

$$MC = P = MU.$$

But if both the MC of beef and the MU of beef are equal to the same price, P, then they must surely be equal to each other. That is, it must be true that the quantity of beef produced and consumed in a perfectly competitive market satisfies the equation

$$MC = MU,$$

which is precisely our rule for efficient output selection. Since the same must be true of every other product supplied by a competitive industry, we conclude that:

Under perfect competition, the unco-ordinated decisions of producers and consumers can be expected to produce *automatically* a quantity of each good that satisfies the $MC = MU$ rule for efficiency in deciding what to produce. That is, under the idealized conditions of perfect competition, the market mechanism, *without any government intervention*, is capable of allocating society's scarce resources efficiently.

The Invisible Hand at Work

This is truly a remarkable result. How can the price mechanism automatically satisfy all the exacting requirements for efficiency—requirements that no central planner can hope to handle because of the masses of statistics and the enormous calculations they require? The conclusion seems analogous to the rabbit that is suddenly pulled from the magician's hat. But, as always, rabbits come out of hats only if they were hidden there in the first place. What really is the machinery by which our act of magic works?

The secret is that the price system lets consumers and producers pursue their own best interests—something they are probably very good at doing. Prices are the dollar costs of commodities to consumers. So, in pursuing their own best interests, consumers will buy the commodities that give them the most satisfaction *per dollar*. As we learned in Chapter 19, this means that each consumer will continue to buy beef until the marginal utility of beef is equal to the market price. And since every consumer pays the same price in a perfectly competitive market, the market mechanism ensures that *every* consumer's MU will be equal to this common price.

Turning next to the producers, we know from Chapter 23 that competition equates prices with marginal costs. And, once again, since every producer faces the same market price, the force of competition will bring the MC of *every* producer into equality with this common price. Since MC measures the resource cost (in every firm) of producing one more unit of the good and MU measures the money value (to every consumer) of consuming one more unit, then when $MC = MU$ *the cost of the good to society is exactly equal to the value that consumers place on it*. Therefore:

When all prices are set equal to marginal costs, the price system is giving the correct cost signals to consumers. It has set prices at levels that induce consumers to use the resources of society with the same care they devote to watching their own money.

This is the magic of the invisible hand. Unlike central planners, consumers need not know how difficult it is to manufacture a certain product or how scarce are the inputs required by the production process. Everything the consumer needs to know to make his or her decision is embodied in the market price, which, under perfect competition, accurately reflects marginal costs.

A Graphic Exposition of Efficiency

Figure 24–2 illustrates the logic behind the MU = MC rule for determining society's efficient level of production. It shows the demand and supply curves for a particular commodity that is produced competitively. Remember that the demand curve represents households' marginal utility schedule for this commodity, while the supply curve represents the producing firms' marginal cost. Assume that initially in this market, the price is not free to adjust; it is fixed at an amount given by distance OF by a law stipulating that amount as the maximum price allowed. We now examine how this law creates inefficiency for the economy.

Initially, the quantity produced is OJ, and there is an unsatisfied demand equal to JL. The MU = MC rule for efficiency in output selection is not satisfied, since marginal utility is JB, which is greater than marginal cost (JG).

Now consider what happens if the maximum price law is removed. Price will rise to level OC, and quantity will increase to level OK. Marginal utility and marginal cost will then be equal, at a value of OC. Let us now explicitly calculate the gain to society of moving to the level of output at which MU = MC.

By being able to consume the JK additional units of the commodity, consumers have a gain in total satisfaction (as measured by their willingness to pay) equal to area $JKEB$. But households must make an additional payment to firms for this extra amount of the good; this additional payment is equal to area $JKED$. After subtracting this additional payment to firms, the net gain in consumer surplus (which comes from their consuming the additional JK units) is area BDE.

As just noted, firms receive extra revenue equal to area $JKED$ for the sale of the additional JK units of the good. But firms had to incur additional costs to produce this extra output; these additional costs are equal to area $JKEG$. After subtracting these

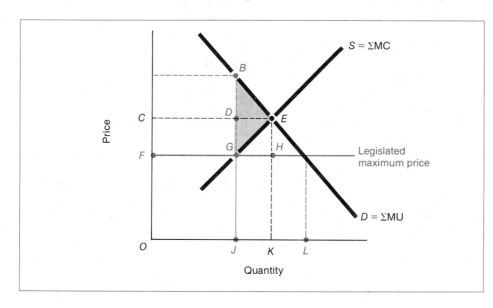

FIGURE 24–2
Efficiency in Output Selection (MU = MC Rule)

When the price ceiling, distance *OF*, is removed, the price level rises to *OC*, and quantity produced rises from *OJ* to *OK*, the level of output at which marginal utility equals marginal cost. The additional benefit to society at this efficient output level is equal to the shaded area, *GEB*.

costs, we see that the additional profit (producer surplus) is area *GDE*. The additional benefit to society as a whole is equal to the sum of the consumers' net gain (*BDE*) and the producers' net gain (*GDE*)—a total of area *GEB*. The initial level of output, *OJ*, was not optimal, since when output increases to level *OK*, the gain in utility exceeds the additional costs to society by amount *GEB*.

Now consider the *OJ* units that were produced in the first place. They are still being purchased by consumers but, without the maximum price law, households now pay area *OJDC*, not just *OJGF*, for these units. Thus, consumers lose area *FGDC* from what was previously consumer surplus. This amount is now producer surplus; it is simply transferred to firms, not lost to society *as a whole*. That is why area *GEB* remains the correct measure of what the society loses overall by producing at a level for which MU does not equal MC.

Of course, in addition to the efficiency problem, there is a distributional issue at stake here. As we have just explained, the total amount of material welfare to be had by everyone, taken together, increases when the maximum price law is removed (by amount *GEB*). This is the efficiency point. But to obtain this aggregate gain, there is a transfer from consumers to producers of amount *FGDC*, which many regard as an undesirable distribution effect. One of our 12 **Ideas for Beyond the Final Exam** focusses on the trade-off between efficiency and equality, and this trade-off is at the heart of the issue of whether prices should be set by a planner or allowed to be determined by market forces. In Part Seven, we consider how income can be redistributed toward low-income earners in ways that minimize the degree of interference with the goal of efficiency.

Other Roles of Prices: Income Distribution and Fairness

So far we have stressed the role of prices most emphasized by economists: Prices guide the allocation of resources. But, as we have just noted, a different role of prices often commands the spotlight in public discussions: Prices influence the distribution of income between buyers and sellers. A concrete example of this issue is high rents, which often make tenants poorer and landlords richer, and lead to the implementation of rent controls.

This rather obvious role of prices draws the most attention from the public, politicians, and regulators, and it is one we should not lose sight of. Markets serve only those demands that are backed up by consumers' desire *and ability* to pay. Though the market system may do well in serving a poor family, giving that family more food and clothing than a less efficient economy would provide, it offers far more to the family of a millionaire. Many observers object that such an arrangement represents a great injustice, however efficient it may be.

Often, recommendations made by economists for improving the economy's efficiency are opposed on the grounds that they are unfair. For example, economists frequently advocate higher prices for transportation facilities at the time of day when they are most crowded. They propose a pricing arrangement called *peak/off-peak pricing*, under which prices for public transportation are higher during rush hours than during other hours.

The rationale for this proposal should be clear from our discussion of efficiency and from the boxed example about airport congestion earlier in this chapter (page 527). A seat on a train is a much scarcer resource during rush hours than during other times of the day, when the trains run fairly empty. Thus, according to the principles of efficiency outlined in this chapter, seats should be more expensive during rush hours to discourage consumers from using the trains during peak periods. The same notion applies to other services. Charges for nighttime long-distance telephone calls are lower than those in the daytime and, in some places, electricity is sold more cheaply at night, when demand does not strain the supplier's generating capacity.

Yet the proposal that higher fares should be charged for public transportation during peak hours—say, from 8:00 A.M. to 9:30 A.M., and from 4:30 P.M. to 6 P.M.—often runs into stiff opposition on the grounds that most of the burden will fall on lower-income working people, who have no choice about the timing of their trips. In this case, people simply find the efficient solution unfair and so refuse to adopt it. (It must be noted, however, that in many other cases it seems that proposals promoting efficiency are rejected simply because people do not understand the concept—witness the cartoon on this page!)

Economics alone cannot decide the appropriate trade-off between equity and efficiency. It cannot even pretend to judge which pricing arrangements are fair and which are unfair. But it can and should indicate whether a particular pricing decision, proposed because it is considered fair, will impose heavy inefficiency costs upon the community. Economic analysis also can and should indicate how to evaluate these costs, so that the issues can be decided on the basis of an understanding of the facts.

Sometimes it is possible to design policies that, as a package, *promote both efficiency and equity simultaneously*. We return to the trade-off between the objectives of equity and efficiency in Chapter 28, and then again in Part Seven of this book.

"They should move Christmas to January—everything's cheaper."

Toward Assessment of the Price Mechanism

Our analysis of the case for laissez faire is not meant to imply that the free-enterprise system is an ideal of perfection, without flaw or room for improvement. In fact, it has a number of serious shortcomings, which we will examine in subsequent chapters. But recognition of these imperfections should not conceal the enormous accomplishments of the price mechanism.

We have shown that, given the proper circumstances, it is capable of meeting the most exacting requirements of allocative efficiency, requirements that go well beyond the capacity of any central-planning bureau. The market mechanism has provided an abundance of goods unprecedented in human history. No one has invented an instrument for directing the economy that can replace the price mechanism, which no one ever designed or planned for, but which simply grew by itself, a child of the processes of history. Even centrally planned economies have started to turn to the market in recent years. We shall now discuss the experience of some of these economies in greater detail.

Economic Planning

Alternative Economic Systems: What Are the Choices?

No one will ever forget 1989, the year the Berlin Wall crumbled—both literally and figuratively. For decades, the rivalry between Western **capitalism** and Soviet-style **socialism** dominated the world's geopolitical scene. This competition had important military and ideological dimensions; for example, the yearning for individual freedom surely played a major role in the breakup of the Soviet empire. However, the miserable performance of the Soviet economic system was certainly a decisive factor.

The economic and political transformations now taking place in Eastern Europe and the Soviet Union dramatize the importance of choosing the right economic system. And there *are* choices to be made. Citizens of the Soviet Union and Eastern Europe are now debating and experimenting with the merits of different economic institutions (see the boxed insert on page 538). To a less dramatic extent, similar debates and experiments are under way in Latin America and elsewhere.

Here in North America, we tend to take economic institutions as given and immutable. But they are not. In fact, there are many ways to practise capitalism, as the

Capitalism is a method of economic organization in which private individuals own the means of production, either directly or indirectly through corporations.

Socialism is a method of economic organization in which the state owns the means of production.

East Meets West in Europe: Behind the Former Iron Curtain

When the Soviet Union loosened its grip on Eastern Europe, both political democracy and free markets broke out with astonishing speed. Poland and Hungary were in the vanguard. By 1990, both had freely elected governments and were headed toward market capitalism, though by different routes. The following two excerpts from *The Wall Street Journal* provide some insight into these developments.

Poland's Big Bang

The communists left behind an economy in which per-capita gross national product had declined to less than one-fifth of the Western European level. Inflation was raging at several thousand percent per year. The shops were empty.

Solidarity's economic team ... eschewed piecemeal reform, in favor of a comprehensive program to create a market economy.... In just 75 days, some stunning successes have been achieved.... Hyperinflation has stopped dead.... With prices now free to balance supply and demand, products [have] returned to the shops ... [and] the six-hour gas lines of December have vanished.... In industry, scarce and vitally needed materials ... are suddenly arriving from Sweden, Finland, and Germany.

But these great successes are matched by grave risks. State firms are no longer coddled.... Absenteeism has fallen in half as workers fear for their jobs.... Yet, with much of the work force in uncompetitive companies and in unneeded sectors, unemployment and plant closings have started to soar. Unemployment could jump by as much as 10 percent of the labor force in the coming months....

Factories ... have been cut off from markets for 40 years [and] know next to nothing about ... export markets. Even when their technology is adequate and their workers skilled, after four decades of socialism, Poland's enterprises lack one key factor of production: skilled managers who know how to operate in a market environment....

SOURCE: Excerpted from Jeffrey Sachs, "Management Positions Available: Call Warsaw," *The Wall Street Journal*, March 21, 1990. *Note:* Professor Sachs has been the major Western economic adviser to Solidarity.

Hungary's Dual System

A thin brick wall dividing a big factory building still separates East from West in this light-industrial town near Hungary's border with Yugoslavia.

On one side of the building, two-thirds of state-owned Texcoop's obsolete knitting machines sit idle for lack of orders. The rest churn out frumpy 100%-acrylic sweaters for the Soviet Union. The plant, greasy and gloomy, has lost money ever since it opened.

On the other side of the building, a freshly scrubbed, brightly lit Levi Strauss factory hums to piped-in jazz. Dozens of women hunch over new American sewing machines and swiftly affix pockets, sew up inseams, and attach zippers.... The women, all of whom worked for Texcoop until last year, now earn more than twice as much money. The plant was profitable from Day One. Levi earned back its total investment in less than a year.

Eastern Europe still has far more factories like Texcoop's than like Levi's, but every day more ventures bringing Western management, cash, and free-market fervor are being planned. Not only will they make jeans, light bulbs, and bicycles, but, economists say, the competition they create will eventually force state companies to either shape up, sell out, or close....

The test of this theory is furthest along in Hungary, the first East bloc country to allow joint ventures on realistic terms with the West, the first to allow its people to own private property, the first to establish an embryonic stock exchange....

SOURCE: Excerpted from Philip Rezvin, "Ventures in Hungary Test Theory That West Can Uplift East Bloc," *The Wall Street Journal*, April 5, 1990.

---

differing economic structures of Japan and Western Europe illustrate. A century ago, our country had no social welfare system, no income tax, no central bank, no competition laws, and hardly any labour unions. More than likely, the structure of the

Canadian economy will change at least as much in the next century as it did in the last. But in which directions?

In this part of the chapter we examine how a society might choose among *alternative economic systems*, and describe some of the actual choices that have been made in the contemporary world. We consider the evolving economic structures of the Soviet Union and the People's Republic of China, two socialist nations in which serious economic problems have precipitated major institutional change. Then we turn to a notable example of a successful capitalist country that does things rather differently than we do: Japan.

The Soviet Economy: Historical Background

In November 1917, a determined group of Bolsheviks led by V. I. Lenin overthrew a short-lived democratic government, and Russia became the first country in the world to establish a communist government. Ironically, this first triumph of communism contradicted the Marxian prophecy that socialism would grow out of a decaying, advanced capitalist system. Instead, it came first to a land that had barely emerged from feudalism. This simple historical fact is important to remember as the U.S.S.R. grapples with its political and economic future: Unlike some of its Eastern European neighbours, the Soviet Union has little experience with either political democracy or market capitalism.

The Russian system of state planning emerged from the dire circumstances of an economy torn by civil war. Once his Red Army had won control, a pragmatic Lenin reacted to the chaotic legacy of the war by permitting substantial amounts of both capitalist ownership and market organization under his New Economic Policy (NEP). The NEP was a success, and it helped rebuild the badly battered Russian economy. After Lenin's death, there were both a fierce struggle for power within the Communist party and a vigorous policy debate over basic economic strategy. Joseph Stalin won both contests and ruthlessly set the Soviet Union on a course that it followed, more or less, until the ascendancy to power of Mikhail Gorbachev in 1985.

Stalin's strategy called for single-minded application of Soviet resources to the goal of rapid *industrial* development with emphasis on *heavy* industry, particularly *armaments*. To achieve such rapid growth and industrialization, it was necessary to limit consumption severely; so the Soviet consumer was asked—or rather forced—to make major sacrifices. To feed the urban labourers needed for industrial expansion, the Soviet Union's backward agricultural peasants were forced—at extremely high human and economic costs—onto collective farms, where they were required to sell their food at low prices and to work for pitifully low wages. Poverty and low productivity remain the key problems associated with Soviet agriculture.

The structure of the Soviet central-planning system is in many ways similar to the hierarchy of a giant corporation. At the top may be a single strong man or a ruling clique. The political leadership plays the role of chairman of the board, setting overall policy objectives, but has much more absolute authority than does the chairman of any corporation.

Communications within the hierarchy are predominantly vertical. Orders designed to implement the overall economic plan flow down from top to bottom, while data flow up from bottom to top. Since the data requirements are so immense, and the layers within the bureaucracy so numerous, the problems of accurate data transmission and processing are monumental.[4] It is precisely this problem, of course, that the market mechanism solves so neatly: Prices convey most of the information that anyone needs.

---

[4]Giant corporations have similar problems in handling and transmitting large amounts of data. However, not even the largest corporation approaches the size and scope of the Soviet economy.

Markets and Prices in Soviet Economic Life

Although central planning has certainly dominated Soviet economic life, the U.S.S.R. has used the market mechanism for some purposes.

For at least some consumer goods, Soviet planners try to set prices to ration the quantity demanded down to the level of production specified in the plan. This usually requires setting consumer prices far above production costs, with the difference made up by the so-called *turnover tax*, the main source of government revenue.

But planners often fail to equate quantities supplied and demanded, and any visitor to the Soviet Union is struck by the frequency with which long lines appear in front of stores. Consumers do exercise free choice among the available goods, but they are far from sovereign. Indeed, they have few mechanisms for communicating their wants back to producers.

The price system is used even more extensively in the labour market. Given the plan for industrial output, Soviet planners try to set wages to attract workers to the right industries and the right regions. With some exceptions, Soviet workers now have considerable freedom to work where they please—a far cry from the situation in Stalin's day. Partly as a result of the strong desire to direct labour to the areas assigned top priority by the plan, wage differentials among Soviet blue-collar workers are quite large. According to most observers, they are at least as large as those in North America, and they lead to considerable inequality in the distribution of labour income. Of course, income from property is negligible in the U.S.S.R., and the gap between blue-collar and white-collar incomes is far smaller than it is here. Thus, the *overall* distribution of income is much more equal than in North America.

Performance and Problems of Soviet Planning

Most observers rate the Soviet performance as good on growth, at least until recent years, but as poor on economic efficiency. Rigorous economic planning quickly brought the backward Soviet economy of the 1920s into the modern age. Postwar economic growth averaged about 7 percent in the 1950s and somewhat more than 5 percent in the 1960s. However, like the Western economies, the Soviet economy has experienced a growth retardation in recent years. The Soviet growth rate slipped into the 3 percent range—about the same as the U.S. growth rate—during the 1970s and seems to have been barely positive in the 1980s.

There are several reasons for this slowdown in Soviet economic growth. For one thing, part of the rapid early growth was achieved by borrowing advanced technology from the West; this obviously could not last forever.

For another, the Soviet Union (like the Western countries) achieved part of its industrial growth through the migration of peasants to the cities—which also could not last forever.

A third factor was the increasing outcry of the Soviet citizenry for more and better consumer goods. Only in recent years has the regime been willing to accommodate these demands, and this required cutting back on investment.

Finally, the plain fact is that the Soviet economic mechanism does not function smoothly and seems to be growing increasingly arthritic. The rigorous system of central planning that worked in Stalin's day, when the economic goals were simple and well defined, seems ill-suited to the more sophisticated modern Soviet economy, with its complex and diverse goals. Greater flexibility is perhaps the central goal of Gorbachev's reform proposals.

Both Western and Soviet observers agree that the Soviet Union's economic problems are manifold. One perennial problem is the tremendous *burden of information transmission* required by the central planning apparatus. Many millions of pieces of information must pass up and down the hierarchy each year. The result is that

Problems of Central Planning

... In 1986, before *perestroika* was officially formulated, Gosplan, the highest planning commission in the Soviet Union, issued two thousand sets of instructions for major "product groups," such as construction materials, metals, and automotive vehicles. Gossnab, the State Material and Technical Supply Commission, then divided these product groups into fifteen thousand categories—lumber, copper, and trucks, for instance—and the various ministries in charge of the categories in turn subdivided them into fifty thousand more finely detailed products (shingles, beams, laths, boards) and then into specific products in each category (large, medium, and small shingles). These plans then percolated down through the hierarchy of production, receiving emendations or protests as they reached the level of plant managers and engineers, and thereafter travelled back up to the ministerial level. In this Byzantine process, perhaps the most difficult single step was to establish "success indicators"—desired performance targets—for enterprises. For many years, targets were given in physical terms—so many yards of cloth or tons of nails—but that led to obvious difficulties. If cloth was rewarded by the yard, it was woven loosely to make the yarn yield more yards. If the output of nails was determined by their number, factories produced huge numbers of pinlike nails; if by weight, smaller numbers of very heavy nails. The satiric magazine *Krokodil* once ran a cartoon of a factory manager proudly displaying his record output, a single gigantic nail suspended from a crane.

The difficulty, of course, was that the inevitable mismatches and mistakes could not be set to rights by the decisions of platoon sergeants or regimental commanders who were able to see that the campaign was not going as expected. [Nikolai] Shmelev and [Vladimir] Popov [two very well known Soviet economists, whose recently published "The Turning Point" gives a scathing account of Russian economic problems] tell of the Kurgan Bus Factory, to which the Gorky Automotive Factory shipped chassis assemblies. These assemblies had extra parts attached to them, suitable for the trucks that the Gorky factory produced but not for the buses that the Kurgan plant produced. The Kurgan workers then took sledgehammers and converted the truck chassis into bus chassis. "It is much harder to change GOST [State All-Union Standards] than to swing a sledgehammer," the authors comment.

SOURCE: Excerpted from Robert Heilbroner, "Reflections: After Communism," *The New Yorker*, September 10, 1990, pages 91–100.

Soviet planners are often overwhelmed or misinformed, and make correspondingly incorrect decisions.

A second, and related, problem is that *enterprises strive to obtain low production quotas* that will be easy to meet or surpass. Why? Because their success is measured not by profits or sales, but by their ability to meet the quotas. So plant managers may deliberately mislead their superiors and understate their productive capacity—which, of course, makes the information problem that much worse.

The system of production targets based on physical quantities rather than on profits or sales often leads to *huge stockpiles of unwanted and inferior goods and equally huge waiting lines for other goods.* For example, since automobile factories generally have quotas stated in terms of cars, there is an almost legendary shortage of spare parts in the Soviet Union. Manufacturers simply do not want to produce things that do not help fulfill their quotas. The accompanying boxed insert vividly illustrates such problems of central planning.

Because government policy has generally led to shortages of most consumer goods, managers of enterprises producing these goods have been able to turn out *low-quality merchandise*, knowing that eager consumers will buy up almost anything. In addition, they need not fear competitors' turning out superior products.

The absence of competition and the concern with meeting production quotas *stifle innovation.* Innovation carries risks, and Russian managers worry more about not fulfilling their plan than about being creative. They also realize that a brilliant production performance this year will lead to a tougher quota next year. With no competition to spur them on, Soviet managers have been slow to adopt the latest innovations.

All these problems would arise even if planners did their jobs flawlessly. But, in fact, as we explained earlier in the chapter (pages 530–32), accurate input–output analysis is simply not feasible on such a vast scale.

The Bumpy Road to Reform

By the mid-1980s, these and other problems were weakening the Soviet economy, causing rising discontent, widening the technological lag behind the West, and threatening the U.S.S.R.'s ability to compete militarily with the United States. A reform-minded Mikhail Gorbachev decided that things had to change.

In 1987, he introduced his first set of reforms, aimed at streamlining Soviet industry, increasing its efficiency, and improving product quality. While maintaining state ownership of the means of production (a key tenet of communism), the reforms gave plant managers the authority to make their own production plans, choose their own suppliers, and respond to what they perceived as market forces. Private enterprise on a small scale was also permitted.

Despite objections from hard-liners, Gorbachev persisted with his economic reforms. But they fared poorly: By 1990 the Soviet economy was teetering, not prospering. Why? History may provide a better answer than we can at this early date, but some aspects of the answer are already clear.

After more than 70 years of central direction, Soviet workers and managers possess little of the initiative and the intuitive understanding of market behaviour that have come to characterize their counterparts in the West. In addition, neither the Communist party bureaucracy nor the Soviet people are totally convinced that a capitalist market system is best for their country. And because communist ideology frowns on the accumulation of personal wealth, successful fledgling "capitalists" may find themselves scorned or even attacked. Finally, Gorbachev's original reforms took a cautious, piecemeal, and not always coherent approach to remaking the Soviet economy. For example, macroeconomic management was neglected even though large budget deficits were leading to rapid increases in the money supply.

In 1990, rather than abandon liberalization, Gorbachev stepped up its pace. The Soviet Union adopted a comprehensive plan to introduce market elements into its economy in stages over the course of the next six years. And, in an astounding denial of its own former dogma, the Communist party declared that:

... The existence of individual property, including ownership of the means of production, does not contradict the modern stage in the country's economic development....
   One of the most difficult aspects of the economic reform is finding an organic combination of plan and market methods to regulate economic activity....[5]

Then the party translated these words into a concrete plan of action.

In the first stage of the plan, the Soviet Union is to begin closing down inefficient enterprises, developing a banking system, and broadening citizens' rights to hold private property. In the next stage, collective farms and unprofitable state enterprises are to be broken up, business loans are to be made at competitive interest rates, and prices of consumer goods are to be determined in free markets. After that, Western-style monetary policy will to be used to control inflation, competition laws will be created to guard against monopoly, and the ruble may even become a convertible currency.

All this, however, makes Soviet economic reform seem far more rational and organized than it actually is. In fact, at this writing (autumn 1990), there is considerable chaos in Soviet political and economic life. Just how far and how fast the U.S.S.R. will travel along the road from rigid central planning to a free-market system remains to be seen. The path is full of perils, and few have gone before to point the way.

---

[5] From the platform of the Central Committee, as quoted in *The New York Times*, February 18, 1990.

The Chinese Economy

The People's Republic of China makes a good case study for this chapter because the Chinese have spent much of the last forty years groping to find an economic model that suits them. In the process, they have vividly confronted the fundamental question of this chapter—decentralized markets or central planning?—and have come up with different answers at different times.

After the Communist takeover in 1949, the Chinese economy was patterned on the Soviet model and developed with Soviet economic aid and technical expertise. In particular, the Chinese economy was very much a command economy, perhaps even more so than the Soviet. Also, China's emphasis on rapid economic growth, particularly industrial growth, was similar to that of the U.S.S.R.

But there were also important differences stemming in part from ideology and in part from the fact that the Soviet model was not quite suitable to China. Probably the most important of these differences was the decision by Mao Tse-tung *not* to rely on **material incentives** to motivate the work force. Mao and the Chinese leadership looked with disdain at this "bourgeois" practice and preferred to motivate Chinese workers by exhortation, appeals to patriotism, and, where necessary, force. The U.S.S.R. bent its socialist doctrine somewhat to accommodate human nature. But Chinese communism for many years seemed determined to bend human nature to accommodate Maoist doctrine—to create "the new man in the new China," an effort that has now been abandoned.

A second, less important, difference is that Chinese planning has always been less centralized than Soviet planning. Local and industrial authorities have more power and discretion than they do in the U.S.S.R. This decentralization was probably dictated by China's immense size and economic backwardness in 1949. Without modern communications (and perhaps even *with* them), there was no way for planners in Beijing to hope to control economic activity in the outlying provinces. Even today, this remains a problem for Beijing.

Chinese economic growth under the Communist regime has proceeded in fits and starts, not least as a result of Mao's abrupt changes of mind as to the emphasis he placed on ideology as opposed to technical planning. Although it was not the first major reversal of policy, the Great Proletarian Cultural Revolution (1965–69) is a dramatic example. During this period, Mao decided that the ideologically pure "Reds" were in and the technocratic "experts" were out as never before. The infamous Red Guards (later assisted by the army) were sent out to purge rightist elements from Chinese society, organize revolutionary cadres, and spread the teachings of Chairman Mao. If anyone worried about economic productivity in this environment, it did not show. By the summer of 1967, the Chinese economy and other elements of Chinese society were in utter disarray. National output fell substantially.

Things began to change again in the 1970s. The period until Mao's death in 1976 was one of consolidation and economic growth. The Chinese revolutionary fever receded, and the "experts" were rehabilitated. There was a restoration of material incentives and of rational economic calculation—both of which had been considered reactionary during the Cultural Revolution. In general, politics and ideology were de-emphasized, and economic growth was promoted.

China since Mao

Since the death of Mao, the Chinese economic system has continued to change rapidly. The leaders who succeeded Mao have shown themselves to be far less interested in doctrine and far more interested in results.

The technicians and scientists who fell into disgrace during Mao's Cultural Revolution were rehabilitated and put into positions of influence. In a startling reversal, it was Mao and the revolutionaries whose wisdom was now being questioned.

Late in the 1970s, the Chinese began a series of reforms that eventually amounted to stepping away from the Soviet model and adopting important features of the market economy in its place. China, long closed to the West, began to welcome Western tourism, trade, and technology. Chinese managers, engineers, and economists visited Western nations to study modern business techniques.

These trends accelerated in the early 1980s, as market forces were allowed to supplement central planning more and more. Farmers were given land to do with as they pleased—once they paid a fixed amount of produce to the state. Markets, and even limited amounts of local entrepreneurship, were allowed to flourish in the form of private shops and other small businesses. Foreign companies were invited to set up operations in China, and the Chinese seemed eager to learn the ways of Western business.

In the late 1980s, however, two problems arose. While allowing markets to gradually replace planning, the government failed to implement sound macroeconomic management. Consequently, China experienced high inflation for the first time since the Communist takeover. At about the same time, the Chinese people began to demand political freedoms to accompany their new-found economic freedoms. A struggle within the Chinese leadership ensued, which hard-liner Li Peng and his supporters won after having brutally suppressed a massive popular revolt in Tiananmen Square in June 1989.

Since then, the economic liberalization of China seems to have been put on hold, although it has not been reversed. The fundamental dilemma facing the current leaders is that the individual freedom that they refuse to grant their people (for political reasons) is necessary to facilitate the desired market-oriented reforms and more rapid economic growth. Given China's volatile past, no one can predict what will happen next.

The Amazing Japanese Economy

People all over the world today view Japan the way they once viewed the United States —with a mixture of awe and resentment. The Japanese are admired as producers and feared as competitors. Their efficiency seems matchless; their ability to export, boundless. "How do the Japanese do it?" is a question frequently asked, with barely concealed wonderment.

The reality is somewhat different. We learned in Chapter 18, for example, that economy-wide productivity in Japan is still below that in North America. Average standards of living lag even farther behind our own, in part because so many Japanese live in tiny dwellings. And Japan's retail and service industries are such marvels of inefficiency that many Japanese goods cost more in Tokyo than they do in New York!

Yet the Japanese economy is certainly *the* most outstanding success story of the period since World War II. From 1955 (when Japan began its productivity-enhancement campaign) to 1989, real GNP in Japan rose by an astounding 836 percent. (The corresponding expansion of the U.S. economy—the usual world standard—was only 177 percent.) Japan's automobile, electronics, and semiconductor industries, to name just a few, lead the world in technological and manufacturing prowess. Its banks and other financial institutions are the world's largest. As an economic power, Japan has truly come of age.

But how? Many say that Japan succeeded by adopting free-market capitalism— but it must be acknowledged that both free markets and capitalism look quite different in Japan than they do in North America.

Export-Led Growth

Japan is a crowded island nation, far removed from the world's major markets. Almost totally devoid of natural resources, it must import large amounts of raw materials, energy, and foodstuffs just to survive. And yet, by concentrating on manufacturing and exporting, it has managed not just to prosper but to propel itself into the forefront of nations.

One of the secrets of Japan's economic success has certainly been its emphasis on both high levels of investment and **export-led growth**. From 1955 to 1989, Japanese exports grew by an astounding 3227 percent in real terms. How has Japan done it? There is no simple answer. High levels of investment have certainly facilitated the adoption of the latest technology. And Japanese industry is clearly outward-looking in a way that North American industry is not. Many organizations, such as the fabled Ministry of International Trade and Industry (MITI) and the Japan External Trade Organization, work to promote exports. Japanese business has also shown a remarkable ability to adapt to changing world markets. As one industry (say, shipbuilding) declines, the Japanese shift rapidly into another (say, consumer electronics), whose star is rising. Above all, the major Japanese companies seek always to grow—and that means exporting.

> **Export-led growth** refers to the strategy of emphasizing the production of goods for export.

"Japan, Inc."

Japan has no tradition of enforcing competition laws. Indeed, at times, the Japanese government has seemed to promote rather than oppose bigness, perhaps as a way to catch up to the West. Consequently, Japanese industry is far more concentrated than American industry. Industrial concentration, barriers to imports, and inefficient retailing combine to keep domestic prices of consumer goods high. The cozy relationship between the big Japanese corporations (*kaisha*) and the Japanese government has acquired the nickname "Japan, Inc.," suggestive of an economic policy geared more to the interests of producers than of consumers.

Japanese industrial organization also looks different from *inside* the corporation. An industrial giant like Toyota may be surrounded by satellite companies that supply parts and help it operate its famous "just-in-time" inventory system (*kanban*)—a highly efficient way of organizing the factory floor to minimize delays. These smaller companies live at the mercy of the large *kaisha* and act as shock absorbers when demand declines.

In addition, members of Japan's manufacturing combines (*keiretsu*) own chunks of one another's stock and forge tight links with the world's largest banks. This gives Japanese industry access to cheap, "patient" capital—funds from lending institutions that are willing to wait for a return on their investment. Japanese managers pay scant attention to daily movements of the stock market and never worry about hostile takeovers. All this helps Japanese industry maintain its long-run focus.

Japan's System of Labour–Management Relations

Japan also differs from North America in the way that its work force is organized and paid. For one thing, many employees of large Japanese corporations have *lifetime employment* guarantees that protect them from being laid off. Such features help align the interests of labour and management, build loyalty to the company, and make Japanese workers less resistant to change than are their North American counterparts. For example, if a Japanese plant introduces automation, most employees know they will not only keep their jobs but share in any gains automation may bring.

The workplace is less hierarchical in Japan than in North America. Pay differentials between executives and workers are much smaller there, and the distribution of income is consequently much more equal. Managers eat in the same cafeterias, drink in the same bars, and sometimes even wear the same uniforms as blue-collar workers. Japanese workers are also consulted closely on how the factory is to be run. Decision-making is by consensus—even if consensus takes a long time to develop. North American management, by contrast, exercises more "top-down" control.

For these reasons, and perhaps also because of strong conformist tendencies within Japanese society, labour–management relations are less adversarial and more co-operative in Japan than they are in North America.

Is Japan a Planned Economy?

All this did not happen by means of the invisible hand alone. The system was consciously designed to raise industrial productivity, keep it growing, and turn Japan into an industrial powerhouse that would equal the Western nations. Many Japanese innovations, such as *kanban*, originated in the private sector. But the government—through the Japan Productivity Center, the Economic Planning Agency, the powerful Ministry of Finance, and MITI—played an active role in promoting what it saw as good ideas, discouraging those it considered bad, and, in general, lending a helping and guiding hand.

The role of the government, and especially of MITI, in Japan's economic success is highly controversial. Ardent free-marketeers downplay its contribution and point to episodes in which MITI clearly got in the way (one such episode was its ill-conceived attempt to drive several companies out of the automobile business in the 1960s). Protectionists seeking to limit Japanese imports exaggerate the role of MITI and portray "Japan, Inc." as a monolith (which it certainly is not). In their eyes, Japan's industrial policy is the key to its success.[6]

It is somewhat difficult to strike a balanced view of the matter, especially since few Westerners can fathom the cliquish ways of Japanese businesses. But a few things seem clear. First, the Ministry of Finance and the Bank of Japan (the central bank) have exercised a more comprehensive control over their financial system than is the custom here. Second, Japanese industrial policy, while far from infallible, seems to have had considerable success in assisting winners and shutting down losers. Third, Japanese industry benefits enormously from a work force that may be the best educated and most co-operative in the world; this is certainly a substantial achievement of government.

The Japanese have learned much from American industry (their famed "quality circles," for example, originated in the United States), and they continue to do so. As we noted in Chapter 18, economy-wide productivity continues to be higher in the United States than it is in Japan. Nonetheless, there are important industries—such as the automobile, robotics, and semiconductor industries—in which the Japanese seem to be the technological leader. In these areas, North Americans can "play catch up" by observing the Japanese, just as they did years ago by observing us.

Many people believe, however, that the most important things we can learn from the Japanese are not the latest innovations in robotics or chip manufacturing, but rather their ways of organizing and motivating people—from their education system, which has virtually abolished illiteracy, to their unique labour-relations system, to *kanban* and other management techniques.

Some observers predict that, as the Japanese get richer, their behaviour will come to resemble that of North Americans more closely. Already, for example, there are signs that Japanese households are saving less and that Japanese workers are changing jobs more frequently than they used to. Other observers, however, stress that basic cultural differences are likely to militate against rapid change, if not preclude significant change altogether.

A more general, and more controversial, hypothesis is that the Japanese "corporatist" style of doing business is better suited to the modern world of international competition than is the American "individualist" style. The two brands of capitalism are indeed different. Is the Japanese brand the wave of the future and the American the wave of the past? Only time will tell.

---

[6]Industrial policy (or industrial strategy) was discussed in Chapter 18, page 388.

Postscript

This chapter should be viewed as the first half of a two-part answer to the question "What does the market do well and what does it do poorly?" Many observers underestimate the very real contribution market forces can make to achieving high levels of material welfare. In an attempt to counter that view, we have stressed in this chapter that it is almost impossible to overstate the advantages of the market for achieving economic efficiency. Our brief review of countries that have suppressed market forces supports the analytical material. But this is only half the story. In the next two chapters we analyze various forms of monopoly, then devote Chapter 27 to an account of the negative half of the story. Reserve judgment in your own evaluation of the market mechanism until then.

Summary

1. Resource allocation is considered *inefficient* if it wastes opportunities to change the use of the economy's resources in any way that would make consumers better off. Conversely, it is called *efficient* if there are no such wasted opportunities.

2. Resource allocation involves three basic co-ordination tasks: (a) How much of each good to produce, (b) What quantities of the available inputs to use in producing the different goods, and (c) How to distribute the goods among different consumers.

3. Under perfect competition, the free-market mechanism adjusts prices so that the resulting resource allocation is efficient. It induces firms to buy and use inputs in ways that yield the most valuable outputs per unit of input; it distributes products among consumers in ways that match individual preferences; and it produces commodities whose value to consumers exceeds the cost of producing them.

4. Efficient decisions about what goods to produce require that the marginal cost (MC) of producing each good be equated to its marginal utility (MU) to consumers. If the MC of any good differs from its MU, then society can improve resource allocation by changing the level of production.

5. Because the market system induces firms to set MC equal to price and induces consumers to set MU equal to price, it automatically guarantees that the MC = MU condition is satisfied.

6. Sometimes improvements in efficiency require some prices to increase in order to stimulate supply or to prevent waste in consumption. This is why price increases can sometimes be beneficial to consumers.

7. In addition to allocating resources, prices also influence the distribution of income between buyers and sellers.

8. The workings of the price mechanism can be criticized on the grounds that it is unfair because of the preferential treatment it accords wealthy consumers. The most direct answer to this criticism is to redistribute income rather than to restrict the workings of the price mechanism. By this means we can avoid both the inefficiencies of central planning and the undesirable income-distribution effects of the market.

9. Free markets seem to do a good job of selecting the bill of goods and services to be produced and at choosing the most efficient techniques for producing these goods and services. Planned systems have difficulties with both these choices, as well as with stimulating inventiveness in the absence of the profit motive.

10. Market economies, however, do not guarantee an equitable distribution of income and are often plagued by business fluctuations. In these two areas, planning seems to have the advantage.

11. Planning in the U.S.S.R. has been bureaucratic and hierarchical and has encountered monumental difficulties in transmitting accurate information, equating supply and demand for the various inputs, motivating both workers and managers, and achieving satisfactory agricultural productivity.

12. While Soviet consumers are free to spend their money as they please, there is no consumer sovereignty. Planners, not consumers, decide what will be produced. The labour market, however, operates in much the same way as it does in Canada—using wage rates to equate supply and demand.

13. Currently, the Soviet Union is moving away from central planning toward a more market-oriented economy in which private ownership of capital is permitted and prices are determined by supply and demand. No one knows how far or how fast this liberalization will go.

14. The Chinese economic system has changed several times since the Communist takeover in 1949, passing through several periods of intense revolutionary fervour and little economic progress. Planning there has been similar to that in Russia, although somewhat less centralized.

15. In the course of the decade from the late 1970s to the

late 1980s, the Chinese introduced important aspects of the market economy into their economic system. In 1989, however, this liberalization came to a halt.

16. Japan has used export-led growth to propel itself to the forefront of nations; but lately its single-minded concentration on exporting has been a source of international tension.

17. Compared with the United States in particular, Japan has more industrial concentration, a less adversarial system of labour–management relations, tighter links between manufacturing companies and banks, and more active co-operation between government and industry. Observers disagree about the relative importance of each of these influences in accounting for Japan's industrial success.

Concepts for Review

Efficient allocation of resources
Co-ordination tasks: output selection, production planning, distribution of goods
Laissez faire

Input–output analysis
MC = P requirement of perfect competition
MC = MU efficiency requirement
Consumer sovereignty

Capitalism
Socialism
Planning
Export-led growth
Industrial policy

Questions for Discussion

1. What are the possible social advantages of price rises in each of the two following cases?
   a. Charging higher prices for electrical power on very hot days when many people use air conditioners.
   b. Raising water prices in drought-stricken areas.

2. Discuss the fairness of the two preceding proposals.

3. Discuss the nature of the inefficiency in each of the following cases:
   a. An arrangement that makes available relatively little coffee and much tea to people who prefer coffee and that accomplishes the reverse for tea lovers.
   b. An arrangement in which skilled mechanics are assigned to ditch-digging and unskilled labourers to repairing cars.
   c. An arrangement that produces a large quantity of trucks and few cars, assuming both cost about the same to produce and to run but most people in the community prefer cars to trucks.

4. In reality, which of the following circumstances might give rise to each of the preceding problem situations?
   a. Regulation of output quantities by a government.
   b. Rationing of commodities.
   c. Assignment of soldiers to different jobs in an army.

5. We have said that the economy's three co-ordination tasks are output selection, production planning, and product distribution. Which of these is done badly in the case described in Question 3(a)? in 3(b)? in 3(c)?

6. In a free market, how will the price mechanism deal with each inefficiency described in Question 3?

7. Suppose a given set of resources can be used to make either one handbag or two wallets, and the MC of a handbag is $23 while the MC of a wallet is $9. If the MU of a wallet is $9 and the MU of a handbag is $30, what can be done to improve resource allocation? What can you say about the gain to consumers?

8. If you were the leader of a small, developing country, what are some of the factors that would weigh heavily in your choice of an economic system?

9. If you were a plant manager under old-style Soviet planning, what are some of the things you might do to make your life easier and more successful? (Use your imagination. Soviet plant managers did!)

10. What are some special problems encountered when a country tries to make the transition from central planning to markets? (*Hint:* What kinds of difficulties can arise when some markets are tightly controlled while others are free?)

11. The Soviet Union has tentatively decided to take a gradual path toward markets and capitalism. Poland, by contrast, has decided to make the leap all at once. What are some of the pros and cons of gradualism versus the "big bang" approach? (*Note:* Poland's "big bang" came in January 1990. You can read about its progress regularly in newspapers and magazines.)

12. Do you think the Canadian government should take a more active role in guiding industry? Do you consider Japan to be a good or a poor model? Explain your answer.

Appendix

The Invisible Hand in the Distribution of Goods and in Production Planning

On pages 532–35 we offered a glimpse of the way economists analyze the workings of the invisible hand by showing how the market handles the problem of efficiency in one of the three tasks of resource allocation: the selection of outputs. We explained the MC = MU rule that must be followed for a set of outputs to be efficient and showed how a free market can induce people to act in a way that satisfies that rule. In this appendix we complete the story, examining how the price mechanism handles the two other tasks of resource allocation: the distribution of goods among consumers and the planning of production.

Efficient Distribution of Commodities: Who Gets What?

While decisions about distribution among consumers depend critically on value judgments, a surprising amount can be said purely on grounds of efficiency. For example, consumers' desires are not being served efficiently if large quantities of milk are given to someone whose preference is for apple cider, while numerous litres of cider are assigned to a milk lover. Deciding how much of which commodity goes to whom is a matter that requires delicate calculation. It causes great difficulties during wartime when planners must ration goods. They generally end up utilizing a crude egalitarianism: the same amount of butter to everyone, the same amount of coffee to everyone, and so on. This may be justified, to paraphrase the statement of a high official in another country, by an "unwillingness to pander to acquired tastes," but it is easy to see that such fixed rations are unlikely to produce an efficient result.

The analysis of the efficient distribution of the economy's different products among its many consumers turns out to be quite similar to our previous analysis of efficient output selection. Suppose there are two individuals, Mr. Steaker and Ms. Chop, and that Steaker wants lots of beef and little lamb, while the opposite is true of Chop. Suppose each is getting one kilogram of lamb and one kilogram of beef per week. It is then possible to make *both* people better off without increasing their total consumption of two kilograms of beef and two kilograms of lamb if Mr. Steaker trades some of his lamb to Ms. Chop in return for some beef. The initial distribution of goods was not efficient because it left room for trades that yield *mutual* gains.

It is easy enough to think of allocations of commodities among consumers that are *inefficient*—simply assign to each person only what he or she does not like. But how does one recognize an allocation that *is* efficient? After all, there are many of us whose preferences have much in common. If two individuals both like beef and lamb, how shall the available amounts of the two commodities be divided between them? We will now show that, as in the analysis of efficient output selection, there is a simple rule that must be satisfied by *any* efficient distribution of products among consumers. Consider any two commodities in the economy, such as beef and lamb, and any two consumers, like Steaker and Chop, each of whom likes to eat some of each type of meat. Then:

The basic rules for the efficient distribution of beef and lamb between Steaker and Chop are that

$$\text{Steaker's MU of beef} = \text{Chop's MU of beef}$$

and

$$\text{Steaker's MU of lamb} = \text{Chop's MU of lamb.}$$

Analogous equations must be satisfied for every other pair of individuals, and for every other pair of products.

Why are these equalities required for efficiency? Recall that a distribution of commodities among consumers can be efficient only if it has taken advantage of every potential gain from trade. That is, if two people can trade in a way that makes them *both* better off, then the distribution cannot be efficient. We can show that if *either* of the previous equations is not satisfied, then such trades are possible.

Suppose, for example, that the following are the relevant marginal utilities:

$$\text{Steaker's MU of beef} = \$40$$
$$\text{Chop's MU of beef} = \$20$$

$$\text{Steaker's MU of lamb} = \$10$$
$$\text{Chop's MU of lamb} = \$10.$$

In such a case a mutually beneficial exchange of beef and lamb can be arranged. For example, if Steaker gives Chop three kilograms of lamb in return for one kilogram of beef, they will both be better off. Steaker loses three kilograms of lamb, which are worth $30 to him, and gets a kilogram of beef, which is worth $40 to him. So he winds up $10 ahead. Similarly, Chop gives up one kilogram of beef, which is worth $20 to her, and gets in return three kilograms of lamb, worth $30 to her. So she also gains $10. Such a mutually beneficial exchange is possible here because the two consumers have different marginal utilities for beef. Each can benefit by giving up what he or she considers less valuable in exchange for something valued more highly. The initial position in which the two equations were not both satisfied was therefore not efficient because *without any increase in the total amounts of beef and lamb available to them, both could be made better off.* The lesson of this example is quite general:

Any time that two persons have unequal MUs for any commodity, the welfare of both parties can be increased by an exchange of commodities. Efficiency requires that any two individuals have the same MUs for any pair of goods.

The great virtue of the price system is that it induces people to carry out *voluntarily* all opportunities for mutually beneficial swaps. Without the price system, Steaker and Chop might not make the trade because they do not know each other. But the price system enables them to trade with each other by trading with the market. Remember from our discussion of consumer choice in Chapter 19 that it pays any consumer to buy any commodity up to the point where the good's money marginal utility is just equal to its price. In other words, in equilibrium:

Mr. Steaker's MU of beef = Price of beef
= Ms. Chop's MU of beef.

This is so because, if, say, Mr. Steaker's MU of beef were greater than the price of beef, he could improve his lot by exchanging more of his money for beef. And the reverse could be true if Steaker's MU of beef fell short of the price of beef. For the same reason, since the price of lamb is the same to both individuals, each will choose voluntarily to buy quantities of lamb at which:

Mr. Steaker's MU of lamb = Price of lamb
= Ms. Chop's MU of lamb.

Thus, we see that as long as both consumers face the same prices for lamb and beef, their independent decisions *must* satisfy our criterion for efficient distribution of beef and lamb between them:

Steaker's MU of beef = Chop's MU of beef
Steaker's MU of lamb = Chop's MU of lamb.

Given any prices for two commodities, each consumer, acting only in accord with his or her preferences and with no necessary consideration of the effects on the other person, will automatically make the purchases that efficiently serve the mutual interests of both purchasers.

This time, where have we sneaked the rabbit into our price system argument? The answer is that the market acts as an intermediary between any pair of consumers. Given the prices offered by the market, each consumer will use his or her dollars in a way that exhausts all opportunities for gains from trade *with the market.* Mr. Steaker and Ms. Chop each take advantage of every such opportunity to gain by trading with the market, and in the process they automatically take advantage of every opportunity for advantageous trades between themselves.

Efficient Production Planning: Allocation of Inputs

Finally, we note briefly that a similar analysis shows how the price system leads to an efficient allocation of inputs among the different production processes—the third of our allocative issues. For precisely the same reasons as in the case of the distribution of products among consumers:

Efficient use of two inputs (say, labour and fertilizer) in the production of two goods (say, wheat and corn) requires that

$$\frac{MPP_{\text{wheat, fertilizer}}}{MPP_{\text{wheat, labour}}} = \frac{MPP_{\text{corn, fertilizer}}}{MPP_{\text{corn, labour}}},$$

where, for example, "$MPP_{\text{wheat, fertilizer}}$" means "the marginal physical product of fertilizer when it is employed in wheat production."

By the same logic as before, we can show that if these equations do not hold, it is possible to produce more corn and more wheat without using more labour and fertilizer than before merely by redistributing the quantities of the two inputs between the two crops.[7] But we learned in Chapter 21 that maximum profits require each wheat farmer to hire so much labour and so much fertilizer that the ratio of their marginal physical products equals the ratio of their prices. That is,

$$\frac{MPP_{\text{wheat, fertilizer}}}{MPP_{\text{wheat, labour}}} = \frac{P_{\text{fertilizer}}}{P_{\text{labour}}}$$

[7]See Discussion Question 2 at the end of this appendix.

(where, for example, "$P_{\text{fertilizer}}$" means "price of fertilizer"). The same relationship must also hold true for every profit-maximizing corn producer:

$$\frac{\text{MPP}_{\text{corn, fertilizer}}}{\text{MPP}_{\text{corn, labour}}} = \frac{P_{\text{fertilizer}}}{P_{\text{labour}}} .$$

Since in a competitive industry such as agriculture, wheat farmers and corn farmers must pay the same prices for each of their inputs such as labour and fertilizer, it follows that the ratio of the marginal physical product of fertilizer and labour must be the same in wheat growing, corn growing, and in every other competitive industry that uses these two inputs, just as the formula for efficient production planning requires.

Thus, we conclude that by making the independent choices that maximize their own profits, and without necessarily considering the effects on anyone else, each farmer (firm) will *automatically* act in a way that satisfies the efficiency condition for the allocation of inputs among different products.

Summary

1. The condition for efficient distribution of commodities among consumers is that every consumer have the same marginal utility (MU) for every product. If this condition is not met, then two consumers can arrange a swap that makes both of them better off.
2. In a free market, all consumers pay the same prices. So, if they pursue their own self-interest by setting $MU = P$, they automatically satisfy the condition for efficient distribution of commodities.
3. The condition for efficient allocation of inputs to the various production processes is that the ratio of the marginal physical products (MPP) of any pair of inputs be the same in every industry.
4. Since all producers pay the same prices for inputs under perfect competition, if each firm pursues its own self-interest by setting the ratio of the marginal physical products of any two of its inputs equal to the ratio of the prices of these inputs, the condition for efficient production planning will be satisfied automatically.

Questions for Discussion

1. Show that commodities are not being distributed efficiently if Mr. Olson's marginal utilities of a kilogram of tomatoes and a kilogram of potatoes are, respectively, 80 cents and 40 cents, while Mr. Johnson's are, respectively, 60 cents and 50 cents.

2. Suppose the marginal revenue product of a litre of petroleum in the trucking industry is 50 cents while the marginal revenue product of petroleum in the auto-racing industry is 28 cents. Show that petroleum inputs are being allocated inefficiently. How would a market system tend to prevent this situation from occurring?

25

Monopoly

The price of monopoly is upon every occasion the highest which can be got.

ADAM SMITH*

I n Chapters 23 and 24 we described an idealized market system in which all industries are perfectly competitive, and we extolled the beauty of that system. In this chapter, we turn to one of the blemishes—the possibility that some industries may be monopolized—and to the consequences of such monopolization.

We begin by defining *monopoly* precisely and investigating some of the reasons for its existence. Then, using the tools of Chapter 22, we consider the monopolist's choice of an optimal price–output combination. As we shall see, while it is possible to analyze how much a monopolist will choose to produce, a monopolist has no "supply curve" in the usual sense. This and other features of monopolized markets require basic modification of our supply–demand analysis of the market mechanism. That modification leads us to the central message of this chapter—that monopolized markets do not match the ideal performance of perfectly competitive ones. In particular, we will see that in the presence of monopoly the market mechanism no longer allocates society's resources efficiently. This observation opens up the possibility that government actions to constrain monopoly may actually improve the workings of the market—a possibility we will study in detail in Chapter 28.

Application: Monopoly and Pollution Charges

We begin, as usual, with a real-life problem. Chapter 1 noted that most economists want to control pollution by charging polluters heavily, making them pay more money the more pollution they emit. Making it sufficiently expensive for firms to pollute, it is said, will force them to cut their emissions.[1]

A common objection to this proposal is that it simply will not work when the polluter is a monopolist: "The monopoly firm can just raise the price of its product, pass the pollution charge on to its customers, and go on polluting as before, with total impunity." After all, if a firm is a monopoly, what is to stop it from raising its price when it is hit by a pollution charge?

Yet observation of the behaviour of firms threatened with pollution charges suggests that there is something wrong with this objection. If the polluter could escape the penalty completely, we would expect him to acquiesce or to put up only token opposition. Yet wherever it has been proposed to levy a charge on the emission of pollutants, the outcries have been enormous, even among firms with no important rivals. Lobbyists are dispatched at once to do their best to stop the legislation. In fact, rather than agree to being charged for their emissions, firms usually indicate a

---

*But Adam Smith's statement is incorrect! See Discussion Question 7 at the end of the chapter.

[1] Details on this method of pollution control are provided in Chapter 32.

preference for direct controls that *force* them to adopt specific processes that are less polluting than the ones they are now using—that is, the firms seem to prefer having government tell them what they must do!

In this chapter we will see how to analyze the issue and learn why monopolies cannot make their customers pay the pollution charge—or at least not all of it.

Monopoly Defined

A pure monopoly is an industry in which there is only one supplier of a product for which there are no close substitutes, and in which it is very hard or impossible for another firm to co-exist.

Pure monopoly was defined in Table 23-1 on page 504, and the definition is quite stringent. First, there must be only one firm in the industry—the monopolist must be "the only supplier in town." Second, there must be no close substitute for the monopolist's product. Thus, even the sole provider of natural gas in a city would not be considered a pure monopoly, since other firms offer close substitutes like heating oil and coal. Third, there must be some reason why survival of a potential competitor is extremely unlikely, for otherwise monopolistic behaviour and its excessive profits could not persist.

These rigid requirements make pure monopoly a rarity in the real world. The local telephone company and the post office are good examples of one-firm industries that face little or no effective competition. But most firms face competition from substitute products. Even if only one airline serves a particular town, it must compete with bus lines, trucking companies, and railways. Similarly, the producer of a particular brand of beer may be the only supplier of that specific product but is not a monopolist by our definition. Since many other beers are close substitutes for its product, the company will lose much of its business if it tries to raise its price much above the prices of other brands.

And there is one further reason why the unrestrained pure monopoly of economic theory is rarely encountered in practice. We will learn in this chapter that pure monopoly can have a number of undesirable features. As a consequence, in markets where pure monopoly might otherwise prevail, the government has intervened to prevent monopolization or to limit the discretion of the monopolist to set its price.

If we do not study pure monopoly for its descriptive realism, why do we study it? Because, like perfect competition, pure monopoly is a market form that is easier to analyze than the more common market structures that we will consider in the next chapter. Thus, pure monopoly is a stepping stone toward models of greater reality. Also, the "evils of monopoly" stand out most clearly when we consider monopoly in its purest form, and this greater clarity will help us understand why governments have rarely allowed unfettered monopoly to exist.

Causes of Monopoly:
Barriers to Entry and Cost Advantages

The key element in preserving a monopoly is keeping potential rivals out of the market. One possibility is that some specific impediment prevents the establishment of a new firm in the industry. Economists call such impediments **barriers to entry**. Some examples are:

1. *Legal restrictions.* Canada Post has a monopoly position because Parliament has given it one. Private companies that might want to compete with the post office are prohibited from doing so by law. Local monopolies of various kinds are sometimes established either because government grants some special privilege to a single firm (for example, the right to operate a food concession in a municipal stadium) or prevents other firms from entering the industry (for instance, by licensing only a single local radio station).

2. *Patents.* A special, but very important, legal impediment to entry is the **patent**. To encourage inventiveness, the government gives exclusive production rights for a

period of time to the inventor of certain products. As long as the patent is in effect, the firm has a protected position and is a monopoly. For example, Xerox had for many years (but no longer has) a monopoly in plain-paper copying.

3. *Control of a scarce resource or input.* If a certain commodity can be produced only by using a rare input, a company that gains control of the source of that input can establish a monopoly position for itself.

4. *Deliberately erected entry barriers.* A firm may deliberately attempt to make entry difficult for others. One way to do so is to start costly lawsuits against new rivals, sometimes on trumped-up charges. Another is to spend exorbitant amounts on advertising, thus forcing any potential entrant to match that expenditure.

Obviously, such barriers can keep rivals out and ensure that an industry is monopolized, but monopoly can also occur in the absence of barriers to entry if a single firm has important cost advantages over its potential rivals. Two examples of this are:

5. *Technical superiority.* A firm whose technological expertise vastly exceeds that of potential competitors can, for a period of time, maintain a monopoly position. For example, IBM for many years had very little competition in the computer business mainly because of its technological virtuosity. Eventually, however, competitors began to catch up.

6. *Economies of scale.* If mere size gives a large firm a cost advantage over a smaller rival, it is likely to be impossible for anyone to compete with the largest firm in the industry.

Natural Monopoly

This last type of cost advantage is important enough to merit special attention. In some industries, economies of large-scale production or economies from simultaneous production of a large number of items (for example, car motors and bodies, truck parts, and so on) are so extreme that the industry's output can be produced at far lower cost by a single firm than by a number of smaller firms. In such cases, we say there is a **natural monopoly**, because once a firm gets large enough relative to the size of the market for its product, its natural cost advantage may well drive the competition out of business, whether or not anyone in the relatively large firm has evil intentions.

A monopoly need not be a large firm if the market is small enough. *What matters is the size of a single firm relative to the total market demand for the product.* Thus, a small bank in a rural town or a gasoline station at a lightly travelled intersection may both be natural monopolies even though they are very small firms.

Figure 25–1 shows the sort of average-cost (AC) curve that leads to natural monopoly. Suppose that any firm producing widgets would have this AC curve and that, initially, the industry has two firms, one large and one small. Suppose also that the large firm is producing two million widgets at an average cost of $2.50, and the small firm is producing one million widgets at an average cost of $3. Clearly, the large firm can drive the small firm out of business by offering its output for sale at a price below $3 (so the small firm can match the price only by running a loss) but above $2.50 (so the large firm can still make a profit). The managers of the large firm will be smart enough to realize this possibility, and hence a monopoly will arise "naturally" even in the absence of barriers to entry. Once the monopoly is established (producing, say, 2.5 million widgets) the economies of scale act as a very effective deterrent to entry because no new entrant can hope to match the low average cost ($2) of the existing monopoly firm. Of course, the public interest may be well served if the firm with a natural monopoly uses its low cost to keep its prices low. The danger, however, is that the firm may raise its price once rivals have left the industry.

Many public utilities are permitted to operate as *regulated* monopoly suppliers

A natural monopoly is an industry in which the advantages of large-scale production make it possible for a single firm to produce the entire output of the market at lower average cost than a number of firms each producing a smaller quantity.

FIGURE 25-1
Natural Monopoly

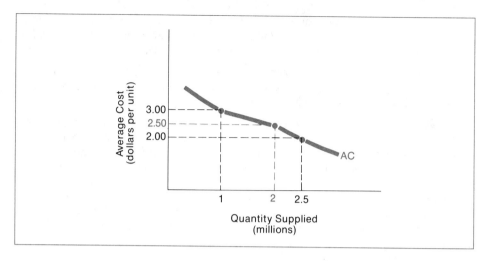

When the average-cost curve of
a firm is declining, as depicted
here, natural monopoly may result. A firm producing two million
widgets will have average costs
of $2.50, which are well below
those of a smaller competitor
producing one million widgets
(average cost = $3). The larger
firm can cut its price to a level
(lower than $3) that its competi-
tor cannot match and thereby
drive the competitor out of
business.

for exactly such reasons. It is believed that the technology of producing or distributing their output enables them to achieve substantial cost reductions when they produce large quantities. It is therefore often considered desirable to permit these firms to obtain the lower costs they achieve by having the entire market to themselves and to subject them to regulatory supervision, rather than break them up into a number of competing firms. The issue of regulating natural monopolies will be examined in detail in Chapter 31. To summarize this discussion:

There are two basic reasons why a monopoly may exist: barriers to entry, such as legal restrictions and patents, and cost advantages of large-scale operation that lead to natural monopoly. It is generally considered undesirable to break up a large firm whose costs are low as a result of scale economies. In contrast, barriers to entry are usually considered contrary to the public interest unless, as in the case of patents, they are believed to offer offsetting advantages.

The rest of this chapter will analyze how a monopoly can be expected to behave if its freedom of action is not limited by the government.

The Monopolist's Supply Decision

A monopoly firm does not have a "supply curve," as we usually define the term. It does not just observe the market price of a product and then decide what quantity to produce. Unlike a perfect competitor, a monopoly is not at the mercy of the market; the firm does not have to take the market price as given and react to it. Instead, it has the power to set the price, or rather to select the price–quantity combination on the demand curve that suits its interests best.

Put differently, a monopolist is not a *price taker* who must simply adapt to whatever price the forces of supply and demand decree. Rather, the monopolist is a *price maker* who can, if so inclined, raise the product's price. For any price that the monopolist might choose, the demand curve for the product indicates how much consumers will buy. Thus, the standard supply–demand analysis described in Chapter 3 does not apply to the determination of price or output in a monopolized industry.

The monopolist's demand curve, unlike that of a perfect competitor, is normally downward sloping, not horizontal. This means that a price rise will not cause the monopoly to lose all its customers. But any increase will cost it *some* business. The higher the price, the less the monopolist can expect to sell.

It is because of the downward-sloping demand curve that the sky is not the limit in pricing by a monopolist. Some price increases are not profitable. In deciding what

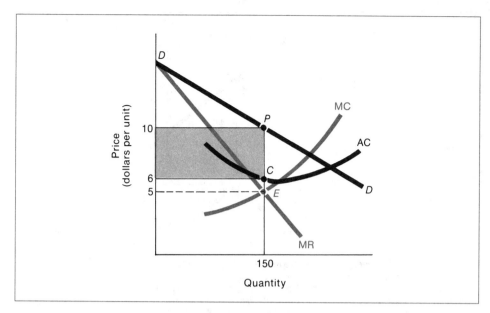

FIGURE 25-2
**Profit-Maximizing
Equilibrium for a
Monopolist**
This monopoly has the cost
structure indicated by the black
average-cost (AC) curve and
the green marginal-cost (MC)
curve. Its demand curve is the
black line labelled *DD*, and its
marginal-revenue curve is the
green line labelled MR. The monopoly maximizes profits by producing 150 units, because at
this level of production MC =
MR (point *E*). The price the monopoly charges is $10 per unit
(as given by point *P* on the demand curve). Since the average
cost per unit ($6) is given by
point *C* on the AC curve, the
monopoly's total profit is indicated by the shaded rectangle.

price best serves the firm's interests, the monopolist must consider whether profits
can be increased by raising or lowering the product's price.

In our analysis, we shall assume that the monopolist wants to maximize profits.
We note two things about that. First, even a monopoly firm is not guaranteed a
positive profit. If the demand for its product is low or the firm is inefficient, it may
lose money and may eventually be forced to go out of business. Second, if a monopoly
firm does earn a positive profit, it may be able to keep on doing so even in the long run
if entry of new competitors on profitable terms is difficult or impossible. This is so
because absence of entry can permit the monopoly firm to keep its price well above its
average cost.

The methods of Chapter 22 can be used to determine which price the profit-
maximizing monopolist will prefer. To maximize profits, the monopolist must compare marginal revenue (the addition to total revenue resulting from a one-unit rise in
output) with marginal cost (the addition to total cost resulting from that additional
unit). For this purpose, a marginal-cost (MC) curve and a marginal-revenue (MR)
curve for a typical monopolist are drawn in Figure 25–2, which also contains the
monopolist's demand curve (*DD*).

The Monopolist's Price and Marginal Revenue

Notice that the marginal-revenue curve is always *below* the demand curve, meaning
that MR is always less than price (*P*). This is an important fact and is easy to explain.
A monopoly normally must charge the same price to all of its customers. So, if the
monopoly firm wants to increase sales by one unit, it must lower its price somewhat to
all of its customers. When the price is cut to attract new sales, all previous customers
also benefit. Thus, the *additional* revenue that the monopoly firm takes in when sales
increase by one unit (*marginal revenue*) is the price the firm collects from the new
customer *minus the revenue it loses by cutting the price paid by all of its old customers*. This means that MR is necessarily *less* than price; graphically, it implies that
the MR curve is *below* the demand curve, as in Figure 25–2.

Figure 25–3 illustrates the relationship between price and marginal revenue in a
specific example. Suppose a monopoly is initially selling 15 units at a price of $2.10 per
unit (point *A*), and the monopolist wishes to increase sales by one unit. The demand
curve indicates that in order to sell the 16th unit, the firm must reduce the price to $2

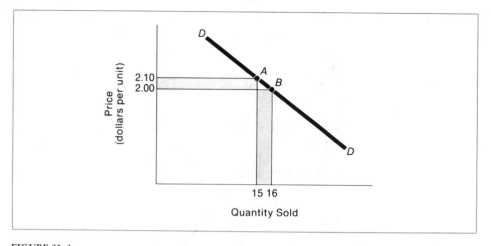

FIGURE 25–3

The Relationship between Marginal Revenue and Price

Line *DD* is the demand curve of a monopoly. In order to raise sales from 15 to 16 units, the firm must cut its price from $2.10 (point *A*) to $2 (point *B*). If it does this, its revenues *go up* by the $2 price it charges the buyer of the 16th unit (the area of the tall green rectangle) but *go down* by the 10-cent price reduction it offers to its previous customers (the area of the flat grey rectangle). The monopoly's marginal revenue, therefore, is the difference between these two areas. Since the price is the area of the green rectangle, it follows that marginal revenue is less than price for a monopolist.

(point *B*). How much revenue will be gained from this increase in sales; that is, how large is the monopolist's marginal revenue?

As we know, *total revenue* at point *A* is the area of the rectangle whose upper right-hand corner is point *A*, or $2.10 × 15 = $31.50. Similarly, total revenue at point *B* is the area of the rectangle whose upper right-hand corner is point *B*, or $2 × 16 = $32. The *marginal revenue* of the 16th unit is, by definition, total revenue when 16 units are sold minus total revenue when 15 units are sold, or $32 – $31.50 = $0.50.

In Figure 25–3, marginal revenue appears as the area of the tall green rectangle ($2) *minus* the area of the flat grey rectangle ($1.50). We can see that MR is less than price by observing that the price is shown in the diagram by the area of the green rectangle.[2] Clearly, the price (area of the green rectangle) must exceed the marginal revenue (area of the green rectangle *minus* area of the grey rectangle), as was claimed.[3]

Determining the Profit-Maximizing Output

We return now to the supply decision of the monopolist depicted in Figure 25–2. Like any other firm, the monopoly maximizes its profits by setting marginal revenue (MR) equal to marginal cost (MC). It selects point *E* in the diagram, where output is 150 units. But point *E* does not tell us the monopoly price because, as we have just seen, price exceeds MR for a monopolist. To learn what price the monopolist charges, we must use the demand curve to find the price at which consumers are willing to purchase 150 units. The answer, we see, is given by point *P*. The monopoly price is $10 per unit, which naturally exceeds both MR and MC (which are equal at $5).

The monopoly firm depicted in Figure 25–2 is earning a tidy profit. This profit is shown in the graph by the shaded rectangle, whose height is the difference between

---

[2]Because the width of this rectangle is one unit, its area is height × width = ($2 per unit) × (1 unit) = $2.

[3]There is another way to arrive at this conclusion. Recall that the demand curve is the curve of *average revenue*. Since the average revenue is declining as we move to the right, it follows from one of the rules relating marginals and averages (see the appendix to Chapter 22) that the marginal-revenue curve must always be below the average.

TABLE 25-1
A Profit-Maximizing Monopolist's Price–Output Decision

| DEMAND CURVE | | REVENUE | | COST | | TOTAL PROFIT |
(1) Q	(2) P	(3) TR = P × Q	(4) MR	(5) TC	(6) MC	(7) TR − TC
0	—	$ 0		$ 10		$−10
1	$140	140	$140	70	$60	70
2	107	214	74	120	50	94
3	92	276	62	166	46	110
4	80	320	44	210	44	110
5	66	330	10	253	43	77
6	50	300	−30	298	45	2

price (point P) and average cost (point C) and whose width is the quantity produced (150 units). In the example, profits are $4 per unit, or $600. The monopolist has the power to raise price above $10 per unit, but chooses not to, since doing so would lower profits.

To study the decisions of a profit-maximizing monopolist, we must:

1. Find the output at which MR = MC, to select the profit-maximizing output level;

2. Find the height of the demand curve at that level of output, to determine the corresponding price;

3. Compare the height of the demand curve with that of the AC curve at that output to see whether the net result is a profit or a loss.

A monopolist's profit-maximization calculation can also be shown numerically. In Table 25–1, the first two columns show the price and quantity figures that constitute a monopolist's demand curve. Column 3 shows total revenue (TR), which is the product of price and quantity, for each output. Thus, for three units of output we have TR = $92 × 3 = $276. Column 4 shows marginal revenue (MR). For example, when output rises from 3 to 4 units, TR increases from $276 to $320 so MR is $320 − $276 = $44. Column 5 gives the monopolist's total costs for each level of output. Column 6 derives marginal cost (MC) from total cost (TC) in the usual way. Finally, by subtracting TC from TR for each level of output, we derive total profit in column 7.

This table brings out a number of important points. We note first (columns 2 and 3) that a cut in price sometimes raises total revenue. For example, when output rises from 1 to 2, P falls from $140 to $107 and TR rises from $140 to $214. But sometimes a fall in P reduces TR; when (between 5 and 6 units of output) P falls from $66 to $50, TR falls from $330 to $300. Next, by comparing columns 2 and 4, we observe that, after the first unit, price always exceeds marginal revenue. Finally, from columns 4 and 6, we see that MC = MR = $44 when Q is 4 units, indicating that this is the level of output that maximizes the monopolist's total profit. That is confirmed in the last column of the table, which shows that at that output profit reaches its highest level, $110, for any of the output quantities considered in the table.

Comparison of Monopoly and Perfect Competition

This completes our analysis of the monopolist's price–output decision. At this point it is natural to wonder whether there is anything distinctive about monopoly, and whether its consequences are desirable or undesirable. For the purpose of finding out, we need a standard of comparison. Perfect competition provides this standard because, as we learned in Chapters 23 and 24, it is a benchmark of ideal performance against which other market structures can be judged. By comparing the results of monopoly with those of perfect competition, we will see why economists since Adam Smith have condemned monopoly as inefficient.

Monopoly Profit Persists

The first difference between competition and monopoly is a direct consequence of the absence of barriers to entry in the former. Profits such as those shown in Figure 25–2 would be competed away by free entry in a competitive market. In the long run, a competitive firm must earn zero economic profit; that is, it can earn only enough to cover its costs, including the opportunity cost of the owner's capital and labour. But higher profits can persist under monopoly—if the monopoly is protected by barriers to entry. The fates can be kind to a monopolist and allow him to grow wealthy at the expense of the consumer. Because people find such accumulations of wealth objectionable, monopoly is widely condemned and, when monopolies are regulated by government, limitations are usually placed on the profits monopolists can earn.

Monopoly Restricts Output to Raise Price

Excess monopoly profits may be a problem, but the second difference between competition and monopoly is even more worrisome in the opinion of economists:

As compared with the perfectly competitive ideal, the monopolist restricts output and charges a higher price.

To see that this is so, let us conduct the following thought experiment. Suppose there is a competitive industry whose operation is shown in Figure 25–4. For the moment ignore everything except the demand and supply curves. We see that these industry demand and supply curves intersect at point A. Since the industry supply curve is the horizontal summation of all the marginal-cost curves of the individual factories (above minimum average variable costs) and since point A is on that supply curve, price equals marginal cost at point A.

Now suppose one firm takes over the industry and operates the same set of plants, so that cost curves are not affected. Holding a monopoly, this firm will now calculate the marginal-revenue curve that is associated with the industry demand

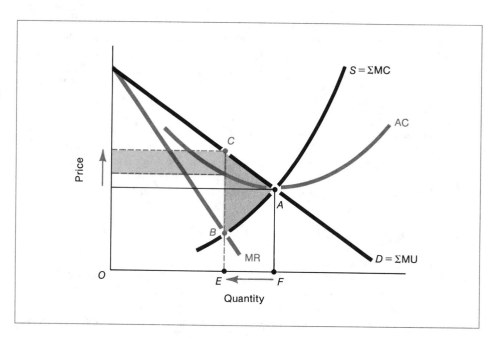

FIGURE 25–4
Comparison of a Monopoly and a Competitive Industry
The monopoly price–output combination is point C (at which MC = MR), while that of the competitive industry is point A (where P = MC, and AC is at the minimum level possible). The *net* loss to society as a result of losing output amount EF is equal to area ABC in every period during which a monopoly prevails.

curve, and operate at the output level given by point *B*, since this is where marginal revenue equals marginal cost. The corresponding point on the demand curve, and hence the price the monopolist will charge, is therefore *C*. By comparing points *A* and *C*, we can clearly see that the monopolist sells a smaller quantity of the good to buyers and charges a higher price per unit than does the corresponding competitive industry. Excess profits are earned (indefinitely, given barriers to entry), and inefficiency exists, as we can see, since the unit cost of production (that is, average cost) is no longer minimized. Thus, the detrimental effects of monopoly involve dimensions of both equity and efficiency.

Monopoly Leads to Inefficient Resource Allocation

We conclude, then, that a monopoly will charge a higher price and produce a smaller output than will a competitive industry with the same demand and cost conditions. Why do economists find this situation so objectionable? Because, as you will recall from Chapter 24, a competitive industry devotes "just the right amount" of society's scarce resources to the production of its particular commodity. Therefore, if a monopoly produces less than a competitive industry, it must be producing too little.

Remember from Chapter 24 that efficiency in resource allocation requires that the marginal utility (MU) of each commodity be equal to its marginal cost, and that perfect competition guarantees that:

$$MU = P \quad \text{and} \quad MC = P, \quad \text{so} \quad MU = MC.$$

Under monopoly, consumers continue to maximize their own welfare by setting MU equal to *P*. But the monopoly producer, we have just learned, sets MC equal to MR. Since MR is *below* the market price, *P*, we conclude that in a monopolized industry:

$$MU = P \quad \text{and} \quad MC = MR < P, \quad \text{so} \quad MU > MC.$$

Because MU exceeds MC, too small a share of society's resources are being used to produce the monopolized commodity. Adam Smith's invisible hand is sending out the wrong signals. Consumers are willing to pay an amount for an additional unit of the good (its MU) that exceeds what it costs to produce that unit (its MC). But the monopoly refuses to increase production, for if it raises output by one unit, the revenue it will collect (the MR) will be less than the price the consumer will pay for the additional unit (*P*). So the monopolist does not increase production and resources are allocated inefficiently. To summarize:

Because it is protected from the entry of other firms, a monopoly firm may earn profits in excess of the opportunity cost of capital. At the same time, monopoly breeds inefficiency in resource allocation by producing too little output and charging too high a price. For these reasons, some virtues of laissez faire evaporate if an industry becomes monopolized.

The inefficiency caused by monopoly can actually be measured from Figure 25–4. How much would it cost society to increase the output of this industry from the monopoly level, amount *OE*, to the competitive level, amount *OF*? The answer is given by *the area under the marginal-cost curve* within the range of additional production (*EF*); that is, area *EFAB*. This is so because we can get the overall increase in cost by adding together all the marginal costs of each unit as output is increased from *OE* to *OF*.

How much does society gain if output is increased in this way? The answer can be had by considering people's overall willingness to pay for this extra output, which is reflected by *the area under the demand curve* within the range of the additional purchases (*EF*); that is, by area *EFAC*. This is so because we get the overall increase in utility by adding together all the marginal utilities of each unit as output is increased from *OE* to *OF*. The demand curve is the summation of all individuals' marginal utility schedules.

The excess of benefits over costs is the difference between the two areas *EFAB* and *EFAC*. The *net* benefit of moving back to the competitive outcome is therefore area *ABC*—the shaded green triangle in Figure 25–4. Once these curves have been estimated with actual data in particular cases, economists directly measure areas such as *ABC* to calculate the loss to society that is incurred in *every* period during which a monopoly prevails.

Can Anything Good Be Said about Monopoly?

Except for the case of natural monopoly, where a single firm offers important cost advantages, or the case of a monopoly obtained through an inventor's patent, which is designed to encourage innovation, it is not easy to find arguments in favour of monopoly. But the comparison between monopoly and perfect competition in the real world is not quite as clean as it is in our example.

Monopoly May Shift Demand

For one thing, we have assumed that the market-demand curve is the same whether the industry is competitive or monopolized. But is this necessarily so? The demand curve will be the same if the monopoly firm does nothing to expand its market, but that hardly seems likely.

Under perfect competition, purchasers consider the products of all suppliers in an industry to be identical, and so no single supplier has any reason to advertise. A farmer who sells apples through one of the major markets has absolutely no motivation to spend money on advertising because he can sell all the apples he wants to at the going price.

When a monopoly firm takes over, however, it may very well pay to advertise. If management believes that advertising can make consumers' hearts beat faster as they rush to the market to purchase the apples whose virtues have been extolled on television, the firm will allocate a substantial sum of money to accomplish this feat. This should shift the demand curve outward; after all, that is the purpose of these expenditures. The monopoly's demand curve and that of the competitive industry will then no longer be the same. The higher demand curve for the monopoly's product will perhaps induce it to expand its volume of production and to reduce the difference between the competitive and the monopolistic output levels indicated in Figure 25–4. It may also, however, make it possible for the monopoly firm to charge even higher prices, so the increased output may not constitute a net gain for consumers.

Monopoly May Shift Cost Curves

Similarly, the advent of a monopoly may produce shifts in the average- and marginal-cost curves. One reason for higher costs is the advertising we have just been discussing. Another is that the sheer size of the monopolist's organization may lead to bureaucratic inefficiencies, co-ordination problems, and the like. On the other hand, the monopolist may be able to eliminate certain types of duplication that are unavoidable for a number of small independent firms: One purchasing agent may do the job where many buyers were needed before, and a few large machines may replace many small items of equipment in the hands of the competitive firms. In addition, the large scale of the monopoly firm's input purchases may permit it to take advantage of quantity discounts not available to small competitive firms.

If the unification achieved by monopoly does succeed in producing a downward shift in the marginal-cost curve, monopoly output will thereby tend to move up closer to the competitive level, and the monopoly price will tend to move down closer to the competitive price.

Monopoly May Aid Innovation

In addition to this, some economists, most notably Joseph Schumpeter, have argued that it is potentially misleading to compare the cost curves of a monopoly and a competitive industry *at a single point in time*. Because it is protected from rivals and therefore sure to capture the benefits from any cost savings it can devise, a monopoly has a particularly strong motivation to invest in research, they argue. If this research bears fruit, then the monopolist's costs will be lower than those of a competitive industry in the long run, even if they are higher in the short run. Monopoly, according to this view, may be the handmaiden of innovation. While the argument is an old one, it remains controversial. The statistical evidence is decidedly mixed.

Natural Monopoly—Where Single-Firm Production Is Cheapest

Finally, we must remember that the monopoly depicted in Figure 25–4 is not a natural monopoly. But some of the monopolies you find in the real world are. Where the monopoly is natural, costs of production would, by definition, be higher and possibly much higher if the single large firm were broken up into many smaller firms. In such cases, it may be in society's best interest to allow the monopoly to exist so that consumers can benefit from the economies of large-scale production. But then it may be appropriate to place legal limitations on the monopolist's ability to set a price; that is, to *regulate* the monopoly. Regulation of business is an issue that will occupy our attention in Chapter 31.

Monopoly Policy

Monopoly raises both an efficiency issue (since with a monopolist MU > MC) and an equity issue (since positive economic profits persist indefinitely and are not competed away). Often, the use of a single policy instrument improves one problem but exacerbates the other. For example, if a monopoly firm is hit with an excise tax, its profit will be reduced. But the tax will shift its marginal-cost curve up, causing it to reduce its output level even *further* below what would obtain in a competitive environment. Thus, the excise tax compounds the efficiency problem.

Since there are two dimensions to the monopoly problem, two policy instruments are needed. One policy *package* that can help solve the problem is to increase fixed costs by levying a licence fee (thereby decreasing profits without causing any change in price or output) and, at the same time, to decrease variable cost by paying a per-unit-of-output subsidy (thereby shifting the marginal-cost curve down and so increasing output and lowering price). As long as the licence fee is high enough, profits will be reduced despite the subsidy. The effects of this policy package are shown in Figure 25–5. Initially, the monopolist is producing output level *OA* and earning profits *CD*. The per-unit subsidy pivots the total-cost curve down, and the licence fee shifts the total-cost curve up in a parallel fashion. If the two effects are combined perfectly, as shown in Figure 25–5, the monopolist could be pushed to point *E*— offering more output to the market but earning no economic profit.

One problem with this policy package is that a large licence fee adds to the barriers to entry. If only small barriers to entry exist in the first place, the licence fee is not an appealing option. But if they are already large, the package can, at least in principle, solve both the equity and the efficiency aspects of the monopoly problem.

In later chapters, we consider the following three policy approaches to the monopoly problem: (1) regulation, (2) laws and their enforcement through the courts, and (3) the discipline of the market. The idea behind this third alternative is to make more substitutes for the monopolist's product available to the public (say, by decreasing tariffs and forcing the firm into competition with foreign suppliers). To make this last point more explicit, it is useful at this stage to derive the formula for a monopolist's price "mark-up." This derivation follows from a manipulation of the MR = MC condition for profit maximization.

FIGURE 25–5

Tackling Both the Equity and Efficiency Problems of Monopoly

Without any tax or subsidy, the monopolist chooses output *OA*. A per-unit subsidy *pivots* TC down (leading to higher output and lower price), and a licence fee shifts TC up in a parallel fashion (since it represents an increase in fixed costs). The licence fee drives profits down (to zero at point *E* in this diagram) without driving the price up or causing output to decline.

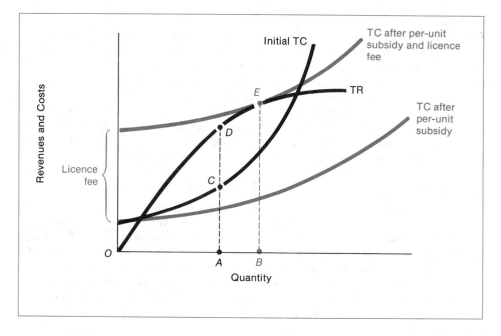

Recall that, by definition, marginal revenue equals $\Delta \text{TR}/\Delta Q$. Now, since total revenue equals price times quantity, PQ, and since $\Delta(PQ) = P\Delta Q + Q\Delta P$,

$$\text{MR} = \frac{\Delta \text{TR}}{\Delta Q} = \frac{\Delta PQ}{\Delta Q} = \frac{P\Delta Q}{\Delta Q} + \frac{Q\Delta P}{\Delta Q} = P\left(1 + \frac{Q\Delta P}{P\Delta Q}\right).$$

But the elasticity of demand, E, equals $-(\Delta Q/Q)/(\Delta P/P)$. When this definition is substituted into the expression for marginal revenue, it becomes:

$$\text{MR} = P(1 - 1/E).$$

For profit maximization, $\text{MR} = \text{MC}$, so this equation becomes:

$$\text{MC} = P(1 - 1/E).$$

Finally, by cross-division, we arrive at the monopolist's price mark-up formula:

$$\frac{P}{\text{MC}} = \frac{1}{1 - 1/E}.$$

Clearly, the closer an industry comes to perfect competition—that is, as the elasticity of demand facing each individual firm approaches infinity, making E very high—the more the mark-up shrinks toward zero. In this case, the mark-up formula reduces to $P = \text{MC}$. Economists believe that anything that can be done to raise demand elasticities is a good anti-monopoly policy. Raising the availability of substitutes is the most obvious way of accomplishing this objective, and this is one of the appealing aspects of free trade.

Monopoly and the Shifting of Pollution Charges

We conclude our discussion of monopoly by returning to the application that began this chapter—the effectiveness of pollution charges as a means of reducing emissions. Recall that the question is whether a monopoly can raise its price enough to cover any

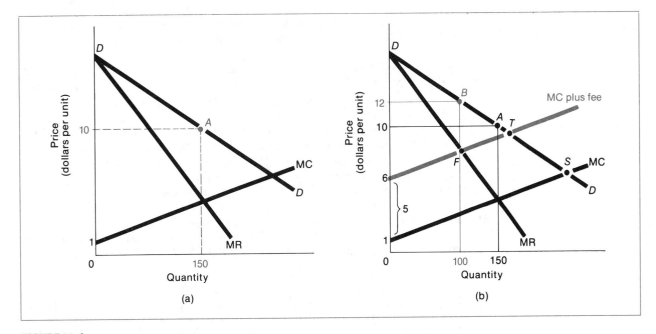

FIGURE 25–6

Monopoly Price and Output with and without a Pollution Charge

Part (a) shows the monopoly equilibrium without a pollution charge, with price equal to $10 and quantity equal to 150 units. In part (b), a $5 fee is levied on each unit of polluting output. This raises the marginal-cost curve by the amount of the fee, from the black to the green line. As a result, the output at which MC = MR falls from 150 to 100 units. Price rises from $10 to $12. Note that this $2 price rise is less than the $5 pollution fee, so the monopolist will be stuck with the remaining $3 of the charge.

pollution fees, thus shifting these charges entirely to its customers and evading them altogether.

The answer is that any firm or industry can usually shift *part* of the pollution charge to its customers. Economists argue that this shifting is a proper part of a pollution-control program since it induces consumers to redirect their purchases from goods that are highly polluting to goods that are not. For example, a significant increase in taxes on leaded gasoline with, perhaps, a simultaneous decrease in the tax on unleaded gasoline will send more motorists to the unleaded-gas pumps, and that will reduce dangerous lead emissions.

But more important for our discussion here is the other side of the matter. While some part of a pollution charge is usually paid by the consumer, *the seller will usually be stuck with some part of the charge, even if he is a monopolist.* Why? Because of the negative slope of the demand curve. If the monopoly firm raises the price of its product, it will lose customers, and that will eat into its profits. The monopoly firm will therefore do better by absorbing *some* of the charge itself rather than trying to pass all of it on to its customers.

This is illustrated in Figure 25–6. In part (a) we show the monopolist's demand, marginal-revenue, and marginal-cost curves. As in Figure 25–2, equilibrium output is 150 units—the point at which marginal revenue (MR) equals marginal cost (MC). And price is again $10—the point on the demand curve corresponding to 150 units of output (point *A*).

Now, let a charge of $5 per unit be put on the firm's polluting output, shifting the marginal-cost curve up uniformly to the curve labelled "MC plus fee" in Figure 25–6(b). Then the profit-maximizing output falls to 100 units (point *F*), for here MR = MC + pollution fee. The new output, 100 units, is lower than the precharge output, 150 units. Thus, the charge leads the monopoly firm to restrict its polluting output. The price of its product rises to $12 (point *B*), the point on the demand curve corresponding to 100 units of output. But the rise in price from $10 to $12 is less than half the $5 pollution charge per unit. Thus:

The pollution charge *does* hurt the polluter even if the polluter is a profit-maximizing monopolist, and it *does* force the monopoly to cut its polluting outputs.

No wonder the polluters' lobbyists fight so vehemently! Polluters realize that they will often be far better off with direct controls that impose a financial penalty *only* if they are caught in a violation, prosecuted, and convicted—and even then the fines are often negligible, as we will see in Chapter 32.[4]

We may note, finally, that *any* rise in a monopoly's costs will hurt its profits. The reason is exactly the same as in the case of a pollution charge. Even though the firm is a monopoly, it cannot simply raise its price and make up for any cost increase. For consumers can and will respond by buying less of the monopoly's commodity—after all, that is what the negative slope of the demand curve means.

If a monopoly already charges the price that maximizes its profits, a rise in cost will always hurt because any attempt to offset it by a price increase must reduce profit. The monopolist cannot pass on the entire burden of the cost increase to consumers.

[4]It is interesting to compare the reaction of a monopolist to a pollution fee with that of a competitive industry in the short run. Using Figure 25-6(b) to represent a situation of perfect competition with the same demand and cost conditions, we see that the industry outcome point moves from point *S* before the fee to point *T* after the fee. By comparing the gap between points *S* and *T* and the gap between points *A* and *B*, we see that the pollution fee can cut back output more in the competitive case, since *more* of the tax is passed on through higher prices in the competitive case.

Summary

1. A pure monopoly is a one-firm industry producing a product for which there are no close substitutes.
2. Monopoly can persist only if there are important cost advantages to single-firm operation or barriers to free entry. These barriers may be legal impediments (patents, licensing), some unique advantage the monopoly acquires for itself (control of a scarce resource), or the result of "dirty tricks" designed to make things tough for an entrant.
3. One important case of cost advantages is natural monopoly: instances where only one firm can survive because of important economies of large-scale production.
4. A monopoly has no supply curve. It maximizes its profit by producing an output at which its marginal revenue equals its marginal cost. Its price is given by the point on its demand curve corresponding to that output.
5. In a monopolistic industry, if demand and cost curves are the same as those of a competitive industry and if the demand curve has a negative slope and the supply curve a positive slope, output will be lower and monopoly price will be higher than those of the competitive industry. Economists regard this as an undesirable inefficiency.
6. Advertising may enable a monopoly to shift its demand curve above that of a comparable competitive industry; and through economies such as large-scale input purchases, it may be able to shift its cost curves below those of a competitive industry.
7. If a pollution charge is imposed on the product of a profit-maximizing monopoly, that monopoly will raise its price, but normally not by the full amount of the charge. That is, the monopolist will end up paying part of the pollution fee.
8. Any rise in costs generally hurts a monopolist. Because of the negatively sloping demand curve, a monopolist cannot simply pass the increase on to consumers.

Concepts for Review

Pure monopoly
Barriers to entry
Patents

Natural monopoly
Monopoly profits
Inefficiency of monopoly

P/MC mark-up
Shifting of pollution charges

Questions for Discussion

1. Which of the following industries are pure monopolies?
   a. The only supplier of water in an isolated desert town.
   b. The only supplier of Esso gas in town.
   c. The only supplier of instant cameras.
   Explain your answers.

2. Suppose a monopoly industry produces less output than a similar competitive industry. Discuss why this may be considered "socially undesirable."

3. If a competitive firm earns zero economic profits, explain why anyone would invest money in it. (*Hint:* What is the role of the opportunity cost of capital in economic profit?)

4. The following are the demand and *total*-cost schedules for Company Town Water Company, a local monopoly.

OUTPUT (litres)	PRICE (dollars per litre)	TOTAL COST (dollars)
50,000	0.14	3,000
100,000	0.13	6,500
150,000	0.11	11,000
190,000	0.10	16,000
250,000	0.08	23,000
300,000	0.06	32,000

   How much output will Company Town produce, and what price will it charge? Will it earn a profit? How much? (*Hint:* You will first have to compute its MR and MC schedules.)

5. Show from the preceding table that for the water company, marginal revenue (per 50,000-litre unit) is always less than price.

6. Suppose a tax of $12 is levied on each item sold by a monopolist, and as a result she decides to raise her price by exactly $12. Why may this decision be against her own best interest?

7. Use Figure 25–2 to show that Adam Smith was wrong when he claimed that the price a monopoly would charge is always "the highest which can be got."

8. Explain fully why you either agree or disagree with each of the following propositions. When necessary, assume constant returns to scale.
   (a) An increase in fixed costs will raise prices in a competitive industry, but not in a monopoly.
   (b) A larger portion of an excise tax is passed on to consumers in a perfectly competitive industry than in a monopoly.
   (c) It does not matter whether it is the buyers or the seller(s) that are hit with an excise tax—the real burden is the same for each group in either case. This statement is true for both perfect competition and monopoly.

9. Each team in the NHL has a monopoly in its own region for selling tickets to its games. Assume that the demand curve for tickets is a downward-sloping straight line and that the *marginal* cost of catering to another ticket buyer is zero. Assuming that only one ticket price can be set, how should that price be determined to maximize profits? Does it make sense to keep the price so high that some seats remain empty? Suppose there is an increase in the players' salaries. How would this change your answer to the preceding questions?

26

Between Competition and Monopoly

I was grateful to be able to answer promptly, and I did. I said I didn't know.

MARK TWAIN

Most productive activity in Canada, as in any advanced industrial society, can be found between the two theoretical poles considered so far: perfect competition and pure monopoly. Thus, if we want to understand the workings of the market mechanism in a real, modern economy, we must look between competition and monopoly, at the hybrid market structures first mentioned in Chapter 23: *monopolistic competition* and *oligopoly*.

Monopolistic competition is a market structure characterized by many small firms selling somewhat different products. Each firm's output is so small relative to the economy's total output of closely related and, hence, rival products that it does not expect its rivals to respond to or even to notice changes in its own behaviour. Monopolistic competition or something close to it is widespread in the retail sector of our economy; shoe stores, restaurants, and gasoline stations are good examples. We will use the theory of the firm described in Chapter 22 to analyze the price–output decision of a monopolistically competitive firm, and then consider industry-wide adjustments, as we did in Chapter 23.

Oligopoly is a market structure in which a few large firms dominate the market. Industries like steel, automobiles, and tobacco are good examples of oligopoly in our economy. The critical feature distinguishing an oligopolist from either a monopolist or a perfect competitor is that the oligopolist cares very much about what other firms in that industry do. And the resulting interdependence of decisions, we will see, makes oligopoly very hard to analyze. Consequently, economic theory contains not one but many models of oligopoly (some of which will be reviewed in this chapter), and it is often hard to know which model to apply in any particular situation. But we can say that the case for laissez faire is weakened by the existence of either monopolistic competition or oligopoly.

Some Puzzling Observations

It is easy to see that we need to study the hybrid market structures considered in this chapter, for many things we observe in the real world defy understanding within the framework of either perfect competition or pure monopoly. Here are two examples:

1. *Advertising.* While some advertising is primarily informative (for example, help-wanted ads), much of the advertising that bombards us on TV and in magazines is part of a competitive struggle for our business. Many big companies use advertising as the principal weapon in their battle for customers, and advertising budgets can constitute a very large share of their expenditures. Yet oligopolistic industries containing a few giant firms are often accused of being "uncompetitive," while farming is considered as close to perfect competition as any industry in our

economy, even though most individual farmers spend nothing at all on advertising.[1] Why do the allegedly "uncompetitive" oligopolists make such heavy use of advertising while very competitive farmers do not?

2. **Excessive number of firms.** We have all seen intersections with three or four gasoline stations in close proximity. Often, two or three of them may have no cars waiting to be served and the attendants are unoccupied. There seem to be more gas stations than the available amount of traffic warrants, with a corresponding waste of labour time, equipment, and other resources. Why do they all stay in business?

Among other things, this chapter will offer some answers to these two questions.

Monopolistic Competition

For years, most economic theorists dealt with only two workable models of the behaviour of firms: the monopoly model and the perfectly competitive model. This gap was partially filled, and the realism of economic theory was thereby greatly increased, by the work of Edward Chamberlin of Harvard University and Joan Robinson of Cambridge University during the 1930s. The market structure they analyzed is called **monopolistic competition**.

A market is said to operate under conditions of *monopolistic competition* if it satisfies four conditions, three of which are the same as those that define perfect competition: (1) *numerous participants*—that is, many buyers and sellers, all of whom are small; (2) *freedom of exit and entry*; (3) *perfect information*; and (4) *heterogeneity of products*—as far as the buyer is concerned, each seller's product is at least somewhat different from every other's.

Notice that monopolistic competition differs from perfect competition in only one respect (item 4 in the definition). While all products are identical under perfect competition, under monopolistic competition products differ from seller to seller—in quality, in packaging, or in supplementary services offered (for example, length of the guarantee, car-window washing by a gas station, and so on). The factors that serve to differentiate products need not be "real" in any objective or scientific sense. For example, differences in packaging or in associated services can and do distinguish products that are otherwise identical. On the other hand, two products may perform quite differently in quality tests, but if consumers know nothing about this difference, it is irrelevant for the market outcome.

Since products under monopolistic competition are not identical, there is no reason to expect the price of any firm's product to remain unchanged when the quantity supplied varies. Each seller, in effect, deals in a market slightly separated from the others and caters to a set of customers who vary in their "loyalty" to the particular product. If one firm raises its price somewhat, it will drive some but not all of its customers into the arms of its competitors. If it lowers its price, it may expect to attract some trade from its rivals. But since the firm's product is not a perfect substitute for its rivals' products, if the firm undercuts them slightly it will not attract away *all* their business as it would in the perfectly competitive case.

Thus, if Harriet's Hot Dog House reduces its price slightly, it will attract those customers of Sam's Sausage Shop who were nearly indifferent between the two. A bigger price cut by Harriet will bring in some customers who have a slightly greater preference for Sam's product. But even a big cut in Harriet's price will not bring her the hard-core sausage lovers who hate hot dogs. So the monopolistic competitor's

---

[1] But farmers' associations and agricultural marketing boards do spend money on advertising. Furthermore, where marketing boards and similar agencies exist and impose price controls or production quotas, competition among farmers is reduced.

demand curve is negatively sloped, like that of a monopolist, rather than horizontal, like that of a perfect competitor.

Since each product is distinguished from all others, a monopolistically competitive firm appears to have something akin to a small monopoly. Can we therefore expect it to earn more than zero economic profit? As with a perfect competitor, perhaps this is possible in the short run. But in the long run, high economic profits will attract new entrants into a monopolistically competitive market—not entrants with products *identical* to an existing firm's, but those with products sufficiently similar to hurt.

If one ice-cream parlour's location enables it to do a thriving business, it can confidently expect another, selling a *different* brand, to open nearby. When one seller adopts a new, attractive package, rivals will soon follow suit, with a slightly different design and colour of their own. In this way, freedom of entry ensures that the monopolistically competitive firm earns no higher return on its capital in the long run than it could earn elsewhere. Just as under perfect competition, price will be driven to the level of average cost, including the opportunity cost of capital. In this sense, though its product is somewhat different from that of everyone else, the firm under monopolistic competition has no more monopoly power than does a firm operating under perfect competition.

Let us now examine the process that assures that economic profits will be driven to zero in the long run, even under monopolistic competition.

Price and Output Determination under Monopolistic Competition

The short-run equilibrium of the firm under monopolistic competition differs little from the case of monopoly. Since the firm faces a downward-sloping demand curve (labelled D in Figure 26–1), its marginal-revenue (MR) curve will lie below its demand curve. Profits are maximized at the output level at which marginal revenue and marginal cost (MC) are equal. In Figure 26–1, the profit-maximizing output for a hypothetical gasoline station is 20,000 litres per week, and it sells this output at a price of 50 cents per litre (point P on the demand curve).

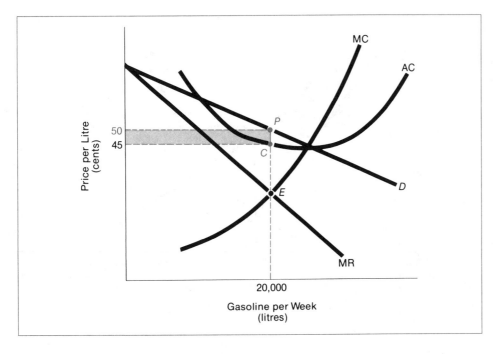

FIGURE 26–1
Short-Run Equilibrium of the Firm under Monopolistic Competition
Like any firm, a monopolistic competitor maximizes profits by equating marginal cost (MC) and marginal revenue (MR). In this example, the profit-maximizing output level is 20,000 litres per week and the profit-maximizing price is 50 cents per litre. The firm is making a profit of 5 cents per litre, which is depicted by the vertical distance from C to P.

This diagram, you will note, looks much like Figure 25–2 (page 557) for a monopoly. The only difference is that the demand curve of a monopolistic competitor is likely to be much flatter than the pure monopolist's because there are many close substitutes for the monopolistic competitor's product. If our gas station raises its price to 60 cents per litre, most of its customers will go across the street. If it lowers its price to 40 cents per litre, it will have long lines at its pumps.

The gas station depicted in Figure 26–1 is making economic profits. Since average cost at 20,000 litres per week is only 45 cents per litre (point C), the station is making a profit on gasoline sales of 5 cents per litre, or $1000 per week in total (the shaded rectangle). Under monopoly, such profits can persist. But under monopolistic competition they cannot, because new firms will be attracted into the market. While the new stations will not offer the identical product, they will offer products that are close enough to take away some business from our firm (for example, they may sell Sunoco or Shell gasoline instead of Esso).

When more firms share the market, the demand curve facing any individual firm must fall. But how far? The answer is basically the same as it was under perfect competition: until the most that the profit-maximizing firm can earn is zero economic profit, for only then will entry cease.

Figure 26–2 depicts the same monopolistically competitive firm as in Figure 26–1 *after* the adjustment to the long run is complete. The demand curve has been pushed down so far that when the firm equates MC and MR in order to maximize profits (point E), it simultaneously equates price (P) and average cost (AC) so that profits are zero (point P). As compared with the short-run equilibrium depicted in Figure 26–1, price in long-run equilibrium is *lower* (47 cents per litre versus 50 cents per litre), there are *more firms* in the industry, and each firm is producing a *smaller* output (15,625 litres versus 20,000 litres) at a *higher* average cost per litre (47 cents versus 45 cents).[2] In general:

Long-run equilibrium under monopolistic competition requires that the firm's demand curve be tangent to its average-cost curve.

[2]EXERCISE: Show that if the demand curve fell still further, the firm would incur a loss. What would then happen in the long run?

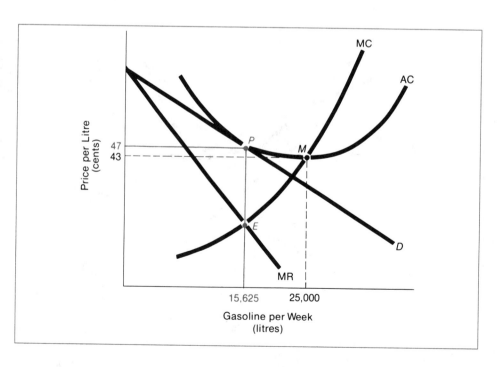

FIGURE 26–2
Long-Run Equilibrium of the Firm under Monopolistic Competition
In this diagram the cost curves are identical to those of Figure 26–1, but the demand curve (and hence also the MR curve) has been depressed by the entry of new competitors. When the firm maximizes profits by equating marginal revenue and marginal cost (point E), its average cost is equal to its price (47 cents), so economic profits are zero. For this reason, the diagram depicts a *long-run* equilibrium position.

Why? Because if the two curves intersected, there would be output levels at which price exceeded average cost, which means that economic profits could be earned and there would be an influx of new substitute products. Similarly, if the average-cost curve failed to touch the demand curve altogether, the firm would be unable to obtain returns equal to those that its capital can get elsewhere, and firms would leave the industry.

This analysis of entry is quite similar to the perfectly competitive case. Moreover, the notion that firms under monopolistic competition earn exactly zero economic profits seems to correspond fairly well to what we see in the real world. Filling-station operators, whose market has the characteristics of monopolistic competition, do not earn notably higher profits than do small farmers, who operate under conditions closer to perfect competition.

The Excess-Capacity Theorem and Resource Allocation

But there is one important difference between perfect and monopolistic competition. Look at Figure 26–2 again. The tangency point between the average-cost and demand curves, point P, occurs along the *negatively sloping portion* of the average-cost curve, since only there does the AC curve have the same (negative) slope as the demand curve. If the AC curve is U-shaped, the tangency point must therefore lie above and to the left of the *minimum point* on the average-cost curve, point M. By contrast, under perfect competition the firm's demand curve is horizontal, so tangency must take place at the minimum point on the average-cost curve, as is easily confirmed by referring back to Figure 23–9(a) on page 516. This observation leads to the following important conclusion:

Under monopolistic competition, the firm in the long run will tend to produce an output lower than that which minimizes its unit costs, and hence unit costs of the monopolistic competitor will be higher than is necessary. Since the level of output corresponding to minimum average cost is naturally considered to be the firm's optimal capacity, this result has been called the **excess-capacity theorem of monopolistic competition**.

It follows that if every firm under monopolistic competition were to expand its output, cost per unit of output would be reduced. But we must be careful about jumping to policy conclusions from that observation. It does *not* follow that *every* monopolistically competitive firm *should* produce more. After all, such an overall increase in industry output would mean that a smaller portion of the economy's resources would be available for other uses, and from the information at hand we have no way of knowing whether that would leave us ahead or behind in terms of social benefits.

Yet the situation represented in Figure 26–2 can still be interpreted to represent a substantial *inefficiency*. While it is not clear that society would gain if *every* firm were to achieve lower costs by expanding its production, society *can* save resources if firms combine into a smaller number of larger companies that produce the same total output. For example, suppose that in the situation shown in Figure 26–2 there are 32 monopolistically competitive firms each selling 15,625 litres of gas per week. The total cost of this output, according to the figures given in the diagram, would be

$$\text{(Number of firms)} \times \text{(Output per firm)} \times \text{(Cost per unit)}$$
$$= 32 \times 15,625 \times \$0.47 = \$235,000.$$

If, instead, the number of stations were cut to 20, and each sold 25,000 litres, total production would be unchanged. But total costs would fall to $20 \times 25,000 \times \$0.43 = \$215,000$, a net saving of $\$20,000$ *for the same total output.*

This result is not dependent on the particular numbers used in our illustration. It follows directly from the observation that lowering the cost per unit must always reduce the total cost of producing any *given* industry output. The excess-capacity theorem explains one of the puzzles mentioned at the start of this chapter. The intersection with four filling stations, where two could serve the available customers with little increase in delays and at lower costs, is a practical example of excess capacity.

The excess-capacity theorem seems to imply that there are too many sellers in monopolistically competitive markets and that society would benefit from a reduction in their numbers. However, such a conclusion would be a bit hasty. Even if a smaller number of larger firms could reduce costs, society may not benefit from the change because it would leave consumers a smaller range of choice. Since all products are at least slightly different under monopolistic competition, a reduction in the number of firms means that the number of different products falls as well. We achieve greater efficiency at the cost of greater standardization. In some cases consumers may agree that this trade-off represents a net gain, particularly where the variety of products available was initially so great that it served only to confuse them. But for some products, many consumers might argue that the diversity of choice is worth the extra cost involved. After all, we would probably save money on clothing if every student were forced to wear the same uniform. But since the uniform is likely to be too hot for Student A, too cool for Student B, and aesthetically displeasing to everyone, would the cost saving really be a net benefit?

Oligopoly

In terms of the dollar value of all manufactured goods produced in our economy, first place must be assigned to our final market form—**oligopoly**. An *oligopoly* is a market dominated by a few sellers, at least several of which are large enough relative to the total market to be able to influence the market price.

An **oligopoly** is a market dominated by a few sellers, at least several of which are large enough relative to the total market to be able to influence the market price.

In highly developed economies, it is not monopoly, but oligopoly, that is virtually synonymous with "big business." Any oligopolistic industry includes a group of giant firms, each of which keeps a watchful eye on the actions of the others.[3] It is under oligopoly that rivalry among firms takes its most direct and active form. Here one encounters such actions and reactions as the frequent introduction of new products, free samples, and aggressive—if not downright nasty—advertising campaigns. One firm's price decision is likely to elicit a cry of pain from its rivals, and firms are engaged in a continuing battle in which strategies are planned day by day and each major decision can be expected to induce a direct response.

The manager of a large oligopolistic firm who has occasion to study economics is somewhat taken aback by the notion of perfect competition, because it is devoid of all harsh competitive activity as he knows it. Remember that under perfect competition the managers of firms make no price decisions—they simply accept the price dictated by market forces and adjust their output accordingly. As we observed at the beginning of the chapter, a competitive firm does not advertise; it adopts no sales gimmicks; it does not even know who most of its competitors are. But since oligopolists are not as dependent on market forces, they do not enjoy such luxuries. They worry about prices, spend fortunes on advertising, and try to understand their rivals' behaviour patterns.

The reasons for such divergent behaviour should be clear. First, a perfectly competitive firm can sell all it wants at the current market price. So why should it waste money on advertising? By contrast, Ford and Chrysler cannot sell all the cars they want at the current price. Since their demand curves are negatively sloped, if they

---

[3]Notice that nothing is said in the definition about the degree of product differentiation. Some oligopolies sell products that are essentially identical (such as steel plate from different steelmakers), while others sell products that are quite different in the eyes of consumers (for example, Chevrolets, Fords, and Plymouths).

want to sell more, they must either reduce prices or advertise more (to shift their demand curves outward).

Second, since the public believes that the products supplied by firms in a perfectly competitive industry are identical, if Firm A advertises its product, the advertisement is just as likely to bring customers to Firm B. Under oligopoly, however, products are usually not identical. Ford advertises to try to convince consumers that its automobiles are better than GM's or Toyota's. And if the advertising campaign succeeds, GM and Toyota will be hurt and probably will respond with more advertising of their own. Thus, it is the firm in an oligopoly with differentiated products that is forced to compete via advertising, while the perfectly competitive firm gains little or nothing by doing so.

Why Oligopolistic Behaviour Is So Hard to Analyze

The relative freedom of choice in pricing of at least the largest firms in an oligopolistic industry and the necessity for them to take direct account of their rivals' responses are potentially troublesome. Producers that are able to influence the market price may find it expedient to adjust their outputs to secure more favourable prices. As in the case of monopoly, such actions are likely to be at the expense of the consumer and detrimental to the economy's efficient use of resources.

It is not easy to reach definite conclusions about resource allocation under oligopoly, however. The reason is that oligopoly is much more difficult to analyze than the other forms of economic organization. The difficulty arises from the interdependent nature of oligopolistic decisions. For example, Ford's management knows that its actions will probably lead to reactions by General Motors, which in turn may require a readjustment in Ford's plans, thereby producing a modification in GM's response, and so on. Where such a sequence of moves and countermoves may lead is difficult enough to ascertain. But the fact that Ford executives know all this in advance and may take it into account in making their initial decision makes even that first step difficult, if not impossible, to analyze and predict.

The truth is that almost anything can happen under oligopoly, and sometimes does. Early American railway kings went so far as to employ gangs of hoodlums who engaged in pitched battles to try to prevent the operation of rival lines. At the other extreme, overt or more subtle forms of collusion have been employed to avoid rivalry altogether—to transform an oligopolistic industry, at least temporarily, into a monopolistic one. Arrangements designed to make it possible for the firms to live and let live have also been utilized: Price leadership (see below) is one example; an agreement allocating geographic areas among firms is another.

Because of this rich variety of behaviour patterns it is not surprising that economists have been unable to agree on a single, widely accepted model of oligopoly behaviour. Nor should they. Since oligopolies in the real world are so diverse, oligopoly models in the theoretical world should also come in various shapes and sizes. The theory of oligopoly contains some really remarkable pieces of economic analysis, some of which we will review in the following sections.

A Shopping List

An introductory course cannot hope to explain all the different models of oligopoly; nor would that serve any purpose but to confuse you. Since economists differ in their opinions about which approaches to oligopoly theory are the most interesting and promising, we offer in this section a quick catalogue of some models of oligopoly behaviour. Then, in the remainder of the chapter, we will describe in greater detail a few other models.

Ignore Interdependence
One simple approach to the problem of oligopolistic interdependence is to assume

that the oligopolists themselves ignore it: that they behave as if their actions will not elicit reactions from their rivals. It *is* possible that an oligopolist, finding the "if they think that we think that they think" chain of reasoning too complex, will decide to ignore rivals' behaviour. The firm may then just maximize profits on the assumption that its decisions will not affect those of its rivals. In this case, the analysis of oligopoly is identical to the analysis of monopoly in the previous chapter.

Strategic Interaction

While it is possible that *some* oligopolies ignore interdependence *some* of the time, it is very unlikely that such models offer a general explanation for the behaviour of *most* oligopoly behaviour *most* of the time. The reason is quite simple. Because they operate in the same market, the price and output decisions of the makers of Brand X and Brand Y detergent *really are* interdependent. Suppose, for example, that the management of Brand X, Inc., decides to cut its price to $1.05 per box (on the assumption that Brand Y, Inc., will continue to charge $1.12 per box), to manufacture five million boxes per year, and to spend $1 million per year on advertising. It may find itself surprised when Brand Y, Inc., cuts its price to $1 per box, raises production to eight million boxes per year, and sponsors the Stanley Cup. If so, Brand X's profits will suffer, and the company will wish it had not cut its price. Most important for our purposes here, it will learn not to ignore interdependence in the future. For many oligopolies, then, competition resembles military operations involving tactics, strategies, moves, and countermoves. Thus it seems imperative to consider models that deal explicitly with oligopolistic interdependence. We will study several such models, probably the most notable of them being those provided by the theory of games.

Cartels

The opposite end of the spectrum from ignoring interdependence is for all the firms in an oligopoly to collude overtly with one another, thereby transforming the industry into a giant monopoly—a **cartel**.

A **cartel** is a group of sellers of a product who have joined together to control its production, sale, and price in the hope of obtaining the advantages of monopoly.

    A notable example of the formation of a cartel is the Organization of Petroleum Exporting Countries (OPEC), which first began to make decisions in unison in 1973. OPEC, for a while, was one of the most spectacularly successful cartels in history. By restricting output, the member nations managed to quadruple the price of oil in 1973–74. Then, unlike most cartels, which come apart in internal bickering or for other reasons, OPEC held together through two worldwide recessions and a variety of unsettling political events, and struck again with huge price increases in 1979–80; only in the mid-1980s did it run into trouble.

    But the story of OPEC is not the norm. Cartels are not easy to organize and are even more difficult to preserve. Firms find it hard to agree on such things as the amount by which each will reduce its output in order to help push up the price. Yet for a cartel to survive, each member must agree to produce no more than some level of output that has been assigned to it by the group of colluding firms. Once price is driven up and profitability increased, however, it becomes tempting for each seller to offer secret discounts in order to lure some of the profitable business away from other members of the cartel. Indeed, some of this happened to OPEC in the early 1980s. When this happens or is even suspected by cartel members, it is often the beginning of the end of the collusive arrangement. Each member begins suspecting the others and is tempted to cut price first, before the others beat it to the punch.

    Therefore, cartels usually adopt elaborate policing arrangements, in effect spying on each member firm to make sure it does not sell more than it is supposed to or at a price lower than that chosen by the cartel. This means that cartels are unlikely to succeed or to last very long if the firms sell many varied products whose prices are difficult to compare and whose outputs are difficult to keep track of. In addition, if prices are often negotiated customer by customer and special discounts are frequent, a cartel may be almost impossible to arrange.

Many economists consider cartels to be one of the least desirable forms of market organization. If a cartel is successful, it may end up charging the monopoly price and obtaining monopoly profits. But because the firms do not actually combine their operations but continue to produce separately, the cartel offers the public no offsetting benefits in the form of economies of large-scale production. For these and other reasons, open collusion among firms is illegal in Canada, as we will see in Chapter 31, and outright cartel arrangements are rarely found. There are some exceptions: firms are allowed to collude in making export arrangements, and collusion is in some cases essentially enforced through the government regulation process. In many other countries, though, cartels are common.

Price Leadership and Tacit Collusion

Though overt collusion is quite rare, some observers think that *tacit collusion* is quite common among oligopolists in our economy. Oligopolists who do not want to rock what amounts to a very profitable boat may seek to develop some indirect way of communicating with one another and signalling their intentions. Each tacitly colluding firm hopes that if it behaves in a way that does not make things too difficult for its competitors, then its rivals will return the favour.

One common example of tacit collusion is **price leadership**, an arrangement in which one firm in the industry is, in effect, assigned the task of making pricing decisions for the entire group. It is expected that other firms will adopt the prices set by the price leader, even though there is no explicit agreement, only tacit consent. Often the price leader will be the largest firm in the industry. But in some price-leadership arrangements the role of leader may rotate from one firm to another.

Price leadership *does* overcome the problem of oligopolistic interdependence, though it is not the only possible way of doing so. If Brand X, Inc., is the price leader for the detergent industry, it can predict how Brand Y, Inc., will react to any price increases it announces. (Brand Y will match the increases.) Similarly, Brand Z executives will be able to predict Brand Y's behaviour as long as the price-leadership arrangement holds up.

But one problem besetting price leadership is that, while the oligopolists as a group may benefit by avoiding a damaging **price war**, one of them may benefit more than the others. The firm that is the price leader is clearly in a better position to maximize its own profits than are any of the rival firms, which must simply fall in line. It is thus the responsibility of the price leader to take into account its rivals' welfare when making its price decision—or else it may find itself dethroned! For this reason, a price-leadership arrangement, if effective, can lead to the same sort of price and production decisions as would a cartel. Alternatively, leadership can break down entirely.

> Under **price leadership**, one firm sets the price for the industry and the others follow.

> In a **price war** each competing firm is determined to sell at a price that is lower than the prices of its rivals, usually regardless of whether that price covers the pertinent cost. Typically, in such a price war Firm A cuts its price below Firm B's; then Firm B retaliates by undercutting Firm A, and so on and on until one or more of the firms surrender and let themselves be undersold.

Sales Maximization

Early in our analysis of the theory of the firm, we discussed the hypothesis that firms try to maximize profits and noted that other objectives are possible (see pages 483–84). Among these alternative goals, the one that has achieved the most attention is **sales maximization**.

Modern industrial firms are managed and owned by entirely different groups of people. The managers are paid executives who work for the company on a full-time basis and may grow to identify their own welfare with that of the company. The owners may be a large and diffuse group of shareholders, most of whom own only a tiny fraction of the outstanding stock, take little interest in the operations of the company, and do not feel that the company is "theirs" in any real sense. In such a situation, it is not entirely implausible that the company's decisions will be influenced more heavily by management's goals than by the goal of the owners (which is, presumably, to maximize profit).

FIGURE 26-3
Sales-Maximization
Equilibrium

A firm that wishes to maximize sales revenue will expand output until marginal revenue (MR) is zero—point *B* in the diagram, where output is 3.75 million boxes per year. This is a greater output level than it would choose if it were interested in maximizing profits. In that case, it would select point *A*, where MC = MR, and produce only 2.5 million boxes. Since the demand curve is downward sloping, the price corresponding to point *B* (75 cents) must be less than the price corresponding to point *A* ($1).

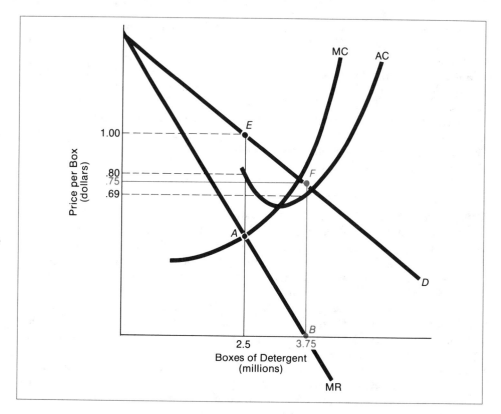

There is some statistical evidence, for example, that managers' salaries and prestige may be tied more directly to the company's *size*, as measured by its dollar sales volume, than to its *profits*. Therefore, the firm's managers may select a price–output combination that maximizes sales rather than profits. But does sales-revenue maximization lead to different decisions than does profit maximization? We shall see now that the answer is yes.

Figure 26–3 is a diagram that should be familiar by now. It shows the marginal-cost (MC) and average-cost (AC) curves for a firm—in this case Brand X, Inc.—along with its demand and marginal-revenue (MR) curves. We have used such diagrams before and know that if the company wants to maximize profits, it will select point *A*, where MC = MR. This means that it will produce 2.5 million boxes of detergent per year and sell them at a price of $1 each (point *E*). Since average cost at this level of output is only 80 cents per box, profit per unit is 20 cents. Total profits are therefore $0.20 × 2,500,000 = $500,000 per year. This is the highest attainable profit level for Brand X, Inc.

Now what if Brand X wants to maximize sales revenue instead? In this case, it will want to keep producing until MR is depressed to *zero*; that is, it will select point *B*. Why? By definition, MR is the *additional* revenue obtained by raising output by one unit. If the firm wishes to maximize revenue, then any time it finds that MR is positive it will want to increase output further, and any time it finds that MR is negative it will want to decrease output. Only when MR = 0 can the maximum sales revenue have possibly been achieved.[4]

Thus if Brand X, Inc. is a sales maximizer, it will produce 3.75 million boxes of detergent per year (point *B*), and charge 75 cents per box (point *F*). Since average costs at this level of production are only 69 cents per box, profit per unit is 6 cents and, with 3.75 million units sold, total profit is $225,000. Naturally, this level of profit is

---

[4]The logic here is exactly the same as the logic that led to the conclusion that a firm maximizes *profits* by setting *marginal profit* equal to zero. If you need review, consult Chapter 22, especially pages 488–89.

less than what the firm can achieve if it reduces output to the profit-maximizing level. But this is not the firm's goal. Its sales revenue at point B is 75 cents per unit times 3.75 million units, or $2,812,500, whereas at point A it was only $2,500,000 (2.5 million units at $1 each). What we conclude, then, is that:

If a firm is maximizing sales revenue, it will produce more output and charge a lower price than it would if it were maximizing profits.

We see clearly in Figure 26–3 that this result holds for Brand X, Inc. But does it always hold? The answer is yes. Look again at Figure 26–3, but ignore the numbers on the axes. At point A, where $MR = MC$, marginal revenue must be positive because it is equal to marginal cost (which, we may assume, is *always* positive). At point B, MR is equal to zero. Since the marginal-revenue curve is negatively sloped, the point where it reaches zero (point B) must necessarily correspond to a higher level of output than the point where it cuts the marginal-cost curve (point A). Thus, sales-maximizing firms always produce more than profit-maximizing firms and, to sell this greater volume of output, they must charge a lower price.

There are other differences between sales-revenue-maximizing firms and profit-maximizing firms; for example, they can react differently when confronted by certain taxes. One of the questions at the end of this chapter will lead you to appreciate some of the implications of these differences for tax policy.

Game Theory

Game theory, contributed in 1944 by mathematician John von Neumann (1903–1957) and economist Oskar Morgenstern (1902–1977), adopts a more imaginative approach than any other analysis of oligopoly. It attacks the issue of interdependence directly by assuming that each firm's managers proceed on the assumption *that their rivals are extremely ingenious decision-makers*. In this model, each oligopolist is seen as a competing player in a game of strategy. Since managers believe their opponents will always adopt the most profitable countermove to any move they make, they seek the optimal defensive strategy.

Two fundamental concepts of game theory are the *strategy* and the *payoff matrix*. A strategy represents an operational plan for one of the participants. In its simplest form it may refer to just one of a participant's possible decisions—for example, "I will add to my product line a car with a TV set that the driver can watch," or "I will cut the price of my car to $9500." Since much of the game-theoretic analysis of oligopoly has focussed on an oligopoly of two firms—a *duopoly*—we illustrate the payoff matrix for a two-person game in Table 26–1.

This matrix is a table of numbers reporting the profits that each of two rival firms, the Atlantic (A) and Pacific (P) companies, can expect to earn, depending on the pricing strategy that each adopts (not knowing the secret price the other is offering customers). The table is read like a mileage chart. For example, the upper left-

TABLE 26–1
A Payoff Matrix

		Pacific's Strategy			
		High Price		Low Price	
Atlantic's Strategy	High Price	A gets 10	P gets 10	A gets -2	P gets 12
	Low Price	A gets 12	P gets -2	A gets 3	P gets 3

At the Frontier: Game Theory and Entry Deterrence

Game theory has moved toward domination of research on the theory of oligopoly. An example is the game-theory model of strategic decisions by firms already inside an industry ("old firms") whose primary purpose is to prevent the entry of new rivals ("new firms"). One way in which this can be done is for the old firm to build a bigger factory than it would want to construct otherwise, in the belief that the output of the excessive factory capacity will force prices down and, in the process, make entry unprofitable. The old firm recognizes that it is giving up some profit compared to what it would earn if no new firm even threatened to enter. However, it hopes that it will be better off than if entry did occur.

Some hypothetical numbers and a graph typical of those used in game theory will make the story clear. The old firm has two options: to build a small factory or a big one. The potential new firm also has two options: to open for business (that is, to enter) or not to enter. The accompanying graph shows the four possible combinations of decisions and the consequent profits or losses the two firms may expect in each case.

The graph shows (fourth line) that the best arrangement of all for the old firm is one in which it builds a small factory and the new firm decides not to enter. In that case, the old firm will earn $6 million while the new firm (since it never starts up) will earn nothing. However, if the old firm does decide to build a small factory (third line), it can be pretty sure the new firm *will* open up for business because then that new firm will earn $2 million (rather than zero), and in the process, it will reduce the old firm's profits to $2 million.

On the other hand, if the old firm selects its other option and builds a big factory, the increased output will depress prices and profits. The old firm will now earn only $4 million even if the new firm stays out (second line), while *each* firm will *lose* $2 million (first line) if the new firm enters. Obviously, if the old firm builds a big factory, the new firm will be better off staying out of the business rather than subjecting itself to a $2 million loss.

What size factory, then, will it pay the old firm to build? When one considers the matter, it becomes clear that it will be profitable for the old firm to build the large factory with its excessive capacity. Then it can expect the new firm to stay out, and the big factory will enable the old firm to earn $4 million. In contrast, if a small factory is built, the new firm will open for business and reduce the old firm's profit to $2 million.

Thus, taking the new firm's strategic choices into account, it is obvious that it pays the old firm to build the oversized factory and take the $4 million in profits it thereby earns by deterring the other firm from entering. *Moral:* Wasting money on excess capacity may not be wasteful in terms of the oligopolist's self-interest.

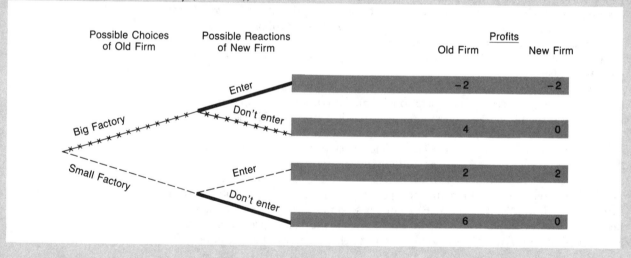

This graph shows the possible choices of an old firm and the possible responses of a potential entrant. If the old firm builds a big factory, the entrant will avoid $2 million in losses by staying out, leaving the old firm with $4 million in profit (asterisk lines). On the other hand, if the old firm builds a small factory, the new firm will enter (dashed lines), so the old firm would be worse off, with only $2 million in profit.

hand cell indicates that, if both firms decide to charge high prices, both A and P will earn $10 million.

The choice open to each firm is to charge either a "high price" or a "low price," and the payoff matrix reports the profits each of the firms can expect to earn, given its own pricing choice and that of its rival. We see that, if either firm succeeds in charging a low price when the other does not, the price cutter will actually raise its profit to $12 million (presumably by capturing enough of the market) and drive its rival to a $2 million loss. However, if *both* firms offer low prices, each will be left with a modest $3 million profit.

How does game theory analyze optimal strategy choice? We may envision the management of say, firm A, reasoning as follows: "If I choose a high-price strategy, the worst that can happen to me is that my competitor will select the low-price counter-strategy, which will cut my return to minus $2 million. Similarly, if I select a low-price strategy, the worst outcome for which I must be prepared is $3 million."

How can the management of firm A best protect itself from trouble in these circumstances? Game theory suggests that A should select among strategies on the basis of the *minimum* payoff to each, just as described above. It should pick the strategy whose minimum payoff is higher than that for any other strategy. This is called the **maximin criterion**: one seeks the *maxi*mum of the *mini*mum payoffs to the various available strategies. In this case, the maximin strategy for each firm is to offer a low price and earn a profit of $3 million.

Notice that, in this case, fear of what its rival will do virtually forces each firm to offer a low price and to forgo the high ($10 million) profit each could earn if it could trust the other to stick to a high price. This example illustrates why many observers conclude that, particularly where the number of firms is small, firms should not be permitted to confer about or exchange information on prices. The same sort of analysis also helps to explain how competition limits profits and benefits consumers, and why price-cartel arrangements are fragile.

A payoff matrix with a pattern like that in Table 26–1 has many other interesting applications. It is used to show how people make each other (and themselves) worse off by driving polluting cars in the absence of laws requiring emission controls. Each does so because he or she does not trust other drivers to install emission controls voluntarily, and this is the analytical basis for making emission controls compulsory.

There is still another interpretation, one that gave this matrix the name by which it is known to game theorists: "the prisoners' dilemma." Here, instead of a two-firm industry, the underlying scenario is that of a pair of burglars captured by the police and taken for interrogation into two separate rooms. Each has two strategy options: to deny the charge or to confess. If both deny it, both go free, for the police have no other evidence. But if one confesses and the other does not, the silent partner can expect the key to his cell to be thrown away. The maximin solution, then, is for both to confess and receive the moderate sentence that this option would elicit.

There is, of course, a great deal more to game theory than we have been able to suggest in a few paragraphs. We have sought only to suggest a little of its flavour. Game theory provides, for example, an illuminating analysis of coalitions, indicating, for cases involving more than two firms, which firms would do well to align themselves together against which others. The theory of games has also been used to analyze a variety of complicated problems outside the realm of oligopoly theory. It has been employed in management-training programs and by a number of government agencies. It is used in political science and in formulating military strategy. It has been presented here to offer the reader a glimpse of the type of work that is taking place on the frontiers of economic analysis and to suggest how economists think about complex analytical problems.

Monopolistic Competition, Oligopoly, and Public Welfare

How good or bad, from the viewpoint of the general welfare, is the performance of firms that are monopolistically competitive or oligopolistic?

We have seen that their performance *can* leave much to be desired. For example, the excess-capacity theorem showed us that monopolistic competition can lead to

The New Theory of Contestable Markets

Perfect competition has long been used as a standard for the structure and behaviour of an industry, though it is widely recognized to be unattainable in reality. Recently, some economists have tried to supplement this concept with the aid of a generalized criterion, called a *perfectly contestable market*. Some markets that contain a few relatively large firms may be highly contestable, though they are certainly not perfectly competitive. Because perfect competition requires a large number of firms, all of them negligible in size relative to the size of the industry, no industry with economies of large-scale production can be perfectly competitive.

A market is defined as perfectly contestable if firms can enter it and, if they choose, exit without losing the money they invested. Note that the crucial issue is not the amount of capital that is required to enter the industry but whether or not an entrant can get his investment out if he wishes—whether that expenditure is a *sunk* cost. For example, if entry involves investing in highly mobile capital—such as airplanes, barges, or cars—the entrant may be able to exit quickly and cheaply. If a car-rental agency enters the Vancouver market and finds business disappointing, it can easily transfer its cars to, say, Winnipeg.

A profitable market that is contestable is, therefore, attractive to *potential* entrants. Because of the absence of barriers to entry or exit, firms undertake little risk by going into such a market. If their entry turns out to have been a mistake, they can move to another market without significant loss.

Performance of Contestable Markets

The constant threat of entry elicits good performance by oligopolists, or even by monopolists, in a perfectly contestable market. In particular, highly contestable markets have at least two desirable characteristics.

First, profits exceeding the opportunity cost of capital are eliminated in the long run by freedom of entry, just as they are in a perfectly competitive market. If the current opportunity cost of capital is 12 percent while the firms in a contestable market are earning a return of 18 percent, new firms will enter the market, expand the industry's outputs, and drive down the prices of its products to the point where all excess profit has been removed. To avoid this outcome, established firms must expand to a level that precludes excess profit.

Second, inefficient enterprises cannot survive in a perfectly contestable industry because cost inefficiencies invite replacement of the incumbents by entrants who can provide the same outputs at lower cost and lower prices. Only firms operating at the lowest possible cost, using the most efficient techniques, can survive.

In sum, firms in a perfectly contestable market will be forced to operate as efficiently as possible and to charge prices as low as long-run financial survival permits. Soon after the contestable-market theory was first published, the idea became widely used by courts and government agencies concerned with the performance of business firms. This occurred because the theory provides workable guidelines for improved or acceptable behaviour in industries in which economies of scale mean that only a small number of firms can or should operate.

The concept is particularly relevant for Canada, if considered in the context of tariff policy. The government can ensure that many markets within Canada become contestable if it lowers existing tariffs. Indeed, if the government established a record of behaviour along these lines, even the *threat* of tariff reduction might make other markets contestable.

---

inefficiently high production costs. Similarly, because market forces may not be sufficiently powerful to restrain oligopolists' behaviour, their prices and outputs may differ substantially from those that are socially optimal. Moreover, there are those who believe that misleading advertising by corporate giants often distorts the judgments of consumers, leading them to buy things they do not need and would otherwise not want. Others argue that much advertising simply cancels out advertising by rival brands. Thus, even if consumer choices are not significantly distorted, many resources may simply be wasted. It is also said that such corporate giants wield political power, economic power, and power over the minds of consumers—and that all of these undermine the beneficent workings of Smith's invisible hand. Finally, because many large firms in Canada are foreign owned, it is sometimes feared that the way in which they operate is even more likely to ignore the general welfare of this country.

Because oligopolistic behaviour is so varied, we cannot generalize with confidence. Since one oligopolist decides on price, output, and advertising in a manner very different from another, the implications for social welfare vary from case to case.

Yet, recent analysis has provided one theoretical case in which both the behaviour and the quality of performance of an oligopolistic or monopolistically competitive firm can be predicted and judged unambiguously. This is the case in which entry into or exit from the market is costless and unimpeded. In such a case, called a **perfectly contestable market** (see the boxed insert opposite), the constant threat of entry forces even the largest firm to behave well—to produce efficiently and never to overcharge. For if that firm is inefficient or sets its prices too high, it will be threatened with replacement by an entrant who offers to serve customers more inexpensively.

A market is **perfectly contestable** if entry and exit are costless and unimpeded.

Of course, no industry is perfectly contestable, and many are not even nearly so. But in those industries that are highly contestable—that is, in which entry and exit costs are negligible—market forces can do a good job of forcing business to behave in the manner that most effectively promotes the public interest. And where an industry is not very contestable but there are ways to reduce entry and exit costs, the new theory of contestable markets suggests that this may sometimes be a more promising approach than any attempt by government to interfere with the behaviour of the oligopolistic firms in order to improve their performance.

Summary

1. Under monopolistic competition, there are numerous small buyers and sellers; each firm's product is at least somewhat different from every other firm's product—that is, each firm has a partial "monopoly" of some product characteristics and thus a downward-sloping demand curve; there is freedom of entry and exit; and there is perfect information.
2. In long-run equilibrium under monopolistic competition, free entry eliminates economic profits by forcing the firm's demand curve into a position of tangency with its average-cost curve. Therefore, output will be below the point at which average cost is lowest. This is why monopolistic competitors are said to have "excess capacity."
3. An oligopolistic industry is composed of a few large firms selling similar products in the same market.
4. Under oligopoly, each firm carefully watches the major decisions of its rivals and will often plan counterstrategies. As a result, rivalry is often vigorous and direct, and the outcome is difficult to predict.
5. One model of oligopolistic behaviour assumes that the oligopolists ignore interdependence and simply maximize profits or sales revenue. Another assumes that they join together to form a cartel and thus act like a monopoly. A third possibility is price leadership, where one firm sets prices and the others follow suit. A fourth is that each firm assumes that its rivals will adopt the optimal countermove to any move it makes.
6. A firm that maximizes sales revenue will continue producing up to the point where marginal revenue is driven down to zero. Consequently, a sales maximizer will produce more than a profit maximizer and will charge a lower price.
7. Game theory provides new tools for analyzing business strategies under conditions of oligopoly.
8. Monopolistic competition and oligopoly can be harmful to the general welfare. But these harmful effects can be limited if the market is contestable, that is, if entry and exit are not too costly. The threat of entry can lead to fairly small departures from optimal performance.

Concepts for Review

Monopolistic competition	Cartel	Maximin criterion
Excess-capacity theorem	Price leadership	Perfectly contestable markets
Oligopoly	Sales maximization	
Oligopolistic interdependence	Game theory	

Questions for Discussion

1. How many real industries can you name that are oligopolies? How many that operate under monopolistic competition? Perfect competition? Which of these is hardest to find in reality? Why do you think this is so?

2. Consider some of the products that are widely advertised on TV. By what kind of firm is each produced—a perfectly competitive firm, an oligopolistic firm, or what? How many major products can you think of that are *not* advertised on TV?

3. In what ways may the small retail sellers of the following products differentiate their goods from those of their rivals to make themselves monopolistic competitors: hamburgers, radios, cosmetics?

4. Discussion Question 4 at the end of Chapter 25 presented cost and demand data for a monopolist and asked you to find the profit-maximizing solution. Use these same data to find the sales-maximizing solution. Are the answers different? Explain.

5. Suppose that both the profit-maximizing firm and the sales-revenue-maximizing firm in the preceding question are hit with a licence fee of $1000. Explain how their responses will differ.

6. Explain why you either agree or disagree with the following statement: "If a monopoly firm were found to be operating at a price–quantity combination on the *inelastic* portion of its demand curve, we would know that the firm must be a sales-revenue maximizer, not a profit maximizer.

7. Explain how the "prisoners' dilemma" concept can shed light on the issues of arms build-up and disarmament.

8. A new entrant, Bargain Airways, cuts air fares between Eastwich and Westwich by 20 percent. Biggie Airlines, which has been operating on this route, responds by cutting fares by 35 percent. What does Biggie hope to achieve?

9. If air transportation is perfectly contestable, why will Biggie fail to achieve the ultimate goal of its price cut?

10. If there were no regulation, which of the following industries would be most likely to be contestable?
    a. Aluminum production.
    b. Barge transportation.
    c. Automobile manufacturing.
    d. Air transportation.
    Explain your answers.

11. Some unions operate like sales-revenue maximizers—they demand a wage that maximizes the total income of their workers. If the demand for a union's labour is given by the function of $4 - w/3$, where w is the wage rate, what value of the wage maximizes total income?

27

The Market Mechanism: Shortcomings and Remedies

What does the market do well, and what does it do poorly? These questions constitute the central theme of our study of microeconomics, and we are by now well on our way toward getting some answers. We began in Chapters 23 and 24 by explaining and extolling the workings of Adam Smith's invisible hand—the mechanism by which a perfectly competitive economy allocates resources efficiently without any guidance from government. While the theoretical model studied there was an idealized one, observation of the real world confirms the accomplishments of the market mechanism. Free-market economies have achieved levels of output, productive efficiency, variety in available consumer goods, and general prosperity that are unprecedented in history and that are now the envy of economies that had once relied primarily on central planning.

Yet the market mechanism also displays some glaring weaknesses. One of these—the fact that large and powerful business firms can interfere with the invisible hand in a way that leads to both concentration of wealth and misallocation of resources—was the subject of Chapters 25 and 26. Now we take a more comprehensive view of the failures of the market and at some of the things that can be done to remedy these failures.

That the market cannot do everything we would like it to do is quite apparent. Amid the outpouring of goods and services, we find areas of depressing poverty, cities choked with traffic and pollution, and educational institutions and artistic organizations in serious financial trouble. Our economy, although capable of yielding an overwhelming abundance of material wealth, seems far less capable of eradicating social ills and controlling environmental damage. In this chapter, we will examine the reasons for the market's failings in these areas and indicate specifically why the price system *by itself* may be incapable of dealing with them.

What Does the Market Do Poorly?

While it is probably impossible to come up with an exhaustive list of the imperfections of the market mechanism, we can identify seven major areas in which the market has been accused of failing:

1. Market economies suffer from severe business fluctuations.
2. The market distributes income rather unequally.
3. Where markets are monopolized, they allocate resources inefficiently.
4. The market deals poorly with the incidental side effects of many economic activities.
5. The market cannot provide public goods, such as national defence.

6. The market may do a poor job of allocating resources between the present and the future.
7. The market mechanism causes public and personal services to become increasingly expensive, often inducing the government to take countermeasures that can be socially detrimental.

The first three of these issues—business fluctuations, income inequality, and monopoly—have already been discussed or will be discussed in detail later. The remaining four items constitute the subject matter of this chapter. Each of these, like monopoly, represents an instance in which the efficiency of the market mechanism is compromised. Therefore, to help us analyze these problems, we offer a brief review of the concept of efficient resource allocation, which was discussed in detail in Chapter 24.

Efficient Resource Allocation: A Review

The basic problem of resource allocation is deciding how much of each commodity the economy should produce. At first glance, it may seem that the solution is simple: the more the better; so we should produce as much of each good as we can. But careful thinking tells us that this is not necessarily the right decision.

Outputs are not created out of thin air. They are produced from the available supplies of labour, fuel, raw materials, and machinery. And if we use these scarce resources to produce, say, more handkerchiefs, we must take them away from some other product, such as hospital linens. So, to decide whether increasing the production of handkerchiefs is a good idea, we must compare the utility of that increase with the loss of utility caused by having to produce less hospital linens. The increased output will be a good thing only if society considers the additional handkerchiefs more valuable than the forgone hospital linens.

Opportunity Cost and Resource Allocation
Here it is worth remembering the concept of *opportunity cost*, one of our 12 **Ideas for Beyond the Final Exam**. The opportunity cost of an increase in the output of some product is the value of the other goods and services that must be forgone when inputs (resources) are taken away from their production in order to increase the output of the product in question. In our example, the opportunity cost of the increased handkerchief output is the decrease in output of hospital linens that results when resources are reallocated from the latter to the former. The general principle is that an increase in some output represents a *misallocation* of resources if the utility of that increased output is less than its opportunity cost.

To illustrate this idea, we repeat a graph encountered several times in earlier chapters—a *production possibilities frontier*—but we put it to a somewhat different use. Curve *ABC* in Figure 27-1 is a production possibilities frontier showing the alternative combinations of handkerchiefs and hospital linens the economy can produce by allocating its resources to the production of one good or the other in varying proportions. For example, point *A* amounts to allocation of all the resources to handkerchief production, so that 100 million of these items and no hospital linens are produced. Point *C* represents the reverse situation, with all resources allocated to hospital linens and none to handkerchiefs. Point *B* represents an intermediate allocation, resulting in the production of 8 million metres of linen and 60 million handkerchiefs.

Suppose now that point *B* represents the *optimal* resource allocation—that is, the only combination of outputs that best satisfies the wants of society among all the possibilities that are *attainable* (given the technology and resources as represented by the production frontier). Two questions are pertinent to our discussion of the price system:

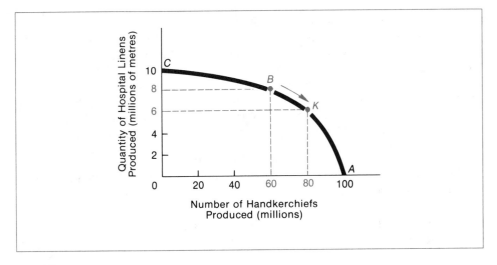

FIGURE 27-1

The Economy's Production Possibilities Frontier for the Production of Two Goods

This graph shows all combinations of outputs of the two goods that the economy can produce with the resources available to it. If *B* is the most desired output combination among those that are possible, it will correspond to a market equilibrium in which each good's price is equal to its marginal cost. If the price of linens is above their marginal cost, or the price of a handkerchief is below its marginal cost, then linen output will be inefficiently small and handkerchief output inefficiently large (point *K*).

1. What prices will get the economy to select point *B*; that is, what prices will yield an *efficient* allocation of resources?
2. How can the wrong set of prices lead to a misallocation of resources?

The first question was discussed extensively in Chapter 24. There we saw that:

An efficient allocation of resources requires that each product's price be equal to its marginal cost; that is:

$$P = \text{MC}.$$

The reasoning, in brief, is as follows. In a free market, the price of any good reflects the money value to consumers of an additional unit; that is, its *marginal utility* (MU). Similarly, if the market mechanism is working well, the *marginal cost* (MC) measures the value (the opportunity cost) of the resources needed to produce an additional unit of the good. Hence, if prices are set equal to marginal costs, then consumers, by using *their own money* in the most effective way to maximize *their own* satisfaction, will automatically be using *society's resources* in the most effective way. That is, as long as the market mechanism sets prices equal to marginal costs, it automatically satisfies the MC = MU rule for efficient resource allocation that we studied in Chapter 24.[1] In terms of Figure 27-1, this means that if *P* = MC for both goods, the economy will automatically gravitate to point *B*, which we assumed to be the optimal point.

This chapter is devoted mainly to the second question: How can the "wrong" prices cause a *mis*allocation of resources? The answer is not too difficult, and we can use the case of monopoly as an illustration.

The "law" of demand tells us that a rise in the price of a commodity will normally reduce the quantity demanded. Suppose, now, that the linen industry is a monopoly, so the price of linens exceeds their marginal cost.[2] This will decrease the

[1]If you need review, consult pages 533-34.

[2]To review why price under monopoly may be expected to exceed marginal cost, you may want to reread pages 557-62.

quantity of linens demanded below the eight million metres that we have assumed to be socially optimal (point B in Figure 27–1). So the economy will move from point B to a point like K, where too few linens and too many handkerchiefs are being produced for maximal consumer satisfaction. By setting the "wrong" prices, then, the market fails to achieve the most efficient use of the economy's resources. With the prices being "wrong," the market is sending the wrong signals to individual consumers. Thus, while consumers still maximize their own individual satisfaction, this does not lead to the optimal resource allocation for the society.

In sum, if the price of a commodity is above its marginal cost, the economy will tend to produce less of that item than maximizes consumer benefits. The opposite will occur if an item's price is below its marginal cost.

In the remainder of this chapter, we will encounter several other instances in which the market mechanism may set the "wrong" prices.

Externalities

We come now to the fourth item on our list of market failures—one of the least obvious, yet one of the most consequential of the imperfections of the price system. Many economic activities provide incidental benefits to others for whom they are not specifically intended. For example, a homeowner who plants a beautiful garden in front of her house incidentally and unintentionally provides pleasure to her neighbours and to those who pass by—people from whom she receives no payment. We say then that her activity generates a **beneficial externality**.

Similarly, there are activities that indiscriminately impose costs on others. For example, the operator of a motorcycle repair shop, from which all sorts of noise besieges the neighbourhood and for which he pays no compensation to others, is said to produce a **detrimental externality**. Pollution constitutes the classic illustration of a detrimental externality.

To see why the presence of externalities causes the price system to misallocate resources, we need only recall that the system achieves efficiency by rewarding producers who serve consumers well—that is, at as low a cost as possible. This argument breaks down, however, as soon as some of the costs and benefits of economic activities are left out of the profit calculation.

When a firm pollutes a river, it uses up some of society's resources just as surely as when it burns coal. However, if it pays for coal but not for the use of water, it is natural for management to be economical in its use of coal and wasteful in its use of water. Similarly, a firm that provides benefits to others for which it receives no payment is unlikely to be generous in allocating resources to the activity, no matter how socially desirable it may be.

In an important sense, the source of the difficulty is to be found in the definition of "property rights." Coal mines are *private property*; their owners will not let anyone take coal without paying for it. Thus, coal is costly and so is not used wastefully. But waterways are not private property. Since they belong to everyone in general, they belong to no one in particular. They can therefore be used free of charge as dumping grounds for wastes by anyone who chooses to do so. Because no one pays for the use of the oxygen in a public waterway, that oxygen will be used wastefully. That is the source of detrimental externalities.

Externalities and Inefficiency

Using these concepts, we can see precisely why an externality has undesirable effects on the allocation of resources. In discussing externalities, it is crucial to distinguish

An activity is said to generate a **beneficial** or **detrimental externality** if that activity causes incidental benefits or damages to others, and no corresponding compensation is provided to or paid by those who generate the externality.

between *social* and *private* marginal cost. We define **marginal social cost** (MSC) as the sum of two components: (1) **marginal private cost** (MPC), which is the share of marginal cost caused by an activity that is paid for by the people who carry out the activity; and (2) *incidental cost*, which is the share of the marginal cost that is borne by others.

If increased output by a firm increases the amount of smoke it emits, then, in addition to its direct private costs as recorded in the company accounts, expansion of its production imposes incidental costs on others in the form of increased laundry bills, medical expenditures, and outlays for air conditioning and electricity, as well as the unpleasantness of living in a cloud of noxious fumes. These are all part of the activity's marginal *social* cost.

Where the firm's activities generate detrimental externalities, its marginal social cost will be greater than its marginal private cost. In symbols, MSC > MPC. This must be so because, in equilibrium, the market will yield an output at which consumers' marginal utility (MU) is equal to the firm's marginal private cost (MU = MPC). It follows that marginal utility is *smaller* than marginal social cost. Society would then necessarily benefit if output of that product were *reduced*: It would lose the marginal utility but save the marginal social cost. And, since "MSC > MU" means that the production of the marginal unit of the good entails a cost to society larger than the benefit contributed by that unit, society would come out ahead. We conclude that:

Where the firm's activity causes detrimental externalities, free markets will leave us in a situation where marginal benefits are less than marginal social costs. Smaller outputs than those that maximize private profits will therefore be socially desirable.

We have already indicated why this is so. Private enterprise has no motivation to take into account costs that it creates for others but for which it does not have to pay. So goods that cause such externalities will be produced in undesirably large amounts by private firms. For precisely analogous reasons:

Where the firm's activity generates beneficial externalities, free markets will produce too little output. Society would be better off with larger output levels.

These principles can be illustrated with the aid of Figure 27–2. This diagram repeats the two basic curves needed for the analysis of the equilibrium of the firm: a

The marginal social cost of an activity is the sum of marginal private cost plus the incidental cost (positive or negative) that is borne by others.

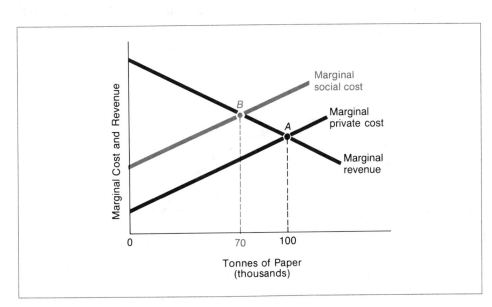

FIGURE 27–2
Equilibrium of a Firm Whose Output Produces Detrimental Externalities (Pollution)
The firm's profit-maximizing output, at which its marginal private cost and its marginal private revenue are equal, is 100,000 tonnes. But if the firm paid all the social costs of its output instead of shifting some of them to others, its marginal-cost curve would be the curve labelled "marginal social cost." Then it would pay the firm to reduce its output to 70,000 tonnes, thereby reducing the pollution it causes.

marginal-revenue curve and a marginal-cost curve (see Chapter 22). These represent the *private* costs and revenues accruing to a particular firm (in this case, a paper mill). The mill's maximum profit is attained with 100,000 tonnes of output corresponding to the intersection of the marginal-cost and the marginal-revenue curves (point *A*).

Now suppose that the factory's wastes pollute a nearby waterway, so that its production creates a detrimental externality whose cost the owner does not himself pay. Then marginal social cost must be higher than marginal private cost, as shown in the diagram, and the socially desirable level of output (70,000 tonnes) is at point *B* rather than point *A*.

Notice that if instead of being able to impose the external costs on others the mill's owner were forced to pay them himself, his own private marginal-cost curve would correspond to the higher of the two curves shown. His output of the polluting commodity would then fall to 70,000 tonnes, corresponding to point *B*, the intersection between the marginal-revenue curve and the marginal-*social*-cost curve. But because the firm does not in fact pay for the pollution damage its output causes, it produces an output (100,000 tonnes) that is larger than the output it would produce if the cost imposed on the community were instead borne by the firm (70,000 tonnes).

The same sort of diagram can be used to show that the opposite relationship will hold when the firm's activity produces beneficial externalities. The firm will produce less of its beneficial output than it would if it were rewarded fully for the benefits that its activities yield. Beneficial externalities arise when the activities of Firm A create incidental benefits for Firm B or Individual C (and perhaps for many others as well) or when A's activities *reduce* the costs of others' activity. For example, Firm A's research laboratories, while making its own products better, may also incidentally discover new research techniques that reduce the research costs of other firms in the economy.

But these results can perhaps be seen more clearly with the help of a production possibilities frontier diagram similar to that in Figure 27–1. In Figure 27–3 we see the frontier for two industries: electricity generation, which causes air pollution (a detrimental externality), and tulip growing, which makes an area more attractive (a beneficial externality). We have just seen that detrimental externalities make marginal social cost greater than marginal private cost. Hence, if the electric company charges a price equal to its own marginal (private) cost, that price will be less than the true marginal (social) cost. Similarly, in tulip growing, a price equal to marginal private cost will be above the true marginal cost to society.

We saw earlier in the chapter that an industry that charges a price above marginal cost will reduce quantity demanded through this high price, and so it will produce an output too small for an efficient allocation of resources. The opposite will

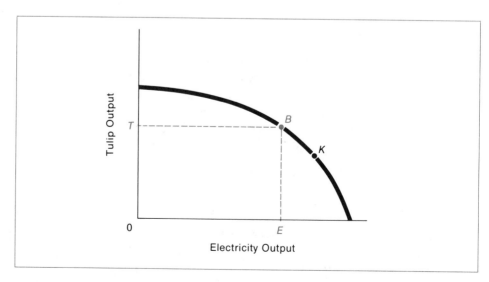

FIGURE 27–3
Externalities, Market Equilibrium, and Efficient Resource Allocation
Because electricity producers emit smoke (a detrimental externality), they do not bear the true marginal social cost of their output. So electricity price will be below marginal social cost, and electricity output will be inefficiently large (point *K*, not point *B*). The opposite is true of tulip production. Because they generate beneficial externalities, tulips will be priced above the marginal social cost and tulip output will be inefficiently small.

be true for an industry whose price is below marginal social cost. In terms of Figure 27–3, suppose point B again represents the efficient allocation of resources, involving the production of E kilowatt hours of electricity and T dozen tulips. Because the polluting electric company charges a price below marginal social cost, it will produce more than E kilowatt hours of electricity. Similarly, because tulip growers generate external benefits, and so charge a price above marginal social cost, they will produce less than T dozen tulips. The economy will end up with the resource allocation represented by point K rather than that represented by point B. There will be too much smoky electricity production and too little attractive tulip growing. More generally:

An industry that generates detrimental externalities will have a marginal social cost higher than its marginal private cost. If its price is equal to its own marginal private cost, that price will, therefore, be below the true marginal cost to society. The market mechanism thereby tends to encourage inefficiently large outputs of products that cause detrimental externalities. The opposite is true of products that cause beneficial externalities—private industry will provide inefficiently small quantities of these products.

Externalities Are Universal

Externalities occur throughout the economy. Many are beneficial. A factory that hires unskilled or semiskilled labourers gives them on-the-job training and provides the external benefit of better workers to future employers. Benefits to others are also generated when firms produce useful but unpatentable products or even patentable products that can be imitated by others to some degree.

Detrimental externalities are also widespread. The emission of air and water pollutants by factories, cars, and airplanes is the source of some of our most pressing environmental problems. The abandonment of buildings causes the quality of a neighbourhood to deteriorate and is the source of serious externalities in some cities. Externality represents a common form of market failure simply because there are so many areas in which property rights are not clearly established.

Externalities

Externalities lie at the heart of some of society's most pressing problems: the problems of the environment, research policy, and a variety of other critical issues. For this reason, the concept of externalities is one of our 12 **Ideas for Beyond the Final Exam**. It is a subject that will recur again and again in this book as we discuss some of these problems in greater detail.

Government Policy and Externalities

Because of the market's inability to cope with externalities, governments have found it appropriate to support activities that are felt to generate external benefits. Education is subsidized not only because it helps promote equal opportunity for all citizens, but also because it is believed to generate beneficial externalities. For example, educated people normally commit fewer crimes than uneducated people do, so the more we educate people, the less we will spend on crime prevention. Also, academic research that has been provided partly as a by-product of the educational system often benefits the entire population and has, indeed, been judged to be a major contributor to the nation's economic growth. We have consequently come to believe that if education were offered only by profit-making institutions, the output of these beneficial services would be provided at less than the optimal level.

Similarly, governments have recently begun to impose fines on companies that contribute heavily to air and water pollution. This approach to policy is in fact suggested by the economist's standard analysis of the effects of externalities on resource allocation. The basic problem is that, in the presence of externalities, the price system fails to allocate resources efficiently. Resources are used up without any price being charged for them, and benefits are supplied without financial compensation to the provider. As a result, the market will produce excessive quantities of outputs that pollute or create other detrimental externalities because these outputs are, in effect, produced at a bargain price that does not cover their entire marginal social cost. Consequently:

> One effective way to deal with externalities may be through the use of taxes and subsidies, making polluters pay for the costs they impose on society, and paying the generators of beneficial externalities for the incidental benefits of their activities (which can be considered an offset or deduction from the social cost of the activity).

For example, firms that generate beneficial externalities should be given a subsidy per unit of their output equal to the difference between their marginal social costs and their marginal private costs. Similarly, firms that generate detrimental externalities should be taxed at levels that effectively make them pay the entire marginal social cost. In terms of Figure 27–2, when the firm pays the tax, its marginal-private-cost curve shifts up until it coincides with the marginal-social-cost curve; the market price is then set in a manner consistent with efficient resource allocation.

While there is much to be said for this approach in principle, it is often difficult to implement it in practice. Social costs are rarely easy to estimate, partly because they are so widely diffused throughout the community (everyone in the area is affected by pollution) and partly because many of the costs and benefits (effects on health, unpleasantness of living in smog) are not readily assessed in monetary terms. The pros and cons of this approach and the alternative policies available for the control of externalities will be discussed in greater detail in Chapter 32, which considers environmental problems.

Public Goods

A public good is a commodity or service whose benefits are *not depleted* by an additional user and for which it is generally difficult or *impossible to exclude* people from its benefits, even if they are unwilling to pay for them. In contrast, a **private good** is characterized by both excludability and depletability.

A commodity is **depletable** if it is used up when someone consumes it.

A commodity is **excludable** is someone who does not pay for it can be kept from enjoying it.

Another area in which the market fails to perform adequately is in the provision of **public goods**. These are commodities that are valuable socially but whose provision, for reasons we will now explain, cannot be financed by private enterprise. Thus, government must pay for the public goods if they are to be provided at all. Standard examples range from national defence to the services of lighthouses.

It is easiest to explain the nature of public goods by contrasting them with **private goods**, commodities at the opposite end of the spectrum. *Private goods are characterized by two important attributes.* One can be called **depletability**. If you eat a steak or use a litre of gasoline, there is that much less beef or fuel in the world available for others to use. Your consumption depletes the supply available for other people, either temporarily or permanently.

But a pure public good is like the legendary widow's jar of oil, which always remained full no matter how many people used it. Once the snow has been removed from a street, the improved driving conditions are available to every driver who uses the street, whether 10 or 1000 cars pass that way. One passing car does not make the road less snow-free for another. The same is true of the spraying of swamps near a town to kill disease-bearing mosquitoes. The cost of the spraying is the same whether the town contains 10,000 or 20,000 persons. A resident of the town who benefits from this service does not deplete its advantages to others.

The other property that characterizes private goods but not public goods is **excludability**, meaning that anyone who does not pay for the good can be excluded from enjoying its benefits. If you do not buy a ticket, you are excluded from the ball game. If you do not pay for an electric guitar, the storekeeper will not give it to you.

But some goods or services are such that, if they are provided to anyone, they automatically become available to many other persons, whom it is difficult, if not impossible, to exclude from the benefits. If a street is cleared of snow, everyone who uses the street benefits, regardless of who paid for the snowplough. If a country provides a strong military establishment, everyone receives its protection, even persons who do not happen to want it.

A public good is defined as a good that lacks depletability. Very often, it also lacks excludability. Notice two important implications.

First, since non-paying users usually cannot be excluded from enjoying a public good, suppliers of such goods will find it *difficult or impossible to collect fees* for the benefits they provide. This is the so-called "free rider" problem. How many people, for example, will *voluntarily* cough up $2000 a year to support our national defence establishment? Yet this is roughly what it costs per Canadian family. Services like national defence and public health, which are not depletable and with regard to which excludability is simply impossible, *cannot* be provided by private enterprise because no one will pay for something that can be had for free. Since private firms are not in the business of giving services away, the supply of public goods must be left to government authorities and non-profit institutions.

The second thing we notice is that, since the supply of a public good is not depleted by an additional user, *the marginal (opportunity) cost of serving an additional user is zero.* With zero marginal cost, the basic principle of optimal resource allocation calls for provision of public goods and services to anyone who wants them *at no charge.* In a word, not only is it often *impossible* to charge a market price for a public good, it is often *undesirable* to do so as well. Any non-zero price would discourage some users from enjoying the public good; this would be inefficient, since one more person's enjoyment of the good costs society nothing. To summarize:

It is usually not *possible* to charge a price for a pure public good because people cannot be excluded from enjoying its benefits. It may also be *undesirable* to charge a price for it because that would discourage some people from using it even though using it does not deplete its supply. For both these reasons we find government supplying many public goods. Without government intervention, public goods simply would not be provided.

Referring back to our example in Figure 27–1, if hospital linens were a public good and their production were left to private enterprise, the economy would end up at point *A* on the graph, with zero production of hospital linens and far more output of handkerchiefs than is called for by efficient allocation (point *B*). Usually, communities have not been content to let that happen; today, a quite substantial proportion of government expenditure—indeed, the bulk of municipal budgets—is devoted to the financing of public goods or services believed to generate substantial external benefits. National defence, public health, police and fire protection, and research are among the services provided by governments because they offer beneficial externalities or because they are public goods.

Allocation of Resources between Present and Future

When a society invests, more resources are devoted to building up a capacity to produce consumer goods in the future. But the inputs that go into building new plant and equipment are unavailable for consumption now. Fuel used to make steel for a factory cannot be used to heat homes or drive cars. Thus, the allocation of inputs between current consumption and investment—that is, their allocation between present and future—determines how fast the economy grows.

In principle, the market mechanism should be as efficient in allocating resources between present and future uses as it is in allocating resources among different outputs at any given time. If future demands for a particular commodity—say, computers for the home—are expected to be higher than they are today, it will pay manufacturers to plan now to build the necessary plant and equipment so they will be ready to turn out the computers when the expanded market materializes. More resources are thereby allocated to future consumption.

The allocation of resources between present and future can be analyzed with the aid of a production possibilities frontier diagram, such as that in Figure 27-1. Suppose the issue is how much labour and capital to devote to producing consumer goods and how much of those inputs to devote to the construction of factories that will produce output in the future. Instead of handkerchiefs and linens, the graph will show consumer goods and number of factories on its axes, but otherwise it will be exactly the same as Figure 27-1. Such a graph appears in Figure 27-4.

The profit motive directs the flow of resources between one time period and another just as it handles resource allocation among different industries in a given period. The lure of profits directs resources to products that command high prices *and to time periods* in which high prices promise to make output most profitable. But at least one feature of the process of allocation of resources among different time periods distinguishes it from the process of allocation among industries. This is the special role that the *interest rate* plays in allocation among time periods.

If the receipt of a given amount of money is delayed until some time in the future, the recipient suffers an *opportunity cost*—the interest that the money could have earned if it had been received earlier and invested. For example, if the rate of interest is 9 percent and you can persuade someone who owes you money to make a $100 payment one year earlier than originally planned, you come out $9 ahead. Put the other way, if the rate of interest is 9 percent and the payment to you of $100 is postponed one year, you lose the opportunity to earn $9. Thus, the rate of interest determines the size of the opportunity cost to a recipient who gets money at some date in the future instead of now. For this reason, as we saw in Chapter 6:

Low interest rates will persuade people to invest more now, since the future benefits of the investment are still attractive in view of the moderate opportunity cost involved. Thus, more resources will be devoted to the future if interest rates are low. Conversely, high interest rates make investment, with its benefits in the future, less attractive. And so high interest rates will tend to increase the use of resources for current output at the expense of reduced future outputs.

FIGURE 27-4
Production Possibilities Frontier between Present and Future

With a given quantity of resources, the economy can produce one million cars for immediate use and build no factories for the future (point *A*). Alternatively, at the opposite extreme (point *B*), it can build 10 factories where products will become available in the future, while producing no cars for current consumption. At points in between on the frontier, such as *C*, the economy will produce a combination of some cars for present consumption and some factories for future use.

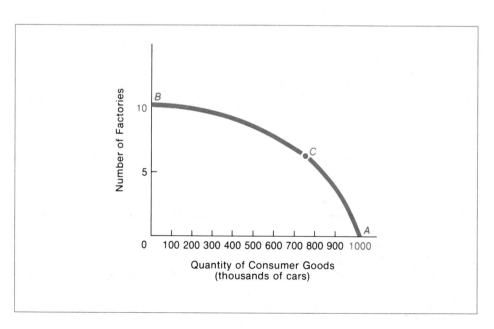

On the surface, it seems that the price system can allocate resources among different time periods in the way consumers prefer, for the supply of and the demand for loans, which determine the interest rate, reflect the public's preferences between present and future. Suppose, for example, that the public suddenly became more interested in future consumption (say, people wanted to save more for their old age). The supply of funds available for borrowing would increase and interest rates would tend to fall. This would stimulate investment and add to the future output of goods at the expense of current consumption.

But several questions have been raised about the effectiveness, in practice, of the market mechanism's allocation of resources among different time periods.

One thing that makes economists uneasy is that the rate of interest, which is the price that controls allocation over time, is also used for a variety of other purposes. As we saw in Chapter 13, in large countries like the United States, the interest rate is manipulated by means of fiscal and monetary policy in an attempt to control business fluctuations. In the process, policy-makers seem to give little thought to the effects on the allocation of resources between present and future, and so one may well worry whether the resulting interest rates are the most appropriate ones. Also, for countries like Canada, whose bonds must compete in international financial markets to be sold, the level of interest rates is largely determined by conditions in the rest of the world.

Second, it has been suggested that even in the absence of government manipulation of the interest rate, the market may devote too many resources to immediate consumption. One British economist, A. C. Pigou, argued simply that people suffer from "a defective telescopic faculty"—that they are too short-sighted to give adequate weight to the future. A "bird in the hand" point of view leads people to care so much about the present that they sacrifice the legitimate interests of the future. As a result, too much goes into today's consumption and too little into investment for tomorrow.

A third reason that the free market may not ensure sufficient investment for the future is that investment projects, such as the construction of a new factory, are much greater risks to the investor than they are to the community. Even if a factory falls into someone else's hands through bankruptcy, it will probably go on turning out goods. But the profits will not go to the investors or their heirs. Therefore, the loss to the individual investor will be far greater than the loss to society. For this reason individual investment for the future may fall short of the amounts that are socially optimal. Investments too risky to be worthwhile to any group of private individuals may nevertheless be advantageous to society as a whole.

Fourth, our economy shortchanges the future when it despoils irreplaceable natural resources, exterminates whole species of plants and animals, floods canyons, "develops" attractive areas into potential slums, and so on. Worst of all, industry, the government, and individuals bequeath a ticking time bomb to the future when they leave behind lethal and slow-acting residues, such as nuclear wastes, which may remain dangerous for hundreds or even thousands of years and whose disposal containers are likely to fall apart long before their contents lose their lethal properties.

Such actions are essentially *irreversible*. If a factory is not built this year, the deficiency in facilities provided for the future can be remedied by building it next year. But a canyon, once destroyed, can never be replaced. For this reason:

Many economists believe that **irreversible decisions** have a very special significance and must *not* be left entirely in the hands of private firms and individuals.

However, some observers question the general conclusion that the free market cannot be relied upon to ensure sufficient investment for the future. They point out that the prosperity of our economy has grown fairly steadily from one decade to the next, and that there is every reason to expect future generations to have real incomes and an abundance of consumer goods far greater than our own. Pressures to increase investment for the future may, in their view, be akin to taking from the poor to give to the rich—a sort of backward Robin Hood redistribution of income.

Some Other Sources of Market Failure

With the exception of a special problem, which we examine later in the chapter, we have now completed our survey of the most important imperfections of the market mechanism. But our list is not complete, and it can never be. In this imperfect world nothing ever works out ideally, and by examining anything with a sufficiently powerful microscope one can always detect some more blemishes. However, some of the items we have omitted from our list are also important, and we now provide a brief description of three of them.

Imperfect Information

The analysis of the virtues of the market mechanism in Chapter 24 assumed that consumers and producers have all the information they need in order to make their decisions. But in reality things are very different. When buying a house or a second-hand car, or when selecting a doctor, consumers are vividly reminded of how little they know about what they are purchasing. The old motto "Let the buyer beware" applies. Obviously, if participants in the market are ill-informed, they will not always make the optimal decisions described in our theoretical models.

Yet, not all economists agree that imperfect information is really a failure of the market mechanism. They point out that information, too, is a commodity that costs money to produce. Neither firms nor consumers have complete information because it would be irrational for them to spend the enormous amounts needed to get it. As always, the optimum is a compromise. One should, ideally, stop buying information at the point where the marginal utility of further information is no greater than its marginal cost. With this amount of information, the business executive or the consumer is able to make what have been referred to as "optimally imperfect" decisions.

Rent-Seeking

Rent-seeking refers to unproductive activity in the pursuit of economic profit; that is, profit in excess of competitive earnings.

An army of lawyers, expert witnesses, and business executives crowd our courtrooms and pile up enormous costs. Business firms seem to sue each other at the slightest provocation, wasting vast resources and delaying business decisions. Why? Because it is possible to make money by means of such unproductive activities—that is, by means of legal battles over profit-making opportunities.

Rent-seeking has become an important issue in takeover battles, where some outside group tries to gain control of a corporation by buying up a large percentage of its shares. Since the new owners are likely to fire the firm's current management, the latter group may fight hard to prevent the takeover, even if the new arrangement would benefit the company's shareholders.

In general, any source of unusual profit, such as that which exists under monopoly, is a temptation for firms to waste economic resources in an effort to obtain control of the source of profits. This process, called **rent-seeking** by economists (meaning that the firms hope to obtain earnings without contributing to production), has been judged by some observers to be a major source of inefficiency in our economy.[3]

Moral Hazard

Another widely discussed problem of the market mechanism is associated with insurance. Insurance—the provision of protection against risk—is viewed by economists as a useful commodity like shoes or the provision of information. But it also creates a problem by encouraging the very risks against which it provides protection. For example, if an individual has valuables that are fully insured against theft, she has little motivation to take steps to protect them against burglars. She may, for example,

HERMAN

"I need as much fire insurance as I can get by next Friday night."

[3]Recall our discussion of takeovers in Chapter 10, pages 220–21. For a more detailed discussion of rent-seeking, see Chapter 29, pages 642–48.

At the Frontier: Asymmetric Information, Lemons, and Agents

Have you ever wondered why a six-month-old car sells for so much less than a new one? One explanation is offered by economists, who have recently intensified their study of the effects of imperfect information on markets.

The problem is that some small proportion of automobiles are "lemons"; that is, they are constantly subject to mechanical troubles. The new-car dealer must sell *all* his cars, and, in any event, he probably knows no more than the buyer whether a particular car is a lemon. The two parties, therefore, have *symmetric* information, and the chances that a car purchased from a new-car dealer will turn out to be a lemon are relatively small. In the second-hand market, however, information is *asymmetric*. The seller knows whether the car is a lemon, but the buyer does not. Moreover, a seller who wants to get rid of a fairly new car is likely to be doing so only because it is a lemon. Potential buyers realize that. Hence, if someone is forced to sell a good new car because of an unexpected need for cash, she too will be stuck with a low price because she cannot *prove* that her car is in fact reliable. The moral is that asymmetric information tends to harm not only buyers, but honest sellers as well.

Problems relating to asymmetric information are not restricted to sales outlets. They pervade most economic relationships and lead to what are called *principal-agent problems*, the analysis of which has been a major concern of recent economic research. The issue arises from the necessity of delegating many critical tasks to others. Shareholders in a corporation delegate the running of the firm to its management team; Canadian citizens delegate lawmaking to their federal and provincial parliaments; union members delegate many decisions to their union leadership. In such cases, the people who give away part of their decision-making powers are called *principals*, and those who exercise those powers are called *agents*. In effect, the principals hire agents to do the jobs in question.

Asymmetric information is crucial here. The principals know only imperfectly whether their agents are serving their interests faithfully and efficiently or are instead neglecting or even acting against their interests to pursue selfish interests of their own. Misuse of principals' property, embezzlement, and political corruption are extreme examples of such dereliction of duty by agents, but, unfortunately, they seem to occur with increasing regularity. Among other things, economic analysis studies ways of remedying or at least alleviating such problems through forms of compensation for agents that bring the agents' interests more closely into line with those of the principals. For example, if the salaries of corporate managers depend heavily on company profits or on the market value of company shares, then managers can make themselves better off only by promoting the welfare of shareholders. And shareholders, even though they know only imperfectly what the management team are doing, can have a fair degree of confidence that they will try to serve their interests well.

fail to lock them up in a safety deposit box, and this failure makes burglary a more attractive and lucrative profession. This problem—the tendency of insurance to encourage the source of risk—is called **moral hazard**, and it constrains private profit-seeking insurance firms from providing the socially optimal amount of insurance. Critics of the unemployment-insurance system are referring to this concept when they argue that the system raises unemployment above the level it would be otherwise.

> **Moral hazard** refers to the tendency of insurance to discourage policy-holders from protecting themselves from risk.

Market Failure and Government Failure

Having pointed out some of the most noteworthy failures of the invisible hand, we seem forced to conclude that a market economy, if left entirely to itself, is likely to produce results that are, at least in some respects, far from ideal. In our discussion we have noted either directly or by implication some of the things government can do to correct these deficiencies. But the fact that government often *can* intervene in the operation of the economy in a constructive way does not always mean that it will actually succeed in doing so. The fact is that governments cannot be relied upon to behave ideally any more than business firms can.

It is apparently hard to make this point in a way that is suitably balanced. Commentators too often stake out one extreme position or the other. Those who think the market mechanism is inherently unfair and biased by the greed of those who run its enterprises seem to think of government as the saviour that can cure all economic ills. Those who deplore government intervention are prone to consider the public sector as the home of every sort of inefficiency, graft, and bureaucratic stultification. The truth, as usual, lies somewhere in between.

Governments are inherently imperfect, like the humans who constitute them. The political process leads to compromises that sometimes bear little resemblance to rational decisions—for example, the prolonged use of rent controls (see Chapter 3). Yet the problems engendered by an unfettered economy are often too serious to be left to the free market. The problems of inflation, environmental decay, and the provision of public goods are cases in point. In such instances, government intervention is likely to yield substantial benefits to the general public. However, even when it is fairly clear that *some* government action is warranted, it may be difficult (if not impossible) to calculate the optimal degree of government intervention. There is a danger of intervention so excessive that society might have been better off without it.

But in other areas the market mechanism is likely to work reasonably well, and the small imperfections that are present do not constitute sufficient justification for intervention. In any event, *even where government intervention is appropriate, it is essential to consider marketlike instruments as the means to correct the deficiencies in the workings of the market mechanism.* The tax incentives described in our discussion of externalities are an outstanding example of what we have in mind.

The Cost Disease of the Service Sector

The last problem to be considered in this chapter is *not* a failure of the market mechanism. However, in this case, the market's behaviour creates that illusion and therefore often leads to ill-advised government action that does not in fact serve the general welfare. The problem is this: While private standards of living have increased and material possessions have grown, the community has simultaneously been forced to cope with deterioration in a variety of services, both public and private.

Throughout the world, streets and subways have grown increasingly dirty. Public safety has declined as crimes of violence have become more commonplace in almost every major city. Public transit and railway services have been reduced. In the mid-nineteenth century in suburban London, there were twelve mail deliveries per day on weekdays and one on Sundays. We all know what has happened to postal services since then.

There have been parallel cutbacks in the quality of private services. Doctors have become increasingly reluctant to visit patients at home; in many areas, the house call has become something that occurs only in a life-and-death emergency, if even then. Another example, though undoubtedly a matter of lesser concern, is what has happened to restaurants. Although they are reluctant to publicize the fact, a great number of restaurants, including some of the most elegant and expensive, serve preprepared, frozen, and reheated meals. They charge high prices for what amount to little more than TV dinners.

There is no single explanation for all these matters. It would be naïve to offer a cut-and-dried hypothesis that purports to account for phenomena as diverse as the rise in crime and violence throughout Western society and the deterioration in postal services. Yet at least one common influence underlies all these problems of deterioration in service quality—an influence that is economic in character and that may be expected to grow more serious with the passage of time. The issue has been called the **cost disease of the personal services**, in reference to the fact that the costs of all basic services such as health care and education have risen so dramatically in recent decades.

But what accounts for these ever-increasing costs? Are they attributable to

HERMAN

"We only have to empty it once a month."

inefficiencies in government management? Perhaps, in part. But there is another reason—one that could not be avoided by any administration, no matter what its integrity and efficiency, and that affects private industry just as severely as it does the public sector.

The problem stems from the basic nature of services. Many services require direct contact between those who consume the service and those who provide it. Fire-fighters, teachers, and librarians are all engaged in activities that require direct person-to-person contact. Moreover, the quality of the service deteriorates if fire-fighters, teachers, and librarians provide less time to each user of their services.

In contrast, the buyer of an automobile usually has no idea who worked on it, and, provided it operates well, could not care less how much labour time went into its production. A labour-saving innovation in auto production need not imply a reduction in product quality. As a result, it has proved far easier for technological change to save labour in manufacturing than in providing services. While output per hour of labour in manufacturing and agriculture went up in the period after World War II at an average rate of close to 3 percent a year, the number of teacher hours per pupil actually *increased* because classes became smaller.

These disparate performances in productivity have grave consequences for prices. If both wages and productivity in manufacturing rise 3 percent, the cost of manufactured products is not affected because increased productivity makes up for the rise in wages. But the nature of services makes it very difficult to introduce labour-saving devices in the service sector. So a 3 percent rise in the wages of teachers or police officers is not offset by higher productivity and must lead to an equivalent rise in government budgets. Similarly, a 3 percent rise in the wages of hairdressers must lead beauty salons to raise their prices.

The Cost Disease of the Personal Services

In the long run, wages and salaries throughout the economy tend to go up and down together, for otherwise the activity whose wage rate falls seriously behind will tend to lose its labour force. Thus, auto workers and police officers will see their wages rise at roughly the same rate in the long run. But if productivity on the assembly line advances while productivity in the patrol car does not, then police protection must grow ever more expensive as time goes on.

This phenomenon is another of our 12 **Ideas for Beyond the Final Exam.** Because productivity improvements are very difficult to achieve in most services, the cost of services can be expected to rise faster, year in, year out, than does the cost of manufactured goods. Over a period of several decades, this difference in the growth rates of the two sectors' costs compounds to make services enormously more expensive relative to manufactured goods.

If services continue to grow ever more expensive in comparison with goods, the implications for life in the future are profound indeed. This analysis portends a world in which the typical home, while containing luxuries and furnishings that we can hardly imagine, is surrounded by garbage and perhaps by violence. It portends a future in which the services of doctors, teachers, and police are limited and impersonal, and in which arts and crafts are supplied largely by amateurs because the cost of professional work in these fields has become too high.

If this is the shape of the economy a hundred years from now, it will be significantly different from our own, and some people will undoubtedly question whether the quality of life has increased commensurately with the increased material prosperity. Some may even ask whether it has increased at all.

Is this future inevitable? Is there anything that can be done to escape it? The answer is that it is by no means inevitable. To see why, we must first recognize that the source of the problem, paradoxically, is the growth in productivity of our economy—or rather, the *unevenness* of that growth. Trash-removal costs go up not because garbage collectors become less efficient but because labour in car manufacturing becomes *more* efficient, thus enhancing the sanitation worker's potential value as an employee on the automotive assembly line. His wages must go up to keep him at his job of garbage removal.

But increasing productivity can never make a nation poorer. It can never make it unable to afford things it was able to afford in the past. Increasing productivity means that we can afford more of *all* things—medical care and education as well as TV sets and electric toothbrushes.

The role of services in our future depends on how we order our priorities. If we value services sufficiently, we can have more and better services—at *some* sacrifice in the rate of growth of manufactured goods. Whether that is a good choice for society is not for economists to say. But it is important to recognize that society *does* have a choice, and that if it fails to exercise it, matters are very likely to proceed relentlessly in the direction they are now headed—toward a world in which there is an enormous abundance of material goods and a great scarcity of many of the things that most people now consider primary requisites for a high quality of life.

How does the cost disease relate to the central topic of this chapter—the performance of the market and its implications for the economic role of government? Here the problem is the reverse of those discussed earlier in the chapter. The cost disease is a case in which the market *does* give the appropriate price signals, but they are likely to be misunderstood by government and to lead to decisions that do not promote the public interest most effectively.

Health care is a suggestive example. The cost disease is capable of causing the costs of health care (say, per patient day) to rise faster than the economy's rate of inflation because hospital care cannot be standardized enough to permit the productivity gains offered by automation and assembly lines. Thus, to prevent standards of care from falling, it is not enough to allow hospital budgets to grow at the *same* rate as the economy's rate of inflation. Those budgets must actually grow *faster* to prevent quality from declining. For example, when the inflation rate is 4 percent per year, it may be necessary to raise hospital budgets by 6 percent annually.

In these circumstances, something will surely seem amiss to a provincial government that increases the budget of its hospitals 5 percent per year. Responsible legislators will doubtless be disturbed by the fact that the budget is growing steadily in real terms and yet standards of quality are constantly slipping. If the legislators do not realize that the cost disease is the cause of the problem, they can be expected to look for villains—greedy doctors, hospital administrators who are inefficient, and so on. The net result, all too often, is a set of wasteful rules that hamper the freedom of action of hospitals and doctors inappropriately or that tighten hospital budgets below the level that demands and costs would require if they were determined by the market mechanism rather than by government.

In sum, the cost disease is not a case of poor market performance. But it is a case in which the market *appears* to misbehave by singling out particular sectors for exceptionally large cost increases. And because the market *seems* to be working badly, it is likely to lead to government reaction that can be highly detrimental to the public interest.[4]

---

[4]Governments have also been induced to intervene in the operation of some private sectors affected by the cost disease. For example, they control the prices of automobile insurance policies, which pay for such things as medical care of accident victims and repair of damaged automobiles, both of which are susceptible to the disease.

Evaluative Comments

This chapter, like Chapter 24, has offered a rather unbalanced assessment of the market mechanism. We spent Chapter 24 extolling the market's virtues, and this chapter cataloguing its vices. We come out, as in the nursery rhyme, concluding that the market is either very, very good, or horrid.

There seems to be nothing moderate about the performance of a market system. As a means of achieving efficiency in the production of ordinary consumer goods and responding to changes in consumer preferences, it is unparalleled. It is, in fact, difficult to overstate the accomplishments of the price system in these areas.

On the other hand, it has proven itself unable to cope with business fluctuations, income inequality, and the consequences of monopoly. It has proved to be a very poor allocator of resources among outputs that generate external costs and external benefits, and it has shown itself completely incapable of arranging for the provision of public goods. Some of the most urgent problems that plague our society—the despoliation of our atmosphere, the social unrest attributable to poverty—can be ascribed in part to one or another of these shortcomings of the market system.

Most economists conclude from these observations that while the market mechanism is virtually irreplaceable, considerable modifications in the way it works are required. Proposals designed to deal directly with the problems of poverty, monopoly, and resource allocation over time abound in the economic literature. All of them call for the government to intervene in the economy, either by supplying directly those goods and services that, it is believed, private enterprise does not supply in adequate amounts, or by seeking to influence the workings of the economy more indirectly through regulation or other policies. Many of these programs have been discussed in earlier chapters; others will be encountered in chapters to come.

Summary

1. There are at least seven major imperfections associated with the workings of the market mechanism: inequality of income distribution, fluctuations in economic activity (inflation and unemployment), monopolistic output restrictions, beneficial and detrimental externalities, inadequate provision of public goods, misallocation of resources between present and future, and finally, deteriorating quality and rising costs of services.

2. Efficient resource allocation is basically a matter of balancing the benefits of producing more of one good against the benefits of devoting the required inputs to the production of some other good.

3. A detrimental externality occurs when an economic activity incidentally does harm to others; a beneficial externality occurs when an economic activity incidentally creates benefits for others.

4. When an activity causes a detrimental externality, the marginal social cost of the activity (including the harm it does to others) must be greater than the marginal private cost to those who conduct the activity. The opposite will be true for a beneficial externality.

5. If manufacture of a product causes detrimental externalities, its price will generally not include all the marginal social cost it causes, since part of the cost will be borne by others. The opposite is true for beneficial externalities.

6. The market will therefore tend to overallocate resources to the production of goods that cause detrimental externalities and underallocate resources to the production of goods that create beneficial externalities. This is one of the 12 **Ideas for Beyond the Final Exam**.

7. A public good is defined by economists as a commodity that (like clean air) is not depleted by additional users and from whose use it is difficult to exclude anyone, even those who refuse to pay for it. A private good, in contrast, is characterized by both excludability and depletability.

8. Free-enterprise firms generally will not produce a public good even if it is extremely useful to the community, because they cannot charge money for the use of the good.

9. Many observers feel that the market often shortchanges the future, particularly when it makes irreversible decisions that destroy natural resources.

10. Because personal services—such as education, medical care, and police protection—are not amenable to labour-saving innovations, they suffer from a "cost disease": Their costs tend to rise considerably faster than do costs in the economy as a whole. This can lead to a distortion in the supply of such services by government because their rising cost is misinterpreted as the result of mismanagement and waste. The cost disease of the service sector is another of our 12 **Ideas for Beyond the Final Exam**.

Concepts for Review

Opportunity cost

Resource misallocation

Production possibilities frontier

Price above or below marginal cost

Externalities (detrimental and beneficial)

Marginal social cost and marginal private cost

Public goods

Private goods

Depletability

Excludability

Cost disease of the personal services

Irreversible decisions

Rent-seeking

Moral hazard

Asymmetric information

Principals and agents

Questions for Discussion

1. Specifically, what is the opportunity cost to society of a chair? Why may the price of that chair not adequately represent that opportunity cost?

2. Suppose that because of a new disease that attacks coffee plants, far more labour and other inputs are required to raise a pound of coffee than were required before. How might that affect the efficient allocation of resources between tea and coffee? Why? How would the prices of coffee and tea react in a free market?

3. Give some examples of goods whose production causes detrimental externalities and some examples of goods that create beneficial externalities.

4. Compare cleaning an office building with cleaning the atmosphere of a city. Which is a public good and which is a private good? Why?

5. Give some other examples of public goods, and discuss in each case why additional users do not deplete them and why it is difficult to exclude people from using them.

6. Think about the goods and services that your local government provides. Which of these are "public goods" as economists use the term?

7. Explain why the services of a lighthouse are considered an example of a public good.

8. Explain why education is not a very satisfactory example of a public good.

9. In recent decades, university tuition costs have risen faster than the general price level even though the wages of professors have failed to keep pace with the price level. Can you explain why?

10. A firm holds a patent that is estimated to be worth $20 million. The patent is repeatedly challenged in the courts by a large number of (rent-seeking) firms, each hoping to grab away the patent. In what sense may the rent-seekers be "competing perfectly" for the patent? In that sense, how much will end up being spent in the legal battles? (*Hint*: Under perfect competition, should firms expect to earn any economic profit?)

28

Comparative Advantage: The Question of Free Trade

Lower trade barriers yield higher productivity, larger plant sizes, and longer production runs.

ECONOMIC COUNCIL OF
CANADA

For many years Canada's strategy for economic development has involved the use of tariff barriers, and this has fostered the growth of various industries within the country. But as a result of Canada's tariff barriers and those imposed by other countries against our manufactured goods, Canadian producers have had to limit the scale of their operations to the small domestic market. This has meant operating at relatively low volume, with relatively high unit costs and just a few firms in each industry. We have tried to control monopoly practices through direct *regulation* and competition *laws*. But as we shall see in Chapter 31, these policies have met with only limited success, and many economists argue that we should rely instead on the discipline of the *market*. This discipline can be enforced by exposing firms that operate in Canada to more competition with firms already existing elsewhere in the world. As Canada cuts its tariffs, our producers are forced to expand operations (in order to reduce unit costs) and to sell a significant part of their output on world markets, or to get out of business.

The *benefits* of a tariff-reduction policy are rather obvious: Canadian consumers are able to buy a host of products at reduced prices, since the increased competition forces producers to more closely approximate the efficiency gains that exist in a perfectly competitive economy. To many people, however, especially Canadian workers, the *costs* of this policy are equally obvious. They fear that our producers are not able to compete with the low prices charged by those employing "cheap foreign labour." These opponents of tariff cuts think that many business failures and a large increase in unemployment follow any cut in tariffs. Thus, they argue that we simply cannot afford to lower our trade barriers unilaterally. Many economists disagree, and we explain why in this chapter.

To be complete, our investigation into the cost of tariff cuts must take a rather circuitous route. First, we explain the purposes of foreign trade and the ways in which governments seek to influence or limit it. Second, we study the crucial *law of comparative advantage*, which determines what commodities a country finds advantageous to export and what commodities it finds advantageous to import. This principle shows that even if there are *no* economies of large-scale production, both trading countries benefit from increased international exchange. Third, we see how the prices of goods traded between countries are determined by supply and demand. Finally, we examine the pros and cons of tariffs and other devices designed to protect a country's industries from foreign competition, and we discuss Canada's Free Trade Agreement with the United States in this context. In the end, we will have exposed the fallacy behind the view that "cheap foreign labour" necessitates tariff barriers.

At the close of this chapter, in the section entitled Microeconomic Policy: A Review and a Preview, we return to the theme of equality versus efficiency—one of our 12 **Ideas for Beyond the Final Exam**. This final section of the chapter serves as a link between Part Six, on the pros and cons of a decentralized market system, and Part Seven, which concerns itself with the problems of income distribution, economic power, pollution, and resource depletion. Free trade is the issue around which competing views on economic efficiency and unfair distributional effects have been most heatedly debated in recent years. For this reason, it is an ideal subject through which to focus once again on the equity–efficiency trade-off, before proceeding to Part Seven.

Issue: The Competition of "Cheap Foreign Labour"

When analyzing international trade, common sense can be extremely valuable; indeed, there is no substitute for it. Yet, in the absence of factual confirmation and careful analysis, conclusions based on common sense can be misleading.

One important example is the argument that buying products made by cheap foreign labour is unfair and destructive to domestic interests. Some Canadian business people and most union leaders argue that imports take bread out of the mouths of Canadian workers and depress standards of living in this country. According to this view, cheap foreign goods cause job losses and put pressure on Canadian businesses to lower wages. As this book goes to press (autumn 1990), this very concern is frequently heard expressed in the news media with regard to the impending U.S.–Mexican free-trade deal. Because Canada is already involved in a free-trade arrangement with the United States, this further deal naturally affects us. Union leaders have been vocal about the damage that imports produced by cheap Mexican labour would inflict on Canadian industries and workers.

But the facts are not consistent with this scenario. Many of Canada's imports come from Western Europe and Japan. Since the early 1960s, wages have risen far more dramatically in these other countries than they have here, yet we continue to import such items as Volkswagens, Volvos, and Toyotas in large numbers. More important, the rise in these foreign wages relative to Canadian wages has *not* strengthened Canada's position in the international marketplace. Conversely, back in the 1950s, when European and Japanese wages were far below those in Canada, we had no trouble marketing our products abroad. Clearly, cheap foreign labour does not necessarily create a crucial obstacle to Canadian sales abroad, as a "common-sense" view of the matter suggests. In this chapter we will see what is wrong with that view.

Why Trade?

The main reason that countries trade with one another rather than try to run completely independent economies is that the earth's resources are not equally distributed across its surface. Canada has an abundant supply of forests and fresh water, resources that are quite scarce in most of the rest of the world. Saudi Arabia has very little land that is suitable for farming, but it sits atop a huge pool of oil. Because of this seemingly whimsical distribution of vital resources, every nation must trade with others to acquire what it lacks. In general, the more varied the endowment of a particular country, the less it will have to depend on others to make up for its deficiencies.

Even if countries had all the resources they needed, other differences in natural endowments—such as climate, terrain, and so on—would lead them to engage in trade. Canadians *could*, with great difficulty, grow their own banana trees and coffee shrubs in hothouses, but these items are much more efficiently grown in such places as Honduras and Brazil, where the climate is appropriate. On the other hand, wheat grows in Canada with little difficulty, while mountainous Switzerland is not a good place to grow either bananas or wheat.

The skills of a country's labour force also play a role. If New Zealand has a large group of efficient farmers but few workers with industrial experience while the opposite is true in Great Britain, it makes sense for New Zealand to specialize in agriculture and for Great Britain to concentrate on manufacturing.

This last point suggests a very important reason why countries choose to trade—the many advantages of **specialization**. If one country were to try to produce everything, it would end up with a number of industries whose scale of operation was too small to permit the use of mass-production techniques, specialized training facilities, and other arrangements that give a cost advantage to large-scale operations. Even now, despite the considerable volume of world trade, this problem seems to arise for some countries, whose operation of their own international airlines or their own steel mills, for example, seems explainable only in political rather than economic terms. Inevitably, small nations that insist on operating in industries that are economical only when their scale of operation is large find that these enterprises can survive only with the aid of large government subsidies. To summarize:

International trade is essential for the prosperity of the trading nations for at least three reasons: (1) every country lacks some vital resources that it can get only by trading with others; (2) each country's climate, labour force, and other endowments make it a relatively efficient producer of some goods and an inefficient producer of other goods; and (3) specialization permits larger outputs and can therefore offer economies of large-scale production.

> **Specialization** means that a country devotes its energies and resources to only a small proportion of the world's productive activities.

Mutual Gains from Trade

Many people believe that one nation can gain from trade only at the expense of another. Centuries ago, early writers on international trade argued that because nothing is produced by the act of trading, the total collection of goods in the hands of the two parties at the end of an exchange is no greater than it was before the exchange took place. Therefore, they concluded (fallaciously), if one country gains from a swap, the other country must necessarily lose.

One of the consequences of this mistaken view was a policy prescription calling for each country, in the interests of its citizens, to do its best to act to the disadvantage of its trading partners—in Adam Smith's terms, to "beggar its neighbours." The idea that one nation's gain must be another's loss means that a country can promote its own welfare only by harming others.

Yet, as Adam Smith and others after him emphasized, in any *voluntary exchange*, unless there is misunderstanding or misrepresentation of the facts, both parties *must* gain (or at least expect to gain) something from the transaction. Otherwise, why would both parties agree to the exchange?

But how can mere exchange, in which no production takes place, actually leave both parties better off? The answer is that although trade does not increase the quantity of goods available, it does allow each party to acquire items better suited to its needs and tastes. Suppose Brian has four sandwiches and nothing to drink, while David has four cartons of milk and nothing to eat. A trade of two of Brian's sandwiches for two of David's cartons of milk does not increase the total supply of either food or beverages, but it clearly produces a net increase in the welfare of both boys.

By exactly the same logic, both Canada and the United States must be better off if Canada voluntarily ships timber to the United States in return for chemicals.

Mutual Gains from Voluntary Exchange
Both parties must expect to gain from any *voluntary exchange.* Trade brings about mutual gains by redistributing products in such a way that both participants end up holding a combination of goods that is better adapted to their preferences than the goods they held before. This principle, which is one of our 12 **Ideas for Beyond the Final Exam**, applies to nations just as it does to individuals.

Comparative Advantage:
The Fundamental Principle of Specialization

Some of the reasons trade can be beneficial to both parties are obvious. We now turn to an important source of mutual benefit that is far from obvious.

We know that coffee can be produced in Colombia using less labour and smaller quantities of other inputs than would be needed to grow it in Canada. And we know that Canada can produce passenger aircraft at a lower resource cost than can Colombia. We say then that Colombia has an **absolute advantage** over Canada in coffee production, and Canada has an absolute advantage over Colombia in aircraft production.

A numerical example will illustrate the idea. According to Table 28–1, one year of labour time in Canada can produce either 50 kilograms of coffee or 1/20 of an airplane. By contrast, one year of labour time in Colombia can produce 300 kilograms of coffee or 1/100 of an airplane. Thus, six years of labour input would be required to produce 300 kilograms of coffee in Canada, whereas Colombia could do the job with only one year's worth of labour. On the other hand, it would take Colombia 100 years of labour to produce an airplane, a job Canada could do in only 20 years.

One country is said to have an **absolute advantage** over another in the production of a particular good if it can produce that good using smaller quantities of resources than can the other country.

TABLE 28–1
Alternative Outputs from One Year of Labour Input

	IN CANADA	IN COLOMBIA
Coffee (kilograms)	50	300
Airplanes	1/20	1/100

Obviously, if Canada wants coffee and Colombia wants airplanes, each can save resources by specializing in what it does best and trading with the other. Each exports the good in which it has an absolute advantage.

Suppose, however, that one country is more efficient than another in producing *every* item. Can they still gain by trading? The surprising answer is *definitely yes*, and a simple parable will help explain why.

The work of a highly paid business consultant frequently requires computer analysis. Suppose the consultant began her career as a computer operator doing her own data entry and was extremely good at it. In her current position she may grow impatient with the slow, sloppy work of some of the low-paid support staff who work for her and at times be tempted to do all the work herself. Good judgment tells her, however, that though she is better *both* at giving business advice *and* at data entry than are her employees, it is foolish to devote any of her valuable time to the low-skilled job. That is because the opportunity cost of an hour devoted to data entry is an hour less devoted to business consulting—a far more lucrative activity.

One country is said to have a **comparative advantage** over another in the production of a particular good relative to other goods it can produce if it produces that good least inefficiently as compared with the other country.

This is an example of the principle of **comparative advantage** at work. The consultant specializes in business advice despite her absolute advantage in data entry because she has a greater absolute advantage in her role as a business consultant. She suffers some direct loss by not doing her own data entry, but that loss is more than compensated for by the earnings she makes selling her consulting services to clients.

This example brings out the fundamental principle that underlies the economic analysis of patterns of specialization and exchange among different nations. This principle is called the *law of comparative advantage*, and it is one of our **12 Ideas for Beyond the Final Exam.** It was discovered by David Ricardo, one of the giants in the history of economic analysis.

The Law of Comparative Advantage

Even if one country is at an absolute *disadvantage* relative to another country in the production of *every* good, it is said to have a *comparative advantage* in making the good in the production of which it is *least inefficient* compared with the other country.

Ricardo's basic finding was that two countries can still gain by trading even if one country is more efficient than another in the production of *every* commodity (that is, it has an absolute advantage in every commodity).

In determining the most efficient patterns of production, what matters is *comparative* advantage, not *absolute* advantage. Thus, one country will often gain by importing a certain good even if that good can be produced at home more efficiently than it can be produced abroad. Such imports will be profitable if the country is even more efficient at producing the goods that it exports in exchange.

The Arithmetic of Comparative Advantage

Let's see precisely how this works using numbers based on Ricardo's original example. Suppose labour is the only input used to produce wine and cloth in two countries, England and Portugal. Suppose further that Portugal has an absolute advantage in both goods, as indicated in Table 28–2. In this example, a week's worth of labour can produce either 12 metres of cloth or 6 barrels of wine in Portugal, but only 10 metres of cloth or 1 barrel of wine in England. So Portugal is the more efficient producer of both goods. Nonetheless, as our multitalented-consultant example suggests, it pays for Portugal to specialize in wine production and to trade with England.

We verify that this is so in two steps. First, we note that Portugal has a comparative advantage in wine while England has a comparative advantage in cloth. Then we show that both countries can gain if Portugal specializes in producing wine, England specializes in producing cloth, and the two countries trade with one another.

TABLE 28–2
Alternative Outputs from One Week of Labour Input

	IN ENGLAND	IN PORTUGAL
Cloth (metres)	10	12
Wine (barrels)	1	6

According to the numbers in Table 28–2, Portugal is 20 percent more efficient than England in producing cloth; it can produce 12 metres with a week's labour, whereas England can produce only 10 metres. However, Portugal is six times as efficient as England in producing wine; it can produce 6 barrels per week rather than 1. Thus Portugal's competitive edge is far greater in wine than in cloth. That is precisely what we mean by saying that Portugal has a *comparative advantage* in wine. From the British perspective, these same numbers indicate that England is only slightly less efficient than Portugal in cloth production but drastically less efficient in wine production. So England's *comparative advantage* is in cloth. According to Ricardo's law of comparative advantage, the two countries can benefit if Portuguese wine is traded for English cloth.

Let us check that this is true. Suppose Portugal transfers a million weeks of labour out of the textile industry and into winemaking. According to the figures in Table 28–2, its cloth output falls by 12 million metres while its wine output rises by 6 million barrels. (See Table 28–3.) Suppose, at the same time, England transfers 2 million weeks of labour out of winemaking (thereby losing 2 million barrels of wine) and into clothmaking (thereby gaining 20 million metres of cloth). Table 28–3 shows

Biographical Note: David Ricardo (1772–1823)

David Ricardo was born four years before publication of Adam Smith's *Wealth of Nations*. Descended from a wealthy Jewish family of Portuguese origins, he had about twenty brothers and sisters. Ricardo's formal education ended at the age of 13, so he was largely self-educated. He began his career by working in his father's brokerage firm in London. At age 21, Ricardo married a Quaker woman and decided to become a Unitarian, a sect then considered "little better than atheist." By Jewish custom, Ricardo's father formally broke off relations with him, though apparently the two remained friendly.

Ricardo then decided to go into the brokerage business on his own and was enormously successful. During the Napoleonic Wars he regularly scored business coups over leading British and foreign financiers, including the Rothschilds. After gaining a huge profit on government securities that he had bought just before the Battle of Waterloo, Ricardo decided to retire from business when he was just over 40 years old.

He purchased a country estate, Gatcomb (now owned by the royal family), where a brilliant group of intellectuals met regularly. Particularly remarkable for the period was the number of women included in the circle, among them Maria Edgeworth, the novelist (who wrote of Ricardo's mind with extravagant praise), and Jane Marcet, an author of textbooks, one of which was probably the first textbook in economics. Ricardo's close friends included the economists T. R. Malthus and James Mill, father of John Stuart Mill, the noted philosopher–economist. Malthus remained a close friend of Ricardo even though they disagreed on many subjects and continued their arguments in personal correspondence and in their published works.

James Mill persuaded Ricardo to go into Parliament. As was then customary, Ricardo purchased his seat by buying a piece of land that entitled its owner to a seat in

Parliament. There he proved to be a noteworthy advocate of many causes that were against his personal interests.

James Mill also helped persuade Ricardo to write his masterpiece, *The Principles of Political Economy and Taxation*, which may have been the first book of pure economic theory ever to be published. It is noteworthy that Ricardo, the most practical of practical men, had little patience with empirical economics and preferred to rest his analysis explicitly and exclusively on theory. His book made considerable contributions to the analysis of pricing, wage determination, and the effects of various types of taxes, among many other subjects. It also gave us the law of comparative advantage. In addition, the book described what has come to be called the Ricardian rent theory—even though Ricardo did not discover the analysis and explicitly denied having done so.

Ricardo died in 1823 at the age of 51. He seems to have been a wholly admirable person—honest, charming, witty, conscientious, brilliant—almost too good to be true.

---

us that these transfers of resources in the two countries increase the world's production of both outputs!

Together, the two countries now have 4 million additional barrels of wine and 8 million additional metres of cloth—surely a nice outcome. But there seems to be some sleight-of-hand here. All that has taken place is an exchange; yet somehow Portugal and England have gained both cloth and wine. How can such gains in physical output be possible?

The explanation is that the trade process we have just described involves more than just a swap of a fixed bundle of commodities. It is also a *change in the production*

TABLE 28–3
Example of the Gains from Trade

	ENGLAND	PORTUGAL	TOTAL
Cloth (millions of metres)	+20	–12	+8
Wine (millions of barrels)	– 2	+ 6	+4

arrangements, with some of England's wine production taken over by the more efficient Portuguese wine producers and with some of Portugal's cloth production taken over by English weavers, who are *less inefficient* at producing cloth than English vintners are at producing wine.

When every country does what it can do best, all countries can benefit because more of every commodity can be produced without increasing the amounts of labour used.

If this result still seems a bit mysterious, the concept of *opportunity cost* will help remove the remaining mystery. If the two countries do not trade, Table 28–2 shows that England can acquire a barrel of wine on its own only by giving up 10 metres of cloth. Thus, the opportunity cost of a barrel of wine in England is 10 metres of cloth. But in Portugal the opportunity cost of a barrel of wine is only 2 metres of cloth (again, see Table 28–2). Thus, in terms of real resources forgone, it is cheaper—for either country—to acquire wine in Portugal. By a similar line of reasoning, the opportunity cost of cloth is higher in Portugal than in England, so it makes sense for both countries to acquire their cloth in England.[1]

The Graphics of Comparative Advantage

The gains from trade can also be displayed graphically, and doing so helps us understand how these gains arise.

The lines *UK* and *PG* in Figure 28–1 are the *production possibilities frontiers* of the two countries, drawn on the assumption that each country has 6 million weeks of labour available.[2] For example, Table 28–2 tells us that with 6 million weeks of labour, England can produce 6 million barrels of wine and no cloth (point *K*), 60 million metres of cloth and no wine (point *U*), or any combination in between (the line *UK*). Similar reasoning shows that *PG* is Portugal's production possibilities frontier.

Note that Portugal's production possibilities frontier lies *above* England's throughout the diagram. That is because Portugal is the more efficient producer of *both* commodities. With the same amount of labour, it can obtain more wine and more cloth than England can. Thus, the higher position of Portugal's frontier is the graph's way of showing Portugal's *absolute* advantage in both wine and cloth.

Portugal's comparative advantage in wine production and England's comparative

[1] EXERCISE: Provide this line of reasoning.

[2] For simplicity in this numerical example, we assume no diminishing returns in either economy. To review the concept of the production possibilities frontier, see Chapter 2.

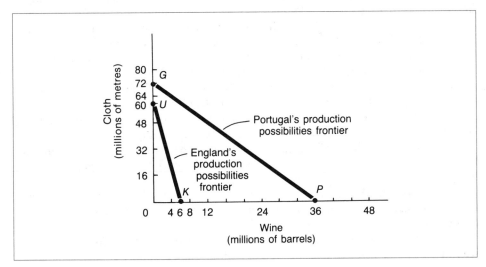

FIGURE 28–1

Absolute and Comparative Advantage Shown by Two Countries' Production Possibilities Frontiers

Portugal's absolute advantage is shown by its ability to produce more of every commodity using the same quantity of labour as does England. Therefore, Portugal's production possibilities frontier, *PG*, is higher than England's *UK*. But Portugal has a comparative advantage in wine production, in which it is six times as productive as England. It can produce 36 million barrels (point *P*), compared with England's 6 million barrels (point *K*). On the other hand, Portugal is only 20 percent more productive in cloth production (point *G*) than England (point *U*). Thus, England is less inefficient in producing cloth, where it consequently has a comparative advantage.

advantage in cloth production are shown in a different way—by the relative *slopes* of the two production possibilities frontiers. Portugal's frontier is not only higher than England's; it is also flatter. What does this mean economically? One way of looking at the difference is to remember that while Portugal can produce six times as much wine as England (compare points *P* and *K*), it can produce only 20 percent more cloth than England (compare points *G* and *U*). England is, relatively speaking, much better at cloth production than at wine production. That is what is meant when we say it has a *comparative* advantage in the former.

We can express this difference more directly in terms of the slopes of the two lines. The slope of Portugal's production possibilities frontier is $0G/0P = 72/36 = 2$. This means that if Portugal reduces its wine production by one barrel it will obtain two metres of cloth. Thus, the *opportunity cost* of a barrel of wine in Portugal is two metres of cloth, as we observed earlier.

Now turning to the case of England, the slope of the production possibilities frontier is $0U/0K = 60/6 = 10$. That is, if England reduces wine production by one barrel, it gets 10 additional metres of cloth. So in England, the *opportunity cost* of a barrel of wine is 10 metres of cloth.

One country's absolute advantage in production over another country is shown by its having a higher production possibilities frontier. The difference in the comparative advantages of the two countries is shown by the difference in the slopes of their frontiers.

Because opportunity costs differ in the two countries, gains from trade are possible. How these gains are divided between the two countries depends on the prices for wine and cloth that emerge from world trade, which is the subject of the next section. But we already know enough to see that world trade must leave a barrel of wine costing less than 10 metres of cloth and more than 2 metres. Why? Because if a barrel of wine cost more than 10 metres of cloth (its opportunity cost in England), England would be better off producing its own wine rather than trading with Portugal. Similarly, if a barrel of wine fetched less than 2 metres of cloth (its opportunity cost in Portugal), Portugal would prefer to produce its own cloth rather than trade with England.

We conclude, therefore, that if both countries are to benefit from trade, the rate of exchange between cloth and wine must be somewhere between 10 to 1 and 2 to 1. To illustrate the gains from trade in a concrete example, suppose the world price ratio settles at 4 to 1; that is, 1 barrel of wine costs 4 metres of cloth. How much, precisely, do England and Portugal gain from world trade?

Figure 28-2 is designed to help us see the answer. Production possibilities frontiers *UK* in part (a) and *PG* in part (b) are the same as in Figure 28-1. But England can do better than *UK*. Specifically, with a world price ratio of 4 to 1, England can buy a barrel of wine by giving up only 4 metres of cloth rather than 10 metres (which is the opportunity cost of wine in England). Hence, if England produces only cloth [point *U* in Figure 28-2(a)] and buys its wine from Portugal, England's *consumption possibilities* will be as indicated by the green line that begins at point *U* and has a slope of 4—indicating that each additional barrel of wine costs England 4 metres of cloth. Since trade allows England to choose a point on *UN* rather than on *UK*, trade opens up consumption possibilities that were simply not available before.

The story is similar for Portugal. If the Portuguese produce only wine [point *P* in Figure 28-2(b)], they can acquire 4 metres of cloth from England for each barrel of wine they give up as they move along the green line *PR* (whose slope is 4). This is better than they can do on their own, since a sacrifice of one barrel of wine yields only 2 metres of cloth in Portugal. Hence world trade enlarges Portugal's consumption possibilities from *PG* to *PR*.

Figure 28-2 shows graphically that gains from trade arise to the extent that world prices (4 to 1 in our example) differ from domestic opportunity costs (10 to 1

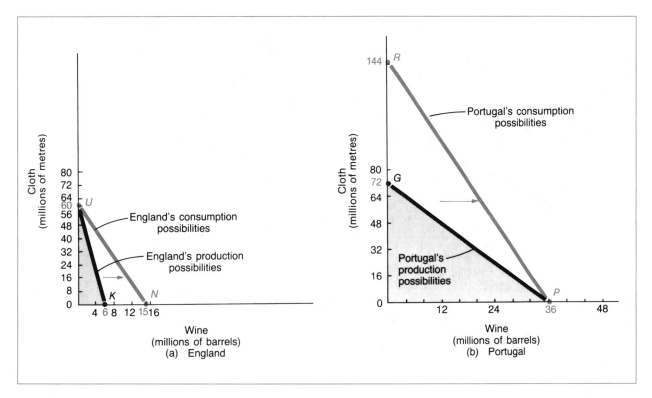

FIGURE 28–2
The Gains from Trade
In this diagram, we suppose that trade opens up between England and Portugal and that the world price of wine is four times the world price of cloth. Now England's consumption possibilities are all the points on line *UN* (which starts at *U* and has a slope of 4), rather than just the points on its own production possibilities frontier, *UK*. Similarly, Portugal can choose any point on line *PR* (which begins at *P* and has a slope of 4), rather than just points on *PG*. Thus both nations gain from trade.

and 2 to 1 in our example). So it is a matter of some importance to understand how prices in international trade are established. Supply and demand is a natural place to start.

Supply–Demand Equilibrium and Pricing in Foreign Trade

When applied to international trade, the supply–demand model runs into several complications we have not encountered before. First, it involves at least two demand curves: that of the exporting country and that of the importing country. Second, it may also involve two supply curves, since the importing country may produce some part of what it consumes. The third and final complication is that equilibrium does not occur at the intersection point of *either* pair of supply–demand curves. Why? Because if there is any trade, the exporting country's quantity supplied must be *greater* than its quantity demanded, while the quantity supplied by the importing country must be *less* than its quantity demanded.

These complications are illustrated in Figure 28–3, where we show, in part (a), the supply and demand curves of a country that exports wine and, in part (b), the supply and demand curves of a country that imports wine. For simplicity, we assume that these countries do not deal in wine with anyone else.

Where will the two-country wine market reach equilibrium? Ignoring transport costs, the equilibrium price in a free market must satisfy two requirements:

1. The price of wine must be the same in both countries.

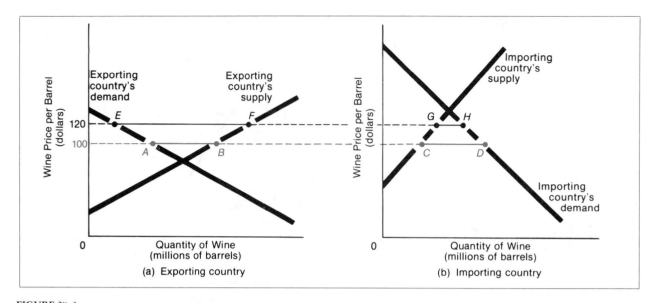

FIGURE 28-3

Supply–Demand Equilibrium in the International Wine Trade

Equilibrium requires that net exports, *AB* (that is, the exporting country's quantity supplied, *B*, minus its quantity demanded, *A*), exactly balance imports, *CD*, by the importing country. At $100 per barrel of wine, there is equilibrium. But at a higher price, say $120, there is disequilibrium because net export supply, *EF*, exceeds net import demand, *GH*.

2. The quantity of wine exported (the excess of the exporting country's quantity supplied over its quantity demanded) must equal the quantity of wine imported (the excess of the importing country's quantity demanded over its quantity supplied).

   In Figure 28–3, this happens at a price of $100 per barrel. At that price, the distance *AB* between what the exporting country produces (point *B*) and what it consumes (point *A*) equals the distance *CD* between the quantity demanded of the importing country (point *D*) and its quantity supplied (point *C*). At a price of $100 per barrel, the amount the exporting country has available to sell abroad is exactly equal to the amount the importer wants to buy. So matters are in balance, and $100 per barrel is the market price.

   At any price higher than $100, producers in both countries will want to sell more and consumers in both countries will want to buy less. For example, if the price rises to $120 per barrel, the exporting country's quantity supplied will rise from *B* to *F*, and its quantity demanded will fall from *A* to *E*, as shown in Figure 28–3(a). As a result, there will be a rise in the amount available for export, from *AB* to *EF*. For exactly the same reason, the price increase will cause higher production and lower sales in the import-ing country, leading to a shrinkage in the amount the importing country wants to import—from *CD* to *GH* in part (b). This means that the new price, $120 per barrel, cannot be sustained if the international market is free and competitive. With export supply *EF* far greater than import demand *GH*, there must be a downward pressure on price and a move back toward the $100 equilibrium price. Similar reasoning shows that prices of less than $100 also cannot be sustained.

   We can now see the straightforward role of supply–demand equilibrium in international trade:

   In international trade, the equilibrium price must be at a level at which the amount the exporting country wants to export is exactly equal to the amount the importing country wants to import. Equilibrium will thus occur at a price at which the horizontal distance *AB* in Figure 28–3(a) (the excess of the exporter's quantity supplied over its quantity demanded) equals the horizontal distance *CD* in Figure 28–3(b) (the excess of the importer's quantity demanded over its quantity supplied). At this price, the *world's* quantity demanded is equal to the *world's* quantity supplied.

Comparative Advantage and Competition of "Cheap Foreign Labour"

The principle of comparative advantage takes us a good part of the way toward an explanation of the fallacy in the "cheap foreign labour" argument described earlier in the chapter. Given the assumed productive efficiency of Portuguese labour and the inefficiency of British labour in Ricardo's example, we would expect wages to be much higher in Portugal than in England. In these circumstances, one can expect Portuguese workers to be apprehensive about an agreement to permit trade between the countries—"How can we hope to meet the unfair competition of those underpaid British workers?" And British labourers are also likely to be concerned—"How can we hope to meet the competition of those Portuguese, who are so efficient in producing everything?"

The principle of comparative advantage shows us that both fears are unjustified. As we have just seen, when trade is opened up between Portugal and England, *workers in both countries will be able to earn higher real wages than they did before* because of the increased productivity that comes about through specialization.

Figure 28–2 shows this fact directly. We have seen from our illustration that, with trade, England can end up with more wine and more cloth than it had before, and so the living standards of its workers can rise even though they have been left vulnerable to the competition of the superefficient Portuguese. Portugal can also end up with more wine and more cloth, so the living standards of its workers can rise even though they have been exposed to the competition of cheap British labour. These higher living standards should be reflected in higher real wages earned by workers in both countries.

The lesson to be learned here is that nothing helps raise standards of living more than does a greater abundance of goods.

Tariffs, Quotas, and Other Interferences with Trade

Despite the mutual gains obtainable, international trade has historically been subjected to unrelenting pressure for government interference. In fact, until the rise of a free-trade movement in England at the end of the eighteenth and the beginning of the nineteenth centuries (with such economists as Adam Smith and David Ricardo at its vanguard), it was taken for granted that one of the essential tasks of government was the imposition of regulations to impede trade, presumably in the national interest.

There were many who argued then (and some who still argue today) that a nation's wealth consists of the amount of gold or other moneys at its command. Consequently, the proper aim of government policy is to do everything it can to promote exports (in order to increase the amount foreigners owe to it) and to discourage imports (in order to decrease the amount the country owes to foreigners).

Obviously, there are limits to carrying out this policy. A country *must* import vital foodstuffs or critical raw materials that it cannot supply for itself; if it does not, it must suffer a severe fall in living standards. Moreover, it is mathematically impossible for *every* country to sell more than it buys—one country's exports *must* be some other country's imports. If everyone competes in this game and cuts imports to the bone, obviously exports must go the same way. The result will be that everyone is deprived of the mutual gains that trade can provide.

In more recent times, notably in the United States during the first three decades of the twentieth century, there was a return to an active policy to reduce competition from foreign imports. Since then, however, Western countries have attempted to promote freedom of trade, and barriers have gradually been reduced, although, during the 1980s, there was some pressure to move back the other way. In the United States, a combination of high unemployment rates and a deterioration of the country's competitive position led to strong political pressures to reduce imports.

Modern governments use three main devices to control trade: tariffs, quotas, and export subsidies. A **tariff** is simply a tax on imports. An importer of wine, for example, may be charged $10 for each barrel of wine he brings into the country. A **quota** is a legal limit on the amount of a good that may be imported. For example, the government might allow no more than 5 million barrels of wine to be imported in a year. In some cases, governments ban the importation of certain goods outright, in effect imposing a quota of zero. An **export subsidy** is a payment by the government to an exporter. By reducing exporters' costs, such subsidies permit them to lower their selling prices and compete more effectively in world trade. Export subsidies are used extensively by some foreign governments to assist their industries—a practice that provokes Canadian manufacturers to complain bitterly about "unfair competition." American manufacturers voice similar complaints about Canadian practices. Since we have more generous government-funded social policies than do the Americans, and since these policies indirectly lower labour costs for Canadian firms, Americans regard programs such as our unemployment-insurance scheme and our provincial health plans as export subsidies—that is, as "unfair trade practices."

How Tariffs and Quotas Work

Both tariffs and quotas restrict supplies coming from abroad and drive up prices. A tariff works by raising prices and hence cutting the demand for imports, while the sequence associated with a quota goes the other way—restriction in supply forces prices up.

Let us use our international trade diagrams to see what a quota does. The supply and demand curves in Figure 28–4 are like those in Figure 28–3. Just as in Figure 28–3, equilibrium in a free international market occurs at a price of $100 per barrel of wine (in both countries). At this price, the exporting country produces 10 million barrels [point B in part (a)] and consumes 5 million barrels (point A), so that exports are 5 million barrels—the distance AB. Similarly, the importing country consumes 8 million barrels [point D in part (b)] and produces only 3 million (point C), so that imports are also 5 million barrels (the distance CD).

Now suppose the government of the importing nation imposes an import quota of (no more than) 3 million barrels. The free-trade equilibrium is no longer possible. Instead, the market must reach equilibrium at a point where both exports and imports are 3 million barrels. As Figure 28–4 indicates, this requires different prices in the two countries.

Imports in part (b) will be 3 million—the distance QT—only when the price of wine in the importing nation is $110 per barrel, because only at this price will quantity demanded exceed domestic quantity supplied by 3 million barrels. Similarly, exports in part (a) will be 3 million barrels—the distance RS—only when the price in the exporting country is $95 per barrel. At this price, quantity supplied exceeds domestic quantity demanded by 3 million barrels in the exporting country. Thus, the quota raises the price in the importing country to $110 and lowers the price in the exporting country to $95. In general:

An import quota on a product will normally reduce the volume of that product traded, raise its price in the importing country, and reduce its price in the exporting country.

The same restriction of trade can be accomplished through a tariff. In the example we have just completed, a quota of 3 million barrels resulted in a price that was $15 higher in the importing country than in the exporting country ($110 – $95).

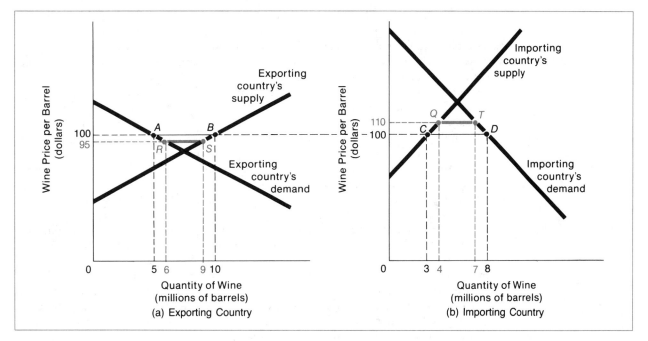

FIGURE 28-4
Quotas and Tariffs in International Trade
Under free trade, the equilibrium price of wine is $100 per barrel. The exporting country, in part (a), sends *AB*, or 5 million barrels, to the importing country (distance *CD*). If the importing country imposes a quota of 3 million barrels, these two distances must shrink to 3 million barrels. The solution is shown by distance *RS* for exports and distance *QT* for imports. Exports and imports are equal, as must be the case, but the quota forces prices to be unequal in the two countries. Wine sells for $110 per barrel in the importing country but only $95 per barrel in the exporting country. A tariff achieves the same result differently. It *requires* that the prices in the two countries be $15 apart. And this, as the graph shows, dictates that exports (= imports) will be equal at 3 million barrels.

Suppose that, instead of a quota, the importing nation posts a $15 per barrel tariff. International trade equilibrium then must satisfy the following two requirements:

1. The price that consumers in the importing country pay for wine must exceed the price that suppliers in the exporting country receive by $15 (the amount of the tariff).

2. The quantity of wine exported must equal the quantity of wine imported.

By consulting the graphs in Figure 28–4, you can see exactly where these two requirements are satisfied. If the exporter produces at *S* and consumes at *R*, while the importer produces at *Q* and consumes at *T*, then exports and imports are equal (at 3 million barrels) and the two domestic prices differ by exactly $15. (They are $110 and $95.) What we have just discovered is a very general result of international trade theory:

Any restriction of imports that is accomplished by a quota can normally also be accomplished by a tariff.

In this case, the tariff corresponding to an import quota of 3 million barrels is $15 per barrel.

Tariffs versus Quotas

Although tariffs and quotas can accomplish the same reduction in international trade and lead to the same domestic prices in the two countries, there *are* some important differences between the two types of restrictions.

First, under a quota, profits from the price increases in the importing country usually go into the pockets of the foreign and domestic sellers of the product. Because supplies are limited by quotas, customers in the importing country must pay more for the product. So the suppliers, be they foreign or domestic, receive more for every unit they sell. For example, the Canadian quota on imports of Japanese automobiles has raised the profit margins of both Canadian and Japanese automakers.

On the other hand, when trade is restricted by a tariff, the profits from the resulting price increase go to the *government* of the importing country as tax revenues. In effect, the government increases its tax revenues partly at the expense of its citizens and partly at the expense of foreign exporters, who must accept a reduced price because of the resulting decrease in quantity demanded in the importing country. (Domestic producers again benefit, because they are exempt from the tariff.) In this respect, a tariff is certainly a better proposition than a quota from the viewpoint of the country that enacts it.

Another important distinction between the two measures is the difference in their implications for productive efficiency and long-run prices. A tariff handicaps all foreign suppliers equally. It still awards sales to the firms and nations that are most efficient and can therefore supply the goods most cheaply. A quota, on the other hand, necessarily awards its import licences more or less capriciously—perhaps on a first-come, first-served basis or in proportion to past sales or by some other arbitrary standard or even on the basis of political criteria. There is not the slightest reason to expect the most efficient and least costly suppliers to get the import permits. In the long run, the population of the importing country is likely to end up with significantly higher prices, poorer products, or both.

The Canadian quota on Japanese cars illustrates all of these effects. Japanese automakers responded to the limit on the number of small cars by shipping bigger models equipped with more "optional" equipment, and many more Japanese trucks. And the newer, smaller Japanese automakers—like Subaru—found it difficult to compete in the Canadian market because their quotas were so much smaller than those of Toyota, Nissan, and Honda.

One interesting example that concerns the distribution of revenues created by trade impediments is provided by the dispute that occurred in the late 1980s between Canada and the United States over softwood lumber products. The Americans wanted to raise employment and profits in their lumber industry by making the Canadian products more expensive to buy in the United States. They felt that Canadian softwood lumber was priced "unfairly" low because Canadian provinces did not charge Canadian firms much tax to cut timber on provincial government lands. Interpreting these low taxes as "subsidies" to the Canadian lumber firms, the Americans threatened to place a large tariff on softwood lumber imports. Canada tried to stop this action. But once it was clear that this attempt would fail, Canada gave up and satisfied the Americans by increasing the domestic taxes imposed on producers. The Canadian government decided that since the Canadian producers were going to lose sales (by being forced to charge higher prices south of the border), Canadians—instead of Americans—might just as well collect the extra revenue involved.

If trade restrictions must be used, there are two important reasons for preferring tariffs over quotas: (1) some of the resulting financial gains from tariffs go to the government, rather than to foreign and domestic producers; and (2) unlike quotas, tariffs offer no special benefits to inefficient exporters.

Why Inhibit Trade?

To state that tariffs are a better way to inhibit international trade than quotas leaves open a far more basic question: Why limit trade in the first place? There are two primary reasons for adopting measures that restrict trade: First, they may help the importing country get more advantageous prices for its goods, and second, they protect particular industries from foreign competition.

Shifting Prices in Your Favour

How can a tariff make prices more advantageous for the importing country if it raises consumer prices there? The answer is that it forces foreign exporters to sell more cheaply. Because their market is restricted by the tariff, they will be left with unsold goods unless they cut their prices. Suppose, as in Figure 28–4(b), that a $15 tariff on wine raises the price of wine in the importing country from $100 to $110 a barrel. This rise in price drives down imports from an amount represented by the length of the black line CD to the smaller amount represented by the green line QT. And to the exporting country, this means an equal reduction in exports [see the change from AB to RS in Figure 28–4(a)].

As a result, the price at which the exporting country can sell its wine is driven down (from $100 to $95 in the example) while producers in the importing country— being exempt from the tariff—can charge $110 per barrel. In effect, such a tariff amounts to government intervention to rig prices in favour of domestic producers and to exploit foreign sellers by forcing them to sell more cheaply than they otherwise would.

This technique works, however, only as long as foreigners accept tariff exploitation passively. And they rarely do. Instead, they retaliate, usually by imposing tariffs or quotas of their own on their imports from the country that first began the tariff game. This can easily lead to a trade war in which no one gains in terms of more favourable prices and everyone loses in terms of the resulting reductions in overall trade. Something like this happened to the world economy in the 1930s and helped prolong the worldwide depression.

Even if there is no retaliation, the tariff or quota can rig prices in favour of domestic producers only if the country imposing the tariff is a significant part of the world demand for that commodity. This requirement is not satisfied in Canada's case. Indeed, we often represent an insignificant portion of world demand for many of our imports. As a result, Canada is essentially in the same position as an individual firm in a perfectly competitive industry. We are a price taker on the world market for our imports.

With this realistic simplification, our analysis of tariffs can be accomplished without the two-part diagram used above. In Figure 28–5, the demand curve and the supply curve of the importing country are shown precisely as they were in Figure 28–4(b). Also, the world supply curve of this commodity (wine) to the small economy is shown as the horizontal line at the price of $100 per barrel. The world supply curve is perfectly elastic at the going world price, since a small country can purchase whatever quantity it desires and have no effect on the world price.

In our example, before any tariff is levied, the country produces 3 million barrels of wine, consumes 8 million barrels and imports 5 million barrels (as indicated by distance CD in Figure 28–5). If world suppliers must pay a $15 per barrel tariff to sell within this economy, the world supply curve shifts up to the $115 point on the price axis. Just as before, equilibrium requires a $15 per barrel gap between the going world price and the price of wine in the country that levies the tariff. However, when the importing country is small, its price rises by the *full amount of the tariff*, and the world price is not forced down at all. This is shown in Figure 28–5, since, after the tariff, domestic production increases to 4.5 million barrels, purchases fall to 6.5 million barrels, and imports fall to 2 million barrels (given by distance VW in the diagram). Our analysis simply verifies the common-sense notion that a small country cannot rig world prices in its favour.

We conclude that ours is too small a country to shift world prices of imports in our favour. Thus, even without considering retaliation, we can state that the price-setting argument for tariffs and quotas is inapplicable to Canada.

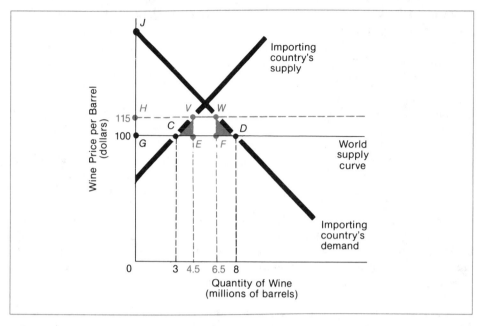

FIGURE 28-5

Quotas and Tariffs When the Importing Country Is Small

Canada is too small to affect the world price of wine, which is $100 per barrel in this example. Under free trade, Canada produces 3 million barrels, consumes 8 million barrels and imports 8 - 3 = 5 million barrels (distance *CD*). This amount is an insignificant portion of world production. If a tariff of $15 per barrel is imposed in Canada, our price rises by the full amount, from $100 to $115 per barrel. Price is unaffected in the rest of the world. Domestic production increases to 4.5 million barrels, consumption falls to 6.5 million barrels, and imports fall to 6.5 - 4.5 = 2 million barrels (distance *VW*). Consumer surplus falls by area *GDWH*, the profits of domestic firms rise by *GCVH*, and government revenue rises by *EFWV*. The net losses to the nation as a whole are shown by the areas of the two green triangles.

We must note, however, that a tariff that fails to rig world prices in our favour not only results in our losing out on a possible benefit, but also causes a greater loss to the nation, which can be calculated as follows. In our wine example, Canadians were consuming 8 million barrels each period before the tariff. Since the demand curve represents the marginal utility schedule for this wine, we know that, in Figure 28–5, the total utility that Canadians derive from the 8 million barrels of wine is the area under this demand curve, up to point *D*. But since Canadians were able to purchase this wine for only $100 per barrel, the amount paid was less than the total utility obtained. The difference is given by area *GDJ*. In Chapter 19 (pages 411–14) we called this free benefit *consumer surplus*. By focussing on this concept here, we can appreciate the costs of a tariff for Canada.

In our example, after the tariff is imposed, Canadians pay $115 per barrel for the decreased quantity of 6.5 million barrels. Consumer surplus is now reduced to area *HWJ*. So the buyers of wine lose area *GDWH* in consumer surplus. Some of this loss is a transfer to domestic firms, and some is a transfer to the government. Domestic firms receive more than they did before the tariff, but their costs have increased as well. The net increase for domestic firms (that is, the increase in their profits) is given by the area *above* their marginal-cost curve (that is, above the domestic supply curve). This is shown by area *GCVH* (the portion of the area between the old and the new price lines that is above the cost curve). The government's revenue is given by area *EFWV* (since the tariff is $15 per barrel times the 2 million barrels imported). The difference between the loss to wine consumers and the gains to domestic producers and the government is the sum of the two triangles that are shown in green in Figure 28–5. In this example, the sum is $22.5 million. So the nation as a whole loses this amount *in every period* as a result of the tariff.

Incidentally, because economists have estimated the elasticities of demand and supply for most traded commodities, we can estimate the sum of the net-loss triangles for all the commodities for which Canada restricts imports. Using this method, and estimating the benefits following from certain economies of scale, the annual gains to Canada of free trade with the United States have been estimated to be an amount equal to about 3 percent of our GDP. These little triangles add up.

Protecting Particular Industries

The second and probably more common reason that countries restrict trade is to protect particular industries from foreign competition. If foreigners can produce steel or watches or shoes more cheaply, domestic businesses and unions in these industries are quick to demand protection, and their government is often reluctant to deny it to them. It is here that the cheap-foreign-labour argument is most likely to be invoked.

The fact is, however, that the firms that are unable to compete in the market are the ones whose relative inefficiency does not permit them to beat foreign exporters at their own game. In Ricardo's example of comparative advantage, one can well imagine the complaints from Portuguese clothmakers as the opening of trade leads to increased importation of English cloth. At the same time, the English grape growers would likely express equal concern over the flood of imported wine from Portugal. Protective tariffs and quotas are designed to undercut harsh competition coming from abroad, yet it is precisely this competition that gives consumers the benefits of international specialization.

When an industry feels threatened by foreign competition, it usually argues that some form of protection against imports is needed to prevent loss of jobs. But we know from our discussion of macroeconomics in Part Three that there are better ways to stimulate employment. Yet it must be admitted that any program that limits foreign competition will, in the short run, preserve jobs in the protected industry. It will work, but often at a very considerable cost to consumers (in the form of higher prices) and to the economy (in the form of inefficient use of resources). For example, several recent American studies have estimated that tariffs and import quotas cost consumers in the United States about $750,000 for each job saved in the steel industry, $105,000 for each job saved in the automobile industry, $100,000 for each job saved in the book manufacturing industry, and $42,000 for each job saved in the textile industry.[3] Similarly, each job in Canadian agriculture that is preserved by means of such trade restrictions costs our government $100,000.

Nevertheless, union complaints over proposals to reduce a tariff or a quota are justified unless something is done to ease the cost to individual workers of switching to those lines of production that trade has now made profitable.

The argument for free trade between countries cannot be considered airtight if there is no adequate program to assist the minority of citizens in each country who will be harmed whenever patterns of production change drastically, as would happen, for example, if tariff and quota barriers were suddenly brought down.

Owners of wineries in Britain and of textile mills in Portugal might see heavy investments suddenly rendered unprofitable, as would workers who invested in acquiring special skills and training that were no longer marketable. Nor are the costs to displaced workers only monetary. Often they have to move to new locations as well as to new industries, uprooting their families, losing old friends and neighbours, and so on. That the *majority* of citizens will undoubtedly gain from free trade is no consolation to those who are its victims. To help alleviate this problem, it is often argued that Canada should expand its **trade adjustment assistance** programs to help workers who

Trade adjustment assistance provides special unemployment benefits, loans, retraining programs, or other aid to workers and firms that are harmed by foreign competition.

[3] Gary C. Hufbauer, Diane T. Berliner, and Kimberly Ann Elliott, *Trade Protection in the United States: 31 Case Studies* (Washington, D.C.: Institute for International Economic Studies, 1986), Table 1.2.

Business Subsidies Should Go to Future Jobs, Not to Saving Dying Ones

During 1986, General Motors, the world's largest manufacturing company, was spending billions of dollars on numerous projects but claimed it could not afford to modernize a plant in Ste-Thérèse, Quebec, and so would close it. The Canadian government stopped this market-based decision by giving GM large amounts of money to keep the plant running. The reaction of Peter Cook, of *The Globe and Mail*, is excerpted below.

The second article here presents an interesting contrast: an alternative kind of assistance policy that Deborah McGregor, writing for the Financial Times News Service, says truly aids adjustment. The example she describes is a Toyota plant built in Kentucky with the aid of a $65 million contribution by the state government.

GM in Quebec

...If there is any company that is looking at investing on its own and taking a real risk, it is acting dumb. The commitment that has been given that government aid will be forthcoming is open-ended. Get in line, please, Ford, Chrysler and whoever else.

The only requirement is that the plant you are going to threaten to shut down to get your investment money is of sufficient size and located in a sufficiently politically sensitive region to scare the politicians.

This kind of thing used to be known as corporate blackmail. Now, in Canada, it is respectable corporate behaviour sanctified by the country's political parties, all of whom back the Ste-Thérèse bailout.

Preventing companies, such as GM, from making rational economic decisions is a high-priced game for governments. Short-term bail-outs for workers can lead to long-term problems for everyone. For politicians, the price of saying no can be costly. But not nearly as costly as the price of saying yes—with dumb subsidies.

SOURCE: Peter Cook, *The Globe and Mail*, April 2, 1987, page B3.

Toyota in Kentucky

Toyota makes all the corporate decisions: what line of cars to produce, how the plant will be run, how many workers are needed. Kentucky's "subsidy" is, in fact, limited to developing the workforce at the plant.

The $65 million is a fund for training and it will work this way: Toyota is expecting 250,000 people to apply for the 3,000 jobs at the plant, which is scheduled to open in late 1988. Of those applications, 9,000 will be selected—if it were a basketball team, these people would be said to have made the "first cut."

The 9,000 people will go through a screening and interview process, and they will be paid $5 an hour for their trouble. Of these, 6,000 prospective workers will be selected—the "second cut." They will undergo further scrutiny and, again, will be paid $5 an hour.

At the end of this lengthy screening, 3,000 workers will be offered jobs. Of those, 600 will be sent to Japan for training. One-half of them will go twice. And 100 instructors will be brought from Japan to train the rest of the workers at the site.

The state of Kentucky picks up the whole bill. It also pays the workers' salaries for a probationary period of six months.

The scheme benefits both Toyota and Kentucky. Toyota is not chained to production or investment agreements that could limit its corporate flexibility. Kentucky has targeted its aid directly to the 3,000 workers who will emerge with new, highly competitive skills. It's not even a bad deal for the 6,000 who don't make the final cut but do make $5 an hour while being exposed to some new rules of the employment game.

SOURCE: Deborah McGregor, *The Hamilton Spectator*, December 18, 1986, page A7.

---

have lost jobs because of the changing patterns of world trade. Sometimes, however, these policies provide too much assistance and actually hinder adjustment. The newspaper excerpts in the accompanying boxed insert give examples.

Other Arguments for Protection

National Defence and Other Non-economic Considerations

There are times when a tariff or some other measure to interfere with trade may be justified on non-economic grounds. If a country considers itself vulnerable to military attack, it may be perfectly rational to keep alive industries whose outputs can be obtained more cheaply abroad but whose supplies might be cut off during an emergency. For example, airplane production by small countries makes sense only on these grounds.

The danger is that many industries, even those with the most peripheral relationship to defence, are likely to invoke this argument on their own behalf. For instance, the U.S. watchmaking industry claimed protection for itself for many years on the grounds that its skilled workers would be invaluable in wartime. Perhaps so, but a technicians' training program probably could have done the job more cheaply and even more effectively by teaching exactly the skills needed for military purposes.

The Infant-Industry Argument

Another common argument for protectionism is the so-called infant-industry argument. Promising new industries often need breathing room to flourish and grow; if we expose these infants to the rigours of international competition too soon, the argument goes, they may never develop to the point of being able to survive on their own in the international marketplace.

The argument, while valid in certain instances, is less defensible than it may at first appear. It makes sense only if the industry's prospective future gains are sufficient to repay the social losses incurred while it is being protected. But if the industry is likely to be so profitable in the future, why doesn't private capital rush in to take advantage of the prospective net profits? The annals of business are full of cases in which a new product or a new firm lost money at first but profited handsomely later. Only where funds are not available, for some reason, to a particular industry, despite its glowing profit prospects, does the infant-industry argument for protection stand up to scrutiny. And even then it may make more sense to provide a government loan than to provide trade protection.

It is hard to think of examples where the infant-industry argument applies. But even in cases where it is a legitimate argument, another real danger exists—namely, that the industry might remain in diapers forever. Too often, the time to withdraw the protection awarded to an industry never arrives. The Canadian textile industry comes to mind. In the late 1980s, Canada's solicitor general signed thirty bilateral trade-restraint agreements with foreign textile suppliers—arrangements that would raise every Canadian family's clothing costs by about $60 per year. Afterwards, the solicitor general said that the policy was not designed to shield Canadian industry from imports! Rather, he claimed, the aim was to give more security to the Canadian industry *while it modernized*—in other words, while it grew up. We must be wary of infant industries that *never* grow up.

Strategic Trade Policy

A new argument for protectionism has become popular in recent years. Advocates of this argument agree that free trade for all is the best system. But they point out that we live in an imperfect world in which many nations refuse to play by the rules of the free-trade game. And they fear that a nation that pursues free trade in a protectionist world is likely to lose out. It therefore makes sense, they argue, to threaten to protect your markets unless other nations agree to open theirs.

This argument is hard for economists to deal with. While it accepts the superiority of free trade, it argues that threatening protectionism is the best way to establish free trade. Such a strategy might work, but it clearly involves great risks. If threats that Canada will turn protectionist induce other countries to scrap existing protectionist policies, then the gamble will have succeeded. But if the gamble fails, the world ends up with even more protection than before. As we have already noted, however, if Canada were to make such threats, they would probably have little effect on other countries, so this is not a compelling argument with regard to Canadian tariffs. For the United States, on the other hand, it could be a worthwhile strategy.

There is a rather obvious analogy here to arms negotiations in the Cold War era.

Suppose, for example, that the Americans had threatened to install new missiles unless the Soviets agreed to dismantle some of theirs. If the Soviets had agreed, the world would have been a safer place and everyone would have been better off. But, if they had not, the arms race would have accelerated and everyone would have been worse off. Would the American threat to build new missiles therefore have been a wise or a foolish policy? There is no agreement on this question, so we should not expect agreement on the advisability of using protectionist measures in a strategic way.

The Development of Trade Policy

In the late 1870s, Sir John A. Macdonald devised a policy of high tariffs for Canada, in the aim of stimulating the growth of the manufacturing sector. Although the policy was meant to unify the country, it turned out to be divisive: It alienated both the Western and the Maritime provinces, which had to share in paying the costs of the high tariffs, despite the fact that there was little chance that their own manufacturing industries would develop as a result. By 1890, the average tariff rate in Canada was about 21 percent; a century later, it had dropped to about 5 percent. The average tariff rate declined reasonably steadily throughout the century, although it did increase somewhat during the depression years of the 1930s.

In 1947, Canada was one of 23 countries that signed the General Agreement on Tariffs and Trade (GATT), which established an organization dedicated to arranging for member nations to legislate reductions in tariffs. All observers agree that this co-operation stimulated much world trade and, therefore, employment growth. But the co-operation has been breaking down in recent years.

The earliest exceptions to GATT's rules were made in the areas of agriculture and textiles. Now, trade arrangements for these items, as well as for steel, are handled largely outside GATT. For the textiles trade, for example, Canada is an active participant in the Multi-Fibre Arrangement, a now-permanent feature of international policy involving discriminatory restraints that are a complete contradiction of GATT rules. Canada is also involved in many arrangements pertaining to agricultural commodities, as well as in voluntary export deals pertaining to automobiles, that also go beyond GATT rules. By 1986, a full $68 billion of U.S. imports was covered by restraints of one kind or another that violated GATT agreements.

For an example of how such trade restraints escalate, consider what happened when Spain and Portugal joined the European Community (the Common Market) in March 1986. These countries were obliged to switch to EC member nations for many of their imports and to bring their own trade restrictions in line with those of other EC countries. For example, Spain had to replace its 20 percent tariff on corn and sorghum with the common EC levy of more than 100 percent. The United States filed a complaint, claiming compensation for its lost exports; when that was denied, the Americans set out to produce a comparable loss of trade by erecting equivalent barriers to EC exports.

In recent years there have been some signs that trade restrictions on agricultural commodities may once again be negotiated on a worldwide basis, but concrete plans have yet to appear. All Western nations now offer their farmers subsidies in an attempt to make them competitive internationally. To this end, as of 1990, some $240 billion was being spent annually by the major Western countries, and most of these expenditures served only to cancel out the effects of the other countries' subsidies.

During the 1980s, Canada faced new tariffs or quotas imposed by the United States in all the following areas: sugars and syrups, carbons and certain steel-alloy products, specialty steel products, dried salted codfish, raspberries, hogs and pork, sewer grates and construction castings, cedar shakes and shingles, Atlantic groundfish, gas- and oil-well steel products, salmon and herring fisheries, softwood lumber, carnations, brass sheets and strips, potash, and natural gas. Then, in 1988, the U.S. Congress passed what is known as the Omnibus Trade Bill, which enshrines in legislative form the American practice of identifying countries that are believed to be restricting imports from the United States. The act stipulates that a **countervailing duty** should be applied on the corresponding exports from such countries to the United States. This trade bill has serious repercussions for Canada, since 80 percent of Canadian exports go to the United States.

A **countervailing duty** is a tariff levied on imports to offset the effects of what are perceived as unrealistically low prices set by producers in the exporting country.

The Canada–U.S. Free Trade Agreement

The Benefits

The Free Trade Agreement (FTA), which Canada signed with the United States on January 1, 1989, in many ways represents a defensive policy on Canada's part. Since we export more than one-quarter of our national product, and since 80 percent of that trade is with the United States, our economy is vulnerable to fundamental disruption by American protectionist policies. It was hoped that the FTA would safeguard us against such policies.

A second rationale for the FTA was Canada's need for secure access to a larger market, which would justify longer production runs and provide the gains in productive efficiency that come only with the increased degree of specialization facilitated by large-scale operations. How could Canadian producers, who were supplying a large variety of products for a domestic market of only 26 million people, hope to compete with the United States, Japan, and the European Community, with their very much larger domestic (and therefore tariff-free) markets? (The European Community, for example, represents a combined domestic market of about 320 million people.) A similar reaction to the problems created by small domestic markets is evident among the six countries that comprise the European Free Trade Association (EFTA)—Austria, Finland, Iceland, Norway, Sweden, and Switzerland. This group, with a combined population of 32 million, has never been part of the EC; rather, it has long been the EC's largest single trading partner (just as Canada has been in relation to the United States). As this book went to press, the EFTA was applying for membership within the EC.

To gain full free access to one of the world's largest markets, Canada has had to accept the costs of cutting its own tariffs—namely, the important adjustment costs that must be paid by formerly protected workers and firms. Conversely, however, benefits come to Canadians from the Americans' cutting their tariffs on *our* exports. As we noted earlier, these benefits flow from three sources—comparative advantage, the increased specialization resulting from larger-scale operations, and lower monopoly markups—and have been estimated to equal about 3 percent of GDP every year. This ongoing flow of benefits is what Canada would have thrown away had we not signed the FTA.

The largest share of these estimated benefits is expected to come from the cost reductions that accompany large-scale production. For these gains to materialize, however, firms operating within Canada must make major investments to reorient their operations. Some critics of the FTA doubt that sufficient investment will occur, because, even with the FTA, such investments are risky: Because either side can abrogate the agreement with only six months' notice, large investments in plant and equipment in Canada could suddenly become worth very little. However, the threat of possible abrogation seems to have waned over time, and the necessary investment expenditures will probably be forthcoming.

The Costs

Let us now consider some of the costs that must be incurred to acquire the higher standard of living that free trade promises. Critics often raise the concern that the FTA will strip Canada's exports down to raw materials alone, because, they argue, our manufacturing and processing industries will be forced to contract as a result of free trade. Two responses to this concern are in order. First, if our comparative advantage is in the area of natural resources, why would we wish to lower incomes just to keep factory jobs? Second, it must be remembered that the FTA removes both Canadian *and* American tariffs. Thus, while the removal of our tariffs does hurt some Canadian manufacturers, the removal of U.S. tariffs helps other Canadian manufacturers. In other words, it is not at all clear that, on balance, our manufacturing industries will have to contract. Indeed, many firms in southern Ontario, for example, are better situated to serve the important markets in the northeastern United States than are many U.S. manufacturers.

During the first year after the FTA was signed, it seemed that every plant closure in Canada was blamed on free trade. It is important to remember, however, that job losses make news stories, while new investments by manufacturing firms tend not to. This imbalance in media coverage is due in part to the fact that it takes longer to expand a plant or to build a new one than it does to close one. It should also be recognized that Canada's job losses in 1990 were due largely to the recession of that year. This recession was caused by a slowdown in the United States, as well as by the record-high levels of both real interest rates and the Canadian dollar that prevailed during that period. Since the unemployment rate rose by no more than the amount one would expect in a recession of this magnitude, its rise cannot reasonably be attributed to the FTA. In other words, if free trade caused job losses, it must have been generating a similar number of new jobs at the same time. Otherwise, the unemployment rate would have to have been significantly higher.

Another issue of concern regarding the FTA is adjustment costs: Critics stress how painful it is for workers to shift from industries that decline as a result of free trade to those that promise to expand. These costs are real, and there is no question that affected workers should receive assistance. Nonetheless, the magnitude of adjustment costs is often exaggerated. The FTA is being phased in gradually over ten years, and it may prove to be the case that much of the necessary adjustment will occur as part of the ongoing pattern of job changing that is already taking place. Many people are surprised to learn that, on average, almost one out of every five Canadian workers changes jobs every year. Also, it is interesting to note how quickly the adjustments took place when other free-trade areas were created. The Treaty of Rome created the European Economic Community in 1958; two years later, those involved were so pleased with the low level of actual adjustment costs that the plan's implementation speed was tripled.

How Will Disputes Be Settled?

A third criticism of the FTA is that it could lead to a loss in the degree of Canada's political independence, in that our domestic policies could come to be sacrificed for the survival of the agreement. Critics fear, for example, that if a domestic policy were deemed by the United States to constitute an "unfair subsidy," our government might be compelled to alter the policy. It is difficult to respond to this concern, since we do not yet know how the so-called unfair subsidies (which must be assumed to exist within both countries) will be formally defined. (The agreement requires that a clear definition be established by 1996.) We must also bear in mind that American countervailing duties had forced Canada to alter domestic policies even before the FTA was signed (recall our example of softwood lumber on page 616). If the dispute-settlement mechanism that is finally negotiated by the two countries actually lessens the United States' ability to impose its protectionist desires on Canada, we will have gained independence. But many expect that it may in fact provide the Americans with a greater power to dictate which domestic policies within Canada are or are not acceptable to them.

Some analysts also expect pressure for an erosion of Canada's social and medical assistance programs, which are more comprehensive, and therefore more expensive, than their counterparts in the United States. The argument is that increased competition with American firms, which pay much less to help finance such programs than do Canadian firms, will cause Canadian firms to lobby for a reduction in the amounts that are collected from them. Thus, according to this argument, our social programs could be forced down to the level of those in the United States. But historical evidence does not seem to support this argument. After all, most of our social programs were developed during the years when our tariffs were being significantly *reduced*. Furthermore, there is a noticeable range in the scope of social programs across the different states south of the border (and, from the perspective of the individual states, their own country is, in effect, a free-trade area). Similarly, there are significant differences among the social policies of various countries within the European Community.

Nonetheless, as we noted earlier, the dispute-settlement mechanism associated with the FTA will remain unsatisfactory until a sensible definition of unfair trade practices is developed. (The existing dispute-settlement scheme requires only that each country satisfy an independent five-person tribunal that its *own* existing trade laws are being applied properly.) Furthermore, our bargaining power in the dispute-settlement negotiations is admittedly small, given the much larger size of our partner in those negotiations. And unlike member countries of the EC, we have no other small partners to whom we can appeal for support. Indeed, our bargaining power could shrink even farther over time, because the more resources our industries invest in their adjustment to free trade, the more costly the consequences of abrogation will be for the country. Again, although the same principle would hold for the United States, the relative impact of the costs involved would be much smaller because that economy is so much larger than ours.

The first trade dispute to be considered after the signing of the FTA is a case in point. The dispute concerned Canada's pork exports, and hinged on the definition of an "unfair subsidy": Canada operates a government-assisted income-stabilization program for its pork producers. The United States won this dispute and, in 1989, imposed a countervailing duty on Canadian pork imports. Canada's exports of pork to the United States represented a full 25 percent of our producers' sales, but only 3 percent of the American market. This example clearly illustrates that the costs of losing these disputes are much higher for Canada than for the United States, and that there is good reason for the concern that Canada may not have secured as open an access to American markets as was hoped. Those who support the FTA trust that progress in negotiating a more satisfactory dispute-settlement mechanism can be expected soon. Supporters also note that our vulnerability to developments within the United States can be lessened if we push hard for further multilateral tariff and quota reductions through the GATT. (The FTA does not limit our negotiations in this regard.)

The Ethics of Competition

Proponents of the FTA are frustrated by the fact that many Canadians see the issue as one that pits materialism against moral justice. For example, in 1988, Canada's major Christian churches submitted a joint statement to the parliamentary committee that was considering the FTA. This statement claimed that free trade was "morally unacceptable" because it would "require a number of human sacrifices on the altar of the almighty dollar." Many economists, concerned with the alarming extent of poverty in the less developed countries, disagree. They see the development of free trade throughout the world as the only possible hope for limiting human sacrifices in those countries. Foreign-aid programs have proved not to be a viable option, because they typically have so many strings attached that the receiving nations are kept in a position of dependence. The experience of the newly industrialized countries in Asia (such as Taiwan and Korea) shows that foreign trade can lead to a vast reduction in poverty, *without* creating an ongoing relationship of dependence. Hence, it would seem that if one is genuinely concerned about worldwide poverty, there is no better option than to support freer trade.

Unfair Foreign Competition

Satire and ridicule are often more persuasive than logic and statistics. Exasperated by the spread of protectionism to so many industries under the prevailing Mercantilist philosophy, French economist Frédéric Bastiat decided to take the protectionist argument to its illogical conclusion. His fictitious petition of the French candlemakers to the Chamber of Deputies, written in 1845 and excerpted below, has become a classic in the battle for free trade.

We are subject to the intolerable competition of a foreign rival, who enjoys, it would seem, such superior facilities for the production of light, that he is enabled to *inundate* our *national market* at so exceedingly reduced a price, that, the moment he makes his appearance, he draws off all custom for us; and thus an important branch of French industry, with all its innumerable ramifications, is suddenly reduced to a state of complete stagnation. This rival is no other than the sun.

Our petition is, that it would please your honorable body to pass a law whereby shall be directed the shutting up of all windows, dormers, skylights, shutters, curtains, in a word, all openings, holes, chinks, and fissures through which the light of the sun is used to penetrate our dwellings, to the prejudice of the profitable manufactures which we flatter ourselves we have been enabled to bestow upon the country....

We foresee your objections, gentlemen; but there is not one that you can oppose to us ... which is not equally opposed to your own practice and the principle which guides your policy....

Labor and nature concur in different proportions, according to country and climate, in every article of production.... If a Lisbon orange can be sold at half the price of a Parisian one, it is because a natural and gratuitous heat does for the one what the other only obtains from an artificial and consequently expensive one....

Does it not argue the greatest inconsistency to check as you do the importation of coal, iron, cheese, and goods of foreign manufacture, merely because and even in proportion as their price approaches *zero*, while at the same time you freely admit, and without limitation, the light of the sun, whose price is during the whole day at *zero*?

SOURCE: F. Bastiat, *Economic Sophisms* (New York: G. P. Putnam's Sons, 1922).

What Import Prices Benefit a Country?

Dumping means selling goods in a foreign market at lower prices than those charged in the home market.

One of the most curious features of the protectionist position is the fear of low prices charged by foreign sellers. Countries that subsidize exports are accused of **dumping**— of getting rid of their goods at unconscionably low prices. For example, in the last few years Japan has frequently been accused of dumping various goods (such as semiconductors) on the Canadian and American markets, and Europe has been accused of dumping its agricultural goods.

A moment's thought should indicate why this fear must be considered curious. As a nation of consumers, we should be indignant when foreigners charge us *high* prices, not *low* ones. That is the common-sense rule that guides every consumer, and the consumers of imported commodities should be no exception. Only from the topsyturvy viewpoint of an industry seeking protection from competition are high prices seen as being in the public interest.

Ultimately, it must be in the best interest of a country to get its imports as cheaply as possible. It would be ideal for Canada if the rest of the world were willing to provide its exports to us free or virtually so. We could then live in luxury at the expense of the rest of the world.

The notion that low import prices are bad for a country is a fitting companion to the idea—so often heard—that it is good for a country to export much more than it imports. True, this means that foreigners will end up owing us a good deal of money. But it also means that we will have given them large quantities of our products and have gotten relatively little in foreign products in return. That surely is not an ideal way for a country to reap gains from international trade.

Our gains from trade do not consist of accumulations of gold or of heavy debts owed us by foreigners. Rather, our gains are composed of the goods and services that others provide minus the goods and services we must provide them in return.

The preceding discussion should indicate the fundamental fallacy in the argument that Canadian workers have to fear "cheap foreign labour." If workers in other countries are willing to supply their products to us with little compensation, this must ultimately *raise* the standard of living of the average Canadian worker. As long as the government's monetary and fiscal policies succeed in maintaining high levels of employment at home, how can we lose by getting the products of the world at bargain prices?

There are, however, some important qualifications to this prognosis. First, our employment policy may not be effective. If Canadian workers who are displaced by foreign competition cannot find jobs in other industries, they will indeed suffer from international trade. But that is a shortcoming of the government's employment program, not of its international trade policies.

Second, we have noted that an abrupt stiffening of foreign competition, resulting, say, from a major innovation in another country or from a discovery of a new and better source of raw materials or from a sharp increase in export subsidies by a foreign country, *can* hurt Canadian workers by not giving them an adequate chance to adapt gradually to the new conditions. The more rapid the change, the more painful it will be. If change occurs fairly gradually, workers can retrain and move on to the industries that now require their services. If the change is even more gradual, no one may have to move. People who retire or leave the threatened industry for other reasons simply need not be replaced. But competition that inflicts its damage overnight is certain to impose very real costs on the affected workers, costs that are no less painful for being temporary.

But these are, after all, minor qualifications to an overwhelming argument. They call for intelligent monetary and fiscal policies and for transitional assistance to unemployed workers, not for abandonment of free trade and permission for monopoly power to flourish behind protection.

In the long run, labour will be "cheap" only where it is not very productive. Wages will tend to be highest in those countries in which high labour productivity keeps costs down and permits exporters to compete effectively despite high wages.

We note that in this matter it is absolute advantage, not comparative advantage, that counts. The country that is most efficient in every output can pay its workers more in every industry.

We started this chapter by noting that tariff cuts involve both benefits and costs. The benefits are that consumers acquire goods at lower prices and that the anti-competitive behaviour of firms can be limited without having to rely on regulations and attempted prosecutions. (These methods, which are used in an attempt to enforce competition policy, have met with quite limited success, as we explain in Chapter 31.) The costs of tariff cuts are the jobs that many expect would be lost to "cheap foreign labour." This chapter has shown that these costs are very much exaggerated in popular discussion. This is because the principle of comparative advantage is not generally appreciated and because the problems associated with increased competition can be better solved by appropriate monetary, fiscal, and adjustment assistance policies.

Microeconomic Policy: A Review and a Preview

The Proper Assignment of Policies to Goals

At many points throughout this book, we have stressed the unfortunate trade-off between two of the fundamental goals of economic policy: efficiency and equality. Indeed, this trade-off is one of our **12 Ideas for Beyond the Final Exam**. It is useful at this stage to generalize the discussion of policy goals and instruments, in order to clarify how the terms of this trade-off can be kept as appealing as possible. After all, would it not be desirable to sacrifice as little efficiency as possible in our pursuit of equity—that is, of greater economic equality?

To start, let us group our major economic policy goals into three main categories:

Goal 1: Efficiency.   To achieve a high level of average income.

Goal 2: Equality.   To redistribute some income from the rich to the poor.

Goal 3: Stabilization.   To minimize the swings in unemployment and inflation caused by variations in the GDP gap.

Once again, to facilitate our discussion, let us group into three broad categories the many policies that the government can either adopt or reject in its pursuit of our economic goals:

Policy A: Market Controls.   For example, tariffs, quotas, minimum-wage laws.

Policy B: An Egalitarian Tax/Transfer System.   A general income tax with significant tax relief for low-income earners and very few tax shelters for the rich.

Policy C: Macroeconomic and Adjustment Assistance Policies.   For example, temporary variations in government spending, taxes, and the money supply or the exchange rate to limit recessionary and inflationary gaps, and the legislation of ongoing stabilizers, such as unemployment insurance and grants for retraining and relocation.

Our fundamental objective is to assign policy instruments to goals in a way that minimizes the trade-offs involved. Most economists are convinced that the optimal assignment is to pair:

> Goal 1 with the rejection of Policy A
>
> Goal 2 with the adoption of Policy B
>
> Goal 3 with the adoption of Policy C

In more specific terms, this assignment calls for rejecting market controls, such as tariffs, on the grounds that they impair the efficiency of the market system, which works well only when the necessary decentralized market signals are allowed to operate. If the goal of efficiency is not pursued, average income is lowered. As far as our objective of equality is concerned, we should redistribute income in ways that involve the fewest possible disincentive effects. For example, welfare programs that encourage people not to work (and therefore prevent them from acquiring skills through experience—see Chapter 30) and minimum-wage laws (which increase the unemployment rate for unskilled workers) are undesirable since they *lower* the overall level of income in the course of attempting to redistribute it. This is the rationale for pairing Goal 2 with the adoption of Policy B. It is true that our pursuit of efficiency can lead to more inequality if we accomplish that efficient outcome by rejecting such measures as tariffs and minimum-wage laws. But we can make up for this reduction in equality *more effectively* by having our general income tax system redistribute more income from the rich to the poor than by giving up the benefits of, for example, freer trade *indefinitely*. In short, the adoption of Policy B has a comparative advantage in achieving the goal of equity, while the rejection of Policy A has a comparative advantage in achieving the goal of efficiency. If we assign policies to goals improperly —for example, by trying to use market controls for income redistribution and a plethora of taxes and subsidies to guide the allocation of resources—we end up scoring lower with respect to both equity and efficiency objectives.

A similar argument can help to explain why our stabilization objectives should be pursued through macroeconomic policy adjustment and the use of policies that increase labour mobility. For example, if we are attempting to relieve unemployment, it makes no sense to use a *permanent* tariff, which imposes permanent losses on all citizens, just to avoid a *temporary* disruption, which could be addressed with a more appropriate set of policy instruments.

Many individuals argue for the use of market controls to pursue *both* equity and stabilization objectives (Goals B and C). These individuals seem to regard economic efficiency (Goal A) as not particularly important. (The prevalence of the argument that free trade is bad because it involves some job losses attests to the popularity of this point of view.) Economists have two general responses to such arguments: First, if society has three broad goals in the economic arena, and three independent classes of policy options, it is counterproductive not to use *all* three kinds of policies in a co-ordinated way. To do otherwise—for example, to try to achieve more than one goal with only one policy instrument—will tend to maximize the trade-offs that we have to face. Second, there is much evidence to suggest that the issue of efficiency matters more than many people think it does. As we shall see in Chapter 30, our gradual progress in reducing poverty in Canada was halted during the 1980s by the major recession that occurred at that time. It is a simple fact of history that most people are unwilling to participate in a redistribution of income toward the poor if their own incomes are not showing signs of growth. In short, if we care about equality, we cannot afford not to care about efficiency.

Summary

1. Countries trade because differences in their natural resources and other inputs create discrepancies in the efficiency with which they can produce different goods, and because specialization may offer them greater economies of large-scale production.

2. Voluntary trade will generally be advantageous to both parties in an exchange. This is one of our 12 **Ideas for Beyond the Final Exam.**

3. International trade is more complicated than trade within a nation because of political factors, different national currencies, and impediments to the movement of labour and capital across national borders.

4. Both countries will gain from trade if each one exports goods in which it has a comparative advantage. That is, even a country that is generally inefficient will benefit by exporting the goods in the production of which it is least inefficient. This is another of the 12 **Ideas for Beyond the Final Exam.**

5. When countries specialize and trade, each can enjoy consumption possibilities that exceed its production possibilities.

6. The prices of goods traded between countries are determined by supply and demand, but one must consider explicitly the demand curve and the supply curve of *each* country involved. Thus, in international trade, the equilibrium price must occur where the excess of the exporting country's quantity supplied over its domestic quantity demanded is equal to the excess of the importing country's quantity demanded over its quantity supplied.

7. The "cheap foreign labour" argument ignores the principle of comparative advantage, which shows that real wages can rise in both the importing and the exporting country as a result of specialization.

8. Tariffs and quotas are designed to protect a country's industries from foreign competition. Such protection may sometimes be advantageous to that country, but not if foreign countries adopt tariffs and quotas of their own as a means of retaliation, and not if the country constitutes a small share of the world market.

9. While a tariff and a quota can accomplish the same restriction of trade, tariffs offer at least two advantages to

the country that imposes them: (1) some of the gains go to the government rather than to foreign producers, and (2) there is greater incentive for efficient production.

10. When a nation shifts from protection to free trade, some industries and their workers will lose out. Equity demands that these people and firms be compensated in some way. Adjustment assistance programs (rather than the rejection of free trade) offer the optimal solution to this problem.

11. Several arguments for protectionism, under the right circumstances, have some validity. These include the national-defence argument, the infant-industry argument, and the strategic-trade-policy argument. Unfortunately, each of these rationales is frequently abused.

12. Since a reduction in tariffs is beneficial even if domestic industries are competitive (as illustrated by the principle of comparative advantage), it is doubly appealing if domestic industries are non-competitive. Thus, tariff cuts represent a significant element in a country's competition policy.

13. Canada's Free Trade Agreement (FTA) with the United States is predicted to raise our average income level by an estimated 3 percent on an ongoing basis. Some studies forecast higher gains; others estimate smaller ones. This uncertainty exists because it is as yet unclear whether Canada will gain secure and full access to U.S. markets. An accurate assessment will be possible only when a definition of what constitutes an "unfair subsidy" has been agreed upon by the two countries.

14. We have three broad goals in economics—efficiency, equality, and stabilization. If we do not properly assign the three available policy instruments to these three goals, we are likely to face very severe trade-offs. Experience shows that the trade-offs are minimized when market controls such as tariffs are rejected as a means of promoting efficiency, and when the general income tax system is used to achieve the desired degree of economic equality. Finally, macroeconomic and labour mobility policies should be used to counter any short-term unemployment problems that may arise as a result of the removal of market controls.

Concepts for Review

Imports	Comparative advantage	Export subsidy
Exports	"Cheap foreign labour" argument	Trade adjustment assistance
Specialization	Tariff	Infant-industry argument
Mutual gains from trade	Non-tariff barriers	Countervailing duty
Absolute advantage	Quota	Dumping

Questions for Discussion

1. Country A has mild weather and plenty of rain, plentiful land, and an unskilled labour force. What sorts of products do you think it is likely to produce? What are the characteristics of countries with which you would expect it to trade?

2. In the eighteenth century, some writers argued that one party in a trade could be made better off only by gaining at the expense of the other. Explain the fallacy in the argument.

3. Upon removal of a quota on semiconductors, a Canadian manufacturer of semiconductors goes bankrupt. Discuss the pros and cons of the quota removal in the short run and in the long run.

4. The table below describes the number of red socks and the number of white socks that can be produced with an hour of labour in two different cities:

	IN BOSTON	IN CHICAGO
Red socks (pairs)	3	2
White socks (pairs)	3	1

a. If there is no trade, what is the price of white socks relative to red socks in Boston?

b. If there is no trade, what is the price of white socks relative to red socks in Chicago?

c. Suppose each city has 1000 hours of labour available per year. Draw the production possibilities frontier for each city.

d. Which city has an absolute advantage in the production of which good(s)? Which city has a comparative advantage in the production of which good(s)?

e. If the cities start trading with each other, which city will specialize in, and export, which good?

f. What can be said about the prices at which trade will take place?

5. Suppose that Canada and Mexico are the only two countries in the world. In Canada a worker can produce 12 bushels of wheat *or* 1 barrel of oil a day. In Mexico, a worker can produce 2 bushels of wheat *or* 2 barrels of oil a day.

a. What will be the price ratio between the two commodities (i.e., the price of oil in terms of wheat) in each country if there is no trade?

b. If free trade is allowed and there are no transportation costs, what commodity would Canada import? What about Mexico?

c. In what range will the price ratio have to fall under free trade? Why?

d. Picking one possible post-trade price ratio, show clearly how it is possible for both countries to benefit from free trade.

6. The table below presents the demand and supply curves for microcomputers in Japan and Canada.

a. Draw the demand and supply curves for Canada on one diagram and those for Japan on another one.

b. If there is no trade between Canada and Japan, what are the equilibrium price and quantity in the computer market in Canada? In Japan?

c. Now suppose trade is opened up between the two countries. What will be the equilibrium price of computers in the world market? What has happened to the price of computers in Canada? In Japan?

d. Which country will export computers? How many?

e. When trade opens, what happens to the quantity of computers produced, and therefore to employment, in the computer industry in Canada? In Japan? Who benefits and who loses *initially* from free trade?

7. Under current trade law, the president of the United States must report periodically to Congress on countries engaging in unfair trade practices that inhibit U.S. exports. How would you define an "unfair" trade practice? Suppose that Canada exported much more to the United States than it imported from that country, year after year. Would that constitute evidence that Canada's trade practices were unfair? What would constitute such evidence?

8. Suppose the United States finds Canada guilty of unfair trade practices and penalizes it with import quotas, so that Canada's exports to the United States fall. Suppose, further, that Canada does not alter its trade practices in any way. Is the United States better or worse off? What about Canada?

PRICE PER COMPUTER (thousands of dollars)	QUANTITY DEMANDED IN CANADA (thousands)	QUANTITY SUPPLIED IN CANADA (thousands)	QUANTITY DEMANDED IN JAPAN (thousands)	QUANTITY SUPPLIED IN JAPAN (thousands)
0	100	0	100	0
1	90	10	90	25
2	80	20	80	50
3	70	30	70	70
4	60	40	60	80
5	50	50	50	90
6	40	60	40	100
7	30	70	30	110
8	20	80	20	120
9	10	90	10	130
10	0	100	0	140

PART VII

Microeconomic Issues

29

Pricing the Factors of Production: Income Distribution

Masters are always and every where in a sort of tacit, but constant and uniform combination, not to raise the wages of labour.

ADAM SMITH

I'm especially grateful, as I have no other marketable skills.

JOHNNY CARSON [on signing a new NBC contract for an estimated $5 million a year]

Much of this book has been devoted to examining the things the free-market system does well and the things it does poorly. We mentioned in Chapter 27 that the market mechanism cannot be counted on to distribute income in accordance with ethical notions of "fairness" or "justice," and we listed this failing as one of the market's shortcomings. But there is much more to be said about how income is distributed in a market economy and about how governments alter this distribution process. These are the subjects of this and the next chapter.

The broad outlines of how the market mechanism distributes income are familiar to all of us. Each person owns some **factors of production**—the inputs used in the production process. Many of us have only our own labour, but some of us also have funds that we can lend, land that we can rent, or natural resources that we can sell. These factors are sold on markets at prices determined by supply and demand. So the distribution of income in a market economy is determined by the level of employment of the factors of production and by their prices. For example, if wages are rather high and are fairly equal among workers and if unemployment is low, then few people will be poor. But if wages are low and unequal and unemployment is high, then many people will be poor.

For purposes of discussion, the factors of production may be grouped into five broad categories: labour, capital, land, exhaustible natural resources, and a rather mysterious input called entrepreneurship. Exhaustible natural resources will be studied in Chapter 32. In this chapter, we will study the payments made for the use of the other four factors: the wages paid to labour, the interest paid to capital, the rent of land, and the profits earned by entrepreneurs.

Since this chapter focusses on the *theories* of factor pricing, it may be useful first to have a brief look at how much these inputs earn in *reality*. According to Canadian data on net domestic income at factor cost for 1989, interest payments accounted for about 10 percent of national income, land rents and non-corporate profits for a mere 7 percent, and corporate profits for about 12 percent. In total, the returns to these factors of production amounted to slightly less than 30 percent of national income. Where did the rest of it go? The answer is that about 70 percent of national income was composed of employee compensation—wages and salaries.

The distribution of income is perhaps the one area in economics in which any one individual's interests almost inevitably conflict with another's. By definition, if a larger share of the total income is distributed to me, a smaller share will be left for you. It is also a topic around which emotions run high, often causing the logic or the facts of the issues to be ignored. In this chapter, we will encounter several examples of people's misunderstandings of the facts and their unwillingness to face up to the undesirable consequences of income controls.

The chapter is divided into three main sections. The first explores marginal productivity theory, and notes a number of criticisms that have been levelled at that approach and at mainstream economics generally. This section covers the basic material that all students should read. The final two sections discuss, in greater detail, the determination of interest and profit incomes and the operation of labour markets, respectively. These two sections can be omitted in a brief course.

Marginal Productivity Theory

The Principle of Marginal Productivity

The **marginal physical product** (MPP) of an input is the increase in output that results from a one-unit increase in the use of the input, holding the amounts of all other inputs constant.

The **marginal revenue product** (MRP) of an input is the additional sales revenue the firm takes in by selling the marginal physical product of that input.

By now it will not surprise you to learn that factor prices are analyzed in terms of supply and demand. The supply sides of the markets for the various factors differ enormously from one another, which is why each factor market must be considered separately. But one basic principle, the **principle of marginal productivity**, has been used to explain the demand for every input. Before restating the principle, it will be useful to recall two concepts that were introduced in Chapter 21: **marginal physical product** (MPP) and **marginal revenue product** (MRP).[1]

Table 29–1 helps us review these two concepts by recalling the example of Farmer Pfister, who had to decide how much fertilizer to apply to his fixed plot of land. The marginal *physical* product (MPP) column tells us how many additional bushels of corn each additional tonne of fertilizer yields. For example, according to the table, the fourth tonne increases the crop by 300 bushels. The marginal *revenue* product (MRP) column tells us how many dollars this marginal physical product is worth. In the example in the table, corn is assumed always to sell at $2 per bushel, so the marginal revenue product of the fourth tonne of fertilizer is $2 per bushel times 300 bushels, or $600. We can now state the marginal productivity principle formally:

The marginal productivity principle states that when factor markets are competitive it always pays a profit-maximizing firm to hire that quantity of any input at which the marginal revenue product is equal to the price of the input.

The basic logic behind the principle is both simple and powerful. If the input's marginal revenue product is, for example, greater than its price, it will pay the firm to

[1] To review these concepts see Chapter 21, pages 454 and 456.

TABLE 29–1
Marginal Physical Products and Marginal Revenue Products of Farmer Pfister's Fertilizer

FERTILIZER (tonnes)	MARGINAL PHYSICAL PRODUCT (bushels)	MARGINAL REVENUE PRODUCT (dollars)
1	250	500
2	300	600
3	350	700
4	300	600
5	250	500
6	150	300
7	50	100
8	0	0
9	−50	−100

hire more and more of it because an additional unit of input brings the firm (via the output it contributes) an addition to revenue that is greater than the cost of that unit of input. Consequently, if MRP is greater than the input price, the firm should expand the quantity of the input it purchases. It should increase the quantity purchased up to the amount at which diminishing returns reduce the MRP to the level of the input's price. Conversely, if MRP is less than price, the firm is using too much of the input. Let us use Table 29-1 to demonstrate how the marginal productivity principle works.

Suppose the firm is using four tonnes of fertilizer at a cost of $350 per tonne. Since the table tells us that a fifth tonne has a marginal revenue product of $500, the firm could obviously add $150 to its profit by buying a fifth tonne. Only when the firm has used so much fertilizer that (because of diminishing returns) the MRP of still another tonne is less than $350 does it pay to stop expanding the use of fertilizer. In this example, five tonnes is the optimal amount to use.

One corollary of the principle of marginal productivity is obvious: The quantity of the input demanded depends on its price. The lower the price of fertilizer, the more of it it pays a firm to use. In the example of the previous paragraphs, it pays the firm to use five tonnes when the price of fertilizer is $350 per tonne. But if fertilizer were more expensive, say $550 per tonne, that price would exceed the value of the marginal product of the fifth tonne. It would, therefore, pay the firm to stop after the fourth tonne. Thus, *marginal productivity analysis shows that the quantity demanded of an input normally will decline as the price of the input rises.* The "law" of demand applies to inputs just as it applies to consumer goods.

The Derived Demand Curve for an Input

We can, in fact, be much more specific than this, for the marginal productivity principle tells us precisely how the demand curve for any input is derived from its marginal revenue product (MRP) curve.

Figure 29-1 presents graphically the MRP schedule from Table 29-1. Recall that, according to the marginal productivity principle, the quantity demanded of the input is determined by setting MRP equal to the input's price. Figure 29-1 considers three different possible prices for a tonne of fertilizer: $600, $500, and $300. At a price of $600 per tonne, we see that the quantity demanded is four tonnes (point A) because at that point MRP equals price. Similarly, if the price of fertilizer drops to $500 per tonne, quantity demanded rises to five tonnes (point B). Finally, if the price falls all the

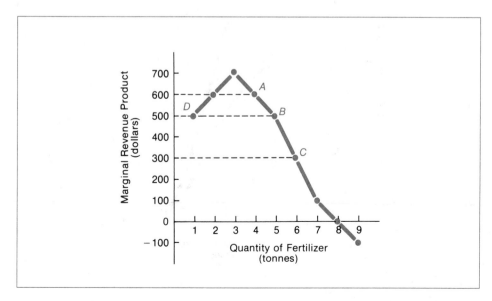

FIGURE 29-1
A Marginal Revenue Product Schedule
This diagram depicts the data in Table 29-1, which show how the marginal revenue product (MRP) of fertilizer first rises and then declines as more and more fertilizer is used. Since the optimal purchase rule is to keep applying fertilizer until MRP is reduced to the price of fertilizer, the *downward-sloping portion* of the MRP curve is Farmer Pfister's demand curve for fertilizer.

way to $300 per tonne, the quantity demanded is six tonnes (point C). Points A, B, and C are therefore three points on the demand curve for fertilizer. Thus:

The demand curve for any input is the downward-sloping portion of its marginal revenue product curve.

Note that we restrict ourselves to the *downward-sloping* portion of the MRP curve. The logic of the marginal productivity principle dictates this. For example, if the price of fertilizer is $500 per tonne, there are two input quantities for which MRP is $500: one tonne (point D) and five tonnes (point B). But point D cannot be the optimal stopping point because the MRP of a second tonne ($600) is greater than the cost of the second tonne ($500). The marginal productivity principle applies only in the range where returns are diminishing.

The demand for fertilizer (or for any other input) is called a **derived demand** because it is derived from the underlying demand for the final product (corn in this case). For example, suppose that a surge in demand drove the price of corn to $4 per bushel. Then, at each level of fertilizer usage, the MRP would be twice as large as when corn fetched $2 per bushel. This is shown in Figure 29–2 as an *upward* shift of the (derived) demand curve for fertilizer, from D_0D_0 to D_1D_1.[2] We conclude that, in general:

An outward shift in the demand curve for any commodity causes an outward shift of the derived demand curve for all factors utilized in the production of that commodity. Conversely, an inward shift in the demand curve for a commodity leads to inward shifts in the demand curves for factors used in producing that commodity.

[2]To make the diagram easier to read, the (irrelevant) upward-sloping portion of each curve has been omitted.

FIGURE 29–2
A Shift in the Demand Curve for Fertilizer
If the price of corn goes up, the marginal *revenue* product curve shifts upward—from D_0D_0 to D_1D_1 in the diagram—even though the marginal *physical* product curve has not changed. In this sense, a greater demand for corn leads to a greater *derived* demand for fertilizer.

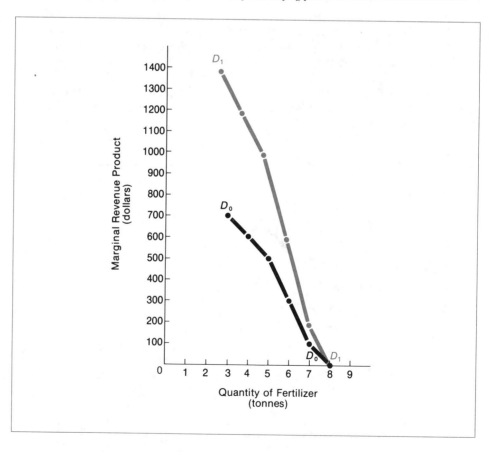

We have almost completed our introductory discussion of the marginal productivity principle and how it serves as a general explanation of the *demand* for any and all inputs. We will now use this theory in our discussion of the determination of two rather different forms of income: wages paid for unskilled labour and rents received for scarce land. Applying the tools of demand *and* supply in these two areas will allow us to clarify the important principles of income determination and to outline the useful (and the less useful) methods available to the government for altering income distribution—the subject of our next chapter.

The Basic Determinants of Income Distribution

If we consider a factor of production that is very plentiful throughout the economy, we know that the supply curve for that factor in a supply and demand diagram must be drawn far over to the right. We also know that the supply curve will intersect the demand curve (the marginal revenue product schedule) at a point where the MRP is very low, since if a large quantity of any factor is employed, then diminishing returns have set in to a very great extent. This tells us that the payment received for the use of an abundant factor is likely to be very low. It follows logically that if a person owns only a small amount of that one abundant factor, that person will be poor. Similar reasoning leads to the conclusion that people who own factors of production that are very scarce will have high incomes (since the supply curves for scarce factors intersect their demand curves at very high levels of payment). The basic point to follow from marginal productivity theory, then, is that:

High incomes go to the owners of scarce factors, and low incomes go to the owners of abundant factors.

This outcome suggests three ways in which the distribution of income can be influenced by governments:

Option 1. By redefining who owns the various factors of production;

Option 2. By intervening in the market's determination of factor prices;

Option 3. By leaving factor ownership and market signals alone, but redistributing income according to the directives of the general tax system.

Option 1 has been the choice of revolutionary governments, and flows from the basic principles of Marxist economics. However, the various affirmative-action programs that have been implemented in capitalist countries to counter discrimination against minority groups in the labour market are a mild form of this sort of income-redistribution strategy. (We discuss discrimination and pay equity in Chapter 30.)

Generally speaking, economists have a strong preference for Option 3 over Option 2. The main reason for this preference is the tendency of the market's "invisible hand" to fight back, producing a variety of undesirable outcomes, when market forces are tampered with (recall our discussion in Chapter 3). The more *general* the mechanism for income redistribution (such as progressive income taxation, with gradual increases in the tax rates and few tax shelters), the better are the chances that redistribution will occur *without* counterproductive disincentive effects.

We are now in a position to tackle the subjects of minimum-wage laws and the taxation of economic rents, which will allow us to clarify the issue of incentive effects. In the next chapter, we will discuss our overall tax and welfare systems with a view to explaining how our existing anti-poverty programs might be improved.

Issue: The Minimum Wage and Unemployment

Unemployment is always higher among the young than it is in the labour force as a whole. Figure 29-3 shows the record. It indicates that whenever unemployment rates

FIGURE 29-3
**The Youth
Unemployment Problem**
Youth unemployment rates
have consistently been much
higher than overall
unemployment rates.
SOURCE: Statistics Canada

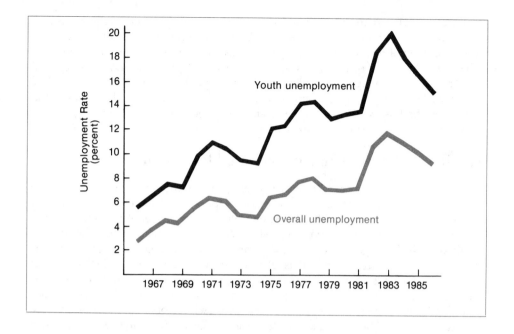

have gone down in the economy as a whole, they have almost always decreased for the young. However, young workers have always suffered more from unemployment than has the average worker. When things are generally bad, things are much, much worse for the young. Despite numerous "opportunities for youth" programs, there has been little relative improvement in youth unemployment in recent years.

Many economists are less surprised than other concerned people about the intractability of this problem. They maintain that despite all the legislation that has been adopted to improve the position of the young and inexperienced, there is a law on the books that, though apparently designed to protect low-skilled workers, is actually an impediment to any attempt to improve job opportunities for the young. As long as this law remains in effect, the young, the inexperienced, and those with educational disadvantages will continue to find themselves handicapped on the job market, and attempts to eliminate their more serious unemployment problems will stand only a limited chance of success.

What is the law? None other than the **minimum-wage law**. We will now explain the grounds on which many observers argue that this law has such pernicious— and presumably unintended—effects.

The labour market is really composed of many sub-markets for labour of different types, each with its own supply and demand curves. To understand the possible effects of minimum-wage legislation, it suffices to consider two such markets, which we call for convenience "skilled" and "unskilled" labour and which are portrayed in the two parts of Figure 29-4. As drawn, the demand curve for skilled workers is higher than that for unskilled workers. The reason is obvious: Skilled workers have higher productivity. Conversely, we have drawn the supply curve of skilled workers farther to the left than the supply curve of unskilled workers to reflect the greater scarcity of skilled workers. The consequence, as we can see in Figure 29-4, is that the equilibrium wage is much higher for skilled workers. In the example, the equilibrium wages are $8 per hour for skilled workers and $2.50 per hour for unskilled workers.

Now suppose the government, seeking to protect unskilled workers, imposes a legal minimum wage of $3.50 per hour (the heavy coloured line in both parts of Figure 29-4). Turning first to part (a), we see that the minimum wage has no effect in the market for skilled workers (such as carpenters and electricians). Since wages in that market are well above $3.50 per hour, a law prohibiting the payment of wage rates below $3.50 cannot possibly matter.

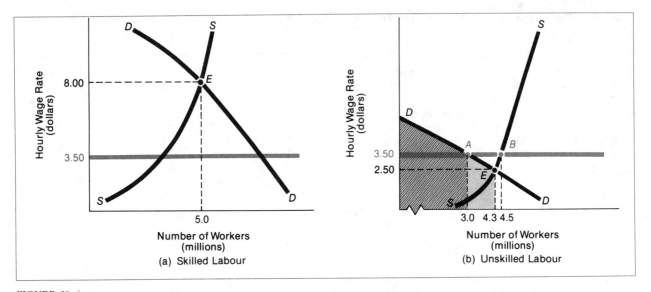

FIGURE 29-4

Possible Effects of Minimum-Wage Legislation

(a) Imposing a minimum wage of $3.50 per hour does not affect the market for skilled labour because the equilibrium wage there ($8 per hour) is well above the legal minimum. (b) However, the minimum-wage legislation does have important effects in the market for unskilled labour. There the equilibrium wage ($2.50 per hour) is below the minimum, so the minimum wage makes the quantity supplied (4.5 million workers) exceed the quantity demanded (3.0 million workers). The result is unemployment of unskilled labour.

But the effects of the minimum wage may be pronounced in the market for unskilled labour—and presumably quite different from those that the government intended. Figure 29–4(b) indicates that at the $3.50 minimum wage, firms want to employ only 3 million unskilled workers (point *A*) whereas employment of unskilled workers would have been 4.3 million (point *E*) in a free market. Although the 3 million unskilled workers lucky enough to retain their jobs do indeed earn a higher wage ($3.50 instead of $2.50 per hour) in this hypothetical example, 1.3 million of their compatriots earn no wage at all because they have been laid off. The job-losers will clearly be the workers whose productivity was lowest, since the minimum wage effectively bans the employment of workers whose marginal revenue product is less than $3.50 per hour.

Although the minimum wage leads to higher wages for those unskilled workers who retain their jobs, it also restricts employment opportunities for unskilled workers.

An additional point warrants emphasis. Before the minimum wage is introduced in this example, the total income generated by the employment of the 4.3 million unskilled workers is equal to the green shaded area in Figure 29–4(b). This is because the *total* revenue generated by these workers' employment is equal to the area under their *marginal* revenue product curve (which is the demand curve for their services). The workers receive the wage bill (the green rectangle below the $2.50 wage line) and their employers receive the amount represented by the triangular green area above the $2.50 wage line. After the minimum wage of $3.50 is imposed and employment of unskilled workers drops to 3.0 million, the total revenue generated by employment in this sector is reduced to the grey shaded area in Figure 29–4(b). Proponents of minimum wages often argue that higher wages mean increased buying power for products, so employment should go up with such minimums in place. But this argument confuses workers' wage rates with their total income (which is wage rate times the number of workers employed). The argument also ignores non-labour (employers') income. As the diagram makes clear (compare the green and the grey

Minimum-Wage Law No Help to Unskilled

... How can we test the economic principle that high minimum-wage levels lead to relatively increased unemployment rates for unskilled workers? One way is to calculate the unemployment rates of youthful Canadians as a percentage of those of the more highly productive adult employees in this nation, and then compare this figure with the minimum-wage levels which apply in each of the provinces. (We choose workers between 20 and 24 as our control because this is the youngest group subject to the "adult" minimum-wage law.)

The results are painfully obvious. Manitoba, with the highest minimum-wage level ($4.30) has the largest unemployment rate for its young workers, relative to the general population (289%). Saskatchewan, with the next greatest level ($4.25), weighs in with the second biggest relative unemployment rate for youth (257%). And at the bottom of the pack in terms of the disenfranchisement of their young people come B.C. and Alberta, with two of the country's lowest minimum-wage levels.

SOURCE: Walter Block, *The Financial Post*, August 17, 1985, reprinted in the *Fraser Forum*, August 1985, pages 4–5.

NOTE: By 1989, the minimum wage had risen to $4.25 in

	UNEMPLOYMENT RATE FOR 20–24 YEAR OLDS RELATIVE TO EMPLOYEES AGED 25+ (percent)	PROVINCIAL MINIMUM-WAGE LEVEL, 1985 (dollars)
Alberta	182	3.80
British Columbia	190	3.65
Newfoundland	204	4.00
Quebec	206	4.00
Nova Scotia	213	4.00
New Brunswick	237	3.80
Ontario	251	4.00
Saskatchewan	257	4.25
Manitoba	289	4.30
Prince Edward Island	n.a.	3.75

SOURCE: Statistics Canada, Labour Department, May 1985

Newfoundland; to $4.50 in Alberta, British Columbia, New Brunswick, Nova Scotia, and Saskatchewan; to $4.70 in Manitoba; to $5.00 in Ontario, Quebec, and the Northwest Territories; and to $5.39 in the Yukon (Source: Labour Canada).

---

areas), total income—that is, overall buying power—*must* fall with higher wages.[3]

Finally, minimum wages may have particularly pernicious effects on those who are the victims of discrimination. Because of the minimum wage, as Figure 29–4(b) shows, employers of unskilled labour have more applicants than job openings. Consequently, they are able to pick and choose among the available applicants and may, for example, discriminate against gender, racial, or ethnic groups whose members have been prevented by past discrimination from acquiring the skills required for admission to the higher-paid portion of the labour force.

For these reasons, many economists feel that the youth unemployment problem and especially the unemployment problem of minority groups will be very difficult to solve as long as the minimum wage remains in effect. Obviously, the minimum wage is not the only culprit. But statistical studies—and even analyses as simple as the one reported in the boxed insert on this page—support the conclusion that forced over-pricing of unskilled labour contributes significantly to unemployment. It is analysis of this sort that induces most economists to reject attempts to repeal the laws of supply and demand in the aim of redistributing income. As we noted earlier, the preferred approach will be outlined in the next chapter.

The Determination of Rent

We turn our attention now to the market for land—the one factor of production whose quantity supplied is roughly the same at every possible price. Indeed, the

---

[3] While it is total income that is relevant for the overall-buying-power argument, the diagram makes clear that the total-labour-income component *could* increase as a result of the minimum wage. This would occur if the income of the 3.0 million workers who are still employed increased by more than the loss of wages suffered by the 1.3 million who lost their jobs because of the minimum-wage law. But for such a significant wage increase to occur, the demand for unskilled labour would have to be inelastic—which it is not, since it is so easy to replace unskilled workers in the production process. In any event, we should not ignore the buying power of those receiving the income shown by the triangle above the wage line.

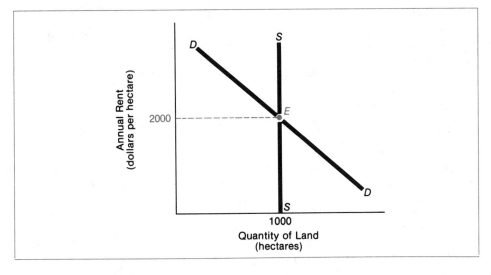

FIGURE 29-5
Determination of Land Rent in Littletown
The supply curve of land, *SS*, is vertical, meaning that 1000 hectares are available in Littletown regardless of the level of rent. The demand curve for land slopes downward for the usual reasons. Equilibrium is established at point *E*, where the annual rental rate is $2000 per hectare.

classical economists used this notion as the working definition of land. And the definition seems to fit, at least approximately. Although people may accumulate landfill, clear land, drain its swamps, fertilize it, build on it, or convert it from one use (a farm) to another (a housing development), it is very difficult for human effort to make a great deal of change in the total supply of land.

What does this fact tell us about the determination of land rents? Figure 29-5 helps to provide an answer. The vertical supply curve *SS* represents the fact that no matter what the level of rents, there are still 1000 hectares of land in a small hamlet called Littletown. The demand curve *DD* is a typical marginal revenue product curve, predicated on the notion that the use of land, like everything else, is subject to diminishing returns. The free-market price is determined, as usual, by the intersection of the supply and demand curves. In this example, each hectare of land in Littletown rents for $2000 per year. The interesting feature of this diagram is that, because quantity supplied is rigidly fixed at 1000 hectares whatever the price:

The market level of rent is entirely determined by the demand side of the market.

If, for example, the relocation of a major university to Littletown attracts more people who want to live there, the *DD* curve will shift outward, as depicted in Figure 29-6. Equilibrium in the market will shift from point *E* to point *A*; there will still be only

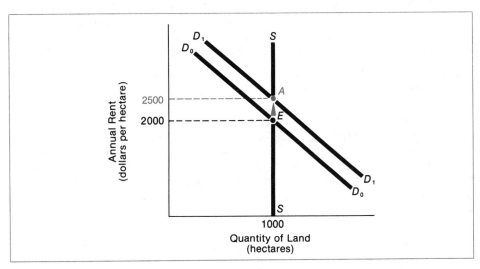

FIGURE 29-6
A Shift in Demand with a Vertical Supply Curve
Now imagine that something happens to increase the demand for land—that is, to shift the demand curve from D_0D_0 to D_1D_1. Quantity supplied cannot change, but the rental rate can, and does. In this example, the annual rental for a hectare of land increases from $2000 to $2500.

1000 hectares of land, but now each hectare will command a rent of $2500. The landlords will collect more rent, though they themselves have done nothing productive. And society will obtain no additional land from the landlords in return for its additional rent payment.

The same process also works in reverse, however. Should the university shut its doors and the demand for land decline as a result, the landlords will suffer even though they have in no way contributed to the decline in the demand for land. (To see this, simply reverse the logic of Figure 29-6. The demand curve begins at D_1D_1 and shifts to D_0D_0.)

This discussion shows the special feature of rent that leads economists to distinguish it from payments to other factors of production: An *economic rent* is a payment for a factor of production (such as land) that does not change the amount of that factor that is supplied.

If every parcel of land were of identical quality, this would be all there was to the theory of land rent. But, of course, plots of land do differ—in quality of soil, in topography, in access to sun and water, in proximity to marketplaces, and in other ways. The classical economists realized this, of course, and took it into account in their analysis of rent determination—a remarkable piece of economic logic formulated late in the eighteenth century and still considered valid today.

The basic notion is that funds invested in any piece of land must yield the same return as funds invested in any other piece of land that is actually used. Why? If it were not so, capitalists would bid against one another for the more profitable pieces of land until the rents of these parcels were driven up to a point where their advantages over other parcels had been eliminated.

Suppose that on one piece of land a given crop is produced for $160,000 per year in labour, fertilizer, fuel, and other non-land costs, while the same crop is produced for $120,000 on a second piece of land. The rent on the second parcel must be *exactly* $40,000 per year higher than the rent on the first, because otherwise production would be cheaper on one plot than on the other. If, for example, the rent difference were only $30,000 per year, it would be $10,000 cheaper to produce on the second plot of land. No one would want to rent the first plot, and every grower would instead bid for the second plot. Obviously, rent on the first plot would be forced down by a lack of customers, and rent on the second would be driven up by eager bidders. These pressures would come to an end only when the rent difference reached $40,000, so that both plots became equally profitable.

Land that is just on the borderline of being used is called **marginal land**.

At any given time, there are some pieces of land of such low quality that it does not pay to use them at all—remote deserts are a prime example. Any land that is exactly on the borderline of being used is called **marginal land**. By definition, marginal land earns no rent because if any rent were charged for it, there would be no takers.

We now combine these two observations—that the difference between the costs of producing on any two pieces of land must equal the difference between their rents, and that zero rent is charged on marginal land—to conclude that:

Rent on any piece of land will equal the difference between the cost of producing the output on that land and the cost of producing it on marginal land.

That is, competition for the superior plots of land will permit the landlords to charge prices that capture the full advantages of their superior parcels.

A useful feature of this analysis is that it helps us to understand more completely the effects of an outward shift in the demand curve for land. Suppose there is an increase in the demand for land because of a rise in population. Naturally, rents will rise. But we can be more specific than this. In response to an outward shift in the demand curve, two things will happen:

1. *It will now pay to employ some land whose use was formerly unprofitable.* The land that was previously on the zero-rent margin will no longer be on the

borderline, and some land that is so poor that it was formerly not even worth considering will now just reach the borderline of profitability. The settling of the West illustrates this process quite forcefully. Land that once could not be given away is now quite valuable.

2. *People will begin more intensive use of the land that was already in use.* Farmers will use more labour and fertilizer to squeeze larger crops out of their land, as has happened in recent decades. Urban real estate on which two-storey buildings previously made most sense will now be used for highrises.

Rents will be increased in a predictable way by these two developments. Since the land that is marginal *after* the change must be inferior to the land that was marginal previously, rents must rise by the difference in yields between the old and the new marginal lands.

But there is a second factor pushing up land rents—the increased intensity of use of land that was already in cultivation. As farmers apply more fertilizer and labour to their land, the marginal productivity of land increases, just as factory workers become more productive when they are given better equipment. Once again, the landowner is able to capture this increase in productivity in the form of higher rents. (If you do not understand why, refer back to Figure 29–6 and remember that the demand curves are marginal revenue product curves.) Thus, we can summarize the classical theory of rent as follows:

As the use of land increases, landlords receive higher payments from two sources:

1. Increased demand leads the community to employ land previously not good enough to use; the advantage of previously used land over the new marginal land increases, and rents go up correspondingly.

2. Land is used more intensively; the marginal revenue product of land rises, thus increasing the ability of the producer who uses the land to pay rent.

As late as the end of the nineteenth century, this analysis still exerted a powerful influence beyond technical economic writings. An American journalist, Henry George, was nearly elected mayor of New York in 1886, running on the platform that all government should be financed by "a single tax"—a tax on landlords, who, he said, are the only ones who earn incomes while contributing nothing to the productive process and who reap the fruits of economic growth without contributing to economic progress.

Generalization: What Determines Wayne Gretzky's Salary?

Land is not the only scarce input whose supply is fixed, at least in the short run. Toward the beginning of this century some economists realized that the economic analysis of rent can be applied to inputs other than land. As we will see, this extension yielded some noteworthy insights.

Consider as an example the earnings of Wayne Gretzky. Performers such as Gretzky might seem to have little in common with plots of land in downtown Toronto. Yet, to an economist, the same analysis—the theory of rent—explains the incomes of these two factors of production. To understand why, we first note that there is only one Wayne Gretzky. That is, he is a scarce input whose supply is fixed just like the supply of land. Because he is in fixed supply, the price of his services must be determined in a way similar to the determination of land rents. Hence, economists arrived at a more general definition of **economic rent** as *any payment made to a factor above the amount necessary to keep that factor in its present employment.*

To understand the concept of economic rent, it is useful to divide the payment for

Economic rent is said to be earned whenever a factor of production receives a reward that exceeds the minimum amount necessary to keep the factor in its present employment.

any input into two parts. The first part is simply the minimum payment needed to acquire the input: the cost of equipment or the compensation for the unpleasantness, hard work, and loss of leisure involved in performing labour. The second part of the payment is a bonus that does not go to every input, but only to those that are of particularly high quality. Payments to workers with exceptional natural skills are a good example. These bonuses are like the extra payment for a better piece of land and so are called *economic rents*.

Notice that only the first part of the factor payment is essential to induce the owner to supply the input. If workers are not paid at least this first part, they will not supply their labour. But the additional payment—the economic rent—is pure gravy. The skilful worker is happy to have it as an extra, but it is not the deciding consideration in his or her choice of whether or not to work.

A moment's thought shows how this general notion of rent applies both to land and to Wayne Gretzky. The total quantity of land available for use is the same whether rent is high, low, or zero; no payments to landlords are necessary to induce land to be supplied to the market. So, by definition, the payments to landholders for their land are entirely economic rent—payments that are not necessary to induce the provision of the land to the economy. Wayne Gretzky is (almost) similar to land in this respect. He has hockey talents that are rare and that cannot be reproduced. What determines the income of such a factor? Since the quantity supplied of such a unique, non-reproducible factor is absolutely fixed, and therefore unresponsive to price, the analysis of rent determination summarized in Figure 29–5 applies. *The position of the demand curve determines the price.*

Figure 29–7 summarizes the "Wayne Gretzky market." Vertical supply curve *SS* represents the fact that no matter what wage he is paid there is only one Wayne Gretzky. Demand curve *DD* is a marginal productivity curve of sorts, but not quite the kind we encountered earlier in the chapter. Since the question "What would be the value of a second unit of Wayne Gretzky?" is nonsensical, the demand curve is constructed by considering only the *portion* of his time demanded at various wage levels. The curve indicates that at an annual salary of $8 million, no employer can

FIGURE 29–7
Hypothetical Market for Wayne Gretzky's Services
At an annual wage of $8 million or more, no one is willing to bid for his time. At a somewhat lower wage, $4 million, two-thirds of his time will be demanded (point G). Only at an annual wage no higher than $2 million will all of Gretzky's available time be demanded (point E).

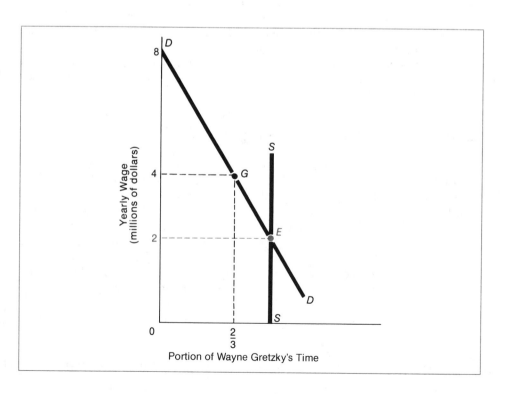

afford even a little bit of Wayne Gretzky. At a lower salary of, say, $4 million per year, however, there are enough profitable uses to absorb two-thirds of his time. At $2 million per year, Gretzky's full time is demanded, and at lower wage rates, the demand for Gretzky's time exceeds the amount of it that is for sale.

Equilibrium is at point E in the diagram, where the supply of and the demand for Gretzky's time are equal. His annual salary in our numerical example is, then, $2 million. Now we can ask: How much of Wayne Gretzky's salary is economic rent? According to the economic definition of rent, his entire $2 million salary is rent. Since, according to the vertical supply schedule, Gretzky's financial reward is unnecessary to get him to supply his services, every penny he earns is rent.

This is why we said that stars like Gretzky are *almost* good examples of pure rent. For, in fact, if his salary were low enough, Gretzky might well prefer to stay home rather than work. Suppose, for example, that $100,000 per year is the lowest salary at which Gretzky will offer even one minute of his services, and that his labour supply then increases with his wage up to an annual salary of $500,000, at which point he is willing to work full time. Then, while his equilibrium salary will still be $2 million per year, not all of it will be rent, because some of it, at least $100,000, is required to get him to supply any services at all.

This same analysis applies to any factor of production whose supply curve is not horizontal, as in Figure 29–8. There we see that at any price above $5 suppliers would be willing to provide some units of the input. Yet the supply–demand equilibrium point yields a price of $7—well above the minimum price at which some input supply would be forthcoming. The difference must constitute a rent to suppliers of the input. The overall earnings of this factor of production are shown by the green rectangle in Figure 29–8; the portion that is rent is shown by the grey shaded triangle. Any such factor earns some rent—or gets paid more than the minimum amount that would induce it to work. Almost all employees earn some rent. What sorts of factors earn no rent? Those that can be exactly reproduced by a number of producers at constant cost. No supplier of ball bearings will ever receive any rent on a ball bearing, at least in the long run, because any desired number of them can be produced at (roughly) constant cost. If one supplier tried to charge a price that included rent, someone else would undercut her and take her customers away. That is, if it costs 50 cents to produce a ball bearing, no matter how many or how few are provided, then none will be supplied at a price below 50 cents, and competition will prevent the price from exceeding that figure, so the price will include no rent.

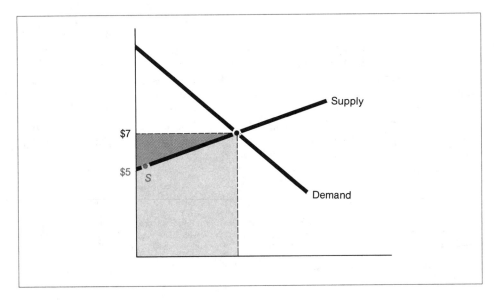

FIGURE 29–8
Rent When the Supply Curve Is Not Vertical
Some of the input would be supplied (point S) at a price of $5 (or a bit more), but the equilibrium price is $7, so the units of input to the left of the equilibrium amount must be earning a rent of up to $2. The total rent is represented by the grey shaded triangle.

At the Frontier: Rent-Seeking

Current research uses the rent concept to analyze such common phenomena as lobbying by industrial groups, lawsuits between rival firms, and battles over exclusive licences (as for a TV station). Such interfirm battles can waste economic resources, such as the time that is expended by executives, bureaucrats, judges, lawyers, and economists. Because this valuable time could have been used in production, such activities entail a large *opportunity cost*. The new analysis offers insights into the reasons for these battles, and provides a way to assess the *quantity* of resources that are wasted.

The opportunity to earn economic rent is extremely attractive to many individuals and firms. Consequently, when a rent-earning opportunity becomes available (a relatively common occurrence), a number of parties are usually prepared to fight over it. The search for such opportunities and the battles over them are called "rent-seeking." The theory of rent-seeking gives us some idea of the extent of society's resources that are wasted in such a process.

Consider a race for a monopoly cable TV licence, which, once awarded, will keep competitors out of the field. There is nothing to prevent competitors from entering the race to *grab* the licence. Anyone can hire the lobbyists and the lawyers or offer the bribes needed in the battle. Thus, while the cable business itself is not competitive, the process of fighting for the licence is.

We know from the analysis of long-run equilibrium under perfect competition, however, that economic profit approximates zero—revenues just cover costs. So, if the cable licence is expected to yield, say, $900 million in rent over its life, rent-seekers are likely to waste something near that amount in the fight for the licence.

Why? Suppose there are ten bidders, each with an equal chance at the prize. Then, to each bidder, that chance should be worth about $90 million. If the average bidder has so far spent only, say, $70 million on the battle, there will still be an expected economic profit of $90 million − $70 million = $20 million to the rent-seeking activity. This will tempt an eleventh bidder to enter and raise the ante to, say, $80 million in lobbying fees, hoping to grab the rent. For risk-neutral participants, this process stops only when a sum equal to the total expected economic rent to be gained from the cable licence has been wasted on the rent-seeking process.

Rent Controls: The Misplaced Analogy

Why is the analysis of economic rent important? Because only economic rent can be taxed away without reducing the quantity of the input supplied. And here common English gets in the way of sound reasoning. Many people feel that the *rent* that they pay to their landlord is economic rent. After all, their apartments will still be there if they pay $500 per month, or $300, or $100. This view, while true in the short run, is quite myopic.

Like the ball-bearing producer, the owner of a building cannot expect to earn *economic* rent because there are too many other potential owners whose costs of construction are roughly the same as his own. If he tried to charge a price that included some economic rent—that is, a price that exceeded his production costs plus the opportunity cost of his capital—other builders would undercut him. Thus, far from being in perfectly *inelastic* (vertical) supply, like raw land, buildings come rather close to being in perfectly *elastic* (horizontal) supply, like ball bearings. As we have learned from the theory of rent, this means that builders and owners of buildings cannot collect economic rent in the long run. Since apartment owners collect very little economic rent, the payments that tenants make in a free market must be just enough to keep those apartments on the market. (This is the definition of zero economic rent.) If rent controls push these prices down, the apartments will start to disappear from the market.[4]

---

[4]None of this is meant to imply that temporary rent controls in certain locations cannot have salutory effects in the short run. In the short run, the supply of apartments and houses really is fixed, and large shifts in demand would hand windfall gains to landlords—gains that are true economic rents. Controls that eliminate such windfalls should not cause serious problems. But knowing when the "short run" fades into the "long run" can be a tricky matter. "Temporary" rent-control laws have a way of lasting for quite a time, as we saw in Chapter 3 (pages 57–59).

Criticisms of Marginal Productivity Theory and Mainstream Economics

The theory of factor pricing described in this chapter is another example of supply–demand analysis. Its special feature is its heavy reliance on the principle of marginal productivity to derive the shape and position of the demand curve. For this reason, the analysis is often rather misleadingly called *the marginal productivity theory of income distribution*. Over the years this analysis has been subject to attack on many grounds.

In general, those who criticize mainstream economics are often called "radical economists." They do not limit their criticism to marginal productivity theory; indeed, they maintain that, as a rule, mainstream economists are asking all the wrong questions and using the wrong set of tools (economic models) to provide the answers. In the sections that follow, we investigate some of these claims.

Justification of the Status Quo

One frequent accusation, which is largely (but not entirely) groundless, is the assertion that:

Marginal productivity theory is merely an attempt to justify the distribution of income that the capitalist system yields—that is, it is a piece of pro-capitalist propaganda.

According to this argument, when marginal productivity theory claims that each factor is paid exactly its marginal revenue product (MRP), this is only a sneaky way of asserting that each factor is paid exactly what it deserves. These critics claim that the theory legitimizes the gross inequities of the system—the poverty of many and the great wealth of the few.

The argument is straightforward but wrong. Payments are made not to *factors of production* but to the people who happen to own them. If land earns $2000 because that is its MRP, this does not mean the payment is *deserved* by the landlord, who may even have acquired it by fraud.

Second, an input's MRP depends not only on "how hard it works" but also on how much of it happens to be employed—for, according to the "law" of diminishing returns, the more that is employed the lower its MRP. Thus, that factor's MRP is not (and cannot legitimately be interpreted as) a measure of the intensity of its "productive effort." In any event, what an input deserves may be taken to depend on more than what it does in the factory. A worker may be held to deserve funds because he is sick, because he has many children, or because of many reasons other than his productivity. On these and other grounds, no economist today claims that marginal productivity analysis shows that distribution under capitalism is either just or unjust. It is simply wrong to claim that marginal productivity theory is pro-capitalist propaganda. The marginal productivity principle is just as relevant to organizing production in a socialist society as it is in a capitalist one.

Narrowness of Focus

One of the more general criticisms levelled by the radical economists against the mainstream approach is that:

Conventional economists typically narrow their field of inquiry so much that they are incapable of addressing the important questions.

For one thing, in contrast to Marx's teachings, modern economics is *ahistorical*. It is very much based on the here and now, with scant attention paid to the origins of the current system or the directions in which it may be headed. Perhaps as a consequence of this narrow scope, mainstream economics *accepts institutions as given and (tacitly) as immutable*. Little attention is paid to how institutions change.

Amplifying the attack, the radicals chide conventional economists for their preoccupation with analysis of *marginal* changes, using the celebrated tools of marginal analysis that we have described in earlier chapters. This, they argue, makes economics incapable of dealing with the really big issues: the institution of private property, poverty and discrimination, unemployment, and alienation. For example, Professor John Gurley of Stanford University, who converted from conventional to radical economics many years ago, scoffed at a prominent economist who expressed the belief that reducing unemployment would do more good things for the distribution of income than any measure he could imagine.

Well, any radical economist can imagine a direct measure that would do even better things—expropriation of the capitalist class and turning over of ownership of capital goods and land to all the people. That, of course, sounds wild—unimaginable—to anyone who does not question the existing system.[5]

The consequence of this disciplinary narrowness, radicals contend, is that economists become, whether deliberately or unwittingly, apologists for the present system, supporters of the propertied class, and defenders of the status quo.

Most economists are prepared to plead guilty to the charge of disciplinary narrowness. As Yale's Nobel Prize winner James Tobin put it:

Most contemporary economists feel ill at ease with respect to big topics—national economic organization, interpretation of economic history, relations of economic and political power, origins and functions of economic institutions. The terrain is unsuitable for our tools. We find it hard even to frame meaningful questions, much less to answer them.[6]

But mainstream economists tend to view their inadequacy in this area as a misdemeanour, not a felony. They point out, in their defence, that a narrow focus is imperative if progress in analysis is to be made. And they are quite proud of the achievements of economic science compared with those of the more diffuse social sciences, such as sociology and political science. They counter that radicals try to paint with such broad strokes that everything becomes necessarily superficial and imprecise. And they argue that the radicals, with their very clear political biases, are hardly in a position to question the objectivity of other economists.

Acceptance of Tastes and Motivation as Given

Just as they do with institutions, conventional economists accept the tastes of consumers and the motivations of workers and managers as given and unchangeable: "just human nature." Radicals, on the other hand, argue that:

Consumers are manipulated. Not only are they bombarded by advertising; they are also brainwashed in the school system, influenced by politicians, and subtly moulded by other social institutions.

This argument is broadened further by the assertion that the need for material incentives to motivate both workers and managers is culturally acquired rather than innate, a product of capitalism rather than a cause of it.

[5] J. G. Gurley, "The State of Political Economics," *American Economic Review* (May 1971), page 59.

[6] J. Tobin, book review of Lindbeck's *The Political Economy of the New Left, Journal of Economic Literature* (December 1972), page 1216.

Naturally, mainstream economists do not really believe that tastes are God-given. Everyone realizes that they are acquired and influenced by many things. The question is: What are we to do about this? Lacking a theory of taste formation, basic economic analysis proceeds on the assumption that consumer tastes are to be respected *regardless* of how they became what they are. If we forsake this principle we find ourselves on some dangerous ground: If consumers do not know what's good for them, who does? Still, most economists would willingly concede that more research into taste formation is desirable, and some have worked on this. The radicals have no doubt pushed the profession in a healthy direction.

Obsession with Efficiency Rather Than Equality

At several points in this book we have emphasized the fundamental trade-off between efficiency and equality. All mainstream economists appreciate and understand this principle, and a great many—in their role as private citizens—advocate greater equality. However, the radicals are quite right to complain that:

The preponderant majority of economic analysis and research is concerned with efficiency, not with equality.

Many conventional economists agree with this criticism.[7] But the radicals do not ask simply for a change in emphasis; they also want a change in the economist's tool kit. The marginal productivity theory of income distribution, they argue, is irrelevant. They maintain that to understand the distribution of income in contemporary market economies, we must first understand the distribution of *power*, which is largely determined by who controls the means of production.

Here the conventional and the radical economists part company. The conventional economist wants to know just how this "power" is measured. Are there statistical studies showing that "power" influences the distribution of income? In short, mainstream economics treats this approach to distribution theory as rhetoric, not as science.

Myopic Concentration on Quantity Rather Than Quality

The radical left is critical of mainstream economists' preoccupation with policies designed to increase the gross domestic product. They argue that a great deal of this output is no more than junk, and that using society's resources to produce such things is patently irrational. They also point to the spoliation of the environment caused by modern industrial production, though at least some radicals concede that conventional economics has some solutions to these problems (see Chapter 32). And they are dismayed that a system that is so good at producing private consumer goods should be so pathetically bad at feeding the hungry, housing and clothing the poor, and providing public services of all kinds. Radicals add one further element to this indictment:

In addition to ruining the quality of the environment, capitalist production ruins human beings.

It makes them aggressive, competitive, even dehumanized, by forcing them into a rat race for material gain. In Marxian terms, workers have little voice in determining the nature of their productive activities and so become *alienated* from their work rather than being proud of their accomplishments.

Are the outputs of the system really that bad? As Prof. Robert Solow of M.I.T. notes, it is hard to disagree with the radicals' disparaging remarks about essentially

---

[7] Alice M. Rivlin, "Income Distribution—Can Economists Help?" *American Economic Review* (May 1975), pages 1–15; Robert Aaron Gordon, "Rigor and Relevance in a Changing Institutional Setting," *American Economic Review* (March 1976), pages 1–14.

unnecessary products, from pungent deodorants to ostentatiously useless gadgets, "without appearing boorish." Yet such products are not only part of the wasteful expenditures of the idle rich. It must be remembered that the median family income in Canada is not excessively high—it is currently less than $40,000 per year. And, by definition, fully *half* of Canadian families earn less than this. Are they squandering their money on frivolities, or are these the things that the Canadian people really want? Solow concludes that:

[The radicals'] attitudes toward ordinary consumption remind one of the Duchess who, upon acquiring a full appreciation of sex, asked the Duke if it were perhaps too good for the common people.[8]

As for alienation, it is safe to say that conventional economists have never known what to make of the notion. If this is an important way in which capitalism has damaged the quality of life, then conventional economics surely has been blind to it. As with "power," however, no one has yet figured out a way to measure alienation. And, as for the alleged dehumanization of the labour force, this seems to be a side effect of modern industrial activity—whether that activity is conducted under capitalism or under socialism. The radicals, however, hope that we can reform the basic structure of society by arranging a *participatory* system in which workers have some real control over what they do and how they do it (not one in which orders flow only from the top down). These changes, radicals believe, would make workers both happier and more productive.

Naïve Conception of the State

Radical economists maintain that mainstream economists hold a naïve and sentimental view of the state. In this view, government is available to set things right when the market system fails (as in the case of income distribution or externalities, for example), and in so doing, allows its decisions to be dictated by the broad public interest. By contrast:

The State, in the radical view, operates ultimately to serve the interest of the controlling class in a class society. Since the "capitalist" class fundamentally controls capitalist societies, the state functions in capitalist societies to serve that class. It does so either directly, by providing services only to members of that class, or indirectly, and probably more frequently, by helping preserve and support the system of basic institutions which support and maintain the power of that class.[9]

This *subservience of the state to the capitalists* manifests itself in several ways. First, since capitalists are driven by competition to accumulate capital continually and to expand production, more and bigger markets are necessary in which to sell this bountiful output. As a result, capitalist nations turn to *imperialist ventures* to secure new markets. Second, in order to maintain domestic demand at high levels, the military–industrial complex promotes a *war economy*, which, if not actually at war, is continually spending inordinate sums on armaments. Third, according to this view, even reforms that appear to be pro-labour, such as minimum wages, social-welfare programs, unemployment insurance, and the like, are really intended to *"buy off"* the *working class* so that it will not rise up in revolt, as radical economists imply Marx had predicted. In this view, for example, the social and economic programs initiated as a

[8] Robert M. Solow, "The New Industrial State or Son of Affluence," *The Public Interest*, no. 9 (Fall 1967), page 108. Copyright © 1967 by National Affairs, Inc.

[9] D. M. Gordon, *Theories of Poverty and Underemployment* (Lexington, Mass.: D. C. Heath & Company, 1972), page 61.

result of the Great Depression were not motivated by a desire to help the working class, but rather by a desire to forestall the coming revolution.

Mainstream economists admit to a certain political naïvete. Yet most economists are unimpressed by the radicals' view of the state. Without denying that corporations often curry political favour and often succeed, mainstream economists wonder how the radical model can explain progressive income taxation, inheritance taxes, competition policy, anti-discrimination regulations, universal health insurance, the "baby bonus," and many, many more laws that the preponderance of the wealthy opposed bitterly at the time they were enacted. Furthermore, they point out, the policy prescriptions that conventional economists offer to improve the functioning of markets are intended as just that—prescriptions for improvement, not predictions about what government will actually do. Economists are not *that* naïve.

This completes our presentation of the core material of this chapter. We have explained marginal productivity theory, used this theory to understand minimum-wage laws and the concept of economic rent, and discussed the radical critique of mainstream economics and that critique's emphasis on marginal analysis. In shorter courses, instructors may choose to move directly to Chapter 30 and its analysis of income redistribution by governments at this point. The two remaining parts of this chapter provide further discussion of factor pricing, covering the determination of interest and profit incomes and the operation of the labour market in greater detail.

Interest and Profit

The Issue of Usury Laws: Are Interest Rates Too High?

The rate of interest is the price at which funds can be rented (borrowed). And, like other factor prices, the rate of interest is determined by supply and demand. However, this is one area in which many people have been dissatisfied with the outcome of the market process. Fears that interest rates, if left unregulated, would climb to exorbitant levels have made usury laws quite popular in many times and places. In a related development, in the late 1980s, some Canadian politicians called for limits on the amount that banks could charge on credit-card loans. However, this sort of intervention, and usury laws generally, interfere with the operation of supply and demand and are often harmful to economic efficiency.

Funds are loaned (rented to users) in many ways: home mortgages, corporation or government bonds, consumer credit, and so on. On the demand side of these credit markets are borrowers—people or institutions that, for one reason or another, wish to spend more than they currently have.

In business, loans are used primarily to finance investment. To the business executive who "rents" (borrows) funds in order to finance an **investment** and pays interest in return, the funds really represent an intermediate step toward the acquisition of the machines, buildings, inventories, and other forms of physical **capital** that the firm will purchase.

Though the words "investment" and "capital" are often used interchangeably in everyday parlance, it is important to keep the distinction in mind. The relation between investment and capital has an analogy in the filling of a bathtub: The accumulated water in the tub is analogous to the stock of capital, while the flow of water from the tap (which adds to the tub's water) is like the flow of investment. Just as the tap must be turned on in order for more water to accumulate, the capital stock increases only when there is investment. If investment ceases, the capital stock stops growing. Notice that when investment is *zero*, the capital stock *remains constant*; it does not fall to zero any more than a bathtub suddenly becomes empty when you turn off the tap.

Investment is the *flow* of resources into the production of new capital. It is the labour, steel, and other inputs devoted to the *construction* of factories, warehouses, railways, and other pieces of capital during some period of time.

Capital refers to an inventory (a stock) of plant, equipment, and other productive resources held by a business firm, an individual, or some other organization.

The process of building up capital by investing, and then using this capital in production, can be divided into five steps:

Step 1. The firm decides to enlarge its stock of capital.

Step 2. It raises the funds with which to finance its expansion.

Step 3. It uses these funds to hire the inputs, which are put to work building factories, warehouses, and the like. This step is the act of *investment*.

Step 4. After the investment is completed, the firm ends up with a larger stock of *capital*.

Step 5. The capital is used (along with other inputs) either to expand production or to reduce costs. At this point the firm starts earning *returns* on its investment.

Notice that what investors put into the investment process is *money*, either their own or funds borrowed from others. The funds are then transformed, in a series of steps, into a physical input suitable for use in production. If the funds were borrowed, the investor will someday return them to the lender with some payment for their use. This payment is called **interest**, and it is calculated as a percentage per year of the amount borrowed. For example, if the *interest rate* is 12 percent per year and $1000 is borrowed, the annual interest payment is $120.

The marginal productivity principle governs the quantity of funds demanded just as it governs the quantity of fertilizer demanded:

Firms will demand the quantity of borrowed funds that makes the marginal revenue product of the investment financed by the funds just equal to the interest payment charged for borrowing.

Capital has one noteworthy feature that distinguishes it from other inputs, like fertilizer, however. The fertilizer applied by Farmer Pfister is used once and then it is gone, but a blast furnace, which is part of a steel company's capital, normally lasts many years. The furnace is a *durable* good, and because it is durable it contributes not only to today's production, but also to future production. This fact makes calculating the marginal revenue product more complex for a capital good than for other inputs.

To determine whether the MRP of a capital good is greater than the cost of financing it (that is, to decide whether an investment is profitable), we need a way to compare money values received at different times. To make such comparisons, economists and business people use a calculation procedure called **discounting**. Discounting was explained in detail in the appendix to Chapter 6, but it is not important that you master this technique in an introductory course. There are really only two important points to learn:

1. A sum of money received at a future date is worth less than a sum of money received today.

2. This difference in values between money today and money in the future is greater when the rate of interest is higher.

It is not difficult to understand why this is so. Consider what you could do with a dollar that you received today as opposed to one that you might receive a year from today. If the annual rate of interest is 10 percent, you could lend it out (for example, by putting it in a bank account) and receive $1.10 in a year's time—your original $1 plus 10 cents interest. For this reason, money received today is worth more than the same number of dollars received later. Specifically, at a rate of interest of 10 percent per year, $1.10 to be received a year from today is equivalent to $1 of today's money. This illustrates the first of our two points.

Now suppose the annual rate of interest is 15 percent instead. In this case $1

Interest is the payment for the use of funds employed in the production of capital; it is measured as a percentage per year of the value of the funds tied up in the capital.

invested today would grow to $1.15 (rather than $1.10) in a year's time, which means that $1.15 (not $1.10) received a year from today would be equivalent to $1 received today, and that $1.10 one year in the future must be worth less than $1 today. This illustrates the second point.

The Market Determination of Interest Rates

Let us now return to the way in which interest rates are determined in the market. We are concerned about the level of interest rates because they play a crucial role in determining the economy's level of investment—that is, in selecting the amount of current consumption that consumers will forgo in order to use resources to build machines and factories that can increase the output of consumers' goods in the future. Thus, the interest rate is crucial in determining the allocation of society's resources between present and future.

The Downward-Sloping Demand Curve for Funds

The two attributes of discounting discussed in the previous section are all we need to explain why the quantity of funds demanded declines when the interest rate rises, or why the demand curve for funds has a negative slope.

Remember that the demand for borrowed funds is a *derived demand*, derived from the desire to invest in capital goods. But part, and perhaps all, of the marginal revenue product of a machine or a factory is received in the future. Hence, the value of this MRP *in terms of today's money* shrinks as the rate of interest rises. Why? Because future returns must be *discounted more heavily* when the interest rate rises. The consequence of this shrinkage is that a machine that appears to be a good investment when the rate of interest is 10 percent may look like a terrible investment when the rate of interest is 15 percent.[10]

As the rate of interest on borrowing rises, more and more investments that previously looked profitable start to look unprofitable. The demand for borrowing for investment purposes, therefore, is lower at higher rates of interest.

An example of a derived demand schedule for borrowing is given in Figure 29–9, and

[10] You may wish to review the material on discounting in the appendix to Chapter 6, pages 148–50.

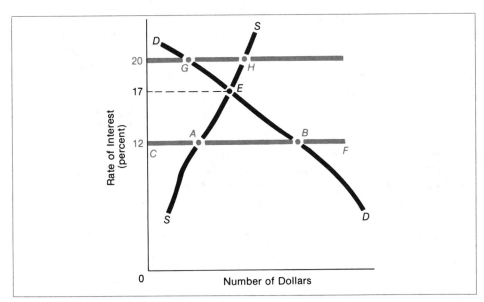

FIGURE 29-9
Equilibrium in the Market for Loans
If there is no foreign lending, the free-market interest rate is 17 percent. At this interest rate, the quantity of loans supplied is equal to the quantity demanded. However, if an interest-rate ceiling is imposed at, say, 12 percent, the quantity of funds supplied (point A) will be smaller than the quantity demanded (point B).

is labelled *DD*. Its negative slope illustrates the conclusion we have just stated—the higher the interest rate, the less money people and firms will want to borrow to finance their investments.

The Supply of Funds

Similar principles apply on the supply side of the market for funds—where the *lenders* are consumers, banks, and other types of business firms. Funds lent out are usually returned to the owner (with interest) only over a period of time. Loans will look better to lenders when they bear higher interest rates, so it is natural to think of the supply schedule for loans as being upward sloping—at higher rates of interest, lenders supply more funds—as shown by the curve *SS* in Figure 29–9.

It is interesting to note, incidentally, that some lenders may have supply curves that do not slope uphill to the right the way curve *SS* does. Suppose, for example, that Jones is saving to buy a $10,000 boat in three years and that if he lends money out at interest in the interim, at current interest rates he must save $3000 a year to reach his goal. If interest rates were higher, he could save less than $3000 each year and still reach his $10,000 goal. (The higher interest payments would, of course, contribute the difference.) So his saving (and lending) might decline. But this argument applies only to savers like Jones who have a fixed accumulation goal.

Generally, we do expect the quantity of loans supplied from domestic sources to rise when the interest reward rises, so the domestic supply curve has a positive slope, like *SS* in Figure 29–9. The equilibrium rate of interest is at point *E*, where quantity supplied and quantity demanded are equal. Thus, if our loan market operates in isolation from the rest of the world, we conclude that the equilibrium interest rate on loans is 17 percent.

Ceilings on Interest Rates

Let us now assume that Figure 29–9 refers to the supply of loans by banks to consumers. Consider what happens if there is a usury law that prohibits interest of more than 12 percent per annum on consumer loans. At this interest rate, the quantity supplied (point *A*) falls short of the quantity demanded (point *B*). This means that many applicants for consumer loans are being turned down even though the banks consider them to be creditworthy.

Who generally gains and who loses as a result of this usury law? The gainers are easiest to identify: those lucky consumers who are able to get loans at 12 percent even though they would have been willing to pay 17 percent. The law represents a windfall gain for them. The losers come on both the supply side and the demand side. First, there are the consumers who would have been willing and able to get credit at 17 percent but who are not lucky enough to get it at 12 percent. Then there are the banks (or, more accurately, bank shareholders) who could have made profitable loans at rates of up to 17 percent if there were no interest-rate ceiling.

This analysis helps explain the political popularity of usury laws. Few people sympathize with bank shareholders; indeed, it is the widespread feeling that banks are "gouging" their borrowers that provides much of the impetus for usury laws. The consumers who get loans at lower rates will, naturally, be quite pleased with the result of the law. The others, who would like to borrow at 12 percent but cannot because quantity supplied is less than quantity demanded, are quite likely to blame the bank for refusing to lend, rather than blame the government for outlawing some mutually beneficial transactions.

This analysis has little good to say about usury ceilings, and economists generally oppose them. However, interest-rate ceilings can play a constructive role when there is a monopoly over credit. If there is a monopoly lender, the analysis of Chapter 25 leads us to expect that firm to restrict its "output" (the volume of loans) by raising its "price" (the interest rate). Under such circumstances, an interest-rate ceiling may conceivably make sense.[11] But *may* is not *will*. Most economists believe that, except for isolated instances, the credit market is far closer to the competitive model than it is to the monopoly model.

The Importance of Foreign Lending for Interest-Rate Determination

The existence of foreign lending makes the supply curve of loans horizontal at the height given by existing foreign interest rates. This case is most relevant for Canada, since our financial markets are so integrated with those in the rest of the Western world. In particular, Canadians regularly borrow in the United States, and the total of our borrowing is very small relative to the overall size of their loan market. This makes Canadian sellers of bonds perfectly competitive sellers on the world bond market—they can sell whatever quantity they wish at the going price (that is, interest rate). Thus, the world demand curve for our bonds (which is the same as the foreign supply curve of loan funds to Canada) is horizontal at the interest-rate value observed in the United States.

Suppose the American interest rate is 12 percent. Since Canadian savers have the option of lending their funds in the United States at 12 percent, the Canadian supply of funds in Figure 29–9 is no longer SS. Only the part above 12 percent is relevant, so the supply curve becomes *CAE*. The foreign supply curve is *CF*. Given this foreign supply, domestic borrowers can obtain all the funds they want at 12 percent and so choose point *B*. In this case, point *A* indicates the proportion of loans that comes from domestic sources and the quantity of foreign borrowing that takes place (amount *AB*).

This analysis shows that a tax on foreign interest earnings in Canada and an increase in U.S. interest rates have exactly the same effects on Canadian interest rates. Both events raise the horizontal line indicating foreign willingness to lend in Canada. Suppose a tax or a hike in U.S. interest rates raises the horizontal line to *GH* in Figure 29–9. Canadian borrowing (demand for funds) will drop to the level indicated by point *G*, and Canadian savers will lend abroad an amount given by distance *GH*. Canadian interest rates will rise along with American rates, to 20 percent in this example. We can now appreciate why U.S. interest-rate increases are so unpopular in Canada, except among Canadians with money to lend. The analysis shows that our interest rates must rise along with U.S. rates, with the result that many of our firms' investment projects become unprofitable. The end result is lower employment in Canada. Perhaps the more surprising conclusion to follow from the analysis is that a tax on foreign interest income in Canada has the same result. Often, the politicians who express the most concern over high interest rates are the same ones who most favour increased taxes on foreigners who earn income in Canada!

Issue: Are Profits Too High or Too Low?

We turn next to business profits, a subject whose discussion seems to elicit more passion than logic. With the exception of some economists, almost no one thinks that the rate of profit is at about the right level. Critics on the left point accusingly at the billion-dollar profits of some giant corporations and argue that they are unconscionably high. They call for much stiffer taxes on profits. On the other hand, Chambers of Commerce, the Canadian Manufacturers' Association, and other business groups complain that regulations and "ruinous" competition keep profits too low, and they are constantly petitioning the government for tax relief.

The public has many misconceptions about the nature of the economy, but probably none is more severe than the popular view of the amount of profit that corporations earn. We suggest to you the following experiment. Ask five of your

---

[11] Chapter 25 of the *Study Guide* that accompanies this book contains an exercise exploring the effects of a maximum price law on a monopolist. Review your answer to that question now; it provides a more precise version of the argument given here.

friends who have never had an economics course what fraction of our national income they imagine is accounted for by profits. While the correct answer varies from year to year, in 1989 corporate profits represented only 12 percent of national income (and in 1983, just over 10 percent). A comparable percentage of the prices you pay represents before-tax profit. Most people assume that this figure is much, much higher. (See the boxed insert at the top of the next page.)

As you have no doubt noticed by now, economists are reluctant to brand factor prices as "too low" or "too high" in some moral or ethical sense. Rather, they are likely to ask first: What is the market equilibrium price? And then they will ask whether there are any good reasons to interfere with the market solution. This analysis, however, is not so easy to apply to the case of profits, since it is hard to use supply and demand analysis when you do not know what factor of production earns profit.

In both a bookkeeping and an economic sense, *profits are the residual*: They are what remains from the selling price after all other factors have been paid.

But what factor of production receives this reward? What factor's marginal productivity constitutes the profit rate?

What Accounts for Profits?

Economic profit, it will be recalled from Chapter 23, is the amount a firm earns *over and above* the payments for all other inputs, including the interest payments for the capital it uses and the opportunity cost of any capital provided by the owners of the firm. The profit rate and the interest rate are closely related. In an imaginary (and uninteresting) world in which everything was certain and unchanging, capitalists who invested money in firms would simply earn the market rate of interest on their funds. Profits beyond this level would be competed away. Profits below this level could not persist because capitalists would withdraw their funds from the firms and deposit them in banks. Capitalists in such a world would be mere money-lenders.

But the real world is not at all like this. Some capitalists are much more than money-lenders and the amounts they earn often exceed the interest rate by a considerable margin. Those activist capitalists who seek out or even create earnings opportunities are called **entrepreneurs**. They are the ones who are responsible for the constant change that characterizes business firms and who prevent the operations of the firms from stagnating. Since they are always trying to do something new, it is difficult to provide a general description of their activities. However, we can list three primary ways in which entrepreneurs are able to drive profits above the level of interest rates.

Entrepreneurship is the act of starting new firms, introducing new products and technological innovations, and, in general, taking the risks that are necessary in seeking out business opportunities.

Exercise of monopoly power. If the entrepreneur can establish a monopoly over some or all of her products, even for a short while, she can use the monopoly power of her firm to earn monopoly profits. The nature of these monopoly earnings was analyzed in Chapter 25.

Risk-bearing. The entrepreneur may engage in risky activities. For example, when a firm prospects for oil, it will drill an exploratory shaft hoping to find a pool of petroleum at the bottom. But a high proportion of such attempts produce only dry holes, and the cost of the operation is wasted. Of course, if the investor is lucky and does find oil, he may be rewarded handsomely. The income he obtains is a payment for bearing risk.

Obviously, a few lucky individuals make out well in this process, while most suffer heavy losses. How well can we expect risk-takers to do on the average? If, on the average, one exploratory drilling out of ten pays off, do we expect its return to be exactly ten times as high as the interest rate, so that the *average* firm will earn exactly the normal rate of interest? The answer is that the payoff will be *more* than ten times

Public Opinion on Profits

Most people think corporate profits are much higher than they actually are. A recent public-opinion poll, for example, found that the average citizen thought that corporate profits *after* tax amounted to 32 percent of sales for the typical manufacturing company. The actual profit rate at the time was only 3.8 percent! Interestingly, when a previous poll asked how much profit was "reasonable," the response was 26 cents on every dollar of sales—more than six times as large as profits actually were.

SOURCE: "Public Attitudes Toward Corporate Profits," *Public Opinion Index*, Opinion Research Corporation, Princeton, N.J., August 1986.

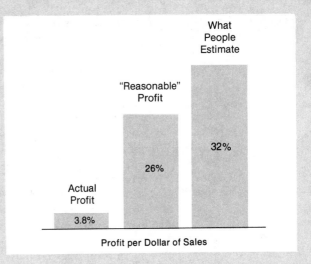

the interest rate if investors dislike gambling; that is, if they prefer to avoid risk. Why? Because investors who dislike risk will be unwilling to put their money into a business in which nine firms out of ten lose out unless there is some compensation for the financial peril to which they expose themselves.

In reality, however, there is no certainty that things always work out this way. Some people love to gamble, and these people tend to be overoptimistic about their chances of coming out ahead. They may plunge into projects to a degree unjustified by the odds. If there are enough such gamblers, the average payoff to risky undertakings may end up below the interest rate. The successful investor will still make a good profit, just like the lucky winner in Las Vegas. But the average participant will have to pay for the privilege of bearing risk.

Returns to innovation. The third major source of profits is perhaps the most important of all from the point of view of social welfare. The entrepreneur who is first to market a desirable new product or to employ a new cost-saving machine or to innovate in some other way will receive a special profit as his reward. **Innovation** is different from **invention**. Invention is the act of generating a new idea; innovation is the next step, the act of putting the new idea into practical use. Business people are rarely inventors, but they are often innovators.

When an entrepreneur innovates, even if her new product or her new process is not protected by patents, she will be one step ahead of her competitors. She will be able to capture much of the market either by offering customers a better product or by supplying the product more cheaply. In either case she will temporarily find herself with some monopoly power left by the weakening of her competitors, and monopoly profit will be the reward for her initiative.

However, this monopoly profit, the reward for innovation, will only be temporary. As soon as the success of the idea has demonstrated itself to the world, other firms will find ways of imitating it. Even if they cannot turn out precisely the same product or use precisely the same process, they will have to find ways to supply close substitutes if they are to survive. In this way, new ideas are spread through the economy. And in the process the special profits of the innovator are brought to an end. The innovator can resume earning special profits only by finding still another promising idea.

Entrepreneurs are forced to keep searching for new ideas, to keep instituting innovations, and to keep imitating those that they have not been the first to put into

> Invention is the act of generating a new idea. Innovation, the next step, is the act of putting the new idea into practical use.

operation. This process is at the heart of the growth of the capitalist system. It is one of the secrets of its extraordinary dynamism.

The Issue of Profits Taxation

So profits in excess of the market rate of interest can be considered as the return on entrepreneurial talent. But this is not really very helpful, since no one can say exactly what entrepreneurial talent is. Certainly we cannot measure it; nor can we teach it in a college course (though business schools try!). Therefore, we do not know how the observed profit rate relates to the minimum reward necessary to attract entrepreneurial talent into the market—a relationship that is crucial for the contentious issue of profits taxation.

Consider a windfall profits tax on oil companies as an example. If oil company profit rates are well above this minimum necessary reward, they contain a large element of economic rent. In that case, we could tax away these excess profits (rents) without fear of reducing oil production. On the other hand, if the profits being earned by oil companies do not contain much economic rent, then the windfall profits tax might seriously curtail exploration and production of oil.

This example illustrates the general problem of deciding how heavily profits should be taxed. Critics of big business who call for high profits taxes believe that profits are mostly economic rent. But if they are wrong, if most of the observed profits are necessary to attract people into entrepreneurial roles, then a high profits tax can be dangerous. It can threaten the very lifeblood of the capitalist system. Business lobbying groups predictably claim that this is the case. Unfortunately, neither group has offered much evidence for its conclusion.

The Labour Market

The Supply of Labour

The economic analysis of labour supply is based on the following simple observation: Given the fixed amount of time in a week, one's decision to *supply labour* to firms is simultaneously a decision to *demand leisure* time for oneself. Assuming that after necessary time for eating and sleeping is deducted a worker has 90 usable hours in a week, a decision to spend 40 of those hours working is simultaneously a decision to demand 50 of them for other purposes.

This suggests that we can analyze the *supply* of this particular input—labour—with the same tools we used in Chapter 19 to analyze the *demand* for commodities. In this case, the commodity is leisure. A consumer "buys" her own leisure time, just as she buys bananas, or back scratchers, or pizzas. In Chapter 19 we observed that any price change has two distinct effects on quantity demanded: an income effect and a substitution effect. Let us review these two effects and see how they operate in the context of the demand for leisure (that is, the supply of labour).

1. *Income effect.* Higher wages make consumers richer. We expect this increased wealth to raise the demand for most goods, leisure included.

The income effect of higher wages probably leads most workers to want to work less.

2. *Substitution effect.* Consumers "purchase" their own leisure time by giving up their hourly wage, so the wage rate is the "price" of leisure. When the wage rate rises, leisure becomes more expensive relative to other commodities that consumers might buy. Thus, we expect a wage increase to induce them to buy *less* leisure time and *more* goods.

The substitution effect of higher wages probably leads most workers to want to work more.

Putting these two effects together, we are led to conclude that some workers may react to an increase in their wage rate by working more, while others may react by working less. Still others will have little or no discretion over their hours of work. In terms of the market as a whole, therefore, higher wages could lead to either a larger or a smaller quantity of labour supplied.

Statistical studies of this issue have reached the conclusions that (a) the response of labour supply to wage changes is not very strong for most workers; (b) for low-wage workers the substitution effect seems clearly dominant, so they work more when wages rise; and (c) for high-wage workers the income effect just about offsets the substitution effect, so they do not work more when wages rise. Figure 29-10 depicts these approximate "facts." It shows labour supply rising (slightly) as wages rise up to point *A*. Thereafter, labour supply is roughly constant as wages rise.

It is even possible that when wages are raised sufficiently high, further increases in wages will lead workers to purchase more leisure and therefore to work less. The supply curve of labour is then said to be "backward-bending," as illustrated by the broken portion of the curve above point *B*.

An Application: The Labour-Supply Paradox

Labour-supply analysis helps explain the following puzzling observation. Throughout the twentieth century, wages have generally been rising, both in number of dollars paid per hour and in the quantity of goods those dollars can buy. Yet labour has asked for and received *reductions* in the length of the work day and the work week. At the beginning of the century, a work week of five and a half days and a work day of ten or more hours were standard, making for a work week of fifty to sixty hours (and there were virtually no vacations). Since then, labour hours have generally declined. Today the standard work week is down to thirty-five to forty hours. Where has the common-sense view of the matter gone wrong? Why, as hourly wages have risen, have workers not sold more of the hours they have available instead of pressing for a shorter and shorter work week?

Part of the answer becomes clear when one recalls that any wage increase sets in motion *both* a substitution effect *and* an income effect. If only the substitution effect operated, then rising wages would indeed cause people to work longer hours because

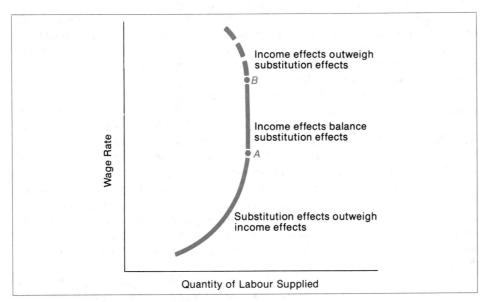

FIGURE 29-10
A Typical Labour Supply Schedule
The labour supply schedule depicted here has a positive slope up to point *A*, as substitution effects outweigh income effects. At higher wages, however, income effects become just as important as substitution effects, and the curve becomes roughly vertical. At still higher wages (above point *B*), income effects might overwhelm substitution effects.

the high price of leisure makes leisure less attractive. But this reasoning leaves out the income effect. As higher wages make workers richer, they will want to buy more of most commodities, including vacations and other leisure-time activities. Thus, the income effect of increasing wages induces workers to work fewer hours.

It is the strong income effect of rising wages that may account for the fact that labour supply has responded in the "wrong" direction, with workers working ever-shorter hours despite their rising real wages. If so, the long-run supply curve of labour is indeed backward-bending.

The Demand for Labour and the Determination of Wages

There is not much to be said about the demand for labour that has not already been said about the demand for other inputs. Like any factor of production, labour has a marginal revenue product curve from which a downward-sloping demand curve for labour is derived. If there are no interferences with the operation of a free market in labour (such as minimum wages or unions), equilibrium will occur at point where the supply and demand curves intersect (as we assumed in our discussion of minimum wages).

Why Wages Differ

But, of course, there is not one labour market but many—each with its own supply and demand curves and its own equilibrium wage. We all know that certain groups in our society (the young, the uneducated) earn relatively low wages, and that some of our most severe social ills (poverty, crime, drug addiction) are related to this fact. But why are some wages so low while others are so high?

Supply and demand analysis at once tells us everything and nothing about this question. It implies that wages are relatively high in markets where demand is great and supply is small, while wages are comparatively low in markets where demand is weak and supply is high. This can hardly be considered startling news. But to make the analysis useful, we need to breathe some life into the supply and demand curves.

We begin our discussion on the demand side. Why is the demand for labour greater in some markets than in others? The marginal productivity principle teaches us that there are two types of influences to be considered. Since a worker's marginal revenue product depends both on his *marginal physical product* and on the *price of the product* he produces, variables that influence either of these will influence his wage.

The determinants of the prices of commodities were discussed at some length in earlier chapters, and there is no need to repeat the analysis here. It is sufficient to remember that because the demand for labour is a *derived demand*, anything that raises or lowers the demand for a particular product will tend to raise or lower the wages of the workers who produce that product.

A worker's marginal physical product depends on several things, including, of course, his own *abilities* and *degree of effort* on the job. But sometimes these characteristics are less important than the *other factors of production* that he has to work with. Workers in Canadian industry are more productive than workers in many other countries because they have generous supplies of machinery, natural resources, and technical know-how to work with. As a consequence, they earn high wages.

Turning next to the supply of labour, it is clear that the *size of the available working population* relative to the magnitude of industrial activity in a given area is of major importance. This helps to explain why wages rose so high in the sparsely populated North when exploration for Arctic oil created many new jobs, and why wages have been and remain so low in Atlantic Canada, where industry is relatively dormant.

Second, it is clear that the *non-monetary attractiveness* of any job will also influence the supply of workers to it. (The monetary attractiveness is the wage itself, which governs movements *along* the supply curve.) Jobs that people find pleasant and satisfying will attract a large supply of labour and will consequently pay a relatively low wage. In contrast, a premium will have to be paid to attract workers to jobs that are onerous, disagreeable, or dangerous—such as washing the windows of skyscrapers.

Finally, the amount of ability and training needed to enter a particular job or profession is relevant to its supply of labour. Brain surgeons and professional football quarterbacks earn generous incomes because there are few people as highly skilled as they are and because it is time consuming and expensive to acquire these skills even for those who have the ability.

In addition to all this, it is important to recognize that adjustments in the labour market are slow in comparison with those for other inputs or commodities. Workers, for example, are reluctant to move their homes from a low-wage geographic area to a higher-wage area, so wage differentials may persist longer than price differentials in other markets do. In the labour markets, long-run equilibrium takes a long time to attain, particularly where substantial retraining and relocation are required to eliminate differences in wages among jobs.

Ability and Earnings

In considering the effects of ability on earnings, it is useful to distinguish between skills that can be duplicated easily and skills that cannot. If Jones has an ability that Smith cannot acquire even if he undergoes extensive training, then the wages that Jones earns will contain an element of *economic rent*, just as in the case of Wayne Gretzky. Virtually anyone with moderate athletic ability can be taught to shoot a hockey puck at a net. But in most cases, no amount of training will teach the player to play hockey the way Gretzky does. His high salary is a reward for his unique ability.

But many of the abilities that the market rewards generously—such as the skills of doctors and lawyers—clearly are duplicable. Here the theory of rent does not apply, and we need a different explanation for the high wages that these skilled professionals earn. Once again, however, part of our analysis from earlier in this chapter finds an immediate application because the acquisition of skills, through formal education and other forms of training, has much in common with business investment decisions. Why? Because the decision to undertake more education in the hope of increasing future earnings involves a sacrifice of *current* income for the sake of *future* gain— precisely the hallmark of an investment decision.

Investment in Human Capital

That education is an investment is a concept familiar to most college and university students. You made a conscious decision to go to school rather than to enter the labour market, and you are probably acutely aware that this decision is now costing you money—lots of money. Your tuition payments may be only a minor part of the total cost of going to college or university. Think of a high school friend who chose not to go on to postsecondary education and who is now working. The salary that he or she is earning could, perhaps, have been yours. You are deliberately giving up this possible income in order to acquire more education.

In this sense, your education can be thought of as an *investment* in yourself—a *human investment*. Like a firm that devotes some of its money to building a plant that will yield profits at some future date, you are investing in your own future, hoping that your postsecondary education will help you earn more than what your high school educated friend can earn or that it will enable you to find a more pleasant or prestigious job when you graduate. Economists call activities like obtaining a postsecondary degree **investments in human capital** because such activities give the human being many of the attributes of a capital investment.

Doctors and lawyers earn such high salaries partly because of their many years of training. That is, part of their wages can be construed as a *return on their (educa-*

tional) investments, rather than as economic rent. Unlike the case of Wayne Gretzky, there are a number of people who conceivably *could* become surgeons if they found the job sufficiently attractive to endure the long years of training that are required. Few, however, are willing to make such a large investment of their own time, money, and energy. Consequently, the few who do become surgeons earn very generous incomes.

Economists have devoted quite a bit of attention to the acquisition of skills through human investment. There is an entire branch of economic theory—called **human-capital theory**—that analyzes an individual's decisions about education, training, and so on in exactly the same way as we have analyzed a firm's decision to buy a machine or build a factory. Though educational decisions can be influenced by love of learning, desire for prestige, and a variety of other preferences and emotions, human-capital theorists find it useful to analyze a schooling decision as though it had been made purely as a business plan. The optimal approach to education, from this point of view, is to stay in school until the marginal revenue (in the form of increased future income) of another year of schooling is exactly equal to the marginal cost.

One implication of human-capital theory is that postsecondary graduates should earn enough more than high school graduates to compensate them for their extra investments in schooling. Do they? Will your investment pay off? Many generations of college and university students have supposed that it would, and for years studies of the incomes earned by graduates indicated that they were right. These studies showed that the income differentials earned by postsecondary graduates provided a good "return" on the tuition payments and sacrificed earnings that they had "invested" in their schooling. But education investments turned a bit sour in the 1970s. The reason was the obvious one: Relative to high school graduates, the supply of college and university graduates expanded much more rapidly than did the demand.

This, of course, does not mean that only fools go to community colleges and universities. What it does mean is that the financial incentive *alone* is not what it used to be. If you simply enjoy the experience or want to acquire knowledge for its own sake or attend because you think it will help to get you a more pleasant job, obtaining a postsecondary degree can still be a perfectly rational decision. It does not, however, offer quite the financial bonanza that it once did.

Human-capital theory stresses that jobs that require more education *must* pay higher wages if they are to attract enough workers, because people insist on a financial return on their human investments. But the theory does not address the other side of the question: What is it about more-educated people that makes firms willing to pay them higher wages? To put the point differently, the theory explains why the quantity of educated people *supplied* is limited but does not explain why the quantity *demanded* is substantial even at high wages.

Most human-capital theorists complete their analyses by assuming that students in high schools, colleges, and universities are acquiring particular skills that are productive in the marketplace. In this view, educational institutions are factories that take less-productive workers as their raw materials, apply doses of training, and produce more-productive workers as outputs. It is a view of what happens in schools that makes educators happy and accords well with common sense. However, a number of social scientists doubt that this is how schooling raises earning power.

Education and Earnings: Dissenting Views

Just why is it that jobs with stiffer educational requirements typically offer higher wages? The common-sense view that educating people makes them more productive is not universally accepted.

Education as a sorting mechanism. One alternative view denies that the educational process teaches students anything directly relevant to their subsequent performance on the job. Rather, it holds that people differ in ability when they enter the school system and differ in more or less the same way when they leave. What the educational system does, according to this theory, is to *sort* individuals by ability. Skills like intelligence and self-discipline that lead to success in schools, it is argued, are closely related to the skills that lead to success in jobs. As a result, more-able individuals stay in school longer and perform better. Prospective employers know this and consequently seek to hire those whom the school system has suggested will be the most productive workers.

The radical view of education. Many radical economists question whether the educational system really sorts people according to ability. The rich, they note, are better situated to buy the best education and to keep their children in school regardless of ability. Thus, education may be one of the instruments by which a more-privileged family passes its economic position on to its heirs while making it appear that there is a legitimate reason for firms to give them higher earnings. As radicals see it, education sorts people according to their social class, not according to their ability.

Radicals also hold a different idea about what happens inside schools to make workers more "productive." They believe that, instead of serving primarily as instruments for the acquisition of knowledge and improved ability to think, schools primarily teach people discipline—how to show up five days a week at 9:00 A.M., how to speak in turn and respectfully, and so on. These characteristics, radicals claim, are what business firms prefer and what cause them to seek more-educated workers. They also suggest that the schools teach docility and acceptance of the capitalist status quo, and that this, too, makes schooling attractive to business.

The dual labour market theory. A third view of the linkages among education, ability, and earnings is part of a much broader theory of how the labour market operates—the theory of **dual labour markets**. Proponents of this theory suggest that there are two very different types of labour markets, with relatively little mobility between them.

The "primary labour market" is where most of the economy's "good jobs" are—jobs like computer programming, business management, and skilled crafts that are interesting and offer considerable possibilities for career advancement. The educational system helps decide which individuals get assigned to the primary labour market, and, for those who make it, greater educational achievement does indeed offer financial rewards.

The privileged workers who wind up in the primary labour market are offered opportunities for additional training on the job; they augment their skills by experience and by learning from their fellow workers, and they progress in successive steps to more-responsible, better-paying positions. Where jobs in the primary labour market are concerned, dual labour market theorists agree with human-capital theorists that education really is productive. But they agree with the radicals that admission to the primary labour market depends in part on social position and that firms probably care more about steady work habits and punctuality than about reading, writing, and arithmetic.

Everything is quite different in the "secondary labour market"—where we find all the "bad jobs." Jobs like domestic service and fast-food service offer low rates of pay, few fringe benefits, and virtually no training to improve the workers' skills. They are dead-end jobs offering little or no hope for promotion or advancement. As a result, lateness, absenteeism, and thievery are expected as a matter of course, so that workers in the secondary labour market tend to develop bad work habits that confirm the prejudices of those who assigned them to inferior jobs in the first place.

In the secondary labour market, increased education leads neither to higher wages nor to increased protection from unemployment—benefits that generally come with increased schooling elsewhere in the labour market. For this reason, workers in the secondary market have little incentive to invest in education.

In sum, we have a well-established fact—that people with more education generally earn higher wages—but very little agreement on the theory accounting for this fact. There is probably some truth to each of the proposed explanations, and each of them consequently has some relevance for the workings of the labour market in reality.

Unions and Collective Bargaining

Thus far, our analysis of labour markets has ignored one rather important fact: The supply of labour is not at all competitive in many labour markets; instead, it is controlled by a labour monopoly, a **union**.

While unions are important, only about 30 percent of Canada's non-agricultural workers belong to unions. Union membership seems much more significant than this to the public because unions are large, and therefore newsworthy, institutions.

Unions are less prevalent in the United States, where only about 16 percent of the workers are unionized, but they are more prevalent in some other industrialized countries. For example, about 43 percent of British workers and about 90 percent of Swedish workers belong to unions.

The Development of Unionism in Canada

There is no doubt that industrial working conditions were terrible before unions were formed and these conditions created widespread support among workers for the labour movement. Just fifty years ago, working conditions remained poor (see the boxed insert on the next page), and significant management resistance to the organization of unions existed.

The original unions in Canada, which appeared in the early 1800s, were formed by workers in particular crafts or trades. These **craft unions** were the first to appear for two reasons: The relatively small number of members in each of the unions meant that organization costs were small, and there were few substitutes for the services offered by these skilled workers. This meant that the threat of a strike represented a much bigger problem for employers than would have been the case with easily replaced unskilled workers.

Early union history included a number of ugly incidents. Sometimes employers would hire men to intimidate union leaders or strike organizers, and often violent incidents were arranged to cast the labour leaders as the trouble-makers. Another problem that limited union growth was the treatment of unions in the courts. Initially the courts interpreted the withholding of services for higher wages as a form of restraint of trade.

In the late 1800s, the Canadian affiliate of the Knights of Labour, a powerful American union, attempted to organize Canada's less-skilled workers along industry rather than craft lines. The Knights of Labour stressed the broader political issues concerning the role of labour in society. As it turned out, however, the workers cared more about what they saw as bread-and-butter issues, and union membership began to decline after 1886. The Knights of Labour and some smaller Marxist-oriented unions in British Columbia continued to exert some influence until about 1930.

The first widely successful confederation of labour in Canada was the Trades and Labor Congress of Canada (TLC), founded in 1883, which became the Canadian affiliate of the American Federation of Labor (AFL). The TLC reverted to an emphasis on skilled workers, organizing them on a country-wide basis by craft. The union devoted its efforts to the day-to-day issues of pay, work week, working and safety conditions, and related problems.

Another attempt to include unskilled workers took place with the formation of the Canadian Congress of Labour (CCL) in 1940. This organization was the Canadian affiliate of the United States' Congress of Industrial Organizations (CIO). It resembled the Knights of Labour in that its aim was to organize all workers by plant and industry rather than by craft. However, the CCL, like the TLC, avoided the broad political emphasis that characterized the Knights of Labour, and the two main wings of the

Working Conditions Fifty Years Ago: One Worker's Account

I started work for Stelco in 1940, and one of the jobs we had will give you an idea of conditions.

When the brick lining on the big open hearths would go down, all the labour gangs from all over the plant were called over to tear them down and to rebuild them. I was on the labour gang at the slag dump, and the foreman would come along about 4:00 in the afternoon and say: "You go home now and be back here at 6:00 and report over to open hearth." They didn't give you a chance to object at all. The inference was there—if you're not there at 6:00, don't bother to come back at all.

These furnaces had just been shut down, and they were still hot—I mean red hot, not white hot. The company didn't want to waste time. They didn't make any money when the furnaces were down.

You wore big wooden clogs on your feet, because your boots would start to burn if you didn't wear these clogs, and you wrapped a scarf around your ears and your ears would start to burn. You'd stand outside the door, and spot a brick. You'd spot the brick, because if you got in there and started to fish around, you started to burn. You couldn't stay in there any longer than 30 seconds or your clothes would start to smoulder. So you made up your mind—that's the brick right

there! You had a big pair of tongs, and you made a lunge, and grabbed that brick, and ran right out. I've seen big, strong husky men—the heat would make them drop like flies. But there was a job that had to be done.

SOURCE: From *Baptism of a Union: Stelco Strike of 1946*, W. Roberts (ed.), Department of Labour Studies, McMaster University.

---

labour movement merged in 1956, forming the Canadian Labour Congress (CLC). A similar merger took place in the United States, creating the AFL–CIO.

It is interesting to compare the growth of unions in Canada and the United States. Strong membership growth occurred earlier in the United States, mainly because of legal differences. By 1935, American workers had acquired the legal right to strike, and in the same year it became illegal for employers to fire pro-union employees. In Canada, such firings were not made illegal until 1939, and it was only later, during the war, that workers gained official recognition of their right to organize. As a result, union membership grew rapidly from 1935 to 1945 in the United States and from 1940 to 1950 in Canada.

The favourable public attitude toward unions in the United States soured somewhat after World War II, perhaps because of the rash of strikes that took place in 1946. One result of these strikes was the Taft-Hartley Act of 1947, which specified and outlawed certain "unfair labour practices" by unions. Specifically, the act severely limited the extent of the "closed shop" (under which only union members can be hired) and permitted state governments, at their discretion, to ban the "union shop" (an arrangement that requires employees to join the union). These so-called right-to-work laws have since been adopted by quite a number of American states.

A rather different legal decision took place in Canada. In 1945 there was a long strike involving the workers of the Ford Motor Company of Canada over the issue of union security. The dispute was finally resolved by an arbitration decision within the Supreme Court. The resulting rules, which came to be known as the **Rand formula** (after the Supreme Court judge), made it illegal for workers to be forced to join a union, but at the same time made it compulsory for them to pay union dues, whether or not they were members. This court decision had the effect of solidifying union rights. Various versions of the Rand formula have been adopted in collective agreements involving public-sector workers in many provinces, and its use is compulsory for many private-sector contracts.

Canadian Unions: Problems and Issues

The 1982 Charter of Rights is seen by many as limiting labour's rights. So far each Supreme Court judgment defining how the Charter is to be interpreted has stressed *individual* rights. In a series of much-noted decisions in 1987, the Court ruled that "the modern rights to bargain collectively and to strike are not fundamental rights and freedoms." Thus, the Court has not interpreted "freedom of association" to include strike or bargaining and has ruled that governments have the right to curtail collective bargaining for public-sector workers by limiting salary increases, prohibiting strikes and lockouts, and imposing compulsory arbitration. The judgment is based on the proposition that restricting the right to strike is justified when "the effect of a strike would be especially injurious to the economic interests of a third party." The labour movement's reaction has been to try to arrange an amendment to the Charter specifying that its references to "everyone" include not only "individuals" and "corporations" but also labour's bargaining units.

A second discouraging set of developments for Canadian unions springs from trends in organized labour in other countries, as well as in the nature of jobs generally. The union movement was considerably weakened in the United States and Great Britain by the policies of Ronald Reagan and Margaret Thatcher, respectively. In addition, there has been a growing trend toward part-time work, which has not only kept average employment income from rising, but has also made it increasingly difficult for unions to organize workers.

Another impediment to Canadian unions is the general move toward freer trade and deregulation. Both require that the productivity of Canadian workers be increased through adjustments to production methods, such as increased use of robotics and computer-assisted design methods. But unions have tended to be suspicious of such changes.*

Unions and Economic Nationalism

It is interesting to consider how labour's views on economic nationalism have changed over the years, as described in the following passages from an article by Prof. Samuel Bowles of the University of Massachusetts:**

A century ago there was a clear connection in the West between nationalism and political ideology. Conservatives were nationalists—businessmen warned their employees and fellow citizens against foreign agitators. Progressives and the labour movement, meanwhile, were internationalists.

Today it is business, not labour, that thinks in international terms. We find the labour movement, and the pro-gressive political community in general, reeling before the challenges posed by the globalization of production.

Recognizing the gains to be made by redistributing income within a national economy, labour has increasingly embraced a nationalist position since the Second World War, while business, recognizing the profit opportunities in global capitalism, has tended to adopt internationalist positions.

The emergence of the welfare state defined national boundaries as the limits of redistribution....

Both the economic effectiveness of the welfare state and the power of the labour movement required national boundaries, for in a world of cheap transport and cheap labour, the free movement of goods and labour jeopardizes the material gains of unions and social-program beneficiaries. A truly global system of economic competition would eventually force wage restraint and even concessions on the more well-to-do segments of the world's working class....

As a result, multinational corporations are now portrayed as unpatriotic, and their global operations are the targets of uncommon criticism from labour. Asia-bashing has also seeped into labour's rhetoric.

From an egalitarian viewpoint, there are practical and moral problems with populist jingoism. It may promote tariffs and gain some short-run job protection, but it is divisive because it pits the interests of (often low-income) consumers of imported goods against those of workers....

Tariff protection ... is an unlikely foundation for a long-term populist coalition. As long as wages, working conditions and environmental protection in other parts of the world fall far short of North American standards, workers here will always be threatened with losing their jobs when their plants pack up and head overseas. Tariff protection can (and should) be used to promote smooth long-term economic adjustments, but it cannot protect the living standards of domestic workers in the long run.

Doing this requires two things: the maintenance of a high level of worldwide demand for developed countries' goods and services, and the spread of democratic and union rights and environmental protection throughout the world. Neither objective can be realized if workers in leading capitalist countries (and those who speak for them) adopt a "blame the Koreans" attitude.

---

*This issue was discussed in greater detail in Chapter 18 (page 383).
**Excerpted from Samuel Bowles, "Different Wavelengths," *The Globe and Mail*, December 8, 1988, page A7. Professor Bowles' article was originally published in *Tikkun*, a journal of political and social criticism based in Oakland, California. Reprinted by permission.

The net result of the two countries' different laws and legal precedents is that only about 16 percent of American workers are union members, a much lower proportion than in Canada. Another difference between the two labour movements is that Canadian unions have maintained their historical involvement with general political reforms in a more direct way than have their American counterparts. The third and most immediate difference is that, today, public-sector unions are far more extensive in Canada than they are in the United States. One reason for this is that many more government employees, at all levels of government, are permitted to unionize in this country.

The largest membership growth in Canada since 1960 has been in the public sector. But this growth has just compensated for declining membership in other areas. Membership has fallen because there is now a lower percentage of workers in the heavy industries (where unions have been popular) and also because a larger percentage of the work force is young and female, and a growing number of workers want part-time employment. These groups seem less attracted to unions. Finally, the deep recession of the early 1980s and the widespread public frustration with visible public-sector unions such as the Canadian Union of Postal Workers have made unions less popular.

Unions as a Labour Monopoly

Unions require that we alter our economic analysis of the labour market in much the same way that monopolies required us to alter our analysis of the goods market. You will recall that in a monopolized product market the firm selects the point on its demand curve that maximizes its profits. Much the same idea applies to unions, which are, after all, monopoly sellers of labour. They too face a demand curve—derived this time from the marginal productivity schedules of firms—and can choose the point on it that suits them best.

The problem for the economist trying to analyze union behaviour—and perhaps also for the union leader trying to select a course of action—is how to decide which point on the demand curve is "best." Unlike the case of the business firm, there is no obvious goal analogous to profit maximization that clearly delineates what the union should do. Instead, a number of *alternative* goals are plausible, partly because union members themselves differ in their objectives, particularly in the trade-off between higher wages and job security. If older workers are protected from being fired by **seniority rules** that require those who have held jobs longest to be the last to be dismissed, these older workers may give greater priority to high wages and pensions than younger workers do. Younger workers may be more concerned about job security, health and safety provisions, and working hours. The policy pursued by union leaders may depend on the relative power of the different groups of members in the union.

Alternative Union Goals and Strategies

Differences in union goals can be illustrated with the aid of Figure 29–11, which

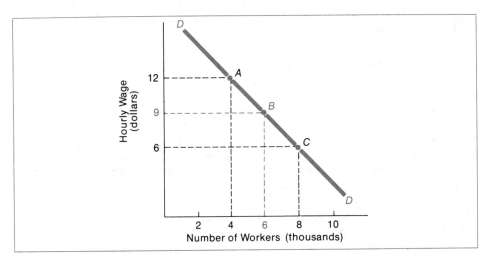

FIGURE 29–11
Alternative Goals for a Union
Line *DD* is the demand curve for labour in a market that becomes unionized. Point *C* is the equilibrium point before the union, when wages were $6 per hour. If the union wants to push wages higher, it normally will have to sacrifice some jobs. Points *A* and *B* show two of its many alternatives.

depicts a demand curve for labour, labelled *DD*. The union leadership must decide which point on the curve is best. One possibility is to treat the size of the union as fixed and force employers to pay the highest wage they will pay and still employ all the union members. If, for example, the union has 4000 members, this would be point *A*, with a wage of $12 per hour. But this is a high-risk strategy for a union. Firms forced to pay such high wages will be at a competitive disadvantage compared with firms that have non-union labour, and may even be forced to shut down.

Alternatively, union leaders may be interested in increasing the size of their unions. As an extreme case of this, they might try to make employment as large as possible without pushing the wage below the competitive level. If the competitive wage were $6 per hour in the absence of the union, this strategy would correspond to selecting point *C*, with employment for 8000 workers. In this case the existence of the union has no effect on wages or on employment.

An intermediate strategy that has often been suggested is that the union maximize the total income of all workers. This would dictate choosing point *B*, with a wage of $9 per hour and jobs for 6000 workers (since point *B* is where the demand elasticity is unity in this numerical example). Other possible strategies can also be imagined, but these suffice to make the basic point clear.

Unions, as monopoly sellers of labour, have the power to push wages above the competitive levels. However, since the demand curve for labour is downward sloping, such increases in wages can normally be achieved only by reducing the number of jobs. Just as a monopoly firm must limit its output to push up its price, so the union must restrict employment to push wages up.

This can be seen clearly by comparing points *B* and *A* with point *C* (the competitive solution). If the union selects point *B*, it raises wages by $3 per hour, but at the cost of 2000 jobs. If it goes all the way to point *A*, wages are raised to twice the competitive level, but employment is cut in half.

What do unions actually try to do? There are probably as many different choices as there are unions. Some seem to pursue a maximum-employment goal much like point *C*, raising wages very little. Others seem to push for the highest possible wages, much like point *A*. Most probably select an intermediate route. This implies, of course, that the effects of unionization on wage rates and employment will differ markedly among industries.

How would a union that has decided to push wages above the competitive level accomplish this task? One approach is to *restrict supply*. By keeping out some of the workers who would like to enter the industry or occupation, it shifts the supply curve of labour inward. This sort of behaviour is often encountered in craft unions, which may require a long period of apprenticeship. Such unions sometimes offer only a small number of new memberships each year, largely to replace members who have retired or died. Membership in such a union is very valuable and is sometimes offered primarily to children of current members. Restricting supply is also practised within the medical profession (whose association operates like a union), by limiting enrolment in medical schools. Many other professional associations also perform the functions of unions for their members.

Instead of restricting supply, the union can simply *set a high wage rate*. In this case, it is the employers who will restrict entry into the job, because with wages so high they will not want to employ many workers. This second strategy is more typically employed by industrial unions, like those representing automobile or mine workers. Either method can be used to achieve the desired point on the demand curve. Wages are raised only by reducing employment in either case.

In some exceptional cases, however, a union may be able to achieve wage gains without sacrificing employment. To do this, the union must be able to exercise effective control over the demand curve for labour. Union actions try to push the demand curve outward, simultaneously raising both wages and employment. This is usually difficult to do. One way to do it is by *featherbedding*—forcing management to employ more workers than are really needed.[12] Quite the opposite technique is to institute a campaign to raise worker productivity, which some unions seem to have been able to do. Alternatively, the union can try to raise the demand for the company's product either by flexing its political muscle (for example, by obtaining legislation to reduce foreign competition) or by appealing to the public to buy union products.

Have Unions Really Raised Wages?

The theory of unions as monopoly sellers of labour certainly suggests that unions have some ability to raise wages, but it also shows that they may be hesitant to use this ability for fear of reducing employment. To what extent do union members actually earn higher wages than non-members?

The consensus that has emerged from economic research on this question would probably surprise most people. A recent study by H. Gregg Lewis[13] has estimated that most union members earn wages about 15 percent higher than those earned by non-members (who are otherwise identical in skill level, geographical location, and so on). While this figure is certainly not negligible, and while there are indications that it has been rising slightly, the differential can hardly be considered huge. This does not mean, however, that unions have raised wages by no more than 15 percent. Some observers believe that union activity has also raised the wages of non-unionized workers by forcing non-union employers to compete harder for their workers. If so, the differential between union and non-union workers must be less than the amount by which unions have raised wages overall. In addition, unions have improved the situations of their members, and perhaps of all workers, in other areas—for example, working conditions, health and safety measures, and the provision of pensions—which do not show up in pay cheques but do raise the cost of labour to the employer.

Monopsony and Bilateral Monopoly

While the analysis we have just presented has its applications, it oversimplifies matters in several important respects. For one thing, it envisions a market situation in which one powerful union is dealing with many powerless employers: The labour market is assumed to be monopolized on the selling side but competitive on the buying side. There are industries that more or less fit this model. The giant Teamsters' union negotiates with a trucking industry that comprises thousands of firms, most of them quite small and powerless. Similarly, most of the unions in the construction industry are much larger than the firms with which they bargain.

But there are many cases that simply do not fit the model. The "Big Four" automakers do not stand idly by while the UAW picks its favourite point on the demand curve for auto workers. Nor does the Steelworkers' union sit across the bargaining table from representatives of a perfectly competitive industry. In these and other industries, while the union certainly has a good deal of monopoly power over labour supply, the firms also have some **monopsony** power over the labour demand. Just as a monopoly union on the selling side of the labour market does not passively sell labour at the going wage, a monopsony firm on the buying side does not passively purchase labour at the going wage or at the wage suggested by the labour union. Analysts find it difficult to predict the wage and employment decisions that will

Monopsony refers to a market situation in which there is only one buyer.

---

[12] The best-known example of featherbedding involved the railway unions, which for years forced management to keep "firemen" in the cabs of diesel engines, in which there were no burning fires. Similarly, the musicians' union requires the O'Keefe Centre in Toronto to hire a "house minimum" of 20 musicians each night, even if fewer are needed for a particular performance. Of course, it is not only labour that has tried to create an artificial demand for its services. Lawyers, doctors, and business firms, among others, have sought ways to induce consumers to buy more of their products and services. *EXERCISE:* Can you think of ways in which they have done this?

[13] H. G. Lewis, *Union Relative Wage Effects: A Survey* (Chicago: University of Chicago Press, 1986).

emerge when both the buying and the selling sides of a market are monopolized—a situation called **bilateral monopoly**.

The difficulties here are similar to those we encountered in considering the behaviour of oligopolistic industries in Chapter 26. Just as one oligopolist, in planning his strategy, is acutely aware that his rivals are likely to react to anything he does, a union dealing with a monopsony employer knows that any move it makes will elicit a countermove by the firm. And this knowledge makes the first decision that much more complicated.

Still, it is possible to say something a bit more concrete about the outcome of the wage-determination process under bilateral monopoly. Where the demand for labour is highly competitive, we have seen that a union can generally achieve a higher wage rate only by paying the price—a reduction in employment. However, where the employer is a monopsonist, a union may be able to induce the firm both to raise wages and to increase employment. While the details of the analysis are left to a more advanced course (or, perhaps, to classroom discussion), the underlying logic is simple enough to be explained here.

A monopsonist employer unrestrained by a union will use its market power to force wages down below the competitive level, just as a monopoly seller uses its market power to force prices higher. The monopsonist employer forces wages down by reducing its demand for labour below what would otherwise be the profit-maximizing amount, thereby cutting both wages and number of workers employed. However, a union may be able to prevent this from happening. It can deliberately set a floor on wages, pledging its members not to work at all at any wage level below this floor. If the union's threat is credible to the employer, the firm will lose the incentive to cut its demand for labour, since that attempt will no longer force wages down. Consequently, the presence of a union may force the monopsony firm to pay higher wages and, simultaneously, to employ more workers than it would otherwise have done.

Even though it is hard to think of industries that are pure monopsonists in their dealings with labour, these conclusions are nonetheless of some importance in reality. The fact is that large oligopolistic firms often do engage in one-on-one wage bargaining with their employees' unions, and there is reason to believe that the resulting bargaining process resembles to a considerable degree the workings of the bilateral monopoly model that we have just described.[14]

Collective Bargaining and Strikes

The process by which unions and management settle upon the terms of a labour contract is called **collective bargaining**. Unfortunately, nothing as straightforward as a supply–demand diagram exists in reality to tell us what wage level will emerge from a collective-bargaining session. Furthermore, actual collective-bargaining sessions range over many more issues than wages. For example, fringe benefits—such as pensions, health and life insurance, paid holidays, and the like—may be just as important as wages to both labour and management. Wage premiums for overtime work and seniority privileges are also commonly negotiated. Similarly, work conditions, such as the speed with which the assembly line should move, can be crucial issues. Many labour contracts specify in great detail the rights of labour and management to set work conditions—and also provide elaborate procedures for resolving grievances and disputes. The list could go on and on. The final contract that emerges from collective bargaining may well run to many pages of fine print.

With the issues so varied and complex and with the stakes so high, it is no

[14]Of course, even in the absence of a union (a monopoly seller), an increase in wages *can* lead to higher employment where a monopsonist employer is involved. This contrasts with the outcome in the competitive situation discussed earlier in this chapter, where a minimum-wage law was shown to cause lower employment. Thus, in a monopsony situation, a minimum-wage law need not involve a trade-off, since both wages and employment can be increased by such a policy.

wonder that both labour and management employ skilled professionals who specialize in preparing for and carrying out these negotiations, and each side enters a collective-bargaining session armed with reams of evidence supporting its positions.

The bargaining in these sessions is often heated, with outcomes riding as much on the personalities and skills of the negotiators as on cool-headed logic and economic facts. Negotiations may last well into the night, with each side seeming to try to wear the other out. Each side may threaten the other with grave consequences if it does not accept its terms. Unions, for their part, generally threaten to strike or to carry out a work slow-down. Firms counter with the threat that they would rather face a strike than give in or that they might even close the plant without a strike (an action that is called a "lockout").

Mediation and Arbitration

Where the public interest is seriously affected or when the union and firm reach an impasse, government agencies may well send in a **mediator**, whose job is to try to speed up the negotiation process. This impartial observer sits down with each side separately to discuss its problems and tries to persuade each to yield a bit to the other. At some stage, when an agreement looks possible, the mediator may call the two sides back together for another bargaining session in his or her presence.

A mediator, however, has no power to force a settlement. Success hinges on his or her ability to smooth ruffled feathers and to find common ground for agreement. Sometimes, in cases where the union and the firm simply cannot agree and where neither wants a strike, differences are finally settled by **arbitration**—the appointment of an impartial individual empowered to settle the issues that negotiation could not resolve. In fact, in some vital sectors where a strike is too injurious to the public interest, the labour contract or the law may stipulate that there must be *compulsory arbitration* if the two parties cannot agree. However, both labour and management are normally reluctant to accept this procedure.

Strikes

Most collective-bargaining situations do not lead to strikes. But the right to strike and to take a strike remain fundamentally important for the bargaining process. Imagine, for example, a firm bargaining with a union that was prohibited from striking. It seems likely that the union's bargaining position would be quite weak. On the other hand, a firm that always capitulated rather than suffer a strike would be virtually at the mercy of the union. So strikes (or more precisely, the possibility of strikes) serve an important economic purpose.

For the families involved, work stoppages clearly represent major dislocations. Despite this and despite the headline-grabbing nature of major strikes, however, the total amount of work-time lost to strikes is small—far less, for example, than the time lost to coffee breaks! It is noteworthy, though, that Canada's record of time lost to strikes is not good in comparison with that of other countries. In recent years, for example, Canada has lost about half a day per worker per year due to strikes. The comparable figures for several other countries are as follows: Italy, four-fifths of a day per worker per year; Great Britain, two-fifths of a day; the United States and France, approximately one-tenth of a day; and Japan, one one-hundredth of a day.

Collective Bargaining in the Public Sector

We have argued that strikes serve an important function in private-sector bargaining as a way of dividing the fruits of economic activity between big labour and big business. But does the same rationale for strikes apply to the public sector, where strikes or work stoppages have become increasingly common among postal workers, garbage collectors, teachers, and others?

It is not clear that it does. In most private-sector strikes, labour and management are inflicting harm upon each other in a battle for the "survival of the fittest." Consumers normally suffer only mild inconveniences. When General Motors is on strike, many potential car buyers may be disappointed, but they can turn to Fords, Chryslers, or many imports. Similarly, when other private products disappear from the shelves because of strikes, the consumer can easily replace them with close substitutes. Thus, in many cases, we can think of consumers as being relatively unharmed spectators when large unions and large private firms slug it out.

But public-sector bargaining is different. Here, management does not represent the interests of capital against those of labour; rather, it represents the public. And there is no pool of profits to be divided between the union and the shareholders. Instead, what management agrees to give the union comes out of the pockets of taxpayers.

Finally, it is quite clear that the public is not just a spectator in such strikes, but the primary victim. When police or fire-protection services are reduced, when mail delivery ceases, when public schools or airports shut down, consumers cannot find substitutes for these services. In a very real sense, then, strikes in the public sector are strikes against citizens, not strikes against management. They pit representatives of a particular group of workers against representatives of taxpayers as a whole.

For these reasons, the right of public employees to strike was traditionally more severely limited than the corresponding right of private-sector workers. Nevertheless, employees in the federal government's jurisdiction were given the right to strike in the late 1960s. Partly as a result of this, the biggest growth in union membership has been in the public sector.

Corporatism and Industrial Democracy

Discussion of public-sector unions raises the more general issue of sectional interests. Trade unions are not the only institutions trying to acquire market power for the benefit of their restricted membership. Professional associations (such as those for doctors and lawyers) have the same purpose, as do firms that engage in takeovers and mergers to increase market share. All these institutions attempt to increase the general support for their actions by claiming that they act in the public interest. For example, firms are simply "trying to achieve the economies of large-scale operations" and the unions are "fighting a general battle for the working class."

The market mechanism limits the power of these institutions, since it facilitates the introduction of cheaper substitutes, such as goods from abroad or labour-saving production inputs. It is perfectly rational for self-seeking institutions to use the political process to limit the market's ability to undermine their market power. This is why both firms and unions call for increased protection through foreign tariffs and quotas, and why unions support minimum-wage legislation. If market power exists and the political process is used to maintain it, what is the prognosis for the price system?

One suggested solution is corporatism or tripartism. It was tried in England in the early 1970s by Prime Minister Edward Heath, when he asked employers and unions to "share fully with the government the benefits and obligations involved in running the national economy." The idea was to blunt the forces of special interest by making big business and big labour truly responsible for the public interest. For instance, it was hoped that this co-operative approach would reduce the excessive wage increases of particular labour groups (all of which had been justified by reference to the public interest). Margaret Thatcher's government discarded this approach, arguing that tripartism simply enabled private groups to strengthen their ability to use the political process for their own purposes.

Industrial democracy is another suggested institutional change that might solve these problems. It is based on the assumption that it is simply not feasible to dismantle the power of large firms and unions. Instead, workers should be allowed fuller participation in management decisions. The reasoning behind this suggestion is that only under a system of worker self-management will workers be forced to appreciate and accept the constraints of the market that employers normally face. There are several successful examples of this arrangement in Canada. Critics of industrial democracy worry that entrepreneurial drive would not be rewarded under such a system, and that it would consequently be diminished. The current state of Canadian labour relations suggests that these issues will continue to be actively debated.

Summary

1. A person's income depends on the factors of production that he or she owns and on the prices that those factors command in the market. Short of redefining the ownership of factors, we can change the distribution of income by changing factor prices (an approach that can have undesirable side effects) or by transferring income from the rich to the poor by means of a very general tax system that does not differentiate among the alternative sources of income. We discuss factor pricing in this chapter, and general income redistribution in the next.

2. A profit-maximizing firm purchases the quantity of any input at which the price of the input equals its marginal revenue product.

3. The demand curve for labour, like the demand curve for any factor of production, is derived from the marginal revenue product curve. It slopes downward because of the "law" of diminishing marginal returns.

4. One reason that youth suffers from such high unemployment rates is that minimum-wage laws militate against the employment of low-productivity workers.

5. Increased demand for a good that needs land to produce it will drive up the prices of land either because inferior land will be brought into use or because land will be used more intensively.

6. Economic rent is any payment to the supplier of a factor of production that is greater than the minimum amount needed to induce the desired quantity of the factor to be supplied.

7. Factors of production that are unique in quality and difficult or impossible to reproduce will tend to be paid relatively high economic rents because of their scarcity. Factors of production that are easy to produce at a constant cost and that are provided by many suppliers will earn little or no economic rent.

8. Radical economists view marginal productivity theory as an instrument that promotes the interests of the capitalist class. They also criticize mainstream economists for having an unduly narrow focus; for accepting consumer tastes and human nature as "givens" rather than treating them as the results of the economic system; for stressing efficiency rather than equality as an economic goal; and for concentrating on increasing the quantity of output rather than the quality of life.

9. Interest rates are determined by the supply of and the demand for funds. The demand for funds is a derived demand, since these funds are used to finance business investment. Thus the demand for funds depends on the marginal productivity of capital.

10. A dollar obtainable sooner is worth more than a dollar obtainable later because of the interest that dollar can earn in the interim.

11. Economic profits over and above the cost of capital are earned (a) by exercise of monopoly power, (b) as a payment for bearing risk, and (c) as the earnings of successful innovation.

12. The desirability of increased taxation of profits depends on its effects on the supply of entrepreneurial talent. If most profits are economic rents, then higher profits taxes will have few detrimental effects. But if most profits are necessary to attract entrepreneurs into the market, then higher profits taxes can threaten the capitalist system.

13. The supply of labour is determined by free choices made by individuals. Because of conflicting income and substitution effects, the quantity of labour supplied may rise or fall as a result of an increase in wages. Historical data show that hours of work per week have fallen as wages have risen, suggesting that income effects may be dominant in the long run.

14. In a free market, the wage rate and the level of employment are determined by the interaction of supply and demand. Workers in great demand or short supply will command high wages, and, conversely, low wages will be assigned to workers in abundant supply or with skills that are not in great demand.

15. Human-capital theory assumes that people make educational decisions in much the same way that businesses make investment decisions and tacitly assumes that people learn things in school that increase their productivity in jobs.

16. Other theories of the effects of education on earnings deny that schooling actually raises productivity. One view is that the educational system primarily sorts people according to their abilities. Another view holds that schools sort people according to their social class and teach them discipline and obedience.

17. According to the theory of dual labour markets, there are two distinct types of labour markets with very little mobility between them. The primary labour market contains the "good" jobs, where wages are high, prospects for advancement are good, and higher education pays off. The secondary labour market contains the

"bad" jobs, with low wages, little opportunity for promotion, and little return to education.

18. About one-third of all Canadian workers belong to unions, which can be thought of as monopoly sellers of labour.

19. Analysis of union behaviour is complicated by the fact that a union can have many goals. For the most part, unions probably force wages to be higher and employment to be lower than they would be in a competitive labour market. However, there are exceptions.

20. Strikes (or at least the threat of strikes) play an important role in collective bargaining as a way of dividing the fruits of economic activity between big business and big labour. Strikes in the public sector, however, take on a different character because the adversaries are no longer "labour" versus "capital" but rather a particular group of labourers versus the general public.

Concepts for Review

Factors of production	Economic rent	Dual labour markets
Marginal productivity principle	Entrepreneurs	Union
Derived demand	Risk-bearing	Rand formula
Minimum-wage law	Invention versus innovation	Monopsony
Investment	Income and substitution effects	Bilateral monopoly
Capital	Backward-bending supply curve	Collective bargaining
Interest	Investments in human capital	Mediation
Discounting	Human-capital theory	Arbitration

Questions for Discussion

1. A profit-maximizing firm expands its purchase of any input up to the point where diminishing returns have reduced the marginal revenue product so that it equals the input price. Why does it not pay the firm to "quit while it is ahead," buying so small a quantity of the input that diminishing returns do not set in?

2. Which of the following inputs do you think include a relatively large economic rent in their earnings?
   a. Nuts and bolts.
   b. Petroleum.
   c. A champion racehorse.
   Use supply–demand analysis to explain your answer.

3. Three machines are employed in an isolated area. They each produce 1000 units of output per month, the first requiring $17,000 in raw materials, the second $21,000, and the third $23,000. What would you expect to be the monthly charge for the first and second machines if the services of the third machine can be hired at a price of $9000 a month? What part of the charges for the first two machines is economic rent?

4. Economists conclude that a tax on the profits of firms will be shifted in part to consumers of the products of those firms, in the form of higher product prices. However, they believe that a tax on the rent of land usually cannot be shifted. What explains the difference?

5. Many economists argue that a tax on apartment houses is likely to reduce the supply of apartments but that a tax on all land, including the land on which apartment houses stand, will not reduce the supply of apartments. Can you explain the difference? How does your answer to this question relate to your answer to Question 4?

6. If you have a contract under which you will be paid $10,000 two years from now, why do you become richer if the rate of interest falls?

7. What is the difference between interest and profit? Who earns interest, in return for what contribution to production? Who earns economic profit, in return for what contribution to production?

8. Explain the difference between an invention and an innovation. Give an example of each.

9. "Marginal productivity does not determine how much a worker will earn—it only determines how many workers will be hired at a given wage. Therefore, marginal productivity analysis is a theory of demand for labour, not a theory of distribution." What, then, do you think determines wages? Does marginal productivity affect their level? If so, how?

10. In Canada today, the first $100,000 of income that an individual earns in capital gains is tax free. Some politicians argue that this tax shelter should be removed. Use supply–demand diagrams to determine the likely effects of such a tax change on the levels of savings, investment, and the rate of interest for both a closed and an open economy.

11. Universities are known to pay rather low wages for student labour. Can this be explained by the operation of supply and demand in the local labour market? Is the concept of monopsony of any use? How might things differ if students formed a union?

12. University professors are highly skilled (or at least highly educated!) labour. Yet their wages are not very high. Is this a refutation of the marginal productivity theory?

13. The following table shows the number of pizzas that can be produced by a large pizza parlour employing various numbers of pizza chefs.

NUMBER OF CHEFS	NUMBER OF PIZZAS PER DAY
1	40
2	64
3	82
4	92
5	100
6	92

a. Find the marginal physical product schedule of chefs.

b. Assuming a price of $5 per pizza, find the marginal revenue product schedule.

c. If chefs are paid $70 per day, how many chefs will this pizza parlour employ? How would your answer change if wages rose to $95 per day?

d. Suppose the price of a pizza rises from $5 to $6. Show what happens to the derived demand curve for pizza chefs.

14. "Strikes are simply intolerable and should be outlawed." Comment.

15. "Public employees should have the same right to strike as private employees." Comment.

16. In which of the following industries is wage determination most plausibly explained by the model of perfect competition? the model of pure monopoly? the model of bilateral monopoly?

a. Odd-job repairs in private homes.

b. Manufacturing of low-priced clothing for women.

c. Steel manufacturing.

17. In the bitter strike battle between Eastern Airlines and several of its unions, it was clear from the beginning that the airline was in serious financial trouble, with its survival and the survival of the jobs it provided apparently in question. Discuss what might nevertheless have led the unions to hold out so tenaciously.

18. Can you think of some types of workers whose marginal products were probably raised by computerization? Are there any whose marginal products were probably reduced? Can you characterize the difference between the two types of jobs in general terms?

30

The Tax System and Income Inequality

The hardest thing in the world to understand is income tax.

ALBERT EINSTEIN

C hapter 27 examined several reasons why the government might want to interfere with the workings of the market mechanism. Some of these interferences involve levying taxes; for example, we noted that taxes may be useful in correcting misallocations of resources caused by externalities. Other interferences involve direct spending by government—the provision of public goods is a good example—and this spending, in turn, requires that taxes be levied to raise the necessary revenue. These, then, are two of the main reasons for taxes: to improve resource allocation and to raise revenue to pay for government expenditures. The third reason for levying taxes is to change the distribution of income. This objective can be accomplished in two ways: by imposing higher rates of taxation on the rich than on the poor, and by paying some of the tax revenue back (in the form of transfer payments) to citizens whose market income is deemed to be inadequate.

Our discussion in this chapter proceeds in four stages. First, we examine the general tax system in Canada. We consider the effects that our current taxes have on the allocation of resources and the distribution of income, and the principles that distinguish "good" from "bad" taxes. An understanding of these principles allows us to evaluate some of the federal government's recent tax reforms, such as the new goods and services tax (GST).

The balance of the chapter is devoted to a broader exploration of the problem of income inequality. In the second major section, we consider the problem of poverty in Canada and explore the workings of our country's welfare system. Then, in the third section, we examine the issue of discrimination—a root cause of some of our problems of income inequality and one of the reasons that those problems cannot be solved fundamentally by means of transfer payments alone. Finally, in the last section of the chapter, we offer a full explanation of one of the 12 **Ideas for Beyond the Final Exam**: *the fundamental trade-off between economic equality and economic efficiency.* Taking it for granted that equality and efficiency are both important social goals, we shall learn why policies that promote greater income equality (or less poverty or less discrimination) often threaten to interfere with economic efficiency. We shall explain *why* this is so and *what* can be done about it.

In a brief course, the two middle sections of the chapter (on welfare problems and discrimination, respectively, pages 698–712) may be omitted without loss of continuity. In other words, if necessary, the reader may move directly from the discussion of taxes in the first section to the examination of the trade-off between equality and efficiency in the last section.

Taxes in Canada

Some Facts and Definitions

By international standards, Canadians are taxed to about the same extent as the citizens of Finland and Spain. Figure 30-1 compares the fraction of income paid in taxes in Canada with that paid by residents of other industrialized nations. Canadians are not heavily taxed in comparison with the Swedes or the Dutch, but we do pay more taxes than the Americans and the Japanese.

Progressive, Proportional, and Regressive Taxes

A progressive tax is one in which the average tax rate paid by an individual rises as his income rises. A proportional tax is one in which the average tax rate is the same at all income levels. A regressive tax is one in which the average tax rate falls as income rises.

Economists classify taxes as *progressive*, *proportional*, or *regressive*. Under a **progressive tax**, the fraction of income paid in taxes *rises* as a person's income increases. Under a **proportional tax**, this fraction is constant. And under a **regressive tax**, the fraction of income paid to the tax collector *declines* as income rises. Since the fraction of income paid in taxes is called the **average tax rate**, these definitions can be formulated as they are in the margin.

Often, however, the *average* tax rate is less interesting than the **marginal tax rate**, which is the fraction of each *additional* dollar that must be paid to the tax collector. The reason, as we will see, is that the *marginal* tax rate, not the *average* tax rate, most directly affects economic incentives.

The **average tax rate** is the ratio of taxes to income.

The **marginal tax rate** is the fraction of each *additional* dollar of income that is paid in taxes.

Direct versus Indirect Taxes

Another way to classify taxes is to divide them into two broad categories: **direct taxes** and **indirect taxes**. Direct taxes are levied directly on *people*. Primary examples are *income taxes* and *inheritance taxes*, though the notoriously regressive *poll tax*—which charges every person the same amount—is also a direct tax. In contrast, indirect taxes are levied on goods and services, such as buying gasoline, using the telephone, owning a home, and so on. *Sales taxes* and *property taxes* are the most important indirect taxes in Canada. Many countries also rely heavily on the *value-added tax*, of which

FIGURE 30-1

The Burden of Taxation in Selected Countries, 1987

Canadians are not heavily taxed in comparison with the citizens of the Netherlands and Sweden, but we do pay more tax than the Americans and the Japanese.

SOURCE: *Revenue Statistics of OECD Member Countries, 1965–1988* (Paris: OECD, 1989).

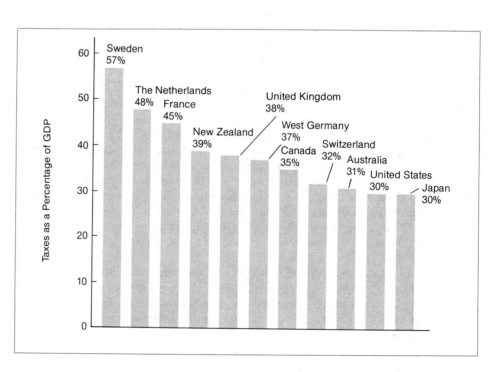

Canada's GST is one version.[1] As a broad generalization, one can say that the Canadian and U.S. governments rely more heavily on direct taxation than do the governments of most other countries.

Direct taxes are taxes levied directly on people. **Indirect taxes** are taxes levied on specific economic activities.

The federal government has relied heavily on direct taxes, while, in comparison, the provincial and municipal governments have depended more on indirect taxes and on transfers from the federal government. The three big direct taxes used by the federal government are the personal income tax, the corporate profits tax, and the payroll tax. Together, these taxes represented 60 percent of the overall tax revenue collected by all levels of government in 1989. The provincial governments have relied largely on sales taxes and related sources, such as natural-resource revenues and profits from liquor sales. The municipal governments depend on property taxes and grants from the provinces. A more complete breakdown of government revenue sources is given in Figure 30–2. Let us now look at the major taxes in some detail.

The Personal Income Tax

The tax on individual incomes began during World War I, and it is now the government's biggest revenue raiser. It is well known that the personal income tax is progressive. Table 30–1 contains an abbreviated version of the tax table for 1989, showing only the rates for the amounts payable to the federal government. (Total income-tax rates vary by province.[2]) The progressivity is reflected in the way the average tax rate rises as income rises. In 1989, there were only three "tax brackets" in Canada: Incomes of $27,500 or less were taxed at the rate of 17 percent; incomes between $27,501 and $55,000, at 26 percent; and incomes of more than $55,000, at 29 percent.

[1] The concept of value-added was defined and explained in Appendix A of Chapter 4. The value-added tax simply taxes each firm on the basis of its value-added, as explained more fully later in this chapter.

[2] For example, Ontario's income tax for each individual equals roughly half of his or her federal taxes. Nine provinces and the two territories allow the federal government to collect their income-tax revenue for them. Quebec continues to levy and collect its own taxes and does not participate in the intergovernmental tax-collection agreements.

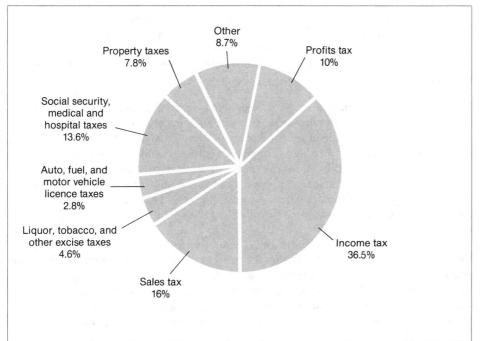

FIGURE 30–2
The Composition of the Overall Tax Bill, 1989
This diagram shows the share of each major tax in the overall tax bill for 1989.
SOURCE: The Fraser Institute.

TABLE 30–1
Federal Personal Income-Tax Rates for the 1989 Tax Year*

TAXABLE INCOME (dollars)	LEGISLATED AVERAGE TAX RATE† (percent)	MARGINAL TAX RATE (percent)	ACTUAL AVERAGE TAX RATE (1987)† (percent)
25,000	9	17	11
45,000	16	26	15
75,000	21	29	16

* This example involves a family of four, with two young children and only one parent working outside the home.

† The legislated tax rate is taken from the tax form. The actual rate is calculated by dividing total taxes paid by total taxable income earned by all income-tax filers at that income level. For many individuals the actual tax rate is lower, since they can use various tax shelters.

SOURCE: Canadian Tax Foundation, *The National Finances*.

A **tax shelter** is a special provision in the Income Tax Act that reduces or defers taxation if certain conditions are met.

A **capital gain** is the profit made from the sale of an asset at a higher price than was paid for it.

The last column of Table 30–1 shows that the personal income tax is not as progressive as the legislated rate structure suggests. These actual average tax rates are calculated by dividing all income-tax filers into a set of income classes. Then, for each income class, the total tax actually paid by this group is divided by the group's total taxable income. Unfortunately, as this book went to press, the most recent year for which these data were available was 1987; the figures in the last column of Table 30–1 are therefore not perfectly comparable with those in the first three columns. This lack of comparability matters most for low-income earners because, effective in 1988, the tax system was changed to provide more relief at low income levels. (We explain how the system was changed on pages 688–89.) But for the point we are stressing here, it is sufficient to focus on the bottom two rows of Table 30–1. There we see that the actual average tax rates are lower than the legislated ones because individuals can use various **tax shelters**. Overall, the table shows what many have suspected for a long time: that lower-income earners are not able to take advantage of tax shelters as effectively as higher-income earners. Let us see what some of the tax shelters are.

Capital gains and dividend income.   Canadian tax laws exempt from income tax the first $100,000 of **capital gains** earned during an individual's lifetime; above this amount, capital gains are taxed at only two-thirds of the usual rate. Dividend income is also taxed at favourable rates. Most capital gains and dividends accrue to people in the upper income groups, so this tax shelter is the preserve of the rich. Why did the government create such a thing? The main reason is to encourage people to save and to invest in risky ventures.

Tax benefits for homeowners.   Many individuals think that our income-tax system should allow homeowners to deduct their payments of mortgage interest and property tax when calculating taxable income. After all, it is argued, such deductions are allowed in the United States and certain European countries, and it seems fair to treat homeowners in a way similar to shopkeepers. The fault in this reasoning is that unlike shopkeepers, homeowners already receive a tax shelter by *not* having to declare the income they earn by incurring these expenses. This is because the "income" from owning a home accrues not in the form of cash but in the form of living without paying rent.

An example will make things clear. Mutt and Jeff are neighbours. Each earns $30,000 a year, and each has just won a lottery and received $100,000 in cash. Mutt uses his winnings to buy a $100,000 house for cash. Thus, he has no mortgage or rent payments, but must pay $2000 per year in property tax. Jeff uses his winnings to buy a bond that yields 10 percent interest. Thus, his interest income is $10,000. Jeff rents the house next door to Mutt's, which is exactly the same and which rents for $12,000 per year. Most observers would agree that Mutt and Jeff *should* pay the same income tax.

TABLE 30–2
Owning versus Renting a Home

ITEM	MUTT (owner)		JEFF (renter)	
Income	$30,000		$30,000	
Interest income	—		10,000	
Property tax		2,000		—
Rent		—		12,000
Taxable income	$30,000		$40,000	

But, ignoring other deductions and exemptions, Mutt's taxable income is $30,000, while Jeff's is $40,000 (see Table 30–2).

How could this disparity be rectified? One way would be to allow *both* home-owners *and* renters to deduct their expenses. This would make Mutt's taxable income fall by $2000 to $28,000, and it would allow Jeff's taxable income to fall by $12,000 to $28,000. Another way would be to force homeowners to add their "imputed rent" to their income. In this example, Mutt would have to add the implicit rental income of $12,000 (that he is receiving from himself), but he would be allowed to deduct the expenses involved (the property tax of $2,000). Thus, his taxable income would be $40,000, just like Jeff's. The fact that the implicit rental income of homeowners is not taxed represents a major tax shelter that favours the well-to-do. Homeowners get a further break since capital gains obtained from the sale of one's principal residence are exempt from taxation.

We could go on listing more tax shelters, but enough has been said to illustrate the point:

Our personal income tax has offered many opportunities to avoid payment of tax through tax shelters. Since most shelters are beneficial mainly to rich people, they have eroded the progressivity of the income tax quite seriously.

Sales and Excise Taxes

Most provincial governments levy a broad-based sales tax on the purchase of goods and services. There are exceptions, such as food, children's clothing, services, and housing rents, so that slightly less than 50 percent of consumer expenditure is exempt. In 1989, sales-tax rates ranged from zero in Alberta to 12 percent in Newfoundland. In addition, most provinces have special **excise taxes** on such things as tobacco products, liquor, gasoline, and luxury items. The federal government has, in the past, levied a general manufacturers' sales tax (MST), which in 1989 stood at a rate of 13.5 percent. It has also imposed excise taxes on a hodgepodge of miscellaneous goods and services, including cigarettes, oil and gasoline, and liquor, and on many imported products (in the form of tariffs and duties).

One of the major issues of Canadian government policy in 1990 was the federal government's proposal to replace the MST with a more general goods and services tax (the GST), a variation on the **value-added tax (VAT)** that is in place in many countries around the world.

With a VAT, each firm is taxed only on the excess of its sales over the costs incurred in buying materials at earlier stages in the production process. Hence, there is a built-in incentive for compliance, since all participants have an interest in reporting to the government the full price of what they had to pay for partly fabricated products. In addition, a VAT is flexible, so exports can easily be exempted. Finally, the tax can be broadly based (that is, levied on a wide variety of goods and services, at primary, intermediate, and final production stages), and the more products it is levied on, the lower the tax rate can be to achieve the same revenue.

An **excise tax** is a tax levied on a particular commodity or service, as a fixed amount of money per unit of product sold or as a fixed percentage of the purchase price.

The main drawback of increased reliance on *any* form of sales tax is that sales taxes are regressive, meaning that they are unfair to low-income families. Since poor families cannot afford to save as much as richer families, they spend a larger proportion of their incomes on goods and services; hence, if the items they buy are taxed, they pay a larger proportion of their incomes in sales tax. When the federal government proposed the GST, however, it called for a personal income-tax credit for low-income families to go hand-in-hand with the new tax. According to government estimates, the two changes in the tax system, taken together, have the effect of lessening the overall tax burden on families earning up to about $30,000 (in 1989), and increasing the tax burden on families with higher incomes. But the promised progressivity of this tax package would come entirely from its tax-credit component; by itself, as we have already stated, a sales tax is regressive.

Why Replace the MST with the GST?*

As its name suggests, the MST was a tax levied on the sale of manufactured items. The problems caused by this tax stemmed largely from the fact that in a modern economy, the production process is divided into many stages. What is a final manufactured product for one company is, in fact, an input to production for another company; hence, the MST amounted, in many cases, to a tax on business inputs. Consequently, the MST effectively raised the costs of production for Canadian manufacturers. In 1989 the Department of Finance estimated that 49 percent of MST revenues actually came from taxing business inputs.

Because other countries do not tax manufacturing inputs in this way, the MST effectively put Canadian firms at a cost disadvantage in relation to the foreign producers of our imports. (Indeed, the MST was often referred to as a "job killer.") Thus, despite the controversy surrounding the introduction of the GST, analysts agreed that the MST had to be changed. They were in favour of eliminating features of the tax system that limited the market's ability to create jobs, especially since no other industrialized country was imposing such an impediment on its own economy.

Short-run job creation was not the only thing at stake in this debate. In the longer term, labour income can be increased only if labour becomes more productive. And for this to occur, firms must invest in new plant and equipment to give labour more-productive capital to work with. In this regard, the usual argument in support of sales taxes as opposed to income taxes is that income taxes discourage saving and therefore restrict the funds available to finance firms' investments. Conversely, sales taxes, because they are paid only when income is spent (not when it is saved), encourage saving and result in more funds being made available to finance firms' investment expenditures. Compared with income taxes, then, sales taxes are supposed to raise the level of the country's future capital stock and increase potential GDP and per-capita incomes in the future. But because the MST taxed business inputs, which resulted in the taxation of about one-third of firms' investment expenditures, it failed to deliver this desirable outcome and instead restricted growth in potential GDP and labour earnings. The GST was designed to solve this problem.

Another undesirable feature of the MST was its unreliability as a source of revenue for the government. As of 1989, only about 70,000 firms actually paid some part of the tax, and 22,000 "special rulings" exempting firms from the tax or modifying its terms had been arranged with the Department of Finance. This administrative morass was a classic example of what can occur when a tax fails as a general scheme that all market participants must confront on an equal footing.

As a general value-added tax, the GST goes a long way toward solving these problems. Some goods and services, such as basic groceries, prescription drugs, medical devices, residential rents, legal-aid services, day-care services, and many health, dental,

---

*At the time of writing (fall 1990), the controversy over the proposed GST was at its height, and it appeared that the legislation might be blocked in the Senate. Our discussion assumes, however, that the GST will indeed have been implemented on January 1, 1990, as proposed.

and educational services, are exempt from the tax. Where the tax does apply, it works as follows: If a household buys an item—say, a dishwasher—it pays the sales tax. If a business buys an item to be used as an input—say, a restaurant buys a dishwasher—it too pays the tax, but it can later claim a refund called an "input tax credit." This is how the GST avoids placing Canadian manufacturers at the competitive disadvantage that existed under the MST.

One problem with the GST is that it requires a great deal of paperwork. At the end of each accounting period, all firms must calculate the total GST that they have collected for the government in the course of making sales. They must also subtract the amount of the GST that they have paid on business inputs to other firms, for which they can claim a GST refund.

Hence, while it is true that 19 of the 24 most highly industrialized countries of the world had a VAT in place well before Canada introduced its GST, the GST is among the most cumbersome of such schemes to implement. This would not have been the case if the government's early attempts to design a co-ordinated federal and provincial sales-tax program had succeeded. Under such a program, both federal and provincial sales taxes would have been collected with the aid of the same administrative machinery. In the face of provincial resistance to the plan, however, the federal government felt compelled to proceed on its own, in the hope that the provinces would agree to co-ordinate as time passed. By the fall of 1990, only Quebec had moved in this direction: Starting in 1991, all goods taxed by the GST will be taxed by Quebec as well, and to compensate for this increase in the tax base, the provincial tax rate will be reduced from 9 percent to 7 percent.

SUMMARY

The main advantages of the GST are:

1. It replaces an inefficient tax. By taxing business inputs, the MST led to job losses in the export sector and in the import-competing sector, and it restricted investment spending by firms. The GST, on the other hand, stimulates growth in potential output, and thus provides the main benefit expected of a sales tax.

2. On democratic grounds, a visible tax is better than a hidden one; and since it is paid at the retail level, the GST is highly visible.

The main disadvantages of the GST are:

1. Like any sales tax, if it were not supplemented by a program such as the income-tax credit for low-income earners, the GST would contribute to regressivity in the overall tax system. This is because the ratio of consumption to income is highest for low-income earners, so any type of sales tax scores well on efficiency grounds but poorly on equity grounds.

2. Many analysts have argued that the early 1990s—a period of economic slowdown —was not the time for implementing the GST, because, as we explained in Chapter 8, increases in sales taxes are stagflationary in the short run.

3. Many individuals are opposed to the GST on the grounds that it could become an instrument facilitating a major "tax grab" by the government in the future.

The last two disadvantages are related. If we could assume that the government would *not* raise the GST rate in the future, we could safely conclude that the GST would not prove to be a strongly inflationary measure. In other words, since government revenues from the GST (minus expenditures on the accompanying tax-credit program) simply replace the revenues lost through the elimination of the MST, the GST should cause no increase in the overall payout by the private sector or in the overall cost of producing goods and services. But if the GST rate were to be raised in the future, the reform package would no longer be revenue-neutral, and inflationary consequences would have to be expected. Can we, then, predict whether or not the GST rate will be raised in the near future?

The experience of other countries can be cited in support of either possibility. For example, while New Zealand implemented a 10 percent VAT in 1986 and increased it to 12.5 percent by 1989, Spain and Greece implemented similar tax schemes at the same time and have not increased their rates since. A number of other countries, such as Germany and the United Kingdom, have had VAT schemes in place for many years and have raised their rates significantly over time. Brazil's VAT, on the other hand, has remained virtually constant for 25 years. Thus, it is difficult to speculate on the implications of Canada's GST for the future.

Other Taxes

Corporate Profits Tax

The tax on corporate profits is considered a "direct" tax because corporations are seen as fictitious "persons" in the eyes of the law. The general federal tax rate is 28 percent of income, and the provincial rate varies from 10 to 17 percent. But the corporate tax rates are lower for manufacturing firms and small businesses. Corporate investments in certain depressed regions also qualify firms for a lower rate.

There are many tax shelters that permit large corporations to reduce their tax obligations. For example, some companies set up subsidiaries in other countries that have low corporate-tax rates. Such companies then adjust the prices of their products or services among their various affiliates in such a way that most of their profits are officially recorded in the countries with the lowest tax rates. We shall discuss some of the difficulties that arise in taxing profits later in this chapter (pages 695–96).

Property Taxes

Municipalities raise revenue by taxing the value of properties, such as houses and office buildings. (Exemptions include educational institutions and church property. For some of these, the province makes grants to municipalities to make up for "lost" taxes.) The usual procedure assigns each taxable property an *assessed value* (originally intended to be an estimate of its market value), and then imposes a tax rate, based on the community's total assessed value, that will yield enough revenue to cover expenditures on local services. Because properties are reassessed much less frequently than market values change and because market values are usually estimated by crude rules of thumb, certain inequities arise. For example, one person's house may be assessed at almost 100 percent of its true market value while another's may be assessed at little more than 50 percent.

The property tax is among the most controversial in the tax system. Some economists view it as a tax on one particular type of wealth—real estate. In this view, since families with higher incomes generally own much more real estate than do families with low incomes, the property tax is *progressive* relative to income; that is, the ratio of property tax to income rises as we move up the income scale. However, other economists view the property tax as an excise tax on rents; since expenditures on rent generally account for a larger fraction of the incomes of the poor than of the rich, this makes it seem *regressive* relative to income.

There is also political controversy over the property tax. Municipal property-tax revenues (along with provincial grants) have been the traditional source of financing for public schools. As a result, wealthy communities with a lot of expensive real estate have been able to afford higher-quality schools than have poor communities. The reason is made clear with a simple arithmetical example. Suppose that real estate holdings in a wealthy municipality average $300,000 per family, while in a poor municipality they average only $100,000 per family. If both municipalities levy a 2 percent property tax to pay for their schools, the wealthy municipality will generate $6000 per family in tax receipts, while the poor one will generate only $2000.

Payroll Taxes and Social Benefits

Canada has two important payroll taxes: contributions to the Canada (or Quebec) Pension Plan and contributions to the unemployment-insurance program. The unemployment-insurance account is supposed to run a surplus during years of reasonable economic growth, and a deficit during years of recession. However, the recession of the early 1980s was so severe and protracted that the government was compelled to supplement the unemployment-insurance fund from general revenues—a practice that has continued ever since. As we explained in Chapter 4 (page 89), however, the government decided in 1990 to try to cut back on these commitments by raising the eligibility requirements for UIC benefits and by decreasing the period of payments.

The other major payroll tax—employer and employee contributions to the Canada Pension Plan—is paid into another fund, which operates somewhat differently from the trust funds associated with most private pension plans. In the private plans, you pay in money while you are working, it accumulates at compound interest, and then you withdraw it bit by bit in your retirement years. The solvency of such a plan is not in doubt, since it does not involve a commitment to pay out more to the individual than he or she has put in, plus the accumulated interest.

With the Canada Pension Plan, however, people who are now retired receive funds from the contributions of those who are currently working. So the solvency of the system depends on changes in the patterns of economic and population growth. The proportion of the Canadian population aged 65 or older rose from 6.5 percent in the 1940s to 9.5 percent in the 1980s, and is expected to rise to more than 11 percent in the 1990s. Unless economic growth occurs at a rapid rate, payroll taxes will have to be raised or pension levels will have to be cut if the Canada Pension Plan is to remain solvent. Although this is not an immediate problem, since the surplus in the pension plan account is still increasing as the interest earned on the loans to provincial governments compounds, few economists expect sufficient economic growth in the longer term to counteract the underlying demographic trends.

The other federal government programs for retirement are the Old Age Security and the Guaranteed Income Supplement schemes. These are not financed by payroll-tax contributions to trust funds but are paid for out of the federal government's current general revenues. There are, however, some provincially levied payroll taxes: workers' compensation in all provinces and health-insurance premiums in Ontario, British Columbia, and Alberta.

Fiscal Federalism

Grants from the federal government are a major source of revenue for provincial and municipal governments. In addition, grants from the provinces are vital to municipal governments. This system of transfers from one level of government to the next is referred to as **fiscal federalism** and has a long history in Canada.

Under the Constitution, most government-funded social programs fall within the jurisdiction of the junior levels of government. Health care, education, and welfare programs are the most notable. As a result, the junior-level governments have faced an ongoing squeeze between the growth in their expenditure requirements and available revenues. The federal government has relieved this squeeze in several ways: by reducing federal government income-tax rates (to "make room" for provincial tax-rate increases), by making transfer payments to the provincial governments, and by directly undertaking income-security programs (such as the Canada Pension Plan and the unemployment-insurance program).

While the provinces have welcomed revenues from the federal government, they have often resented the loss of provincial discretion that is involved. Before 1977,

Fiscal federalism refers to the system of transfer payments from one level of government to the next.

there was a complicated set of transfer payments called **conditional grants**. Under these schemes, the federal government matched provincial government spending, according to various formulae, *if* the provinces spent their money in specified ways. The provinces often argued that the funds should have "no strings attached." The federal government discontinued conditional grants, because it objected to the power that this system gave the provinces in determining the size of the grants. The provinces received more **unconditional grants** and an increased share of the personal income tax in return. (Other aspects of federal–provincial co-ordination leave the federal government with some control over certain transfers.)

As the name implies, unconditional grants involve transfers from the federal government to the provinces, with "no strings attached." The grants are paid out of general federal revenues, and many go only to provinces that would have to levy very high tax rates in order to raise per-capita revenues equal to the national average. Many different taxes are involved in these schemes, and the arrangements are revised every few years. In recent years, seven of the ten provinces (excepting British Columbia, Alberta, and Ontario) have received unconditional grants. The negotiations associated with revising these "equalization payments" are often the major source of dispute at federal–provincial conferences.

The Concept of Equity in Taxation

Taxes are judged on the basis of two criteria: *equity* (is the tax fair?) and *efficiency* (does it interfere unduly with the workings of the market economy?). It is curious that economists have been concerned mostly with the latter, while public discussions about tax proposals almost always focus on the former. Let us, therefore, begin our discussion by investigating the concept of equitable taxation.

Horizontal Equity

Horizontal equity is the notion that equally situated individuals should be taxed equally.

There are three distinct concepts of tax equity. The first is **horizontal equity**, which simply asserts that equally situated individuals should be taxed equally. When the principle is stated in this way, few would quarrel with it. But it is often quite difficult to apply this principle in practice, and violations of horizontal equity can be found throughout Canadian tax laws.

Consider, for example, the personal income tax. Horizontal equity calls for two families with the same income to pay the same tax. But what if one family has eight children and the other has one child? Well, you answer, we must define "equally situated" to include equal family sizes, so only families with the same number of children can be compared on grounds of horizontal equity. But what if one family has unusually high medical expenses, while the other has none? Are they still "equally situated"? By now the point should be clear: Determining when two families are "equally situated" is no simple task. In fact, the Canadian tax provisions involve many requirements that must be met before two families are construed to be "equal."

A tax exemption permits the reduction of an individual's or a firm's taxable income by some amount.

Another set of issues concerns the specific measures used to achieve horizontal equity in taxation. For example, if the goal is to ensure that families with many children are taxed fairly compared to smaller families, is it better to give relief to the former through a **tax exemption**—reducing taxable income by some amount—or through a **tax credit**—reducing the tax that is due by some amount? Some of the government's 1987 tax reforms focussed on just this issue, and as a result of the new legislation, credits replaced exemptions in our tax system.

A tax credit directly reduces an individual's or a firm's tax obligation by a given amount that is independent of the tax rate. Some individual tax credits are *refundable*; if they reduce the tax owed to an amount less than zero, the government transfers that amount to the individual.

The importance of this change is best explained with the aid of a numerical example. Consider two Ontario families, each with an employed father, a mother who does not work outside the home, and two young children. The families are alike in every way except that one has a gross income of $75,000, and the other, a gross income of $30,000. Under the pre-1988 system, the personal exemptions for a basic income earner, his or her spouse, and two children totalled roughly $10,000, so the taxable incomes for our two families would have been reduced to $65,000 and $20,000, respectively. The combined federal and provincial marginal tax rate would have been about 50 percent for the richer family and 20 percent for the poorer one. Thus, although the exemption of $10,000 would have reduced each family's tax base by the same amount, it would have saved the richer family $5000 in taxes and the poorer family only $2000.

Under the new credit system, the government may still give a total of $7000 in tax relief, but it distributes the funds differently. With credits, taxes are first calculated on the full amount of gross income—$75,000 and $30,000 in our example—but the amount of tax actually to be collected is reduced by the tax credit. If the credit were set at $3500 for a four-person family, then both the high- and the low-income families would receive the *same* relief.

In brief, by removing the preferential treatment given to high-income earners under an exemption system, tax credits increase the progressivity of the tax system. (This is the change to which we referred in our discussion of Table 30–1 earlier in this chapter.) In addition, tax credits set up an obvious and automatic mechanism for a system of *negative income tax*, a method of transferring funds to the poor that some people think would be easier and more equitable than are existing social-assistance schemes. Under a negative-income-tax scheme, almost every adult (not just those who owe tax) would fill out a tax form; tax credits and/or lack of income would result in some of them "owing" a negative amount, which would be paid to them by the government. The negative-income-tax proposal is discussed fully later in this chapter.

Vertical Equity

The second concept of fair taxation seems to flow naturally from the first. If equals are to be treated equally, it appears that unequals should be treated unequally. This precept is known as **vertical equity**.

Just saying this, of course, does not get us very far. For the most part, vertical equity has been translated into the **ability-to-pay principle**, according to which those most able to pay should pay the highest taxes. But this still leaves a definitional problem similar to the problem of defining "equally situated": How do we measure ability to pay? The nature of each tax often provides a straightforward answer. In income taxation, we measure ability to pay by income; in property taxation, we measure it by property value; and so on.

A thornier problem arises when we try to translate the notion into concrete terms. Consider the three alternative income-tax plans listed in Table 30–3. Under all three plans, families with higher incomes pay higher income taxes. So all three plans could be said to operate on the ability-to-pay concept of vertical equity. Yet the three are quite different in their distributive consequences. Plan 1 is a progressive tax, something like the personal income tax in Canada: The average tax rate is higher for richer families. Plan 2 is a proportional tax: Every family pays 10 percent of its income. Plan 3 is quite regressive: Since tax payments rise more slowly than income, the tax rate for richer families is lower than that for poor families.

Which plan comes closest to the ideal notion of vertical equity? Many people find that Plan 3 offends their sense of "fairness," for it makes the distribution of income

Vertical equity is the notion that differently situated individuals should be taxed differently in a way that society deems to be fair.

The **ability-to-pay principle** is the idea that people with greater ability to pay taxes should pay higher taxes.

TABLE 30–3
Three Alternative Income-Tax Plans

INCOME	TAX PAYMENTS (dollars)			AVERAGE TAX RATES (percent)		
	PLAN 1	PLAN 2	PLAN 3	PLAN 1	PLAN 2	PLAN 3
10,000	300	1,000	1,000	3	10	10
50,000	8,000	5,000	3,000	16	10	6
250,000	70,000	25,000	7,500	28	10	3

Should We Move toward the Benefits Principle of Taxation?

Immediately following its election in 1984, the government of Prime Minister Brian Mulroney commenced a review of Canada's social-assistance programs, to see whether the principle of *universal access* should be reconsidered. All but our public health-care programs were examined, to see whether access should be restricted.

This exercise has not resulted in any changes (perhaps for political reasons), but it does illustrate the fundamental trade-off between equity and efficiency. Even for health care, a strong case can be made on efficiency grounds for an increased use of the benefits principle. To an economist, the dramatic increase in health-care costs that we have observed is a predictable result of there being no service charge involved in the public health-care program.

As we stressed in Chapter 19 (page 413), the key feature of our current programs is that the *marginal private cost* of medical care is *zero* for *all* users, while the *true marginal social* cost is high. As a result, there is no mecha-

nism to encourage people to economize on the use of medical services, and therefore no mechanism to induce doctors to consider more cost-effective techniques. Some sort of user charge (that is, application of the benefits principle of taxation) is necessary if the runaway increase in medical costs is to be controlled without a deterioration in service.

To protect the poor, the government would still have to pay the user charges for those with insufficient income. It seems that many people find it objectionable to have free medical care available only to those with lower incomes. They feel it should be a "right" for everyone, so that those with lower incomes should not have to face a demoralizing means test just to gain access to basic health care. The sad truth, however, is that *noticeable inefficiency* costs appear to be necessary to maintain this *equity* principle. Economists *cannot* say whether we should pay these costs, but it *is* their job to ensure that policy-makers and voters are informed about the terms of the equity–efficiency trade-off.

---

after taxes even more unequal than the distribution *before* taxes. But there is much less agreement over the relative merits of Plan 1 (progressive taxation) and Plan 2 (proportional taxation). Very often, in fact, the notion of vertical equity is taken to be synonymous with progressivity. Other things being equal, progressive taxes are seen as "good" taxes in some ethical sense because they make the distribution of income more equal. Conversely, regressive taxes are seen as "bad." On these grounds, advocates of greater equality of incomes support progressive income taxes and oppose sales taxes.

The Benefits Principle

The benefits principle of taxation holds that people who derive the benefits from the service should pay the taxes that finance it.

Whereas the principles of horizontal and vertical equity, for all their ambiguities and practical problems, at least do not conflict with each other, the third principle of fair taxation often violates commonly accepted notions of vertical equity. According to the **benefits principle of taxation**, which is often applied when the proceeds from certain taxes are earmarked for specific public services, those who reap the benefits from government services should pay the taxes.

One clear example is admission fees to national parks. Most people seem to find the use of the benefits principle fair in such cases. But in other contexts—such as public schools, hospitals, and libraries—the body politic has been loath to apply the benefits principle because it clashes so dramatically with common notions of fairness. So these services are normally financed out of general tax revenues, rather than by direct charges for their use.

The Concept of Efficiency in Taxation

The concept of economic *efficiency* is the central notion of Parts Five through Seven of this book. The economy is said to be *efficient* if it has used every available opportunity to make someone better off without making someone else worse off. In this sense, taxes almost always introduce *inefficiencies*. That is, if the tax were removed, some people could be made better off without anyone being harmed.

However, a comparison of a world with taxes to a world without taxes is not terribly pertinent. The government does, after all, need to raise revenues to pay for the

---

goods and services it provides. For this reason, when economists discuss the notion of "efficient" taxation, they are usually looking for the taxes that cause the *least* amount of inefficiency.

To explain the concept of efficient taxation, we need to introduce one new term. Economists define the **burden of a tax** as the amount of money taxpayers would have to be given to make them just as well off in the presence of the tax as they would be in its absence. An example will clarify this notion and also make clear why *the burden of a tax normally exceeds the revenues it raises.*

Suppose the government, in the interest of energy conservation, decides to levy a high tax on the biggest gas-guzzling cars, with progressively lower taxes on smaller cars.[3] For example, a simple tax schedule might be the following:

CAR TYPE	TAX
Cadillac	$1000
Firebird	$ 500
Pony	0

The **burden of a tax** on individuals is the amount of money they would have to be given to make them just as well off with the tax as they were without it.

Sandra has a taste for big cars and has always bought Cadillacs. (Sandra is clearly no pauper.) Once the new tax takes effect, she has three options. She can still buy a Cadillac Seville and pay $1000 in tax, she can switch to a Firebird and avoid half the tax, or she can switch to a Pony and avoid the entire tax.

If Sandra chooses the first option, we have a case in which the burden of the tax is exactly equal to the amount of tax the person pays. Why? Because if Sandra's rich aunt gives her $1000, Sandra winds up exactly as well off as she was before the tax was enacted. In general:

When a tax induces no change in economic behaviour, the burden of the tax can be measured accurately by the revenue collected.

However, this is not what we normally expect to happen. And it is certainly not what the government intends by levying a tax on big cars. Normally, we expect taxes to induce some people to alter their behaviour in ways that reduce or avoid tax payments. So let us look into Sandra's other two options.

If she decides to purchase a Firebird, Sandra pays only $500 in tax. But this is an inadequate measure of the burden of the new tax because Sandra is greatly chagrined by the fact that she no longer drives a Cadillac. How much money would it take to make Sandra just as well off as she was before the tax? Only Sandra knows for sure. But we do know that it is more than the $500 tax that she pays. Why? Because, even if someone were to give Sandra the $500 needed to pay her tax bill, she would still be less happy, owing to the switch from a Cadillac to a Firebird, than she was before the tax was introduced. Whatever the (unknown) burden of the tax is, the amount by which it exceeds the $500 tax bill is called the **excess burden** of the tax.

Sandra's final option makes the importance of understanding excess burden even clearer. If she switches to buying a Pony, Sandra will pay no tax. Are we therefore to say she has suffered no burden? Clearly not, for she longs for the Cadillac that she no longer has. The general principle is:

Whenever a tax induces people to change their behaviour—that is, whenever it "distorts" their choices—the tax has an excess burden. This means that the revenue collected by the tax systematically understates the true burden of the tax.

The **excess burden** of a tax to an individual is the amount by which the burden of the tax exceeds the tax that is paid.

[3] Some provinces differentiate automobile licence fees in this way.

The excess burdens that arise from tax-induced changes in economic behaviour are precisely the inefficiencies we referred to at the outset of this discussion. And the basic precept of efficient taxation is to try to devise a tax system that *minimizes* these inefficiencies.[4] In particular:

In comparing two taxes that raise the same total revenue, the one that produces less excess burden is the more efficient.

Notice the proviso that the two taxes being compared must yield the *same* revenue. We are really interested in the *total* burden of each tax. Since

Total burden = Tax collections + Excess burden,

only when tax collections are equal can we unambiguously state that the tax with less *excess* burden is more efficient. Since excess burdens arise when consumers and firms alter their behaviour on account of taxation, this precept of sound tax policy can be restated in the following way:

In devising a tax system to raise revenue, try to raise any given amount of revenue through taxes that induce the smallest changes in behaviour.[5]

Shifting the Burden of Taxation: Tax Incidence

The incidence of a tax is an allocation of the burden of the tax to specific individuals or groups.

When economists speak of the **incidence of a tax**, they are referring to who actually bears the burden of the tax. In discussing the tax on gas-guzzling autos, we have adhered, so far, to what has been called the *flypaper theory of tax incidence*: that the burden of any tax sticks where the government puts it. In this case, the theory holds that the burden stays on Sandra. But often things do not work out this way.

Consider, for example, what will happen if the government levies a $1000 tax on luxury cars like Cadillacs. Figure 30–3 shows this tax as a $1000 vertical shift of the

[4] Another way of putting the same point is to say that the goal is to devise a tax system that minimizes the aggregate loss in consumer surplus. By recalling pages 411–14 in Chapter 19, you can see that as long as an industry has constant long-run average costs (so that the supply curve is horizontal), the excess burden of a sales tax is precisely measured as the loss in consumer surplus that results from the tax.

[5] Sometimes a tax is levied not primarily as a revenue raiser but as a way of inducing individuals or firms to alter their behaviour. This possibility will be discussed in a later section.

FIGURE 30–3
The Incidence of an Excise Tax
When the government imposes a $1000 tax on luxury cars, the supply curve relating quantity supplied to the price *inclusive of tax* shifts upward from S_0S_0 to S_1S_1. The equilibrium price in this example rises from $30,000 to $30,500, so the burden of the tax is shared equally between car sellers (who receive $500 less) and car buyers (who pay $500 more, including the tax). In general, how the burden is shared depends on the elasticities of demand and supply.

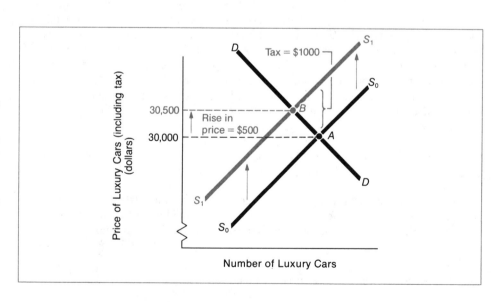

supply curve. If the demand curve does not shift, the market equilibrium moves from point *A* to point *B*. The quantity of luxury cars declines as Sandras all over Canada react to the higher price by buying fewer luxury cars. Notice that the price rises from $30,000 to $30,500, an increase of $500. So people who continue buying luxury cars bear a burden of only $500—just half the tax that they pay!

Does this mean that the tax imposes a *negative* excess burden? Certainly not. What it means is that consumers who refrain from buying the taxed commodity have managed to *shift* part of the burden of the tax away from consumers as a whole, including those who continue to buy luxury cars. Who are the victims of this **tax shifting**? In our example, there are two main candidates. First are the car manufacturers or, more precisely, their shareholders. Shareholders bear the burden to the extent that the tax, by reducing car sales, cuts into their profits. The other principal candidates are auto workers. To the extent that their reduced production leads to layoffs or to lower wages, the automobile workers bear part of the burden of the tax.

> **Tax shifting** occurs when the economic reactions to a tax cause prices and outputs in the economy to change, thereby shifting part of the burden of the tax onto others.

People who have never studied economics almost always believe in the flypaper theory of tax incidence, which holds that sales taxes are borne by consumers, property taxes by homeowners, taxes on corporations by shareholders, and so on. Perhaps the most important lesson to follow from our discussion of taxes is that:

The flypaper theory of tax incidence is often wrong.

Failure to grasp this basic point has led to all sorts of misguided tax legislation in which governments, *thinking* they were placing a tax burden on one group of people, inadvertently placed it squarely on another. Of course, there are cases where the flypaper theory of tax incidence comes very close to being correct. So let us consider some specific examples of tax incidence.

The Incidence of Excise Taxes

Excise taxes have already been covered in our automobile example—Figure 30-3 could represent any commodity that is taxed.[6] The basic finding is that *part* of the burden will fall on consumers of the taxed commodity (including those who stop buying it because of the tax), and part will be shifted to the firms and the workers who produce the commodity.

The amount that is shifted depends on the slopes of the demand and supply curves. We can understand intuitively how this works. If consumers are so loyal to the taxed commodity that they will continue to buy almost the same quantity no matter what the price, it is clear that they will be stuck with most of the tax bill because they have left themselves vulnerable to it. Thus, we expect that:

The more inelastic the demand for the product, the larger is the share of the tax that consumers will pay.

Similarly, if suppliers are determined to supply the same amount of the product no matter how low the price, most of the tax will be borne by suppliers. That is:

The more inelastic the supply curve, the larger is the share of the tax that suppliers will pay.

One extreme case arises if no one stops buying luxury cars when their price rises. The demand curve becomes vertical, like the demand curve *DD* in Figure 30-4. In this case, there can be no tax shifting. The price of a luxury car (inclusive of tax) rises by the full amount of the tax—from $30,000 to $31,000, so consumers bear the entire burden.

---

[6]Although we did not use the term "incidence," excise taxes were analyzed in detail in Chapter 20. If you need a review, see pages 431–34.

FIGURE 30-4

FIGURE 30-4

An Extreme Case of Tax Incidence

If the quantity demanded is totally insensitive to price (completely *inelastic*), the demand curve will be vertical. As the diagram shows, the price inclusive of tax rises, to $31,000 in this case, so buyers bear the entire burden of the tax. Since price exclusive of tax remains at $30,000, none of the burden falls on the sellers.

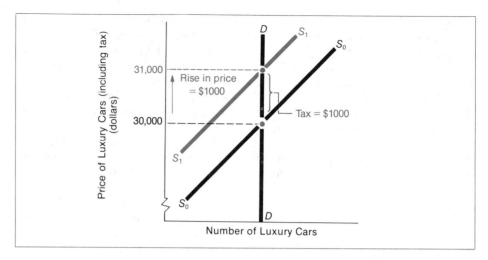

FIGURE 30-5

Another Extreme Case of Tax Incidence

If the quantity supplied is totally insensitive to price, then the supply curve *SS* will be vertical and will not shift when a tax is imposed. The sellers will bear the entire burden, because the price that they receive (here, $29,000) is reduced by the full amount of the tax.

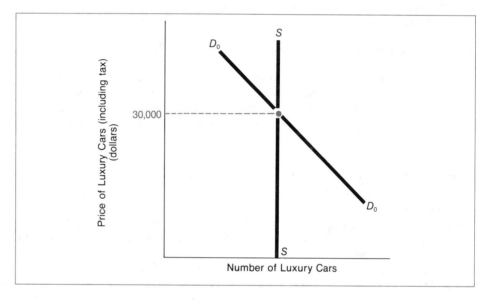

The other extreme case arises when the supply curve is totally inelastic (see Figure 30-5). Since the number of luxury cars supplied is the same at any price, the supply curve will not shift when a tax is imposed. Consequently, car manufacturers must bear the full burden of any tax that is placed on their product. Figure 30-5 shows that the tax does not change the market price (including tax), which, of course, means that the price received by sellers must fall by the full amount of the tax.

Demand and supply schedules for most goods and services are not as extreme as those depicted in Figures 30-4 and 30-5, so the burden is shared by consumers and suppliers. Precisely how it is shared depends on the elasticities of the supply and demand curves.

The Incidence of the Payroll Tax

A payroll tax may be thought of as an excise tax on the employment of labour. As we mentioned earlier, the Canadian payroll tax comes in two parts: Some of it is levied on the employees (through payroll deductions) and the rest on employers. A fundamental point, which people who have never studied economics often fail to grasp, is that:

The incidence of a payroll tax is the same whether it is levied on employers or employees.

A simple numerical example can illustrate why this is so. Consider an employee earning $100 a day with a 14 percent payroll tax that is "shared" equally between the employer and the employee. How much does it cost the firm to hire this worker? It costs $100 in wages paid to the worker plus $7 in taxes paid to the government, for a total of $107 a day. How much does the worker receive? She gets $100 in wages paid by the employer less $7 deducted and sent to the government, or $93 a day. The difference between wages paid and wages received is $107 – $93 = $14.

Now suppose the government tries to "shift" the burden of the tax entirely onto firms by raising the employer's tax to $14 while lowering the employee's tax to zero. At first, the daily wage is fixed at $100, so firms' total labour costs (including tax) rise to $114 per day and workers' net incomes rise to $100 per day. The government seems to have achieved its goal.

But this is not an equilibrium situation. With the daily wage at $114 for firms and $100 for workers, the quantity of labour *demanded* by firms will be *less* and the quantity of labour *supplied* by the workers will be *more* than when the two wages were $107 and $93. There will, therefore, be a *surplus of labour* on the market (an excess of quantity supplied over quantity demanded), and this surplus will put downward pressure on wages.

How far will wages have to fall? It is easy to see that a wage of $93 will restore equilibrium. If the daily wage is $93, labour will cost firms $107 per day, just as it did before the tax change. So firms will demand the same quantity as they did when the payroll tax was shared. Similarly, workers will receive the same $93 net wage as they did previously; so quantity supplied will be the same as it was before the tax change. Thus, in the end, the market will completely frustrate the intent of the government.

The payroll tax is an excellent example of a case in which the government, misled by the flypaper theory of tax incidence, thinks it is "taxing firms" when it raises the employer's share and that it is "taxing workers" when it raises the employee's share. In truth, who is really paying depends on the incidence of the tax. But no difference results from a change in the employee's and the employer's shares.

Who, then, really bears the burden of the payroll tax? Like any excise tax, the incidence of the payroll tax depends on the elasticities of the supply and demand schedules. In the case of labour supply, a large body of empirical evidence points to the conclusion that the quantity of labour supplied is not very responsive to price for most population groups. The supply curve is almost vertical, like that shown in Figure 30-5. The result is that workers as a group are able to shift very little of the burden of the payroll tax.

But employers *can* shift it in most cases. Firms view their share of the payroll tax as an additional cost of using labour. So when payroll taxes go up, firms try to substitute cheaper factors of production (capital) for labour wherever they can. This reduces the quantity of labour demanded, lowering the wage received by workers. And this is how market forces shift part of the tax burden from firms to workers.

To the extent that the supply curve of labour has some positive slope, the quantity of labour supplied will fall when the wage goes down, and in this way workers can shift some of the burden back onto firms. But the firms, in turn, can shift that burden onto consumers by raising their prices. As we know from Part Five, prices in competitive markets generally rise when costs (such as labour costs) increase. It is doubtful, therefore, that firms bear any of the burden of the payroll tax. Here, the flypaper theory of tax incidence could not be farther from the truth. Even though the tax is collected by the firm, it is really borne by workers and consumers.

The Incidence of the Tax on Capital

The corporate profits tax is difficult to analyze since it is partly a tax on pure economic profit and partly an excise tax on the employment of capital equipment. Also, as we noted in Chapter 9 (page 204), the Canadian profits tax can have no effect on profits, or the earnings of capital, when it is levied on multinationals that receive a tax credit

FIGURE 30-6

The Incidence of a Tax on Mobile Capital

Before the domestic tax is imposed, the supply of capital is perfectly elastic at a 10 percent rate of return, the return assumed available in the rest of the world. If a 50 percent tax is imposed in Canada, capital owners require a 20 percent return before tax, so the supply curve shifts from $S_0 S_0$ to $S_1 S_1$, and the owners of capital bear none of the tax.

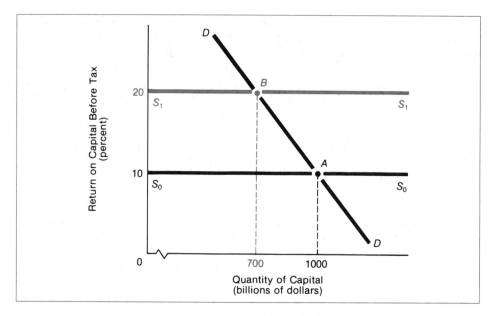

in their home country equal to the taxes paid in Canada. In the case of the multinationals, the burden of any unsheltered Canadian profits tax is squarely on the government (and therefore on the citizens) of the foreign country where the company is based. Our corporate tax simply lowers the tax revenue of the company's home country, dollar for dollar, as long as the company does not avoid paying the taxes to both governments. (Large corporations can avoid paying taxes by transferring portions of profits out of both Canada and the United States—which is usually the relevant home country—to affiliates in third countries where corporate tax rates are low.) Even for purely domestic firms that cannot escape taxes in this way, the flypaper theory of tax incidence is again far from the truth.

In the case of domestic firms, we can learn much about the incidence of the profits tax by treating it as a tax on the earnings of capital. The supply of capital to the Canadian economy is very elastic. If Canadian owners of capital cannot obtain an after-tax return in Canada equal to what is available elsewhere, they will invest elsewhere. Capital is far more mobile internationally than labour, and for a country as small as Canada, the minimum acceptable rate of return for capital is determined outside. Thus, we investigate the incidence of the tax on capital on the assumption that the supply is perfectly elastic, as shown in Figure 30-6.

Before the domestic tax is imposed, the supply of capital is perfectly elastic at a 10 percent rate of return (the return that we assume, for the purposes of this discussion, to be available in the rest of the world). Equilibrium in the capital market is initially at point *A*. If a 50 percent tax is imposed in Canada, capital owners require a 20 percent before-tax return to continue to employ their capital in Canada. Thus, the supply curve shifts upward from $S_0 S_0$ to $S_1 S_1$, and the equilibrium position after the tax is levied is given by point *B*. Since the before-tax rate of return rises by the full amount of the tax, the owners of capital completely escape the tax. The burden falls entirely on consumers and on the labour employed by the firms.

The conclusion is that it is difficult to impose a tax that sticks on the owners of capital.

When Taxation Can Improve Efficiency

We have spent much of this chapter discussing the kinds of inefficiencies and excess burdens that arise from taxation. Before we finish this discussion, two things must be pointed out.

First, economic efficiency is not society's only goal. For example, the tax on gas-guzzling cars causes inefficiencies if it changes people's behaviour patterns. But this, presumably, was exactly what the government sought to accomplish. The government wanted to reduce the number of big cars on the road to conserve energy, and it was willing to tolerate some economic inefficiency to accomplish this end. We can, of course, argue whether this was a good idea—whether the conservation achieved was worth the efficiency loss. But the general point is that:

Some taxes that introduce economic inefficiencies are nonetheless good ideas, because they help achieve some other goal.

A second, and more fundamental, point is that:

Some taxes that change economic behaviour may lead to efficiency *gains* rather than to efficiency *losses*.

As you might guess, this can happen only when there is an inefficiency in the system prior to the tax. In that case, an appropriate tax may help set things right. One important example of this phenomenon will occupy much of the last chapter of this book. There we will see that because firms and individuals who despoil clean air and clean water often do so without paying any price, these precious resources are used inefficiently. A corrective tax on pollution can remedy this problem.

Equity, Efficiency, and the Optimal Tax

In a perfect world, the ideal tax would reflect society's views on equity in taxation without inducing changes in economic behaviour and therefore without creating excess burden. Unfortunately, there is no such tax.

On the contrary, the taxes with the smallest excess burdens can be the most regressive. For instance, one option that has long been suggested is the head tax, which would, in principle, charge every person the same number of dollars. Although such a tax would be very regressive, it would also be quite efficient: Since there is no change in economic behaviour that would enable anyone to avoid the tax, there would be no reason for anyone to change his or her behaviour.[7] As we have already noted, the regressive payroll tax also seems to have small excess burdens.

Fortunately, however, there is a tax that, while not ideal, scores very high on both the equity and the efficiency criteria: a comprehensive personal income tax with few shelters.

While it is true that income taxes can be avoided by earning less income, we have already observed that in reality the supply of labour is changed little by taxation. Investing in relatively safe assets (such as government bonds) rather than risky ones (such as common shares) is another possible reaction that would reduce tax bills, since less risky assets pay lower rates of return. But it is not clear that the income tax actually induces such behaviour because, while it taxes away some of the profits when investments turn out well, it also offers a tax deduction when investments turn sour.

The main argument against an income tax is that it reduces the return on saving. As noted earlier, many economists have worried that income taxes discourage saving and thus retard economic growth. This is the reason that many tax analysts in Canada

---

[7]In practice, because of the way head taxes are normally implemented, they do induce a change in behaviour. They are often called poll taxes because they are imposed on everyone listed to vote in elections. People can avoid the tax by giving up the opportunity to vote; if they do so, an excess burden exists after all.

In Great Britain, Margaret Thatcher's Conservative government imposed a poll tax in 1990 to pay for a reduction in property taxes. This tax substitution raises the tax burden on individuals who own low-valued property, unless they remove themselves from the voters' list. Given that a large percentage of the voters so affected have not traditionally supported Mrs. Thatcher's party, it is doubtful that she regards such a change in behaviour as a burden.

favour the GST (which taxes only income that is spent, not income that is saved) and schemes such as extending the limits for tax-deductible contributions to registered retirement savings plans. However, other analysts doubt that the effect of the disincentive to save that accompanies income taxes is in fact large enough to cause concern. Consequently, they favour income taxes over sales taxes. Thus, although there are still unresolved questions, and research is continuing:

Many studies suggest that a comprehensive personal income tax with no unintended tax shelters induces few behavioural reactions that would reduce consumer well-being, and thus has a rather small excess burden.

On efficiency grounds, sales taxes score somewhat higher than does a general income tax. But on equity grounds, unless a sales tax is combined with a wealth tax (for example, an inheritance tax), it scores poorly. We know that personal income taxes can be made as progressive as society deems desirable, though if marginal tax rates on rich people get extremely high, some of the potential efficiency losses might get more serious than they now seem to be. On both efficiency and equity grounds, then, many economists—including both liberals and conservatives—view a comprehensive personal income tax as one of the best ways for a government to raise revenue.

The Real versus the Ideal

That seems to be a cheerful conclusion, because the personal income tax is the biggest tax in the Canadian revenue system. Unfortunately, however, our actual tax system does not much resemble an ideal, comprehensive income tax. For one thing, tax shelters make the income tax less progressive than it seems to be; for another, they make it far less efficient than it could be. The reason follows directly from our analysis of the incidence of taxation.

When different income-earning activities are taxed at different marginal rates, economic choices are distorted by tax considerations; this impairs economic efficiency.

Our present tax system encourages people to devote more time and energy to lightly taxed sources of income (such as capital gains) and less to heavily taxed activities (such as earning wages). Consequently, economic activity is distorted. The result is that the personal income tax, which could *in principle* raise a lot of revenue with little excess burden, *in fact* imposes considerable excess burdens on society. As a result, proposals for tax reform are continually being debated, as the controversial GST illustrates.

Poverty and the Welfare System

Poverty: The Facts

The dividing line between the poor and the non-poor is called the **poverty line**. It is defined as the level of income at which a person or a family spends 59 percent of that income on the essentials of life (food, clothing, and shelter). (The average Canadian family spends 39 percent of income on these essentials.) For 1990, this definition meant that the poverty line for an individual was an income of $8760 per year in rural areas and $12,870 per year in a large city. For a family of four, the corresponding low-income cut-offs were $17,380 and $25,525, respectively. Using these National Council of Welfare definitions, slightly less than 15 percent of Canadian families were poor at the end of the 1980s.

Substantial progress toward eliminating poverty was made during the 1970s; the percentage of persons in Canada living below the poverty line fell from 23 percent to

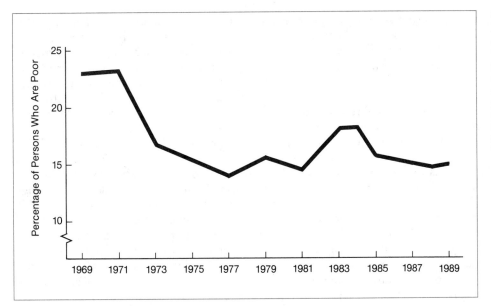

FIGURE 30–7
Progress in the Reduction of Poverty
This figure charts the decline in the percentage of Canadians classified as "poor" by official definitions. While substantial progress has been made, 15 percent of all Canadians remain below the poverty line.
SOURCE: National Council of Welfare.

15 percent (see Figure 30–7). However, because of the severe recession of the early 1980s, the poverty rate at the end of the 1980s was no better than it had been at the beginning of the decade. One in every seven Canadians was living below the poverty line in 1989! This fact has worried many people. But some critics have argued that the official data may overstate the incidence of poverty, since the official definition is based only on cash income. A number of goods are received by the poor in kind: for example, public education, public housing, and health care.

This debate raises the fundamental question of how we define "the poor." Continuing economic growth will eventually pull almost everyone above any arbitrarily established poverty line. Does this event mark the end of poverty? Some would say yes. But others would insist that the biblical injunction is right: "The poor ye have always with you."

There are two ways to define poverty. The more optimistic definition uses an *absolute concept of poverty*: If you fall short of a certain minimum standard of living, you are poor; once you pass this standard, you are no longer poor. The second definition is based on a *relative concept of poverty*: The poor are those who fall too far behind the average income.

Each definition has its pros and cons. The basic problem with the absolute-poverty concept is that it is arbitrary. Who sets the line? Most of the people of Bangladesh would be delighted to live a bit below the Canadian poverty line and would consider themselves quite prosperous. Similarly, the standard of living that we now call "poor" would probably not have been considered so in Canada in 1780 and certainly not in Europe during the Middle Ages. Different times and different places apparently call for different poverty lines.

The fact that the concept of poverty is culturally, not physiologically, determined suggests that it must be a relative concept. For example, the Canadian Council on Social Development defines the poverty line as one-half of the national average income. This way, the poverty line automatically rises as the nation grows richer.

In contrast, the Fraser Institute, a pro-market research group based in Vancouver, is critical of the relative concept of poverty. The Institute has argued as follows:[8] the poverty line for a family of four was only $3500 in 1961, and if that figure

[8] *Fraser Forum*, April 1986, page 15.

were projected allowing only for increases in the cost of living since that time, the 1990 low-income cut-off would be $15,525 for a family of four rather than $25,525, as is currently estimated. The Institute prefers to use this absolute concept to measure the progress of the war on poverty, and using it, concludes that while 26 percent of families were below the poverty line in 1961, only 10 percent were in that position toward the end of the 1980s. The Fraser Institute also notes that of those officially counted as poor, 40 percent are homeowners; it feels that poverty should not be measured by income levels without any reference to household assets.

How can we achieve some perspective on whether official estimates of the poverty line should be regarded as too low or too high? One way of providing an answer is to consider the Gallup poll taken in March 1986, which asked respondents what they considered the least amount of money a family of four needed to get along. The average answer was almost exactly equal to the official poverty line for 1986. Another standard of reference is provided by minimum-wage legislation. In most provinces, a full-time worker receiving the minimum wage earns an income below the poverty line. While this suggests that the poverty line may be a bit high, it must be remembered that *most* poor people earn incomes *significantly* below the poverty line.

Once we start moving away from an absolute concept of poverty toward a relative concept, the sharp distinction between the poor and the non-poor starts to evaporate. Instead, it is more constructive to think of a parade of people from the poorest soul to the richest millionaire. The "poverty problem," then, seems to be that the disparities in income are "too large" in some sense. The poor are so poor because the rich are so rich. If we follow this line of thought far enough, we are led away from the narrow problem of *poverty* toward the broader problem of *inequality of income*.

Inequality: The Facts

There is nothing in the market mechanism that works to prevent large differences in incomes. On the contrary, it tends to breed inequality, for the basic source of the great efficiency of the market mechanism is its system of rewards and penalties. The market is generous to those who are successful in operating efficient enterprises that are responsive to consumer demands, and it is ruthless in penalizing those who are unable or unwilling to satisfy consumer demands efficiently. Its financial punishment of those who try and fail can be particularly severe. At times it even brings down the great and powerful.

Most people have a good idea that the income distribution is quite spread out—that the gulf between the rich and the poor is a wide one. But few have any concept of where they stand in the distribution. In Table 30–4, you will find some statistics on the

TABLE 30–4
Distribution of Family Income in Canada, 1988

INCOME RANGE (dollars)	PERCENTAGE OF ALL FAMILIES IN THIS RANGE	PERCENTAGE OF FAMILIES IN THIS AND LOWER RANGES
Under 10,000	3.3	3.3
10,000 to 19,999	13.3	16.6
20,000 to 29,999	15.1	31.7
30,000 to 39,999	16.4	48.1
40,000 to 49,999	15.0	63.1
50,000 to 64,999	16.9	80.0
65,000 and more	20.0	100.0

If your family's income falls close to one of the end points of the ranges indicated here, you can approximate the fraction of families with income *lower* than yours just by looking at the last column.
SOURCE: Statistics Canada 13-210.

1988 income distribution in Canada (the most recent data available when this book went to press). But before looking at these, try the following experiment. First, write down your family's before-tax income in 1988. (If you do not know, take a guess.) Next, try to guess what percentage of Canadian families had incomes *lower* than this. Finally, if we divide Canada into three broad income classes—rich, middle class, and poor—to which group do you think your family belongs?

Once you have written down answers to these three questions, look at the income distribution data for 1988 in Table 30–4. If you are like most postsecondary students, these figures will contain a few surprises for you. First, if we adopt the tentative definitions that the lowest 20 percent are the "poor," the highest 20 percent are the "rich," and the middle 60 percent are the "middle class," many fewer of you belong to the celebrated "middle class" than thought so. In fact, the cut-off point that defined membership in the "rich" class in 1988 was about $65,000 before taxes, an income level exceeded by the families of many students. (Your family may be shocked to learn that it is rich!)

Next, use Table 30–4 to estimate the fraction of Canadian families that have incomes lower than your family's. Most students who come from households of moderate prosperity have an instinctive feeling that they stand somewhere near the middle of the income distribution; so they estimate about half, or perhaps a little more. In fact, if your family earned a pre-tax income of $60,000 in 1988, more than 75 percent of Canadian families are poorer than yours!

This exercise has perhaps brought us down to earth. Let us now look past the average level of income and see how the pie is divided. Table 30–5 shows the shares of

TABLE 30–5
Income Shares in Selected Years

INCOME GROUP	1988	1985	1982	1979	1973	1965
Lowest fifth	6.5	6.3	6.3	6.1	6.1	6.2
Second fifth	12.4	12.3	12.6	13.0	12.9	13.1
Middle fifth	17.9	17.9	18.0	18.4	18.1	18.0
Fourth fifth	24.0	24.1	24.1	24.3	23.9	23.6
Highest fifth	39.2	39.4	38.9	38.3	38.9	39.0

SOURCE: Statistics Canada 13–210.

"*There is a perfect example of what is wrong with this country today.*"

"*There is a perfect example of what is wrong with this country today.*"

income accruing to each fifth of the population in 1988 and several earlier years. In a perfectly equal society, all the numbers in this table would be "20 percent" since each fifth of the population would receive one-fifth of the income. In fact, as the table shows, this is certainly not the case. In 1988, for example, the poorest fifth of all families had only 6.5 percent of the total income, while the richest fifth had 39.2 percent—six times as much.

Depicting Income Distributions: The Lorenz Curve

Statisticians and economists use a convenient tool to portray data like those in Table 30–5 graphically. The device, called a **Lorenz curve**, is shown in Figure 30–8. To construct a Lorenz curve, we first draw a square whose vertical and horizontal dimensions both represent 100 percent. Then we record the percentage of families (or persons) on the horizontal axis and the percentage of income that these families (or persons) receive on the vertical axis, using all the data that we have. For example, point C in Figure 30–8 depicts the fact (known from Table 30–5) that the bottom 60 percent (the three lowest fifths) of Canadian families in 1988 received 36.8 percent of the total income. Similarly, points A, B, and D represent the other information contained in Table 30–5. We can list four important properties of a Lorenz curve:

1. It begins at the origin, because zero families naturally have zero income.

2. It always ends at the upper-right corner of the square, since 100 percent of the nation's families must necessarily receive all the nation's income.

3. If income were distributed equally, the Lorenz curve would be a straight line connecting these two points (the thin solid line in Figure 30–8). With everybody equal, the bottom 20 percent of the families would receive 20 percent of the income, the bottom 40 percent would receive 40 percent, and so on.

4. In a real economy, with significant income differences, the Lorenz curve will "sag" downward from this line of perfect equality. It is easy to see why this is so. If there is any inequality at all, the poorest 20 percent of families must get less than 20 percent of all the income. This corresponds to a point below the equality line, such as point A. Similarly, the bottom 40 percent of families must receive less than 40 percent of the income (point B), and so on.

FIGURE 30–8
A Lorenz Curve for Canada

This Lorenz curve for Canada is based on the 1988 distribution of income given in Table 30–5. The percentage of families is measured along the horizontal axis, and the percentage of income that these families receive is measured along the vertical axis. Thus, for example, point C indicates that the bottom 60 percent of Canadian families received 36.8 percent of the total income in 1988.

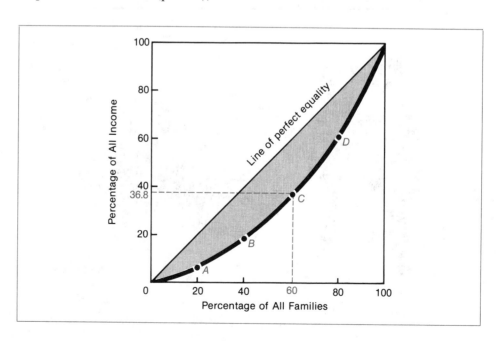

In fact, the size of the area between the line of perfect equality and the Lorenz curve (the shaded area in Figure 30–8) is often used as a handy measure of inequality. The larger this area, the more unequal is the income distribution. For Canadian family incomes, this so-called area of inequality usually fills up about one-third of the total area underneath the equality line.

Standing by itself, the Lorenz curve tells us rather little. To interpret it, we must know what it looked like in earlier years or what it looks like in other countries. The historical data in Table 30–5 show that *the Canadian Lorenz curve has not moved much at all in the last quarter century*. To some, this remarkable stability in the income distribution is deplorable. To others, it suggests some immutable law of the capitalist system. In fact, neither view is correct. The apparent stability in the income distribution is the result of a standoff between certain demographic forces that were pushing the Lorenz curve outward (such as more young people, more old people, and more families headed by women) and other forces that were pulling it inward (such as government anti-poverty programs).

Comparing Canada with other countries is much harder, since no two countries use precisely the same definition of income distribution. In 1976, the Organization for Economic Cooperation and Development (OECD) made a heroic effort to standardize the income distribution data of its member countries so they could be compared.[9] In this analysis, Japan stood out as the industrialized country with the most equal income distribution, with Australia, West Germany, the Netherlands, and Sweden bunched closely in second place. Canada placed between this group and France and the United States, which seemed to have the most inequality. Before extrapolating from these findings, it should be pointed out that only twelve industrial countries were compared. Israel, which is often thought to have the most equal income distribution in the non-communist world, is not in the OECD. Neither are any of the less developed countries, which are generally found to have much more inequality than the developed ones.

Policies to Combat Poverty

Let us take it for granted that the nation has a commitment to reduce the amount of poverty. What are some policies that can promote this goal? Which of these does the least harm to economic incentives and is hence most efficient? The traditional approach to poverty fighting in Canada has utilized a variety of programs collectively known as *social assistance*. The best-known of these is the welfare system administered by the municipalities.

Our welfare system has been attacked as a classic example of an inefficient redistributive program. Why? One reason is that it provides little incentive for a welfare recipient to get a job and earn income. Only by acquiring skills on the job can welfare recipients ever break out of the unemployment–poverty circle. The following example was used by the Economic Council of Canada in its 1983 *Annual Review*: If a single mother with two dependent children works regularly as a sales clerk at half the average industrial wage, the family would still qualify for some welfare. However, for each dollar earned, welfare is reduced by 75 cents. Also, the woman would have to make contributions to unemployment insurance and to the Canada Pension Plan. Furthermore, her taxable income would have increased enough to cross the income-tax threshold. When all these reductions in transfer payments and increases in taxes and contributions are added up, the effective tax rate on the women's earnings from the job would be 110 percent! The family's income position would actually be reduced by working. Furthermore, even today, working at the minimum wage brings in less than does welfare in most provinces. Such disincentive effects make it essentially impossible for many individuals to escape the poverty trap. Some attempts have been made to

[9]Malcolm Sawyer, "Income Distribution in OECD Countries," *OECD Occasional Studies* (July 1976), pages 3–36.

ease this transition from welfare to paid employment but very few individuals have been able to participate in the pilot projects.

Equally alarming is the fact that our existing federal legislation precludes any requirement that individuals engage in some work as part of their welfare program. This means that we cannot implement "workfare" programs such as those that have been in place in the United States for some years. In a workfare program, the government finds a job for the welfare recipient, and welfare payments continue only as long as the individual reports for work. Five-year studies have found that welfare rates dropped by one-third among individuals involved in these programs. It turned out that simply by being in a social setting with other working individuals and by developing contacts and skills, one-third of the welfare recipients found better jobs and dropped off the welfare rolls entirely.

In Canada, the federal government funds the provincial welfare schemes through the Canada Assistance Plan. The legislation that defines this plan states explicitly that provinces cannot require individuals to engage in a program of work as a prerequisite for receiving welfare assistance.

The welfare system is not the only government program directed toward the relief of poverty. As explained in Chapter 4 (pages 88–89), the unemployment-insurance system plays a role. Also, many of the poor are provided with a number of important goods and services either at no charge or at prices that are well below market levels. Subsidized day care, free prescription drugs, and subsidized public housing are some notable examples. These programs significantly enhance the living standards of the poor. However, most of them offer benefits that decline as family income rises. As a result, these anti-poverty programs accentuate the basic problem—that many poor families are *worse* off if their earnings *rise*. *With an effective tax rate of more than 100 percent, there is a powerful incentive not to work.*

The Negative Income Tax

These problems and others like them have contributed to the "welfare mess" and have led to frequent calls to scrap the whole system and replace it with a simple structure designed to get income into the hands of the poor without providing such adverse incentives. The solution suggested most frequently, at least by economists, is the so-called **negative income tax (NIT)**. The Macdonald Commission, a federal royal commission of the mid-1980s charged with studying the country's economic affairs, endorsed this proposal, calling it the Universal Income Security Program.

The name "negative income tax" derives from the scheme's similarity to the regular (positive) income tax. Let us illustrate how NIT would work. To describe a particular NIT plan we require two numbers: a minimum income level below which no person or family is allowed to fall (the "guaranteed annual income"), and a rate at which benefits are "taxed away" as income rises. Consider a plan with a $6000 guaranteed income (for an individual) and a 50 percent tax rate. A person with no earnings would then receive a $6000 payment (a "negative tax") from the government. A person earning $2000 would have the basic benefit reduced by 50 percent of his or her earnings. Since half of the earnings is $1000, the individual would receive $5000 from the government plus the $2000 earned income for a total income of $7000 (see Table 30–6).

Notice in Table 30–6 that with a 50 percent tax rate, the increase in total income as earnings rise is always half of the increase in earnings. There is always *some* incentive to work under an NIT system. Notice also that there is a "break-even" level of income at which benefits cease. In this case, the break-even level is $12,000. This is not another number that policy-makers can arbitrarily select in the way they select the guarantee level and the tax rate. Rather, it is dictated by the choice of the guarantee level and the tax rate. In our example, $6000 is the maximum possible benefit and benefits are reduced by 50 cents for each $1 of earnings. Hence, benefits will be

TABLE 30-6
Illustration of a Negative-Income-Tax Plan

EARNINGS (dollars)	BENEFITS PAID (dollars)	TOTAL INCOME (dollars)
0	6,000	6,000
2,000	5,000	7,000
4,000	4,000	8,000
6,000	3,000	9,000
8,000	2,000	10,000
10,000	1,000	11,000
12,000	0	12,000

reduced to zero when 50 percent of earnings is equal to $6000. This occurs when earnings are $12,000 in our example. The general relation is:

$$\text{Guarantee} = \text{Tax rate} \times \text{Break-even level.}$$

The fact that the break-even level is completely determined by the guarantee level and the tax rate creates an annoying problem. If we are truly to make a dent in the poverty population through an NIT system, the guarantee will have to come fairly close to the poverty line. But then, if we are to keep the tax rate moderate, the break-even level will have to be much above the poverty line. This means that families that are not considered "poor" (though they are certainly not rich) will also receive benefits. For example, a low tax rate of 33.3 percent means that some benefits will be paid to families whose income is as high as three times the guarantee level.

But if we raise the tax rate to bring the guarantee and break-even levels closer together, the incentive to work—and with it, the principal rationale for the NIT in the first place—shrinks. So the NIT is no magic cure-all. Difficult choices must still be made.

The Negative Income Tax and Work Incentives

For people now covered by welfare programs, the NIT would increase the incentive to work. However, we have just seen that it is virtually inevitable that a number of families who are now too well off to collect welfare would become eligible for NIT payments. For these people, the NIT would impose work disincentives, both because it would provide them with more income and because it would subject them to the relatively high NIT tax rate, reducing their after-tax wage rate.[10]

These possible disincentive effects have worried both social reformers and legislators, so in the late 1960s the government initiated a series of social experiments to estimate the effect of the NIT on the supply of labour. Families in several communities in Manitoba were offered negative-income-tax payments in return for allowing social scientists to monitor their behaviour. A matched set of "control" families, who were not given NIT payments, were also observed. The idea was to measure how the behaviour of the families receiving NIT payments differed from that of the families that did not receive them or received conventional welfare payments.

The experiments, like more extensive ones undertaken in the United States, lasted about a decade. They showed clearly that the net effects of the NIT on labour supply were small—but certainly not zero. Members of families receiving NIT benefits did work slightly less than the others, but some obtained higher-paying jobs. The fears of those who predicted that NIT payments would induce widespread withdrawals from the labour force were unfounded. This, combined with the fact that some

---

[10] For a review of income and substitution effects in labour-supply analysis, refer to Chapter 29, pages 660–62.

individuals were inspired to obtain higher-paying work, led many economists to conclude that the NIT should be adopted. After all, the only way to beat the poverty problem in the long run is to encourage people to acquire skills on the job that will improve their productivity.

Other Tax and Expenditure Programs

If we take the broader view that society's objective is not just to eliminate poverty but to reduce income disparities, then the fact that many non-poor families would receive benefits from the NIT is perhaps not a serious drawback. After all, unless the plan were outlandishly generous, these families would still be well below the average income. Still, in popular discussions the NIT is largely thought of as an anti-poverty program, not as a tool for general income equalization.

By contrast, the personal income tax *is* thought to be a means of promoting equality. Indeed, it is probably given more credit for this than it actually deserves. The reason is that the income tax is widely known to be *progressive*. The fact that the tax is progressive means that incomes *after* tax are distributed more equally than incomes *before* tax, because the rich turn over a larger share of their incomes to the tax collector. This is illustrated by the two Lorenz curves in Figure 30–9. These curves, however, are not drawn accurately to scale. If they were, they would lie almost on top of each other because the degree of equalization that can be attributed to the tax system is very modest—one reason being the existence of tax shelters (which were discussed earlier in this chapter).

There are many other taxes in the Canadian system, and most experts agree that the remaining taxes as a group are decidedly regressive. Since low-income earners *spend* a larger portion of their incomes than do high-income earners, and since an especially high proportion of their incomes is spent on housing, both sales and property taxes can be quite regressive. On balance, the evidence suggests that when the effects of these taxes are combined with those of the income tax, the tax system as a whole is only very slightly progressive.

It is more difficult to measure the income distribution effects of government expenditure programs. Nevertheless, studies have been done to estimate which income classes benefit most from individual expenditure schemes, such as those that finance highways, postsecondary education, the protection of private property, and so

Figure 30–9
The Effect of Progressive Income Taxation on the Lorenz Curve
Since a progressive income tax takes proportionately more income from the rich than from the poor, it reduces income inequality. Graphically, this means that society's Lorenz curve shifts in the manner shown here. The magnitude of the shift, however, is exaggerated to make the graph more readable. In reality, the Canadian income tax has only a very small effect on the Lorenz curve.

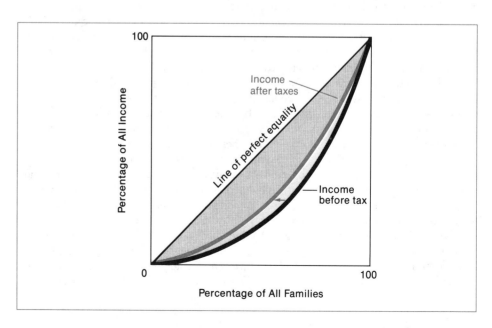

on. These studies show that higher-income classes benefit to such an extent that government expenditures as a whole are regressive. In fact, they are so regressive that they outweigh the mildly progressive effect of total taxes, so that the overall income distribution effect of the entire set of government-sector initiatives is estimated to be slightly *regressive*.

As noted earlier in this chapter, one set of government transfer policies does not involve individuals directly. Instead, these schemes redistribute funds from the "have provinces" to the "have-not provinces." The most important of these is the equalization program that involves grant payments from federal government revenues to all provincial governments except Ontario, British Columbia, and Alberta.

Finally, there are numerous regional programs offering incentives to companies that locate or expand in the so-called depressed regions. Unfortunately there is a dearth of research on the effectiveness of these regional policies. Some economists have argued that transfers to the have-not regions have significantly reduced out-migration from these areas. This leaves the depressed regions with an excess supply of labour, with low wages, and with the slow growth that is usually associated with a state of dependency on the federal government. Other economists argue that the regional redistribution payments have stimulated much local economic activity, thereby lessening the general poverty problem. Further research is very much needed in this area.

Discrimination

Some of the factors that lead to income differentials are widely accepted as "just." For example, few quarrel with the idea that it is fair for people who work longer hours to receive higher incomes. However, almost no one is willing to condone income inequalities that arise strictly because of discrimination.

Discrimination: The Facts

The facts about discrimination are not easy to come by. We define **economic discrimination** as occurring when equivalent factors of production receive different payments for equal contributions to output. But this definition is hard to apply in practice because we cannot always tell when two factors of production are "equivalent."

Probably no one would call it "discrimination" if a woman with only a high school diploma received a lower salary than a man with a university degree (though one might legitimately ask whether discrimination helps to explain the difference in their educational attainments). Even if they have the same education, the man may have ten more years of work experience than the woman. If they receive different wages for this reason, are we to call that "discrimination"?

Similar ambiguities plague discussions about racial discrimination. For example, if a native Indian receives less pay than a white when working in a "same job," it may be that the white has had more education and training, which make him more productive. Thus, it is not clear that the employer is discriminating. It may be that discrimination exists at the schooling level, and that this is what caused the skill differential assumed in our example. But discrimination within the educational system is not the fault of an individual employer.

Ideally, we would compare men and women, or natives and whites, whose *productivities* are equal. In this case, if women receive lower wages than men, or if natives receive lower wages than whites, we would clearly call it discrimination. But discrimination normally takes much more subtle forms than paying unequal wages for equal work. For instance, employers can simply keep women or natives relegated to inferior jobs, thus justifying the lower salaries they pay them.

One clearly *incorrect* way to measure discrimination is to compare the typical incomes of different groups. For example, in 1988, women's average earnings were

Economic discrimination is defined as occurring when equivalent factors of production receive different payments for equal contributions to output.

about 71 percent of men's. Virtually everyone agrees that existing levels of discrimination are smaller than these differentials suggest, but far greater than zero. Precisely how much greater is a topic of continuing economic research. Several studies in the United States suggest that at least half of the observed wage differential between white women and white men is caused by discrimination in the labour market (though more might be due to discrimination in education, and so on). Other studies have reached somewhat different conclusions. While no one denies the existence of discrimination, its quantitative importance is a matter of ongoing controversy and research.

Discrimination: The Theory

Let us see what economic theory tells us about discrimination. In particular, consider the following two questions:

1. Must the existence of *prejudice*, which we define as arising when one group dislikes associating with another group, always lead to *discrimination* (unequal pay for work of equal value)?

2. Are there "natural" economic forces that tend either to erode or to exacerbate discrimination over time?

As we shall see now, the analysis we have provided in previous chapters sheds light on both these issues.

Discrimination by Employers

Most attention seems to focus on discrimination by employers, so let us start there. What happens if, for instance, some firms refuse to hire women for certain positions? Figure 30–10 will help us find the answer. Part (a) pertains to firms that discriminate; part (b) pertains to firms that do not. The supply and demand curves for labour in both parts are based on the analysis of Chapter 29. We suppose the two demand curves to be identical. However, the supply curve in part (b) must be farther to the right than the supply curve in part (a), because men *and* women can work in part (b), whereas

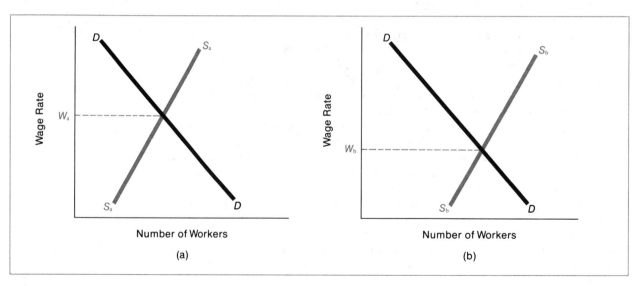

FIGURE 30–10
Wage Discrimination
Part (a) depicts supply and demand curves for labour among discriminatory firms; part (b) shows the same for non-discriminatory firms. Since only men can work in part (a), while both sexes can work in part (b), the supply curve in part (b) is farther to the right than the supply curve in part (a). Consequently, the wage rate in part (b), W_b, winds up below the wage rate in part (a), W_a.

only men can work in part (a). The result is that wages will be lower in part (b) than in part (a). Since all the women are forced into part (b), their wages are lower than the average wage of the men in parts (a) and (b), so we conclude that there is discrimination against women.

But now consider the situation from the point of view of the employers. Firms in part (a) of Figure 30–10 are paying more for labour; they are paying for the privilege of discriminating against women. The non-discriminatory firms in part (b) have a cost advantage. As we learned in earlier chapters, if there is effective competition, these non-discriminatory firms will tend to capture more and more of the market. The discriminators will gradually be driven out of business. If, on the other hand, many of the firms in part (a) have protected monopolies, they will be able to remain in business. But they will pay for the privilege of discriminating by earning lower monopoly profits than they otherwise could (because they pay higher wages than they have to).

Discrimination by Fellow Workers

Competitive forces will tend to reduce discrimination over time if employers are the source of discrimination. Such optimistic conclusions cannot necessarily be reached, however, if it is workers who are prejudiced. Consider what happens if, for example, men do not like to have women as their supervisors. If men do not give their full co-operation, female supervisors will be less effective than their male counterparts and, hence, will earn lower wages. Here prejudice does lead to discrimination, even in the long run.

Statistical Discrimination

A final type of discrimination, called **statistical discrimination**, may be the most stubborn of all and can exist even where there is no prejudice. Here is an important example. It is, of course, a fact that only women can have babies. It is also a fact that many, though certainly not all, working women who have babies quit their jobs (at least for a while) to care for their newborns. Employers know this. What they cannot know, however, is *which* women of child-bearing age are likely to drop out of the labour force for this reason.

Suppose three candidates apply for a job that requires a long-term commitment. Susan plans to quit after a few years to raise a family. Jane does not plan to have any children. Jack is a man. If the employer knew all the facts, he would prefer either Jane or Jack to Susan but would be indifferent between Jane and Jack. Instead, he presumes that both Jane and Susan, being young women, are more likely to quit to raise a family than Jack is; so he hires Jack, even though Jane is just as good a prospect. Jane is discriminated against.[11]

Statistical discrimination is said to occur when the productivity of a particular worker is estimated to be low just because that worker belongs to a particular group (such as women).

With regard to the two questions with which we began this section, then, we conclude that different types of *discrimination* lead to different answers. Prejudice often but not always leads to economic discrimination. And discrimination may occur in the absence of prejudice. Finally, the forces of competition tend to erode some, but not all, of the inequities caused by discrimination. And, as we have seen, the victims of discrimination are not the only losers; society as a whole loses whenever discriminatory practices impair economic efficiency. Hence, most observers feel that we should not rely on market forces *alone* to combat discrimination. The government has a clear role to play.

---

[11] Lest it be thought that this example justifies discrimination against women, it should be pointed out that women generally have less job turnover and absenteeism for non-pregnancy health reasons than men do. Furthermore, it can be argued that because society attaches utility to the species' continuing, women produce external economies by having children and therefore are entitled to compensation by society in excess of their productivity within a firm.

Policies to Combat Discrimination

The policies that we considered earlier in this chapter for combatting poverty or reducing income inequality are all based on taxes and transfer payments—on moving dollars from one set of hands to another. This has not been the approach used to fight discrimination. Instead, governments have decided to make it *illegal* to discriminate.

Originally, it was thought that the problem could best be attacked by outlawing discrimination in rates of pay and in hiring standards—and by devoting resources to enforcement of these provisions. While progress toward the elimination of discrimination according to race and sex was made during the 1960s and 1970s and will undoubtedly continue in the context of the Canadian Charter of Rights and Freedoms, some people have felt the pace has been too slow. One reason is that discrimination in the labour market has proved to be more subtle than was first thought. Officials can rarely find proof that unequal pay is being given for work of equal value, because determining when work is "of equal value" has turned out to be a formidable task.

In the early 1970s in the United States, a new wrinkle was added. Firms and other organizations with a suspiciously small representation of minority groups or women in their work forces are required not only to end discriminatory practices, but also to demonstrate that they are taking **affirmative action** to remedy this imbalance. That is, they have to *prove* that they are making efforts to locate members of minority groups and females and to hire them if they prove to be qualified.

This approach to fighting discrimination is highly controversial. Critics claim that affirmative action really means hiring quotas and compulsory hiring of unqualified workers simply because they are female or members of a minority group. Proponents counter that, without affirmative action, discriminatory employers would simply claim they could not find qualified minority or female employees. The difficulty revolves around the impossibility of deciding, on *purely objective criteria*, who is "qualified" and who is not. What one person sees as government coercion to hire an unqualified applicant to fill a quota, another sees as a discriminatory employer being forced to mend his ways. Nothing in this book—or anywhere else—will teach you which view is correct in any particular instance.

A number of people have concluded that affirmative action will never put appreciable numbers of women into "men's jobs" and have sought to combat sex discrimination by setting wage rates according to some standard of **pay equity**. The argument, which has sparked acrimonious debate in recent years, runs as follows. Women are frequently discriminated against by being relegated to low-paying occupations while men get the better-paid jobs. To remedy the resulting wage disparities, the government should use job evaluations to decide which men's and women's jobs are comparable and then insist that employers pay equal wages to jobs judged to be of comparable worth.

Critics of pay equity scoff at the idea that the government can decide the relative values of different jobs on objective criteria. The forces of supply and demand described in Chapter 29, they argue, are the only sensible way to set relative wages. The wages that emerge from the marketplace reflect both the marginal revenue products in the various occupations and the availability of labour to each. Any other wages invite shortages in some occupations, and cause others to be besieged by a surplus of applicants.

The controversies over affirmative action and pay equity are excellent examples of the trade-off between equality and efficiency. Without a doubt, giving more high-paying jobs to members of minority groups and to women, or raising the wages of low-paid workers, would move society's Lorenz curve in the direction of greater equality. Supporters of pay equity and affirmative action seek this result. But if affirmative action disrupts industry and requires firms to replace "qualified" workers with "less qualified" workers, the nation's productivity may fall. And if pay equity creates chronic surpluses in some occupations and shortages in others, economic efficiency may suffer. Opponents of these policies are greatly troubled by these

Affirmative action refers to active efforts to locate and hire members of minority groups.

Pay equity involves classifying jobs by objective criteria and forcing employers to pay equal wages for the jobs judged to be of comparable worth.

Ontario's Experiment with Pay Equity

Ontario is now being closely watched by the world as the first major jurisdiction to require private businesses to devise and implement standards of comparable worth. The task is not easy, and it has yet to be seen whether the scheme proves to be sufficiently comprehensive and whether it achieves its intended results. Nonetheless, the attempt itself is new and dramatic enough to capture world attention, as evidenced by the following article from the influential *Wall Street Journal*.

It seems [as though] nurses and pastry chefs wouldn't have much in common. But at one suburban Toronto hospital, they have been deemed equally valuable, and therefore will get paid the same.

Because of a new Ontario law on "pay equity," employers in the province are wrestling with how to compare jobs as diverse as secretaries and warehouse workers, janitors and telephone operators....

While many Ontario employers have come up with workable pay-equity plans, others have stumbled, failing to meet the deadline or angering employees. The suburban Toronto nurses, for instance, were annoyed at being equated with chefs. In a few cases, some strange new inequities have been created.

"When you compare secretaries to truck drivers, both are offended. There's nothing more sensitive than a person's self-esteem," said Belinda Morin, a Toronto consultant who has helped companies draw up pay-equity plans.

... There have been comparable-worth pay disputes in Canada and the U.S. before, but most have been dealt with in the courts through employee lawsuits, not legislation....

... Under the [new] law, if "women's jobs" pay less than "men's jobs" of equal value, then the women must get raises.... Ontario's Pay Equity Commission reckons that raises at most companies will total about 3% or 4% of current payroll....

... Determining the "worth" of dissimilar jobs is so daunting that the provincial government itself failed to meet the Jan. 1 deadline for posting a plan. So did about 20% of the private employers....

potential losses. How far should such policies be pushed? A good question, but one without a good answer.

Some evidence on how pay equity works can be had by considering the experience of other countries. Australia has had equal-pay legislation since 1969; since that time women's pay has risen from 66 percent to more than 85 percent of men's (even though the legislation was phased in gradually over several years in the early 1970s). Major labour-market imbalances do not seem to have emerged. One thing that has helped the success of the Australian policy is that the country's wage-setting was already very centralized, so an institutional structure that permitted the government to co-ordinate with firms and unions concerning job classifications was already in place. In contrast to Australia is the European Community, which has required member countries to have pay-equity legislation for both public and private sectors since 1975. But the European countries have few enforcement mechanisms, so the wage gap between men and women remains about equal to that observed in North America. Some changes are occurring, however. In Britain, for example, Prime Minister Margaret Thatcher toughened pay-equity laws in 1983 after the European court ruled that the country was not complying with the European Community requirements. In 1988, Ontario introduced the most thorough pay-equity laws in the world (see the accompanying boxed insert). The provincial act stipulates that government departments and

"I am an equal opportunity employer. That's why I've decided to give all the other employers an equal opportunity at your services."

agencies, along with the 700 private-sector companies in the province that employ more than 500 workers, must submit their detailed implementation plans in 1990, and that pay equity must be achieved within five years.

While it remains to be seen how the pros and cons of particular pay-equity laws work out, a more definite analysis can be given concerning other policies aimed at women's rights on the job market. For example, paternity leave should be as available as maternity leave. With only the institution of maternity leave, the demand for female labour is reduced because the relative cost of employing women is increased.

Equality versus Efficiency

The Politics and Economics of Inequality

It is apparent that the trade-off between equality and efficiency is not widely understood. Social reformers often argue that society should adopt even the most outlandish programs to increase income equality or eradicate poverty, regardless of the potential side effects these policies might have. Defenders of the status quo, for their part, often seem so obsessed with these undesirable side effects—whether real or imagined—that they ignore the benefits of redistribution programs.

The continuing debate over supply-side economics is a good illustration. Many of the tax incentives supported by supply-siders, such as the elimination of taxes on the first $100,000 of capital gains, are clearly of greatest benefit to the wealthy. The poor, after all, do not own much corporate stock. On the other hand, measures such as this one are designed to increase the incentives to save and invest, and if they are successful, the whole nation will benefit from the resulting increase in productivity. The more zealous advocates of supply-side initiatives trumpet the hoped-for gains in productivity and show little appreciation of the harmful effects on income equality. Some of their opponents vocally decry the widening of income differentials and show little concern for increasing the nation's productivity. Each side claims to have a monopoly on virtue. Neither one has.

Economists try not to paint these issues in black and white. They prefer to phrase things in terms of trade-offs—to reap gains on one front, you must often make sacrifices on another. A policy is not necessarily ill-conceived simply because it has an undesirable effect on income inequality, *if* it makes an important enough contribution to productivity. On the other hand, policies with very bad distributive consequences may deserve to be rejected, even if they would raise GDP.

Admitting that there is a trade-off between equality and efficiency—that while supply-side tax cuts may help solve the productivity problem, they may also increase income inequality—may not be the best way to win votes, but it does face the facts. And in that way the admission helps us make the inherently political decisions about what should be done.

The Optimal Amount of Inequality

We have seen that substantial income inequality exists in Canada and have noted some reasons for it. Let us now ask a question that is loaded with value judgments, but to which economic analysis has something to contribute nonetheless: *How much inequality is the ideal amount?* We shall not, of course, be able to give a numerical answer to this question. No one can do that. Our objective is rather to see the type of analysis that is relevant to answering the question. We begin in a simple setting in which the answer is easily obtained. Then we shall see how the real world differs from this simple model.

Consider a world in which there are two people, Smith and Jones, and suppose

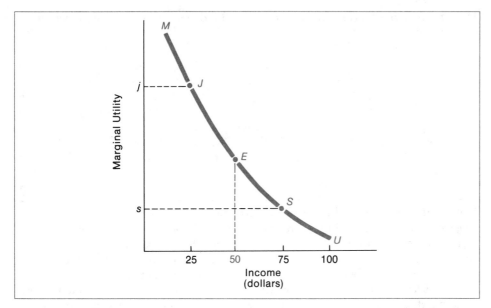

FIGURE 30–11
The Optimal Distribution of Income
If Smith and Jones have the identical marginal utility schedule (the curve *MU*), then the optimal way to distribute $100 between them is to give $50 to each (point *E*). If income is not distributed this way, then their marginal utilities will be unequal, so that a redistribution of income can make society better off. This is illustrated by points *J* and *S*, representing an income distribution in which Jones gets $25 (and hence has marginal utility *j*), while Smith gets $75 (and hence has marginal utility *s*).

that we want to divide $100 between them in the way that yields the most *total utility*. Suppose further that Smith and Jones are alike in their ability to enjoy money; technically, we say that their *marginal utility* schedules are identical.[12] This identical marginal utility schedule is depicted in Figure 30–11. We can prove the following result: *The optimal distribution of income is to give $50 to Smith and $50 to Jones*, which is point *E* in Figure 30–11.

To prove it, we show that if the income distribution is unequal, we can improve things by moving closer to equality. So suppose that Smith has $75 (point *S* in the figure) and Jones has $25 (point *J*). Then, as we can see, because of the law of diminishing marginal utility, Smith's *marginal* utility (which is *s*) must be *less* than Jones's (which is *j*). If we take $1 away from Smith, Smith *loses* the low marginal utility, *s*, of a dollar to him. Then, when we give it to Jones, Jones *gains* the high marginal utility, *j*, that a dollar gives him. On balance, then, society's total utility must rise by *j* − *s* because Jones's gain exceeds Smith's loss. Therefore, a distribution with Smith getting only $74 is better than one in which he gets $75. Since the same argument can be used to show that a $73–$27 distribution is better than $74–$26, and so on, we have established our result that a $50–$50 distribution—point *E*—is best.

Now in this argument there is nothing special about the fact that we assumed only two people or that exactly $100 was available. Any number of people and dollars would do as well. What really *is* crucial is our assumption that the same amount of money would be available no matter how we chose to distribute it. Thus we have proved the following general result:

To maximize total utility, the best way to distribute any fixed amount of money among people with identical marginal utility schedules is to divide it equally.

The Trade-Off between Equality and Efficiency

If we seek to apply this analysis to the real world, two major difficulties arise. First, people are different and have different marginal utility schedules. Thus *some* inequality can probably be justified.[13] The second problem is much more formidable.

[12] If you need to refresh your memory about marginal utility, see Chapter 19, especially pages 407–408.

[13] It can be shown, however, that if we know that people differ but cannot tell who has the higher marginal utility schedule, then the best way to distribute income is still in equal shares.

The total amount of income in our society is *not* independent of the ways in which we try to distribute it.

To see this in an extreme form, ask yourself the following question: What would happen if we tried to achieve perfect equality by putting a 100 percent income tax on all workers and then dividing the tax receipts equally among the population? No one would have any incentive to work, to invest, to take risks, or to do anything else to earn money, because the rewards for all such activities would disappear. The gross domestic product would fall drastically. While the example is extreme, the same principle applies to more moderate policies to equalize incomes; indeed, it is the basic idea behind supply-side economics.

The Trade-Off between Equality and Efficiency
Policies that redistribute income reduce the rewards of high-income earners while raising the rewards of low-income earners. Hence they reduce the incentive to earn high income. This gives rise to a trade-off that is one of the most fundamental in all of economics and one of our **12 Ideas for Beyond the Final Exam**.

Measures taken to increase the amount of economic equality will often reduce economic efficiency—that is, lower the gross domestic product. In trying to divide the pie more equally, we may inadvertently reduce its size.

Because of this trade-off, the result that equal incomes are always optimal does not apply to the real world. On the contrary:

The optimal distribution of income will always involve *some* inequality.

But this does not mean that attempts to reduce inequality are always misguided. What we should learn from this analysis are two things:

1. There are better and worse ways to promote equality. In pursuing further income equality (or fighting poverty), we should seek policies that do the least possible harm to incentives.
2. Equality is bought at a price. Thus, like any commodity, we must decide rationally how much to purchase. We will probably want to spend some of our potential income on equality, but not all of it.

Figure 30–12 illustrates both these lessons. The curve *abcde* represents possible combinations of GDP and income equality that are obtainable under the present system of taxes and transfers. If, for example, point *c* is the current position of the economy, raising taxes on the rich to finance more transfers to the poor might move us downward to the right, toward point *d*. Equality increases, but GDP falls as the rich react to higher marginal tax rates by producing less. Similarly, reducing both taxes and social-welfare programs might move us upward to the left, toward point *b*. Notice that, to the left of point *b*, GDP falls as inequality rises. This might be because very poorly paid workers are less productive due to inadequate investments in human capital, poor nutrition, or just a general sense of disaffection. The curve *ABCDE* represents possible combinations of GDP and equality under some new, more efficient, redistributive policy. It is more efficient in the sense that, for any desired level of equality, we can get more GDP with the policy represented by *ABCDE* than with the policy represented by *abcde*.

The first lesson is that we should stick to the higher of the two curves. Any point chosen on curve *abcde* can be improved upon by moving to the corresponding point on curve *ABCDE*. By picking the more efficient redistributive policy, we can have more equality *and* more GDP.

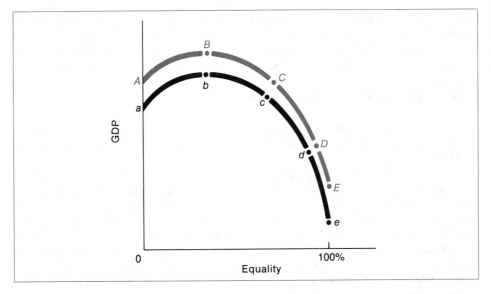

FIGURE 30-12
The Trade-Off between Equality and Efficiency
This diagram represents the fundamental trade-off between equality and efficiency. If the economy is initially at point c, then movements toward greater equality (to the right) normally can be achieved only by reducing economic efficiency, and thus reducing the gross national product. The movements from points C and c toward points D and d represent two alternative policies for equalizing the income distribution. The policy that leads to D is preferred since it is more efficient.

The second lesson is that neither point B nor point E would normally be society's optimal choice. At point B we are seeking the highest possible GDP with utter disregard for whatever inequality might accompany it. At point E we are forcing complete equality, even if work incentives vanish and a very low GDP is the result.

It is astonishing how much confusion is caused by a failure to understand these two lessons. Proponents of measures that further economic equality often feel obligated to deny that their programs will have any harmful effects on incentives. At times these vehement denials are so obviously unrealistic that they undermine the very case that the egalitarians are trying to defend. Conservatives who oppose these policies also undercut the strength of their case by making outlandish claims about the efficiency losses that are likely to arise from greater equality. Neither side, it seems, is willing or able to acknowledge the basic trade-off between equality and efficiency depicted in Figure 30-12. And hence the debate generates more heat than light. Since these debates are sure to continue for the next ten or twenty years, and probably for the rest of your lives, we hope that some understanding of this trade-off stays with you well **Beyond the Final Exam**.

But just understanding the terms of the trade-off will not tell you what the right answer is. By looking at Figure 30-12, we know that the optimal amount of equality lies between points B and E, but we do not know what it actually is. Is it something like point D, with more equality and less GDP than we now have? Or is it a movement back toward point B? Everyone will have a different answer to this question, because it is basically a question of value judgment. Just how much is more equality worth to you?

We noted earlier in this chapter that many economists recommend a negative income tax (NIT) system. In terms of Figure 30-12, they believe that it would be more efficient to redistribute income through an NIT system than through the existing welfare system. The NIT is curve *ABCDE*, while the present system is curve *abcde*. If this view is correct, then by replacing the current welfare system with the NIT, we could have more equality *and* more efficiency at the same time. But this does not mean that equalization would become costless. The curve *ABCDE* still slopes downward—by increasing equality, we still diminish the GDP.

The late Arthur Okun, an influential American economist, used the following analogy to illustrate the issue. Imagine that money is liquid and that you have a bucket you can use to transport money from the rich to the poor. The problem is that the bucket is leaky. As you move the money, some gets lost. Will you use the bucket if only one cent is lost for each one dollar you move? Probably everyone would say yes. But what if each dollar taken from the rich results in only 10 cents for the poor? Only the most extreme egalitarians will still say yes. Now try the hard questions. What if 20 cents to 40 cents is lost for each dollar that you move? If you can answer questions like these, you can decide how far down the hill from point *B* you think society should travel, for you will have expressed your value judgments in quantitative terms.

Postscript on the Distribution of Income

Now that we have completed our analysis of the distribution of income, it may be useful to see how it all relates to our central theme: What does the market do well, and what does it do poorly?

We have learned that a market economy uses the marginal productivity principle to assign an income to each individual. In so doing, the market attaches high prices to scarce factors and low prices to abundant ones and thus guides firms to make *efficient* use of society's resources. This is one of the market's great strengths. However, by attaching high prices to some factors and low prices to others, the market mechanism often creates a distribution of income that is quite unequal; some people wind up fabulously rich while others wind up miserably poor. For this reason, the market has been widely criticized for centuries for doing a rather poor job of distributing income in accord with commonly held notions of *fairness* and *equity*.

On balance, most observers feel that the criticism is justified: The market mechanism is extraordinarily good at promoting efficiency but rather bad at promoting equality. As we said at the outset, the market has both virtues and vices.

Summary

1. Because of tax shelters, the personal income tax has not been as progressive as it might be. Nonetheless, it is a progressive tax. Many other taxes, by contrast, are regressive.

2. Sales taxes are more efficient than income taxes, since income taxes discourage saving. With lower saving, firms invest less in new plant and equipment, which results in lower per-capita incomes in the future. The disadvantage of the sales tax, however, is that it is regressive.

3. The controversial goods and services tax (GST) was designed to replace the manufacturers' sales tax (MST) —a tax that raised the cost of business inputs and so put Canadian producers at a cost disadvantage in relation to foreign firms. The new tax is supplemented by an income-tax credit scheme, making the package less regressive than a sales tax is on its own. Nevertheless, the GST has remained very unpopular, because most Canadians regard it as a mechanism that could facilitate a big tax grab on the part of the government in the future.

4. There are three concepts of fair or "equitable" taxation that occasionally conflict. Horizontal equity simply calls for equals to be treated equally. Vertical equity, which calls for unequals to be treated unequally, has often been translated into the ability-to-pay principle—that people who are more able to pay taxes should be taxed more heavily. The benefits principle of tax equity ignores ability to pay and seeks to tax people according to the benefits they receive.

5. The burden of a tax is the amount of money an individual would have to be given to make her as well off with the tax as she was without it. This burden normally exceeds the taxes that are paid; the difference between the two is called the excess burden of the tax.

6. Excess burden arises when a tax induces some people or firms to change their behaviour. Excess burdens represent economic inefficiencies, so the basic principle of efficient taxation is to utilize taxes that have small excess burdens.

7. When people change their behaviour in response to a tax, they often shift the burden of the tax onto someone else. This is why the "flypaper theory of tax incidence" —the belief that the burden of any tax always stays where government puts it—is often incorrect.

8. The burden of a sales or excise tax is normally shared between suppliers and consumers. The manner in which it is shared depends on the elasticities of supply and demand.

9. A payroll tax is like an excise tax on labour services. Since the supply of labour is much less elastic than the demand for labour, workers bear most of the burden of the payroll tax. This includes both the employer's "share" and the employee's "share" of the tax.

10. The corporate profits tax can be treated like an excise tax on capital's services. Since the supply of capital is much more elastic than the demand for capital, buyers of the products produced by capital bear most of the burden of the tax.

11. Sometimes, "inefficient" taxes—that is, taxes that cause a good deal of excess burden—are nonetheless desirable because the changes in behaviour they induce further some other social goal.

12. When there are inefficiencies in the system for reasons other than the tax system (for example, externalities), taxation can improve efficiency.

13. When both equity and efficiency are considered, many economists feel that a general personal income tax is one of the best ways to raise revenue. A sales tax may be superior on efficiency grounds (since it does not involve a disincentive for saving), but in the absence of a wealth tax (such as an inheritance tax), the sales tax is inferior on equity grounds.

14. Substantial progress toward eliminating poverty was made during the 1970s; the percentage of families living below the poverty line fell from 23 percent to 15 percent. However, because of the severe recession of the early 1980s, the poverty rate did not improve during that decade.

15. The difficulty in agreeing on a sharp dividing line between the poor and the non-poor leads one to broaden the problem of poverty into the problem of inequality in incomes.

16. In Canada in 1988, the richest 20 percent of families received 39.2 percent of the income, while the poorest 20 percent of families received just above 6.5 percent. These numbers have changed little over the past twenty years and represent an average level of inequality when compared with other advanced industrial nations.

17. Individual incomes differ for many reasons, one of which is discrimination. Prejudice against members of a minority group or against women may lead to discrimination in rates of pay, or to segregation in the workplace, or to both. However, discrimination may also arise even when there is no prejudice (this is called statistical discrimination).

18. There is a trade-off between the goals of reducing inequality and enhancing economic efficiency: Policies that help on the equality front normally harm efficiency, and vice versa. This is one of the 12 **Ideas for Beyond the Final Exam.**

19. Because of this trade-off, there is an optimal degree of inequality for any society. Society finds this optimum in the same way that a consumer decides how much to buy of different commodities: The trade-off tells us how costly it is to "purchase" more equality, and preferences then determine how much should be "bought." However, since people differ in their value judgments about the importance of equality, there will inevitably be disagreement over the ideal amount of equality.

20. There may, however, be some hope of reaching agreement over the policies to use in pursuit of whatever goal for equality is selected. This is because more-efficient redistributive policies let us buy any amount of equality at a lower price in terms of lost output. Economists claim on these grounds, for example, that a negative income tax is preferable to our current welfare system.

21. Even the negative income tax, though, is no panacea. Its primary virtue lies in the way it preserves incentives to work. But if this is done by keeping the tax rate low, then either the minimum guaranteed level of income will have to be very low or many non-poor families will become eligible to receive benefits.

22. The goal of income equality is also pursued through the tax system, especially through the progressive income tax. However, because of tax shelters, the equalization achieved by this tax is much less than is commonly believed. In addition, taxes other than income taxes are typically regressive, as are many government expenditure programs, so the government sector as a whole is slightly regressive.

Concepts for Review

Progressive, proportional, and regressive taxes	Property tax	Poverty line
Corporate profits tax	Fiscal federalism	Absolute and relative concepts of poverty
Excise tax	Horizontal and vertical equity	Lorenz curve
Direct and indirect taxes	Tax deductions and credits	Economic discrimination
Value-added tax	Ability-to-pay principle	Statistical discrimination
Personal income tax	Benefits principle of taxation	Optimal amount of inequality
Payroll tax	Burden of a tax	Trade-off between equality and efficiency
Average and marginal tax rates	Excess burden	Negative income tax (NIT)
Tax shelters	Incidence of a tax	Pay equity
Capital gain	Flypaper theory of tax incidence	Affirmative action
	Tax shifting	

Questions for Discussion

1. "If the federal government continues to raise taxes as it has been doing, it will ruin the country." Comment.

2. Using the following hypothetical income-tax table, compute the marginal and average tax rates. Is the tax progressive, proportional, or regressive?

INCOME (dollars)	TAX (dollars)
10,000	0
20,000	2,400
30,000	4,800
40,000	7,200

3. Which concept of tax equity, if any, seems to be served by each of the following?
   a. The progressive income tax.
   b. The excise tax on liquor.
   c. The property tax.

4. Think of some tax that you personally pay. What steps have you taken or could you take to reduce your tax payments? Is there an excess burden on you? Why or why not?

5. Suppose the supply and demand schedules for cigarettes are as follow:

PRICE PER PACK (dollars)	QUANTITY DEMANDED (millions of packs per year)	QUANTITY SUPPLIED (millions of packs per year)
3.00	360	160
3.25	330	180
3.50	300	200
3.75	270	220
4.00	240	240
4.25	210	260
4.50	180	280
4.75	150	300
5.00	120	320

   a. What is the equilibrium price and equilibrium quantity?
   b. Now the government levies a $1.25 per pack excise tax on cigarettes. What is the equilibrium price paid by consumers, price received by producers, and quantity now?
   c. Explain why it makes no difference whether the government levies the $1.25 tax on the consumer or the producer. (Relate your answer to the discussion of the payroll tax on pages 694–95 of the text.)
   d. Suppose the tax is levied on the producers. How much of the tax are they able to shift onto consumers? Explain how they manage to do this.
   e. Is there any excess burden from this tax? Why? Who bears this excess burden?
   f. By how much does cigarette consumption decline on account of the tax? Why might the government be happy about this outcome, despite the excess burden?

6. The country of Taxmania produces only two commodities: rice and caviar. The poor spend all their income on rice, while the rich purchase both goods. Both demand for and supply of rice are quite inelastic. In the caviar market, both supply and demand are quite elastic. Which good would be heavily taxed if Taxmanians cared most about efficiency? What if they cared most about vertical equity?

7. Using the leaky-bucket analogy (pages 715–16), explain why economists believe that replacing the present welfare system with a negative income tax would help reduce the leak.

8. Suppose you were to design a negative-income-tax system for Canada. Pick a guaranteed income level and a tax rate that seem reasonable to you. What break-even level of income is implied by these choices? For the plan you have just devised, construct a corresponding version of Table 30–6 (page 705).

9. Below is a complete list of the distribution of income in Canada's Wonderland. From these data, construct a Lorenz curve for Canada's Wonderland.

NAME	INCOME
Fred Flintstone	$100,000
Barney Rubble	172,000
Ticket taker	16,000
Yogi Bear	68,000
Boo-Boo	44,000

How different is this from the Lorenz curve for Canada (Figure 30–8, on page 702)?

10. Suppose you were assigned the task of defining the poor. Would you choose an absolute or a relative concept of poverty? Why? What would be your specific definition of poverty?

11. Discuss the concept of the "optimal amount of inequality." What are some of the practical problems in determining how much inequality really is optimal? Use the issue of capital gains taxation as an example to make your answer more specific.

31

Regulation of Industry and Competition Policy

The free enterprise system is absolutely too important to be left to the voluntary action of the marketplace.

A U.S. CONGRESSMAN (1979)

Because the market system may not function ideally in monopolistic or oligopolistic industries, governments have frequently intervened in these areas. In Canada, such intervention has followed two basic patterns. The Competition Act seeks to prohibit the acquisition of monopoly power and to ban certain monopolistic practices. In addition, some firms have been subjected to **regulation**, which constrains their pricing policies and other decisions.

In the first part of this chapter, we discuss the reasons for, and the effectiveness of, regulation. We find that despite the good intentions of its designers, the regulatory mechanism, particularly in the form it took before the 1980s, was criticized on the grounds that while its cost to the consuming public was high, it did not protect their interests effectively. We explain the nature of the problems involved and the steps, many of them suggested by simple economic theory, that have been taken since the late 1970s to remedy those problems. We also discuss some recent moves toward deregulation (that is, reducing the number of regulations and the powers of the regulatory agencies) and privatization (that is, reversing earlier policy decisions to nationalize certain firms). Much of our discussion deals with regulatory restrictions of *pricing* by the firm under regulatory control. Regulators control a variety of economic activities other than pricing, as we note, but price-setting rules and their consequences for economic welfare are most easily analyzed with the help of the tools studied in previous chapters of this book.

The second part of the chapter explores our Competition Act. This piece of legislation—the main instrument of the government's **competition policy**—attempts to control the growth of monopoly and to prevent firms from engaging in "undesirable" practices. Firms violating competition laws risk a lawsuit from the federal government, which can seek a ruling that both prevents the practice from recurring and punishes the offender by imposing fines or even prison terms. As in the first part of the chapter, on regulation, we reach the conclusion that government policy in this area has not been very successful.

Regulation of industry is a process established by law that restricts or controls some specified decisions made by the affected firms. Regulation is usually carried out by a special government agency assigned the task of administering and interpreting the law. That agency also acts as a court in enforcing the regulatory laws.

Monopoly, Regulation, and Nationalization

In the Western economies, certain industries have traditionally been run as monopolies. These include postal services, electricity generation, transportation, and gas supply. Since there are no competitive pressures to protect the interests of consumers from monopolistic exploitation in these cases, it is generally agreed that some substitute form of protection from excessive prices and restricted outputs is needed.

Most of Western Europe has adopted **nationalization** as its solution, which means that the state owns and operates certain monopolistic industries. In Canada, we seem to have been reluctant to go as far as the Europeans, but we have nonetheless had significant elements of nationalization. For example, most cities run their own public transportation systems, and numerous Crown corporations either exist today (for example, Via Rail) or have existed until recently (for example, Air Canada).

The main instrument of control of public utility industries in Canada, however, is the regulatory agency. The federal and provincial governments have created a large number of agencies that regulate prices, standards of service, provisions for safety, and a variety of other aspects of the operations of telephone companies, radio and television stations, electric utilities, airlines, trucking companies, and firms in many other industries (such as car insurance, where, in some provinces, companies must comply with no-fault provisions). Many of these industries are not pure monopolies but include firms that are nevertheless suspected of possessing so much market power that their regulation is considered to be in the public interest.

A Puzzle: Industry Opposition to Deregulation

An observer who knew nothing about regulated industries might expect that deregulation would be welcomed by the firms affected. After all, regulations curb their freedom of decision-making in many ways.

Yet most companies—and their unions—fight bitterly against proposals for deregulation. Later, we will discuss some of the reasons for this opposition. But already we may surmise from this observation that regulation may, inadvertently or deliberately, have been serving the interests of some of the regulated firms, rather than making life harder for them.

The Degree of Regulation in Canada

Regulation is extensive in Canada: The proportion of national product that is subject to direct regulation is 29 percent, and this figure does not record the share in GDP of the industries that are "self-regulated." (Self-regulated industries are those that the elected bodies—in most cases provincial legislatures—have given *carte blanche* to set their own rules of practice, and in many cases, their own charges. Industries that are self-regulated include medicine, law, and dentistry.)

In 1980, the Bureau of Competition Policy in the federal department of Consumer and Corporate Affairs established a Regulated Sector Branch. The staff of this branch appear before federal and provincial regulatory bodies to argue on behalf of greater competition. They have, for example, argued for greater recognition of the costs that agricultural marketing boards impose on the consumer.

Agricultural marketing boards are pervasive in Canada. The products they affect include chickens, turkeys, tobacco, and well over a *hundred* others. If it were not for the existence of the provincial marketing boards, which set quotas for individual suppliers, these agricultural industries would be competitive. Hence, in these cases, the whole point of regulation is to *create* monopoly power, so that total market supply can be managed. The purpose of this policy is to create higher and more stable incomes for farmers. While consumers lose from this policy, and there are often calls to do away with agricultural marketing boards, these boards seem destined to survive until more-efficient and more-equitable methods of maintaining farm incomes are broadly understood to be available.

We limit our discussion of agricultural marketing boards to the boxed insert on pages 722–23, since, in this chapter, we wish to concentrate on government regulation that is at least *intended* to *reduce* monopoly practices.

Why Regulation?

As we learned in Chapters 21 and 25, one main reason for regulation of industry is the phenomenon of **natural monopoly**. In some industries it is apparently far cheaper to have production carried out by one firm than by a number of different firms. This situation may occur for several reasons.

Economies of Scale and Scope

One reason why this may occur is because of economies of large-scale production. An example of such **economies of scale** is a railroad track, which can carry 100 trains a day with total cost hardly higher than when it carries one. Here is a case in which savings are made possible by expanding the volume of an activity—a case of economies of scale. As we saw in Chapter 22, scale economies lead to an average-cost curve that goes downhill as output increases (see Figure 31–1). This means that a firm with a large output can cover its costs at a price lower than that of a firm whose output is smaller. In Figure 31–1 point A represents the larger firm, whose AC is $5, while B is the smaller firm, with AC = $7.

> **Economies of scale** are savings that are acquired through increases in quantities produced.

Another reason a single large firm may have a cost advantage over a group of small firms is that it is sometimes cheaper to produce a number of *different commodities together* than to turn them out separately, each by a different firm. The saving made possible by simultaneous production of many different products is called **economies of scope**. An example of economies of scope is the manufacture of both cars and trucks by the same producer. The techniques employed in producing both commodities are sufficiently similar to make specialized production by different firms impractical.

> **Economies of scope** are savings that are acquired through simultaneous production of many different products.

In industries where there are great economies of scale *and* scope, society will obviously incur a significant cost penalty if it insists on maintaining a large number of firms. Supply by a number of smaller competing firms will be far more costly and use up far larger quantities of resources than will supply by a monopoly. Moreover, in the presence of strong economies of scale and scope, society *will not be able to preserve free competition, even if it wants to*. The large, multiproduct firm will have so great a cost advantage over its rivals that the small firms will simply be unable to survive. We say in such a case that free competition is *not sustainable*.

Where monopoly production is cheapest and where free competition is not sustainable, the industry is a natural monopoly. Because monopoly is cheaper, society may not

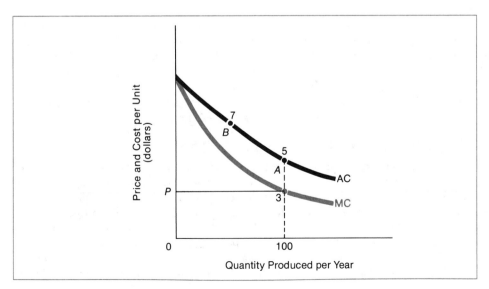

FIGURE 31–1
Economies of Scale
Economies of scale imply that the average-cost (AC) curve is declining, and therefore that the marginal-cost (MC) curve is below the average-cost curve. In such a case, the first firm to become large has the lowest costs and drives others out of business. If a regulator forces the remaining large firm to produce 100 units and charge a price equal to its marginal cost ($3 per unit), then that firm will take in $300 in revenues. But, since its average cost at 100 units is $5 per unit, its total cost will be $500, and the firm will lose money.

Agricultural Marketing Boards

The thrust of the government's overall regulatory program is to reverse or forestall monopoly behaviour—that is, to force prices and profit levels down. Similarly, the Competition Act itself, which we study later in this chapter, is intended to stop firms from colluding and operating like a monopolist. But concern for low incomes in agriculture has led to the opposite approach in the regulation of many agricultural industries. In this area, our laws permit firms to band together as a monopoly in what are known as marketing boards. If a majority of firms producing a particular farm product vote in favour of the formation of a marketing board, *all* such firms are required by law to sell through the board and to obey the quotas on sales that it imposes.

To see why a marketing board always establishes and enforces quotas, consider the accompanying diagram. Panel (a) depicts the demand and supply curves of a given competitive industry, while panel (b) shows the situation of one of the numerous firms within that industry. Assume that the competitive industry is in full long-run equilibrium—at point *A* in both diagrams—before the marketing board is formed.

Now suppose the producers band together and the executive of the newly formed marketing board decides to dictate a higher price, indicated by the horizontal green line in the diagram. This rise in price causes buyers of the industry's product to decrease their quantity demanded (to point *B* in panel [a]), so that industry output and sales are cut in half. To make sure that this cutback in production occurs, the marketing board imposes a quota on the output of each individual firm in the industry. The quota for each firm is equal to the horizontal distance from the origin to the vertical green line in panel (b). Each firm then operates at point *B*, and earns above-normal profits (indicated by the shaded rectangle).

Without the quotas, such profits could not persist. For one thing, price exceeds marginal cost at the output level given by point *B*, so firms that are already in the industry would, under normal circumstances, expand output. With all firms acting in this manner, the market price would be driven back down. A second consideration is that new firms, in the hope of acquiring a share of the above-normal profits that result from the quotas, would be tempted to enter the industry. Such an influx of new firms would also have the effect of driving the market price back down. However, the quota system is designed to preclude this possibility: New entry will *not* occur, because only the pre-existing firms are assigned a positive quota.

In recent years, agricultural marketing boards have come under attack, most commonly for the following four reasons. First, as in other industries, consumers prefer to have access to more goods at lower prices—that is, they dislike monopolies. Second, the imposition of quotas can have certain consequences that do not meet with public support—for example, millions of "unwanted" eggs and large quantities of cheese are known to have been destroyed when quotas were exceeded. The third reason frequently cited in support of eliminating marketing boards is that their existence makes it very difficult for Canada to be taken seriously when we argue in trade negotiations with other countries that *they* are indulging in too much protection of their agricultural industries. For example, in international negotiations pertaining to the wheat industry (an industry in which we have no marketing boards), Canada has been a leader in calling for all countries to reduce government subsidization of farmers. But our credibility is undermined—and any hope for improvements for our wheat farmers therefore severely threatened—when other countries can justifiably argue that Canadian authorities intervene extensively in other areas of agriculture in Canada through our system of marketing boards.

The fourth problem with marketing boards that makes them vulnerable to criticism is that, in the long run, they in

want to have competition; if free competition is not sustainable, society will not even have a choice in the matter.

But even if society reconciles itself to monopoly, it will generally not want to let the monopoly firm do whatever it wants to with its market power. Therefore, it will consider either regulation or nationalization of these firms.

Universal Service and Rate Averaging

A second reason for regulation is the desire for "universal service"; that is, the availability of service at "reasonable prices" even to small communities where the small scale of operation makes costs extremely high. In such cases, regulators have sometimes encouraged a public utility to supply services to some consumers at a financial loss. But a loss on some sales is financially feasible only when the firm is permitted to make up for it by obtaining higher profits on its other sales.

Rate averaging or **cross subsidization** means selling one product at a loss, which is balanced by higher profits on another product.

This process of **rate averaging** of gains and losses, also referred to as **cross subsidization**, is possible only if the firm is protected from price competition and free fact *fail* to raise producer incomes. Let us consider why this is so. Quotas are typically attached to farm properties; consequently, when a farm is sold, it goes for a higher price once a quota is part of the package. Competition forces the price of the property up to include the present value of the stream of extra profits that is generated by the quota—a value, for each period, equal to the shaded profit area in the diagram. This higher purchase price raises the new owner's fixed costs, causing the farm's AC curve to move up to the level at which it will cross through point *B*. Hence, those who buy into the industry *after* the quotas have been assigned get no financial benefits from them; the only beneficiaries of the quota system are the individuals who owned their farms at the time that the marketing board was originally established. And these original owners benefit from the system only in their role as landowners; as current producers, they gain nothing because their AC curves (which are based on opportunity costs) have been pushed up just as much as have those of the new farm owners. Hence, the quota system provides a one-time windfall gain for the pre-existing farm owners; as producers in any year thereafter, they do not benefit at all. Ultimately, then, the quota system is difficult to defend: It imposes real costs on society, yet fails to benefit current farmers in their role as producers.

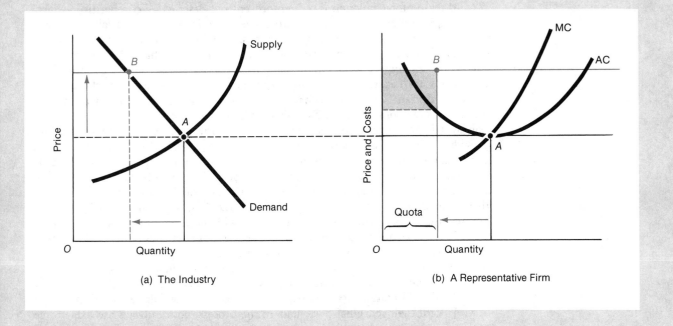

(a) The Industry

(b) A Representative Firm

entry of new competitors in its more profitable markets. If no such protection is provided by a regulatory agency, potential competitors will sniff out the profit opportunities in the markets where service is supplied at a price well above cost. Many new firms will enter the business and cause prices to be driven down in those markets. This practice is referred to as "cream skimming." The entrants choose to enter only into the profitable markets and skim away the cream of the profits for themselves, leaving the unprofitable markets (the skimmed milk) to the supplier who had attempted to provide universal service. This phenomenon is one reason regulatory rules, until recently, made it very difficult or impossible for new firms to enter when and where they saw fit.

Airlines and telecommunications are two industries in which these issues have arisen. In both cases, fears have been expressed that without regulation of entry and rates or the granting of special subsidies, less populous communities would effectively be isolated, losing their airline services and obtaining telephone service only at cripplingly high rates. Many economists question the validity of this argument for regulation, which, they say, calls for a hidden subsidy of rural consumers by all other consumers. In the United States, the airline deregulation act provided for government subsidies to help small communities attract airline service. In fact, what has happened is that this market has been taken over to a considerable extent by specialized "commuter" airlines flying much smaller aircraft than do the major airlines, which have withdrawn from many such routes.

A similar issue affects our postal service, which charges the same price to deliver a letter anywhere within the country, regardless of the distance or the special difficulties and costs of a particular route. To maintain this pricing scheme, the law must protect Canada Post from direct competition in many of its activities; otherwise, its extreme form of uniform pricing would soon deprive it of its most profitable routes.

We conclude that the goal of "universal service" leads to regulatory control of entry and exit, and not just to control of prices.

Self-Destructive Competition

A third reason for regulation is to help prevent **self-destructive competition**, which, for example, economies of scale make possible. In an industry such as rail transportation, equipment—including roadbeds, tracks, switching facilities, locomotives, and cars—is extremely expensive. Suppose that two railways, having been built and equipped, are competing for some limited business that happens to be insufficient to use their total facilities to anything near capacity. That is, to meet this level of consumer demand, each railway may have to run only 40 percent as many trains over the track as can conveniently be scheduled over that route. The management of each railway will feel that, with its unused capacity, any business will be worthwhile, provided that it covers more than its short-run marginal costs—fuel, labour, and expenses other than plant and equipment. If the short-run marginal cost of shipping an additional tonne of, say, coal is $5, then either railway will be happy to lure coal-shipping customers away from the other at a price of, say, $7 per tonne, even though that price may not cover the entire cost of track and equipment. Each tonne of business that pays $7 when marginal cost is $5 will put the railway $2 ahead of where it would have been without the business. The new business does not contribute much to the cost of the tracks or locomotives or other equipment, which must be paid for whether that business is acquired or not. Thus, even if the new business pays only for its own marginal cost and a little more, it seems financially desirable.

But the temptation to accept business on such terms will drive both firms' prices down toward their marginal costs, and, in the process, both railways are likely to go broke. If there are no customers paying for the track, the roadbed, and the equipment, the railway will simply be unable to go on. Thus, there are those who believe that regulation of rates can be sensible, even in industries subject to competitive pressures, simply to protect the firms from themselves. Without this regulation, self-destructive competition could end up sinking those industries financially, and the public would thereby be deprived of vital services.

Management of a Public Resource

A fourth reason often given for public regulation is that some industries base their operations on a public resource of limited capacity, so that a public agency must intervene to ration out that resource "fairly." The most notable example of the need for this type of rationing is radio and television broadcasting. The frequency spectrum that is currently used for broadcasting is limited, so it must be divided up among the users. If it were not divided up, and entry were not limited, the airwaves might become crowded and interference of broadcasters with one another's transmissions would undermine the quality of reception and perhaps even make the airwaves totally useless.

Many economists have argued that government has no business allocating scarce resources like the radio and TV spectrum among commercial users who employ such public resources for a profit. These economists argue that government rationing of the airwaves is a giveaway of public resources to favoured individuals, who then grow rich at the public's expense—even though the CRTC, in return, does retain some right to regulate the content of broadcasts. Rather, it is proposed that firms be required to bid against one another for licences to run radio and TV stations. In that way the licences would go to those who could make the best use of them—an ability that would be determined by their bids. The profits would then go into the public treasury rather than into private pockets, and could be used to finance non-profit public-interest activities such as public broadcasting.

Protection against Misinformation

A final reason for regulation is the danger that consumers will be misinformed or cheated; that consumers, employees, or the environment will be threatened by unscrupulous sellers; or that even conscientious sellers will be forced to keep up with the questionable practices of less-scrupulous rivals. Because some of these issues will be illustrated and examined in detail in Chapter 32 on environmental protection, the subject will not be discussed further in this chapter.

SUMMARY

There are five basic reasons for the activities of regulatory agencies:

1. The desire to prevent excess profits and other undesirable practices in an industry that is considered to be a natural monopoly.

2. The desire for universal service—that is, the desire to provide service at relatively low rates to customers whom it is particularly expensive to serve, and to do so without government subsidy.

3. The desire to prevent self-destructive price competition in multifirm industries with large capital costs and low marginal costs.

4. The desire to allocate public resources or facilities of limited capacity fairly.

5. The desire to protect customers, employees, and the environment from damage resulting from inappropriate behaviour by firms.

Why Regulators Sometimes Raise Prices

It has been suggested that regulation sometimes results in prices higher than consumers would pay in its absence. One of the most widely publicized illustrations of this tendency was the difference in U.S. air fares between San Francisco and Los Angeles and between Washington, D.C., and New York City before the United States deregulated airlines. The former fare was never regulated by the Civil Aeronautics Board because the flight is contained entirely within the state of California, whereas the board did control the interstate flight between New York and Washington, D.C. The California flight is nearly twice as long as the East Coast flight, and neither route is sparsely travelled nor beset by any other noteworthy features that would make for substantial differences in cost. Yet at the time of deregulation, fares were a little higher than $40 for the long California trip and a little higher than $50 for the short Washington–New York trip.

Why would regulators ever push for a price floor rather than a price ceiling? (This relates to the puzzle mentioned near the beginning of this chapter.) The answer is that they typically do so when they want to introduce or preserve competitors in an industry. We saw earlier that strong economies of scale and scope make it impossible for a number of smaller firms to survive. The largest firm in the industry will have such cost advantages over its competitors that it will be able to drive them out of the market while still operating at prices that are profitable. Most observers applaud low prices and price cuts that reflect such cost advantages. However, a firm that wants the market for itself may conceivably engage in price-cutting even when such cuts are not justifiable in terms of cost.

The reason such price-cutting may not reduce the overall profits of a regulated firm is that regulation often imposes an upper limit on the amount of profit a firm is permitted to earn. To see the connection, consider a regulated firm that produces two commodities, A and B, and that is setting each price below its profit-maximizing level in order to limit profits to the allowable ceilings. The firm may be able, without loss of profit, to cut the price of A even below its marginal cost and make up for any resulting decrease in profit by a sufficient rise in the price of B. In other words, the firm has instituted a *cross subsidy* from the consumers of product B to the consumers of product A. Consumers of B are paying an excessive amount for their purchase in order to make up for the deficit in the sale of product A.

Why would any firm want to do this? Suppose A is threatened by competition while B has no competitors on the horizon. Then, a cross subsidy from B to A may be a way of preventing the entry of the potential competitors of A or even of driving some current competitors out of the field.

But regulation sometimes goes beyond the prevention of cross subsidy. Firms that feel they are hurt by competitive pressures will complain to regulatory commissions that the prices charged by their rivals are "unfairly" low. The commission, afraid that unrestrained pricing will reduce the number of firms in the industry, then attempts to "equalize" matters by imposing price floors that permit all the firms in the industry to operate profitably.

Many economists maintain that this approach to pricing is a perversion of the idea of competition. The virtue of competition is that, where it occurs, firms force one another to supply consumers with products of high quality at *low* prices. Any firm that cannot do this is driven out of business by market forces. If competition does not do this, it loses its purpose, because, to the economist, it is a means to an end, not an end in itself.

An arrangement under which firms are enabled to co-exist only by *preventing* them from competing with one another preserves the appearance of competition but destroys its substance.

Some Pricing Issues

Consider the natural monopoly depicted in Figure 31–2. If this firm is left unregulated, it will choose to operate at output level *OA*, since this is the point at which MR = MC. This firm will charge a price equal to *OF*, and earn an amount of profit equal to the grey shaded area in the graph. Let us compare this unregulated outcome with the outcomes that would follow from several possible price-setting rules.

1. Average-Cost Pricing

Suppose the regulator stipulates that price can be no higher than the level that just permits the firm to earn a normal rate of profit. In the economist's language, this regulation allows zero economic profits, meaning that the stipulated price is equal to average cost. This price is shown by the height of the horizontal green line connecting points *E* and *G* in Figure 31–2. The monopoly firm is forced to operate at the price and quantity given by point *G*. Consumers appear to be better off with this outcome than with the one that occurs *without* regulation, since price is lower (distance *OE* is less than distance *OF*) and the quantity of the good available for consumption is greater (distance *OB* is greater than distance *OA*). Furthermore, society's sense of fairness is more likely to be satisfied, since monopoly profits are eliminated.

There are three problems with this average-cost pricing approach, however. The first is simply a problem of implementation. Consider that almost every company produces a number of different varieties and qualities of some product, and many

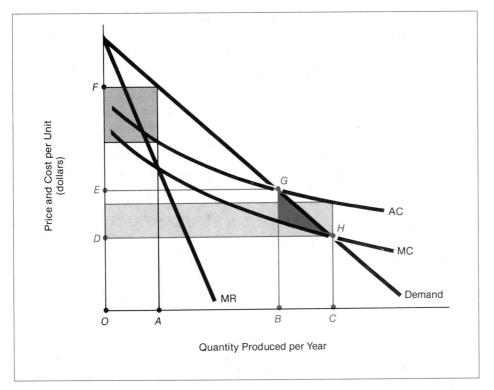

FIGURE 31-2

Alternative Regulations for a Natural Monopoly

An unregulated natural monopoly obeys the MR = MC rule, setting price to equal distance *OF* and quantity produced to equal distance *OA*, and earning profits equal to the shaded grey area. If regulated and subject to the rules of average-cost pricing, the firm is allowed to earn no more than normal (that is, zero) economic profits; it must therefore set its price equal to distance *OE* and produce a quantity equal to distance *OB*. Alternatively, if the firm is subject to the rules of marginal-cost pricing (facing a *P* = MC constraint), society's optimal-resource-allocation rule (MU = MC) is satisfied, but the firm must be subsidized by an amount equal to the area of the pale green rectangle.

firms produce thousands of different products, each with its own price. Even General Motors, a fairly specialized firm, produces many makes and sizes of cars and trucks in addition to refrigerators, washing machines, and quite a few other things. In a multiproduct firm, we cannot even define AC = TC/Q, since to calculate Q (total output) we would have to add up all the apples and oranges (and all the other different items) the firm produces. But we know that one cannot add up apples and oranges. So, since we cannot calculate AC for a multiproduct firm, it is hardly possible for the regulator to require P = AC for each of the firm's products, though regulators sometimes *think* they can do so.

Even if we ignore this implementation issue, there is a second problem. It is that the maximum-profit constraint removes the incentive for firms to invest in cost-saving innovations. After all, if whenever the firm successfully lowers the position of its AC and MC curves, the regulator automatically lowers the allowed-price line (to continue to satisfy the P = AC rule), the firm gains nothing from investing in the cost-saving innovation. This means that our comparison of the regulated firm and the unregulated firm in Figure 31–2 is somewhat misleading, in that the unregulated firm could conceivably lower its cost curves enough that it could charge a lower price and produce a higher quantity than the price and quantity levels that occur with regulation.

Here again, an actual implementation issue arises. In a number of regulated industries, a proposed change in rates is likely to take a minimum of several months before it gets through the regulatory machinery. This phenomenon, known as **regulatory lag**, is perhaps the main reason that profit regulation has not eliminated all rewards for efficiency and all penalties for inefficiency.

Suppose, for example, that the regulatory commission approves a set of prices calculated to yield exactly the "fair rate of return" to the company—say, 10 percent. If management then invests successfully in new processes, which reduce its costs sharply, the rate of return under the old prices may rise to, say, 12 percent. If it takes two years for the regulators to review the prices they previously approved and adjust them to the new cost levels, the company will earn a 2 percent bonus reward for its efficiency during the two years of regulatory lag. Similarly, if management makes a series of bad decisions, which reduce the company's return to 7 percent, the firm may well apply to the regulator for some adjustments in prices to permit it to recoup its losses. If the regulator takes eighteen months to act, the firm suffers a penalty for its inefficiency. It may be added that where mismanagement is *clearly* the cause of losses, regulators will be reluctant to permit the regulated firm to make up for such losses by rate adjustments. But in most cases it is difficult to pinpoint responsibility for a firm's losses.

All in all, those who have studied regulated industries have come away deeply concerned about the effects of regulation upon economic efficiency. Although some regulated firms seem to operate very efficiently, others seem to behave in quite the opposite way.

Although regulatory lag does permit some penalty for inefficiency and some reward for superior performance by the regulated firm, the arrangement works only in a rough-and-ready manner. It leaves unsolved one of the fundamental problems of regulation—the provision of incentives for efficiency.

The third problem with average-cost pricing is that, even if it did not involve a disincentive effect on investment in cost-saving innovations or any implementation difficulties with regard to multiproduct firms, its outcome would still be inefficient. The reason for this will become clear in the following discussion of an alternative regulation strategy—marginal-cost pricing.

2. Marginal-Cost Pricing

As noted in Chapter 25, economic efficiency requires that MU equal MC, but at point G in Figure 31–2 (the outcome point under average-cost pricing), MU exceeds MC. This inefficiency can be eliminated only by expanding output to amount OC. It seems clear, then, that the regulator should set the maximum price at the level indicated by the green line connecting points D and H in Figure 31–2. We can also see that at this price, society would benefit from the increase in quantity produced that is represented by distance BC. The value of this extra output to consumers is equal to the area below the demand curve between points B and C. And since it costs society only the amount equal to the area below the *marginal-cost* curve between points B and C to produce the extra output, the benefits to society of this higher level of output exceed the costs by an amount equal to the dark green triangular-shaped area in the graph. Thus, marginal-cost pricing is indeed preferable to average-cost pricing.

There is, however, a problem with marginal-cost pricing for a firm with a natural monopoly. Since the MC curve is forever below the AC curve, the firm would be forced to cease operation if it were confronted by this regulation. To operate at $P = MC$ would cause the firm to incur losses (equal to the area of the pale green rectangle in Figure 31–2). Thus, if marginal-cost pricing is to be pursued in a natural monopoly situation, the private firm must be either subsidized or replaced by a Crown corporation that would continue to operate at a loss.

3. The Ramsey Pricing Rule

In recent years economists have been attracted to a very imaginative third approach to the problem of pricing in regulated industries that produce a multiplicity of products. This approach derives its name from its discoverer, Frank Ramsey, a brilliant English mathematician who died in 1930, at the age of 26, after making several enduring contributions to both mathematics and economics.

The basic idea of Ramsey's pricing principle can be explained in a fairly straightforward manner. As we just explained, prices must be set *above* marginal costs if a firm with increasing returns to scale is to break even. But how much above? In effect, Ramsey argued as follows: The reason we do not like prices to be above marginal costs is that such high prices distort the choices made by consumers, leading them to buy "too little" of the goods whose prices are set way above MC. Yet, it is necessary to set prices somewhat above marginal costs to allow the firm to survive. Therefore it makes sense to raise prices *most* above marginal cost where consumers will respond the *least* to such price increases; that is, where the *elasticity of demand* is the lowest, so that price rises will create the least distortion of demand. This line of argument led Ramsey to formulate the following rule:

Ramsey Pricing Rule: Where prices must exceed marginal cost in order to permit the regulated firm to break even, the ratios of *P* to MC should be largest for those products whose elasticities of demand are the smallest.

Many economists accept this pricing rule as the correct conclusion on theoretical grounds. It has even been proposed for postal and telephone pricing.

4. Constrained Market Pricing and Stand-Alone Cost Ceilings

In the regulation of railways in the United States, that country's Interstate Commerce Commission has recently adopted a new approach to regulation explicitly derived from the theory of contestability that we mentioned in Chapter 26 (see page 582). In its decisions, the commission has recognized the value of the Ramsey pricing rule as a general guideline for policy. But the commissioners felt it was not practical to calculate statistically and update constantly all the demand-elasticity numbers and marginal-cost figures that use of the Ramsey rule requires. Instead they decided to adopt a four-part rule known as **constrained market pricing**. The intent was to compel the U.S. railways to set the prices they would have set if all of their activities were contestable— that is, to set prices as if entry into freight transportation were everywhere sufficiently easy to subject the railways to a perpetual and constant threat of new competition. The four parts of the rule are as follows:

1. For types of freight and routes where competition happens to be substantial and effective, the railways should be deregulated; that is, market forces should be allowed to do the job of policing the railways' behaviour.

2. Where competition is inadequate, a floor and a ceiling should be set for each and every railway price, with the railway companies left free to select any price level they wish within those bounds.

3. The price floor should be the lowest level to which price could fall in the long run under perfectly competitive conditions. This provision, in effect, prohibits a railway from adopting any price below marginal cost. It is designed to provide adequate and defensible protection to any railway's rivals against any attempt at unfair competitive price-cutting.

4. The price ceiling should be the cost that a *hypothetical* (that is, imaginary) efficient entrant would have to bear to supply each specific service. In other words, for activities where entry is difficult or impossible, the idea is to prohibit the railways from charging more than they could get away with if entry were easy and cheap. The hypothetical cost figure for the efficient entrant is called the **stand-alone cost** of the service. It is the cost that would be required if an efficient entrant were to

supply only the service or group of services in question. This provision is intended to protect the interests of railway customers, guaranteeing them prices no higher than those that might be charged if the markets were effectively competitive.

Most economists who have studied the issue seem to approve of this new approach to rate regulation, though there are still some disputes about details of its operation. Given the historical similarity between the American and Canadian approaches to regulation, we may expect this approach to receive attention in Canada.

Reactions to the Problems of Regulation

Deregulation plus Increased Competition

One of the most widespread approaches to solving the problems of regulation is to have regulators get out of the business, leaving much more (if not all) of the task of looking after consumer interests to the natural forces of competition. This approach is promising in areas of the economy in which competition can be expected to survive without government intervention—for example, in freight transportation, airlines, and pipelines. As a consequence, a number of economists representing a broad range of political views have been advocating at least some deregulation in these fields.

Throughout the 1980s, a significant amount of deregulation took place within the United States, and some occurred in Canada as well. It is interesting to note one aspect of this experience: In a number of cases, we observed both an increase in quantity of service and a decrease in price. Our analysis has shown that this combination of results can be explained by only two possibilities:

1. that the incentive to avoid cost-saving innovations under regulation is quantitatively important;

2. that new firms successfully entered these deregulated industries. This development proves that the industries in question were not natural monopoly situations after all. In such instances, the regulatory board must have functioned as a *preserver* of monopoly power, which would explain why firms in these industries resisted deregulation. This provides one answer to the puzzle of industry opposition to deregulation, which we noted at the beginning of this chapter.

In a number of cases, then, deregulation has been deemed successful.

Of course, deregulation will not work in industries in which self-destructive competition is likely to occur in the absence of government regulation. The experience of the U.S. airlines after the industry was deregulated offers some evidence to support this assertion. While considerable competition continues to prevail, many of the new airlines established since the end of regulation have gone bankrupt or have been purchased by the older firms. On many routes, the number of competitors has decreased sharply. This has given rise to concerns about the ability of competition to continue to protect consumer interests, at least on some of the routes. In other industries, competition is considered sufficiently weak that many think some continued regulation is indispensable. So the question remains: Which controls in those fields will not destroy incentives for efficiency?

Performance Criteria for the Permitted Rate of Return

The argument for deregulation addresses itself to all of the problems discussed in the previous section, but there are other proposals that are concerned with only one or another of these problems. We turn now to proposals designed to prevent profit controls from discouraging efficiency.

Some observers have advocated that the legally permitted rate of return not be set at a fixed number—say, 10 percent—but that it be varied from firm to firm depending on the firm's record of efficiency and performance. That is, if some measure of quality of performance can be agreed on (a measure that should take account of cost efficiency as well as product and service quality), then the better the performance score of the regulated firm, the more it would be permitted to earn. A firm that performed well in a given year might be permitted 12 percent profits for that year, whereas a firm that did badly might be allowed only 8 percent, and a firm that performed abominably might be permitted only 4 percent.

However, financial incentives cannot easily be built into rate-of-return formulas that contain no good objective criteria of performance (for example, in the railway industry, the number of minutes that trains come in behind schedule). Moreover, it is difficult to balance incentives for different aspects of performance. For example, if the formula assigns too much weight to product quality and too little to low cost, the firm will be encouraged to incur costs that are unjustifiably high from the point of view of public welfare in order to turn out products of slightly higher quality.

Institutionalized Regulatory Lag

The previous edition of this book described a third alternative, which, in the intervening three years, has been adopted in Great Britain for airport services and in the United States for telephone rates. The basic idea is for regulation to consciously take advantage of the incentive for efficiency provided by regulatory lag. Under this program, the regulators assign ceilings (*price caps*) for the product prices of the firms they oversee.

However, the price caps (measured in inflation-adjusted *real* terms) are lowered each year at a rate based on the rate of cost reduction (productivity growth) previously achieved by the regulated firm. Thus, if in the future the regulated firm can manage to achieve cost savings (by innovation or other means) greater than those it obtained in the past, the firm's real costs will fall faster than its real prices and it will be permitted to keep the resulting profits as its reward for having implemented cost-reduction programs. Of course, the catch for the regulated firm is that if it proves able to reduce its costs by, say, 2 percent per year (in real terms), but has its regulatory price cap cut by 3 percent per year on the basis of its past record, it will lose profits. Consumers, however, will continue to benefit from the cuts in real prices. Thus, in order to earn economic profits, management is constantly forced to look for ever more economical ways of doing things.

This approach clearly gives up any attempt to limit the profit of the regulated firm. Nonetheless, it protects the consumer by controlling the firm's prices—indeed, it makes those prices lower and lower, in real terms.

The Patent System

One form of incentive that government has long employed is the **patent** system, which rewards innovative firms by granting them a temporary monopoly. The patent restricts imitation and is designed to offer small-firm innovators the same advantages from their research activities as are enjoyed by innovators in industries that contain no competitors ready to erode profits by imitation. The idea is that, with the incentive of patent protection, these smaller firms will dare to challenge the larger, more monopolistic firms. Thus, somewhat ironically, while government tries to limit existing monopolies, it also creates and guarantees monopoly power for other firms. A patent acts as a temporary barrier to entry, thereby providing society with the benefits of firms' increased expenditures on innovation while protecting it from the costs associated with long-term monopoly power. Of course, sometimes the protected firms themselves grow big with the help of the protection. Once-small firms like Polaroid and Xerox grew into industrial giants with the help of government protection through the patent laws.

Questions have been raised about the effectiveness of patents in promoting expenditure on R & D, and the evidence certainly does not provide overwhelming

A **patent** is a temporary grant of monopoly rights over an innovation.

support for the view that patents constitute a strong stimulus for innovation. Questions have also been raised about the desirability of granting an innovator an unrestricted monopoly for twenty years, as the patent program now does in Canada. Similar issues have been raised about copyright (and related) laws, which restrict reproduction of written and artistic works, trademarks, and registered industrial designs.

Some Effects of Deregulation

Deregulation of industries is much more advanced in the United States than it is in Canada, although even there, it is too early to reach a final evaluation of its consequences. Nonetheless, several conclusions are becoming clear from the American experience of the past decade, and these should be borne in mind when considering the pros and cons of deregulation in Canada.

1. *Effects on prices and local services.* The first key effect of deregulation (which we have already noted above) is that prices have decreased significantly. Originally, it was feared that smaller and more isolated communities would be deprived of service because the small number of customers and the new, lower, prices would make service unprofitable. It was said that airlines, railways, and telephone companies would withdraw from such communities once they were no longer forced to stay there by the regulators.

   These worries have largely proved groundless. True, the larger airlines have left the smaller communities, as predicted. But they have usually been replaced by smaller commuter airlines that have provided, on the average, more frequent service than did their regulated predecessors. Of course, a few communities have been left without service or with service of poorer quality, but other locations have benefited considerably.

2. *Effects on profits.* Just as deregulation went into effect in the United States, a severe recession hit the North American economy. The profits of the older firms in the industry fell sharply and in many cases turned into losses. Whether deregulation or recession or both are responsible is very much disputed. Some experienced observers argue that without deregulation, losses would have been even worse, but no one can be sure.

   What was surprising was that deregulation turned out, even during the recession, to be profitable to many new entrants. A number of new airlines, trucking companies, and telephone companies either showed a profit almost at once or showed promise of becoming profitable very soon. Indeed, in airlines, trucking, and bus transportation it turned out that the new entrants, instead of suffering from a cost handicap, often had a substantial cost advantage over the older firms. The reason was that the older firms had agreed to costly union contracts under regulation.

3. *Effects on the unions.* Deregulation has badly hurt unions such as the Teamsters (of the trucking industry) and the Airline Pilots Association. In the new competitive climate, firms have been forced to make sharp cuts in their work forces and to resist wage increases and other costly changes in working conditions. Indeed, there has been strong pressure for retrenchment on all these fronts.

4. *Concentration and mergers.* Particularly in aviation and rail-freight transportation, deregulation in the United States was followed by a wave of mergers in which two firms agreed to join together or one firm agreed to be bought out by another.

   That this has happened should not be surprising since, as we saw earlier in the chapter, industries with important economies of scale are the most likely targets for regulation. It was to be expected that, once freed from regulatory constraints, firms in such industries would try to take advantage of the opportunity to achieve cost reductions through rapid expansion or by means of mergers.

Evaluations of the merger movement have differed sharply. Some observers have concluded that mergers threaten to increase monopoly power and exploit the public. Others have argued that indirect competitive pressures (for example, barges and trucks are rivals of large railways) remain strong and that economies of scale resulting from the mergers will be passed on to the consuming public.

Critics of deregulation have placed a good deal of emphasis on such things as reduced passenger comfort in the airline industry, but economists argue that competition would not bring such results unless passengers as a group preferred lower fares to the greater standards of luxury that preceded them.

In addition, some observers have been concerned about the safety effects of deregulation, suggesting, for example, that the incidence of airline accidents may increase because of it, as airlines may cut expenditures on safety to keep prices low. Despite the fact that the U.S. evidence displays no such trend for the years since deregulation was introduced, special vigilance may nonetheless be required to guard against neglect of safety as a cost-cutting measure. The expense of additional governmental inspection can be considered a required cost of deregulation.

A Word on Nationalization

As we indicated at the beginning of the chapter, in industries in which monopoly or near monopoly offers cost advantages to society over competition, there is an alternative to regulation. This alternative is *nationalization*—that is, government ownership and operation of the firms in such industries. A number of cities operate their own public transport facilities, collect their own garbage, and offer other services that elsewhere are provided by private enterprise.

It is an almost instinctive reaction among people in Canada to consider such public enterprises as being prone to extreme mismanagement and waste. And the near-legendary problems of Canada Post do seem to support this supposition. However, here too, one should be careful not to jump to conclusions. It is true that for many years visitors found the nationalized French telephone system a model of chaos and mismanagement. But at the same time, the Swedish telephone system, which is also nationalized, has consistently been smooth-working and efficient. And the French government-supplied electricity system has set world standards in its use of the most modern analytic techniques of economics and engineering and has adopted innovative pricing policies that promote efficiency.

Despite these accomplishments, nationalized industries continue to be beset by weak incentives for efficiency. First, governments virtually never permit a nationalized firm to go bankrupt and, as a result, the firm's management is deprived of one of the most powerful motivations for the minimization of costs. Second, no one has yet found a systematic incentive mechanism for efficiency that can do for nationalized industries what the profit motive does for private enterprise. Where the market is unsparing in its rewards for accomplishments and in its penalties for poor performance, one can be quite sure that a firm's inefficiency will not readily be tolerated. But nationalized industries have no such automatic mechanism to hand out rewards and penalties dependably and impartially. We have seen, however, that there are analogous problems under regulation; where profits are controlled by the regulator, the rewards for efficiency are also far from automatic. Hence, the relative efficiency of a nationalized firm versus a regulated private firm is far from clear.

By now there have been several dozen studies comparing the efficiency of private unregulated, private regulated, and nationalized firms.[1] While a majority conclude that the costs of unregulated private firms are the lowest, they find considerably more

---

[1] For a good survey of these studies, see Yair Aharoni, *The Evolution and Management of State Owned Enterprises* (Cambridge, Mass.: Ballinger Publishing Company, 1986), pages 197–204.

variation in the relative performance of nationalized and private regulated firms. Results seem to vary by type of industry, by country, and by size of enterprise.

One industry that has been studied is residential garbage collection, a relatively homogeneous service that is carried out by both government and private firms and thus seems particularly well suited for comparing the costs of competition, private monopoly, and government monopoly. A study of the relative costs of private and public collection of garbage in about 300 municipalities in the United States found that collection costs were about the same whether the job was done by government or by a group of competing firms.[2] Competition was expensive because each firm served only scattered customers, and there was much duplication of routes. On the other hand, the costs of both government collection and competitive private collection were some 34 percent higher than the costs of service by a private monopoly collector working under contract to the municipal government. The government services typically had significantly larger crews, higher rates of employee absenteeism, smaller trucks, and less frequent use of incentive systems than did the private collectors.

Another study, however, compared the costs of thirty-three private electric utilities and twenty-three public ones in the United States.[3] On the basis of a sophisticated statistical analysis, the authors concluded that publicly owned electric utilities perform better than their privately owned regulated counterparts. The costs of the government-owned firms were 24 to 33 percent lower than those of the private firms, a difference similar to that found in other studies of the issue. Thus, at least for the electric utilities they studied, the authors judged that public ownership is a better choice than production by regulated private firms.

In sum, it is by no means clear that the regulatory approach always serves the public better than does nationalization. In both cases, much seems to depend on the rules employed by the pertinent government agency.

The Movement toward Privatization

In a number of countries, a trend moving sharply away from nationalization has been apparent. Among free-market economies, Great Britain is the prime example. The Conservative government of Margaret Thatcher **privatized** about 40 percent of the industries that were nationalized between 1945 and 1979. The list includes telecommunications; oil and gas production; airports and airlines; trucking; rail hotels; seaports; shipbuilding; and the aerospace, automobile, and semiconductor industries. Under "Thatcherism," bus and coach routes were also deregulated; local governments began to contract services out to private contractors; privatization of pension plans, health care, and education increased; and more than a million public housing units were sold to tenants. Television broadcasting, formerly the exclusive province of the BBC, a government-owned corporation, went increasingly into private hands. The results of privatization are still the subject of heated debate.

However, it is in the formerly centrally planned economies of Eastern Europe that the movement away from nationalization has come to sound like a stampede. Plans, and actions already taken, to transform the economies of Poland, Hungary, Czechoslovakia, Lithuania, and what was formerly East Germany into free-market systems imply extreme disillusionment with the performance of government-owned industry. As this is being written, there is too much turmoil to permit any sensible guesses about the future of this movement. But the rejection of nationalized enterprise in favour of privatization by the public of Eastern Europe seems unambiguous.

[2] E. S. Savas, "Evaluating the Organization of Service Delivery: Solid Waste Collection and Disposal: A Summary," Center for Government Studies, Graduate School of Business, Columbia University, New York, April 1978.

[3] See D. R. Pescatrice and J. M. Trapani III, "The Performance and Objectives of Public and Private Utilities Operating in the United States," *Journal of Public Economics* 13 (1980), pages 259–78.

Sell Revenue Canada and Collect Taxes as the Romans Did

The following newspaper article was written by Professor Trevor Hodge of Carleton University. Besides being amusing, it shows that the nationalization-versus-privatization debate has been waged for many years.

... There is one simple and obvious way of reforming the tax system, a way that would be agreeable to business, welcome to taxpayers and pleasing to Conservatives, a way that Finance Minister Michael Wilson probably hasn't even considered. Privatize it. Sell off Revenue Canada, and entrust tax collection to the private sector.

Mr. Wilson may be forgiven for not having looked at this attractive option, but anyone with the benefit of a classical education can tell you that was how the ancient Romans did it. And given the fractious state of national unity, no lessons from a prosperous multicultural empire that lasted 1000 years are to be sneezed at.

... It worked like this.... The government set the tax rates and every year auctioned off to the highest bidder the right to collect them. The actual collection was done by private companies in competition (and sometimes in cahoots) with each other. Shares in them were traded publicly. You could buy into a tax company and ... the more tax that was wrung out of the taxpayers, the better a dividend you got.

In theory, a profit margin of half a percent was built into the contract price. In reality, you bid as high as you dared to land the contract and then stung the taxpayers for every cent you could get, since everything over the contract price was gravy.

In the provinces, where you were not dealing with Roman citizens, this meant that claims for a refund were often settled by the tax inspector arriving on the doorstep accompanied ... by half a dozen goons from the Roman army barracks down the road. In this healthy demonstration of the spirit of free enterprise, an amicable settlement would be reached right speedily.

As with all private ventures, there was, of course, a risk. To avoid the trap of overbidding, you had to have some idea of how much blood really could be squeezed from the stone. Most companies accordingly ran a kind of private intelligence service, with agents reporting on how the harvest was shaping up, and other potential plums for the picking....

But man is fallible, and sometimes an incautiously high bid led to a situation distressingly reminiscent of Dome Petroleum, de Havilland Aircraft, Maislin trucking and other familiar names on the Canadian economic scene. In 59 BC, the Roman government found itself faced with an appeal from the tax-collecting companies operating in the province of Asia. They had committed themselves to what they now saw was a grossly optimistic contract and, if held to it, they were staring bankruptcy in the face. Speakers urged that ... a contract was a contract, but students of political economy won't be surprised to learn the companies were bailed out by remission of one-third of the debt.

... What the ordinary taxpayer thought of it all is perhaps summed up in one word. The Latin term for the tax companies and their representatives was *publicani*. All it really means is "public servants," but it normally appears in the New Testament as "publicans" (and it's not necessary to read very far to find what kind of reputation they enjoyed among their friends and neighbours).

SOURCE: Excerpted from A. Trevor Hodge, "Sell Revenue Canada and Collect Taxes as the Romans Did," *The Globe and Mail*, June 18, 1987, page 7.

The Canadian government is similarly convinced that some of the country's nationalized firms should be privatized. Since the mid-1980s, it has sold off a number of companies, of which Air Canada, sold in 1989, is perhaps the most notable. Other firms, such as PetroCanada, are also planned to be privatized.

Cynics claim that the only reason for these sales is to provide funds to reduce the budget deficit. In fact, not many funds can be provided in this way. When a company is sold by the government, the government has to subtract the asset's book value from the sale proceeds before it can apply the remaining funds to reducing the deficit. Instead, in promoting the principle of privatization, the government offers the following five reasons in support of its choice:

1. The economic environment has changed. In Canada's early years, state intervention was deemed necessary for opening the country to commerce (through the development of canals, railways, a national broadcasting system, and so on); today, this involvement is no longer necessary.

2. The test of market competition can improve efficiency.

3. A number of Crown corporations need sizable amounts of funds to expand and meet competition. The government cannot afford to raise these funds, and the firms themselves, as Crown corporations, are precluded from acquiring equity funds elsewhere.

4. Management style in the private sector is more conducive to risk-taking.

5. It is unfair to use tax dollars raised in the private sector to fund Crown corporations that compete directly with private firms.

Some Canadians agree with these government beliefs. Others disagree—in principle or with respect to specific cases. No doubt these views will be fully debated over the coming years.

The Competition Act

Competition cases in the courts are likely to be well publicized because the accused firms are often household names. For example, in the last three years, each of the following companies has been found guilty of either misleading advertising or some improper pricing practice: The Brick, Commodore Business Machines, Chrysler, K Mart, Krazy Kelly's, Sears, Toshiba, and Zellers. But the vast majority of competition cases investigated by the government do not even come to trial, let alone receive a conviction. A classic example of the lags and expenses involved in the pursuit of cases of unfair competition was the government's attempted prosecution of five major moving companies for price fixing. The combines investigation began in 1966, but a guilty plea *without trial* was entered only on December 14, 1983.

What are the specific purposes of our competition laws? And how well has the government's competition policy program succeeded in practice? These questions are the main concerns of the remainder of this chapter. Starting with a little history, we describe how competition policy has fared over the century since its inception. We outline the activities that are currently prohibited by law and how the recent revisions to the Competition Act have changed the nature of our competition policy. Then we re-examine the role of monopoly in the economy and the pros and cons of the competition policy program from the viewpoint of economic analysis.

The Origin and Development of Competition Policy

In 1888, a Select Committee of the House of Commons investigating alleged combinations (monopolies and mergers) in the manufacturing, trade, and insurance industries reported that combines existed in thirteen commodities or industries in Canada (including, for example, sugar, groceries, coal, and stoves). As a result, in 1889, the Parliament of Canada passed into law An Act for the Prevention and Suppression of Combinations in Restraint of Trade. Thus, Canada's formal competition policy predated that of the United States—the Sherman Act—by one year.

The Canadian act was part of the criminal code and provided that:

Every person who conspires, combines, agrees or arranges with any other person ... unlawfully ... to restrain or injure trade or commerce in relation to any ... article or commodity; to unduly prevent ... [its] manufacture or production ..., to unreasonably enhance [its] price ... or to unduly prevent or lessen competition in [its] production, manufacture, purchase, barter, sale, transportation or supply ... is guilty of a misdemeanor and liable on conviction to a penalty not exceeding $4,000 and not less than $200, or to imprisonment for any term not exceeding 2 years. And if a corporation, it is liable on conviction to a penalty not exceeding $10,000 and not less than $1,000.

Note the words "unduly" and "unreasonably." They still exist in important sections of current legislation and have been the cause of great concern because, in criminal law, it is necessary to prove guilt beyond a reasonable doubt—a difficult task considering the vagueness of these words.

In any case, the original act was not effective because no machinery was set up to secure evidence. Not until 1910, at the peak of a merger movement in Canada, was a formal process of investigation enacted. Under the terms of the legislation, six citizens could apply to a judge to appoint a board of investigation. This board, if approved, would submit a report and could recommend fines. However, the mere publication of a report was considered to be the main punishment. For example, in 1923, Mackenzie King asked the House of Commons:

What is the power of the criminal code to prosecute some particular person or group of persons in comparison with the power of spreading broadcast throughout the land accurate and true information with regard to a situation which is inimical to the public interest, and which the people themselves are certain to be concerned in remedying?[4]

Over the years a number of amendments were made to the existing legislation, which by the 1970s had been renamed the **Combines Investigation Act**. However, the government remained dissatisfied with the legislation because the rules relied on criminal, rather than civil, law (the implications of which will be explained shortly). As a result, the government was losing *all* of its major cases. In 1971, in an attempt to rectify this and a number of other weaknesses, the government introduced a new bill that was intended to facilitate the prosecution of major forms of anti-competitive behaviour. The introduction of the bill sparked one of the largest lobbying efforts in Canadian history. The business community, in particular, opposed any strengthening of the law and in the end was at least partially successful. After more than three years, the government split the legislation into two parts (Stage 1 and Stage 2) and passed only the first (less controversial) stage into law in 1976. Stage 2 did not become law until 1986; hence our current **Competition Act** is indeed a very recent law, and is therefore only now in the process of being interpreted through judicial decisions.

Current Legislation

The Competition Act deals with events that change the structure of the economy, such as mergers or monopolization, and with conduct in business that is considered not to be to the benefit of the economy as a whole. Examples of such conduct include agreements to restrict competition and certain problematic pricing, distribution, and sales practices.

Monopoly

Only *one* conviction had been obtained, after trial, under the monopoly section of the old Combines Investigation Act. In 1952, the Eddy Match company was found guilty of monopolizing the market for wooden matches over a twenty-year period. It had maintained its monopoly by buying up rivals and carrying out industrial spying, among other things.

Nine other cases were brought to trial under the old act and in five of them the companies were acquitted. In one of the remaining four, the company pleaded guilty without trial. In the other three, the companies involved agreed to the terms of a *prohibition order* (an order forbidding the repetition or continuation of an offence) without admitting guilt.

Generally, prosecutions failed under the old act because, while the government

[4]*House of Commons Debate, Second Session,* 1923, page 262S.

could often show that monopolies existed, it was not able to *prove* that monopolies were operating *to the detriment of the public*. As a result, in the K. C. Irving case, the company was found innocent even though, from 1944 to 1971, it had acquired all five of the English-language daily newspapers in New Brunswick. Because of such problems, our new act contains no awkward "detriment-of-the-public" clause. Instead, the Competition Act defines a *monopoly* as *any abuse of a dominant position*. Explicitly included as abuses are the following practices:

Squeezing ... the margin available ... for the purpose of impeding or preventing entry into or expansion in a market; ... pre-emption of scarce facilities or resources required by a competitor for the operation of a business; ... adoption of product specifications that are incompatible with products produced by any other person and are designed to prevent his entry into, or to eliminate him from, a market; requiring or inducing a supplier to sell only or primarily to certain customers, or to refrain from selling to a competitor, with the object of preventing a competitor's entry [into], or expansion in, a market; and selling articles at a price lower than the acquisition cost for the purpose of disciplining or eliminating a competitor.

Another problem with the old act was that its monopoly provisions were part of the criminal code, as opposed to the civil law. Criminal law requires that guilt be proved beyond a reasonable doubt, a requirement unsuited to economic issues. Whether competition has been *unduly* eliminated is always a matter of judgment, resting on a comparison of the advantages of possible economies of scale and superior competitive performance and the disadvantages of possible anti-competitive behaviour. Furthermore, the empirical information on which such a comparison must be based is normally quite limited. In civil law, the Crown must establish only a balance of probability that competition has been significantly lessened.

One final problem that limited effectiveness of the old Combines Investigation Act was that the fines were very small compared with the benefits that could be had from breaking the law.

Mergers

Mergers have long been regarded with suspicion by competition-policy authorities. Particularly when a merger is **horizontal**, it is often feared that because the number of competing firms in the industry is reduced (that is, concentration is increased), competition will decline.

The authorities do not wish to impede mergers that seem likely to increase efficiency by improving the co-ordination of production activities, permitting economies of scale, getting one of the firms out of financial difficulties, or facilitating operations in a variety of other ways. But the authorities do want to prevent mergers that threaten to reduce competition.

Though by no means unanimous on the subject, most economists agree that mergers *sometimes* reduce competition, particularly in a market that is not contestable,[5] so that threats of entry do not prevent the merged firm from raising prices above competitive levels. This danger is particularly acute if the number of firms is sufficiently small to make collusion a real possibility.

On the other hand, where there is reason to believe that a merger would *not* reduce competition, many economists would oppose impediments to it, arguing that mergers that are not undertaken to reduce competition have only one purpose—to achieve greater efficiency. For example, the larger firm that results from the merger may enjoy substantial economies of scale not available to smaller firms. The two merging companies may learn special skills from one another, or they may offset one another's risks. Mergers have sometimes proved disappointing and have brought little

A **merger** occurs when two previously independent firms are combined under a single owner or group of owners. A **horizontal merger** is a merger of two firms producing similar products, as when one toothpaste manufacturing firm purchases another. A **vertical merger** involves the joining of two firms, one of which supplies an ingredient of the other's product, as when an auto-maker acquires a tire manufacturing firm. A **conglomerate merger** is the union of two unrelated firms, as when a defence industry firm joins a firm that produces phonograph records.

[5] See Chapter 26, pages 582–83, for a definition and discussion of this concept.

cost saving. But a recent U.S. study of roughly 22,000 large manufacturing establishments, of which 1100 had been purchased and merged ("taken over") between 1981 and 1986, found that the merged manufacturing plants subsequently had rates of productivity growth some 14 percent higher than the others in the same industry.[6]

In Canada, because of the relatively small size of the market, government policy has long been favourable to the existence of large firms, and a reflection of this general policy can be seen in the results of attempts to prosecute certain mergers under the terms of the old Combines Investigation Act. In the years up to 1986, only six merger prosecutions were undertaken. One resulted in a guilty plea before trial while the remainder resulted in acquittals.

The reason for the lack of success in prosecutions and for the apparent unwillingness of the government to initiate new cases under the old act can be found in the courts' interpretation of the law. Just as in the case of monopoly, a finding of guilty under the old law required proof that because of a merger, competition was or was likely to be lessened *to the detriment of the public*. The courts interpreted the latter phrase to mean the existence of a virtual monopoly. Thus, in the case of British Columbia Sugar, even though it was shown that the company, through merger, had gained a near monopoly over sugar sales in the four Western provinces, the presiding judge decided that the Eastern sugar companies presented a viable source of potential competition.

Shortly after the proclamation of the new act, there was a merger conviction: A funeral-home company in Hamilton pleaded guilty to limiting competition by buying up funeral homes in the area until it controlled 70 percent of the Protestant market. The company was fined $200,000.

Under the new act, mergers come under the jurisdiction of the Competition Tribunal, which is composed of federal judges and laypeople appointed by the government. Decisions by the tribunal cannot be appealed to the Cabinet—only to the Federal Court of Appeal. As we have noted in earlier chapters, it is difficult to determine what output levels are required for firms to realize fully the economies of larger-scale operation. Thus, it is fortunate that the new act shifted mergers from a criminal to a civil offence. The wording of the act carefully notes that mergers have both costs and benefits, and these contradictory features make the civil law jurisdiction absolutely necessary. The tribunal must judge the relative size of the gains in efficiency and international competitiveness (which are particularly stressed in the opening clause of the act) versus the increase in industry concentration within the domestic market. Section 68 of the Competition Act states:

The Tribunal shall not make an order ... if it finds that the merger or proposed merger ... is likely to bring about gains in efficiency that will be greater than, and will offset, the effects of any prevention or lessening of competition that will result or is likely to result from the merger.

Under the new act, the Bureau of Competition Policy must be notified before a merger occurs if the parties have Canadian assets or sales of more than $400 million or if the deal itself involves assets or sales of more than $35 million. As a result, 3700 mergers were recorded by the bureau during the first three and a half years after the passage of the new act.

Agreements to Restrict Competition

Section 32 of the Competition Act provides that:

Everyone who conspires, combines, agrees or arranges with another person ... to ...

---

[6]Frank Lichtenberg and David Siegel, "The Effects of Leveraged Buyouts on Productivity and Related Aspects of Firm Behavior," NBER Working Paper no. 3022, 1989.

restrain or injure competition unduly . . . is guilty of an indictable offence and is liable to imprisonment for five years or a fine of one million dollars or to both.

Under the old Combines Investigation Act, the government was successful in approximately 75 percent of the nearly 100 cases brought under Section 32. At a certain point, however, two cases—those of Aetna and of Atlantic Sugar—produced judgments that made successful prosecution virtually impossible thereafter. The problem arose in the added requirement of *proof of double intent*. Prior to these cases, it was sufficient for the government to prove that the parties in the conspiracy *intended to enter an agreement*. It was not necessary to show that they *intended to limit competition*. After the precedent had been set with the Aetna and the Atlantic Sugar cases, both conditions were required for a conviction. The presiding judge in the Atlantic Sugar case held that although the companies shared virtually the entire market (each having had a constant market share for a quarter of a century), they should be acquitted of conspiracy charges because "the reason for maintaining traditional market shares was to avoid a price war which would have resulted had the accused taken the only method of increasing them by price cutting through excessive discounts."[7] Notice that there was no mention of consumer interest.

Under the new Competition Act, agreements to limit competition are still classified as offences under the criminal code, but now only proof of single intent is required; for example, all the government has to prove is that price-fixing occurred, not that prices were being fixed for a particular reason.

Consumer advocates also welcomed the raising of the maximum fine, although the nature of this change can still be criticized on two counts. First, in principle, the fines should bear some relationship to the economic cost to consumers of the anti-competitive behaviour. Second, the maximum fines are hardly ever imposed. During the year ending March 31, 1989 (the last complete year for which data were available when this book went to press), 23 criminal court cases were concluded. Fifteen of these cases resulted in a conviction, with an average fine of $202,000—an amount that some firms may still regard as a reasonable cost of doing business. More recently, however, larger fines *have* been levied: In late 1990, Canada's three largest flour-milling companies were each fined $1 million for price-rigging. This is consistent with the Bureau of Competition Policy's recently stated objective to "get the fines up to a level that is more than a permit or fee for companies to break the law."[8]

Pricing Practices

The Competition Act deals with several pricing practices that are assumed to reduce competition.

Resale price maintenance involves forcing retailers to keep the price of a product at or above that specified by the wholesaler.

Resale price maintenance.   This pricing practice typically involves the manufacturer's forcing retailers to maintain the price of a product at, or at least not below, some specified amount. If a retailer refuses to carry out the manufacturer's wishes, the manufacturer normally cuts off the supply of the product. This practice has been illegal in Canada since 1952, despite many analysts' expressed concern that this part of the law may actually lessen competition. These analysts note that the discounters who undercut the manufacturer's stipulated price cut corners in customer service, offering little help in product selection, installation, or repair. Also, the discounters make it difficult for full-service retailers to survive. Potential customers go to a full-service department store for product information and then buy the item from a discounter.

[7]See G. Kaiser, *World Law of Competition, Vol. 3A: Canada* (New York: Matthew Bender, 1982) for an account of this and other relevant cases.

[8]Howard Wetston, Director of the Bureau of Competition Policy, as quoted in Jock Ferguson and Drew Fagan, "Mills Fined for Rigging CIDA Bids," *The Globe and Mail*, December 8, 1990, pages A1, A9.

The final result, it is claimed, can be a decrease in competition, as the full-service retailer is forced out of the particular business. Given the ambiguity that surrounds the question of whether resale price maintenance is indeed a reprehensible practice, it is ironic that, in contrast to other sections of the old Combines Investigation Act, prosecutions against resale price maintenance were generally successful. Fines were usually assessed, and prohibition orders often issued. As we shall see later on, the power of the new act to limit resale price maintenance has yet to be determined.

Predatory pricing. This term refers to price cuts by existing firms when such cuts are effected in an attempt to keep other firms from entering the industry. Unfortunately, a crucial element in this section of the act states that prices cannot be "unreasonably low." In addition, to obtain a conviction it has to be proved that the predatory-pricing practice is part of a policy and that competition is or can be threatened or destroyed by that policy.

Predatory pricing refers to price cuts that are undertaken only to keep other firms from entering the industry.

Three major cases falling under this section of the act have reached full trial. In one of these, the Hoffman–La Roche case, the company was found guilty because for a six-month period it had adopted a policy of giving away one of its products (Valium) to hospitals in order to build up a consumer preference. It was noted at trial that a zero price was certainly a large drop from regular prices. In a second case, Consumers Glass Company, a producer of cup lids, was charged with lowering prices unreasonably in order to drive out a competitor. However, the company successfully argued that due to excess capacity in the industry it was merely lowering its prices to make the maximum possible recovery of its fixed costs. That is, given the market situation, it was "loss minimizing" by charging a price greater than average variable cost but less than what was called average total cost.

Price discrimination. The intent of this section of the act is to ensure that a seller does not sell products of like quality to competing buyers at different prices. Such a practice confers an undue advantage to the buyer paying the lower price. This section of the old act was not utilized to a great extent because of difficulties in dealing with matters such as whether the buyers are competitors (which involves defining relevant markets). In fact only two cases were brought to trial under the old act, with one conviction and one acquittal being recorded.

Price discrimination involves charging different prices, relative to costs, to different buyers of the same product.

Many economists find the legal definition of price discrimination misleading. Suppose, for instance, that one person lives on a mountaintop far from the place where a good is produced and another customer is located in an area that enjoys easy access to the good in question. Economists would say that it is not discriminatory to charge each a different price. On the contrary, economists hold that in such cases it is discriminatory to charge both customers the same price, because one price would not account for the substantial difference in the two delivery costs.

Even more important than this definitional argument, though, is the issue of the desirability or undesirability of discrimination. The word *discrimination* is what has been called a "persuasive term"—in this case, a word that automatically implies gross misconduct. But, in fact, price discrimination can sometimes be beneficial to all parties to a transaction.

Suppose, for example, that a commodity is available to the poor only if it is sold at a relatively low price, though one that still more than covers the good's marginal cost (the cost incurred in expanding into the lower-income market). In this case, the contribution from the lower-income market may permit *some* reduction in price to the rich, since the firm might not be able to cover its total cost if it were to charge the rich the *same* low price necessary for entry into the low-income market. The result is that everyone—the poor, the wealthy, and the selling firm—will benefit from this discriminatory pricing.

The pricing practices of doctors before the existence of universal medicare offer an example of the situation described above. At that time, doctors were known to charge higher fees to their wealthy patients than to their poor ones. The reduced fees presumably permitted more poor patients to visit them, and doctors may thus have been able to earn an even better income than they could by charging a uniformly high fee to everyone. Even the fee to the rich may have gone down in the process because of the doctors' increased earnings from their enlarged pool of poor patients. Discrimination led to lower fees for everyone and all parties were made better off. It is therefore difficult to understand why the government should prohibit such behaviour. It should also be noted that it is this sort of ambiguity that makes it difficult to obtain a judgment "beyond reasonable doubt," as is required under criminal law—the domain within which these cases continue to be tried.

Distribution Practices

The following distribution practices are subject to review by the Competition Tribunal: tied selling, exclusive dealing, consignment selling, refusal to supply, and market restriction. Being "reviewable" means that these practices are not considered to be offences under the Competition Act. There is basically no appeal from a decision by the tribunal, and it may issue only remedial orders.

These practices deal generally with **vertical marketing** arrangements, which are considered harmful to competition in that they might allow the wholesaler or retailer to gain a local monopoly on the sale of a product or permit the supplier to abuse a monopoly position.

Two cases will illustrate the nature of these practices. In the case of Bombardier Ltée., the company's exclusive dealing practices in snowmobiles were brought under review. The company admitted that it had supplied dealers with its snowmobiles under the explicit condition that they would not handle any other brand of snowmobiles. Eight dealers had had their franchises terminated for breaching this contract. Although the Restrictive Trade Practices Commission, the precursor of the Competition Tribunal, agreed that Bombardier controlled a substantial share of the snowmobile market (50 percent in Quebec, Ontario, and Atlantic Canada), it found that this fact had not produced a substantial lessening of competition. Accordingly, the case was dismissed.

In a case dealing with tied selling, the results were different. The BBM (Bureau of Broadcast Measurement) is a major supplier of television rating services and the sole supplier of radio rating services in Canada. The company had a requirement that anyone desiring its radio ratings, over which it had a monopoly, would also have to purchase its television ratings. The commission held that this practice was unfair to an existing competitor and would impede entry into or expansion within the ratings market. It therefore issued a prohibition order in this matter.

Misleading Advertising and Unfair Trade Practices

Other sections of the Competition Act contain provisions dealing with misleading advertising and deceptive marketing practices. It is important that any violations in these areas be prosecuted in order to protect a fundamental principle on which our economic system is based: the assumption that the buyer is "knowledgeable."

These sections have spawned more prosecutions and convictions since 1976 than have any other sections of the Competition Act. For example, in his annual report for the year ending March 31, 1989, the Director of Investigation and Research under the auspices of the Bureau of Competition Policy reported that 111 cases dealing with misleading advertising and deceptive marketing practices had been completed. Unfortunately, however, about 4000 of the approximately 13,000 complaints regarding misleading or deceptive advertising that come in each year have to be defined as low priority. The lack of resources in the department precludes investigation into all cases.

Penalties and Exemptions

When guilty verdicts are obtained, competition policy is enforced by one or more of the penalties provided for in various sections of the Competition Act:

1. Fines—the limit varies with the section of the act and is unlimited in some sections of the act.
2. Divestiture—convicted companies are forced to sell some of their assets.
3. Prohibition orders—the order prohibits the repetition or continuation of an offence.
4. Restitution—payment of a sum to certain persons identified by the court.
5. Interim injunctions—the order prevents certain activities pending a trial.
6. Post-conviction reporting.
7. Declaring invalid patents or trademarks.
8. Imprisonment to a maximum of five years.

In addition, private damage actions can be based on a breach of the Competition Act. However, class actions, which are available in the United States, are not provided for in the Canadian act.

While this list of penalties sounds imposing, it must be remembered that the government has achieved *very few* prosecutions, except under the resale price maintenance and unfair trade practices sections of the act. In addition to this, many activities are currently exempt from the act, including:

1. The formation of labour unions.
2. Any association between fishermen and fish processors.
3. The operation of shipping conferences (cartels of ship owners who collude on prices).
4. Competition-reducing agreements in the professions.
5. The conduct of firms that are effectively regulated.
6. Monopoly behaviour of firms holding a valid patent or trademark.
7. With some exceptions, agreements among exporters.

It was only with the passage of the new act in 1986 that banks and Crown corporations came under the jurisdiction of competition policy.

The Administration of Competition Policy

The federal minister charged with the responsibility of administering competition policy in Canada is the Minister of Consumer and Corporate Affairs. The day-to-day administration of this program is carried out by the Director of Investigation and Research under the auspices of the Bureau of Competition Policy (one of the three bureaus in Consumer and Corporate Affairs Canada). The bureau had an authorized strength of 260 person-years in 1989. The majority of these personnel were situated at headquarters in Hull, Quebec, while the remainder comprised the field staff of the Marketing Practices Branch.

An inquiry into any alleged violation of the Competition Act can be initiated in one of three ways: at the direction of the minister, in response to a formal request by six Canadian residents,[9] or by the director. In fact, the vast majority of inquiries are initiated by the director, often in response to complaints by companies or individuals regarding alleged violations.

In general, a preliminary inquiry into a complaint is carried out by the staff of the bureau, and if the preliminary evidence gives the director reason to believe that a

---

[9]For example, if you felt it necessary to initiate an inquiry into a case of misleading advertising or deceptive marketing practices, you and five friends could do so by writing to the following address: Marketing Practices Branch, Bureau of Competition Policy, Consumer and Corporate Affairs, 50 Victoria Street, 19th floor, Hull, Quebec, K1A 0C9 (phone: (819) 997-4282). You could also contact one of the regional offices, located in major centres across Canada.

violation has in fact been committed, he initiates a formal inquiry. Once an inquiry has become formal, evidence can be obtained by searching premises, formally requesting data, or holding hearings under the auspices of the Competition Tribunal.

If the formal investigation finds sufficient evidence of wrongdoing, the director can refer the case either to the Competition Tribunal, if the alleged offence is reviewable, or to the Attorney General of Canada, to be considered for the laying of criminal charges (since some prohibitions under the act are still criminal issues).

The Attorney General reviews the case (a time-consuming process ranging from several months to several years) and decides either to drop it or to lay formal charges. (Note that it is the Attorney General and *not* the Director of Investigation and Research who lays charges and formally prosecutes the cases.) Once charges are laid, cases travel along the normal route of criminal justice in Canada.

Judicial Interpretations of the Competition Act

Several years have now passed since the new Competition Act became law, and we are starting to see how the courts are interpreting its provisions. In our legal system, these precedent-setting decisions are very important in determining whether the new law will represent any real increase in effectiveness over the former legislation—the Combines Investigation Act. Unfortunately, several decisions to date suggest that it may not.

In April 1990, the Quebec Superior Court struck down some of the key sections of the act that empowered the new Competition Tribunal to stop mergers that it believed would lessen competition. The judgment stated that the tribunal was unconstitutional because its proceedings would limit the accused's right to a fair and impartial hearing—something that is guaranteed by the Charter of Rights and Freedoms. A related, but earlier, decision had argued that the Charter limited the tribunal's ability to investigate a company's files. In July 1990, the Federal Court of Appeal ruled against the tribunal in the latter's attempt to file a contempt charge against Chrysler Canada Ltd. for ignoring an order it had issued. In explaining the Court's decision, the Chief Justice said,

I cannot find ... a clear expression of an intention to confer on the tribunal the power to punish for contempt those who fail to comply with the tribunal's order.... Granted it might be desirable that the tribunal possess such a power, but it seems that Parliament thought otherwise.[10]

Clearly, without this authority, the tribunal is close to useless.

As this book went to press, all of these rulings were being appealed by the federal government. But if the appeals are lost, the power and the intended flexibility that were foreseen for the Competition Tribunal will fail to materialize. Growing concern about such an eventuality is clearly evident in the article featured in the boxed insert on page 745. The article is based on an interview with the director of the Bureau of Competition Policy.

The government did, however, receive some good news in late 1990. The NutraSweet case—the first to come to trial under the new Abuse of Dominant Position section of the Competition Act—was completed, and the government won a conviction against the firm. After NutraSweet's Canadian patent on aspartame (an artificial sweetener) had expired, the company was alleged to have engaged in a series of unfair trade practices to maintain its 95 percent share of the Canadian market. Unfortunately, even this victory for the government is somewhat mixed. Many of the hearings in the prolonged case were conducted in secrecy, since much of what was being examined (for example, corporate pricing and sales strategies) could not be

---

[10] As quoted in *The Globe and Mail*, July 11, 1990, page A1.

Corporate Watchdog Finds Teeth Blunter

It's been anything but a tranquil year for Howard Wetston.

Since taking over as the director of the federal government's Bureau of Competition Policy last Oct. 30, he has been buffeted by judicial decisions that have trimmed his powers and led to concerns that the four-year-old Competition Act may already be in need of an overhaul....

... Mr. Wetston plans to intervene more often in regulatory matters to push for greater competition in areas such as broadcast policy and marketing boards.

As well, efforts to reduce the mystery surrounding bureau processes have led to the circulation of discussion papers on how officials should examine such issues as price discrimination.

The biggest step in opening up the bureau will come with the distribution in early 1991 of merger guidelines that will provide fairly specific information on when takeovers might be expected to be challenged by the bureau on competition grounds.

In recent months, Mr. Wetston's attention has been turned to a series of constitutional challenges that, unless overturned on appeal, would make thin gruel of the much-praised Competition Act.

Already, a Nova Scotia Supreme Court judge has found unconstitutional the heart of the legislation, the key conspiracy section that protects consumers from business collusion and price fixing.

That decision is being used to challenge search warrants as the competition bureau continues to try to enforce the law. And the Nova Scotia ruling sets an important precedent as lawyers for major drugstore chains in Quebec facing criminal charges of price fixing on birth-control pills seek to have those charges quashed....

Mr. Wetston agrees it would be "a disaster" if the Nova Scotia decision was upheld by the Supreme Court of Canada....

In the other major Charter setback in recent months, a Quebec Superior Court judge struck down the sweeping powers of the quasi-judicial Competition Tribunal to block or alter mergers. The judge found that a company's right to freedom of association would be violated....

... Mr. Wetston has general reservations about the way courts have traditionally dealt with competition cases—arguing that judges "have not been receptive enough to the importance of competition law as an instrument for the dynamic growth of the economy."

That concern was a major reason why large parts of the ineffective Combines Investigation Act were rewritten in the new legislation, making some prohibited practices such as monopolistic activity the subject of regulatory review rather than criminal charges.

But as one competition specialist said: "The courts have now begun their cutting and slicing on constitutional grounds."...

[It took] years for the new legislation to be written and the Conservative government did not want the controversy of a re-evaluation. But if the Supreme Court of Canada upholds the Nova Scotia or Quebec rulings, that is just what will face the Tory cabinet. And probably right around the time of the next election.

SOURCE: Excerpted from Drew Fagan, "Corporate Watchdog Finds Teeth Blunter," *The Globe and Mail*, October 30, 1990, pages B1–B2.

---

made public beyond the members of the tribunal. Therefore, the Court's reasoning behind its final decision could not be given in detail in the written account of the case. This in itself may limit the usefulness of the NutraSweet case as a legal precedent.

Issues in Concentration of Industry

Having reviewed our competition policy and its interpretation by the courts, we have reached the conclusion that it has not been very successful. One very rough way to measure the success of anti-combines legislation, especially on the merger–monopoly front, is to look at what has happened to the share of Canadian business in the hands of the largest firms.

First, we can compare the degree of domination by large firms in the Canadian economy with that in other countries. A second method of evaluation involves observations of firms over a long period of time. Some observers, particularly Marxist economists, have predicted that capitalism will have a basic tendency toward **concentration of industry**. They argue that because small firms are increasingly driven out of business, especially during economic crises, large firms consequently acquire ever-larger shares of the market. One can therefore investigate whether such a tendency has been observed in Canada. If, in fact, concentration has not increased, someone who holds these views might be led to surmise that competition policy has had a hand in preventing the growth of monopoly. But first, we should consider what might have been expected to happen to concentration in Canada in the absence of any counter-measures by government. Is there good reason to expect an inexorable trend toward bigness, as the Marxists suggest?

There are two basic reasons why the larger firms in an industry may triumph over the small. First, larger firms may obtain monopoly power, which they can use to their advantage. They can force sellers of equipment, raw materials, and other inputs to give them better terms than are available to small competitors, and they can also force retailers to give preference to their products. These are, of course, the sorts of advantages to bigness that the anti-combines laws are intended to eliminate.

The second reason an industry's output may tend to be divided among fewer and larger firms with the passage of time has to do with technology. In some industries, fairly small firms can produce as cheaply as, or more cheaply than, large ones, while in other industries only rather large firms can achieve minimum costs. By and large, the difference in the number of firms from one industry to another has tended to correspond to the size of firm that is least costly. Automobile, steel, and airplane manufacturing are all industries in which tiny companies cannot hope to produce economically, and indeed, these are all industries made up of a relatively few large firms. In clothing production and many personal-service industries, matters go the other way.

Frequently, innovation seems to have increased the plant size that minimizes costs. Such examples as automated processes or assembly lines suggest that new techniques always call for gigantic equipment, but this is not always true. For example, the introduction of truck transportation took much of the freight-shipping market away from the giant railways and gave it to much smaller trucking firms. Technological change also seems to have favoured the establishment of small electronics firms. Similarly, the continuing development of cheaper and smaller computers is likely to provide a competitive advantage to smaller firms in many other industries. Furthermore:

If innovation provides increased cost advantages to larger firms, the growth of firms will be stimulated. But a fall in the number of firms in the industry need not inevitably result. If demand for the industry's output grows faster than does the optimal size of the firms, we may end up with a larger number of firms, each of them bigger than before but each having a smaller share of an expanded market.

For example, suppose in some industry a new process is invented that requires a far larger scale of operation than is currently typical. Specifically, suppose that the least costly plant size becomes twice as large. If demand for the industry's product increases only a little, we can expect a decrease in the number of firms. But if demand for the industry's product happens to triple at the same time, then the optimal number of firms will in fact increase to one and a half times the original number—each firm will be twice as big as before, so that together they serve three times the volume. In such a case, each firm's share of industry output will in fact have declined.

In the twentieth century, technological developments do seem to call for larger firms, which are best adapted to take advantage of the resulting economies of scale. Perhaps this has somewhat outstripped the rate of growth in output—that is, the growth of GDP. If so, we should expect some fall in the number of firms in a typical industry, somewhat as many Marxists expect. However, as was just noted, not all technological change has worked in this direction. For example, many firms in the electronics industry are relatively small, and there are observers who argue that new techniques will permit smaller firms to supply some telecommunications services without incurring high costs. We must turn to the evidence to judge whether or not Canadian industry has grown more concentrated.

Evidence on Concentration in Industry

There have been many statistical studies of concentration in Canadian industry. One common way of measuring concentration is to calculate the share of the industry's output produced by the four largest firms in an industry, the so-called **concentration ratio**. Of course, there is no theoretical reason why the three or five or ten largest firms could not be used for the purpose, but conventionally four firms are used as the standard. In Canada, the use of four firms is also dictated by the Statistics Act, which, for reasons of confidentiality, does not permit more detailed information regarding individual companies to be published.

Four-firm concentration ratios in Canada range from 99 (for tobacco products manufacturers and breweries), 93 (for motor vehicle manufacturers), 77 (for makers of major appliances), and 62 (for petroleum refining) to 33 (for bakeries), 21 (for logging), and 6 (for machine shops and women's clothing factories). But only comparisons over time and by geographic area can reveal the most significant implications of these figures. Here, the available evidence suggests that concentration in Canadian industry is somewhat higher than it is in the United States and the United Kingdom. The relatively small size of the Canadian market (which has been somewhat insulated from world markets by tariffs and quotas) and the virtual absence of an effective Canadian merger policy have been put forward as two major explanations for this fact. However, some of the differences are also likely to be the result of different methods of measurement.

In Canada there has been no trend whatsoever in the *average* four-firm concentration ratio over time: It has been stuck at 50 for decades. In a frequently quoted statement concerning a similar phenomenon in the United States, M. A. Adelman, a noted authority on the subject, concluded, "Any tendency either way, if it does exist, must be at the pace of a glacial drift."[11] Or, as a more recent report interprets similar findings for the United States, "Almost all observers of the industrial scene . . . agree that . . . the evidence fails to support a claim that competition has declined. While concentration has increased in some areas, decreases have occurred elsewhere, leaving the overall structure unaffected."[12]

> A concentration ratio is the percentage of an industry's output produced by its *four* largest firms. It is intended to measure the degree to which the industry is dominated by large firms; that is, how closely it approximates a monopoly.

Concentration and Market Power

Why should anyone care about concentration ratios? One should care about them if they are a good measure of market power. **Market power** is the ability of a firm to raise its price significantly above the competitive price level and to maintain this high price profitably for a considerable period. The question, then, is this: If an industry becomes more concentrated, will the firms necessarily increase their ability to institute a profitable rise in price above the competitive level?

Many economists have concluded that this does not necessarily happen. Specifically, the following three conclusions are now widely accepted:

1. If, after an increase in concentration, an industry still has a very low concentration ratio, then its firms are very unlikely to have any market power either before or after the rise in concentration.

2. If circumstances in the industry are in other respects favourable for successful price collusion (tacit or explicit agreement on price), then a rise in concentration will facilitate market power. It will do so by reducing the number of firms that need to be consulted in arriving at an agreement and by decreasing the number of firms that have to be watched to make sure they do not betray the collusive agreement.

> **Market power** is the ability of a firm to raise its price significantly above the competitive price level and to maintain this high price profitably for a considerable period.

[11] M. A. Adelman, "The Measurement of Industrial Concentration," *Review of Economics and Statistics*, vol. 33 (November 1951), pages 295–96.
[12] P. W. McCracken and T. G. Moore, "Competition and Market Concentration in the American Economy," Subcommittee on Antitrust and Monopoly, U.S. Senate, March 29, 1973.

3. Where entry into and exit from the industry are easy and costless—that is, where the market is highly *contestable*—then even when concentration increases, market power will not be enhanced. This is because an excessive price will attract new entrants, who will soon force the price down.

As long as barriers to foreign trade do not preclude foreign firms entering Canadian markets, the openness of the economy should permit many of our markets to be contestable. Tariffs and quotas limit this process, however, and so they raise the likelihood that high concentration truly does represent significant market power. Thus, tariff cuts can be used as a substitute for the traditional legal and regulatory approaches to competition policy that we have considered in this chapter. And given that the latter approaches have met with quite limited success, as we have just learned, many economists *favour* the free-trade approach. It relies on the internal discipline of competition rather than on the externally imposed discipline of the regulator or the legal system.

Summary

1. Regulation has three primary purposes: to put brakes on the decisions of industries with monopoly power; to contribute to public health and safety; or to manage market supply so that producer incomes (for example, those of farmers) can be raised and stabilized.

2. Agriculture, railways, trucking, telecommunications, and gas and electricity supply are among the industries that are directly regulated in Canada.

3. In recent years there has been a major push toward reduction of regulation, except in agriculture and self-regulated areas such as law and medicine.

4. Many agricultural products are sold through marketing boards—that is, monopoly sales outlets that set quotas for all individual producers. While other government regulatory agencies are intended to limit and reduce monopoly power, marketing boards are designed to create and maintain monopoly power.

5. Among the major reasons given for regulation are: (a) economies of scale and scope, which make industries into natural monopolies; (b) the danger of self-destructive competition in industries with low (short-run) marginal costs; (c) the desire to provide service to isolated areas where supply is expensive and unprofitable; (d) the desire for fair allocation of scarce resources (such as radio and television air space); and (e) the protection of consumers, employees, and the environment.

6. The standard rule for reaching the optimal allocation of society's resources—that is, that quantity produced in each industry should be set at the level given by MU = MC—cannot be applied in the case of a natural monopolist. Since AC exceeds MC, the marginal-cost pricing rule would cause such a firm to operate at a loss.

7. Price regulations that limit firms to a normal rate of profit remove the incentive for them to invest in cost-reducing innovations. Deregulation is one approach to this problem, and institutionalized regulatory lag is another.

8. Deregulation in the United States has clearly reduced costs and prices. However, it has also reduced "frills" in service to customers and has been followed by a substantial number of mergers.

9. Nationalized (government-run) industries are frequently suspected of being wasteful and inefficient, but the evidence is not uniform and there are cases in which nationalized firms seem more efficient than similar regulated firms.

10. Competition policy refers to programs designed to control the growth of monopoly and to prevent big business from engaging in "undesirable" practices.

11. The Combines Investigation Act was replaced by the Competition Act in 1986. The most important revisions to the competition policy laws were:
   a. Changing many of the laws to civil rather than criminal provisions.
   b. Changing the legal interpretation of monopoly mergers so that "complete elimination" of competition is not a requirement for prosecution.
   c. Raising the fines involved for breaking the competition laws.

12. By 1990, the new Competition Act had run into several constitutional challenges. While the government has appealed these challenges, they represent a serious threat to the power and flexibility that were envisioned for the new Competition Tribunal.

13. The evidence indicates that there has been no significant increase in the concentration of individual Canadian industries into larger firms during the twentieth century. Direct evidence as to whether competition policy has been effective in preventing monopoly is inconclusive, but it is generally agreed that Canada has not had an effective merger policy.

14. High concentration ratios for domestic industries do not necessarily mean that the larger firms in those industries wield excessive market power, since markets can still be contestable through the elimination of foreign trade barriers.

Concepts for Review

Nationalization
Natural monopoly
Economies of scale
Economies of scope
Cross subsidy
Self-destructive competition
Average-cost pricing
Marginal-cost pricing

Ramsey Pricing Rule
Regulatory lag
Privatization
Combines Investigation Act
Competition Act
Resale price maintenance
Predatory pricing
Price discrimination

Vertical merger
Horizontal merger
Conglomerate merger
Concentration of industry
Concentration ratio
Patent
Market power

Questions for Discussion

1. Why is a hydroelectric company in a city usually considered to be a natural monopoly? What would happen if two competing hydroelectric companies were established? How about telephone companies?

2. In some regulated industries, prices are prevented from falling by the regulatory agency and, as a result, many firms open up business in that industry. In your opinion, is this competitive or anti-competitive? Is it a good idea or a bad one?

3. List some industries with regulated rates whose services you have bought. What do you think of the quality of their service?

4. In which, if any, of the regulated industries mentioned in your previous answer is there competitive rivalry? Why is regulation appropriate in these cases? (Or is it inappropriate in your opinion, and if so, why?)

5. Do you think it is appropriate for local users of telephone service to be cross subsidized by other telephone users?

6. Can you think of a way in which a new rural telephone subscriber contributes a beneficial externality? If so, does it make sense to provide a subsidy to rural subscribers? Who should pay the subsidy?

7. How might one go about distinguishing "predatory" from "non-predatory" pricing?

8. To provide incentives for increased efficiency, several regulatory agencies in the United States have eliminated ceilings on the profits of the regulated firm but instead put caps on their prices. Suppose a regulated

firm manages to cut its prices in half but in the process doubles its profits. Should rational consumers consider this to be a good or a bad development? Why?

9. Suppose Sam lives in the central city while Fran's home is far away, so that it requires much more gas to deliver newspapers to Fran than to Sam. Yet the newspaper charges them exactly the same amount. Would the courts consider this to be price discrimination? Would an economist? Would you? Why?

10. A shopkeeper sells her store and signs a contract that restrains her from opening another store in competition with the new owner. The courts have decided that this contract is a *reasonable* restraint of trade. Can you think of any other types of restraint of trade that seem reasonable? Any that seem unreasonable?

11. Why do you think some industries are highly concentrated?

12. Do you think it is in the public interest to launch a combines suit that costs a billion dollars? What leads you to your conclusions?

13. In Japan and a number of European countries, the competition laws are much less severe than those in the United States. Do you think this helps or harms American industry in its efforts to compete with foreign producers? Why?

14. Do you think government authorities should interfere more than they do now in corporate takeover activities? What are some of the pros and cons?

32

Environmental Protection and Resource Conservation

We learned in Chapter 27 that *externalities* (the incidental benefits or damages imposed upon people not directly involved in an economic activity) can cause the market mechanism to malfunction. The first part of this chapter takes up a particularly important application of the analysis of externalities—the problem of environmental deterioration. The second half addresses the closely related subject of natural-resource depletion and the interwoven questions of energy use and environmental decay.

Environmental protection is one of the critical issues of our era, and one in which there is naturally a great deal of public interest. As concerned citizens, you will be called upon to participate, in one way or another, in the global effort to curb the growing problems in this area, and your understanding of the economic principle of externalities and of the related issue of property rights will enable you to come to a better-informed and more-responsible position on the subject. We have chosen to end our textbook with this chapter precisely because it so clearly embodies our belief that you will be able to apply the ideas you have learned here "beyond the final exam."

The Economics of Environmental Protection

Environmental problems are by no means new. What *is* new and different is the amount of attention the community is now prepared to give them. Perhaps much of this increased interest can be attributed to rising incomes, which have freed people from the more urgent concerns about food, clothing, and shelter, allowing them the luxury of concentrating on the next level of needs—the *quality* of their lives.

Economic thought on the environment preceded the outburst of public concern about the subject by nearly half a century. In 1911, a noted British economist, A. C. Pigou, wrote a remarkable book called *The Economics of Welfare*, which offered an explanation of the market economy's poor environmental performance that is still generally accepted by economists today. What is more, that same book outlined an approach to environmental policy that is still favoured by most economists and that is beginning to win over lawmakers as well. Pigou suggested that a system of charges on emissions would be an effective and efficient means of controlling pollution. In this way, the price mechanism can remedy one of its own shortcomings.

The most common method for controlling water and air pollution in Canada is for the provincial governments to issue specific discharge limits for each individual firm. Often, each firm in an area or an industry is required to reduce its pollution by the same percentage amount. The analysis in this chapter will enable us to see why this assignment of equal percentage reductions is both inefficient and inequitable.

"The picture's pretty bleak, gentlemen.... The world's climates are changing, the mammals are taking over, and we all have a brain about the size of a walnut."

The Environment in Perspective: Is Everything Getting Steadily Worse?

Much of the discussion of environmental problems in the popular press leaves the reader with the impression that matters have been growing steadily worse, and that pollution is largely a product of the profit system and modern industrialization. As we will see, there are environmental problems today that are both enormous and pressing, but in fact pollution is nothing new. Medieval cities were pestholes—the streets and rivers were littered with garbage and the air stank of rotting wastes. At the beginning of the eighteenth century, a German traveller reported that to get a view of London from the tower of St. Paul's, one had to get there very early in the morning "before the air was full of coal smoke." And early in the twentieth century the automobile was hailed as a source of major improvement in the cleanliness of city streets, where until then a losing battle against the proliferation of horse dung had been fought.

Since 1960 there has been progress in solving some pollution problems, much of it the result of concerted efforts to protect the environment. The quality of the air in most Canadian cities has improved. In Toronto, for example, the concentration of suspended particulates, or soot, in the air has fallen dramatically since the Grey Cup "Smog Bowl" of 1962. On that weekend, the air pollution index rose to 155. To put this figure in perspective, it should be noted that the current health advisory level for the index is 32. At a level of 58, people with chronic respiratory diseases may be affected. At 100, even healthy people may be affected by prolonged conditions, and those with cardiac and respiratory diseases could suffer severe effects. Depending on weather conditions, readings in excess of 50 can trigger a first alert and cause industrial operations to be curtailed. At 100, the air pollution threat is considered serious and the province can order a stoppage of all operations not essential to public health and safety.

Such regulations are improving the situation. Recently in Toronto, for example, the index has exceeded 32 on fewer than half a dozen days annually. Similar improvements have occurred elsewhere in Canada and in other industrialized countries. Even the famous, or rather infamous, "fogs" of London are almost a thing of the past. There have been two high readings of particular note in the British capital: in 1959 (when the index rose to 275 and there was a 10 percent increase over the normal number of deaths) and in 1962 (when the index rose to 575 and there was a 20 percent increase in mortality). But more recently, London's cleaner air has resulted in an astounding 50 percent increase in the number of hours of winter sunshine. In short, pollution problems are not a uniquely modern phenomenon, nor is every part of the environment deteriorating relentlessly.

Environmental problems do not occur exclusively in capitalist economies. For example, in the People's Republic of China, coal soot from factory smokestacks in Beijing envelops the city in a thick black haze. Similarly, smoke from brown-coal furnaces pollutes the air almost everywhere in Eastern Europe. The Polish government recently declared Bogomice and four other towns "unfit for human habitation," because of heavy-metal particles suspended in the air and deposited in the soil by emissions from nearby copper-smelting plants, and it has been estimated that a third of Poland's citizens live in areas of "ecological disaster." In December 1987, the Soviet newspaper *Pravda* stated that the industrial city of Ufa, with a population of nearly one million, had also become unfit for human beings. The citizens of Leipzig, a major industrial city in what was formerly East Germany, have a life expectancy a full six years shorter than the national average. The Iset and Volga rivers in the Soviet Union are so filled with chemicals that they have actually caught fire!

In the preceding discussion we have tried to put matters into perspective, but we do not mean to suggest that all is well with the environment in market-oriented economies or that there is nothing more to do. While there have been some improvements, serious problems remain. Our world is now subject to a number of new pollutants, most of which are far more dangerous than those we have reduced, even though they may be less visible and less malodorous.

A variety of highly toxic substances—PCBs (polychlorinated biphenyls), chlorinated hydrocarbons, dioxins, heavy metals, and radioactive materials—are dumped carelessly, left to cause cancer and threaten life and health in other ways. Some of these substances linger in the environment so long that they are likely to constitute a threat for many thousands of years. The accumulation of these and other by-products of modern technology may well cause damage that is all but irreversible. Ironically, although successful clean-up of conventional water pollutants has returned fishlife to some previously "dead" waterways, those fish are sometimes inedible because they are so contaminated with toxic substances. This is true of the Great Lakes, where vast quantities of toxic pesticides and other chemicals remain trapped in bottom sediments. But even these problems pale in comparison with the environmental issues discussed in the boxed insert on pages 756–57. There, we consider acid rain, the problem of carbon dioxide buildup in the earth's atmosphere (and the resulting increase in global temperatures that some scientists predict), the expanding hole in the ozone layer of the atmosphere, and toxic wastes.

While environmental problems are neither new nor confined only to capitalist, industrialized economies, these facts are not legitimate grounds for complacency. The potential damage that we are inflicting on ourselves and on our surroundings is very real and very substantial.

The Law of Conservation of Matter and Energy

The physical law of conservation of matter and energy tells us there is no way that objects can be made to disappear—at most they can be changed into something else. Oil, for instance, can be transformed into heat (and smoke) or into plastic—but it will never vanish. After a raw material has been used, either it must be used again (recycled) or it becomes a waste product that must somehow be disposed of.

If any input used in the production process is not recycled, it *must* ultimately become a waste product. It may end up on the garbage heap of some municipal dump. It may literally go up in smoke, contributing its bit to the pollution of the atmosphere. Or it may even be transformed into heat, warming up adjacent waterways and killing aquatic life in the process. The laws of physics tell us there is nothing we can do to make used inputs disappear altogether from the earth.

In fact, only a small proportion of the economy's inputs are made up of recycled materials, and although recycling rates for such commonly used materials as aluminum, paper, and glass appear to be rising in many industrial countries, only one country—the Netherlands—recovers more than half of these products, which are relatively easy to recycle. Canada's current recycling rates are among the worst in the industrialized world; we recycle only about 3 percent of such goods, on average. Things are improving, however. During the 1980s, more than 250 Canadian municipalities (about 200 of them in Ontario) launched voluntary recycling programs. A more aggressive approach is being adopted in the United States. There, at least 30 states have adopted laws requiring the recycling of wastes. Recycling laws and municipal garbage fees are hitting people where it hurts: in the pocketbook. In one town, for instance, noncompliance with recycling rules results in fines of up to $500. In another, residents must pay by the bag to have their garbage taken away, instead of paying a flat annual fee for whatever amount of trash they produce. The switch to the pay-by-the-bag system has reduced trash volume by 25 percent, as people are induced to recycle, compost, and perhaps refrain from purchasing "over-packaged" products. These examples are typical of what is starting to happen in many communities.

Nevertheless, as we discussed in Chapter 3, the recent public enthusiasm for recycling has created a glut of recycled items, with the result that the existing system does not have the capacity to process all of them, and some portion is simply dumped as usual (see page 56). Hence, average recycling rates of 25 percent are considered very successful. And although this does represent an important step in the right direction, we must realize that, with output growing over time and with input use consequently increasing, waste disposal and pollution are virtually certain to be growing problems.

Many people think of industry as the primary villain in environmental damage. But although private firms have done their share in harming the environment, private individuals and government have also been prime contributors. The emissions of private passenger cars play an important role in the air pollution problems of most major cities; wastes from residential washing machines contribute to their water pollution problems. Governments are guilty as well. Major hydroelectric power projects usually alter entire ecosystems fundamentally, and the wastes of municipal sewage-treatment plants are a major source of water pollution. Worse still, many municipalities continue to dump untreated sewage into lakes and rivers. Consider conditions in Quebec: In 1990, only one-sixth of that province's towns and cities were equipped with sewage-treatment plants, and less than half of Montreal's sewage was being treated. (To keep matters in perspective, we should note that this problem is not exclusive to Canada: 70 percent of the cities on the Mediterranean pump unprocessed sewage into the sea. If the governments of the developed world have such poor records, what can we reasonably expect of the less developed countries?) Even more threatening than inadequate sewage treatment, however, are government-run nuclear power plants that produce radioactive materials, which are among the most dangerous of all wastes. And the problem of their disposal is far from solved.

Environmental Damage as an Externality

We have already indicated that our very existence means that some environmental damage is inevitable. Products of the earth must be used up, and wastes must be generated in the process of creating the means of subsistence.

There is no question of reducing environmental damage to zero. As long as the human race survives, complete elimination of such damage is impossible. *Indeed, it is not even desirable to get as close as possible to zero damage.* Some pollutants in small quantities are quickly dispersed and rendered harmless by natural processes, and it is not worth the opportunity cost to eliminate others whose damage is slight. Use of a large quantity of resources for this purpose could so limit their supply that there would not be materials available for the construction of hospitals, schools, and other things more important to society than the elimination of some pollutants.

The real issue, then, is not whether pollution should exist at all, but whether environmental damage in an unregulated market economy tends to be more serious and widespread than the public interest can tolerate. This issue immediately raises three key questions. First, why do economists believe that environmental damage is unacceptably severe *in terms of the public interest*? And how do they measure "the public interest"? Second, why does the market mechanism, which is so good at providing about the right number of toasters and trucks, generate too much pollution? What goes wrong with the system? And, third, what can we do about it?

Economists do not claim any special ability to judge what is good for the public interest. They normally prefer to accept the wishes of the members of the public as adequate indicators of "the public interest." When the economy reflects these wishes as closely as it can, given the resources and technology available, economists conclude that it is working effectively. When it operates in a way that frustrates the desires of the people, they conclude that the economy is functioning improperly. Why, then, do economists believe that the market mechanism generates "too much" pollution?

To answer this, we must deal with the fundamental analysis of A. C. Pigou, to which we referred at the beginning of this chapter. In Chapter 27 we discussed some of the failures of the market mechanism and singled out externalities as a primary cause. An *externality*, it will be recalled, is an incidental consequence of some economic activity that is either beneficial or detrimental to someone who neither controls the activity nor is intentionally served by it. The emission of pollutants constitutes one of the most clear-cut examples of a detrimental externality. The smoke from a chemical plant affects people other than the management of the plant or its customers. Because the incidental damage done by the smoke does not enter the financial accounts of the firm whose plant produces the emissions, the owners of the firm have no financial incentive to restrain those emissions, particularly since emission control costs money. Instead, they will find it profitable to produce their chemical product and to emit their smoke as though it caused no external damage to the community.

One way to look at the matter is as *a failure of the pricing system*. Through the smoke externality, the business firm is able to use up some of the community's clean air without paying for the privilege. Just as the firm would undoubtedly use oil and electricity wastefully if they were obtainable at no charge, the firm uses the community's air wastefully, despoiling it with smoke far beyond the level that the public interest can justify. Rather than being at the (low) socially desirable level, the quantity of smoke is at whatever (usually high) level is necessary to save as much money as possible for the firm that emits it, because the external damage caused by the smoke costs the firm nothing.

The achievement of any solution to this externality problem is particularly difficult when the smoke crosses political boundaries. This represents a very large problem for Canada, as the boxed insert on pages 756–57 indicates.

Externalities

Externalities play a crucial role affecting the quality of life. They show why the market mechanism, which is so efficient in supplying consumers' goods, has a much poorer record in terms of its effects on the environment. The problem of pollution illustrates the importance of externalities for public policy and indicates why their analysis is one of our 12 **Ideas for Beyond the Final Exam**.

Supply–Demand Analysis of Environmental Problems

Basic supply–demand analysis can be used to explain both how externalities lead to environmental problems and how these problems can be cured. As an illustration, let us look at the problem of solid wastes—and the damage that the massive generation of garbage is doing to our environment.

In Figure 32–1 (on page 758) we see a demand curve, *DE*, for garbage removal. As usual, this curve has a negative slope, meaning that if the price of garbage removal is set sufficiently high, people will become more sparing in the amount of garbage removal they order. They may more often bring papers, bottles, and cans to recycling centres and public dumps; they may repair broken items rather than throw them out; and so on. In short, a higher price for garbage removal can be expected to reduce the quantity demanded of garbage-removal services.

The graph also shows the supply curve, *SS*, that we can expect to prevail in an ideal market for garbage removal. Garbage disposal is expensive to society—it requires people and trucks to haul it away; garbage dumps occupy valuable land; and the use of fire or other means to get rid of the garbage creates pollution that, as we have seen, has a high real cost to the community. As we saw in our analysis of competitive

The Threatened Environment

In recent years we have come to realize that several threats to the environment are fundamental. One is acid rain, which is created by the millions of tonnes of sulphur dioxide and nitrogen oxides spewed out of North American smokestacks and automobile exhaust pipes (globally, more than 4.5 billion tonnes of carbon are injected into the earth's atmosphere each year). The oxides mix with water vapour in the air to form weak sulphuric and nitric acid, which later falls as acid rain. The result is increased acidity in lakes, which has curtailed the ability of many fish to reproduce, and in the soil, which has slowed the growth of trees and increased their vulnerability to disease. The taller the smokestacks and the stronger the prevailing winds, the farther away from the source of the pollution the damage is likely to occur. Fifty percent of the acid rain that falls in Canada comes from American sources, and about 10 percent of the acid rain that falls in the eastern United States comes from Canada.

Canadian authorities have taken major steps in coming to grips with the problem of acid rain in recent years. For example, the federal government set a requirement that polluters reduce sulphur-dioxide emissions below 1980 levels by 25 percent by 1990 and by a further 25 percent by 1994. Research has indicated that these reductions, along with similar cutbacks in the United States, would maintain acid deposits at an "acceptable" level. But this reduction program is very costly for the Americans, since it involves their reducing emissions by 12 billion tonnes per year (Canada has to cut back by only 2.3 billion tonnes). In addition, many of the benefits of this expenditure by the Americans would flow to Canada—a classic externality situation. It was only in 1990 that the U.S. government made a substantial commitment to the emission-reduction program.

Clearly, one reason that pollution issues are so difficult to solve is that they are rife with problems of externality, which stem from the fact that clear property rights do not exist. Who owns the air or the rivers: the general public or the owners of the firms that discharge the waste? It is very difficult to come to an agreement that establishes such prop-

erty rights, especially when more than one country is involved.

When problems are fairly localized, agreements are more feasible. For example, the governments of Ontario, New York state, Canada, and the United States have agreed to cut pollution in the Niagara River by 50 percent by 1996. But when more jurisdictions are involved—as is the case in Europe—agreements are more difficult to come by. For example, West Germany and Austria regularly complain of acid rain and river contamination from Czechoslovakia, yet nothing has been done to eliminate the problem.

With every news report, the externality dimension of environmental problems seems to become clearer. For instance, it was recently reported that Lapp villagers in northern Sweden and Norway were forbidden to eat local reindeer meat after their herds became contaminated by fallout from the nuclear accident at Chernobyl in far-off Ukraine. (This episode highlights another difficulty: that a single accident can have such lasting effects.) Similarly, Canadian wildlife scientists have found high levels of PCBs and other contaminants in polar-bear livers.

The lack of established property rights is an age-old

industries (Chapter 23), the position of the market's supply curve depends on the marginal cost of garbage removal. If suppliers have to pay the full costs of garbage removal, the supply curve will be comparably high (as drawn in the graph) and have a positive slope, meaning that the marginal cost of garbage disposal rises as the quantity rises. We see that, for the community depicted in the graph, the price of garbage removal will be P dollars per tonne, and at that price 10 million tonnes will be generated (point A).

But what if the community's government decides to remove garbage "free"? Of course, that means the government is really charging the consumer for the service in the form of taxes, but not in a way that makes each consumer pay for the quantity of garbage that he or she produces. The result is that the supply curve is no longer SS. Rather, it becomes the green line, TT, which lies along the horizontal axis, because any household can increase the garbage it throws away and still face a zero cost. Now the intersection of the supply and demand curves is no longer point A. Rather it is point E, at which the price is zero and the quantity of garbage generated is 25 million tonnes—

factor in the destruction of common resources. When European settlers moved across the plains of North America, their cow herds, being privately owned, were not killed off. The buffalo were publicly owned, however, so it was in no particular hunter's interest to preserve the herds. It is therefore not surprising that the buffalo no longer roam.

It may be that people are becoming increasingly aware of the need to establish property rights for the environment. No-smoking areas are spreading at a rapid rate, as people understand more about the effects of second-hand smoke.

But some pollution problems involve such dramatic externalities that the whole world is affected. One example is the greenhouse effect. The steadily rising and essentially irreversible concentration of carbon dioxide in the earth's atmosphere causes it to trap increasing amounts of the heat radiated by the planet. The general warming trend is expected to have disastrous effects, including mass starvation in some less developed countries, flooding of entire coastal areas, and severe droughts on the Canadian prairies, perhaps within the next fifty years.

Another worldwide threat is in the upper atmosphere—the thinning of the layer of ozone, a bluish gas that shields the earth from the sun's ultraviolet rays. Synthetic chemicals called chlorofluorocarbons (CFCs) are depleting the ozone layer. One estimated result is that the chance of getting skin cancer is now 8 to 16 percent greater than it was in 1950. The Montreal Protocol, an international treaty ratified by Canada and 46 other nations (effective January 1, 1989), calls for a 50 percent reduction in the production and use of CFCs by 1998, and for a total halt in their production two years later.

Hazardous wastes (such as those from nuclear plants, industrial manufacturing, laboratories, and medical institutions) represent yet another critical environmental problem: improperly disposed, they can threaten all forms of organic life. Unfortunately, little has been done so far to solve this problem. Indeed there are many instances in which industrialized countries have literally just shipped the problem off to the poorest of the less developed countries—countries unequipped with the necessary storage and treatment facilities, and certainly too poor to deal with the serious environmental problems that will follow. For example, in 1988 the government of Guinea-Bissau signed a contract with two British firms to receive 15 million tonnes of pharmaceutical wastes over a five-year period. While this arrangement was very inexpensive from the firms' point of view, the payments to Guinea-Bissau totalled more than four times that country's national product. It makes it difficult to solve the problem when parts of the world are so poor that they are forced to regard such transactions as "good deals."

The users of the world's resources simply must be made to take the external costs of their actions into consideration when making their decisions. The people who are hacking down the world's rain forests at the rate of 1200 hectares an hour are literally cutting away the lungs of the earth, since rain forests contribute a large percentage of the oxygen in the earth's atmosphere. But these individuals are not necessarily evil: in many cases, they are forced to overuse the environment for their own or their country's immediate survival. For example, some developing countries' needs for foreign exchange to pay for imports compel them to cut timber faster than it can be regenerated. They simply cannot afford to worry about the future.

Obviously, many of these problems cannot be solved without political decisions to redistribute income to the less developed countries, and to define property rights. But the right kinds of political and institutional changes will be forthcoming only if they are rooted in an understanding of the externality dimension of environmental issues.

Countries in the developed world must therefore learn to co-operate in order to devise a sufficiently comprehensive program of income redistribution to the less developed countries. Without help from the developed world, these poorer countries cannot possibly make the sacrifices that the human race must make *collectively* to reverse the deterioration of the environment.

It is clear that the degree of global income redistribution required is vast, and that we must consequently ensure that the pollution-abatement strategies we adopt involve the *least possible costs* in terms of job and income losses. That is why we argue so forcefully later on in this chapter for the most efficient pollution-abatement schemes available.

---

an amount substantially greater than would be produced if those who made the garbage had to pay the cost of getting rid of it.

Similar problems occur if the community offers the oxygen of its waterways and the purity of its atmosphere without charge to all who choose to utilize them. The amount that will be wasted and otherwise used up is likely to be enormously greater than it would be if users had to pay for the cost of their actions to society. And that, in the view of economists, is one major reason for the severity of our environmental problems. Several conclusions follow:

1. The magnitude of our pollution problem is attributable in large part to the fact that the market lets individuals, firms, and government agencies deplete such resources as oxygen in the water and pure air without financial charge.

2. One way of dealing with pollution problems is to charge those who emit pollution (or despoil the environment in other ways) a price commensurate with the costs they impose on society.

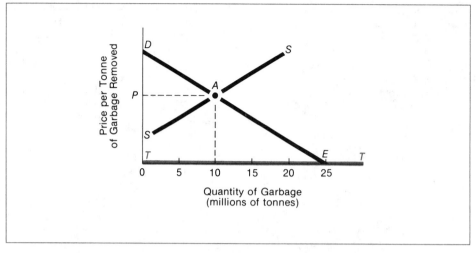

FIGURE 32-1

Free Dumping of Pollutants as an Inducement to Environmental Damage
Whether wastes are solid, liquid, or gaseous, they impose costs upon the community. If the emitter is not charged for the damage, the resulting wastes are effectively being removed at zero charge to the polluter (green removal supply curve *TT*). The polluter is thus induced to pollute a great deal (25 million tonnes in the figure). If the charges to him reflected the true cost to the community (supply curve *SS* of waste removal), it would pay to emit a much smaller amount (10 million tonnes in the figure).

3. This is another instance in which higher prices—on environmentally damaging activities—can be beneficial to the community.

Basic Approaches to Environmental Policy

In broad terms, three general methods have been proposed for the control of activities that damage the environment.

1. *Voluntary programs*, such as non-mandatory investment in pollution control equipment by firms that decide to act in a manner that meets their social responsibilities, or voluntary separation of solid wastes by consumers for recycling.

2. *Direct controls*, which either impose legal ceilings on the amount any polluter is permitted to emit or specify how particular activities must be carried on—for example, they may prohibit backyard incinerators or the use of high-sulphur coal or require smokestack "scrubbers" to capture the emissions of electricity-generating installations.

3. *Taxes on emissions*, or the use of other monetary incentives or penalties to make it financially unattractive for emitters of pollutants to continue to pollute as usual.

Each of these methods has its place. If used appropriately, together they can constitute an effective and efficient environmental program. Let us consider each of them in turn.

Voluntarism

Voluntary control of pollution has usually proved to be weak and unreliable. Voluntary programs for the collection and separation of garbage into different and easily recyclable materials have rarely managed to reroute more than a small fraction of a community's wastes from the garbage dump to the recycling plants. Some business people with strong consciences have manifested good intentions and made sincere attempts to improve the practices of their companies. Yet competition has usually prevented them from spending more than token amounts for this purpose. No business, whatever its virtues, can long afford to have the prices of its products undercut by rival suppliers. As a result, voluntary business programs have often been more helpful to the companies' public relations activities than to the environment. Firms with a real interest in environmental protection have called for legislation that *requires* all firms, including competitors, to undertake the same measures, thereby subjecting all firms in the industry to similar handicaps.

Yet voluntary measures do have their place. They are appropriate where alternative measures are not readily available. Where surveillance and, consequently, enforcement are impractical, as in the prevention of littering by campers in isolated areas, there is no choice but an appeal to people's consciences. And in brief but serious emergencies, in which there is no time to plan and enact a systematic program, there may also be no good substitute for voluntary compliance. Several major cities have, for example, experienced periods of temporary but dangerous concentrations of pollutants and the authorities were forced to appeal to the public to avoid activities that would aggravate the problem. One can easily cite cases in which the public response to appeals requiring co-operation for short periods was enthusiastic and gratifying. To summarize:

Voluntary programs are not dependable ways to protect the environment. However, in brief, unexpected emergencies or where effective surveillance is impossible, the policy-maker may have no other choice. Sometimes in these cases voluntary programs work.

Incidentally, government spending policies can create incentives for voluntary action in the private sector (or at least minimize private-sector resistance to non-voluntary changes). A recent example from Australia illustrates the point. In that country, the departments of the federal government collectively use enough paper that their demand alone can justify a very large pulp mill. The government has announced that it will use only unbleached paper (it is the bleaching process that produces the dioxins and furans that are the environmental culprits in the pulp and paper industry). The Australian government policy effectively undercuts industry arguments that a shift to unbleached paper is unaffordable (on profitability and job-creation grounds).

Direct Controls

Direct controls have been the chief instrument of environmental policy in Canada. Under the constitution, legislative authority for the environment is shared between the provincial and federal governments. The job of enforcing federal standards often falls to the provinces. Probably the best-known of these controls are automobile emissions standards. The federal government establishes emissions standards for new vehicles being sold in Canada, but the provincial governments are responsible for the control of pollution after the vehicles have been sold.

Control measures in provincial legislation, such as Ontario's Environmental Protection Act, include control orders, stop orders, and program approvals. These restrictions focus on the *results* of pollution. Such was the case on October 13, 1970, when the Ontario government ordered forty-eight firms and institutions in Toronto and Hamilton to reduce operations because the air pollution index exceeded 50.

Since then, major operations such as Ontario Hydro, Inco, Falconbridge and Algoma Steel have co-operated with a 1986 Ontario statute that requires them to reduce sulphur-dioxide pollution by 67 percent in stages between 1986 and 1994. This step is significant since these four companies produce 80 percent of the acid gas pollution in the province.

Taxes on Emissions

Most economists agree that a nearly exclusive reliance on direct controls is a mistake and that, in most cases, financial penalties on polluters can do the same job more dependably, more effectively, and more economically. The most common suggestion is that firms be permitted to pollute all they want but be forced to pay a tax for the privilege, to make them *want* to pollute less. A tax on emissions requires the polluter to install a meter that records emissions in the same way that a hydro meter records the use of electricity. At the end of the month the government automatically sends the polluter a bill charging a stipulated amount for each litre of waste (the amount must also vary with the quality of the wastes—a higher tax rate being imposed on wastes that are more dangerous or unpleasant). Thus, the more damage the polluter does, the more he must pay. Such taxes are deliberately designed to *encourage* the use of a glaring loophole—polluters *can* reduce the tax they pay by decreasing the amount they emit. In terms of Figure 32–1, if the tax is used to increase the payment for waste emissions from zero (green supply line TT) and instead forces the polluter to pay their true cost to society, emissions will automatically be reduced from 25 million to 10 million tonnes.

Firms do respond to such taxes. The most widely publicized example comes from the Ruhr River basin in Germany, where emissions taxes have been used for more than three decades. Though the Ruhr is one of the world's most concentrated industrial centres, those of its rivers that are protected by taxes are sufficiently clean to be usable for fishing and other recreational purposes. Firms have found it profitable to avoid the taxes by extracting pollutants from their liquid discharges and recycling. Almost 40 percent of the industrial acids used in the Ruhr are recovered in this way.

It is encouraging that Finance Minister Michael Wilson has reflected publicly about using taxes as a lever to achieve environmental goals. It is hoped that his officials have studied the success of such schemes as Singapore's charging of a toll on vehicles entering the downtown area with fewer than four passengers. The day the policy went into effect in Singapore, there was a 50 percent drop in the number of cars entering the city. In the absence of such a scheme, Toronto's ground-level ozone readings in 1988 exceeded federal maximum guidelines on more than 100 occasions.

Emissions Taxes versus Direct Controls

It is important to see why taxes on emissions may prove more effective and reliable than direct controls. Direct controls rely essentially on the enforcement mechanism of the criminal justice system. Rules are set up that the polluter must obey. If the polluter violates those rules, he must be caught. Then the regulatory agency must decide whether it has enough evidence to prosecute. Next, it must win its case before the courts. And, finally, the courts must impose a penalty that is more than a token gesture. If any one of these steps does not occur, the polluter gets away with damaging activities.

Enforcement Issues

The enforcement of direct controls requires vigilance and enthusiasm by the regulatory agency, which must assign the resources and persons needed to carry out the task of enforcement. Yet experience indicates that regulatory vigour is far from universal and often evaporates as time passes and public concern recedes. In many cases the resources devoted to enforcement are pitifully small. Also, there are often lags in the court process, and legislation has typically prescribed ridiculously light penalties for violators.

The following facts illustrate some of these problems. The province of Quebec has some of the toughest environmental laws in Canada, with fines ranging up to $1 million per day, but little effort seems to go into enforcing the law. For example, in 1987 fewer than half the companies required by law to submit a report complied. In Ontario, surveys by the Ministry of the Environment showed that half the province's industries and one-third of the municipal sewage plants violated water pollution guidelines in 1988. The Ontario government did obtain 176 convictions in 343 court cases during 1988–89, but the total fines involved only $2 million. However, some progress is being made: in 1989 Ontario became the first province to jail a corporate executive for a pollution-related offence (the firm repeatedly ignored a court order to curtail emissions). Since corporate executives are directly responsible for actual decision-making, the threat of imprisonment is one aspect of the legal approach that might indeed represent a more effective disincentive than do the prevailing, relatively small, fines and penalties.

But even when the legal machinery is set in motion, the laws often seem rigged in favour of polluters. For example, early in 1990, an arsonist set fire to 15 million used tires at the five-hectare Tyre King dump in Hagersville, Ontario. The fire—the largest of its kind in North American history—burned for seventeen days, and forced the evacuation of the area. A major component of tires is a petroleum-based substance that is highly flammable and almost impossible to extinguish once it catches fire. The flames release toxic gases and a dioxin-laced oil that contaminates the water system. In 1987, Tyre King had been issued a control order to stack the tires in hundreds of piles separated by fire lanes, and to fence the site. The company appealed the order, and three years later, when the fire broke out, a hearing date had yet to be set. By allowing the activity in question to continue until an appeal is heard, current laws give polluters an incentive to appeal rather than to obey the law.

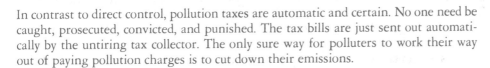

In contrast to direct control, pollution taxes are automatic and certain. No one need be caught, prosecuted, convicted, and punished. The tax bills are just sent out automatically by the untiring tax collector. The only sure way for polluters to work their way out of paying pollution charges is to cut down their emissions.

Efficiency in Clean-Up

A second difference between direct controls and taxes is worth noting. Suppose there is a ruling under a program of direct controls that Filth, Ltd., must cut its emissions by 50 percent. That firm has absolutely no motivation to go one drop further. Why should it cut its emissions by 55 or even 52 percent when the law offers it neither reward nor encouragement for going beyond the selected quota? Under a system of emission taxes, however, the more the firm cuts back on its pollution, the more it saves in tax payments.

A third important difference between direct controls and taxes on emissions is the greater efficiency of the latter in the use of resources. The tax approach can probably do the job far more cheaply, saving labour, fuel, and raw materials, which can instead be used to build, say, schools, hospitals, and housing for low-income groups. Statistical estimates for several pollution-control programs suggest that the cost of doing the job through direct controls can easily be twice as high as under the tax alternative.

Why should there be such a difference? The answer is that under direct controls the job of cutting back emissions is apportioned among the various polluters on the basis of some principle (usually intended to approximate some standard of fairness) selected by the regulators. This approach rarely assigns the task in accordance with the firm's ability to carry it out cheaply and efficiently. Suppose it costs Firm A only 2 cents a litre to reduce emissions while Firm B must spend 10 cents a litre to do the same job. If both firms spew out 2000 litres of pollution a day, a 50 percent reduction in pollution can be achieved by ordering both firms to limit emissions to 1000 litres a day. This may or may not be fair, but it is certainly not efficient. The social cost will be 1000 times 2 cents, or $20, to Firm A and 1000 times 10 cents, or $100, to Firm B—a total of $120.

If, instead, a tax of 5-cents-per-litre is imposed, all the work will be done by Firm A—which can do it more cheaply. Firm A will cut its emissions out altogether, paying the 2 cents a litre this requires, to avoid the 5-cent-per-litre tax. Firm B will probably go on polluting as before, because it is cheaper to pay the tax than the 10 cents a litre it costs to control its pollution. In this way, under the tax, *total daily emissions will still be cut by 2000 litres a day*. But the entire job will be done by the polluter who can do it more cheaply, and the total daily cost of the program will therefore be $40 (2 cents × 2000 litres) instead of the $120 it would cost under direct controls.

The secret of the efficiency induced by a tax on pollution is straightforward. Only polluters who can reduce emissions cheaply and efficiently can afford to take advantage of the built-in loophole—the opportunity to save on taxes by reducing emissions. The tax approach simply assigns the job to those who can do it most effectively.

Equity Issues

Under direct controls the authorities usually aim at an *equitable* assignment of emissions quotas. For example, they may require all polluters to reduce their discharges by the same percentage. However, the attempt to put this rule into practice almost always results in complaints, political pressures, renegotiation of quotas, and a consequent set of assignments that seem to have been designed with the aid of a roulette wheel rather than a deliberate decision-making process.

Why are equal percentage reductions in emissions not generally equitable? We have already seen one reason: Costs of reduction are not the same for all industries or all plants in an industry. For example, the cost for a typical beet sugar plant to reduce its emissions (as measured in terms of the oxygen these wastes use up) is only about one-sixth as large as an equivalent reduction for a petroleum refinery. A modern paper plant can usually decrease its discharges at much less cost than can an antiquated plant in the same industry. Is it really *fair* to require all these firms to cut back their emissions by the same amounts when, through no fault of their own, the resulting financial burden and loss of jobs is so different?

There are even clearer examples of the potential inequity in equal percentage reductions. Consider two companies, one run by a conscientious environmentalist who has voluntarily installed substantial amounts of equipment to cleanse and reduce emissions, and the other by an irresponsible management that has continued to allow as much garbage to pour into the public waterways as maximum profitability requires. Is it really fair for both these firms to be told to cut back equally?

Once such problems and others like them are recognized, and an attempt is made to reassign emissions quotas accordingly, it will become clear that each emitter is a special case requiring special treatment. The regulator is almost forced to proceed case by case, and the resulting quotas end up following complex patterns that are at best difficult to defend in terms of equity or efficiency.

The pollution tax avoids these problems by leaving to the individual firm the choice of whether to pollute and pay the tax or to clean up.

Advantages and Disadvantages

Given all these advantages of the tax approach, why would anyone want to use direct controls?

There are three general and important situations in which direct controls have a clear advantage:

1. *Where an emission is so dangerous that it is decided to prohibit it altogether.* Here there is obviously nothing to be gained by installing complicated procedures for the collection of taxes that will never be paid because there will be no emissions for which payment is required.

2. *Where a sudden change in circumstances—for example, a dangerous air quality crisis—calls for prompt and substantial changes in conduct, such as temporary reductions in the use of cars or incinerators.* It is difficult and clumsy to change tax rules, and direct controls will usually do a better job here.

3. *Where effective and dependable metering devices have not been invented or are prohibitively costly to install and operate.* In such cases there is no way to operate an effective tax program; if the amount of wastes the polluting firm has emitted cannot be determined, its tax bill cannot be calculated. In that case the only effective option may be to *require* it to use "clean" fuel or to install emissions-purification equipment.

In reality there is often no device analogous to a gas or water meter that can be used to measure pollution emissions cheaply and effectively. For example, to evaluate emissions in waterways, the standard procedure is to take samples, bring them to a laboratory, and subject them to a series of complicated tests (which often take weeks to carry out) to determine the chemical contents of the emissions. For a polluter whose emissions are very large, this may be worth doing. But for the emitter who spews out only a few litres of pollutants a day, the cost of such a complex process is likely to exceed the benefits. Whatever their other inefficiencies, direct controls are likely to do the job of controlling such sources of pollution more cheaply. On the other side of the argument, however, is the possibility that the widespread adoption of emissions charges and the resulting rise in demand for metering devices could lead to research and development that produces cheaper and more effective meters.

Other Financial Devices to Protect the Environment

The basic idea underlying the emissions-tax approach to environmental protection is that it provides financial incentives for polluters to reduce the damage they do to the environment. But emissions taxes are not the only form of financial inducement that has been proposed. There are at least two others that deserve consideration: *subsidies for reduced emissions* and the requirement of *emissions permits* for polluters, each permit authorizing the emission of a specified quantity of pollutant. Such permits would be offered for sale in limited quantities fixed by the authorities, at prices set by demand and supply.

Subsidies

Subsidies are already in use. Their advocates say that financial inducements can be just as effective when they take the form of a reward for good behaviour as when they take the form of a penalty (taxes) for harmful behaviour. One can induce a donkey to move forward by dangling a carrot in front of its nose just as surely (and with much less unpleasantness) as by applying a stick to its rump. Environmental subsidies usually take one of two forms:

1. Partial payment of the cost of installation of some sort of pollution-control equipment.
2. The offer of a fixed reward for every reduction in emissions from some base level, usually some amount that the polluter emitted in the past.

A subsidy to help defray the cost of control equipment can be effective when the purchaser of the equipment was considering doing it anyhow but did not because of the high cost. This may be the case for a municipality that wants to treat its wastes more thoroughly but has not found a way to afford the cost. It may also be the case in private industry, where collection of the wastes can yield products that are valuable and reusable but the equipment required for the process is too costly. But where the polluter gains nothing from such control, a partial subsidy for the purchase of control equipment is not likely to be very effective. It simply reduces the cost of something he does not want to do in any event.

The second type of subsidy—a reward based on quantity of reduced emissions—does indeed have the same sort of incentive effects for *individual* polluters as does a tax. In both cases the more polluters emit, the worse off they are financially, either because they receive a smaller subsidy payment or because their tax bill is higher. But as far as the *industry* is concerned, there is a world of difference between the effect of a tax and the effect of a subsidy. *A tax discourages the output of commodities whose production causes pollution, whereas a subsidy encourages such output to expand.* Consider the difference between the tax and the subsidy approaches in the case of automotive emissions. A tax will increase the cost of operating cars, thereby encouraging the use of public transportation (which produces far lower quantities of emissions per passenger-kilometre travelled than does the automobile). On the other hand, a subsidy for the installation of emissions-control devices will tend to encourage the use of autos at the expense of public transportation by keeping down the price of cars.

It is a paradox that a subsidy intended to induce an industry to reduce its emissions can actually *increase* the size of the industry's output and consequently *increase* its total emissions.

This paradox is readily illustrated with the help of a standard supply–demand diagram for a competitive industry. We see in Figure 32–2 that a tax on polluting output will raise the costs of the industry and hence raise the price of whatever quantity it supplies. Thus, a tax will shift the supply curve upward to the curve labelled "supply after tax." Similarly, the subsidy will reduce dollar costs to the industry and so will shift the supply curve downward to the curve labelled "supply after subsidy." So, under a tax on emissions, the equilibrium point will move from point E to point T, reducing the output of the polluting product from e to t. But the subsidy, which moves the supply–demand equilibrium point from E to S, will actually *increase* the output of the polluting industry, from e to s! How does this happen? While the pollution-reduction subsidy will induce each firm to decrease its emissions somewhat, it will also attract new polluting firms into the industry; as the graph shows, the net result may be that the subsidy will backfire, and instead of reducing pollution, as it is intended to do, it will actually increase it.

The main advantage of subsidies over taxes as a financial inducement to decrease pollution is that subsidies attract less opposition and are therefore more easily adopted through the political process. Obviously, industry always prefers a subsidy to a tax. But the rest of the community may well be worse off if a subsidy is selected instead of an emissions tax.

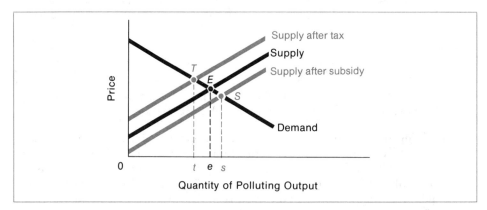

FIGURE 32–2
Supply–Demand Equilibrium in a Competitive Polluting Industry
A tax on pollution raises costs and so shifts the supply curve upward; that is, a higher price is needed to elicit a given quantity supplied. This causes equilibrium output to fall from *e* to *t* and succeeds in its purpose—reducing pollution. But a subsidy to those who decrease their polluting output reduces costs and shifts the supply curve downward. By reducing costs, it attracts more firms into the industry. Paradoxically, output of the polluting product must actually increase from *e* to *s*.

Putting Ivory-Tower Theory to the Test

As indicated in the text, one remedy for pollution long advocated by economists as an alternative to direct controls is the issuance of a limited number of pollution permits to be sold on a free market. About fifteen years ago, the U.S. Environmental Protection Agency (EPA), motivated by theoretical studies suggesting huge savings in pollution-control costs and under pressure from approaching deadlines for air pollution standards, began to experiment with a program of emissions trading. The four components of this program—netting, offsets, bubbles, and banking—work together as a market in emissions permits.

Netting was introduced in 1974. It allows a company to create a new source of pollution in a factory if it cuts emissions from another source within the same factory, thus effecting an internal trade of emissions. Next came *offsets*, which allow *new* factories or other new sources of air pollution to be constructed in areas where pollution standards have not been met, so long as their emissions are more than offset by reductions in pollution from elsewhere. This program permits external trades. For example, firm A can open for business if it can induce firm B to adopt pollution controls that cut down B's emissions by an amount at least equal to A's proposed emissions.

So far, few offset transactions have worked out quite this way. Instead, most firms have obtained permits to build new plants by means of internal offsets—that is, by reducing emissions from other plants they own. In some cases, offsetting reductions in emissions have been undertaken by government agencies. For example, state officials in Pennsylvania switched to non-polluting road-paving materials on the state's highways to offset the pollution from a new Volkswagen auto assembly plant in New Stanton.

The *bubble* program, introduced in 1979, is similar to the offsets program but applies to firms already in operation rather than to newly established plants or firms. With the old direct controls, each pollution-discharge point in a factory or plant was regulated. But under the bubble concept, all operations of the firm are considered to be encased in an imaginary bubble with a single discharge point; the firm is permitted to satisfy the air pollution ceiling for its bubble in any way it finds most economical. The EPA does not care what goes on inside the bubble—that is, whether emissions come from one point or another—as long as emissions from the entire bubble stay within the required limits.

Banking, the last element in the EPA's emissions-trading program, permits firms whose total emissions fall below the required limits to sell their unused emission rights to

Classified advertisement in *The Wall Street Journal*, June 5, 1986, page 32.

other firms whose bubbles are not performing so well, or to store these extra rights in an emission-reduction "bank" for future use or trade.

The level of activity within each of these programs has varied widely. Netting has been the best-received, accounting for between 5000 and 12,000 transactions through the mid-1980s. About 2000 offset trades have taken place, though only 10 percent of them have been external offsets. Fewer than 150 bubbles have been approved, and there has been almost no banking. Nevertheless, one expert concluded that the emissions-trading program has "clearly afforded many firms flexibility in meeting emission limits, and this flexibility has resulted in significant aggregate cost savings—in the billions of dollars."*

*Robert W. Hahn, "Economic Prescriptions for Environmental Problems: How the Patient Followed the Doctor's Orders," *Journal of Economic Perspectives*, vol. 3, no. 2 (Spring 1989), page 101.

Emissions Permits

A third type of financial inducement strongly advocated by some economists is the sale of *marketable emissions permits*. Under this arrangement, the environmental agency decides what quantity of emissions per unit of time (say, per month) is tolerable and then issues a batch of permits authorizing (altogether) just that amount of pollution.

The permits are offered for sale to the highest bidders. Their price is therefore determined by demand and supply. It will be high if the number of permits offered for sale is small and there is a large number of industrial firms that must use the permits. Similarly, the price of a permit will be low if many permits are issued but the number of polluters demanding them is small.

In many ways the emissions permit works the way a tax does—it simply makes it too expensive for polluters to continue emitting as much as they would have without it. In addition, the permit offers two clear advantages over the tax approach. First, it reduces uncertainty about the quantity that will be emitted. Under a tax we cannot be sure about this in advance, since it depends on the extent to which polluters respond to the tax rate that is selected. In the case of permits, the ceiling on emissions is decided in advance by the environmental authorities, who enforce the ceiling simply by issuing permits authorizing a specific total quantity of emissions.

Second, any given tax on emissions will be eroded and made ineffective by inflation. For example, a tax of X dollars will become insignificant as inflation erodes the value of the dollar, even though it may have been effective when it was first enacted and the price level was much lower. With an emissions-permit system, however, as long as there is no change in the quantity of emissions authorized by licence, inflation will obviously have no effect on the amount of pollution. It will simply raise the price of a licence along with the prices of other commodities.

A shortcoming of the pollution-licence idea is its apparent political unattractiveness: Many people react indignantly to the notion of "licences to pollute." Yet the Environmental Protection Agency in the United States has introduced some compromise measures that are close approximations to a market in emissions permits (see the boxed insert on page 765). These measures have been embraced by several international conferences on pollution problems in recent years.

Two Cheers for the Market

We have seen that protecting the environment is one task that cannot be left to the free market; because of the important externalities involved, the market will systematically allocate too few resources to the job. This problem is particularly difficult to solve politically when the pollution extends beyond political boundaries. However, if pollution is localized, the market failure does not imply that the price mechanism must be discarded. On the contrary, we have seen that a legislated market solution—based on pollution charges—may well be the best way to protect the environment. At least in this case, the power of the market mechanism can be harnessed to correct its own failings.

The Economics of Energy and Natural Resources

We turn now, in the second half of this chapter, to the case of natural resources, where the market mechanism also plays a crucial role. The "energy crisis" of the 1970s, during which the price of oil leapt dramatically upward, had profound effects throughout the world—one of which was a marked change in our tendency to think that unlimited stocks of natural resources are simply ours for the taking. Indeed, in the mid-1970s there was near-panic about the prospect of running out of a number of commodities. In fact, humanity has a long history of panicking about imminent exhaustion of natural resources. In the thirteenth century a large part of Europe's forests was cut down, primarily for use in metalworking (much of it for armour). Wood prices rose, and there was a good deal of talk about the depletion of fuel stocks.

In this part of the chapter, we will try to sort such matters out. On the one hand, natural resources have always been scarce, and one can argue with good reason that they have been used wastefully. On the other hand, we are *not* about to run out of most vital resources, and there is reason to be optimistic about the availability of substitutes.

A Puzzle: Those Resilient Resource Supplies

It is a plain fact that the earth is endowed with only finite quantities of such vital resources as oil, copper, lead, coal, and many others. This fact has fascinated pessimists through the years. In 1972, extreme pessimism assumed its most scientific guise in a publication by the Club of Rome called *The Limits to Growth*. Using computers to project future world conditions, the authors concluded "with some confidence" that if there is "no major change in the present system ... industrial growth will certainly stop within the next century, at the latest." At the core of the problem, they said, would be our running out of resources.[1]

Table 32–1 shows the sort of data that are frequently used to support such doomsday forecasts. The bottom line of the table shows for four minerals the number of years of consumption (assuming unchanged rates of use) that could be met by known reserves of these resources as of 1980. Reading this table without knowing what lies behind it can indeed be alarming. It seems to say that we will run out of all of these vital minerals by the year 2051.

But now compare the two rows of the table. Surely something mysterious is going on! We see that in 1960 only about a twenty-four-year supply of zinc apparently remained. Yet twenty years later, despite all the zinc that had been used in the meantime, the reserves of zinc were estimated to last another forty-two years! Each of the other resources also had *larger* reserves in 1980 than in 1960, even though rates of consumption had risen in the interim. This does seem a funny way to keep score.

In part, this puzzle is ascribable to the misleading nature of figures on "known reserves," though these are the sorts of statistics on resource depletion that are commonly cited by pessimists. But economic principles also help a great deal in clearing up the mystery.

The Free Market and Pricing of Depletable Resources

If figures on known reserves behave as peculiarly as those we have just seen, one begins to doubt their ability to indicate whether we are really coming uncomfortably close to running out of certain resources. Is there some other indicator of growing scarcity that seems more reliable? Most economists agree that there is—that the *price of the resource* serves this function well.

As a resource becomes scarcer, we expect its price to rise for several reasons. One is that for most resources the process of depletion is not simply a matter of gradually using up the supply of a homogeneous product, every unit of which is equally available. Rather, the most accessible and highest-quality deposits of the resource are generally

[1]Donella H. Meadows et al., *The Limits to Growth* (New York: Universe Books, 1972), pages 125–26.

TABLE 32–1
Expected Life (in Years) of Some World Mineral Reserves, 1960 and 1980 Estimates

	ZINC	NICKEL	LEAD	COPPER
1960	24	43	19	37
1980	42	71	47	59

Notice that we had more years' supply of each of these depletable resources in 1980 than in 1960, despite twenty years of consumption!
SOURCE: Bureau of Mines, U.S. Department of the Interior, *The Domestic Supply of Critical Minerals*, 1983, page 21.

---

used up first; then industry turns to less accessible locations and/or deposits of lower purity or quality, and then finally to deposits that are still harder or more costly to extract or of still poorer quality. Oil is a clear example of this. First, Canadians relied primarily on the most easily found domestic oil wells. Then they turned to imports from South America and elsewhere, with their higher transport costs. At that point it was not yet profitable to embark on the dangerous and extremely costly process of bringing up oil from the ocean floor off Newfoundland. We know that Canada still possesses huge stocks of petroleum embedded in the Alberta tar sands and in the Arctic, but until recently they have been too difficult and, therefore, too costly to get at.

Increasing scarcity of a resource such as oil is not usually a matter of imminent and total disappearance. Rather, it takes the form of exhaustion of the most accessible and cheapest sources so that new supplies become more costly.

A second reason for rising resource prices is hidden in the operation of the supply–demand mechanism. To see how it works, let us consider the simpler (if less realistic) case in which extraction of a resource does not grow increasingly difficult as its reserves dwindle. That is, we envision the earth's supplies of a mythical mineral, Zipthon, all of identical quality, which can be extracted and delivered to market with negligible extraction and transportation costs. How quickly will the reserves of Zipthon be used up, and what will happen to the price of the mineral with the passage of time?

If the market for Zipthon is perfectly competitive, we can provide a remarkably concrete answer about the behaviour of prices. The answer, which was discovered by the American economist Harold Hotelling, tells us that as long as the supply of Zipthon lasts, its price must rise at a rate equal to the rate of interest. That is, if in 1990 the price of Zipthon is $100 per tonne and the rate of interest is 10 percent, then its price in 1991 must be $110.

Under perfect competition the price of a depletable resource whose costs of transportation and extraction are negligible must rise at the rate of interest. If the rate of interest is 10 percent, the price of the resource must rise 10 percent every year.

Why is this so? The answer is simple. People who have money tied up in inventories of Zipthon must earn exactly as much per dollar of investment as they would by putting their money into, say, a government bond. Suppose that $100 invested in bonds would next year rise in value to $112, while $100 in Zipthon would grow only to $110, and suppose the two investments were equally risky. What would happen? People who owned Zipthon would obviously find it profitable to sell the Zipthon and put their money into bonds instead.

But as more Zipthon was dumped on the market, it would become increasingly abundant today and increasingly scarce tomorrow. So its expected *future* price would rise while its actual *current* price would fall. This and other associated changes in Zipthon prices and bond prices would continue until there was no further advantage in the one investment against the other—that is, until both offered the same rate of return per dollar of investment.

The same process, working in reverse, would apply if Zipthon prices were rising faster than the rate of interest. Investors would switch from bonds to Zipthon, and with more Zipthon held for investment rather than released for current consumption, current prices of Zipthon would rise. At the same time the abundance of future stocks would be increased and thus expected future prices would fall.

Following this fundamental principle about the pricing of a scarce resource with fixed extraction costs, let us see what will happen to the price of $100 worth of Zipthon over the course of, say, four years. We have the following pattern of Zipthon prices:

INITIAL DATE	ONE YEAR LATER	TWO YEARS LATER	THREE YEARS LATER	FOUR YEARS LATER
$100	$110	$121	$133.10	$146.41

These prices follow from the fact that $110 is 10 percent higher than $100, $121 is 10 percent higher than $110, and so on. What is to be noted is that because of the compounding effect, the dollar amount of the price increase is greater and greater each year. Zipthon rises in value by $10 in the first year, $11 in the second year, $12.10 in the third, $13.31 in the fourth, and so on indefinitely. Thus we conclude:

The basic law of pricing of a depletable resource tells us that as its stocks are used up its price in a perfectly competitive market will rise every year by greater and greater dollar amounts.

Notice that we have been able to make these predictions about the price of Zipthon without any knowledge about the supply of Zipthon or consumer demand for it. This is really remarkable. But if we want to go on to determine what will happen to the consumption of Zipthon—the rate at which its inventory will be used up—we need to know something about supply and demand.

In Figure 32–3(a) there is a demand curve for Zipthon, *DD*, which shows the amount people want to use up *per year* at various price levels. On the vertical axis we show how the price must rise from year to year in the pattern we have just calculated—from $100 per tonne in the initial year to $110 in the next year, and so on. Because of the negative slope of the demand curve, it follows that each year consumption of Zipthon will fall. That is, *if there is no shift in the demand curve*, consumption will fall from 100,000 tonnes initially, to 95,000 tonnes in the next year, and so on.

FIGURE 32–3

Consumption over Time of a Depletable Resource

The price of the resource must rise, year after year (from $100 to $110 to $121, and so on). If the demand curve does not shift [part (a)], quantity demanded will be reduced every year. Even if the demand curve does shift outward [as in part (b)], the increasing price will keep any rise in quantity demanded lower than it would otherwise have been.

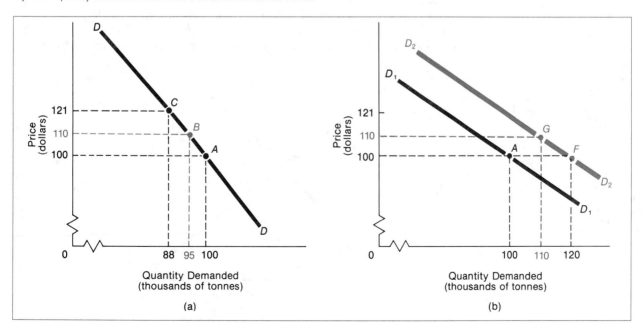

(a)   (b)

But in reality such demand curves rarely do stay still. As the economy grows and population and per-capita incomes increase, demand curves can be expected to shift outward. And there is every reason to believe that this has been true of the demand for most scarce resources. Shifts in the demand curve naturally tend to increase consumption, thereby offsetting at least part of the reduction in quantity demanded that results from rising prices. Nevertheless, it remains true that rising prices do help to cut back consumption growth relative to what it would have been if price had remained constant. In Figure 32–3(b) we depict an outward shift in demand from curve D_1D_1 in the initial period to curve D_2D_2 a year later. If price had remained constant at the initial value, \$100 per tonne, quantity consumed per year would have risen from 100,000 tonnes to 120,000 tonnes. But since, in accord with the basic principle, price must rise to \$110, quantity demanded increases only to 110,000 tonnes—which is smaller than 120,000 tonnes. Thus, whether or not the demand curve shifts, we conclude:

The ever-rising prices that accompany increasing scarcity of a depletable resource discourage consumption (encourage conservation). Even if quantity demanded is growing, it will grow less rapidly than if prices were not rising.

How do the facts match up with this theoretical analysis? Their correspondence is very poor indeed. For example, the real prices of zinc and lead (that is, after the effects of general inflation or deflation have been eliminated) have remained roughly constant during this century, while other resource prices, such as the price of crude oil, have experienced large shifts (both up *and* down) every few years. Thus, in reality, resource prices have not risen steadily, as our simple theory might have led us to expect.

How does one explain the actual behaviour of the prices of finite resources, which surely are being used up, even if only gradually? What this price behaviour indicates is that reality is much more complicated than our simple analytic model and that sometimes the complications grow so extreme that prices behave very differently from what simple theory predicts. Of these complications, we mention only three:

1. *Unexpected discoveries of reserves whose existence was previously not suspected.* If we were to stumble on a huge and easily accessible reserve of Zipthon, which came as a complete surprise to the market, the price of Zipthon would obviously fall. This is illustrated in Figure 32–4, where we see that people originally believed the available supply curve to be that represented by curve S_1S_1. The discovery of the new Zipthon reserves leads them to recognize that the supply is much larger than

FIGURE 32–4
Price Effects of a Discovery of Additional Reserves
A discovery causes a rightward shift in the supply curve of the resource. Because the cost to suppliers of any given quantity of the resource is reduced by the discovery, it will pay them to supply a larger quantity at any given price. This must lead to a price fall (from P_1 to P_2).

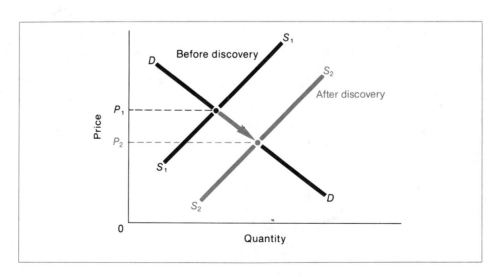

they had thought (curve S_2S_2). Like any outward shift in a supply curve, this can be expected to cause a fall in price.

2. *The invention of new methods of mining or refining that may significantly reduce extraction costs.* This, too, can lead to a rightward shift in the supply curve as it becomes profitable for suppliers to deliver a larger quantity at any given price. The situation can also be represented by Figure 32–4, only it is now a reduction in cost, not a discovery of new reserves, that shifts the supply curve to the right.

3. *A government subsidy.* From the point of view of the supplier, a government subsidy is exactly the same as a reduction in mining or processing costs—either technological improvement or a handout from the government will decrease the cost per tonne of supplying the resource. Thus the supply curve will shift to the right (from S_1S_1 to S_2S_2 in Figure 32–4) and the price will fall.

Yet, despite these influences, which postpone the price rises in depletable resources predicted by the theory, both logic and evidence indicate that in the long run, as a resource really becomes scarce and costly to obtain, its price must ultimately rise.

The Free Market and Resource Depletion

Popular views of the process of depletion of a vital resource envision a scenario in which consumption grows year after year and stocks of the item dwindle as a result until, one day, quantity supplied can no longer keep up with quantity demanded. From then on, the nation faces a history of steady shortfalls, with rationing or chaos the inevitable result. Economists pay little attention to such scenarios. Though it seems implausible to anyone who has not studied economics, it is nevertheless true that:

In a free market, quantity demanded can never exceed quantity supplied, even if a finite resource is undergoing rapid depletion. The reason is simple: In any free market, quantity demanded must always equal quantity supplied, for price will automatically adjust to eliminate any difference between them.

In fact, there have been cases of real shortages in the past. For example, twice during the 1970s the quantities of gasoline supplied were, in many parts of the United States, lower than the quantities demanded, and chaos did indeed result. There were long lines of cars at those gas stations that remained open, and huge amounts of petroleum and time were wasted in the process as the cars inched forward (sometimes for hours) toward the gas pumps. During World War II, meat, sugar, and other commodities were in short supply, and there was a period in the 1970s when supplies of paper, copper, and other commodities were inadequate to meet demand. But in every such case there were regulations or laws that prohibited full adjustment of prices. In a sense, then, it was these price regulations, and not any disappearance of resources, that were responsible for the shortages.

In theory, any shortage—any excess of quantity demanded over quantity supplied—must be artificial; that is, it must be ascribed to a decision to prevent the price mechanism from doing its job.

To say that the cause is artificial does not, of course, settle the basic issue—whether freedom of price adjustments is desirable when resource depletion is under way, or whether interference with the pricing process is justified. We will see that there are, in fact, valid grounds on which to question the desirability of completely unrestricted freedom of pricing in such circumstances.

Many economists, however, believe that this is another of those cases in which the cure—deregulation of prices—is better than the disease—shortages and the resulting dislocations in the economy. They hold that the general public is misguided in its clamour against the rising prices that must ultimately accompany depletion of a resource, and that people are mistaken in regarding these price rises as the problem when in fact they are part of the cure.

It is, of course, easy to understand why no consumer loves a price rise. And it is also easy to understand why many consumers ascribe any such price rise to a plot—to a conspiracy by greedy suppliers who somehow deliberately arrange shortages in order to force prices upward. Sometimes, this view is correct. For example, the members of OPEC have openly and frankly undertaken to influence the flow of oil in order to increase the price they receive for it. But it is important to recognize from the principles of supply and demand that when a resource grows scarce, its price will tend to rise automatically, even without any conspiracies or plots.

Let us first see how economists can possibly say that rising prices for scarce resources are good for the economy. Then we will consider some valid reservations about the desirability of an unfettered-market solution as we discuss the controversy over Canadian energy policy.

On the Virtues of Rising Prices

Rising prices help control the process of resource depletion in three basic ways:

1. They discourage consumption and waste and provide an inducement for conservation.

2. They stimulate more efficient use of the resource by industry, providing incentives for the employment of processes that are more sparing in their use of the resource or that use substitute resources.

3. They encourage innovation—the discovery of other, more abundant resources that can do the job and of new techniques that permit these other resources to be used economically.

Let us examine each of these a bit more carefully.

It used to be said that consumer demand for oil was highly *inelastic*—that prices would never make a significant dent in consumption of petroleum. Recent events seem to have proved otherwise. With rising fuel prices people have begun to insulate their homes, to keep home temperatures lower, to take fewer shopping trips, and to buy smaller automobiles. Moreover, in the long run, we can expect even more demand adjustment—that is, the long-run demand curve for oil is probably more elastic than the short-run curve. As the nation's fleet of cars wears out, they will gradually be replaced by vehicles that economize on fuel. New homes will be built more snugly to save on heat, and they will be located closer to the workplace to save on fuel in transportation.

Evidence indicating how much difference price can make is provided by the pattern of fuel consumption in Europe. There, fuel taxes have long habituated the public to high gasoline prices, and fuel consumption per capita is much less than it is in North America.

The second way in which a price increase helps to conserve a scarce resource is through its effect on industrial usage. Like a final consumer, a business firm can economize on its use of a resource. It can use more fuel-efficient means of transportation and more insulation. It can locate its new plants in ways that reduce the need for transportation. And it can substitute labour and other inputs for scarce resources. The use of a pick and shovel involves the employment of more labour to save the fuel that might have been used by a bulldozer. Farmers who gather manure save the fuel necessary to produce chemical fertilizers. U.S. oil-consumption data provide clear evidence of the overall responsiveness of the demand for oil to its price. Between 1960 and 1973, U.S. demand increased by more than 75 percent, but after the OPEC price increases, from 1973 to 1985, demand declined by 10 percent.

Finally, rising prices help to slow the disappearance of a resource by stimulating the production of substitutes and even by inducing more production of the resource itself. The last statement is paradoxical—if a resource is finite, how can more be produced? Certainly it can be extracted and sold faster, but that only hastens the process of depletion. How can we get *more* of a *finite* resource? Of course, we cannot. But rising prices make it feasible to use repositories of the resource that otherwise would have been considered not worth the effort. It has recently become economically feasible, for example, to extract oil from Canada's tar sands—formations that it was formerly too expensive to exploit. Similarly, piping natural gas from the Arctic has long been talked about, but only higher prices will make it feasible.

Higher prices of a vanishing resource also stimulate research and development leading to the emergence of substitute products. It is high oil prices that will transform solar energy, wind energy, and biomass energy from romantic notions, which cynics can deride as impractical, into effective sources of fuel that may someday make substantial contributions to the economy's energy flows. At the oil prices in effect during the 1960s, these sources simply could not compete.

A final word on the price mechanism and resource conservation is in order. One often hears about the rape of our natural resources by greedy owners who rush to exchange them for profits without any thought for the needs of the future. But the price mechanism has built-in incentives to prevent this from happening. We have seen how a resource's price can be expected to rise automatically as its stocks dwindle. Obviously, when the price rise is sufficiently rapid, it becomes more profitable to leave more of the resource underground for future extraction than to sell it now at today's lower prices. One may legitimately object to this for many reasons, but surely *not* on the grounds that oil supplies are being squandered by excessive and irresponsible rates of extraction.

Freedom of pricing of a dwindling resource induces conservation by consumers and by industry; it encourages the introduction of substitute products; and it induces moderation in rates of extraction by the owners of the resources.

Growing Reserves of Exhaustible Resources: Our Puzzle Revisited

We began the second part of this chapter with a brief discussion of the more pessimistic views about future resource supplies, including an estimate made in 1960 that by 1985 we would have run out of zinc and lead and would have only eighteen years of nickel reserves and twelve years of copper reserves left. Yet in Table 32–1 (page 767) we saw that between 1960 and 1980 the reserves of all of these finite resources actually increased.

This paradox, as we have seen, has a straightforward economic explanation: Rising reserves are a tribute to the success of exploration activity that took place in the meantime. Minerals are not discovered by accident. They are discovered by difficult and costly work requiring the services of geologists and engineers and the use of extremely expensive machinery. Exploration requires an enormous expenditure, which industry does not find worth making when reserves are high and when mineral prices are low.

Consequently, over the course of the twentieth century proven reserves have not changed very much. Every time some mineral's known reserves fell, particularly if its price therefore tended to rise, exploration increased until the decline was offset.

Controversies over Canadian Resource Policy

Depletable Resources

Let us now consider how some of these arguments apply to the Canadian experience. Our 1974–84 controversy over oil prices stemmed from four basic facts. First, many Canadian consumers of oil felt that the high world price was *artificial*. It had been caused by a monopolistic cartel in foreign lands. Since Canada has the resources to be self-sufficient in oil, many felt that we should not be "held to ransom" by such monopoly practices. After all, the only reason we import oil in the East and export it in the West is that we lack sufficient pipeline facilities. It was argued that if we could solve this problem, our self-sufficiency in oil would permit a lower, "made in Canada" price.

The second major influence in the oil price debate was the *fear of unemployment* expressed by many workers in manufacturing firms in central Canada and in the energy industries of the West. The concern in central Canada was that large increases in energy prices would force firms to lay off some of their workers. We learned in Chapter 8 that this reasoning is correct: Rising costs of energy cause an inward shift of the aggregate supply curve, leading simultaneously to a rise in the overall price level and to a fall in real GDP (review Figure 8–2 and pages 164–67 if necessary). But the decrease in output for the country as a whole would be much smaller than that which would occur in central Canada. Meanwhile, energy workers in the West feared that low prices for energy in Canada would eliminate the profit incentive for their employers, so that exploration and other activities would diminish, with a consequent loss of jobs in the West. We learned earlier in this chapter that this reasoning is also correct. Thus, fear of unemployment and lower incomes boiled down to a *distribution problem*: Whose incomes should the governments protect—those of workers in central Canada or those of workers in the West?

The third major issue in the oil price discussions was the fight between the federal and provincial (mainly Alberta) governments concerning tax revenue. *Both levels of government wanted the tax revenue that could stem from higher oil prices.* Natural resources are owned by the provinces, which can impose various taxes (known as royalties) on producers operating on provincial lands. But the federal government has jurisdiction over international and interprovincial trade, so it can levy export and import taxes and subsidies as oil crosses provincial and international borders. The two levels of government were forced to negotiate, because there is a limit to the total amount of tax that can be imposed. If taxes are very high, consumer prices must also skyrocket to provide some operating revenue to the producer. So the total tax is bounded by concern for both consumers and producers.

The fourth important factor in the oil price issue was the high degree of *foreign ownership* in the energy industry. Approximately 70 percent of the shares of oil companies operating in Canada were foreign-owned. The federal government thought a low oil price was a good idea because it would limit the profits of these companies and so preclude a large transfer of income from Canadians to foreigners.

How did the energy policy of the Liberal federal government accommodate these four concerns? The Canadian price of oil was allowed to increase, but only very *gradually*, so that by 1981 it was at only half the level of world oil prices. This pricing policy followed from two considerations: (1) the federal government's sympathy with the view that Canadian resource endowments give us the right and ability to ignore world prices, and (2) its view that potential unemployment in manufacturing operations in Ontario was more important, on political grounds, than potential unemployment in the energy industries in the West. The government's attempt to overcome the problem of there being no pipeline to Atlantic Canada involved imposing export taxes on oil and gas from the West to pay for an import subsidy for foreign oil purchased in the East.

Concerning the distribution of energy tax revenues between Ottawa and the provinces, the federal government simply saw the world price developments as an opportunity to tap a lucrative new tax source. It imposed the Petroleum and Natural Gas Revenue Tax at such a level that producer returns became *negative*.[2] This forced

---

[2] See Brian L. Scarfe, "The National Energy Program After Three Years: An Economic Perspective," *Western Economic Review*, 1984.

provincial governments (principally Alberta) to reduce their taxes, just to try to stimulate economic activity within their own regions.

Two components of the federal National Energy Program were directed at the issue of foreign profits. One was direct purchases of oil operations from foreigners (this included such measures as the creation of PetroCanada), and the other involved levying a tax on producing firms that was designed to avoid limiting the return on *new* exploration and development. The idea in this case was to tax oil discovered before 1981 much more heavily than that found later. The "old" oil is produced at much lower cost than that from recent operations. Thus, economic rents exist on these older operations, since the going market price is sufficient to make viable the more recent, more expensive extractions. From a microeconomic point of view, the attempt to tax only rents made sense, as long as the tax was not set too high (review Chapter 29, pages 642–48, if necessary).

How did the federal government's decisions turn out? Were they consistent with sound economic analysis? Again, let us consider each part of the problem in turn. Of course, our energy supplies made it *possible* for Canadians to pay a price below world levels. Nevertheless, the option of selling at the world price was available, so it represented the true opportunity cost of Canadians' using domestic energy. (Consuming energy resources domestically means that we cannot sell those resources to foreigners at the world price. The world price therefore represents the buying power that we forgo.) A lower price simply prevented the "correct" signals of relative scarcities from reaching individual Canadian decision-makers. Only if the high world price could have been viewed as very temporary (say, because of an expectation that OPEC would collapse as a result of internal struggles over production quotas for member countries) would it have made sense to insulate our economy from a needless series of adjustments.

The federal government's views concerning unemployment in central Canada versus unemployment in the West appear to have been somewhat short-sighted. Job prospects are not enhanced in Canadian manufacturing if artificially low energy prices encourage the perpetuation of production techniques that are inefficient by international standards. Finally, unemployment in central Canada was increased when the depressed energy industry in the West sent fewer orders back East for industrial equipment and when job-seekers ceased their migration to the West.

Some "Canadianization" of the energy industry did follow from the National Energy Program, but any contribution this might have made to establishing "security of supply" was certainly nullified in the short run by the cutbacks in exploration and development that stemmed from low producer prices and high taxes. Unfortunately, the nationalization program and the retroactive taxing of the oil industry's most profitable operations (involving "old" oil) came at a most inopportune time—just as deregulation was occurring in the United States. Combined with the negative returns, this was enough to cause a significant shift in economic activity to the United States.

In summary, with the passage of time, any validity of the "made in Canada" oil price diminished. By late 1984, Canadian prices were roughly in line with world prices, but the lag in getting there had been too long. Among the problems that resulted from this lag were a cutback in oil development, a delay in moving toward less energy-intensive production methods, and a setback in federal–provincial co-operation. When the Conservatives came to federal power in 1984, they reversed many of the Liberal policies. By 1986, all of the major components of the National Energy Program had been dismantled.

Renewable Resources

As we enter the 1990s, it seems that more attention is being paid to several other Canadian resources—fisheries, fresh water, and forests. In principle, these are all renewable resources, but there is serious concern that, in practice, depletion is foreseeable in these areas as well. For example, our fishery stocks are certainly being run down and, again, a fundamental externality problem is involved. To protect the size of the stocks in the future, we need government regulations today limiting the size of current catches. But property rights cannot be easily defined, since the fish swim on both sides of the boundary that separates Canadian and international waters. In 1990, for example, the countries of the European Community decided to take three times more fish from the international waters off Newfoundland than the amount recommended by the North Atlantic Fisheries Organization, a 17-member international agency to which the European Community belongs. There is no mechanism allowing Canada to appeal this sort of transgression. Hence, to ensure our resources of fish are protected for the future, our government has little option but to impose stiffer quotas on domestic fishing. For some communities in Atlantic Canada, the effect of these developments is devastating.

Similar problems plague our supply of fresh water. The Saint Lawrence River—the source of drinking water for about half of Quebec's 6.7 million people—is so polluted that beluga whales are dying at a rapid rate. Similarly, in British Columbia, Greenpeace calls the Fraser River "the biggest sewer line" in the province.

With regard to forests, public concern had become so great by 1990 that proposals for a significant slowdown in the rate of future development of our forestry resources were under serious consideration. One example of the problems involved comes from Alberta. In an attempt to prevent the province's economy from becoming too dependent on a single resource—oil—the Alberta government sold forest-cutting rights on a grand scale: Between 1987 and 1990, rights for an area almost the size of Great Britain were sold off. In addition to the threat of deforestation, other environmental concerns ensued. In 1990 the federal government intervened in the provincial government's activities to investigate the environmental impact of a large pulp-mill complex that was planned on the Athabasca River about 100 kilometres northeast of Edmonton. Pulp mills introduce hundreds of chemical compounds known collectively as organochlorines—a major source of dioxins—into the water system.

The dispute over this kind of resource development represents the classic trade-off: short-run job creation versus potentially long-term environmental damage (in this case, to drinking water and native fisheries). Central Canada could ease the terms of this trade-off for Alberta—and the similar trade-off facing Atlantic Canada that we discussed earlier—by facilitating the diversification of those regional economies. If the more environmentally friendly economic activities that are currently more prevalent in central Canada were encouraged throughout the country, the burden of protecting our resource stocks would be more evenly distributed, and would consequently be made more manageable.

Serious Problems Remain

We close this chapter with some thoughts about the future. First, we might note that there are some grounds for optimism about the availability of energy. Past history and research already under way suggest that new techniques will become feasible as higher prices encourage the development of alternative energy sources. Already solar heating has become economically viable in certain cases (especially for private homes in sunny climates) and its use can be expected to spread. Also, scientists are studying the use of geothermal energy, and nuclear fusion promises a virtually unlimited supply of energy if we can learn to harness it. In all these ways, then, higher prices will lead to a lower quantity demanded and a greater quantity supplied of energy, thus helping to avert an "energy crisis."

Yet we certainly do not want to paint too rosy a picture. Adjustment to higher relative prices can be painful, as owners of gas-guzzling cars and fuel-inefficient homes have already found out. In peering into the crystal ball, we can see that goods and services that rely either directly or indirectly on fossil fuels are likely to be relatively more expensive. This can hardly be considered good news. But the point to emphasize is that we *can* see an end to this process. And this end is not a cataclysmic one in which we run out of energy and industrial activity ceases. Instead, it is one in which new technology based on non-depletable energy resources, such as the sun and the atom, takes over the business of powering vehicles, heating homes, and turning the wheels of industry. Energy will probably be more expensive than it is today, but it *will* be available.

The truly cataclysmic possibilities that follow from natural-resource use are not generally problems of *availability*; rather, they are the *effects on the environment* of using these resources. For example, earlier in this chapter, we mentioned that burning fossil fuels is raising the concentration of carbon dioxide in the earth's atmosphere, thereby increasing global temperatures (the greenhouse effect). As we noted, many observers now predict that, within fifty years, gradually increasing temperatures may well have disastrous effects on crops, will begin to melt the polar icecaps (causing massive flooding along coastlines), and will have other calamitous consequences. The reason we cannot expect the market mechanism to prevent these problems automatically is because of the *externalities* involved.

Alternatives for the Future

We hope that the analysis contained in this chapter will help you come to a reasoned view on these very serious issues. The global nature of externality effects and the magnitude of the income redistribution to the less developed countries that must occur if those countries are to take part in the limiting of pollution are cause for great concern. But there is no point in *not* doing whatever it is possible to do *now*, and in this regard the most fundamental decision confronting us is whether the very nature of our economic system is at fault.

Many observers, including scientist, author, and broadcaster David Suzuki, argue that our environmental problems call for an entire reorientation of human nature and economic life. According to this widespread view, we must:

1. purge our system of its dependence on human greed as a motivating factor;

2. reject economic growth as a goal for society;

3. reject mainstream economics as a useful discipline in the area of environmental protection.

For example, David Suzuki writes:

Economists consider the environment to be essentially limitless, endless, self-renewing, and free....
  Economic growth has become an end in itself, a mindless goal that is sought by every country in the world and the very measure of progress. Yet any thoughtful person knows that it is a deadly notion that cannot be sustained in a finite world.[3]

Not surprisingly, many economists think that this criticism of their discipline goes too far. It is true that only fairly recently have people—including economists—appreciated how far-reaching and essentially irreversible some of our environmental and resource-conservation problems are. But we must also appreciate that some economic growth is required to enable the less developed countries to take their very necessary part in the solution to these problems.

Thus, we have chosen to end this book with a boxed insert that presents excerpts from one of the published responses to critics such as David Suzuki. The article is by

[3] David Suzuki, "Reflections: You Can't Put a Price on Earth," *The Hamilton Spectator*, September 9, 1989.

Economics and the Environment: A Reconciliation?

... Most people see an unbridgeable chasm between the desire of ecologists and environmentalists to have clean air and water and to control toxic wastes, on the one hand, and the pursuits of economists and business people concerned with economic development and prosperity, on the other hand. These two views are seen as impossible to reconcile, and the attitude of most people is that one of them has to give way to the other. I suggest that it is possible to reconcile the two—a reconciliation that upholds the goals of environmentalists but not necessarily their means. ...

The first principle [that guides this analysis] is that of private property and the incentives engendered thereby. ...

[Take] ... the case of Soviet agriculture. In the pre-*perestroika* days ... on the 98 percent of the land that was communally owned, only 75 percent of the crops were produced. On the 2 percent of the land that was privately owned in the form of small gardens around the workers' houses, fully 25 percent of the crops were grown. This illustrates the difference in incentives that operates when something is privately owned versus when it is publicly owned. ...

The second principle is the tragedy of the commons. One way to illustrate this is to suppose that we are all shepherds, grazing our sheep on a common meadow. Some public-spirited citizen decides that the grass is being grazed too closely by the sheep. He takes his sheep elsewhere, at some expense, in order to preserve the meadow. But what typically happens is that other people then allow their sheep to graze on the meadow that has just been vacated by this public-spirited citizen, and the grass is not saved. As you can see, there is very little incentive to act in a public-spirited way in a common meadow. If you owned the entire meadow and saw that it was becoming overgrazed, you would stop the sheep from grazing there and let that grass build up while they grazed elsewhere. That you will not do so under the institution of public property is the tragedy of the commons.

Perhaps a more direct illustration of this principle is to imagine four or five children age 10 or 12, each sipping a soda pop. They each have their own can and are drinking at their own rates. That is scenario one. In scenario two, we take the soda pop cans away from them, pour all the soda into a common cup, and give each child a straw. Then we

watch them go at it. What differences are we likely to see? These little kids are going to be sucking up the pop at a much greater rate. Those of you who have children will realize that the rate of drinking will be very different. In scenario two, if you don't drink it very quickly, you can't have it later; someone else will grab it in the meanwhile. ...

Let us now consider species extinction. Thanks to the modern miracle of television we have all seen the results of actions of poachers in Africa, the herds of elephants left to die with their tusks cut off with a chain saw. Pregnant cows

economist Walter Block of the Fraser Institute in Vancouver, an economic research and educational institution dedicated to directing public attention to the positive contribution competitive markets can make to economic well-being. Some readers will find Block's enthusiasm for unfettered private markets to be somewhat exaggerated. The important thing is that, by now, you will have developed an understanding of the issues and arguments involved, and of the ways in which mainstream economics can contribute to sorting them out.

Our problems in the areas of pollution and resource conservation are indeed serious, but as a method of scientific inquiry, the discipline of economics does *not* are killed, the meat and leather go to waste, and the tusks don't get their true market value but only their black market value. Entire herds of elephants have been killed in this fashion.

Here we have a problem of the tragedy of the commons and a lack of the incentives that only private ownership can supply. The poachers are aided and abetted in their activities by the villagers because these elephants are not privately owned. Villagers cannot profit from the elephants. Instead, the central governments of these African republics expropriate the value. The poachers in the African jungle see these animals as predators. The elephants destroy the crops of the villagers. So there are costs to the villagers of the elephants but no gains for them. The incentive is to encourage poachers to slaughter elephants. . . .

Several African countries have . . . allowed privatization of the animals. Hunting rights are sold to the native peoples, who can then rent them out to people who want to join safaris. These countries have given an incentive to their people to preserve the elephants because now they have a value to them. Under such conditions, elephant herds are actually increasing. . . .

Some people say that the reason the elephant is being hunted to extinction is because of its highly valued ivory tusk or, in the case of the rhinoceros, because of its horn. This is true under a regime of non-ownership. But when these animals are privately owned, the ivory tusk is the reason for their preservation. When people have an incentive and can profit from the existence of the elephant, they will protect it and make sure that pregnant females are not killed. Are the cow, goat, and chicken harmed to the point of extinction because of their value to us? On the contrary, they are preserved because of this value. . . .

Let's now look briefly at recycling and hazardous wastes. Here, again, the market is blamed. People point to plastic foam cups and plastic bags and other items that are not biodegradable [or] environmentally friendly and suggest it is an evil chase after the "unholy buck" that explains their presence. I would like to offer a different assessment of this problem. . . .

. . . The . . . government has engaged in nationalizing or municipalizing or socializing the solid waste management industry. It costs you no more to put plastic into your curbside garbage can than it does to put in paper. . . .

Suppose private enterprise was in total control of the disposal of solid wastes. Then the person with whom you contract to pick up your garbage at the curbside would say to you: "If I accept your plastic—and I am willing to do that—when I bring it to the dump, the dump owner will charge me me for the plastic because it will ruin his land, so I will have to charge you more for it, householder." Under this scenario, the next time you are faced with the choice of a plastic or paper bag, the true costs of your choice will impinge upon you, and you will act environmentally rationally or at least you will tend in that direction. Right now there is no financial incentive to do so. . . .

The next issue I'd like to address is the greenhouse effect and the ozone layer. . . .

One proposed solution to the greenhouse effect is to maintain large acreages devoted to forests because trees take in carbon dioxide and give off oxygen. This raises the question of why our forests are disappearing. I think the culprit is government ownership of forest preserves, not greed and profits, as people like David Suzuki maintain. . . .

If a forestry company owns a hundred square miles of forest and cuts it all down without replanting, the present discounted value of that land plummets. If a company does that once too often, it risks courting bankruptcy. In sharp contrast, suppose the government owns the land and gives the company a contract to do with that land as it wishes for six months. In this situation it is in the best interests of the company to clear cut, and the economic incentives to reforest are greatly attenuated. . . .

There are many serious environmental groups with impeccable credentials that have seen that the best way to preserve woodlands is to buy them and administer them. The Audubon Society has a vast holding in Alabama and oil was discovered on it. Instead of saying that oil is evil and we're not going to have anything to do with it, they made a deal with an oil company to exploit this resource, in a very clean way, so they could buy more property for wildlife preserves. People open to the evidence will eventually be convinced that there is a case to be made for employing the tools and analysis of economics in the marketplace to preserve these holdings.

SOURCE: Walter E. Block, "Environment Problems, Free Market Solutions," *Fraser Forum* (February 1990), pages 4–17.

perpetuate these problems. On the contrary, by focussing as they do on incentive mechanisms, economists can make, and have made, very constructive suggestions about the ways in which some of our laws and our tax system might usefully be changed. Indeed, as we have tried to demonstrate throughout this book, experience has shown that the public interest is best served when we accept human nature as we know it and when we design our laws and institutions in such a way that private interests and the public interest are made to coincide.

Summary

1. Pollution is as old as human history, and both planned and market economies suffer from substantial environmental problems.

2. The production of commodities *must* cause waste-disposal problems unless everything is recycled. Even recycling processes cause pollution (and use up energy).

3. Industrial activity causes environmental damage, but so does the activity of private individuals (as when they drive cars that emit pollutants). Government agencies also damage the environment (as when municipal sewage is dumped untreated or a hydroelectric project floods large areas).

4. Pollution is an externality—when a factory emits smoke, it may damage the health of people who neither work for the factory nor buy its products. Hence, pollution control cannot be left to the free market. This is one of our **12 Ideas for Beyond the Final Exam**.

5. Pollution can be controlled by voluntary programs, direct controls, taxes on emissions, or other monetary incentives for the reduction of emissions. Most economists believe that the tax approach (or the related but more flexible emissions-permit system) is the most efficient and effective way to control detrimental externalities.

6. The quantity demanded of a scarce resource can exceed the quantity supplied only if something prevents the market mechanism from operating freely.

7. As a resource grows scarce on a free market, its price will rise, inducing increased conservation by consumers, increased exploration for new reserves, and increased substitution of other items that can serve the same purpose.

8. In fact, in the twentieth century the relative prices of many resources have remained roughly constant, largely because of the discovery of new reserves and because of cost-saving innovations.

9. The price mechanism and rationing are the only known alternatives to chaos in the allocation of scarce resources.

10. In the 1970s, OPEC succeeded in raising the relative price of petroleum, but the rise in price led to a substantial decline in world demand as well as to an increase in production in countries outside OPEC.

11. Canada's energy policy during the late 1970s and early 1980s kept domestic energy prices below world levels, while producers were heavily taxed. Energy consumers obtained a short-term benefit, but longer-run costs included a cutback in exploration and development and reduced investment in energy-efficient production techniques in Canadian manufacturing.

12. Some commentators argue that concern for the environment and acceptance of mainstream economic analysis are somehow incompatible. According to this view, environmental problems cannot be solved until the existing focus on private profit is eliminated and individuals are persuaded to care more about the "public good." Mainstream economics rejects this view, arguing that success in solving these problems is facilitated by *harnessing* the profit motive rather than wishing it were not with us. The goal of mainstream economic policy is to arrange our laws in such a way that the public interest and private interests complement, rather than compete with, each other.

Concepts for Review

Externality
Direct controls

Pollution charges (taxes on emissions)
Tradeable emissions permits

Paradox of growing reserves of finite resources

Questions for Discussion

1. What sorts of pollution problems would you expect in a small African village? In a city in India? In communist China? In Toronto?

2. Suppose you are assigned the task of drafting a law to impose a tax on the emission of smoke. What provisions would you put into the law?
   a. How would you decide the size of the tax?
   b. What would you do about smoke emitted by a municipal electricity plant?
   c. Would you use the same tax rate in densely and sparsely settled areas?
   What information would you need to collect before determining what you would do about each of the preceding provisions?

3. Production of commodity X creates 10 kilograms of emissions for every unit of X produced. The demand and supply curves for X are described by the following table:

PRICE (dollars)	QUANTITY DEMANDED	QUANTITY SUPPLIED
10	80	100
9	85	95
8	90	90
7	95	85
6	100	80
5	105	75

What are the equilibrium price and quantity, and how much pollution will be emitted?

4. If the price of X to consumers is $9 and the government imposes a tax of $2 per unit, show that because suppliers get only $7 they will produce only 85 units of output, not the 95 units of output they would produce if they received the full $9 per unit.

5. Show that, with this tax, the equilibrium price is $9 and the equilibrium quantity demanded is 85. How much pollution will not be emitted?

6. Compare your answers to Questions 3 and 5 and show how large a reduction in pollution emissions occurs because of the $2 tax on the polluting output.

7. Discuss some valid and some invalid objections to letting rising prices eliminate shortages of supplies of scarce resources.

8. Describe what must be done by a government agency that is given the job of rationing a scarce resource.

9. Some observers believe that a program of rationing may work fairly satisfactorily for a few months or for one or two years, particularly during an emergency period when patriotic spirit is strong. However, they believe that over longer periods and when there is no upsurge of patriotism it is likely to prove far less satisfactory. Do you agree or disagree? Why?

Glossary

Numbers in parentheses indicate pages in the text where the terms are discussed.

Ability-to-pay principle of taxation The idea that persons with greater ability to pay taxes should pay higher taxes. (689)

Absolute advantage Said of one country over another in the production of a particular good if the first country can produce that good using smaller quantities of resources than can the other country. (606)

Abstraction Ignoring many details in order to focus on the most important factors in a problem. (10)

Affirmative action Active efforts to locate and hire members of minority groups. (710)

Aggregate demand The total amount that all consumers, business firms, government agencies, and foreigners are willing to spend on final goods and services. (114)

Aggregate demand curve Graphic presentation of the quantity of national product that is demanded at each possible value of the price level. (74, 141)

Aggregate supply The total amount that all business firms are willing to produce. (164)

Aggregate supply curve Graphic presentation, for each possible price level, of the quantity of goods and services that all the nation's businesses are willing to produce at given factor prices. (74, 164)

Aggregation Combining many individual markets into one overall market. Economic aggregates are the focus of macroeconomics. (72)

Allocation of resources The decision on how to divide the economy's scarce input resources among the different outputs produced in the economy and among the different firms or other organizations that produce those outputs. (30)

Appreciation (of a nation's currency) Is said to occur when exchange rates change so that a unit of its own currency can buy more units of foreign currency. (253)

Asset An item of value that an individual or a firm owns. (236)

Automatic stabilizer Any arrangement that automatically supports aggregate demand when it would otherwise sag and holds down aggregate demand when it would otherwise surge ahead; thus it reduces the sensitivity of the economy to shifts in demand. (288)

Autonomous increase in consumption An increase in consumer spending without any increase in incomes. Represented graphically as a shift of the entire consumption function. (157)

Average-cost curve Shows, for each output, the cost per unit, that is, total cost divided by output. (458)

Average physical product (APP) Total physical product (TPP) divided by the quantity of input utilized. (453)

Average propensity to consume (APC) The ratio of overall consumption to disposable income. (123)

Average propensity to save (APS) The ratio of overall savings to disposable income. (123)

Average revenue (AR) Total revenue (TR) divided by quantity. (485)

Balance of payments See Deficit, balance of payments; Surplus, balance of payments.

Balance sheet An account statement listing the values of all assets on the left-hand side and of all liabilities and net worth on the right-hand side. (237)

Bank of Canada Canada's central bank. (247)

Bank rate The rate of interest charged by the Bank of Canada when reserves are loaned to the chartered banks (advances from the central bank). It is used as a signal of the direction of monetary policy. (252)

Barter A system of exchange in which people directly trade one good for another, without using money as an intermediate step. (228)

Benefits principle of taxation The idea that people who derive benefits from a service should pay the taxes that finance it. (690)

Bilateral monopoly Market situation in which there is both a monopoly on the selling side and a monopsony on the buying side. (672)

Bond A corporation's promise to pay the holder a fixed sum of money at the specified *maturity* date and some other fixed amount of money (the *coupon* or *interest payment*) every year up to the date of maturity. (214)

Brain drain Occurs when the educated natives of a less developed country emigrate to wealthier nations. (400)

Budget deficit Amount by which the government's expenditures exceed its receipts during a specified period of time, usually one year. (330)

Budget line Graphic representation of all the possible combinations of two commodities that a household can purchase, given the prices of the commodities and some fixed amount of money at its disposal. (417)

Burden of a tax The amount of money individuals would have to be given to make them just as well off with the tax as they were without it. (691)

Capital Inventory (stock) of plant, equipment, and other productive resources held by a business firm, an individual, or some other organization. (653)

Capital gain An increase in the market value of a piece of property that occurs between the time it is bought and the time it is sold. (202, 682)

Capital good An item that is used to produce other goods and services in the future, rather than being consumed today. (35)

Capital loss A decrease in the market value of a piece of property that occurs between the time it is bought and the time it is sold. (202)

Capitalism Method of economic organization in which private individuals own the means of production, either directly or indirectly through corporations. (537)

Cartel Group of sellers of a product who have joined together to control its production, sale, and price in the hope of obtaining the advantages of monopoly. (576)

Central bank A bank for banks. The central bank of Canada is the Bank of Canada. (247)

Commodity money An object used as a medium of exchange that also has a substantial value in alternative (non-monetary) uses. (230)

Common stock A piece of paper that gives the holder a share in the ownership of a corporation. (214)

Comparative advantage Said of one country over another in the production of a particular good relative to other goods it can produce if the first country produces that good least inefficiently compared with the other country. (606)

Competition policy Government policy that attempts to control the growth of monopoly and to prevent firms from engaging in "undesirable" practices through the use of legislation and various programs. (719, 736)

Complements Two goods are called complements if an increase in the price of one reduces the quantity demanded of the other, all other things remaining constant. (441)

Concentration of industry The share of the industry's total output (in money terms) supplied by some given number (usually four) of its largest firms. (745)

Concentration ratio Percentage of an industry's output produced by its *four* largest firms. It is intended to measure the degree to which the industry is dominated by large firms; that is, how closely it approximates a monopoly. (747)

Consumer expenditure (consumption) The total amount spent by consumers on newly produced goods and services (excluding purchases of new homes, which are considered investment goods). Symbolized by the letter C. (114)

Consumer Price Index The most popular index number for the price level. Its weights are based on the spending patterns of a typical urban household. (110)

Consumer sovereignty Consumer preferences determine what goods shall be produced, and in what amounts. (529)

Consumer surplus The amount by which an individual's total willingness to pay for an item exceeds what he or she has to pay to buy it. (412)

Consumption function Relationship between total consumer expenditure and total disposable income in the economy, holding all other determinants of consumer spending constant. (122)

Consumption good An item that is available for immediate use by households and that satisfies wants of members of households without contributing directly to future production by the economy. (35)

Corporation A firm with the legal status of a fictional individual. It is owned by shareholders and run by elected officers and a board of directors, whose chairman often influences the firm's affairs. (212)

Correlation A relationship between two variables such that they tend to go up or down together. Correlation need not imply causation. (13)

Cost disease of personal services Tendency of the cost of services such as auto repair and legal counsel to rise faster than the economy's overall inflation rate because it is difficult to increase productivity (output per person hours) in these services. (599)

Countervailing duty A tariff levied on imports to offset the effects of what are perceived as unrealistically low prices set by producers in the exporting country. (623)

Cross elasticity of demand For product X to a change in the price of another product, Y, is the ratio of the percentage change in quantity demanded of product X to the percentage change in the price of product Y that brings about the change in quantity demanded. (442)

Cross subsidization (rate averaging) Selling one product at a loss, which is balanced by higher profits on another product. (722)

Crowding out Occurs when deficit spending by the government forces private investment spending or exports to contract. (342)

Cyclically adjusted budget Hypothetical budget we *would have* if the economy were operating with an average level of unemployment. (336)

Deficit, balance of payments Amount by which the quantity supplied of foreign exchange (per year) falls short of the quantity demanded. Such deficits arise whenever the value of foreign exchange is pegged at an artificially low level; that is, whenever the value of the *domestic*

currency is pegged at an artificially high level. (255)

Deflating (by a price index) Dividing some nominal magnitude by a price index in order to express that magnitude in dollars of constant purchasing power. (111)

Deflation A sustained decrease in the general price level. (80)

Demand curve A graph showing how the quantity demanded of some product during a specified period of time will change as the price of that product changes, holding all other determinants of quantity demanded constant. (46)

Demand, law of States that a lower price generally increases the amount of a commodity that people in a market are willing to buy. Thus, for most goods, demand curves have a negative slope. (430)

Demand schedule A table showing how the quantity demanded of some product during a specified period of time changes as the price of that product changes, holding all other determinants of quantity demanded constant. (45)

Depletability An attribute of private goods, as opposed to public goods. A commodity is depletable if it is used up when someone consumes it. (592)

Deposit creation Process by which the banking system turns a dollar of reserves into several dollars of deposits. (238)

Deposit insurance A system that guarantees that depositors will not lose money even if their bank goes bankrupt. (236)

Depreciation (of capital goods) The value of the portion of the nation's capital equipment that is used up within the year. It indicates how much output is needed just to keep the economy's capital stock intact. (105)

Depreciation (of a nation's currency) Is said to occur when exchange rates change so that a unit of its own currency can buy fewer units of foreign currency. (253)

Depreciation allowances Tax deductions that businesses may claim when they spend money on investment goods. (133)

Direct taxes Taxes levied directly on people. (681)

Discounting Process of determining the present worth of a quantity of money receivable or payable at some future date. (148, 654)

Discouraged worker An unemployed person who gives up looking for work and is therefore no longer counted as part of the labour force. (85)

Discrimination, economic Occurs when equivalent factors of production receive different payments for equal contributions to output. (707)

Discrimination, statistical Occurs when the productivity of a particular worker is estimated to be low just because that worker belongs to a particular group. (709)

Disguised unemployment Occurs when tasks are carried out by a number of persons larger than the number that can complete them most efficiently. (399)

Disposable income The sum of the incomes of all the individuals in the economy after all taxes have been deducted. (108, 115)

Diversification An increase in the number and *variety* of stocks, bonds, and other such items in an individual's portfolio of investments. (216)

Division of labour Breaking up a task into a number of smaller, more specialized tasks so that each worker can become more adept at his or her particular job. Division of labour creates efficiency and increases productivity. (37)

Dual labour market theory A theory asserting that workers generally work in one of two types of jobs—those which offer opportunities for acquisition of skills and promotions, and "dead end jobs" which offer little scope for improvement. (665)

Dumping Selling goods in a foreign market at lower prices than those charged in the home market. (626)

Economic growth Occurs when an economy is able to produce more goods and services for each consumer. (34)

Economic model A representation of a theory or a part of a theory, often for the purpose of illuminating some aspect of the economy. Economic models are often expressed in equations, by graphs, or in words. (13)

Economic profit The total revenue a firm or an industry derives from the sale of its products minus the total cost of its inputs, including the opportunity cost of any inputs supplied by the proprietors. (484, 517)

Economic rent What is said to be earned whenever a factor of production receives a reward that exceeds the minimum amount necessary to keep the factor in its present employment. (645)

Economies of scale Savings acquired through increases in quantities produced. (470, 721)

Economies of scope Savings acquired through simultaneous production of many different products. (721)

Efficiency The absence of waste, achieved primarily by gains in productivity resulting from specialization, division of labour, and a system of exchange. (36)

Efficient allocation of resources One that takes advantage of every opportunity to make some individuals better off in their own estimation while not worsening the lot of anyone else. (525)

Elasticity of demand, price Ratio of the *percentage* change in quantity demanded to the *percentage* change in price that brings about the change in quantity demanded. (434)

Entrepreneurship The act of starting new firms, introducing new products and technological innovations, and, in general, taking the risks necessary in seeking out business opportunities. (658)

Equation of exchange Statement that the money value of GDP transactions must be equal to the product of the average stock of money times velocity ($M \times V = P \times Y$). (276)

Equilibrium A situation in which there are no inherent forces that produce change. Changes away from an equilibrium position occur only as a result of "outside events" that disturb the status quo. (49, 135)

Equilibrium level of GDP (on the demand side) Level of GDP which makes aggregate demand equal to production. (136)

Equilibrium price Price at which quantity demanded and quantity supplied are equal. This common quantity is called the equilibrium quantity. (49)

Excess burden of a tax The amount by which the burden of the tax exceeds the tax that is paid. (691)

Excess capacity theorem Asserts that monopolistic competitive firms will tend to produce outputs lower than those that minimize average costs; that is, that they will tend to produce less than their capacity. (573)

Excess reserves Reserves held in excess of the legal minimum. (238)

Exchange A mechanism by which workers can trade the various products resulting from specialization and the division of labour. (37)

Exchange controls Laws restricting the exchange of one nation's currency for that of another. (319)

Exchange rate The price at which one currency can be bought, stated in terms of another currency. (62, 167, 253)

Exchange rates, fixed Rates set by government decisions and maintained by central bank actions. (255)

Exchange rates, floating or flexible Rates determined in free markets by the law of supply and demand. (254)

Excise tax A tax levied on a particular commodity or service, as a fixed amount of money per unit of product sold or as a fixed percentage of the purchase price. (431, 683)

Excludability An attribute of private goods, as opposed to public goods. A commodity is excludable if someone who does not pay for it can be kept from enjoying it. (592)

Expansion path The locus of a firm's cost-minimizing input combinations for all relevant output levels. (480)

Exponential growth Growth at a constant percentage rate. (386)

Export subsidy Payment by the government to exporters to permit them to reduce the selling price of their goods so they can compete more effectively in foreign markets. (614)

Externality Result of an activity that causes incidental benefits or damages to others with no corresponding compensation provided to or paid by those who generate the externality. (588)

Fiat money Money decreed as such by the government. It has little value as a commodity, but it maintains its value as a medium of exchange because people have faith that the issuer will stand behind the pieces of printed paper and limit their production. (230)

Final goods and services Those that are purchased by their ultimate users. (76)

Fiscal federalism The system of transfer payments from one level of government to the next. (687)

Fiscal policy The government's plan for spending and taxation, designed to steer aggregate demand in some desired direction. (185)

Fixed cost Unavoidable overhead

costs that do not vary when the firm's output level changes. (460)

A 45⁰ line A ray through the origin with a slope of +1. It marks off points where the variables measured on each axis have equal values, assuming that both variables are measured in the same units. (20)

Fractional reserve banking A system under which bankers keep in their vaults as reserves only a fraction of the funds they hold on deposit. (235)

Game theory Analyzes the behaviour of competing firms mathematically, treating it as analogous to the strategies of rival players in a competitive game. (579)

Gold-exchange system (Bretton Woods system) International monetary system that prevailed from 1944 to 1971. Under this system, the United States fixed the value of the dollar in terms of gold, and other countries fixed the values of their currencies in terms of the U.S. dollar. (318)

Gold standard System in which exchange rates are set in terms of gold and pegged by buying or selling gold as necessary. (316)

Government purchases All the goods and services purchased by all levels of government. Transfer payments to individuals (such as welfare benefits) and payments from one level of government to another are not included. Symbolized by the letter *G*. (114)

Gross domestic product (GDP) The sum of the money values of all final goods and services produced by the economy during a specified period, usually one year. (75, 103)

Gross domestic product, nominal The economy's total output valued at current prices. (75)

Gross domestic product, real The economy's total output valued at the prices that prevailed in some agreed-upon year (currently 1981). (76)

Gross domestic product per capita The economy's total output divided by the number of people among whom it will be distributed—that is, the economy's population. (376)

Gross domestic product deflator Price index obtained by dividing nominal GDP by real GDP. (111)

Gross national product The total income created by the employment of all factors of production owned by a nation's people. In contrast, *gross domestic product* is the amount of employment-creating production activity that takes place within the nation. (107)

Growth, disembodied Increases in an economy's output which can occur without being accompanied by (embodied in) additional capital stock. (390)

Growth, embodied Increases in an economy's output which are made possible by increased or improved plant, equipment, or other forms of capital. (390)

Growth, export-led Strategy of emphasizing the production of goods for export. (545)

Horizontal equity The notion that equally situated persons should be taxed equally. (688)

Human capital theory A theory interpreting education as an investment in a human being's earning power, just as an improvement in a factory is an investment in the factory's earning capacity. (664)

Incidence of a tax An allocation of the burden of the tax to specific individuals or groups. (692)

Income effect A portion of the change in quantity demanded of a good when its price changes. A rise in price cuts the consumer's purchasing power (real income), which leads to a change in the quantity demanded of that commodity. That change is the income effect. (414)

Income–expenditure diagram (45⁰ line diagram) A plotting of total real expenditure (on the vertical axis) against real income (on the horizontal axis). The 45⁰ line marks off points where income and expenditure are equal. (139)

Incomes policy Variety of measures to curb inflation *without* reducing aggregate demand. (367)

Incomes policy, tax-based Use of the tax system to provide incentives favouring non-inflationary behaviour. (369)

Increasing costs, principle of As the production of one good expands, the opportunity cost of producing another such unit generally increases. (32)

Indexing Provisions in a law or contract whereby monetary payments are automatically adjusted whenever a specified price index changes; sometimes called *escalator clauses.* (370)

Index number A number indicating the percentage change in some variable (such as the price level) between the base period and some other period. Typically, the value of the index number in the base period is arbitrarily set to 100. (109)

Indifference curve Line connecting all combinations of commodities that are equally desirable to the consumer. (419)

Indirect taxes Taxes levied on specific economic activities. (681)

Induced increase in consumption An increase in consumer spending that stems from an increase in consumer incomes. Represented graphically as a movement along a fixed consumption function. (157)

Induced investment That part of investment spending that rises when GDP rises and falls when GDP falls. (137)

Inferior good A commodity whose quantity demanded falls when the purchaser's real income rises, all other things remaining equal. (414)

Inflation A sustained increase in the general price level. (74)

Inflation, creeping Inflation that proceeds for a long time at a moderate and fairly steady pace. (100)

Inflation, expected rate of Forecasted rate of price change. Also, the difference between the nominal interest rate and the real interest rate. (97)

Inflation, galloping Inflation that proceeds at an exceptionally high rate, perhaps for only a relatively brief period. This type of inflation is generally characterized by accelerating inflation rates, so that the inflation rate is higher this month than last month. (100)

Inflation accounting Adjusting standard accounting procedures for the fact that inflation lowers the purchasing power of money. (334)

Inflationary gap The amount by which equilibrium real GDP exceeds the full-employment level of GDP. (143)

Innovation The act of putting a new idea into practical use. (659)

Input Any item that the firm uses in its production process. Inputs, also called the means of production, are the natural resources, labour, and produced plant and equipment used to make outputs. (29, 453)

Interest Payment for the use of funds

employed in the production of capital; measured as a percentage per year of the value of the funds tied up in the capital. (654)

Intermediate good One that is bought for resale or for use in producing another good. (76)

International Monetary Fund (IMF) International organization set up originally to police and manage the gold-exchange system. (318)

Invention The act of generating a new idea. (659)

Investment Flow of resources into the production of new capital. (103, 653)

Investment, gross private domestic Sum of business investment expenditures on plant and equipment, residential construction expenditures, and inventory change. (103)

Investment good See Capital good.

Investment schedule Table or curve showing how investment spending depends on GDP. (137)

Investment spending The sum of the expenditures of business firms on new plant and equipment, and inventories, plus the expenditures of households on new homes. Financial "investments" and resales of existing physical assets are not included. Symbolized by the letter *I*. (114)

Isoquant (sometimes called a *production indifference curve*) A curve in a graph showing quantities of *inputs* on its axes. Each isoquant indicates *all* combinations of input quantities capable of producing a *given* quantity of output. (476)

Labour force The number of people employed or seeking employment. (84)

Labour productivity See Productivity of labour.

Laissez faire A program of minimal interference with the workings of the market system. (528)

Less developed countries (LDCs) Countries whose share of output composed of agricultural products, mining, and the like is relatively high, which engage in relatively little industrial high-technology activity, and whose per capita incomes are generally comparatively low. (375, 392)

Liability An item of value that an individual or a firm owes; collectively, liabilities are known as *debts*. (237)

Liability, limited Legal obligation of a firm's owners to pay back company debts only with the money they have already invested in the firm. (212)

Liability, unlimited Legal obligation of a firm's owners to repay company debts with whatever resources they own. (210)

Liquidity, of an asset The ease with which it can be converted into cash. (234)

Long run Period of time long enough for all the firm's sunk commitments to come to an end. (463)

Lorenz curve Graph depicting the distribution of income. (702)

M1 The narrowly defined money supply, which is the sum of all coins and paper money in circulation, plus pure chequing deposits at chartered banks. (233)

M2 The broadly defined money supply, which is the sum of currency in public hands, plus chequing and all savings deposits at chartered banks. (233)

Macroeconomics The study of the behaviour of entire economies. (72)

Marginal-cost curve Shows, for each output, the increase in the firm's total cost required if it increases its output by an additional unit. (458)

Marginal land Land that is just on the borderline of being used. (644)

Marginal physical product (MPP) Increase in total output that results from a one-unit increase in an input, holding the amounts of all other inputs constant. (454, 636)

Marginal private cost (MPC) See Marginal social cost.

Marginal profit The addition to total profit resulting from one more unit of output. (488)

Marginal propensity to consume (MPC) Ratio of the change in consumption to the change in disposable income that produces the change in consumption. On a graph, it appears as the slope of the consumption function. (122)

Marginal propensity to save (MPS) Graphically, the slope of the saving function, which indicates how much more consumers will save if disposable income rises by one unit. (123)

Marginal rate of substitution In relation to two commodities, the maximum amount of one commodity the consumer is willing to give up in exchange for one more unit of the other commodity; it is represented by the *slope of an indifference curve*. (421)

Marginal returns, law of diminishing Asserts that if the quantities of all other inputs are held constant, the employment of additional quantities of any one input by a firm or an industry will eventually yield smaller and smaller (marginal) increases in output. (456)

Marginal revenue (MR) The *addition* to total revenue resulting from the addition of one more unit to total output. Geometrically, marginal revenue is the *slope* of the total revenue curve. (485)

Marginal revenue product (MRP) Additional revenue earned as a result of increased sales when an additional unit of an input is used. (456, 636)

Marginal social cost (MSC) The sum of *marginal private cost (MPC)*, which is the share of marginal cost caused by an activity that is paid for by the persons who carry out the activity, and *incidental cost*, which is the share borne by others. (589)

Marginal utility, law of diminishing Asserts that additional units of a commodity are worth less and less to a consumer in money terms. As the individual's consumption increases, the marginal utility of each additional unit declines. (408)

Market The set of all sale and purchase transactions that affect the price of some commodity. (504)

Market-demand curve Shows how the total quantity demanded of some product during a specified period of time changes as the price of the product changes, other things being constant. (429)

Market power The ability of a firm to raise its price significantly above the competitive price level and to maintain this high price profitably for a considerable period. (747)

Market system A form of organization of the economy in which decisions on resource allocation are left to the independent decisions of individual producers and consumers acting in their own best interest without central direction. (39)

Maximin criterion Selecting the strategy that yields the maximum payoff, on the assumption that your opponent will do as much damage to you as he can. (581)

Merger The combining of two previously independent firms under a single owner or group of owners. A **horizontal merger** involves two firms producing similar products. A

vertical merger involves two firms, one of which supplies an ingredient of the other's product. A **conglomerate merger** is the union of two unrelated firms. (738)

Microeconomics The study of the behaviour of individual decision-making units, such as farmers or consumers. (72)

Minimum-wage law Requires all employees (with some specified exceptions) to be paid at least some fixed given dollar amount per hour. (640)

Monetarism Mode of analysis that uses the equation of exchange to organize macroeconomic data. (279)

Monetary policy Actions that the Bank of Canada takes to change the equilibrium of the money market; that is, to alter either the money supply or the exchange rate. (261)

Monetizing the deficit The effect of the central bank's purchasing the bonds that the government issues. (340)

Money Medium of exchange; that is, the standard object used in exchanging goods and services. (229)

Money fixed asset Asset with a face value fixed in terms of dollars, such as money itself, government bonds, and corporate bonds. (125)

Monopolistic competition Competition among firms, each of which has products that are somewhat different from those of its rivals. (570)

Monopoly, natural Industry in which advantages of large-scale production make it possible for a single firm to produce the entire output of the market at lower average cost than a number of firms each producing a smaller quantity. (555)

Monopoly, pure Industry in which there is only one supplier of a product for which there are no close substitutes, and in which it is difficult or impossible for another firm to coexist. (554)

Monopsony Market situation in which there is only one buyer. (671)

Moral hazard Tendency of insurance to discourage policy-holders from protecting themselves from risk. (597)

Multinational corporations Corporations whose production activities occur in a number of different countries. (396)

The multiplier The ratio of the change in equilibrium GDP (Y) divided by the original change in spending that causes the change in GDP. (151)

National debt The federal government's total indebtedness, which has resulted from previous deficits. (330)

National income The sum of the incomes of all individuals in the economy earned in the forms of wages, interest, rents, and profits. It excludes transfer payments and is calculated before any deductions are taken for income taxes. (107, 114)

National income accounting Bookkeeping and measurement system for national economic data. (103)

National product The total production of a nation's economy. (72)

Nationalization Government ownership and operation of business firms. (733)

Near moneys Liquid assets that are close substitutes for money. (234)

Negative income tax (NIT) Transfer program under which families with incomes below a certain threshold (the "breakeven level") would receive cash benefits from the government; these benefits would decline as income rose. (704)

Net exports The excess of foreign expenditures on our products over our purchases of their goods (Canadian exports minus Canadian imports). Symbolized by $X - IM$. (114)

Net worth The value of all assets minus the value of all liabilities. (237)

Oligopoly Market dominated by a few sellers, at least several of which are large enough relative to the total market to be able to influence the market price. (574)

Open-market operations The Bank of Canada's purchase or sale of government securities through transactions in the open market. (250)

Opportunity cost The forgone value of the next best alternative that is not chosen. (29)

Origin The lower left-hand corner of a graph where the two axes meet. In two-variable diagrams, both variables equal zero at the origin. (16)

Output The goods and services that consumers want to acquire and that firms produce; also, the quantity of the good or service that a firm produces. (29, 453)

Paradox of thrift The fact that an effort by a nation to save more may simply reduce national income and fail to raise total saving. (159)

Partnership A firm whose ownership is shared by a fixed number of proprietors. (211)

Patent A temporary grant of monopoly rights over an innovation. (731)

Pay equity Classifying jobs by objective criteria and forcing employers to pay equal wages for the jobs judged to be of comparable worth. (710)

Perfectly contestable market One in which entry and exit are costless and unimpeded. (583)

Personal income A measure of income derived by subtracting corporate profits, retained earnings, and payroll taxes from national income, then adding in transfer payments. Personal income measures the income that actually accrues to individuals. (107)

Phillips curve Graph depicting the rate of unemployment on the horizontal axis and either the rate of inflation or the rate of change of money wages on the vertical axis; normally downward sloping, indicating that higher inflation rates are associated with lower unemployment rates. (353)

Phillips curve, vertical (long run) Shows the menu of inflation/unemployment choices available to society in the long run; a vertical straight line at the natural rate of unemployment. (357)

Potential gross domestic product The real GDP the economy would produce if its labour and other resources were fully employed. (90)

Poverty line Amount of income below which a family is considered "poor." (698)

Predatory pricing Price cuts that take place only to keep other firms from entering the industry. (741)

Price ceiling Legal maximum price that may be charged. (56)

Price discrimination Charging different prices, relative to costs, to different buyers of the same product. (741)

Price floor Legal minimum price that may be charged. (60)

Price leadership One firm sets the price for the industry and the others follow. (577)

Price war Each competing firm is determined to sell at a price that is lower than the prices of its rivals, usually regardless of whether that price covers the pertinent cost. (577)

Private good Commodity or service whose benefits are depleted by an additional user and for which other people are excluded from its benefits. (592)

Production function Indicates the *maximum* amount of product that can be obtained from any specified *combination* of inputs, given the current state of knowledge. (467)

Production possibilities frontier A graphical presentation of the different combinations of various goods that a producer can turn out, given the available resources and existing technology. (30)

Productivity The amount of output produced by a unit of input. (167)

Productivity of labour The amount of output produced per hour (or week or year) of labour input. It can be measured as total national output (GDP) in a given year divided by the total number of hours of work performed for pay in the country during that year. That is, labour productivity is defined as GDP per labour hour. (376)

Profit-sharing A system of compensating labour in which workers receive both a fixed base wage and a share of the firm's profits. (370)

Progressive tax One in which the average tax rate paid by an individual rises as his income rises. (680)

Property tax Tax on assessed value of real property. (686)

Proportional tax One in which the average tax rate is the same at all income levels. (680)

Public good Commodity or service whose benefits are *not depleted* by an additional user and for which it is generally difficult or *impossible to exclude* people from its benefits, even if they are unwilling to pay for them. (592)

Purchasing power The purchasing power of a given sum of money is the volume of goods and services it will buy. (92)

Purchasing-power parity theory (of exchange rates) Theory that the exchange rate between any two national currencies adjusts to reflect differences in the price levels of the two nations. (312)

Quantity theory of money A simple theory of aggregate demand based on the idea that velocity is constant, so that nominal GDP is proportional to the money stock. (276)

Quota Specification of the maximum amount of a good that is permitted into the country from abroad per unit of time. (614)

Random walk The time path of a variable, such as the price of a stock, when its magnitude in one period equals its value in the preceding period plus a completely random number. (223)

Rate averaging *See* Cross subsidization.

Rate of interest, nominal The percentage by which the money the borrower pays back exceeds the money that he borrowed, making no adjustment for any fall in the purchasing power of this money that results from inflation. (97)

Rate of interest, real The percentage increase in purchasing power that the borrower pays to the lender for the privilege of borrowing. It indicates the increased ability to purchase goods and services that the lender earns. (97)

Rational decision A decision that best serves the objective of the decision-maker, whatever the objective may be. The term "rational" connotes neither approval nor disapproval of the objective. (29)

Rational expectations Forecasts that, while not necessarily correct, are the best that can be made given the available data. If expectations are rational, forecasting errors are pure random numbers. (363)

Ray through the origin (or ray) A straight line emanating from the origin, or zero point on a graph. (20)

Real wage rate The wage rate adjusted for inflation. It indicates the volume of goods and services that the money wage will buy. (92)

Recession A period during which the total output of the economy declines. (75)

Recessionary gap The amount by which the equilibrium level of real GDP falls short of potential GDP. (143)

Regressive tax One in which the average tax rate falls as income rises. (680)

Regulation of industry A process established by law that restricts or controls some specified decisions made by the affected firms. (719)

Relative price The price of an item in terms of some other item, rather than in terms of dollars. (94)

Rent seeking Unproductive activity in the pursuit of economic profit. (596)

Required reserves The minimum amount of reserves (in cash or the equivalent) required by law. Required reserves are usually proportional to the volume of deposits. (236)

Resale price maintenance Forcing retailers to keep the price of a product at or above that specified by the wholesaler. (740)

Research and development (R & D) Systematic efforts undertaken to invent new or improved products or productive techniques and to make them ready to market or for use in production processes. (379)

Resources The instruments provided by nature or by people that are used to obtain the goods and services humans want. Three types are often referred to as "land" (natural resources), "labour," and "capital" (resources made by people, such as factories and machines). (28)

Retained earnings (ploughback) The portion of a corporation's profits that management decides to keep and reinvest in the firm's operations rather than pay out directly to shareholders in the form of dividends. (213)

Run on a bank An event that occurs when many depositors withdraw cash from their accounts simultaneously. (228)

Sales-maximizing firm One whose objective is to sell as much of its output as possible (measured in terms of the revenue it brings in) rather than to maximize the company's profit. (577)

Scatter diagram Graph showing the relationship between two variables. Each year is represented by a point in the diagram. The co-ordinates of each year's point show the value of the two variables in that year. (119)

Self-correcting mechanism The economy's way of curing inflationary or recessionary gaps automatically via inflation or deflation. (176)

Service industry One that does not turn out physical products. (380)

Shortage An excess of quantity demanded over quantity supplied. When a shortage exists, buyers cannot purchase the quantities they desire. (48)

Short run A period of time shorter than the long run so that some, but not all, of the firm's sunk commitments will have ended. (463)

Slope of a budget line Amount of one commodity the market requires an individual to give up in order to obtain one additional unit of another commodity without any change in the amount of money spent. (421)

Slope of a curved line At any particular point, the slope of the straight line that is tangent to the curved line at that point. (19)

Slope of an indifference curve *See* Marginal rate of substitution.

Slope of a straight line The ratio of the vertical change to the corresponding horizontal change as we move to the right along the line. The ratio of the "rise" over the "run." (17)

Socialism Method of economic organization in which the state owns the means of production. (537)

Sole proprietorship A business firm owned by a single person. (210)

Specialization The process whereby a country devotes its energies and resources to only a small proportion of the world's productive activities. (605)

Speculation Investment in risky assets in the hope of obtaining a profit from expected changes in the prices of these assets. (222)

Stabilization policy The name given to government programs designed to prevent or shorten recessions and to counteract inflation (that is, to *stabilize* prices). (83)

Stagflation Inflation that occurs while the economy is growing slowly ("stagnating") or having a recession. (82, 172)

Store of value An item used to store wealth from one point in time to another. (229)

Substitutes Two goods are called substitutes if an increase in the price of one raises the quantity demanded of the other, all other things remaining constant. (442)

Substitution effect Change in quantity demanded of a good resulting from a change in its relative price, exclusive of whatever change in quantity demanded may be attributable to the associated change in real income. (415)

Sunk cost A cost to which a firm is precommitted for some limited period, either because it has signed a contract to make the payments or because it has already paid for some durable item and cannot get its money back except by using that item to produce output for some period of time. (463)

Supply curve A graph showing how the quantity supplied of some product during a specified period of time will change as the price of that product changes, holding all other determinants of quantity supplied constant. (47)

Supply–demand diagram Diagram showing both a supply curve and a demand curve. (48)

Supply schedule A table showing how the quantity supplied of some product during a specified period of time changes as the price of that product changes, holding all other determinants of quantity supplied constant. (47)

Surplus An excess of quantity supplied over quantity demanded. When there is a surplus, sellers cannot sell the quantities they desire to supply. (48)

Surplus, balance of payments Amount by which the quantity supplied of foreign exchange (per year) exceeds the quantity demanded. Such surpluses arise whenever the value of foreign exchange is pegged at an artificially high level; that is, when the value of the *domestic* currency is pegged at an artificially low level. (255)

Tariff Tax on imports. (197, 614)

Tax credit Reduction of an individual's or firm's tax obligation by a given amount that is independent of the tax rate. Some individual tax credits are *refundable*; if they reduce the tax owed to an amount less than zero, the government transfers that amount to the individual. (688)

Tax exemption Removal of an amount from an individual's or firm's tax base (taxable income). (688)

Tax rate, average Ratio of taxes to income. (680)

Tax rate, marginal Fraction of each *additional* dollar of income that is paid in taxes. (680)

Tax shelter A special provision in the Income Tax Act that reduces or defers taxation if certain conditions are met. (682)

Tax shifting Occurs when the economic reactions to a tax cause prices and outputs in the economy to change, thereby shifting part of the burden of the tax onto others. (693)

Theory A deliberate simplification of factual relationships whose purpose is to explain how those relationships work. (12)

Time-series graph A type of two-variable diagram that depicts the change in a variable over time. The horizontal axis always represents time. (21)

Total-cost curve Shows, for each possible quantity of output, the total amount that the firm must spend for its inputs to produce that amount of output plus any opportunity cost incurred in the process. (458)

Total expenditure schedule Illustration of how total spending varies with the level of national income (GDP). (137)

Total physical product curve Shows what happens to the quantity of the firm's output as one changes the quantity of one of the firm's inputs while holding the quantities of all other inputs unchanged. (453)

Trade adjustment assistance Special unemployment benefits, loans, retraining programs, and other aid provided to workers and firms that are harmed by foreign competition. (619)

Transfer payments Sums of money that certain individuals receive as grants from the government, rather than as payments for services rendered to employers. (104, 116, 687)

Transfer payments, regional A variety of programs for redistributing funds from the federal government to the provinces, especially the poorer ones. (688)

Unemployment, cyclical The portion of unemployment that is attributable to a decline in the economy's total production. Cyclical unemployment rises during recessions and falls as prosperity is restored. (86).

Unemployment, frictional Unemployment resulting from the normal workings of the labour market. It includes people who are temporarily between jobs because they are moving or changing occupations, or for similar reasons. (86)

Unemployment, natural rate of Also referred to as the "full-employment" unemployment rate. The specific rate of unemployment toward which the economy's self-correcting mechanism tends to push the unemployment rate. (357)

Unemployment, structural Unemployment of workers who have lost their jobs because they have been displaced by automation, because their skills are no longer in demand, or for similar reasons. (86)

Unemployment insurance Government program under which some, but not all, unemployed workers receive transfer payments. (88)

Unemployment rate The number of unemployed people, expressed as a percentage of the labour force. (84)

Unit of account The standard unit for quoting prices. (229)

Utility, marginal Of a commodity to a consumer (measured in money terms) the maximum amount of money he or she is willing to pay for *one more unit* of it. (407)

Utility, total Of a quantity of goods to a consumer (measured in money terms) the maximum amount of money he or she is willing to give in exchange for it. (407)

Value added The value added by a company is its revenue from selling a product minus the amounts paid for goods and services purchased from other firms. (105)

Value judgment A proposition that cannot be proven true or false; it simply is or is not consistent with a particular moral code. (14)

Variable An object, such as price, whose magnitude is measured by a number, and for which one wishes to study what happens when the size of that number changes (varies). (16)

Variable cost Any cost that is not a fixed cost. (460)

Velocity Number of times per year that an "average dollar" is spent on goods and services; the ratio of nominal GDP to the number of dollars in the money stock. (275)

Vertical equity The notion that differently situated persons should be taxed differently in a way that society deems fair. (689)

Wage–price controls Legal restrictions on the ability of industry and labour to raise wages and prices. (368–69)

Index

Elasticity of demand, cross, 441-443
Elasticity of demand, income, 441, 444
Elasticity of demand, price, 434-446
Elasticity of supply, price, 441
Embodied growth, 390
Emission offsets program, 765
Emissions permits/trading, 765-766
Emissions taxes, 759-763, 764
    See also Pollution charges
Employment
    full, 86-87, 90
    See also Labour; Unemployment
Energy, economics of, 766-779
Energy policy, in Canada, 773-776
Energy prices, 355, 767-768, 771, 772,
    773-775, 776-777
    and aggregate supply, 166
    and productivity growth, 379-380
    and stagflation, 177-178
    See also Oil prices
Energy sources, 776-777
Engels, Friedrich, 505
Entrepreneurship, 387, 399, 544, 635,
    658-660, 675
Entry of firms to industry,
    barriers to, 554-556, 557, 560, 561,
        563, 580, 731
    freedom of, 505, 514-518, 570-571,
        572-573, 582, 583, 730, 748
    See also Contestable markets
Environmental issues, 390, 391-392,
    598, 651, 751-766, 777-779
    See also Externalities; Pollution
Environmental Protection Act (Ont.),
    759
Environmental Protection Agency
    (EPA), U.S., 765
Equality vs. efficiency, 536, 603-604,
    628-629, 651, 679, 690, 710-711,
    712-716
    See also Equity
Equalization payments, 688, 707
Equation of exchange, 276, 279
Equilibrium, 49, 135
    demand-side, 131-146
    industry, 513-517
    in international trade, 195-197
    in the labour market, 662-663
    long-run, 514-519, 572-573
    in money market, 260-266
    profit-maximizing, 506-508, 557
    short-run, 506-508, 509, 513-514,
        571-572
    supply–demand, 47-50, 168-169,
        349-350, 611-612
    supply-side, 163-181
    unemployment, 142-144
Equilibrium GDP, 131-146, 171, 186,
    189, 191, 196
Equilibrium income, 135
    and government purchases (*G*),
        186-187, 189, 190, 191
    and tax policy, 189-191
Equilibrium output, 136-139

Equilibrium price, 48, 49, 50, 513-514,
    517, 611-613
Equilibrium quantity, 48, 50, 517
Equity,
    and environmental issues, 762
    horizontal, 688-689
    and monopoly, 560, 561, 563
    pay, 710-712
    and taxation, 688-690, 697-698
    vertical, 689-690
    See also Equality
*An Essay on the Principle of
    Population* (Malthus), 385
*Ethical Reflections on the Economic
    Crisis* (Canadian Conference of
    Catholic Bishops), 371
Ethiopia, 393
European Community, 221, 249,
    322-323, 622, 623, 624, 625, 711,
    776
European Free Trade Association
    (EFTA), 623
European Monetary System (EMS),
    322-323
Excess burden of a tax, 691-692, 697,
    698
Excess-capacity theorem, 573-574, 581
Excess profits, regulation of, 730-731
Excess reserves, 238, 244, 251, 261
Exchange
    equation of, 276, 279
    money as medium of, 229
    mutual gains from, 5, 37, 38, 396,
        413, 549-550, 605-606
Exchange controls, 319
Exchange-rate policy, 250, 253, 303,
    305, 628
Exchange rates
    and aggregate demand, 197
    and aggregate supply, 167, 302-303
    and Bank of Canada, 261, 263
    and crowding out, 342
    defined, 253
    determination in a free market,
        254-255, 311-315
    and economic activity, 314-315
    fixed (pegged), 62, 82, 253, 255-258,
        263-264, 316-321
    flexible (floating), 253, 254, 255,
        264-266, 303-305, 311-315
    and inflation, 312-315
    and interest rates, 314-315
    and international trade, 197, 253
    and multiplier, 156
Excise taxes, 431-434, 563, 683, 686,
    692-694, 695
    See also Sales taxes
Excludability of commodities, 592-593
Exhaustible resources. *See* Depletable
    resources
Expansionary policy. *See* Fiscal policy,
    expansionary; Monetary
    policy, expansionary
Expansion path, 478-479

Expectations
    consumer, 126-127, 200
    inflationary, 361-363, 368
    rational, 363-366
Expected rate of inflation, 97,
    278-279, 361-363, 371
Experimental economics, 57
Exploration, resource, 203
Exponential population growth,
    386-387
Export-led growth, 544-545
Exports, 197, 257, 400, 577
    and competition policy, 603, 743
    and equilibrium income, 195-197
    net, 114
    See also International trade
Export subsidies, 614, 626, 627
Export taxes, 774
Externalities, 6-7, 588-592, 754-755,
    776, 777-779
    See also Environment; Pollution

F

Factor payments, 104-105
Factors of production,
    ownership of, 76, 639, 650
    pricing of, 635-675
    See also Capital; Entrepreneurship;
        Inputs; Labour; Land
Farm-income problem, 444, 503,
    519-520, 720, 722-723
Featherbedding, 671
Federalism, fiscal, 687-688
Federal vs. provincial-municipal
    revenues and spending, 681-686,
    687, 774-775
Fiat money, 230, 235
Final goods and services, 76, 103-104,
    105
Finland, 623, 680
Fiscal federalism, 687-688
Fiscal policy, 185-205, 270, 273,
    290-293, 301, 303
    and aggregate demand, 295-297,
        301, 305, 364, 365
    and aggregate supply, 302, 305
    and budget, 329-330, 336
    contractionary, 199, 200, 305, 319,
        343-345, 358-359, 363, 367, 369,
        371
    defined, 185
    and exchange rates, 295-297, 301,
        305
    expansionary, 198-199, 200, 201,
        248, 295-297, 302-303, 319, 323,
        336, 340-341, 345
    and inflation, 358-359, 364, 365,
        366
    and interest rates, 280-281
    and international trade, 627
    and Keynesian model, 280-281
    and monetarism, 280
    vs. monetary policy, 344-345
    restrictive. *See* Fiscal policy,

Value added, 105-106
Value-added taxes, 680-681, 683-686
Value judgments, 14-15, 540
Vancouver Stock Exchange, 218
Variable costs, 380, 460-461, 509, 510, 563
Variables, 16
Velocity of circulation, 275-279
Vertical axis, 16
Vertical equity, 689-690
Vertical marketing arrangements, 742
Vertical mergers, 738
Vertical Phillips curve
    long-run, 356, 357
    short-run, 362, 364
Via Rail, 720
Voluntarism, and environmental
    issues, 758-759
Voluntary exchange, 5, 37, 38, 396, 413, 549-550, 605-606
von Neumann, John, 579

W

Wachtel, Paul, 391
Wage premiums, 672
Wage and price controls, 367-369, 371
Wage rate, 92, 165-166
Wages
    and ability, 662, 663, 664-665
    determination of, 635, 639-642, 645-647, 660-674
    and education, 663-666
    and GDP, 104-105, 106
    and income distribution, 540, 635, 700, 703, 707-712
    and inflation, 92-94, 353, 360, 369-370, 370
    and inflationary expectations, 361-363
    and international trade, 604, 627
    and labour supply, 660-662
    money, 92, 93, 111, 167, 171, 361-363, 370
    and national income, 116
    and population, 385
    and prices, 92-94
    and productivity, 175, 382-384, 662
    real, 92, 111, 361-363
    and recessionary gaps, 174-176
    and taxation, 695, 698
    and unions, 669-672
    See also Discrimination;
        Minimum-wage laws; Salaries
Wars, 385, 387, 549, 652
Wastes/waste disposal, 390, 391, 595, 753-754, 755-757, 758-759, 763, 779
Water pollution. See Environmental
    issues; Pollution
Wealth, 124-125, 542
    and economic growth, 390-391, 392
    and international trade, 613
    and monopoly, 560
    real, 125
    and taxation, 686, 698

The Wealth of Nations (Smith), 37, 38
Welfare state, 668
Welfare system, 679, 687, 703-707
    See also Social programs
West Germany, 249, 325, 347, 377, 378, 380, 393, 680, 703, 756
White, Robert, 383
Workers' compensation, 687
Worker self-management, 674-675
"Workfare" programs, 704
World economy. *See* International
    monetary system
World War II, 78, 79, 80, 82, 163, 317, 331, 342-343

Z

Zero economic growth, 392
Zero economic profit, 484, 516, 517-518, 560, 571, 572-573, 648
Zero population growth, 386
Zero user fees, 413

Credits and Permissions

Illustrations

Pages 10, 11: Perly's Maps Ltd.; p. 11: Ministère des Transports du Québec; p. 14: London School of Economics and Political Science; p. 21: Surveys and Mappings Branch, Energy, Mines and Resources Canada; p. 38: Brown Brothers; p. 40: Loblaw International Merchants; p. 45: Historical Pictures Service, Chicago; p. 56: Paguin/Publiphoto; p. 64: Health and Welfare Canada; p. 81: Canada, Department of National Defence/National Archives of Canada/PA-035132; p. 89: Brian Willer; p. 92: Canapress Photo Service; p. 94: From *The Wall Street Journal*, permission Cartoon Features Syndicate; p. 100: Camera Press—PHOTO TRENDS; p. 133: Brown Brothers; p. 145: Diakopolilos/Stock, Boston; p. 204: Reprinted with permission—The Toronto Star Syndicate; p. 224: KAL © 1990 Cartoonists & Writers Syndicate; p. 230: By permission of Johnny Hart and Creators Syndicate; p. 231: Currency Museum, The Bank of Canada; loon coin courtesy of the Royal Canadian Mint; p. 232: The University Museum, The University of Pennsylvania; p. 245: Canapress Photo Service; p. 249: Roussel/Image Bank; p. 265: The Bank of Canada; p. 290: Argos Football Club; p. 313: McDonald's Corporation; p. 320: *The New Yorker*; p. 325: Canapress Photo Service; p. 344: Canapress Photo Service; p. 371: Courtesy Canadian Conference of Catholic Bishops; p. 383: Canapress Photo Service; p. 395: HBJ; p. 416: Harvard University; p. 443: AP/Wide World Photo; p. 467: Photo Centre/Phototheque; p. 527: Miller Comstock Inc.; p. 537: *Herman*, © 1989 Jim Unger. Reprinted with permission of Universal Press Syndicate; p. 538: AP/Wide World Photo; p. 596: *Herman*, © 1989 Jim Unger. Reprinted with permission of Universal Press Syndicate; p. 597: Bryce Flynn/Stock, Boston; p. 598: *Herman*, © 1990 Jim Unger. Reprinted with permission of Universal Press Syndicate; p. 599: *Herman*, © 1989 Jim Unger. Reprinted with permission of Universal Press Syndicate; p. 608: Culver Pictures; p. 626: Culver Pictures; p. 646: Canapress Photo Service; p. 667: Wood engraving by Rosemary Kilbourn. From William Kilbourn, *The Elements Combined: A History of The Steel Company of Canada* (Toronto: Clarke, Irwin & Company, 1960). Reprinted with permission of the author; p. 701: *The New Yorker*; p. 711: Canapress Photo Service; p. 711: *Herman*, © 1986 Jim Unger. Reprinted with permission of Universal Press Syndicate; p. 752: *The Far Side*, © 1985 Universal Press Syndicate. Reprinted with permission; p. 754: Beaulieu/Publiphoto; p. 756: Bilderberg/SABA; p. 761: Ed Regan/*The Globe and Mail*; p. 765: Miller Comstock Inc.; p. 778 (top): Fontaine/Publiphoto; p. 778 (bottom): Canapress Photo Service.

Note

Every effort has been made to obtain permission for copyright material used in this book and to acknowledge all such indebtedness accurately. For reasons beyond our control, permission for the use of data from Statistics Canada publications has not been secured for this edition. This and any other errors or omissions brought to our attention will be corrected in future printings.

To the Owner of this Book

We are interested in your reaction to W. Baumol, A. Blinder, and W. Scarth's **Economics: Principles and Policy**, Third Canadian Edition. Through feedback from you, we may be able to improve this book in future editions.

1. What was your reason for using this book?

_____ college course

_____ university course

_____ continuing education

_____ other (specify)

2. If you used this text for a program, what was the name of that program?

3. Which chapters or sections were omitted from your course?

4. Have you any suggestions for improving this text?

Fold here

- -

Tape shut

Canada's Balance of Payments and the Value of the Canadian Dollar

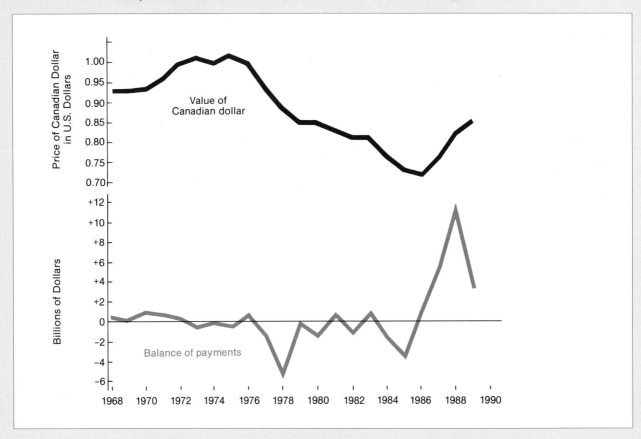

Canadian and U.S. Interest Rates and the Expected Appreciation of the U.S. Dollar, 1962–1989

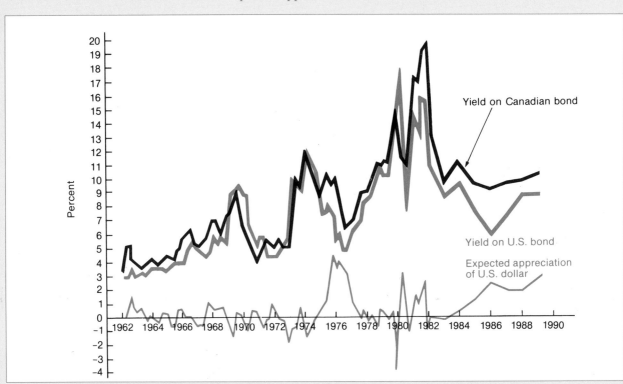